Volume

I

SEVENTH EDITION

The Humanistic Tradition

Prehistory to the Early Modern World

Volume

I

SEVENTH EDITION

The Humanistic Tradition

Prehistory to the Early Modern World

Gloria K. Fiero

Boston Burr Ridge, IL Dubuque, IA New York San Francisco St. Louis
Bangkok Bogotá Caracas Kuala Lumpur Lisbon London Madrid Mexico City
Milan Montreal New Delhi Santiago Seoul Singapore Sydney Taipei Toronto

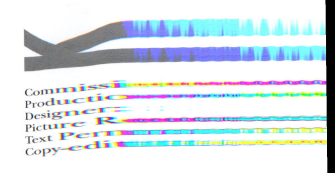

THE HUMANISTIC TRADITION, VOLUME I
PREHISTORY TO THE EARLY MODERN WORLD
SEVENTH EDITION

Published by McGraw-Hill Education, 2 Penn Plaza, New York, NY 10121. Copyright 2015 by
McGraw-Hill Education. All rights reserved. Printed in the United States of America. Previous
edition © 2011, 2006, 2002, 1998, 1995, 1992. No part of this publication may be reproduced
or distributed in any form or by any means, or stored in a database or retrieval system, without
the prior consent of McGraw-Hill Education, including, but not limited to, in any network or
other electronic storage or transmission, or broadcast for distance learning.

Some ancillaries, including electronic and print components, may not be available to
customers outside the United States.

This book is printed on acid-free paper.

1 2 3 4 5 6 7 8 9 0 DOW/DOW 1 0 9 8 7 6 5

ISBN 978-1-259-36066-4
MHID 1-259-36066-0

Senior Vice President, Products & Markets: *Kurt L. Strand*
Vice President, General Manager, Products & Markets: *Michael Ryan*
Vice President, Content Design & Delivery: *Kimberly Meriwether David*
Managing Director: *William Glass*
Brand Manager: *Sarah Remington*
Director, Product Development: *Meghan Campbell*
Marketing Manager: *Kelly Odom*
Director of Development: *Dawn Groundwater*
Digital Product Developer: *Betty Chen*
Director, Content Design & Delivery: *Terri Schiesl*
Program Manager: *Debra Hash*
Content Program Manager: *Sheila Frank*
Buyer: *Susan K. Culbertson*
Printer: *R. R. Donnelley*

Permissions Acknowledgments appear on page 505,
and on this page by reference.

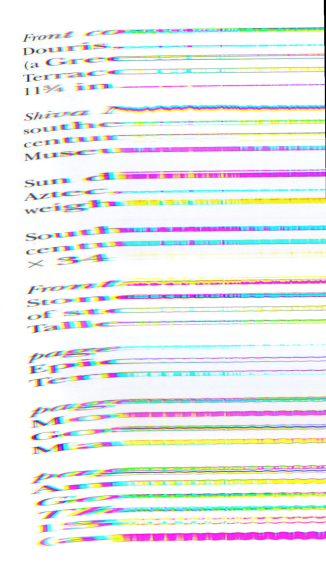

 Library of Congress Cataloging-in-Publication Data

Fiero, Gloria K.
  The humanistic tradition / Gloria K. Fiero. – Seventh edition.
     volumes cm
  Includes bibliographical references and index.

  Contents: BOOK 1. The First Civilizations and the Classical Legacy – BOOK 2. Medieval
Europe and the World Beyond – BOOK 3. The European Renaissance, the Reformation,
and Global Encounter – BOOK 4. Faith, Reason, and Power in the Early Modern World –
BOOK 5. Romanticism, Realism, and the Nineteenth-Century World – BOOK 6. Modernism,
Postmodernism, and the Global Perspective – VOLUME I. Prehistory to the Early Modern
World – VOLUME II. The Early Modern World to the Present.

  ISBN 978-1-259-36066-4 (volume 1 : acid-free paper) – ISBN 1-259-36066-0 (volume 1 :
acid-free paper) – ISBN 978-1-259-35168-6 (volume 2 : acid-free paper)) – ISBN 1-259-35168-8
(volume 2 : acid-free paper) – ISBN 978-0-07-337666-0 (looseleaf : book 1 : acid-free paper) –
ISBN 0-07-337666-3 (looseleaf : book 1 : acid-free paper) – ISBN 978-1-259-35209-6 (looseleaf
: book 2 : acid-free paper) – ISBN 1-259-35209-9 (looseleaf : book 2 : acid-free paper) –
ISBN 978-1-259-35210-2 (looseleaf : book 3 : acid-free paper) – ISBN 1-259-35210-2 (looseleaf
: book 3 : acid-free paper) – ISBN 978-1-259-35539-4 (looseleaf : book 4 : acid-free paper) –
ISBN 1-259-35539-X (looseleaf : book 4 : acid-free paper) – ISBN 978-1-259-35540-0 (looseleaf
: book 5 : acid-free paper) – ISBN 1-259-35540-3 (looseleaf : book 5 : acid-free paper) –
ISBN 978-1-259-35211-9 (looseleaf : book 6 : acid-free paper)

1. Civilization, Western–History–Textbooks. 2. Humanism–History–Textbooks. I. Title.
  CB245.F47 2015
  909'.09821–dc23

                        2014037553

The Internet addresses listed in the text were accurate at the time of publication. The
inclusion of a website does not indicate an endorsement by the author or McGraw-Hill
Education, and McGraw-Hill Education does not guarantee the accuracy of the information
presented at these sites

www.mhhe.com

Volume

I

SEVENTH EDITION

The Humanistic Tradition

Prehistory to the Early Modern World

Gloria K. Fiero

Boston   Burr Ridge, IL   Dubuque, IA   New York   San Francisco   St. Louis
Bangkok   Bogotá   Caracas   Kuala Lumpur   Lisbon   London   Madrid   Mexico City
Milan   Montreal   New Delhi   Santiago   Seoul   Singapore   Sydney   Taipei   Toronto

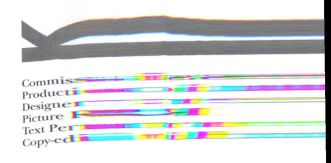

THE HUMANISTIC TRADITION, VOLUME I
PREHISTORY TO THE EARLY MODERN WORLD
SEVENTH EDITION

Published by McGraw-Hill Education, 2 Penn Plaza, New York, NY 10121. Copyright 2015 by McGraw-Hill Education. All rights reserved. Printed in the United States of America. Previous edition © 2011, 2006, 2002, 1998, 1995, 1992. No part of this publication may be reproduced or distributed in any form or by any means, or stored in a database or retrieval system, without the prior consent of McGraw-Hill Education, including, but not limited to, in any network or other electronic storage or transmission, or broadcast for distance learning.

Some ancillaries, including electronic and print components, may not be available to customers outside the United States.

This book is printed on acid-free paper.

1 2 3 4 5 6 7 8 9 0 DOW/DOW 1 0 9 8 7 6 5

ISBN 978-1-259-36066-4
MHID 1-259-36066-0

Senior Vice President, Products & Markets: *Kurt L. Strand*
Vice President, General Manager, Products & Markets: *Michael Ryan*
Vice President, Content Design & Delivery: *Kimberly Meriwether David*
Managing Director: *William Glass*
Brand Manager: *Sarah Remington*
Director, Product Development: *Meghan Campbell*
Marketing Manager: *Kelly Odom*
Director of Development: *Dawn Groundwater*
Digital Product Developer: *Betty Chen*
Director, Content Design & Delivery: *Terri Schiesl*
Program Manager: *Debra Hash*
Content Program Manager: *Sheila Frank*
Buyer: *Susan K. Culbertson*
Printer: *R. R. Donnelley*

Permissions Acknowledgments appear on page 505, and on this page by reference.

Library of Congress Cataloging-in-Publication Data

Fiero, Gloria K.
  The humanistic tradition / Gloria K. Fiero. – Seventh edition.
    volumes cm
  Includes bibliographical references and index.

  Contents: BOOK 1. The First Civilizations and the Classical Legacy – BOOK 2. Medieval Europe and the World Beyond – BOOK 3. The European Renaissance, the Reformation, and Global Encounter – BOOK 4. Faith, Reason, and Power in the Early Modern World – BOOK 5. Romanticism, Realism, and the Nineteenth-Century World – BOOK 6. Modernism, Postmodernism, and the Global Perspective – VOLUME I. Prehistory to the Early Modern World – VOLUME II. The Early Modern World to the Present.

  ISBN 978-1-259-36066-4 (volume 1 : acid-free paper) – ISBN 1-259-36066-0 (volume 1 : acid-free paper) – ISBN 978-1-259-35168-6 (volume 2 : acid-free paper)) – ISBN 1-259-35168-8 (volume 2 : acid-free paper) – ISBN 978-0-07-337666-0 (looseleaf : book 1 : acid-free paper) – ISBN 0-07-337666-3 (looseleaf : book 1 : acid-free paper) – ISBN 978-1-259-35209-6 (looseleaf : book 2 : acid-free paper) – ISBN 1-259-35209-9 (looseleaf : book 2 : acid-free paper) – ISBN 978-1-259-35210-2 (looseleaf : book 3 : acid-free paper) – ISBN 1-259-35210-2 (looseleaf : book 3 : acid-free paper) – ISBN 978-1-259-35539-4 (looseleaf : book 4 : acid-free paper) – ISBN 1-259-35539-X (looseleaf : book 4 : acid-free paper) – ISBN 978-1-259-35540-0 (looseleaf : book 5 : acid-free paper) – ISBN 1-259-35540-3 (looseleaf : book 5 : acid-free paper) – ISBN 978-1-259-35211-9 (looseleaf : book 6 : acid-free paper)

  1. Civilization, Western–History–Textbooks. 2. Humanism–History–Textbooks. I. Title.
  CB245.F47 2015
  909'.09821–dc23

2014037553

The Internet addresses listed in the text were accurate at the time of publication. The inclusion of a website does not indicate an endorsement by the author or McGraw-Hill Education, and McGraw-Hill Education does not guarantee the accuracy of the information presented at these sites

www.mhhe.com

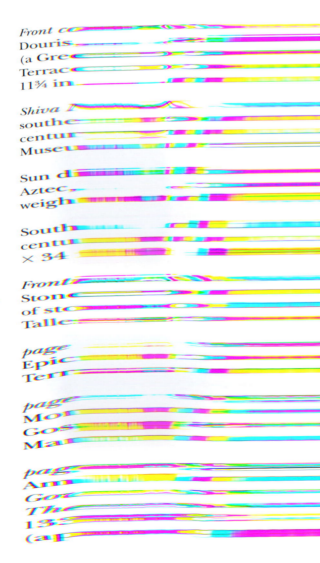

Volume

I

SEVENTH EDITION

The Humanistic Tradition

**Prehistory to the
Early Modern World**

Gloria K. Fiero

McGraw Hill Education

Boston   Burr Ridge, IL   Dubuque, IA   New York   San Francisco   St. Louis
Bangkok   Bogotá   Caracas   Kuala Lumpur   Lisbon   London   Madrid   Mexico City
Milan   Montreal   New Delhi   Santiago   Seoul   Singapore   Sydney   Taipei   Toronto

THE HUMANISTIC TRADITION, VOLUME I
PREHISTORY TO THE EARLY MODERN WORLD
SEVENTH EDITION

Published by McGraw-Hill Education, 2 Penn Plaza, New York, NY 10121. Copyright 2015 by McGraw-Hill Education. All rights reserved. Printed in the United States of America. Previous edition © 2011, 2006, 2002, 1998, 1995, 1992. No part of this publication may be reproduced or distributed in any form or by any means, or stored in a database or retrieval system, without the prior consent of McGraw-Hill Education, including, but not limited to, in any network or other electronic storage or transmission, or broadcast for distance learning.

Some ancillaries, including electronic and print components, may not be available to customers outside the United States.

This book is printed on acid-free paper.

1 2 3 4 5 6 7 8 9 0 DOW/DOW 1 0 9 8 7 6 5

ISBN 978-1-259-36066-4
MHID 1-259-36066-0

Senior Vice President, Products & Markets: *Kurt L. Strand*
Vice President, General Manager, Products & Markets: *Michael Ryan*
Vice President, Content Design & Delivery: *Kimberly Meriwether David*
Managing Director: *William Glass*
Brand Manager: *Sarah Remington*
Director, Product Development: *Meghan Campbell*
Marketing Manager: *Kelly Odom*
Director of Development: *Dawn Groundwater*
Digital Product Developer: *Betty Chen*
Director, Content Design & Delivery: *Terri Schiesl*
Program Manager: *Debra Hash*
Content Program Manager: *Sheila Frank*
Buyer: *Susan K. Culbertson*
Printer: *R. R. Donnelley*

Permissions Acknowledgments appear on page 505,
and on this page by reference.

Library of Congress Cataloging-in-Publication Data

Fiero, Gloria K.
  The humanistic tradition / Gloria K. Fiero. – Seventh edition.
     volumes cm
  Includes bibliographical references and index.

  Contents: BOOK 1. The First Civilizations and the Classical Legacy – BOOK 2. Medieval Europe and the World Beyond – BOOK 3. The European Renaissance, the Reformation, and Global Encounter – BOOK 4. Faith, Reason, and Power in the Early Modern World – BOOK 5. Romanticism, Realism, and the Nineteenth-Century World – BOOK 6. Modernism, Postmodernism, and the Global Perspective – VOLUME I. Prehistory to the Early Modern World – VOLUME II. The Early Modern World to the Present.

  ISBN 978-1-259-36066-4 (volume 1 : acid-free paper) – ISBN 1-259-36066-0 (volume 1 : acid-free paper) – ISBN 978-1-259-35168-6 (volume 2 : acid-free paper)) – ISBN 1-259-35168-8 (volume 2 : acid-free paper) – ISBN 978-0-07-337666-0 (looseleaf : book 1 : acid-free paper) – ISBN 0-07-337666-3 (looseleaf : book 1 : acid-free paper) – ISBN 978-1-259-35209-6 (looseleaf : book 2 : acid-free paper) – ISBN 1-259-35209-9 (looseleaf : book 2 : acid-free paper) – ISBN 978-1-259-35210-2 (looseleaf : book 3 : acid-free paper) – ISBN 1-259-35210-2 (looseleaf : book 3 : acid-free paper) – ISBN 978-1-259-35539-4 (looseleaf : book 4 : acid-free paper) – ISBN 1-259-35539-X (looseleaf : book 4 : acid-free paper) – ISBN 978-1-259-35540-0 (looseleaf : book 5 : acid-free paper) – ISBN 1-259-35540-3 (looseleaf : book 5 : acid-free paper) – ISBN 978-1-259-35211-9 (looseleaf : book 6 : acid-free paper)

  1. Civilization, Western–History–Textbooks. 2. Humanism–History–Textbooks. I. Title.
  CB245.F47 2015
  909'.09821–dc23

                        2014037553

www.mhhe.com

Volume

I

SEVENTH EDITION

The Humanistic Tradition

**Prehistory to the
Early Modern World**

Gloria K. Fiero

Boston Burr Ridge, IL Dubuque, IA New York San Francisco St. Louis
Bangkok Bogotá Caracas Kuala Lumpur Lisbon London Madrid Mexico City
Milan Montreal New Delhi Santiago Seoul Singapore Sydney Taipei Toronto

This book was designed and produced by Laurence King Publishing Ltd., London
www.laurenceking.com

Commissioning Editor: *Kara Hattersley-Smith*
Production: *Simon Walsh*
Designer: *Ian Hunt*
Picture Researcher: *Louise Thomas*
Text Permissions: *Rachel Thorne*
Copy-editor: *Rosanna Lewis*

THE HUMANISTIC TRADITION, VOLUME I
PREHISTORY TO THE EARLY MODERN WORLD
SEVENTH EDITION

1 2 3 4 5 6 7 8 9 0 DOW/DOW 1 0 9 8 7 6 5

ISBN 978-1-259-36066-4
MHID 1-259-36066-0

Senior Vice President, Products & Markets: *Kurt L. Strand*
Vice President, General Manager, Products & Markets: *Michael Ryan*
Vice President, Content Design & Delivery: *Kimberly Meriwether David*
Managing Director: *William Glass*
Brand Manager: *Sarah Remington*
Director, Product Development: *Meghan Campbell*
Marketing Manager: *Kelly Odom*
Director of Development: *Dawn Groundwater*
Digital Product Developer: *Betty Chen*
Director, Content Design & Delivery: *Terri Schiesl*
Program Manager: *Debra Hash*
Content Program Manager: *Sheila Frank*
Buyer: *Susan K. Culbertson*
Printer: *R. R. Donnelley*

Permissions Acknowledgments appear on page 505, and on this page by reference.

Library of Congress Cataloging-in-Publication Data

Fiero, Gloria K.
  The humanistic tradition / Gloria K. Fiero. – Seventh edition.
    volumes cm
  Includes bibliographical references and index.

  Contents: BOOK 1. The First Civilizations and the Classical Legacy – BOOK 2. Medieval Europe and the World Beyond – BOOK 3. The European Renaissance, the Reformation, and Global Encounter – BOOK 4. Faith, Reason, and Power in the Early Modern World – BOOK 5. Romanticism, Realism, and the Nineteenth-Century World – BOOK 6. Modernism, Postmodernism, and the Global Perspective – VOLUME I. Prehistory to the Early Modern World – VOLUME II. The Early Modern World to the Present.

  ISBN 978-1-259-36066-4 (volume 1 : acid-free paper) – ISBN 1-259-36066-0 (volume 1 : acid-free paper) – ISBN 978-1-259-35168-6 (volume 2 : acid-free paper)) – ISBN 1-259-35168-8 (volume 2 : acid-free paper) – ISBN 978-0-07-337666-0 (looseleaf : book 1 : acid-free paper) – ISBN 0-07-337666-3 (looseleaf : book 1 : acid-free paper) – ISBN 978-1-259-35209-6 (looseleaf : book 2 : acid-free paper) – ISBN 1-259-35209-9 (looseleaf : book 2 : acid-free paper) – ISBN 978-1-259-35210-2 (looseleaf : book 3 : acid-free paper) – ISBN 1-259-35210-2 (looseleaf : book 3 : acid-free paper) – ISBN 978-1-259-35539-4 (looseleaf : book 4 : acid-free paper) – ISBN 1-259-35539-X (looseleaf : book 4 : acid-free paper) – ISBN 978-1-259-35540-0 (looseleaf : book 5 : acid-free paper) – ISBN 1-259-35540-3 (looseleaf : book 5 : acid-free paper) – ISBN 978-1-259-35211-9 (looseleaf : book 6 : acid-free paper)

  1. Civilization, Western–History–Textbooks. 2. Humanism–History–Textbooks. I. Title.
  CB245.F47 2015
  909'.09821–dc23

                    2014037553

Front cover (clockwise from left)
Douris, interior of a red-figured kylix (a Greek drinking cup), ca. 480 B.C.E. Terracotta, height 4⅜ in., diameter 11¾ in.

Shiva Nataraja, Lord of the Dance, from southern India, Chola period, eleventh century. Bronze, 35 × 28 in. Dallas Museum of Art.

Sun disk, known as the "Calendar Stone," Aztec, fifteenth century. Diameter 13 ft., weight 24½ tons.

South rose and lancets, thirteenth century. Chartres Cathedral. 57 ft. 6¾ in. × 34 ft. 7¾ in.

Frontispiece and page xvi
Stonehenge trilitons (lintel-topped pairs of stones at center), ca. 3000–1800 B.C.E, Tallest upright 22 ft. (including lintel).

page xix
Epictetus, cup (detail), ca. 510 b.c.e. Terracotta, diameter 13 in.

page 181
Monogram XPI, first page of Matthew's Gospel, Book of Kells (detail), ca. 800. Manuscript illumination, 13 × 9½ in.

page 355
Ambrogio Lorenzetti, *Effects of Good Government in the City and the Country*, from *The Allegory of Good Government* (detail), 1338–1339. Fresco, total length 46 ft. (approx.)

Volume I Contents

Series Contents

Letter from the Author

The Humanistic Tradition originated more than two decades ago. As a long-time humanities instructor, I recognized that the Western-only perspective was no longer adequate to understanding the cultural foundations of our global world. However, none of the existing humanities textbooks served my needs. The challenge was daunting—covering the history of Western literature, philosophy, art, music, and dance was already an ambitious undertaking for a humanities survey; how could I broaden the scope to include Asia, Africa, and the Americas without over-loading the course?

I found the solution in my classroom: Instead of assuming a strictly historical approach to the past, (as I did in my history classes), I would organize my humanities lectures topically, focusing on universal themes, major styles, and significant movements—gods and rulers, classicism, imperialism, the Romantic hero, racial and sexual equality, globalism—as they reflected or shaped the culture of a given time or place. What evolved was *The Humanistic Tradition*, a thematic, yet global and chronological approach to humanities, one that provokes thought and discussion without burying students under mountains of encyclopedic information.

Now in its seventh edition, *The Humanistic Tradition* continues to celebrate the creative mind by focusing on how the arts and ideas relate to each other, what they tell us about our own human nature and that of others on our planet. Its mission remains relevant to the present, and essential (I would hope) to enriching the future of each student who reads its pages.

The Seventh Edition of *The Humanistic Tradition*

To the seventh edition of *The Humanistic Tradition* I have added a new feature: **Looking Into** is a diagrammatic analysis of key works, such as Neolithic stone circles (including the latest archeological discoveries in Southeast Turkey), the Parthenon, the sonnets of Petrarch and Donne, *Shiva: Lord of the Dance*, Jan van Eyck's *Arnolfini Double Portrait*, and Judy Chicago's *Dinner Party*.

The new edition expands two popular features that promote critical thinking: **Exploring Issues**, which focuses on controversial ideas and current debates (such as the battle over the ownership of antiquities, and creationism versus evolution); and **Making Connections**, which brings attention to contrasts and continuities between past and present. To **Exploring Issues**, I have added the debate over the origins of India's Vedic culture (chapter 3). To **Making Connections** I offer a novel illustration of the contemporary affection for Chinese landscape painting (chapter 14).

The chapter-by-chapter integration of literary, visual, and aural primary sources remains a hallmark of *The Humanistic Tradition*. In an effort to provide the most engaging and accessible literary works, some selected readings in this edition appear in alternate translations. **Marginal logos** have been added to direct students to additional literary resources that are discussed but not included in the text itself.

Additions to the art program include the Nebra Sky Disk, Hellenistic mosaics, Delacroix's *Women of Algiers*, Oceania's art of tattoo, Japan's Amida Buddha, Charles Willson Peale's *Portrait of Yarrow Mamout* (the earliest known portrait of a Muslim in America), Ai Wei Wei's *Forever Bicycle*, Ernesto Neto's *Anthropodino*, and Zaha Hadid's Heydar Aliyev Center. Chapters 37 and 38, which treat the Information Age and Globalism, have been updated to present a cogent overview of contemporary issues, including terrorism, ecological concerns, ethnic conflict, and the digital arts.

The Humanistic Tradition pioneered a flexible six-book format in recognition of the varying chronological range of humanities courses. Each slim volume was also convenient for students to bring to classes, the library, and other study areas. The seventh edition continues to be available in this six-book format, as well as in a two-volume set for the most common two-term course configuration.

In preparing the seventh edition, I have depended on the excellent editorial and production team led by Donald Dinwiddie at Laurence King Publishing. Special thanks also go to Kara Hattersley-Smith at LKP and Sarah Remington at McGraw-Hill Higher Education.

Gloria K. Fiero

The Humanistic Tradition—a personalized learnin

Each generation leaves a creative legacy, the sum of its ideas and achievements. This legacy represents the response to our effort to ensure our individual and collective survival, our need to establish ways of living in harmony with others, and our desire to understand our place in the universe. Meeting the challenges of *survival*, *communality*, and *self-knowledge*, we have created and transmitted the tools of science and technology, social and political institutions, religious and philosophic systems, and various forms of personal expression—the totality of which we call **culture**. Handed down from generation to generation, this legacy constitutes the humanistic tradition, the study of which is called *humanities*.

Understanding that a global humanities course is taught in varying ways, Gloria Fiero redefines the discipline for greater flexibility via a variety of innovative digital tools. Enhanced by McGraw-Hill Education's LearnSmart and SmartBook, Fiero delivers a learning experience tailored to the needs of each institution, instructor, and student. With the ability to incorporate new extended readings, streaming music, and artwork, *The Humanistic Tradition* renews the understanding of the relationship between world cultures and humankind's creative legacy.

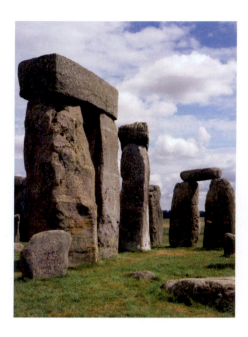

Personalized Learning Experience

In **Connect Humanities**, you can access all of the art and music from *The Humanistic Tradition* on your computer or mobile device. Music logos (right) that appear in the margins of the text refer to listening selections available for streaming.

As part of McGraw-Hill Education's Connect Humanities, LearnSmart is an adaptive learning program designed to personalize the learning experience. LearnSmart helps students learn faster, study smarter, and retain more knowledge for greater success. Distinguishing what students know from what they don't, and touching on concepts they are most likely to forget, LearnSmart continuously adapts to each students' needs by building a personalized learning path. LearnSmart is proven to strengthen memory recall, keep students in class, and boost grades. By helping students master core concepts ahead of time, LearnSmart enables instructors to spend more meaningful time in the classroom.

SMARTBOOK™

Enhanced by LearnSmart, SmartBook is the first and only adaptive reading experience currently available.

- **Making It Effective** SmartBook creates a personalized reading experience by highlighting the most impactful concepts a student needs to learn at that moment in time. This ensures that every minute spent with SmartBook is returned to the student as the most valuable minute possible.
- **Make It Informed** Real-time reports quickly identify the concepts that require more attention from individual students—or the entire class.

Personalized Teaching Experience

Personalize and tailor your teaching experience to the needs of your humanities course with Create, Insight, and instructor resources.

Create What You've Only Imagined

No two humanities courses are the same. That is why Gloria Fiero has personally hand-picked additional readings that can be added easily to a customized edition of *The Humanistic Tradition*. Marginal icons (right) that appear throughout this new edition indicate additional readings, a list of which is found at the end of the Table of Contents.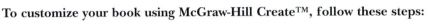

To customize your book using McGraw-Hill Create™, follow these steps:
1. Go to http://create.mheducation.com and sign in or register for an instructor account.
2. Click Collections (top, right) and select the "Traditions: Humanities Readings Through the Ages" Collection to preview and select readings. You can also make use of McGraw-Hill's comprehensive, cross-disciplinary content as well as other third-party resources.
3. Choose the readings that are most relevant to your students, your curriculum, and your own areas of interest.
4. Arrange the content in a way that makes the most sense for your course.
5. Personalize your book with your course information and choose the best format for your students—color, black-and-white, or ebook. When you are done, you will receive a free PDF review copy in just minutes.

Or contact your McGraw-Hill Education representative, who can help you build your unique version of *The Humanisitic Tradition*.

Powerful Reporting on the Go

The first and only analytics tool of its kind, Connect Insight is a series of visual data displays—each framed by an intuitive question—that provide at-a-glance information regarding how your class is doing.
- **Intuitive** You receive an instant, at-a-glance view of student performance matched with student activity.
- **Dynamic** Connect Insight puts real-time analytics in your hands so you can take action early and keep struggling students from falling behind.
- **Mobile** Connect Insight travels from office to classroom, available on demand wherever and whenever it's needed.

Instructor Resources

Connect Image Bank is an instructor database of images from select McGraw-Hill Education art and humanities titles, including *The Humanistic Tradition*. It includes all images for which McGraw-Hill has secured electronic permissions. With Connect Image Bank, instructors can access a text's images by browsing its chapters, style/period, medium, and culture, or by searching with key terms. Images can be easily downloaded for use in presentations and in PowerPoints. The download includes a text file with image captions and information. You can access Connect Image Bank on the library tab in Connect Humanities (http://connect.mheducation.com).

Various instructor resources are available for *The Humanistic Tradition*. These include an instructor's manual with discussion suggestions and study questions, music listening guides, lecture PowerPoints, and a test bank. Contact your McGraw-Hill sales representative for access to these materials.

Studying humanities engages us in a dialogue with primary sources: works original to the age in which they were produced. Whether literary, visual, or aural, a primary source is a text; the time, place, and circumstances in which it was created constitute the context; and its various underlying meanings provide the subtext. Studying humanities from the perspective of text, context, and subtext helps us understand our cultural legacy and our place in the larger world.

Text

The *text* of a primary source refers to its medium (that is, what it is made of), its form (its outward shape), and its content (the subject it describes).

Literature: Literary form varies according to the manner in which words are arranged. So, *poetry*, which shares rhythmic organization with music and dance, is distinguished from *prose*, which normally lacks regular rhythmic patterns. Poetry, by its freedom from conventional grammar, provides unique opportunities for the expression of intense emotions. Prose usually functions to convey information, to narrate, and to describe.

Philosophy (the search for truth through reasoned analysis) and *history* (the record of the past) make use of prose to analyze and communicate ideas and information.

In literature, as in most forms of expression, content and form are usually interrelated. The subject matter or form of a literary work determines its *genre*. For instance, a long narrative poem recounting the adventures of a hero constitutes an *epic*, while a formal, dignified speech in praise of a person or thing constitutes a *eulogy*.

The Visual Arts: The visual arts employ a wide variety of media, ranging from the traditional colored pigments used in painting, to wood, clay, marble, and (more recently) plastic and neon used in sculpture, to a wide variety of digital media, including photography and film. The form or outward shape of a work of art depends on the manner in which the artist manipulates the elements of color, line, texture, and space. Unlike words, these formal elements lack denotative meaning.

The visual arts are dominantly spatial, that is, they operate and are apprehended in space. Artists manipulate form to describe or interpret the visible world (as in the genres of portraiture and landscape), or to create worlds of fantasy and imagination. They may also fabricate texts that are nonrepresentational, that is, without identifiable subject matter.

Music and Dance: The medium of music is sound. Like literature, music is durational: it unfolds over the period of time in which it occurs. The major elements of music are melody, rhythm, harmony, and tone color—formal elements that also characterize the oral life of literature. However, while literary and visual texts are usually descriptive, music is almost always nonrepresentational: it rarely has meaning beyond sound itself. For that reason, music is the most difficult of the arts to describe in words.

Dance, the artform that makes the human body itself the medium of expression, resembles music in that it is temporal and performance-oriented. Like music, dance exploits rhythm as a formal tool, and like painting and sculpture, it unfolds in space as well as in time.

Studying the text, we discover the ways in which the artist manipulates medium and form to achieve a characteristic manner of execution or expression that we call *style*. Comparing the styles of various texts from a single era, we discover that they usually share certain defining features and characteristics. Similarities between, for instance, ancient Greek temples and Greek tragedies, or between Chinese lyric poems and landscape paintings, reveal the unifying moral and aesthetic values of their respective cultures.

Context

The *context* describes the historical and cultural environment of a text. Understanding the relationship between text and context is one of the principal concerns of any inquiry into the humanistic tradition. To determine the context, we ask: In what time and place did our primary source originate? How did it function within the society in which it was created? Was it primarily decorative, didactic, magical, or propagandistic? Did it serve the religious or political needs of the community? Sometimes our answers to these questions are mere guesses. For instance, the paintings on the walls of Paleolithic caves were probably not "artworks" in the modern sense of the term, but, rather, magical signs associated with religious rituals performed in the interest of communal survival.

Determining the function of the text often serves to clarify the nature of its form, and vice-versa. For instance, in that the Hebrew Bible, the *Song of Roland*, and many other early literary works were spoken or sung, rather than read, such literature tends to feature repetition and rhyme, devices that facilitate memorization and oral delivery.

Subtext

The *subtext* of a primary source refers to its secondary or implied meanings. The subtext discloses conceptual messages embedded in or implied by the text. The epic poems of the ancient Greeks, for instance, which glorify prowess and physical courage, suggest an exclusively male perception of virtue. The state portraits of the seventeenth-century French king Louis XIV bear the subtext of unassailable and absolute power. In our own time, Andy Warhol's serial adaptations of Coca-Cola bottles offer wry commentary on the commercial mentality of American society. Examining the implicit message of the text helps us determine the values of the age in which it was produced, and offers insights into our own.

The First Civilizations and the Classical Legacy

Prehistory and the Birth of Civilization

ca. 7 million B.C.E.–1500 B.C.E.

*"But, after all, who knows, and who can say
whence it all came, and how creation happened?"*
Rig Veda

Figure 0.1 Spotted horses and negative hand prints, Pech-Merle caves, Lot, France, ca. 15,000–10,000 B.C.E. Length 11 ft. 2 in.

The first chapters in the history of human life are often regarded as the most challenging. They present us with a gigantic puzzle that requires scientists and historians to piece together various fragments of information, most of which, like buried treasure, have been dug out of the earth. Reassembled, they reveal the progress of humankind from its earliest beginnings; they track a record of the genetic and behavioral adaptation of human beings to their natural (and often hostile) surroundings. The story of modern humans is the last chapter in a long history that begins with the simplest forms of life that thrived in the primeval seas hundreds of millions of years ago. To understand that story, we must turn to the evidence provided by prehistory.

Prehistory

The study of history before the appearance of written records, an enterprise that originated in France around 1860, is called **prehistory**. In the absence of written records, prehistorians depend on information about the past provided by the disciplines of geology, paleontology, anthropology, archeology, and ethnography. For instance, using instruments that measure the radioactive atoms remaining in the organic elements of the earth's strata, geologists have determined that our planet is approximately 4.5 billion years old. Paleontologists record the history of fossil remains and that of the earth's earliest living creatures. Anthropologists study human biology, society, and cultural practices, while archeologists uncover, analyze, and interpret the material remains of past societies. Finally, a special group of cultural anthropologists known as ethnographers study surviving preliterate societies. All of these specialists contribute to producing a detailed picture of humankind's earliest environment and the prehistoric past.

The earliest organic remains in the earth's strata are almost four billion years old. From one-celled organisms that inhabited the watery terrain of our planet, higher forms of life very gradually evolved. Some hundred million years ago, dinosaurs stalked the earth, eventually becoming extinct—possibly because they failed to adapt to climatic change. Eighty million years ago, mammals roamed the earth's surface. Although even the most approximate dates are much disputed, it is generally agreed that between ten and five million years ago ancestral humans first appeared on earth, probably in eastern and southern Africa. The exact genealogy of humankind is still a matter of intense debate. However, in the last fifty years, anthropologists have clarified some aspects of the relationship between human beings and earlier primates—the group of mammals that today includes monkeys, apes, and human beings. Fossil evidence reveals structural similarities between human beings and chimpanzees (and other apes). More recent research in molecular biology indicates that the DNA of chimpanzees is approximately 99 percent identical to human DNA, suggesting that humans are more closely related to chimpanzees than domestic cats are to lions.

Paleolithic ("Old Stone") Culture*
(ca. 7 million–10,000 B.C.E.)**

Early in the twentieth century, anthropologists discovered the first fossil remains of the near-human or proto-human creature known as **hominid**, who lived some five or more million years ago. Hominids lived in packs; they gathered seeds, berries, wild fruits, and vegetables, and possibly even hunted the beasts of the African savannas. Hominid footprints found in South Africa in the mid-1990s and fossil remains uncovered since 2002 in Central Africa and near the Black Sea suggest that hominids may have walked upright as early as six million years ago. What is the relationship between modern humans and their now-extinct relatives? Molecular biologists have analyzed fossil DNA and determined that the human family tree has numerous branches. Diverse groups of the genus *Homo* left Africa at different times, some co-existing before dying out. The branch that represents our ancestors, that is, modern humans (*Homo sapiens*) departed from Africa some 66,000 years ago. However, many human species preceded us.

About three million years ago, a South African variety of hominid known as *Australopithecus* was using sharp-edged pebbles for skinning animals and for chopping. Creating the first stone and bone tools and weapons, *Homo habilis* ("tool-making human") met the challenge of survival with problem-solving ingenuity. Stone-tipped spears were in use some 500,000 years ago. Anthropologists have long considered tool-making the distinguishing feature of modern humans. Tool-making represents the beginnings of **culture**, which, in its most basic sense, proceeds from the manipulation of nature; and the appearance of tools and weapons—humankind's earliest technology—constitutes the initial act of extending control over nature. Co-existing with *Homo habilis* for half a million years in parts of Africa and East Asia, hunter-gatherers known as *Homo erectus* ("upright human") made tools that were more varied and efficient than those of their predecessors. These tools included hand-axes, cleavers, chisels, and a wide variety of choppers. The hand-ax became the standard tool for chopping, digging, cutting, and scraping. Fire, too, became an important part of the early culture of humankind, providing safety, warmth, and a means of cooking food. Although it is still not certain how long ago fire was first

---

*The terms Paleolithic and Neolithic do not describe uniform time periods, but, rather, cultures that appeared at different times in different parts of the world.

**Dates are signified as B.C.E., "Before the Christian (or common) era," or C.E., "Christian (or common) era."

used, archeologists confirm that fire was a regular feature in the hearths of most *Homo erectus* dwellings.

Some 100,000 years ago, a group of humanoids with anatomical features and brain size similar to our own appeared in the Neander Valley near Düsseldorf, Germany. The burial of human dead (their bodies dyed with red ocher) among Neanderthals and the practice of including tools, weapons, food, and flowers in Neanderthal graves are evidence of the self-conscious, symbol-making human known as *Homo sapiens*. Characterized by memory and foresight, these now-extinct cousins of modern-day humans were the first to demonstrate—by their ritual preparation and disposal of the deceased—a self-conscious concern with human mortality. That concern may have involved respect for, or fear of, the dead and the anticipation of life after death.

The development of the primate brain in both size and complexity was integral to the evolution of *Homo sapiens*: over millions of years, the average brain size of the human being grew to roughly three times the size of the gorilla's brain. Equally critical was the growth of more complex motor capacities. Gradually, verbal methods of communication complemented the nonverbal ones shared by animals and proto-humans. Over time, modern humans came to use spoken language as a medium for transmitting information. Communication by means of spoken language distinguished *Homo sapiens* from other primates. Chimpanzees have been known to bind two poles together in order to reach a bunch of bananas hanging from the top of a tree, but, short of immediate physical demonstration, they have developed no means of passing on this technique to subsequent generations of chimpanzees. *Homo sapiens*, on the other hand, have produced symbol systems that enable them to transmit their ideas and inventions. Thus, in the fullest sense, culture requires both the manipulation of nature and the formulation of a symbolic language for its transmission.

Paleolithic culture evolved during a period of climatic fluctuation called the Ice Age. Between roughly three million and 10,000 years ago, at least four large glacial advances covered the area north of the equator. As hunters and gatherers, Paleolithic people were forced either to migrate or to adapt to changing climatic conditions. It is likely that more than fifteen species of human co-existed with one another, and all but *Homo sapiens* became extinct. Ultimately, the ingenuity and imagination of *Homo sapiens* were responsible for the fact that they fared better than many other creatures.

Early modern humans devised an extensive technology of stone and bone tools and weapons that increased their comfort and safety, and almost certainly their confidence. A 7-foot stone-tipped spear enabled a hunter to attack an animal at a distance of 6 or more yards. Other devices increased the leverage of the arm and thus doubled that range. Spears and harpoons, and—toward the end of the Ice Age—bows and arrows, extended the efficacy and safety of Paleolithic people, just as axes and knives facilitated their food-preparing abilities.

Figure 0.2 Hall of Bulls, left wall, Lascaux caves, Dordogne, France, ca. 15,000–10,000 B.C.E. Paint on limestone rock, length of individual bulls 13–16 ft.

Science and Technology

2,500,000 B.C.E.	first stone tools are utilized in East Africa[†]
500,000 B.C.E.	in China, *Homo erectus* uses fire for domestic purposes
24,000 B.C.E.	fish hooks and lines are utilized in Europe
20,000 B.C.E.	bows and arrows are in use in North Africa and Spain; oil lamps, fueled by animal fat, come into use
13,000 B.C.E.	devices to hurl harpoons and spears are in use

†*All dates in this introduction are approximate.*

Cave Art

Since 1875 archeologists have found painted, drawn, and engraved images on cave walls in Europe, Africa, Australia, and North America. The most recent of these discoveries was made at the El Castillo cave in northwestern Spain, where painted disks, clublike symbols, and hundreds of handprints, at least 37,000 years old, appear to be the world's oldest known wall-paintings. Handprints, probably made by blowing or splattering earth pigments through a hollow reed as the hand rested against the wall, are commonly found in most prehistoric caves (Figure **0.1**). The hand, an essential ally in the creation of tools and weapons, as well as in the depiction of imagery, held an obviously prized place in Paleolithic culture.

At Lascaux, a site discovered in southern France in 1940, a magnificent array of animals and symbols is now tragically disappearing under the ruinous attack of algae, bacteria, and fungi (the caves have been closed to the public since 1963). While Lascaux features a variety of commonly hunted species—bison, reindeer, elk, mammoths, and zebras—caves at Cosquer and Chauvet on the southern coast of France, found in the early 1990s, depict an even wider variety of Paleolithic creatures: rhinoceros, horses, bears, lions, panthers, hyenas, and sea birds. Executed between 30,000 and 10,000 years ago, the images at these various sites were skillfully painted with **polychrome** mineral pigments. The animals, shown standing or running, often wounded by spears or arrows, are strongly **naturalistic**: shaded with bitumen and burnt coal, and sometimes protruding from the uneven rock surface, they appear three-dimensionally lifelike (Figure **0.2**).

What was the purpose or function of so-called cave art? Scholars have long debated this question. Some hold that it served as part of a hunting ritual. Others contend that the creatures pictured on cave walls were **clan totems** (heraldic tribal emblems) or symbols of male and female forces. Still others read certain abstract markings on cave walls as lunar calendars, notational devices used to predict seasonal change or the seasonal migration of animals. Long associated with the procreative womb and cosmic underworld, the cave itself may have served as a ceremonial chamber, shrine, or council room in which rituals were orchestrated by **shamans**, that is, mediators between the natural and the spiritual worlds. In the preliterate societies of Native America, Africa, and Polynesia, shamans have traditionally made use of animals as message-bearers, clan totems, and spirit guides; the animals painted on prehistoric cave walls may have served in similar ways.

Located in the most inaccessible regions of the caves, and usually drawn one over the other with no apparent regard for clarity, it is unlikely that cave paintings served as formal decoration or as records of actual hunts. Nevertheless, the association between cave art and hunting remains convincing. It is supported by ethnographic evidence of hunting rituals practiced in the African Congo as recently as the early twentieth century. At such rituals, leaders of the hunt make sand drawings of the animals they are about to hunt, then fire arrows into the drawings. If the hunt is successful, they smear the images with the blood and fur of their prey. Such rituals constitute a form of *sympathetic magic* whereby power is gained over a person, animal, or object by capturing it visually (in the painted mark), orally (in the proper combination of words, chanted or sung), or by way of prescribed gestures and body movements (dance).

It has been argued that some of the animals depicted in the Chauvet cave were never or rarely hunted; however, archeologists confirm that extinct species of panther, jaguar, and lion were indeed hunted by early humans, not exclusively for food, but because such animals were predators—Paleolithic people were as much preyed upon as they were themselves predators—and competitors for smaller game. Some animals, such as the wooly mammoth, were hunted for their bones, which were used for weapons, musical instruments, and the construction of Ice Age huts, at least seventy of which have been found in Ukraine and parts of Russia (Figure **0.3**). Sympathetic magic has characterized religious ritual throughout the history of humankind, but it was especially important in the prehistoric world, where mastery of nature was crucial to physical survival. While we may never know its exact function, cave art, like tools and weapons, surely served the communal well-being of a hunting-gathering culture.

Mother Earth

It is likely that shared responsibility characterized humankind's earliest societies. Women probably secured food by gathering fruits and berries; they also acted as healers and nurturers. Since the female (in her role as child-bearer) assured the continuity of the tribe, she assumed a special importance. As life-giver, she was identified with the mysterious powers of procreation and exalted as Mother Earth. Her importance in the prehistoric community is confirmed by the great number of female statuettes uncovered by archeologists throughout the world. A good many of these objects show the female nude with pendulous breasts, large buttocks, and a swollen abdomen, indicating pregnancy (Figure **0.4**).

Figure 0.3 Reconstruction of a mammoth-bone house, Mezhirich, Ukraine, ca. 16,000–10,000 B.C.E.

Figure 0.4 "Venus" of Willendorf, from Lower Austria, ca. 25,000–20,000 B.C.E. Limestone, height 4⅜ in.

Neolithic ("New Stone") Culture (ca. 10,000–4000 B.C.E.)

Paleolithic people lived at the mercy of nature. However, toward the end of the Ice Age, between 10,000 and 8,000 B.C.E., as the glaciers covering the Northern hemisphere melted, and grassy plains and forests replaced regions once covered with ice and snow, there occurred a transition from nomadic, hunting-gathering culture to a sedentary one marked by settled, food-producing communities. The domestication of wild animals, the production of polished stone tools and weapons, the construction of mud or brick and timber dwellings and huge stone ceremonial centers, and the development of more sophisticated forms of social organization were some of the main features of this transition. But the defining event of the Neolithic culture was the development of agriculture: the discovery that wild grains and fruits might be planted to grow food. The transition to Neolithic culture occurred gradually and at different stages in different regions.

Science and Technology

12,000 B.C.E.	domesticated dogs (descended from Asian wolves) appear
10,000 B.C.E.	goats are domesticated; herding begins in Asia and Africa
8000 B.C.E.	clay tokens are used in Mesopotamia to tally goods
7000 B.C.E.	cloth is woven in Anatolia (now Turkey)
5000 B.C.E.	crop irrigation is first employed in Mesopotamia

Figure 0.5 Saharan rock-painting, Tassili, Algeria, ca. 8000–4000 B.C.E. Copy of the original. Men and women are shown herding domestic cattle.

The rock art paintings discovered at Tassili in Africa's Sahara Desert—once fertile grasslands—tell the story of a transition from hunting to herding and the domestication of cattle and camels (Figure **0.5**). Gradually, over a period of centuries, as hunters, gatherers, and herdsmen became farmers and food producers, the dynamic Neolithic culture emerged. Food production freed people from a nomadic way of life. They gradually settled permanent farm communities, raising high-protein crops such as wheat and barley in Asia, rice in China, and maize in the Americas. They raised goats, pigs, cattle, and sheep that provided regular sources of food and valuable by-products, such as wool and leather. The transition from the hunting-gathering phase of human subsistence to the agricultural-herding phase was a revolutionary development in human social organization, because it marked the shift from a nomadic to a sedentary way of life.

Neolithic sites excavated in Southwest Asia (especially Israel, Jordan, Turkey, Iran, and Iraq), East Asia (China and Japan), and (as late as 1000 B.C.E.) in Meso-America center on villages consisting of a number of mud- and limestone-faced huts—humankind's earliest architecture (Figure **0.6**). At Jericho, in present-day Israel, massive defense walls surrounded the town, while tombs held the ornamented remains of local villagers. At Jarmo, in northern Iraq, a community of more than 150 people harvested wheat with stone sickles. Polished stone tools, some designed especially for farming, replaced the cruder tools of Paleolithic people. Ten thousand years before plant cultivation and agriculture came to China, communities in the southern part of the country were producing pottery in the form of simple concave ceramic vessels. But it is in Southwest Asia that some of the finest examples of painted pottery have come to light. Clay vessels, decorated with abstract motifs such as the long-necked birds that march around the rim of a beaker from Susa (Figure **0.7**), held surplus foods for the lean months of winter, and woven rugs and textiles provided comfort against the wind, rain, and cold. Homemakers, artisans, and shepherds played significant roles in Neolithic society.

Agricultural life stimulated a new awareness of seasonal change and a profound respect for those life-giving powers, such as sun and rain, that were essential to the success of the harvest. The earth's fertility and the seasonal cycle were the principal concerns of the farming culture. The overwhelming number of female statuettes found

Figure 0.6 Isometric reconstruction of a Neolithic house at Hassuna, Mesopotamia (level 4). Originally mud and limestone.

in Neolithic graves suggests that Mother Earth may have become increasingly important in the transition from food gathering to food production, when fertility and agricultural abundance were vital to the life of the community. Nevertheless, as with cave art, the exact meaning and function of the so-called mother goddesses remain a matter of speculation: they may have played a role in the performance of rites celebrating seasonal regeneration, or they may have been associated with fertility cults that ensured successful childbirth. The symbolic association between the womb and Mother Earth played an important part in almost all ancient societies. In contrast with the Paleolithic "Venus" of Willendorf (see Figure 0.4), whose sexual characteristics are boldly exaggerated, the marble statuettes produced in the Cyclades, the Greek islands of the Aegean Sea, are as streamlined and highly stylized as some modern sculptures (Figure **0.8**). Although lacking the pronounced sexual characteristics of the "Venus," the Cycladic figure probably played a similar role in rituals that sought the blessings of Mother Earth.

Figure 0.8 Female figure, early Cycladic II, Late Spedos type, ca. 2600–2400 B.C.E. Marble, height 24¾ in.

Figure 0.7 Beaker painted with goats, dogs, and long-necked birds, from Susa, southwest Iran, ca. 5000–4000 B.C.E. Baked clay, height 11¼ in.

Neolithic Earthworks

Almost all early cultures regarded the dead as messengers between the material world and the spirit world, hence the need for careful burial. Neolithic peoples marked graves with **megaliths** (literally, "great stones"), upright stone slabs roofed by a capstone to form a stone tomb or **dolmen** (Figure **0.9**). At some sites, the tomb was covered over with dirt and rubble to form a mound (Figure **0.10**), symbolic of the sacred mountain (the abode of the gods) and the procreative womb (the source of regenerative life). The shape prevails in sacred architecture ranging from the Meso-American temple (see Figure 3.11) to the Buddhist shrine (see chapter 9). The dolmen tomb made use of the simplest type of architectural construction: the **post-and-lintel** principle.

At ceremonial centers and burial sites, megaliths might be placed upright in circles or multiple rows and capped by horizontal slabs. The oldest of such Neolithic earthworks are those found recently in southeastern Turkey (see LOOKING INTO, Figures 0.11 and 0.12). At a site known as Göbekli Tepe ("Potbelly Hill"), located between the Tigris and Euphrates rivers at the northwestern rim of the Fertile Crescent (see Map 0.1), archeologists have uncovered a series of at least four stone circles dating from ca. 9000 B.C.E.

The best-known Neolithic earthwork, however, is the sanctuary at Stonehenge in southern England, where a group of concentric stone circles, constructed in stages over a period of 2000 years, forms one of the most mysterious and impressive ritual spaces of the prehistoric world (see LOOKING INTO, Figures 0.13 and 0.14). It is probable that Stonehenge, a hub for neighboring Neolithic towns such as Amesbury, served as a celestial calendar, predicting the movements of the sun and moon, clocking the seasonal cycle, and thus providing information that would have been essential to an agricultural society. However, since excavations of the fifty-six pits that circle the rim of the henge have revealed numerous cremated human remains, it is likely that Stonehenge served as a major burial site.

Recent excavations at nearby Durrington Walls confirm that Stonehenge probably functioned as the site of funerary rituals for the cremated dead. Dated at around 2600 B.C.E., the huge settlement at Durrington consists

Figure 0.10 Burial site. Dolmen (upright stones supporting a horizontal slab), Crucuno, north of Carnac, France, Neolithic period.

of hundreds of houses, as well as a ceremonial complex featuring concentric timber rings. Buildings thought by archeologists to have housed religious shrines stand along a wide avenue built on the "solstice axis" that may have served as a processional highway connecting Durrington and Stonehenge.

Some scholars speculate that the model for Stonehenge may be found at yet another recently uncovered Neolithic earthwork: the settlement on the Scottish islands of Orkney. This waterside site, known as the Ness of Brodgar ("Brodgar Promontory"), includes ceremonial stone circles and earthwork walls dating from 3500 B.C.E. Excavations in 2011 brought to light polished stone tools, clay pottery, and the first evidence of building surfaces covered with red and yellow painted designs. Ongoing excavation will no doubt unlock more of the mysteries of this and other monumental Neolithic landmarks.

The Birth of Civilization

Around 4000 B.C.E., a new chapter in the history of humankind began: Neolithic villages grew in population and size. They produced surplus food and goods that might be traded with neighboring villages. The demands of increased production and trade went hand in hand with changes in division and specialization of labor, which rapidly enhanced economic efficiency. Advances in technology, such as the invention of the wheel, the plow, and the solar calendar, occurred in the earliest known civilizations of Sumer and Egypt. Wheeled carts transported people, food, and goods overland, and sailboats used the natural resource of wind for travel by water. Large-scale farming required artificial systems of irrigation, which, in turn, required cooperative effort and a high degree of communal organization. Neolithic villages grew in complexity to become the bustling cities of a new era. The birth of civilization (the word derives from the Latin *civitas*, or "city") marks the shift from rural/pastoral to urban/commercial

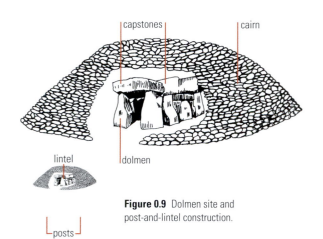

Figure 0.9 Dolmen site and post-and-lintel construction.

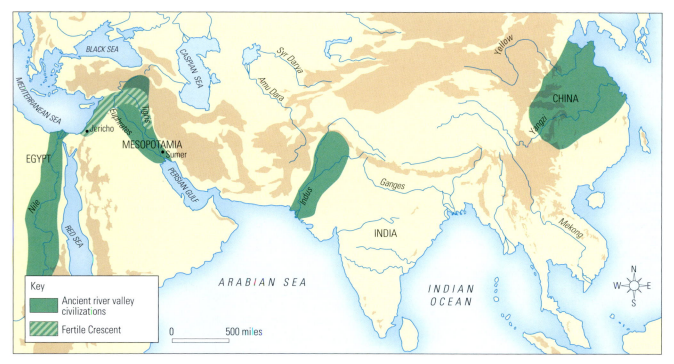

Map 0.1 Ancient River Valley Civilizations. In the four great river valleys shown on the map, agriculture flourished to support the rise of cities and the beginnings of civilization. The Nile valley regions are the site of modern-day Egypt and the Sudan. The area designating Mesopotamia and the Fertile Crescent is shared by modern-day Iraq, Iran, Syria, Israel, Lebanon, Kuwait, Bahrain, and Saudi Arabia. The Indus valley civilization was located primarily in modern-day Pakistan, northwestern India, and parts of Iran and Afghanistan.

culture; or, more specifically, the transition from simple village life to the more complex forms of social, economic, and political organization associated with urban existence.

The first civilization of the ancient world emerged in Mesopotamia, a fertile area that lay between the Tigris and Euphrates rivers of the Southwest Asian landmass (Map **0.1**). Mesopotamia formed the eastern arc of the Fertile Crescent, which stretched westward to the Nile delta. At the southeastern perimeter of the Fertile Crescent, about a dozen cities collectively constituted Sumer, the earliest civilization known to history. Shortly after the rise of Sumer, around 3500 B.C.E., Egyptian civilization emerged along the Nile River in Northeast Africa. In India, the earliest urban centers appeared in the valley of the Indus River that runs through the northwest portion of the Indian subcontinent. Chinese civilization was born in the northern part of China's vast central plain, watered by the Yellow River. The appearance of these four civilizations was not simultaneous. Fully a thousand years separate the birth of civilization in Sumer from the rise of cities in China. Two newly discovered sites, dating from ca. 3000 B.C.E., in Lima on the west coast of Peru, may be added to those of the river valley civilizations. While no evidence of writing has been found in these early American cultures, other hallmarks of civilization are evident (see chapter 3).

By comparison with the self-sustaining Neolithic village, the early city reached outward. Specialization and the division of labor stimulated productivity and encouraged trade, which, in turn, enhanced the growth of the urban economy. Activities related to the production and distribution of goods could not be committed entirely to memory; rather, they required an efficient system of accounting and record keeping.

The Evolution of Writing

Writing made it possible to preserve and transmit information. More a process than an invention, writing evolved from counting. As early as 7500 B.C.E., people used tokens—pieces of clay molded into shapes to represent specific commodities: a cone for a unit of grain, an egg shape for a unit of oil, and so on. Tokens were placed in hollow clay balls that accompanied shipments of goods. Upon arrival at their destination, the balls were broken open and the tokens—the "record" of the shipment—were counted. Eventually, traders began to stamp the tokens into wet clay to identify the content and quantity of the traded goods. By 3100 B.C.E. these pictorial symbols, or **pictographs**, had replaced the tokens, and other graphic

---

Science and Technology

4500 B.C.E.	sailboats are used in Mesopotamia
4200 B.C.E.	the first known calendar (365 days) is devised in Egypt
4000 B.C.E.	copper ores are mined and smelted by Egyptians; bricks are fired in Mesopotamian kilns
3600 B.C.E.	bronze comes into use in Mesopotamia
3500 B.C.E.	the plow, wheeled cart, potter's wheel, tokens with pictographic impressions, and fermentation processes for wine and beer are all introduced in Sumer

Neolithic Stone Circles

The circles at Göbekli Tepe, consisting of 10- to 16-ton limestone megaliths adorned with low-relief sculptures of lions, foxes, snakes, scorpions, wild boars, spiders, carrion birds, and human body parts (Figure **0.11**), belong to a larger complex (Figure **0.12**) that probably served as a religious sanctuary. Since only 5 percent of the site has been excavated, its significance for unraveling the history of our human origins is still to be determined. But the presence of such a ceremonial center in an area lacking evidence of farm-based villages suggests that open-air shrines may have preceded the more complex agricultural communities historically associated with Neolithic culture.

It is likely that Stonehenge also served as a ceremonial center. To this windswept site, 20-foot-high megaliths, some weighing 25–50 tons each, were dragged from a quarry 20 miles away, then shaped and assembled without metal tools to form a huge outer circle and an inner horseshoe of post-and-lintel stones. In the center, arranged in two additional circles, were eighty 4–6-ton bluestones transported from southwest Wales, 170 miles away (Figures **0.13** and **0.14**, and p. ii). A 35-ton **stele** (known as the Heel Stone) stands apart from the complex, marking the point—visible from the exact center of the inner circle—at which the sun rises at the summer solstice (the longest day of the year).

Figure 0.11 Göbekli Tepe pillar with low-relief animal. The T-shaped stones (ranging from 9 to 19 ft. in height) resemble stylized human beings, while the animals are visibly male, and may have served as totems.

Figure 0.12 Reconstruction of Göbekli Tepe. No burial remains have been uncovered yet; however, evidence indicates that every few decades, an earlier circle was buried, and a new one constructed. This building program seems to have terminated around 8200 B.C.E.

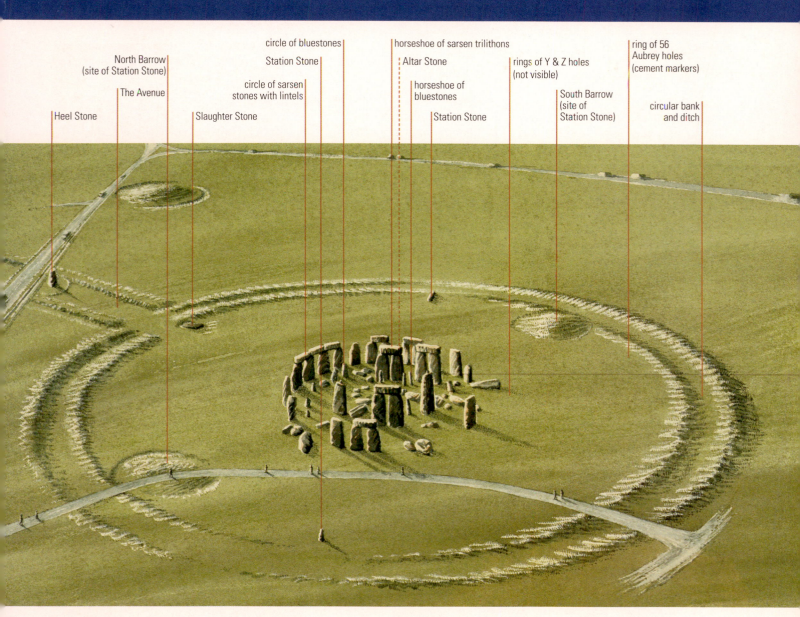

circle of bluestones

North Barrow
(site of Station Stone)

Station Stone

horseshoe of sarsen trilithons

Altar Stone

rings of Y & Z holes
(not visible)

ring of 56
Aubrey holes
(cement markers)

The Avenue

circle of sarsen
stones with lintels

horseshoe of
bluestones

South Barrow
(site of
Station Stone)

circular bank
and ditch

Heel Stone

Slaughter Stone

Station Stone

Figure 0.13 Stonehenge, Salisbury Plain, Wiltshire, England, ca. 3000–1800 B.C.E. Stone, diameter of circle 97 ft., tallest height 22 ft.

Figure 0.14 Hypthetical construction of Stonehenge. Above: raising the megaliths into an upright position by way of levers, ropes, and piled logs. Below: raising a lintel to the top of two sarsens by way of a working platform of stacked timbers.

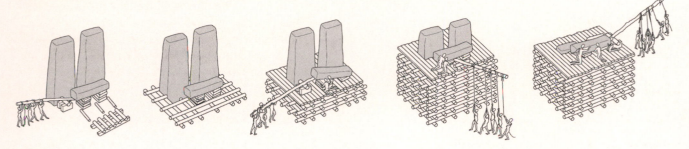

Earliest pictographs (3000 B.C.E.)	Denotation of pictographs	Pictographs in rotated position	Cuneiform signs ca. 1900 B.C.E.	Basic logographic values	
				Reading	Meaning
	head and body of a man			lú	man
	head with mouth indicated			ka	mouth
	bowl of food			ninda	food, bread
	mouth + food			kú	to eat
	stream of water			a	water
	mouth + water			nag	to drink
	fish			kua	fish
	bird			mušen	bird
	head of an ass			anše	ass
	ear of barley			še	barley

Figure 0.15 The development of Sumerian writing from a pictographic script to cuneiform script to a phonetic system.

Figure 0.16 Reverse side of a pictographic tablet from Jamdat Nasr, near Kish, Iraq, ca. 3000 B.C.E. Clay, 2⅕ × 2½ × 1½ in . The tablet lists accounts involving animals and various commodities, including bread and beer.

3100 B.C.E. cuneiform, the earliest known form of script, appears in Sumer; an early form of hieroglyphics appears in Egypt

3000 B.C.E. candles are manufactured in Egypt; cotton fabric is woven in India; Sumerian math evolves based on units of 60 (60 becomes the basic unit for measuring time)

2600 B.C.E. Imhotep (Egyptian) produces the first known medical treatise

2600 B.C.E. a lost-wax method of bronze casting is used in east Mesopotamia

2500 B.C.E. the beginning of systematic standards in weights and measurement emerges in Sumer

1600 B.C.E. Nebra Sky Disk configures the heavens

symbols (for people and places) were added to produce a total of some 1500 early pictographs. Pictographs were often combined to express an idea. For instance, the signs for "mouth" and for "food" were combined to form an **ideogram** (a sign that represents an idea or thing) meaning "to eat" (Figure **0.15**). Inscribed on tablets of wet clay, pictographs assumed a more angular and wedged shape. **Cuneiform** (from *cuneus*, the Latin word for "wedge"), a form of writing used throughout the Near East for well over 3000 years, ushered in the world's first Information Age (Figure **0.16**). Thousands of clay tablets have survived. The earliest of them come from Sumer in Mesopotamia. Most bear notations concerning production and trade, while others are inventories and business accounts, historical records, myths, prayers, and genealogies of local rulers.

In Egypt, a set of "sacred signs" known as **hieroglyphs** answered similar needs (see Figure 2.4). Ancient Egyptian writing remained a mystery to the world until 1822, when the Rosetta Stone (a black basalt slab discovered in 1799 in the Egyptian town of Rashid, or "Rosetta") was deciphered (Figure **0.17**). The stone's inscription, written in two different types of Egyptian script and one Greek script, arranged in tiers, was understood only after a number of scholars, and ultimately Jean-François Champollion (1790–1832), matched the hieroglyphs for certain Egyptian rulers (such as Cleopatra) with their names in Greek. As Champollion showed, hieroglyphic writing combined ideograms and **phonograms** (signs that represent sounds).

The development of a written language is often cited as the defining feature of a "civilized" society, but, in fact, some complex urban cultures (such as those of the pueblo communities and Andean peoples in the ancient Americas) have existed without writing systems. Writing was only one of many inventions mothered by necessity

Hieroglyphic script   Demotic script

Hence, bronze weapons were costly and available only to a small and well-to-do minority of the population. This minority formed a military elite who wielded power by virtue of superior arms. As the victory monument pictured in Figure **0.18** indicates, Sumerian warriors were outfitted with bronze shields, helmets, and lances.

The technology of bronze casting spread throughout the ancient world. Mesopotamians of the third millennium B.C.E. were among the first to use the **lost-wax** method of casting (Figure **0.19**). Spreading eastward into the Indus valley, the lost-wax technique became popular for the manufacture of jewelry, musical instruments, horse fittings, and toys (Figure **0.20**). The ancient Chinese cast the separate parts of bronze vessels in sectional clay molds, and then soldered the parts together. Master metallurgists, the Chinese transformed the techniques of bronze casting into one of the great artforms of the ancient world (see chapter 3).

The European Bronze Age, evolving during the second millennium B.C.E., left tangible evidence of ancient astronomy in the form of the Nebra Sky Disk, humankind's oldest known representation of the heavens (Figure **0.21**). This extraordinary artifact, one that until recently was thought to be a forgery, is a 5-pound, twelve-and-a-half-inch bronze disk inlaid with gold symbols representing the sun, a crescent moon, and stars. Found in the Saxon-Anhalt region of Germany and dated to ca. 1600 B.C.E., it may have functioned as a portable calendar or navigational tool.

Figure 0.17 Rosetta Stone, 196 B.C.E. Basalt, height 3 ft. 9 in. The same information is inscribed in hieroglyphic (a pictographic script), demotic script (a simplified form of hieroglyphic), and Greek.

on the threshold of the urban revolution. Technology itself would undergo dramatic transformation.

Metallurgy

At about the same time that systems of writing emerged in Mesopotamia, metal began to replace stone and bone tools. Metallurgy, which was first practiced around Asia Minor in about 4000 B.C.E., afforded humans a significant extension of control over nature by providing them with harder and more durable tools and weapons. At first, copper ore was extracted from surface deposits, but eventually metalsmiths devised sophisticated methods of mining and smelting ores. The result was bronze, an alloy of copper and tin that proved far superior to stone or bone in strength and durability. Since copper and tin were often located far apart, travel and trade were essential to Bronze Age cultures. (The discovery in 1995 of Caucasian mummies in graves found in East Asia's Gobi Desert argues for the existence of long-distance trade and cross-cultural contact.) Metallurgy was a time-consuming process that required specialized training and the division of labor.

Figure 0.18 The king of Lagash leads his phalanx into battle. Detail of Eannatum's Stele of Victory, Tello, formerly Girsu, ca. 2450 B.C.E. Limestone, 5 ft. 10⅞ in. × 4 ft. 3⅝ in.

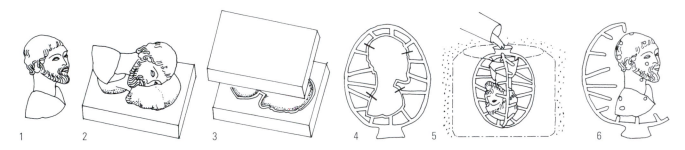

1   2   3   4   5   6

Figure 0.19 (above) The lost-wax process of bronze casting developed in Mesopotamia, third millennium B.C.E. A positive model (1) is used to make a negative mold (2), which is then coated with wax. Cool fireclay is poured into the wax shell; the mold is then removed (3). Metal rods are added to hold the layers in place, as are wax vents for the even flow of bronze (4). The whole structure is immersed in sand; the wax is burned out. Investment ready for molten bronze (5). Bronze head, ready for removal of gates and metal rods (6).

Figure 0.20 (left) Chariot from Daimabad, Maharashtra, ca. 1500 B.C.E. Bronze, 8⅝ × 20½ × 6⅞ in. Similar models of carts and chariots are found in shrines and tombs in Syria and elsewhere in West Asia, dating from the third millennium B.C.E., an era in which domesticated animals were used to transport goods on land. Along with bronze technology, wheeled vehicles gave urban communities a leading edge at the beginning of civilization.

People and Nature

Like their prehistoric ancestors, the inhabitants of the earliest civilizations lived in intimate association with nature. They looked upon the forces of nature—sun, wind, and rain—as vital and alive, indeed, as inhabited by living spirits—a belief known as **animism**. Just as they devised tools to manipulate the natural environment, so they devised strategies by which to understand and control that environment. In ancient belief systems, the living spirits of nature assumed human qualities and characteristics. They might be vengeful or conciliatory, ugly or beautiful, fickle or reliable. They might become a family of superhumans—gods and goddesses who very much resembled humans in their physical features and personalities, but whose superior strength and intelligence far exceeded that of human beings. The gods were also immortal, which made them the envy of ordinary humans. The enactment of rituals honoring one or more of the gods accompanied seasonal celebrations, and almost every other significant communal event. In the early history of civilization, goddesses seem to have outnumbered gods, and local deities reigned supreme within their own districts. By means of specially appointed priests and priestesses, who mediated between human and divine realms, ancient people forged contractual relationships with their gods: in return for divine benefits, they lived as they believed the gods would wish.

Myth and the Quest for Beginnings

Today, no less than thousands of years ago, humans are driven to explain the origins of the universe and define their place in it. While modern speculation on the origins of life usually draws on science, ancient societies formulated their answers in the shape of myth. In everyday speech, the word "myth" describes a popular fiction accepted as truth or half-truth. Historically, however, myths constitute a body of speculation that reflects the collective beliefs of a society. Myths of creation are stories that rationalize and explain the unknown. Often fantastic, they are usually grounded in the evidence of the senses, and are thus rich in visual imagery. They are closely linked to the moral values and religious systems of a given culture, since what is considered true is also often held sacred.

Figure 0.21 Nebra Sky Disk, bronze, diameter 12½ in. The golden arcs along the side and bottom were probably added later and are variously interpreted.

Almost every culture has produced a creation myth. Such myths were probably associated with rituals of seasonal renewal. The creation myths of various cultures show remarkable similarities, the most notable of which is the primacy of water as the medium for the genesis of life—a notion that modern science now supports as fact. The following four creation myths represent only a small sample of those generated over thousands of years.

The first, a hymn from the *Rig Veda*—the oldest religious literature of India—locates our beginnings in a watery darkness (see chapter 3). The second is but one example drawn from the huge fund of creation stories told by African tribal people and transmitted orally for centuries. It situates the origins of life in the slender grasses that grow in wet, marshy soil. The third, an account of creation from the *Popol Vuh* ("Sacred Book") of Central America's Maya Indians, links creation to light, thought, and language itself. Finally, from the Native American Iroquois Federation, a Mohawk tale recounts how the Good Spirit fashioned humankind in its diversity (see chapter 18).

READING 0.1 Creation Tales

"The Song of Creation" from the *Rig Veda*

Then even nothingness was not, nor existence.   1
   There was no air then, nor the heavens beyond it
   What covered it? Where was it? In whose keeping?
   Was there then cosmic water, in depths unfathomed?
Then there were neither death nor immortality,   5
   nor was there then the torch of night and day.
   The One breathed windlessly and self-sustaining.
   There was that One then, and there was no other.
At first there was only darkness wrapped in darkness.
   All this was only unillumined water.   10
   That One which came to be, enclosed in nothing,
   arose at last, born of the power of heat.
In the beginning desire descended on it—
   that was the primal seed, born of the mind.
   The sages who have searched their hearts with wisdom   15
   know that which is, is kin to that which is not.
And they have stretched their cord across the void,
   and know what was above, and what below.
   Seminal powers made fertile mighty forces
Below was strength, and over it was impulse.   20
But, after all, who knows, and who can say
   whence it all came, and how creation happened?
   The gods themselves are later than creation,
   so who knows truly whence it has arisen?
Whence all creation had its origin,   25
   he, whether he fashioned it or whether he did not,
   he, who surveys it all from highest heaven,
   he knows—or maybe even he does not know.

(India)

An African Creation Tale

. . . It is said all men sprang from Unkulunkulu, who sprang   1
up first. The earth was in existence before Unkulunkulu. He
had his origin from the earth in a bed of reeds.

All things as well as Unkulunkulu sprang from a bed of reeds—everything, both animals and corn, everything came into being with Unkulunkulu.

He looked at the sun when it was finished (worked into form as a potter works clay) and said: "There is a torch which will give you light, that you may see." He looked down on the cattle and said: 10
"These are cattle. Be ye broken off, and see the cattle and let them be your food; eat their flesh and their milk." He looked on wild animals and said: "That is such an animal. That is an elephant. That is a buffalo." He looked on the fire and said: "Kindle it, and cook, and warm yourself; and eat meat when it has been dressed by the fire." He looked on all things and said: "So and so is the name of everything."

Unkulunkulu said: "Let there be marriage among men, that there may be those who can intermarry, that children may be born and men increase on earth." He said, "Let there be black   20 chiefs; and the chief be known by his people, and it be said, 'That is the chief: assemble all of you and go to your chief.'"

(Amazulu)

From the *Popol Vuh*

This is the account of how all was in suspense, all calm, in   1 silence; all motionless, still, and the expanse of the sky was empty.

This is the first account, the first narrative. There was neither man, nor animal, birds, fishes, crabs, trees, stones, caves, ravines, grasses, nor forests; there was only the sky.

The surface of the earth had not appeared. There was only the calm sea and the great expanse of the sky.

There was nothing brought together, nothing which could make a noise, nor anything which might move, or tremble, or   10 could make noise in the sky.

There was nothing standing; only the calm water, the placid sea, alone and tranquil. Nothing existed.

There was only immobility and silence in the darkness in the night. Only the Creator, the Maker, Tepeu, Gucumatz, the Forefathers, were in the water surrounded with light. They were hidden under green and blue feathers, and were therefore called Gucumatz [the Feathered Serpent: Aztec Quetzalcoatl; Maya Kukulkan]. By nature they were great sages and great thinkers. In this manner the sky existed and also the   20 Heart of Heaven, which is the name of God and thus He is called.

Then came the word. Tepeu and Gucumatz came together in the darkness, in the night, and Tepeu and Gucumatz talked together. They talked then, discussing and deliberating; they agreed, they united their words and their thoughts.

Then while they meditated, it became clear to them that when dawn would break, man must appear. Then they planned the creation, and the growth of the trees and the thickets and the birth of life and the creation of man. Thus it was arranged   30 in the darkness and in the night by the Heart of Heaven who is called Huracán.

Then Tepeu and Gucumatz came together; then they conferred about life and light, what they would do so that there would be light and dawn, who it would be who would provide food and sustenance.

Thus let it be done! Let the emptiness be filled! Let the water recede and make a void, let the earth appear and

become solid; let it be done. Thus they spoke. Let there be
light, let there be dawn in the sky and on the earth! There shall 40
be neither glory nor grandeur in our creation and formation
until the human being is made, man is formed. So they spoke.

Then the earth was created by them. So it was, in truth,
that they created the earth. Earth! . . . they said, and instantly
it was made. . . .

(Maya)

A Native American Creation Tale, "How Man Was Created"

After Sat-kon-se-ri-io, the Good Spirit, had made the 1
animals, birds, and other creatures and had placed them to
live and multiply upon the earth, he rested. As he gazed
around at his various creations, it seemed to him that there
was something lacking. For a long time the Good Spirit
pondered over this thought. Finally he decided to make a
creature that would resemble himself.

Going to the bank of a river he took a piece of clay, and out
of it he fashioned a little clay man. After he had modeled it, he
built a fire and, setting the little clay man in the fire, waited 10
for it to bake. The day was beautiful. The songs of the birds
filled the air. The river sang a song and, as the Good Spirit
listened to this song, he became very sleepy. He soon fell
asleep beside the fire. When he finally awoke, he rushed to
the fire and removed the clay man. He had slept too long.
His little man was burnt black. According to the Mohawks,
this little man was the first Negro. His skin was black. He had
been overbaked.

The Good Spirit was not satisfied. Taking a fresh piece of
clay, he fashioned another man and, placing him in the fire, 20
waited for him to bake, determined this time to stay awake

and watch his little man to see that he would not be
overbaked. But the river sang its usual sleepy song. The Good
Spirit, in spite of all he could do, fell asleep. But this time he
slept only a little while. Awakening at last, he ran to the fire
and removed his little man. Behold, it was half baked.
This, say the Mohawks, was the first white man. He was
half baked!

The Good Spirit was still unsatisfied. Searching along the
riverbank he hunted until he found a bed of perfect red clay. 30
This time he took great care and modeled a very fine clay man.
Taking the clay man to the fire, he allowed it to bake.
Determined to stay awake, the Good Spirit stood beside the
fire, after a while Sat-kon-se-ri-io removed the clay man.
Behold, it was just right—a man the red color of the sunset sky.
It was the first Mohawk Indian.

(Mohawk)

Q What do all the creation myths in this reading have in common? How do they differ?

Civilization emerged not as a fleeting moment of change, but as a slow process of urban growth. By the operation of an increasingly refined abstract intelligence, and by means of ingenuity, imagination, and cooperation, the earliest human beings took the first steps in perpetuating their own survival and the security of their communities. Technology provided the tools for manipulating nature, while mythology and the arts lent meaning and purpose to nature's mysteries. By such cultural achievements, the earliest human beings laid the foundations for the humanistic tradition.

Glossary

animism the belief that the forces of nature are inhabited by spirits

clan a group that traces its descent from a common ancestor

culture the sum total of those things (including traditions, techniques, material goods, and symbol systems) that people have invented, developed, and transmitted

cuneiform ("wedge-shaped") one of humankind's earliest writing systems, consisting of wedge-shaped marks impressed into clay by means of a reed stylus

dolmen a stone tomb formed by two posts capped by a lintel

hieroglyph (Greek, "sacred sign") the pictographic script of ancient Egypt

hominid any of a family of bipedal primate mammals, including modern humans and their ancestors, the earliest of which is *Australopithecus*

ideogram a sign that represents an idea or thing

lost wax (also French, *cire-perdu*) a method of metal casting in which a figure is modeled in wax, then enclosed in a clay mold that is fired; the wax melts, and molten metal is poured in to replace it; finally, the clay mold is removed and the solid metal form is polished (see Figure 0.19)

megalith a large, roughly shaped stone, often used in ancient architectural construction

naturalism a descriptive approach to the visual world that seeks to imitate natural appearance

phonogram a sign that represents a sound

pictograph a pictorial symbol used in humankind's earliest systems of writing

polychrome having many or various colors

post-and-lintel the simplest form of architectural construction, consisting of vertical members (posts) and supporting horizontals (lintels) (see Figure 0.9)

prehistory the study of history before written records

shaman a priestly leader or healer who mediates between the natural and the spiritual worlds

stele an upright stone slab or pillar

totem a heraldic emblem of a tribe, family, or clan

Chapter 1

Mesopotamia: Gods, Rulers, and the Social Order

ca. 3500–330 B.C.E.

"From the days of old there is no permanence.
The sleeping and the dead, how alike they are, they are like a painted death."
The Epic of Gilgamesh

Figure 1.1 Winged human-headed bull from Khorsabad, Iraq, ca. 720 B.C.E. Limestone, height 13 ft. 10 in. (approx.). Hybrid creatures bearing the features of the monarch guarded the gateways of the Assyrian palace at Khorsabad in present-day Iraq.

Mesopotamia, literally "the land between the two rivers," was the stage upon which many civilizations rose and fell. Rather than tell the story of each, we will explore their cultural legacies by way of three principal themes: gods, rulers, and social organization. The first deals with the belief systems that linked the secular and spiritual realms; the second focuses on the establishment of leadership within the earliest urban communities; and the third examines the nature of the social order as revealed in law and other forms of cultural expression. These three themes, which dominate the visual and literary works of humankind's earliest civilizations, reflect universal concerns that remain with us today. Religious beliefs and political and social practices differ from culture to culture, but all belief systems and social practices reflect the human effort to come to terms with the unknown, to master the perils of the environment, to achieve communal cooperation, and to understand the destiny and purpose of humankind.

The Land Between the Two Rivers

The land between the Tigris and Euphrates rivers formed part of a fertile crescent that occupied the western end of Asia (Map **1.1**). Sumer, the first of Mesopotamia's many civilizations, arose some time around 3500 B.C.E., at the point at which the Tigris and Euphrates empty into the Persian Gulf. Watered by the rivers, the rich soil at the southeastern tip of the Fertile Crescent promoted agricultural activity and supported the growth of humankind's first cities: Uruk, Ur, Kish, Nippur, and Lagash. However, the rivers upon which life depended overflowed unpredictably, often devastating whole villages and cities. Mesopotamians also suffered fierce changes in weather, ranging from violent rainstorms, wind, and hail, to long periods of drought.

Compounding these conditions of insecurity, the region experienced repeated attacks by tribal nomads, who, attracted by the fertile lands along the rivers, descended from the mountainous areas to the north, bringing an end to the history of one civilization, and establishing a new civilization that often absorbed the culture of the previous one.

Sumer consisted of small groups of self-ruling city-states. Other civilizations, such as the Assyrian, founded great empires, while the people of still another, the Hebrews, remained nomadic for centuries before forming a political state. No one language or single, continuous form of government united these various Mesopotamian peoples; yet they shared a common world-view and, with the exception of the Hebrews, a common belief system based in **polytheism**, the worship of many gods.

Map 1.1 Mesopotamia, 3500–2000 B.C.E. This area of Southwest Asia is often referred to as the "Near East" or "Middle East," the latter a Eurocentric term coined by the British ca. 1900. The region of the Hittite Empire is modern-day Turkey. For the other modern-day countries in these territories, see the legend to Map 0.1.

The Gods of Mesopotamia

Mesopotamia's gods and goddesses were associated with the forces of nature. Like its climate, its divinities were fierce and capricious, its mythology filled with physical and spiritual woe, and its cosmology based on the themes of chaos and conflict. *The Babylonian Creation*, humankind's earliest cosmological myth, illustrates all these conditions. A Sumerian poem recorded early in the second millennium B.C.E., and recited during the festival of the New Year, it celebrates the birth of the gods and the order of creation. It describes a universe that originated by means of spontaneous generation: at a moment when there was neither heaven nor earth, the sweet and bitter waters "mingled" to produce the first family of gods.

As the story unfolds, chaos and discord prevail amid the reign of Tiamat, the Great Mother of the primeval waters, until Marduk, hero-god and offspring of Wisdom, takes matters in hand: he destroys the Great Mother and proceeds to establish a new order. Marduk founds the holy city of Babylon (literally, "home of the gods") and creates human beings, whose purpose it is to serve heaven's squabbling divinities.

READING 1.1 From *The Babylonian Creation*

When there was no heaven,   1
no earth, no height, no depth, no name,
   when Apsu[1] was alone,
the sweet water, the first begetter; and Tiamat[2]
   the bitter water, and that   5
return to the womb, her Mummu,[3]
   when there were no gods—

   When sweet and bitter
mingled together, no reed was plaited, no rushes
   muddied the water,   10
the gods were nameless, natureless, futureless, then
   from Apsu and Tiamat
in the waters gods were created, in the waters
   silt precipitated,

Lahmu and Lahamu,[4]   15
were named; they were not yet old,
   not yet grown tall
when Anshar and Kishar[5] overtook them both,
   the lines of sky and earth
stretched where horizons meet to separate   20
   cloud from silt.

   Days on days, years

[1] The primeval sweet waters.
[2] The primeval bitter waters.
[3] One of the primordial beings of the universe.
[4] Male and female primordial beings.
[5] The horizon of the sky (male) and the horizon of the earth (female).

on years passed till Anu,[6] the empty heaven,
   heir and supplanter,
first-born of his father, in his own nature   25
   begot of Nudimmud-Ea[7]
intellect, wisdom, wider than heaven's horizon,
   the strongest of all the kindred.

Discord broke out among the gods although they were
brothers, warring and jarring in the belly of Tiamat,   30
heaven shook, it reeled with the surge of the dance.
Apsu could not silence the clamor. Their behavior was
bad, overbearing, and proud. . . .

[Ea kills Apsu; Marduk is born, and Tiamat spawns serpents and monsters to make war on the gods.]

When her labor of creation was ended, against her children   1
Tiamat began preparations of war. This was the evil she did to
requite Apsu, this was the evil news that came to Ea.

When he had learned how matters lay he was stunned, he sat in
black silence till rage had worked itself out; then he remembered
the gods before him. He went to Anshar, his father's father, and
told him how Tiamat plotted,

   "She loathes us, father, our mother Tiamat has raised up
that Company, she rages in turbulence and all have joined her,
all those gods whom you begot,   10

   "Together they jostle the ranks to march with Tiamat, day
and night furiously they plot, the growling roaring rout, ready
for battle, while the Old Hag, the first mother, mothers a new
brood. . . ."

[The gods make Marduk Supreme Commander of the wars; he leads the attack on Tiamat.]

Then Marduk made a bow and strung it to be his own weapon,   1
he set the arrow against the bow-string, in his right hand he
grasped the mace and lifted it up, bow and quiver hung at his
side, lightnings played in front of him, he was altogether an
incandescence.

He netted a net, a snare for Tiamat; the winds from their
quarters held it, south wind, north, east wind, west, and no
part of Tiamat could escape. . . .

He turned back to where Tiamat lay bound, he straddled the
legs and smashed her skull (for the mace was merciless), he   10
severed the arteries and the blood streamed down the north
wind to the unknown ends of the world.

When the gods saw all this they laughed out loud, and they
sent him presents. They sent him their thankful tributes.

The lord rested; he gazed at the huge body, pondering how to

[6] God of the sky (the offspring of Anshar and Kishar).
[7] Another name for Ea, god of wisdom (the offspring of Anu).

use it, what to create from the dead carcass. He split it apart like a cockle-shell; with the upper half he constructed the arc of sky, he pulled down the bar and set a watch on the waters, so they should never escape. . . .

[Marduk makes Babylon "the home of the gods" and proceeds to create Man.]

Now that Marduk has heard what it is the gods are saying, he   1
is moved with desire to create a work of consummate art. He
told Ea the deep thought in his heart.

> Blood to blood
> I join,
> blood to bone
> I form
> an original thing,
> its name is MAN,
> aboriginal man   10
> is mine in making.
> All his occupations
> are faithful service,
> the gods that fell
> have rest,
> I will subtly alter
> their operations,
> divided companies
> equally blest.

Ea answered with carefully chosen words, completing the   20
plan for the gods' comfort. He said to Marduk,
     "Let one of the kindred be taken; only one need die for the
new creation. Bring the gods together in the Great Assembly;
there let the guilty die, so the rest may live."

Q **How does this creation myth compare with those in Reading 0.1?**

From Matriarchy to Patriarchy

Marduk's destruction of the Great Mother Tiamat reflects the shift from matriarchy to patriarchy in the polytheistic history of the ancient world. Whereas many early cultures venerated female divinities, ancient civilizations gradually came to give primacy to male deities. Some of the earliest literature from Sumer celebrates the colorful "Queen of Heaven" known as Inanna (or Ishtar), goddess of chaos and love, associated with fertility, the moon, and the planet Venus (Figure **1.2**). She seems to have held priestly authority in the ancient city of Uruk. The most famous of the myths surrounding Inanna recounts her descent to the underworld, where she consigns her mate (her husband or brother) Dumuzi to the shadowy realm of darkness. The descent myth, which appears in the literature of a great many ancient agricultural societies, including those of Egypt and Greece, was probably associated with seasonal celebrations involving the cycles of vegetation: the "birth" of the crops in spring and their "death" in winter, when vegetation disappears from the earth.

Principal Mesopotamian Gods

Name	Role
Adad	storm and rain god
Anu	father of the gods, god of heaven
Apsu	god of the primeval sweet waters
Dumuzi (Tammuz)	god of vegetation, fertility, and the underworld; husband of Ishtar
Ea	god of wisdom and patron of the arts
Enlil	god of earth, wind, and air
Ishtar (Inanna)	goddess of love, fertility, and war; Queen of Heaven
Ninhursag	mother goddess, creator of vegetation; wife of Enlil
Nisaba	goddess of grain
Shamash	god of the sun; judge and law-giver; god of wisdom
Sin (Nanna)	goddess of the moon

The Search for Immortality

The theme of human vulnerability and the search for everlasting life are the central motifs in the *Epic of Gilgamesh*, the world's first epic. An **epic**, that is, a long narrative poem that recounts the deeds of a hero in quest of meaning and identity, embodies the ideals and values of the culture from which it comes. The *Epic of Gilgamesh* was recited orally for centuries before it was recorded at Sumer in the late third millennium B.C.E. It may have been chanted or sung to the accompaniment of a harp, such as those found in the royal graves at Ur (Figures **1.3** and **1.4**). As literature, it precedes the Hebrew Bible and all the other major writings of antiquity. Its hero is a semihistorical figure who probably ruled the ancient Sumerian city of Uruk around 2800 B.C.E. Described as two-thirds god and one-third man, Gilgamesh is blessed by the gods with beauty and courage. But when he spurns the affections of the Queen of Heaven, Ishtar, he is punished with the loss of his dearest companion, Enkidu. Despairing over Enkidu's death, Gilgamesh undertakes a long and hazardous quest in search of everlasting life. He meets Utnapishtim, a mortal who (like Noah of the Hebrew Bible) has saved humankind from a devastating flood. As a reward he (unlike Noah) has received the secret Gilgamesh seeks: eternal life. Utnapishtim warns Gilgamesh that all classes of people—the master and the slave—are equal in death. Nevertheless, he guides Gilgamesh to the plant that miraculously restores lost youth. Although Gilgamesh retrieves the plant, he guards it carelessly: while he sleeps, it is snatched by a serpent (whose ability to shed its skin made it an ancient symbol of rebirth).

Figure 1.2 The "Queen of Heaven," Babylonian goddess, southern Iraq, 1800–1750 B.C.E. Painted terracotta plaque, height 19½ in (approx.). Scholars identify this winged figure as Inanna (or Ishtar). She wears a horned headdress and holds the rod and ring of authority in each hand. She stands on a pair of lions, symbols of power, and is flanked by owls, symbols of wisdom. The plaque has lost most of its brightly painted colors.

Figure 1.3 Gilgamesh between two human-headed bulls (top portion). Soundbox of a harp, from Ur, Iraq, ca. 2600 B.C.E. Wood with inlaid gold, lapis lazuli, and shell, height 12 in (approx.). Some of the other images that figure in the epic, such as the Man-Scorpion, appear in the other registers of the soundbox of the harp. The meaning of these figures is obscure; they may illustrate nonsurviving portions of the epic, or they may refer to popular fables.

Figure 1.4 Harp (reconstructed) from Ur, ca. 2600 B.C.E. Wood and inlays of gold, lapis lazuli, and shell, height 3 ft. 6 in.

READING 1.2 From the *Epic of Gilgamesh*

O Gilgamesh, Lord of Kullab,[1] great is thy praise. This was [1]
the man to whom all things were known; this was the king
who knew the countries of the world. He was wise, he saw
mysteries and knew secret things, he brought us a tale of the
days before the flood. He went on a long journey, was weary,
worn-out with labor, and returning engraved on a stone the
whole story.

When the Gods created Gilgamesh they gave him a perfect
body. Shamash the glorious sun endowed him with beauty,
Adad the god of the storm endowed him with courage, the [10]
great gods made his beauty perfect, surpassing all others.
Two thirds they made him god and one third man.

In Uruk[2] he built walls, a great rampart, and the temple of
blessed Eanna for the god of the firmament Anu, and for Ishtar
the goddess of love [see Figure 1.2].

*[Gilgamesh and his bosom companion, Enkidu, destroy Humbaba,
the guardian of the cedar forest, and perform other heroic deeds.
But Gilgamesh spurns the affections of Ishtar, and in revenge, she
takes Enkidu's life.]*

Bitterly Gilgamesh wept for his friend Enkidu; he wandered
over the wilderness as a hunter, he roamed over the plains;
in his bitterness he cried, "How can I rest, how can I be at
peace? Despair is in my heart. What my brother is now, that
shall I be when I am dead. Because I am afraid of death I will [20]
go as best I can to find Utnapishtim whom they call the
Faraway, for he has entered the assembly of the gods." So
Gilgamesh traveled over the wilderness, he wandered over the
grasslands, a long journey, in search of Utnapishtim, whom the
gods took after the deluge; and they set him to live in the land
of Dilmun,[3] in the garden of the sun; and to him alone of men
they gave everlasting life.

At night when he came to the mountain passes Gilgamesh
prayed: "In these mountain passes long ago I saw lions, I was
afraid and I lifted my eyes to the moon; I prayed and my [30]
prayers went up to the gods, so now, O moon god Sin, protect
me." When he had prayed he lay down to sleep, until he was
woken from out of a dream. He saw the lions round him
glorying in life; then he took his ax in his hand, he drew
his sword from his belt, and struck and destroyed and
scattered them.

So at length Gilgamesh came to that great mountain whose
name is Mashu, the mountain which guards the rising and the
setting sun. Its twin peaks are as high as the wall of heaven
and its paps reach down to the underworld. At its gate the [40]
Scorpions stand guard, half man and half dragon; their glory is
terrifying, their stare strikes death into men, their shimmering
halo sweeps the mountains that guard the rising sun. When
Gilgamesh saw them he shielded his eyes for the length of a
moment only; then he took courage and approached. When
they saw him so undismayed the Man-Scorpion called to his
mate, "This one who comes to us now is flesh of the gods."
The mate of the Man-Scorpion answered, "Two thirds is god
but one third is man."

Then he called to the man Gilgamesh, he called to the child [50]
of the gods: "Why have you come so great a journey; for what
have you traveled so far, crossing the dangerous waters; tell

me the reason for your coming?" Gilgamesh answered, "For
Enkidu; I loved him dearly, together we endured all kinds of
hardships; on his account I have come, for the common lot of
man has taken him. I have wept for him day and night, I would
not give up his body for burial, I thought my friend would come
back because of my weeping. Since he went, my life is
nothing; that is why I have traveled here in search of
Utnapishtim my father; for men say he has entered the [60]
assembly of the gods, and has found everlasting life. I have
a desire to question him concerning the living and the dead."
The Man-Scorpion opened his mouth and said, speaking to
Gilgamesh, "No man born of woman has done what you have
asked, no mortal man has gone into the mountain; the length
of it is twelve leagues[4] of darkness; in it there is no light, but
the heart is oppressed with darkness. From the rising of the
sun to the setting of the sun there is no light." Gilgamesh said,
"Although I should go in sorrow and in pain, with sighing and
with weeping, still I must go. Open the gate of the mountain." [70]
And the Man-Scorpion said, "Go, Gilgamesh, I permit you to
pass through the mountain of Mashu and through the high
ranges; may your feet carry you safely home. The gate of the
mountain is open."

When Gilgamesh heard this he did as the Man-Scorpion
had said, he followed the sun's road to his rising, through the
mountain. When he had gone one league the darkness
became thick around him, for there was no light, he could see
nothing ahead and nothing behind him. After two leagues the
darkness was thick and there was no light, he could see [80]
nothing ahead and nothing behind him. After three leagues
the darkness was thick, and there was no light, he could see
nothing ahead and nothing behind him. After four leagues
the darkness was thick and there was no light, he could see
nothing ahead and nothing behind him. At the end of five
leagues the darkness was thick and there was no light, he
could see nothing ahead and nothing behind him. At the end
of six leagues the darkness was thick and there was no light,
he could see nothing ahead and nothing behind him. When he
had gone seven leagues the darkness was thick and there was [90]
no light, he could see nothing ahead and nothing behind him.
When he had gone eight leagues Gilgamesh gave a great cry,
for the darkness was thick and he could see nothing ahead
and nothing behind him. After nine leagues he felt the north
wind on his face, but the darkness was thick and there was
no light, he could see nothing ahead and nothing behind him.
After ten leagues the end was near. After eleven leagues the
dawn light appeared. At the end of twelve leagues the sun
streamed out.

There was the garden of the gods; all round him stood [100]
bushes bearing gems. Seeing it he went down at once, for
there was fruit of carnelian with the vine hanging from it,
beautiful to look at; lapis lazuli leaves hung thick with fruit,
sweet to see. For thorns and thistles there were hematite and

[1] Part of Uruk, a city located in Sumer.
[2] Gilgamesh was the fifth ruler in the dynasty of Uruk after the flood.
[3] The Sumerian paradise, a mythical land resembling the Garden of
Eden described in the Hebrew Bible.
[4] Approximately 36 miles.

rare stones, agate, and pearls from out of the sea. While Gilgamesh walked in the garden by the edge of the sea Shamash[5] saw him, and he saw that he was dressed in the skins of animals and ate their flesh. He was distressed, and he spoke and said, "No mortal man has gone this way before, nor will, as long as the winds drive over the sea." And to Gilgamesh he said, "You will never find the life for which you are searching." Gilgamesh said to glorious Shamash, "Now that I have toiled and strayed so far over the wilderness, am I to sleep, and let the earth cover my head forever? Let my eyes see the sun until they are dazzled with looking. Although I am no better than a dead man, still let me see the light of the sun." 110

[Gilgamesh meets Siduri, the maker of wine, who advises him to give up his search and value more highly the good things of the earth. Gilgamesh prepares to cross the Ocean and, with the help of the ferryman Urshanabi, finally reaches Dilmun, the home of Utnapishtim.]

"Oh, father Utnapishtim, you who have entered the assembly of the gods, I wish to question you concerning the living and the dead, how shall I find the life for which I am searching?" 120

Utnapishtim said, "There is no permanence. Do we build a house to stand for ever, do we seal a contract to hold for all time? Do brothers divide an inheritance to keep for ever, does the flood-time of rivers endure? It is only the nymph of the dragonfly who sheds her larva and sees the sun in his glory. From the days of old there is no permanence. The sleeping and the dead, how alike they are, they are like a painted death. What is there between the master and the servant when both have fulfilled their doom? When the Annunaki, the judges, come together, and Mammetun the mother of destinies, together they decree the fates of men. Life and death they allot but the day of death they do not disclose." 130

Then Gilgamesh said to Utnapishtim the Faraway, "I look at you now, Utnapishtim, and your appearance is no different from mine; there is nothing strange in your features. I thought I should find you like a hero prepared for battle, but you lie here taking your ease on your back. Tell me truly, how was it that you came to enter the company of the gods and to possess everlasting life?" Utnapishtim said to Gilgamesh, "I will reveal to you a mystery, I will tell you a secret of the gods." 140

[Utnapishtim relates the story of the flood.]

In those days the world teemed, the people multiplied, the world bellowed like a wild bull, and the great god was aroused by the clamor. Enlil heard the clamor and he said to the gods in council, "The uproar of mankind is intolerable and sleep is no longer possible by reason of the babel." So the gods in their hearts were moved to let loose the deluge; but my lord Ea warned me in a dream. He whispered their words to my house of reeds. . . . "Tear down your house, I say, and build a boat. These are the measurements of the barque as you shall build her: let her beam equal her length, let her deck be roofed like the vault that covers the abyss; then take up into the boat the seed of all living creatures. . . ." 150

For six days and six nights the winds blew, torrent and tempest and flood overwhelmed the world, tempest and flood

raged together like warring hosts. When the seventh day dawned the storm from the south subsided, the sea grew calm, the flood was stilled; I looked at the face of the world and there was silence, all mankind was turned to clay. The surface of the sea stretched as flat as a roof-top; I opened a hatch and the light fell on my face. Then I bowed low, I sat down and I wept, the tears streamed down my face, for on every side was the waste of water. 160

[Utnapishtim leads Gilgamesh to Urshanabi the Ferryman.]

Then Gilgamesh and Urshanabi launched the boat onto the water and boarded it, and they made ready to sail away; but the wife of Utnapishtim the Faraway said to him, "Gilgamesh came here wearied out, he is worn out; what will you give him to carry him back to his own country?" So Utnapishtim spoke, and Gilgamesh took a pole and brought the boat in to the bank. 170 "Gilgamesh, you came here a man wearied out, you have worn yourself out; what shall I give you to carry you back to your own country? Gilgamesh, I shall reveal a secret thing, it is a mystery of the gods that I am telling you. There is a plant that grows under the water, it has a prickle like a thorn, like a rose; it will wound your hands, but if you succeed in taking it, then your hands will hold that which restores his lost youth to a man."

When Gilgamesh heard this he opened the sluices so that a sweet-water current might carry him out to the deepest channel; he tied heavy stones to his feet and they dragged him 180 down to the water-bed. There he saw the plant growing; although it pricked him he took it in his hands; then he cut the heavy stones from his feet, and the sea carried him and threw him on the shore. Gilgamesh said to Urshanabi the ferryman, "Come here, and see this marvelous plant. By its virtue a man may win back all his former strength. I will take it to Uruk of the strong walls; there I will give it to the old to eat. Its name shall be 'the Old Men are Young Again'; and at last I shall eat it myself and have back all my lost youth." So Gilgamesh returned by the gate through which he had come, Gilgamesh 190 and Urshanabi went together. They traveled their twenty leagues and then they broke their fast; after thirty leagues they stopped for the night.

Gilgamesh saw a well of cool water and he went down and bathed; but deep in the pool there was lying a serpent,[6] and the serpent sensed the sweetness of the flower. It rose out of the water and snatched it away, and immediately it sloughed its skin and returned to the well. Then Gilgamesh sat down and wept, the tears ran down his face, and he took the hand of Urshanabi; "O Urshanabi, was it for this that I toiled with 200 my hands, is it for this I have wrung out my heart's blood? For myself I have gained nothing; not I, but the beast of the earth has joy of it now. Already the stream has carried it twenty leagues back to the channels where I found it. I found a sign and now I have lost it. Let us leave the boat on the bank and go."

Q **What makes Gilgamesh an epic hero? Are there any comparable figures in contemporary literature or life?**

---

5 The Semitic sun god.
6 More literally "earth lion" or "chameleon."

The *Epic of Gilgamesh* is important not only as the world's first epic poem, but also as the earliest known literary work that tries to come to terms with death, or nonbeing. Its subtext is the profound human need for an *immortality ideology**—a body of beliefs that anticipates the survival of some aspect of the self in a life hereafter. Typical of the mythic hero, Gilgamesh is driven to discover his human limits, to bring about change through human ingenuity, but his quest for personal immortality is frustrated and his goals remain unfulfilled.

The Rulers of Mesopotamia

The area collectively known as Sumer was a loosely knit group of city-states, that is, urban centers that governed the neighboring countryside. Here, men and women produced humankind's earliest Bronze Age technology and refined the cuneiform script that became the first written language. They began the use of a base-60 number system that is the origin of the seconds and minutes still used today in telling time. In each of the city-states of Sumer, individual priest-kings ruled as agents of one or another of the gods. The priest-king led the army, regulated the supply and distribution of food, and provided political and religious leadership. From the temple at his palace, he conducted the services that were designed to win the favor of the gods.

Disunited and rivalrous, the city-states of Sumer were vulnerable to invasion. Around 2350 B.C.E., a gifted Akkadian warlord named Sargon I (Figure **1.5**) conquered Sumer and united the city-states under his command. For fifty-six years, he reigned as **theocratic monarch** (sole ruler and representative of the gods). Consolidating various peoples and language groups, Sargon created the world's first multi-ethnic **empire**, extending his authority from Elam (see Map 1.1) to the Mediterranean Sea. By 2000 B.C.E., however, his dynasty collapsed under the attacks of nomadic tribespeople from the north. The invaders—establishing the pattern that dominated all of Mesopotamian history—built on the accomplishments of the very states they conquered. So, theocratic monarchy, religious polytheism, and established traditions of trade and barter would prevail from civilization to civilization. The myths and legends, indeed the *Epic of Gilgamesh* itself, would be transmitted from century to century to be transcribed in ever more refined versions of cuneiform script.

The Social Order

In the newly formed civilizations of the ancient world, community life demanded collective effort in matters of production and distribution, as well as in the irrigation of fields and the construction of roads, temples, palaces, and military defenses. Specialization of labor and the complexity of urban life encouraged the development of social classes with different kinds of training, different

Figure 1.5 Head of the Akkadian ruler Sargon I, from Nineveh, Iraq, ca. 2350 B.C.E. Bronze, height 12 in. Iraq Museum, Baghdad.

---

* The phrase is from Ernest Becker. *The Denial of Death.* New York: The Free Press, 1973.

The Standard of Ur

The Standard of Ur constitutes a visual text that sheds light on class divisions and royal authority in ancient Mesopotamian culture. On the side of the panel generally called "War," the lowest register records a battle in which four-wheeled chariots trample the enemy; in the middle register, prisoners are stripped of their clothes; and in the top register, they are paraded before the ruler and his officials. The top register of the panel known as "Peace" depicts a victory banquet: the ruler and six of his officials, entertained by a harpist, raise their goblets. The middle register shows a procession of servants herding animals that will probably serve as culinary fare or as sacrificial tribute; on the bottom register, foreigners (probably prisoners of war) carry bundles on their backs.

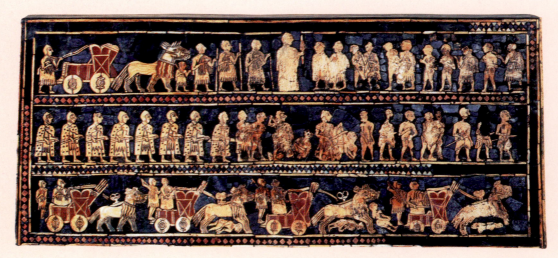

Figure 1.6 The Standard of Ur, ca. 2700 B.C.E. Double-sided panel inlaid with shell, lapis lazuli, and red limestone, 8 × 19 in. (approx.). Leonard Woolley, the early twentieth-century British archeologist who excavated Ur, imagined that the object was carried on a pole as a battle standard. More recently, scholars have suggested that the panels belong to the soundbox of a musical instrument.

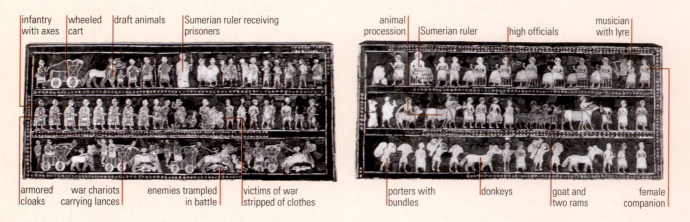

infantry with axes | wheeled cart | draft animals | Sumerian ruler receiving prisoners

armored cloaks | war chariots carrying lances | enemies trampled in battle | victims of war stripped of clothes

animal procession | Sumerian ruler | high officials | musician with lyre

porters with bundles | donkeys | goat and two rams | female companion

responsibilities, and different types of authority. In the first civilizations, the priest who prepared the wine in the ritual vessel, the soldier who protected the city, and the farmer who cultivated the field represented fairly distinct classes of people with unique duties and responsibilities to society as a whole.

The social order and division of labor that prevailed in Mesopotamia around 2700 B.C.E. are depicted in the "Standard of Ur," a double-sided wooden panel found in the royal tombs excavated at the city of Ur (see LOOKING INTO, Figure **1.6**). The panel, ornamented in **mosaic** consisting of mother-of-pearl, red limestone, and **lapis lazuli** (a semiprecious blue stone), appears to commemorate a Sumerian victory. Leonard Woolley, the early twentieth-century British archeologist who excavated Ur, imagined that the object was carried on a pole as a battle standard, but more recently scholars have suggested that the panels belong to the soundbox of a musical instrument.

Law and the Social Order in Babylon

Shortly after 2000 B.C.E., rulers of the city-state of Babylon unified the neighboring territories of Sumer to establish the First Babylonian Empire. In an effort to unite these regions politically and provide them with effective leadership, Babylon's sixth ruler, Hammurabi, called for a systematic codification of existing legal practices. He sent out envoys to collect the local statutes and had them consolidated into a single body of law. Hammurabi's Code—a collection of 282 clauses engraved on a 7-foot-high stele— is our most valuable index to life in ancient Mesopotamia (Figure **1.7**). The Code is not the first example of recorded law among the Babylonian kings; it is, however, the most extensive and comprehensive set of laws to survive from ancient times. Although Hammurabi's Code addressed primarily secular matters, it bore the force of divine decree. This fact is indicated in the prologue to the Code, where Hammurabi claims descent from the gods. It is also manifested visually in the low-relief carving that appears at the top of the stele: here, in a scene that calls to mind the story of the biblical Moses on Mount Sinai, Hammurabi is pictured receiving the law (symbolized by a staff) from the sun god Shamash.

Written law represented a landmark advance in the development of human rights in that it protected the individual from the capricious decisions of monarchs. Unwritten law was subject to the hazards of memory and

Figure 1.7 Stele of Hammurabi, first Babylonian dynasty, ca. 1750 B.C.E. Basalt, entire stele 7 ft. 4½ in. × 25½ in. (approx.). Wearing a conical crown topped with bull's horns, and discharging flames from his shoulders, the god Shamash sits enthroned atop a sacred mountain symbolized by triangular markings beneath his feet.

Science and Technology

1800 B.C.E.	multiplication tables are devised in Babylon[†]
1750 B.C.E.	mathematicians in Babylon develop quadratic equations, square roots, cube roots, and an approximate value of *pi*
1700 B.C.E.	windmills are employed for irrigation in Babylon

[†]*All dates in this chapter are approximate.*

the eccentricities of the powerful. Written law, on the other hand, permitted a more impersonal (if more objective and impartial) kind of justice than did oral law. It replaced the flexibility of the spoken word with the rigidity of the written word. It did not usually recognize exceptions and was not easily or quickly changed. Ultimately, recorded law shifted the burden of judgment from the individual ruler to the legal establishment. Although written law necessarily restricted individual freedom, it safeguarded the basic values of the community.

Hammurabi's Code covers a broad spectrum of moral, social, and commercial obligations. Its civil and criminal statutes specify penalties for murder, theft, incest, adultery, kidnapping, assault and battery, and many other crimes. More importantly for our understanding of ancient culture, it is a storehouse of information concerning the nature of class divisions, family relations, and human rights. The Code informs us, for instance, on matters of inheritance (clauses 162 and 168), professional obligations (clauses 218, 219, 229, and 232), and the individual's responsibilities to the community (clauses 109 and 152). It also documents the fact that under Babylonian law, individuals were not regarded as equals. Human worth was defined in terms of a person's wealth and status in society. Violence committed by one free person upon another was punished reciprocally (clause 196), but the same violence committed upon a lower-class individual drew considerably lighter punishment (clause 198), and penalties were reduced even further if the victim was a slave (clause 199). Similarly, a principle of "pay according to status" was applied in punishing thieves (clause 8): the upper-class thief was more heavily penalized or fined than the lower-class one. A thief who could not pay at all fell into slavery or was put to death. Slaves, whether captives of war or victims of debt, had no civil rights under law and enjoyed only the protection of the household to which they belonged.

In Babylonian society, women were considered intellectually and physically inferior to men and—much like slaves—were regarded as the personal property of the male head of the household. A woman went from her father's house to that of her husband, where she was expected to bear children (clause 138). Nevertheless, as indicated by the Code, women enjoyed commercial freedom (clause 109) and considerable legal protection (clauses 134, 138, 209, and 210), their value as child-bearers and housekeepers clearly acknowledged. Clause 142 is an astonishingly early example of no-fault divorce: since a husband's neglect of his spouse was not punishable, neither party to the marriage was legally "at fault."

READING 1.3 From Hammurabi's Code (ca. 1750 B.C.E.)

. . . Hammurabi, the shepherd, named by Enlil am I, who increased plenty and abundance. The ancient seed of royalty, the powerful king, the sun of Babylon, who caused light to go forth over the lands of Sumer and Akkad . . . the favorite of Inanna [Ishtar] am I. When Marduk sent me to rule the people

and to bring help to the land, I established law and justice in the language of the land and promoted the welfare of the people.

Clause 8 If a man has stolen an ox, or sheep or an ass, or a pig or a goat, either from a god or a palace, he shall pay thirty-fold. If he is a plebeian,[1] he shall render ten-fold. If the thief has nothing to pay, he shall be slain.

14 If a man has stolen a man's son under age, he shall be slain.

109 If rebels meet in the house of a wine-seller and she does not seize them and take them to the palace, that wine-seller shall be slain.

129 If the wife of a man is found lying with another male, they shall be bound and thrown into the water; unless the husband lets his wife live, and the king lets his servant live.

134 If a man has been taken prisoner, and there is no food in his house, and his wife enters the house of another; then that woman bears no blame.

138 If a man divorces his spouse who has not borne him children, he shall give to her all the silver of the bride-price, and restore to her the dowry which she brought from the house of her father; and so he shall divorce her.

141 If a man's wife, dwelling in a man's house, has set her face to leave, has been guilty of dissipation, has wasted her house, and has neglected her husband; then she shall be prosecuted. If her husband says she is divorced, he shall let her go her way; he shall give her nothing for divorce. If her husband says she is not divorced, her husband may espouse another woman, and that woman shall remain a slave in the house of her husband.

142 If a woman hate her husband, and says "Thou shalt not possess me," the reason for her dislike shall be inquired into. If she is careful and has no fault, but her husband takes himself away and neglects her; then that woman is not to blame. She shall take her dowry and go back to her father's house.

143 If she has not been careful, but runs out, wastes her house, and neglects her husband; then that woman shall be thrown into the water.

152 If, after that woman has entered the man's house, they incur debt, both of them must satisfy the trader.

154 If a man has known his daughter, that man shall be banished from his city.

157 If a man after his father has lain in the breasts of his mother, both of them shall be burned.

162 If a man has married a wife, and she has borne children, and that woman has gone to her fate; then her father has no claim upon her dowry. The dowry is her children's.

168 If a man has set his face to disown his son, and has said to the judge, "I disown my son," then the judge shall look into his reasons. If the son has not borne a heavy crime which would justify his being disowned from filiation, then the father shall not disown his son from filiation.

195 If a son has struck his father, his hand shall be cut off.

196 If a man has destroyed the eye of a free man,[2] his own eye shall be destroyed.

198 If he has destroyed the eye of a plebeian, or broken the bone of a plebeian, he shall pay one mina[3] of silver.

199 If he has destroyed the eye of a man's slave, or broken the bone of a man's slave, he shall pay half his value.

209 If a man strike the daughter of a free man, and causes her fetus to fall; he shall pay ten shekels[4] of silver for her fetus.

210 If that woman die, his daughter shall be slain.

213 If he has struck the slave of a man, and made her fetus fall; he shall pay two shekels of silver.

214 If that slave die, he shall pay a third of a mina of silver.

218 If a doctor has treated a man with a metal knife for a severe wound, and has caused the man to die, or has opened a man's tumor with a metal knife, and destroyed the man's eye; his hands shall be cut off.

219 If a doctor has treated a slave of a plebeian with a metal knife for a severe wound, and caused him to die, he shall render slave for slave.

229 If a builder has built a house for a man, and his work is not strong, and if the house he has built falls in and kills the householder, that builder shall be slain.

232 If goods have been destroyed, he shall replace all that has been destroyed; and because the house that he built was not made strong, and it has fallen in, he shall restore the fallen house out of his own personal property.

282 If a slave shall say to his master, "Thou are not my master," he shall be prosecuted as a slave, and his owner shall cut off his ear.

Q **What does Hammurabi's Code tell us about women in ancient Babylon?**

---

[1] A member of the lower class, probably a peasant who worked the land for the ruling class.

[2] Above the lower-class peasant, the free man who rented land owed only a percentage of the produce to the ruling class.

[3] A monetary unit equal to approximately 1 pound of silver.

[4] 60 shekels = 1 mina.

The Arts in Mesopotamia

The royal graves found at Ur and elsewhere in Mesopotamia have yielded artifacts of great beauty. Jewelry, weapons, household goods, and musical instruments testify to the wealth of Mesopotamia's princely rulers (see Figures 1.3 and 1.4). Rather than building elaborate homes for the dead, however, the inhabitants of Sumer and Babylon raised temple-towers that might bring them closer to heaven. The **ziggurat**—a massive terraced tower made of rubble and brick—was the spiritual center of the Mesopotamian city-state. Serving as both a shrine and a temple, and also possibly as a burial site, it symbolized the sacred mountain that linked the realms of heaven and earth (Figure **1.8**; see also Figure 3.12). At the top level of a series of platforms joined by a steep stairway stood a sanctuary dedicated to local deities. Tended by priests and priestesses, the shrine rooms of the sanctuary stored clay tablets inscribed with cuneiform records of the city's economic activities, its religious customs, and its rites. At Tell Asmar in Sumer the shrine room also housed a remarkable group of statues representing men and women of various sizes, with large, staring eyes and hands clasped across their chests (Figure **1.9**). Carved out of soft stone, alabaster, and marble, some of these cult images may represent the gods, but it is more likely that they are votive (devotional) figures that represent the townspeople of Tell Asmar in the act of worshiping their local deities. The larger figures may be priests, and the smaller figures, laypersons. Rigid and attentive, they stand as if in perpetual prayer. Their enlarged eyes, inlaid

Figure 1.8 Ziggurat at Ur (partially reconstructed), third dynasty of Ur, Iraq, ca. 2150–2050 B.C.E.

Figure 1.9 Statuettes from the Abu Temple, Tell Asmar, Iraq, ca. 2900–2600 B.C.E. Marble, tallest figure ca. 30 in.

with shell, lapis lazuli, and black limestone, convey the impression of dread and awe, visual testimony to the sense of human apprehension in the face of divine power. These images express the insecurity of a people whose vulnerability was an ever-present fact of life.

The Iron Age

During the course of the second millennium B.C.E., all of Mesopotamia felt the effects of a new technology: iron was introduced into Asia Minor (present-day Turkey) by the Hittites, tribal nomads who built an empire that lasted until ca. 1200 B.C.E. Cheaper to produce and more durable than bronze, iron represented new, superior technology. In addition to their iron weapons, the Hittites made active use of horse-drawn war chariots, which provided increased speed and mobility in battle. The combination of war chariots and iron weapons gave the Hittites clear military superiority over all of Mesopotamia.

As iron technology spread slowly throughout the Near East, it transformed the ancient world. Iron tools contributed to increased agricultural production, which in turn supported an increased population. In the wake of the Iron Age, numerous small states came to flower, bringing with them major cultural innovations. By 1500 B.C.E., for instance, the Phoenicians, an energetic seafaring people who lived on the Mediterranean Sea (see Map 1.1), had developed an alphabet of twenty-two signs. These signs eventually replaced earlier forms of script and became the basis of all Western

alphabets. In Asia Minor, the Lydians, successors to the Hittites, began the practice of minting coins. And along the arid coast of the eastern Mediterranean, a nomadic people known as the Hebrews founded a theocratic state based on a unique belief system that would become the wellspring of three great world religions: Judaism, Christianity, and Islam.

The Hebrews

Archeologists have traced the origins of the tribal people called by their neighbors *habiru* or "Hebrews" to the region of Sumer. While their history originates around 2000 B.C.E., the books from which we reconstruct that history (known collectively as the Bible, from the Greek word *biblia*, meaning "books") were written some 1000 years later. The beginnings of Hebrew history are associated with the name Abraham of Ur, the patriarch who is believed to have led the Hebrews westward across the Fertile Crescent to settle in Canaan (ancient Israel, see Map 1.1). In Canaan, according to the first book of the Bible (Genesis), a special bond or **covenant** was forged between God and Abraham ("I will be your God, you will be my people," Genesis 17:7). In return for their unswerving obedience and loyalty, God would protect Abraham's descendants, giving them "all the land of Canaan for an everlasting possession" in order that they might become "a great nation" (Genesis 17:8).

Some time after 1700 B.C.E., the Hebrews migrated into Egypt, there to prosper until, during a period of political and military instability, they were reduced to the status of state slaves. Their liberation occurred under the leadership of the patriarch Moses (ca. 1250 B.C.E.), who led the Hebrews across the Red Sea (then probably a reed swamp); the event became the basis for the second book of the Hebrew Bible, Exodus (literally, "going out"). Since the "promised land" of Canaan was occupied by local tribes with sizable military strength, the Hebrews settled in the Sinai desert near the Dead Sea. Here, during a forty-year period that archeologists place some time between 1300 and 1150 B.C.E., the Hebrews forged the fundamentals of their faith: **monotheism**, the belief in a single, all-powerful creator-god,* and the renewal of the covenant binding them to their god in exchange for divine protection. The terms of the covenant required obedience to a set of ethical and spiritual obligations, delivered by Moses, and known as the Ten Commandments (the Decalogue). These moral laws define the proper relationship between God and the faithful; they also define the ethical obligations between and among the members of the Hebrew community.

Hebrew Monotheism

Monotheism first appeared in the ancient world around 1350 B.C.E. In Egypt, the pharaoh Amenhotep IV (Akhenaten) advanced the worship of the sun god Aten as the country's sole deity, more powerful than all the other Egyptian gods (see chapter 2). But Hebrew monotheism differed from that of Egypt, for while Aten was elevated above the other gods of the Egyptian pantheon, the Hebrews perceived their god as the one and *only* god. Moreover, while Aten (like other ancient gods) was associated with a specific natural phenomenon, in his case the sun, the god of the Hebrews was said to transcend nature and all natural phenomena. Hebrew religious beliefs also stood apart from those of other Mesopotamian societies. As Supreme Creator, the Hebrew god did not descend from nature or from other gods, but preceded the physical universe. Unlike the Babylonian universe, described as spontaneously generated and perpetually chaotic, the Hebrew Creation (see Reading 1.4a) was divinely planned and invested with moral order by a benevolent, all-knowing Being. Finally, in contrast to the Babylonian world, where squabbling gods made human beings their servants, the Hebrew universe was the gift given by its Creator to his supreme creation: humankind.

The Hebrew belief system stands apart from other ancient concepts of divine power in yet another dimension: its ethical charge. *Ethical monotheism*, the veneration of a single god as moral monitor, was unique in the ancient world. Its practice dignified individual moral judgment and became the most lasting of the Hebrew contributions to world culture.

---

* In the Hebrew Bible, God's name is written with four consonants (the Latinized letters YHWH), pronounced "Yahweh." This ancient name was considered too sacred to speak or write; other names for God (such as *Elohim*) found in the Hebrew Bible probably reflect different aspects of God's divinity. Greek transcriptions of the Bible replaced the Hebrew YHWH with *Kyrios* ("Lord"), while medieval Latin bibles translated God's name as "Jehovah."

The Hebrew Bible

The excerpts that follow belong to the Hebrew Bible (often called the Old Testament to distinguish it from the Christian canon known as the New Testament). Like the *Epic of Gilgamesh*, the stories that make up the early history of the Hebrews were passed orally from generation to generation, and recorded in the centuries following the founding of the first Hebrew state in 1000 B.C.E. The first five books of the Bible, known as the **Torah** (literally "instruction"), were assembled from four main sources some time between the tenth and seventh centuries B.C.E. Parts of the text in the first book of the Torah, Genesis, belong to a common context: the world and lore of ancient Sumer. The story of the Flood, for instance, appears in both Genesis and the *Epic of Gilgamesh*, as well as in other Mesopotamian texts. Like the *Epic of Gilgamesh*, the Bible conflates centuries of fact and legend. Its significance as great literature is unquestionable, but its value as a historical document remains in question. It is held by many as the revealed word of God, and is regarded as sacred scripture by the adherents of Judaism, Christianity, and Islam.

READING 1.4a From the Hebrew Bible (Genesis 1, 2)

Chapter 1
The Creation

[26]Then God said, "Let us make man in our image, according to our likeness; and let them rule over the fish of the sea and over the birds of the sky and over the cattle and over all the earth, and over every creeping thing that creeps on the earth."

[27]God created man in his own image, in the image of God he created him; male and female he created them.

[28]God blessed them; and God said to them, "Be fruitful and multiply, and fill the earth, and subdue it; and rule over the fish of the sea and over the birds of the sky and over every living thing that moves on the earth." [29]Then God said, "Behold, I have given you every plant yielding seed that is on the surface of all the earth, and every tree which has fruit yielding seed; it shall be food for you; [30]and to every beast of the earth and to every bird of the sky and to every thing that moves on the earth which has life, I have given every green plant for food"; and it was so. [31]God saw all that he had made, and behold, it was very good. And there was evening and there was morning, the sixth day.

Chapter 2
The Creation of man and woman

[1]Thus the heavens and the earth were completed, and all their hosts. [2]By the seventh day God completed his work which he had done, and he rested on the seventh day from all his work which he had done. [3]Then God blessed the seventh day and sanctified it, because in it he rested from all his work which God had created and made.

[4]This is the account of the heavens and the earth when they were created, in the day that the Lord God made earth and heaven.

[5]Now no shrub of the field was yet in the earth, and no plant of the field had yet sprouted, for the Lord God had not sent rain upon the earth, and there was no man to cultivate the ground. [6]But a mist used to rise from the earth and water the whole surface of the

Translating the Hebrew Bible

One's understanding and interpretation of the Hebrew Bible depends to a large extent on which translation one reads. Generated over a thousand-year period, the largest portion of the Bible was written in ancient Hebrew, while some of the later chapters were written in Aramaic. A Greek version of the Hebrew Bible did not appear until the second century B.C.E. (see chapter 8). The first Latin translation was made by Jerome, a fourth-century church father who was versed in Greek, Hebrew, and Aramaic. In the course of this and later translations, the Hebrew Bible was Christianized. For example, Jerome translated the Hebrew word *nefesh*, meaning "life breath" or "life," as the Latin word *anima*. Subsequent translations, such as the seventeenth-century authorized English translation known as the King James Bible, translated *anima* as "soul," suggesting a

Christian body/soul dualism (with implications of an afterlife) that is absent from the early portions of the Hebrew Bible.

A second example: the King James Bible translates the Hebrew *Sheol* as the English word "Hell." *Sheol*, however, describes a shadowy underworld, the common grave of the good and bad alike (see the Book of Job, 14:13, Reading 1.4d). There is no explicit designation of Heaven and Hell as places or conditions of reward and punishment in the Hebrew Bible. The first reference to the "Kingdom of God," taken by some to suggest Heaven, occurs in the Book of Daniel, written in Aramaic in the second century B.C.E. While the accurate translation of the Bible may not be crucial to belief, it remains critical to scholarly debate concerning the meaning and interpretation of the West's primary scripture.

---

ground. ⁷Then the Lord God formed man of dust from the ground, and breathed into his nostrils the breath of life; and man became a living being.

⁸The Lord God planted a garden toward the east, in Eden; and there he placed the man whom he had formed. ⁹Out of the ground the Lord God caused to grow every tree that is pleasing to the sight and good for food; the tree of life also in the midst of the garden, and the tree of the knowledge of good and evil.

¹⁰Now a river flowed out of Eden to water the garden; and from there it divided and became four rivers. ¹¹The name of the first is Pishon; it flows around the whole land of Havilah, where there is gold. ¹²The gold of that land is good; the bdellium* and the onyx** stone are there. ¹³The name of the second river is Gihon; it flows around the whole land of Cush. ¹⁴The name of the third river is Tigris; it flows east of Assyria. And the fourth river is the Euphrates.

¹⁵Then the Lord God took the man and put him into the garden of Eden to cultivate it and keep it. ¹⁶The Lord God commanded the man, saying, "From any tree of the garden you may eat freely; ¹⁷but from the tree of the knowledge of good and evil you shall not eat, for in the day that you eat from it you will surely die."

¹⁸Then the Lord God said, "It is not good for the man to be alone; I will make him a helper suitable for him." ¹⁹Out of the ground the Lord God formed every beast of the field and every bird of the sky, and brought them to the man to see what he would call them; and whatever the man called a living creature, that was its name. ²⁰The man gave names to all the cattle, and to the birds of the sky, and to every beast of the field, but for Adam there was not found a helper suitable for him. ²¹So the Lord God caused a deep sleep to fall upon the man, and he slept; then he took one of his ribs and closed up the flesh at that place. ²²The Lord God fashioned into a woman the rib which he had taken from the man, and brought her to the man. ²³The man said,

---

* Variously interpreted as a deep-red gem or a pearl.
**A semiprecious red stone (carnelian).

"This is now bone of my bones,
And flesh of my flesh;
She shall be called Woman,
Because she was taken out of Man."

²⁴For this reason a man shall leave his father and his mother, and be joined to his wife; and they shall become one flesh.

²⁵And the man and his wife were both naked and were not ashamed.

Q **How does this creation story differ from those in Readings 0.1 and 1.1?**

The Hebrew Laws

Two groups of laws are represented below. In the first group, which is framed in the negative, the consequences of violating the law are left unspecified. There is no promise of reward for obedience, no promise of heaven, no threat of hell; only the terrible warning that God will punish those who fail to keep the commandments to the third generation. That is, the fault of the parents will fall on their children, grandchildren, and great-grandchildren (Exodus 20:5).

The legal practices in the second excerpt, which belongs to a much larger body of Hebrew laws, resemble those of Hammurabi (Reading 1.3). These, which deal primarily with social obligations, prescribe specific penalties for their violation. Some so closely parallel the laws of the First Babylonian Empire that scholars believe both look back to a common source. It is worth noting, however, a major difference between the laws of the Hebrews and those of Babylon: among the Hebrews, punishment was not levied according to social class. This is not to say that class distinctions did not exist in Hebrew society, but rather that the law was meant to apply equally to all classes, with the exception of slaves. The humanitarian bias of the Hebrew laws is best reflected in God's frequent reminder to the Hebrews that since they themselves were once aliens and slaves, they must treat even the lowest members of the social order as worthy human beings. If Babylonian law prized economic prosperity and political stability, it was the unity of religious and moral life that formed the core of the Hebrew message.

READING 1.4b From the Hebrew Bible (Exodus 20:1–21; 21:1–2, 18–27, 37; 23:1–9)

The Ten Commandments (The Decalogue)
[1]Then God spoke all these words, saying, [2]"I am the LORD your God, who brought you out of the land of Egypt, out of the house of slavery.

[3]"You shall have no other gods before me.

[4]"You shall not make for yourself an idol, or any likeness of what is in heaven above or on the earth beneath or in the water under the earth.

[5]You shall not worship them or serve them; for I, the LORD your God, am a jealous God, visiting the iniquity of the fathers on the children, on the third and the fourth generations of those who hate me, [6]but showing loving kindness to thousands, to those who love me and keep my commandments.

[7]"You shall not take the name of the LORD your God in vain, for the LORD will not leave him unpunished who takes his name in vain.

[8]"Remember the sabbath day, to keep it holy. [9]Six days you shall labor and do all your work, [10]but the seventh day is a sabbath of the LORD your God; in it you shall not do any work, you or your son or your daughter, your male or your female servant or your cattle or your sojourner who stays with you. [11]For in six days the LORD made the heavens and the earth, the sea and all that is in them, and rested on the seventh day; therefore the LORD blessed the sabbath day and made it holy.

[12]"Honor your father and your mother, that your days may be prolonged in the land which the LORD your God gives you.

[13]"You shall not murder.

[14]"You shall not commit adultery.

[15]"You shall not steal.

[16]"You shall not bear false witness against your neighbor.

[17]"You shall not covet your neighbor's house; you shall not covet your neighbor's wife or his male servant or his female servant or his ox or his donkey or anything that belongs to your neighbor."

[18]All the people perceived the thunder and the lightning flashes and the sound of the trumpet and the mountain smoking; and when the people saw it, they trembled and stood at a distance. [19]Then they said to Moses, "Speak to us yourself and we will listen; but let not God speak to us, or we will die." [20]Moses said to the people, "Do not be afraid; for God has come in order to test you, and in order that the fear of him may remain with you, so that you may not sin." [21]So the people stood at a distance, while Moses approached the thick cloud where God was.

Ordinances for the people
[1]"Now these are the ordinances which you are to set before them: [2]If you buy a Hebrew slave, he shall serve for six years; but on the seventh he shall go out as a free man without payment."

Personal injuries
[18]"If men have a quarrel and one strikes the other with a stone or with his fist, and he does not die but remains in bed, [19]if he gets up and walks around outside on his staff, then he who struck him shall go unpunished; he shall only pay for his loss of time, and shall take care of him until he is completely healed.

[20]"If a man strikes his male or female slave with a rod and he dies at his hand, he shall be punished. [21]If, however, he survives a day or two, no vengeance shall be taken; for he is his property.

[22]"If men struggle with each other and strike a woman with child so that she gives birth prematurely, yet there is no injury, he shall surely be fined as the woman's husband may demand of him, and he shall pay as the judges decide. [23]But if there is any further injury, then you shall appoint as a penalty life for life, [24]eye for eye, tooth for tooth, hand for hand, foot for foot, [25]burn for burn, wound for wound, bruise for bruise.

[26]"If a man strikes the eye of his male or female slave, and destroys it, he shall let him go free on account of his eye. [27]And if he knocks out a tooth of his male or female slave, he shall let him go free on account of his tooth."

. . . .

Theft of animals
[37]"When someone steals an ox or a sheep and slaughters or sells it, he shall restore five oxen for the one ox, and four sheep for the one sheep."

Sundry laws
[1]"You shall not bear a false report; do not join your hand with a wicked man to be a malicious witness. [2]You shall not follow the masses in doing evil, nor shall you testify in a dispute so as to turn aside after a multitude in order to pervert justice; [3]nor shall you be partial to a poor man in his dispute.

[4]"If you meet your enemy's ox or his donkey wandering away, you shall surely return it to him. [5]If you see the donkey of one who hates you lying helpless under its load, you shall refrain from leaving it to him, you shall surely release it with him.

[6]"You shall not pervert the justice due to your needy brother in his dispute.

[7]Keep far from a false charge, and do not kill the innocent or the righteous, for I will not acquit the guilty. [8]"You shall not take a bribe, for a bribe blinds the clear-sighted and subverts the cause of the just.

[9]"You shall not oppress a stranger, since you yourselves know the feelings of a stranger, for you also were strangers in the land of Egypt."

Q **Why are many of the Commandments framed in the negative?**

Q **How do these laws differ from those in Hammurabi's Code?**

The Hebrew State and the Social Order

Under the military leadership of the patriarch Joshua, the Hebrews returned to Canaan, gradually wresting control of the "promised land" from powerful tribes of Philistines ("People of the Sea"). The new Hebrew state consisted

Figure 1.10 Reconstruction of Solomon's Temple.

city of Jerusalem (see Map 1.1) by constructing a royal palace and a magnificent temple (Figure **1.10**) to enshrine the Ark of the Covenant. Lacking the raw materials for this enterprise, he established trade relations with the wealthy neighboring state of Phoenicia, which provided timber from nearby Lebanon. Ornamentation of the Temple was abstract or symbolic, owing to the biblical injunction against carved images (Exodus 20:4). Prohibiting the representation of three-dimensional form did not so much reflect a fear that the Hebrews might worship pagan idols; rather, it asserted that human efforts to create lifelike images disrespected God as Supreme Creator. Early **synagogues** (houses of worship) were embellished with symbols of the faith, such as the curtained enclosure that sheltered the Torah, the **menorah** (a seven-branched candelabrum), and a **shofar** (ram's horn used to call the faithful to prayer) (Figure **1.11**).

The social order of the Hebrews was shaped by biblical precepts. Between Hebrew kings and their people, there existed a covenant—protection in exchange for loyalty and obedience—similar to that which characterized the relationship between God and the Hebrews. This same patriarchal bond also prevailed between Jewish fathers and their families. Hebrew kings were considered the divinely appointed representatives of God; and Hebrew wives and children came under the direct control of the male head of the household and were listed among his possessions. In short, the covenant between God and the Hebrews, as

of twelve tribes, each descended from one of the sons of Jacob, whom God had named "Israel." Under the rule of the Hebrew kings Saul (ca. 1040–1000 B.C.E.), David (ca. 1000–960 B.C.E.), and Solomon (ca. 960–920 B.C.E.), Canaan became a powerful state defended by armies equipped with iron war chariots. As related in the Book of Kings, the scriptural history of the Hebrew rulers descended from David, Solomon embellished the capital

Figure 1.11 The Ark of the Covenant and sanctuary implements, Hammath, near Tiberias, fourth century. Mosaic, 6 ft. 7 in. × 16 ft. 5 in. The stone tablets bearing the Ten Commandments are said to have been carried back to Canaan in a secure container known as the Ark of the Covenant. In modern synagogues, the Ark houses the Torah.

expressed in the laws, established the model for both secular and familial authority.

The Hebrew Prophets

Toward the end of his reign, Solomon divided the Hebrew state into two administrative divisions: the northern portion, retaining the name Israel with its capital at Samaria, and the southern portion, called Judah (from which comes the name "Jews") with its capital at Jerusalem. While the commercial pursuits of the Hebrew nation brought them wealth and material comforts, the less rigorous cults of Canaanite fertility gods and goddesses lured Hebrews away from strict adherence to their moral obligations. By the eighth century B.C.E., the voices of reform grew loud. A group of religious zealots, known as **prophets** (literally "spokespersons") claimed to have heard words of divine disapproval, indeed, anger. Warning that the violations of the covenant would invite harsh punishment, the prophets Amos, Hosea, and Isaiah urged the Hebrews to return to the laws of the Torah. A century after the fall of Jerusalem to the Assyrians in 722 B.C.E., the prophet Jeremiah urged the Hebrews to reaffirm the covenant, citing the Assyrian assault on Judah as divine chastisement, an expression of God's wrath. Nowhere is the Hebrew concept of destiny as being divinely directed more clearly illustrated than in Jeremiah's message: God rewards and punishes not in a life hereafter, but here on earth.

READING 1.4c From the Hebrew Bible (Jeremiah 11: 1–14)

The broken covenant

[1]The word which came to Jeremiah from the Lord, saying, [2]"Hear the words of this covenant, and speak to the men of Judah and to the inhabitants of Jerusalem; [3]and say to them, Thus says the Lord, the God of Israel, Cursed is the man who does not heed the words of this covenant [4]which I commanded your forefathers in the day that I brought them out of the land of Egypt, from the iron furnace, saying, Listen to my voice, and do according to all which I command you; so you shall be my people, and I will be your God, [5]in order to confirm the oath which I swore to your forefathers, to give them a land flowing with milk and honey, as it is this day." Then I said, "Amen, O Lord." [6]And the Lord said to me, "Proclaim all these words in the cities of Judah and in the streets of Jerusalem, saying, 'Hear the words of this covenant and do them. [7]For I solemnly warned your fathers in the day that I brought them up from the land of Egypt, even to this day, warning persistently, saying, "Listen to my voice." [8]Yet they did not obey or incline their ear, but walked, each one, in the stubbornness of his evil heart; therefore I brought on them all the words of this covenant, which I commanded them to do, but they did not.'"

[9]Then the Lord said to me, "A conspiracy has been found among the men of Judah and among the inhabitants of Jerusalem. [10]They have turned back to the iniquities of their ancestors who refused to hear my words, and they have gone after other gods to serve them; the house of Israel and the house of Judah have broken my covenant which I made with their fathers." [11]Therefore thus says the Lord, "Behold I am bringing disaster on them which they will not be able to escape; though they will cry to me, yet I will not listen to them. [12]Then the cities of Judah and the inhabitants of Jerusalem will go and cry to the gods to whom they burn incense, but they surely will not save them in the time of their disaster.

[13]For your gods are as many as your cities, O Judah; and as many as the streets of Jerusalem are the altars you have set up to the shameful thing, altars to burn incense to Baal.

[14]"Therefore do not pray for this people, nor lift up a cry or prayer for them; for I will not listen when they call to me because of their disaster."

Q **For what failings does Jeremiah chastise the Hebrews?**

The Babylonian Captivity and the Book of Job

In 586 B.C.E., Judah fell to Chaldean armies led by the mighty King Nebuchadnezzar (ca. 630–562 B.C.E.). Nebuchadnezzar burned Jerusalem, raided the Temple, and took the inhabitants of the city into captivity. In the newly restored city of Babylon, with its glazed brick portals (Figure 1.12), its resplendent "hanging" gardens, its towering ziggurat—the prototype for the Tower of Babel

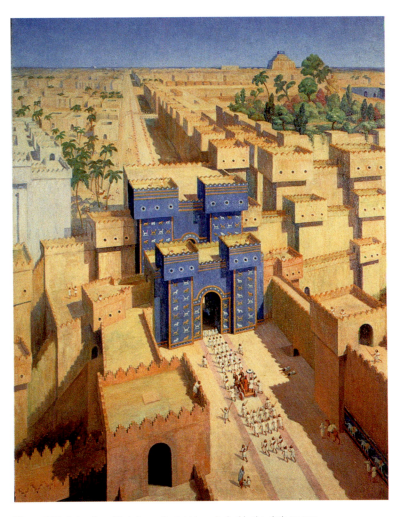

Figure 1.12 A drawing of Babylon as it might have looked in the sixth century B.C.E. The Ishtar Gate, one of Babylon's eight monumental portals, spanned the north entrance route into the city. Faced with deep blue glazed bricks, it is the earliest example of a round arch employed on a colossal scale. The palace of Nebuchadnezzar II and the Hanging Gardens lie behind and to its right. On the horizon and the east bank of the Euphrates looms the Marduk Ziggurat.

described in Genesis—the Hebrews experienced almost fifty years of exile (586–538 B.C.E.). Their despair and doubt in the absolute goodness of God are voiced in the Book of Job, probably written in the years after the Babylonian Captivity. The finest example of wisdom literature in the Hebrew Bible, the Book of Job raises the question of unjustified suffering in a universe governed by a merciful god. The "blameless and upright" Job has obeyed the Commandments and has been a devoted servant of God throughout his life. Yet he is tested unmercifully by the loss of his possessions, his family, and his health. His wife begs him to renounce God, and his friends encourage him to acknowledge his sinfulness. But Job defiantly protests that he has given God no cause for anger. Job asks a universal question: "If there is no heaven (and thus no justice after death), how can a good man's suffering be justified?" or simply phrased, "Why do bad things happen to good people?"

READING 1.4d From the Hebrew Bible (Job 1; 2; 3:1–5; 7:17–21; 14; 38:1–18; 42:1–6)

The Book of Job

Chapter 1: Job's character and wealth

[1]There was a man in the land of Uz whose name was Job; and that man was blameless, upright, fearing God and turning away from evil. [2]Seven sons and three daughters were born to him. [3]His possessions also were 7,000 sheep, 3,000 camels, 500 yoke of oxen, 500 female donkeys, and very many servants; and that man was the greatest of all the men of the east. [4]His sons used to go and hold a feast in the house of each one on his day, and they would send and invite their three sisters to eat and drink with them. [5]When the days of feasting had completed their cycle, Job would send and consecrate them, rising up early in the morning and offering burnt offerings according to the number of them all; for Job said, "Perhaps my sons have sinned and cursed God in their hearts." Thus Job did continually.

[6]Now there was a day when the sons of God came to present themselves before the Lord, and Satan also came among them. [7]The Lord said to Satan, "From where do you come?" Then Satan* answered the Lord and said, "From roaming about on the earth and walking around on it." [8]The Lord said to Satan, "Have you considered my servant Job? For there is no one like him on the earth, a blameless and upright man, fearing God and turning away from evil." [9]Then Satan answered the Lord, "Does Job fear God for nothing? [10]Have you not made a hedge about him and his house and all that he has, on every side? You have blessed the work of his hands, and his possessions have increased in the land. [11]But put forth your hand now and touch all that he has; he will surely curse you to your face." [12]Then the Lord said to Satan, "Behold, all that he has is in your power, only do not put forth your hand on him." So Satan departed from the presence of the Lord.

Satan allowed to test Job

[13]Now on the day when his sons and his daughters were eating

* Literally, "adversary."

and drinking wine in their oldest brother's house, [14]a messenger came to Job and said, "The oxen were plowing and the donkeys feeding beside them, [15]and the Sabeans attacked and took them. They also slew the servants with the edge of the sword, and I alone have escaped to tell you." [16]While he was still speaking, another also came and said, "The fire of God fell from heaven and burned up the sheep and the servants and consumed them, and I alone have escaped to tell you." [17]While he was still speaking, another also came and said, "The Chaldeans formed three bands and made a raid on the camels and took them and slew the servants with the edge of the sword, and I alone have escaped to tell you." [18]While he was still speaking, another also came and said, "Your sons and your daughters were eating and drinking wine in their oldest brother's house, [19]and behold, a great wind came from across the wilderness and struck the four corners of the house, and it fell on the young people and they died, and I alone have escaped to tell you."

[20]Then Job arose and tore his robe and shaved his head, and he fell to the ground and worshiped. [21]He said,

"Naked I came from my mother's womb,
And naked I shall return there.
The Lord gave and the Lord has taken away.
Blessed be the name of the Lord."

[22]Through all this Job did not sin nor did he blame God.

Chapter 2: Job loses his health

[1]Again there was a day when the sons of God came to present themselves before the Lord, and Satan also came among them to present himself before the Lord. [2]The Lord said to Satan, "Where have you come from?" Then Satan answered the Lord and said, "From roaming about on the earth and walking around on it." [3]The Lord said to Satan, "Have you considered my servant Job? For there is no one like him on the earth, a blameless and upright man fearing God and turning away from evil. And he still holds fast his integrity, although you incited me against him to ruin him without cause." [4]Satan answered the Lord and said, "Skin for skin! Yes, all that a man has he will give for his life. [5]However, put forth your hand now, and touch his bone and his flesh; he will curse you to your face." [6]So the Lord said to Satan, "Behold, he is in your power, only spare his life."

[7]Then Satan went out from the presence of the Lord and smote Job with sore boils from the sole of his foot to the crown of his head. [8]And he took a potsherd to scrape himself while he was sitting among the ashes. [9]Then his wife said to him, "Do you still hold fast your integrity? Curse God and die!" [10]But he said to her, "You speak as one of the foolish women speaks. Shall we indeed accept good from God and not accept adversity?" In all this Job did not sin with his lips.

[11]Now when Job's three friends heard of all this adversity that had come upon him, they came each one from his own place, Eliphaz the Temanite, Bildad the Shuhite and Zophar the Naamathite; and they made an appointment together to come to sympathize with him and comfort him. [12]When they lifted up their eyes at a distance and did not recognize him, they raised their voices and wept. And each of them tore his robe and they threw dust over their heads toward the sky. [13]Then they sat down on the ground with him for seven days and seven nights with no one speaking a word to him, for they saw that his pain was very great.

Chapter 3: Job's lament

[1]Afterward Job opened his mouth and cursed the day of his birth. [2]And Job said,

> [3]"Let the day perish on which I was to be born,
> And the night which said, 'A boy is conceived.'
> [4]"May that day be darkness;
> Let not God above care for it,
> Nor light shine on it.
> [5]"Let darkness and black gloom claim it;
> Let a cloud settle on it;
> Let the blackness of the day terrify it."

Chapter 7: Job's life seems futile

> [17]"What is man that you magnify him,
> And that you are concerned about him,
> [18]That you examine him every morning
> And try him every moment?
> [19]"Will you never turn your gaze away from me,
> Nor let me alone until I swallow my spittle?
> [20]"Have I sinned? What have I done to you,
> O watcher of men?
> Why have you set me as your target,
> So that I am a burden to myself?
> [21]"Why then do you not pardon my transgression
> And take away my iniquity?
> For now I will lie down in the dust;
> And you will seek me, but I will not be."

Chapter 14: Job speaks of the finality of death

> [1]"Man, who is born of woman,
> Is short-lived and full of turmoil.
> [2]"Like a flower he comes forth and withers.
> He also flees like a shadow and does not remain.
> [3]"You also open your eyes on him
> And bring him into judgment with yourself.
> [4]"Who can make the clean out of the unclean?
> No one!
> [5]"Since his days are determined,
> The number of his months is with you;
> And his limits you have set so that he cannot pass.
> [6]"Turn your gaze from him that he may rest,
> Until he fulfills his day like a hired man.
> [7]"For there is hope for a tree,
> When it is cut down, that it will sprout again,
> And its shoots will not fail.
> [8]"Though its roots grow old in the ground
> And its stump dies in the dry soil,
> [9]At the scent of water it will flourish
> And put forth sprigs like a plant.
> [10]"But man dies and lies prostrate [cast face down].
> Man expires, and where is he?
> [11]"As water evaporates from the sea,
> And a river becomes parched and dried up,
> [12]So man lies down and does not rise.
> Until the heavens are no longer,
> He will not awake nor be aroused out of his sleep.
> [13]"Oh that you would hide me in Sheol,**

** The shadowy underworld.

> That you would conceal me until your wrath returns to you,
> That you would set a limit for me and remember me!
> [14]"If a man dies, will he live again?
> All the days of my struggle I will wait
> Until my change comes.
> [15]"You will call, and I will answer you;
> You will long for the work of your hands.
> [16]"For now you number my steps,
> You do not observe my sin.
> [17]"My transgression is sealed up in a bag,
> And you wrap up my iniquity.
> [18]"But the falling mountain crumbles away,
> And the rock moves from its place;
> [19]Water wears away stones,
> Its torrents wash away the dust of the earth;
> So you destroy man's hope.
> [20]"You forever overpower him and he departs;
> You change his appearance and send him away.
> [21]"His sons achieve honor, but he does not know it;
> Or they become insignificant, but he does not perceive it.
> [22]"But his body pains him,
> And he mourns only for himself."

Chapter 38: God speaks now to Job

[1]Then the Lord answered Job out of the whirlwind and said,

> [2]"Who is this that darkens counsel
> By words without knowledge?
> [3]"Now gird up your loins like a man,
> And I will ask you, and you instruct me!
> [4]"Where were you when I laid the foundation of the earth?
> Tell me, if you have understanding,
> [5]Who set its measurements? Since you know.
> Or who stretched the line on it?
> [6]"On what were its bases sunk?
> Or who laid its cornerstone,
> [7]When the morning stars sang together
> And all the sons of God shouted for joy?
> [8]"Or who enclosed the sea with doors
> When, bursting forth, it went out from the womb;
> [9]When I made a cloud its garment
> And thick darkness its swaddling band,
> [10]And I placed boundaries on it
> And set a bolt and doors,
> [11]And I said, 'Thus far you shall come, but no farther;
> And here shall your proud waves stop'?"

God's mighty power

> [12]"Have you ever in your life commanded the morning,
> And caused the dawn to know its place,
> [13]That it might take hold of the ends of the earth,
> And the wicked be shaken out of it?
> [14]"It is changed like clay under the seal;
> And they stand forth like a garment [in splendor].
> [15]"From the wicked their light is withheld,
> And the uplifted arm is broken.
> [16]"Have you entered into the springs of the sea
> Or walked in the recesses of the deep?
> [17]"Have the gates of death been revealed to you,
> Or have you seen the gates of deep darkness?

¹⁸"Have you understood the expanse of the earth?
Tell me, if you know all this."

Chapter 42: Job's confession
¹Then Job answered the Lord and said,
²"I know that you can do all things,
And that no purpose of yours can be thwarted.
³'Who is this that hides counsel without knowledge?'
Therefore I have declared that which I did not understand,
Things too wonderful for me, which I did not know."
⁴"Hear, now, and I will speak;
I will ask you, and you instruct me."
⁵"I have heard of you by the hearing of the ear;
But now my eye sees you;
⁶Therefore I retract,
And I repent in dust and ashes."

— **Q** Why is the Book of Job called "wisdom literature"?

— **Q** Why is this book essential to an understanding of the Hebrew covenant?

God's answer to Job is an eloquent vindication of unquestioned faith: God's power is immense and human beings cannot expect rational explanations of the divine will. Proclaiming the magnitude of divine power and the fragility of humankind, the Book of Job confirms the pivotal role of faith (the belief and trust in God) that sustains the Hebrew covenant. The anxious sense of human vulnerability that pervades the Book of Job recalls the *Epic of Gilgamesh.* Job and Gilgamesh are tested by superhuman forces, and both come to realize that misfortune and suffering are typical of the human condition. Gilgamesh seeks but fails to secure personal immortality; Job solicits God's promise of heavenly reward but fails to secure assurance that once dead, he might return to life. Just as Utnapishtim tells Gilgamesh, "There is no permanence," so Job laments that man born of woman "Like a flower he comes forth and withers. He also flees like a shadow and does not remain" (Job 14.2). Such pessimism was not uncommon in Mesopotamia, the region in which both the *Epic of Gilgamesh* and the Hebrew Bible originated. The notion of life after death (so prominent in Egyptian religious thought; see chapter 2) is as elusive a concept in Hebraic literature as it is in Mesopotamian myth. Job anticipates a final departure to an underworld, an abode of the dead known among the Hebrews as *Sheol* or Shadowland. Yet, even without the promise of reward, Job remains stubbornly faithful to the covenant. His tragic vision involves the gradual but dignified acceptance of his place in a divinely governed universe.

The Book of Psalms

In 538 B.C.E., the Jewish remnant returned to Jerusalem to rebuild the Temple of Solomon. The post-exile age—the period following the Babylonian Captivity—was marked by apocalyptic hopes and the renewal of the covenant. This era also produced one of the best-loved books of the Hebrew Bible. The Book of Psalms (or "Psalter," from

The Hebrew Bible

The Torah	Genesis	Numbers
	Exodus	Deuteronomy
	Leviticus	
The Prophets	Joshua	Isaiah
	Judges	Jeremiah
	Samuel I & II	Ezekiel
	Kings I & II	Twelve Minor Prophets
The Writings	Psalms	Ecclesiastes
	Proverbs	Esther
	Job	Daniel
	Song of Songs	Ezra
	Ruth	Nehemiah
	Lamentations	Chronicles I & II

the Greek word *psalterion*, a stringed instrument) is a collection of 150 songs of praise, thanksgiving, confession, and supplication. Traditionally attributed to King David, whose name was associated with leadership in religious music, the psalms were transmitted orally for more than half a century. In Hebrew culture, music was closely tied to prayer and worship. **Cantors** chanted biblical passages as part of the Hebrew **liturgy** (the rituals for public worship), and members of the congregation participated in the singing of psalms. Both prayers and psalms might be performed in the **responsory** style, in which the congregation answered the voice of the cantor, or in the **antiphonal** manner, in which the cantor and the congregation sang alternate verses. Sung in public worship, the psalms forge a link between the individual and the Hebrew community, as reflected in the line: "O magnify the Lord with me, and let us exalt his name together!" (Ps. 34:3). Psalm 8, reproduced below, is one of the most eloquent songs of praise in the Hebrew Bible.

— **READING 1.4e** From the Hebrew Bible (Psalms 8: 1–9)

The Lord's glory and man's dignity
¹O Lord, our Lord,
How majestic is your name in all the earth,
Who have displayed your splendor above the heavens!

²From the mouth of infants and nursing babes you have established strength
Because of your adversaries,
To make the enemy and the revengeful cease.

³When I consider your heavens, the work of your fingers,
The moon and the stars, which you have ordained;
⁴What is man that you take thought of him,
And the son of man that you care for him?

⁵Yet you have made him a little lower than God,
And you crown him with glory and majesty!

⁶You make him to rule over the works of your hands;
You have put all things under his feet,

⁷All sheep and oxen,
And also the beasts of the field,
⁸The birds of the heavens and the fish of the sea,
Whatever passes through the paths of the seas.

⁹O Lord, our Lord,
How majestic is your name in all the earth!

Q How does this song of praise compare with "The Hymn to the Aten" (Reading 2.1)?

The Hebrew Bible played a major role in shaping the humanistic tradition in the West. It provided the religious and ethical foundations for Judaism, and, almost 2000 years after the death of Abraham, for Christianity and Islam. Biblical teachings, including the belief in a single, personal, caring god who intervenes on behalf of a faithful people, have become fundamental to Western thought. Bible stories—from Genesis to Job—have inspired some of humankind's greatest works of art, music, and literature. And the Book of Psalms, along with the later books of the Bible (see Box above), have had a profound influence on the religious history of the West.

Empires of the Iron Age

Iron technology encouraged the rise of large and powerful empires. Cheaper and stronger weapons meant larger,

more efficient armies: war was no longer the monopoly of the elite. Equipped with iron weapons, the Assyrians (ca. 750–600 B.C.E.), Chaldeans (ca. 600–540 B.C.E.), and Persians (ca. 550–330 B.C.E.) followed one another in conquering vast portions of Mesopotamia. Each of these empires grew in size and authority by imposing military control over territories outside their own natural boundaries—a practice known as *imperialism.*

The Assyrian Empire

The first of the Iron Age empire builders, the Assyrians earned a reputation as the most militant civilization of ancient Mesopotamia. Held together by a powerful army that systematically combined engineering and fighting techniques, the Assyrians turned their iron weapons against most of Mesopotamia. In 721 B.C.E., they conquered Israel and dispersed its population. By the middle of the seventh century B.C.E., they had swallowed up most of the land between the Persian Gulf and the Nile valley. Assyrian power is reflected in the imposing walled citadel of Khorsabad, located some 10 miles from Nineveh (see Map 1.1). Covering 25 acres, this walled complex featured a ziggurat and an elaborate palace with more than 200 rooms: a maze of courtyards, harem quarters, treasuries, and state apartments (Figure **1.13**). The palace walls were adorned with low-relief scenes of war and pillage and with cuneiform inscriptions celebrating Assyrian military victories. One seventh-century B.C.E. relief shows the imperial armies of King Ashurbanipal (668–627 B.C.E.) storming the battlements of an African city

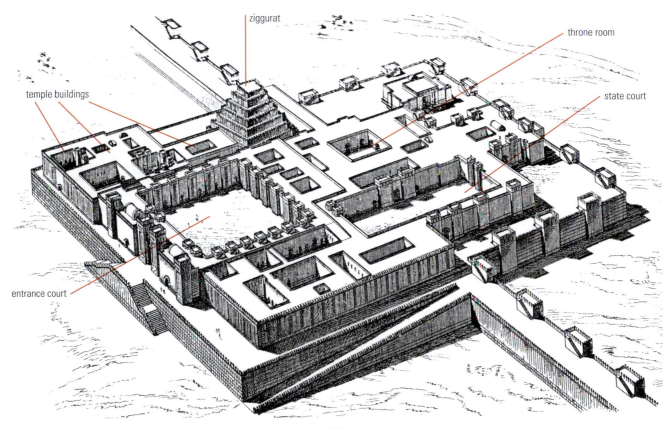

Figure 1.13 Reconstruction of the walled citadel at Khorsabad, Assyria (Iraq), ca. 720 B.C.E.

Figure 1.15 King Ashurnasirpal II killing lions, from the Palace of King Ashurnasirpal II, Nimrud, ca. 883–859 B.C.E. Alabaster relief, 3 ft. 3 in. × 8 ft. 4 in. The most militant of the iron-wielding empires of Mesopotamia, the Assyrians carved low-relief depictions of royal hunts that pitted the courage of the king against the lion, a traditional symbol of power.

(Figure **1.14**). In the lower left, male captives (their chieftains still wearing the feathers of authority) are led away, followed in procession by women, children, and the spoils of war.

Flanking the scenes of military conquest on the palace walls at Nineveh and Nimrud are depictions of the royal lion hunt. Hunting and war, two closely related enterprises, were ideal vehicles by which to display the ruler's courage and physical might. In Assyrian reliefs, the lion, a traditional symbol of power throughout the ancient world, is depicted as the adversary of the king. Ceremonial lion hunts symbolized the invincibility of the monarch, who, in earlier times, might have proved his prowess by

Figure 1.14 Ashurbanipal besieging an Egyptian city, 667 B.C.E. Alabaster relief, 2 ft. 11 in. × 7 ft. 4¼ in.

combating wild animals in the field—in the manner of the legendary Gilgamesh (see Figure 1.3). One dramatic relief from Nimrud depicts a wounded lion fiercely pursuing the royal chariot as it speeds away, while another beast lies dying before the wheels of the king's chariot (Figure **1.15**). Spatial depth is indicated by superimposing the chariot wheels over the rear lion's legs. Yet the heads and legs of the horses are shown on a single plane, and clarity of design required that the second wounded lion, crouching in pain, fit precisely within the space between the front and rear legs of the prancing steeds. The balance between figures (positive shapes) and ground (negative or "empty" space) results in a brilliant formal composition. The Assyrian reliefs—housed in large numbers at the British Museum in London—are superb examples of the artist's ability to infuse violent subject matter with narrative grandeur. If the lion-hunt reliefs made implicit reference to the ruler's invincibility, colossal sculpture clearly manifested his superhuman status. Thirteen-foot-tall hybrid beasts guarded the gateways of Assyrian palaces (see Figure 1.1). Bearing the facial features of the monarch, these colossi united the physical attributes of the bull (virility), the lion (physical strength), and the eagle (predatory agility). The winged, human-headed bulls from the citadel at Khorsabad were power-symbols designed to inspire awe and fear among those who passed beneath their impassive gaze. Clearly, the art of Assyria was visual propaganda, designed not only to celebrate Assyrian rulership, but also to intimidate its enemies.

The Persian Empire

The Persian Empire, the last and the largest of the empires of Mesopotamia, was brought to its peak by Cyrus II (ca. 585–ca. 529 B.C.E.), called "the Great" for his conquests over territories ranging from the frontiers of India to the Mediterranean Sea. The linguistic and ethnic diversity of this empire made it the first multicultural civilization of the ancient world. At Persepolis, its capital and ceremonial center, the Persians built a huge stone palace ornamented with carved reliefs of the king's royal guard.

The powerful monarchs of Persia (modern-day Iran), aided by a large cadre of administrators, oversaw a vast network of roads connecting the major cities of the Empire. Across some 1600 miles of terrain, fresh horses (located at post stations 14 miles apart) carried couriers "unhindered by snow, or rain, or heat, or by the darkness of night," according to the Greek historian Herodotus, who (unwittingly) provided the motto for the United States Postal Service.

The Persians devised a religion based on the teachings of the prophet Zoroaster (ca. 628–ca. 551 B.C.E.). Denying the nature gods of earlier times, Zoroaster exalted the primal spirit Ahura-Mazda ("Wise Lord"), who, opposing the evil spirit Angra Mainyu, demanded good thoughts, good works, and good deeds. As described in hymns known as the Gathas, Zoroaster (also known as Zarathustra) taught that life was a battlefield on which the dual forces of light and darkness contended for supremacy. Human beings took part in this cosmic struggle by way of their freedom to

Figure 1.16 Achaemenid (Persian) gold vessel, fifth to third century B.C.E. 6¾ × 9 in.

Chronology

ca. 3200–2350 B.C.E.	Sumerian city-states
ca. 2360–2000 B.C.E.	Sargon's Empire
ca. 2000–1600 B.C.E.	Babylonian Empire (Hammurabi reign: 1792–1750 B.C.E.)
ca. 1800–1200 B.C.E.	Hittite Empire
ca. 1300–700 B.C.E.	Era of Small States (Phoenicia, Lydia, Hebrew)
ca. 750–600 B.C.E.	Assyrian Empire
ca. 600–540 B.C.E.	Chaldean (Neo-Babylonian) Empire
ca. 550–330 B.C.E.	Persian Empire

choose between good and evil, the consequences of which would determine their fate at the end of time. According to Zoroaster, a Last Judgment would consign the wicked to everlasting darkness, while the good would live eternally in an abode of luxury and light: the Persian *pairidaeza*, from which the English word "paradise" derives. Zoroastrianism came to influence the moral teachings of three great world religions: Judaism, Christianity, and Islam (see chapters 8 and 10).

At Persepolis, artists perpetuated the architectural and sculptural traditions of Assyria. The Persians also brought to perfection the art of metalworking that had flourished in Mesopotamia since the beginning of the Bronze Age. Utensils, vessels, and jewelry produced by Persian crafts-people display some of the most intricate and sophisticated techniques of goldworking known to the history of that medium (Figure **1.16**). Many of these techniques would be practiced for centuries to come.

LOOKING BACK

The Land Between the Two Rivers

- The Tigris and Euphrates rivers formed part of a fertile crescent at the western end of Asia; here, agricultural activity encouraged the rise of Sumer, humankind's earliest civilization.
- Mesopotamia's geographic vulnerability contributed to invasion and instability. In the history of its rapid turnover of civilizations, language and government were as versatile and varied as the civilizations themselves.

The Gods of Mesopotamia

- The deities of Mesopotamia were associated with the forces of nature. According to *The Babylonian Creation*, Marduk, hero-god and offspring of Wisdom, destroyed the Great Mother, founded the city of Babylon, and created human beings.

- The *Epic of Gilgamesh*, the world's first heroic epic, follows the semihistorical ruler of Uruk on his quest for everlasting life. The epic reflects the sense of human vulnerability that prevailed in Mesopotamian culture.

The Rulers of Mesopotamia

- Individual priest-kings ruled Sumerian city-states as agents of the gods; they led the army, regulated the supply and distribution of food, provided political and religious leadership, and conducted services designed to win the favor of the gods.
- Around 2350 B.C.E., the Akkadian warlord Sargon I conquered the Sumerian city-states and ruled over them as a theocratic monarch.

The Social Order

- The social order and division of labor that prevailed in Mesopotamia around 2700 B.C.E. are depicted in the Standard of Ur; the ruler and his officials are shown in the top register, soldiers and servants below, and victims of war or slaves at the bottom.
- After 2000 B.C.E., rulers of the city-state of Babylon established the First Babylonian Empire. Its sixth king, Hammurabi, called for a written code of law covering a broad spectrum of moral, social, and commercial obligations.
- Mesopotamian women were considered intellectually and physically inferior to men and were regarded as personal property; however, as indicated by Hammurabi's Code, women enjoyed commercial freedom and gained considerable legal protection.

The Arts in Mesopotamia

- Artifacts from Mesopotamia, including jewelry, weapons, household goods, and musical instruments, testify to the wealth of its early civilizations.
- The ziggurat, the culture's most notable architectural symbol, was the spiritual center of the Mesopotamian city-states. Both a shrine and a temple, it symbolized the sacred mountain that linked heaven and earth.

The Iron Age

- During the second millennium B.C.E., iron was introduced into Asia Minor by the Hittites, tribal nomads who built an empire that lasted until ca. 1200 B.C.E.
- Cheaper and more durable than bronze, iron represented a new, superior technology. Iron tools contributed to increased agricultural production, facilitating the rise of small states, such as Phoenicia and Lydia, while iron weapons and chariots expedited the militant expansion of empires.

The Hebrews

- Archeologists trace the beginnings of Hebrew history to the region of Sumer around 2000 B.C.E. The Hebrew Bible cites Abraham of Ur as the patriarch who led the Hebrews westward across the Fertile Crescent into Canaan.
- The first book of the Hebrew Bible (Genesis) recounts the covenant by which the Hebrew god promised to protect Abraham's descendants in return for their unswerving obedience.
- Hebrew monotheism holds that there is only one god. Believed to transcend nature and all natural phenomena, this god differed from those of other ancient societies.
- The first five books of the Hebrew Bible, collectively known as the Torah, were written down between the tenth and seventh centuries B.C.E.
- The Decalogue, or Ten Commandments, is said to have been handed directly from God to Moses after the Hebrew exodus from Egypt. This set of moral and spiritual obligations is fundamental to ethical monotheism, the belief in God as the sole moral monitor.
- The first Hebrew state was forged under the theocratic rules of Saul, David, and Solomon; it came under successive attacks by Mesopotamia's aggressive empires.
- The writings of the prophets and the Book of Job reflect the Hebrew history of insecurity and exile. The Hebrew Bible provided the religious and ethical foundations for Judaism, Christianity, and Islam.

Empires of the Iron Age

- Equipped with iron weapons, the Assyrians, Chaldeans, and Persians followed one another in conquering large portions of Mesopotamia, creating vast empires.
- The Assyrians combined fighting techniques and engineering ingenuity to swallow up most of the land between the Persian Gulf and the Nile valley by 721 B.C.E.
- The Persian Empire, the last and largest of Mesopotamia's empires, was a multicultural civilization that reached its peak in the sixth century B.C.E. The Persian prophet Zoroaster imagined a cosmic struggle between the forces of good and evil, and warned of a Last Judgment that consigned souls to abodes of light or darkness.

Glossary

antiphonal a type of music in which two or more groups of voices or instruments alternate with one another

cantor the chief singer of the liturgy

covenant contract; the bond between the Hebrew people and their god

empire a state achieved militarily by the unification of territories under a single sovereign power

epic a long narrative poem that recounts the deeds of a legendary or historical hero in his quest for meaning or identity

lapis lazuli a semiprecious blue stone

liturgy the rituals for public worship

menorah a seven-branched candelabrum

monarch a single or sole ruler

monotheism the belief in one and only one god

mosaic a medium by which small pieces of glass or stone are used to ornament a flat surface

polytheism the belief in many gods

prophet (Greek, "one who speaks for another"), a divinely inspired teacher

responsory a type of music in which a single voice answers another voice or a chorus

shofar a trumpet made of a ram's horn, used to summon Jews to prayer

synagogue the Jewish house for worship and religious study

theocracy rule, by god or god's representative

Torah (Hebrew, "instruction," "law," or "teaching"), the first five books of the Hebrew Bible: Genesis, Exodus, Leviticus, Numbers, and Deuteronomy

ziggurat a terraced tower of rubble and brick that served ancient Mesopotamians as a temple-shrine

Africa: Gods, Rulers, and the Social Order

ca. 3100–330 B.C.E.

"The barges sail upstream and downstream too, for every way is open at your rising."
The Hymn to the Aten

Figure 2.1 Sphinx at Gizeh, Egypt, ca. 2540–2514 B.C.E. Limestone, length 240 ft., height 65 ft. The Sphinx looks to the East: the place of revival and rebirth associated with the rising sun, a natural life force deified by the ancient Egyptians.

In Africa, as in Mesopotamia, the forces of nature challenged the rise of civilization. The sun that nourished a bountiful harvest, the winds that swept away whole villages, the rains that caused rivers to flood the land—all these affected daily life, even as they do in our own time. Among our ancestors, however, for whom survival was a day-to-day struggle, such forces and the gods that represented them assumed supreme importance. The success

of ancient Africa's first civilization depended on a shared view of the earthly order as god-given and as immutably fixed in nature, on strong leadership, and on communal cooperation. As in Mesopotamia, the bonds between the divine and secular realms governed social and moral life. So, "gods, rulers, and the social order" remains the threefold focus of our survey.

Africa: Ancient Egypt

Ancient Egyptian civilization emerged along the banks of the Nile River in Northeast Africa. From the heart of Africa, the thin blue thread of the Nile flowed some 4000 miles to its fan-shaped delta at the Mediterranean Sea. Along this river, agricultural villages thrived, coming under the rule of a sole ruler around 3150 B.C.E. Surrounded by sea and desert, Egypt was relatively invulnerable to foreign invasion (Map **2.1**), a condition that lent stability to Egyptian history. Unlike Mesopotamia, home to many different civilizations, ancient Egypt enjoyed a fairly uniform religious, political, and cultural life that lasted for almost 3000 years. Its population shared a common language and a common perception of reality.

The Gods of Ancient Egypt

Geography, climate, and the distinctive features of the natural environment worked to shape the world-views and religious beliefs of all ancient peoples. In the hot, arid climate of Northeast Africa, where ample sunlight made possible the cultivation of crops, the sun god held the place of honor. Variously called Amon, Rē (Ra), or Aten, this god was considered greater than any other deity in the Egyptian pantheon. His cult dominated the polytheistic belief system of ancient Egypt for three millennia. Equally important to Egyptian life was the Nile, the world's longest river. Egypt, called by the Greek historian Herodotus "the gift of the Nile," depended on the annual overflow of the Nile, which left fertile layers of rich silt along its banks. The 365-day cycle of the river's inundation became the basis of the solar calendar and the primary source of Egypt's deep sense of order. In the regularity of the sun's daily cycle and the Nile's annual deluge, ancient Egyptians found security. From the natural elements—the sun, the Nile, and the largely flat topography of North Africa—they also constructed their **cosmology**, that is, their theory of

Map 2.1 Ancient Egypt. The Nile River begins in the mountains of modern-day Ethiopia and southern Sudan. It flows north for more than 4000 miles to the delta, where it empties into the Mediterranean Sea. Ancient Egypt flourished along the 750-mile stretch from Aswan to the Mediterranean. The terms "Upper Egypt" and "Lower Egypt" reflect the fact that the Nile flows from highlands in the south to the lowlands of the north.

the origin and structure of the universe. Egyptian myths of creation describe the earth as a flat platter floating on the waters of the underworld. At the beginning of time, the Nile's primordial waters brought forth a mound of silt, out of which emerged the self-generating sun god; and from that god, the rest of Egypt's gods were born.

Ancient Egyptians viewed the sun's daily ascent in the east as symbolic of the god's "rebirth"; his daily resurrection signified the victory of the forces of day, light, purity, goodness, and life over those of night, darkness, ignorance, evil, and death. In the cyclical regularity of nature evidenced by the daily rising and setting of the sun, the ancient Egyptians perceived both the inevitability of death and the promise of birth. The cult of the sun dominated the religious history of ancient Egypt. In the earliest hymns of the Old Kingdom, Rē (or Ra) was celebrated as the self-generating life force. Like other ancient deities, he was known by many names, each of which described a different aspect of his power: Amun or Amon (giver of the breath

Principal Egyptian Gods

Name	Role	Depicted As
Amon	sun god, creator of heaven and earth	falcon, sun rays
Anubis	patron of embalmers, god of cemeteries	jackal
Aten	god of the solar disk	solar disk
Bes	helper of women in childbirth, protector against snakes	lion-faced dwarf
Hapi	god of the Nile	bull
Hathor	mother, wife, and daughter of Ra, sky goddess	cow
Horus	son of Isis and Osiris, sky god	falcon
Isis	wife of Osiris, mother of Horus, fertility goddess	female
Maat	goddess of truth and universal order	head-feather
Osiris	god of the underworld	mummified king
Ptah	creator of humans, patron of craftspeople	mummified man
Set	brother of Osiris, god of storms and violence	pig, ass, hippopotamus
Thoth	inventor of writing, patron of scribes	ibis

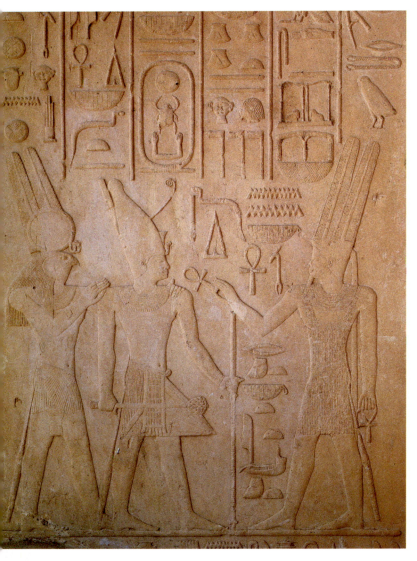

Figure 2.2 Amon receives Sesostris (Senusret) I, pillar relief, White Chapel, Karnak, ca. 1925 B.C.E. The god Amon, on the right, grants everlasting life (in the form of the *ankh*) to the Middle Kingdom pharaoh Sesostris. Behind the pharaoh stands the protective falcon-headed god Horus.

of life), Atum (the setting sun), and Aten (the disk of the sun; see Reading 2.1). Hymns of praise were probably accompanied by rituals of renewal honoring the pharaoh, the divinely appointed representative of the sun:

Praise to thee, O Rē, when thou settest, Atum . . .
Divine divinity that came into being of himself,
Primeval god, that existed at the beginning.

The transfer of power from the sun god to the pharaoh was frequently shown in Egyptian tombs and temples. In a carved relief from the White Chapel at Karnak, the pharaoh Sesostris, wearing the combined crowns of Upper and Lower Egypt, and holding the scepter and staff of authority, receives from Amon the symbol of life known as the *ankh* (Figure **2.2**).

Second only to the sun as the major natural force in Egyptian life was the Nile River. Ancient Egyptians identified the Nile with Osiris, ruler of the underworld and god of the dead. According to Egyptian myth, Osiris was slain by his evil brother, Set, who chopped his body into pieces and threw them into the Nile. But Osiris' loyal wife, Isis, Queen of Heaven, gathered the fragments and restored Osiris to life. The union of Isis and the resurrected Osiris produced a son, Horus, who ultimately avenged his father by overthrowing Set and becoming ruler of Egypt. The Osiris myth vividly describes the idea of resurrection that was central to the ancient Egyptian belief system. Although the cult of the sun in his various aspects dominated the official religion of Egypt, local gods and goddesses—more than 2000 of them—made up the Egyptian pantheon. These deities, most of whom held multiple powers, played protective roles in the daily lives of the ancient Egyptians. However, the following invocation to Isis, found inscribed on a sculpture of the goddess, suggests her central role among the female deities of Egypt:

> Praise to you, Isis, the Great One
> God's Mother, Lady of Heaven,
> Mistress and Queen of the Gods.

The Rulers of Ancient Egypt

Local rulers governed the Neolithic villages along the Nile until roughly 3150 B.C.E., when they were united under the authority of Egypt's first pharaoh, Narmer (also known as Menes). This important political event—the union of Upper and Lower Egypt—is commemorated on a 2-foot-high slate object known as the Palette of King Narmer (see LOOKING INTO, Figure **2.4**, see page 48), and initiated Egypt's first **dynasty**. For some 2500 years to follow, ancient Egypt was ruled by a succession of dynasties, the history of which was divided into chronological periods by an Egyptian priest of the third century B.C.E.

Civil dissent marked the intermediate period between the Old and Middle kingdoms, while the era between the Middle and New kingdoms (the second intermediate period) withstood the invasion of the Hyksos, warlike tribes who introduced the horse and chariot into Egypt. Following the expulsion of the Hyksos, New Kingdom pharaohs (the word means "great house" in the sense of "first family") created Egypt's first empire, extending royal authority far into Syria, Palestine, and Nubia. The last eleven Egyptian dynasties (XXI–XXXI) struggled through centuries of political volatility. Foreign invasions, ending with the conquest of Egypt by Alexander the Great in 332 B.C.E., finally brought the 3000-year-old civilization to an end.

Throughout their long history, ancient Egyptians viewed the land as sacred. It was owned by the gods, ruled by the pharaohs, and farmed by the peasants with the assistance of slaves. The fruits of each harvest were shared according to the needs of the community. This divinely sanctioned way of life, known as *theocratic socialism*, provided Egypt with an abundance of food and a surplus that encouraged widespread trade. The land itself, however, passed from generation to generation not through the male but through the female line, that is, from the king's daughter to the man she married. For the pharaoh's son to come to the throne, he would have to marry his own sister or half-sister (hence the numerous brother–sister marriages in Egyptian dynastic history). This tradition, probably related to the practice of tracing parentage to the child-bearer, lasted longer in Egypt than anywhere else in the ancient world. In the free-standing sculpture of the Old Kingdom pharaoh Mycerinus, the queen stands proudly at his side, one arm around his waist and the other gently touching his arm (Figure **2.3**). A sense of shared purpose is conveyed by

Figure 2.3 Pair statue of Mycerinus and Queen Kha-merer-nebty II, Gizeh, Mycerinus, fourth dynasty, ca. 2599–1571 B.C.E. Slate schist, height 4 ft. 6½ in. (complete statue).

Chronology

Early dynastic period	ca. 3100–2700 B.C.E.	(Dynasties I–II)
Old Kingdom	ca. 2700–2150 B.C.E.	(Dynasties III–VI)
Middle Kingdom	ca. 2050–1785 B.C.E.	(Dynasties XI–XII)
New Kingdom	ca. 1575–1085 B.C.E.	(Dynasties XVIII–XX)

The Palette of King Narmer

The back of the slate palette (right) shows the triumphant Narmer seizing a fallen enemy by the hair. Below his feet lie the bodies of the vanquished. To his left, a slave (represented smaller in size than Narmer) dutifully carries his master's sandals. At the upper right is the victorious falcon, symbol of the god Horus. Horus/Narmer holds by the leash the now-subdued lands of Lower Egypt, symbolized by a severed head and **papyrus**, the reedlike plants that grow along the Nile. On the front (left), the top register bears a victory procession flanked by rows of defeated soldiers, who stand with their decapitated heads between their legs.

Figure 2.4 The Palette of King Narmer (front and back), ca. 3100 B.C.E. Slate, height 25 in.

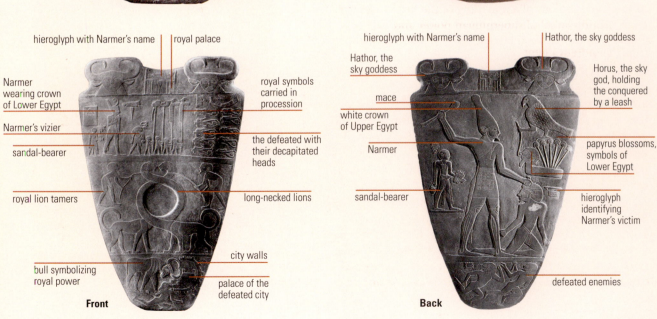

hieroglyph with Narmer's name

royal palace

Narmer wearing crown of Lower Egypt

royal symbols carried in procession

Narmer's vizier

sandal-bearer

the defeated with their decapitated heads

royal lion tamers

long-necked lions

bull symbolizing royal power

city walls

palace of the defeated city

Front

hieroglyph with Narmer's name

Hathor, the sky goddess

Hathor, the sky goddess

Horus, the sky god, holding the conquered by a leash

mace

white crown of Upper Egypt

Narmer

papyrus blossoms, symbols of Lower Egypt

sandal-bearer

hieroglyph identifying Narmer's victim

defeated enemies

Back

their lifted chins and confident demeanor. While Egypt's rulers were traditionally male, women came to the throne three times. The most notable of all female pharaohs, Hatshepsut (ca. 1500–1447 B.C.E.), governed Egypt for twenty-two years. She is often pictured in male attire, wearing the royal wig and false beard, and carrying the crook and the flail—traditional symbols of rulership.

Egyptian Theocracy

From earliest times, political power was linked with spiritual power and superhuman might. The Egyptians held that divine power flowed from the gods to their royal agents. In this theocracy, reigning monarchs represented heaven's will on earth. While the pharaoh ruled in the name of the immortal and generative sun god, he was also identified with the falcon-headed god Horus, the avenging son of Osiris and Isis (see Figure 2.2). So close was the association between rulers and the gods that Egyptian hymns honoring the pharaoh address him in terms identical with those that supplicate the gods.

In the visual arts, rulers and gods alike were depicted with the attributes and physical features of powerful animals. Such is the case with the Great Sphinx, the recumbent creature that guards the entrance to the ceremonial complex at Gizeh (see Figure **2.1**). This haunting figure, antiquity's largest and earliest surviving colossal statue, bears the portrait head of the Old Kingdom pharaoh Khafre and the body of a lion, king of the beasts. As such, it is a hybrid symbol of superhuman power and authority.

Law in Ancient Egypt

In ancient Egypt, long-standing customs and unwritten rules preceded the codification and transcription of civil and criminal law. Indeed, Egyptian law consisted of the unwritten decrees of the pharaoh (passed down orally until they were transcribed during the New Kingdom). An inscription on an Old Kingdom tomb wall sums up this phenomenon as follows: "The law of the land is the mouth of the pharaoh." In Egypt, no written laws have been preserved from any period before the fourth century B.C.E. When one considers that toward the end of the thirteenth century B.C.E. the pharaoh Rameses II ruled approximately three million people, it is clear that the oral tradition—the verbal transmission of rules, conventions, and customs—played a vital part in establishing political continuity.

The Cult of the Dead

Ancient Egyptians venerated the pharaoh as the living representative of the sun god. They believed that on his death, the pharaoh would join with the sun to govern Egypt eternally. His body was prepared for burial by means of a special ten-week embalming procedure that involved removing all his internal organs (with the exception of his heart) and filling his body cavity with preservatives. His intestines, stomach, lungs, and liver were all embalmed separately; the brain was removed and discarded. The king's corpse was then wrapped in fine linen and placed in an elaborately ornamented coffin (Figure **2.5**), which was floated down the Nile on a royal barge to a burial site at Gizeh, near the southern tip of the Nile delta (see Map 2.1). The earliest Egyptian tombs—homes for the dead—were probably modeled on Egypt's domestic dwellings. These rectangular single-story mud-brick tombs, called **mastabas**, consisted of an offering chamber, a room that held a statue of the dead, and a shaft that descended to the burial chamber some 100 feet below the ground. Stacking five mastabas of decreasing size one on top of another, the third-dynasty architect Imenhotep produced the impressive stepped pyramid for King Zoser, who ruled shortly before 2600 B.C.E. (Figure **2.6**). The pyramidal shape may have been inspired by the mythical mound of silt from which the primordial sun god was said to have risen. With the fourth-dynasty pharaohs of the Old Kingdom, the true geometric **pyramid** took shape.

Figure 2.5 Egyptian mummy and coffin, ca. 1000 B.C.E.

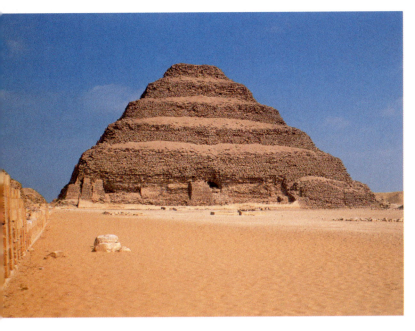

Figure 2.6 Stepped pyramid of King Zoser, Saqqara, ca. 2630 B.C.E.

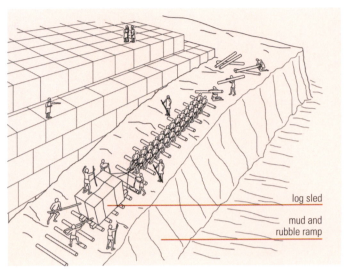

Figure 2.7 Pyramid construction. Some historians speculate that the vast stone building-blocks were hauled into position using log sleds and inclined ramps made of packed sand.

Constructed between 2600 and 2500 B.C.E., the pyramids are technological wonders, as well as symbols of ancient Egypt's endurance through time. A workforce of some 50,000 men (divided into gangs of twenty-five) labored for almost thirty years to raise the Great Pyramid of Khufu. According to recent DNA analysis of the workers found buried at Gizeh, the pyramid builders were Egyptians, not foreign slaves as was previously assumed. This native workforce quarried, transported, and assembled thousands of mammoth stone blocks, most weighing between 2 and 50 tons. These they lifted from tier to tier by means of levers—although some historians speculate that they were slid into place on inclined ramps of sand and rubble (Figure 2.7). Finally, the laborers faced the surfaces of the great tombs with finely polished limestone. All these feats were achieved with copper saws and chisels, and without pulleys or mortar.

The Great Pyramid of Khufu, which stands as part of a large walled burial complex at Gizeh (Figures 2.8 and 2.9), consists of more than two million stone blocks rising to a height of approximately 480 feet and covering a base area of 13 acres. The royal burial vault, hidden within a

Figure 2.8 Great pyramids of Gizeh: from left to right, Menkure, ca. 2575 B.C.E., Khufu (Khefren), ca. 2650 B.C.E., Khafre, ca. 2600 B.C.E. Top height 480 ft. (approx.).

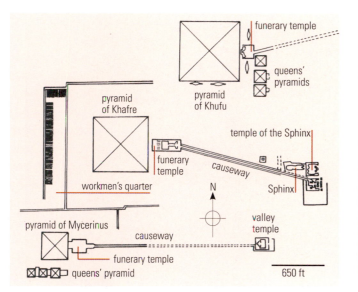

Figure 2.9 Reconstruction of the pyramids of Khufu and Khafre at Gizeh, ca. 2650–2600 B.C.E.

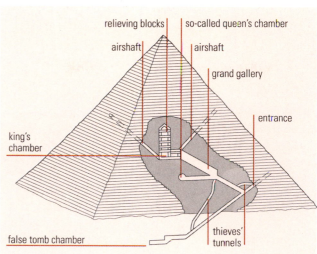

Figure 2.10 Burial chambers within a typical pyramid.

series of chambers connected to the exterior by tunnels (Figure **2.10**), was prepared as a home for eternity—a tribute to communal faith in the eternal benevolence of the pharaoh. Its chambers were filled with his most cherished possessions: priceless treasures of jewelry, weapons, and furniture, all of which he might require in the life to come. The walls of the chamber were painted with colored pigments, a technique known as **fresco secco** (dry fresco), or carved in **relief** with images visualizing sacred rituals and daily activities (see Figure 2.18). Hieroglyphs formed an essential component of pictorial illustration, narrating the achievements of Egypt's rulers, listing the grave goods, and offering perpetual prayers for the deceased (see also Figures 2.2, 2.4, and 2.13). Carved and painted figures representing important royal officials, such as administrators and scribes, accompanied the pharaoh to the afterlife (Figure **2.11**). Other figures representing servants carried provisions such as bread, fowl, beer, and linens.

The carved images may have served as surrogates for servants and slaves who, in earlier times, went to the grave with their masters. Death masks or "reserve" portrait heads of the pharaoh might be placed in the tomb to provide the king's *ka* (life force or divine essence) with safe and familiar dwelling places.

Intended primarily as homes for the dead, the pyramids were built to assure the ruler's comfort in the afterlife. However, in the centuries after their construction, grave robbers greedily despoiled them, and their contents were largely plundered and lost. Middle and Late Kingdom pharaohs turned to other methods of burial, including interment in the rock cliffs along the Nile and in unmarked graves in the Valley of the Kings, west of Thebes. In time, these too were pillaged. One of the few royal graves to have escaped vandalism was that of a minor fourteenth-century B.C.E. ruler named Tutankhamen (ca. 1345–1325 B.C.E.). Uncovered by the British archeologist Howard

Figure 2.11 Seated scribe, Saqqara. Fifth dynasty, ca. 2400 B.C.E. Painted limestone, height 21 in. The scribe was one of the highest officials in ancient Egypt. Trained in reading, writing, law, religion, and mathematics, scribes often ranked as scholars and priests. The eyes of this limestone figure were once inlaid with rock crystal, calcite, and magnesite mounted in copper.

Figure 2.12 Cover of the coffin of Tutankhamen (ca. 1345–1325 B.C.E.) (detail), from the Valley of the Kings. Gold with inlay of enamel, carnelian, lapis lazuli, and turquoise, height 6 ft.

Figure 2.13 Throne with Tutankhamen (ca. 1345–1325 B.C.E.) and Queen (detail of the back), late Marana period, New Kingdom, eighteenth dynasty. Wood, plated with gold and silver, inlays of glass paste, 12 × 12 in. (approx.). The rays of the sun god shine down on Tutankhamen and his consort. Both wear lavish crowns that symbolize authority over Upper and Lower Egypt.

Carter in 1922, the tomb housed riches of astonishing variety, including the pharaoh's solid-gold coffin, inlaid with semiprecious carnelian and lapis lazuli (Figure **2.12**), and a lavish throne depicting Tutankhamen and his wife (Figure **2.13**). Standing below the shining disk of the sun god, the queen, in an ankle-length gown, tenderly straightens her consort's collar. Above them the sun disk's rays end in human hands, some of which carry the *ankh*.

The promise of life after death seems to have dominated at all levels of Egyptian culture. The most elaborate homes for the dead were reserved for royalty and members of the aristocracy, but recent excavations of the lower cemetery at Gizeh reveal at least 700 graves of workmen and artisans. In the coffins of ancient Egypt's dead are found papyrus scrolls inscribed with prayers and incantations to guide the soul in the afterlife. The *Book of the Dead*, a collection of funerary prayers originating as far back as 4000 B.C.E., prepared each individual for final judgment.

In the presence of the gods Osiris and Isis, the dead souls were expected to recite a lengthy confession attesting to their purity of heart, including:

I have not done iniquity.
I have not robbed with violence.
I have not done violence [to any man].
I have not committed theft.
I have not slain man or woman.
I have not made light the bushel.
I have not acted deceitfully.
I have not uttered falsehood.
I have not defiled the wife of a man.
I have not stirred up strife.
I have not cursed the god.
I have not behaved with insolence.
I have not increased my wealth, except with such things as are my own possessions.

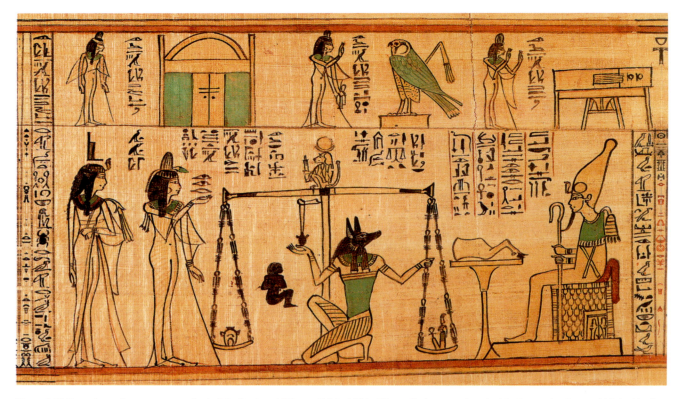

Figure 2.14 Scene from a funerary papyrus, *Book of the Dead*, ca. 1285 B.C.E. Height 11¾ in. Princess Entiu-ny stands to the left of a set of scales on which Anubis, the jackal-headed god, weighs her heart against the figure of Truth, while Osiris, Lord of the Dead, judges from his throne. His wife, Isis, stands behind the princess.

A painted papyrus scroll from the *Book of the Dead* brings to life the Last Judgment itself: the enthroned Osiris, god of the underworld (far right), and his wife, Isis (far left), oversee the ceremony in which the heart of the deceased Princess Entiu-ny is weighed against the figure of Truth (Figure **2.14**). Having made her testimony, the princess watches as the jackal-headed god of death, Anubis, prepares her heart for the ordeal. "Grant thou," reads the prayer to Osiris, "that I may have my being among the living, and that I may sail up and down the river among those who are in thy following." If the heart is not "found true by trial of the Great Balance," it will be devoured by the monster Ament, thus meeting a second death. If pure, it might sail with the sun "up and down the river," or flourish in a realm where wheat grows high and the living souls of the dead enjoy feasting and singing. An image of this heavenly domain is depicted on the walls of the tomb of Sennudjem: the "fields of the blessed" are bordered by beneficent gods (top) and flourishing fruit trees (bottom) (Figure **2.15**). Here, death is a continuation of daily life in a realm that floats eternally on the primordial waters—indicated by the jagged blue lines that frame the registers.

Akhenaten's Reform

Throughout the dynastic history of Egypt, the central authority of the pharaoh was repeatedly contested by local temple priests, each of whom held religious and political sway in their own regions along the Nile. Perhaps in an effort to consolidate his authority against priestly encroachment, the New Kingdom pharaoh Amenhotep IV (ca. 1353–1336 B.C.E.) defied the tradition of polytheism by elevating Aten (god of the sun disk) to a position of supremacy over all other gods. "The Hymn to the Aten," which is based on earlier Egyptian songs of praise, dates from the reign of Amenhotep IV.

READING 2.1 From "The Hymn to the Aten"

(ca. 1352–1336 B.C.E.)

You rise in perfection on the horizon of the sky   1
    living Aten,[1] who started life.
Whenever you are risen upon the eastern horizon
    you fill every land with your perfection.
      You are appealing, great, sparkling, high over every land;   5
    your rays hold together the lands as far as everything you have made.
Since you are Rē,[2] you reach as far as they do,
    and you curb them for your beloved son.
Although you are far away, your rays are upon the land;
    you are in their faces, yet your departure is not observed.   10
Whenever you set on the western horizon,
    the land is in darkness in the manner of death.
They sleep in a bedroom with heads under the covers,
    and one eye does not see another.
      If all their possessions which are under their heads were stolen,   15
    they would not know it.

---

[1] The sun disk.
[2] Another name for the sun god, associated with his regenerative powers.

Figure 2.15 Illustration of Spell 110 from the *Book of the Dead* in the burial chamber of Sennudjem, ca. 1279 B.C.E. Frescoes like this one were preserved by Egypt's dry climate. The blue color (a compound of calcium copper tetrasilicate) used in frescoes like this one is believed to be the world's oldest artificial pigment.

Every lion who comes out of his cave
    and all the serpents bite,
    for darkness is a blanket.
The land is silent now, because he who made them   20
    is at rest on his horizon

But when day breaks you are risen upon the horizon,
    and you shine as the Aten in the daytime.
When you dispel darkness and you give forth your rays
    the two lands[3] are in festival,   25
    alert and standing on their feet,
    now that you have raised them up.
Their bodies are clean,
    and their clothes have been put on;
    their arms are [lifted] in praise at your rising.   30
The entire land performs its work:
    all the cattle are content with their fodder,
    trees and plants grow,
    birds fly up to their nests,
    their wings [extended] in praise for your Ka.[4]   35
All the Kine[5] prance on their feet;
    everything which flies up and alights,
    they live when you
    have risen for them.
The barges sail upstream and downstream too,   40
    for every way is open at your rising.
The fishes in the river leap before your face
    when your rays are in the sea.

You who have placed seed in woman
    and have made sperm into man,   45
    who feeds the son in the womb of his mother,
    who quiets him with something to stop his crying;
    you are the nurse in the womb,
    giving breath to nourish all that has been begotten.

**Q Which of Aten's powers are glorified
     in this hymn?**

Changing his own name to Akhenaten ("Shining Spirit of Aten"), the pharaoh abandoned the political capital at Memphis and the religious center at Thebes to build a new palace midway between the two at a site called Akhetaten ("Place of the Sun Disk's Power") (see Map 2.1).

Akhenaten's chief wife, Queen Nefertiti, along with her mother-in-law, assisted in organizing the affairs of state. The mother of six daughters, Nefertiti is often pictured as Isis, the goddess from whom all Egyptian queens were said to have descended. Nefertiti's confident beauty inspired numerous sculpted likenesses, some of which are striking in their blend of realism and abstraction (Figure **2.16**). Akhenaten's monotheistic reform lasted only as long as his reign, and in the years following his death, Egypt's conservative priests and nobles returned to the polytheism of their forebears.

---

[3] Upper and Lower Egypt.
[4] The governing spirit or soul of a person or god.
[5] Cows.

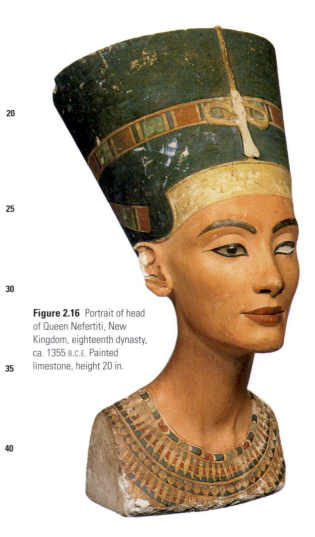

Figure 2.16 Portrait of head of Queen Nefertiti, New Kingdom, eighteenth dynasty, ca. 1355 B.C.E. Painted limestone, height 20 in.

The Social Order

Like all ancient civilizations, Egypt could not have existed without a high level of cooperation among those whose individual tasks—governing, trading, farming, fighting—contributed to communal survival. Powerful families, tribes, and clans, usually those that had proved victorious in battle, established long-standing territorial claims. Such families often claimed descent from, or association with, the gods. Once royal authority was entrenched, it was almost impossible to unseat. The ruling dynasty, in conjunction with a priestly caste that supervised the religious activities of the community, formed an elite group of men and women who regulated the lives of the lower classes: merchants, farmers, herders, artisans, soldiers, and servants. Nevertheless, the class structure in ancient Egypt seems to have been quite flexible. Ambitious individuals of any class were free to rise in status, usually by way of education.

For well over 2000 years, Egypt was administered by the pharaoh's vast bureaucracy, members of which collected taxes, regulated public works, and mobilized the army. In the social order, these individuals, along with large landowners and priests, constituted the upper classes. As in all ancient societies, power was not uniformly distributed but descended from the top rung of the hierarchy in diminishing degrees of influence. Those closest to the pharaoh participated most fully in his authority and prestige. Other individuals might advance their positions and improve their status through service to the pharaoh.

At the top of the bureaucratic pyramid stood the vizier. Essential to the administration and the security of the state, the vizier was in charge of appointing members of the royal bureaucracy and dispatching the local officials. He oversaw the mobilization of troops, the irrigation of canals, and the taking of inventories, and, with the assistance of official scribes, he handled all litigation for the Egyptian state. Merchants, traders, builders, and scribes made up a prosperous middle class, who ranked in status just below the aristocracy. At the base of the social pyramid, the great masses of peasants constituted the agricultural backbone of ancient Egypt. Aided by slaves, peasant men and women worked side by side to farm the land. Even in the afterlife, husbands and wives shared the tasks of reaping and plowing (see Figure 2.15). Class status seems to have extended into the afterlife: in the cemeteries recently uncovered at Gizeh, artisans received separate and more elaborate burials than common laborers. Slaves constituted a class of unfree men and women. In the ancient world, slaves were victims of military conquest. Enslaving one's enemy captives was a humane alternative to executing them. Some people became slaves as punishment for criminal acts, and still others as a result of falling into debt. Slaves might be sold or traded like any other form of property, but in Egypt and elsewhere in the ancient world, it appears that some slaves were able to acquire sufficient wealth to buy their own or their children's freedom.

Egyptian Women

Possibly because all property was inherited through the female line, Egyptian women seem to have enjoyed a large degree of economic independence, as well as civil rights and privileges. Women who could write and calculate might go into business. Women of the pharaoh's harem oversaw textile production, while others found positions as shopkeepers, midwives, musicians, and dancers (Figure 2.17). Nevertheless, men were wary of powerful women, as is indicated in a Middle Kingdom manual of good conduct, which offers the husband this advice concerning his wife: "Make her happy while you are alive, for she is land profitable to her lord. Neither judge her nor raise her to a position of power . . . her eye is a stormwind when she sees."

The Arts in Ancient Egypt

Literature

Ancient Egypt did not produce any literary masterpieces. Nevertheless, from tomb and temple walls, and from papyrus rolls, come prayers and songs, royal decrees and letters, prose tales, and texts that served to educate the young. One school text, which reflects the fragile relationship between oral and written traditions, reads: "Man decays, his corpse is dust,/ All his kin have perished;

Figure 2.17 Procession of female musicians with instruments, including a harp, double pipes, and a lyre, Tomb of Djeserkarasneb, Thebes, ca. 1580–1314 B.C.E. Copy of the original.

/ But a book makes him remembered,/ Through the mouth of its reciter." The so-called wisdom literature of Egypt, which consists of words of advice and instruction, anticipates parts of the Hebrew Bible.

During the Middle Kingdom, as Egypt's government grew in size, increasing emphasis was placed on the importance of keeping written records. *The Satire on Trades*, a standard exercise for student scribes, argues that the life of a government clerk is preferable to that of a farmer, baker, soldier, metalworker, or priest. "Behold," it concludes, "there is no profession free of a boss—except for the scribe: he is the boss!"

From the New Kingdom came a very personal genre of poetry that would come to be called **lyric** (literally, accompanied by the **lyre** or harp, see Figure 2.17). In the following three poems, two in a male voice and one female (from a group of poems known as "songs of the Birdcatcher's Daughter"), images from nature are freely employed to evoke sentiments of love and desire. Lines 5 to 7 of the second poem illustrate the effective use of **simile**, while the third poem operates as an extended **metaphor**.

READING 2.2 Egyptian Poetry

I will lie down inside,	1
and there I will feign illness.	
Then my neighbours will enter to see,	
and then my sister[1] will come with them.	
She'll put the doctor to shame,	5
for she will understand	
my illness.	

—◆—

My sister has come,	1
my heart exults,	
My arms spread out	
to embrace her;	
My heart bounds	5
in its place,	
Like the red fish	
in its pond.	
O night, be mine forever,	
Now that my lady has come!	10

—◆—

The voice of the goose complains,	1
when it is caught by the bait.	
Your love takes me (to you),	
and I cannot loose it.	
I must abandon my nets.	5
What shall I say to my mother,	
to whom I go back every day,	
laden with my birds?	
'You have set no trap to-day?'	
I am the captive of your love.	10

Q **How do simile and metaphor operate to enrich these poems?**

---

[1] Meaning "mistress" or "lady."

The Visual Arts

Egyptian art comes almost exclusively from tombs and temples. Such art was not intended as decoration; rather, it was created to replicate the living world, to benefit or honor the dead. Perhaps for that reason, the Egyptians found a unique way to express the deep sense of order that dominated ancient Egyptian life. For 3000 years, Egypt followed a set of conventions that dictated the manner in which subjects should be depicted. In representations of everyday life, figures are usually sized according to a strict hierarchy, or graded order: upper-class individuals are shown larger than lower-class ones, and males usually outsize females and servants (Figure **2.18**). In monumental sculptures of royalty, however, the chief wife of the pharaoh is often shown the same size as her husband (see Figure 2.3). The same is true in frescoes illustrating the *Book of the Dead*, where men and women share the task of reaping wheat (see Figure 2.14).

Very early in Egyptian history, artists developed a **canon** (or set of rules) by which to represent the human form. The proportions of the human body were determined according to a **module** (or standard of measurement) represented by the width of the clenched fist (Figure **2.19**). More generally, Egyptian artists adhered to a set of guidelines by which they might "capture" the most characteristic and essential aspects of the subject matter: in depicting the human figure, the upper torso is shown from the front, while the lower is shown from the side; the head is depicted in profile, while the eye and eyebrow are frontal. This method of representation is *conceptual*—that is, based on ideas—rather than *perceptual*—that is, based on visual evidence.

The Egyptian artist's approach to space was also conceptual. Spatial depth is indicated by placing one figure above (rather than behind) the next, often in horizontal registers, or rows. Cast in timeless space, Egyptian figures share the symbolic presence of the hieroglyphs by which they are framed (see Figure 2.2). Nowhere else in the ancient world do we see such an intimate and intelligible conjunction of image and word—a union designed to immortalize ideas rather than imitate reality.

This is not to say that Egyptian artists ignored the world of the senses, nor that they were incapable of naturalistic representation. The painted limestone figure of the seated scribe (see Figure 2.11) assumes a lifelike presence. His fleshy torso contrasts with the more stylized physique of the pharaoh Mycerinus pictured in Figure 2.3. Realistic detail also enlivens many Egyptian frescoes. For instance, in the New Kingdom tomb of the scribe Neb-amon (himself depicted in a stylized and conventional pose), the figures are surrounded by marsh birds so accurately rendered that ornithologists have been able to identify them by species (see Figure 2.18). It is in the union of the particular and the general that Egyptian art achieves its timeless quality.

New Kingdom Temples

Temples were built by the Egyptians from earliest times, but most of those that have survived date from the

Figure 2.18 Scene of fowling, from the tomb of Neb-amon at Thebes, Egypt, ca. 1400 B.C.E. Fragment of a fresco secco, height 32¼ in. Neb-amon, an Egyptian scribe and grain-counter, stands on a light papyrus raft that floats on the shallow waters of a marsh. He holds three birds (possibly stuffed decoys) in his right hand and a throw-stick shaped like a snake in his left. (The stick acts like a boomerang to break the neck of his prey.) He is accompanied by his wife and by his daughter, who crouches between his legs, gently steadying his stance.

Figure 2.19 The Egyptian canon of proportion.

New Kingdom. The basic plan of the temple mirrored the central features of the Egyptian cosmos: the **pylons** (two truncated pyramids that made up the gateway) symbolized the mountains that rimmed the edge of the world, while the progress from the open courtyard through the **hypostyle** hall into the dark inner sanctuary housing the cult statue represented a voyage from light to darkness (and back) symbolic of the sun's cyclical journey (Figure **2.20**). Oriented on an east–west axis, the temple received the sun's morning rays, which reached through the sequence of hallways into the sanctuary. The Great Temple of Amon-Ra at Karnak was the heart of a 5-acre religious complex that included a sacred lake, a sphinx-lined causeway, and numerous **obelisks** (commemorative stone pillars). The temple's hypostyle hall is adorned with painted reliefs that cover the walls and the surfaces of its 134 massive columns shaped like budding and flowering papyrus—these plants were identified with the marsh of creation (Figure **2.21**). Decorated with stars and other celestial images, the ceiling of the hall symbolized the heavens. Such sacred precincts were not intended for communal assembly—in fact, commoners were forbidden to enter. Rather, Egyptian temples were sanctuaries in which priests performed daily rituals of cosmic renewal on behalf of the pharaoh and the people. Temple rituals were celebrations of the solar cycle, associated not only with the birth of the sun god but also with the regeneration of the ruler upon whom cosmic order depended.

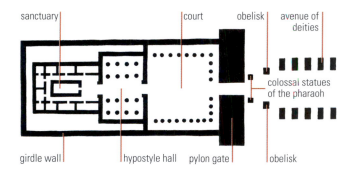

sanctuary   court   obelisk   avenue of deities

colossal statues of the pharaoh

girdle wall   hypostyle hall   pylon gate   obelisk

Figure 2.20 Plan of a typical pylon temple.

Music in Ancient Egypt

Tomb paintings reveal much about ancient Egyptian culture. They are, for example, our main source of information about ancient Egyptian music and dance (see Figure 2.17). It is clear that song and poetry were interchangeable (hymns like those praising the Aten were chanted, not spoken). Musical instruments, including harps, small stringed instruments, pipes, and sistrums (a type of rattle)—often found buried with the dead—accompanied song and dance. Greek sources indicate that Egyptian music was based in theory; nevertheless, we have no certain knowledge how that music actually sounded. Visual representations confirm, however, that music had a special place in religious rituals, in festive and funeral processions, and in many aspects of secular life.

Africa: The Sudan

Northern Sudan: Nubia

The ancient civilization of Nubia arose along the Nile in what is now known as northern Sudan (see Map 2.1). Located between the first and sixth cataracts of the Nile, this independent kingdom was the first literate urban civilization to appear in Africa south of the Sahara. It was probably populated by peoples from the south and southwest portions of Africa as early as the third millennium B.C.E., as the Sahara Desert became too arid to support human settlements. Famous for its large quantities of gold—the name "Nubia" may derive from the Egyptian word *nub*, meaning "gold"—the area became a trade corridor between the upper and lower regions of the Nile. Nubia provided its northern neighbors with cattle and a variety of luxury goods, including ivory, ebony, and incense. Royal officials of Old Kingdom Egypt made frequent expeditions to Nubia to report on political conditions there and to arrange for the importation of desirable tribute, such as elephant tusks, panther skins, and gold jewelry. While Nubia came under Egyptian jurisdiction during the Middle Kingdom, its rulers continued to oversee trade between Egypt and sub-Saharan Africa.

Figure 2.21 Hypostyle hall, Great Temple of Amon-Ra, Karnak, ca. 1220 B.C.E.

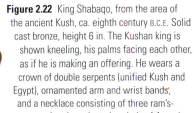

Figure 2.22 King Shabaqo, from the area of the ancient Kush, ca. eighth century B.C.E. Solid cast bronze, height 6 in. The Kushan king is shown kneeling, his palms facing each other, as if he is making an offering. He wears a crown of double serpents (unified Kush and Egypt), ornamented arm and wrist bands, and a necklace consisting of three ram's-head pendants (symbols of Amon) surmounted by a serpent crest and sun disk.

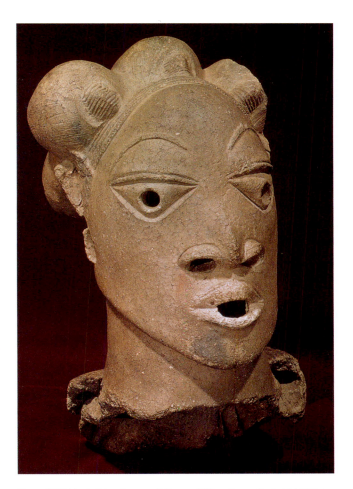

Figure 2.23 Head, Nok culture, ca. 500 B.C.E.–200 C.E. Terracotta, height 14³⁄₁₆ in.

Around 1550 B.C.E., the powerful state of Kush in Nubia defeated the Egyptian army. The conquerors adopted many aspects of Egyptian culture, including the practice of pyramid building. While New Kingdom Egypt reestablished its authority over the region, by the ninth century B.C.E. Kush came to govern all of southern (Upper) Egypt. For at least a century, Nubian artists crafted objects of great technical sophistication. This is especially visible in the area of metalworking, as reflected, for instance, in the bronze statue of the Kushan king Shabaqo (Figure **2.22**). In this small but forceful portrait, Nubia anticipated the birth of an African tradition in portraiture that began in western Sudan as early as 500 B.C.E. and continued to flourish for at least a thousand years.

Western Sudan: Nok Culture

While East Africa's ancient civilizations were known to the world as early as the eighteenth century, the western parts of the continent were not fully investigated by archeologists until the mid-twentieth century. In 1931, near a farming village called Nok, on the Niger River in western Sudan (see Map 2.1), tin miners accidentally uncovered a large group of terracotta sculptures (Figure **2.23**). Dating from the first millennium B.C.E., these hand-modeled figures, representing people and animals, are the earliest known three-dimensional artworks of sub-Saharan Africa. They are the first evidence of a long tradition of naturalistic portraiture in African art. The Nok heads, many of which display clearly individualized personalities, probably represent tribal rulers or revered ancestors.

LOOKING BACK

Africa: Ancient Egypt

- The Nile River, flowing from the heart of Africa to its fan-shaped delta at the Mediterranean Sea, provided the ideal setting for the rise of Egyptian civilization.
- Surrounded by sea and desert, and blessed with a stable climate, ancient Egypt flourished for almost 3000 years.

The Gods of Ancient Egypt

- The geography, climate, and topography of ancient Egypt played an important part in the shaping of the civilization's world-views and religious beliefs. Egyptian myth held that at the beginning of time, the Nile brought forth a mound of silt, out of which emerged the sun god called Amon or Rē (Ra), from whom the rest of Egypt's gods were born.
- The pharaohs of Egypt were the divinely appointed representatives of the sun god, a sharing of power depicted frequently in Egyptian tombs and temples.

The Rulers of Ancient Egypt

- Upper and Lower Egypt were united in ca. 3150 B.C.E. under the rule of Egypt's first pharaoh, Narmer.
- Egypt's theocratic monarchs required elaborate burials that ensured their well-being in the afterlife. Royal graves were filled with frescoes, relief carvings, and precious goods that reflect the Egyptian cult of the dead.
- A belief that the land was owned by the gods supported a way of life known as theocratic socialism, by which Egypt's population shared in the production and distribution of agricultural harvests.
- Egyptian rulers followed a matriarchal lineage by which land passed through the female line. For the pharaoh's son to come to the throne, he would have to marry his own sister or half-sister.
- In an effort to consolidate his power, the New Kingdom pharaoh Akhenaten denied all gods except Aten (god of the sun disk); his reforms did not outlast him.

The Social Order

- The class structure in ancient Egypt was flexible. Ambitious individuals of any class were free to rise in status, usually by way of education.
- A huge bureaucracy administered Egypt's affairs; its appointees collected taxes, regulated public works, and mobilized the army. Along with large landowners and priests, they constituted the upper classes.
- Merchants, traders, builders, and scribes made up a prosperous middle class. At the base of the social pyramid, peasants constituted Egypt's agricultural backbone.
- Egyptian women seem to have enjoyed a large degree of economic independence, as well as civil rights and privileges.

The Arts in Ancient Egypt

- Egyptian literature included manuals of instruction and advice, and lyric poetry, much of which appear in texts that served to educate the young.
- Egyptian art comes almost exclusively from tombs and temples. For 3000 years, Egypt followed a set of pictorial conventions that dictated the manner in which subjects should be depicted.
- The plan of the Egyptian temple mirrored the central features of the Egyptian cosmos and the daily "voyage" of the sun.
- Poems were sung or chanted at Egypt's religious and secular events. Musical instruments, including harps, pipes, and sistrums, accompanied song and dance.

Africa: The Sudan

- Nubia, an ancient civilization that arose along the Nile in what is now known as northern Sudan, was the first urban civilization to appear in Africa south of the Sahara.
- Around 1550 B.C.E., the powerful state of Kush in Nubia defeated the Egyptian army. The conquerors adopted many aspects of Egyptian culture, including the practice of pyramid building. During the ninth century B.C.E., Kush came to govern all of Upper Egypt.
- In 1931, archeologists found evidence of cultures in Africa's western Sudan near a farming village called Nok. Terracotta sculptures representing people and animals anticipate the long tradition of naturalistic portraiture in African art.

Glossary

canon a set of rules or standards used to establish proportions

cosmology the theory of the origins, evolution, and structure of the universe

dynasty a sequence of rulers from the same family

fresco secco (Italian, "fresh," "dry") a method of painting on walls or ceilings surfaced with moist lime plaster

hypostyle a hall whose roof is supported by columns

lyre any one of a group of plucked stringed instruments; usually made of tortoise shell or horn and therefore light in weight

lyric literally "accompanied by the lyre," hence, verse that is meant to be sung rather than spoken; usually characterized by individual and personal emotion

mastaba an early rectangular Egyptian tomb with sloping sides and a flat roof

metaphor a figure of speech in which two unlike things are compared without the use of the words "like" or "as"

module a unit of measurement used to determine proportion

obelisk a tall, four-sided pillar that tapers to a pyramidal apex

papyrus a reedlike plant from which the ancient Egyptians made paper

pylon a massive gateway in the form of a pair of truncated pyramids

pyramid a four-sided structure rising to a peak

relief a sculptural technique in which figures or forms are carved either to project from the background surface (raised relief) or cut away below the background level (sunk relief); the degree of relief is designated as high, low, or sunken

simile a figure of speech in which two unlike things are compared

India, China, and the Americas

ca. 3500–500 B.C.E.

"He knows peace who has forgotten desire.
He lives without craving:
Free from ego, free from pride."
The Bhagavad-Gita

Figure 3.1 "Baby" Figure, Mexico, Olmec, twelfth to ninth century B.C.E. Ceramic, height 13⅜ in. Hundreds of pudgy, nearly life-sized human baby sculptures like this one have been found in Olmec graves.

The civilizations of India and China emerged somewhat later than those of Mesopotamia and ancient Egypt. Both are among the only continuous civilizations in world history: their language, belief systems, and many of their cultural practices flourish today in much the same form as they took in ancient times. Independent of the West, India and China produced works of literature, philosophy, art, and music that rank with those of their Western contemporaries. The Asian world-view differs somewhat from that of Western cultures. In India, for instance, religion is grounded in **pantheism**, the belief that an all-pervading divine spirit infuses all aspects of the universe. The identification of the divine with the unvarying rhythms of nature is also common to ancient Chinese culture. For the Chinese, the natural order dominated secular and spiritual life.

India and China shared a holistic view of the cosmos, one that perceived an organic and intimate interrelationship between gods, rulers, and the social order.

The ancient history of the Americas is not as well understood as that of the two Asian civilizations. This is partly because of the number and variety of cultures that flourished in the third to first millennia B.C.E., and partly because these cultures—lacking written records—are available to us only by way of artifacts, many of which remain the object of archeological analysis. Nevertheless, similarities between the cultures of the Americas and the civilizations of the ancient world invite our examination— if only to anticipate the wealth of information that still lies buried in unexcavated ruins.

Ancient India

Indus Valley Civilization (ca. 2700–1500 B.C.E.)

India's earliest known civilization was located in the lower Indus valley, in an area called Sind— from which the words "India" and "Hindu" derive (Map **3.1**). At Mohenjo-daro ("Mound of the Dead") and Harappa (in modern-day Pakistan), a sophisticated Bronze Age culture flourished before 2500 B.C.E. India's first cities were planned communities: Mohenjo-daro's wide streets, lined with fired-brick houses, were laid out in a grid pattern, and their covered drains, bathing facilities, and sewage systems were unmatched in other parts of the civilized world. Bronze Age India also claimed a form of written language, although the 400 pictographic signs that constitute the earliest script are still undeciphered. At Mohenjo-daro there is little evidence of temples or tombs; while first excavated in 1921, only 10 percent of the site has been uncovered. Nevertheless, there existed a vigorous sculptural tradition in both bronze and stone. The lively female dancer pictured in Figure **3.2** is one of many objects (see also Figure 0.20) that reflect India's mastery of the lost-wax method of working bronze. In the medium of stone, the powerful portrait of a bearded man (possibly a priest or ruler) distinguished by an introspective expression anticipates the meditative images of India's later religious art (Figure **3.3**).

The Vedic Era (ca. 1500–500 B.C.E.)

India's oldest devotional texts, the *Vedas* (literally, "sacred knowledge"), give their name to the thousand-year period after 1500 B.C.E. The *Vedas* are a collection of prayers, sacrificial formulae, and hymns, one example of which appears in Reading 0.1 in the Introduction. Transmitted orally for centuries, these sacred hymns reflect a blending of the native folk traditions of the Indus valley along with those of the Aryan populations. Among the chief Vedic deities were the sky gods Indra and Rudra (later known as Shiva), the fire god Agni, and the sun god Vishnu. The *Vedas* provide a wealth of information concerning astronomical phenomena. The study of the stars, along with the practice of surgery and dissection, mark the beginnings of scientific inquiry in India.

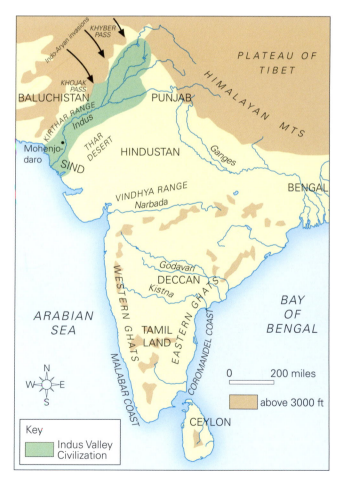

Map 3.1 Ancient India, ca. 2700–1500 B.C.E.

The Vedic Era also saw the institution of the **caste system**, a societal division based on differences in wealth, rank, occupation, and possibly skin color. While a hierarchical order marked the social systems of all ancient civilizations, India developed the most rigid kind of class stratification, one that prevailed until modern times. By 1000 B.C.E., four principal castes existed: priests and scholars; rulers and warriors; artisans and merchants; and unskilled workers. Slowly, these castes began to subdivide according to occupation. At the very bottom of the social order—or, more accurately, outside it—lay those who held the most menial and degrading occupations. They became known as Untouchables.

Some time around 1500 B.C.E., Sanskrit became the classic language of India. The bards of India recounted stories of the bitter tribal wars between rivalrous clans. These stories were the basis for India's two great epics—the *Mahabharata* (*Great Deeds of the Bharata Clan*) and the *Ramayana* (*Song of Prince Rama*)—which were transmitted orally for generations but not recorded until the eighth century B.C.E. The *Mahabharata*—the world's longest folk epic—recounts a ten-year struggle for control of the Ganges valley, occurring around the year 1000 B.C.E. Along with the *Ramayana*, this epic assumed a role in the cultural history of India not unlike that of the *Iliad* and the *Odyssey* in Hellenic history. Indeed, the two epics have been treasured resources for much of the poetry, drama, and art produced throughout India's long history.

Figure 3.3 Bearded man, from Moherjo-daro, Indus valley, ca. 2000 B.C.E. Limestone, height 7 in. The inward gaze of this figure suggests the practice of meditation that would come to characterize Hinduism in ancient India.

Hindu Pantheism

From the Indus valley civilization came the most ancient of today's world religions: Hinduism. Hinduism is markedly different from the religions of the West. It identifies the sacred not as a superhuman personality, but as an objective, all-pervading Cosmic Spirit called **Brahman**. Pantheism, the belief that divinity is inherent in all things, is basic to the Hindu view that the universe itself is sacred. While neither polytheistic nor monotheistic in the traditional sense, Hinduism venerates all forms and manifestations of the all-pervasive Brahman.

Hence, Hindus embrace all the Vedic gods, a multitude of deities who are to this day perceived as emanations of the divine (see chapter 14). In the words of the *Rig Veda*, "Truth is one, but the wise call it by many names."

Hinduism is best understood by way of the religious texts known as the *Upanishads*, some 250 prose commentaries on the *Vedas*. Like the *Vedas* themselves, the *Upanishads* were orally transmitted and recorded in Sanskrit between the eighth and sixth centuries B.C.E. While the *Vedas* teach worship through prayer and sacrifice, the *Upanishads* teach enlightenment through meditation. They predicate the concept of the single, all-pervading Brahman. Unlike the nature deities of Mesopotamia and Egypt, Brahman is infinite, formless, and ultimately unknowable. Unlike the

Figure 3.2 Dancing girl, from Mohenjo-daro, Indus valley, ca. 2300–1750 B.C.E. Bronze, height 4¼ in.

The "Out of India" Debate

Two theories dominate the narrative of India's early history: The traditional one holds that warlike seminomadic foreigners speaking Indo-European languages and calling themselves Aryans ("nobles") invaded the Indus valley around 1500 B.C.E., enslaving or removing the native Dravidian population and initiating the unique cultural developments of Sanskrit (India's classic language) and the caste system. More recently, revisionist scholars have argued that the Aryans in fact migrated gradually from Central to South Asia during the second millennium B.C.E., blending with the native peoples of the Indus valley to form a single population that generated India's cultural traditions.

Supporters of the revisionist "Out of India" theory hold that a series of natural disasters and environmental changes (rather than military conquest) was responsible for the decline of Indus valley civilization between 1700 and 1500 B.C.E. They maintain that India's unique culture and its devotional texts, the *Vedas*, emerged before ca. 1500 B.C.E., when Sanskrit became the dominant language; that the caste system grew out of tribelike social and economic organization; and that India's great epics were the product of native tribal warfare. Traditionalists, however, point to the fact that the *Vedas* themselves refer frequently to military conflict between Aryans and native peoples. To date, the available evidence—archeological, linguistic, and genetic—is insufficient to resolve the question of India's origins. The subject remains hotly debated.

Hebrew god, Brahman assumes no personal and contractual relationship with humankind. Brahman is the Uncaused Cause and the Ultimate Reality.

In every human being, there resides the individual manifestation of Brahman: the Self, or **Atman**, which, according to the *Upanishads*, is "soundless, formless, intangible, undying, tasteless, odorless, without beginning, without end, eternal, immutable, [and] beyond nature." Although housed in the material prison of the human body, the Self (Atman) seeks to be one with the Absolute Spirit (Brahman). The spiritual (re)union of Brahman and Atman—a condition known as *nirvana*—is the goal of every Hindu. This blissful reabsorption of the Self into Absolute Spirit must be preceded by one's gradual rejection of the material world, that is, the world of illusion and ignorance, and by the mastery of the techniques of meditation and through a system of spiritual exercises known as **yoga**. Yoga (literally "to yoke") seeks the joining of one's Atman to Brahman through control of the mind and body. A complex combination of physical positions and breathing exercises, which was not codified until the second century B.C.E., yoga (and its manifold schools) developed as one of the many Hindu ascetic disciplines aimed at achieving liberation of the Self and union with the Supreme Spirit.

A literature of humility, the *Upanishads* offer no guidelines for worship, no moral laws, and no religious dogma. These texts neither exalt divine power, nor interpret it. They do, however, instruct the individual Hindu on the subject of death and rebirth. The Hindu anticipates a succession of lives: that is, the successive return of the Atman in various physical forms. The physical form, whether animal or human and of whatever species or class, is determined by the level of spiritual purity the Hindu has achieved by the time of his or her death. The Law of **Karma** holds that the collective spiritual energy gained from accumulated deeds determines one's physical state in the next

life. Reincarnation, or the Wheel of Rebirth, is the fate of Hindus until they achieve *nirvana*. In this ultimate state, the enlightened Atman is both liberated and absorbed—a process that may be likened to the dissolution of a grain of salt in the vast waters of the ocean.

The *Bhagavad-Gita*

The fundamental teachings of Hinduism are lyrically expressed in one of India's most popular religious poems: the *Bhagavad-Gita* (*Song of God*), which constitutes one episode from the *Mahabharata*. In this most famous part of the poem, a dialogue takes place between Arjuna, the warrior-hero, and Krishna, the incarnation of the god Vishnu and a divine manifestation of Brahman. Facing the prospect of shedding the blood of his own kinsmen in the battle to come, Arjuna seeks to reconcile his material obligations with his spiritual quest for selflessness. Krishna's answer to Arjuna—a classic statement of resignation—represents the essence of Hindu thought as distilled from the *Upanishads*. Although probably in existence earlier, the *Bhagavad-Gita* was not recorded until some time between the fifth and second centuries B.C.E.

READING 3.1 From the *Bhagavad-Gita*

He knows bliss in the Atman	1
And wants nothing else.	
Cravings torment the heart:	
He renounces cravings.	
I call him illumined.	5
Not shaken by adversity,	
Not hankering after happiness:	
Free from fear, free from anger,	
Free from the things of desire,	
I call him a seer, and illumined.	10

The bonds of his flesh are broken.
He is lucky, and does not rejoice:
He is unlucky, and does not weep.
I call him illumined.

. . . .

Thinking about sense-objects
Will attach you to sense-objects;   15
Grow attached, and you become addicted;
Thwart your addiction, it turns to anger;
Be angry, and you confuse your mind;
Confuse your mind, you forget the lesson of experience;   20
Forget experience, you lose discrimination;
Lose discrimination, and you miss life's only purpose.
When he has no lust, no hatred,
A man walks safely among the things of lust and hatred.
To obey the Atman   25
Is his peaceful joy:
Sorrow melts
Into that clear peace;
His quiet mind
Is soon established in peace.   30
The uncontrolled mind
Does not guess that the Atman is present:
How can it meditate?
Without meditation, where is peace?
Without peace, where is happiness?   35
The wind turns a ship
From its course upon the waters:
The wandering winds of the senses
Cast man's mind adrift
And turn his better judgment from its course.   40
When a man can still the senses
I call him illumined.
The recollected mind is awake
In the knowledge of the Atman
Which is dark night to the ignorant: 45
The ignorant are awake in their sense-life
Which they think is daylight:
To the seer it is darkness.
Water flows continually into the ocean
But the ocean is never disturbed: 50
Desire flows into the mind of the seer
But he is never disturbed.
The seer knows peace:
The man who stirs up his own lusts
Can never know peace.   55
He knows peace who has forgotten desire.
He lives without craving:
Free from ego, free from pride.
This is the state of enlightenment in Brahman:
A man who does not fall back from it   60
Into delusion.
Even at the moment of death
He is alive in that enlightenment:
Brahman and he are one. . . .

Q **What are the obstacles to the state of enlightenment, according to Krishna?**

The Hindu view of the relationship between people and gods differs significantly from the religious views of the Mesopotamians and the ancient Egyptians. While these two cultures regarded human beings as separate from the gods, Hindus, guided by the *Upanishads* and the *Bhagavad-Gita*, asserted the oneness of matter and spirit. Where Western religions emphasize the imperishability of individual consciousness, Hinduism aspires to its sublimation, or rather, its reabsorption into the spiritual infinite. Although Hinduism still embraces the vast pantheon of Vedic gods and goddesses (see chapter 14), it has remained relatively unaffected by the religious precepts of Western Judaism and Christianity. Unlike the latter, Hinduism has no institutional forms of worship and no doctrinal laws. On the other hand, since the nineteenth century, Hinduism's holistic view of nature has increasingly influenced Western thought and belief. And since the last decades of the twentieth century, Hindu techniques of deep meditation have made a notable impact on the disciplines of religion, philosophy, and medical science.

Ancient China

Ancient Chinese civilization emerged in the fertile valleys of two great waterways: the Yellow and the Yangzi* rivers (Map **3.2**). As early as 3500 B.C.E., the Neolithic villages of China were producing silk, a commodity that would bring wealth and fame to Chinese culture.

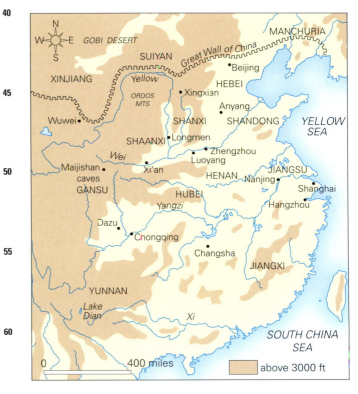

Map 3.2 Ancient China.

* All transcriptions of Chinese names appear in the system known as Hanyu Pinyin.

It is likely that China's early dynasties flourished for some four centuries before the appearance of writing. The first dynasty described in ancient Chinese historical records, the Xia (originating ca. 2200 B.C.E.), has only recently been excavated. Near Luoyang (see Map 3.2), archeologists have uncovered a city with a large palace-type structure, pottery workshops, and a bronze foundry. Such evidence gives credibility to age-old legends honoring Xia's dynastic founder, King Yu, who is said to have reduced the flooding of the Yellow River by authorizing the construction of canals along its tributaries.

The Shang Dynasty (ca. 1766–1027 B.C.E.)

The warrior tribe known as the Shang initiated the first fully developed urban culture in Bronze Age China. Shang rulers were hereditary monarchs who ruled, like the pharaohs of Egypt, by divine right. They claimed their authority from the Lord on High (Shang-di). Royal authority was symbolized by the dragon, a hybrid beast that stood for strength, fertility, and life-giving water (Figure 3.4). Occupants of the "dragon throne," China's early monarchs defended their position by way of a powerful bureaucracy (the landholding nobility) and huge armies of archer-warriors recruited from the provinces. The king's soldiers consisted of peasants, who, in peacetime, farmed the land with the assistance of slaves captured in war.

The Chinese social order is clearly articulated in Shang royal tombs, where the king is surrounded by the men and women who served him in his lifetime. Royal graves also contain several hundred headless bodies, probably those

of the slaves who built the tombs. As in Mesopotamia and Egypt, China's royal tombs were filled with treasures—a vast array of ritual and grave goods that include silk fabrics, ceramic sculptures, jade artifacts, bronze vessels (Figure 3.5), and objects of personal adornment. Unlike the tombs of ancient Egypt, China's graves were rarely plundered. Nevertheless, the early history of China is still largely hidden from us. Some of the richest discoveries have taken place in only the last few decades. For instance, in 1986, archeologists working in Sichuan province (an area beyond the rule of the Shang) uncovered graves that contained gold and silver objects, along with more than 200 bronze objects, including the earliest life-sized human figures in Chinese art (Figure 3.6).

Beginning in Neolithic times and continuing throughout ancient Chinese history, large numbers of jade objects—especially finely carved jade disks (see Figure 3.4)—were placed in royal graves. The meaning and function of these objects is a matter of some speculation. The Chinese used jade for tools, but also for carved insignias and talismans probably related to ceremonial ritual. Jade was prized by the Chinese for its durability, its musical qualities, its subtle, translucent colors, and its alleged protective powers—it was thought to prevent fatigue and delay the decomposition of the body. Jade disks were usually placed at the center of the body in the tomb. In the tombs of later rulers, the deceased were often encased in shrouds made up of thousands of carved jade plaques sewn with gold wire (see Figure 7.6).

Chinese pictograms, probably identifying individual clans, were incised on pottery as early as the second half of the third millennium B.C.E. But by 1750 B.C.E., the Chinese developed a pictographic writing system employing characters that stood for specific things or concepts. To a special group of priests fell the

Figure 3.4 Ritual disk, Zhou dynasty, fifth to third century B.C.E. Jade, diameter 6½ in. Jade disks such as this, placed on the body of the deceased, may have served as cosmic talismans that ensured protection from evil and decay.

responsibility for foretelling future events: whether the harvest would be bountiful, whether to declare or delay war, and so on. Shang diviners etched such questions with sharp tools on turtle shells and animal bones (Figure **3.7**). These were then heated to produce cracks that the priests might read and interpret. Not deciphered until the early twentieth century, "oracle bone script" provides a valuable record of Shang rulers, giving us vital information about their ceremonies, wars, and administrative history. The script also discloses intriguing details about weather, disease, and other routine topics relating to ancient Chinese life.

Eventually, the Chinese technique for writing script, known as **calligraphy**, became an artform in itself. Executed by means of a pliant brush filled with ink,

Figure 3.5 Ceremonial vessel with a cover, late Shang dynasty, China, ca. 1000 B.C.E. Bronze, height 20¹⁄₁₆ in. The surface of this ritual object is adorned with a complex pattern of dragons, birds, and geometric motifs arranged symmetrically. The object is a text that reflects its context: the ancient Chinese perception of the cosmos as both animated and regulated by a natural order.

Figure 3.6 Standing figure, late Shang dynasty, ca. 1300–1100 B.C.E., from Pit 2 at Sanxingdui, Guanghan, Sichuan province. Bronze, height 8 ft. 7 in. This barefooted figure was found among more than fifty bronze heads and twenty bronze masks. Holes in his earlobes suggest that he was adorned with earrings. His hands once grasped a cylindrical object, possibly an ivory tusk.

Figure 3.7 Inscribed oracle bone, China, ca. 1500–1000 B.C.E. 7 × 4½ in. Chinese characters were inscribed in columns and read from top to bottom.

place in society. Within the natural hierarchy, those with greater intellectual abilities should govern, and those with lesser abilities should fulfill the physical needs of the state. Exactly how those with greater abilities were distinguished from those with lesser abilities is difficult to discern. Nevertheless, between the twelfth and eighth centuries B.C.E., when the Zhou kings took control of most of civilized China, the principle of the natural hierarchy already provided the basis for China's political and social order. Since the Zhou rulers delegated local authority to aristocrats of their choosing, it is probable that the assumptions of superiority and inferiority among people came after the fact of a division of labor among the members of society. Nevertheless, well before the second century B.C.E., the Chinese put into practice the world's first system whereby individuals were selected for government service on the basis of merit and education. Written examinations tested the competence and skill of those who sought government office. Such a system persisted for centuries and became the basis for an aristocracy of merit that has characterized Chinese culture well into modern times.

Repeated attacks by Central Asian tribes forced the Zhou dynasty into decline. In 771 B.C.E., the Zhou capital was moved eastward to Luoyang (see Map 3.2). While the Eastern Zhou dynasty would continue until 256 B.C.E., its rulers faced political turbulence and decades of warfare (see chapter 7).

Spirits, Gods, and the Natural Order

The agricultural communities of ancient China venerated an assortment of local spirits associated with the natural forces, and with rivers, mountains, and crops. Regulating the natural order of the universe was the creative principle known interchangeably as the Lord on High (Shang-di) and as Heaven (*Tian*). Chinese mythology describes cosmic unity as the marriage of Heaven (*Tian*) and Earth (*Kun*), the receptive principle. Although not anthropomorphic like the gods of Mesopotamia and Egypt, these celestial deities oversaw the workings of the universe, impartially guiding human destiny. But the most powerful personalized spirits of ancient China were those of deceased ancestors, the members of an extended familial community (Figure **3.8**). According to the Chinese, the spirits of their ancestors continued to exist in Heaven, where they assumed their role as mediators between Heaven and Earth. Since the ancestors exerted a direct influence upon

Chinese writing grew to some 4500 characters, many of which are still used today. Indeed, Chinese characters represent the world's oldest continuous writing system. Combining pictographic and phonetic elements, Chinese characters became the basis for writing throughout East Asia.

The Western Zhou Dynasty (1027–771 B.C.E.)

The sacred right to rule was known in China as the Mandate of Heaven. Although the notion of divine-right kingship began in the earliest centuries of China's dynasties, the concept of a divine mandate was not fixed until early in the Zhou Era, when the rebel Zhou clan justified their assault on the Shang by claiming that Shang kings had failed to rule virtuously; hence, Heaven (*Tian*) had withdrawn its mandate. Charged with maintaining the will of Heaven on earth, the king's political authority required obedience to established moral law, which, in turn, reflected the natural order.

According to the Chinese, nature determined human intelligence and ability, as well as the individual's proper

Figure 3.8 Mask, Shang dynasty, ca. 1500–1600 B.C.E. Bronze, 10 × 9¼ in.

Science and Technology

3500 B.C.E.	silk manufacture begins in China
2700 B.C.E.	first experiments in acupuncture and herbal medicine are made in China
2296 B.C.E.	first reported sighting of a comet occurs in China
1350 B.C.E.	decimal numerals are introduced in China
1000 B.C.E.	the Chinese introduce an early version of the abacus

human affairs, their eternal welfare was of deep concern to ancient Chinese families. They buried their dead in richly furnished tombs, regularly made sacrifices to them, and brought offerings of food and wine to their graves. One of the earliest odes in China's classic *Book of Songs* (*Shi jing*) celebrates the veneration of ancestors of both sexes:

> Rich is the year with much millet and rice;
> And we have tall granaries
> With hundreds and thousands and millions of sheaves.
> We make wind and sweet spirits
> And offer them to our ancestors, male and female;
> Thus to fulfill all the rites
> And bring down blessings in full.

The Chinese Classics

The perception of an inviolable natural order dominated all aspects of Chinese culture. Its earliest expression is found in China's oldest known text, the *Book of Changes* (*I jing*). This classic text, a collection of ancient cosmic principles, is a guide for interpreting the workings of the universe. It centers on the principle that order is achieved through the dynamic balance of opposites. Originating in the Shang Era, but not recorded until the sixth century B.C.E., the *Book of Changes* consists of cosmological diagrams by means of which diviners were able to predict the future and advise others on the inevitability of change. The aim of such divination was to bring into balance that which had fallen out of balance—a key concept in Chinese thought, and one that continues to dominate Chinese medicine.

Basic to the natural order is the condition of balance between the four seasons, the five elements (wood, fire, earth, metal, and water), and the five creative powers (heat, cold, dryness, moisture, and wind). It is symbolized by way of abstract symbols, the square and the circle, often represented on Shang bronzes. It is evident in the holistic idea that universal energy, called **qi** (pronounced "chee"), pervades all things, including the human body, to which balance is essential. And it is graphically expressed in the unity of opposites known as *yin/yang*. This principle, which ancient Chinese emperors called "the foundation of the entire universe," interprets all nature as the dynamic product of two interacting cosmic forces, or modes of energy, commonly configured as twin interpenetrating shapes enclosed within a circle (Figure 3.9). The interaction of *yang*, the male principle (associated with lightness, hardness, brightness, warmth, and the sun), and *yin*, the female principle (associated with darkness, softness, moisture, coolness, the earth, and the moon), describes the creative energy of the universe and the natural order itself. For the Chinese, this order is inherent in the balance between the complementary yet opposing forces of hot and cold, day and night, heaven and earth, male and female.

Moral order, calling for subjects to obey their rulers and local landlords, and social order, emphasizing the value of family and the proper performance of religious rites, followed the basic precepts of the natural order. These were enshrined in documents that (along with the *Book of Changes*) became China's classic texts: the *Book of History* (*Shu jing*), the *Book of Songs* (*Shi jing*), and the *Book of Rites* (*Li jing*) (see chapter 7). Compiled after 600 B.C.E., these literary treasures preserve fragments of China's ancient past. The *Book of History*, for instance, records speeches from the Xia, Shang, and Zhou eras, while many of the 300 odes in the *Book of Songs* capture the intimate family loyalties of the Zhou period.

Figure 3.9 The *yin* and the *yang* as interpenetrating shapes in a circle, a figure with no beginning and no end.

Daoism

The most mystical expression of the natural order as it relates to humankind is preserved in the ancient Chinese belief system known as Daoism. As much a philosophy as a religion, Daoism embraces a universal and natural principle—the Dao, or "Way." While the Dao is ineffable—indeed, it resists all intellectual analysis—it manifests itself in the harmony of things. It may be thought of as the unity underlying nature's multiplicity; and it is understood only by those who live in total simplicity and in harmony with nature. Daoists seek to cultivate tranquility, spontaneity, compassion, and spiritual insight. Like the Hindu, the Daoist practices meditation and breath control, along with dietary and other physical means of prolonging and enriching life.

Daoism existed in China as early as 1000 B.C.E., but its basic text, the *Dao de jing* (*The Way and its Power*), did not appear until the sixth century B.C.E. This modest "scripture" of some 5000 words is associated with the name Lao Zi ("the Old One"), who may or may not have ever actually existed. The following poem, one of the eighty-one chapters of the *Dao de jing*, conveys the Daoist idea of nature's unity. It uses a series of simple images to illustrate the complementary and harmonious function of positive and negative elements in ordinary things, as in nature. Like all Daoist teaching, it relies on subtle wit and paradox as springboards to enlightenment.

READING 3.2 From the *Dao de jing* (ca. 550 B.C.E.)

Thirty spokes will converge	1
In the hub of a wheel;	
But the use of the cart	
Will depend on the part	
Of the hub that is void.	5
With a wall all around	
A clay bowl is molded;	
But the use of the bowl	
Will depend on the part	
Of the bowl that is void.	10
Cut out windows and doors	
In the house as you build;	
But the use of the house	
Will depend on the space	
In the walls that is void.	15
So advantage is had	
From whatever is there;	
But usefulness rises	
From whatever is not.	

Q **What images in this poem convey the idea of the Dao as a unity of opposites?**

The Americas

It is likely that the first Americans arrived 30,000 to 20,000 years ago, as successive waves of Asian nomads migrated across a land bridge that once linked Siberia and Alaska at the Bering Strait. Recent evidence suggests the possibility of other migrations by way of Scandinavian ice sheets or via small boats that brought settlers to various parts of the Pacific coast. Some archeologists suggest that Ice Age Europeans may have arrived at North America's east coast by way of boats that hugged the edges of the great ice sheets stretching west from Greenland. While debate continues on the details of this subject, it is clear that over a long period of time a mosaic of migrant peoples came to settle in North, South, and Middle ("Meso") America: parts of present-day Mexico and Central America. By the fifteenth century, when Europeans first made contact with the Americas, some 1000 agricultural societies flourished, and a number of new "American" civilizations had left the world their unique cultural legacies.

Ancient Peru

Until recently, it was believed that the earliest civilizations in the Americas dated from the middle of the second millennium B.C.E. In the first decade of the twenty-first century, however, archeologists established a dating of 3500 to 2600 B.C.E. for two ancient Peruvian sites, Caral and Sechin Bajo. Located in the coastal region northwest of Lima, these sites (only two of many recently uncovered in the area) are as old as, or older than, the Egyptian pyramids.

Caral, a site with six pyramids, wide plazas, numerous residences, and a sunken amphitheater, probably supported a population that exceeded 3000 people (Figure **3.10**). The remains of cotton nets suggest that fishing complemented native agricultural production. Other artifacts, such as flutes made of bird bones and cornets (horns) made from deer and llama bones, suggest a music-loving culture.

At Chankillo, a third site north of Lima, archeologists have identified a group of thirteen stone towers as a 2300-year-old solar observatory. Part of a heavily fortified complex that includes a stone temple, these monumental towers—resembling prehistoric teeth—appear to have functioned in a manner similar to the megalithic alignments at Stonehenge (see Figures 0.13 and 0.14), and other Neolithic European sites.

On the plains of southwestern Peru, archeologists continue to study a number of huge **geoglyphs** in the shape of geometric figures, insects, animals, reptiles, and birds (Figure **3.13**). Created by the removal of surface stones to expose the yellow soil beneath, these enormous images are fully visible only from very far above. While their exact function remains the subject of speculation, it is possible that they served as skymaps or calendars designed, like Stonehenge (see Figure 0.13), to mark seasonal change and help ancient farmers determine favorable times for planting crops. The recent discovery of a 2½-mile-long labyrinth and small stone platforms at this site suggests that these earthworks played a role in religious rituals.

Clearly, current research in Peru and elsewhere in the Americas raises many questions concerning the origins and development of ancient societies in the Western hemisphere. Capable of erecting mammoth temple complexes, the inhabitants of Caral clearly reached a level of political and social complexity beyond that of any typical

Figure 3.10 Amphitheater, Caral, Peru, ca. 2627 B.C.E.

MAKING CONNECTIONS

The largest of Caral's pyramids, the size of four football fields, boasts a wide, steep stairway leading to a ceremonial atrium and fire pit (Figure **3.11**). This type of stepped pyramid, the spiritual focus of a larger ceremonial complex, prevailed for centuries in the civilizations of the Olmec, Maya, Aztec, and Inca cultures, the last of which flourished some 3000 years later in Peru. There are striking similarities between the ziggurats of Mesopotamia (Figure **3.12**) and the stepped pyramids of the Americas. Whether both served similar purposes, and whether there exists any historical link between the two, remain as matters of speculation. Doubtless, however, those who ascended the steep stair of these sacred mounds saw themselves as moving closer to the heavens.

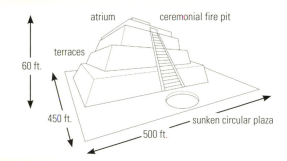

Figure 3.11 The largest of the Caral pyramids, a site of religious rituals, near Lima, Peru, ca. 2627 B.C.E.

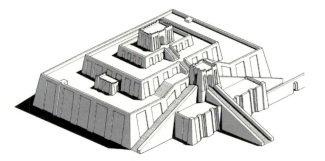

Figure 3.12 Reconstruction of the ziggurat at Ur, Mesopotamia (Iraq), ca. 2100 B.C.E.

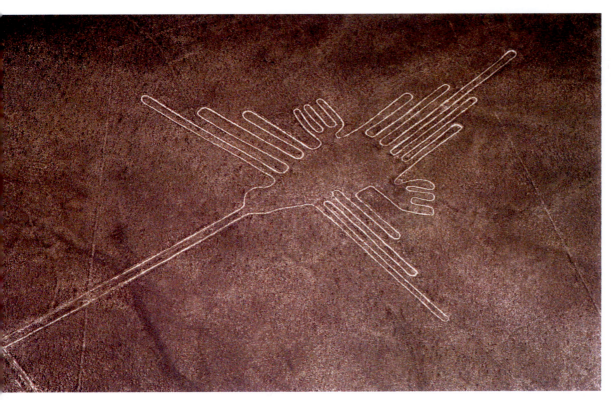

Figure 3.13 Giant hummingbird, Nasca culture, southwest Peru, ca. 200 B.C.E.–200 C.E. Wingspan 900 ft. This geoglyph was created by scraping away the weathered surface of the desert and removing stones. The giant hummingbird is one of eighteen bird images pictured on the Peruvian plain.

Neolithic village. Yet, at Caral, no draft animals, no wheeled vehicles, no evidence of writing, and no metal tools or weapons have been found. Although gold was mined in Peru as early as 2000 B.C.E., copper and bronze did not come into use in the Americas until the ninth century C.E. While Peru may prove to be the birthplace of civilization in the Americas, its culture differs dramatically from that of the first civilizations in Mesopotamia, Africa, India, and China. Ongoing excavation at Caral and nearby sites will surely continue to shape the historical record.

The Olmecs

Around 1300 B.C.E., Meso-America produced one of its largest and most advanced native cultures, that of the Olmecs (literally "rubber people," the name given by the Aztecs to those living among trees that produced this substance). On the coast of the Gulf of Mexico, south of the modern-day Mexican city of Veracruz, the Olmecs established urban centers. Here, priestly rulers governed on behalf of the gods. This elite cadre oversaw the spiritual life of the community—a population consisting of farmers and artisans at the lower end of the social order, and a ruling nobility at the upper end.

The Olmecs raised temple-pyramids on clay platforms fitted with elaborate drainage systems. They created a calendrical system, developed portraiture and mirror-making, and practiced rituals involving human sacrifice. They honored their rulers by carving colossal stone heads, which they placed facing outward from their ceremonial precincts (Figure **3.14**). The production of such massive sculptures and the building of monumental civic precincts required the labor of thousands, as well as a high degree of civic organization. Olmec culture flourished until ca. 400 B.C.E., but its political, religious, and artistic traditions survived for centuries in the civilizations of the Mayans and the Aztecs (see chapter 18).

One of the intriguing mysteries of Olmec culture is the existence of hollow ceramic "baby-face" figurines (see Figure 3.1). These nude, sexless, chubby figures, with oversized heads and puffy, slit eyes, often wear helmets similar to those on the colossal stone heads (see Figure 3.14). Found in graves and in household refuse, they may represent ancient Olmec deities, or may have served as substitutes for victims of infant sacrifice.

Figure 3.14 Olmec head, from San Lorenzo, Veracruz, Mexico, ca. 1000 B.C.E. Basalt, height 5 ft. 10⅞ in. Colossal heads like this one, weighing between 12 and 24 tons, range in height from 5 to 12 feet.

Ancient India

- India's earliest known civilization, located in the lower Indus valley, experienced a flourishing Bronze Age (ca. 2700–1500 B.C.E.) that featured planned communities, advanced sewage systems, and a pictographic script.
- During the Vedic Era (ca. 1500–500 B.C.E.), India's caste system, established by Aryan invaders, divided its people into four distinct castes: priests and scholars; rulers and warriors; artisans and merchants; and unskilled workers. Outside the social order lay those with the most degrading occupations: the Untouchables.
- The Aryans introduced Sanskrit, India's classic language, its early epics (the *Mahabharata* and the *Ramayana*), and its oldest devotional texts, the *Vedas*. Hinduism, the most ancient of today's world religions, came from this era. Markedly different from earlier religions, pantheistic Hinduism identified the sacred as an objective, all-pervading cosmic Spirit (Brahman).
- The goal of the ancient Hindu was *nirvana*: the union of Brahman with its individual manifestation (Atman), and release from the Wheel of Rebirth, achieved through meditation and the stilling of the senses.
- The fundamental teachings of pantheistic Hinduism are expressed in one of India's most popular religious poems: the *Bhagavad-Gita*.

Ancient China

- Early Chinese civilizations emerged between the Yellow and Yangzi rivers. As early as 3500 B.C.E., China was producing pottery, bronze, and silk, the commodity that would bring wealth and fame to Chinese culture.
- The Shang dynasty (1766–1027 B.C.E.), a warrior tribe, initiated the first fully developed urban culture and the earliest calligraphic script. Shang rulers ruled by divine right and were buried in elaborate tombs filled with bronze and jade artifacts.
- The Zhou clan eventually defeated the Shang, claiming that Shang kings had failed to rule virtuously, thus violating their right to rule: the Mandate of Heaven. The Western Zhou dynasty (1027–771 B.C.E.) put into practice the world's first administrative system whereby individuals were selected for government service on the basis of merit and education.
- According to the Chinese, the spirits of deceased ancestors continued to exist in Heaven, where they acted as mediators between Heaven and Earth.
- The idea of "balance," expressed by the cosmological principle known as *yin/yang*, dominated ancient Chinese spirituality. The *Book of Changes* (*I jing*) consists of cosmological diagrams used for divination and the interpretation of the natural order.
- Daoism, the most eloquent expression of the natural order, taught the individual to embrace the "Way" (Dao), a path to spiritual awareness that emphasized simplicity, meditation, and strict dietary practice.

The Americas

- It is likely that the first Americans arrived at least 20,000 years ago, as groups of Asian nomads migrated across a land bridge that once linked Siberia and Alaska at the Bering Strait, or by way of Scandinavian ice bridges.
- Archeologists recently established a dating of 3500 to 2600 B.C.E. for two ancient Peruvian cultures, Caral and Sechin Bajo (located in the coastal region northwest of Lima), that erected mammoth temple complexes as old as, or older than, the Egyptian pyramids.
- Between 1300 and 400 B.C.E., on Mexico's Gulf coast, the Olmecs raised temple-pyramids, created a calendar system, erected massive sculptures, and established political, religious, and artistic traditions that survived in the later civilizations of the Americas.

Glossary

Atman the Hindu name for the Self; the personal part of Brahman

Brahman the Hindu name for the Absolute Spirit; an impersonal World Soul that pervades all things

calligraphy (Greek, "beautiful writing") stylized or elegant writing usually executed with pen or brush and ink

caste system a rigid social stratification in India based on differences in wealth, rank, or occupation

geoglyph a large design or motif inscribed or imposed on the ground or on natural elements in the landscape

karma (Sanskrit, "deed") the law that holds that one's deeds determine one's future life in the Wheel of Rebirth

nirvana (Sanskrit, "liberation" or "extinction") the blissful reabsorption of the Self into the Absolute Spirit (Brahman): release from the endless cycle of rebirth (see also Buddhism, chapters 8 and 9)

pantheism the belief that a divine spirit pervades all things in the universe

qi (Chinese, "substance" or "breath") the material substance or vital force of the universe

yoga (Sanskrit, "to yoke or join") a system of spiritual exercises aimed at joining the Self and the One through control of mind and body

Greece: Humanism and the Speculative Leap

ca. 3000–332 B.C.E.

"I say that Athens is the school of Hellas, and that the individual Athenian in his own person seems to have the power of adapting himself to the most varied forms of action with the utmost versatility and grace."
Thucydides

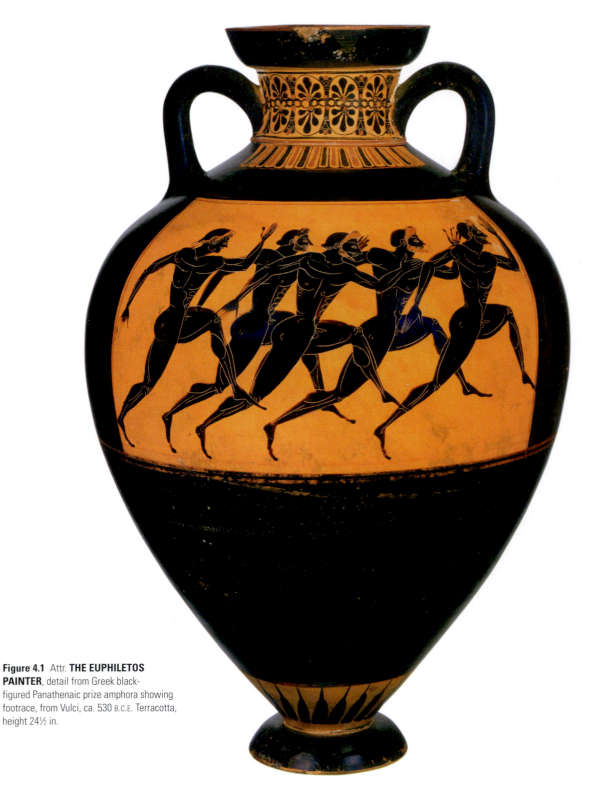

Figure 4.1 Attr. **THE EUPHILETOS PAINTER**, detail from Greek black-figured Panathenaic prize amphora showing footrace, from Vulci, ca. 530 B.C.E. Terracotta, height 24½ in.

"We are all Greeks," proclaimed the nineteenth-century British poet Percy Bysshe Shelley. He meant by this that modern individuals—profoundly influenced by the Hellenic ideals of reason, beauty, and the good life on earth—bear the indelible stamp of ancient Greece. To the Greeks, we owe the refinement of almost all the basic forms of literary expression (including drama, lyric poetry, and historical narrative), the fundamentals of philosophic and scientific inquiry, and the formulation of a set of aesthetic values in art and music that—having persisted for well over a thousand years—have come to be called "Classical."

Greek urban life originated at the western end of the Asian landmass, north and west of the civilizations of ancient Mesopotamia and Egypt. During the second millennium B.C.E., the first Greek city-states emerged on islands and peninsulas in the Aegean Sea, the coast of Asia Minor, at the southern tip of Italy, and in Sicily (Map **4.1**). This ancient civilization called itself "Hellas" and its people "Hellenes" (the name "Greece" came into use later, from the Latin *Graecus*).

Few civilizations have been so deeply concerned with the quality of human life as that of the ancient Greeks. And few have been so committed to exploring human intellect and action, as they affect the individual and the community. Because Hellenic culture reflects a concern with life as it is lived here on earth, the Greeks have been called the humanists of the ancient world. The robust optimism of ancient Greece is apparent even in its formative stages, which are set in the Bronze Age civilizations of the Aegean Sea.

Bronze Age Civilizations of the Aegean (ca. 3000–1200 B.C.E.)

The Bronze Age culture of Mycenae was not known to the world until the late nineteenth century, when an amateur German archeologist named Heinrich Schliemann uncovered the first artifacts of ancient Troy (see Map 4.1). Schliemann's excavations brought to light the civilization of an adventuresome tribal people, the Mycenaeans, who had established themselves on the Greek mainland around 1600 B.C.E. In the first decade of the twentieth century, the British archeologist Sir Arthur Evans uncovered an even earlier pre-Greek civilization on the island of Crete in the Aegean Sea. He called it "Minoan" after the legendary King Minos, celebrated in ancient Greek legend. This maritime civilization flourished between 2000 and 1400 B.C.E., when it seems to have been absorbed or destroyed by the Mycenaeans.

Map 4.1 Ancient Greece, ca. 1200–332 B.C.E. Located in the eastern Mediterranean Sea, ancient Greece consisted of a group of islands and peninsulas, including Crete, the Cyclades (the islands of the Aegean Sea), the coast of Asia Minor, Sicily, and the southern tip of Italy. The entire area was smaller than the state of Maine.

Figure 4.2 Palace of Minos, Knossos, Crete, ca. 1500 B.C.E.

Minoan Civilization (ca. 2000–1400 B.C.E.)

Centered on the Palace of Minos at Knossos on the island of Crete (Figure **4.2**), Minoan culture was prosperous and seafaring. The absence of protective walls around the palace complex suggests that the Minoans enjoyed a sense of security. The three-story palace at Knossos was a labyrinthine masonry structure with dozens of rooms and corridors built around a central courtyard. The interior walls of the palace bear magnificent frescoes illustrating natural and marine motifs (Figure **4.3**), ceremonial processions, and other aspects of Cretan life.

The most famous of the palace frescoes, the so-called bull-leaping fresco, shows two women and a man, the latter vigorously somersaulting over the back of a bull (Figure **4.4**). Probably associated with the cult of the bull—an ancient symbol of virility (see Figures 1.1 and 2.4)—the ritual game prefigures the modern bullfight, the "rules" of which were codified in Roman times by Julius Caesar. Since 1979, when modern archeologists uncovered evidence of human sacrifice in Minoan Crete, historians have speculated on the meaning of ancient bull-vaulting (a sport still practiced in Portugal), and its possible relationship to

Figure 4.3 The queen's quarters, Palace of Minos, Knossos, Crete, ca. 1450 B.C.E.

Figure 4.4 Bull-leaping fresco from the Palace of Minos, Knossos, Crete, ca. 1500 B.C.E. Height 32 in.

rituals of blood sacrifice. Nevertheless, the significance of the representation lies in the authority it bestows upon the players: human beings are pictured here not as pawns in a divine game, but, rather, as challengers in a contest of wits and physical agility.

The Minoans developed a hieroglyphic script by 2000 B.C.E. Neither it nor a second type of writing (called by Evans "Linear A") have been deciphered; however, a later version of the script ("Linear B") found on mainland

Greece appears to be an early form of Greek. Deciphered in the 1950s, Linear B was a language used for bureaucratic and administrative purposes. Some 4600 tablets are inscribed with lists of people, produce, animals, and manufactured goods. The search for more extensive archives containing poetry and other texts continues.

Modern archeologists were not the first to prize Minoan culture; the Greeks immortalized the Minoans in myth and legend. The most famous of the legends describes a

MAKING CONNECTIONS

Many Minoan artifacts suggest the persistence of ancient fertility cults honoring gods traditionally associated with procreation. The small statue of a bare-breasted female brandishing snakes may represent a popular fertility goddess; or it may depict a priestess performing specific cult rites, such as those accompanying ancient Greek dances that featured live snakes (Figure **4.5**). Because the head of the figure and the snake in her left hand are modern fabrications, recent scholarship has questioned the authenticity of this reconstruction, as well as the authenticity of related "snake goddess figurines." Nevertheless, statuettes and pendants similar to this figure are very common to second-millennium B.C.E. cultures of the eastern Mediterranean. Fabricated in ivory, gold, and other precious materials, they depict goddesses wearing a serpentine coil, holding or flanked by snakes (Figure **4.6**). Such figures are identified as agricultural deities, associated with the regenerative powers of the snake, an ancient symbol of rebirth.

Figure 4.5 Priestess with snakes, Minoan, ca. 1600 B.C.E. Faience, height 13½ in.

Figure 4.6 Goddess of growth (Astarte?) with two serpents (pendant). Ugarit, Phoenicia, fifteenth century B.C.E. Gold, 2⅝ × 1⅛ in.

Minotaur—a monstrous half-man, half-bull born of the union of Minos' queen and a sacred white bull. According to the story, the clever Athenian hero Theseus, aided by the king's daughter Ariadne, threaded his way through the Minotaur's labyrinthine lair to kill the monster, thus freeing Athens from its ancient bondage to the Minoans. Around 1700 B.C.E., some three centuries before mainland Greece absorbed Crete, an earthquake brought devastation to Minoan civilization.

Mycenaean Civilization (ca. 1600–1200 B.C.E.)

By 1600 B.C.E., the Mycenaeans had established themselves in the Aegean. By contrast with the Minoans, the Mycenaeans were a militant and aggressive people: their warships challenged other traders for control of the eastern Mediterranean. On mainland Greece at Tiryns and Mycenae (see Map 4.1), the Mycenaeans constructed heavily fortified citadels and walls so massive that later generations thought they had been built by a mythical race of giants known as the Cyclops. These "cyclopean" walls were guarded by symbols of royal power: in the triangular arch above the entrance gate to the citadel, two 9-foot-high stone lions flank a column that rests on a Minoan-style altar (Figure 4.7).

Master stonemasons, the Mycenaeans buried their rulers in beehive-shaped tombs. The royal graves, uncovered by Schliemann in 1876, are filled with weapons and jewelry fit for an Egyptian pharaoh. These items, and in particular the gold death mask that once covered the face of the deceased, Schliemann identified as belonging to Agamemnon (Figure 4.8), the legendary king who led the ancient Greeks against the city of Troy. This tale is immortalized in the first of the Greek epic poems, the *Iliad*. Although later archeologists have proved Schliemann wrong—the tombs are earlier than he thought—the legends and the myths of the Greek world would flower in Mycenaean soil.

Around 1200 B.C.E., the Mycenaeans attacked Troy ("Ilion" in Greek), a commercial stronghold on the northwest coast of Asia Minor. The ten-year-long war between Mycenae and Troy would provide the historical context for both the *Iliad* and the *Odyssey*, the other great epic poem of the ancient Greeks.

The Heroic Age (ca. 1200–750 B.C.E.)

Soon after 1200 B.C.E., more powerful, iron-bearing tribes of Dorians, a Greek-speaking people from the north, destroyed Mycenaean civilization. During the long period of darkness that followed, storytellers kept alive the history of early Greece, the adventures of the Mycenaeans, and the tales of the Trojan War, passing them orally from generation to generation. It was not until at least the ninth century B.C.E. that these stories were transcribed; and it was yet another 300 years before they reached their present form. The *Iliad* and the *Odyssey* became the "national"

Figure 4.7 Lion Gate, citadel at Mycenae, ca. 1500–1300 B.C.E. Limestone, height of relief 9 ft. 6 in. Huge rock-cut blocks of stone were set in projecting layers to hold in place the triangular relief above the entranceway. Heraldic lions, symbols of power, flank the central column. Carved separately, the heads of the lions are missing.

Figure 4.8 Funerary mask, once believed to be that of Agamemnon, ca. 1500 B.C.E. Gold, height 12 in.

The *Odyssey* recounts the long, adventure-packed sea journey undertaken by Odysseus, a resourceful hero of the Trojan War, in his effort to return to his home and family, and reassume his authority as king of Ithaca. Like the *Epic of Gilgamesh*, the *Iliad* and the *Odyssey* belong to the oral tradition of a heroic age, but whereas the *Epic of Gilgamesh* takes as its theme the pursuit of everlasting life, the Greek epics give voice to the quest for individual honor and glory.

Almost 16,000 lines long, the *Iliad* is a robust tale of war (Figure 4.10), but its true subject is Achilles, the offspring of Peleus, king of Thessaly, and the sea goddess Thetis. (Later legends report that Thetis, having dipped her infant son in the River Styx, made him invulnerable except for the heel by which she held him.) Like Gilgamesh, Achilles is part-god and part-man, but the Greek superhero is a more psychologically complex character than Gilgamesh; the emotions he exhibits—anger, love, rage, and grief—are wholly human. The plot of the *Iliad* turns on Achilles' decision to take action that will bring glory to his warriors and to himself. The importance of heroic action in proving virtue, or excellence (the Greek

Figure 4.9 EUPHRONIOS and **EUXITHEOS**, *Death of Sarpedon*, ca. 515 B.C.E. Ceramic krater with red-figure decoration, height 18 in. The legendary warrior and Trojan ally, Sarpedon, was killed by Patroclus in the course of the war. He is shown on this **krater** (a vessel used for mixing wine and water) being carried from the battlefield by the winged figures of Hypnos (Sleep) and Thanatos (Death). Central to the lyrically balanced composition is the figure of Hermes, messenger of the gods, who guides the dead to the underworld.

poems of ancient Greece, uniting Greek-speaking people by giving literary authority to their common heritage. Although much of what is known about the early history of the Greeks comes from these epic poems, little is known about the blind poet Homer, to whom they are traditionally attributed. Scholars are not sure when or where he lived, or, indeed, if he existed at all. It is unlikely that he composed the poems, although legend has it that he actually memorized the whole of each poem. The only fact of which we can be fairly certain is that Homer represents the culmination of a long and vigorous tradition in which oral recitation—possibly to instrumental accompaniment—was a popular kind of entertainment.

The *Iliad* takes place in the last days of the Trojan War. It is the story of the Achaean (ancient Greek) hero Achilles (or Achilleus), who, moved to anger by an affront to his honor, refuses to join the battle against Troy alongside his Achaean comrades. Wearing Achilles' armor, his dearest friend, Patroclus, goes forth to rout the Trojans, slaying many of their allies (Figure 4.9). Only after Patroclus is killed by Hector, leader of the Trojan forces, does Achilles finally, and vengefully, go to war. In a dramatic battle, he confronts and kills Hector, stripping him of his armor and dragging his nude corpse before the walls of Troy. Following this great indignity to the body and the memory of the Trojan prince, Hector's father, King Priam, humbles himself before Achilles and begs for the return of his son. The epic closes with Hector's funeral.

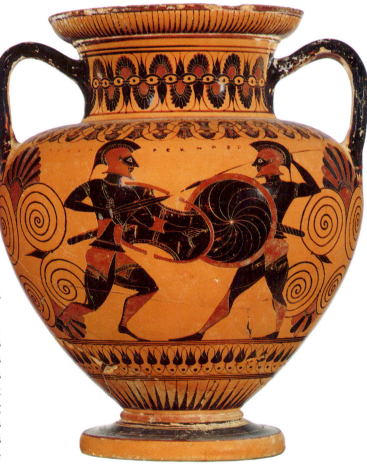

Figure 4.10 By the "**BOTKIN CLASS**," *Contest of Two Warriors*, ca. 540–530 B.C.E. Attic black-figured amphora, ceramic, 11$\frac{9}{16}$ × 9½ in. Two black-figured warriors are shown on this **amphora** (a Greek vessel used for storing wine or oil). Both wear traditional Greek helmets and greaves (leg armor worn below the knee). Both are protected by handheld shields; one soldier is armed with a short sword, the other with a spear.

word *arete* connotes both), is central to the *Iliad* and to the male-dominated culture of the Heroic Age (see Figure 4.10). To the ancient Greeks, moral value lay in proper action, even if the consequence of that action was death. Indeed, death in battle was a sure path to honor.

The language of the *Iliad*, no less than its theme, is charged with heroic vigor. It makes use of vivid similes (anger "blinds like smoke"), graphic **epithets** ("the bronze-armed Achaeans"), and lengthy **catalogs** of particulars. Its majestic poetry and its heroic personalities have inspired generations of Western writers, including Virgil and Milton (discussed in later chapters). The following excerpts from the *Iliad*, rendered in a 1990 translation by Robert Fagles, illustrate the qualities that have made the work a classic.

READING 4.1 From the *Iliad* (ca. 850 B.C.E.)

(Book 18, ll. 1–42, 82–150; Book 19, ll. 423–77; Book 24, ll. 471–707)

So the men fought on like a mass of whirling fire   1
as swift Antilochus raced the message toward Achilles.
Sheltered under his curving, beaked ships he found him,
foreboding, deep down, all that had come to pass.
Agonizing now he probed his own great heart:
"Why, why? Our long-haired Achaeans[1] routed again,
driven in terror off the plain to crowd the ships, but why?
Dear gods, don't bring to pass the grief that haunts my heart—
the prophecy that mother revealed to me one time . . .
she said the best of the Myrmidons[2]—while I lived—   10
would fall at Trojan hands and leave the light of day.
And now he's dead, I know it: Menoetius' gallant son,[3]
my headstrong friend! And I told Patroclus clearly,
'Once you have beaten off the lethal fire, quick,
come back to the ships—you must not battle Hector!'"

As such fears went churning through his mind
the warlord Nestor's son drew near him now,
streaming warm tears, to give the dreaded message:
"Ah son of royal Peleus, what you must hear from me!
What painful news—would to god it had never happened!   20
Patroclus has fallen. They're fighting over his corpse.
He's stripped, naked—Hector with that flashing helmet,
Hector has your arms!"
So the captain reported.
A black cloud of grief came shrouding over Achilles.
Both hands clawing the ground for soot and filth,
he poured it over his head, fouled his handsome face
and black ashes settled onto his fresh clean war-shirt.
Overpowered in all his power, he sprawled in the dust.
Achilles lay there, fallen . . .
tearing his hair, defiling it with his own hands.   30

---

[1] The Mycenaeans, who inhabited the kingdom near Thessaly, and, more broadly, the Greek army that besieged Troy.

[2] The name by which the subject warriors of Peleus and Achilles are known in Homer. It derives from the Greek word for ants, the creatures out of which Zeus was said to have created the inhabitants of the island of Aegina, ruled by Peleus.

[3] Patroclus, Achilles' favorite companion and friend.

And the women he and Patroclus carried off as captives
caught the grief in their hearts and keened and wailed,
out of the tents they ran to ring the great Achilles,
all of them beat their breasts with clenched fists,
sank to the ground, each woman's knees gave way.

Antilochus kneeling near, weeping uncontrollably,
clutched Achilles' hands as he wept his proud heart out—
for fear he would slash his throat with an iron blade.
Achilles suddenly loosed a terrible, wrenching cry
and his noble mother heard him, seated near her father,   40
the Old Man of the Sea[4] in the salt green depths,
and she cried out in turn.

. . . .

As he groaned from the depths his mother rose before him
and sobbing a sharp cry, cradled her son's head in her hands
and her words were all compassion, winging pity: "My child—
why in tears? What sorrow has touched your heart?
Tell me, please. Don't harbor it deep inside you.
Zeus has accomplished everything you wanted,
just as you raised your hands and prayed that day.
All the sons of Achaea are pinned against the ships   50
and all for want of you—they suffer shattering losses."

And groaning deeply the matchless runner answered,
"O dear mother, true! All those burning desires
Olympian Zeus has brought to pass for me—
but what joy to me now? My dear comrade's dead—
Patroclus—the man I loved beyond all other comrades,
loved as my own life—I've lost him—Hector's killed him,
stripped the gigantic armor off his back, a marvel to behold—
my burnished gear! Radiant gifts the gods presented Peleus
that day they drove you into a mortal's marriage bed . . .   60
I wish you'd lingered deep with the deathless sea-nymphs,
lived at ease, and Peleus carried home a mortal bride.
But now, as it is, sorrows, unending sorrows must surge
within your heart as well—for your own son's death.
Never again will you embrace him striding home.
My spirits rebel—I've lost the will to live,
to take my stand in the world of men—unless,
before all else, Hector's battered down by my spear
and gasps away his life, the blood-price for Patroclus,
Menoetius' gallant son he's killed and stripped!"   70

But Thetis answered, warning through her tears,
"You're doomed to a short life, my son, from all you say!
For hard on the heels of Hector's death your death
must come at once—"
"Then let me die at once"—
Achilles burst out, despairing—"since it was not my fate
to save my dearest comrade from his death! Look,
a world away from his fatherland he's perished,
lacking me, my fighting strength, to defend him.
But now, since I shall not return to my fatherland . . .
nor did I bring one ray of hope to my Patroclus,   80

---

[4] A sea god, the "Old Man" of the sea and father of some 50–100 daughters, including Thetis, mother of Achilles.

nor to the rest of all my steadfast comrades,
countless ranks struck down by mighty Hector—
No, no, here I sit by the ships . . .
a useless, dead weight on the good green earth—
I, no man my equal among the bronze-armed Achaeans,
not in battle, only in wars of words that others win.
If only strife could die from the lives of gods and men
and anger that drives the sanest man to flare in outrage—
bitter gall, sweeter than dripping streams of honey,
that swarms in people's chests and blinds like smoke—   90
just like the anger Agamemnon[5] king of men
has roused within me now . . .

        Enough.
Let bygones be bygones. Done is done.
Despite my anguish I will beat it down,
the fury mounting inside me, down by force.
But now I'll go and meet that murderer head-on,
that Hector who destroyed the dearest life I know.
For my own death, I'll meet it freely—whenever Zeus
and the other deathless gods would like to bring it on!
Not even Heracles fled his death, for all his power,   100
favorite son as he was to father Zeus the King.
Fate crushed him, and Hera's savage anger.
And I too, if the same fate waits for me . . .
I'll lie in peace, once I've gone down to death.
But now, for the moment, let me seize great glory!—
and drive some woman of Troy or deep-breasted Dardan
to claw with both hands at her tender cheeks and wipe away
her burning tears as the sobs come choking from her throat—
they'll learn that I refrained from war a good long time!
Don't try to hold me back from the fighting, mother,   110
love me as you do. You can't persuade me now."

   .   .   .   .

*[Hephaestus (Hephaistos), god of fire and of metalworking,
has forged a special set of arms for Achilles. In the following
lines from Book 19, Achilles prepares to lead the Achaeans
into battle.]*

Thick-and-fast as the snow comes swirling down from Zeus,
frozen sharp when the North Wind born in heaven blasts it on—
so massed, so dense the glistening burnished helmets shone,
streaming out of the ships, and shields with jutting bosses,
breastplates welded front and back and the long ashen spears.
The glory of armor lit the skies and the whole earth laughed,
rippling under the glitter of bronze, thunder resounding
under trampling feet of armies. And in their midst
the brilliant Achilles began to arm for battle . . .   120
A sound of grinding came from the fighter's teeth,
his eyes blazed forth in searing points of fire,
unbearable grief came surging through his heart
and now, bursting with rage against the men of Troy,
he donned Hephaestus' gifts—magnificent armor
the god of fire forged with all his labor.
First he wrapped his legs with well-made greaves,
fastened behind his heels with silver ankle-clasps,

next he strapped the breastplate round his chest
then over his shoulder Achilles slung his sword,   130
the fine bronze blade with its silver-studded hilt,
then hoisted the massive shield flashing far and wide
like a full round moon—and gleaming bright as the light
that reaches sailors out at sea, the flare of a watchfire
burning strong in a lonely sheepfold up some mountain slope
when the gale-winds hurl the crew that fights against them
far over the fish-swarming sea, far from loved ones—
so the gleam from Achilles' well-wrought blazoned shield
shot up and hit the skies. Then lifting his rugged helmet
he set it down on his brows, and the horsehair crest   140
shone like a star and the waving golden plumes shook
that Hephaestus drove in bristling thick along its ridge.
And brilliant Achilles tested himself in all his gear,
Achilles spun on his heels to see if it fit tightly,
see if his shining limbs ran free within it, yes,
and it felt like buoyant wings lifting the great captain.
And then, last, Achilles drew his father's spear
from its socket-stand—weighted, heavy, tough.
No other Achaean fighter could heft that shaft,
only Achilles had the skill to wield it well;   150
Pelian ash it was, a gift to his father Peleus
presented by Chiron[6] once, hewn on Pelion's crest
to be the death of heroes.

        Now the war-team—
Alcimus and Automedon worked to yoke them quickly.
They clinched the supple breast-straps round their chests
and driving the bridle irons home between their jaws,
pulled the reins back taut to the bolted chariot.
Seizing a glinting whip, his fist on the handgrip,
Automedon leapt aboard behind the team and behind
him Achilles struck his stance, helmed for battle now,   160
glittering in his armor like the sun astride the skies,
his ringing, daunting voice commanding his father's horses:
"Roan Beauty and Charger, illustrious foals of Lightfoot!
Try hard, do better this time—bring your charioteer
back home alive to his waiting Argive comrades
once we're through with fighting. Don't leave Achilles
there on the battlefield as you left Patroclus—dead!"

   .   .   .   .

*[After Achilles defeats Hector, Priam, Hector's father and king
of Troy, comes to the Achaean camp. In the following lines
from Book 24, Priam begs for the return of his son's body.]*

. . . the old king went straight up to the lodge
where Achilles dear to Zeus would always sit.
Priam found the warrior there inside . . .   170
many captains sitting some way off, but two,
veteran Automedon and the fine fighter Alcimus
were busy serving him. He had just finished dinner,
eating, drinking, and the table still stood near.
The majestic king of Troy slipped past the rest
and kneeling down beside Achilles, clasped his knees
and kissed his hands, those terrible, man-killing hands

---

[5] King of Mycenae, who led the Greek forces in the Trojan War.

[6] A centaur (half-man, half-horse), one of the creatures driven from
Mount Pelion by the Lapiths (see Figure 5.23).

that had slaughtered Priam's many sons in battle.
Awesome—as when the grip of madness seizes one
who murders a man in his own fatherland and flees   180
abroad to foreign shores, to a wealthy, noble host,
and a sense of marvel runs through all who see him—
so Achilles marveled, beholding majestic Priam.
His men marveled too, trading startled glances.
But Priam prayed his heart out to Achilles:
"Remember your own father, great godlike Achilles—
as old as I am, past the threshold of deadly old age!
No doubt the countrymen round about him plague him now,
with no one there to defend him, beat away disaster.
No one—but at least he hears you're still alive   190
and his old heart rejoices, hopes rising, day by day,
to see his beloved son come sailing home from Troy.
But I—dear god, my life so cursed by fate . . .
I fathered hero sons in the wide realm of Troy
and now not a single one is left, I tell you.
Fifty sons I had when the sons of Achaea came,
nineteen born to me from a single mother's womb
and the rest by other women in the palace. Many,
most of them violent Ares cut the knees from under.
But one, one was left me, to guard my walls, my people—   200
the one you killed the other day, defending his fatherland,
my Hector! It's all for him I've come to the ships now,
to win him back from you—I bring a priceless ransom.
Revere the gods, Achilles! Pity me in my own right,
remember your own father! I deserve more pity . . .
I have endured what no one on earth has ever done before—
I put to my lips the hands of the man who killed my son."

    Those words stirred within Achilles a deep desire
to grieve for his own father. Taking the old man's hand
he gently moved him back. And overpowered by memory   210
both men gave way to grief. Priam wept freely
for man-killing Hector, throbbing, crouching
before Achilles' feet as Achilles wept himself,
now for his father, now for Patroclus once again,
and their sobbing rose and fell throughout the house.
Then, when brilliant Achilles had his fill of tears
and the longing for it had left his mind and body,
he rose from his seat, raised the old man by the hand
and filled with pity now for his gray head and gray beard,
he spoke out winging words, flying straight to the heart: 220
"Poor man, how much you've borne—pain to break the spirit!
What daring brought you down to the ships, all alone,
to face the glance of the man who killed your sons,
so many fine brave boys? You have a heart of iron.
Come, please, sit down on this chair here . . .
Let us put our griefs to rest in our own hearts,
rake them up no more, raw as we are with mourning.
What good's to be won from tears that chill the spirit?
So the immortals spun our lives that we, we wretched men
live on to bear such torments—the gods live free of sorrows.   230
There are two great jars that stand on the floor of Zeus's halls
and hold his gifts, our miseries one, the other blessings.
When Zeus who loves the lightning mixes gifts for a man,
now he meets with misfortune, now good times in turn.
When Zeus dispenses gifts from the jar of sorrows only,

he makes a man an outcast—brutal, ravenous hunger
drives him down the face of the shining earth,
stalking far and wide, cursed by gods and men.
So with my father, Peleus. What glittering gifts
the gods rained down from the day that he was born!   240
He excelled all men in wealth and pride of place,
he lorded the Myrmidons, and mortal that he was,
they gave the man an immortal goddess for a wife.
Yes, but even on him the Father piled hardships,
no powerful race of princes born in his royal halls,
only a single son he fathered, doomed at birth,
cut off in the spring of life— and I, I give the man
care as he grows old since here I sit in Troy,
no far from my fatherland, a grief to you, a grief
to all your children. And you too, old man, we hear   250
you prospered once: as far as Lesbos, Macar's
kingdom, bounds to seaward, Phrygia east and
upland, the Hellespont vast and north— that entire
realm, they say, you lorded over once, you excelled
all men, old king, in sons and wealth. But then the
gods of heaven brought this agony on you—ceaseless
battles round your walls, your armies slaughtered.
You must bear up now. Enough of endless tears,
the pain that breaks the spirit.
Grief for your son will do no good at all.   260
You will never bring him back to life—
sooner you must suffer something worse."

    But the old and noble Priam protested strongly:
"Don't make me sit on a chair, Achilles, Prince,
not while Hector lies uncared-for in your camp!
Give him back to me, now, no more delay—
I must see my son with my own eyes.
Accept the ransom I bring you, a king's ransom!
Enjoy it, all of it—return to your own native land,
safe and sound . . . since now you've spared my life."   270
    A dark glance—and the headstrong runner answered,
"No more, old man, don't tempt my wrath, not now!
My own mind's made up to give you back your son.
A messenger brought me word from Zeus—my mother,
Thetis who bore me, the Old Man of the Sea's daughter.
And what's more, I can see through you, Priam—
no hiding the fact from me: one of the gods
has led you down to Achaea's fast ships.
No man alive, not even a rugged young fighter,
would dare to venture into our camp. Never—   280
how could he slip past the sentries unchallenged?
Or shoot back the bolt of my gates with so much ease?
So don't anger me now. Don't stir my raging heart still more.
Or under my own roof I may not spare your life, old man—
suppliant that you are—may break the laws of Zeus!"

    The old man was terrified. He obeyed the order.
But Achilles bounded out of doors like a lion—
not alone but flanked by his two aides-in-arms,
veteran Automedon and Alcimus, steady comrades,
Achilles' favorites next to the dead Patroclus.   290
They loosed from harness the horses and the mules,
they led the herald in, the old king's crier,

and sat him down on a bench. From the polished wagon
they lifted the priceless ransom brought for Hector's corpse
but they left behind two capes and a finely-woven shirt
to shroud the body well when Priam bore him home.
Then Achilles called the serving-women out:
"Bathe and anoint the body—bear it aside first.
Priam must not see his son." He feared that,
overwhelmed by the sight of Hector, wild with   300
grief, Priam might let his anger flare and Achilles
might fly into fresh rage himself, cut the old man
down and break the laws of Zeus. So when the
maids had bathed and anointed the body sleek with
olive oil and wrapped it round and round in a braided
battle-shirt and handsome battle-cape, then Achilles
lifted Hector up in his own arms and laid him down
on a bier, and comrades helped him raise the bier
and body onto the sturdy wagon . . . Then with a
groan he called his dear friend by name: "Feel no   310
anger at me, Patroclus, if you learn— even there
in the House of Death—I let his father have
Prince Hector back. He gave me worthy ransom
and you shall have your share from me, as always,
your fitting, lordly share."

So he vowed and brilliant Achilles strode
back to his shelter, sat down on the well-carved
chair that he had left, at the far wall of the room,
leaned toward Priam and firmly spoke the words
the king had come to hear: "Your son is now set free,
old man, as you requested. Hector lies in state.   320
With the first light of day you will see for yourself
as you convey him home. Now, at last, let us turn
our thoughts to supper."

Q **How would you describe the personality of Achilles?**

Q **How do Achilles and Gilgamesh compare as epic heroes?**

The Greek Gods

The ancient Greeks envisioned their gods as a family of immortals who intervened in the lives of human beings. Originating in the cultures of Crete and Mycenae, the Greek pantheon exalted Zeus, the powerful sky god, and his wife, Hera, as the ruling deities. Among the lesser gods were Poseidon, god of the sea; Apollo, god of light, medicine, and music (Figure **4.11**); Dionysus, god of wine and vegetation; Athena, goddess of wisdom and war; and Aphrodite, goddess of love, beauty, and procreation. Around these and other deities there emerged an elaborate mythology.

Many Greek myths look back to the common pool of legends and tales that traveled throughout the Mediterranean and the Near East. In the *Theogony* (*The Birth of the Gods*), a poem recounting the history and genealogy of the gods, Homer's contemporary Hesiod (fl. 700 B.C.E.) describes the origins of the universe in a manner reminiscent of *The Babylonian Creation:*

First of all, the Void came into being, next broad-bosomed Earth, the solid and eternal home of all, and Eros [Desire], the most beautiful of the immortal gods, who in every man and every god softens the sinews and overpowers the prudent purpose of the mind. Out of Void came Darkness and black Night, and out of Night came Light and Day, her children conceived after union in love with Darkness. Earth first produced starry Sky, equal in size with herself . . .

The Greeks also had their own version of the Isis/Osiris myth. When Hades, god of the underworld, abducts the beautiful Persephone, her mother, Demeter, rescues her; tricked by Hades, however, this goddess of vegetation is forced to return annually to the underworld, leaving the earth above barren and desolate. Cults based in myths of death and rebirth offered their devotees the hope of personal regeneration.

The Greeks traced their origins to events related to the fury of Zeus: angered by human evil, Zeus decided to destroy humankind by sending a flood. Deucalion, the Greek Noah, built a boat for himself and his wife and obeyed an oracle that commanded them to throw the "bones" of Mother Earth overboard. From these stones sprang up human beings, the first of whom was Hellen, the legendary ancestor of the Greeks, or "Hellenes."

Principal Greek Gods

Greek Name	Roman Name	Signifies
Aphrodite	Venus	love, beauty, procreation
Apollo	Phoebus	solar light, medicine, music
Ares	Mars	war, strife
Artemis	Diana	hunting, wildlife, the moon
Athena	Minerva	war, wisdom
Demeter	Ceres	agriculture, grain
Dionysus	Bacchus	wine, vegetation
Eros	Amor/Cupid	erotic love, desire
Hades	Pluto	underworld
Helios	Phoebus	sun
Hephaestus	Vulcan	fire, metallurgy
Hera	Juno	queen of the gods
Heracles	Hercules	strength, courage
Hermes	Mercury	male messenger of the gods
Hestia	Vesta	hearth, domestic life
Nike	Victoria	victory
Persephone	Proserpina	underworld
Poseidon	Neptune	sea
Selene	Diana	moon
Zeus	Jupiter	king of the gods, sky

Although immortal, the Greek gods were much like the human beings who worshiped them: they were amorous, adulterous, capricious, and quarrelsome. They lived not in some remote heaven, but (conveniently enough) atop a mountain in northern Greece—that is, among the Greeks themselves. From their home on Mount Olympus, the gods might take sides in human combat (as they regularly do in the *Iliad*), seduce mortal women, and meddle in the lives of those they felt were worthy of their attention. The Greek gods were not always benevolent or just. Unlike the Hebrew god, they set forth no clear principles of moral conduct and no guidelines for religious worship. Priests and priestesses tended the temples and shrines and oversaw rituals, including human and animal sacrifices performed to win the favor of the gods.

Popular Greek religion produced no sacred scripture and no doctrines—circumstances that may have contributed to the freedom of intellectual inquiry for which the Greeks became famous. Equally famous, at least in ancient times, was the oracle at Delphi, the shrine of Apollo and the site that marked for the Greeks the center of the universe and the "navel" of the earth. Here the priestess of Apollo sat on a tripod over a fissure in the rock, and, in a state of ecstasy (which recent archeologists attribute to hallucinogenic fumes from narcotic gases in two geologic faults below) uttered inscrutable replies to the questions of supplicants from near and far. The oracle at Delphi remained the supreme source of prophecy and mystical wisdom until the temple-shrine was destroyed in late Roman times.

The Greek City-State and the Persian Wars (ca. 750–480 B.C.E.)

Toward the end of the Homeric Age, the Greeks formed small rural colonies that gradually grew into urban communities, mainly through maritime trade. Geographic conditions—a rocky terrain interrupted by mountains, valleys, and narrow rivers—made overland travel and trade difficult. At the same time, Greek geography (see Map 4.1) encouraged the evolution of the independent city-state (in Greek, *polis*). Ancient Greece consisted of a constellation of some 200 city-states, a few as large as 400 square miles and others as tiny as 2 square miles. Many of these (Athens, for instance) were small enough that a person might walk around their walls in only a few hours. Although all the Greek city-states shared the same language, traditions, and religion, each *polis* governed itself, issued its own coinage, and provided its own military defenses. The autonomy of the Greek city-states—so unlike the monolithic Egyptian state—fostered fierce competition and commercial rivalry. However, like the squabbling members of a family who are suddenly menaced by aggressive neighbors, the Greek city-states, confronted by the rising power of Persia, united in self-defense.

By the sixth century B.C.E., the Persian Empire had conquered most of the territories between the western frontier of India and Asia Minor. Advancing westward, Persia annexed Ionia, the Greek region on the coast of Asia Minor (see Map 4.1), a move that clearly threatened mainland Greece. Thus, when in 499 B.C.E. the Ionian cities revolted against Persian rule, their Greek neighbors came to their aid. In retaliation, the Persians sent military expeditions to punish the rebel cities of the Greek mainland. In 490 B.C.E., on the plain of Marathon, 25 miles from Athens, a Greek force of 11,000 men met a Persian army with twice its numbers and defeated them, losing only 192 men. Persian casualties exceeded 6000. The Greek warrior who brought news of the victory at Marathon to Athens died upon completing the 26-mile run. (Hence the word "marathon" has come to designate a long-distance endurance contest.) But the Greeks soon realized that without a strong navy even the combined land forces of all the city-states could not hope to oust the Persians. They thus proceeded to build a fleet of warships, which, in 480 B.C.E., ultimately defeated the Persian armada at Salamis, one of the final battles of the Persian Wars.

Herodotus

Much of what we know about the Persian Wars comes to us from the world's first known historian, Herodotus (ca. 485–425 B.C.E.), the "father of history." Writing not as an eyewitness to the wars, but a half-century later, Herodotus nevertheless brought keen critical judgment to sources that included hearsay as well as record. His sprawling narrative is filled with fascinating anecdotes and colorful digressions, including a "travelogue" of his visits to Egypt and Asia—accounts that remain among our most detailed sources of information about ancient African and West Asian life. Here, for instance, is our earliest information on Scythian royal burials and on the use of hemp as a hallucinogen. The chapters on Africa, filled with numerous comparisons between Greek and Egyptian social practices and religious beliefs, show Herodotus as an early investigator of what would today be called "comparative culture."

By presenting various (and often contradictory) pieces of evidence and weighing them against one another before arriving at a conclusion, Herodotus laid the basis for the historical method. Following the Homeric epics by some 300 years, the nine-volume *History of the Persian Wars* is not only the West's first historical narrative, it is the first major literary work written in prose. Like the Homeric epics, and designed (as Herodotus claimed) "to preserve the memory of the past," the *History* shaped the Greek national identity.

Athens and the Greek Golden Age (ca. 480–430 B.C.E.)

Although all the city-states had contributed to expelling the Persians, it was Athens that claimed the crown of victory. Indeed, in the wake of the Persian Wars, Athens assumed political dominion among the city-states, as well as commercial supremacy in the Aegean Sea. The defeat of Persia inspired a mood of confidence and a spirit of vigorous chauvinism. This spirit ushered in an age of drama, philosophy, music, art, and architecture. In fact, the period between 480 and 430 B.C.E., known as the Greek Golden Age, was one of the most creative in the history of the world. In Athens, it was as if the heroic idealism of the *Iliad* had bloomed into civic patriotism.

Athens, the most cosmopolitan of the city-states, was unique among the Greek communities, for the **democratic** government that came to prevail there was the exception rather than the rule in ancient Greece. In its early history, Athens—like most of the other Greek city-states—was an **oligarchy**, that is, a government controlled by an elite minority. But a series of enlightened rulers who governed Athens between roughly 600 and 500 B.C.E. introduced reforms that placed increasing authority in the hands of its citizens. The Athenian statesman, poet, and legislator Solon (ca. 638–558 B.C.E.) fixed the democratic course of Athenian history by abolishing the custom of debt slavery and encouraging members of the lower classes to serve in public office. By broadening the civic responsibilities of Athenians, Solon educated citizens of all classes in the activities of government. By 550 B.C.E., the Popular Assembly of Citizens (made up of all citizens) was operating alongside the Council of Five Hundred (made up of aristocrats who handled routine state business) and the Board of Ten Generals (an annually elected executive body). When, at last, in the year 508 B.C.E., the Popular Assembly acquired the right to make laws, Athens became the first direct democracy in world history.

The word "democracy" derives from Greek words describing a government in which the people (*demos*) hold power (*kratos*). In the democracy of ancient Athens, Athenian citizens exercised political power directly, thus—unlike in the United States, where power rests in the hands of representatives of the people—the citizens of Athens themselves held the authority to make the laws and approve state policy. Athenian democracy was, however, highly exclusive. Its citizenry included only landowning males over the age of eighteen. Of an estimated population of 250,000, this probably constituted some 40,000 people. Women, children, resident aliens, and slaves did not qualify as citizens. Athenian women could not inherit or own property and had few legal rights. (Slaves, as in earlier civilizations, arrived at their unfree condition as a result of warfare or debt, not race.) Clearly, in the mind of the Athenian, Hellenes were superior to non-Greeks (or outsiders, whom the Greeks called *barbaros*, from which comes the English word "barbarians"), Athenians were superior to non-Athenians, Athenian males were superior to Athenian females, and all classes of free men and women were superior to slaves.

Fundamental to Athenian democracy was a commitment to the legal equality of its participants: one citizen's vote weighed as heavily as the next. Equally important to Athenian (as to any) democracy was the hypothesis that individuals who had the right to vote would do so, and, moreover, were willing to take responsible action in the interest of the common good. (Such ideals are still highly valued in many parts of the modern world.) The small size of Athens probably contributed to the success of its unique form of government. Although probably no more than 5000 Athenians attended the Assembly that met four times a month to make laws in the open-air marketplace (the

Agora) located at the foot of the Acropolis, these men were the proponents of a brave new enterprise in governing.

Golden Age Athens stands in vivid contrast to those ancient civilizations whose rulers—the incarnate representatives of the gods—held absolute power while citizens held none. Athens also stands in contrast to its rival, Sparta, the largest *polis* on the Peloponnesus (see Map 4.1). In Sparta, an oligarchy of five officials, elected annually, held tight reins on a society whose male citizens (from the age of seven on) were trained as soldiers. All physical labor fell to a class of unfree workers called *helots*, the captives of Sparta's frequent local wars. Spartan soldiers were renowned for their bravery; their women, expected to live up to the ideals of a warrior culture, enjoyed a measure of freedom that was unknown in Athens. Yet, the history of Sparta would be one in which a strict social order left little room for creativity, in government or in the arts.

Pericles' Glorification of Athens

The leading proponent of Athenian democracy was the statesman Pericles (ca. 495–429 B.C.E.) (Figure **4.12**), who dominated the Board of Ten Generals for more than thirty years until his death. An aristocrat by birth, Pericles was a democrat at heart. In the interest of broadening the democratic system, he initiated some of Athens' most sweeping domestic reforms, such as payment for holding public office and a system of public audit in which the finances of outgoing magistrates were subject to critical scrutiny. In

Figure 4.12 Bust inscribed with the name of Pericles, from Tivoli. Roman copy after a bronze original of 450–425 B.C.E. Marble, height 23 in. The helmet resting on Pericles' head signifies his role as a military general in the campaigns of the Peloponnesian Wars.

Pericles' time, many public offices were filled by lottery—a procedure that invited all citizens to seek governmental office, and one so egalitarian as to be unthinkable today.

Pericles' foreign policy was even more ambitious than his domestic policies. In the wake of the Persian Wars, he encouraged the Greek city-states to form a defensive alliance against future invaders. At the outset, the league's collective funds were kept in a treasury on the sacred island of Delos (hence the name "Delian League"). But, in a bold display of chauvinism, Pericles moved the fund to Athens and expropriated its monies to rebuild the Athenian temples that had been burned by the Persians.

Pericles' high-handed actions, along with his imperialistic efforts to dominate the commercial policies of league members, led to antagonism and armed dispute between Athens and a federation of rival city-states led by Sparta. The ensuing Peloponnesian Wars (431–404 B.C.E.), which culminated in the defeat of Athens, brought an end to the Greek Golden Age. Our knowledge of the Peloponnesian Wars is based mainly on the account written by the great historian Thucydides (ca. 460–400 B.C.E.), himself a general in the combat. Thucydides went beyond merely recording the events of the war to provide insights into its causes and a firsthand assessment of its political and moral consequences. Thucydides' terse, graphic descriptions and his detached analyses of events distinguish his style from that of Herodotus.

The following speech by Pericles, excerpted from Thucydides' *History of the Peloponnesian War*, was presented on the occasion of a mass funeral held outside the walls of Athens to honor those who had died in the first battles of the war. Nowhere are the concepts of humanism and individualism more closely linked to civic patriotism than in this speech. Pericles reviews the "principles of action" by which Athens rose to power. He describes Athens as "the school of Hellas"; that is, it is the model and the teacher for all the other Greek communities. The greatness of Athens, according to Pericles, lies not merely in its military might and in the superiority of its political institutions, but in the quality of its citizens, their nobility of spirit, and their love of beauty and wisdom. Pericles' views, which were shared by most Athenians as primary articles of faith, reflect the spirit of civic pride that characterized Hellenic culture at its peak.

READING 4.2 From Thucydides' *Peloponnesian War* (ca. 410 B.C.E.)

Pericles' Funeral Speech

"I will speak first of our ancestors, for it is right and becoming that now, when we are lamenting the dead, a tribute should be paid to their memory. There has never been a time when they did not inhabit this land, which by their valor they have handed down from generation to generation, and we have received from them a free state. But if they were worthy of praise, still more were our fathers, who added to their inheritance, and after many a struggle transmitted to us their sons this great empire. And we ourselves assembled

1

here today, who are still most of us in the vigor of life, have chiefly done the work of improvement, and have richly endowed our city with all things, so that she is sufficient for herself both in peace and war. Of the military exploits by which our various possessions were acquired, or of the energy with which we or our fathers drove back the tide of war, Hellenic or barbarian, I will not speak; for the tale would be long and is familiar to you. But before I praise the dead, I should like to point out by what principles of action we rose to power, and under what institutions and through what manner of life our empire became great. For I conceive that such thoughts are not unsuited to the occasion, and that this numerous assembly of citizens and strangers may profitably listen to them.

"Our form of government does not enter into rivalry with the institutions of others. We do not copy our neighbors, but are an example to them. It is true that we are called a democracy, for the administration is in the hands of the many and not of the few. But while the law secures equal justice to all alike in their private disputes, the claim of excellence is also recognized; and when a citizen is in any way distinguished, he is preferred to the public service, not as a matter of privilege, but as the reward of merit. Neither is poverty a bar, but a man may benefit his country whatever be the obscurity of his condition. There is no exclusiveness in our public life, and in our private intercourse we are not suspicious of one another, nor angry with our neighbor if he does what he likes; we do not put on sour looks at him which, though harmless, are not pleasant. While we are thus unconstrained in our private intercourse, a spirit of reverence pervades our public acts; we are prevented from doing wrong by respect for authority and for the laws, having an especial regard to those which are ordained for the protection of the injured as well as to those unwritten laws which bring upon the transgressor of them the reprobation of the general sentiment.

"And we have not forgotten to provide for our weary spirits many relaxations from toil; we have regular games[1] and sacrifices throughout the year; at home the style of our life is refined; and the delight which we daily feel in all these things helps to banish melancholy. Because of the greatness of our city the fruits of the whole earth flow in upon us; so that we enjoy the goods of other countries as freely as of our own.

"Then, again, our military training is in many respects superior to that of our adversaries. Our city is thrown open to the world, and we never expel a foreigner or prevent him from seeing or learning anything of which the secret if revealed to an enemy might profit him. We rely not upon management or trickery, but upon our own hearts and hands. And in the matter of education, whereas they from early youth are always undergoing laborious exercises which are to make them brave, we live at ease, and yet are equally ready to face the perils which they face. And here is the proof. The Lacedaemonians[2] come into Attica not by themselves, but with their whole confederacy following; we go alone into a neighbor's country; and although our opponents are fighting for their homes and

10

20

30

40

50

60

we on a foreign soil, we have seldom any difficulty in overcoming them. Our enemies have never yet felt our united strength; the care of a navy divides our attention, and on land we are obliged to send our own citizens everywhere. But they, if they meet and defeat a part of our army, are as proud as if they had routed us all, and when defeated they pretend to have been vanquished by us all.

"If then we prefer to meet danger with a light heart but without laborious training, and with a courage which is gained by habit and not enforced by law, are we not greatly the gainers? Since we do not anticipate the pain, although, when the hour comes, we can be as brave as those who never allow themselves to rest; and thus too our city is equally admirable in peace and in war.

"For we are lovers of the beautiful, yet with economy, and we cultivate the mind without loss of manliness. Wealth we employ, not for talk and ostentation, but when there is a real use for it. To avow poverty with us is no disgrace; the true disgrace is in doing nothing to avoid it. An Athenian citizen does not neglect the state because he takes care of his own household; and even those of us who are engaged in business have a very fair idea of politics. We alone regard a man who takes no interest in public affairs, not as a harmless, but as a useless character; and if few of us are originators, we are all sound judges of a policy. The great impediment to action is, in our opinion, not discussion, but the want of that knowledge which is gained by discussion preparatory to action. For we have a peculiar power of thinking before we act and of acting too, whereas other men are courageous from ignorance but hesitate upon reflection. And they are surely to be esteemed the bravest spirits who, having the clearest sense both of the pains and pleasures of life, do not on that account shrink from danger. In doing good, again, we are unlike others; we make our friends by conferring, not by receiving favors. . . . We alone do good to our neighbors not upon a calculation of interest, but in the confidence of freedom and in a frank and fearless spirit.

"To sum up: I say that Athens is the school of Hellas, and that the individual Athenian in his own person seems to have the power of adapting himself to the most varied forms of action with the utmost versatility and grace. This is no passing and idle word, but truth and fact; and the assertion is verified by the position to which these qualities have raised the state. For in the hour of trial Athens alone among her contemporaries is superior to the report of her. No enemy who comes against her is indignant at the reverses which he sustains at the hands of such a city; no subject complains that his masters are unworthy of him. And we shall assuredly not be without witnesses; there are mighty monuments of our power which will make us the wonder of this and of succeeding ages; we shall not need the praises of Homer or of any other panegyrist whose poetry may please for the moment, although his representation of the facts will not bear the light of day. For we have compelled every land and every sea to open a path for our valor, and have everywhere planted eternal memorials of our friendship and of our enmity. Such is the city for whose sake these men nobly fought and died; they could not bear the thought that she might be taken from them; and every one of us who survive should gladly toil on her behalf.

70

80

90

100

110

120

---

[1] Athletic games were part of many Greek festivals, the most famous of which was the Panhellenic Festival (see below).

[2] Citizens of the city-state of Sparta, ideologically opposed to Athens.

"I have dwelt upon the greatness of Athens because I want to show you that we are contending for a higher prize than those who enjoy none of these privileges, and to establish by manifest proof the merit of these men whom I am now commemorating. Their loftiest praise has been already spoken. For in magnifying the city I have magnified them, and men like them whose virtues made her glorious." 130

Q **In what way does Pericles find Athens unique?**

Q **What does he mean by saying "Athens is the school of Hellas"?**

The Olympic Games

Pericles makes proud to the "regular games" that provide Athenians with "relaxations from toil." But, in fact, the most famous of the "games" were athletic contests in which all the city-states of Greece participated. These games were the chief feature of the Panhellenic ("all-Greek") Festival, instituted in 776 B.C.E. in honor of the Greek gods. Located in Olympia, one of the great religious centers of Greece, the festival took place at midsummer every four years, even during wartime: a sacred truce guaranteed safe conduct to all visitors. So significant were the games that they became the basis for the reckoning of time. While Mesopotamia and Egypt calculated time according to the rule of dynasties and kings, the ancient Greeks marked time in "Olympiads," four-year periods beginning with the first games, in 776 B.C.E. The central event of the games was a 200-yard sprint (see Figure **4.1**) called the *stadion* (hence our word "stadium"). But there were also many other contests: a footrace of one and a half miles, the discus throw (Figure **4.13**), the long jump, wrestling, boxing, and other games that probably looked back to Minoan tradition (see Figure 4.4). Greek athletes competed in the nude—from the Greek word *gymnos* ("naked") we get "gymnasium." Winners received amphoras filled with olive oil, garlands of wild olive or laurel leaves, and the enthusiastic acclaim of Greek painters and poets (see Reading 5.3), but no financial reward.

Figure 4.13 MYRON, *Discobolus* (*Discus Thrower*), reconstructed Roman marble copy of a bronze Greek original of ca. 450 B.C.E. Height 5 ft. 1 in.

Although women were not permitted to compete in the Olympics, they could hold games of their own. Prowess rather than cunning was valued in all games: in wrestling, hair-pulling and finger-bending were permitted, but biting and finger-breaking were forbidden. A match terminated when either wrestler gave up, lost consciousness, or fell dead. True "sport" was that which gave athletes an opportunity to rival the divinity of the gods. Nevertheless, the Olympics were a national event that, typically, promoted both individual excellence and communal pride.

The Individual and the Community

Greek Drama

While the Olympic Games were held only once in four years, theatrical performances in the city of Athens occurred twice annually. Like the games, Greek drama was a form of play that addressed the relationship between the individual, the community, and the gods. The ancient Greeks were the first masters in the art of drama. The literary genre that tells a story through the imitation of action, drama grew out of a complex of rituals associated with the worship of Dionysus, god of wine, vegetation, and seasonal regeneration. In early Homeric times, religious rites performed in honor of Dionysus featured a dialogue between two choruses or between a leader (originally perhaps the shaman or priest) and a chorus (the worshipers or ritual participants). With the advent of the poet Thespis (fl. 534 B.C.E.), actor and chorus (the performers) seem to have become separate from those who witnessed the action (the audience). At some point, dramatic action assumed two principal forms: *tragedy* and *comedy*. Although the origins of each are still the subject of speculation among scholars, tragedy probably evolved from fertility rituals surrounding the death and decay of the crops, while comedy seems to have developed out of village revels celebrating seasonal rebirth. It is possible, as well, that such performances had something to do with the healing cults of ancient Greece: the great theater at Epidaurus (Figure **4.14**) was dedicated to Asclepius, the god of medicine. Like the more ancient

Figure 4.14 POLYCLEITUS THE YOUNGER, theater at Epidaurus, Greece, ca. 350 B.C.E. Greek theaters like this one were typically great in size (13,000 capacity). Nevertheless, actors and chorus could be heard even from the top row.

theater of Dionysus in Athens, it stood adjacent to a chief sanctuary for the worship of the god of healing.

The two annual festivals dedicated to Dionysus were the occasion for the performances of tragedies and comedies, and on each occasion (lasting several days) the author of the best play in its category received a prize. By the fifth century B.C.E., Greece had become a mecca

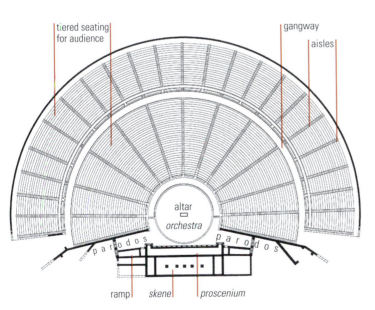

Figure 4.15 Plan of the theater at Epidaurus.

for theater, and while hundreds of plays were performed during the century in which Athenian theater flourished, only forty-four have survived.* They are the products of but four playwrights: Aeschylus (ca. 525–456 B.C.E.), Sophocles (496–406 B.C.E.), Euripides (480–406 B.C.E.), and Aristophanes (ca. 450–ca. 388 B.C.E.). Their plays were staged in the open-air theaters built into the hillsides at sacred sites throughout Greece. These acoustically superb structures, which seated between 13,000 and 27,000 people, featured an *orchestra* (the circular "dancing space" in front of the stage), a *skene* (an area that functioned as a stage set or dressing room), and an *altar* dedicated to the god Dionysus (Figure **4.15**). The *proscenium*, a raised stage in front of the *skene*, came into use somewhat later, in the Hellenistic era (see chapter 5). Music, dance, and song were essential to dramatic performance; scenery and props were few; and actors (all of whom were male) wore elaborate costumes, along with masks that served to amplify their voices.

The tragedies of Aeschylus, Sophocles, and Euripides deal with human conflicts as revealed in Greek history, myth, and legend. Since such stories would have been generally familiar to the average Greek theater-goer, it fell to the playwright to develop the story in an interesting manner. Dramatic action progressed from a specific moment

---

* All the Greek plays in English translation may be found at the website http://classics.mit.edu.

of friction between the individual and fate, the gods, or the community. The events of the play unfolded by way of dialogue spoken by individual characters, but also through the commentary of the chorus. Aeschylus, the author of the oldest surviving Western tragedy, introduced a second actor and gave the chorus a principal role in the drama. He brought deep religious feeling to his tragedies, the most famous of which is the series of three plays, or trilogy, known as the *Oresteia* (the plays of Orestes). These plays deal with the history of the family of Agamemnon, who led the Greeks to Troy, and whose murder at the hands of his wife upon his return from Troy is avenged by their son, Orestes.

While Aeschylus advanced the story of the play by way of sonorous language, Sophocles, the second of the great tragedians, developed his plots through the actions of the characters. He modified the ceremonial formality of earlier Greek tragedies by individualizing the characters and introducing moments of great psychological intimacy. Euripides, the last of the great tragedians, brought even greater realism to his characters. Plays such as *Medea* and *Electra* offer striking psychological portraits that explore the human soul in its experience of grief.

Tragedy, which gave formal expression to the most awful kinds of human experience—disaster and death—invited the spectator to participate vicariously in the dramatic action, thus undergoing a kind of emotional liberation. Comedy, on the other hand, drew its ability to provoke laughter from incongruity and the unexpected. Originating in association with fertility rites, and revels honoring Dionysus, comedy involved satire and parody of sexual union and erotic play of the kind found to this day in seasonal festivals and carnivals such as Mardi Gras. Obscene jokes, grotesque masks, fantastic costumes, and provocative dance and song were common to ancient comedy, as they are in various forms of modern slapstick and burlesque.

In the history of ancient Greek drama, the only comic plays to survive are those of Aristophanes. His inventive wit, sharply directed against Athenian politics and current affairs, is best revealed in the comedy *Lysistrata*, the oldest of his eleven surviving works. In this play, written in the wake of the bitter military conflict between Athens and Sparta, the playwright has the leading character—the wife of an Athenian soldier—launch a "strike" that will deprive all husbands of sexual satisfaction until they agree to refrain from war. As timely today as it was in ancient Athens, *Lysistrata* is a hilarious attack on the idealized, heroic image of armed combat.

The Case of *Antigone*

The drama that is most relevant to the theme of this chapter is Sophocles' *Antigone*, the third of a group of plays that includes *Oedipus the King* and *Oedipus at Colonus*. The story of *Antigone* proceeds from the last phase of the history of Thebes, a history with which most Athenians would have been familiar, since it recalled the ancient ascendancy of Athens over Thebes: following the death of Oedipus, king of Thebes, his sons Polynices and Eteocles kill each other in a dispute over the throne, thus leaving the crown to Creon, the brother-in-law of Oedipus and the only surviving male member of the ill-fated royal family. Upon becoming king, Creon forbids the burial of Polynices, contending that Eteocles had been the rightful ruler of Thebes. Driven by familial duty and the wish to fulfill the divine laws requiring burial of the dead, Oedipus' daughter Antigone violates Creon's decree and buries her brother Polynices. These circumstances provoke further violence and tragic death.

Antigone is a play that deals with many issues: it explores the conflict between the rights of the individual and the laws of the state; between dedication to family and loyalty to community; between personal and political obligations; between female willpower and male authority; and, finally, between human and divine law. It reflects Sophocles' effort to reconcile human passions, the will of the gods, and the sovereignty of the *polis*.

READING 4.3 From Sophocles' *Antigone* (ca. 440 B.C.E.)

Characters

Antigone, daughter of Oedipus and Iocasta

Ismene, her sister

Creon, King of Thebes, brother of Iocasta

Haemon, his son

A guard

Messenger

Eurydice, wife to Creon

Chorus of Theban elders

Guards, Attendants, etc.

Enter, from the palace, Antigone and Ismene

    Antigone: Ismene, my own sister, dear Ismene, how many   **1**
miseries our father caused! And is there one of them that
does not fall on us while yet we live? Unhappiness,
calamity, disgrace, dishonor—which of these have you
and I not known? And now again: there is the order which
they say brave Creon has proclaimed to all the city. You
understand? Or do you not yet know what outrage threatens
one of those we love?

    Ismene: Of them, Antigone, I have not heard good news or
bad—nothing, since we two sisters were robbed of our two   **10**
brothers on one day when each destroyed the other. During
the night the enemy has fled: so much I know, but nothing
more, either for grief or joy.

    Antigone: I knew it; therefore I have brought you here,
outside the doors, to tell you secretly.

    Ismene: What is it? Some dark shadow is upon you.

    Antigone: Our brother's burial.—Creon has ordained
honor for one, dishonor for the other. Eteocles, they say,
has been entombed with every solemn rite and ceremony
to do him honor in the world below; but as for Polyneices,   **20**

Creon has ordered that none shall bury him or mourn for him; he must be left to lie unwept, unburied, for hungry birds of prey to swoop and feast on his poor body. So he has decreed, our noble Creon, to all the citizens: to you, to me. To me! And he is coming to make it public here, that no one may be left in ignorance; nor does he hold it of little moment: he who disobeys in any detail shall be put to death by public stoning in the streets of Thebes. So it is now for you to show if you are worthy, or unworthy, of your birth. 30

Ismene: O my poor sister! If it has come to this what can I do, either to help or hinder?

Antigone: Will you join hands with me and share my task?

Ismene: What dangerous enterprise have you in mind?

Antigone: Will you join me in taking up the body?

Ismene: What? Would you bury him, against the law?

Antigone: No one shall say *I* failed him! I will bury my brother—and yours too, if you will not.

Ismene: You reckless girl! When Creon has forbidden?

Antigone: He has no right to keep me from my own! 40

Ismene: Think of our father, dear Antigone, and how we saw him die, hated and scorned, when his own hands had blinded his own eyes because of sins which he himself disclosed; and how his mother-wife, two names in one, knotted a rope, and so destroyed herself. And, last of all, upon a single day our brothers fought each other to the death and shed upon the ground the blood that joined them. Now you and I are left, alone; and think: if we defy the King's prerogative and break the law, our death will be more shameful even than 50 theirs. Remember too that we are women, not made to fight with men. Since they who rule us now are stronger far than we, in this and worse than this we must obey them. Therefore, beseeching pardon from the dead, since what I do is done on hard compulsion, I yield to those who have authority; for useless meddling has no sense at all.

Antigone: I will not urge you. Even if you should wish to give your help I would not take it now. Your choice is made. But I shall bury him. And if I have to die for this pure crime, I am content, for I shall rest beside him; 60 his love will answer mine. I have to please the dead far longer than I need to please the living; with them, I have to dwell for ever. But you, if so you choose, you may dishonor the sacred laws that Heaven holds in honor.

Ismene: I do them no dishonor, but to act against the city's will I am too weak.

Antigone: Make that your pretext! I will go and heap the earth upon the brother whom I love.

Ismene: You reckless girl! I tremble for your life.

Antigone: Look to yourself and do not fear for me. 70

Ismene: At least let no one hear of it, but keep your purpose secret, and so too will I.

Antigone: Go and denounce me! I shall hate you more if you keep silent and do not proclaim it.

Ismene: Your heart is hot upon a wintry work!

Antigone: I know I please whom most I ought to please.

Ismene: But can you do it? It is impossible!

Antigone: When I can do no more, then I will stop.

Ismene: But why attempt a hopeless task at all?

Antigone: O stop, or I shall hate you! He will hate you too, 80 for ever, justly. Let me be, me and my folly! I will face the danger that so dismays you, for it cannot be so dreadful as to die a coward's death.

Ismene: Then go and do it, if you must. It is blind folly—but those who love you love you dearly.

.   .   .   .

Creon: My lords: for what concerns the state, the gods who tossed it on the angry surge of strife have righted it again; and therefore you by royal edict I have summoned here, chosen from all our number. I know well how you revered the throne of Laius; and then, when Oedipus 90 maintained our state, and when he perished, round his sons you rallied, still firm and steadfast in your loyalty. Since they have fallen by a double doom upon a single day, two brothers each killing the other with polluted sword, I now possess the throne and royal power by right of nearest kinship with the dead. There is no art that teaches us to know the temper, mind, or spirit of any man until he has been proved by government and lawgiving. A man who rules a state and will not ever steer the wisest course, but is afraid, and says not what 100 he thinks, that man is worthless; and if any holds a friend of more account than his own city, I scorn him; for if I should see destruction threatening the safety of my citizens, I would not hold my peace, nor would I count that man my friend who was my country's foe, Zeus be my witness. For be sure of this: it is the city that protects us all; she bears us through the storm; only when she rides safe and sound can we make loyal friends. This I believe, and thus will I maintain our city's greatness.—Now, conformably, of Oedipus' two sons 110 I have proclaimed this edict: he who in his country's cause fought gloriously and so laid down his life, shall be entombed and graced with every rite that men can pay to those who die with honor; but for his brother, him called Polyneices, who came from exile to lay waste his land, to burn the temples of his native gods, to drink his kindred blood, and to enslave the rest, I have proclaimed to Thebes that none shall give him funeral honors or lament him, but leave him there unburied, to be devoured by dogs and birds, mangled most hideously. 120 Such is my will; never shall I allow the villain to win more honor than the upright; but any who show love to this our city in life and death alike shall win my praise.

Chorus: Such is your will, my lord; so you requite our city's champion and our city's foe. You, being sovereign, make what laws you will both for the dead and those of us who live.

Creon: See then that you defend the law now made.

Chorus: No, lay that burden on some younger men.

Creon: I have appointed guards to watch the body. 130

Chorus: What further charge, then, do you lay on us?

Creon: Not to connive at those that disobey me.

Chorus: None are so foolish as to long for death.

Creon: Death is indeed the price, but love of gain has often lured a man to his destruction.

Enter a guard

Guard: My lord: I cannot say that I am come all out of breath with running. More than once I stopped and thought and turned round in my path and started to go back. My mind had much to say to me. One time it said "You fool! Why do you go to certain punishment?" Another time "What? Standing still, you wretch? You'll smart for it, if Creon comes to hear from someone else." And so I went along debating with myself, not swift nor sure. This way, a short road soon becomes a long one. At last this was the verdict: I must come and tell you. It may be worse than nothing; still, I'll tell you. I can suffer nothing more than what is in my fate. There is my comfort!

Creon: And what is this that makes you so despondent?

Guard: First for myself: I did not see it done, I do not know who did it. Plainly then, I cannot rightly come to any harm.

Creon: You are a cautious fellow, building up this barricade. You bring unpleasant news?

Guard: I do, and peril makes a man pause long.

Creon: O, won't you tell your story and be gone?

Guard: Then, here it is. The body: someone has just buried it, and gone away. He sprinkled dry dust on it, with all the sacred rites.

Creon: What? Buried it? What man has so defied me?

Guard. How can I tell? There was no mark of pickaxe, no sign of digging; the earth was hard and dry and undisturbed; no wagon had been there; he who had done it left no trace at all. So, when the first day-watchman showed it to us, we were appalled. We could not see the body; it was not buried but was thinly covered with dust, as if by someone who had sought to avoid a curse. Although we looked, we saw no sign that any dog or bird had come and torn the body. Angry accusations flew up between us; each man blamed another, and in the end it would have come to blows, for there was none to stop it. Each single man seemed guilty, yet proclaimed his ignorance and could not be convicted. We were all ready to take hot iron in our hands, to walk through fire, to swear by all the gods we had not done it, nor had secret knowledge of any man who did it or contrived it. We could not find a clue. Then one man spoke: it made us hang our heads in terror, yet no one could answer him, nor could we see much profit for ourselves if we should do it. He said "We must report this thing to Creon; we dare not hide it"; and his word prevailed. I am the unlucky man who drew the prize when we cast lots, and therefore I am come unwilling and, for certain, most unwelcome: nobody loves the bringer of bad news.

Chorus: My lord, the thought has risen in my mind: do we not see in this the hand of the gods?

Creon: Silence! or you will anger me. You are an old man: must you be a fool as well? Intolerable, that you suppose the gods should have a single thought for this dead body. What? should they honor him with burial as one who

served them well, when he had come to burn their pillared temples, to destroy their treasuries, to devastate their land and overturn its laws? Or have you noticed the gods prefer the vile? No, from the first there was a muttering against my edict, wagging of heads in secret, restiveness and discontent with my authority. I know that some of these perverted others and bribed them to this act. Of all vile things current on earth, none is so vile as money. For money opens wide the city-gates to ravishers, it drives the citizens to exile, it perverts the honest mind to shamefulness, it teaches men to practice all forms of wickedness and impiety. These criminals who sold themselves for money have bought with it their certain punishment; for, as I reverence the throne of Zeus, I tell you plainly, and confirm it with my oath: unless you find, and bring before me, the very author of this burial-rite mere death shall not suffice; you shall be hanged alive, until you have disclosed the crime, that for the future you may ply your trade more cleverly, and learn not every pocket is safely to be picked. Ill-gotten gains more often lead to ruin than to safety.

Guard: May I reply? Or must I turn and go?

Creon: Now, as before, your very voice offends me.

Guard: Is it your ears that feel it, or your mind?

Creon: Why must you probe the seat of our displeasure?

Guard: The rebel hurts your mind; I but your ears.

Creon: No more of this! You are a babbling fool!

Guard: If so, I cannot be the one who did it.

Creon: Yes, but you did—selling your life for money!

Guard: It's bad, to judge at random, and judge wrong!

Creon: You judge my judgment as you will—but bring the man who did it, or you shall proclaim what punishment is earned by crooked dealings.

Guard: Gods grant he may be found! But whether he be found or not—for this must lie with chance—you will not see me coming *here* again. Alive beyond my hope and expectation, I thank the gods who have delivered me.

Creon goes into his house

Chorus: Wonders are many, yet of all things is Man the most wonderful. He can sail on the stormy sea though the tempest rage, and the loud waves roar around, as he makes his path amid the towering surge. Earth inexhaustible, ageless, he wearies, as backwards and forwards, from season to season, his ox-team drives along the ploughshare. He can entrap the cheerful birds, setting a snare, and all the wild beasts of the earth he has learned to catch, and fish that teem in the deep sea, with nets knotted of stout cords; of such inventiveness is man. Through his inventions he becomes lord even of the beasts of the mountain: the long-haired horse he subdues to the yoke on his neck, and the hill-bred bull, of strength untiring. And speech he has learned, and thought so swift, and the temper of mind to dwell within cities, and not to lie bare amid the keen, biting frosts or cower beneath pelting rain; full of resource against all that comes to him is Man. Against Death alone he is left with no defence. But painful sickness he can cure by his own skill. Surpassing belief, the device and cunning that Man has attained, and it bringeth him now to evil, now to good. If he observe Law, and tread the righteous path the gods ordained, honored is he; dishonored, the man whose reckless heart 250 shall make him join hands with sin: may I not think like him, nor may such an impious man dwell in my house.

The guard reappears leading Antigone

Chorus: What evil spirit is abroad? I know her well: Antigone. But how can I believe it? Why, O you unlucky daughter of an unlucky father, what is this? Can it be you, so mad and so defiant, so disobedient to a King's decree?
Guard: Here is the one who did the deed, this girl; we caught her burying him.—But where is Creon?
Chorus: He comes, just as you need him, from the palace.

Creon comes from the house

Creon: How? What occasion makes my coming timely? 260
Guard: Sir, against nothing should a man take oath, for second thoughts belie him. Under your threats that lashed me like a hailstorm, I'd have said I would not quickly have come here again; but joy that comes beyond our dearest hope surpasses all in magnitude. So I return, though I had sworn I never would, bringing this girl detected in the act of honoring the body. This time no lot was cast; the windfall is my very own. And so, my lord, do as you please: take her yourself, examine her, cross-question her. I claim the right of free and final quittance. 270
Creon: Why do you bring this girl? Where was she taken?
Guard: In burying the body. That is all.
Creon: You know what you are saying? Do you mean it?
Guard: I saw her giving burial to the corpse you had forbidden. Is that plain and clear?
Creon: How did you see and take her so red-handed?
Guard: It was like this. When we had reached the place, those dreadful threats of yours upon our heads, we swept aside each grain of dust that hid the clammy body, leaving it quite bare, and sat down on a hill, to the 280 windward side that so we might avoid the smell of it. We kept sharp look-out; each man roundly cursed his neighbor, if he should neglect his duty. So the time passed, until the blazing sun reached his mid-course and burned us with his heat. Then, suddenly, a whirlwind came from heaven and raised a storm of dust, which blotted out the earth and sky; the air was filled with sand and leaves ripped from the trees. We closed our eyes and bore this visitation as we could. At last it ended; then we saw the girl. She raised a bitter cry, as will a bird returning to its nest and finding it 290 despoiled, a cradle empty of its young. So, when she saw the body bare, she raised a cry of anguish mixed with imprecations laid upon those who did it; then at once brought handfuls of dry dust, and raised aloft a shapely vase of bronze, and three times poured the funeral libation for the dead. We rushed upon her swiftly, seized our prey, and charged her both with this offence and that. She faced us calmly; she did not disown the double crime. How glad I was!—and yet how sorry too; it is a painful thing to bring a friend to ruin. Still, for me, my own escape comes 300 before everything.
Creon: You there, who keep your eyes fixed on the ground, do you admit this, or do you deny it?
Antigone: No, I do not deny it. I admit it.
Creon [*to Guard*]: Then you may go; go where you like. You have been fully cleared of that grave accusation.

Exit Guard

You: tell me briefly—I want no long speech: did you not know that this had been forbidden?
Antigone: Of course I knew. There was a proclamation.
Creon: And so you dared to disobey the law? 310
Antigone: It was not Zeus who published this decree, nor have the Powers who rule among the dead imposed such laws as this upon mankind; nor could I think that a decree of yours—a man—could override the laws of Heaven unwritten and unchanging. Not of today or yesterday is their authority; they are eternal; no man saw their birth. Was I to stand before the gods' tribunal for disobeying *them*, because I feared a man? I knew that I should have to die, even without your edict; if I die before my time, why then, I count it gain; to one who lives as I do, ringed 320 about with countless miseries, why, death is welcome. For me to meet this doom is little grief; but when my mother's son lay dead, had I neglected him and left him there unburied, that would have caused me grief; this causes none. And if you think it folly, then perhaps I am accused of folly by the fool.
Chorus: The daughter shows her father's temper—fierce, defiant; she will not yield to any storm.
Creon: But it is those that are most obstinate suffer the greatest fall; the hardest iron, most fiercely tempered 330 in the fire, that is most often snapped and splintered. I have seen the wildest horses tamed, and only by the tiny bit. There is no room for pride in one who is a slave! This girl already had fully learned the art of insolence when she transgressed the laws that I established; and now to that she adds a second outrage— to boast of what she did, and laugh at us. Now she would be the man, not I, if she defeated me and did not pay for it. But though she be my niece, or closer still than all our family, she shall not escape the direst 340 penalty; no, nor shall her sister: I judge her guilty too; she played her part in burying the body. Summon her. Just now I saw her raving and distracted within the palace. So it often is: those who plan crime in secret are betrayed despite themselves; they show it in their faces. But this is worst of all: to be convicted and then to glorify the crime as virtue.
Antigone: Would you do more than simply take and kill me?
Creon: I will have nothing more, and nothing less.
Antigone: Then why delay? To me no word of yours is 350

pleasing—gods forbid it should be so!—and everything in
me displeases you. Yet what could I have done to win
renown more glorious than giving burial to my own brother?
These men too would say it, except that terror cows them
into silence. A king has many a privilege: the greatest,
that he can say and do all that he will.

    Creon: You slander the race of Cadmus;[1] You are the only one in
Thebes to think it!

    Antigone: These think as I do—but they dare not speak.

    Creon: Have you no shame, not to conform with others?   360

    Antigone: To reverence a brother is no shame.

    Creon: Was he no brother, he who died for Thebes?

    Antigone: One mother and one father gave them birth.

    Creon: Honoring the traitor, you dishonor *him*.

    Antigone: He will not bear this testimony, in death.

    Creon: Yes! if the traitor fare the same as he.

    Antigone: It was a brother, not a slave who died!

    Creon: He died attacking Thebes; the other saved us.

    Antigone: Even so, the god of Death demands these rites.

    Creon: The good demand more honor than the wicked.   370

    Antigone: Who knows? In death they may be reconciled.

    Creon: Death does not make an enemy a friend!

    Antigone: Even so, I give both love, not share their hatred.

    Creon: Down then to Hell! Love there, if love you must. While
I am living, no woman shall have rule.

*Ismene is led from the King's house by two attendants. She tries to
share responsibility for Antigone's deed, but Antigone refuses. The
Chorus laments the fate of Antigone. Haemon, Creon's son, comes
before his father.*

    Creon: Soon we shall know, better than seers can tell us.
My son: you have not come in rage against your father
because your bride must die? Or are you still my loyal son,
whatever I may do?

    Haemon: Father, I am your son; may your wise judgment   380
rule me, and may I always follow it. No marriage shall
be thought a greater prize for me to win than your
good government.

    Creon: So may you ever be resolved, my son, in all things
to be guided by your father. It is for this men pray that
they may have obedient children, that they may requite
their father's enemy with enmity and honor whom their
father loves to honor. One who begets unprofitable
children makes trouble for himself, and gives his foes
nothing but laughter. Therefore do not let your pleasure   390
in a woman overcome your judgment, knowing this,
that if you have an evil wife to share your house, you'll find
cold comfort in your bed. What other wound can cut so
deep as treachery at home? So, think this girl your enemy;
spit on her, and let her find her husband down in Hell!
She is the only one that I have found in all the city disobedient.
I will not make myself a liar. I have caught her; I will kill her.
Let her sing her hymns to Sacred Kinship! If I breed
rebellion in the house, then it is certain there'll be no lack
of rebels out of doors. No man can rule a city uprightly   400
who is not just in ruling his own household. Never will I

[1] The ancestor of the noble families of Thebes.

approve of one who breaks and violates the law, or
would dictate to those who rule. Lawful authority must be
obeyed in all things, great or small, just and unjust alike;
and such a man would win my confidence both in command
and as a subject; standing at my side in the storm of battle
he would hold his ground, not leave me unprotected. But there
is no greater curse than disobedience. This brings destruction
on a city, this drives men from hearth and home, this brings
about a sudden panic in the battle-front. Where all goes well,   410
obedience is the cause. So we must vindicate the law; we
must not be defeated by a woman. Better far be overthrown,
if need be, by a man than to be called the victim of a woman.

    Chorus: Unless the years have stolen away our wits,
all you say is said most prudently.

    Haemon: Father, it is the gods who give us wisdom; no gift of
theirs more precious. I cannot say that you are wrong, nor would
I ever learn that impudence, although perhaps another might
fairly say it. But it falls to me, being your son, to note what
others say, or do, or censure in you, for your glance   420
intimidates the common citizen; he will not say, before
your face, what might displease you; I can listen freely,
how the city mourns this girl. "No other woman",
so they are saying, "so undeservedly has been
condemned for such a glorious deed.
When her own brother had been slain in battle
she would not let his body lie unburied to be devoured
by dogs or birds of prey. Is not this worthy of a crown of
gold?"—such is the muttering that spreads everywhere.
Father, no greater treasure can I have than your   430
prosperity; no son can find a greater prize than his own
father's fame, no father than his son's. Therefore
let not this single thought possess you: only what
you say is right, and nothing else. The man
who thinks that he alone is wise, that he is best
in speech or counsel, such a man brought to
the proof is found but emptiness. There's no
disgrace, even if one is wise, in learning more, and
knowing when to yield. See how the trees that grow
beside a torrent preserve their branches, if they bend;   440
the others, those that resist, are torn out, root and
branch. So too the captain of a ship; let him refuse
to shorten sail, despite the storm— he'll end his
voyage bottom uppermost. No, let your anger cool,
and be persuaded. If one who is still young can
speak with sense, then I would say that he does
best who has most understanding; second best,
the man who profits from the wisdom of another.

    Chorus: My lord, he has not spoken foolishly;
you each can learn some wisdom from the other.   450

    Creon: What? Men of our age go to school again
and take a lesson from a very boy?

    Haemon: If it is worth the taking. I am young,
but think what should be done, not of my age.

    Creon: What should be done! To honor disobedience!

    Haemon: I would not have you honor criminals.

    Creon: And is this girl then not a criminal?

    Haemon: The city with a single voice denies it.

    Creon: Must I give orders then by their permission?

    Haemon: If youth is folly, this is childishness.   460

Creon: Am I to rule for them, not for myself?

Haemon: That is not government, but tyranny.

Creon: The king is lord and master of his city.

Haemon: Then you had better rule a desert island!

Creon: This man, it seems, is the ally of the woman.

Haemon: If you're the woman, yes! I fight for you.

Creon: Villain! Do you oppose your father's will?

Haemon: Only because you are opposing Justice.

Creon: When I regard my own prerogative?

Haemon: Opposing the gods', you disregard your own.   470

Creon: Scoundrel, so to surrender to a woman!

Haemon: But not to anything that brings me shame.

Creon: Your every word is in defence of her.

Haemon: And me, and you—and of the gods below.

Creon: You shall not marry her this side the grave!

Haemon. So, she must die—and will not die alone.

Creon: What? Threaten me? Are you so insolent?

Haemon: It is no threat, if I reply to folly.

Creon: The fool would teach me sense! You'll pay for it.

Haemon: I'd call you mad, if you were not my father.   480

Creon: I'll hear no chatter from a woman's plaything.

Haemon: Would you have all the talk, and hear no answer?

Creon: So? I swear to the gods, you shall not bandy words with me and not repent it! Bring her out, that loathsome creature! I will have her killed at once, before her bridegroom's very eyes.

Haemon: How can you think it? I will not see that, nor shall you ever see my face again. Those friends of yours who can must tolerate your raging madness; I will not endure it.   490

Haemon rushes away.

. . . .

Antigone engages in an impassioned lament over her destiny. Creon will not relent, and the guards lead Antigone to the tomb. The blind prophet Teiresias warns Creon that his actions have brought "sickness" to the state. Creon responds rudely to the Seer's claim that "it is the stubborn man who is the fool." The Chorus sings a hymn in praise of Dionysus. Then, a Messenger appears from the direction of the plain.

. . . .

Messenger: You noblemen of Thebes, how insecure is human fortune! Chance will overthrow the great, and raise the lowly; nothing's firm, either for confidence or for despair; no one can prophesy what lies in store. An hour ago, how much I envied Creon! He had saved Thebes, we had accorded him the sovereign power; he ruled our land supported by a noble prince, his son. Now all is lost, and he who forfeits joy forfeits his life; he is a breathing corpse. Heap treasures in your palace, if you will, and wear the pomp of royalty; but if you have no happiness,   500
I would not give a straw for all of it, compared with joy.

Chorus: What is this weight of heavy news you bring?

Messenger: Death!—and the blood-guilt rests upon the living.

Chorus: Death? Who is dead? And who has killed him? Tell me.

Messenger: Haemon is dead, and by no stranger's hand.

Chorus: But by his father's? Or was it his own?

Messenger: His own—inflamed with anger at his father.

Chorus: Yours was no idle prophecy, Teiresias!   510

Messenger: That is my news. What next, remains with you.

Chorus: But look! There is his wife, Eurydice; she is coming from the palace. Has she heard about her son, or is she here by chance?

Eurydice comes from the house.

Eurydice: You citizens of Thebes, I overheard when I was standing at the gates, for I had come to make an offering at the shrine of Pallas, and my hand was on the bar that holds the gate, to draw it; then there fell upon my ears a voice that spoke of death. My terror took away my strength; I fell into my servants' arms and   520
swooned away. But tell it me once more; I can endure to listen; I am no stranger to bad news.

Messenger: Dear lady, I was there, and I will tell the truth; I will not keep it back from you. Why should Igloss it over? You would hear from someone else, and I should seem a liar. The truth is always best.
I went with Creon up to the hill where Polyneices' body still lay, unpitied, torn by animals. We gave it holy washing, and we prayed to Hecate and Pluto[2]   530
that they would restrain their anger and be merciful. And then we cut some branches, and we burned what little had been left, and built a mound over his ashes of his native soil. Then, to the cavern, to the home of death, the bridal-chamber with its bed of stone. One of us heard a cry of lamentation from that unhallowed place; he went to Creon and told him. On the wind, as he came near, cries of despair were borne. He groaned aloud in anguish: "O, and are my fears come true?   540
Of all the journeys I have made, am I to find this one the most calamitous? It is my son's voice greets me. Hurry, men; run to the place, and when you reach the tomb creep in between the gaping stones and see if it be Haemon there, or if the gods are cheating me." Upon this desperate order we ran and looked. Within the furthest chamber we saw her hanging, dead; strips from her dress had served her for a rope. Haemon we saw embracing her dead body and lamenting his loss, his father's deed, and her   550
destruction. When Creon saw him he cried out in anguish, went in, and called to him: "My son! my son! O why? What have you done? What brought you here? What is this madness? O come out, my son, come, I implore you!" Haemon glared at him with anger in

---

[2] Hecate is the goddess of the crossroads and transitions—such as that between life and death. Pluto is another name for Hades, the Greek god of the underworld, the shadowy realm where the souls of the dead were thought to rest.

his eyes, spat in his face, said nothing, drew his
double-hiked sword, but missed his aim as Creon
leapt aside. Then in remorse he leaned upon the
blade and drove it half its length into his body.
While yet the life was in him he embraced the girl   560
with failing arms, and breathing hard poured out his
life-blood on to her white face. So side by side they lie,
and both are dead. Not in this world but in the world
below he wins his bride, and shows to all mankind
that folly is the worst of human evils.

Eurydice goes into the house.

    Chorus: What can we think of this? The Queen is gone
without one word of good or evil omen.
    Messenger: What can it mean? But yet we may sustain
the hope that she would not display her grief in public,
but will rouse the sad lament for Haemon's death among   570
her serving-women inside the palace. She has true
discretion, and she would never do what is unseemly.
    Chorus: I cannot say, but wild lament would be
less ominous than this unnatural silence.
    Messenger: It is unnatural; there may be danger.
I'll follow her; it may be she is hiding some secret purpose
in her passionate heart.

*The Messenger enters the house. As he goes, Creon comes into
the open place before the house with attendants carrying the
shrouded body of Haemon on a bier.*

    Chorus: Look, Creon draws near, and the burden he bears
gives witness to his misdeeds; the cause lies only in his
blind error.   580
    Creon: Alas! The wrongs I have done by ill-counselling!
Cruel and fraught with death. You behold, men of Thebes,
the slayer, the slain; a father, a son. My own stubborn ways
have borne bitter fruit. My son! Dead, my son!
So soon torn from me, so young, so young!
The fault only mine, not yours, O my son.
    Chorus: Too late, too late you see the path of wisdom.
    Creon: Alas! A bitter lesson I have learned! The god
coming with all his weight has borne down on me,
and smitten me with all his cruelty; my joy overturned,   590
trampled beneath his feet. What suffering besets the
whole race of men!

The Messenger comes from the house.

    Messenger: My master, when you came you brought a burden
of sorrow with you; now, within your house, a second store
of misery confronts you.
    Creon: Another sorrow come to crown my sorrow?
    Messenger: The Queen, true mother of her son, is dead;
in grief she drove a blade into her heart.
    Creon: Alas! Thou grim hand of death, greedy and
unappeased, why so implacable? Voice of doom, you who   600
bring such dire news of grief, O, can it be true?
What have you said, my son? O, you have slain the slain!
Tell me, can it be true? Is death crowning death?

My wife! my wife! My son dead, and now my wife taken too!

*The doors of the King's house are opened, and the corpse of
Eurydice is disclosed.*

    Chorus: But raise your eyes: there is her lifeless body.
    Creon: Alas! Here is a sorrow that redoubles sorrow.
Where will it end? What else can Fate hold in store?
While yet I clasp my dead son in my arms before me
there lies another struck by death. Alas cruel doom!
the mother's and the son's.   610
    Messenger: She took a sharp-edged knife, stood by the
altar, and made lament for Megareus who was killed of old,
and next for Haemon. Then at last, invoking evil upon you,
the slayer of both her sons, she closed her eyes in death.
    Creon: A curse, a thing of terror! O, is there none
will unsheathe a sword to end all my woes with one
deadly thrust? My grief crushes me.
    Messenger: She cursed you for the guilt of Haemon's death
and of the other son who died before.
    Creon: What did she do? How did she end her life?   620
    Messenger: She heard my bitter story; then she put
a dagger to her heart and drove it home.
    Creon: The guilt falls on me alone; none but I have slain her;
no other shares in the sin. 'Twas I dealt the blow.
This is the truth, my friends. Away, take me away, far from
the sight of men! My life now is death. Lead me away
from here.
    Chorus: That would be well, if anything is well.
Briefest is best when such disaster comes.
    Creon: O come, best of all the days I can see,   630
the last day of all, the day that brings death.
O come quickly! Come, thou night with no dawn!
    Chorus: That's for the future; here and now are duties
that fall on those to whom they are allotted.
    Creon: I prayed for death; I wish for nothing else.
    Chorus: Then pray no more; from suffering that has been
decreed no man will ever find escape.
    Creon: Lead me away, a rash, a misguided man,
whose blindness has killed a wife and a son.
O where can I look? What strength can I find?   640
On me has fallen a doom greater than I can bear.

Creon is led into his house as the Chorus speaks.

    Chorus: Of happiness, far the greatest part
is wisdom, and reverence towards the gods.
Proud words of the arrogant man, in the end,
meet punishment, great as his pride was great,
till at last he is schooled in wisdom.

Q **Who is the tragic figure in this play: Antigone or
Creon?**

Q **How does the play illustrate "heroic idealism"
and the conflict between personal and communal
obligations?**

The tragic action in *Antigone* springs from the irreconcilability of Antigone's personal idealism and Creon's hardheaded political realism. Creon means well by the state; he is committed to the exercise of justice under the law. As a king newly come to power, he perceives his duty in terms of his authority: "whoever the city shall appoint to rule," says Creon, "that man must be obeyed, in little things and in great things, in just things and unjust; for the man who is a good subject is the one who would be a good ruler . . ." But Creon ignores the ancient imperatives of divine law and familial duty. His blind devotion to the state and his unwillingness to compromise trap him into making a decision whose consequences are disastrous.

In Greek tragedy, the weakness or "tragic flaw" of the **protagonist** (the leading character) brings that character into conflict with fate or with the **antagonist** (one who opposes the protagonist), and ultimately to his or her fall. Creon's excessive pride (in Greek, *hubris*) results in the loss of those who are dearest to him. But Antigone is also a victim of self-righteous inflexibility. In an age that confined women to the domestic household and expected them to conform to male opinion, Antigone was unique. In ancient Greece, a girl in her early teens might marry a man considerably older than she. Along with the other female members of the household, she oversaw the daily chores associated with child-rearing, food preparation, and the production of clothing—spinning, weaving, and sewing. She could not inherit or own property and could not choose to divorce her husband (although he could divorce her); hence she was subordinate to her husband, as she had been to her father. While there were exceptions to this pattern (usually among courtesans and prostitutes), it seems clear that by challenging male authority, Antigone threatened the status quo: "*She* is the man," Creon angrily objects, "if she can carry this off unpunished." Antigone's sister, Ismene, argues, "We must remember we were born women, not meant to strive with men." But Antigone persists: her heroism derives from her unswerving dedication to the ideals of divine justice and to the duty of the individual to honor family, even if it challenges the laws of the state.

Sophocles perceived the difficulties involved in reconciling public good and private conscience. In *Antigone*, he offers a moving plea for sound judgment and rational action, and for harmony between the individual and the community.

Aristotle on Tragedy

In modern parlance, the word "tragedy" is often used to describe a terrible act of fate that befalls an unwitting individual. With regard to drama, however, the word (and the form it describes) has a very different meaning. As a literary genre, tragedy deals not so much with catastrophic events as with *how* these events work to affect individuals in shaping their character and in determining their fate. The protagonist becomes a tragic hero not because of what befalls him, but rather as a result of the manner in which he confronts his destiny. In the *Poetics*, the world's first treatise on literary criticism, the Greek philosopher Aristotle

(384–322 B.C.E.) describes tragedy as an imitation of an action involving incidents that arouse pity and fear. Tragic action, he argues, should involve an error in judgment made by an individual who is "better than the ordinary man" but with whom the audience may sympathize.

The *Poetics* further clarifies the importance of "proper construction": the play must have a balanced arrangement of parts, and the action of the story should be limited to the events of a single day. The plot should consist of a single action made up of several closely connected incidents (without irrelevant additions). If we apply Aristotle's aesthetic principles of tragedy to Sophocles' *Antigone*, we discover the so-called unities of action and time that characterize Classic Greek tragedy. (Seventeenth-century playwrights added "unity of place" to Neoclassical drama.) In *Antigone*, the action rests on a single incident: the rash decision of Creon. The events of the play occur within a single place, and they are acted out within a time span comparable to their occurrence in real life. Every episode in the play is relevant to the central action. Proportion and order apply to the writing of drama, suggests Aristotle, even as they must apply to the conduct and the fate of the tragic hero.

Finally, Aristotle addresses the function of tragedy as a genre. It must arouse in the spectator a mixture of fear and pity; it must effect a **catharsis**, that is, a cleansing or purification that provokes change in the spectator's emotional life. Tragedy, the theatrical rendering of human frailty and its consequences, was—in the Greek world as in our own—no mere entertainment, but a vehicle for self-knowledge.

READING 4.4 From Aristotle's *Poetics* (ca. 340 B.C.E.)

. . . let us now consider the proper construction of the Fable   1
or Plot, as that is at once the first and the most important
thing in Tragedy. We have laid it down that a tragedy is an
imitation of an action that is complete in itself, as a whole
of some magnitude; for a whole may be of no magnitude to
speak of. Now a whole is that which has beginning, middle,
and end. A beginning is that which is not itself necessarily
after anything else, and which has naturally something else
after it; an end is that which is naturally after something itself,
either as its necessary or usual consequent, and with nothing   10
else after it; and a middle, that which is by nature after one
thing and has also another after it. A well-constructed Plot,
therefore, cannot either begin or end at any point one likes;
beginning and end in it must be of the forms just described.
Again: to be beautiful, a living creature, and every whole
made up of parts, must not only present a certain order in
its arrangement of parts, but also be of certain definite
magnitude. Beauty is a matter of size and order, and therefore
impossible either (1) in a very minute creature, since our
perception becomes indistinct as it approaches instantaneity;   20
or (2) in a creature of vast size—one, say, 1000 miles long—
as in that case, instead of the object being seen all at once,
the unity and wholeness of it is lost to the beholder. Just in the
same way, then, as a beautiful whole made up of parts, or a
beautiful living creature, must be of some size, but a size to be

taken in by the eye, so a story or Plot must be of some length, but of a length to be taken in by the eye, so a story or Plot must be of some length, but of a length to be taken in by the memory. . . . The truth is that, just as in the other imitative arts one imitation is always of one thing, so in poetry the 30 story, as an imitation of action, must represent one action, a complete whole, with its several incidents so closely connected that the transposal or withdrawal of any one of them will disjoin and dislocate the whole. For that which makes no perceptible difference by its presence or absence is no real part of the whole. . . . The perfect Plot, accordingly, must have a single, and not (as some tell us) a double issue; the change in the hero's fortunes must be not from misery to happiness, but on the contrary from happiness to misery; and the cause of it must lie not in any depravity, but in some 40 great error on his part; . . . As Tragedy is an imitation of personages better than the ordinary man, we in our way should follow the example of good portrait-painters, who reproduce the distinctive features of a man, and at the same time, without losing the likeness, make him handsomer than he is. . . .

Q Why does Aristotle require the length of a play to be equivalent to the course of its plot in real life?

Q How does a "great error" figure in the plot of a tragedy?

Greek Philosophy: The Speculative Leap

During the sixth century B.C.E., a small group of Greek thinkers introduced methods of intellectual inquiry that combined careful observation, systematic analysis, and the exercise of pure reason. These individuals, whom we call philosophers (literally, "lovers of wisdom"), laid the foundations for Western science and philosophy. While they lived at a time in which most people viewed earthquakes, windstorms, and floods as expressions of divine anger, they theorized that such disasters might have natural, not supernatural, causes. Challenging all prevailing myths, the Greek philosophers made the speculative leap from supernatural to natural explanations of the unknown.

Naturalist Philosophy: The Pre-Socratics

The earliest of the Greek philosopher-scientists lived just prior to the time of Socrates in the city of Miletus on the Ionian coast of Asia Minor (see Map 4.1). Although their senses reported a world of constant change, they reasoned that there must be a single unifying substance that formed the basic "stuff" of nature. They asked, "What is everything made of?," "How do things come into existence?," and "What permanent substance lies behind the world of appearance?" Thales (ca. 625–ca. 547 B.C.E.), history's first philosopher, held that water was the fundamental substance and source from which all things proceeded. Water's potential for change (from solid to liquid to gas) and its pervasiveness on earth convinced him that water formed the primary matter of the universe. His followers challenged this view: "Air," said one, "Fire," countered another,

and still others identified the basic substance as a mixture of the primordial elements. The concept that a single unifying substance underlay reality drew opposition from some of the pre-Socratics. The universe, argued Heraclitus of Ephesus (ca. 540–ca. 480 B.C.E.), has no permanence, but, rather, is in constant process of flux. Heraclitus defended the idea that change itself was the basis of reality. "You cannot step twice into the same river," he wrote, "for fresh waters are ever flowing in upon you." Yet, Heraclitus believed that an underlying Form or Guiding Force (in Greek, *logos*) permeated nature, an idea that resembles Hindu pantheism and anticipates the Christian concept (found in the Gospel of John) of a Great Intelligence governing the beginning of time. For Heraclitus the Force was impersonal, universal, and eternal.

Around 500 B.C.E., Leucippus of Miletus theorized that physical reality consisted of minute, invisible particles that moved ceaselessly in the void. These he called *atoms*, the Greek word meaning "indivisible." Democritus (ca. 460–370 B.C.E.), a follower of Leucippus and the best known of the naturalist philosophers, developed the atomic theory of matter. For Democritus, the mind consisted of the same indivisible physical substances as everything else in nature. According to this materialist view, atoms moved constantly and eternally according to chance in infinite time and space. The atomic theory survived into Roman times, and, although forgotten for 2000 years thereafter, it was validated by physicists of the early twentieth century.

Pythagoras

Yet another pre-Socratic thinker, Pythagoras (ca. 580–ca. 500 B.C.E.), advanced an idea that departed from both the material and nonmaterial views of the universe. Pythagoras believed that proportion, discovered through number, was the true basis of reality. According to him, all universal relationships may be expressed through numbers, the truths of which are eternal and unchanging. The formula in plane geometry that equates the square of

Science and Technology

600 B.C.E.	Thales of Miletus produces an accurate theory of the solar eclipse; he also advances the study of deductive geometry[†]
540 B.C.E.	Anaximander claims that life evolved from beginnings in the sea and that man evolved from a more primitive species
530 B.C.E.	Pythagoras argues for a spherical earth around which five planets revolve; he also develops the "Pythagorean Theorem"
500 B.C.E.	Leucippus theorizes that all matter is composed of "atoms"
480 B.C.E.	Anaxagoras postulates that the sun is a large, glowing rock; he explains solar eclipses

†All dates in this chapter are approximate

the hypotenuse in right-angle triangles to the sum of the square of the other two sides—a theorem traditionally associated with Pythagoras—is an example of such an unchanging and eternal truth, as is the simplest of mathematical equations: $2 + 2 = 4$. Pythagoras was the founding father of pure mathematics. He was also the first to demonstrate the relationship between musical harmonics and numbers. His view that number gives order and harmony to the universe is basic to the principles of balance and proportion that dominate Classical art and music (see chapter 5).

In contrast with the Mesopotamians and Egyptians, who deified the sun, the rivers, and other natural elements, the pre-Socratics stripped nature of supernatural associations. They made accurate predictions of solar and lunar eclipses, plotted astronomical charts, and hypothesized on the processes of regeneration in plants and animals. Yet, in the areas of geometry, astronomy, and mathematics, it is likely that they inherited a large body of practical and theoretical data from the astrologists and palace engineers of Babylon, who knew how to solve linear and quadratic equations, and from the pyramid builders and calendar keepers of Egypt. It is also likely that the philosophic and religious theories originating in China and India influenced the speculative systems of Heraclitus, Pythagoras, and other pre-Socratics. Ideas, along with goods like silk, ivory, and cotton, moved back and forth along the overland trade routes that linked East Asia to the Mediterranean. For example, the Pythagorean proscription against eating animal flesh and certain plants suggests Greek familiarity with the Hindu belief in reincarnation and the transmigration of souls (see chapter 3).

Hippocrates

The Chinese association between illness and an imbalance of vital body energy seems to have made its way westward into the purview of Hippocrates. Hippocrates (ca. 460–377 B.C.E.), the most famous of the Greek physicians and so-called father of medicine, investigated the influence of diet and environment on general health and advanced the idea that an imbalance among bodily "humors"—blood, phlegm, black bile, and yellow bile—was the cause of

disease. He insisted on the necessary relationship of cause and effect in matters of physical illness, and he raised questions concerning the influence of the mind on the body. He may also be deemed the "father of medical ethics": to this day, graduating physicians are encouraged to practice medicine according to the precepts of the Hippocratic Oath (probably not written by Hippocrates himself), which binds them to heal the sick and abstain from unprofessional medical practices.

The separation of the natural from the supernatural was as essential to the birth of medical science as it was to speculative philosophy. And although no agreement as to the nature of reality was ever reached among the pre-Socratics, these intellectuals laid the groundwork and the methodology for the rational investigation of the universe. Their efforts represent the beginnings of Western science and philosophy as formal disciplines.

Humanist Philosophy

The Sophists

The naturalist philosophers were concerned with describing physical reality in terms of the unity that lay behind the chaos of human perceptions. The philosophers who followed them pursued a different course: they turned their attention from the world of nature to the realm of the mind, from physical matters to moral concerns, and from the gathering of information to the cultivation of wisdom. Significantly, these thinkers fathered the field of inquiry known as metaphysics (literally, "beyond physics"), that branch of philosophy concerned with abstract thought. They asked not simply "*What* do we know (about nature)?" but "*How* do we know what we know?" The transition from the examination of matter to the exploration of mind established the humanistic direction of Greek philosophy for at least two centuries.

The first humanist philosophers were a group of traveling scholar-teachers called Sophists. Masters of formal debate, the Sophists were concerned with defining the limits of human knowledge. The Thracian Sophist Protagoras (ca. 485–410 B.C.E.) believed that knowledge could not exceed human opinion, a position summed up in his memorable dictum: "Man is the measure of all things." His contemporary Gorgias (ca. 483–ca. 376 B.C.E.) tried to prove that reality is incomprehensible and that even if one could comprehend it, one could not describe the real to others. Such skepticism was common to the Sophists, who argued that truth and justice were relative: what might be considered just and true for one individual or situation might not be just and true for another.

Socrates and the Quest for Virtue

Athens' foremost philosopher, Socrates (ca. 470–399 B.C.E.), vigorously opposed the views of the Sophists. Insisting on the absolute nature of truth and justice, he described the ethical life as belonging to a larger set of universal truths and an unchanging moral order. For Socrates, virtue was not discovered by means of clever

Science and Technology

470 B.C.E.	Greek physicians practice dissection in the study of human anatomy
430 B.C.E.	Democritus argues that atoms move freely in space and are eternal
400 B.C.E.	Hippocrates' treatises on medicine include a study of epidemics, a description of phobias, and an examination of the effects of the environment on health
330 B.C.E.	Agnodike, a female physician, successfully challenges the law that prohibits women from practicing medicine in Athens

Figure 4.16 Portrait bust of Socrates, supposedly created by **LYSIPPOS**. Roman marble copy of an original bronze, ca. 350 B.C.E., height 13 in. (approx.)

but misleading argumentation—a kind of reasoning that would come to be called (after the Sophists) *sophistry*, nor was it relative to individual circumstances. Rather, virtue was a condition of the *psyche**, the seat of both the moral and intellectual faculties of the individual. Hence, understanding the true meaning of virtue was preliminary to acting virtuously: to know good is to do good.

The question of right conduct was central to Socrates' life and teachings. A stonemason by profession, Socrates preferred to roam the streets of Athens and engage his fellow citizens in conversation and debate (Figure **4.16**). Insisting that the unexamined life was not worth living, he challenged his peers on matters of public and private virtue, constantly posing the question, "What is the greatest good?" In this pursuit, Socrates employed a rigorous question-and-answer technique known as the **dialectical method**. Unlike the Sophists, he refused to charge fees for teaching: he argued that wealth did not produce excellence; rather, wealth derived *from* excellence. Socrates described himself as a large horsefly, alighting upon and pestering the well-bred but rather sluggish horse—that is, Athens. So Socrates "alighted" on the citizens of Athens, arousing, persuading, and reproaching them and—most importantly—demanding that they give rational justification for their actions.

Socrates established philosophy as a lived experience, rather than a set of doctrines. His style of cross-examination, the question-and-answer method, proceeded from his first principle of inquiry, "Know thyself," while the

progress of his analysis moved from specific examples to general principles, and from particular to universal truths, a type of reasoning known as *inductive*. The inductive method demands a process of abstraction: a shift of focus from the individual thing (the city) to all things (cities) and from the individual action (just or unjust) to the idea of justice. Central to Socratic inquiry was discourse (Figure **4.17**). The notion that talk itself humanizes the individual is typically Greek and even more typically Socratic. Indeed, the art of conversation—the dialectical exchange of ideas—united the citizens of the *polis*.

As gadfly, Socrates won as many enemies as he won friends. The great masses of Greek citizens found comfort in the traditional Greek gods and goddesses. They had little use for Socrates' religious skepticism and stringent methods of self-examination. Outspoken in his commitment to free inquiry, Socrates fell into disfavor with the reactionary regime that governed Athens after its defeat in the Peloponnesian Wars. Although he had fought bravely in the wars, he vigorously opposed the new regime and the moral chaos of postwar Athens. In the year 399 B.C.E., when he was over seventy years old, he was brought to trial for subversive behavior, impiety, and atheism. The Athenian jury found him guilty by a narrow margin of votes and sentenced him to death by drinking hemlock, a poisonous herb.

In his lifetime, Socrates wrote no books or letters: what we know of him comes mainly from his students' writings.

Figure 4.17 DOURIS, interior of a red-figured *kylix* (a Greek drinking cup), ca. 480 B.C.E. Terracotta, height 4⅜ in., diameter 11¾ in. The scene recreates a moment of conversation between a teacher and a student; scholars interpret the painting to depict an older man propositioning a younger one. The artist, Douris, is said to have ornamented some 10,000 pieces of pottery in the course of his career.

---

* "Psyche" is often translated as "soul," "spirit," or "mind," as distinguished from "body" or "matter."

The dialogue called *Crito* (written by Plato) narrates the last events of Socrates' life: Crito, Socrates' friend and pupil, urges him to escape from prison, but the old philosopher refuses. He explains that to run away would be to subvert the laws by which he has lived. His escape would represent an implicit criticism of the democratic system and the city-state that he had defended throughout his life. For Socrates, the loyalty of the citizen to the *polis*, like that of the child to its parents, is a primary obligation. To violate the will of the community to which he belongs would constitute dishonor. Like Antigone, Socrates prefers death to dishonor. In the excerpt from *Crito*, Socrates explains why right action is crucial to the destiny of both the individual and the community. These words reaffirm the Hellenic view that immortality is achieved through human deeds, which outlast human lives.

─ READING 4.5 From Plato's *Crito* (ca. 390 B.C.E.)

Crito: ... O my good Socrates, I beg you for the last time to listen to me and save yourself. For to me your death will be more than a single disaster: not only shall I lose a friend the like of whom I shall never find again, but many persons who do not know you and me well will think that I might have saved you if I had been willing to spend money, but that I neglected to do so. And what reputation could be more disgraceful than the reputation of caring more for money than for one's friends? The public will never believe that we were anxious to save you, but that you yourself refused to escape.   10

Socrates: But, my dear Crito, why should we care so much about public opinion? Reasonable men, of whose opinion it is worth our while to think, will believe that we acted as we really did.

Crito: But you see, Socrates, that it is necessary to care about public opinion, too. This very thing that has happened to you proves that the multitude can do a man not the least, but almost the greatest harm, if he is falsely accused to them.

Socrates: I wish that the multitude were able to do a man the greatest harm, Crito, for then they would be able to do   20 him the greatest good, too. That would have been fine. But, as it is, they can do neither. They cannot make a man either wise or foolish: they act wholly at random. Consider it in this way. Suppose the laws and the commonwealth were to come and appear to me as I was preparing to run away (if that is the right phrase to describe my escape) and were to ask, "Tell us, Socrates, what have you in your mind to do? What do you mean by trying to escape but to destroy us, the laws, and the whole state, so far as you are able? Do you think that a state can exist and not be overthrown, in which the decisions of   30 law are of no force, and are disregarded and undermined by private individuals?" How shall we answer questions like that, Crito? Much might be said, especially by an orator, in defense of the law which makes judicial decisions supreme. Shall I reply, "But the state has injured me by judging my case unjustly." Shall we say that?

Crito: Certainly we will, Socrates.

Socrates: And suppose the laws were to reply, "Was that our agreement? Or was it that you would abide by whatever judgments the state should pronounce?" And if we were   40 surprised by their words, perhaps they would say, "Socrates, don't be surprised by our words, but answer us; you yourself are accustomed to ask questions and to answer them. What complaint have you against us and the state, that you are trying to destroy us? Are we not, first of all, your parents? Through us your father took your mother and brought you into the world. Tell us, have you any fault to find with those of us that are the laws of marriage?" "I have none," I should reply. "Or have you any fault to find with those of us that regulate the raising of the child and the education which you, like   50 others, received? Did we not do well in telling your father to educate you in music and athletics?" "You did," I should say. "Well, then, since you were brought into the world and raised and educated by us, how, in the first place, can you deny that you are our child and our slave, as your fathers were before you? And if this be so, do you think that your rights are on a level with ours? Do you think that you have a right to retaliate if we should try to do anything to you? You had not the same rights that your father had, or that your master would have had if you had been a slave. You had no right to retaliate if   60 they ill-treated you, or to answer them if they scolded you, or to strike them back if they struck you, or to repay them evil with evil in any way. And do you think that you may retaliate in the case of your country and its laws? If we try to destroy you, because we think it just, will you in return do all that you can to destroy us, the laws, and your country, and say that in so doing you are acting justly—you, the man who really thinks so much of excellence? Or are you too wise to see that your country is worthier, more to be revered, more sacred, and held in higher honor both by the gods and by all men of   70 understanding, than your father and your mother and all your ancestors; and that you ought to reverence it, and to submit to it, and to approach it more humbly when it is angry with you than you would approach your father; and either to do whatever it tells you to do or to persuade it to excuse you; and to obey in silence if it orders you to endure flogging or imprisonment, or if it sends you to battle to be wounded or die? That is just. You must not give way, nor retreat, nor desert your station. In war, and in the court of justice, and everywhere, you must do whatever your state and your   80 country tell you to do, or you must persuade them that their commands are unjust. But it is impious to use violence against your father or your mother; and much more impious to use violence against your country." What answer shall we make, Crito? Shall we say that the laws speak the truth, or not?

Crito: I think that they do.

Socrates: "Then consider, Socrates," perhaps they would say, "if we are right in saying that by attempting to escape you are attempting an injustice. We brought you into the world, we raised you, we educated you, we gave you and   90 every other citizen a share of all the good things we could. Yet we proclaim that if any man of the Athenians is dissatisfied with us, he may take his goods and go away wherever he pleases; we give that privilege to every man who chooses to avail himself of it, so soon as he has reached manhood, and sees us, the laws, and the administration of our state. No one of us stands in his way or forbids him to take his goods and go wherever he likes, whether it be to an Athenian colony, or to any foreign country, if he is dissatisfied with us and with the state. But we say that every man of you who remains here, seeing how we administer justice, and how we govern the state in other matters, has agreed, by the very fact of remaining here, to do whatsoever we tell him. And, we say, he who disobeys us acts unjustly on three counts: he disobeys us who are his parents, and he disobeys us who reared him, and he disobeys us after he has agreed to obey us, without persuading us that we are wrong. Yet we did not tell him sternly to do whatever we told him. We offered him an alternative; we gave him his choice either to obey us or to convince us that we were wrong; but he does neither. "These are the charges, Socrates, to which we say that you will expose yourself if you do what you intend; and you are more exposed to these charges than other Athenians." And if I were to ask, "Why?" they might retort with justice that I have bound myself by the agreement with them more than other Athenians. They would say, "Socrates, we have very strong evidence that you were satisfied with us and with the state. You would not have been content to stay at home in it more than other Athenians unless you had been satisfied with it more than they. You never went away from Athens to the festivals, nor elsewhere except on military service; you never made other journeys like other men; you had no desire to see other states or other laws; you were contented with us and our state; so strongly did you prefer us, and agree to be governed by us. And what is more, you had children in this city, you found it so satisfactory. Besides, if you had wished, you might at your trial have offered to go into exile. At that time you could have done with the state's consent what you are trying now to do without it. But then you gloried in being willing to die. You said that you preferred death to exile. And now you do not honor those words: you do not respect us, the laws, for you are trying to destroy us; and you are acting just as a miserable slave would act, trying to run away, and breaking the contracts and agreement which you made to live as our citizen. First, therefore, answer this question. Are we right, or are we wrong, in saying that you have agreed not in mere words, but in your actions, to live under our government?" What are we to say, Crito? Must we not admit that it is true?

Crito: We must, Socrates. . . .

Q **What reasons does Socrates give for refusing to escape from prison?**

Q **How does this reading illustrate the relationship between the individual and the community?**

Plato and the Theory of Forms

Socrates' teachings were an inspiration to his pupil Plato (ca. 428–ca. 347 B.C.E.). Born in Athens during the Peloponnesian Wars, Plato reaped the benefits of Golden Age culture along with the insecurities of the postwar era. In 387 B.C.E., more than a decade after the death of his master, he founded the world's first school of philosophy, the Academy. Plato wrote some two dozen treatises, most of which were cast in the dialogue or dialectical format that Socrates had made famous. Some of the dialogues may be precise transcriptions of actual conversations, whereas others are clearly fictional, but the major philosophical arguments in almost all Plato's treatises are put into the mouth of Socrates. Since Socrates himself wrote nothing, it is almost impossible to distinguish between the ideas of Plato and those of Socrates.

Plato's most famous treatise, the *Republic,* asks two central questions: "What is the meaning of justice?" and "What is the nature of a just society?" In trying to answer these questions, Plato introduces a theory of knowledge that is both visionary and dogmatic. It asserts the existence of a two-level reality, one consisting of constantly changing particulars available to our senses, the other consisting of unchanging eternal truths understood by way of the intellect. According to Plato, the higher reality of eternal truths, which he calls Forms, is distinct from the imperfect and transient objects of sensory experience, which are mere copies of Forms. Plato's Theory of Forms proposes that all sensory objects are imitations of the Forms, which, like the simplest mathematical equations, are imperishable and forever true. For example, the circle and its three-dimensional counterpart, the sphere, exist independent of any *particular* circle and sphere. They have always existed and will always exist. But the beach ball I toss in the air, an imperfect copy of the sphere, is transitory. Indeed, if all the beach balls in the world were destroyed, the Universal Form—Sphere—would still exist. Similarly, suggests Plato, Justice, Love, and Beauty (along with other Forms) stand as unchanging and eternal models for the many individual and particular instances of each in the sensory world.

According to Plato, Forms descend from an ultimate Form, the Form of the Good. Plato never located or defined the Ultimate Good, except by analogy with the sun. Like the sun, the Form of the Good illuminates all that is intelligible and makes possible the mind's perception of Forms as objects of thought. The Ultimate Good, knowledge of which is the goal of dialectical inquiry, is the most difficult to reach.

In the *Republic,* Plato uses a literary device known as **allegory** to illustrate the dilemma facing the psyche in its ascent to knowledge of the imperishable and unchanging Forms. By way of allegory—the device by which the literal meaning of the text implies a figurative or "hidden"

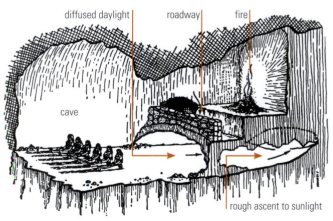

diffused daylight roadway fire

cave

rough ascent to sunlight

Figure 4.18 "Allegory of the Cave," from *The Great Dialogues of Plato.*

meaning—Plato describes a group of ordinary mortals chained within an underground chamber (the psyche imprisoned within the human body). Their woeful position permits them to see only the shadows on the walls of the cave (the imperfect and perishable imitations of the Forms that occupy the world of the senses), which the prisoners, in their ignorance, believe to be real (Figure **4.18**). Only when one of the prisoners (the philosopher-hero) ascends to the domain of light (true knowledge, or knowledge of the Forms) does it become clear that what the cave-dwellers perceive as truth is nothing more than shadows of Reality. This intriguing parable is presented as a dialogue between Socrates and Plato's older brother, Glaucon.

READING 4.6 From the "Allegory of the Cave" from Plato's *Republic* (ca. 375 B.C.E.)

Next, said [Socrates], here is a parable to illustrate the 1
degrees in which our nature may be enlightened or
unenlightened. Imagine the condition of men living in a sort of
cavernous chamber underground, with an entrance open to the
light and a long passage all down the cave. Here they have
been from childhood, chained by the leg and also by the neck,
so that they cannot move and can see only what is in front of
them, because the chains will not let them turn their heads.
At some distance higher up is the light of a fire burning behind
them; and between the prisoners and the fire is a track[1] with 10
a parapet built along it, like the screen at a puppet-show, which
hides the performers while they show their puppets over the top.

    I see, said he.

    Now behind this parapet imagine persons carrying along various
artificial objects, including figures of men and animals in wood or
stone or other materials, which project above the parapet.
Naturally, some of these persons will be talking, others silent.[2]

    It is a strange picture, he said, and a strange sort of 20
prisoners.

    Like ourselves, I replied; for in the first place prisoners so
confined would have seen nothing of themselves or of one
another, except the shadows thrown by the firelight on the
wall of the Cave facing them, would they?

    Not if all their lives they had been prevented from moving
their heads.

    And they would have seen as little of the objects
carried past.

    Of course. 30

    Now, if they could talk to one another, would they not

---

[1] The track crosses the passage into the Cave at right angles and is above the parapet built along it.

[2] A modern Plato would compare his Cave to an underground cinema, where the audience watch the play of shadows thrown by the film passing before a light at their backs. The film itself is only an image of "real" things and events in the world outside the cinema. For the film Plato has to substitute the clumsier apparatus of a procession of artificial objects carried on their heads by persons who are merely part of the machinery, providing for the movement of the objects and the sound whose echo the prisoners hear. The parapet prevents these persons' shadows from being cast on the wall of the Cave.

suppose that their words referred only to those passing
shadows which they saw?

    Necessarily.

    And suppose their prison had an echo from the wall facing
them? When one of the people crossing behind them spoke,
they could only suppose that the sound came from the shadow
passing before their eyes.

    No doubt.

    In every way, then, such prisoners would recognize as 40
reality nothing but the shadows of those artificial objects.

    Inevitably.

    Now consider what would happen if their release from the
chains and the healing of their unwisdom should come about
in this way. Suppose one of them were set free and forced
suddenly to stand up, turn his head, and walk with eyes lifted
to the light; all these movements would be painful, and he
would be too dazzled to make out the objects whose shadows
he had been used to see. What do you think he would say,
if someone told him that what he had formerly seen was 50
meaningless illusion, but now, being somewhat nearer to
reality and turned toward more real objects, he was getting a
truer view? Suppose further that he were shown the various
objects being carried by and were made to say, in reply to
questions, what each of them was. Would he not be perplexed
and believe the objects now shown him to be not so real as
what he formerly saw?

    Yes, not nearly so real.

    And if he were forced to look at the firelight itself, would
not his eyes ache, so that he would try to escape and turn 60
back to the things which he could see distinctly, convinced
that they really were clearer than these other objects now
being shown to him?

    Yes.

    And suppose someone were to drag him away forcibly up
the steep and rugged ascent and not let him go until he had
hauled him out into the sunlight, would he not suffer pain and
vexation at such treatment, and, when he had come out into
the light, find his eyes so full of its radiance that he could not
see a single one of the things that he was now told were 70
real?

    Certainly he would not see them all at once.

    He would need, then, to grow accustomed before he could
see things in that upper world. At first it would be easiest to
make out shadows, and then the images of men and things
reflected in water, and later on the things themselves. After
that, it would be easier to watch the heavenly bodies and the
sky itself by night, looking at the light of the moon and stars
rather than the Sun and the Sun's light in the day-time.

    Yes, surely. 80

    Last of all, he would be able to look at the Sun and
contemplate its nature, not as it appears when reflected
in water or any alien medium, but as it is in itself in its own
domain.

    No doubt.

    And now he would begin to draw the conclusion that it is
the Sun that produces the seasons and the course of the year
and controls everything in the visible world, and moreover is in
a way the cause of all that he and his companions used to see.

    Clearly he would come at last to that conclusion. 90

Then if he called to mind his fellow prisoners and what passed for wisdom in his former dwelling-place, he would surely think himself happy in the change and be sorry for them. They may have had a practice of honoring and commending one another, with prizes for the man who had the keenest eye for the passing shadows and the best memory for the order in which they followed or accompanied one another, so that he could make a good guess as to which was going to come next. Would our released prisoner be likely to covet those prizes or to envy the men exalted to honor and power in the Cave? Would he not feel like Homer's Achilles, that he would far sooner "be on earth as a hired servant in the house of a landless man"[3] or endure anything rather than go back to his old beliefs and live in the old way?

Yes, he would prefer any fate to such a life.

Now imagine what would happen if he went down again to take his former seat in the Cave. Coming suddenly out of the sunlight, his eyes would be filled with darkness. He might be required once more to deliver his opinion on those shadows, in competition with the prisoners who had never been released, while his eyesight was still dim and unsteady; and it might take some time to become used to the darkness. They would laugh at him and say that he had gone up only to come back with his sight ruined; it was worth no one's while even to attempt the ascent. If they could lay hands on the man who was trying to set them free and lead them up, they would kill him.[4]

Yes, they would.

Every feature in this parable, my dear Glaucon, is meant to fit our earlier analysis. The prison dwelling corresponds to the region revealed to us through the sense of sight, and the firelight within it to the power of the Sun. The ascent to see the things in the upper world you may take as standing for the upward journey of the soul into the region of the intelligible; then you will be in possession of what I surmise, since that is what you wish to be told. Heaven knows whether it is true; but this, at any rate, is how it appears to me. In the world of knowledge, the last thing to be perceived and only with great difficulty is the essential Form of Goodness. Once it is perceived, the conclusion must follow that, for all things, this is the cause of whatever is right and good; in the visible world it gives birth to light and to the lord of light, while it is itself sovereign in the intelligible world and the parent of intelligence and truth. Without having had a vision of this Form no one can act with wisdom, either in his own life or in matters of state.

So far as I can understand, I share your belief.

Then you may also agree that it is no wonder if those who have reached this height are reluctant to manage the affairs of men. Their souls long to spend all their time in that upper world—naturally enough, if here once more our parable holds true. Nor, again, is it at all strange that one who comes from the contemplation of divine things to the miseries of human life should appear awkward and ridiculous when, with eyes still dazed and not yet accustomed to the darkness, he is compelled, in a law court or elsewhere, to dispute about the shadows of justice or the images that cast those shadows, and to wrangle over the notions of what is right in the minds of men who have never beheld Justice itself.

It is not at all strange.

No; a sensible man will remember that the eyes may be confused in two ways—by a change from light to darkness or from darkness to light; and he will recognize that the same thing happens to the soul. When he sees it troubled and unable to discern anything clearly, instead of laughing thoughtlessly, he will ask whether, coming from a brighter existence, its unaccustomed vision is obscured by the darkness, in which case he will think its condition enviable and its life a happy one; or whether, emerging from the depths of ignorance, it is dazzled by excess of light. If so, he will rather feel sorry for it; or, if he were inclined to laugh, that would be less ridiculous than to laugh at the soul which has come down from the light.

That is a fair statement.

If this is true, then, we must conclude that education is not what it is said to be by some, who profess to put knowledge into a soul which does not possess it, as if they could put sight into blind eyes. On the contrary, our own account signifies that the soul of every man does possess the power of learning the truth and the organ to see it with; and that, just as one might have to turn the whole body round in order that the eye should see light instead of darkness, so the entire soul must be turned away from this changing world, until its eye can bear to contemplate reality and that supreme splendor which we have called the Good. Hence there may well be an art whose aim would be to effect this very thing, the conversion of the soul, in the readiest way; not to put the power of sight into the soul's eye, which already has it, but to ensure that, instead of looking in the wrong direction, it is turned the way it ought to be.

Yes, it may well be so.

It looks, then, as though wisdom were different from those ordinary virtues, as they are called, which are not far removed from bodily qualities, in that they can be produced by habituation and exercise in a soul which has not possessed them from the first. Wisdom, it seems, is certainly the virtue of some diviner faculty, which never loses its power, though its use for good or harm depends on the direction toward which it is turned. You must have noticed in dishonest men with a reputation for sagacity the shrewd glance of a narrow intelligence piercing the objects to which it is directed. There is nothing wrong with their power of vision, but it has been forced into the service of evil, so that the keener its sight, the more harm it works.

Quite true.

And yet if the growth of a nature like this had been pruned from earliest childhood, cleared of those clinging overgrowths which come of gluttony and all luxurious pleasure and, like leaden weights charged with affinity to this mortal world, hang upon the soul, bending its vision downward; if, freed from these, the soul were turned round toward true reality, then this same power in these very men would see the truth as keenly as the objects it is turned to now.

---

[3] This verse, spoken by the ghost of Achilles, suggests that the Cave is comparable with Hades, the Greek underworld.

[4] An allusion to the fate of Socrates.

Yes, very likely.

Is it not also likely, or indeed certain after what has been said, that a state can never be properly governed either by the uneducated who know nothing of truth or by men who are allowed to spend all their days in the pursuit of culture? The ignorant have no single mark before their eyes at which they must aim in all the conduct of their own lives and of affairs of state; and the others will not engage in action if they can help it, dreaming that, while still alive, they have been translated to the Island of the Blest.

Quite true.

It is for us, then, as founders of a commonwealth, to bring compulsion to bear on the noblest natures. They must be made to climb the ascent to the vision of Goodness, which we called the highest object of knowledge; and, when they have looked upon it long enough, they must not be allowed, as they now are, to remain on the heights, refusing to come down again to the prisoners or to take any part in their labors and rewards, however much or little these may be worth.

Shall we not be doing them an injustice, if we force on them a worse life than they might have?

You have forgotten again, my friend, that the law is not concerned to make any one class specially happy, but to ensure the welfare of the commonwealth as a whole. By persuasion or constraint it will unite the citizens in harmony, making them share whatever benefits each class can contribute to the common good; and its purpose in forming men of that spirit was not that each should be left to go his own way, but that they should be instrumental in binding the community into one.

True, I had forgotten.

You will see, then, Glaucon, that there will be no real injustice in compelling our philosophers to watch over and care for the other citizens. We can fairly tell them that their compeers in other states may quite reasonably refuse to collaborate: there they have sprung up, like a self-sown plant, in despite of their country's institutions; no one has fostered their growth, and they cannot be expected to show gratitude for a care they have never received. "But," we shall say, "it is not so with you. We have brought you into existence for your country's sake as well as for your own, to be like leaders and king-bees in a hive; you have been better and more thoroughly educated than those others and hence you are more capable of playing your part both as men of thought and as men of action. You must go down, then, each in his turn, to live with the rest and let your eyes grow accustomed to the darkness. You will then see a thousand times better than those who live there always; you will recognize every image for what it is and know what it represents, because you have seen justice, beauty, and goodness in their reality; and so you and we shall find life in our commonwealth no mere dream, as it is in most existing states, where men live fighting one another about shadows and quarreling for power, as if that were a great prize; whereas in truth government can be at its best and free from dissension only where the destined rulers are least desirous of holding office."

Quite true.

Then will our pupils refuse to listen and to take their turns at sharing in the work of the community, though they may live together for most of their time in a purer air?

No; it is a fair demand, and they are fair-minded men. No doubt, unlike any ruler of the present day, they will think of holding power as an unavoidable necessity.

Yes, my friend; for the truth is that you can have a well-governed society only if you can discover for your future rulers a better way of life than being in office; then only will power be in the hands of men who are rich, not in gold, but in the wealth that brings happiness, a good and wise life. All goes wrong when, starved for lack of anything good in their own lives, men turn to public affairs hoping to snatch from thence the happiness they hunger for. They set about fighting for power, and this internecine conflict ruins them and their country. The life of true philosophy is the only one that looks down upon offices of state; and access to power must be confined to men who are not in love with it; otherwise rivals will start fighting. So whom else can you compel to undertake the guardianship of the commonwealth, if not those who, besides understanding best the principles of government, enjoy a nobler life than the politician's and look for rewards of a different kind?

There is indeed no other choice. . . .

Q **What does each allegorical figure (the Cave, the Sun, and so on) represent?**

Q **How does this education of the psyche contribute (according to Socrates) to the life of a "well-governed society"?**

The "Allegory of the Cave" illustrates some key theories in the teachings of Plato. The first of these is **idealism**, the theory that holds that reality lies in the realm of unchanging Forms, rather than in sensory objects. Platonic idealism implies a dualistic (spirit-and-matter or mind-and-body) model of the universe: the psyche (mind) belongs to the world of the eternal Forms, while the *soma* (body) belongs to the sensory or material world. Imprisoned in the body, the mind forgets its once-perfect knowledge of the Forms. It is, nevertheless, capable of recovering its prenatal intelligence. The business of philosophy is to educate the psyche, to draw it out of its material prison so that it can regain perfect awareness.

Plato's concept of an unchanging force behind the flux of our perceptions looks back to the theories of Heraclitus, while his description of the Forms resembles Pythagorean assertions of the unchanging reality of number. It is not without significance that Plato's Theory of Forms has been hailed in modern physics: the celebrated twentieth-century German physicist Werner Heisenberg argued that the smallest units of matter are not physical objects in the ordinary sense; rather, he asserted, they are "forms," or ideas that can be expressed unambiguously only in mathematical language.

In constructing the Theory of Forms, Plato may also have been influenced by Asian religious thought. The spiritual "spark" with which humans are born, according to Plato, and which must be kindled and cultivated, resembles the Hindu Atman (see chapter 3). And Plato's distinction between the realm of the senses and the ultimate, all-embracing Form recalls the Hindu belief that the illusory world of matter stands apart from Ultimate Being or Brahman. In contrast with Hinduism, however, Plato's teachings do not advocate enlightenment as escape from the material world. Rather, Plato perceives the mind's ascent to knowledge as a prerequisite of individual well-being and the attainment of the good life here on earth. Such enlightenment is essential to achieving a just state and a healthy society.

Plato's *Republic*: The Ideal State

Plato's *Republic* establishes a set of social and moral requirements for everyday life. While this utopian community permits no private property and little family life, it defends a practical system of education by which every citizen might arrive at knowledge of the Good. Education, fundamental to the good society, is available equally to men and women. If women are to be employed in the same duties as men, argues Plato, they must receive the same instruction, which includes music, gymnastics, and military training. In Book 5 of the *Republic*, Socrates explains:

> none of the occupations which comprehend the ordering of the state belong to woman as woman, nor yet to man as man: but natural gifts are to be found here and there in both sexes alike, and so far as her nature is concerned, the woman is admissible to all pursuits as well as the man, though in all of them the woman is weaker than the man.

While all citizens are educated equally, the ability of each determines that person's place within society. Thus the duties of all citizens—laborers, soldiers, or governors—will be consistent with their mental and physical abilities.

Plato had little use for democracy of the kind practiced in Athens. Governing, in his view, should fall to those who are the most intellectually able. That is, those who have most fully recovered a knowledge of the Forms are obliged to act as "king-bees" in the communal hive. (Plato might have been surprised to discover that the ruling bee in a beehive is female.) The life of contemplation carries with it heavy responsibilities, for in the hands of the philosopher-kings lies "the welfare of the commonwealth as a whole." Such views are remarkably compatible with ancient China's premise that a natural hierarchy determines who is fit to govern (see chapter 3).

Aristotle and the Life of Reason

Among Plato's students at the Academy was a young Macedonian named Aristotle, whose contributions to philosophy ultimately rivaled those of his teacher. After a period of travel in the eastern Mediterranean and a brief career as tutor to the young prince of Macedonia (the future Alexander the Great), Aristotle returned to Athens and founded a school known as the Lyceum. Aristotle's habit of walking up and down as he lectured in the *peripatos* ("covered walkway") of the school gave him the nickname the "peripatetic philosopher." His teachings, which exist only in the form of lecture notes compiled by his students,

cover a wider and more practical range of subjects than those of Plato.

Aristotle did not accept Plato's Theory of Forms. For him, the real was not a reflection of ideal Forms, but existed in the objects of the material world. He equated form (or *essence*) with the true nature of a thing, and held that its full possession was achieved by the proper performance of its function. Questioning Plato's theory of an eternal psyche, he theorized that the portion of the soul identified with reason (and with the impersonal force he called the Unmoved Mover) might be immortal.

Aristotle left a vast number of works on some 400 subjects, including biology, physics, politics, poetry, drama, logic, and ethics. To each of his inquiries he brought the habit of systematic classification, identifying each thing according to its essence—its unique and unchanging nature. He also brought to his inquiries the exercise of keen observation. The son of a physician, Aristotle gathered specimens of plant and animal life, and classified them according to their physical similarities and differences. Over 500 different animals, some of which Aristotle himself dissected, are mentioned in his zoological treatises, known as the *Historia Animalium*. Although he did little in the way of modern scientific experimentation, his practice of basing conclusions on very careful observation advanced the **empirical method**—a method of inquiry dependent on direct experience. He brought to his analysis of political life, literature, and human conduct the same principles he employed in classifying plants and animals: objectivity, clarity, and consistency. Before writing the *Politics*, he examined the constitutions of more than 150 Greek city-states. And in the *Poetics* he defined the various genres of literary expression (see chapter 5).

In the fields of biology, astronomy, and physics, Aristotle's conclusions (including many that were incorrect) remained unchallenged for centuries. For instance, Aristotle theorized that in sexual union, the male was the "generator" and the female the "receptacle," while procreation involved the imposition of life-giving form (the male) on chaotic matter (the female). In short, Aristotle's views on female biology and sexuality led centuries of scholars to regard woman as an imperfect and incomplete version of man.

Aristotle's application of scientific principles to the reasoning process was the basis for the science of logic. Aristotelian logic requires the division of an argument into individual terms, followed—in Socratic fashion—by

---

THE SYLLOGISM

All men are mortal.
a:b
Socrates is a man.
c:a
Therefore, Socrates is mortal.
∴ c = b

an examination of the meaning of those terms. Aristotle formulated the **syllogism**, a deductive scheme that presents two premises from which a conclusion may be drawn. As a procedure for reasoned thought without reference to specific content, the syllogism is a system of notation that is similar to mathematics.

Aristotle's *Ethics*

Not the least of Aristotle's contributions was that which he made to **ethics**, that branch of philosophy that sets forth the principles of human conduct. Proceeding from an examination of human values, Aristotle hypothesizes that happiness or "the good life" (the Greek word *eudaimonia* means both) is the only human value that might be considered a final goal or end (*telos*) in itself, rather than a means to any other end. Is not happiness the one goal to which all human beings aspire? If so, then how does one achieve it? The answer, says Aristotle, lies in recognizing one's defining essence, and functioning to fulfill it. The function of the eye is to see; the function of the racehorse is to run fast; the function of a knife is to cut, and so on. How well a thing performs is synonymous with its excellence or virtue (in Greek, the word *arete* denotes both): the excellence of the eye, then, lies in seeing well; the excellence of a racehorse lies in how fast it runs; the excellence of a knife depends on how well it cuts, and so on. The unique function of the human being, concludes Aristotle, is the ability to reason; hence, the excellence of any human creature lies in the exercise of reason.

In the *Ethics*, edited by Aristotle's son Nicomachus, Aristotle examines the Theory of the Good Life and the Nature of Happiness. He explains that action in accordance with reason is necessary for the acquisition of excellence, or virtue. Ideal conduct, suggests Aristotle, lies in the Golden Mean—the middle ground between any two extremes of behavior. Between cowardice and recklessness, for instance, one should seek the middle ground: courage. Between boastfulness and timidity, one should cultivate modesty. The Doctrine of the Mean rationalized the Classical search for moderation and balance. In contrast with the divinely ordained moral texts of other ancient cultures, Aristotle's *Ethics* required individuals to reason their way to ethical conduct.

┌─ **READING 4.7** From Aristotle's *Nicomachean Ethics* (ca. 340 B.C.E.)

The Supreme Good

If it is true that in the sphere of action there is an end which   1
we wish for its own sake, and for the sake of which we wish
for everything else, and that we do not desire all things for the
sake of something else (for, if that is so, the process will go on
ad infinitum, and our desire will be idle and futile), it is clear
that this will be the good or the supreme good. Does it not
follow then that the knowledge of this supreme good is of
great importance for the conduct of life, and that, if we know
it, we shall be like archers who have a mark at which to aim,
we shall have a better chance of attaining what we want?

But, if this is the case, we must endeavor to comprehend,   10
at least in outline, its nature, and the science or faculty to
which it belongs. . . .

It seems not unreasonable that people should derive their
conception of the good or of happiness from men's lives.
Thus ordinary or vulgar people conceive it to be pleasure,
and accordingly approve a life of enjoyment. For there are
practically three prominent lives, the sensual, the political,
and, thirdly, the speculative. Now the mass of men present an
absolutely slavish appearance, as choosing the life of brute
beasts, but they meet with consideration because so many   20
persons in authority share the tastes of Sardanapalus.[1]
Cultivated and practical people, on the other hand, identify
happiness with honor, as honor is the general end of political
life. But this appears too superficial for our present purpose;
for honor seems to depend more upon the people who pay it
than upon the person to whom it is paid, and we have an
intuitive feeling that the good is something which is proper to
a man himself and cannot easily be taken away from him. It
seems too that the reason why men seek honor is that they
may be confident of their own goodness. Accordingly they   30
seek it at the hands of the wise and of those who know them
well, and they seek it on the ground of virtue; hence it is clear
that in their judgment at any rate virtue is superior to honor. . . .

We speak of that which is sought after for its own sake as
more final than that which is sought after as a means to
something else; we speak of that which is never desired as a
means to something else as more final than the things which
are desired both in themselves and as means to something
else; and we speak of a thing as absolutely final, if it is
always desired in itself and never as a means to something   40
else.

It seems that happiness preeminently answers to this
description, as we always desire happiness for its own sake
and never as a means to something else, whereas we desire
honor, pleasure, intellect, and every virtue, partly for their own
sakes (for we should desire them independently of what might
result from them) but partly also as being means to happiness,
because we suppose they will prove the instruments of
happiness. Happiness, on the other hand, nobody desires for
the sake of these things, nor indeed as a means to anything   50
else at all. . . .

Perhaps, however, it seems a truth which is generally
admitted, that happiness is the supreme good; what is wanted
is to define its nature a little more clearly. The best way of
arriving at such a definition will probably be to ascertain the
function of Man. For, as with a flute-player, a statuary, or any
artisan, or in fact anybody who has a definite function and
action, his goodness, or excellence, seems to lie in his
function, so it would seem to be with Man, if indeed he has a
definite function. Can it be said then that, while a carpenter   60
and a cobbler have definite functions and actions, Man,
unlike them, is naturally functionless? The reasonable view is
that, as the eye, the hand, the foot, and similarly each . . . part
of the body has a definite function, so Man may be regarded
as having a definite function apart from all these. What then,
can this function be? It is not life; for life is apparently

---

[1] The legendary king of Assyria, known for his sensuality.

something which man shares with the plants; and it is something peculiar to him that we are looking for. We must exclude therefore the life of nutrition and increase. There is next what may be called the life of sensation. But this, too, is apparently shared by Man with horses, cattle, and all other animals. There remains what I may call the practical life of the rational part of *Man's being*. But the rational part is twofold; it is rational partly in the sense of being obedient to reason, and partly in the sense of possessing reason and intelligence. The practical life too may be conceived of in two ways, viz., *either as a moral state, or as a moral activity*: but we must understand by it the life of activity, as this seems to be the truer form of the conception.

The function of Man then is an activity of soul in accordance with reason, or not independently of reason. . . .

The Golden Mean
Our present study is not, like other studies, purely speculative in its intention; for the object of our inquiry is not to know the nature of virtue but to become ourselves virtuous, as that is the sole benefit which it conveys. It is necessary therefore to consider the right way of performing actions, for it is actions as we have said that determine the character of the resulting moral states. . . .

The first point to be observed then is that in such matters as we are considering[,] deficiency and excess are equally fatal. It is so, as we observe, in regard to health and strength; for we must judge of what we cannot see by the evidence of what we do see. Excess or deficiency of gymnastic exercise is fatal to strength. Similarly an excess or deficiency of meat and drink is fatal to health, whereas a suitable amount produces, augments, and sustains it. It is the same then with temperance, courage, and the other virtues. A person who avoids and is afraid of everything and faces nothing becomes a coward; a person who is not afraid of anything but is ready to face everything becomes foolhardy. Similarly he who enjoys every pleasure and never abstains from any pleasure is licentious; he who eschews all pleasures like a boor is an insensible sort of person. For temperance and courage are destroyed by excess and deficiency but preserved by the mean [middle] state. . . .

The nature of virtue has been now generically described. But it is not enough to state merely that virtue is a moral state, we must also describe the character of that moral state. It must be laid down then that every virtue or excellence has the effect of producing a good condition of that of which it is a virtue or excellence, and of enabling it to perform its function well. Thus the excellence of the eye makes the eye good and its function good, as it is by the excellence of the eye that we see well. Similarly, the excellence of the horse makes a horse excellent and good at racing, at carrying its rider and at facing the enemy. If then this is universally true, the virtue or excellence of man will be such a moral state as makes a man good and able to perform his proper function well. We have already explained how this will be the case, but another way of making it clear will be to study the nature or character of this virtue.

Now in everything, whether it be continuous or discrete, it is possible to take a greater, a smaller, or an equal amount,

and this either absolutely or in relation to ourselves, the equal being a mean between excess and deficiency. By the mean in respect of the thing itself, or the absolute mean, I understand that which is equally distinct from both extremes; and this is one and the same thing for everybody. By the mean considered relatively to ourselves I understand that which is neither too much nor too little; but this is not one thing, nor is it the same for everybody. Thus if 10 be too much and 2 too little we take 6 as a mean in respect of the thing itself; for 6 is as much greater than 2 as it is less than 10, and this is a mean in arithmetical proportion. But the mean considered relatively to ourselves must not be ascertained in this way. It does not follow that if 10 pounds of *meat* be too much and 2 too little for a man to eat, a trainer will order him 6 pounds, as this may itself be too much or too little for the person who is to take it; it will be too little [for instance] for Milo,[2] but too much for a beginner in gymnastics. It will be the same with running and wrestling; *the right amount will vary with the individual*. This being so, everybody who understands his business avoids alike excess and deficiency; he seeks and chooses the mean, not the absolute mean, but the mean considered relatively to ourselves.

Every science then performs its function well, if it regards the mean and refers the works which it produces to the mean. This is the reason why it is usually said of successful works that it is impossible to take anything from them or to add anything to them, which implies that excess or deficiency is fatal to excellence but that the mean state ensures it. Good artists too, as we say, have an eye to the mean in their works. But virtue, like Nature herself, is more accurate and better than any art; virtue therefore will aim at the mean;—I speak of moral virtue, as it is moral virtue which is concerned with emotions and actions, and it is these which admit of excess and deficiency and the mean. Thus it is possible to go too far, or not to go far enough, in respect of fear, courage, desire, anger, pity, and pleasure and pain generally, and the excess and the deficiency are alike wrong; but to experience these emotions at the right times and on the right occasions and toward the right persons and for the right causes and in the right manner is the mean or the supreme good, which is characteristic of virtue. Similarly there may be excess, deficiency, or the mean, in regard to actions. But virtue is concerned with emotions and actions, and here excess is an error and deficiency a fault, whereas the mean is successful and laudable, and success and merit are both characteristics of virtue.

Virtue then is a state of deliberate moral purpose consisting in a mean that is relative to ourselves, the mean being determined by reason, or as a prudent man would determine it. . . .

— **Q** **What, according to Aristotle, is the supreme good?**

— **Q** **How does one arrive at the Golden Mean?**

---

[2] A famous athlete from the Greek city-state of Crotona in southern Italy. As a teenager, he began lifting a calf each day, until, as both his strength and the calf grew, he could lift a fully grown bullock.

Aristotle and the State

While the Golden Mean gave every individual a method for determining right action, Aristotle was uncertain that citizens would put it to efficient use in governing themselves. Like Plato, he questioned the viability of the democratic state. Political privilege, argued Aristotle, was the logical consequence of the fact that some human beings were naturally superior to others: from the hour of their birth some were marked out for subjection and others for rule. Aristotle also insisted that governments must function in the interest of the state, not in the interest of any single individual or group. He criticized democracy because, at least in theory, it put power in the hands of great masses of poor people who might rule in their own interests. He also pointed out that Athenian demagogues were capable of persuading the Assembly to pass less-than-worthy laws. In his *Politics*, the first treatise on political theory produced in the West, Aristotle concluded that the best type of government was a constitutional one ruled by the middle class. Aristotle defined the human being as a *polis*-person (the term from which we derive the word "political"). Humans are, in other words, political creatures, who can reach their full potential only within the political framework of the state. Only beasts and gods, he noted, have no need for the state—he gracefully excluded women from such considerations. Aristotle resolved the relationship between the individual and the state as follows:

> [The] state is by nature clearly prior to the family and to the individual, since the whole is of necessity prior to the part. . . . The proof that the state is a creation of nature and prior to the individual is that the individual, when isolated, is not self-sufficing; and

therefore he is like a part in relation to the whole. But he who is unable to live in society, or who has no need because he is sufficient for himself, must be either a beast or a god: he is no part of a state. A social instinct is implanted in all men by nature, and yet he who first founded the state was the greatest of benefactors.

For man, when perfected, is the best of animals, but, when separated from law and justice, he is the worst of all; since armed injustice is the more dangerous, and he is equipped at birth with arms, meant to be used by intelligence and virtue, he is the most unholy and the most savage of animals, and the most full of lust and gluttony. But justice is the bond of men in states, for the administration of justice, which is the determination of what is just, is the principle of order in political society.

Science and Technology

390 B.C.E.	Plato coins the term "elements" to describe four primary substances: earth, air, fire, and water (earlier introduced by Empedocles)
350 B.C.E.	Aristotle posits a spherical earth based on observations of a lunar eclipse
340 B.C.E.	Eudemus of Rhodes writes the *History of Mathematics*
330 B.C.E.	Aristotle's *Historia Animalium* classifies animals and records details of animal life; other of his writings advance the study of medicine, biology, and physics

LOOKING BACK

Bronze Age Civilizations of the Aegean (ca. 3000–1200 B.C.E.)

- The Aegean civilizations of Crete and Mycenae laid the foundations for much of Greek life and legend. While the Minoans were peace-loving, the militant and aggressive Mycenaeans challenged other traders for control of the eastern Mediterranean.

The Heroic Age (ca. 1200–750 B.C.E.)

- The Homeric epics immortalize the Mycenaean attack on Troy in Asia Minor ca. 1200 B.C.E. and its legendary heroes. Transmitted orally and recorded ca. 800 B.C.E., they became the "national" poems of Greece.
- The *Iliad* follows Achilles and his vengeful fight in the Trojan War as he attempts to reconcile his sense of personal honor and his obligations to his fellow warriors.
- The *Odyssey*, the second great epic of the Heroic Age, recounts the adventures of the Greek commander Odysseus during his long sea journey back to his native Ithaca.
- The Greek pantheon was seen as a family of gods who intervened in the lives of human beings.

The Greek City-State and the Persian Wars (ca. 750–480 B.C.E.)

- Greek geography encouraged the evolution of the *polis*; each of the 200 independent city-states established its own economy, government, and military defenses.
- When the Persian Empire attacked the Greek mainland during the sixth century B.C.E., the city-states formed an alliance and built a strong naval force to defeat the Persians.
- Herodotus, the "father of history," recorded an account of the Persian Wars that remains the Western world's first major work in prose.

Athens and the Greek Golden Age (ca. 480–430 B.C.E.)

- Following the Persian Wars, ancient Greece experienced a Golden Age in cultural productivity, with the city-state of Athens assuming political dominion as well as commercial supremacy in the Aegean Sea.
- When the Popular Assembly of Citizens acquired the right to make laws, in 508 B.C.E., Athens became the first direct democracy in world history.
- Beginning in 776 B.C.E., the Greeks enjoyed athletic contests in the form of the Olympic Games, in which all Greek city-states competed.

The Individual and the Community

- The Greeks were the first masters of the art of drama, presenting the Athenian community with regular theatrical performances and leaving the world its earliest tragedies and comedies.
- Such famous Greek trilogies as the *Oresteia* and *Oedipus* explore the moral dilemma that brings personal choice and action into conflict with the well-being of the community.
- Sophocles' tragedy *Antigone*, in which Oedipus' daughter violates the king's decree and buries her brother's dead body, examines the irreconcilability of personal and political obligations, and the consequences of excessive pride.

Greek Philosophy: The Speculative Leap

- During the sixth century B.C.E., Greek philosophers laid the foundations for Western scientific and philosophic inquiry; they argued for natural causes, using observation and systematic analysis to reach valid conclusions.
- The naturalist philosophers tried to determine the material basis of the universe: Democritus advanced the atomic theory of matter; Pythagoras held that proportion based on number constituted the underlying cosmic order; Hippocrates, the "father of medicine," separated science from superstition by seeking natural causes for disease.

Humanist Philosophy

- The Sophists and the humanist philosophers Socrates, Plato, and Aristotle moved beyond the naturalists to probe the nature of human knowledge, the question of right conduct, and the advance of wisdom.
- The Sophists argued that truth and justice were relative, while their critic Socrates pursued absolute standards for moral conduct.
- Plato's Theory of Forms laid the basis for philosophical idealism and for the separation of mind and matter. In the *Republic*, Plato explained how virtue might be cultivated for the mutual benefit of the individual and the community.
- Aristotle investigated a variety of subjects, ranging from logic and zoology to the art of poetry and the science of stagecraft. In his *Ethics*, Aristotle asserted that the good life was identical to the life of reason, a life guided by the Golden Mean.

Glossary

allegory a literary device in which objects, persons, or actions are equated with secondary, figurative meanings that underlie their literal meaning

amphora a two-handled vessel used for oil or wine (see Figures 4.1, 4.10, and 5.5)

antagonist the character that directly opposes the protagonist in drama or fiction

catalog a list of people, things, or attributes, characteristic of biblical and Homeric literature

catharsis (Greek, "purification" or "cleansing") in drama, an emotional experience that revitalizes the spectator

democracy a government in which supreme power is vested in the people

dialectical method a question-and-answer style of inquiry made famous by Socrates

empirical method a method of inquiry dependent on direct experience or observation

epithet a characterizing word or phrase; in Homeric verse, a compound adjective used to identify a person or thing

ethics that branch of philosophy that sets forth the principles of human conduct

hubris excessive pride; arrogance

idealism (Platonic) the theory that holds that things in the material world are manifestations of an independent realm of unchanging, immaterial ideas of forms (see also Kantian idealism, chapter 25)

krater A vessel used for mixing wine and water

oligarchy a government in which power lies in the hands of an elite minority

protagonist the leading character in a play or story

syllogism a deductive scheme of formal argument, consisting of two premises from which a conclusion may be drawn

Chapter

5

The Classical Style
ca. 700–30 B.C.E.

"Men are day-bound. What is a man? What is he not? Man is a shadow's dream. But when divine advantage comes, men gain a radiance and a richer life."
Pindar

Figure 5.1 KALLICRATES, Temple of Athena Nike, Acropolis, Athens, ca. 427–424 B.C.E. Pentelic marble, 17 ft. 9 in. × 26 ft. 10 in.

The words "classic" and "classical" are commonly used to mean "first-rate" and "enduring." They also describe a style of creative expression marked by clarity, simplicity, balance, and harmonious proportion—features associated with moderation, rationalism, and dignity. This style dominated the arts of ancient Greece. It was brought to its height during the period that followed the Persian Wars (ca. 480–400 B.C.E.). In the visual arts, as well as in literature, philosophy, and music, the Greek "classics" provided a standard of beauty and excellence that was preserved and imitated for centuries. During the fourth century B.C.E., Alexander the Great carried Greek language and culture into North Africa and Central Asia, thus "Hellenizing" a vast part of the civilized world. Thereafter, the Romans absorbed Greek culture and transmitted its

legacy to the West.* Most of the free-standing sculptures of the Greek masters survive only in Roman replicas, and what remains is a fraction of what once existed. The balance fell to the ravages of time and vandals, who pulverized marble statues to make mortar and melted down bronze pieces to mint coins and cast cannons.

Despite these losses, the Classical conception of beauty has had a profound influence on Western cultural expression. Its mark is most visible in the numerous Neoclassical ("new Classical") revivals that have flourished over the centuries, beginning with the Renaissance in Italy (see chapters 16–17).

---

* The Roman contribution to the Classical style is discussed in chapter 6.

The Classical Style

The quest for harmonious proportion was the driving force behind the evolution of the Classical style, even as it was the impetus for the rise of Greek philosophy. In chapter 4, we saw that the naturalist philosophers worked to identify the fundamental order underlying the chaos of human perception. Pythagoras, for example, tried to show that the order of the universe could be understood by observing proportion (both geometric and numerical) in nature: he produced a taut string that, when plucked, sounded a specific pitch; by pinching that string in the middle and plucking either half he generated a sound exactly consonant with (and one **octave** higher than) the first pitch. Pythagoras claimed that relationships between musical sounds obeyed a natural symmetry that might be expressed numerically and geometrically. If music was governed by proportion, was not the universe as a whole subject to similar laws? And, if indeed nature itself obeyed laws of harmony and proportion, then should not artists work to imitate them?

Among Greek artists and architects, such ideas generated the search for a canon, or set of rules, for determining physical proportion. To establish a canon, the artist fixed on a *module*, or standard of measurement, that governed the relationships between all parts of the work of art and the whole. The module was not absolute, but varied according to the subject matter. In the human body, for instance, the distance from the chin to the top of the forehead, representing one-tenth of the whole body height, constituted a module by which body measurements might be calculated. Unlike the Egyptian canon (see Figure 2.19), the Greek canon was flexible: it did not employ a grid on which the human form was mapped, with fixed positions for parts of the body. Nevertheless, the Greek canon made active use of that principle of proportion known as *symmetry*, that is, correspondence of

opposite parts in size, shape, or position, as is evident in the human body.

Although little survives in the way of Greek literary evidence, Roman sources preserve information that helps us to understand the canon that, after three centuries of experimentation, artists of the Greek Golden Age put into practice. Among these sources, the best is the *Ten Books on Architecture* written by the Roman architect and engineer Vitruvius Pollio (?–26 B.C.E.). Vitruvius recorded many of the aesthetic principles and structural techniques used by the ancient Greeks. In defining the Classical canon, he advised that the construction of a building and the relationship between its parts must imitate the proportions of the human body. Without proportion, that is, the correspondence between the various parts of the whole, there can be no design, argued Vitruvius. And without design, there can be no art. The eminent Greek Golden Age sculptor Polycleitus, himself the author of a manual on proportion (no longer in existence), is believed to have employed the canon Vitruvius describes (Figure **5.2**). But it was the Vitruvian model itself that, thanks to the efforts of the Renaissance artist–scientist Leonardo da Vinci (see chapter 17), became a symbol for the centrality of the ideally proportioned human being in an ideally proportioned universe (Figure **5.3**).

READING 5.1 From Vitruvius' *Principles of Symmetry* (ca. 46–30 B.C.E.)

On Symmetry: In Temples and in the Human Body

1 The Design of a temple depends on symmetry, the   1
principles of which must be most carefully observed by the
architect. They are due to proportion.... Proportion is a
correspondence among the measures of the members of
an entire work, and of the whole to a certain part selected
as standard. From this result the principles of symmetry.
Without symmetry and proportion there can be no principles

Figure 5.2 POLYCLEITUS, *Doryphorus* (*Spear-Bearer*), Roman copy after a bronze Greek original of ca. 450–440 B.C.E. Marble, height 6 ft. 11½ in. The figure, who once held a spear in his left hand, strides forward in a manner that unites motion and repose, energy and poise, confidence and grace—the qualities of the ideal warrior-athlete.

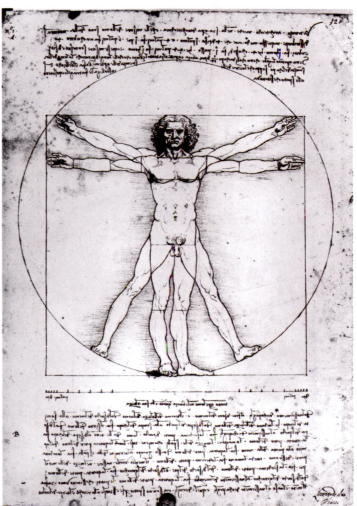

Figure 5.3 LEONARDO DA VINCI, *Proportional Study of a Man in the Manner of Vitruvius*, ca. 1487. Pen and ink, 13½ × 9⅝ in.

in the design of any temple; that is, if there is no precise relation between its members, as in the case of those of a well-shaped man.   10

2 For the human body is so designed by nature that the face, from the chin to the top of the forehead and lowest roots of the hair, is a tenth part of the whole height; the open hand from the wrist to the tip of the middle finger is just the same; the head from the chin to the crown is an eighth, and with the neck and shoulder from the top of the breast to the lowest roots of the hair is a sixth; from the middle of the breast to the summit of the crown is a fourth. If we take the height of the face itself, the distance from the bottom of the chin to the underside of the nostrils is one third of it; the nose from the underside of the   20 nostrils to a line between the eyebrows is the same; from there to the lowest roots of the hair is also a third, comprising the forehead. The length of the foot is one sixth of the height of the body; of the forearm, one fourth; and the breadth of the breast is also one fourth. The other members, too, have their own symmetrical proportions, and it was by employing them that famous painters and sculptors of antiquity attained to great and endless renown.

3 Similarly, in the members of a temple there ought to be the greatest harmony in the symmetrical relations of the different   30 parts to the general magnitude of the whole. Then again, in the human body the central point is naturally the navel. For if a man be placed flat on his back, with hands and feet extended, and a pair of compasses centered at his navel, the fingers and toes of his two hands and feet will touch the circumference of a circle described therefrom. And just as the human body yields a circular outline, so too a square figure may be found from it [see Figure 5.3]. For if we measure the distance from the soles of the feet to the top of the head, and then apply that measure to the outstretched arms, the breadth will be found to be the same as the height, as in the case of plane surfaces which are perfectly square.

4 Therefore, since nature has designed the human body so that its members are duly proportioned to the frame as a whole, it appears that the ancients had good reason for their rule, that in perfect buildings the different members must be in exact symmetrical relations to the whole general scheme. Hence, while transmitting to us the proper arrangements for buildings of all kinds, they are particularly careful to do so in the case of temples of the gods, buildings in which merits and faults usually last forever. . . .

Q Should the proportions of the human body govern architectural design, as Vitruvius suggests?

Humanism, Realism, and Idealism

While proportion and order are guiding principles of the Classical style, other features informed Greek Classicism from earliest times. One of the most apparent is *humanism*. Greek art is said to be humanistic not only because it observes fundamental laws derived from the human physique, but also because it focuses so consistently on the actions of human beings. Greek art is fundamentally *realistic*, that is, faithful to nature; but it refines nature in a process of *idealization*, that is, the effort to achieve a perfection that surpasses nature. Humanism, Realism, and Idealism are hallmarks of Greek art.

Because almost all Greek frescoes have disappeared, decorated vases are our main source of information about Greek painting. During the first 300 years of Greek art—the *Geometric period* (ca. 1200–700 B.C.E.)—artists painted their ceramic wares with angular figures and complex geometric patterns arranged to enhance the shape of the vessel. Scenes from a warrior's funeral dominate the upper register of a krater; the funeral procession, with horse-drawn chariots, occupies the lower register (Figure **5.4**). By the *Archaic period* (ca. 700–480 B.C.E.), scenes from mythology, literature, and everyday life came to inhabit the central zone of the vase (Figure **5.5**; see also Figures 4.1 and 4.10). Water jars, wine jugs, storage vessels, drinking cups, and bowls all record the keen enjoyment of everyday activities among the Greeks: working, dancing, feasting, fighting, and gaming. In these compositions, little if any physical setting is provided for the action. Indeed, in their decorative simplicity, the flat black figures often resemble the abstract shapes that ornament the rim, handle, and foot of the vessel (see Figure 5.5). The principles of clarity and order so apparent in the Geometric style (see

Figure 5.4) remain dominant in the decoration of later black-figured vases, where a startling clarity of design is produced by the interplay of dark and light areas of figure and ground.

During the *Classical period* (480–323 B.C.E.), artists replaced the black-figured style with one in which the human body was left the color of the clay and the ground was painted black (Figure 5.6). They refined their efforts to position figures and objects to complement the shape of the vessel (see also Figures 4.17 and 5.5). However, with the newly developed red-figured style, artists might delineate physical details on the buff-colored surface, thereby making the human form appear more lifelike. Although still flattened and aligned side by side, figures are posed

Figure 5.4 Funerary krater with "Geometric" decoration, ca. 750 B.C.E. Terracotta, height 3 ft. 4½ in. The Greeks used monumental vases like this one as grave markers. The deceased is laid out on the bier, surrounded by his family and a group of mourners. The foot soldiers in the procession below carry full-body ("hourglass") shields and lances.

naturally. *Realism*, that is, fidelity to nature, has overtaken the decorative aspect of the Geometric and Archaic styles. At the same time, artists of the Classical period moved toward aesthetic *idealism*. Socrates is noted for having described the idealizing process: he advised the painter Parrhasius that he must reach beyond the flawed world of appearances by selecting and combining the most beautiful details of many different models. To achieve ideal form, the artist must simplify the subject matter, free it of incidental detail, and impose the accepted canon of proportion. Accordingly, the art object will surpass the imperfect and transient objects of sensory experience. Like Plato's Ideal Forms, the artist's imitations of reality are lifelike in appearance, but they aim to improve upon or perfect sensory reality. Among the Greeks, as among the Egyptians, conception played a large part in the art-making process; with the Greeks, however, the created object was no longer a static sacred sign, but a dynamic, rationalized replica of the physical world.

Figure 5.6 EPICTETUS, cup (detail), ca. 510 B.C.E. Terracotta, diameter 13 in.

The Evolution of the Classical Style

Greek Sculpture: The Archaic Period (ca. 700–480 B.C.E.)

Nowhere is the Greek affection for the natural beauty of the human body so evident as in Hellenic sculpture, where the male nude form assumed major importance as a subject. Free-standing Greek sculptures fulfilled the same purpose as Mesopotamian and Egyptian votive statues: they paid perpetual homage to the gods. They also served as cult statues, funerary monuments, and memorials designed to honor the victors of the athletic games. Since athletes both trained and competed in the nude, the unclothed body was completely appropriate to visual representation. Ultimately, however, the dominance of the nude in Greek art reflects the Hellenic regard for the human body as nature's perfect creation. (The fig leaves that cover the genitals of some Greek sculptures are additions dating from the Christian era.)

In sculpture, as in painting, the quest for realism was balanced by the effort to idealize form. Achieving the delicate balance between real and ideal was a slow process, one that had its beginnings early in Greek history. During the Archaic phase of Greek sculpture, free-standing representations of the male youth (***kouros***) retain the rigid verticality of tree trunks from which earlier Greek sculptures were carved.

Produced some fifty years after the Attica *kouros* (Figure 5.7), the *Calf-Bearer* is more gently and more realistically

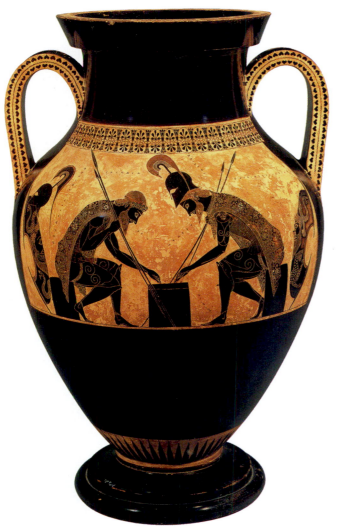

Figure 5.5 EXEKIAS, black-figured amphora with Achilles and Ajax playing dice, ca. 530 B.C.E. Height 24 in.

Greek culture owed much to the ancient Egyptians. That debt is evident in representations of the Greek life-sized male nude. In the Archaic phase of Greek art, the *kouros* is pictured in a frontal pose, with head and body erect; the figure is composed symmetrically around a central axis, and the anatomy of the torso is delineated with geometric precision (Figure **5.7**). As with ancient Egyptian figures (Figure **5.8**), the left leg of the *kouros* is shown in advance, while his arms are locked at the sides. The pose reflects the inflexibility of the medium, but it also lends a sense of dignity and authority to the figure. This life-sized *kouros*, one of the earliest carved in Attica, marked the grave of a young Athenian aristocrat.

Figure 5.8 Statue of Mycerinus (Queen Kha-merer-nebty II cropped out to his left; see Figure 2.3 for full pair statue). Height 4 ft.

Figure 5.7 DIPYLON MASTER, *New York Kouros*, from Attica, ca. 600 B.C.E. Marble, height 6 ft. 4 in.

modeled—note especially the abdominal muscles and the sensitively carved bull calf (Figure **5.9**). The hollow eyes of the shepherd once held inlays of semiprecious stones (mother-of-pearl, gray agate, and lapis lazuli) that would have given the smiling face a strikingly realistic appearance. Such lifelike effects were enhanced by the brightly colored paint (now almost gone) that enlivened the lips, hair, and other parts of the figure. A quarter of a century later, the robust likeness of a warrior named Kroisos (found marking his grave) shows close anatomical attention to knee and calf muscles. Like his Archaic predecessors, he strides aggressively forward, but his forearms now turn in toward his body, and his chest, arms, and legs swell with powerful energy (Figure **5.10**). He also bears the "Archaic blissful

smile" that, in contrast with the awestruck countenances of Mesopotamian votive statues (see Figure 1.9), reflects the buoyant optimism of the early Greeks.

Greek Sculpture: The Classical Period (480–323 B.C.E.)

By the early fifth century B.C.E., a major transformation occurred in Hellenic art. With the *Kritios Boy* (Figure **5.11**), the Greek sculptor had arrived at the natural positioning of the human body that would characterize the Classical style. The sensuously modeled torso turns on the axis of the spine, and the weight of the body shifts from equal distribution on both legs to greater weight on the left leg—a kind of balanced opposition that is at once natural and graceful. (This counterpositioning would be called **contrapposto** by

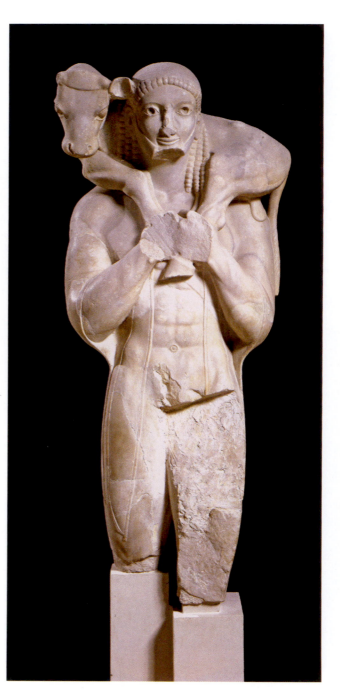

Figure 5.9 *Calf-Bearer*, ca. 575–550 B.C.E. Marble, height 5 ft. 6 in.

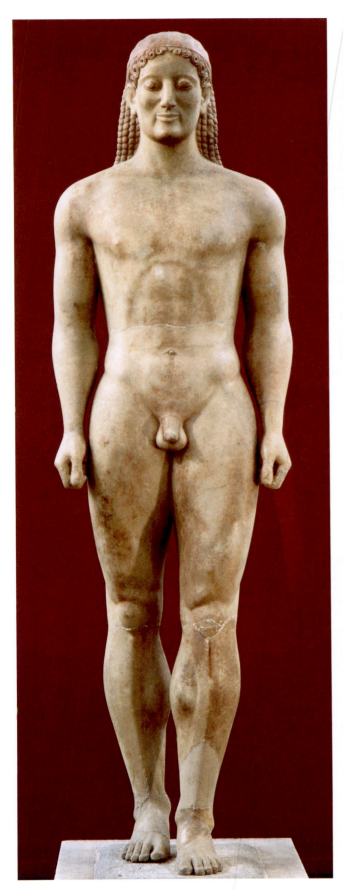

Figure 5.10 Kroisos from Anavyssos, ca. 525 B.C.E. Marble with traces of paint, height 6 ft. 4½ in. Kroisos was a young warrior who died heroically in battle some time before 530 B.C.E. Inscribed on the base of the statue is the inscription, "Stay and mourn at the tomb of dead Kroisos, whom raging Ares destroyed one day as he fought in the foremost ranks."

Figure 5.11 *Kritios Boy*, ca. 480 B.C.E. Marble, height 46¼ in.

Figure 5.12 Zeus (or Poseidon), ca. 460 B.C.E. Bronze, height 6 ft. 10 in. The Greeks did not invent the lost-wax method of bronze casting (see Figure 0.19), but they were the first to employ this technique for large artworks, such as this one. This sophisticated technique allowed artists to depict more vigorous physical action and to include greater detail than was possible in the more restrictive medium of marble.

Italian Renaissance artists.) The muscles of the *Kritios Boy* are no longer geometrically schematized, but protrude subtly; the figure is no longer smiling, but instead solemn and contemplative. The new poised stance, along with the naturalistic treatment of human anatomy and proportion, are features of the High Classical style that flourished between ca. 480 and 400 B.C.E. At midcentury, Polycleitus brought that style to perfection with the *Doryphorus* (*Spear-Bearer*; see Figure 5.2). Known today only by way of Roman copies, the *Doryphorus* is widely regarded as the embodiment of the canon of ideal human proportions (see Reading 5.1).

The Classical Ideal: Male and Female

There is little to distinguish man from god in the bronze statue of Zeus (or Poseidon) hurling a weapon, the work of an unknown sculptor (Figure **5.12**). This nude, which conveys the majesty and physical vitality of a mighty Greek deity, might just as well represent a victor of the Olympic Games. Dynamically posed—the artist has deliberately exaggerated the length of the arms—the god fixes the decisive moment just before the action, when every muscle in the body is tensed, ready to achieve the mark. The sculptor has also idealized the physique in the direction of geometric clarity. Hence the muscles of the stomach are indicated as symmetrical trapezoids, and the strands of the god's hair and beard assume a distinctive pattern of parallel wavy lines.

Greek and Roman sculptors often made marble copies of popular bronze-cast figures. The *Discobolus* (*Discus Thrower*) (see Figure 4.13), originally executed in bronze by Myron around 450 B.C.E., but surviving only in various Roman marble copies, is one example. Like the majestic bronze in Figure 5.12, it captures the instant before the action, the ideal moment when intellect guides performance. The male nudes of the High Classical Age fulfill Aristotle's idea of excellence as the exercise of human will dominated by reason.

The evolution of the female figure (*kore*) underwent a somewhat different course from that of the male. Early on, *korai* were fully clothed; they did not appear in the nude until the fourth century B.C.E. Female statues of the Archaic period were ornamental, columnar, and (like their male counterparts) smiling (Figure **5.13**). Not until the Late Classical Age (400–323 B.C.E.) did Greek sculptors arrive at the sensuous female nude figures that so inspired Hellenistic, Roman, and (centuries later) Renaissance artists. The *Aphrodite of Knidos* (Figure **5.14**) by Praxiteles is the first such figure. It established a model for the ideal female nude: tall and poised, with small breasts and broad hips. Regarded by the Romans as the finest statue in the world, Praxiteles' goddess of love exhibits a subtle counterposition of shoulders and hips, smooth body curves, and a face that bears a dreamy, melting gaze. She is distinguished by the famous Praxitelean technique of carving that coaxed a translucent shimmer from the fine white marble.

Figure 5.13 *Kore* from Chios (?), ca. 520 B.C.E. Marble with traces of paint, height 22 in. (approx., lower part missing).

Figure 5.14 PRAXITELES, *Aphrodite of Knidos*, Roman copy of marble Greek original of ca. 350 B.C.E. Marble, height 6 ft. 8 in. Commissioned by the citizens of the city of Knidos, this image of their patron goddess would become a Classical icon of love and beauty. Imitated in some sixty versions, the celebrated nude is shown holding her robe, having just emerged from her bath, or (according to legend) from the sea foam.

Our brief study of Greek statuary from the Archaic through the Late Classical Age concludes with some important general observations concerning the Classical ideal: its history is one of increasing realism, freed of incidental detail. Human imperfections (wrinkles, warts, blemishes) are purged in favor of a radiant flawlessness. The ideal figure is neither very old nor very young, neither very thin nor very fat. He or she is eternally youthful, healthy, serene, dignified, and liberated from all accidents of nature. This synthesis of Humanism, Realism, and Idealism in the representation of the free-standing figure was one of the great achievements of Greek art. It defined the standard of beauty in Western art for centuries.

The Parthenon

Figure 5.15 **ICTINUS** and **KALLICRATES**, west end of the Parthenon, Athens, 448–432 B.C.E. Pentelic marble, height of columns 34 ft.

The Parthenon represents the apex of a long history of post-and-lintel temple building among the Greeks. The plan of the temple, a rectangle delimited on all four sides by a colonnaded walkway, reflects the typically Classical reverence for clarity, balance, and harmonious proportion (Figure **5.15**). Free-standing columns (each 34 feet tall) make up an exterior colonnade, while two further rows of columns on the east and west ends of the temple provide inner **porticos** (Figure **5.16**). The interior of the Parthenon is divided into two rooms: a central hall (or *cella*), which held the 40-foot-high cult statue of Athena; and a smaller room used as a treasury. It was here that the much-disputed Delian League funds were stored. Entirely elevated on a raised platform, the Parthenon invited the individual to move around it, as if it were a monumental shrine. Indeed, scholars have suggested that the Parthenon was both a shrine to Athena and a victory monument.

Figure 5.16 Plan of the Parthenon, Athens.

portico

cella

statue of Athena

Doric colonnade

treasury

portico

steps   frieze

0   100 ft.

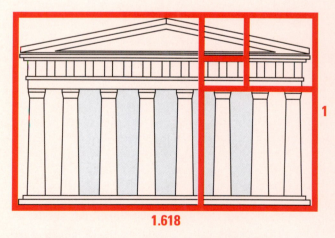

1

1.618

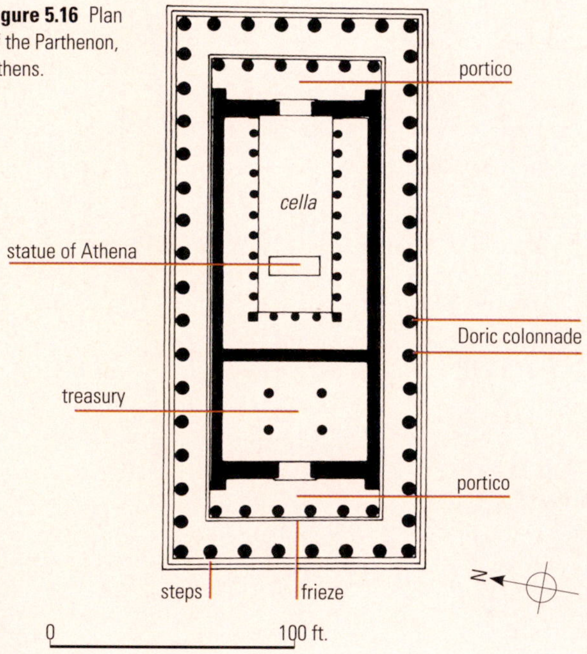

Figure 5.17 Line drawing of the Parthenon elevation with Golden Ratio indicated. Two quantities are in Golden Ratio when their ratio is the same as the ratio of their sum to the maximum. The fundamentals of the Golden Section were formulated by Euclid in the late fourth century B.C.E. (see page 132) and were later enshrined in the Vitruvian canon (see Reading 5.1).

Greek Architecture: The Parthenon

The great monuments of Classical architecture were designed to serve the living, not—as in Egypt—the dead. In contrast with the superhuman scale of the Egyptian pyramid, the Greek temple, as Vitruvius observed, was proportioned according to the human body. Greek theaters (see Figure 4.14) celebrated life here on earth rather than the life in the hereafter, and Greek temples served as shrines for the gods and depositories for civic and religious treasures. Both theaters and temples functioned as public meeting places. Much like the Mesopotamian ziggurat (see Figure 1.8), the Greek temple was a communal symbol of reverence for the gods. However, while the ziggurat enforced the separation of priesthood and populace, the Greek temple united religious and secular domains.

The outstanding architectural achievement of Golden Age Athens is the Parthenon (see LOOKING INTO, Figures **5.15**, **5.16**, and **5.17**), a temple dedicated to Athena, the goddess of war, patron of the arts and crafts, and the personification of wisdom. The name "Parthenon" derives from the Greek *parthenos* ("maiden" or "virgin"), popular epithets for Athena. Built in glittering Pentelic marble upon the ruins of an earlier temple burned during the Persian Wars, and housing a colossal statue of Athena (which no longer exists), the Parthenon overlooks Athens from the highest point on the Acropolis (Figure **5.18**). Athens' preeminent temple was commissioned by Pericles, designed by the architects Ictinus and Kallicrates, and embellished by the sculptor Phidias (fl. ca. 490–430 B.C.E.). Phidias directed and supervised the construction of the temple over a period of more than ten years, from 448 to 432 B.C.E. In the tradition of Egyptian builders,

Greek architects used no mortar. Rather, they employed bronze clamps and dowels to fasten the individually cut marble segments.

The Parthenon makes use of the Doric **order**, one of three programs of architectural design developed by the ancient Greeks (Figure **5.19**). Each of the orders—Doric, Ionic, and (in Hellenistic times) Corinthian—prescribes a fundamental set of structural and decorative parts that stand in fixed relation to one another. Each order differs in details and in the relative proportions of the parts. The Doric order, which originated on the Greek mainland, is simple and severe. In the Parthenon it reached its most refined expression. The Ionic order, originating in Asia Minor and the Aegean Islands, is more delicate and ornamental. Its slender columns terminate in capitals with paired volutes or scrolls. The Ionic order is employed in some of the small temples on the Acropolis (see Figure **5.1**). The Corinthian, the most ornate of the orders, is characterized by capitals consisting of acanthus leaves. It is often found on victory monuments, in **tholos** (circular) sanctuaries and shrines, and in various Hellenistic and Roman structures (see Figure 6.14).

While symmetry and order governed the structural elements of the Parthenon, a similar set of laws determined its proportions. The precise canon of proportion adopted by Phidias for the construction of the Parthenon is still the subject of debate. Nevertheless, most architectural historians agree that a module governed the entire project. It is likely that this module was both geometric and numerical, adhering to a specific ratio: the famous "Golden Section" (see Figure 5.17). The system of proportion known as the "Golden Section" or "Golden Ratio" is expressed

Figure 5.18 Model of the Classical Acropolis at Athens.

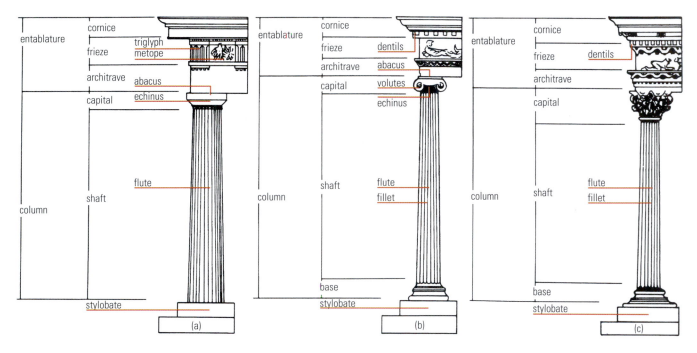

Figure 5.19 The Greek orders: (a) Doric; (b) Ionic; and (c) Corinthian.

numerically by the ratio 1.618:1, or approximately 8:5; it is represented by the Greek letter φ (phi), which derives from the name of the Parthenon's designer, Phidias. This ratio, which governs the proportions of the ground plan of the Parthenon and the relationship between its structural parts, represents an aesthetic ideal found in nature and in the human anatomy.

An analysis of the Parthenon's construction is further complicated by the fact that there are virtually no straight lines in the entire building. Its Doric columns, for instance, swell near the center to counter the optical effect of

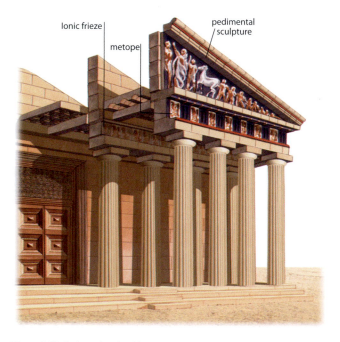

Figure 5.20 Sculptural and architectural detail of the Parthenon. **Frieze**, a decorative band along the top of a wall; metopes, segmented spaces on a frieze; pediment, a gable.

thinning that occurs when the normal eye views an uninterrupted set of parallel lines. All columns tilt slightly inward. Corner columns are thicker than the others to compensate for the attenuating effect produced by the bright light of the sky against which the columns are viewed, and also to ensure their ability to bear the weight of the terminal segments of the superstructure. The top step of the platform on which the columns rest is not parallel to the ground, but rises four and a quarter inches at the center, allowing rainwater to run off the convex surface even as it corrects the optical impression of sagging along the extended length of the platform. Consistently, the architects of the Parthenon corrected negative optical illusions produced by strict conformity to geometric regularity. Avoiding rigid systems of proportion, they took as their primary consideration the aesthetic and functional integrity of the building. Today, the Parthenon stands as a noble ruin, the victim of an accidental gunpowder explosion in the seventeenth century, followed by centuries of vandalism, air pollution, and unrelenting tourist traffic.

The Sculpture of the Parthenon

Between 448 and 432 B.C.E., Phidias and the members of his workshop executed the sculptures that would appear in three main locations on the Parthenon: in the **pediments** of the roof **gables**, on the **metopes** or square panels between the beam ends under the roof, and in the area along the outer wall of the *cella* (Figure **5.20**). Brightly painted, as were the decorative portions of the building, the Parthenon sculptures relieved the stark angularity of the post-and-lintel structure. In subject matter, the temple sculptures paid homage to the patron deity of Athens: the east pediment narrates the birth of Athena with gods and goddesses in attendance (Figures **5.21** and **5.22**). The west pediment shows the contest between Poseidon

The Battle Over Antiquities

Only one-half of the Parthenon's original sculptures survive, and half of these are displayed at the British Museum in London. The rest are in the recently opened Acropolis Museum in Athens.

In 1687, when the Ottoman Turks ruled Greece (see chapter 21), an enemy firebomb ignited the Ottoman gunpowder supply stored in the Parthenon, destroying much of the building's interior. In the early 1800s, England's ambassador to the Ottoman Empire, Thomas Bruce, the seventh earl of Elgin, rescued the sculptures from rubble and ruin, and shipped them to England. A few years later, the trustees of the British Museum purchased the marbles with money given by Parliament. Since achieving independence in 1832, the Greeks have demanded the return of the sculptures. Britain, however, claims legitimate ownership. The issue remains in dispute today.

Similar debates are currently raging over the question of "cultural patrimony." Do antiquities (and other artworks) belong to the country in which they were produced, or do they belong to those individuals and institutions who have bought them for private collections or for public display? The issue is complicated by the fact that many works of art, both ancient and modern, were looted from ancient graves or taken forcibly from their owners during times of war. Some museum curators and art dealers have faced trial for buying and selling objects that were illegally excavated or stolen from ancient tombs. In 2008, the Metropolitan Museum in New York City was forced to return the magnificent Euphronios krater (see Figure 4.9) it had purchased in the early 1970s. While the museum insisted the artifact had a reliable provenance, evidence gathered by the Italian police proved that the piece had been stolen from a tomb in Cerveteri, an Etruscan site north of Rome. How similar cases are resolved will have a major effect on the global art market, and on the availability of visual landmarks for public display in the world's great art collections.

Figure 5.21 Three Goddesses: Hestia, Dione, Aphrodite, from the east pediment of the Parthenon, Athens, ca. 437–432 B.C.E. Marble, over life-sized.

Figure 5.22 A reconstruction of the three goddesses shown above.

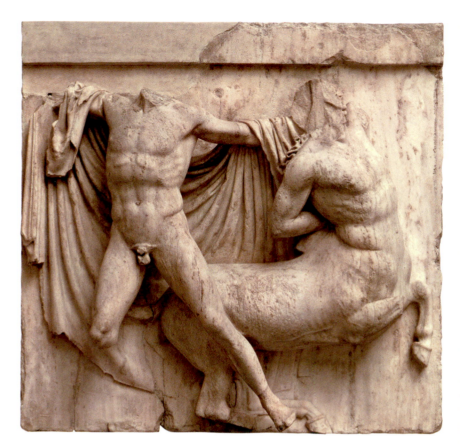

Figure 5.23 Lapith overcoming a centaur, south metope 27, Parthenon, Athens, 447–438 B.C.E. Marble, height 4 ft. 5 in.

of two contestants, one human and the other bestial. Appropriate to a temple honoring the goddess of wisdom, the sculptural program of the Parthenon celebrates the victory of intellect over unbridled passion, hence barbarism.

Completing Phidias' program of architectural decoration for the Parthenon is the continuous frieze that winds around the outer wall of the *cella* where that wall meets the roofline. The 524-foot-long sculptured band is thought by most scholars to depict the Panathenaic Festival, a celebration held every four years in honor of the goddess Athena. (Other interpretations, however, exist, the most recent of which views the frieze as a mythic account of virgin sacrifice by the daughters of Erectheus, legendary king of Athens.) Hundreds of figures—a cavalcade of horsemen (Figure **5.24**), water-bearers,

and Athena for domination of Athens. The ninety-two metopes that occupy the frieze (see Figure 5.20) illustrate the legendary combat between the Greeks (the bearers of civilization) and Giants, Amazons, and Centaurs (the forces of barbarism). Figure **5.23**, for instance, shows one of the Lapiths (an ancient Greek tribe) defeating a centaur (a fabulous hybrid of horse and man) after a group of drunken centaurs tried to abduct the Lapiths' women. Carved in high relief, each metope is a masterful depiction

musicians, and votaries—are shown filing in calm procession toward an assembled group of gods and goddesses (see Figure 4.11). The figures move with graceful rhythms, in tempos that could well be translated into music. Once brightly painted and ornamented with metal details, these noble figures must have appeared impressively lifelike. To increase this effect and satisfy a viewpoint from below, Phidias graded the relief, cutting the marble more deeply at the top than at the bottom. Housed today in the British

Figure 5.24 Group of young horsemen, from the north frieze of the Parthenon, Athens, 447–438 B.C.E. Marble, height 3 ft. 7 in. The horsemen ride bareback. Their bridles and reins, cast originally in metal, are now missing, as are the bright colors with which the frieze was painted.

Museum in London, where it is hung at approximately eye level, the Parthenon frieze loses much of its illusionistic subtlety. Nevertheless, this masterpiece of the Greek Golden Age reveals the harmonious reconciliation of Humanism, Realism, and Idealism that is the hallmark of the Classical style.

The Gold of Greece

The famous statue of Athena that stood in the *cella* of the Parthenon disappeared many centuries ago. However, there are images of the goddess in Hellenic art. One of the most spectacular appears in the form of a gold pendant disk that shows the head of Athena wearing a helmet bearing a sphinx, deer, and griffin heads, and an elaborate triple crest (Figure **5.25**). From Athena's shoulders snakes spring forth, and by her head stands an owl (the symbol of wisdom)—both motifs recalling the powers of the Minoan priestess (see Figure 4.5). Rosettes of gold filigree and enameled buds ornament the complex of looped chains that hang from the disk.

The Greeks gained international acclaim for their gold-working techniques, many of which had been inherited from Persia and from the nomadic Scythians of northern Asia. Gold-rich mining areas of northern Greece provided craftspeople with materials for the manufacture of jewelry. Particularly popular were pendants, earrings, and headpieces in the form of miniature sculptures, some of which (like the pendant of Athena) reproduced familiar images of the gods. Much like today, gold jewelry was a mark of wealth that also bore sentimental and religious value. In Greece and especially in the cities of Asia Minor, men as well as women adorned themselves with stylish earrings and bracelets.

The Classical Style in Poetry

In Classical Greece, as in other parts of the ancient world, distinctions between individual forms of artistic expression were neither clear-cut nor definitive. A combination of the arts prevailed in most forms of religious ritual and in public and private entertainment. In *Antigone*, for instance, choric pantomime and dance complemented dramatic poetry (see Reading 4.3). The intimate relationship between music and poetry is revealed in the fact that many of the words we use to describe lyric forms, such as "**ode**" and "**hymn**," are also musical terms. The word lyric, meaning "accompanied by the lyre," describes verse that was meant to be sung, not read silently. As in ancient Egypt, this genre of poetry gave voice to deep emotions.

Hellenic culture produced an impressive group of lyric poets, the greatest of whom was Sappho (ca. 610– ca. 580 B.C.E.). The details of her personal life remain a mystery. Born into an aristocratic family on the island of Lesbos, she seems to have married and mothered a daughter. On Lesbos, she instructed a group of women, dedicated to the cult of Aphrodite, in the production of lyric poetry. She herself produced some nine books of poems, of which only a fraction remain. Her highly self-conscious lyrics, many of which come to us only as fragments, are filled

Figure 5.25 Gold pendant disk with the head of Athena (one of a pair), from Kul Oba, ca. 400–350 B.C.E. Height 3¹⁹⁄₂₀ in., diameter of disk 1½ in.

with passion and tenderness. They offer only a glimpse of a body of poetry that inspired Sappho's contemporaries to regard her as "the female Homer."

Ancient and modern poets alike admired Sappho for her economy of expression and her inventive combinations of sense and sound—features that are extremely difficult to convey in translation. The first of these features, however, is apparent in the following poem:

> Although they are
> only breath, words
> which I command
> are immortal.

Here, in the space of four short lines, Sappho captures the spirit of confident optimism that marks her poetry and her age: while words are "only breath," they are the tools by which the poet claims her immortality.

In the first of the four poems reproduced below, Sappho expresses her affection for one of the women of the Lesbian community. Romantic bonds between female members of a given circle were commonplace in Greek society, as were homoerotic attachments between men—usually between an older man and a youth (see Figure 4.17). And while Hellenic literature and art offers ample evidence of bisexual and homosexual relationships, Sappho's poems reveal a passionate intensity often missing from other erotic works of art.

The last of the selections below is a pensive but brief meditation on death: it reflects the intense love of life and the generally negative view of death that pervaded the Hellenic world.

READING 5.2 The Poems of Sappho (ca. 590 B.C.E.)

He is more than a hero	1
He is a god in my eyes	
the man who is allowed	
to sit beside you—he	
who listens intimately	5
to the sweet murmur of	
your voice, the enticing	
laughter that makes my own	
heart beat fast. If I meet	
you suddenly, I can't	10
speak—my tongue is broken;	
a thin flame runs under	
my skin; seeing nothing,	
hearing only my own ears	
drumming, I drip with sweat;	15
trembling shakes my body	
and I turn paler than	
dry grass. At such times	
death isn't far from me	

———◆———

With his venom	1
Irresistible	
and bittersweet	
that loosener	
of limbs, Love	5
reptile-like	
strikes me down	

———◆———

I took my lyre and said:	1
Come now, my heavenly	
tortoise shell; become	
a speaking instrument	

———◆———

We know this much	1
Death is an evil;	
we have the gods'	

word for it; they too	
would die if death	5
were a good thing	

Q What themes are treated in these four poems?

Q How do the poems illustrate "economy of expression"?

While lyric poetry conveyed deeply personal feelings, certain types of lyrics, namely odes, served as public eulogies or songs of praise. Odes honoring Greek athletes bear strong similarities to songs of divine praise, such as the Egyptian "Hymn to the Aten" (see chapter 2) and the Hebrew psalms (see chapter 1). But the sentiments conveyed in the odes of the noted Greek poet Pindar (ca. 522–438 B.C.E.) are firmly planted in the secular world. They celebrate the achievements of the athletes who competed at the games held at the great sanctuaries of Olympia, Delphi, Nemea, and elsewhere (see Figure 4.1). Perpetuating the heroic idealism of the *Iliad*, Pindar's odes make the claim that prowess, not chance, leads to victory, which in turn renders the victor immortal. The first lines of his *Nemean Ode VI* honoring Alcimidas of Aegina (winner in the boys' division of wrestling) make the case that gods and men share a common origin. The closest human beings can come to achieving godlike immortality, however, lies in the exercise of "greatness of mind/Or of body." The ode thus narrows the gap between hero-athletes and their divine prototypes.

In his *Pythian Ode VIII* (dedicated to yet another victorious wrestler), Pindar develops a more modest balance of opposites: he sets the glories of youth against the adversities of aging and mortality itself. Although mortal limitations separate human beings from the ageless and undying gods, "manly action" secures the "richer life."

READING 5.3 From Pindar's Odes (ca. 465–445 B.C.E.)

From Nemean Ode VI

Single is the race, single	1
Of men and of gods;	
From a single mother we both draw breath.	
But a difference of power in everything	
Keeps us apart;	5
For the one is as nothing, but the brazen sky	
Stays a fixed habitation for ever.	
Yet we can in greatness of mind	
Or of body be like the Immortals,	
Though we know not to what goal	10
By day or in the nights	
Fate has written that we shall run.	

From Pythian Ode VIII

In the Pythian games	1

you pinned four wrestlers
unrelentingly, and sent
them home in losers' gloom;
no pleasant laughter cheered them as they reached   5
their mothers' sides; shunning ridicule,
they took to alleys, licking losers' wounds.
And he, who in his youth
secures a fine advantage
gathers hope and flies   10
on wings of manly action,
disdaining cost. Men's happiness is early-
ripened fruit that falls to earth
from shakings of adversity.
Men are day-bound. What is a man? What is   15
he *not*? Man is a shadow's dream. But when divine
advantage comes, men gain a radiance and a richer life.

Q **How does Pindar answer his own question
(line 15), "What is a man?"**

Q **How does his answer compare to other
responses to this question in Readings 1.2, 1.4e,
and 4.3, lines 233–49?**

The Classical Style in Music and Dance

The English word *music* derives from *muse*, the Greek word describing any of the nine mythological daughters of Zeus and the goddess of memory. According to Greek mythology, the muses presided over the arts and the sciences. Pythagoras observed that music was governed by mathematical ratios and therefore constituted both a science and an art. As with other arts, music played a major role in Greek life. Both vocal and instrumental music were commonplace, and contests between musicians, like those between playwrights, were a regular part of public life. Nevertheless, we know almost as little about how Greek music sounded as we do in the cases of Sumerian or Egyptian music.

The ancient Greeks did not invent a system of notation with which to record instrumental or vocal sounds. Apart from written and visual descriptions of musical performances, there exist only a few fourth-century B.C.E. treatises on music theory and some primitively notated musical works. The only complete piece of ancient Greek music that has survived is an ancient song found chiseled on a first-century B.C.E. gravestone. It reads: "So long as you live, be radiant, and do not grieve at all. Life's span is short and time exacts the final reckoning." Vase paintings reveal that the principal musical instruments of ancient Greece were the lyre, the **kithara**—both belonging to the harp family and differing only in shape, size, and number of strings (Figure **5.26**)—and the **aulos**, a flute or reed pipe (see Figure 5.6). Along with percussion devices often used to accompany dancing, these string and wind instruments were probably inherited from Egypt.

See Music Listening Selections at end of chapter.

The Greeks devised a system of **modes**, or types of **scale** characterized by fixed patterns of pitch and tempo within the octave. (The sound of the ancient Greek Dorian mode is approximated by playing the eight white keys of the piano beginning with the white key two notes above middle C.) Modified variously in Christian times, the modes were preserved in Gregorian chant and Byzantine church hymnology (see chapter 9). Although the modes themselves may have been inspired by the music of ancient India, the diatonic scale (familiar to Westerners as the series of notes C, D, E, F, G, A, B, C) originated in Greece. Greek music lacked harmony as we know it. It was thus **monophonic**, that is, confined to a single unaccompanied line of melody. The strong association between poetry and music suggests that the human voice had a significant influence in both melody and rhythm.

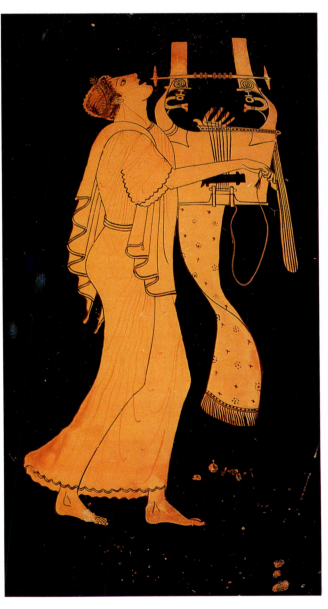

Figure 5.26 THE BERLIN PAINTER, red-figured amphora, ca. 490 B.C.E. Terracotta, height of vase 16⅜ in. Head thrown back, a young man sings to the accompaniment of a kithara, a type of lyre used in public performance and in the recitation of epic poetry. Pictured on the reverse of this amphora is a figure holding a wand—probably the judge of a music competition.

From earliest times, music was believed to hold magical powers and therefore exercise great spiritual influence. Greek and Roman mythology describes gods and heroes who used music to heal or destroy. Following Pythagoras, who equated musical ratios with the unchanging cosmic order, many believed that music might put one "in tune with" the universe. The planets, which Pythagoras described as a series of spheres moving at varying speeds in concentric orbits around the earth, were said to produce a special harmony, the so-called *music of the spheres.* The Greeks believed, moreover, that music had a moral influence. This argument, often referred to as the "Doctrine of Ethos," held that some modes strengthened the will, whereas others undermined it and thus damaged the development of moral character. In the *Republic,* Plato encourages the use of the Dorian mode, which settles the temper and inspires courage, but he condemns the Lydian mode, which arouses sensuality. Because of music's potential for affecting character and mood, both Plato and Aristotle recommended that the type of music used in the education of young children be regulated by law. Such music should reflect the Classical features of balance, harmony, and dignity.

Dance was prized for its moral value, as well as for its ability to give pleasure and induce good health (see Figure 5.6). For Plato the uneducated man was a "danceless" man. Both Plato and Aristotle advised that children be instructed at an early age in music and dancing. However, both men distinguished noble dances from ignoble ones. Dionysian and comic dances were considered unfit for Athenian citizens and therefore inappropriate to the educational curriculum. Nevertheless, such dances are often depicted on vases and in sculptured reliefs (Figure **5.27**). The wildest types of dance, those associated with celebrations honoring Dionysus, the god of vegetation and wine, were performed by cult followers known as *maenads,* whose intoxicated revelries were favorite Hellenic subjects.

Figure 5.27 A *maenad* leaning on a *thyrsos*, Roman copy of Greek original, ca. 420–410 B.C.E. Marble relief, height 56¼ in. The mythical followers of Dionysus, known as *maenads* (or *bacchantes*), were said to roam the forests singing and dancing with ecstatic abandon. This barefoot *maenad* holds a *thyrsos,* a fennel stalk ornamented with berries and ivy leaves, symbolic of vegetation and fertility. The movement of the dance is suggested by the swaying motion of her diaphanous draperies.

The Diffusion of the Classical Style: The Hellenistic Age (323–30 B.C.E.)

The fourth century B.C.E. was a turbulent era marked by rivalry and warfare among the Greek city-states. Ironically, however, the failure of the Greek city-states to live in peace would lead to the spread of Hellenic culture throughout the civilized world. Manipulating the shifting confederacies and internecine strife to his advantage, Philip of Macedonia eventually defeated the Greeks in 338 B.C.E. When he was assassinated two years later, his twenty-year-old son, Alexander (356–323 B.C.E.), assumed the Macedonian throne (Figure **5.28**). A student of Aristotle, Alexander brought to his role as ruler the same far-reaching ambition and imagination that his teacher had exercised in the intellectual realm. Alexander was a military genius: within twelve years, he created an empire that stretched from Greece to the borders of modern India (Map **5.1**). To all parts of his empire, but especially to the cities he founded—many of which he named after himself—Alexander carried Greek language and culture. Greek art and literature made a major impact on civilizations as far east as India, where it influenced Buddhist art and Sanskrit literature (see chapters 9 and 14).

Alexander carved out his empire with the help of an army of 35,000 Greeks and Macedonians equipped with weapons that were superior to any in the ancient world. Siege machines such as catapults and battering rams were used to destroy the walls of the best-defended cities of Asia Minor, Egypt, Syria, and Persia. Finally, in northwest India, facing the prospect of confronting the formidable army of the king of Ganges and his force of 5000 elephants, Alexander's troops refused to go any further. Shortly thereafter, the thirty-two-year-old general died (probably of malaria), and his empire split into three segments: Egypt was governed by the Ptolemy dynasty; Persia came under the leadership of the Seleucid rulers; and Macedonia-Greece was governed by the family of Antigonus the One-Eyed (see Map 5.1, inset).

The era that followed, called Hellenistic ("Greek-like"), lasted from 323 to 30 B.C.E. The defining features of the Hellenistic Age were cosmopolitanism, urbanism, and the blending of Greek, African, and Asian cultures. Trade routes linked Arabia, East Africa, and Central Asia, bringing great wealth to the cities of Alexandria, Antioch, Pergamon, and Rhodes. Alexandria, which replaced Athens as a cultural center, boasted a population of more than one million people and a library of half a million books (the collection was destroyed by fire when Julius Caesar besieged the city in 47 B.C.E.). The Great Library, part of the cultural complex known as the Temple of the Muses (or "Museum"), was an ancient "think tank" that housed both scholars and books. At the rival library of Pergamon (with some 200,000 books), scribes prepared sheepskin to produce "pergamene paper," that is, parchment, the medium that would be used for centuries of manuscript production prior to the dissemination of paper. Textual criticism and the editing of Classical manuscripts produced the scholarly

Figure 5.28 Head of Alexander, from Pergamon, Hellenistic portrait, ca. 200 B.C.E. Marble, height 16 in.

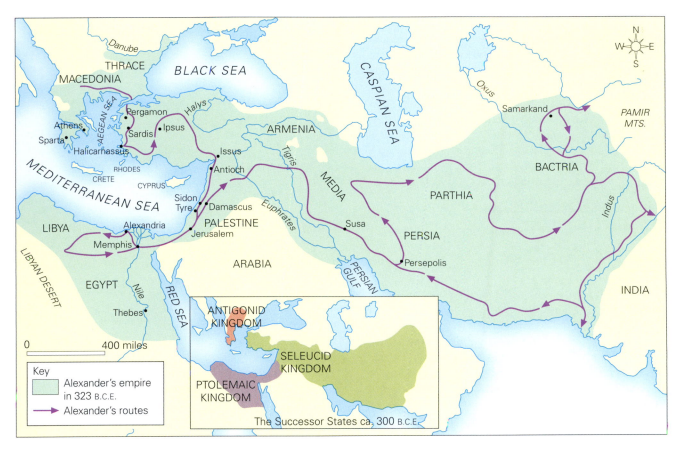

Map 5.1 The Hellenistic World. The cities of Pergamon, Antioch, and Alexandria were vital urban centers of Alexander's empire, which broke into three successor states (located in the regions of Greece, Egypt, and Persia) after Alexander's death.

editions of Homer's epics and other classics that would be passed on to generations of Western readers.

The Hellenistic Age made important advances in geography, astronomy, and mathematics. Euclid, who taught mathematics in Alexandria during the late fourth century B.C.E., produced a textbook of existing geometric learning that systematized the theorems of plane and solid geometry (see Figure 5.17). His contemporary, the astronomer Aristarchus of Samos, proposed that the earth and all the planets revolved around the sun, a theory abandoned by his followers and not confirmed until the seventeenth century.

Archimedes of Syracuse, who flourished a century later, calculated the value of *pi* (the ratio of the circumference of a circle to its diameter). An engineer as well as a mathematician, he invented the compound pulley, a windlass for moving heavy weights, and many other mechanical devices. "Give me a place to stand," he is said to have boasted, "and I shall move the earth." Legend describes Archimedes as the typical absent-minded scientist, who often forgot to eat; upon realizing that the water he displaced in his bathtub explained the law of specific gravity, he is said to have jumped out of the bathtub and run naked through the streets of Syracuse, shouting "*Eureka*" ("I have found it!").

Hellenistic Schools of Thought

The Hellenistic world was considerably different from the world of the Greek city-states. In the latter, citizens identified with their community, which was itself the state; but in Alexander's vast empire, communal loyalties were unsteady and—especially in sprawling urban centers—impersonal. The intellectuals of the Hellenistic Age did not formulate rational methods of investigation in the style of Plato and Aristotle; rather they espoused philosophic schools of thought that guided everyday existence: Skepticism, Cynicism, Epicureanism, and Stoicism.

The Skeptics—much like the Sophists of Socrates' time—denied the possibility of knowing anything with certainty: they argued for the suspension of all intellectual judgment. The Cynics held that spiritual satisfaction was only possible if one renounced societal values, conventions, and material wealth. The Epicureans, followers of

the Greek thinker Epicurus (341–270 B.C.E.), taught that happiness depended on avoiding all forms of physical excess; they valued plain living and the perfect union of body and mind. Epicurus held that the gods played no part in human life, and that death was nothing more than the rearrangement of atoms of which the body and all of nature consisted. Finally, the Stoics found tranquility of mind in a doctrine of detachment that allowed them to accept even the worst of life's circumstances. The aim of the Stoic was to bring the individual will into complete harmony with the will of nature, which they believed was governed by an impersonal intelligence. Stoicism, which became increasingly influential among Roman intellectuals (see chapter 6), also advanced the notion of universal equality. All four of these schools of thought placed the personal needs and emotions of the individual over and above the good of the community at large; in this, they constituted a practical and radical departure from the Hellenic quest for universal truth.

Hellenistic Art

The shift from city-state to empire that accompanied the advent of the Hellenistic Era was reflected in larger, more monumental forms of architecture and in the construction of utilitarian structures, such as lighthouses, theaters, and libraries. Circular sanctuaries and colossal Corinthian temples with triumphant decorative friezes were particularly popular in the fourth century B.C.E. and thereafter. At Pergamon (see Map **5.1**) stood the largest sculptural complex in the ancient world: the Altar of Zeus (Figure **5.29**). Erected around 180 B.C.E. to celebrate the victory of the minor kingdom of Pergamon over the invading tribal Gauls, achieved some fifty years earlier, the altar stands atop a 20-foot-high platform enclosed by an Ionic

Figure 5.29 The Altar of Zeus (reconstructed), Pergamon, ca. 175 B.C.E. Marble. Dedicated to Zeus and Athena, the Great Altar once stood on a hillside above the city. It has been reconstructed by the Pergamon Museum in Berlin. The theatrical stairway ascends some 30 feet to the shrine at the top.

colonnade. A massive stairway reaches upward to the shrine. Around the base of the platform runs a 300-foot-long sculptured frieze depicting the mythological battle between the Olympic gods and the race of giants known as Titans. Its subject matter, alluding to Pergamon's victory over the Gauls (hence, the victory of civilization over barbarism), recalls the program of the Parthenon metopes. However, both the altar and the frieze are far more theatrical in style than anything created in Classical Greece. The drama of the structure itself, which more resembles a stage than a temple, is made emphatic in the frieze, where colossal high-relief figures writhe in rhythmic patterns, engaging one another in fierce combat. The goddess Athena, some 7 feet tall, grasps by the hair a serpent-tailed male, the son of the Earth Mother who rises from the ground on

the lower right (Figure **5.30**). The deeply cut figures produce strong light and dark contrasts; indeed, some seem to break free of the architectural frame. In the Altar of Zeus, Classical restraint has given way to violent passion.

Hellenistic artists brought a similar kind of dramatic energy to mosaics, a medium that employs small bits of colored stone, glass, or marble (see Figure 1.6). Using mosaics as a permanent waterproof medium for walls and floors, they often copied earlier paintings that ornamented homes and palaces. Violent action dominates the turbulent narrative rendering of Alexander's confrontation with the king of Persia at the Battle of Issos (Figure **5.31**). Realistic details, radical foreshortening (note the foreground horse), and careful shading bring the scene vividly and illusionistically to life.

Figure 5.30 Athena battling with Acyoneus, from the frieze of the Altar of Zeus, Pergamon, ca. 180 B.C.E. Marble, height 7 ft. 6 in.

Figure 5.31 *Alexander the Great Confronts Darius III at the Battle of Issos,* detail of a mosaic floor decoration from Pompeii, Italy. First century C.E. Roman copy after a Hellenistic painting of ca. 310 B.C.E. Alexander appears heroically at left, with no helmet, windblown hair, and bare neck.

In free-standing Hellenistic sculpture, the new emphasis on personal emotion gave rise to portraits that were more lifelike and less idealized than those of the Hellenic era. A marble portrait of the ruler Alexander (see Figure 5.28) manifests the new effort to capture fleeting mood and momentary expression.

Hellenistic art is also notable for its celebration of the female nude figure, which, in the tradition of Praxiteles, became an iconic symbol of erotic love (see Figure 5.14). Equally sensuous, however, is the Hellenistic treatment of the male nude, the most famous example of which is the statue known as the *Apollo Belvedere* (Figure 5.32). This Roman copy of a Hellenistic statue was destined to exercise a major influence in Western art from the moment it was recovered in Rome in 1503. A comparison of the *Apollo* with its Hellenic counterpart, the *Spear-Bearer* (see Figure 5.2), reveals the transition from the contained movement of the High Classical style to the more animated, feminized expressionism of the Hellenistic Era.

Moving toward greater naturalism, Hellenistic sculptors broadened the range of subjects to include the young, the elderly, and even deformed people. They refined the long tradition of technical virtuosity in Greek sculpture by introducing new carving techniques that yielded complex patterns of light and dark, dramatic displays of vigorous movement, and a wide range of expressive details. These features are evident in the larger-than-life **Nike** (the Greek personification of victory) erected at Rhodes to celebrate a naval triumph over Syria (Figure 5.33). The deeply cut drapery of the *Nike of Samothrace* clings sensuously to the body as the figure strides, wings extended, into the wind like some gigantic ship's figurehead.

The work that best sums up the Hellenistic aesthetic is *Laocoön and His Sons* (Figure 5.34). This monumental sculpture recreates the dramatic moment, famous in Greek legend, when Laocoön (Trojan priest of Apollo)

and his two sons succumb to the strangling attack of sea serpents (sent by gods friendly to the Achaeans) to punish him for his effort to warn the Trojans of the Greek ruse: a wooden horse filled with Achaean soldiers who would destroy Troy and bring an end to the Trojan War.

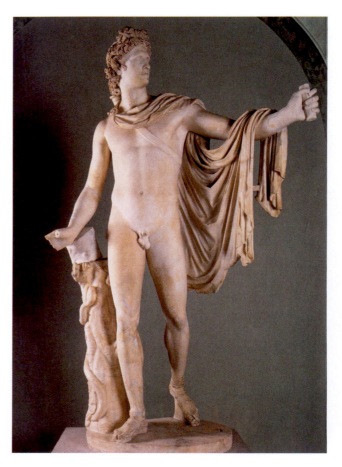

Figure 5.32 *Apollo Belvedere.* Roman marble copy of a Greek original, late fourth century B.C.E. Height 7ft. 4in.

The writing limbs, strained muscles, and anguished expressions of the doomed family contribute to a sense of turbulence and agitation that departs from the dignified restraint of Hellenic art. Indeed, the *Laocoön* is the landmark of an age in which Classical Idealism had already become part of history.

Figure 5.33 PYTHOCRITOS OF RHODES, *Nike of Samothrace*, ca. 190 B.C.E. Marble, height 8 ft.

Figure 5.34 AGESANDER, **POLYDORUS**, and **ATHENODORUS OF RHODES**, *Laocoön and His Sons*, second to first century B.C.E. or a Roman copy of first century C.E. Marble, height 7 ft. 10½ in. Unearthed in 1506, the sculpture had an enormous influence on Michelangelo and other High Renaissance sculptors (see chapter 17). The piece is not carved out of a single block of marble, as was claimed by the Roman writer Pliny the Elder.

LOOKING BACK

The Classical Style

- Classical style reflects the Hellenic quest for rational laws of proportion, order, clarity, and balance.
- The Classical style is characterized by Humanism, a this-worldly belief in the dignity and inherent worth of human beings; by Realism, or fidelity to nature; and by Idealism, that is, the commitment to an underlying standard of perfection.
- The human body and human experience, as evidenced in Greek vase-paintings and in multiple sculptures of the Classical nude, are central to the art of Classical Greece.

The Evolution of the Classical Style

- A study of Greek statuary from the Archaic through the Late Classical Age reflects increasing refinements in Realism and Idealism: all imperfections have been purged in favor of radiant flawlessness. In the Classical nude figure, Hellenic sculptors achieved a balance between realistic and idealized form.
- The monument that best mirrors the Classical style is the Parthenon, the Greek temple built atop the Acropolis to honor Athens' patron goddess of wisdom and war. The Parthenon is notable for its application of the Doric order, the integration of geometric and technical refinements, and the intelligent use of architectural decoration.

The Classical Style in Poetry

- The lyric poetry of Sappho and Pindar makes the human being the measure of earthly experience.
- Sappho conveys deep personal feelings with elegant economy of expression.
- The odes of Pindar celebrate the athletes who competed at the games held in Olympia and elsewhere. Pindar's odes make the claim that ability, not chance, leads to victory, which in turn renders the victor immortal.

The Classical Style in Music and Dance

- In Greek music, where the clarity of the single line of melody prevails, modal patterns of pitch and tempo were held to influence the moral condition of the listener.
- Although music played a major role in Greek life, we know very little about Greek music apart from written and visual descriptions of musical performances, a few remaining treatises on music theory, and some primitively notated musical works.

The Diffusion of the Classical Style: The Hellenistic Age (323–30 B.C.E.)

- During the fourth century B.C.E., Alexander the Great spread Greek language and culture throughout a vast empire that extended from Macedonia to India.
- Metaphysics gave way to practical philosophies such as Skepticism, Cynicism, Epicureanism, and Stoicism; and scientific advances in astronomy, geography, and mathematics were made by Archimedes, Euclid, and others.
- Cosmopolitanism, urbanism, and the blending of Greek, African, and Asian cultures were defining features of the Hellenistic Age. Monumental forms of architecture and utilitarian structures, such as libraries and lighthouses, became landmarks of this era.
- While the Classical style spread to other parts of Asia, Hellenistic art moved toward detailed Realism and melodramatic expressiveness.

Music Listening Selection

- Anonymous, "Epitaph for Seikilos," Greek, ca. 50 C.E.

Glossary

aulos a wind instrument used in ancient Greece; it had a double reed (held inside the mouth) and a number of finger holes and was always played in pairs, that is, with the performer holding one in each hand; a leather band was often tied around the head to support the cheeks, thus enabling the player to blow harder (see Figure 5.6)

contrapposto (Italian, "counterpoised") a position assumed by the human body in which one part is turned in opposition to another part

frieze in architecture, a sculptured or ornamented band

gable the triangular section of a wall at the end of a pitched roof

hymn a lyric poem offering divine praise or glorification

kithara a large version of the lyre (having seven to eleven strings) and the principal instrument of ancient Greek music

kouros (Greek, "youth"; plural *kouroi*) a youthful male figure, usually depicted nude in ancient Greek sculpture; the female counterpart is the *kore* (Greek, "maiden"; plural *korai*)

metope the square panel between the beam ends under the roof of a structure (see Figure 5.17)

mode a type of musical scale characterized by a fixed pattern of pitch and tempo within the octave; because the Greeks associated each of the modes with a different emotional state, it is likely that the mode involved something more than a particular musical scale—perhaps a set of rhythms and melodic turns associated with each scale pattern

monophony (Greek, "one voice") a musical texture consisting of a single, unaccompanied line of melody

Nike the Greek goddess of victory

octave the series of eight tones forming any major or minor scale

ode a lyric poem expressing exalted emotion in honor of a person or a special occasion

order in Classical architecture, the parts of a building that stand in fixed and constant relation to one another; the three Classical orders are the Doric, the Ionic, and the Corinthian (see Figure 5.19)

pediment the triangular space forming the gable of a two-pitched roof in Classical architecture; any similar triangular form found over a portico, door, or window

portico a porch with a roof supported by columns

scale (Latin, *scala*, "ladder") a series of tones arranged in ascending or descending consecutive order; the *diatonic* scale, characteristic of Western music, consists of the eight tones (or series of notes C, D, E, F, G, A, B, C) of the twelve-tone octave; the *chromatic* scale consists of all twelve tones (represented by the twelve piano keys, seven white and five black) of the octave, each a semitone apart

tholos a circular structure, generally in Classical Greek style and probably derived from early tombs

Chapter

6

Rome: The Rise to Empire

ca. 1000 B.C.E.–476 C.E.

". . . remember, Roman,
To rule the people under law, to establish
The way of peace, to battle down the haughty,
To spare the meek. Our fine arts, these forever."
Virgil

Figure 6.1 Detail from Trajan's Victory Column, Rome, 113 C.E. Marble. The 625-foot-long continuous frieze that documents the two Balkan campaigns of the Roman emperor Trajan resembles a documentary war film. The pictorial narrative, in which Trajan appears fifty-nine times, features realistic depictions of the military activities for which the Romans were famous, but it also includes scenes of comradery and suffering (see Figure 6.20).

"In the second century of the Christian Era, the empire of Rome comprehended the fairest part of the earth, and the most civilized portion of mankind. The frontiers of that extensive monarchy were guarded by ancient renown and disciplined valor. The gentle, but powerful, influence of laws and manners had gradually cemented the union of the provinces." So wrote the eighteenth-century historian Edward Gibbon, who voiced universal and abiding respect for the longest-lasting and most complex empire in Western history.

The rise and fall of the Roman Empire is too long a story to be told in these pages. Rather, this chapter explores Rome's imperial presence in Classical antiquity and its enduring contributions in architecture, the visual arts, literature, and law. Along with these achievements, the Romans would transmit to the West the legacy of Classical Greece and the fundamentals of a young religious faith called Christianity.

The Roman Rise to Empire

Rome's Early History

Rome's origins are to be found among tribes of Iron Age folk called Latins, who invaded the Italian peninsula just after the beginning of the first millennium B.C.E. By the mid-eighth century B.C.E., these people had founded the city of Rome in the lower valley of the Tiber River, a spot strategically located for control of the Italian peninsula and for convenient access to the Mediterranean Sea (Map 6.1). While central Italy became the domain of the Latins, the rest of the peninsula received a continuous infusion of eastern Mediterranean people—Etruscans, Greeks, and Phoenicians—who brought with them cultures richer and more complex than that of the Latins. The Etruscans, whose origins are unknown, established themselves in northwest Italy. A sophisticated, Hellenized people with commercial contacts throughout the Mediterranean, they

were experts in the arts of metallurgy, town building, and city planning. The Greeks, who colonized the tip of the Italian peninsula and Sicily, were masters of philosophy and the arts. The Phoenicians, who settled on the northern coast of Africa, brought westward their alphabet and their commercial and maritime skills. From all these people, but especially from the first two groups, the Latins borrowed elements that would enhance their own history.

From the Etruscans, the Romans absorbed the fundamentals of urban planning, chariot racing, the toga, bronze- and gold-crafting, and the most ingenious structural principle of Mesopotamian architecture—the arch. Roman numerals were based on an Etruscan system that was borrowed in turn from the Greeks. And from Etruscan tradition came one of Rome's founding myths by which the twin sons of Mars, Romulus and Remus—abandoned on the Tiber River but suckled by a she-wolf—established the city of Rome in 753 B.C.E. The Etruscans provided their

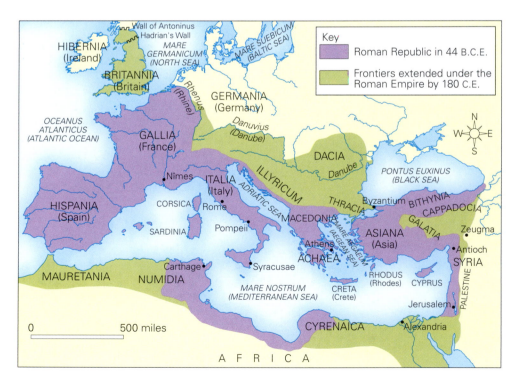

Map 6.1 The Roman Empire in 180 C.E.

Figure 6.2 Sarcophagus from Cerveteri, ca. 520 B.C.E. Painted terracotta, length 6 ft. 7 in. The hands of the couple are positioned in a manner that suggests they are enjoying lively conversation.

dead with tombs designed to resemble the lavish dwelling places of the deceased. On the lids of the **sarcophagi** (stone coffins) that held the remains, Etruscan artists carved portraits of the dead, depicting husbands and wives relaxing and socializing on their dining couch, as if still enjoying a family banquet (Figure **6.2**).

From the Greeks, the Romans borrowed a pantheon of gods and goddesses, linguistic and literary principles, and the aesthetics of the Classical style. A passion for Greek art made the Romans collectors and imitators of Hellenic sculpture; Roman copies of Greek art would fill palaces and public places. As the Latins absorbed Etruscan and Greek culture, so they drew these and other peoples into what would become the most powerful world-state in ancient history.

The Roman Republic (509–133 B.C.E.)

For three centuries, Etruscan kings ruled the Latin population, but in 509 B.C.E. the Latins overthrew the Etruscans. Over the next 200 years, monarchy slowly gave way to a government "of the people" (*res publica*). The agricultural population of ancient Rome consisted of a powerful class of large landowners, the *patricians*, and a more populous class of farmers and small landowners called *plebeians*. The plebeians constituted the membership of a Popular Assembly. Although this body conferred civil and military authority (the *imperium*) upon two elected magistrates (called *consuls*), its lower-class members had little voice in government. The wealthy patricians—life members of the Roman Senate—controlled the lawmaking process. But step by step, the plebeians gained increasing political influence. Using as leverage their service as soldiers in the Roman army and their power to veto laws initiated by the Senate, the plebeians—through their leaders, the *tribunes*—made themselves heard. Eventually, they won the freedom to intermarry with the patricians, the right

to hold executive office, and, finally, in 287 B.C.E., the privilege of making laws. The stern and independent population of Roman farmers had arrived at a *res publica* by peaceful means. But no sooner had Rome become a Republic than it adopted an expansionist course that would erode these democratic achievements.

Obedience to the Roman state and service in its powerful army were essential to the life of the early Republic. Both contributed to the rise of Roman imperialism, which proceeded by means of long wars of conquest similar to those that had marked the history of earlier empires. After expelling the last of the Etruscan kings, Rome extended its power over all parts of the Italian peninsula. By the middle of the third century B.C.E., having united all of Italy by force or negotiation, Rome stood poised to rule the Mediterranean.

A long-standing distrust of the Phoenicians and rivalry with the city of Carthage, Phoenicia's commercial stronghold in northeastern Africa, led Rome into the Punic (Latin for "Phoenician") Wars—a 150-year period of intermittent violence that ended with the destruction of Carthage in 146 B.C.E. With the defeat of that city, Rome assumed naval and commercial leadership in the western Mediterranean, the sea they would come to call *mare nostrum* ("our sea"). But the ambitions of army generals and the impetus of a century of warfare fueled the fire of Roman imperialism. Rome seized every opportunity for conquest, and by the end of the first century B.C.E., the Empire included most of North Africa, the Iberian peninsula, Greece, Egypt, much of Southwest Asia, and the territories constituting present-day Europe as far as the Rhine River (see Map 6.1).

Despite the difficulties presented by the task of governing such far-flung territories, the Romans proved to be efficient administrators. They demanded from their foreign provinces taxes, soldiers to serve in the Roman army, tribute, and slaves. Roman governors, appointed by the Senate from among the higher ranks of the military, ruled within the conquered provinces. Usually, local customs and even local governments were permitted to continue unmodified, for the Romans considered tolerance of provincial customs politically practical. The Romans brought the Latin language and Roman law to the provinces. They built paved roads, freshwater aqueducts, and bridges, and eventually granted the people of their conquered territories Roman citizenship.

Rome's highly disciplined army was the backbone of the Empire. During the Republic, the army consisted of citizens who served two-year terms, but by the first century C.E., the military had become a profession to which all free men might devote twenty-five years (or more) of their lives. Since serving for this length of time allowed a non-Roman to gain Roman citizenship for himself and his children, military service acted as a means of Romanizing foreigners. The Roman army was the object of fear and admiration among those familiar with Rome's rise to power. Josephus (ca. 37–100 C.E.), a Jewish historian who witnessed the Roman destruction of Jerusalem in 70 C.E., described the superiority of the Roman military machine, which he estimated to include more than 300,000 armed men. According to Josephus, Roman soldiers performed as though they "had been born with weapons in their hands." The efficiency of the army, he reported, was the consequence of superior organization and discipline. The following description of a Roman military camp reflects the admiration and awe with which non-Romans viewed Roman might. It also describes the nature of that "perfect discipline" and dedication to duty that characterized the Roman ethos and Roman culture in general.

READING 6.1 Josephus' *Description of the Roman Army* (ca. 70 C.E.)

. . . one cannot but admire the forethought shown in this particular by the Romans, in making their servant class useful to them not only for the ministrations of ordinary life but also for war. If one goes on to study the organization of their army as a whole, it will be seen that this vast empire of theirs has come to them as the prize of valor, and not as a gift of fortune. [1]

For their nation does not wait for the outbreak of war to give men their first lesson on arms; they do not sit with folded hands in peacetime only to put them in motion in the hour of need. On the contrary, as though they had been born with [10] weapons in hand, they never have a truce from training, never wait for emergencies to arise. Moreover, their peace maneuvers are no less strenuous than veritable warfare; each soldier daily throws all his energy into his drill, as though he were in action. Hence that perfect ease with which they sustain the shock of battle: no confusion breaks their customary formation, no panic paralyzes, no fatigue exhausts them; and as their opponents cannot match these qualities, victory is the invariable and certain consequence. Indeed, it would not be wrong to describe their maneuvers as bloodless [20] combats and combats as sanguinary maneuvers.

The Romans never lay themselves open to a surprise attack; for, whatever hostile territory they may invade, they engage in no battle until they have fortified their camp. This camp is not erected at random or unevenly; they do not all work at once or in disorderly parties; if the ground is uneven, it is first leveled; a site for the camp is then measured out in the form of a square. For this purpose the army is accompanied by a multitude of workmen and of tools for building.

The interior of the camp is divided into rows of tents. [30] The exterior circuit presents the appearance of a wall and is furnished with towers at regular intervals; and on the spaces between the towers are placed "quick-firers," catapults, "stone-throwers," and every variety of artillery engines, all ready for use. In this surrounding wall are set four gates, one on each side, spacious enough for beasts of burden to enter without difficulty and wide enough for sallies of troops in emergencies. The camp is intersected by streets symmetrically

laid out; in the middle are the tents of the officers, and precisely in the center the headquarters of the commander-in-chief, resembling a small temple. Thus, as it were, an [40] improvised city springs up, with its marketplace, its artisan quarter, its seats of judgment, where captains and colonels adjudicate upon any differences which may arise. . . .

Once entrenched, the soldiers take up their quarters in their tents by companies, quietly and in good order. All their fatigue duties are performed with the same discipline, the same regard for security; the procuring of wood, food-supplies, and water, as required—each party has its allotted task. . . . The same precision is maintained on the battlefield: the troops [50] wheel smartly round in the requisite direction, and, whether advancing to the attack or retreating, all move as a unit at the word of command.

When the camp is to be broken up, the trumpet sounds a first call; at that none remain idle: instantly, at this signal, they strike the tents and make all ready for departure. The trumpets sound a second call to prepare for the march: at once they pile their baggage on the mules and other beasts of burden and stand ready to start, like runners breasting the cord on the race-course. They then set fire to the encampment, both [60] because they can easily construct another [on the spot], and to prevent the enemy from ever making use of it. . . .

Then they advance, all marching in silence and in good order, each man keeping his place in the ranks, as if in face of the enemy. . . . By their military exercises the Romans instill into their soldiers fortitude not only of body but also of soul; fear, too, plays its part in their training. For they have laws which punish with death not merely desertion of the ranks, but even a slight neglect of duty; and their generals are held in even greater awe than the laws. For the high honors with [70] which they reward the brave prevent the offenders whom they punish from regarding themselves as treated cruelly.

This perfect discipline makes the army an ornament of peacetime and in war welds the whole into a single body; so compact are their ranks, so alert their movements in wheeling to right or left, so quick their ears for orders, their eyes for signals, their hands to act upon them. Prompt as they consequently ever are in action, none are slower than they in succumbing to suffering, and never have they been known in any predicament to be beaten by numbers, by ruse, by [80] difficulties of ground, or even by fortune; for they have more assurance of victory than of fortune. Where counsel thus precedes active operations, where the leaders' plan of campaign is followed up by so efficient an army, no wonder that the Empire has extended its boundaries on the east to the Euphrates, on the west to the ocean,[1] on the south to the most fertile tracts of Libya, on the north to the Ister[2] and the Rhine. One might say without exaggeration that, great as are their possessions, the people that won them are greater still. . . .

Q **What, according to Josephus, are the admirable features of the Roman army?**

---

[1] The Atlantic.
[2] The Roman name for the Danube River.

The Collapse of the Republic (133–30 B.C.E.)

By the beginning of the first millennium C.E., Rome had become the watchdog of the ancient world. Roman imperialism, however, worked to effect changes within the Republic itself. By its authority to handle all military matters, the Senate became increasingly powerful, as did a new class of men, wealthy Roman entrepreneurs (known as *equestrians*), who filled the jobs of provincial administration. The army, by its domination of Rome's overseas provinces, also became more powerful. Precious metals, booty, and slaves from foreign conquests brought enormous wealth to army generals and influential patricians; corruption became widespread. Captives of war were shipped back to Rome and auctioned off to the highest bidders, usually patrician landowners, whose farms soon became large-scale plantations (*latifundia*) worked by slaves. The increased agricultural productivity of the *latifundia* gave economic advantage to large landowners who easily undersold the lesser landowners and drove them out of business. Increasingly, the small farmers were forced to sell their farms to neighboring patricians in return for the right to remain on the land. Or, they simply moved to the city to join, by the end of the first century B.C.E., a growing unemployed population. The disappearance of the small farmer signaled the decline of the Republic.

While Rome's rich citizens grew richer and its poor citizens poorer, the patricians fiercely resisted efforts to redistribute wealth more equally. But reform measures failed and political rivalries increased. Ultimately, Rome fell victim to the ambitions of army generals, who, having conquered in the name of Rome, now turned to conquering Rome itself. The first century B.C.E. was an age of military dictators, whose competing claims to power fueled a spate of civil wars. As bloody confrontations replaced reasoned compromises, the Republic crumbled.

In 46 B.C.E., an extraordinary army commander named Gaius Julius Caesar (Figure **6.3**) triumphantly entered the city of Rome and established a dictatorship. Caesar, who had spent nine years conquering Gaul (present-day France and Belgium), was as shrewd in politics as he was brilliant in war. These campaigns are described in his prose *Commentaries on the Gallic War*. His brief but successful campaigns in Syria, Asia Minor, and Egypt—where his union with the Egyptian queen Cleopatra (69–30 B.C.E.) produced a son—inspired his famous boast: *veni, vidi, vici* ("I came, I saw, I conquered"). A superb organizer, Caesar took strong measures to restabilize Rome: he codified the

Figure 6.3 Bust of Julius Caesar, first century B.C.E. Green schist, height 16⅛ in.

laws, regulated taxation, reduced debts, sent large numbers of the unemployed proletariat to overseas colonies, and inaugurated public works projects. He laid out Rome's first urban center: the Forum, a public meeting place that combined the functions of government, law, commerce, and religion, which would be enlarged and embellished by his imperial followers. Caesar granted citizenship to non-Italians and reformed the Western calendar to comprise 365 days and twelve months (one of which—July—he named after himself). Threatened by Caesar's populist reforms and his contempt for republican institutions, a group of his senatorial opponents, led by Marcus Junius Brutus, assassinated him in 44 B.C.E. Despite his inglorious death, the name *Caesar* would be used as an honorific title by all his imperial successors well into the second century C.E., as well as by many modern-day dictators.

The Roman Empire (30 B.C.E.–180 C.E.)

Following the assassination of Julius Caesar, a struggle for power ensued between Caesar's first lieutenant, Mark Anthony (ca. 80–30 B.C.E.), and his grandnephew (and adopted son) Octavian (63 B.C.E.–14 C.E.). The contest between the two was resolved at Actium in 31 B.C.E., when Octavian's navy routed the combined forces of Mark Anthony and Queen Cleopatra. The alliance between Anthony and Cleopatra, like that between Cleopatra and Julius Caesar, advanced the political ambitions of Egypt's most seductive queen, who sought not only to unite the eastern and western portions of Rome's great empire, but also to govern a vast Roman world-state. That destiny, however, would fall to Octavian. In 43 B.C.E., Octavian usurped the consulship and gained the approval of the Senate to rule for life. Although he called himself "first citizen" (*princeps*), his title of Emperor betrayed the reality that he was first and foremost Rome's army general (*imperator*). The Senate, however, bestowed on him the title *Augustus* ("the Revered One"). Augustus shared legislative power with the Senate, but retained the right to veto legislation. Thus, to all intents and purposes, the Republic was defunct. The future of Rome lay once again in the hands of a military dictator. It is in this guise that Augustus appears in Roman sculpture (Figure **6.4**).

In this free-standing, larger-than-life statue from Primaporta, Octavian raises his arm in a gesture of leadership and imperial authority. He wears a breastplate celebrating his victory over the Parthians in 20 B.C.E. At his feet appear Cupid and a dolphin, reminders of his alleged divine descent from Venus—the mother of Aeneas, Rome's legendary founder. Octavian's stance and physical proportions are modeled on the *Doryphorus* by Polycleitus (see Figure 5.2).

Figure 6.4 Augustus of Primaporta, early first century C.E., after a bronze of ca. 20 B.C.E. Marble, height 6 ft. 8 in.

His handsome face and tall, muscular physique serve to complete the heroic image. In reality, however, the emperor was only 5 feet 4 inches tall—the average height of the Roman male.

Augustus' reign ushered in an era of peace and stability, a *Pax Romana*; from 30 B.C.E. to 180 C.E., the Roman peace prevailed throughout the Empire, and Rome enjoyed active commercial contact with all parts of the civilized world, including India and China. Augustus tried to arrest the tide of moral decay that had swept into Rome: in an effort to restore family values and the begetting of legitimate children, he passed laws (which ultimately failed in their purpose) to curb adultery and to prevent bachelors from receiving inheritances.

The *Pax Romana* was also a time of artistic and literary productivity. An enthusiastic patron of the arts, Augustus commissioned literature, sculpture, and architecture. He boasted that he had come to power when Rome was a city of brick and would leave it a city of marble. In most cases, this meant a veneer of marble that was, by standard Roman building practices, laid over the brick surface. In a city blighted by crime, noise, poor hygiene, and a frequent scarcity of food and water, Augustus initiated many new public works (including three new aqueducts and

Principal Roman Emperors

The Julio-Claudian Dynasty

27 B.C.E.–14 C.E.	Augustus
14–37	Tiberius
37–41	Gaius Caligula
41–54	Claudius
54–68	Nero

The Flavian Dynasty

68–79	Vespasian
79–81	Titus
81–96	Domitian

The "Good Emperors"

96–98	Nerva
97–117	Trajan
117–138	Hadrian
138–161	Antoninus Pius
161–180	Marcus Aurelius

Beginning of Decline

180–192	Commodus

The Severan Dynasty

193–211	Septimius Severus
211–217	Caracalla
222–235	Alexander Severus
235–284	Anarchy
284–305	Diocletian
306–337	Constantine I

some 500 fountains) and such civic services as a police force and a fire department. The reign of Octavian also witnessed the birth of a new religion, Christianity, which, in later centuries, would spread throughout the Empire (see chapters 8 and 9).

Augustus put an end to the civil wars of the preceding century, but he revived neither the political nor the social equilibrium of the early Republic. Following his death, Rome continued to be ruled by military officials. Since there was no machinery for succession to the imperial throne, Rome's rulers held office until they either died or were assassinated. Of the twenty-six emperors who governed Rome during the fifty-year period between 335 and 385 C.E., only one died a natural death. Government by and for the people had been the hallmark of Rome's early history, but the enterprise of imperialism ultimately overtook these lofty republican ideals.

Roman Law

Against this backdrop of conquest and dominion, it is no surprise that Rome's contributions to the humanistic tradition were practical rather than theoretical. The sheer size of the Roman Empire inspired engineering programs, such as bridge and road building, that united all regions under Roman rule. Law—a less tangible means of unification—was equally important in this regard. The development of a system of law was one of Rome's most original and influential achievements.

Roman law (the Latin *jus* means both "law" and "justice") evolved out of the practical need to rule a world-state, rather than—as in ancient Greece—as the product of a dialectic between the citizen and the *polis*. Inspired by the laws of Solon, the Romans published their first civil code, the Twelve Tables of Law, in 450 B.C.E. They placed these laws on view in the Forum. The Twelve Tables of Law provided Rome's basic legal code for almost a thousand years. To this body of law were added the acts of the Assembly and the Senate, and public decrees of the emperors. For some 500 years, *praetors* (magistrates who administered justice) and *jurisconsults* (experts in the law) interpreted the laws, bringing commonsense resolutions to private disputes. Their interpretations constituted a body of "case law." In giving consideration to individual needs, these magistrates cultivated the concept of equity, which puts the spirit of the law above the letter of the law. The decisions of Roman jurists became precedents that established comprehensive guidelines for future judgments. Thus, Roman law was not fixed, but was an evolving body of opinions on the nature and dispensation of justice.

Early in Roman history, the law of the land (*jus civile*) applied only to Roman citizens, but as Roman citizenship was extended to the provinces, so too was the law. Law that embraced a wider range of peoples and customs, the law of the people (*jus gentium*), assumed an international quality that acknowledged compromises between conflicting customs and traditions. The law of the people was, in effect, a law based on universal principles, that is, the law of nature (*jus naturale*). The full body of Roman law came to incorporate the decisions of the jurists, the acts passed by Roman legislative assemblies, and the edicts of Roman emperors. In the sixth century C.E., 200 years after the division of the Empire into eastern and western portions and a hundred years after the collapse of Rome, the Byzantine (East Roman) emperor Justinian would codify this huge body of law, thereafter known as the *Corpus Juris Civilis*. The Roman system of law influenced the development of codified law in all European countries with the exception of England.

The Roman Contribution to Literature

Roman Philosophic Thought

Roman contributions to law were numerous, but such was not the case with philosophy. More a practical than a speculative people, the Romans produced no systems of philosophic thought comparable to those of Plato and Aristotle. However, they preserved the writings of Hellenic and Hellenistic thinkers. Educated Romans admired Aristotle and absorbed the works of the Epicureans and the Stoics. The Latin poet Lucretius (ca. 95–ca. 55 B.C.E.) popularized the materialist theories of Democritus and Leucippus, which describe the world in purely physical terms, denying the existence of the gods and other supernatural beings. Since all of reality, including the human soul, consists of atoms, Lucretius argues in his only work, *On the Nature of Things*, there is no reason to fear death: "We shall not feel because we shall not be."

In the vast, impersonal world of the Empire, many Romans cultivated the attitude of rational detachment popular among the Stoics (see chapter 5). Like their third-century B.C.E. forebears, Roman Stoics believed that an impersonal force (Providence or Divine Reason) governed the world, and that happiness lay in one's ability to accept the will of the universe. Stoics rejected any emotional attachments that might enslave them. The ideal spiritual condition and the one most conducive to contentment, according to the Stoic point of view, depends on self-control and the subjugation of the emotions to reason.

Science and Technology

312 B.C.E.	Consul Appius Claudius orders construction of the "Appian Way," the first in a strategic network of Roman roads
101 B.C.E.	the Romans use water power for milling grain
46 B.C.E.	Caesar inaugurates the "Julian Calendar," on which the modern calendar is based
77 C.E.	Pliny the Elder completes a 37-volume encyclopedia called *Natural History*, which summarized information about astronomy, geography, and zoology
79 C.E.	Pliny the Younger writes a detailed account of the eruption of Mount Vesuvius

The commonsense tenets of Stoicism encouraged the Roman sense of duty. At the same time, the Stoic belief in the equality of all people had a humanizing effect on Roman jurisprudence and anticipated the all-embracing direction of Early Christian thought (see chapter 8). Stoicism was especially popular among such intellectuals as the noted playwright and essayist Lucius Annaeus Seneca (ca. 4 B.C.E.–65 C.E.) and the emperor Marcus Aurelius (121–180 C.E.), both of whom wrote classic treatises on the subject. Seneca's *On Tranquility of Mind*, an excerpt from which follows, argues that one may achieve peace of mind by avoiding burdensome responsibilities, gloomy companions, and excessive wealth. Stoicism offered a reasoned retreat from psychic pain and moral despair, as well as a practical set of solutions to the daily strife between the self and society.

READING 6.2 From Seneca's *On Tranquility of Mind* (ca. 40 C.E.)

. . . our question, then, is how the mind can maintain a consistent and advantageous course, be kind to itself and take pleasure in its attributes, never interrupt this satisfaction but abide in its serenity, without excitement or depression. This amounts to tranquility. We shall inquire how it may be attained. . .

A correct estimate of self is prerequisite, for we are generally inclined to overrate our capacities. One man is tripped by confidence in his eloquence, another makes greater demands upon his estate than it can stand, another burdens a frail body with an exhausting office. Some are too bashful for politics, which requires aggressiveness; some are too headstrong for court; some do not control their temper and break into unguarded language at the slightest provocation; some cannot restrain their wit or resist making risky jokes. For all such people retirement is better than a career; an assertive and intolerant temperament should avoid incitements to outspokenness that will prove harmful.

Next we must appraise the career and compare our strength with the task we shall attempt. The worker must be stronger than his project; loads larger than the bearer must necessarily crush him. Certain careers, moreover, are not so demanding in themselves as they are prolific in begetting a mass of other activities. Enterprises which give rise to new and multifarious activities should be avoided; you must not commit yourself to a task from which there is no free egress. Put your hand to one you can finish or at least hope to finish; leave alone those that expand as you work at them and do not stop where you intend they should.

In our choice of men we should be particularly careful to see whether they are worth spending part of our life on and whether they will appreciate our loss of time; some people think we are in their debt if we do them a service. Athenadorus said he would not even go to dine with a man who would not feel indebted for his coming. Much less would he dine with people, as I suppose you understand, who discharge indebtedness for services rendered by giving a dinner and count the courses as favors, as if their lavishness

was a mark of honor to others. Take away witnesses and spectators and they will take no pleasure in secret gormandizing.

But nothing can equal the pleasures of faithful and congenial friendship. How good it is to have willing hearts as safe repositories for your every secret, whose privity[1] you fear less than your own, whose conversation allays your anxiety, whose counsel promotes your plans, whose cheerfulness dissipates your gloom, whose very appearance gives you joy! But we must choose friends who are, so far as possible, free from passions. Vices are contagious; they light upon whoever is nearest and infect by contact. During a plague we must be careful not to sit near people caught in the throes and burning with fever, because we would be courting danger and drawing poison in with our breath; just so in choosing friends we must pay attention to character and take those least tainted. To mingle the healthy with the sick is the beginning of disease. But I would not prescribe that you become attached to or attract no one who is not a sage. Where would you find him? We have been searching for him for centuries. Call the least bad man the best. You could not have a more opulent choice, if you were looking for good men, than among the Platos and Xenophons[2] and the famous Socratic brood, or if you had at your disposal the age of Cato,[3] which produced many characters worthy to be his contemporaries (just as it produced many unprecedentedly bad, who engineered monstrous crimes. Both kinds were necessary to make Cato's quality understood: he needed bad men against whom he could make his strength effective and good men to appreciate his effectiveness). But now there is a great dearth of good men, and your choice cannot be fastidious. But gloomy people who deplore everything and find reason to complain you must take pains to avoid. With all his loyalty and goodwill, a grumbling and touchy companion militates against tranquility.

We pass now to property, the greatest source of affliction to humanity. If you balance all our other troubles—deaths, diseases, fears, longings, subjection to labor and pain—with the miseries in which our money involves us, the latter will far outweigh the former. Reflect, then, how much less a grief it is not to have money than to lose it, and then you will realize that poverty has less to torment us with in the degree that it has less to lose. If you suppose that rich men take their losses with greater equanimity you are mistaken; a wound hurts a big man as much as it does a little. Bion[4] put it smartly: a bald man is as bothered when his hair is plucked as a man with a full head. The same applies to rich and poor, you may be sure; in either case the money is glued on and cannot be torn away without a twinge, so that both suffer alike. It is less distressing, as I have said, and easier not to acquire money than to lose it, and you will therefore notice that people upon whom Fortune never has smiled are more cheerful than those she has deserted. . . .

---

[1] Private or secret knowledge.
[2] Greek historian and biographer who lived ca. 428–354 B.C.E.
[3] Marcus Porcius Cato (234–149 B.C.E.), known as "the Censor," a Roman champion of austerity and simplicity.
[4] A Greek poet who lived around 100 B.C.E.

All life is bondage. Man must therefore habituate himself to his condition, complain of it as little as possible, and grasp whatever good lies within his reach. No situation is so harsh that a dispassionate mind cannot find some consolation in it. If a man lays even a very small area out skillfully it will provide ample space for many uses, and even a foothold can be made livable by deft arrangement. Apply good sense to your problems; the hard can be softened, the narrow widened, and the heavy made lighter by the skillful bearer. . . .

Q **How, according to Seneca, does one achieve "tranquility of mind"?**

Q **What, in his view, is humanity's greatest source of affliction?**

Latin Prose Literature

Roman literature reveals a masterful use of Latin prose for the purposes of entertainment, instruction, and record keeping. Applying knowledge to practical ends, the Romans found prose the ideal vehicle for compiling and transmitting information. Rome gave the West its first geographies and encyclopedias, as well as some of its finest biographies, histories, and manuals of instruction. In the writing of history, in particular, the Romans demonstrated their talent for the collection and analysis of factual evidence. Although Roman historians tended to glorify Rome and its leadership, their attention to accurate detail often surpassed that of the Greek historians. One of Rome's greatest historians, Titus Livius ("Livy," ca. 59 B.C.E.–17 C.E.), wrote a history of Rome from the eighth century B.C.E. to his own day. Although only a small portion of Livy's original 142 books survive, this monumental work—commissioned by Octavian himself—constitutes our most reliable account of political and social life in the days of the Roman Republic.

The Romans were masters, as well, of **oratory**, that is, the art of public speaking, and in the writing of **epistles** (letters). In both of these genres, the statesman Marcus Tullius Cicero (106–43 B.C.E.) excelled. A contemporary of Julius Caesar, Cicero produced more than 900 letters—sometimes writing three a day to the same person—and more than 100 speeches and essays. Clarity and eloquence are the hallmarks of Cicero's prose style, which Renaissance humanists hailed as the model for literary excellence (see chapter 16). Cicero was familiar with the theoretical works of Aristotle and the Stoics, but his letters reflect a profound concern for the practical realities of his own day. In his lifetime, Cicero served Rome as consul, statesman, and orator; his carefully reasoned speeches helped to shape public opinion. While he praised Julius Caesar's literary style, he openly opposed his patron's dictatorship. Nevertheless, Caesar congenially confessed to Cicero, "It is nobler to enlarge the boundaries of human intelligence than those of the Roman Empire." During the tumultuous years following Caesar's assassination, Cicero too was murdered, and his head and hands put on public display at the Forum. As we see in the following excerpt from his essay *On Duty*, Cicero considered public service the noblest of human activities—one that demanded the

exercise of personal courage equal to that required in military combat.

READING 6.3 From Cicero's *On Duty* (ca. 44 B.C.E.)

. . . that moral goodness which we look for in a lofty, high-minded spirit is secured, of course, by moral, not by physical, strength. And yet the body must be trained and so disciplined that it can obey the dictates of judgment and reason in attending to business and in enduring toil. But that moral goodness which is our theme depends wholly upon the thought and attention given to it by the mind. And, in this way, the men who in a civil capacity direct the affairs of the nation render no less important service than they who conduct its wars: by their statesmanship oftentimes wars are either [10] averted or terminated; sometimes also they are declared. Upon Marcus Cato's[1] counsel, for example, the Third Punic War was undertaken, and in its conduct his influence was dominant, even after he was dead. And so diplomacy in the friendly settlement of controversies is more desirable than courage in settling them on the battlefield; but we must be careful not to take that course merely for the sake of avoiding war rather than for the sake of public expediency. War, however, should be undertaken in such a way as to make it evident that it has no other object than to secure peace. [20]

But it takes a brave and resolute spirit not to be disconcerted in times of difficulty or ruffled and thrown off one's feet, as the saying is, but to keep one's presence of mind and one's self-possession and not to swerve from the path of reason.

Now all this requires great personal courage; but it calls also for great intellectual ability by reflection to anticipate the future, to discover some time in advance what may happen whether for good or for ill, and what must be done in any possible event, and never to be reduced to having to say [30] "I had not thought of that."

These are the activities that mark a spirit strong, high, and self-reliant in its prudence and wisdom. But to mix rashly in the fray and to fight hand to hand with the enemy is but a barbarous and brutish kind of business. Yet when the stress of circumstances demands it, we must gird on the sword and prefer death to slavery and disgrace.

As to destroying and plundering cities, let me say that great care should be taken that nothing be done in reckless cruelty or wantonness. And it is a great man's duty in troublous times [40] to single out the guilty for punishment, to spare the many, and in every turn of fortune to hold to a true and honorable course. For whereas there are many, as I have said before, who place the achievements of war above those of peace, so one may find many to whom adventurous, hot-headed counsels seem more brilliant and more impressive than calm and well-considered measures.

We must, of course, never be guilty of seeming cowardly and craven in our avoidance of danger; but we must also beware of exposing ourselves to danger needlessly. Nothing [50]

---

[1] The Roman senator Cato repeatedly demanded the total destruction of Carthage.

can be more foolhardy than that. Accordingly, in encountering danger we should do as doctors do in their practice: in light cases of illness they give mild treatment; in cases of dangerous sickness they are compelled to apply hazardous and even desperate remedies. It is, therefore, only a madman who, in a calm, would pray for a storm; a wise man's way is, when the storm does come, to withstand it with all the means at his command, and especially when the advantages to be expected in case of a successful issue are greater than the hazards of the struggle. 60

The dangers attending great affairs of state fall sometimes upon those who undertake them, sometimes upon the state. In carrying out such enterprises, some run the risk of losing their lives, others their reputation and the goodwill of their fellow-citizens. It is our duty, then, to be more ready to endanger our own than the public welfare and to hazard honor and glory more readily than other advantages. . . .

Q **According to Cicero, under what circumstances is war justified?**

Q **What are the main duties of a statesman?**

As Cicero suggests, Roman education emphasized civic duty. It aimed at training the young for active roles in civic life. For careers in law and political administration, the art of public speaking was essential. Indeed, in the provinces, where people of many languages mingled, oratory was the ultimate form of political influence. Since the art of public speaking was the distinctive mark of the educated Roman, the practical skills of grammar and rhetoric held an important place in Roman education. One of the greatest spokesmen for the significance of oratory in public affairs was the Roman historian and politician P. Cornelius Tacitus (ca. 56–120 C.E.). Tacitus' *Dialogue on Oratory* describes the role of public speaking in ancient Roman life. It bemoans the passing of a time when "eloquence not only led to great rewards, but was also a sheer necessity."

READING 6.4 From Tacitus' *Dialogue on Oratory*

(ca. 100–105 C.E.)

. . . great oratory is like a flame: it needs fuel to feed it, movement to fan it, and it brightens as it burns. 1

At Rome too the eloquence of our forefathers owed its development to [special] conditions. For although the orators of today have also succeeded in obtaining all the influence that it would be proper to allow them under settled, peaceable, and prosperous political conditions, yet their predecessors in those days of unrest and unrestraint thought they could accomplish more when, in the general ferment and without the strong hand of a single ruler, a speaker's political 10 wisdom was measured by his power of carrying conviction to the unstable populace. This was the source of the constant succession of measures put forward by champions of the people's rights, of the harangues of state officials who almost spent the night on the hustings,[1] of the impeachments of powerful criminals and hereditary feuds between whole

families, of schisms among the aristocracy and never-ending struggles between the senate and the commons.[2] All this tore the commonwealth in pieces, but it provided a sphere for the oratory of those days and heaped on it what one saw were 20 vast rewards. The more influence a man could wield by his powers of speech, the more readily did he attain to high office, the further did he, when in office, outstrip his colleagues in the race for precedence, the more did he gain favor with the great, authority with the senate, and name and fame with the common people. These were the men who had whole nations of foreigners under their protection, several at a time; the men to whom state officials presented their humble duty on the eve of their departure to take up the government of a province, and to whom they paid their respects on their 30 return; the men who, without any effort on their own part, seemed to have praetorships and consulates at their beck and call; the men who even when out of office were in power, seeing that by their advice and authority they could bend both the senate and the people to their will. With them, moreover, it was a conviction that without eloquence it was impossible for anyone either to attain to a position of distinction and prominence in the community, or to maintain it; and no wonder they cherished this conviction, when they were called on to appear in public even when they would rather not, when it 40 was not enough to move a brief resolution in the senate, unless one made good one's opinion in an able speech, when persons who had in some way or other incurred odium, or else were definitely charged with some offence, had to put in an appearance in person, when, moreover, evidence in criminal trials had to be given not indirectly or by affidavit, but personally and by word of mouth. So it was that eloquence not only led to great rewards, but was also a sheer necessity; and just as it was considered great and glorious to have the reputation of being a good speaker, so, on the other hand, it 50 was accounted discreditable to be inarticulate and incapable of utterance. . . .

Q **What role, according to Tacitus, did oratory play in Roman life? Is this true of oratory today?**

Roman Epic Poetry

While the Romans excelled in didactic prose, they also produced some of the world's finest verse. Under the patronage of Octavian, Rome enjoyed a golden age of Latin literature whose most notable representative was Virgil (Publius Vergilius Maro, 70–19 B.C.E.). Rome's foremost poet-publicist, Virgil wrote the semilegendary epic that immortalized Rome's destiny as world ruler. The *Aeneid* was not the product of an oral tradition, as were the Homeric epics; rather, it is a literary epic, undertaken as a work that might rival the epics of Homer. The hero of Virgil's poem is Rome's mythical founder, the Trojan-born Aeneas. As epic hero, Aeneas undertakes a long journey filled with adventures that test his prowess. The first six books of the *Aeneid* recount the hero's voyage from Troy to Italy and his love affair with the beautiful Carthaginian

---

[1] The speaker's platform.
[2] The Popular Assembly.

princess Dido. The second six books describe the Trojan conquest of Latium and the establishment of the Roman state. No summary of the *Aeneid* can represent adequately the monumental impact of a work that would become the foundation for education in the Latin language. Yet, the following two excerpts capture the spirit of Virgil's vision. In the first, Aeneas, pressed to meet his destiny, prepares to take leave of the passionate Dido. Here, his Stoic sense of duty overcomes his desire for personal fulfillment. The second passage, selected from the lengthy monologue spoken by the ghost of Aeneas' father, Anchises, sums up the meaning and purpose of Rome's historic mission.

— **READING 6.5** From Virgil's *Aeneid* (Books Four and Six) (ca. 20 B.C.E.)

[Mercury, the divine herald, urges Aeneas to leave Carthage and proceed to Italy.]

Mercury wastes no time:—"What are you doing,   1
Forgetful of your kingdom and your fortunes,
Building for Carthage? Woman-crazy fellow,
The ruler of the Gods, the great compeller
Of heaven and earth, has sent me from Olympus   5
With no more word than this: what are you doing,
With what ambition wasting time in Libya?
If your own fame and fortune count as nothing,
Think of Ascanius[1] at least, whose kingdom
In Italy, whose Roman land, are waiting   10
As promise justly due." He spoke, and vanished
Into thin air. Appalled, amazed, Aeneas
Is stricken dumb; his hair stands up in terror,
His voice sticks in his throat. He is more than eager
To flee that pleasant land, awed by the warning   15
Of the divine command. But how to do it?
How get around that passionate queen?[2] What opening
Try first? His mind runs out in all directions,
Shifting and veering. Finally, he has it,
Or thinks he has: he calls his comrades to him,   20
The leaders, bids them quietly prepare
The fleet for voyage, meanwhile saying nothing
About the new activity; since Dido
Is unaware, has no idea that passion
As strong as theirs is on the verge of breaking,   25
He will see what he can do, find the right moment
To let her know, all in good time. Rejoicing,
The captains move to carry out the orders.
    Who can deceive a woman in love? The queen
Anticipates each move, is fearful even   30
While everything is safe, foresees this cunning,
And the same troublemaking goddess, Rumor,
Tells her the fleet is being armed, made ready
For voyaging. She rages through the city
Like a woman mad, or drunk, the way the Maenads[3]   35

---

[1] Aeneas' son.
[2] Dido, Queen of Carthage.
[3] "Mad women," the votaries of Bacchus (Dionysus).

Go howling through the night-time on Cithaeron[4]
When Bacchus' cymbals summon with their clashing.
She waits no explanation from Aeneas;
She is the first to speak: "And so, betrayer,
You hoped to hide your wickedness, go sneaking   40
Out of my land without a word? Our love
Means nothing to you, our exchange of vows,
And even the death of Dido could not hold you.
The season is dead of winter, and you labor
Over the fleet; the northern gales are nothing—   45
You must be cruel, must you not? Why, even,
If ancient Troy remained, and you were seeking
Not unknown homes and lands, but Troy again,
Would you be venturing Troyward in this weather?
I am the one you flee from: true? I beg you   50
By my own tears, and your right hand—(I have nothing
Else left my wretchedness)—by the beginnings
Of marriage, wedlock, what we had, if ever
I served you well, if anything of mine
Was ever sweet to you, I beg you, pity   55
A falling house; if there is room for pleading
As late as this, I plead, put off that purpose.
You are the reason I am hated; Libyans,
Numidians, Tyrians, hate me; and my honor
Is lost, and the fame I had, that almost brought me   60
High as the stars, is gone. To whom, O guest—
I must not call you husband any longer—
To whom do you leave me? I am a dying woman;
Why do I linger on? Until Pygmalion,
My brother, brings destruction to this city?   65
Until the prince Iarbas leads me captive?
At least if there had been some hope of children
Before your flight, a little Aeneas playing
Around my courts, to bring you back, in feature
At least, I would seem less taken and deserted."   70
    There was nothing he could say. Jove[5] bade him keep
Affection from his eyes, and grief in his heart
With never a sign. At last, he managed something:—
"Never, O Queen, will I deny you merit
Whatever you have strength to claim; I will not   75
Regret remembering Dido, while I have
Breath in my body, or consciousness of spirit.
I have a point or two to make. I did not,
Believe me, hope to hide my flight by cunning;
I did not, ever, claim to be a husband,   80
Made no such vows. If I had fate's permission
To live my life my way, to settle my troubles
At my own will, I would be watching over
The city of Troy, and caring for my people,
Those whom the Greeks had spared, and Priam's palace   85
Would still be standing; for the vanquished people
I would have built the town again. But now
It is Italy I must seek, great Italy,
Apollo orders, and his oracles
Call me to Italy. There is my love,   90
There is my country. If the towers of Carthage,

---

[4] A mountain range between Attica and Boetia.
[5] Jupiter, the sky god.

The Libyan citadels, can please a woman
Who came from Tyre,[6] why must you grudge the Trojans
Ausonian land?[7] It is proper for us also
To seek a foreign kingdom. I am warned   95
Of this in dreams: when the earth is veiled in shadow
And the fiery stars are burning, I see my father,
Anchises, or his ghost, and I am frightened;
I am troubled for the wrong I do my son,
Cheating him out of his kingdom in the west,   100
And lands that fate assigns him. And a herald,
Jove's messenger—I call them both to witness—
Has brought me, through the rush of air, his orders;
I saw the god myself, in the full daylight,
Enter these walls, I heard the words he brought me.   105
Cease to inflame us both with your complainings;
I follow Italy not because I want to."

[In the Underworld described in Book Six, Aeneas encounters the
soul of his father, Anchises, who foretells the destiny of Rome.]

"Others, no doubt, will better mold the bronze
To the semblance of soft breathing, draw from marble,
The living countenance; and others please   110
With greater eloquence, or learn to measure
Better than we, the pathways of the heavens,
The risings of the stars: remember, Roman,
To rule the people under law, to establish
The way of peace, to battle down the haughty,   115
To spare the meek. Our fine arts, these forever."

— Q **Why does Aeneas abandon Dido?**

— Q **How do Aeneas and Achilles (Reading 4.1)
         compare as epic heroes?**

Roman Lyric Poetry

While Virgil is best known for the *Aeneid*, he also wrote
pastoral poems, or **eclogues**, that glorify the natural landscape and its rustic inhabitants. Virgil's *Eclogues* found
inspiration in the pastoral sketches of Theocritus, a third-
century B.C.E. Sicilian poet. Many Classicists besides Virgil
looked to Hellenic prototypes. The poetry of Catullus
(ca. 84–54 B.C.E.), for instance, reflects familiarity with the
art of Sappho, whose lyrics he admired. The greatest of the
Latin lyric poets, Catullus came to Rome from Verona. A
young man of some wealth and charm, he wrote primarily
on the subjects that consumed his short but intense life:
friendship, love, and sex. His passionate affair with Clodia,
the adulterous wife of a Roman consul, inspired some of his
finest poems, three of which appear below. These trace the
trajectory from the poet's first fevered amorous passions
to his despair and bitterness at the collapse of the affair.
The fourth poem betrays the raw invective and caustic

wit that Catullus brought to many of his verses, including
those with themes of jealousy and possession related to his
bisexual liaisons. Candid and deeply personal, these poems
strike us with the immediacy of a modern, secular voice.

— **READING 6.6** The Poems of Catullus (ca. 60 B.C.E.)

Come, Lesbia,[1] let us live and love,   1
nor give a damn what sour old men say.
The sun that sets may rise again
but when our light has sunk into the earth,
it is gone forever.   5
   Give me a thousand kisses,
then a hundred, another thousand,
another hundred
   and in one breath
still kiss another thousand,   10
another hundred.
   O then with lips and bodies joined
many deep thousands;
   confuse
their number,   15
   so that poor fools and cuckolds (envious
even now) shall never
learn our wealth and curse us
with their
evil eyes.   20

———◆———

He is changed to a god he who looks on her,   1
godlike he shines when he's seated beside her,
immortal joy to gaze and hear the fall of
   her sweet laughter.

All of my senses are lost and confounded;   5
Lesbia rises before me and trembling
I sink into earth and swift dissolution
   seizes my body.

Limbs are pierced with fire and the heavy tongue fails,
ears resound with noise of distant storms shaking   10
this earth, eyes gaze on stars that fall forever
   into deep midnight.

This languid madness destroys you Catullus,
long day and night shall be desolate, broken,
as long ago ancient kings and rich cities   15
   fell into ruin.

———◆———

Lesbia, forever spitting fire at me, is never silent, And now   1
if Lesbia fails to love me, I shall die. Why
do I know in truth her passion burns for me? Because I am
   like her,

---

[6] A maritime city of ancient Phoenicia, ruled by Dido's father.
[7] From Ausones, the ancient name for the inhabitants of middle and
    southern Italy.

[1] The name Catullus gave to Clodia, a reference to Sappho of Lesbos.

because I curse her endlessly. And still, O hear me gods,   5
I love her.

———◆———

Furius, Aurelius, I'll work your own perversions   1
upon you and your persons, since you say my poems
prove that I'm effeminate, deep in homosexual vice.
A genuine poet must be chaste, industrious,
though his verse may give us   5
rich, voluptuous passion to please the
taste of those who read him and not only
delicate boys, but bearded men whose limbs are
stiff and out of practice. And you because my verses
contain many (thousands of) kisses, look at me   10
as though I were a girl. Come at me, and I'll be ready
to defile you and seduce you.

Q How do the poems of Catullus compare with those of Sappho?

The poetry of Catullus notwithstanding, passion and personal feeling were not typical of Latin literature, which inclined more usually toward instruction and satire. One of Rome's most notable poets, Publius Ovidius Naso, or Ovid (43 B.C.E.–17 C.E.), earned centuries of fame for his narrative poem the *Metamorphoses*; this vast collection of stories about Greek and Roman gods develops the theme of supernatural transformation. Ovid himself pursued a career of poetry and love. Married three times, he seems to have been a master in the art of seduction. His witty guide on the subject, *The Art of Love*, brought him into disfavor with Augustus, who (finding the work morally threatening) sent Ovid into exile. Although written with tongue in cheek, *The Art of Love* swelled an already large canon of misogynistic, or antifemale, Classical literature. In this humorous "handbook," Ovid offers vivid glimpses into everyday life in Rome, but he clearly holds that the greatest human crimes issue from women's lust, which, according to the poet, is "keener, fiercer, and more wanton" than men's.

The Poems of Horace

Roman poets were at their most typical when they were moralizing. Octavian's poet laureate, Quintus Haeredes Flaccus, better known as Horace (65–8 B.C.E.), took a critical view of life. Although lacking the grandeur of Virgil and the virtuosity of Ovid, Horace composed verse that pointed up the contradictions between practical realities and philosophic ideals. Having lived through the devastating civil wars of the first century B.C.E., Horace brought a commonsense insight to the subject of war, as we see in the first of the following poems. The second poem exemplifies the Roman taste for **satire**, a literary genre that uses humor to denounce human vice and folly. Satire—Rome's unique contribution to world literature—is a kind of moralizing in which human imperfection is not simply criticized, but rather mocked through biting wit and comic exaggeration. "To Be Quite Frank" is a caustic description of a

middle-aged lady with teenage pretensions, a characterization as unvarnished and true to life as most Roman portraits. Finally, in the third poem below, Horace discloses his Stoic disbelief in human perfection: he advises us to "seize the day" (*carpe diem*) and "learn to accept whatever is to be."

READING 6.7 The Poems of Horace (ca. 30–15 B.C.E.)

Civil War

Why do ye rush, oh wicked folk,   1
 To a fresh war?
Again the cries, the sword, the smoke—
 What for?

Has not sufficient precious blood   5
 Been fiercely shed?
Must ye spill more until ye flood
 The dead?

Not even armed in rivalry
 Your hate's employed;   10
But 'gainst yourselves until ye be
 Destroyed!

Even when beasts slay beasts, they kill
 Some other kind.
Can it be madness makes ye still   15
 So blind?

Make answer! Is your conscience numb?
 Each ashy face
Admits, with silent lips, the dumb
 Disgrace.   20

Murder of brothers! Of all crime,
 Vilest and worst!
Pause—lest ye be, through all of time,
 Accursed.

To Be Quite Frank

Your conduct, naughty Chloris, is   1
 Not just exactly Horace's
Ideal of a lady
 At the shady
Time of life;   5
You mustn't throw your soul away
On foolishness, like Pholoë—
 Her days are folly-laden—
 She's a maiden,
  You're a wife.   10

Your daughter, with propriety,
May look for male society,
 Do one thing and another
 In which mother
  Shouldn't mix;   15

But revels Bacchanalian
Are—or should be—quite alien
    To you a married person,
    Something worse'n
                    Forty-six!   20

Yes, Chloris, you cut up too much,
You love the dance and cup too much,
    Your years are quickly flitting—
    To your knitting
                    Right about!   25
Forget the incidental things
That keep you from parental things—
    The World, the Flesh, the Devil,
    On the level,
                    Cut 'em out!   30

Carpe Diem

Pry not in forbidden lore,   1
    Ask no more, Leuconoë,
How many years—to you?—to me?—
The gods will send us
Before they end us;   5
Nor, questing, fix your hopes
On Babylonian horoscopes.
Learn to accept whatever is to be:
Whether Jove grant us many winters,
Or make of this the last, which splinters   10
Now on opposing cliffs the Tuscan sea.

Be wise; decant your wine; condense
Large aims to fit life's cramped circumference.
We talk, time flies—you've said it!
Make hay today,   15
Tomorrow rates no credit.

— **Q** **How does each of these poems reflect Horace's "critical view of life"?**

The Satires of Juvenal

While Horace's satirical lyrics are, for the most part, genial, those of Rome's most famous satirist, Juvenal (Decimus Junius Juvenalis, ca. 60–130 C.E.), are among the most devastating ever written. Juvenal came to Rome from the provinces. His subsequent career as a magistrate and his experience of poverty and financial failure contributed to his negative perception of Roman society, which he describes in his sixteen bitter *Satires* as swollen with greed and corruption. Juvenal's attack on the city of Rome paints a picture of a noisy, dirty, and crowded urban community inhabited by selfish, violent, and self-indulgent people.

— **READING 6.8a** From Juvenal's "Against the City of Rome" (ca. 110–127 C.E.)

"Rome, good-bye! Let the rest stay in the town if they want to,   1
Fellows like A, B, and C, who make black white at their pleasure,

Finding it easy to grab contracts for rivers and harbors,
Putting up temples, or cleaning out sewers, or hauling off corpses,
Or, if it comes to that, auctioning slaves in the market.   5
Once they used to be hornblowers, working the carneys;
Every wide place in the road knew their puffed-out cheeks and their
    squealing.
Now they give shows of their own. Thumbs up! Thumbs down![1] And
    the killers
Spare or slay, and then go back to concessions for private privies.
Nothing they won't take on. Why not?—since the kindness of Fortune 10
(Fortune is out for laughs) has exalted them out of the gutter.

    .   .   .   .

"If you're poor, you're a joke, on each and every occasion.
What a laugh, if your cloak is dirty or torn, if your toga
Seems a little bit soiled, if your shoe has a crack in the leather,
Or if more than one patch attests to more than one mending!   15
Poverty's greatest curse, much worse than the fact of it, is that
It makes men objects of mirth, ridiculed, humbled, embarrassed.
'Out of the front-row seats!' they cry when you're out of money,
Yield your place to the sons of some pimp, the spawn of some
    cathouse,
Some slick auctioneer's brat, or the louts some trainer has fathered 20
Or the well-groomed boys whose sire is a gladiator.

    .   .   .   .

"Here in town the sick die from insomnia mostly.
Undigested food, on a stomach burning with ulcers,
Brings on listlessness, but who can sleep in a flophouse?
Who but the rich can afford sleep and a garden apartment?   25
That's the source of infection. The wheels creak by on the narrow
Streets of the wards, the drivers squabble and brawl when they're
    stopped,
More than enough to frustrate the drowsiest son of a sea cow.
When his business calls, the crowd makes way, as the rich man,
Carried high in his car, rides over them, reading or writing,   30
Even taking a snooze, perhaps, for the motion's composing.
Still, he gets where he wants before we do; for all of our hurry
Traffic gets in our way, in front, around and behind us.
Somebody gives me a shove with an elbow, or two-by-four
    scantling.[2]
One clunks my head with a beam, another cracks down with
    a beer keg.   35
Mud is thick on my shins, I am trampled by somebody's big feet.
Now what?—a soldier grinds his hobnails into my toes."

— **Q** **What urban ills does Juvenal describe in this poem? Are they exclusive to ancient Rome?**

If Juvenal found much to criticize among his peers, he was equally hostile toward foreigners and women. His sixth *Satire*, "Against Women," is one of the most bitter anti-female diatribes in the history of Western literature. Here, the poet laments the disappearance of the chaste Latin woman whose virtues, he submits, have been corrupted by

---

[1] To turn the thumb down was the signal to kill a wounded gladiator; to turn it up signaled that he should be spared.
[2] A piece of lumber.

life, and the consorts of Rome's rulers often shaped matters of succession and politics by way of their influence on their husbands and sons. Roman records confirm that in addition to the traditional occupations of women in food and textile production and in prostitution, they also held positions as musicians, painters, priestesses, midwives, and gladiators. Nevertheless, in 200 C.E., the emperor Septimius Severus banned female combat, finding it an affront to military dignity.

READING 6.8b From Juvenal's "Against Women" (ca. 110–127 C.E.)

Where, you ask, do they come from, such monsters as these?
In the old days   1
Latin women were chaste by dint of their lowly fortunes.
Toil and short hours for sleep kept cottages free from contagion,
Hands were hard from working the wood, and husbands were
watching,
Standing to arms at the Colline Gate, and the shadow of
Hannibal's looming.[1]   5
Now we suffer the evils of long peace. Luxury hatches
Terrors worse than the wars, avenging a world beaten down.
Every crime is here, and every lust, as they have been
Since the day, long since, when Roman poverty perished.
Over our seven hills,[2] from that day on, they came pouring.   10
The rabble and rout of the East, Sybaris, Rhodes, Miletus,
Yes, and Tarentum[3] too, garlanded, drunken, shameless.
Dirty money it was that first imported among us
Foreign vice and our times broke down with overindulgence.
Riches are flabby, soft. And what does Venus care for   15
When she is drunk? She can't tell one end of a thing from another,
Gulping big oysters down at midnight, making the unguents
Foam in the unmixed wine, and drinking out of a conchhorn
While the walls spin round, and the table starts in dancing,
And the glow of the lamps is blurred by double their number.   20

. . . .

There's nothing a woman won't do, nothing she thinks is disgraceful
With the green gems at her neck, or pearls distending her ear lobes.
Nothing is worse to endure than your Mrs. Richbitch, whose visage
Is padded and plastered with dough, in the most ridiculous manner.
Furthermore, she reeks of unguents, so God help her husband   25
With his wretched face stunk up with these, smeared by her lipstick.
To her lovers she comes with her skin washed clean. But at home
Why does she need to look pretty? Nard[4] is assumed for the lover,
For the lover she buys all the Arabian perfumes.
It takes her some time to strip down to her face, removing the layers 30
One by one, till at last she is recognizable, almost,
Then she uses a lotion, she-asses' milk; she'd need herds

---

[1] In 213 B.C.E., the Carthaginian general Hannibal, Rome's most formidable enemy, was camped only a few miles outside Rome, poised to attack (see Livy, xxvi:10).
[2] The hills surrounding the city of Rome.
[3] Greek cities associated with luxury and vice.
[4] Spikenard, a fragrant ointment.

Figure 6.5 Flavian women, ca. 89 C.E. Marble, life-sized. Elegant hairstyles of this period often involved attaching curls to the front of the head, while the hair in back might be braided and coiled into a bun.

luxury. Indeed, upper-class women were notorious for the luxuries that Rome provided: exquisite jewelry, fine perfumes, and elegant wigs (Figure **6.5**). Although Juvenal's bias against womankind strikes a personal note, it is likely that he was reflecting the public outcry against the licentiousness that was widespread in his own day. Increasingly during the second century, men openly enjoyed concubines, mistresses, and prostitutes. Infidelity among married women was on the rise, and divorce was common, as were second and third marriages for both sexes.

The women of imperial Rome did not have many more civil rights than did their Golden Age Athenian sisters. They could neither vote nor hold public office. However, they did not occupy separate household quarters from males, they could own property, and they were free to manage their own legal affairs. Roman girls were educated along with boys, and most middle-class women could read and write. Some female aristocrats were active in public

Of these creatures to keep her supplied on her northernmost journeys.
But when she's given herself the treatment in full, from the ground base
Through the last layer of mud pack, from the first wash to a poultice, **35**
What lies under all this—a human face, or an ulcer?

Q **What complaints does Juvenal launch against the women of imperial Rome?**

Q **What does he mean by saying Rome suffers "the evils of long peace"?**

Roman Drama

Roman tragedies were roughly modeled on those of Greece. They were moral and didactic in intent, and their themes were drawn from Greek and Roman history. Theatrical performances in Rome did not share, however, the religious solemnity of those in Greece. Rather, they were a form of entertainment offered along with the public games, known as *ludi*, that marked the major civic festivals. Unlike the rituals and athletic contests of the Greeks, *ludi* featured displays of armed combat and other violent amusements. The nature of these public spectacles may explain why many of the tragedies written to compete with them were bloody and ghoulish in character. The lurid plays of the Stoic writer Seneca drew crowds in Roman times and were to inspire—some 1500 years later—such playwrights as William Shakespeare.

The Romans seem to have preferred comedies to tragedies, for most surviving Roman plays are in the comic genre. Comic writers employed simple plots and broad (often obscene) humor. The plays of Plautus (ca. 250–184 B.C.E.) and Terence (ca. 185–159 B.C.E.) are filled with stock characters, such as the good-hearted prostitute, the shrewish wife, and the clever servant. The characters engage in farcical schemes and broad slapstick action of the kind common to today's television situation comedies. In the comic theater of the Romans, as in Roman culture in general, everyday life took precedence over fantasy, and the real, if imperfect, world was the natural setting for down-to-earth human beings.

The Arts of the Roman Empire

Roman Architecture

Rome's architecture reflected the practical needs of a sprawling empire whose urban centers suffered from the congestion, noise, and filth described by Juvenal. To link the provinces that ranged from the Atlantic Ocean to the Euphrates River, Roman engineers built 50,000 miles of paved roads, many of which are still in use today. The need to house, govern, and entertain large numbers of citizens inspired the construction of tenements, meeting halls, baths, and amphitheaters. Eight- and nine-story tenements provided thousands with cheap (if often rat-infested) housing. Roman bridges and tunnels defied natural barriers, while some eighteen aqueducts brought fresh water to Rome's major cities. The aqueducts, some of which

Science and Technology

45 C.E.	the Romans invent the technique of glassblowing
90 C.E.	a system of aqueducts provides water for the city of Rome
122 C.E.	in Roman Britain, the emperor Hadrian begins construction of a wall to protect against invasion from the north
140 C.E.	the Alexandrian astronomer Ptolemy produces the *Almagest*, which posits a geocentric (earth-centered) universe (and becomes the basis for Western astronomy for centuries)
160 C.E.	Claudius Galen writes over 100 medical treatises (despite errors, they become the basis for Western medical practice for centuries)

delivered well over forty million gallons of water per day to a single site, were the public works that the Romans considered their most significant technological achievement.

Superb engineers, the Romans employed the structural advantages of the arch (the knowledge of which they inherited from the Etruscans) to enclose great volumes of uninterrupted space. The arch constituted a clear technical advance over the post-and-lintel construction used by the Greeks in buildings like the Parthenon (see Figure 5.15). The Romans adapted this structural principle inventively: they placed arches back to back to form a barrel **vault**, at right angles to each other to form a cross or groined vault, and around a central point to form a dome (Figure **6.6**). Roman building techniques reveal a combination of practicality and innovation: the Romans were the first to use concrete (an aggregate of sand, lime, brick-and-stone rubble, and water), a medium that made possible cheap large-scale construction. They laid their foundations with concrete, raised structures with brick, rubble, and stone, and finished exterior surfaces with veneers of marble, tile, bronze, or plaster.

Roman architecture and engineering were considered one and the same discipline. Vitruvius' *Ten Books on Architecture* (see chapter 5), the oldest and most influential work of its kind, includes instructions for hydraulic systems, city planning, and mechanical devices. For the Roman architect, the function of a building determined its formal design. The design of villas, theaters, and temples received the same close attention as that given to hospitals, fortresses, and—as Josephus reveals—military camps. One of Rome's most spectacular large-scale engineering projects is the 900-foot-long Pont du Gard, part of a 25-mile-long aqueduct that brought fresh water to the city of Nîmes in southern France (Figure **6.7**). Built of 6-ton stones and assembled without mortar, the structure reflects the practical function of arches at three levels, the bottom row supporting a bridge and the second row undergirding the top channel, through which water ran by gravity to its destination.

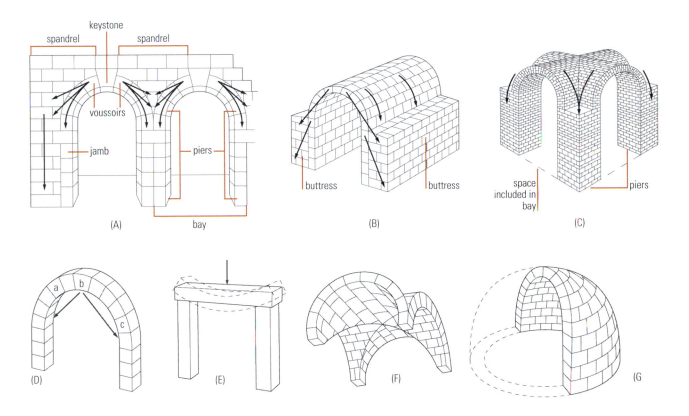

Figure 6.6 Arches and vaults. (**A**) round arch; (**B**) barrel or tunnel vault; (**C**) groin vault;
(**D**) arch consisting of voussoirs, wedge-shaped blocks (a,b,c); (**E**) post-and-lintel; (**F**) inside of groin vault; (**G**) dome.

Figure 6.7 Pont du Gard, near Nîmes, France, ca. 20–10 B.C.E. Stone, height 180 ft., length ca. 900 ft.

Figure 6.8 Reconstruction of fourth-century C.E. Rome. | Circus Maximus | Colosseum

Figure 6.9 Colosseum, Rome (aerial view), 70–82 C.E. By its sheer size, this structure, once surfaced with gleaming marble, advertised the power of Rome and its will to serve the pleasures of its huge urban population.

Figure 6.10 Detail from a fourth-century C.E. mosaic portraying a gladiator fighting a wild beast. Gladiatorial contests were introduced in Rome in 264 B.C.E. Most gladiators were criminals, prisoners of war, or slaves. They were trained in special schools. While they often fought to the death, they might be pardoned (or even win their freedom) if they displayed outstanding valor.

The sheer magnitude of such Roman amphitheaters as the Circus Maximus, which seated 200,000 spectators (Figure **6.8**, foreground), and the Colosseum, which covered 6 acres and accommodated 50,000 (Figure **6.9**), is a reminder that during the first century C.E. Rome's population exceeded one million people. By this time, many Romans were the impoverished recipients of relief in the form of wheat and free entertainment, hence the phrase "bread and circuses." The Roman amphitheaters testify to the popular taste for entertainments that included chariot races, mock sea battles, gladiatorial contests, and a variety of brutal blood sports (Figure **6.10**). At the Colosseum, three levels of seating rose above the arena floor. Beneath the floor was a complex of rooms and tunnels from which athletes, gladiators, and wild animals emerged to entertain the cheering crowd. To provide shade from the sun, an awning at the roof level could be extended by means of a system of pulleys. On each level of the exterior, arches were framed by a series of decorative, or engaged, columns displaying the three Greek orders: Doric (at ground level), Ionic, and Corinthian.

The ingenious combination of arch and post-and-lintel structural elements would be widely imitated for centuries, and especially during the Italian Renaissance. More generally, the long-standing influence of this Roman amphitheater is apparent in the design of the modern sports arena.

Roman architectural genius may be best illustrated by the Pantheon, a temple whose structural majesty depends on the combination of Roman technical ingenuity and dramatic spatial design. Dedicated to the seven planetary deities, the Pantheon was built in the early second century C.E. Its monumental exterior—once covered with a veneer of white marble and bronze—features a portico with eight Corinthian columns originally elevated by a flight of stairs that now lie buried beneath the city street (Figure **6.11**). One of the few buildings from Classical antiquity to have remained almost intact, the Pantheon boasts a 19-foot-thick rotunda that is capped by a solid dome consisting of 5000 tons of concrete (see Figure 6.12). The interior of the dome, once painted blue and gold to resemble the vault of heaven, is pierced by a 30-foot-wide

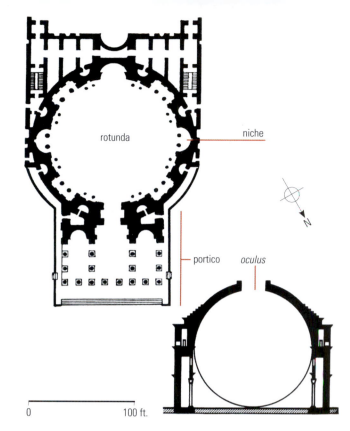

Figure 6.11 Plan and section of the Pantheon.

oculus, or "eye," that admits light and air (Figure **6.14**). The proportions of the Pantheon observe the Classical principles of symmetry and harmony as described by Vitruvius (see Reading 5.1): the height from the floor to the apex of the dome (143 feet) equals the diameter of the rotunda.

The Pantheon is distinctly Roman in spirit; however, other Roman buildings imitated Greek models. The temple in Nîmes, France, for instance, known as the Maison Carrée, stands like a miniature Greek shrine atop a high podium (Figure **6.15**). A stairway and a colonnaded portico accentuate the single entranceway and give the building a frontal "focus" usually lacking in Greek temples. The Corinthian order (see Figure 5.19) appears in the portico, and engaged columns adorn the exterior wall. The epitome of Classical refinement, the Maison Carrée inspired numerous European and American copies. Indeed, the Virginia State Capitol, designed by Thomas Jefferson, offers clear evidence of the use of Classical models to convey

MAKING CONNECTIONS

Figure 6.12 The Pantheon, Rome, ca. 118–125 C.E.

The Pantheon (Figure **6.12**) has inspired more works of architecture than any other monument in Greco-Roman history. It awed and delighted such eminent late eighteenth-century Neoclassicists as Thomas Jefferson, who used it as the model for many architectural designs, including that of his country estate at Monticello in Charlottesville, Virginia, and the Rotunda of the University of Virginia (Figure **6.13**). Jefferson was faithful to the original plan of the Roman temple, which included the stairway leading up to the portico.

Figure 6.13 THOMAS JEFFERSON, the Rotunda, University of Virginia, Charlottesville, Virginia, 1822–1826.

Figure 6.14 GIOVANNI PAOLO PANINI, *The Interior of the Pantheon*, ca. 1734–1735. Oil on canvas, 4 ft. 2½ in. × 3 ft. 3 in. In its sheer size and its uninterrupted interior space, the Pantheon exceeded any previous temple built in antiquity. The difference between its stolid exterior and its breathtaking cylindrical interior is captured in this eighteenth-century painting, which shows the dramatic effects of the *oculus* "spotlight."

Figure 6.15 Maison Carrée, Nîmes, France, ca. 16 B.C.E.

the dignity, stability, and authority that Neoclassicists associated with the world of Greece and Rome.

If temples such as the Pantheon and the Maison Carrée answered the spiritual needs of the Romans, the baths, such as those named for the emperor Caracalla, satisfied some of their temporal requirements. Elaborate structures fed by natural hot springs (Figure **6.16**), the baths provided a welcome refuge from the noise and grime of the city streets. In addition to rooms in which pools of water were heated to varying degrees, such spas often included steam rooms, exercise rooms, art galleries, shops, cafés, reading rooms, and chambers for physical intimacy. Although most baths had separate women's quarters, many permitted mixed bathing. The popularity of the baths is reflected in the fact that by the third century C.E., there were more than 900 of them in the city of Rome.

Roman baths incorporated the **basilica**, a rectangular colonnaded hall commonly used for public assemblies. The basilica was the ideal structure for courts of law, meeting halls, and marketplaces. The huge meeting hall known

Figure 6.16 Great Bath, Roman bath complex, Bath, England, 54 C.E. Part of the finest group of Roman remains in England, this sumptuous pool is still fed by natural hot springs.

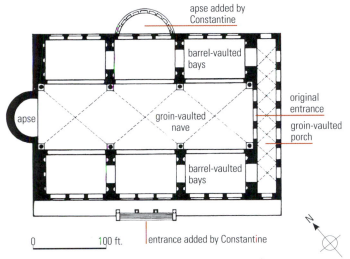

apse added by Constantine

barrel-vaulted bays

apse

groin-vaulted nave

original entrance

groin-vaulted porch

barrel-vaulted bays

N

0   100 ft.   entrance added by Constantine

Figure 6.17 (above) Plan of the Basilica of Maxentius and Constantine.

as the Basilica of Maxentius consisted of a 300-foot-long central nave, four side aisles, and a semicircular recess called an **apse** (Figure **6.17**). The Roman basilica might be roofed by wooden beams or—as in the case of the Basilica of Maxentius (Figures **6.18** and **6.19**)—by gigantic stone vaults. Completed by the emperor Constantine in the fourth century C.E., these enormous vaults rested on brick-faced concrete walls some 20 feet thick. In its floor plan and construction features, the Roman basilica became the model for the Early Christian church in the West.

Figure 6.18 (below) Basilica of Maxentius and Constantine, Rome, begun 306–310 C.E., completed by Constantine after 313 C.E. This basilica was the last and largest of all those commissioned by Rome's emperors. The original central hall (nave) rose to a height of 115 feet. Load-bearing walls 20 feet thick supported the weight of the ceiling. A colossal statue of Constantine (of which only the head remains) once sat in the apse.

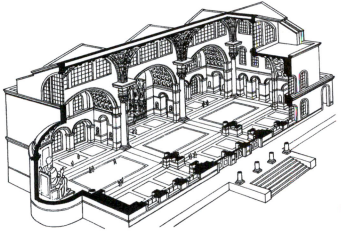

Figure 6.19 The Basilica of Maxentius and Constantine.

Roman Sculpture

Like its imperialistic predecessors, Rome advertised its military achievements in monumental public works of art. These consisted mainly of triumphal arches and victory columns, which, like the obelisks of Egyptian pharaohs, commemorated the conquests of strong rulers. The 100-foot-tall marble column erected in 113 C.E. by Emperor Trajan to celebrate his victory over Dacia (present-day Romania) includes 2500 figures—a huge picture scroll carved in brilliant low relief (Figures **6.1** and **6.20**). Here, a documentary vitality is achieved by the piling up of figures in illusionistic space, and by a plethora of realistic details describing Roman military fortifications and weaponry.

The triumphal arch was the landmark image of Roman imperial victory. More rightly classed with sculpture than with architecture, where arches function mainly to enclose interior space, this distinctive structure—made of concrete and faced with marble—served as visual propaganda. Commemorative arches were first erected by Augustus to celebrate his military triumphs. They also functioned as monumental gateways. Some thirty-four, embellished with sculptures and laudatory inscriptions, were raised in Rome; and many more throughout the Empire bear witness to the power and the geographic reach of the Roman state. The Arch of Titus, marking the upper end of the Roman Forum, commemorates the final days of the Jewish Wars (66–70 C.E.) fought by the emperors Vespasian and Titus (Figure **6.21**). The marble-faced concrete vault of the arch

Figure 6.20 Trajan's Victory Column, Rome, 113 C.E. Marble, height (with base) 125 ft. This column is the sole surviving monument of Trajan's Forum, which once included judicial courts, temples, shops, and two library buildings, one for Greek texts and one for Latin texts. The column, a booklike scroll inspired by the (lost) *Commentaries* of Trajan, stood (approximately) between the Greek and Roman libraries.

Figure 6.21 Arch of Titus, Rome, ca. 81 C.E. Marble, height 50 ft., width 40 ft. (approx.). The Latin inscription on the superstructure declares that the Senate and the Roman people (SPQR) dedicate the arch to Titus, son of Vespasian.

Figure 6.22 *The Spoils of Jerusalem.* Relief from the Arch of Titus, Rome, ca. 81 C.E. Marble, height 7 ft. (approx.).

is elevated between two massive piers that bear engaged Corinthian columns and an **attic** or superstructure carrying a commemorative inscription. Narrative relief panels on the interior sides of the vault depict a typical Roman triumphal procession celebrating the destruction of Jerusalem and the pillage of the Temple of Solomon (Figure **6.22**). Crowned with laurel wreaths of victory, Roman soldiers march through a city gate carrying the menorah and other spoils of victory. Subtly carved in various depths from low to high relief, the scene evokes the illusion of deep space. Even in its damaged state, *The Spoils of Jerusalem* remains a vivid record of conquest and triumph. It is the product of an age that depended on realistic narrative relief—as we today depend on photography and film—to document (and immortalize) key historical events.

While triumphal arches served as visual propaganda for Rome's military exploits, monumental sculpture glorified Roman rulers. The statue of Augustus from Primaporta (see Figure 6.4) is one of the best examples of Roman heroic portraiture. It exemplifies the Classical synthesis of realistic detail (most evident in the treatment of the breastplate and toga) and idealized form (obvious in the handsome face and canonic proportions) that dominated official Roman art, including that found on Rome's mass-produced coins.

During the second century C.E., the tradition of heroic portraiture assumed an even more magisterial stamp in the image of the ruler on horseback: the **equestrian** statue (Figure **6.23**). The equestrian portrait of the Roman

Figure 6.23 Equestrian statue of Marcus Aurelius, ca. 173 C.E. Bronze, height 16 ft. 8 in. Piazza del Campidoglio, Rome. This gilded bronze sculpture by an unknown artist escaped destruction because it was thought to represent the emperor Constantine, the first ruler officially to adopt Christianity. In 1997, the original (pictured here) was moved to the Capitoline Museum in Rome. A copy, made from a mold created with computer-generated photographs, now stands in this Roman square.

Figure 6.24 Roman aristocrat holding portrait busts of his ancestors, late first century B.C.E. Marble, height 5 ft. 5 in.

emperor Marcus Aurelius depicts the general addressing his troops with the traditional gesture of imperial authority. The body of a conquered warrior once lay under the raised right hoof of the spirited charger, whose veins and muscles seem to burst from beneath his bronze skin.

While public portrayal of the ruler usually demanded a degree of flattering idealization, images intended for private use invited naturalistic detail. The Roman taste for Realism is perhaps best illustrated in three-dimensional portraits of Roman men and women, often members of the ruling class or wealthy patricians. In contrast to the idealized portraits of Golden Age Greece (see Figure 4.12), many Roman likenesses reflect obsessive fidelity to nature. So true to life seem some Roman portrait heads that scholars suspect they may have been executed from wax death masks. Roman portrait sculpture tends to reflect the personality and character of the sitter, a fact perhaps related to the ancient custom of honoring the "genius" or in-dwelling spirit of the dead ancestor. The lifelike portrait bust of Julius Caesar, carved in green schist with inset crystal eyes, captures the spirit of resolute determination (see Figure 6.3). It is the record of a particular person at a particular time in his life; as such it conveys a degree of psychological Realism absent from most Classical Greek portraits.

In that portrait sculpture served much as our photographs do today—as physical reminders of favorite relatives and friends—the emphasis on Realism is understandable. The balding patrician who carries two portrait busts of his ancestors (Figure **6.24**) reminds us that the Roman family placed extraordinary emphasis on its lineage, honoring the father of the family (*paterfamilias*) no less devotedly than did the ancient Chinese. Such intimate likenesses of the deceased would have been displayed and venerated at special altars and shrines within the Roman home. Roman women were similarly honored: the portrait of the square-jawed aristocratic female, whose wig or hairdo surely required the fastidious application of the curling iron, discloses the proud confidence of a Roman matron (see Figure 6.5). Whether cast in bronze, or carved in marble, slate, or terracotta, these

Figure 6.25 Atrium, House of the Vetii. Pompeii, Italy, first century C.E.

Figure 6.26 *Seated Woman Playing a Kithara*, Roman, Late Republic, ca. 40–30 B.C.E. Villa of P. Fannius Synistor at Boscoreale. The fresco, which decorated a reception hall, belongs to a set that probably celebrated a dynastic marriage. Both figures wear gold diadems and earrings. The red colors, derived from cinnabar and vermilion, were among the most expensive pigments used in Pompeian wall-painting.

psychologically penetrating studies are often as unflattering as they are honest. In their lack of idealization and their affection for literal detail, they reveal Roman sculpture as a record of commonplace reality.

Roman Painting and Mosaics

Pictorial Realism also dominates the frescoes and mosaics with which the Romans decorated their meeting halls, baths, and country villas (see Figures 5.31 and 6.10). Probably inspired by Greek murals, of which only a few examples survive, Roman artists painted scenes drawn from literature, mythology, and daily life. Among the finest examples of Roman frescoes are those found in and around Pompeii and Herculaneum, two southern Italian cities that attracted a population of wealthy Romans. But even in the outer reaches of the Empire, such as at Zeugma in modern Turkey (uncovered as recently as 1992), the Roman taste for visual representation is evident in magnificently decorated palatial villas. Pompeii and Herculaneum

remain the showcases of Roman suburban life: both cities were engulfed by a mountain of ash from the volcanic eruption of Mount Vesuvius in 79 C.E., but the lava from the disaster preserved many of the area's suburban homes. These residential villas, constructed around an **atrium** (a large central hall open to the sky), are valuable sources of information concerning the lifestyles of upper-class Romans (Figure **6.25**).

At a villa in Boscoreale, about a mile north of Pompeii, floors and walls display fine ornamental motifs and scenes illustrated in mosaic, a technique by which small pieces of stone or glass are embedded into wet cement surfaces or plaster surfaces (see Figure 6.10). The walls of some rooms are painted with frescoes designed to give viewers the impression that they are looking out upon gardens and distant buildings. Others show scenes of everyday life. A handsome Roman matron sits on an elegant wooden chair playing a kithara; her daughter stands behind (Figure **6.26**). Both look at us directly, as though we have interrupted a private moment. Light coming from the right illuminates the figures, which, shaded uniformly on the left, assume a true-to-life presence. Illusionism of this kind, known as *trompe l'oeil* ("fool the eye"), makes use of pictorial devices that render a sense of three-dimensional space on a two-dimensional surface. One such device, famously employed by Roman artists, was empirical perspective. Another was the manipulation of light and shade that seduces the eye into believing that it perceives real objects in deep space. In the extraordinary *Still Life with Eggs and Thrushes*, one of a series of frescoes celebrating food, from a villa at Pompeii, light seems to bounce off the metal pitcher, whose shiny surface contrasts with the densely textured towel and the ceramic plate holding ten lifelike eggs (Figure **6.27**). The objects cast shadows to the right, suggesting a light source coming from the left. Roman artists integrated illusionistic devices in ways that would not be seen again in Western art for a thousand years (see chapter 23). The invention of still life as an independent genre (or type) of art confirmed the Roman fondness for the tangible things of everyday life.

Yet another subject, the natural landscape, reflects Rome's attachment to the world of the senses. Although both the Egyptians and the Greeks used natural settings for human activities, it was the Romans who pioneered landscape as a subject in and of itself. First-century B.C.E. frescoes illustrating the adventures of the Greek hero Odysseus feature spacious landscapes filled with rocky plains, feathery trees, animals, and people (Figure **6.28**). Bathed in light and shade, the naturalistically modeled figures cast shadows to indicate their physical presence in atmospheric space.

Roman landscapes show a deep affection for the countryside and for the pleasures of nature. Arcadia, the mountainous region in the central Peloponnesus (inhabited by the peace-loving shepherds and nymphs of ancient Greek legend), provided the model for the Classical landscape. Described by Virgil as a pastoral paradise, it was celebrated in both Greek and Latin **pastoral** poetry as the setting for a life of innocence and simplicity. The glorification of bucolic freedom—the "Arcadian Myth"—reflected the Roman disenchantment with city life and became a recurring theme in the arts of the West, especially during periods of rising urbanization.

Roman Music

While Roman civilization left abundant visual and literary resources, the absence of surviving examples in music makes it almost impossible to evaluate the Roman contribution in this domain. Passages from the writings of Roman historians suggest that Roman music theory was adopted from that of the Greeks, as were most Roman instruments.

Figure 6.27 *Still Life with Eggs and Thrushes*, from the House (or Villa) of Julia Felix, Pompeii, before 79 C.E. Fresco, 35 × 48 in. In contrast to the fresco secco (dry fresco) technique used in ancient Egypt, Roman wall-paintings were executed on freshly laid plaster; pigments were applied to sections while they were still damp. This technique is known as "true fresco."

Figure 6.28 *Odysseus in the Land of the Lestrygonians,* part of the *Odyssey Landscapes,* second-style ("architectural") wall-paintings from a house in Rome, late first century B.C.E. Height 5 ft. (approx.). Illusionism is heightened by way of the shadows cast by the lively figures, and by the foreshortened figure of the sheep (left foreground) that views its own reflection in a pool of water.

In drama, musical interludes replaced the Greek choral odes—a change that suggests the growing distance between drama and its ancient ritual function. Music was, however, essential to most forms of public entertainment and also played an important role in military life; for the latter, the Romans developed brass instruments, such as trumpets and horns, and drums for military processions.

The Fall of Rome

Why and how the mighty Roman Empire came to collapse in the fifth century C.E. has intrigued scholars for centuries. A great many theories have been advanced, ranging from soil exhaustion and lead poisoning to the malaria epidemic of the third century, and the absence of a system for legitimate succession to the throne. In reality, it is likely that no *one* problem was responsible. Rome's slow decline was probably the result of a combination of internal circumstances: the difficulties of governing so huge an empire, the decline of the slave trade, and the increasing gap between the rich and the poor—during the *Pax Romana,* one-third to one-half of Rome's urban population received some form of public welfare. The Empire's internal problems were made all the worse by repeated barbarian attacks on Rome's borders. The emperors Diocletian (245–316) and Constantine (ca. 274–337) tried, but failed, to arrest the decline. Finally, in 476, a Germanic army commander led a successful attack on Rome and deposed the reigning Roman emperor, Romulus Augustulus. The great Empire had fallen.

The Roman Rise to Empire

- From its Latin beginnings, Rome showed an extraordinary talent for adopting and adapting the best of other cultures: Etruscan and Greek.
- The Romans preserved and transmitted the culture of the Hellenic and Hellenistic world.
- Although the Roman Republic engaged all citizens in government, power rested largely with the wealthy and influential patrician class.
- As Rome built an empire and assumed mastery of the civilized world, the Republic fell increasingly into the hands of military dictators, the greatest of whom was Julius Caesar.
- Caesar's heir, Octavian, ushered in the *Pax Romana*, a time of peace and high cultural productivity.
- Rome's highly disciplined army was the backbone of the Empire.
- The sheer size of the Roman Empire inspired engineering programs, such as bridge and road building, that united all regions under Roman rule. The need to rule a world-state brought about a practical system of law.

The Roman Contribution to Literature

- The Romans produced no original philosophy, but cultivated Hellenistic schools of thought such as Stoicism.
- Roman literature manifests a practical bias for factual information. The Romans gave the world its first encyclopedias, as well as memorable biographies, essays, speeches, histories, and letters.
- The high moral tone and lucid prose of Cicero and Tacitus characterize Latin literature at its best.
- In poetry, Virgil paid homage to the Roman state in the monumental epic the *Aeneid*. Catullus left memorable love lyrics, while Horace and Juvenal both offered a critical view of Roman life in satiric verse.

The Arts of the Roman Empire

- Rome's architectural and engineering projects featured the inventive use of the arch and the techniques of concrete and brick construction. The Romans contributed domed and stone-vaulted types of construction that enclose vast areas of interior space.
- Rome's monumental building projects often served as visual imperial propaganda.
- The Romans imitated and borrowed Hellenic models, but their taste for realistic representation and naturalistic detail dominated relief sculptures, portrait busts, and fresco paintings.
- Roman music theory was adopted from the Greeks, as were most Roman instruments. However, the Romans developed brass instruments, such as trumpets, horns, and drums for military use.

The Fall of Rome

- For almost a thousand years, the Romans ruled a geographically and ethnically diverse realm. Their contribution is imprinted on the language, laws, and architecture of the West.
- The collapse of Rome was hastened by a combination of factors: the overreaching imperial ambitions of its rulers, political and economic problems, and the attacks of Germanic tribes on the borders of the Empire.

Glossary

apse a vaulted semicircular recess at one or both ends of a basilica

atrium the inner courtyard of a Roman house, usually colonnaded and open to the sky

attic the superstructure or low upper story above the main order of a façade

basilica a large colonnaded hall commonly used for public assemblies, law courts, baths, and marketplaces

eclogue a pastoral poem, usually involving shepherds in an idyllic rural setting

epistle a formal letter

equestrian mounted on horseback

imperium (Latin, "command," "empire") the civil and military authority exercised by the rulers of ancient Rome (and the root of the English words "imperialism" and "empire"); symbolized in ancient Rome by an eagle-headed scepter and the *fasces*, an ax bound in a bundle of rods

oratory the art of public speaking

pastoral pertaining to the country, to shepherds, and the simple rural life; also, any work of art presenting an idealized picture of country life

res publica (Latin, "of the people") a government in which power resides in citizens entitled to vote and is exercised by representatives responsible to them and to a body of law

sarcophagus (plural **sarcophagi**) a stone coffin

satire a literary genre that ridicules or pokes fun at human vices and follies

trompe l'oeil (French, "fool the eye") a form of illusionistic painting that tries to convince the viewer that the image is real and not painted

vault a roof or ceiling constructed on the arch principle (see Figure 6.6)

Chapter

7

China: The Rise to Empire

ca. 770 B.C.E.–220 C.E.

"He who learns but does not think is lost.
He who thinks but does not learn is in great danger."
Confucius

Figure 7.1 The Great Wall, near Beijing, China, begun 214 B.C.E. Length 1500 miles, height and width 25 ft. (approx.). Constructed of rubble and earth, and faced with stone, the Great Wall required a labor force of thousands. Watchtowers and military barracks were situated strategically along the wall, which reached its present extent (seen in this photograph) under Ming rulers in the seventeenth century.

In the thousand-year period (ca. 500 B.C.E. to 500 C.E.) during which Greco-Roman civilization flourished in the West, both China and India* brought forth cultures that were definitive and enduring, hence "classical." China and India each generated a body of learning and an artistic heritage that became the cultural bedrock of their respective countries, and served as models for the rest of East Asia. Their legacies, like those of ancient Greece and Rome, reached beyond their time and place to shape the larger humanistic tradition. The focus of this chapter is classical China. China's dynastic development and its rise to empire offer intriguing parallels with the histories of Greece and Rome. The philosophic traditions of both China and Greece were launched by the great thinkers of the fifth and sixth centuries B.C.E. Equally interesting is the comparison between Han China and the Roman Empire. These two great empires, located at either end of the Eurasian landmass, brought political stability and cultural unity to vast stretches of territory. Both were profoundly secular in their approach to the world and to the conduct of human beings. Both inherited age-old forms and practices in religion, law, literature, and the arts; these they self-consciously preserved and transmitted to future generations. The classical legacies of China and Rome would come to shape the respective histories of East and West.

* India's classical history—the birth of Buddhism and the revival of Hindu culture—is surveyed in chapters 8, 9, and 14.

Confucius and the Classics

The Eastern Zhou Dynasty (ca. 771–256 B.C.E.)

After 771 B.C.E., the Zhou dynasty, which had ruled since 1027 B.C.E., slowly disintegrated. Zhou rulers, who had moved their capital eastward, faced perilous attacks by the nomadic Mongol and Turkic horsemen of Central Asia and increasing warfare between independent Chinese states. Nevertheless, trade and urban life continued to flourish, and China developed some of its most significant and lasting material and philosophic traditions. Chopsticks, cast iron, square-holed coins, and finely lacquered objects were all developed during the sixth century B.C.E. At the same time, and parallel with (but totally independent of) the rise of philosophic thought in Greece, China experienced a burst of intellectual creativity: its classical texts date from this period, and with them came the formulation of some of China's oldest moral and religious precepts.

As we saw in chapter 3, the ancient Chinese regarded the natural order as the basis for spiritual life, political stability (witness the Mandate of Heaven), and the social order. To know one's place within the order and to act accordingly were essential to the well-being of both the individual and the community. The Chinese describe this ethical imperative with the word *li*, which translates variously as "propriety," "ritual," and "arrangement." The original meaning of the word *li* is found in the act of ritual sacrifice, that is, the proper performance of traditional Chinese rites. But by the middle of the Zhou Era, *li* had come to refer to the pattern or principles governing appropriate behavior, or action in conformity with the rules of decorum and civility. Formative in the evolution of this concept were the teachings of the philosopher Kongfuzi (551–479 B.C.E.), better known as Confucius, a Latinization of his Chinese name.

Confucius was China's most notable thinker. According to tradition, he was also the compiler and editor of the "Five Chinese Classics" (see chapter 3 and box). A self-educated man, who served as a local administrator, Confucius pursued the career of a teacher and social reformer. Like his Greek counterpart, Socrates, he himself wrote nothing. He earned renown through the force of his teachings, which his disciples transcribed after his death. This collection of writings came to be known as the *Analects*. As eclectic in origin and dating as the Hebrew Bible, the *Analects* embody the words of Confucius on matters as diverse as music, marriage, and death. But they focus on questions of conduct: the proper behavior of the individual in the society at large. They articulate the ancient Chinese conviction that human beings must heed a moral order that is fixed in nature, not in divine pronouncement. Confucius confidently maintained that human character, not birth, determined the worth and status of the individual. He had little to say about gods and spirits; nor did he speculate on the nature of reality (in the manner of the Greek philosophers). Rather, he taught the importance of tradition, filial piety (respect for one's elders), and the exercise of *li*. In doing so, he formulated the first expression of the so-called Golden Rule: "What you do not wish for yourself, do not do to others."

The Five Chinese Classics*

1 *I jing* (*Book of Changes*)—a text for divination

2 *Shu jing* (*Book of History*)—government records: speeches, reports, and announcements by rulers and ministers of ancient China

3 *Shi jing* (*Book of Songs*)—an anthology of some 300 poems: folk songs, ceremonial and secular poems

4 *Li ji* (*Book of Rites*)—a collection of texts centering on rules of conduct for everyday life

5 *Lushi chunqiu* (*Spring and Autumn Annals*)—commentaries that chronicle events up to the fifth century B.C.E.

*A sixth classic, on music, is no longer in existence

The teachings of Confucius preserved social and political ideas as old as the Shang and Zhou dynasties. In that Confucius lived during the turbulent years just prior to the collapse of the Zhou and the era of the Warring States (ca. 403–221 B.C.E.), he worked to ensure the survival of traditional values. Basic to these ideals was the notion that the ruler was the "parent" of the people. The cultivation of character and the successful regulation of the family preceded the ruler's ability to govern. The good influence and high moral status of the ruler—a figure much like Plato's philosopher-king—was of greater political value than physical force or the threat of punishment. If a ruler was not himself virtuous, he could not expect to inspire virtue among his subjects. For Confucius, as for Plato, moral and political life were one. Moral harmony was the root of political harmony, and moral rectitude made government all but unnecessary. Such precepts were basic to humanist thought in China for well over 2000 years.

READING 7.1 From the *Analects* of Confucius

2.1 The Master said: "He who rules by virtue is like the polestar, which remains unmoving in its mansion while all the other stars revolve respectfully around it."

2.2 The Master said: "The three hundred *Poems* are summed up in one single phrase: 'Think no evil.' "

2.3 The Master said: "Lead them by political maneuvers, restrain them with punishments: the people will become cunning and shameless. Lead them by virtue, restrain them with ritual: they will develop a sense of shame and a sense of participation."

2.13 Zigong asked about the true gentleman. The Master said: "He preaches only what he practices."

2.14 The Master said: "The gentleman considers the whole rather than the parts. The small man considers the parts rather than the whole."

2.15 The Master said: "To study without thinking is futile. To think without studying is dangerous."

2.17 The Master said: "Zilu, I am going to teach you what knowledge is. To take what you know for what you know, and what you do not know for what you do not know, that is knowledge indeed."

2.20 Lord Ji Kang asked: "What should I do in order to make the people respectful, loyal, and zealous?" The Master said: "Approach them with dignity and they will be respectful. Be yourself a good son and a kind father, and they will be loyal. Raise the good and train the incompetent, and they will be zealous."

2.24 The Master said: "To worship gods that are not yours, that is toadyism. Not to act when justice commands, that is cowardice."

4.7 The Master said: "Your faults define you. From your very faults one can know your quality."

4.11 The Master said: "A gentleman seeks virtue; a small man seeks land. A gentleman seeks justice; a small man seeks favors."

4.14 The Master said: "Do not worry if you are without a position; worry lest you do not deserve a position. Do not worry if you are not famous; worry lest you do not deserve to be famous."

4.16 The Master said: "A gentleman considers what is just; a small man considers what is expedient."

4.17 The Master said: "When you see a worthy man, seek to emulate him. When you see an unworthy man, examine yourself."

4.19 The Master said: "While your parents are alive, do not travel afar. If you have to travel, you must leave an address."

4.21 The Master said: "Always keep in mind the age of your parents. Let this thought be both your joy and your worry."

4.24 The Master said: "A gentleman should be slow to speak and prompt to act."

12.16 The Master said: "A gentleman brings out the good that is in people, he does not bring out the bad. A vulgar man does the opposite."

12.21 Fan Chi was taking a walk with Confucius under the Rain Dance Terrace. He said: "May I ask how one can accumulate moral power, neutralize hostility, and recognize emotional incoherence?" The Master said: "Excellent question! Always put the effort before the reward: is this not the way to accumulate moral power? To attack evil in itself and not the evil that is in people: is this not the way to neutralize hostility? To endanger oneself and one's kin in a sudden fit of anger: is this not an instance of incoherence?"

15.6 Zizhang asked about conduct. The Master said: "Speak with loyalty and good faith, act with dedication and deference, and even among the barbarians your conduct will be irreproachable. If you speak without loyalty and good faith, if you act without dedication or deference, your conduct will be unacceptable, even in your own village. Wherever you stand, you should have this precept always in front of your eyes; have it carved upon the yoke of your chariot, and only then will you be able to move ahead." Zizhang wrote it on his sash.

15.8 The Master said: "When dealing with a man who is capable of understanding your teaching, if you do not teach him, you waste the man. When dealing with a man who is incapable of understanding your teaching, if you do teach him, you waste your teaching. A wise teacher wastes no man and wastes no teaching."

15.9 The Master said: "A righteous man, a man attached to humanity, does not seek life at the expense of his humanity; there are instances where he will give his life in order to fulfill his humanity."

15.12 The Master said: "A man with no concern for the future is bound to worry about the present."

15.13 The Master said: "The fact remains that I have never seen a man who loved virtue as much as sex."

15.15 The Master said: "Demand much from yourself, little from others, and you will prevent discontent."

15.18 The Master said: "A gentleman takes justice as his basis, enacts it in conformity with the ritual, expounds it with modesty, and through good faith, brings it to fruition. This is how a gentleman proceeds."

15.19 The Master said: "A gentleman resents his incompetence; he does not resent his obscurity."

15.20 The Master said: "A gentleman worries lest he might disappear from this world without having made a name for himself."

15.21 The Master said: "A gentleman makes demands on himself; a vulgar man makes demands on others."

15.24 Zigong asked: "Is there any single word that could guide one's entire life?" The Master said: "Should it not be *reciprocity*? What you do not wish for yourself, do not do to others."

> **Q** **What aspects of moral conduct occupy Confucius in the *Analects*?**
>
> **Q** **What do the *Analects* reveal about ancient Chinese values?**

Confucianism and Legalism

The two centuries following the death of Confucius marked an era of social upheaval inflicted by the armies of China's warring states. *Bing Fa* (*The Art of War*), the world's oldest treatise on military strategy, reflects the spirit of the age. Probably written between 500 and 400 B.C.E., and attributed to Sun Wu, this Chinese classic, which deals with the tactical as well as the psychological aspects of combat—including the use of spies—was prized by China's rulers and by later military strategists, including Napoleon and Winston Churchill.

The instability of the era of the Warring States generated competing schools of thought concerning human nature and, by extension, the ideal form of government. Such speculation took place among the class of China's scholars, who, much like Aristotle, took a practical approach to the investigation of morality. Mencius (372–289 B.C.E.), China's most significant voice after Confucius, expanded Confucian concepts of government as a civilizing force and the ruler as the moral model. Mencius held that human beings are born good; they fall into evil only by neglect or abuse. In defining human nature, Mencius insisted:

> The tendency of human nature to do good is like that of water to flow downward. There is no man who does not tend to do good; there is not water that does not flow downward. Now you may strike water and make it splash over your forehead, or you may even force it up the hills. But is this in the nature of water? It is of course due to the force of circumstances. Similarly, man may be brought to do evil, and that is because the same is done to his nature.

Based on this view of humankind, Mencius envisioned the state as an agent for cultivating the goodness of the individual.

An opposing body of thought challenged this point of view. In contrast to the Confucians, who generally perceived humankind as good, those who came to be called Legalists described the nature of humankind as inherently evil. From this negative premise, the Legalists concluded that the best state was one in which rulers held absolute authority to uphold (strict) laws and dole out punishment to violators. The leading Legalist, Han Fei Zi (?–233 B.C.E.), argued that the rationality of an adult was no more reliable than that of an infant. The innate selfishness of humankind justified strong central authority and harsh punishment. "Now take a young fellow who is a bad character," he writes:

> His parents may get angry at him, but he never makes any change. The villagers may reprove him, but he is not moved. His teachers and elders may admonish him, but he never reforms. The love of his parents, the efforts of the villagers, and the wisdom of his teachers and elders . . . are applied to him, and yet not even a hair on his chin is altered. It is only after the district magistrate sends out his soldiers and in the name of the law searches for wicked individuals that the young man becomes afraid and changes his ways and alters his deeds. So while the love of parents is not sufficient to discipline the children, the severe penalties of the district magistrate are. This is because men become naturally spoiled by love, but are submissive to authority.

The Legalism of Han Fei would become the fundamental philosophy of China's first empire.

The Chinese Rise to Empire

The Qin Dynasty (221–206 B.C.E.)

Even as the great Roman *imperium* came to dominate the Western world, a comparable empire arose on the eastern end of the vast Asian landmass. The first great period of unity in China came about under the Qin (pronounced "chin"), the dynasty from which the English word "China" derives. By the fifth century B.C.E., the different autonomous states into which the Zhou realm had dissolved were in open warfare, vying with one another for supremacy. In 221 B.C.E., King Zheng (ca. 259–210 B.C.E.) of the state of Qin finally succeeded in conquering all the other rival states, unifying their domains under his rule. He declared himself "First Emperor" (Shi Huang Di), and—like the first Roman emperor, Augustus—immediately set about eliminating the possibility of further conflict. Like the Shang and Zhou kings, the Qin emperors held absolute responsibility for maintaining order and harmony. However, the First Emperor took the additional step of replacing the old system of governing based on a landowning aristocracy with a new imperial government centered on his capital, Xianyang (near present-day Xi'an), and organized into a network of provinces and districts governed by nonhereditary officials. By way of these governors, the Qin enforced the laws, collected taxes, and drafted men to defend the newly annexed regions of their former rival states.

This large, salaried bureaucracy worked to centralize political power by various administrative devices. These included a census of China's population (the first of its kind in world history), the standardization of the written Chinese language, the creation of uniform coinage, as well as a system of weights and measures, and the division of China into administrative provinces that exist more or less intact to this day. In a practical move worthy of the Romans, the First Emperor standardized the width of all axles manufactured for Chinese wagons, so that the wagons would fit the existing ruts in Chinese roads (thus speeding travel and trade). Royal promotion of the silk industry attracted long-distance merchants and brought increasing wealth to China; the Romans called the Chinese the Seres ("Silk People"). While imperial policies fostered the private ownership of land by peasant farmers, the new system permitted the governors to tax those farmers, which they did mercilessly. Peasant protest was a constant threat to imperial power, but the most serious challenge to Qin safety came from the repeated invasions by the nomadic Central Asian peoples along China's northern borders. To discourage invasion, the Qin commissioned the construction of the then roughly 3000-mile-long Great Wall, which stretched from northeast to northwest China (see Map 3.2 and Figure **7.1**). This spectacular feat of engineering may be compared with the defensive wall built by the Roman emperor Hadrian: Hadrian's Wall, only 73 miles long, would be raised in the early second century C.E. in an effort to deter barbarian attacks on Roman Britain's northernmost border. Like Hadrian's Wall, the Great Wall of China could not stop an army on foot; rather, it discouraged mounted men, wagons, and the like from making raids across the borders.

The building of the Great Wall required the labor of some 700,000 people. An equal number of workers is said to have labored for eleven years on the emperor's tomb. The entrance to that tomb, part of a 21-square-mile burial site near the Qin capital, provides an immortal record of the Qin military machine. It contains almost 8000 life-sized **terracotta** soldiers, most of which are armed with actual swords, spears, and crossbows (Figure **7.2**).

Standing at strict attention, the huge army of foot soldiers and cavalry guards the tomb itself, which has not yet been excavated. These figures may have served to replace the living sacrifices that went into the graves of the Shang kings (see chapter 3). The bodies of the ceramic warriors were mass-produced from molds, but the faces, no two of which are exactly alike, were individually carved and brightly painted (Figure **7.3**). In their lifelike intensity, these images resemble Roman portrait busts (see Figure 6.3). But while the latter honored the dead among the living, the Chinese figures were designed to serve the dead in the afterlife. Nevertheless, the subterranean legions of the First Emperor glorify an armed force that the Romans might have envied.

Legalist theory provided justification for the stringency of the law under the Qin, as well as for the civil and political oppressiveness of imperial authority. The Legalist First Emperor so feared public opposition and the free exercise of thought that he required all privately owned copies of the Confucian classics burned and all who opposed his government beheaded, along with their families. These policies, compounded by the oppressive taxes levied to pay for imperial projects, brought the Qin Empire to its end.

The Han Dynasty (206 B.C.E.–220 C.E.)

The Qin dynasty survived only fifteen years, but the succeeding Han Empire would last more than four centuries. Just as the Roman Empire marked the culmination of Classical civilization in the West, so the Han dynasty represented the high point and the classical phase of Chinese civilization. The intellectual and cultural achievements of the Han also made an indelible mark on the history of neighboring Korea, Vietnam, and Japan, whose cultures adopted Chinese methods of writing and the Confucian precepts of filial piety and propriety. The Chinese have long regarded the era of the Han as their classical age, and to this day refer to themselves as the "children of the Han." Han intellectual achievements ranged from the literary and artistic to the domains of **cartography**, medicine, mathematics, and astronomy. The invention of paper, block printing, the seismograph, the crossbow, the horse collar, and the wheelbarrow are but a few of the technological advances of the late Han era.

Han rulers tripled the size of the empire they inherited from the Qin. At its height, the Han Empire was roughly equivalent to that of Rome in power and prestige, but

Science and Technology

350 B.C.E.	Shin Shen completes a catalog of some 800 stars
300 B.C.E.	cast iron is produced in China
250 B.C.E.	the crossbow is invented in China
214 B.C.E.	the First Emperor orders construction to begin on the Great Wall (which will not take its final form until the seventeenth century)

Figure 7.2 Terracotta army of soldiers, horses, and chariots, tomb of the First Emperor of the Qin dynasty, 221–206 B.C.E. Some 1000 figures of the 8000 have been excavated. They were painted with earth pigments of green, black, white, and red. Recently, however, conservators identified the unique synthetic compound called "Chinese purple," used in painting the uniforms of some ceramic warriors. This rare pigment was a mark of royalty and wealth.

larger in actual population—a total of 57 million people, according to the census of 2 C.E. (Map **7.1**). Improvements in farming and advances in technology insured economic prosperity, which in turn stimulated vigorous long-distance trade. In exchange for Western linen, wool, glass, and metalware, the Chinese exported silk, ivory, gems, and spices. Spices were essentials in the ancient world, serving not only to flavor food, but also as drugs, perfumes, preservatives, and anesthetics. Trade proceeded by way of Asian intermediaries, who led camel caravans along the vast "Silk Road" that stretched from Asia Minor to the Pacific Ocean. Trade with the peoples of the Silk Road was brought to its height by the great Han emperor Wudi (140–86 B.C.E.). Impressed with the superior mobility of West Asian peoples, he launched military campaigns to capture the large and sturdy steeds the Chinese called "Celestial Horses" (Figure **7.4**). Bred thereafter by the Han, these horses became status symbols for rich merchants and administrators.

In accordance with Confucian thought, China traditionally scorned its merchants (who were perceived as profiting from the labor of others) and regarded its farmers as

Figure 7.3 Terracotta soldier, tomb of the First Emperor of the Qin dynasty, 221–206 B.C.E. Height 4 ft. Carrying bronze and iron weapons, kneeling and standing alongside terracotta horses and actual chariots, the army of the First Emperor of China guarded his tomb.

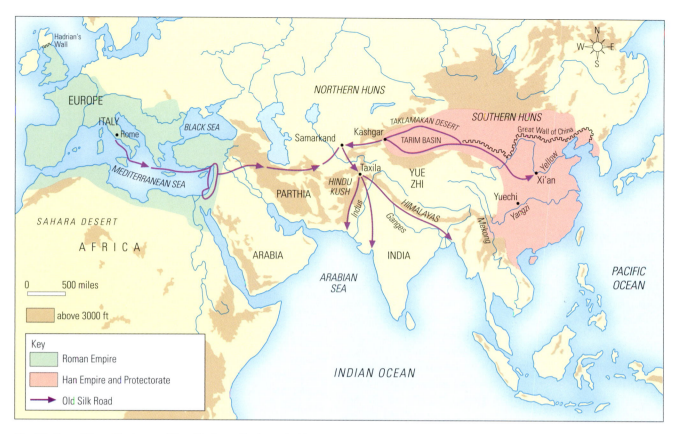

Map 7.1 Han and Roman Empires, ca. 180 C.E. The Roman Empire reached its height by 180 C.E. Two hundred years earlier, Han emperors had extended their authority throughout most of Central Asia and eastward into Korea.

honorable. Nevertheless, while Chinese merchants flourished, Chinese peasants failed to reap the benefits of Han prosperity. Conscripted for repeated wars, they fought the nomadic tribes along the bitterly cold northern frontier. They also served in the armies that conquered western Korea and northern Vietnam. Heavy taxes levied on Chinese farmers to support the Han machinery of state forced many to sell their lands. Wealthy landowners purchased these lands, on which (in a manner reminiscent of the late Roman Republic) bankrupt farmers became tenants or unfree peasants. By the early third century, violent peasant revolts accompanied by "barbarian" incursions led to the overthrow of the Han dynasty. Like the Roman Empire, the great Han Empire fell victim to internal and external pressures it could not withstand.

Figure 7.4 Prancing horse, Eastern Han dynasty, second century C.E. Bronze, 13 × 10 in (approx.). The Chinese believed the larger and finer horses of Central Asia were descendants of celestial horses. They were reported to sweat blood, a condition that may have been caused by parasitic infections that caused swellings that burst and bled.

Science and Technology

150 B.C.E.	iron wheels are designed for shaping jade and reeling silk
110 B.C.E.	the Chinese devise the collar harness (for horses)
100 B.C.E.	the Chinese invent the crank (for turning wheels)
1 B.C.E.	cast iron is used in Chinese suspension bridges

The Literary Contributions of Imperial China

Just as the Romans borrowed the best of the cultural achievements that preceded them, so Han rulers preserved the enduring works of their forebears. These they passed on to future generations as a body of classical learning and thought. Where the Qin rulers had preferred Legalist thought, the Han emperors restored Confucianism to its place at the heart of China's intellectual traditions, and with it came the restoration of Confucian texts and the Confucian scholar/official.

Chinese Prose Literature

The Chinese placed high value on record keeping: the writing of history was one of China's greatest achievements. According to tradition, Chinese court historians kept chronicles of events as far back as 1000 years before the Han Era. Unfortunately, many of these chronicles were lost in the wars and notorious "book-burnings" of the Qin Era. Beginning with the second century B.C.E., however, palace historians kept a continuous record of rulership. Ancient China's greatest historian, Sima Qian (145–90 B.C.E.), the rival of both Thucydides and Livy, produced the monumental *Shi ji* (*Records of the Grand Historian*), a narrative account of Chinese history from earliest times through the lifetime of the author. Sima Qian, himself the son of a palace historian-astronomer, served at the court of the emperor Wudi. After Sima's death, China's first woman historian, Ban Zhao (45–114 C.E.), continued his court chronicle. Ban also won fame for her handbook *Lessons for Women*, which outlined the obligations and duties of the wife to her husband.

The following excerpt from Sima Qian's chapter on "Wealth and Commerce" offers a detailed description of the Han economy, as well as its social and moral life. Whereas economic activity follows the natural order, morals, observes the author, "come as the effects of wealth." In Sima's view, wealth and virtue are interdependent. A flourishing economy will encourage the people to be virtuous, while poverty leads inevitably to moral decay. Stylistically, Sima Qian's *Records* display the economy and vigor of expression that characterize the finest Han prose.

READING 7.2 From Sima Qian's *Records of the Grand Historian* (ca. 100 B.C.E.)

I do not know about prehistoric times before Shennong,[1] but since [Emperor Yu and the Xia dynasty, after the] twenty-second century B.C.E. during the period discussed by the historical records, human nature has always struggled for good food, dress, amusements, and physical comfort, and has always tended to be proud of wealth and ostentation. No matter   1

---

[1] A legendary cultural hero, inventor of agriculture and commerce, ca. 2737 B.C.E.

how the philosophers may teach otherwise, the people cannot be changed. Therefore, the best of men leave it alone, and next in order come those who try to guide it, then those who moralize about it, and then those who try to make adjustments to it, and lastly come those who get into the scramble themselves. Briefly, Shanxi produces timber, grains, linen, ox hair, and jades. Shandong produces fish, salt, lacquer, silks, and musical instruments. Jiangnan [south of the Yangzi] produces cedar, *zi* [a hard wood for making wood blocks], ginger, cinnamon, gold and tin ores, cinnabar, rhinoceros horn, tortoise shell, pearls, and hides. Longmen produces stone for tablets. The north produces horses, cattle, sheep, furs, and horns. As for copper and iron, they are often found in mountains everywhere, spread out like pawns on a chessboard. These are what the people of China like and what provide the necessities for their living and for ceremonies for the dead. The farmers produce them, the wholesalers bring them from the country, the artisans work on them, and the merchants trade on them. All this takes place without the intervention of government or of the philosophers. Everybody exerts his best and uses his labor to get what he wants. Therefore prices seek their level, cheap goods going to where they are expensive and higher prices are brought down. People follow their respective professions and do it on their own initiative. It is like flowing water which seeks the lower level day and night without stop. All things are produced by the people themselves without being asked and transported to where they are wanted. Is it not true that these operations happen naturally in accord with their own principles? *The Book of Zhou*[2] says, "Without the farmers, food will not be produced; without the artisans, industry will not develop; without the merchants, the valuable goods will disappear; and without the wholesalers, there will be no capital and the natural resources of lakes and mountains will not be opened up." Our food and our dress come from these four classes, and wealth and poverty vary with the size of these sources. On a larger scale, it benefits a country, and on a smaller scale, it enriches a family. These are the inescapable laws of wealth and poverty. The clever ones have enough and to spare, while the stupid ones have not enough. . . .   10   20   30   40

Therefore, first the granaries must be full before the people can talk of culture. The people must have sufficient food and good dress before they can talk of honor. The good customs and social amenities come from wealth and disappear when the country is poor. Even as fish thrive in a deep lake and the beasts gravitate toward a deep jungle, so the morals of mankind come as effects of wealth. The rich acquire power and influence, while the poor are unhappy and have no place to turn to. This is even truer of the barbarians. Therefore it is said: "A wealthy man's son does not die in the marketplace," and it is not an empty saying. It is said: 50

> The world hustles
>> Where money beckons.
> The world jostles
>> Where profit thickens.   60

---

[2] The book of documents devoted to the Zhou dynasty (1111–221 B.C.E.)

Even kings and dukes and the wealthy gentry worry about poverty. Why wonder that the common people and the slaves do the same? . . .

[Here follows a long section on the economic products and conditions and the people's character and way of living of the different regions.]

Therefore you see the distinguished scholars who argue at courts and temples about policies and talk about honesty and self-sacrifice, and the mountain recluses who achieve a great reputation. Where do they go? They seek after the rich. The honest officials acquire wealth as time goes on, and the honest merchants become wealthier and wealthier. For wealth is something which man seeks instinctively without being taught. You see soldiers rush in front of battle and perform great exploits in a hail of arrows and rocks and against great dangers, because there is a great reward. You see young men steal and rob and commit violence and dig up tombs for treasures, and even risk the punishments by law, throwing all considerations of their own safety to the winds—all because of money. The courtesans of Zhao and Zheng dress up and play music and wear long sleeves and pointed dancing shoes. They flirt and wink, and do not mind being called to a great distance, irrespective of the age of the men—all are attracted by the rich. The sons of the rich dress up in caps and carry swords and go about with a fleet of carriages just to show off their wealth. The hunters and the fishermen go out at night, in snow and frost, roam in the wooded valleys haunted by wild beasts, because they want to catch game. Others gamble, have cockfights, and match dogs in order to win. Physicians and magicians practice their arts in expectation of compensation for their services. Bureaucrats play hide-and-seek with the law and even commit forgery and falsify seals at the risk of penal sentences because they have received bribes. And so all farmers, artisans, and merchants and cattle raisers try to reach the same goal. Everybody knows this, and one hardly ever hears of one who works and declines pay for it. . . .

— **Q What is Sima Qian's attitude toward wealth?**

— **Q Based on this reading, how might one describe second-century B.C.E. Chinese society?**

Sima Qian's narrative describes the men and women of the Han Era as practical and this-worldly—in fact, as remarkably similar to Romans. This sensibility, which unites a typically Chinese holism with sober realism, is also visible in the large body of Confucianist essays from the Han period. Of these, only one brief example may be cited, for its similarity to the rationalism of Seneca, Lucretius, and other Roman thinkers is striking. *A Discussion of Death* by Wang Chong (17–100 C.E.), offers a skeptical view of the supernaturalism that attracted the vast majority of Chinese people. Wang writes:

Before a man is born he has no consciousness, so when he dies and returns to this original unconscious state how could he still have consciousness? The reason a man is intelligent and understanding is that

he possesses the forces of the five virtues [humanity, righteousness, decorum, wisdom, and faith]. The reason he possesses these is that he has within him the five organs [heart, liver, stomach, lungs, and kidneys]. If these five organs are unimpaired, a man has understanding, but if they are diseased, then he becomes vague and confused and behaves like a fool or an idiot. When a man dies, the five organs rot away and the five virtues no longer have any place to reside. Both the seat and the faculty of understanding are destroyed. The body must await the vital force [*qi*] before it is complete, and the vital force must await the body before it can have consciousness. Nowhere is there a fire that burns all by itself. How then could there be a spirit with consciousness existing without a body?

Chinese Poetry

The writing of poetry has a long and rich history in China. While China's *Book of Songs* drew on an ancient oral tradition (see chapter 3), the poems of the Han Era originated as written works—a circumstance that may have been encouraged by the Chinese invention of paper. Chinese poetry is striking in its simplicity and its refinement. Humanism and common sense are fundamental to Han poetic expression, and Han verse seems to have played an indispensable part in everyday life. As with Greek and Roman lyrics, Chinese poetry took the form of hymns and ritual songs accompanied by the lute or other stringed instruments. Poems served as entertainments for various occasions, such as banquets, and as expressions of affection that were often exchanged as gifts. In contrast with the Greco-Roman world, however, the Chinese produced neither epics nor heroic poems. Their poetry does not so much glorify individual prowess or valorous achievement as it meditates on human experience. Han poetry, much of which takes the form of the "prose-poem," is personal and intimate rather than moralizing and eulogistic. Even in cases where the poem is the medium for social or political complaint, it is more a mirror of the poet's mood than a vehicle of instruction. Notable too is the large number of female poets among the Chinese. The four poems that follow (translated by Burton Watson) are drawn from the

Science and Technology

70 C.E.	China begins building the Grand Canal (eventually 600 miles long)
90 C.E.	the Chinese invent a winnowing device that separates grain from the chaff
100 C.E.	the first insecticide is produced from dried chrysanthemums in China
105 C.E.	cellulose-based paper is first produced in China
132 C.E.	Zhang Heng invents a seismometer that detects the direction of earthquakes

vast corpus of Han poetry. They have been selected not only for their lyric beauty, but also as expressions of some of the deepest concerns of Han poets, such as the practice of bestowing women upon neighboring tribes as "conciliatory" gifts and the conscription of laborers for public works projects. The perceptive reader should discover a number of interesting parallels, as well as contrasts, between these poems and those of the Greeks Sappho and Pindar, and the Romans Virgil, Horace, and Juvenal.

┌── READING 7.3 A Selection of Han Poems

Song of Sorrow

My family has married me   1
  in this far corner of the world,
sent me to a strange land,
  to the king of the Wu-sun.
A yurt[1] is my chamber,   5
  felt is my walls,
flesh my only food,[2]
  kumiss[3] to drink.
My thoughts are all of my homeland,
my heart aches within.   10
Oh to be the yellow crane
  winging home again!

                                   Liu Xijun, ca. 107 B.C.E.

Song: I Watered My Horse at the Long Wall Caves

I watered my horse at the Long Wall caves,   1
water so cold it hurt his bones;
I went and spoke to the Long Wall boss:
"We're soldiers from Tai-yuan—will you keep us here forever?"
"Public works go according to schedule—   5
swing your hammer, pitch your voice in with the rest!"
A man'd be better off to die in battle
than eat his heart out building the Long Wall!
The Long Wall—how it winds and winds,
winds and winds three thousand li;[4]   10
here on the border, so many strong boys;
in the houses back home, so many widows and wives.
I sent a letter to my wife:
"Better remarry than wait any longer—
serve your new mother-in-law with care   15
and sometimes remember the husband you once had."
In answer her letter came to the border:
"What nonsense do you write me now?
Now when you're in the thick of danger,
how could I rest by another man's side?"   20
(HE) If you bear a son, don't bring him up!

---

[1] A circular tent of felt and skins on a framework of poles, the common habitation of the nomads of Mongolia.
[2] Meat was a staple of the Mongol diet.
[3] The fermented milk of a horse, mule, or donkey.
[4] A *li* equals approximately one-third of a mile.

But a daughter—feed her good dried meat.
Only *you* can't see, here by the Long Wall,
the bones of the dead men heaped about!
(SHE) I bound up my hair and went to serve you;   25
constant constant was the care of my heart.
Too well I know your borderland troubles;
and I—can I go on like this much longer?

                                   Chen Lin (d. 217 C.E.)

Two Selections from *Nineteen Old Poems of the Han*

I turn the carriage, yoke and set off,   1
far, far, over the never-ending roads.
In the four directions, broad plain on plain;
east wind shakes the hundred grasses.
Among all I meet, nothing of the past;   5
what can save us from sudden old age?
Fullness and decay, each has its season;
success—I hate it, so late in coming!
Man is not made of metal or stone;
how can he hope to live for long?   10
Swiftly he follows in the wake of change.
A shining name—let that be the prize!

                          Anonymous, late second century C.E.

Man's years fall short of a hundred;   1
a thousand years of worry crowd his heart.
If the day is short and you hate the long night,
why not take the torch and go wandering?
Seek out happiness in season;   5
who can wait for the coming year?
Fools who cling too fondly to gold
earn no more than posterity's jeers.
Prince Qiao,[5] that immortal man—
small hope we have of matching him!   10
                          Anonymous, late second century C.E.

┌─ **Q What personal sentiments are expressed in each of these poems?**

└─ **Q How do these poems compare with those of Sappho, Catullus, and Horace (Readings 5.2, 6.6, and 6.7)?**

The Visual Arts and Music

Because the Chinese built primarily in the impermanent medium of wood, nothing remains of the palaces and temple structures erected during the Han Era, and therefore no monumental architecture survives from China's classical period comparable to that of Rome. Such engineering projects as the Great Wall, however, testify to the high level of Qin and Han building skills.

Some idea of Chinese architecture is provided by the polychromed, glazed earthenware models of traditional multistoried buildings—houses surmounted by

---

[5] According to Chinese legend, a prince who became an immortal spirit.

watchtowers—that are found in Chinese tombs. In the four-story replica fronted by a courtyard (Figure **7.5**), the middle two stories would have been occupied by the family. All levels of the building were roofed by projecting eaves that would become typical of East Asian architecture (see Figure 14.21).

China's royal tombs were replicas of the imperial palace, which was laid out according to a cosmological model: the central building was symmetrical and bisected by a north–south axis. Its foundation was square, symbolizing the earth (*Kun*), and its roof was round, symbolizing Heaven (*Tian*). The plan for tombs, palaces, and cities adhered to the ancient Chinese practice of **feng shui**, by which one seeks to adjust the physical environment in accordance with the five elements (see chapter 3), universal energy (*qi*), and balance (*yin/yang*). The invention of the magnetic compass (see Science and Technology box, page 178) made it possible to bring these "laws of heaven" into conjunction with the needs of the human being. Similar to the Hellenic quest for harmonious proportion, this cosmological practice was less an effort to idealize nature than a means of embracing the natural order. Han royal tombs (many of which still await excavation) held the bodies of rulers and their families, often encased in jade shrouds (Figure **7.6**) and surrounded by their servants. Stone entrances with carved designs combine scenes of everyday life and ritual ceremonies with a variety of protective symbols, all of which reflect the theme of immortality (Figure **7.7**).

Like their forebears, the Han excelled in bronze casting: bronze chariots, horses (see Figure 7.4), weapons, mirrors, and lamps (Figure 7.8) are found in royal burial tombs. Han craftspeople also produced exquisite works in jade and gold, lacquered wood, and silk. But it is in the medium of terracotta—glazed for durability—that the Han left a record of daily life almost as detailed as that found in ancient Egyptian tombs. Scenes of threshing, baking, juggling, music-making, game-playing, and other everyday

Figure 7.5 Tomb model of a house, Eastern Han dynasty, first century C.E. Earthenware with unfired pigments, 52 × 33½ × 27 in. The surface of the exterior is ornamented with geometric designs; to the courtyard exterior, the artist has added trees occupied by birds.

Figure 7.6 Shroud, from the tomb of Liu Sheng at Lingshan, Mancheng, Hebei province, Han dynasty, 206 B.C.E.–24 C.E. Jade and gold wire, length 6 ft. 2 in. Found resting in a lacquered coffin in a cliffside tomb excavated in 1968, the deceased wore a shroud consisting of some 2000 jade wafers (sewn together with golden thread), thought to protect the body from decay and assist in achieving immortality.

Science and Technology

140 C.E. early Chinese compass devised with magnetic silver that always points north–south

190 C.E. Chinese mathematicians use powers of ten to express numbers

200 C.E. the double-yoke harness is invented in China

220 C.E. Chinese make ink from lampblack for early block printing

270 C.E. Chinese alchemists create gunpowder

302 C.E. the stirrup is depicted for the first time in Chinese art

Figure 7.8 Lamp held by kneeling servant-girl. Gilt bronze, height 19 in. From the tomb of Tou Wan (died ca. 113 B.C.E.), Man-ch'eng, Hopei, People's Republic of China. Western Han dynasty. The sleeve and arm of the kneeling servant cleverly become the chimney of this elegant lamp, which was found in the tomb of a Han princess.

Figure 7.7 Reliefs on tomb entrance, Eastern Han dynasty, 25–220 C.E. Stone, height 4ft. (approx.). The top register of the lintel depicts a lively procession of chariots and horses. Beneath are scenes of hunting, while on each side of the portal, figures with weapons and winged ancestral spirits protect the chamber. On the doors appear (top to bottom) phoenixes (symbols of resurrection), beast masks, and raging unicorns.

Figure 7.9 Bells from the tomb of the Marquis Yi of Zeng, Hubei province, fifth century B.C.E. Bronze, height of largest nearly 5 ft.

activities appear routinely in three-dimensional poly-chromed ceramic models recovered from Han funerary chambers. The Han nobility spent so much money on tomb furnishings that the emperors issued edicts to curb excess.

The technical and aesthetic achievements of the Han in the visual arts seem to have been matched in music. Han rulers established an Office of Music in charge of collecting China's folk music—it continued to operate until 1914. They continued the centuries-old practice of burying bronze bells in royal tombs, the most spectacular example of which comes from the late Zhou Era. A set of sixty-five bells, seven large **zithers**, two panpipes, three transverse flutes, three drums, and other musical instruments accompanied the fifth-century B.C.E. Marquis Yi of Zeng to his grave (Figure **7.9**). The instruments (along with the bodies of eight young women and a dog) occupied a subterranean room that replicated the great hall of a palace. Each bell can produce two notes (depending on where the bell is struck), and the name of each note is inscribed in gold on the bell. A set of bells was thus able to range over several octaves, each containing up to ten notes. Whether the bells were used in ceremonial, ritual, or secular events is unclear, but other evidence of other sorts, such as the bronze buckle with dancers holding cymbals (Figure **7.10**), suggests the Han enjoyed a variety of musical entertainments.

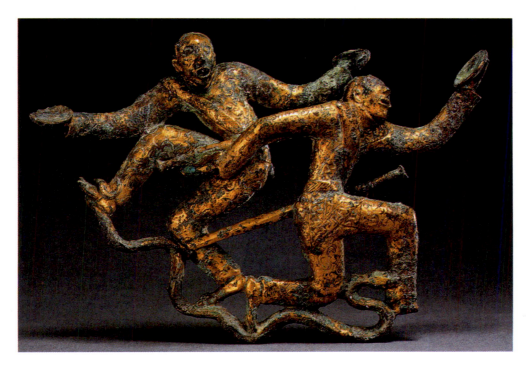

Figure 7.10 Buckle ornament with dancers, Western Han dynasty, 206 B.C.E–8 C.E. Gilt bronze, 4¾ × 7¼ in.

Confucius and the Classics

- During the fifth century B.C.E., Confucius, China's leading thinker, articulated the fundamental rules of proper conduct and proper behavior, which, along with the "Five Chinese Classics," came to provide the basis for Chinese education and culture.
- The two centuries following the death of Confucius brought about an opposing body of thought called Legalism, which challenged Confucius' teachings by describing the nature of humankind as inherently evil.

The Chinese Rise to Empire

- The short-lived, militant Qin dynasty created China's first unified empire. Qin emperors embraced the harsh principles of Legalism, rather than the humanistic teachings of Confucius.
- The Han tripled the size of the empire, which rivaled that of Rome in size and power.
- Han rulers played a vital part in establishing China's classical culture. Over a period of 400 years, an educated bureaucracy revived the teachings of Confucius, while a healthy economy encouraged long-distance trade between East and West.
- Such inventions as the crossbow, the magnetic compass, gunpowder, and paper testify to the high level of Chinese technology.

The Literary Contributions of Imperial China

- Han China produced a body of literature that displays a this-worldly affection for nature and a passion for the good life.
- Ancient China's greatest historian, Sima Qian, wrote the monumental *Shi ji*, a narrative account of Chinese history from earliest times through the lifetime of the author.
- Chinese poetry is striking in its simplicity and its refinement. Humanism and common sense are fundamental to Han poetic expression.

The Visual Arts and Music

- Because the Chinese built primarily in wood, nothing remains of the palaces and temple structures of the Han Era; yet some idea of ancient Chinese architecture is provided by the Great Wall and by earthenware models of traditional buildings.
- China's royal tombs were laid out according to a cosmological model: the central building was symmetrical and bisected by a north–south axis. Its foundation was square, symbolizing the earth, and its roof was round, symbolizing Heaven.
- Grave goods in Han royal tombs reflect China's excellence in bronze casting, silk weaving, jade carving, and the arts of ceramics and lacquered wood. These items, along with spices and other goods, were traded on the Silk Road that stretched from East Asia to the Mediterranean.
- Ancient China's achievements in the visual arts were probably matched in music, as evidenced by the number and variety of musical instruments found in imperial tombs.

Glossary

cartography the art of making maps or charts

feng shui (Chinese, "wind-water") the practice of arranging the physical environment in accordance with the five elements, the balance of nature (*yin/yang*), and universal energy (*qi*)

li (Chinese, "propriety", "ritual," or "arrangement") originally, the proper performance of ritual, but eventually also the natural and moral order, thus, appropriate behavior in all aspects of life

terracotta (Italian, "baked earth") a clay medium that may be glazed or painted; also called "earthenware"

zither a five- or seven-stringed instrument positioned horizontally and usually plucked with a plectrum and the fingertips; the favorite instrument of ancient China

Medieval Europe and the World Beyond

A Flowering of Faith: Christianity and Buddhism

ca. 400 B.C.E.–300 C.E.

"Do not imagine that I have come to abolish the Law or the Prophets. I have come not to abolish but to complete them."
Gospel of Matthew

Figure 8.1 *Crucifixion*, west doors of Santa Sabina, Rome, ca. 430 C.E. Wood, 11 × 15¾ in. This low-relief sculpture is one of a number of fifth-century wood panels depicting scenes from the Old and New Testaments, prepared for the cypress doors of the basilica of Santa Sabina. Often regarded as the earliest depiction of the Crucifixion, it actually shows Jesus (and the two thieves) with arms raised in a position of prayer, common to Early Christian representations found in the catacombs and in liturgical manuscripts (see Figure 9.4).

Shortly after the reign of the Roman emperor Octavian, in the province of Judea (the Roman name for Palestine), an obscure Jewish preacher named Joshua (in Greek, Jesus) brought forth a message that became the basis for a new world religion: Christianity. This fledgling faith came to provide an alternative to the secular focus of Classical culture. It offered the apocalyptic hope of messianic deliverance and eternal life.

As Christianity began to win converts within the Roman Empire, a somewhat older set of religious teachings was spreading in the East. The message of Siddhartha Gautama, the fifth-century B.C.E.* founder of Buddhism, was rooted in the Hinduism of ancient India. Spreading into China and Japan, Buddhism absorbed the older traditions of East Asia, while projecting a deeply personalized spiritual message. By the third century B.C.E., Buddhism had

become India's state religion, and by the fifth century C.E. it was the principal religious faith of China. The similarities and differences between Buddhism and Christianity offer valuable insights into the spiritual communities of the East and West. While no in-depth analysis of either religion can be offered here, a brief look at the formative stages of these two world faiths provides some understanding of their significance within the humanistic tradition.

---

* B.C.E. designates dates "before the Christian (or common) era," while dates from the "Christian (or common) era" are either designated by C.E. where necessary to distinguish them from B.C.E. dates, or are left undesignated.

The Background to Christianity

Both as a religious faith and as a historical phenomenon, Christianity emerged from three distinctly different cultural traditions: Greco-Roman, Near Eastern (West Asian), and Hebraic. All three of these cultures have been examined in the first seven chapters of this book; however, by focusing on the religious life of each at the turn of the first millennium—just prior to the birth of Jesus—we are better able to understand the factors that contributed to the rise of the religion that would become the largest of the world's faiths.

The Greco-Roman Background

Roman religion, like Roman culture itself, was a blend of native and borrowed traditions. Ancient pagan religious rituals marked seasonal change and celebrated seedtime and harvest. Augury, the interpretation of omens (a practice borrowed from the Etruscans), was important to Roman religious life as a means of predicting future events. As with the Greeks, Rome's favorite deities were looked upon as protectors of the household, the marketplace, and the state: Vesta, for instance, guarded the hearth fire, and Mars, god of war, ministered to soldiers. The Romans welcomed the gods of non-Roman peoples and honored them along with the greater and lesser Roman gods. They embraced the Greek gods, who had assumed Latin names (see Table, chapter 4). Tolerance for non-Roman cults and creeds contributed to a lack of religious uniformity, as well as to wide speculation concerning the possibility of life after death. Roman poets pictured a shadowy underworld in which the souls of the dead survived (similar to the Greek Hades and the Hebrew *Sheol*), but Roman religion promised neither retribution in the afterlife nor the reward of eternal life.

Rome hosted a wide variety of religious beliefs and practices, along with a number of quasi-religious Hellenistic philosophies (see chapter 6). Of these, Stoicism and Neoplatonism were the most influential. Stoicism's ethical view of life and its emphasis on equality among human beings offered an idealized alternative to a social order marked by wide gaps between rich and poor, and between citizens and slaves. Neoplatonism, a school of philosophy developed in Alexandria, took as its inspiration some of the principal ideas in the writings of Plato and his followers. It anticipated a mystical union between the individual soul and "the One" or Ultimate Being—comparable with Plato's Form of Goodness. According to Plotinus, a third-century Egyptian-born Neoplatonist, union with the One could be achieved only by the soul's ascent through a series of levels or degrees of spiritual purification. Neoplatonism's view of the soul as eternal and divine, and its perception of the universe as layered in ascending degrees of perfection, would have a shaping influence on Early Christian thought.

Following the decline of the Roman Republic, and in the wake of repeated diplomatic contacts with the royal courts of Persia and Egypt, Rome absorbed a number of uniquely Eastern traditions. Roman emperors came to be regarded as theocratic monarchs and assumed titles such as *dominus* ("lord") and *deus* ("god"). By the second century, Rome enjoyed a full-blown imperial cult that honored the living emperor as semidivine and deified him after his death. At the same time, widespread social, political, and economic unrest fed a rising distrust of reason and a growing impulse toward mysticism.

The Near Eastern Background

In Greece, Egypt, and throughout Southwest Asia, there had long flourished numerous religious cults whose appeal was less intellectual than that of Neoplatonism and far more personal than that of the prevailing Greco-Roman religious philosophies. The promise of personal immortality was the central feature of the "mystery cults," so called because their initiation rituals were secret (in Greek, *mysterios*). The cults of Isis in Egypt, Cybele in Phrygia, Dionysus in Greece, and Mithra in Persia, to name but four, had a heritage dating back to Neolithic times. As we have seen in earlier chapters, ancient agricultural societies celebrated seasonal change by means of symbolic performances of the birth, death, and rebirth of gods and goddesses associated with the regeneration of crops. The mystery cults perpetuated these practices. Their initiates participated in symbolic acts of spiritual death and rebirth, including ritual baptism and a communal meal at which they might consume the flesh or blood of the deity.

The cult of Isis originated in the Egyptian myth of the descent of the goddess Isis into the underworld to find and resurrect her mate, Osiris (see chapter 2). Followers identified Isis as Earth Mother and Queen of Heaven, and looked to her to ensure their own salvation (Figure **8.2**). Initiation into the cult included formal processions, a ritual meal, purification of the body, and a ten-day period of fasting that culminated in the ecstatic vision of the goddess herself. During the second century, in a Latin novel entitled *The Golden Ass*, or *Metamorphoses*, the Roman writer Lucius Apuleius described the initiation rites of the cult of Isis. At the close of the solemn rites, according to Apuleius, the initiate fell prostrate before the image of the Queen of Heaven and recited the prayer that is reproduced in part in the passage that follows. The ecstatic tone of this prayer—a startling departure from the measured restraint of most Greco-Roman literature—reflects the mood of religious longing that characterized the late Classical era.

Figure 8.2 *Isis and Horus Enthroned*, Middle Egyptian, fourth century C.E. Limestone, height 35 in. Sculptures such as this anticipate images of the Mother of God and the baby Jesus popular in Romanesque and Gothic art (see Figures 13.27 and 13.34).

READING 8.1 From Apuleius' *Initiation into the Cult of Isis* (ca. 155)

"O holy and eternal savior of mankind, you who ever   1
bountifully nurture mortals, you apply the sweet affection of
a mother to the misfortunes of the wretched. Neither a day
nor a night nor even a tiny moment passes empty of your
blessings: you protect men on sea and land, and you drive
away the storm-winds of life and stretch forth your rescuing
hand, with which you unwind the threads of the Fates even
when they are inextricably twisted, you calm the storms of
Fortune, and you repress harmful motions of the stars. The
spirits above revere you, the spirits below pay you homage.   10
You rotate the earth, light the sun, rule the universe, and tread
Tartarus[1] beneath your heel. The stars obey you, the seasons
return at your will, deities rejoice in you, and the elements
are your slaves. At your nod breezes breathe, clouds give
nourishment, seeds sprout, and seedlings grow. Your majesty
awes the birds traveling the sky, the beasts wandering upon
the mountains, the snakes lurking in the ground, and the
monsters that swim in the deep. But my talent is too feeble to
speak your praises and my inheritance too meager to bring you
sacrifices. The fullness of my voice is inadequate to express   20
what I feel about your majesty; a thousand mouths and as
many tongues would not be enough, nor even an endless flow
of inexhaustible speech. I shall therefore take care to do the
only thing that a devout but poor man can: I shall store your
divine countenance and sacred godhead in the secret places of
my heart, forever guarding it and picturing it to myself. . . ."

Q **What are the powers of Isis that are praised in this reading?**

Q **How does this compare to "The Hymn to the Aten" (Reading 2.1)?**

While the worship of Isis, Dionysus, and Cybele was peculiar to the Mediterranean, Mithraism, the most popular of the mystery cults, originated in Persia. Mithraism looked back to one of the oldest religious philosophies of the ancient world, Zoroastrianism (see chapter 1). Over the centuries, the ancient hero-god Mithra, who had appeared as judge in the Zoroastrian Judgment ceremony, came to play a major part in this Persian belief system. Associated with the forces of Light and the Good, Mithra's slaughter of the Sacred Bull, one of many heroic "labors," was thought to render the earth fertile (Figure **8.3**). By their personal attachment to Mithra, his devotees looked forward to spiritual well-being and everlasting life. Mithraism featured strict initiation rites, periods of fasting, ritual baptism, and

---

[1] In Greek mythology, a part of the underworld where the wicked are punished.

Figure 8.3 Mithraic relief, early third century C.E. Bronze, 14 × 11⅝ × 1¾ in. Ancient rituals of bull-worship and slaughter, common to Mediterranean cultures (see Figure 4.4), are preserved today in the form of the bullfight (*corrida*).

a communal meal of bread and wine. Mithra's followers celebrated his birth on December 25—that is, just after the sun's "rebirth" at the winter solstice. While Mithraism excluded the participation of women, it quickly became the favorite religion of Roman soldiers, who identified with Mithra's physical prowess and self-discipline.

From Persia, Mithraism spread throughout Europe and North Africa, where archeologists have discovered the remains of numerous Mithraic chapels. Indeed, for the first two centuries of the common era, Mithraism was the chief rival of Christianity. The similarities between Mithraism and Christianity—a man-god hero, ritual baptism, a communal meal, and the promise of deliverance from evil—suggest that some of the basic features of Christianity already existed in the religious history of the ancient world prior to the time of Jesus. It is no surprise that many educated Romans considered Christianity to be an imitation of Mithraism.

Although the mystery cults often involved costly and demanding rituals, they were successful in attracting devotees. The Romans readily accommodated the exotic gods and goddesses of these cults as long as their worship did not challenge the authority of the Roman imperial cult or threaten the security of the Roman state.

The Jewish Background

Judaism, the oldest living religion in the Western world, differed from the other religions and religious cults of this period in its strongly ethical bias, its commitment to monotheism, and its exclusivity—that is, its emphasis on a special relationship (or covenant) between God and the Chosen People, the Jews themselves. As discussed in chapter 1, the early history of the Hebrews is a dramatic narrative of wandering, settlement, and conquest at the hands of foreign powers. Following almost fifty years of exile known as the Babylonian Captivity (586–538 B.C.E.), the Hebrews returned to Jerusalem, rebuilt the Temple of Solomon, and renewed their faith in the Torah. Many, however, in the great dispersion of the Jews known as the **Diaspora**, settled elsewhere. Under the influence of the scholar and teacher Ezra (fl. 428 B.C.E.), the books of the Bible became ever more central in shaping the Hebrew identity. With the eastward expansion of Alexander the Great, the Jews were "Hellenized," and by the second century B.C.E. a Greek translation of Hebrew Scriptures appeared. Called the *Septuagint* ("Seventy"), as it was reputed to have been translated by seventy or seventy-two scholars over a period of seventy-two days, this edition is the first known translation of a sacred book into another language. Repeated contact with Greek and Persian peoples also influenced Hebraic thought. The Book of Daniel, written around 165 B.C.E., makes the first clear reference to resurrection and the afterlife in the Hebrew Bible: "Many of those who sleep in the dust of the earth shall awake, some to everlasting life, and some to shame and everlasting contempt."

The homeland of the Jews became the Roman province of Judea in 63 B.C.E., when the Roman general Pompey (106–48 B.C.E.) captured Jerusalem and the neighboring territories. Imperial taxes and loyalty to Rome were among the traditional demands of the conquerors, but Judaism, a monotheistic faith, forbade the worship of Rome's rulers and Rome's gods. Hence the Roman presence in Jerusalem caused mutual animosity and perpetual discord, conditions that would culminate in the Roman assault on the city and the destruction of the Second Temple in 70 C.E.* (see Figure 6.22). In 135, the Romans renamed Judea "Provincial Syria Palaestina," after the Philistines ("Sea People") who had settled there in the twelfth century B.C.E. Not until 1948, when the independent state of Israel came into being, did Judaism have a primary location in the world. During the first century B.C.E., however, unrest in Judea was complicated by disunity of opinion and biblical interpretation. Even as a special group of **rabbis** (Jewish teachers) met in 90 C.E. to draw up the authoritative list of thirty-six books that would constitute the canonic Hebrew Bible,** there was no agreement concerning the meaning of many Scriptural references. What, for instance, was the destiny of the Jew in the hereafter? What was the nature and the mission of the figure called by the Hebrew prophets the **Messiah** (the "Anointed One")? The Sadducees, a

---

* Hereafter, unless otherwise designated, all dates refer to the Christian (or common) era.

**Following ancient Hebrew tradition, these were grouped into three divisions: the Law (the first five books of instruction, called the Torah), the Prophets, and the Writings—that is, wisdom literature (see chapter 1).

Figure 8.4 *The Good Shepherd*, ca. 425–450 C.E. Mosaic, 6 ft. 10⅔ in. × 12 ft. 1⅔ in. Pictured as a shepherd tending his flock, Jesus wears the purple and gold robes of a Roman emperor—the subtext conflates humility and royal status. The shepherd's crook is replaced by a cruciform staff, a reference to Christ's death by crucifixion.

learned sect of Jewish aristocrats who advocated cultural and religious solidarity among the Jews, envisioned the Messiah as a temporal leader who would consolidate Jewish ideals and lead the Jews to political freedom. Defending a literal interpretation of the Torah, they denied that the soul survived the death of the body. The Pharisees, the more influential group of Jewish teachers and the principal interpreters of Hebrew law, believed in the advent of a messianic redeemer who, like a shepherd looking after his flock, would lead the righteous to salvation (Figure **8.4**). In their view (one that recognized oral tradition along with Scripture), the human soul was imperishable and the wicked would suffer eternal punishment.

In addition to the Sadducees and the Pharisees, there existed in Judea a minor religious sect called the Essenes, whose all-male members lived in monastic communities near the Dead Sea. Renouncing worldly possessions, they practiced **asceticism**—strict self-denial and self-discipline. The Essenes believed in the immortality of the soul and its ultimate release and liberation from the body. They may have been responsible for the copying and preservation of 942 texts, including some of the oldest extant fragments of the Hebrew Bible: the Dead Sea Scrolls, found in 1947 in caves at Qumran near the Dead Sea, which forecast an apocalyptic age marked by the coming of a Teacher of Righteousness. In Judea, where all these groups, along with

scores of self-proclaimed miracle workers and preachers, competed for an audience, the climate of intense religious expectation was altogether receptive to the appearance of a charismatic leader.

The Rise of Christianity

The Life of Jesus

That charismatic leader proved to be a young Jewish rabbi from the city of Nazareth. The historical Jesus is an elusive figure. His name is not mentioned in the non-Christian literature until almost the end of the first century C.E. The Christian writings that describe his life and teachings, known as the Gospels (literally "Good News"), date from at least forty years after his death. And since the authors of the Gospels—the evangelists Matthew, Mark, Luke, and John—gave most of their attention to the last months of Jesus' life, these books are not biographies in the true sense of the word. Nevertheless, the Gospels constitute a body of revelations, beginning with the miraculous birth of Jesus and his baptism by the preacher John at the Jordan River in Galilee: "And when Jesus was baptized, he went up immediately from the water," writes Matthew, "and behold, the heavens were opened and he saw the Spirit of God descending like a dove, and alighting on him; and lo, a voice from heaven saying, 'This is my beloved Son, with whom I am well pleased'" (Matthew 3:16–17).

Written in Greek and Aramaic, the Gospels describe the life of an apocalyptic reformer, who proclaimed his mission to "complete" Hebrew law and fulfill the lessons of the prophets. Word of the preacher from Nazareth and stories of his miraculous acts of healing spread like wildfire throughout Judea. While the Roman authorities viewed his presence in Jerusalem as subversive, the Pharisees and the Sadducees accused him of violating Jewish law and contradicting Scripture. Many questioned his legitimacy as the biblical Messiah. Finally, the Romans condemned him as a threat to imperial stability. By the authority of the Roman governor Pontius Pilate (ruled from 26 to ca. 36), Jesus was put to death by crucifixion, the humiliating and horrific public punishment Rome dispensed to thieves and traitors (see Figure 8.1). All four of the Gospels report that Jesus rose miraculously from the dead on the third day after his death, and that he appeared to his disciples before ascending into heaven. This event, the *resurrection* of Jesus, became fundamental to the religion called Christianity, from the Greek word for Messiah, "*Christos.*" In the earliest representations of Jesus, however, it is not his death on the Cross, nor his reported resurrection, but his role as redeemer and protector—as Good Shepherd—that is immortalized (see Figure 8.4).

The Message of Jesus

While the message of Jesus embraced the ethical monotheism of traditional Judaism, it gave new emphasis to the virtues of pacifism and compassion. It warned of the perils of wealth and the temptations of the secular world. In simple and direct language, embellished with homely parables (stories that illustrated a moral), Jesus urged the renunciation of material possessions, not only as a measure of freedom from temporal enslavement, but as preparation for eternal life and ultimate reward in "the kingdom of heaven." Such teachings represented a new direction in ancient thought, for, with few exceptions, such as the Stoics, the Neoplatonists, and the Essenes, Classical culture was fundamentally materialistic.

Criticizing the Judaism of his time, with its emphasis on strict observance of ritual, Jesus stressed the importance of faith and compassion that lay at the heart of the Hebrew covenant: love of god and love of one's neighbor. He embraced the spirit rather than the letter of Hebrew law, picturing its omnipotent god as stern, but also loving, merciful, and forgiving. In the Sermon on the Mount, as recorded by the **apostle** (disciple) Matthew, Jesus sets forth the injunctions of an uncompromising ethic: love your neighbor as yourself, accept persecution with humility, pass no judgment on others, and treat others as you would have them treat you. This ideal, unconditional love is linked to an equally lofty directive: "You must . . . be perfect, just as your heavenly Father is perfect" (Matthew 5:48).

READING 8.2 From the Gospel of Matthew

(5; 6:1–21; 7:1–14)

The Sermon on the Mount

Chapter 5: The Beatitudes

[1]When Jesus saw the crowds, he went up on the mountain; and after he sat down, his disciples came to him. [2]He opened his mouth and began to teach them, saying,

[3]"Blessed are the poor in spirit,
for theirs is the kingdom of heaven.

[4]"Blessed are those who mourn,
for they shall be comforted.

[5]"Blessed are the gentle,
for they shall inherit the earth.

[6]"Blessed are those who hunger and thirst for righteousness,
for they shall be satisfied.

[7]"Blessed are the merciful,
for they shall receive mercy.

[8]"Blessed are the pure in heart,
for they shall see God.

[9]"Blessed are the peacemakers,
for they shall be called sons of God.

[10]"Blessed are those who have been persecuted for the sake of righteousness,
for theirs is the kingdom of heaven.

[11]"Blessed are you when people insult you and persecute you, and falsely say all kinds of evil against you because of me. [12]Rejoice and be glad, for your reward in heaven is great; for in the same way they persecuted the prophets who were before you.

Disciples and the world

[13]"You are the salt of the earth; but if the salt has become tasteless, how can it be made salty again? It is no longer good for anything,

---

The New Testament

Gospels

Matthew	Luke
Mark	John

Acts of the Apostles

Letters of Paul

Romans	I Thessalonians
I Corinthians	II Thessalonians
II Corinthians	I Timothy
Galatians	II Timothy
Ephesians	Titus
Philippians	Philemon
Colossians	Hebrews

Letters of

James	II John
I Peter	III John
II Peter	Jude
I John	

The Book of Revelations

(The Apocalypse)

except to be thrown out and trampled under foot by men. [14]"You are the light of the world. A city set on a hill cannot be hidden; [15]nor does anyone light a lamp and put it under a basket, but on the lampstand, and it gives light to all who are in the house. [16]Let your light shine before men in such a way that they may see your good works, and glorify your Father who is in heaven.

[17]"Do not think that I came to abolish the Law or the Prophets; I did not come to abolish but to fulfill. [18]For truly I say to you, until heaven and earth pass away, not the smallest letter or stroke shall pass from the Law until all is accomplished. [19]Whoever then annuls one of the least of these commandments, and teaches others to do the same, shall be called least in the kingdom of heaven; but whoever keeps and teaches them, he shall be called great in the kingdom of heaven.

[20]"For I say to you that unless your righteousness surpasses that of the scribes and Pharisees, you will not enter the kingdom of heaven.

Personal relationships

[21]"You have heard that the ancients were told, 'You shall not commit murder' and 'Whoever commits murder shall be liable to the court.' [22]But I say to you that everyone who is angry with his brother shall be guilty before the court; and whoever says to his brother, 'You good-for-nothing,' shall be guilty before the supreme court; and whoever says, 'You fool,' shall be guilty enough to go into the fiery hell. [23]Therefore if you are presenting your offering at the altar, and there remember that your brother has something against you, [24]leave your offering there before the altar and go; first be reconciled to your brother, and then come and present your offering. [25]Make friends quickly with your opponent at law while you are with him on the way, so that your opponent may not hand you over to the judge, and the judge to the officer, and you be thrown into prison. [26]Truly I say to you, you will not come out of there until you have paid up the last cent.

[27]"You have heard that it was said, 'You shall not commit adultery'; [28]but I say to you that everyone who looks at a woman with lust for her has already committed adultery with her in his heart. [29]If your right eye makes you stumble, tear it out and throw it from you; for it is better for you to lose one of the parts of your body, than for your whole body to be thrown into hell. [30]If your right hand makes you stumble, cut it off and throw it from you; for it is better for you to lose one of the parts of your body, than for your whole body to go into hell.

[31]"It was said, 'Whoever sends his wife away, let him give her a certificate of divorce'; [32]but I say to you that everyone who divorces his wife, except for the reason of unchastity, makes her commit adultery; and whoever marries a divorced woman commits adultery.

[33]"Again, you have heard that the ancients were told, 'You shall not make false vows, but shall fulfill your vows to the Lord.' [34]But I say to you, make no oath at all, either by heaven, for it is the throne of God, [35]or by the earth, for it is the footstool of his feet, or by Jerusalem, for it is the city of the great King. [36]Nor shall you make an oath by your head, for you cannot make one hair white or black. [37]But let your statement be, 'Yes, yes' or 'No, no'; anything beyond these is of evil.

[38]"You have heard that it was said, 'An eye for an eye, and a tooth for a tooth.' [39]But I say to you, do not resist an evil person; but whoever slaps you on your right cheek, turn the other to him also. [40]If anyone wants to sue you and take your shirt, let him have your coat also. [41]Whoever forces you to go one mile, go with him two. [42]Give to him who asks of you, and do not turn away from him who wants to borrow from you.

[43]"You have heard that it was said, 'You shall love your neighbor and hate your enemy.' [44]But I say to you, love your enemies and pray for those who persecute you, [45]so that you may be sons of your Father who is in heaven; for he causes his sun to rise on the evil and the good, and sends rain on the righteous and the unrighteous. [46]For if you love those who love you, what reward do you have? Do not even the tax collectors do the same? [47]If you greet only your brothers, what more are you doing than others? Do not even the Gentiles do the same? [48]Therefore you are to be perfect, as your heavenly Father is perfect.

Chapter 6: Giving to the poor and prayer

[1]"Beware of practicing your righteousness before men to be noticed by them; otherwise you have no reward with your Father who is in heaven. [2]So when you give to the poor, do not sound a trumpet before you, as the hypocrites do in the synagogues and in the streets, so that they may be honored by men. Truly I say to you, they have their reward in full. [3]But when you give to the poor, do not let your left hand know what your right hand is doing, [4]so that your giving will be in secret; and your Father who sees what is done in secret will reward you.

[5]"When you pray, you are not to be like the hypocrites; for they love to stand and pray in the synagogues and on the street corners so that they may be seen by men. Truly I say to you, they have their reward in full. [6]But you, when you pray, go into your inner room, close your door and pray to your Father who is in secret, and your Father who sees what is done in secret will reward you.

[7]"And when you are praying, do not use meaningless repetition as the Gentiles do, for they suppose that they will be heard for their many words. [8]So do not be like them; for your Father knows what you need before you ask him. [9]Pray, then, in this way:

Our Father who is in heaven,
Hallowed be your name.
[10]Your kingdom come.
Your will be done,
On earth as it is in heaven.
[11]Give us this day our daily bread.
[12]And forgive us our debts, as we also have forgiven our debtors.
[13]And do not lead us into temptation, but deliver us from evil.

[14]"For if you forgive others for their transgressions, your heavenly Father will also forgive you. [15]But if you do not forgive others, then your Father will not forgive your transgressions."

Fasting; The true treasure; Wealth (Mammon)

[16]"Whenever you fast, do not put on a gloomy face as the hypocrites do, for they neglect their appearance so that they will be noticed by men when they are fasting. Truly I say to you, they have their reward in full. [17]But you, when you fast, anoint your head and wash your face [18]so that your fasting will not be noticed by men, but by your Father who is in secret; and your Father who sees what is done in secret will reward you.

[19]"Do not store up for yourselves treasures on earth, where moth and rust destroy, and where thieves break in and steal. [20]But store up for yourselves treasures in heaven, where neither moth nor rust

destroys, and where thieves do not break in or steal; [21]for where your treasure is, there your heart will be also."

Chapter 7: Judging others

[1]"Do not judge so that you will not be judged. [2]For in the way you judge, you will be judged; and by your standard of measure, it will be measured to you. [3]Why do you look at the speck that is in your brother's eye, but do not notice the log that is in your own eye? [4]Or how can you say to your brother, 'Let me take the speck out of your eye,' and behold, the log is in your own eye? [5]You hypocrite, first take the log out of your own eye, and then you will see clearly to take the speck out of your brother's eye.

[6]"Do not give what is holy to dogs, and do not throw your pearls before swine, or they will trample them under their feet, and turn and tear you to pieces."

Prayer and the Golden Rule

[7]"Ask, and it will be given to you; seek, and you will find; knock, and it will be opened to you. [8]For everyone who asks receives, and he who seeks finds, and to him who knocks it will be opened. [9]Or what man is there among you who, when his son asks for a loaf, will give him a stone? [10]Or if he asks for a fish, he will not give him a snake, will he? [11]If you then, being evil, know how to give good gifts to your children, how much more will your Father who is in heaven give what is good to those who ask him!

[12]"In everything, therefore, treat people the same way you want them to treat you, for this is the Law and the Prophets."

The Narrow and Wide Gates

[13]"Enter through the narrow gate; for the gate is wide and the way is broad that leads to destruction, and there are many who enter through it. [14]For the gate is small and the way is narrow that leads to life, and there are few who find it.

Q **What moral injunctions form the core of this sermon, as recounted by Matthew?**

Q **Which might be the most difficult to fulfill?**

The Teachings of Paul

The immediate followers of Jesus were a group of apostles who anticipated a Second Coming in which all who had followed Jesus would be delivered to the Kingdom of Heaven. Despite their missionary activities, only a small percentage of the population of the Roman Empire— scholarly estimates range from 10 to 15 percent—became Christians in the first hundred years after Jesus' death. And those who did convert came mainly from communities where Jewish tradition was not strong. However, through the efforts of the best known of the apostles, Paul (d. 65), the message of Jesus gained widespread appeal. A Hellenized Jew from Tarsus in Asia Minor, Paul had been schooled in both Greek and Hebrew. Following a mystical experience in which Jesus is said to have revealed himself to Paul, he became a passionate convert to the teachings of the preacher from Nazareth. Paul is generally believed to have written ten to fourteen of the twenty-seven books of the Christian Scriptures called by Christians the "New

Testament," to distinguish it from the Hebrew Bible, which they referred to as the "Old Testament." Paul's most important contributions lie in his having universalized and systematically explained Jesus' message. While Jesus preached only to the Jews, Paul spread his teachings to the gentile (non-Jewish) communities of Greece, Asia Minor, and Rome, thus earning the title "Apostle to the Gentiles." He stressed that the words of Jesus were directed not exclusively to Jews, but to non-Jews as well. Paul explained the messianic mission of Jesus and the reason for his death. He described Jesus as a living sacrifice who died for the sins of humankind, and, specifically, for the sin that had entered the world through Adam's defiance of God in the Garden of Eden. For Paul, the death of Jesus was the act of atonement that "acquitted" humankind of Original Sin. Where Adam's sin had condemned humankind, Jesus—the New Adam—would redeem humankind. His resurrection confirmed the promise of eternal salvation. By their faith in Jesus, promised Paul, the faithful would be rewarded with everlasting life.

These concepts, which indelibly separated Christianity from both its parent faith, Judaism, and the Classical belief in the innate goodness and freedom of human nature, are set forth in Paul's Epistle to the Church in Rome, parts of which follow. Written ten years before his death, the letter imparts the message that those who are "baptized in Christ" will "live a new life." The view of Jesus as a sacrifice for human sin accommodated ancient religious practices in which guilt for communal (or individual) transgressions was ritually displaced onto a living sacrifice. It also rehearsed a basic aspect of the mystery cults: the promise of eternal life as reward for devotion to a savior deity. However, Paul's focus on moral renewal and redemption would set Christianity apart from the mystery religions. So important was Paul's contribution to the foundations of the new faith that he has been called "the co-founder of Christianity."

READING 8.3 From Paul's Epistle to the Church in Rome

(1: 8–15; 2:1–11; 5; 6:1–11; 8:1–8)

Chapter 1: The Gospel Exalted

[8]First, I thank my God through Jesus Christ for you all, because your faith is being proclaimed throughout the whole world. [9]For God, whom I serve in my spirit in the preaching of the gospel of his Son, is my witness as to how unceasingly I make mention of you, [10]always in my prayers making request, if perhaps now at last by the will of God I may succeed in coming to you. [11]For I long to see you so that I may impart some spiritual gift to you, that you may be established; [12]that is, that I may be encouraged together with you while among you, each of us by the other's faith, both yours and mine. [13]I do not want you to be unaware, brethren, that often I have planned to come to you (and have been prevented so far) so that I may obtain some fruit among you also, even as among the rest of the Gentiles. [14]I am under obligation both to Greeks and to barbarians [non-Greeks], both to the wise and to the foolish. [15]So, for my part, I am eager to preach the gospel to you also who are in Rome.

Chapter 2: The impartiality of God

[1]Therefore you have no excuse, everyone of you who passes judgment, for in that which you judge another, you condemn yourself; for you who judge practice the same things. [2]And we know that the judgment of God rightly falls upon those who practice such things. [3]But do you suppose this, O man, when you pass judgment on those who practice such things and do the same yourself, that you will escape the judgment of God? [4]Or do you think lightly of the riches of his kindness and tolerance and patience, not knowing that the kindness of God leads you to repentance? [5]But because of your stubbornness and unrepentant heart you are storing up wrath for yourself in the day of wrath and revelation of the righteous judgment of God, [6]who will render to each person according to his deeds: [7]to those who by perseverance in doing good seek for glory and honor and immortality, eternal life; [8]but to those who are selfishly ambitious and do not obey the truth, but obey unrighteousness, wrath and indignation. [9]There will be tribulation and distress for every soul of man who does evil, of the Jew first and also of the Greek, [10]but glory and honor and peace to everyone who does good, to the Jew first and also to the Greek. [11]For there is no partiality with God.

Chapter 5: Results of justification

[1]Therefore, having been justified by faith, we have peace with God through our Lord Jesus Christ, [2]through whom also we have obtained our introduction by faith into this grace in which we stand; and we exult in hope of the glory of God. [3]And not only this, but we also exult in our tribulations [hardships], knowing that tribulation brings about perseverance; [4]and perseverance, proven character; and proven character, hope; [5]and hope does not disappoint, because the love of God has been poured out within our hearts through the Holy Spirit who was given to us. [6]For while we were still helpless, at the right time Christ died for the ungodly. [7]For one will hardly die for a righteous man; though perhaps for the good man someone would dare even to die. [8]But God demonstrates his own love toward us, in that while we were yet sinners, Christ died for us. [9]Much more then, having now been justified by his blood, we shall be saved from the wrath of God through him. [10]For if while we were enemies we were reconciled to God through the death of his Son, much more, having been reconciled, we shall be saved by His life. [11]And not only this, but we also exult in God through our Lord Jesus Christ, through whom we have now received the reconciliation.

[12]Therefore, just as through one man sin entered into the world, and death through sin, and so death spread to all men, because all sinned—[13]for until the Law sin was in the world, but sin is not imputed when there is no law. [14]Nevertheless death reigned from Adam until Moses, even over those who had not sinned in the likeness of the offense of Adam, who is a type of [prefigured] him who was to come.

[15]But the free gift is not like the transgression. For if by the transgression of the one the many died, much more did the grace of God and the gift by the grace of the one Man, Jesus Christ, abound to the many. [16]The gift is not like that which came through the one who sinned; for on the one hand the judgment arose from one transgression resulting in condemnation, but on the other hand the free gift arose from many transgressions resulting in justification. [17]For if by the transgression of the one, death reigned through the one, much more those who receive the abundance of grace and of the gift of righteousness will reign in life through the One, Jesus Christ.

EXPLORING ISSUES

The Gnostic Gospels

The canon of twenty-seven writings known as the New Testament was established in 325 by the Council of Nicaea. Modern scholars agree that the four canonical Gospels—Matthew, Mark, Luke, and John—were probably written in the first century, but possibly not by first-person witnesses to the life of Jesus. From the late first and second centuries, however, come many apocryphal writings that describe the life and teaching of Jesus. Originally written in Greek and translated into the Egyptian Coptic language in later centuries, these texts are known as the Gnostic Gospels (the Greek *gnosis* meaning "knowledge," that is, knowledge of spiritual truths). Some of these noncanonical writings, such as the Gospel of Thomas, the Gospel of Mary Magdalene, and the Gospel of Judas, record detailed conversations between Jesus and his disciples.

Discovered in the 1970s in an Egyptian cavern, the twenty-six-page Coptic-language version of the Gospel of Judas portrays this disciple as one who served Jesus in planning the course of events that would free the soul in death. In the Gospel of Thomas, written in Greek ca. 140, Jesus is said to have advised his disciple:

"the Kingdom [of Heaven] is inside you and outside you. When you know yourselves, then you will be known, and you will understand that you are children of the living Father. But if you do not know yourselves, then you live in poverty."

The idea (expressed here) that knowledge of Self equals knowledge of the Divine characterized gnostic speculation that flourished in the Jewish community of Jesus' time; it also suggests possible contact between Early Christianity and the westward spread of Buddhist thought (see page 192).

Whether or not the noncanonical Gospels are historically reliable, they offer valuable insights into the beliefs and concerns of Jesus' contemporaries. In an effort to unify and consolidate the young Christian faith, however, early church authorities either rejected or suppressed these writings, some of which, such as the Gospel of Judas, were translated into English only as recently as 2006.

[18]So then as through one transgression there resulted condemnation to all men, even so through one act of righteousness there resulted justification of life to all men. [19]For as through the one man's disobedience the many were made sinners, even so through the obedience of the One the many will be made righteous. [20]The Law came in so that the transgression would increase; but where sin increased, grace abounded all the more, [21]so that, as sin reigned in death, even so grace would reign through righteousness to eternal life through Jesus Christ our Lord.

Chapter 6: Believers are dead to sin, alive to God

[1]What shall we say then? Are we to continue in sin so that grace may increase? [2]May it never be! How shall we who died to sin still live in it? [3]Or do you not know that all of us who have been baptized into Christ Jesus have been baptized into his death? [4]Therefore we have been buried with him through baptism into death, so that as Christ was raised from the dead through the glory of the Father, so we too might walk in newness of life. [5]For if we have become united with him in the likeness of his death, certainly we shall also be in the likeness of his resurrection, [6]knowing this, that our old self was crucified with him, in order that our body of sin might be done away with, so that we would no longer be slaves to sin; [7]for he who has died is freed from sin.

[8]Now if we have died with Christ, we believe that we shall also live with him, [9]knowing that Christ, having been raised from the dead, is never to die again; death no longer is master over him. [10]For the death that he died, he died to sin once for all; but the life that he lives, he lives to God. [11]Even so consider yourselves to be dead to sin, but alive to God in Christ Jesus.

Chapter 8: Deliverance from bondage

[1]Therefore there is now no condemnation for those who are in Christ Jesus. [2]For the law of the Spirit of life in Christ Jesus has set you free from the law of sin and of death. [3]For what the Law could not do, weak as it was through the flesh, God did: sending his own Son in the likeness of sinful flesh and as an offering for sin, He condemned sin in the flesh, [4]so that the requirement of the Law might be fulfilled in us, who do not walk [direct our lives] according to the flesh but according to the Spirit. [5]For those who are [live] according to the flesh set their minds on the things of the flesh, but those who are according to the Spirit, the things of the Spirit. [6]For the mind set on the flesh is death, but the mind set on the Spirit is life and peace, [7]because the mind set on the flesh is hostile toward God; for it does not subject itself to the law of God, for it is not even able to do so, [8]and those who are in the flesh cannot please God.

Q **How does Paul explain the death of Jesus?**

Q **What is his position on sin and salvation?**

The Spread of Christianity

A variety of historical factors contributed to the slow but growing receptivity to Christianity within the Roman Empire. The decline of the Roman Republic had left in its wake large gaps between the rich and the poor. Octavian's efforts to restore the old Roman values of duty and civic pride had failed to offset increasing impersonalism and bureaucratic corruption. Furthermore, as early as the

second century B.C.E., Germanic tribes had been migrating into the West and assaulting Rome's borders (see chapter 11). Repeatedly, these nomadic people put Rome on the defensive and added to the prevailing sense of insecurity. Amid widespread oppression and grinding poverty, Christianity promised redemption from sins, personal immortality, and a life to come from which material adversity was absent. The message of Jesus was easy to understand, free of cumbersome regulations (characteristic of Judaism) and costly rituals (characteristic of the mystery cults), and, in contrast to Mithraism, accessible to all—male and female, rich and poor, free and enslaved. The unique feature of the new faith, however, was its historical credibility, that is, the fact that Jesus—unlike the elusive gods of the mystery cults or the remote Yahweh—had actually lived among Judea's men and women and had practiced the morality he preached. The spread of Christianity was helped by the evangelical fervor of the apostles, the common language of Greek in the eastern part of the Empire, and the fact that the *Pax Romana* facilitated safe travel by land and sea.

Nevertheless, at the outset the new religion failed to win official approval. While both Roman religion and the mystery cults were receptive to many gods, Christianity—like Judaism—professed monotheism. Christians not only refused to worship the emperor as divine but also denied the existence of the Roman gods. Even more threatening to the state was the Christian refusal to serve in the Roman army. While the Romans dealt with the Jews by destroying Jerusalem, how might they annihilate a people whose kingdom was in heaven? During the first century, Christian converts were simply expelled from the city of Rome, but during the late third century—a time of famine, plague, and war—Christians who refused to make sacrifices to the Roman gods of state suffered horrific forms of persecution: they were tortured, burned, beheaded, or thrown to wild beasts in the public amphitheaters. Christian martyrs astonished Roman audiences by going to their deaths joyously proclaiming their anticipation of a better life in the hereafter.

Not until 313, when the emperor Constantine issued the Edict of Milan, did the public persecution of Christians come to an end. The Edict, which proclaimed religious toleration in the West, not only liberated Christians from physical and political oppression, but also encouraged the development of Christianity as a legitimate faith. Christian leaders were free to establish a uniform doctrine of belief, an administrative hierarchy, guidelines for worship, and a vocabulary of religious expression (see chapter 9). By the end of the fourth century, the minor religious sect known as Christianity had become the official religion of the Roman Empire.

The Rise of Buddhism

The Life of the Buddha

The reasons why similar world-historical developments occur at approximately the same time within two remotely related cultures is a mystery never solved by historians. One of the most interesting such parallels is that between the spread of Buddhism in the East and the emergence of Christianity in the West, both of which occurred during the first century of the Christian era. Siddhartha Gautama, known as the Buddha ("Enlightened One"), lived in India some three to five centuries before Jesus—scholars still disagree as to whether his life spanned the years 560–480 or 440–360 B.C.E. Born into a princely Hindu family, Siddhartha was well educated and protected from the experience of pain and suffering. At the age of nineteen, he married his cousin and fathered a son. Legend has it that upon leaving the palace one day, Siddhartha encountered a diseased man, a wrinkled old man, and a rotting corpse. The realization of these three "truths" of existence—sickness, old age, and death— led the twenty-nine-year-old Siddhartha to renounce his wealth, abandon his wife and child, and begin the quest for inner illumination. With shaven head, yellow robe, and

begging bowl, he followed the way of the Hindu ascetic. After six years, however, he concluded that the life of self-denial was futile. Turning inward, Siddhartha sat beneath a bo (fig) tree (Figure **8.5**) and began the work that would bring him to enlightenment—the omniscient consciousness of reality. Meditation would lead Siddhartha to the full perception that the cause of human sufferings is desire, that is, attachment to material things. For the next forty years—he died at the age of eighty—the Enlightened One preached a message of humility and compassion, the pursuit of which might lead his followers to *nirvana*, the ultimate release from illusion and from the Wheel of Rebirth.

The Message of the Buddha

With his earliest sermons, the Buddha set in motion the Wheel of the Law (*dharma*). His message was simple. The path to enlightenment begins with the Four Noble Truths:

1. pain is universal
2. desire causes pain
3. ceasing to desire relieves pain
4. right conduct leads to release from pain.

Right conduct takes the Middle Way, or Eightfold Path: right views, right intention, right speech, right action, right livelihood, right effort, right mindfulness, and right concentration. The Eightfold Path leads to insight and knowledge, and, ultimately, to *nirvana*. The Buddhist's goal is not, as with Christianity, the promise of personal immortality, but rather, escape from the endless cycle of birth, death, and rebirth. For the Buddhist, "salvation" lies in the extinction of the Self.

The Buddha was an eloquent teacher whose concerns, like those of Jesus, were ethical and egalitarian. Just as Jesus criticized Judaism's emphasis on ritual, so Siddhartha attacked the existing forms of Hindu worship, including animal sacrifice and the authority of the *Vedas*. In accord with Hinduism, he encouraged the annihilation of worldly desires and the renunciation of material wealth. But in contrast to the caste-oriented Hinduism of his time, the Buddha held that enlightenment could be achieved by all people, regardless of caste. Renouncing reliance on the popular gods of the *Vedas* (see chapter 3), the Buddha urged his followers to work out their own salvation.

Ultimately, Jesus and Siddhartha were reformers of older world faiths: Judaism and Hinduism. Soon after his enlightenment, Siddhartha assembled a group of disciples, five of whom founded the first Buddhist monastic order. In the years after his death, his life came to be surrounded by miraculous tales, which, along with his sermons, were preserved and recorded by his followers. For instance, legend has it that Siddhartha was born miraculously from the right side of his mother, Queen Maya; and at that very moment, the tree she touched in the royal garden burst into bloom.

The Buddha himself wrote nothing, but his disciples memorized his teachings and set them down during the first century B.C.E. in three main books, the *Pitakas* or "Baskets of the Law." These works, written in Pali and Sanskrit, were divided into instructional chapters known as **sutras** (Sanskrit for "thread"). The most famous of the

Figure 8.5 *Seated Buddha*, from the Gandharan region of northwest Pakistan, ca. 200. Gray schist, 4 ft. 3 in. × 31 in. Born into India's princely Shakya clan, the Buddha was known as Shakyamuni, "sage of the Shakyas." He is shown here wearing the simple robes of a monk; his elongated earlobes are a reference to his princely origins. The iconic Buddha pose is a study in psychic self-containment.

works in the Buddhist canon is the sermon that the Buddha preached to his disciples at the Deer Park in Benares (modern Varanasi in northeast India). The Sermon at Benares, part of which is reproduced here, urges the abandonment of behavioral extremes and the pursuit of the Eightfold Path of right conduct. In its emphasis on modesty, moderation, and compassion, and on the renunciation of worldly pleasures, it has much in common with Jesus' Sermon on the Mount. Comparable also to Jesus' teachings (see Matthew 5:11, for instance) is the Buddha's regard for loving kindness that "commends the return of good for evil"—a concept central to the Sermon on Abuse.

READING 8.4a From the Buddha's Sermon at Benares (recorded ca. 100 B.C.E.)

"There are two extremes, O bhikkhus,[1] which the man who **1** has given up the world ought not to follow—the habitual practice, on the one hand, of self-indulgence which is unworthy, vain, and fit only for the worldly-minded—and the habitual practice, on the other hand, of self-mortification, which is painful, useless, and unprofitable.

"Neither abstinence from fish or flesh, nor going naked, nor shaving the head, nor wearing matted hair, nor dressing in a rough garment, nor covering oneself with dirt, nor sacrificing to Agni,[2] will cleanse a man who is not free from delusions. **10**

"Reading the Vedas, making offerings to priests, or sacrifices to the gods, self-mortification by heat or cold, and many such penances performed for the sake of immortality, these do not cleanse the man who is not free from delusions.

"Anger, drunkenness, obstinacy, bigotry, deception, envy, self-praise, disparaging others, superciliousness, and evil intentions constitute uncleanness; not verily the eating of flesh.

"A middle path, O bhikkhus, avoiding the two extremes, had been discovered by the Tathāgata[3]—a path which opens the **20** eyes, and bestows understanding, which leads to peace of mind, to the higher wisdom, to full enlightenment, to Nirvāna!
"What is that middle path, O bhikkhus, avoiding these two extremes, discovered by the Tathāgata—that path which opens the eyes, and bestows understanding, which leads to peace of mind, to the higher wisdom, to full enlightenment, to Nirvāna?

"Let me teach you, O bhikkhus, the middle path, which keeps aloof from both extremes. By suffering, the emaciated devotee produces confusion and sickly thoughts in his mind. **30** Mortification is not conducive even to worldly knowledge; how much less to a triumph over the senses!

"He who fills his lamp with water will not dispel the darkness, and he who tries to light a fire with rotten wood will fail. And how can any one be free from self by leading a wretched life, if he does not succeed in quenching the fires of

lust, if he still hankers after either worldly or heavenly pleasures. But he in whom self has become extinct is free from lust; he will desire neither worldly nor heavenly pleasures, and the satisfaction of his natural wants will not **40** defile him. However, let him be moderate, let him eat and drink according to the needs of the body.

"Sensuality is enervating; the self-indulgent man is a slave to his passions, and pleasure-seeking is degrading and vulgar.

"But to satisfy the necessities of life is not evil. To keep the body in good health is a duty, for otherwise we shall not be able to trim the lamp of wisdom, and keep our mind strong and clear. Water surrounds the lotus-flower, but does not wet its petals.

"This is the middle path, O bhikkhus, that keeps aloof from **50** both extremes."

And the Blessed One spoke kindly to his disciples, pitying them for their errors, and pointing out the uselessness of their endeavors, and the ice of ill will that chilled their hearts melted away under the gentle warmth of the Master's persuasion.

Now the Blessed One set the wheel of the most excellent law[4] rolling, and he began to preach to the five bhikkhus, opening to them the gate of immortality, and showing them the bliss of Nirvāna. **60**

The Buddha said:

"The spokes of the wheel are the rules of pure conduct: justice is the uniformity of their length; wisdom is the tire; modesty and thoughtfulness are the hub in which the immovable axle of truth is fixed.

"He who recognizes the existence of suffering, its cause, its remedy, and its cessation has fathomed the four noble truths. He will walk in the right path.

"Right views will be the torch to light his way. Right aspirations will be his guide. Right speech will be his **70** dwelling-place on the road. His gait will be straight, for it is right behavior. His refreshments will be the right way of earning his livelihood. Right efforts will be his steps: right thoughts his breath; and right contemplation will give him the peace that follows in his footprints.

"Now, this, O bhikkhus, is the noble truth concerning suffering:

"Birth is attended with pain, decay is painful, disease is painful, death is painful. Union with the unpleasant is painful, painful is separation from the pleasant; and any craving that is **80** unsatisfied, that too is painful. In brief, bodily conditions which spring from attachment are painful.

"This, then, O bhikkhus, is the noble truth concerning suffering.

"Now this, O bhikkhus, is the noble truth concerning the origin of suffering:

"Verily, it is that craving which causes the renewal of existence, accompanied by sensual delight, seeking satisfaction now here, now there, the craving for the gratification of the passions, the craving for a future life, **90** and the craving for happiness in this life.

"This, then, O bhikkhus, is the noble truth concerning the origin of suffering.

---

[1] Disciples.

[2] The Vedic god of fire, associated with sun and lightning.

[3] "The successor to his predecessors in office," another name for the Buddha.

[4] The Wheel of the Law.

"Now this, O bhikkhus, is the noble truth concerning the destruction of suffering:

"Verily, it is the destruction, in which no passion remains, of this very thirst; it is the laying aside of, the being free from, the dwelling no longer upon this thirst.

"This, then, O bhikkhus, is the noble truth concerning the destruction of suffering.

"Now this, O bhikkhus, is the noble truth concerning the way which leads to the destruction of sorrow. Verily! it is this noble eightfold path; that is to say:

"Right views; right aspirations; right speech; right behavior; right livelihood; right effort; right thoughts; and right contemplation.

"This, then, O bhikkhus, is the noble truth concerning the destruction of sorrow.

"By the practice of loving kindness I have attained liberation of heart, and thus I am assured that I shall never return in renewed births. I have even now attained Nirvāna."

And when the Blessed One had thus set the royal chariot wheel of truth rolling onward, a rapture thrilled through the universes. . . .

Q **How does the Buddhist Middle Path compare with Aristotle's Doctrine of the Mean (Reading 4.7)?**

Q **How might a Stoic (Reading 6.2) respond to the Buddha's sermon?**

READING 8.4b From the Buddha's Sermon on Abuse (recorded ca. 100 B.C.E.)

And the Blessed One observed the ways of society and noticed how much misery came from malignity and foolish offenses done only to gratify vanity and self-seeking pride.

And the Buddha said: "If a man foolishly does me wrong, I will return to him the protection of my ungrudging love; the more evil comes from him, the more good shall go from me; the fragrance of goodness always comes to me, and the harmful air of evil goes to him."

A foolish man learning that the Buddha observed the principle of great love which commends the return of good for evil, came and abused him. The Buddha was silent, pitying his folly.

When the man had finished his abuse, the Buddha asked him, saying: "Son, if a man declined to accept a present made to him, to whom would it belong?" And he answered: "In that case it would belong to the man who offered it."

"My son," said the Buddha, "thou has railed at me, but I decline to accept thy abuse, and request thee to keep it thyself. Will it not be a source of misery to thee? As the echo belongs to the sound, and the shadow to the substance, so misery will overtake the evildoer without fail."

The abuser made no reply, and the Buddha continued:

"A wicked man who reproaches a virtuous one is like one who looks up and spits at heaven; the spittle soils not the heaven, but comes back and defiles his own person.

"The slanderer is like one who flings dust at another when

the wind is contrary; the dust does but return on him who threw it. The virtuous man cannot be hurt and the misery that the other would inflict comes back on himself."

The abuser went away ashamed, but he came again and took 30 refuge in the Buddha, the Dharma,[1] and the Sangha[2]. . . .

Q **Based on these sermons, how do the teachings of Jesus (Reading 8.2) and the Buddha compare?**

The Spread of Buddhism

During the third century B.C.E., the emperor Ashoka (273–232 B.C.E.) made Buddhism the state religion of India. Ashoka's role in spreading Buddhism foreshadowed Constantine's labors on behalf of Christianity; but Ashoka went even further. He initiated official policies of non-violence (*ahimsa*), promoted vegetarianism, and defended egalitarianism. He built monuments and shrines honoring the Buddha throughout India; and he sent Buddhist missionaries as far west as Greece and southeast into Ceylon (present-day Sri Lanka). So influential was this remarkable ruler that numerous stories of his humility came to be compiled in a book known as the *Ashokavadana* (*The Legend of King Ashoka*). In spite of Ashoka's efforts to promote a unified faith, the Buddha's teachings generated varying interpretations and numerous factions. By the first century C.E., there were as many as 500 major and minor Buddhist sects in India alone. In general, however, two principal schools of Buddhism emerged: Hinayana ("Lesser Vehicle") Buddhism and Mahayana ("Greater Vehicle") Buddhism. Hinayana Buddhism (also known as Theravada Buddhism) emphasizes the personal pursuit of *nirvana*, and its followers consider that in doing so they remain close to the teachings of the Buddha and his emphasis on self-destiny. Mahayana Buddhism, on the other hand, elevated the Buddha to the level of a cosmic being. It reveres the Buddha himself, and teaches that he came to earth in the form of a man to guide humankind. Mahayana Buddhists regard Siddhartha Gautama as but one of the Buddha's earthly incarnations, of which there have been many in the past and will be many in the future. The gods of other religions, including those of Hinduism, are held to be incarnations of the Buddha, who had appeared in various bodily forms in his previous lives.

Mahayana Buddhism developed a pantheon of celestial Buddhist figures who inhabit the heavens, but also manifest themselves in earthly form in order to help believers attain enlightenment. These "Buddhas-to-be" or *bodhisattvas* (Figure **8.6**) are beings who have reached enlightenment, but who—out of compassion—have held back from entering *nirvana* until every last soul has been brought to enlightenment. *Bodhisattvas* are the heroes of Buddhism; and much like the Christian saints, they became objects of many popular Buddhist cults. The most

---

[1] The Law of Righteousness; the Wheel of the Law.
[2] An assemblage of those who vow to pursue the Buddhist life.

famous *bodhisattva* is Avalokiteshvara (known in Chinese as Guanyin and in Japanese as Kannon). Although *bodhisattvas*, like the Buddha, are beings beyond sexual gender, they are generally depicted as male. However, in East Asia Avalokiteshvara came to be regarded as a goddess of mercy, hence depicted as more feminine (see Figure 14.1) and worshiped much in the way that Roman Catholics and Orthodox Christians honor the Virgin Mary.

Despite Ashoka's efforts, Buddhism never gained widespread popularity in India. The strength of the established Hindu tradition there (like that of Judaism in Judea) and the resistance of the Brahmin caste to Buddhist egalitarianism ultimately hindered the success of the new faith. By the middle of the first millennium, Hinduism was at least as prevalent as Buddhism in India, and by the year 1000, Buddhism was the religion of a minority. Buddhist communities nevertheless continued to flourish in India until the Islamic invasion of northern India in the twelfth and thirteenth centuries (see chapter 14), during which time Buddhism became all but extinct. Buddhism did, however, continue to thrive in lands far from its place of birth. In China, Mahayana Buddhism gained an overwhelming following and influence. From China, the new religion spread also to Korea, Japan, and Vietnam, where its impact was similarly great. Buddhism's tolerance for other religions enhanced its popularity and universal appeal. Mahayana Buddhism brought a message of hope and salvation to millions of people in northern parts of East Asia. Hinayana (Theravada) Buddhism dominated in Ceylon (Sri Lanka), and spread from there to Burma (Myanmar), Thailand, and Cambodia.

Buddhism in China and Japan

Buddhism entered China during the first century C.E. and rose to prominence during the last, turbulent decades of the Han era (see chapter 7). At that time, Buddhist texts were translated into Chinese; over the following centuries, Buddhism was popularized in China by the writings of the Indian poet Asvaghosha (ca. 80–ca. 150). Asvaghosha's Sanskrit description of the life of the Buddha, which became available in the year 420, was the literary medium for Mahayana Buddhism. Here, as in many other parts of Asia, the Buddha was regarded not simply as a teacher or reformer, but as a divine being. Daoism and Buddhism made early and largely amicable contact in China, where their religious traditions would contribute to the formation of a syncretic popular faith. Buddhist "paradise sects" closely resembling the mystery cults of Southwest Asia promised their adherents rebirth in an idyllic, heavenly realm presided over by a heavenly Buddha. The most popular of these came to be the "Pure Land of the West" of Amitabha Buddha.

Still another Buddhist sect, known in China as Chan ("meditation") and in Japan as Zen, rose to prominence in the later centuries of the first millennium. Chan emphasized the role of meditation and visionary insight in reaching *nirvana*. Strongly influenced by Daoist thought, this sect held that enlightenment could not be attained by rational means but, rather, through intense concentration that led to a spontaneous awakening of the mind. Among the tools of Zen masters were such mind-sharpening riddles as: "You know the sound of two hands clapping; what, then, is the sound of one hand clapping?" The Zen monk's attention to such queries forced him to move beyond reason. Legend has it that heavily caffeinated tea was introduced from India to China and Japan as an aid to prolonging meditation, by which practice one might reach a higher state of consciousness.

Figure 8.6 *Standing Bodhisattva*, from the Gandharan region of northwest Pakistan, late second century C.E. Gray schist, height 3 ft. (approx.). Unlike the Buddha, who wears a humble monk's robe, *bodhisattvas* like this one are adorned with rich robes and elaborate jewelry that reflect the worldliness they will ultimately shed.

The Background to Christianity

- Christianity emerged out of three distinctly different cultural traditions: Greco-Roman, Near Eastern (West Asian), and Hebraic.
- Popular Near Eastern mystery cults promised rebirth and resurrection to devotees of fertility gods and goddesses.
- In the Jewish community, Sadducees, Pharisees, and Essenes held differing interpretations of the biblical Messiah.
- Amidst mutual animosity and perpetual discord between Romans and Jews in Roman-occupied Judea, scores of self-proclaimed miracle workers and preachers competed for an audience.

The Rise of Christianity

- The oldest canonical record of the life and teachings of Jesus is the Christian Gospels ("good news"), dating from at least forty years after Jesus' death.
- The message of Jesus emphasized an abiding faith in God, compassion for one's fellow human beings, and the renunciation of material wealth.
- Jesus cast his message in simple and direct language, and in parables that carried moral instruction.

The Teachings of Paul

- The apostle Paul universalized Jesus' message by preaching to non-Jewish communities, thus earning the title "Apostle to the Gentiles." He explained the death of Jesus as atonement for sin and anticipated eternal life for his followers.

- Paul is generally believed to have written ten to fourteen of the twenty-seven books of the Christian Scriptures, or "New Testament."

The Spread of Christianity

- Christianity slowly won converts among populations that experienced poverty and oppression. It promised redemption from sins, personal immortality, and a life to come from which material adversity was absent.
- In contrast with the elusive gods of the mystery cults, Jesus had actually lived among men and women, and had practiced the morality he preached.
- Not until the rule of Constantine, and the Edict of Milan (313), did the public persecution of Christians come to an end. The Edict encouraged the development of Christianity as a legitimate faith.

The Rise of Buddhism

- Siddhartha Gautama was a Hindu prince whose teachings established his role as the Buddha ("the Enlightened One"). He taught that the path to enlightenment begins with the Four Noble Truths: pain is universal, desire causes pain, ceasing to desire relieves pain, and right conduct (the Eightfold Path) leads to release from pain.
- The Buddhist's goal is not the promise of personal immortality, but rather escape from the endless cycle of birth, death, and rebirth. For the Buddhist, "salvation" lies in the extinction of the Self.

- Like Jesus, the Buddha's concerns were profoundly ethical. Preaching the law of compassion and humility (*dharma*), he promised that enlightenment could be achieved by all people, regardless of class.
- The Buddha himself left no written records; his disciples memorized his teachings and wrote them down during the first century B.C.E. in three main books, the *Pitakas*.

The Spread of Buddhism

- During the third century B.C.E., the emperor Ashoka made Buddhism the state religion of India, sending Buddhist missionaries as far west as Greece and southeast into present-day Sri Lanka.
- In spite of Ashoka's efforts to establish a unified faith, the Buddha's teachings generated varying interpretations and numerous factions. By the first century C.E., at least 500 Buddhist sects flourished in India alone. Mahayana Buddhists claimed the Buddha as a divinity who would lead his followers to personal salvation.
- Buddhism entered China during the first century C.E. and rose to prominence during the last decades of the Han Era. Buddhism was popularized in China by the writings of the Indian poet Asvaghosha.
- Given the strength of Hinduism in India, Buddhism never gained widespread popularity there; in China and elsewhere in Southeast Asia, however, it became the faith of millions.

Glossary

apostle one of the twelve disciples chosen by Jesus to preach his Gospel

asceticism strict self-denial and self-discipline

bodhisattva (Sanskrit, "one whose essence is enlightenment") a being who has postponed his or her own entry into *nirvana*

in order to assist others in reaching that goal; worshiped as a deity in Mahayana Buddhism

Diaspora the dispersion of Jews following the Babylonian Captivity

gnosis (Greek, "knowledge") insight into spiritual truths; secret knowledge

Messiah Anointed One, or Savior; in Greek, *Christos*

rabbi a teacher and master trained in the Jewish law

sutra (Sanskrit, "thread") an instructional chapter or discourse in any of the sacred books of Buddhism

Chapter 9

The Language of Faith: Symbolism and the Arts

ca. 300–600 C.E.

"The earthly city loves its own strength as revealed in its men of power; the heavenly city says to its God: 'I will love thee, O Lord, my strength.'"
Augustine of Hippo

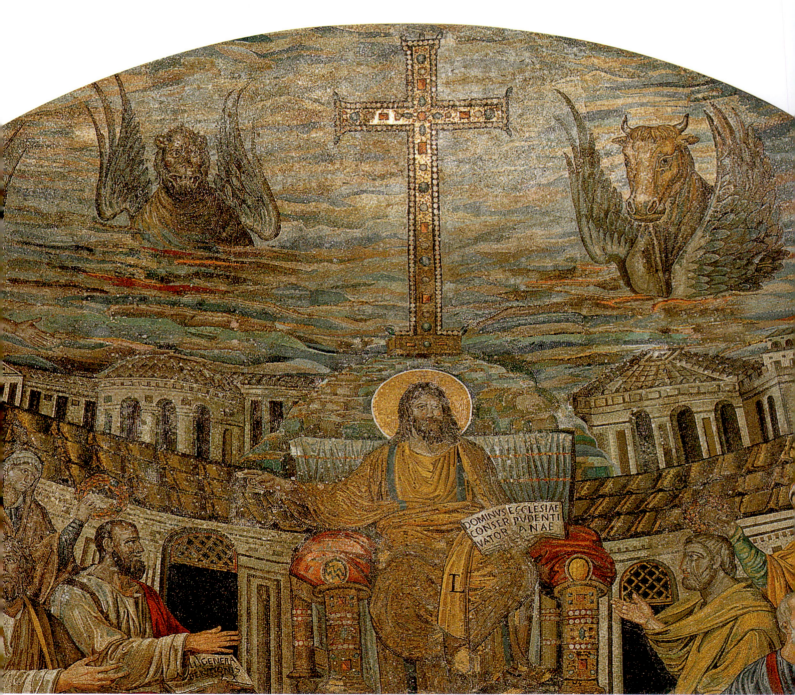

Figure 9.1 *Christ Teaching the Apostles in the Heavenly Jerusalem*, ca. 401–417. Mosaic, height 10 ft. (approx.). Apse of Santa Pudenziana, Rome. Drawing on both Roman and Christian symbolism, Early Christian mosaic masters depict Jesus as Lord of the Universe. Enthroned in the halls of the heavenly Jerusalem, he wears the imperial gold toga with purple trim, and is surrounded by saints, apostles, and apocalyptic symbols taken from the Book of Revelation.

Christianity began its rise to world significance amidst an empire beset by increasing domestic difficulties and the assaults of barbarian nomads (see chapter 11). The last great Roman emperors, Diocletian (245–316) and Constantine (ca. 274–337), made valiant efforts to restructure the Empire and reverse military and economic decline. In order to govern Rome's sprawling territories more efficiently, Diocletian divided the Empire into western and eastern halves and appointed a co-emperor to share the burden of administration and defense. After Diocletian retired, Constantine levied new taxes and made unsuccessful efforts to revive a money economy. By means of the Edict of Milan (313), which proclaimed toleration of all religions (including the fledgling Christianity), Constantine tried to heal Rome's internal divisions. Failing to breathe new life into the waning Empire, however, in 330 he moved the seat of power from the beleaguered city of Rome to the eastern capital of the Empire, Byzantium, which he renamed Constantinople.

While the Roman Empire languished in the West, the East Roman or Byzantine Empire—the economic heart of the Roman world—prospered. Located at the crossroads of Europe and Asia, Constantinople was the hub of a vital trade network and the heir to the cultural traditions of Greece, Rome, and Asia. Byzantine emperors formed a firm alliance with church leaders and worked to create an empire that flourished until the mid-fifteenth century. The Slavic regions of Eastern Europe (including Russia) converted to Orthodox Christianity during the ninth and tenth centuries, thus extending the religious influence of the city that Constantine had designated the "New Rome." As Christians in Rome and Byzantium worked to formulate an effective language of faith, Buddhists in India, China, and Southeast Asia were developing their own vocabulary of religious expression. Buddhism inspired a glorious outpouring of art, architecture, and music that nourished the spiritual needs of millions of people throughout the East, as Early Christian art did in the West.

The Christian Identity

 Between the fourth and sixth centuries, Christianity grew from a small, dynamic sect into a fully fledged religion; and its ministerial agent, the Roman Catholic Church, came to replace the Roman Empire as the dominant authority in the West. The history of these developments sheds light on the formation of the Christian identity.

In the first centuries after the death of Jesus, there was little unity of belief and practice among those who called themselves Christians. But after the legalization of the faith in 313, the followers of Jesus moved toward resolving questions of church hierarchy, **dogma** (prescribed doctrine), and liturgy (the rituals for public worship). From Rome, church leaders in the West took the Latin language, the Roman legal system (which would become the basis for church or **canon law**), and Roman methods of architectural construction. The Church retained the Empire's administrative divisions, appointing archbishops to oversee the provinces, bishops in the dioceses, and priests in the parishes. As Rome had been the hub of the Western Empire, so it became the administrative center of the new faith. When church leaders in Constantinople and Antioch contested the administrative primacy of Rome, the bishop of Rome, Leo the Great (ca. 400–461), advanced the "Petrine Doctrine," claiming that Roman pontiffs inherited their position as the successors to Peter, the First Apostle and the principal evangelist of Rome. As Roman emperors had held supreme authority over the state, so Roman Catholic popes—the temporal representatives of Christ—would govern Western Christendom.

The new spiritual order in the West was thus patterned after imperial Rome.

A functional administrative hierarchy was essential to the success of the new faith; so too was the formulation of a uniform doctrine of belief. As Christianity spread, the story of Jesus and the meaning of his message provoked various kinds of inquiry. Was Jesus human or divine? What was the status of Jesus in relation to God? Such fundamental questions drew conflicting answers. To resolve them, Church officials would convene to hammer out a systematic explanation of the life, death, and resurrection of Jesus. The first **ecumenical** (worldwide) council of churchmen was called by the emperor Constantine. It met at Nicaea (present-day Iznik), Turkey, in 325. At the Council of Nicaea, a consensus of opinion among church representatives laid the basis for Christian dogma. It was resolved—to the objection of some dissenting Eastern churchmen—that Jesus was of one substance (or essence) with God the Father. The council issued a statement of Christian belief known as the Nicene Creed. A version of the Nicene Creed issued in 381 and still used by Eastern Orthodox Christians is reproduced below. It pledges commitment to a variety of miraculous phenomena, including virgin birth, the resurrection of the dead, and a mystical Trinity comprising Jesus, God the Father, and the Holy Spirit. The principal formula of Christian belief, it stands as the turning point between Classical rationalism and Christian mysticism. Challenging reason and the evidence of the senses, it embraces faith and the intuition of truths that transcend ordinary understanding. As such, it anticipates the shift from a homocentric Classical world-view to the God-centered medieval world-view.

We believe in one God the Father All-Sovereign, maker of   1
heaven and earth, and of all things visible and invisible;
    And in one Lord Jesus Christ, the only-begotten Son of God,
Begotten of the Father before all the ages, Light of Light, true
God of true God, begotten not made, of one substance with
the Father, through whom all things were made; who for us
men and for our salvation came down from the heavens, and
was made flesh of the Holy Spirit and the Virgin Mary, and
became man, and was crucified for us under Pontius Pilate,
and suffered and was buried, and rose again on the third day   10
according to the Scriptures, and ascended into the heavens,
and sitteth on the right hand of the Father, and cometh again
with glory to judge living and dead, of whose kingdom there
shall be no end:
    And in the Holy Spirit, the Lord and the Life-giver, that
proceedeth from the Father, who with Father and Son is
worshiped together and glorified together, who spake
through the prophets:
    In one holy Catholic and Apostolic Church:
    We acknowledge one baptism unto remission of sins.   20
We look for a resurrection of the dead, and the life of the age
to come.

Q What is a "creed"?

**Q How does the Nicene Creed illustrate the "leap of
faith" that is basic to all religious belief?**

Christian Monasticism

Even before the coming of Christ, communal asceticism (self-denial) was a way of life among those who sought an environment for study and prayer and an alternative to the decadence of urban life. Such was the case with the Essenes in the West and the Buddhist monks of Asia. The earliest Christian monastics (the word comes from the Greek *monas*, meaning "alone") pursued sanctity in the deserts of Egypt. Fasting, poverty, and celibacy were the essential features of the ascetic lifestyle instituted by the Greek bishop Saint Basil (ca. 329–379) and still followed by monastics of the Eastern Church.

In the West, the impulse to retreat from the turmoil of secular life became more intense as the last remnants of Classical civilization disappeared. In 529, the same year that Plato's Academy closed its doors in Athens, the first Western monastic community was founded at Monte Cassino in southern Italy. Named after its founder, Benedict of Nursia (ca. 480–547), the Benedictine rule (in Latin, *regula*) required that its members take vows of poverty (the renunciation of all material possessions), chastity (abstention from sexual activity), and obedience to the governing **abbot**, or father of the **abbey** (the monastic community). Benedictine monks followed a routine of work that freed them from dependence on the secular world, balanced by religious study and prayer: the daily recitation of the Divine Office, a cycle of prayers that marked eight devotional intervals in the twenty-four-hour period. This

program of *ora et labora* ("prayer and work") gave structure and meaning to the daily routine, and provided a balanced standard best expressed by the Benedictine motto, *mens sana in corpore sano* ("a sound mind in a sound body").

Monastics and church fathers alike generally regarded women as the daughters of Eve, inherently sinful and dangerous as objects of sexual temptation. The Church prohibited women from holding positions of church authority and from receiving ordination as **secular clergy** (priests). However, women were not excluded from joining the ranks of the religious. In Egypt, some 20,000 women—twice the number of men—lived in monastic communities as nuns. In the West, aristocratic women often turned their homes into Benedictine nunneries, where they provided religious education for women of all classes. Saint Benedict's sister Scholastica (d. 543) became abbess of a monastery near Monte Cassino. A refuge for female intellectuals, the convent offered women an alternative to marriage.

From the fifth century on, members of the **regular clergy** (those who follow the rule of a monastic order) played an increasingly important role in Western intellectual history. As Greek and Roman sources of education dried up and fewer men and women learned to read and write, the task of preserving the history and literature of the past fell to the last bastions of literacy: the monasteries. Benedictine monks and nuns hand-copied and illustrated Christian as well as Classical manuscripts, and stored them in their libraries. Over the centuries, Benedictine monasteries provided local education, managed hospices, sponsored sacred music and art, and produced a continuous stream of missionaries, scholars, mystics, and Church reformers. One little-known sixth-century abbot, Dionysius Exiguus (Denis the Little, fl. 525), was responsible for establishing the calendar that is most widely used in the world to this day. In an effort to fix the Church timetable for the annual celebration of Easter, Dionysius reckoned the birth of Jesus at 754 years after the founding of Rome. Although he was inaccurate by at least three years, he applied his chronology to establish the year one as *Anno domini nostri Jesu Christi* ("the Year of Our Lord Jesus Christ"). This method of dating became the standard practice in the West when the English abbot and scholar known as the Venerable Bede (673–735) employed the Christian calendar in writing his monumental history of England.

The Latin Church Fathers

In the formulation of Christian dogma and liturgy in the West, the most important figures were four Latin scholars who lived between the fourth and sixth centuries: Jerome, Ambrose, Gregory, and Augustine. Saint Jerome (ca. 347–420), a Christian educated in Rome, translated into Latin both the Hebrew Bible and the Greek books of the "New Testament." This mammoth task resulted in the Vulgate, the Latin edition of Scripture that became the official Bible of the Roman Catholic Church. Although Jerome considered pagan culture a distraction from the spiritual life, he admired the writers of Classical antiquity and did not hesitate to plunder the spoils of Classicism—and Hebraism—to build the edifice of a new faith.

Like Jerome, Ambrose (339–397) drew on Hebrew, Greek, and Southwest Asian traditions in formulating Christian doctrine and liturgy. A Roman aristocrat who became bishop of Milan, Ambrose wrote some of the earliest Christian hymns for congregational use. Influenced by eastern Mediterranean chants and Hebrew psalms, Ambrose's hymns are characterized by a lyrical simplicity that made them models of religious expression. In the hymn that follows, divine light is the unifying theme. The reference to God as the "Light of light" distinctly recalls the cult of Mithras, as well as Plato's analogy between the Good and the Sun. Culminating in a burst of praise for the triune God, the hymn conveys a mood of buoyant optimism.

READING 9.2 Saint Ambrose's "Ancient Morning Hymn" (ca. 380)

O Splendor of God's glory bright,	1
O Thou who bringest light from light,	
O Light of light, light's living spring,	
O Day, all days illumining!	
O Thou true Sun, on us Thy glance	5
Let fall in royal radiance;	
The Spirit's sanctifying beam	
Upon our earthly senses stream.	
The Father, too, our prayers implore,	
Father of glory evermore,	10
The Father of all grace and might,	
To banish sin from our delight.	
To guide whate'er we nobly do,	
With love all envy to subdue,	
To make ill-fortune turn to fair,	15
And give us grace our wrongs to bear.	
Rejoicing may this day go hence;	
Like virgin dawn our innocence,	
Like fiery noon our faith appear,	
Nor know the gloom of twilight drear.	20
Morn in her rosy car is borne:	
Let him come forth, our perfect morn,	
The Word in God the Father one,	
The Father perfect in the Son.	
All laud to God the Father be;	25
All praise, eternal Son, to Thee;	
All glory, as is ever meet,	
To God the holy Paraclete.[1]	

Q **How does this song of praise compare to "The Hymn to the Aten" (Reading 2.1) and to Psalm 8 (Reading 1.4e)?**

[1] Holy Spirit.

The contribution of the Roman aristocrat Gregory the Great (ca. 540–604) was vital to the development of early church government. Elected to the papacy in 590, Gregory established the administrative machinery by which all subsequent popes would govern the Church of Rome. A born organizer, Gregory sent missionaries to convert England to Christianity, and extended the temporal authority of the Roman Church throughout Western Europe. Despite the lack of historical evidence, his name has long been associated with the codification of the body of chants that became the liturgical music of the early Church.

The most profound and influential of all the Latin church fathers was Augustine of Hippo (354–430). His treatises on the nature of the soul, free will, and the meaning of evil made him the greatest philosopher of Christian antiquity. A native of Roman Africa and an intellectual who came under the spell of both Paul and Plotinan Neoplatonism, Augustine converted to Christianity at the age of thirty-three. Before then, Augustine had enjoyed a sensual and turbulent youth, marked by womanizing, gambling, and fathering an illegitimate child. Augustine's lifelong conflict between his love of worldly pleasures, dominated by what he called his "lower self," and his love of God, exercised by the "higher part of our nature," is the focus of his fascinating and self-scrutinizing autobiography, known as the *Confessions*. Here, Augustine makes a fundamental distinction between physical and spiritual satisfaction, arguing that "no bodily pleasure, however great it might be . . . [is] worthy of comparison, or even of mention, beside the happiness of the life of the saints." The dualistic model of the human being as the locus of warring elements—the "unclean body" and the "purified soul"—drew heavily on the Neoplatonist duality of Matter and Spirit and the Pauline promise that the sin of Adam might be cleansed by the sacrifice of Jesus.

In the extract below from his *Confessions*, Augustine identifies the three temptations that endanger his soul: the lust of the flesh, the lust of the eyes, and the ambition of the secular world. Nowhere is Augustine's motto, "Faith seeking understanding," so intimately reflected as in the self-examining prose of the *Confessions*.

READING 9.3 From Saint Augustine's *Confessions* (ca. 400)

You [God] command me without question to abstain 'from	1
the lust of the flesh and the lust of the eyes and the ambition	
of the secular world'. You commanded me to abstain from	
sleeping with a girl-friend and, in regard to marriage itself,	
you advised me to adopt a better way of life than you have	
allowed. And because you granted me strength, this was	
done even before I became a dispenser of your sacrament.	
But in my memory of which I have spoken at length, there	
still live images of acts which were fixed there by my sexual	
habit. These images attack me. While I am awake they have	10
no force, but in sleep they not only arouse pleasure but even	
elicit consent, and are very like the actual act. The illusory	

image within the soul has such force upon my flesh that false dreams have an effect on me when asleep, which the reality could not have when I am awake. During this time of sleep surely it is not my true self, Lord my God? Yet how great a difference between myself at the time when I am asleep and myself when I return to the waking state. Where then is reason which, when wide-awake, resists such suggestive thoughts, and would remain unmoved if the actual reality were to be presented to it? Surely reason does not shut down as the eyes close. It can hardly fall asleep with the bodily senses. For if that were so, how could it come about that often in sleep we resist and, mindful of our avowed commitment and adhering to it with strict chastity, we give no assent to such seductions? Yet there is a difference so great that, when it happens otherwise than we would wish, when we wake up we return to peace in our conscience. From the wide gulf between the occurrences and our will, we discover that we did not actively do what, to our regret, has somehow been done in us.

It cannot be the case, almighty God, that your hand is not strong enough to cure all the sicknesses of my soul and, by a more abundant outflow of your grace, to extinguish the lascivious impulses of my sleep. You will more and more increase your gifts in me, Lord, so that my soul, rid of the glue of lust, may follow me to you, so that it is not in rebellion against itself, and so that even in dreams it not only does not commit those disgraceful and corrupt acts in which sensual images provoke carnal emissions, but also does not even consent to them. . . .

To this I may add another form of temptation, manifold in its dangers. Beside the lust of the flesh which inheres in the delight given by all pleasures of the senses (those who are enslaved to it perish by putting themselves far from you), there exists in the soul, through the medium of the same bodily senses, a cupidity which does not take delight in carnal pleasure but in perceptions acquired through the flesh. It is a vain inquisitiveness dignified with the title of knowledge and science. As this is rooted in the appetite for knowing, and as among the senses the eyes play a leading role in acquiring knowledge, the divine word calls it 'the lust of the eyes'. Seeing is the property of our eyes. But we also use this word in other senses, when we apply the power of vision to knowledge generally. We do not say 'Hear how that flashes', or 'Smell how bright that is', or 'Taste how that shines' or 'Touch how that gleams'. Of all these things we say 'see'. But we say not only 'See how that light shines', which only the eyes can perceive, but also 'See how that sounds, see what smells, see what tastes, see how hard that is'. So the general experience of the senses is the lust, as scripture says, of the eyes, because seeing is a function in which eyes hold the first place but other senses claim the word for themselves by analogy when they are exploring any department of knowledge.

From this observation it becomes easier to distinguish the activity of the senses in relation to pleasure from their activity in relation to curiosity. Pleasure pursues beautiful objects— what is agreeable to look at, to hear, to smell, to taste, to touch. But curiosity pursues the contraries of these delights with the motive of seeing what the experiences are like, not

with a wish to undergo discomfort, but out of a lust for experimenting and knowing. What pleasure is to be found in looking at a mangled corpse, an experience which evokes revulsion? Yet wherever one is lying, people crowd around to be made sad and to turn pale. They even dread seeing this in their dreams, as if someone had compelled them to look at it when awake or as if some report about the beauty of the sight had persuaded them to see it. The same is true of the other senses, but it would be too long to follow the theme through. To satisfy this diseased craving, outrageous sights are staged in public shows. The same motive is at work when people study the operations of nature which lie beyond our grasp, when there is no advantage in knowing and the investigators simply desire knowledge for its own sake. This motive is again at work if, using a perverted science for the same end, people try to achieve things by magical arts. Even in religion itself the motive is seen when God is 'tempted' by demands for 'signs and wonders' desired not for any salvific[1] end but only for the thrill. . . .

Every day, Lord, we are beset by these temptations. We are tempted without respite. The human tongue is our daily furnace. In this respect also you command us to be continent: grant what you command, and command what you will. In this matter you know the 'groaning' of my heart towards you, and the rivers which flow from my eyes. I cannot easily be sure how far I am cleansed from that plague. I have great fear of my subconscious impulses which your eyes know but mine do not.

In temptations of a different sort I have some capacity for self-exploration, but in this matter almost none. It is simple to see how far I have succeeded in restraining my mind from carnal pleasures and from curious quests for superfluous knowledge; for I do not indulge in these things, either by choice or because they are not available. I then ask myself whether it is more or less vexatious to me not to have them. Riches, moreover, are sought to provide means for one or two or all of the three lusts. If the mind cannot clearly perceive whether it despises the possession of them, that can be simply tested by giving them away.

But how can we live so as to be indifferent to praise, and to be sure of this in experience? Are we to live evil lives, so abandoned and depraved that no one who knows us does not detest us? Nothing more crazy can be suggested or imagined. If admiration is the usual and proper accompaniment of a good life and good actions, we ought not to renounce it any more than the good life which it accompanies. Yet I have no way of knowing whether my mind will be serene or upset to be lacking something unless it is actually absent. . . .

Q. Which temptation does Augustine seem to find the most difficult of resist?

Q. How might he respond to Buddhism's Four Noble Truths?

[1] redemptive.

Augustine's *City of God*

A living witness to the decline of the Roman Empire, Augustine defended his faith against recurrent pagan charges that Christianity was responsible for Rome's downfall. In his multivolume work the *City of God Against the Pagans*, he distinguishes between the earthly city of humankind and the heavenly city that is the eternal dwelling place of the Christian soul. Augustine's earthly abode, a place where "wise men live according to man," represents the Classical world prior to the coming of Jesus. By contrast, the heavenly city—the spiritual realm where human beings live according to divine precepts—is the destiny of those who embrace the "New Dispensation" of Christ.

Augustine's influence in shaping Christian dogma cannot be overestimated. His rationalization of evil as the perversion of the good created by God, and his defense of "just war"—that is, war as reprisal for the abuse of morality—testify to the analytic subtlety of his mind. His description of history as divinely ordered and directed toward a predestined end became fundamental to Christian historiography. Finally, his dualistic model of reality—matter and spirit, body and soul, earth and heaven, Satan and God, state and Church—governed Western thought for centuries to come. The conception of the visible world (matter) as an imperfect reflection of the divine order (spirit) determined the allegorical character of Christian culture. According to this model, matter was the matrix in which God's message was hidden. In Scripture, as well as in every natural and created thing, God's invisible order might be discovered. For Augustine, the Hebrew Bible was a symbolic prefiguration of Christian truths, and history itself was a cloaked message of divine revelation.

The extract from the *City of God* illustrates Augustine's dual perception of reality and suggests its importance to the tradition of Christian allegory. Augustine's description of Noah's ark as symbolic of the City of God, the Church, and the body of Christ exemplifies the way in which a single image might assume various meanings within the language of Christian faith.

READING 9.4 From Saint Augustine's *City of God Against the Pagans* (413–426)

On the character of the two cities, the earthly and the heavenly.

The two cities then were created by two kinds of love: the [1]
earthly city by a love of self carried even to the point of
contempt for God, the heavenly city by a love of God carried
even to the point of contempt for self. Consequently, the
earthly city glories in itself while the other glories in the Lord.[1]
For the former seeks glory from men, but the latter finds its
greatest glory in God, the witness of our conscience. The
earthly city lifts up its head in its own glory; the heavenly city
says to its God: "My glory and the lifter of my head."[2] In the
one, the lust for dominion has dominion over its princes as [10]

well as over the nations that it subdues; in the other, both
those put in charge and those placed under them serve one
another in love, the former by their counsel, the latter by their
obedience. The earthly city loves its own strength as revealed
in its men of power; the heavenly city says to its God: "I will
love thee, O Lord, my strength."[3]

Thus in the earthly city its wise men who live according to
man have pursued the goods either of the body or of their own
mind or of both together; or if any of them were able to know
God, "they did not honor him as God or give thanks to him, but [20]
they became futile in their thinking and their senseless minds
were darkened; claiming to be wise," that is, exalting
themselves in their own wisdom under the dominion of pride,
"they became fools, and exchanged the glory of the immortal
God for images resembling mortal man or birds or beasts or
reptiles," for in the adoration of idols of this sort they were
either leaders or followers of the populace, "and worshiped
and served the creature rather than the creator, who is blessed
forever."[4] In the heavenly city, on the other hand, man's only
wisdom is the religion that guides him rightly to worship the [30]
true God and awaits as its reward in the fellowship of saints,
not only human but also angelic, this goal, "that God may be
all in all."[5] . . .

That the ark which Noah was ordered to make symbolizes Christ and the Church in every detail.

Now God, as we know, enjoined the building of an ark upon
Noah, a man who was righteous and according to the true
testimony of Scripture, perfect in his generation,[6] that is,
perfect, not as the citizens of the City of God are to become in
that immortal state where they will be made equal with the [40]
angels of God, but as they can be during their sojourn here on
earth. In this ark he was to be rescued from the devastation of
the flood with his family, that is, his wife, sons, and daughters-
in-law, as well as with the animals that came to him in the ark
at God's direction. We doubtless have here a symbolic
representation of the City of God sojourning as an alien in this
world, that is, of the church which wins salvation by virtue of the
wood on which the mediator between God and men, the
man Christ Jesus,[7] was suspended.

The very measurements of the ark's length, height, and [50]
breadth symbolize the human body, in the reality of which it
was prophesied that Christ would come to mankind, as, in fact,
he did come. For the length of the human body from top to toe
is six times its breadth from one side to the other and ten times
its thickness measured on a side from back to belly. Thus if you
measure a man lying on his back or face down, his length from
head to foot is six times his breadth from right to left or from
left to right and ten times his elevation from the ground. This is
why the ark was made three hundred cubits in length, fifty in
breadth, and thirty in height. And as for the door that it received [60]
on its side, that surely is the wound that was made when the

---

[1] Cf. 2 Corinthians 10:17.
[2] Psalms 3:3.
[3] Psalms 18:1.
[4] Romans 1:21–23, 25.
[5] 1 Corinthians 15:28.
[6] Cf. Genesis 6:9.
[7] 1 Timothy 2:5.

side of the crucified one was pierced by the spear.[8] This is the way by which those who come to him enter, because from this opening flowed the sacraments with which believers are initiated. Moreover, the order that it should be made of squared beams contains an allusion to the foursquare stability of saints' lives, for in whatever direction you turn a squared object, it will stand firm. In similar fashion, everything else mentioned in the construction of this ark symbolizes some aspect of the church. . . .

Q How is allegory used in this reading?

Q Why was allegory such an important tool in shaping the "New Dispensation"?

Symbolism and Early Christian Art

Christian signs and symbols linked the visible to the invisible world. They worked by analogy, in much the same way that allegory operated in Augustine's *City of God*. Since in Christian art the symbolic significance of a representation is often more important than its literal meaning, the identification and interpretation of the subject matter (a discipline known as **iconography**) is especially important. Before Christianity was legalized in 313, visual symbols served the practical function of identifying new converts to the faith among themselves. Followers of Jesus adopted the sign of the fish because the Greek word for fish (*ichthys*) is an acrostic combination of the first letters of the Greek words "Jesus Christ, Son of God, Savior." They also used the first and last letters of the Greek alphabet, *alpha* and *omega*, to designate Christ's presence at the beginning and the end of time. Roman converts to Christianity saw in the Latin word for peace, *pax*, a symbolic reference to Christ, since the last and first letters could also be read as *chi* and *rho*, the first two letters in the Greek word *Christos*. Indeed, *pax* was emblazoned on the banner under which Constantine supposedly defeated his enemies. Such symbols soon found their way into Early Christian art.

On a sixth-century sarcophagus (stone coffin) of the archbishop Theodorus of Ravenna (Figure **9.2**), the *chi*

Figure 9.2 Sarcophagus of Archbishop Theodorus, sixth century. Marble, length 5 ft., 9in.

[8] Cf. John 19:34.

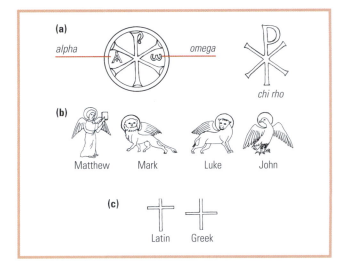

Figure 9.3 (a) Christian monograms; **(b)** symbols of the four evangelists; **(c)** Latin and Greek crosses.

and *rho* and the *alpha* and *omega* have been made into an insignia that resembles both a crucifix (symbolizing Christ as Savior) and a pastoral cross (symbolizing Christ as Shepherd, Figure **9.3**). Three laurel wreaths, traditional Roman imperial symbols of triumph, encircle the medallions on the coffin lid, indicating Christ's victory over death. On either side of the frontal medallion are grapevines designating the wine that represents the blood of Christ. The tiny birds that stand beneath the vines— derived from Greek funerary art—refer to the human soul. Also included in the iconographic program are two popular Southwest Asian symbols of immortality: the peacock or phoenix, a legendary bird that was thought to be reborn from its own ashes, and the rosette, an ancient symbol of Isis in her regenerative role. Taken as a whole, the archbishop's coffin is the vehicle of a sacred language signifying Christ's triumph over death and the Christian promise of resurrection and salvation.

In Early Christian art, music, and literature, almost every number and combination of numbers was thought to bear allegorical meaning. The number 3, for example, signified the Trinity; 4 signified the evangelists; 5 symbolized the wounds of Jesus; 12 stood for the apostles; and so on. The evangelists were usually represented by four winged creatures: the man for Matthew, the lion for Mark, the ox for Luke, and the eagle for John (see Figure 9.3 and the upper portion of Figure 9.1). Prefigured in the Book of Revelation (4:1–8), each of the four creatures came to be associated with a particular Gospel. The lion, for example, was appropriate to Mark because in his Gospel he emphasized the royal dignity of Christ; the heavenward-soaring eagle suited John, who produced the most lofty and mystical of the Gospels. The halo, a zone of light used in Roman art to signify divinity or holiness, became a favorite symbolic device in the visual representation of Jesus, the evangelists, and others whom the Church canonized as holy persons capable of interceding for sinners.

Figure 9.4 *Orans* (praying figure), ca. 300. Fresco. Catacombs of Saint Priscilla, Rome. The figure here is shown wearing the Jewish prayer shawl known as the *tallis* (or *tallit*).

In the centuries following the legalization of Christianity, stories about the life of Jesus came to form two main narrative cycles: the Youth of Christ and the Passion of Christ. Not until the fifth century, however, when the manner of Jesus' death began to lose its ignoble associations, was Jesus depicted on the Cross. One of the earliest of such scenes is that carved in low relief on the wooden west doors of Santa Sabina in Rome (see Figure 8.1). Christ assumes the *orans* in a rigid and static frontal position that also signifies a crucified body. The tripartite composition of the relief includes the smaller (because less important) figures of the thieves who flanked Jesus at the Crucifixion. Despite its narrative content, the image is far from being a representation of the Crucifixion of Jesus. Rather, it is a symbolic statement of Christian redemption.

Early Christians had little use for the Roman approach to art as a window on the world. Roman Realism, with its scrupulous attention to time, place, and personalities, was ill-suited to convey the timeless message of a universal faith and the miraculous events surrounding the life of a savior god. Moreover, Christian artists inherited the Jewish prohibition against "graven images." As a result, very little free-standing sculpture was produced between the second and eleventh centuries; that which was produced, such as the

Some of the earliest evidence of Christian art comes from the **catacombs**, subterranean burial chambers outside the city of Rome. These vast networks of underground galleries and rooms include gravesites whose walls are covered with frescoes illustrating scenes from the Old and New Testaments. One figure is shown in the *orans* position—with arms upraised in an attitude of prayer—an ancient gesture (see Figure 1.2) used in the performance of ritual (Figure **9.4**). Like the story of Noah's ark, "decoded" by Augustine to reveal its hidden significance, Early Christian imagery was multilayered and pregnant with symbolic meaning. For example, the popular figure of Jesus as Good Shepherd, an adaptation of the calf- or lamb-bearing youth of Greco-Roman art (see chapter 5), symbolizes Jesus' role as savior-protector (shepherd) and sacrificial victim (lamb). Featured in catacomb frescoes (Figure **9.5**) and in free-standing sculpture (see Figure 9.6), the Good Shepherd evokes the Early Christian theme of deliverance. But while the message of the catacomb frescoes is one of salvation and deliverance, the style of these paintings resembles that of secular Roman art (see chapter 6): figures are small but substantial and deftly shaded to suggest three-dimensionality. Setting and specific indications of spatial depth are omitted, however, so that human forms appear to float in ethereal space.

Figure 9.5 *Christ as Good Shepherd*, mid-fourth century. Fresco. Catacombs of Saints Pietro and Marcellino, Rome.

Figure 9.6 *The Good Shepherd*, ca. 300. Marble, height 3 ft. (The legs are restored.) One of the most common images of Jesus in Early Christian art shows him as a youthful figure holding a lamb on his shoulders, a theme illustrating the parable of the Good Shepherd (Luke 15:4–7 and John 10:11–16).

fourth-century *Good Shepherd* (Figure **9.6**), retains only the rudimentary features—such as the *contrapposto* stance—of High Classical statuary.

On the other hand, hand-illuminated manuscripts and **diptychs** (two-leaved hinged tablets or panels) designed for private devotional use were produced in great numbers. A sixth-century ivory book cover from Murano, Italy (see LOOKING INTO, Figure **9.7**), is typical of the Early Christian preoccupation with didactic content and surface adornment. Despite its Classical borrowings, the piece abandons Greco-Roman Realism in favor of a language of symbolic abstraction that conveys the Christian triumph over death.

Early Christian Architecture

The legalization of Christianity made possible the construction of monumental houses for public religious worship. In the West, the Early Christian church building was modeled on the Roman basilica (see Figure 6.17). As with the sacred temples of antiquity, the Christian church consisted of a hierarchy of spaces that ushered the devotee from the chaos of the everyday world into the serenity of the sacred chamber, and, ultimately, to the ritual of deliverance. One entered Rome's earliest Christian basilicas, Saint Peter's and Saint Paul's, through the unroofed atrium surrounded on three sides by a covered walkway or **ambulatory**, and on the fourth side (directly in front of the church entrance) by a vestibule, or **narthex**. This outer zone provided a transition between temporal and spiritual realms. Having crossed the vestibule and entered through the west portal, one proceeded down the long, colonnaded central hall or **nave**, flanked by two aisles; the upper wall of the nave consisted of the **gallery** and the **clerestory** (Figure **9.8**). The gallery was often decorated with mosaics or frescoes illuminated by light that entered the basilica through the clerestory windows (Figure **9.9**).

Toward the east end of the church, lying across the axis of the nave, was a rectangular area called the **transept**. The north and south arms of the transept, which might be extended to form a Latin cross, provided entrances additional to the main doorway at the west end of the church. Crossing the transept, one continued toward the triumphal arch that framed the apse, the semicircular space beyond the transept. In the apse, at an altar that stood on a raised platform, one received the sacrament of Holy Communion. As in ancient Egypt, which prized the eastern horizon as the site of the sun's daily "rebirth," so in Christian ritual the most important of the sacraments was celebrated in the east. The Christian pilgrimage from secular to sacred space thus symbolized the soul's progress from sin to salvation.

Early Christian churches served as places of worship, but they also entombed the bones of Christian martyrs, usually beneath the altar. Hence, church buildings were massive shrines, as well as settings for the performance of the liturgy. Their spacious interiors—Old Saint Peter's basilica was approximately 355 feet long and 208 feet wide—accommodated thousands of Christian pilgrims. However, the wood-trussed roofs of these churches made

The Murano Book Cover

On this ivory book cover carved in low relief, scenes of Jesus' miracles are wedged together in airless compartments surrounding the central image of the enthroned Jesus. Pictured smaller than the youthful, elongated Jesus, the figures of Peter and Paul, holding gospel books, stand at either side. A royal canopy flanked by **Latin crosses** (see Figure 9.3) crowns the holy space. In the top register, two angels modeled on Classical *putti* (winged angelic beings) carry a **Greek cross** encircled by a triumphal wreath, while below, biblical miracles of healing and scenes from the life of Jonah ("reborn" from the belly of the whale) make reference to redemption and resurrection in Christ. This extraordinary artifact integrates Greco-Roman, Hebrew, and Early Christian iconography, and illustrates the manner in which Old Testament stories served New Testament teachings.

Figure 9.7 Book cover, from Murano, Italy, sixth century. Ivory, 14 × 12⅕ in.

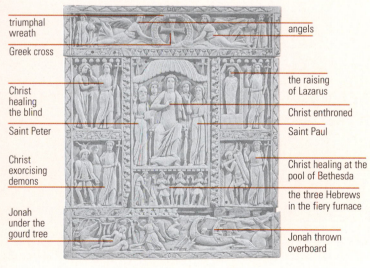

triumphal wreath

Greek cross

Christ healing the blind

Saint Peter

Christ exorcising demons

Jonah under the gourd tree

angels

the raising of Lazarus

Christ enthroned

Saint Paul

Christ healing at the pool of Bethesda

the three Hebrews in the fiery furnace

Jonah thrown overboard

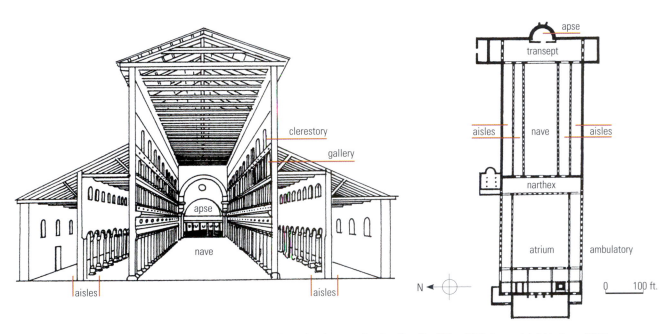

Figure 9.8 Cross section and floor plan of Old Saint Peter's Basilica, Rome, fourth century. Interior of basilica 208 × 355 ft. (approx.), height of nave 105 ft.

Figure 9.9 Interior of the nave of Saint Paul's Outside the Walls, Rome (after reconstruction), begun 386. The chancel arch, supported by Ionic columns and resembling the monumental triumphal arches of the Romans (see Figure 6.21), makes reference to the victory of Christ.

Iconography of the Life of Jesus

THE YOUTH OF CHRIST (principal events)

1 The Annunciation
The archangel Gabriel announces to the Virgin Mary that God has chosen her to bear his son

2 The Visitation
The pregnant Mary visits her cousin Elizabeth, who is pregnant with the future John the Baptist

3 The Nativity
Jesus is born to Mary in Bethlehem

4 The Annunciation to the Shepherds
An angel announces the birth of Jesus to humble shepherds, who hasten to Bethlehem

5 The Adoration of the Magi
Three wise men from the East follow a star to Bethlehem where they present the Christ Child with precious gifts (gold, frankincense, and myrrh)

6 The Presentation in the Temple
Mary and Joseph present Jesus to the high priest at the Temple in Jerusalem

7 The Massacre of the Innocents and the Flight to Egypt
King Herod murders all the newborn of Bethlehem; the Holy Family (Mary, Joseph, and Jesus) flee to Egypt

8 The Baptism
John the Baptist, a preacher in the wilderness of Judea, baptizes Jesus in the Jordan River

9 The Temptation
Jesus fasts for forty days and nights in the wilderness; he rejects the worldly wealth offered to him by the Devil

10 The Calling of the Apostles Near the Sea of Galilee,
Jesus calls the brothers Simon (Peter) and Andrew into his service

11 The Raising of Lazarus
Jesus restores to life Lazarus, the brother of Mary and Martha

12 The Transfiguration
On Mount Tabor in Galilee, among his disciples Peter, James, and John the Evangelist, the radiantly transfigured Jesus is hailed by God as his beloved Son

THE PASSION OF CHRIST (principal events)

1 The Entry into Jerusalem
Jesus, riding on a donkey, enters Jerusalem amidst his disciples and receptive crowds

2 The Last Supper
At the Passover *seder*, Jesus reveals to his disciples his impending death and instructs them to consume the bread (his body) and the wine (his blood)

3 The Agony in the Garden
In the Garden of Gethsemane on the Mount of Olives, while the disciples Peter, James, and John sleep, Jesus reconciles his soul to death

4 The Betrayal
Judas Iscariot, who has been bribed to point Jesus out to his enemies, identifies him by kissing him as he leaves the Garden of Gethsemane

5 Jesus Before Pilate
Jesus comes before the Roman governor of Judea and is charged with treason; when the crowd demands that Jesus be put to death, Pilate washes his hands to signify his innocence of the deed

6 The Flagellation
Jesus is scourged by his captors, the Roman soldiers

7 The Mocking of Jesus
Pilate's soldiers dress Jesus in royal robes and put a crown of thorns on his head

8 The Road to Calvary
Jesus carries the Cross to Golgotha (Calvary), where he is to be executed affixed to a cross raised to stand upright

9 The Crucifixion
At Golgotha, Jesus is crucified between two thieves

10 The Descent from the Cross and the Lamentation
Grief-stricken followers remove the body of Jesus from the Cross; the Virgin, Mary Magdalene, and others grieve over it

11 The Entombment
Mary and the followers of Jesus place his body in a nearby tomb

12 The Resurrection
Three days after his death, Jesus rises from the tomb

---

them especially vulnerable to fire. None of the great Early Christian structures has survived, but the heavily restored basilica of Saint Paul's Outside the Walls offers some idea of the magnificence of the early church interior.

The Latin cross plan (see Figure 9.3) became the model for medieval churches in the West. The church exterior, which clearly reflected the functional divisions of the building's interior, was usually left plain and unadorned, while the interior was lavishly decorated with mosaics consisting of tiny pieces of colored glass or marble set in wet cement. The technique had been used by the Romans to decorate public and private buildings (see Figure 6.10).

In Early Christian art, however, where the mosaic medium was employed to flatten and simplify form, it became the ideal vehicle for capturing the transcendental character of the Christian message. Glass backed with gold leaf provided a supernatural spatial field in which brightly colored figures seemed to float (see Figure 9.18). As daylight or candlelight flickered across church walls embellished with mosaic, images were transformed into sparkling and ethereal apparitions.

In the fifth-century mosaic *Christ Teaching the Apostles* from the apse of Santa Pudenziana in Rome (see Figure **9.1**), the heavenly city unfolds below the hovering image of a magnificent jeweled cross flanked by winged symbols of the four evangelists. The bearded Jesus, here conceived as a Roman emperor, rules the world from atop "the throne set in heaven," as described in Revelation 4. Two female figures, personifications of the Old and New Testaments, offer wreaths of victory to Peter and Paul. Looking like an assembly of Roman senators, the apostles receive the Law, symbolized by the open book, and the **benediction** (blessing) of Jesus.

Byzantine Art and Architecture

In the churches of Byzantium, the mosaic technique reached its artistic peak. Byzantine church architects favored the Greek cross plan, by which all four arms of the structure were of equal length (see Figure 9.3). At the crossing point rose a large and imposing dome. Occasionally, as with the most notable example of Byzantine architecture, Hagia Sophia ("Holy Wisdom"), the longitudinal axis of the Latin cross plan was combined with the Greek cross plan (Figure **9.10**). The crowning architectural glory and principal church of Constantinople, Hagia Sophia (Figures **9.11** and **9.12**) was commissioned in 532 by the East Roman emperor Justinian (481–565). Its massive dome—112 feet in diameter—rises 184 feet above the pavement (40 feet higher than the Pantheon; see chapter 6). Triangular **pendentives** make the transition between the square base of the building and the superstructure (Figure **9.13**). Light filtering through the forty closely set windows at the base of the dome creates the impression that the dome is floating miraculously above the substance of the building.

That light, whose symbolic value was as important to Byzantine liturgy as it was to Saint Ambrose's "Ancient Morning Hymn," illuminated the resplendent mosaics and colored marble surfaces that once filled the interior of the church. After the fall of Constantinople to the Turks in 1453, the Muslims transformed Hagia Sophia into a mosque and whitewashed its mosaics (in accordance with the Islamic prohibition against images). Modern Turkish officials, however, have made the building a museum and restored some of the mosaics.

Hagia Sophia marks the golden age of Byzantine art and architecture that took place under the leadership

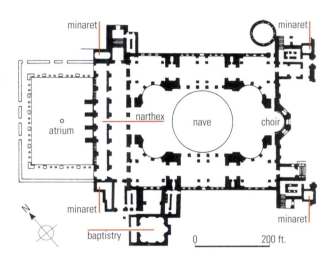

Figure 9.10 Plan of Hagia Sophia, Constantinople (Istanbul), Turkey.

Figure 9.11 ANTHEMIUS OF TRALLES and **ISIDORUS OF MILETUS**, Hagia Sophia, from the southwest, Constantinople, Turkey, 532–537. Dome height 184 ft.; diameter 112 ft. The body of the original church is now surrounded by later additions, including the minarets built after 1453 under the Ottoman Turks. When Justinian saw the completed church, he is said to have boasted, "Solomon, I have surpassed you," a reference to the achievement of the Hebrew king's Temple of Jerusalem.

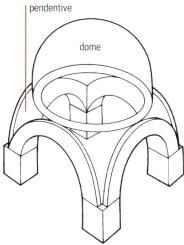

Figure 9.12 Hagia Sophia, Constantinople. Interior showing the central dome, pendentives, and galleries.

pendentive

dome

Figure 9.13 Schematic drawing of the dome of Hagia Sophia, showing pendentives.

Map 9.1 The Byzantine World Under Justinian, 565. This map indicates how much of the old Roman Empire has fallen to the Germanic peoples, who, by the sixth century, had established individual kingdoms in the West.

of the emperor Justinian. Assuming the throne in 527, Justinian envisioned Constantinople as the "New Rome." Supported by his politically shrewd consort, Theodora, he sought to reunify the eastern and western portions of the old Roman Empire (Map **9.1**). Although he did not achieve this goal, he nevertheless restored the prestige of ancient Rome by commissioning one of the monumental projects of his time: the revision and codification of Roman law. The monumental *Corpus juris civilis* (*Collected Civil Law*) consisted of four parts: the *Code*, a compilation of Roman laws; the *Digest*, summaries of the opinions of jurists; the *Institutes*, a legal textbook; and the *Novels*, a collection of laws issued after 533. This testament to the primacy of law over imperial authority would have an enormous influence on legal and political history in the West, especially after the eleventh century, when it became the basis for the legal systems in most of the European states. Justinian's influence was equally important to the Byzantine economy. Legend has it that two of Justinian's ambassadors, Greek Orthodox monks, smuggled silkworm eggs out of China by hiding them in a hollow staff, thus initiating a thriving Byzantine silk industry that came to compete with Eastern markets.

The city that served as Justinian's western imperial outpost was Ravenna, in northwest Italy (see Map 9.1). Here Justinian commissioned the construction of one of the small gems of Byzantine architecture: the church of San Vitale (Figure **9.14**). The drab exterior of this domed octagonal structure hardly prepares one for the radiant interior, the walls of which are embellished with polychrome marble, carved alabaster columns, and some of

Figure 9.15 San Vitale, Ravenna. Apse showing Christ flanked by angels, and seated on the orb that symbolizes his universal dominion. He offers the crown of martyrdom to Saint Vitale on the far right.

Figure 9.14 San Vitale, Ravenna, Italy, ca. 526–547.

the most magnificent mosaics in the history of world art (Figure **9.15**).

The mosaics on either side of the altar show Justinian and Theodora, each carrying offerings to Christ (Figures **9.16** and **9.17**). Justinian is flanked by twelve companions, an allusion to Christ and the apostles. On his right are his soldiers, the defenders of Christ (note the *chi* and *rho* emblazoned on the shield), while on his left are representatives of the clergy, who bear the instruments of the liturgy: the crucifix, the book, and the incense vessel. Justinian himself carries the bowl for the bread of the Eucharist. Robed in the imperial purple, and crowned by a solar disk or halo—a device often used in Persian and late Roman art to indicate divine status—Justinian assumes the sacred

Figure 9.16 *Emperor Justinian and His Courtiers*, ca. 547. Mosaic, 8 ft. 8 in. × 12 ft. San Vitale, Ravenna.

Figure 9.17 *Empress Theodora and Retinue*, ca. 547. Mosaic, 8 ft. 8 in. × 12 ft. San Vitale, Ravenna.

authority of Christ on earth: temporal and spiritual power united in the person of the emperor. The iconography of the Justinian representation illustrates the bond between Church and state that characterized Byzantine history; but the scene has also been interpreted to represent the "Little Entrance" that marks the beginning of the Byzantine liturgy of the Mass. Justinian and the empress reenact the ancient rite of royal donation, a theme underscored by the illustration of the Three Magi on the hem of Theodora's robe (see Figure 9.17).

The style of the mosaic contributes to the solemn formality of the event: Justinian and his courtiers stand grave and motionless, as if frozen ceremonially at attention. They are slender, elongated, and rigidly positioned—like the notes of a musical score—against a gold background that works to eliminate spatial depth. Minimally shaded, these "paper cut-out" figures with small, flipperlike feet seem to float on the surface of the picture plane, rather than stand anchored in real space. A comparison of these mosaics with, for instance, any Roman paintings or sculptural reliefs (see chapter 6) underlines the vast differences between the aesthetic aims and purposes of Classical and Christian art. Whereas the Romans engaged a realistic narrative style to honor temporal authority, the Christians cultivated an abstract language of line and color to celebrate otherworldly glory.

The sixth-century mosaic *Jesus Calling the First Apostles, Peter and Andrew* (Figure **9.18**), found in Sant'Apollinare Nuovo in Ravenna—a Christian basilica ornamented by Roman and Byzantine artisans—provides yet another example of the surrender of narrative detail to symbolic abstraction. In the composition, setting is minimal: a gold background shuts out space and provides a celestial screen against which formal action takes place. The figures, stiff and immovable, lack substance. There is almost no sense

Figure 9.18 *Jesus Calling the First Apostles, Peter and Andrew,* early sixth century. Mosaic, 22½ × 36 in. Detail of upper register of north wall, Sant'Apollinare Nuovo, Ravenna. Adorning the wall of this Early Christian basilica, the highly stylized scene belongs to the earliest surviving mosaic cycle showing events in the life of Jesus.

of muscle and bone beneath the togas of Christ and the apostles. The enlarged eyes and solemn gestures impart a powerful sense of otherworldliness.

The Byzantine Icon

Although religious imagery was essential to the growing influence of Christianity, a fundamental disagreement concerning the role of **icons** (images) in divine worship led to conflict between the Roman Catholic and Eastern Orthodox churches. Most Christians held that visual representations of God the Father, Jesus, the Virgin, and the saints worked to inspire religious reverence. Others, however, adhering to the prohibition of "graven images" in the Hebrew Bible (Exodus 20:4–5), considered images to be no better than pagan idols. During the eighth century, the issue came to a head when the Byzantine emperor Leo III (ruled 717–741) inaugurated a policy of *iconoclasm* ("image-breaking") that called for the wholesale destruction of religious sculpture and the whitewashing of mosaics and wall-paintings. The Iconoclastic Controversy, which remained unresolved until the middle of the ninth century, generated a schism between the Eastern and Western churches. Compounded by other liturgical and theological differences, that schism would become permanent in 1054 (see chapter 12). Nevertheless, both before the Iconoclastic Controversy and in the centuries following its resolution, the Greek Orthodox faith inspired the production of countless religious icons of Jesus, Mary, and the saints. These devotional images are regarded by the faithful as sacred; some are thought to provide miraculous healing or protective powers. The idea of the icon as epiphany or "appearance" is linked to the belief that the image is the tangible confirmation of the saint's miraculous appearance. The anonymity of icon painters and the formulaic quality of the image from generation to generation reflects the unique nature of the icon as an archetypal image—one that cannot be altered by the human imagination.

Executed in glowing colors and gold paint on small, portable panels, Byzantine icons usually featured the Virgin and Child (alone or surrounded by saints) seated frontally in a formal, stylized manner (Figure 9.19; compare Figure 9.17). While such representations look back to portrayals of Mediterranean mother cult deities (see Figure 8.2), they also prefigure medieval representations of the Virgin (see Figures 13.1 and 13.25).

Following the conversion of Russia to Orthodox Christianity in the tenth century, artists brought renewed splendor to the art of the icon, often embellishing the painted panel with gold leaf and semiprecious jewels, or enhancing the garments of the saint with thin sheets of hammered gold or silver. To this day, the icon assumes a special importance in the Eastern Orthodox Church and home, where it may be greeted with a kiss, a bow, and the sign of the Cross.

Figure 9.19 *Virgin and Child with Saints and Angels*, second half of sixth century. Icon: encaustic on wood, 27 × 18⅞ in. Monastery of Saint Catherine, Mount Sinai, Egypt. Tradition held that Saint Luke had painted a portrait of the Virgin and Child that served as a model for icons such as this one. Enthroned in majesty and wearing a purple robe (in the manner of official portraits of the emperor), the Virgin points to the Christ Child as the Way to Salvation. She is flanked by Saints Theodore and George, and by angelic attendants who look toward the ray of light emanating from the hand of God.

Early Christian Music

Early Christians distrusted the sensuous and emotional powers of music, especially instrumental music. Saint Augustine noted the "dangerous pleasure" of music and confessed that on those occasions when he was more "moved by the singing than by what was sung" he felt that he had "sinned criminally." For such reasons, the early Church was careful to exclude all forms of individual expression from liturgical music. Ancient Hebrew religious ritual, especially the practice of chanting daily prayers and singing psalms (see chapter 1), directly influenced church music. Hymns of praise such as those produced by Saint Ambrose were sung by the Christian congregation led by a cantor. But the most important music of Christian antiquity, and that which became central to the liturgy of the Church, was the music of the Mass.

The most sacred rite of the Christian liturgy, the Mass celebrated the sacrifice of Christ's body and blood as enacted at the Last Supper. The service culminated in the sacrament of Holy Communion (or Eucharist), by which Christians ritually shared the body and blood of their Redeemer. In the West, the service called High Mass featured a series of Latin chants known as either plainsong, plainchant, or Gregorian chant—the last because Gregory the Great was said to have codified and made uniform the many types of religious chant that existed in Early Christian times. The invariable or "ordinary" parts of the Mass—that is, those used throughout the year—included "Kyrie eleison" ("Lord have mercy"), "Gloria" ("Glory to God"), "Credo" (the affirmation of the Nicene Creed), "Sanctus" ("Holy, Holy, Holy"), "Benedictus" ("Blessed is He that cometh in the name of the Lord"), and "Agnus Dei" ("Lamb of God"). Eventually, the Sanctus and the Benedictus appeared as one chant, making a total of five parts to the ordinary of the Mass.

One of the oldest bodies of liturgical song still in everyday use, Gregorian chant stands among the great treasures of Western music. Like all Hebrew and Early Christian hymnody, it is monophonic, that is, regardless of the number of voices in the performing group, there is only one line of melody. Sung **a cappella** (without instrumental accompaniment), the plainsong of the Early Christian era was performed by the clergy and by choirs of monks rather than by members of the congregation. Both the Ambrosian hymns and plainsong could be performed in a responsorial style, with the chorus answering the voice of the cantor, or antiphonally, with parts of the choir or congregation singing alternating verses. In general, the rhythm of the words dictated the rhythm of the music. Plainsong might be **syllabic** (one note to one syllable), or it might involve **melismatic** embellishments (many notes to one syllable). Since no method for notating music existed before the ninth century, choristers depended on memory and on **neumes**—marks entered above the words of the text to indicate the rise and fall of the voice. The duration and exact pitch of each note, however, had to be committed to memory.

🎵 See Music Listening Selections at end of chapter.

Lacking fixed meter or climax, the free rhythms of Gregorian chant echoed through Early Christian churches, whose cavernous interiors must have contributed to producing effects that were otherworldly and hypnotic. These effects, conveyed only to a limited degree by modern recordings, are best appreciated when Gregorian chant is performed in large, acoustically resonant basilicas such as the remodeled Saint Peter's in Rome.

The Buddhist Identity

Buddhism, as it spread through India and China, followed a very different path from that of Christianity. Under the leadership of Ashoka (see chapter 8), councils of Buddhist monks tried to organize the Master's teachings into a uniform, official canon; but they did not succeed in creating a single, monolithic interpretation of the Buddha's teachings—one adhered to by the entire Buddhist community, or even a majority thereof. Despite the unifying influence of the Buddha's sermons as collected in the *Pitakas*, Buddhism established no church hierarchy or uniform liturgy—a standardized ritual for public worship—comparable to that of the Roman and Orthodox communities of Christianity. The Buddhist identity was embellished, however, by a large body of folklore and legend, along with stories of the Master's previous lives, known as *jatakas* ("birth-stories"). The heart of Buddhist Scripture, however, is a body of discourses informed by the Master's sermons. Devoted to uncovering "the truth of life," these teachings deal with such subjects as the nature of the Self, the cultivation of infinite consciousness, and the development of proper breathing. The essential element of the Buddhist "creed" calls for adherence to the Law of Righteousness (*dharma*) and the Eightfold Path. In its purist (Hinayana) form, it urges Buddhists to work out their own salvation. In its later (Mahayana) development, it seeks divine help in the quest for enlightenment. Within every Buddhist sect, however, can be found the monastic community—a place for religious retreat and spiritual practice similar to that of the early Benedictine community. The ancient Buddhist monastic complex centered on a hall used for teaching and meditation. An adjacent shrine or pagoda might hold relics or ashes of the Buddha.

While the majority of Buddhists belonged to the laity, the Buddhist monk became the model of religious life. To this day, religious "services" consist only of the chanting of Buddhist texts (mainly the Buddha's sermons), the recitation of hymns and **mantras** (sacred word and sound formulas), meditation, and confession. Despite the deification of the Buddha among Mahayana Buddhists and the popular adulation of *bodhisattvas* who might aid humans to achieve *nirvana*, Buddhism never abandoned its profoundly contemplative character.

Buddhist Art and Architecture in India

Buddhist texts relate that upon his death, the body of the Buddha was cremated and his ashes divided and enshrined

Figure 9.20 West gateway, the Great Stupa, Sanchi, central India, Shunga and early Andhra periods, third century B.C.E. to early first century C.E. Shrine height 50 ft.; diameter 105 ft.

in eight burial mounds or *stupas*. When the emperor Ashoka made Buddhism the state religion of India in the third century B.C.E., he further divided the ashes, distributing them among some 60,000 shrines. These came to house the relics of the Buddha (and his disciples) and mark the places at which he had taught. The most typical of Buddhist structures, the *stupa* is a beehivelike mound of earth encased by brick or stone. Derived from the prehistoric burial mound, it symbolizes at once the World Mountain, the Dome of Heaven, and the hallowed Womb of the Universe. A hemisphere set atop a square base, the *stupa* is also the three-dimensional realization of the cosmic *mandala*—a diagrammatic map of the universe used as a visual aid to meditation. Separating the shrine from the secular world are stone balustrades. Four gates mark the cardinal points of the compass; the walls and gates are carved with symbols of the Buddha and his teachings. As Buddhist pilgrims pass through the east gate and circle the *stupa* clockwise, tracing the path of the sun, they make the sacred journey that awakens the mind to the rhythms of the universe. The spiritual journey of the Early Christian pilgrim is linear (from narthex to apse), marking the movement from sin to salvation, while the Buddhist journey is circular, symbolizing the cycle of regeneration and the quest for *nirvana*.

Begun in the third century B.C.E., the Great Stupa at Sanchi in central India was one of Ashoka's foremost achievements (Figure **9.20**). Elevated on a 20-foot drum and surrounded by a circular stone railing and four stone portals (*toranas*, Figure **9.21**), the shrine is 105 feet in diameter and rises to a height of 50 feet. It is surmounted by a series of *chatras*, umbrellalike shapes that signify the sacred bo tree under which the Buddha reached *nirvana*. The *chatras* also symbolize the levels of human consciousness

Figure 9.21 *Yakshi* (female fertility spirit) bracket figure, east *torana*, Great Stupa, Sanchi, India. Sandstone, height 5 ft. (approx.). The individual figures on these profusely ornamented entrance gates convey a sense of rhythmic vitality that is typical of early Buddhist art.

Figure 9.22 Interior of carved *chaitya* cave, Karli, India, ca. 50. The Buddhist cave-temple was carved from solid rock; however, similar prayer halls were erected as free-standing structures.

through which the soul ascends in seeking enlightenment. Occasionally, *stupas* were enclosed in massive rock-cut caves or placed at the end of arcaded halls adjacent to monastic dwellings (Figures **9.22** and **9.23**). Known as *chaitya* halls, these sacred spaces were not intended for the kind of congregational worship associated with the Early Christian Mass; rather, they were sanctuaries for individual meditation and prayer. Nevertheless, the *chaitya* hall bears a striking resemblance to the Early Christian basilica. As in the basilica, a long colonnaded hall leads the devotee from the veranda at the entrance to the semicircular apse in which the *stupa* is situated. The ceilings of both the Early Christian church and the *chaitya* hall were made of wood, but the latter was usually barrel-vaulted, its curved rafters carrying the eye down toward an ornate frieze or rows of elephants—ancient symbols of royal authority and spiritual strength associated with the Buddha.

Buddhism's prohibition of idolatry influenced art in the first centuries after the Master's death, during which time artists avoided portraying the Buddha in human form. Like the Early Christians, who devised a body of sacred signs to represent the Christos (see Figure 9.3), Buddhists adopted a variety of symbols for the Buddha, such as the fig tree under which he meditated, his footprints, elephants, and, most important, the wheel (signifying both the sun and the Wheel of the Law). These devices, along with scenes from the Buddha's former lives and images of Vedic nature deities, make up the densely ornamented surface of the 34-foot-high stone gateways that mark the entrances to the Great Stupa at Sanchi (see Figure 9.21). Notably different from the Augustinian antagonism of flesh and spirit, and Christianity's general abhorrence of carnal pleasure, Buddhism (like Hinduism) regarded sexuality and spirituality as variant forms of a single, fundamental cosmic force. Hence, Buddhist art—in contrast with Christian art—did not condemn the representation of the nude body. Indeed, Sanchi's voluptuous fertility goddesses, whose globular breasts and tubelike limbs swell with life, celebrate female sexuality as candidly as any Classically carved Venus.

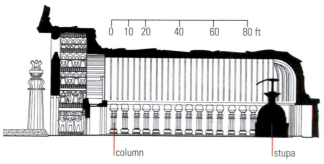

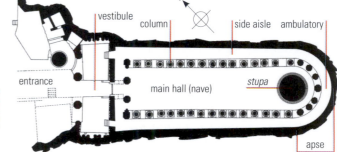

Figure 9.23 Elevation and ground plan of *chaitya* cave, Karli.

Figure 9.24 *Enlightenment*, detail of frieze showing four scenes from the life of the Buddha: *Birth*, *Enlightenment*, *First Preaching*, and *Nirvana*, from the Gandharan region of northwest Pakistan, Kushan dynasty, late second to early third century. Dark gray-blue slate, 26⅜ × 114⅛ × 31³⁄₁₆ in.

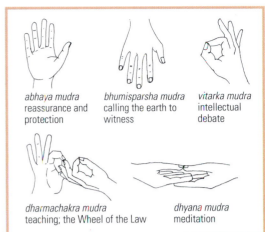

Figure 9.25 *Mudras*. The circles formed by the thumb and index fingers (lower left) represent the turning of the Wheel of the Law.

Mahayana Buddhism, however, glorified the Buddha as a savior, and thus, by the second century C.E., the image of the Buddha himself became important in popular worship. Contact between northwest India (Gandhara) and the West influenced the emergence of a distinctly human Buddha icon inspired by Hellenistic and Roman representations of the god Apollo. Gandharan artists created classically draped and idealized free-standing figures of the Buddha and the *bodhisattvas* (see Figures 8.5 and 8.6). They also carved elaborate stone reliefs depicting the life of the Buddha. One well-preserved frieze shows scenes from this narrative: the birth of the Buddha—shown miraculously emerging from the hip of his mother, Queen Maya; the demonic assault on the Buddha as he achieves enlightenment beneath the Bodhi tree, his right hand touching the earth in the **mudra** (symbolic gesture) that calls the earth to witness his enlightenment (Figures **9.24** and **9.25**); the Buddha preaching the *Sermon at Benares*; and the death of the Buddha. In its union of realistic narrative and abstract symbols, the frieze has much in common with Early Christian devotional images (see Figure 9.7).

Between the fourth and sixth centuries, under the sway of the Gupta Empire, India experienced a golden age in the arts as well as in the sciences. Gupta rulers commissioned Sanskrit prose and poetry that ranged from adventure stories and plays to sacred and philosophical works. Gupta mathematicians were the first to use a special sign for the numeric zero, and Hindu physicians made significant advances in medicine. (As we shall see in chapter 10, the Arabs transmitted many of these innovations to the West.)

In the hands of Gupta sculptors, the image of the Buddha assumed its classic form: a figure seated cross-legged in the position of yoga meditation (Figure **9.26**). The Buddha's oval head, framed by an elaborately ornamented halo, features a mounded protuberance (symbolizing spiritual wisdom), elongated earlobes (a reference to

Figure 9.26 *Teaching Buddha*, from Sarnath, India, Gupta period, fifth century. Sandstone, height 5 ft. 2 in.

Figure 9.27 Palace scene, Cave 17, Ajanta, India, Gupta period, fifth century. Wall-painting. An assortment of ethnic groups and castes are included in the Ajanta paintings.

Siddhartha's princely origins), and a third "eye"—a symbol of spiritual vision—between the eyebrows (see Figure 8.5). His masklike face, with downcast eyes and gentle smile, denotes the still state of inner repose. His hands form a *mudra* that indicates the Wheel of the Law, the subject of the Buddha's first sermon (see Figure 9.25). Wheels, symbolizing the Wheel of the Law, are engraved on the palms of his hands and the soles of his feet. The lotus, a favorite Buddhist symbol of enlightenment (and an ancient symbol of procreativity), appears on the seat of the throne and in the decorative motifs on the halo. Finally, in the relief on the base of the throne is the narrative depiction of the Buddha preaching: six disciples flank the Wheel of the Law, while two rampant deer (foreground) signify the site of the sermon, the Deer Park in Benares (see Reading 8.4a). More stylized than their Gandharan predecessors, Gupta figures are typically full-bodied and smoothly modeled, with details reduced to decorative linear patterns.

The Gupta period also produced some of the earliest surviving examples of Indian painting. Hundreds of frescoes found on the walls of some thirty rock-cut sanctuaries at Ajanta in Central India show scenes from the lives and incarnations of the Buddha (as told in Mahayana literature), as well as stories from Indian history and legend. In the Ajanta frescoes, musicians, dancers, and lightly clad *bodhisattvas* (Figure **9.27**) rival the sensual elegance of the carved goddesses at Sanchi. The Ajanta frescoes are among the best-preserved and most magnificent of Indian paintings. They rank with the frescoes of the Roman catacombs and the mosaic cycles of Early Christian and Byzantine churches, although in their naturalistic treatment of form and in their mythic subject matter (which includes depictions of erotic love), they have no equivalent in the medieval West. They underline the fact that, in Buddhist thought, the divine and the human, the spirit and the body, are considered complementary.

Buddhist Art and Architecture in China

Between the first and third centuries, Buddhist missionaries introduced many of the basic conventions of Indian art and architecture into China. The Chinese adopted the *stupa* as a temple-shrine and place of private worship, transforming its moundlike base and umbrellalike structure into a **pagoda**, or multitiered tower with many roofs. These temple-towers are characterized by sweeping curves and upturned corners similar to those used in ancient watchtowers and multistoried houses (see chapter 7). At the same time, they recreate the image of the spreading pine tree, a beneficent sign in Chinese culture. Favoring timber as the principal building medium, Chinese architects devised complex vaulting systems for the construction of pagodas, of which no early examples have survived.

The earliest dated Buddhist building in China is the twelve-sided brick pagoda on Mount Song in Henan, which served as a shrine for the nearby Buddhist monastery (Figure **9.28**). Constructed in the early sixth century, this pagoda has a hollow interior that may once have held a large statue of the Buddha. Pagodas, whether built in brick or painted wood, became popular throughout Southeast Asia and provided a model for all religious shrines—Daoist and Confucian—as well as for Hindu temples in medieval India (see chapter 14).

Between the fourth and sixth centuries, along the southern arteries of the Silk Road (see Map 7.1), wandering Buddhist monks built hundreds of rock-cut sanctuaries modeled on India's monastic shrines. These grottoes, which continued to be created for centuries, housed numerous holy texts, including the fabled *Diamond Sutra* (see Figure 14.14). Many seventh-century caves were ornamented with sculptured images of the Buddha and his

Figure 9.28 Pagoda of the Song Yue Temple, Mount Song, Henan, China, 523.

Figure 9.29 *Large Seated Buddha with Standing Bodhisattva*, Cave 20, Yungang, Shanxi, China, Northern Wei dynasty, ca. 460–470. Stone, height 44 ft. Similar colossal rock-cut Buddhas were carved in cliffs along caravan routes into Southeast Asia. Splendidly painted and gilded, they were visible to approaching pilgrims and travelers from miles away. In 2001, iconoclastic radical Muslims known as the Taliban destroyed two of the most notable of these shrines at Bamiyan in Afghanistan. Efforts are currently underway to reconstruct the destroyed statues.

Figure 9.30 *The Empress as Donor with Attendants*, from the Binyang cave chapel, Longmen, Henan, China, Northern Wei dynasty, ca. 522. Fine gray limestone with traces of color, 6 ft. 4 in. × 9 ft. 1 in.

Figure 9.31 Altar with Maitreya Buddha, Northern Wei dynasty, 524. Gilt bronze, height 30¼ in. Two *bodhisattvas* flank the central figure, while two more, along with two donors, surround an incense burner below. Infused with ornamental, calligraphic vitality, the shrine was commissioned by a father to commemorate the death of his son.

achieves an ornamental elegance that is as typical of Chinese relief sculpture as it is of Chinese calligraphy and painting (see chapter 14).

By the sixth century, the Maitreya Buddha—the Buddha of the Future—had become the favorite devotional image of Mahayana Buddhism. A messianic successor of the historical Buddha, Maitreya was said to be a *bodhisattva* who would come to earth to deliver his followers to a special place in paradise. In an elegant bronze altarpiece (Figure **9.31**), the Maitreya Buddha raises his right hand in the gesture of reassurance. Standing above a group of *bodhisattvas* and monks, he is framed by a perforated, flame-shaped halo from which sprout winged angelic creatures, each playing a musical instrument. Comparison of this devotional object with one from the Christian West—such as the ivory book cover from Murano (see Figure 9.7)—reveals certain formal similarities: the sacred personages (Jesus and the Buddha) are pictured centrally and physically larger than the accompanying figures, thus indicating their greater importance. Both make use of special symbols, such as the halo and the throne, to indicate divine status; and both favor iconic stylization and abstraction. Such devices, employed by artists East and West, contributed to the language of faith that served both Buddhism and Christianity.

Buddhist Music

Scholars did not begin to survey Buddhist music until the early twentieth century. It seems clear, however, that Buddhist religious practices were based in India's ancient musical traditions, specifically those that involved the intoning of sacred Hindu texts. The recitation of *mantras* and the chanting of Sanskrit prayer were central acts of meditation among Buddhist monks throughout Asia, and the performance of such texts assumed a trancelike quality similar to that of Western plainsong. Buddhist chant was

bodhisattvas, and spectacular murals, executed with walnut and poppy-seed oils—the earliest use of the oil medium known to history.

Once sheltered by a sandstone cave front that collapsed centuries ago, a colossal Buddha and standing *bodhisattva* at Yungang Cave 20 reveal sharply cut, masklike faces and calligraphic folds of clinging drapery (Figure **9.29**). The Chinese preference for abstract patterns and flowing, rhythmic lines also characterizes the relief carvings in the limestone rock walls of late fifth- and sixth-century Buddhist caves at Longmen (Figure **9.30**). Once painted with bright colors, representations of the emperor Xuanwu (483–515) and his consort bearing ritual gifts to the shrine of the Buddha may be compared with the almost contemporaneous mosaics of Justinian and Theodora in San Vitale, Ravenna (see Figures 9.16, 9.17). Both the Ravenna mosaics and the Longmen reliefs are permanent memorials of worldly rulers in the act of religious devotion. Lacking the ceremonial formality of its Byzantine counterpart, the image of *The Empress as Donor with Attendants*

See Music Listening Selections at end of chapter.

monophonic and lacked a fixed beat; but, unlike Western church music, it was usually accompanied by percussion instruments (such as drums, bells, cymbals, and gongs) that imparted a rich rhythmic texture. Complex drumming techniques were among the most notable of Indian musical contributions.

As in India, Buddhist chant in China and Japan was performed in the monasteries. It featured the intoning of statements and responses interrupted by the sounding of percussion instruments such as bells or drums. As the chant proceeded, the pace of recitation increased, causing an overlapping of voices and instruments that produced a hypnotic web of sound.

Sliding, nasal tones characterized the performance of Chinese music. Such tones were achieved both by the voice and by the instruments peculiar to Chinese culture. One of China's oldest and most popular instruments was the zither, a five- or seven-stringed instrument generally plucked with a plectrum and the fingertips (see chapter 7). Associated with ancient religious and ceremonial music, the zither was quickly adopted by Buddhist monks. The vibrato or hum produced by plucking the strings of the zither is audible long after the instrument is touched, a phenomenon that Buddhists found comparable to the pervasive resonance of chant (and to the human breath seeking union with the One).

LOOKING BACK

The Christian Identity

- Rome became the administrative center of the newly unified Christian faith in the West. As Roman emperors had held supreme authority over the state, so Roman Catholic popes—the temporal representatives of Christ—would govern Western Christendom.
- At the Council of Nicaea a consensus of opinion among church representatives laid the basis for Christian dogma, resolving that Jesus was of one substance with God the Father.
- The Benedictine order, the first monastic community in the West, was founded in southern Italy. It required vows of poverty, chastity, and obedience to the governing abbot; it established a routine of work that freed monks from dependence on the secular world.
- The four Latin church fathers, Jerome, Ambrose, Gregory, and Augustine, were responsible for the formulation of Christian dogma and liturgy. Augustine's writings were crucial to the development of the allegorical tradition.

Symbolism and Early Christian Art

- Christian signs and symbols linked the visible to the invisible world. The language of Symbolism came to convey the Christian message of deliverance. Accordingly, a more abstract, ethereal style replaced the worldly Realism of Greco-Roman art.
- In the catacombs outside the city of Rome, vast networks of underground galleries enclose gravesites whose walls are covered with frescoes illustrating scenes from the Old and New Testaments.
- The legalization of Christianity made possible the construction of monumental houses for public religious worship. Early Christian churches in the West were modeled on the Roman basilica, but engaged a Latin cross plan.
- Byzantine church architects favored the Greek cross plan, by which all four arms of the structure were of equal length. At the crossing point rose a large and imposing dome, such as the one crowning Hagia Sophia.
- In the churches of Constantinople and in Ravenna, Italy, the East Roman emperor Justinian commissioned some of Early Christianity's finest mosaics. As with the painted devotional icons popular in Byzantium, these mosaics abandon literal representation in favor of formal abstraction and religious symbolism.

Early Christian Music

- Ancient Hebrew religious ritual, especially the practice of chanting daily prayers and singing psalms, directly influenced church music.
- The sacred rite of the Christian liturgy, the Mass, celebrates the sacrifice of Christ. The service features a series of Latin chants known as plainsong or Gregorian chant.
- Early Christian music features a single line of melody that lacks fixed meter. Since no method for notating music existed before the ninth century, choristers depended on memory or on textual marks known as neumes.

The Buddhist Identity

- Buddhism established no single, monolithic interpretation of the Buddha's teachings, and therefore no church hierarchy or uniform liturgy comparable to that of the Roman and Orthodox Christian communities. The Buddhist identity was embellished by a large body of folklore and legend.
- The Buddhist monk became the model of religious life for the laity; the monastic community centered on a hall used for teaching and meditation.
- The most typical of early Buddhist structures in India, the *stupa*, was a mound-shaped shrine honoring the Buddha. A three-dimensional realization of the cosmic *mandala*—a diagrammatic map of the universe used as a visual aid to meditation—it was circled by Buddhist pilgrims. The rock-cut caves and halls that occasionally enclosed *stupas* provided sanctuaries for individual contemplation.
- Buddhism's prohibition of idolatry influenced art in the first centuries after the Master's death: artists avoided portraying the Buddha in human form, adopting instead a variety of symbols, the most important of which was the Wheel (of the Law).
- Buddhist missionaries introduced the basic conventions of Indian art and architecture into China. The Chinese

adopted the *stupa* as a temple-shrine and place of private worship, transforming its moundlike base and umbrellalike structure into a pagoda.

- Buddhist religious practices were based in India's ancient musical traditions, specifically those that involved the intoning of sacred Hindu texts. The recitation of *mantras* and the chanting of prayers were central acts of meditation among Buddhist monks throughout Asia.

Music Listening Selections

- Gregorian chant, "Alleluya, vidimus stellam," codified 590–604.

- Buddhist chant, Morning prayers (based on the Lotus Scripture) at Nomanji, Japan, excerpt.

Glossary

abbey a monastery or convent

abbot (Latin, "father") the superior of an abbey or monastery for men; the female equivalent in a convent of nuns is called an "abbess"

a cappella choral singing without instrumental accompaniment

ambulatory a covered walkway, outdoors or indoors (see Figures 9.8 and 13.4)

benediction the invocation of a blessing; in art, indicated by the raised right hand with fore and middle fingers extended

canon law the ecclesiastical law that governs the Christian Church

catacomb a subterranean complex consisting of burial chambers and galleries with recesses for tombs

chaitya a sacred space, often applied to arcaded assembly halls that enclose a *stupa*

chatra an umbrellalike shape that signifies the sacred tree under which the Buddha reached *nirvana*

clerestory (also "clerstory") the upper part of the nave, whose walls contain openings for light (see Figure 9.8)

diptych a two-leaved hinged tablet; a two-paneled altarpiece

dogma a prescribed body of doctrines concerning faith or morals, formally stated and authoritatively proclaimed by the Church

ecumenical worldwide in extent; representing the whole body of churches

gallery the area between the clerestory and the nave arcade, usually adorned with mosaics in Early Christian churches (see Figure 9.8)

Greek cross a cross in which all four arms are of equal length

icon (Greek, "likeness") the image of a saint or other religious figure

iconography the study, identification, and interpretation of subject matter in art; also the visual imagery that conveys specific concepts and ideas

Latin cross a cross in which the vertical member is longer than the horizontal member it intersects

mandala a diagrammatic map of the universe used as a visual aid to meditation and as a ground plan for Hindu and Buddhist temple-shrines

mantra a sacred formula of invocation or incantation that is common to Hinduism and Buddhism

melismatic with many notes of music to one syllable

mudra (Sanskrit, "sign") a symbolic gesture commonly used in Buddhist art

narthex a porch or vestibule at the main entrance of a church (see Figure 9.8)

nave the central aisle of a church between the altar and the apse, usually demarcated from the side aisles by columns or piers (see Figure 9.8)

neume a mark or symbol indicating the direction of the voice in the early notation of Gregorian chant

orans a gesture involving the raising of the arms in an attitude of prayer

pagoda an East Asian shrine in the shape of a tower, usually with roofs curving upward at the division of each of several stories

pendentive a concave piece of masonry that makes the transition between the angle of two walls and the base of the dome above (see Figure 9.13)

putto (Italian, "child," plural *putti*) a nude male child, usually winged; related to the Classical Cupid (see chapter 6) and to Greco-Roman images of the angelic psyche or soul

regular clergy (Latin, *regula*, meaning "rule") those who have taken vows to obey the rules of a monastic order; as opposed to secular clergy (see below)

secular clergy (Latin, *seculum*, meaning "in the world") those ordained to serve the Christian Church in the world

stupa a hemispherical mound that serves as a Buddhist shrine

syllabic with one note of music per syllable

torana a gateway that marks one of the four cardinal points in the stone fence surrounding a *stupa*

transept the part of a basilica-plan church that runs perpendicular to the nave (see Figure 9.8)

The Islamic World: Religion and Culture

ca. 570–1300

"Whoever goes aright, for his own soul does he go aright; and whoever goes astray, to its detriment only does he go astray . . ."
The Qur'an

Figure 10.1 *The Slave Market at Zabīd,* Yemen, from the *Maqāmāt of al-Harīrī,* 1237. The woman shown here is veiled with the *hijab* that covers her neck and bosom, as well as part of her face. Customs concerning dress varied locally, with some Muslim communities calling for women to wear the *chador* that covers the body from head to toe. The latter practice is not prescribed in the Qur'an.

Islam, the world's youngest major religion, was born in the seventh century among the people of the Arabian peninsula. The faith of the followers of Muhammad, it became the unifying force in the rise of the first global civilization to flourish following the fall of Rome. Bridging Europe and East Asia, Islam forged the historical link between Classical and early modern civilization. As early as the mid-eighth century, an international Islamic community stretched from Spain (Al-Andalus) across North Africa into India (Map **10.1**).

Just as rising Christianity had absorbed the cultural legacy of the Mediterranean and the Roman world, so, in its expansion, Islam embraced the cultures of Arabia, the Near East, and Persia. Between the eighth and fourteenth centuries, the new faith brought religious unity and cultural cohesiveness to people of a wide variety of languages and customs. Muslim communities in Spain, North Africa, and the Near East cultivated rich traditions in the arts, the sciences, and technology. Muslim scholars in the cities of Baghdad (in present-day Iraq) and Córdoba (in southern Spain) copied Greek manuscripts, creating an invaluable preserve of Classical literature; and Islamic intermediaries carried into the West many of the greatest innovations of Asian culture. These achievements had far-reaching effects on global culture, on the subsequent rise of the European West, and, more broadly, on the global humanistic tradition.

The religion of Islam is practiced today by some one billion people, more than two-thirds of whom live outside of Southwest Asia. In the United States, home to over six million Muslims, Islam is the fastest growing religion. These facts suggest that, despite a decline in Islamic culture after 1350, Islam remains one of the most powerful forces in world history.

The Religion of Islam

Muhammad and Islam

Centuries before the time of Christ, nomadic Arabs known as Bedouins lived in the desert peninsula of Arabia east of Egypt. At the mercy of this arid land, they traded along the caravan routes of Southwest Asia. Bedouin Arabs were an animistic, tribal people who worshiped some 300 different nature deities. Statues of these gods, along with the sacred Black Stone (possibly an ancient meteorite), were housed in the *Kaaba*, a cubical sanctuary located in the city of Mecca (in modern Saudi Arabia). Until the sixth century C.E., the Arabs remained polytheistic and disunited, but the birth of the prophet Muhammad in 570 in Mecca changed these circumstances dramatically.

Orphaned at the age of six, Muhammad received little formal education. He traveled with his uncle on caravan journeys that brought him into contact with communities

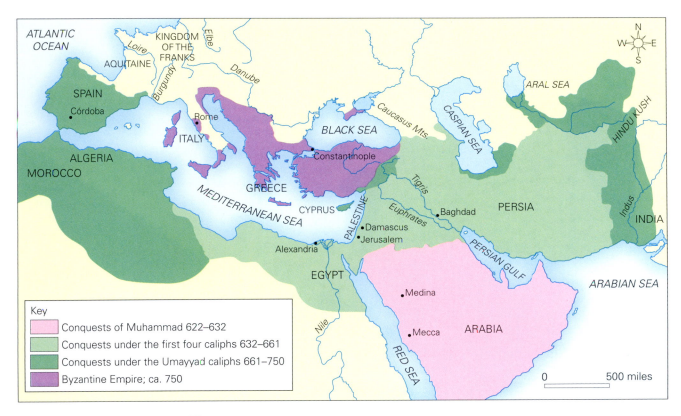

Map 10.1 The Expansion of Islam, 622–ca. 750.

of Jews, Christians, and pagans. At the age of twenty-five he married Khadijah, a wealthy widow fifteen years his senior, and assisted in running her flourishing caravan trade. Long periods of retreat and solitary meditation in the desert, however, led to a transformation in Muhammad's life: according to Muslim teachings, the archangel Gabriel appeared to Muhammad and commanded him to receive the revelation of the one and only Allah (the Arabic word for "God"). Now forty-one years old, Muhammad declared himself the final messenger in a history of religious revelation that had begun with Abraham and continued through Moses and Jesus.

While Muhammad preached no new doctrines, he emphasized the bond between Allah and his followers, and the importance of the community (*umma*) of the faithful, whose unswerving love of God would govern every aspect of their lives and conduct. His message reinforced many of the basic precepts of Christianity and Judaism. Some of Allah's revelations to Muhammad, such as the immortality of the soul, the anticipation of a final judgment, and the certainty of Heaven and Hell, were staples of Early Christianity. Others, such as an uncompromising monotheism, a strict set of ethical and social injunctions, and special dietary laws, were fundamental to Hebraic teaching.

At the outset, Muhammad's message attracted few followers. Since his attack on idolatry threatened Mecca's prominence as a prosperous pilgrimage site, the polytheistic Meccan elite actively resisted the new faith. Tribal loyalties among Meccans ran deep, and armed conflict was common. In 622, after twelve years of indecisive warfare with the Meccan opposition, the Prophet abandoned his native city. Along with some seventy Muslim families, he emigrated to Medina—a journey known as the **hijra** ("migration"). Eight more years marked by sporadic warfare were to elapse before the population of Medina was converted. When Muhammad returned to Mecca with a following of 10,000 men, the city opened its gates to him. Muhammad conquered Mecca and destroyed the idols in the *Kaaba*, with the exception of the Black Stone, the revered ancient cornerstone of the Sacred House. Thereafter, Muhammad assumed spiritual and political authority—establishing a theocracy that bound religious and secular realms in a manner not unlike that of the early Hebrew kings. By the time Muhammad died in 632, the entire Arabian peninsula was united in its commitment to Islam. Since the history of Muhammad's successful missionary activity began with the *hijra* of 622, that date marks the first year of the Muslim calendar.

Figure 10.2 The *Kaaba*, Mecca, Saudi Arabia. According to Muslim tradition, the *Kaaba* was built by Abraham and his son Ishmael; it is also said to mark the sacred spot where, at God's command, Abraham had prepared to sacrifice his son. Muslims are expected to make the *hajj* to the *Kaaba* at least once during their lifetime. Some two million pilgrims throng to Mecca annually to take part in the ritual procession that circles the shrine seven times.

Submission to God

Muhammad's followers—called Muslims ("those who submit to Allah")—honor him as the last of the prophets, human rather than divine in nature. They acknowledge Allah as the one true god, identical with the god of the Jews and the Christians. Fulfilling the Judeo-Christian tradition of deliverance, Islam (literally, "submission to God's will") claims to complete God's revelation to humankind. The declaration of faith in Allah and his Messenger known as the *shahadah* (literally "witness") is the first of the so-called Five Pillars of Muslim practice.

The Qur'an

Muhammad himself wrote nothing, but his disciples memorized his teachings and recorded them some ten years after his death. Written in Arabic, the Qur'an (literally, "recitation") is the holy book of Islam (Figure 10.3). The Muslim guide to spiritual and secular life, the Qur'an consists of 114 chapters (*suras*), each of which opens with the *bismillah* (invocation), "In the name of God, the Lord of Mercy, the Giver of Mercy." As the supreme authority and fundamental source of Muslim ritual, ethics, and laws, the Qur'an provides guidelines for worship and specific moral and social injunctions for everyday conduct. It condemns the drinking of wine, the eating of pork, and all forms of gambling. Islam limits **polygyny** (marriage to several women at the same time) to no more than four wives, provided that a man can support and protect all of them. Although the Qur'an defends the equality of men and women before God (see Sura 4.3–7), it describes men as being "a degree higher than women" (in that they are the providers) and endorses the pre-Islamic tradition requiring women to veil their bodies from public view (Sura 24.31; see Figure 10.1). A husband has unrestricted rights of divorce and can end a marriage by renouncing his wife publicly. Nevertheless, Muhammad's teachings raised the status of women by condemning female infanticide, according women property

rights, and ensuring their financial support, in an age when such protection was not commonly guaranteed.

Muslim Scripture reveals the nature of God and the inevitability of judgment and resurrection. It teaches that human beings are born in the purity of God's design, free from Original Sin. To the righteous—those who practice submission, humility, and reverence for God—it promises a hereafter resembling a garden of paradise, filled with cool rivers and luscious fruit trees. To the wicked and to **infidels** (nonbelievers), it promises the terrifying punishments of Hell—as hot and dusty as the desert itself.

Muslims consider the Qur'an the eternal and absolute word of God. Chanted or recited, rather than read silently, it is often committed to memory by the devout. The Qur'an is the primary text for the study of the Arabic language. It is considered untranslatable, not only because its contents are

Figure 10.3 Kufic calligraphy from the Qur'an, from Persia, ninth to tenth centuries. Ink and gold leaf on vellum, 8½ × 21 in. Qur'ans, like the holy books of Judaism and Early Christianity, were usually handwritten on sheepskin (parchment) or calfskin (vellum) and hand-decorated or "illuminated"—that is, ornamented with gold leaf or gold paint and brightly colored pigments. Arabic script, like Hebrew script, is read from right to left. Kufic calligraphy is notable for its angularity and its horizontal extensions.

Translating the Qur'an

The Qur'an is said to be untranslatable; even non-Arabic-speaking Muslims often learn it in its original language. Nevertheless, this holy book has been translated numerous times—into English and many other languages. Most translations adhere as closely as possible to the classical Arabic used at the time of Muhammad; others attempt to modernize the Arabic. As with all efforts to translate great literature from its original language, clarity and accuracy of meaning are major goals. In the case of works that are said to be divinely revealed, accurate translation is even more crucial (see Translating the Hebrew Bible, Chapter 1). The choice of a single word or phrase may modify the meaning of the text.

The following translations are of the same excerpt from the Qur'an, which appears in a chapter that deals with family relations and the rights and obligations of men and women in achieving proper behavior. Similar to both ancient Jewish and Early Christian cultures, Muslim society was patriarchal. Sura 4:34 offers instruction as to how Muslim men should deal with disobedient wives. The differences between the two translations illustrate the problematic relationship between translation and interpretation.

1) "Men are the protectors and maintainers of women, because Allah has given the one more (strength) than the other, and because they support them from their means. Therefore the righteous women are devoutly obedient, and guard in (the husband's) absence, what Allah would have them guard. As to those women on whose part ye fear disloyalty and ill-conduct, admonish them (first), (next), refuse to share their beds, (and last) beat them (lightly); but if they return to obedience, seek not against them Means (of annoyance): For Allah is Most High, great (above you all)."

Translated by Abdullah Yusuf Ali (1934)

2) "Men are supporters of wives because God has given some of them an advantage over others and because they spend of their wealth. So the ones who are in accord with morality are the ones who are morally obligated, the ones who guard the unseen of what God has kept safe. But those whose resistance you fear, then admonish them and abandon them in their sleeping place then go away from them; and if they obey you, surely look not for any way against them; truly God is Lofty, Great."

Translated by Laleh Bakhtiar (2006)

---

deemed holy, but also because it is impossible to capture in other languages the musical nuances of the original Arabic.

READING 10.1 From the Qur'an

Chapter 5 The Table
In the Name of God, the Most Gracious, the Most Merciful

· · · · · · · · ·

6. Believers, when you rise to pray, wash your faces and your hands up to the elbows and wipe your heads and [wash] your feet up to the ankles. If you are in a state of impurity, take a full bath. Should you be ill or on a journey or when you have just relieved yourselves, or you have consorted with your spouses, purify yourself by bathing. If you can find no water, take some clean sand and rub your faces and hands with it. God does not wish to place any burden on you; he only wishes to purify you and perfect his favor to you, in order that you may be grateful.
7. Remember God's favor to you, and the covenant, which He made with you when you said "We hear and we obey." Fear God. God has full knowledge of the innermost thoughts of men.
8. Believers, be steadfast in the cause of God and bear witness with justice. Do not let your enmity for others turn you away from justice. Deal justly; that is nearer to being God-fearing. Fear God. God is aware of all that you do.
9. God has promised those who believe and do good deeds forgiveness and a great reward; but those who deny the truth and deny Our signs are destined for Hell.

10. Believers, remember the blessings which God bestowed upon you when a certain people were about to lay hands on you and He held back their hands from you. Have fear of God and in God let the believers place their trust.

· · · · · · · · · ·

19. People of the Book,[1] Our Messenger has come to you to make things clear to you after an interval between the messengers, lest you say, "No bearer of glad tidings and no warner has come to us." So a bearer of glad tidings and a warner has indeed come to you. God has the power to do all things.

· · · · · · · · · ·

66. If only the People of the Book would believe and be mindful of God, We would surely pardon their sins and We would surely admit them into the Gardens of Bliss. If they had observed the Torah and the Gospel and what was revealed to them from their Lord, they would surely have been nourished from above and from below. There are some among them who are on the right course; but there are many among them who do nothing but evil.
67. O Messenger, deliver whatever has been sent down to you by your Lord. If you do not do so, you will not have conveyed His message. God will defend you from mankind. For God does not guide those who deny the truth.
68. Say, "People of the Book, you have no ground to stand on until you observe the Torah and the Gospel and what is revealed to you

---

[1] Jews and Christians.

from your Lord." What is revealed to you from your Lord will surely increase many of them in rebellion and in their denial of the truth. But do not grieve for those who deny the truth.

69. Believers, Jews, Sabaeans[2] and Christians—whoever believes in God and the Last Day and does what is right—shall have nothing to fear nor shall they grieve.

70. We made a covenant with the Children of Israel and sent forth messengers among them. But whenever a messenger came to them with a message that was not to their liking, some they accused of lying, while others they put to death,

71. and they imagined that no harm would come to them; and so they became blind and deaf [of heart]. God turned to them in mercy; yet again many of them became blind and deaf. God is fully aware of their actions.

72. Indeed, they are deniers of the truth who say, "God is the Christ, the son of Mary." For the Christ himself said, "Children of Israel, serve God, my Lord and your Lord." If anyone associates anything with God, God will forbid him the Garden and the Fire will be his home. The wrongdoers shall have no helpers.

73. They are deniers of the truth who say, "God is one of three."[3] There is only One God. If they do not desist from so saying, a painful punishment is bound to befall such of them as are bent on denying the truth.

74. Why do they not turn to God and ask for His forgiveness? God is forgiving and merciful.

75. Christ, son of Mary, was no more than a messenger. Many messengers passed away before him. His mother was a virtuous woman; and they both ate food [like other mortals]. See how We make the signs clear to them! See how they turn away!

76. Say, "Do you worship something other than God, that has no power to do you harm or good? God alone is the All Hearing and All Knowing."

77. Say, "People of the Book! Do not go to extremes in your religion and do not follow the whims of those who went astray before you—they caused many to go astray and themselves strayed away from the right path."

. . . .

Chapter 17 The Night Journey
In the Name of God, the Most Gracious, the Most Merciful

. . . .

9. Surely, this Qur'an guides to the most upright way and gives good news to the believers who do good deeds, so that they will have a great reward

10. and warns those who deny the life to come with grievous punishment.

11. Yet man asks for evil as eagerly as he should ask for good. Truly, man is indeed hasty.

12. We have made the night and the day as two signs. We blotted out the sign of night and made the sign of the day illuminating, so that you may seek the bounty of your Lord and learn to compute the seasons and the years. We have set everything forth in detail.

13. We have tied the fate of every man about his neck; and We shall produce a book for him on Resurrection Day that he will find spread open.

14. It will say, "Read your record, today there will be none but yourself to call you to account!"

15. Whoever chooses to follow the right path, follows it for his own good; and whoever goes astray, goes astray at his own peril; no bearer of burdens shall bear the burdens of another. Nor do We punish until We have sent forth a messenger to forewarn them.

16. When We decide to destroy a town, We command the affluent section of its people [to reform], but they transgress therein; thus the word [sentence of punishment] is justified, then We destroy the town utterly.

17. How many generations have We destroyed since Noah's time. Your Lord is well aware of the sins of His servants and observes them all.

18. We give whatever We will to whoever desires immediate gains; but then We have prepared Hell for him which he will enter, disgraced and rejected.

19. Anyone who desires the Hereafter and makes a proper effort to achieve it, being a true believer, shall find favor with God for his endeavors.

20. Upon all, both these [who desire the world] and those [who desire the Hereafter] We bestow the bounty of your Lord: none shall be denied the bounty of your Lord—

21. see how We have exalted some above others [in the present life]. Yet the Hereafter shall be greater in degrees of rank and greater in excellence.

22. Do not set up any other deity beside God, lest you incur disgrace, and be forsaken.

23. Your Lord has commanded that you should worship none but Him, and show kindness to your parents. If either or both of them attain old age with you, say no word of contempt to them and do not rebuke them, but always speak gently to them

24. and treat them with humility and tenderness and say, "Lord, be merciful to them both, as they raised me up when I was little."

25. Your Lord knows best what is in your hearts; if you are righteous, He is most forgiving to those who constantly turn to Him.

26. Give to your relatives their due, and also to the needy and the wayfarer. Yet do not spend extravagantly;

27. spendthrifts are the brothers of Satan, and Satan is ever ungrateful to his Lord—

28. but if, while waiting for your Lord's bounty which you are expecting, you turn them down, then at least speak to them kindly.

29. Be neither miserly, nor so open-handed that you suffer reproach and become destitute.

30. Your Lord gives abundantly to whom He will and sparingly to whom He pleases. He is informed and observant about His servants.

31. You shall not kill your offspring for fear of want. It is We who provide for them, and for you. Indeed, killing them is a great sin.

32. Do not commit adultery, for it is an indecent thing and an evil course.

33. Do not take life which God has made inviolate—except by right. If anyone is killed wrongfully, We have given authority to his heirs to demand retribution, but let them not transgress the prescribed limits in exacting retribution; for then he will be assisted [by the law].

34. Do not go near the orphans' property, except with the best of intentions, until they reach maturity. Keep your promises; you will be called to account for every promise which you have made!

35. Give full measure, when you measure, and weigh with accurate scales. That is fair, and better in the end.

36. Do not follow what you do not know; for the ear and the eye and the heart shall all be called to account.

37. Do not walk proudly on the earth. You cannot cleave the earth, nor can you rival the mountains in height.

38. All this is evil in the sight of your Lord, and is detestable.

. . . .

---

[2] Semitic merchants from the Saba, a kingdom in southern Arabia.
[3] The Trinity.

Chapter 47 Muhammad

In the name of God, the Most Gracious, the Most Merciful

1. God will bring to naught all the good deeds of those who are bent on denying the truth and bar [others] from the path of God.

2. As for those who believe and do good deeds and believe in what has been revealed to Muhammad—and it is the truth from their Lord—God will remove their sins from them and set their condition right.

3. That is because the ones who deny the truth follow falsehood, while those who believe follow the Truth from their Lord. Thus God sets forth comparisons for mankind.

4. When you meet those who deny the truth in battle, strike them in the neck, and once they are defeated, make [them] prisoners, and afterwards either set them free as an act of grace, or let them ransom [themselves] until the war is finally over. Thus you shall do; and if God had pleased, He would certainly have exacted retribution from them, but His purpose is to test some of you by means of others. As for those who are killed in God's cause, He will never let their deeds be in vain;

5. He will guide them and improve their condition;

6. He will admit them into the Garden He has already made known to them.

7. Believers! If you succor[4] God, He will succor you and make your footsteps firm.

8. But as for those who are bent on denying the truth, destruction will be their lot, and [God] will make their deeds come to nothing.

9. It is because they are averse to what God has revealed that He has rendered their deeds futile.

10. Have they not traveled the earth and seen how those before them met their end? God destroyed them utterly: a similar fate awaits those who deny the truth.

11. That is because God is the protector of the believers, and those who deny the truth have no protector at all.

12. God will admit those who believe and do good deeds to Gardens through which rivers flow. Those who deny the truth may take their fill of pleasure in this world, and eat as cattle do, but the Fire will be their ultimate abode.

13. How many towns We have destroyed, greater in strength than your city which has driven you out [Prophet], and there was no one to help them.

. . . .

Chapter 76 Man

In the name of God, the Most Gracious, the Most Merciful

1. Was there not a period of time when man was nothing worth mentioning?[5]

2. We created man from a drop of mingled fluid so that We might try him; We gave him hearing and sight;

3. We showed him the way, whether he be grateful or ungrateful.

4. [Now,] behold, for those who deny the truth, We have prepared chains, iron collars and a blazing fire, but

5. the righteous shall drink from a cup mixed with the coolness of *kafur*,[6]

6. a spring from which God's servants will drink, making it gush forth in branches.

7. They keep their vows and fear a day the woe of which will spread far and wide;

8. they give food, despite their love for it, to the poor and orphans and captives,

9. saying, "We feed you for the sake of God alone, we seek neither recompense nor thanks from you.

10. Truly, we fear from our Lord a woefully grim Day."

11. Therefore, God will ward off from them the woes of that Day, and make them find brightness and joy,

12. and their reward for being patient will be a Garden and silk [clothing].

13. Reclining upon couches, they will find therein neither the heat of the sun nor bitter, biting cold,

14. the shading branches of trees will come down low over them, and their clusters of fruit, will hang down where they are the easiest to reach.

15. Vessels of silver and goblets of pure crystal will be passed round among them

16. and gleaming silver goblets which have been filled to the exact measure,

17. and they will be given a cup to drink flavored with ginger,

18. from a flowing spring called Salsabil.[7]

19. They will be attended by youths who will not age—when you see them you will think them to be like sprinkled pearls—

20. wherever you look, you will see bliss and a great kingdom:

21. they will wear green garments of fine silk and rich brocade. They will be adorned with silver bracelets. And their Lord will give them a pure drink.

22. This is your reward. Your endeavor is fully acknowledged.

23. Truly, it is We who have revealed to you the Qur'an, a gradual revelation.

24. So wait patiently for the command of your Lord, and do not yield to anyone among them who is sinful or ungrateful;

25. and glorify your Lord morning and evening;

26. and during the night prostrate yourself before Him, and extol His glory for a long part of the night.

27. Those people [who are unmindful of God] aspire for immediate gains, and put behind them a Heavy Day.

28. It was We who created them and made their constitution strong, but if We wish we can replace them with others like them.

29. This is a reminder. Let whoever wishes, take the right path to his Lord.

30. But you cannot will it unless God wills [to show you that way]—God is indeed allknowing and wise—

31. He admits whoever He will into His grace and has prepared a painful punishment for the evil doers.

Q How does the Qur'an describe the "People of the Book?"

Q How does the Muslim view of reward and punishment compare with that of other world faiths?

---

[4] Help.

[5] Literally, "Has there not come over man a period of time when he was not mentioned?" This refers to the time before a person is born, the point being that he was nothing, then God created him, just as he will bring him to life again for judgment.

[6] A fragrant herb.

[7] Literally, "Seek the Way"; the word also means "sweet" and "rapid-flowing."

The Muslim Identity

Islam's success in becoming a world faith is explained in part by the fact that, at the outset, religious, political, and military goals were allied. However, other factors were crucial to attracting followers. The new faith offered rules of conduct that were easy to understand and to follow—a timely alternative, perhaps, to the complexities of Jewish ritual and Christian theology. In contrast with Christianity and Judaism, Islam remained free of dogma and liturgy and unencumbered by a priestly hierarchy. Orthodox Muslims regarded the Trinity and the Christian cult of saints as polytheistic; they denied the divinity of Jesus, admiring him as a prophet, like Moses or Muhammad himself. On the other hand, like Jews and Christians ("People of the Book"), the Muslim community was united by a message of piety and faith.

The core Islamic texts, the Qur'an and the *Hadith* (a compilation of Muhammad's words and actions compiled a century after his death), provide an all-embracing code of ethical conduct known as the ***sharia*** (literally "legislation"). Regarded by Muslims as "the path to follow," *sharia* law offers precise guidance in matters as diverse as marriage, dress code, inheritance, and business practice. It is subject to interpretation by Islamic judges (***qadi***), by religious leaders (***imams***), and by scholars trained in Muslim law (***mullahs***). *Mullahs* also function as teachers in Islamic schools (***madrasas***), affiliated with the Muslim place of worship known as the **mosque**.

The Expansion of Islam

Islam unified the tribal population of Arabia in a common religious and ethnic bond that propelled Muslims out of their desert confines into East Asia, Africa, and the West. The young religion assumed a sense of historical mission much like that which drove the ancient Romans. In fact, the militant expansion of Islam was the evangelical counterpart of ***jihad***, fervent religious struggle. Often translated as "holy war," the word signifies all aspects of the Muslim drive toward moral and religious perfection, including the defense and spread of Islam. In Muslim thought and practice, the term denotes both "the lesser *jihad*" (war) and "the greater *jihad*" (self-control: the struggle to contain lust, anger, and other forms of indulgence). Militant Muslims would have agreed with Augustine that a "just cause" made warfare acceptable in the eyes of God (see chapter 9). Indeed, Christian soldiers anticipated heavenly rewards if they died fighting for Christ, while Muslims looked forward to Paradise if they died in the service of Allah.

Generally speaking, early Muslim expansion succeeded not so much by the militant coercion of foreign populations as it did by the economic opportunities Muslims offered conquered people. Unlike Christianity and Buddhism, Islam neither renounced nor condemned material wealth. Jews and Christians living in Muslim lands were taxed but not persecuted. Converts to Islam were exempt from paying a poll-tax levied on all non-Muslim subjects. Into the towns that would soon become cultural oases, Muslims brought expertise in navigation, trade, and commercial exchange. They fostered favorable associations between Arab merchants and members of the ruling elite (in Africa, for instance) and rewarded converts with access to positions of power and authority. While many subject people embraced Islam out of genuine spiritual conviction, others found clear commercial and social advantages in conversion to the faith of Muhammad.

Muhammad never designated a successor; hence, after his death, bitter controversies arose concerning Muslim leadership. Rival claims to authority produced major divisions within the faith and armed conflicts that still exist today; the Sunni (from *sunna*, "the tradition of the Prophet") consider themselves the orthodox of Islam. Representing approximately 90 percent of the modern Muslim world population, they hold that religious rulers should be chosen by the faithful. By contrast, the Shiites or Shiah-i-Ali ("partisans of Ali") (the majority population in present-day Iran and Iraq) claim descent through Muhammad's cousin and son-in-law Ali. They hold that only his direct descendants should rule. Following Muhammad's death, the **caliphs**, theocratic successors to Muhammad, were appointed by his followers. The first four caliphs, who ruled until 661, assumed political and religious authority, and their success in carrying Islam outside of Arabia (see Map 10.1) resulted in the establishment of a Muslim empire. Damascus fell to Islam in 634, Persia in 636, Jerusalem in 638, and Egypt in 640. Within another seventy years, under the leadership of the Umayyad caliphs (661–750), all of North Africa and Spain lay under Muslim rule.

Muslim expansion played a key role in defining the geographic borders of Western Europe. The control of the Mediterranean by Muslim forces snuffed out the waning Western sea trade, isolating the Christian West (see chapter 11). The Muslim advance upon the West encountered only two significant obstacles: the first was Constantinople, where Byzantine forces equipped with "Greek fire" (an incendiary compound catapulted from ships) deterred repeated Arab attacks. The second was in southwest France, near Tours, where, in 732, Frankish soldiers led by Charles Martel (the grandfather of Charlemagne) turned back the Muslims, thus barring the progress of Islam into Europe. Nevertheless, in less than a century, Islam had won more converts than Christianity had gained in its first 300 years.

Islam in Africa

Islam's success in Africa was remarkable. As early as the seventh century, on the edges of the Sahara Desert and in North Africa, the Muslim merchants came to dominate commerce in salt, gold, and slaves (see Figure **10.1**). The volume of slave raids within the native Berber population west of the Nile River was so large as to spark open revolt. Nevertheless, Muslim traders soon commanded the trans-Saharan network that linked West Africa to Cairo and continued through Asia via the Silk Road to China (see chapters 7 and 14).

Islam quickly became Africa's fastest-growing religion, mingling with various aspects of local belief systems as it attracted a following primarily among the ruling elite of the continent's burgeoning kingdoms: in West Africa, Ghana, Mali, and Songhai (see chapter 18). The kings of Mali incorporated Islamic rituals into native African ceremonies; adopted the Arabic language for administrative purposes; hired Muslim scribes and jurists; and underwrote the construction of mosques and universities, the greatest of which was at Timbuktu. In East Africa, as elsewhere, Swahili rulers who converted to Islam did not actively impose the religion on their subjects, so that only the larger African towns and centers of trade became oases of Islamic culture.

Islam in the Middle East

Between 661 and 750, Damascus (in present-day Syria) served as the political center of the Muslim world. However, as Islam spread eastward under the leadership of a new Muslim dynasty—the Abbasids—the capital shifted to Baghdad (in present-day Iraq). In Baghdad, a multi-ethnic city of more than 300,000 people, a golden age would come to flower. Between the eighth and tenth centuries, the city became an international trade center, and expansive commercial activity enriched the growing urban population. Arab merchants imported leopards and rubies from India; silk, paper, and porcelain from China; horses and camels from Arabia; and topaz and cotton cloth from Egypt. The court of the caliph Harun al-Rashid (ruled 786–809) attracted musicians, dancers, writers, and poets. Harun's sons opened a House of Wisdom (*Dar al-Hikmet*) in which scholars prepared Arabic translations of Greek, Persian, Syriac, and Sanskrit manuscripts. In the ninth century, no city in the world could match the breadth of educational instruction or boast a library as large as that of Baghdad. Al-Yaqubi, a late ninth-century traveler, called Baghdad "the navel of the earth" and "the greatest city, which has no peer in the east or the west of the world in extent, size, prosperity, abundance of water, or health of climate. . . ." He continued:

> To [Baghdad] they come from all countries, far and near, and people from every side have preferred Baghdad to their own homelands. There is no country, the peoples of which have not their own quarter and their own trading and financial arrangements. In it there is gathered that which does not exist in any other city in the world. On its flanks flow two great rivers, the Tigris and the Euphrates, and thus goods and foodstuffs come to it by land and water with the greatest ease, so that every kind of merchandise is completely available, from east and west, from

Muslim and non-Muslim lands. Goods are brought from India, Sind [modern Pakistan], China, Tibet, the lands of the Turks, . . . the Ethiopians, and others to such an extent that [products] are more plentiful in Baghdad than in the countries from which they come. They can be procured so readily and so certainly that it is as if all the good things of the world are sent there, all the treasures of the earth assembled there, and all the blessings of creation perfected there. . . . The people excel in knowledge, understanding, letters, manners, insight, discernment, skill in commerce and crafts, cleverness in every argument, proficiency in every calling, and mastery of every craft. There is none more learned than their scholars, better informed than their traditionists, more cogent than their theologians, more perspicuous than their grammarians, more accurate than their [calligraphers], more skillful than their physicians, more melodious than their singers, more delicate than their craftsmen, more literate than their scribes, more lucid than their logicians, more devoted than their worshipers, more pious than their ascetics, more juridical than their [magistrates], more eloquent than their preachers, more poetic than their poets, and more reckless than their rakes.

Almost one hundred years later, the late tenth-century geographer Al-Muqaddasi of Jerusalem described Baghdad as "the metropolis of Islam." It is accurate to say that between the eighth and tenth centuries, the cosmopolitan cities of the Muslim world boasted levels of wealth and culture that far exceeded those of Western Christendom. Even after invading Turkish nomads gained control of Baghdad during the eleventh century, the city retained cultural primacy within the civilized world—although Córdoba, with a library of some 400,000 volumes, came to rival Baghdad as a cultural and educational center. The destruction of Baghdad in 1258 at the hands of the Mongols ushered in centuries of slow cultural decline. However, Mongols and Turks, themselves converts to Islam, carried Islamic culture into India and China. In Egypt, an independent Islamic government ruled until the sixteenth century. The Tunisian historian Ibn Khaldun, visiting fourteenth-century Egypt, called Cairo "the mother of the world, the great center of Islam and the mainspring of the sciences and the crafts." Until the mid-fourteenth century, Muslims continued to dominate a system of world trade that stretched from Western Europe to China. Thereafter, the glories of medieval Muslim culture began to wane, to be revived only in the lavish court of the sixteenth-century Ottoman Turks and then by the Moguls of seventeenth-century India (see chapter 21). The same cannot be said of the religion of Islam: over the centuries of Islamic expansion, millions of people found Islam responsive to their immediate spiritual needs, and in most of the Asiatic and African regions conquered prior to the late seventh century (see Map 10.1), it is still the dominant faith. To date, Islam has experienced less change and remains closer to its original form than any other world religion.

Islamic Culture

From its beginnings, Islam held the status of a state-sponsored religion. Whereas Church and state were interdependent in both Byzantium and the Christian West, in Muslim lands they were inseparable. Theocratic rule brought a strong element of unity to Islamic culture, which is otherwise notable for its ethnic diversity, the product of its assimilation of many different peoples. The principal languages of the Islamic world, for instance, are Arabic, Persian, and Turkish, but dozens of other languages, including Berber, Swahili, Kurdish, Tamil, Malay, and Javanese, are spoken by Muslims. As Islam expanded, it absorbed many different styles from the arts of non-Arab peoples. "Islamic," then, is a term used to describe the culture of geographically diverse regions—Arab and non-Arab—dominated by Islam.

Scholarship in the Islamic World

Following Muhammad's dictum to "seek knowledge," Islam was enthusiastically receptive to the intellectual achievements of other cultures and aggressive in its will to understand the workings of the natural world. At a time when few Westerners could read or write Latin and even fewer could decipher Greek, Arab scholars preserved hundreds of ancient Greek manuscripts—the works of Plato, Aristotle, Archimedes, Hippocrates, Galen, Ptolemy, and others—copying and editing them in Arabic translations. An important factor in this burst of literary creativity was the availability of paper, which originated in China as early as the second century and came into use in Baghdad during the ninth century. In the copying of Classical manuscripts, in the codification of religious teachings (that had heretofore been passed orally), and in the production of new types of literature, such as scientific treatises, cookbooks, poems, and tales (see Readings 10.2–4), paper provided a major advance over parchment and papyrus, expensive materials from whose surfaces ink could easily be erased.

Between the ninth and twelfth centuries, Muslims absorbed and preserved much of the medical, botanical, and astrological lore of the Hellenized Mediterranean. This fund of scientific and technological knowledge, along with Arabic translations of Aristotle's works in logic and natural philosophy, and Muslim commentaries on Aristotle, filtered into the urban centers of Europe. There, in the twelfth century, they stimulated a rebirth of learning and contributed to the rise of Western universities (see chapter 12). Muslim philosophers compared the theories of Aristotle and the Neoplatonists with the precepts of Islam, seeking a unity of truth that would become the object of inquiry among Italian Renaissance humanists.

Crucial to the advancement of learning was the Muslim transmission of Hindu numbers, which replaced cumbersome Roman numerals with so-called Arabic numbers such as those used to paginate this book. Muslims also provided the West with such technological wonders as block printing (after the eighth century) and gunpowder (after the thirteenth century), both of which originated in China. Muslims thus borrowed and diffused the knowledge of Greek, Chinese, and Indian culture as energetically as they circulated commercial goods.

But the scholars of the Islamic world were not merely copyists; they made original contributions in mathematics, medicine, optics, chemistry, geography, philosophy, and astronomy. In the field of medicine, Islamic physicians wrote treatises on smallpox, measles, and diseases transmitted by animals (such as rabies), on the cauterization of wounds, and on the preparation of medicinal drugs (Figure **10.4**). The single most important medieval health handbook, the *Tacuinum Sanitatis*, originated among Arab physicians who examined the effects of various foods, drinks, and clothing on human well-being. Translated into Latin in the eleventh century, this manuscript came into widespread popular use throughout the West. The vast *Canon of Medicine* compiled by the Persian physician and philosopher Ibn Sina (Avicenna, 980–1037) was a systematic repository of medical knowledge in use well into the sixteenth century. Muslim chemists invented the process of

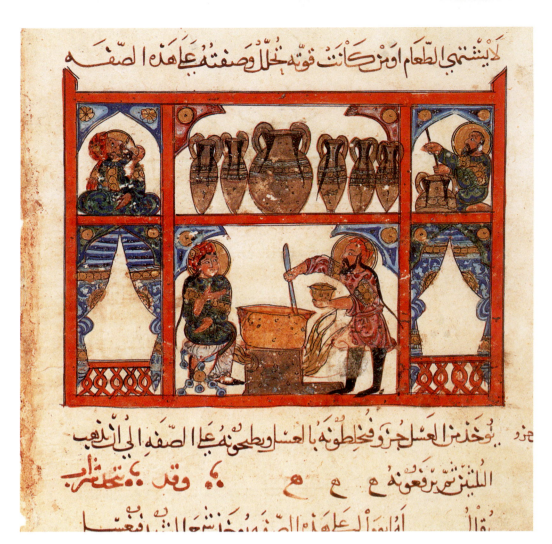

لَا يَشْتَهِي الطَّعَام اوَمن كَانَت قوَّته تُحَلّل وصفتُه عَلى هَذَنَ الصَّفه

Figure 10.4 *Preparing Medicine from Honey*, from an Arabic manuscript of *Materia Medica* by Dioscorides, thirteenth century. Colors and gilt on paper, 12⅜ × 9 in.

يُوخَذ من العَسَل جزوَ فخَلَطونَه بِالعَسَار وطحوَنَه عَلى الصَّفه الى الذَهَب

الليَّن نشَر نَعونَه ع ع م

وقد بتطَلاب

أَوَامِ العَطَه الصَّ مَن خَزنَتها نَعسَل

distillation and produced a volatile liquid (and forbidden intoxicant) called *alkuhl* (alcohol).

At a time when most Europeans knew little of the earth's physical size or shape, geographers in Baghdad estimated with some accuracy the earth's circumference, as well as its shape and curvature. Muslim astronomers made advances in spherical geometry and trigonometry that aided religious observance, which required an accurate lunar calendar and the means of determining the direction of Mecca from any given location. By refining the astrolabe, an ancient instrument for measuring the altitude of heavenly bodies above the horizon (Figure **10.5**), Muslims were able to determine the time of day, hence estimate the correct hours for worship.

Islamic Poetry

In the Islamic literary tradition—a tradition dominated by two highly lyrical languages, Arabic and Persian—poetry played an infinitely more important role than prose. As within the cultures of ancient Greece, Africa, and China, poetry and music were intimately related, and local bards or wandering minstrels were the "keepers" of a popular oral verse tradition. The Bedouin minstrels of pre-Islamic culture celebrated in song themes of romantic love, tribal warfare, and nomadic life. Bedouin songs, like the Arabic language itself, are rich in rhyme, and a single rhyme often dominates an entire poem. No English translation

can capture the musical qualities of Arabic verse, and only some translations succeed in preserving its colorful descriptive imagery. Such is the case with the sixth-century ode by Tarafa in Reading 10.2, which uses vivid similes to convey a memorable portrait of the camel that has captured his heart.

Following the rise of Islam, no literature was prized more highly than the Arabic lyrics that constituted the Qur'an. However, the pre-Islamic affection for secular verse persisted: the dominant themes in Islamic poetry included laments over injustice, elegies for the departed, and celebrations of the physical delights of nature. Romantic love—both heterosexual and homosexual, and often strongly erotic—was a favorite subject, especially among those who came under the influence of Persian literature. The eighth-century "Romance of Antar," a eulogy in honor of a beautiful and bewitching female, attributed to Al-Asmai (740–828), reflects the sensual power of the finest Islamic lyrics. The poet's "ailment" of unrequited love, or "lovesickness," was a popular conceit in Arabic verse and one that became central to the code of courtly

---

* The term "Moor" describes a Northwest African Muslim of mixed Arab and Berber descent. The Moors invaded and occupied Spain in the eighth century and maintained a strong presence there until they were expelled from Granada, their last stronghold, in 1492.

Figure 10.5 ABD AL-KARIM AL-MISRI, Astrolabe, from Cairo, 1235–1236. Brass, height 15½ in.

love in the medieval West. With their frank examination of physical desire and their reverence for female beauty, the poems of Al-Asmai, Ibn Zaydun (1003–1071), and Ibn Abra—the last two representative of Moorish* Islam—influenced the various genres of literature in Western Europe. This includes *troubadour* poetry, the medieval romance (see chapter 11), and the sonnets and songs of the Renaissance poet Petrarch (see chapter 16).

— READING 10.2 Secular Islamic Poems (ca. 800–1300)

From Tarafa's "Praise for His Camel"

. . . .

Yet I have means to fly from grief, when such pursues me,   **1**
    on a lean high beast, which paces swiftly by day and
    by night,
A camel sure of foot, firm and thin as the planks of a bier,
    whom I guide surely over the trodden ways, ways   **5**
    etched in earth as texture is in cloth;
A she-camel, rival of the best, swift as an ostrich. When
    she trots her hind feet fall in the marks of her forefeet
    on the beaten road.
With her white feathery tail she lashes backward and   **10**
    forward. Sometimes the lash falls on her rider,
    sometimes on her own dried udder, where no milk is,
    flaccid as an old bottle of leather.
Firm and polished are her haunches as two worn jambs of
    a castle gate.   **15**

The bones of her spine are supple and well-attached, and
    her neck rises solidly.

When she raises her long neck it is like the rudder of a
    boat going up the Tigris.
She carries her strong thighs well apart, as a carrier of   **20**
    water holds apart his buckets.
Red is the hair under her chin. Strong she is of back, long
    of stride; easily she moves her forelegs.

The marks of the girths on her sides are as the marks of
    water-courses over smooth rock.   **25**
Sometimes the marks unite and sometimes are distinct,
    like the gores in fine linen, well-cut and stitched.
Her long skull is like an anvil, and where the bones unite
    their edges are sharp as the teeth of a file.
Her cheek is smooth as paper of Syria, and her upper lip   **30**
    like leather of Yemen, exactly and smoothly cut.
The two polished mirrors of her eyes gleam in the caverns
    of their sockets as water gleams in rocky pools.

Her ears are sharp to hear the low voices of the night, and
    not inattentive to the loud call,   **35**
Pricked ears, that show her breeding, like those of a lone
    wild bull in the groves of Haumel.
Her upper lip is divided and her nose pierced. When she
    stretches them along the ground her pace increases.
I touch her with my whip and she quickens her step, even   **40**
    though it be the time when the mirage shimmers on
    the burning sands.
She walks with graceful gait, as the dancing girl walks,
    showing her master the skirts of her trailing garment.

From Al-Asmai's "Romance of Antar"

. . . .

The lovely virgin has struck my heart with the arrow of a   **1**
    glance, for which there is no cure.
Sometimes she wishes for a feast in the sandhills, like a
    fawn whose eyes are full of magic.
My disease preys on me; it is in my entrails: I conceal it;   **5**
    but its very concealment discloses it.
She moves: I should say it was the branch of the tamarisk[1]
    that waves its branches to the southern breeze.
She approaches: I should say it was the frightened fawn,
    when a calamity alarms it in the waste.   **10**
She walks away: I should say her face was truly the sun
    when its luster dazzles the beholders.
She gazes: I should say it was the full moon of the night
    when Orion[2] girds it with stars.
She smiles: and the pearls of her teeth sparkle, in which   **15**
    there is the cure for the sickness of lovers.
She prostrates herself in reverence towards her God;
    and the greatest of men bow down to her beauties.
O Abla! when I most despair, love for thee and all its
    weaknesses are my only hope!   **20**

---

[1] A small tree or shrub from the Mediterranean region.
[2] A constellation of bright stars represented by the figure of a hunter with belt and sword.

Ibn Zaydun's "Two Fragments"

I

The world is strange
For lack of you;
Times change their common hue—
The day is black, but very night
With you was shining white.

II

Two secrets in the heart of night
We were until the light
Of busybody day
Gave both of us away.

Ibn Abra's "The Beauty-Spot"

A mole on Ahmad's cheek
Draws all men's eyes to seek
The love they swear reposes
In a garden there.
That breathing bed of roses
In a Nubian's care.

Q What are the principal themes in these poems?

Q What similes and metaphors make these poems distinctive?

Sufi Poetry

One of the richest sources of literary inspiration in Islamic history was the movement known as Sufism. As early as the eighth century, some followers of Muhammad began to pursue a meditative, world-renouncing religious life that resembled the spiritual ideals of Christian and Buddhist ascetics and Neoplatonic mystics. The Sufi, so called for the coarse wool (*suf*) garments they wore, were committed to purification of the soul and mystical union with God through meditation, fasting, and prayer. As the movement grew, Sufism placed increasing emphasis on visionary experience and the practice of intensifying physical sensation through music, poetry, and dance. Religious rituals involving whirling dances (associated with Persian Sufis, known as "dervishes") functioned to transport the pious to a state of ecstasy (Figure **10.6**). The union of the senses and the spirit sought by the members of this ascetic brotherhood is also evident in Sufi poetry.

Sufi poetry, as represented in the works of the great Persian mystic and poet Jalal al-Din Rumi (ca. 1207–1273), draws on the intuitive, nonrational dimensions of the religious experience. In the first of the following three poems, a number of seeming contradictions work to characterize the unique nature of the spiritual master. The body of Sufi instructions outlined in the second poem might be equally appropriate to the Buddhist or the Christian mystic. In the third piece, "The One True Light," from *Love is a Stranger*, Rumi rehearses an ancient parable that illuminates the

unity of God: seeing beyond the dim gropings of the ordinary intellect, the mystic perceives that religions are many, but God is One.

— READING 10.3 The Poems of Rumi (ca. 1250)

The Man of God

The man of God is drunken while sober.	1
The man of God is full without meat.	
The man of God is perplexed and bewildered.	
The man of God neither sleeps nor eats.	
The man of God is a king clothed in rags.	5
The man of God is a treasure in the streets.	
The man of God is neither of sky nor land.	
The man of God is neither of earth nor sea.	
The man of God is an ocean without end.	
The man of God drops pearls at your feet.	10
The man of God has a hundred moons at night.	
The man of God has a hundred suns' light.	
The man of God's knowledge is complete.	
The man of God doesn't read with his sight.	
The man of God is beyond form and disbelief.	15
The man of God sees good and bad alike.	
The man of God is far beyond non-being.	
The man of God is seen riding high.	
The man of God is hidden, Shamsuddin.	
The man of God you must seek and find.	20

Empty the Glass of Your Desire

Join yourself to friends	1
and know the joy of the soul.	
Enter the neighborhood of ruin	
with those who drink to the dregs.	
Empty the glass of your desire	5
so that you won't be disgraced.	
Stop looking for something out there	
and begin seeing within.	
Open your arms if you want an embrace.	
Break the earthen idols and release the radiance.	10
Why get involved with a hag like this world?	
You know what it will cost.	
And three pitiful meals a day	
is all that weapons and violence can earn.	
At night when the Beloved comes	15
will you be nodding on opium?	
If you close your mouth to food,	
you can know a sweeter taste.	
Our Host is no tyrant. We gather in a circle.	
Sit down with us beyond the wheel of time.	20
Here is the deal: give one life	
and receive a hundred.	
Stop growling like dogs,	
and know the shepherd's care.	

Figure 10.6 *Dancing Dervishes*, from a manuscript of the *Diwan* (*Book of Poems*) of Hafiz, Herat School, Persia, ca. 1490. Colors and gilt on paper, 11¾ × 7⅜ in.

You keep complaining about others   25
and all they owe you?
Well, forget about them;
just be in His presence.

When the earth is this wide,
why are you asleep in a prison?   30
Think of nothing but the source of thought.
Feed the soul; let the body fast.

Avoid knotted ideas;
untie yourself in a higher world.
Limit your talk   35
for the sake of timeless communion.

Abandon life and the world,
and find the life of the world.

The One True Light

The lamps are different, but the Light is the same:
    it comes from Beyond.   1
If thou keep looking at the lamp, thou art lost: for thence
    arises the appearance of number and plurality.
Fix thy gaze upon the Light, and thou art delivered from
    the dualism inherent in the finite body.
O thou who art the kernel of Existence, the disagreement
    between Moslem, Zoroastrian, and Jew depends on the
    standpoint.

Some Hindus brought an elephant, which they exhibited
in a dark shed.   5
As seeing it with the eye was impossible, every one felt it
with the palm of his hand.
The hand of one fell on its trunk: he said, "This animal
is like a water-pipe."
Another touched its ear: to him the creature seemed like
a fan.
Another handled its leg and described the elephant as
having the shape of a pillar.
Another stroked its back. "Truly," said he, "this elephant
resembles a throne."   10
Had each of them held a lighted candle, there would
have been no contradiction in their words.

Q What aspects of these poems reflect religious mysticism?

Q Do they also put forth practical insights or advice?

Islamic Prose Literature

Islam prized poetry over prose, but both forms drew on enduring oral tradition and on the verbal treasures of many regions. Unique to Arabic literature was rhyming prose, which brought a musical quality to everyday speech. One of the most popular forms of prose literary entertainment was a collection of eighth-century animal fables, which instructed as they amused. Another, which narrated the adventures of a rogue or vagabond characters, anticipated by five centuries the picaresque novel in the West (see chapter 19).

The rich diversity of Islamic culture is nowhere better revealed, however, than in the collection of prose tales known as *The Thousand and One Nights*. This literary classic, gradually assembled between the eighth and tenth centuries, brought together in the Arabic tongue various tales from Persian, Arabic, and Indian sources. It typifies the narrative technique of the **frame tale**, whereby a main story is composed for the purpose of including a group of shorter stories. The frame derives from an Indian fairy tale: Shahrasad (in English, Scheherazade) marries a king who fears female infidelity so greatly that he kills each new wife on the morning after the wedding night. In order to forestall her own death, Scheherazade entertains the king by telling stories, each of which she carefully brings to a climax just before dawn, so that, in order to learn the ending, the king must allow her to live. Scheherazade—or, more exactly, her storytelling—has a humanizing effect upon the king, who, after a thousand nights, comes to prize his clever wife. *The Thousand and One Nights*, which exists in many versions, actually contains only some 250 tales, many of which have become favorites with readers throughout the world: the adventures of Ali Baba, Aladdin, Sinbad, and other post-medieval stories are filled with fantasy, exotic characters, and spicy romance. The manner in which each tale loops into the next, linking story to story and parts of each story to each other,

resembles the regulating principles of design in Islamic art, which include repetition, infinite extension, and the looping together of motifs to form a meandering, overall pattern (Figure **10.7**).

The story of Prince Behram and the Princess Al-Datma, reproduced below, addresses some of the major themes in Islamic literary culture: the power of female beauty, survival through cunning, and the "battle" of the sexes. While the story provides insight into Islamic notions of etiquette, it confirms the subordinate role of women in this, as in Western, society (see Reading 11.3). Nevertheless, ingenuity (exercised by both of the major characters in their efforts to achieve what they most desire) plays a saving role in both the tale told by Scheherazade and the destiny of the storyteller herself, whose beauty, wit, and verbal powers prove to be a civilizing force.

READING 10.4 From *The Thousand and One Nights* (ca. 850)

"Prince Behram and the Princess Al-Datma"

There was once a king's daughter called Al-Datma who, in her   1
time, had no equal in beauty and grace. In addition to her lovely
looks, she was brilliant and feisty and took great pleasure in
ravishing the wits of the male sex. In fact, she used to boast,
"There is nobody who can match me in anything." And the fact is
that she was most accomplished in horsemanship and martial
exercises, and all those things a cavalier should know.

Given her qualities, numerous princes sought her hand in
marriage, but she rejected them all. Instead, she proclaimed,   10
"No man shall marry me unless he defeats me with his lance and
sword in fair battle. He who succeeds I will gladly wed. But if
I overcome him, I will take his horse, clothes, and arms and brand his
head with the following words: 'This is the freedom of Al-Datma.'"

Now the sons of kings flocked to her from every quarter far
and near, but she prevailed and put them to shame, stripping
them of their arms and branding them with fire. Soon, a son of
the king of Persia named Behram ibn Taji heard about her and
journeyed from afar to her father's court. He brought men and   20
horses with him and a great deal of wealth and royal treasures.
When he drew near the city, he sent her father a rich present,
and the king came out to meet him and bestowed great honors
on him. Then the king's son sent a message to him through his
vizier and requested his daughter's hand in marriage. However,
the king answered, "With regard to my daughter Al-Datma,
I have no power over her, for she has sworn by her soul to marry
no one but him who defeats her in the listed field."

"I journeyed here from my father's court with no other   30
purpose but this," the prince declared. "I came here to woo her and
to form an alliance with you."

"Then you shall meet her tomorrow," said the king.

So the next day he sent for his daughter, who got ready for battle
by donning her armor of war. Since the people of the kingdom had
heard about the coming joust, they flocked from all sides to the
field. Soon the princess rode into the lists, armed head to toe with
her visor down, and the Persian king's son came out to meet her,
equipped in the fairest of fashions.

Figure 10.7 Niche (*mihrab*) showing Islamic calligraphy, from Iran. The rectangle in the center of the niche bears the evocation to Allah with which every chapter of the Qur'an begins: "In the name of Allah, the Lord of Mercy, the Giver of Mercy" (see Reading 10.1). Geometric designs, abstract floral motifs, and calligraphic text combine to ornament the surface.

Then they charged at each other and fought a long time, 40
wheeling and sparring, advancing and retreating, and the
princess realized that he had more courage and skill than she
had ever encountered before. Indeed, she began to fear that he
might put her to shame before the bystanders and defeat her.
Consequently, she decided to trick him, and raising her visor,
she showed her face, which appeared more radiant than the full
moon, and when he saw it, he was bewildered by her beauty.
His strength failed, and his spirit faltered. When she perceived
this moment of weakness, she attacked and
knocked him from his saddle. Consequently, he became like a 50
sparrow in the clutches of an eagle. Amazed and confused, he
did not know what was happening to him when she took his
steed, clothes, and armor. Then, after branding him with fire, she
let him go his way.

When he recovered from his stupor, he spent several days
without food, drink, or sleep. Indeed, love had gripped his heart.
Finally, he decided to send a letter to his father via a messenger,
informing him that he could not return home until he had won
the princess or died for want of her. When his sire
received the letter, he was extremely distressed about his son 60
and wanted to rescue him by sending troops and soldiers. However,
his ministers dissuaded him from this action and advised him to be
patient. So he prayed to Almighty Allah for guidance.

In the meantime, the prince thought of different ways to
attain his goal, and soon he decided to disguise himself as a
decrepit old man. So he put a white beard over his own black
one and went to the garden where the princess used to walk
most of the days. Here he sought out the gardener and said to
him, "I'm a stranger from a country far away, and from my 70
youth onward I've been a gardener, and nobody is more skilled
than I am in the grafting of trees and cultivating fruit, flowers,
and vines."

When the gardener heard this, he was extremely pleased and
led him into the garden, where he let him do his work. So the
prince began to tend the garden and improved the Persian
waterwheels and the irrigation channels. One day, as he was
occupied with some work, he saw some slaves enter the garden
leading mules and carrying carpets and vessels, and he
asked them what they were doing there. 80

"The princess wants to spend an enjoyable afternoon here,"
they answered.

When he heard these words, he rushed to his lodging and
fetched some jewels and ornaments he had brought with him from
home. After returning to the garden, he sat down and spread some
of the valuable items before him while shaking and pretending to be
a very old man.

And Scheherazade noticed that dawn was approaching and
stopped telling her story. When the next night arrived, however,
she received the king's permission to continue her tale and said, 90

In fact, the prince made it seem as if he were extremely
decrepit and senile. After an hour or so a company of damsels
and eunuchs entered the garden with the princess, who looked
just like the radiant moon among the stars. They ran about the
garden, plucking fruits and enjoying themselves, until they
caught sight of the prince disguised as an old man sitting under
one of the trees. The man's hands and feet were trembling from

old age, and he had spread a great many precious jewels and
regal ornaments before him. Of course,
they were astounded by this and asked him what he was 100
doing there with the jewels.

"I want to use these trinkets," he said, "to buy me a wife from
among the lot of you."

They all laughed at him and said, "If one of us marries you, what
will you do with her?"

"I'll give her one kiss," he replied, "and then divorce her."

"If that's the case," said the princess, "I'll give this damsel to you
for your wife."

So he rose, leaned on his staff, staggered toward the
damsel, and gave her a kiss. Right after that he gave her the 110
jewels and ornaments, whereupon she rejoiced and they all went
on their way laughing at him.

The next day they came again to the garden, and they found
him seated in the same place with more jewels and ornaments
than before spread before him.

"Oh sheikh," they asked him, "what are you going to do with all
this jewelry?"

"I want to wed one of you again," he answered, "just as I did
yesterday."

So the princess said, "I'll marry you to this damsel." 120

And the prince went up to her, kissed her, and gave her the
jewels, and they all went their way.

After seeing how generous the old man was to her slave girls,
the princess said to herself, "I have more right to these fine things
than my slaves, and there's surely no danger involved in this game."
So when morning arrived, she went down by herself into the garden
dressed as one of her own damsels, and she appeared all alone
before the prince and said to him, "Old man, the king's daughter has
sent me to you
so that you can marry me." 130

When he looked at her, he knew who she was. So he
answered, "With all my heart and love," and he gave her the
finest and costliest of jewels and ornaments. Then he rose to
kiss her, and since she was not on her guard and thought she
had nothing to fear, he grabbed hold of her with his strong
hands and threw her down on the ground, where he deprived
her of her maidenhead. Then he pulled the beard from his face
and said, "Do you recognize me?"

"Who are you?"

"I am Behram, the King of Persia's son," he replied. "I've 140
changed myself and have become a stranger to my people, all
for your sake. And I have lavished my treasures for your love."

She rose from him in silence and did not say a word to him.
Indeed, she was dazed by what had happened and felt that it was
best to be silent, especially since she did not want to be shamed.
All the while she was thinking to herself, "If I kill myself, it will be
senseless, and if I have him put to death, there's nothing that I'd
really gain. The best thing for me to do is to elope with him to his
own country."

So, after leaving him in the garden, she gathered together 150
her money and treasures and sent him a message informing him
what she intended to do and telling him to get ready to depart with
his possessions and whatever else he needed. Then they set a
rendezvous for their departure.

---

[1] Chief justice.

At the appointed time they mounted racehorses and set out under cover of darkness, and by the next morning they had traveled a great distance. They kept traveling at a fast pace until they drew near his father's capital in Persia, and when his father heard about his son's coming, he rode out to meet him with his troops and was full of joy.   160

After a few days went by, the king of Persia sent a splendid present to the princess's father along with a letter to the effect that his daughter was with him and requested her wedding outfit. Al-Datma's father greeted the messenger with a happy heart (for he thought he had lost his daughter and had been grieving for her). In response to the king's letter, he summoned the kazi[1] and the witnesses and drew up a marriage contract between his daughter and the prince of Persia. In addition, he bestowed robes of honor on the envoys from the king of Persia and sent his daughter her marriage   170 equipage. After the official wedding took place, Prince Behram lived with her until death came and sundered their union.

No sooner had Scheherazade concluded her tale than she said, "And yet, oh king, this tale is no more wondrous than the tale of the three apples."

Q Does this tale have a "moral"? If so, what does it teach?

Islamic Art and Architecture

Five times a day, at the call of ***muezzins*** (criers) usually located atop **minarets** (tall, slender towers; see Figure 9.11), Muslims are summoned to interrupt their activities to kneel and pray facing Mecca. Such prayer is required whether believers are in the heart of the desert or in their homes. The official Muslim place of worship, however, is the mosque: a large, columned hall whose square or rectangular shape derives from the simple urban house made of sun-dried bricks. The design of the mosque is not, as with the Early Christian church, determined by the needs of religious liturgy. Rather, the mosque is first and foremost a place of prayer. Every mosque is oriented toward Mecca, and that direction (***qibla***) is marked by a niche (***mihrab***) located in the wall (Figure **10.8**). Occasionally, the niche holds a lamp that symbolizes Allah as the light of the heavens and the earth (Sura 24.35). To the right of the *mihrab* is a small, elevated platform (***minbar***) at which the Qur'an may be read.

The Great Mosque in Córdoba, Spain, begun in 784 and enlarged over a period of 300 years, is one of the noblest examples of early Islamic architecture. Its interior consists of more than 500 double-tiered columns that originally supported a wooden roof. The floor plan of the Great Mosque (now a Catholic cathedral), with its seemingly

Figure 10.8 The *mihrab* of the Great Mosque at Córdoba, Spain, eleventh century. Gold and glass mosaic on marble. Lavishly ornamented with gold and mosaic glass, the horseshoe arch opens onto the *mihrab*, the niche that marks the direction of Muslim prayer (toward Mecca).

infinite rows of columns (Figure **10.9**), represents a sharp contrast with the design of the Early Christian basilica, which moves the worshiper in a linear fashion from portal to altar. At Córdoba, horseshoe-shaped arches consisting of contrasting wedges of white marble and red sandstone crown a forest of ornamental pillars (Figure **10.10**). Such arches seem to "flower" like palm fronds from their column "stems." In some parts of the structure, multilobed arches are set in "piggyback" fashion, creating further ornamental rhythms. The dome of the *mihrab*, constructed on eight intersecting arches and lavishly decorated with mosaics, is clear evidence of Muslim proficiency in mathematics, engineering, and artistic virtuosity.

Islam was self-consciously resistant to image-making. Like the Jews, Muslims condemned the worship of pagan idols and considered making likenesses of living creatures an act of pride that "competed" with the Creator God. Therefore, in Islamic religious art, there is almost no three-dimensional sculpture, and, with the exception of occasional scenes of the Muslim Paradise, no pictorial representations of the kind found in Christian art. Islamic art also differs from Christian art in its self-conscious avoidance of symbols. But such self-imposed limitations did not prevent Muslims from creating one of the richest bodies of visual ornamentation in the history of world art. Three types of motif dominate the Islamic decorative repertory: *geometric, floral,* and *calligraphic.* Geometric designs, drawn largely from a Classical repertory, were developed in complex and variegated patterns. Abstract, interlocking shapes often enclose floral motifs that feature the **arabesque**, a type of ornamentation based on plant and flower forms inspired by Byzantine and Persian art (see Figure 10.7). Calligraphy, that is "beautiful writing," completes the vocabulary of ornamentation. In Islamic art, where the written word takes precedence, calligraphy assumes a sacramental character. Most calligraphic inscriptions were drawn from the Qur'an. In carved, painted, and enameled surfaces, the Word of Allah, written in elegant **Kufic**, the earliest form of Arabic script (originating in the Iraqi town of Kufa), plays an essential part in both embellishment and revelation. Whether calligraphic, floral, or geometric, Islamic motifs are repeated in seemingly infinite rhythmic extension, bound only by the borders of the frame. This device may be viewed as the visual equivalent of the frame tale, in which many individual stories are incorporated into the whole. "Meander and frame"—an expression of the universal theme of variety and unity in nature—is a fundamental principle of the Islamic decorative tradition and (as noted earlier) of Islamic aesthetics. The aesthetic of infinite extension sees Truth as intuitive and all-pervasive, rather than (as in Western Christian thought) as apocalyptic and self-fulfilling.

The bold use of color is one of the key features of Islamic art and architecture. Complex surface designs executed in mosaics and polychrome patterned glazed tiles transform the exteriors of mosques and palaces into shimmering veils of light and color. At the Dome of the Rock (Figures **10.11** and **10.12**), the earliest surviving Islamic sanctuary, Qur'anic inscriptions in gold mosaic cubes on a blue ground wind around the spectacular

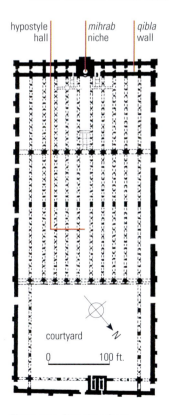

Figure 10.9 Plan of the Great Mosque, Córdoba. The additions of 832–848 and 961 are shown, but not the final enlargement of 987.

Figure 10.10 Columns in the Moorish part of the Great Mosque, Córdoba, 784–987. White marble and red sandstone.

Figure 10.11 Dome of the Rock, Jerusalem, Israel, ca. 687–691. Lying below the Dome is the sacred rock that some identify as the foundation stone of Solomon's Temple. Islamic maps identified this spot in the city of Jerusalem as the "center of the world."

octagon. Constructed on a 35-acre plateau in east Jerusalem, the sanctuary (also known as the Mosque of Omar) is capped by a **gilded** dome. While much of the exterior has been refaced with glazed pottery tiles, the interior still shelters the original dazzling mosaics. In both its harmonious proportions and its lavishly ornamented surfaces, the structure is a landmark of the Muslim faith. It is believed to crown the site of the creation of Adam and mark the spot from which Muhammad ascended to Heaven. It is also said to be the site of the biblical Temple of Solomon. Hence, the Dome of the Rock is a sacred shrine whose historical significance—like that of Jerusalem itself—is shared, but also bitterly contested, by Jews, Muslims, and Christians.

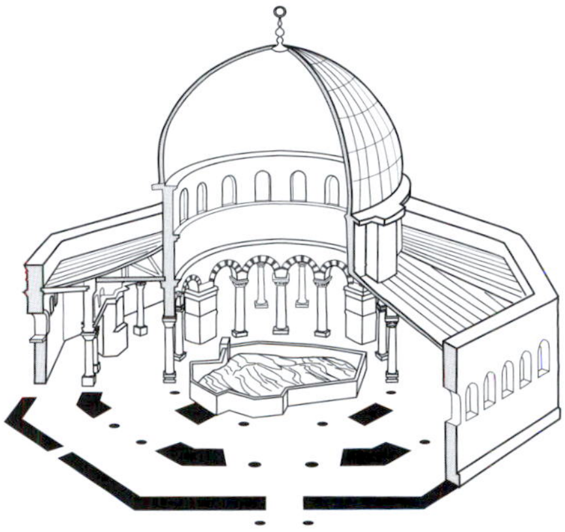

A lavish combination of geometric, floral, and calligraphic designs distinguishes Islamic frescoes, carpets, ivories, manuscripts, textiles, and ceramics. Occasionally, however, calligraphy alone provides ornamentation. Along the rim of a tenth-century earthenware bowl, for instance, elegant Kufic script imparts Muhammad's injunction: "Planning before work protects one from regret; prosperity and peace" (Figure **10.13**). Here, as on the pages of an early **illuminated manuscript** of the Qur'an (see Figure 10.3),

Figure 10.12 Schematic cutaway drawing of the Dome of the Rock showing its interior plan.

fluid calligraphic strokes (with red and yellow dots to indicate vowels) provide the sole "decoration."

While figural subjects are avoided in religious art, they abound in secular manuscripts, and especially in those produced after 1200 (see Figure 10.1). Travel tales, fables, romances, chronicles, and medical treatises (see Figure 10.4) are freely illustrated with human and animal activities. In one miniature from an illustrated manuscript of Sufi poetry, dervishes (some of whom have succumbed to vertigo), musicians, and witnesses congregate in a tapestrylike landscape filled with flowers and blooming trees (see Figure 10.6).

Islamic art and architecture often feature the garden and garden motifs as symbolic of the Muslim Paradise (which is mentioned in the Qur'an no fewer than 130 times). Like the biblical Garden of Eden and the Babylonian Dilmun (see Reading 1.2), the paradisal garden is a place of spiritual and physical refreshment. Watered by cool rivers and filled with luscious fruit trees, the Garden of the Afterlife takes its earthly form in Islamic architecture. Luxuriant palaces throughout

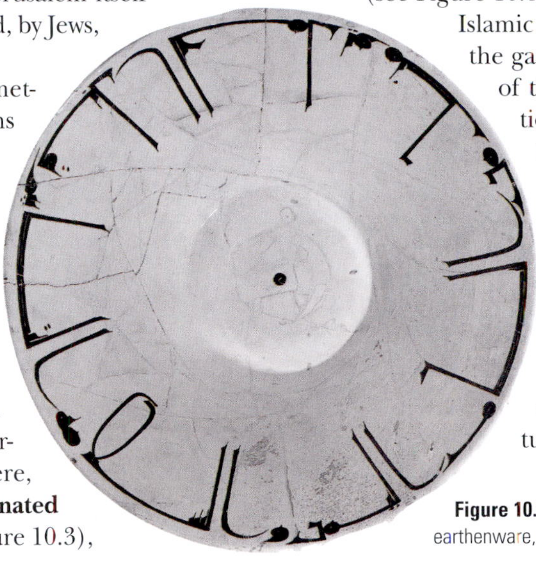

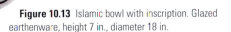

Figure 10.13 Islamic bowl with inscription. Glazed earthenware, height 7 in., diameter 18 in.

Figure 10.14 Court of the Lions, the Alhambra, Granada, Spain, fourteenth century. Central to the courtyard here, as to that of the Islamic mosque, is the fountain with cool running waters, symbolic of the paradise garden and essential relief from the hot, dry climate.

its sensual powers were celebrated by Sufi mystics. During Islam's golden age, secular music flourished in the courts of Córdoba and Baghdad, and, even earlier, Arab song mingled with the music of Persia, Syria, Egypt, and Byzantium.

The music of the Islamic world originated in the songs of the desert nomads—songs featuring the solo voice and unmeasured rhythms. (The meter of one type of caravan song, however, is said to resemble the rhythm of the camel's lurching stride.) As in ancient Greece, India, and China, the music of Arabia consisted of a single melodic line, either unaccompanied or with occasional instrumental accompaniment. It was also modal (each mode bearing association with a specific quality of emotion). Two additional characteristics of Arab music (to this day) are its use of microtones (the intervals that lie between the semitones of the Western twelve-note system) and its preference for improvisation (the performer's original, spur-of-the-moment variations on the melody or rhythm of a given piece). Both of these features, which also occur in modern jazz, work to give Arab music its unique sound. The melodic line of the Arab song weaves and wanders, looping and repeating themes in a kind of aural arabesque; the voice slides and intones in subtle and hypnotic stretches. In its linear ornamentation and in its repetitive rhythmic phrasing, Arab music has much in common with literary and visual forms of Islamic expression. This vocal pattern, resembling Hebrew, Christian, or Buddhist chant, is not unlike the sound of the *muezzin* calling Muslims to prayer.

Instrumental music took second place to the voice everywhere in the Islamic world, except in Persia, where a strong pre-Islamic instrumental tradition flourished. Lyres, flutes, and drums—all light, portable instruments—were used to accompany the songs of Bedouin camel drivers, while bells and tambourines might provide percussion for dancing. At the end of the sixth century, the Arabs developed the lute (in Arabic, *ud*, meaning "wood"), a half-pear-shaped wooden string instrument that was used to accompany vocal performance (Figures **10.15** and **10.16**). The forerunner of the guitar, the lute has a right-angled neck and is played with a small quill.

the Muslim world—real-life settings for the fictional Scheherazade—as well as royal tombs like the Taj Mahal (see chapter 21) normally feature gardens and park pavilions with fountains and water pools. At the oldest well-preserved Islamic palace in the world, the Alhambra in Granada, Spain, rectangular courtyards are cooled by clear, reflecting pools of water and bubbling central fountains from which flow (in the cardinal directions) the four "paradisal rivers" (Figure **10.14**). This fourteenth-century palace—the stronghold of Muslim culture in the West until 1492—makes use of polychrome **stucco** reliefs, glazed tiles, lacy arabesque designs, and lush gardens simulating Heaven on earth.

Music in the Islamic World

For the devout Muslim, there was no religious music other than the sound of the chanted Qur'an and the *muezzin's* call to prayer. Muslims regarded music as a forbidden pleasure and condemned its "killing charm" (as *The Thousand and One Nights* describes it). Nevertheless, the therapeutic uses of music were recognized by Arab physicians and

See Music Listening Selections at end of chapter.

Some time after the eighth century, Muslim musicians in Spain began to compose larger orchestral pieces divided into five or more distinct movements, to be performed by string and wind instruments, percussion, and voices. It is possible that the Western tradition of orchestral music, along with the development of such instruments as oboes, trumpets, viols, and kettledrums, originated among Arab musicians during the centuries of Muslim rule in Spain. Indeed, the renowned ninth-century musician Ziryab (known because of his dark complexion as "the Blackbird") traveled from Baghdad through North Africa to Córdoba to become the founder of the first conservatory of music and patriarch of Arabo-Andalusian musical art. Music composition and theory reached a peak between the ninth and eleventh centuries, when noted Islamic scholars wrote almost 200 treatises on musical performance and theory. They classified the aesthetic, ethical, and medicinal functions of the modes, recommending specific types of music to relieve specific illnesses. One Arab writer, Al-Isfahani (897–967), compiled the *Great Book of Songs*, a twenty-one-volume encyclopedia that remains the most important source of information about Arab music and poetry from its beginnings to the tenth century. The wide range of love songs, many with motifs of complaint and yearning, would have a distinct influence on both the secular and the religious music of the Western Middle Ages and the Renaissance.

Figure 10.15 Lute with nine strings. Spanish miniature from the Cantigas de Santa Maria, 1221–1289. The figure on the left plays a type of medieval viol known as a rebec (see Figure 13.37).

Figure 10.16 Drawing of a lute.

See Music Listening Selections at end of chapter.

LOOKING BACK

The Religion of Islam

- In seventh-century Arabia, Islam emerged as the third of the monotheistic world faiths. Divine revelation came by way of the archangel Gabriel, who instructed Muhammad to declare himself the Prophet of Allah, the last in a line of prophets beginning with the biblical Abraham.
- Muhammad's migration (*hijra*) from Mecca to Medina in 622 marks the first year of the Muslim calendar. After his return to Mecca, Muhammad assumed spiritual and political authority, establishing a theocracy that bound religious and secular realms. By his death in 632, the entire Arabian peninsula was united in its commitment to Islam.
- The Five Pillars of religious practice govern the everyday life of Muslims ("those who submit to Allah"). The

faithful can expect the reward of eternal life, while those who disbelieve or stray from Allah's law are doomed to the punishments of Hell.
- The Qur'an, a record of Muhammad's recitations set down by his disciples ten years after the Prophet's death, is the Holy Book of Islam. The Muslim guide to spiritual and secular life, it consists of 114 chapters that offer guidance on Muslim rituals, ethics, and laws.
- Islam's success in becoming a world faith owes much to the alliance of its early religious, political, and military goals. Islam also offered rules of conduct, and ritual practices that resembled those of Christianity and Judaism.

The Expansion of Islam

- Early Muslim expansion succeeded not so much by the militant coercion

of foreign populations as it did by the economic opportunities Muslims offered conquered people.
- In that Muhammad did not designate a successor, disputes concerning the leadership of Islam followed his death. Here began the splintering of Islam into Shiite and Sunni partisans.
- The first four deputies (caliphs) carried Islam outside of Arabia, initiating the rise of a Muslim empire. The Umayyad caliphs took the faith west, across North Africa into Spain. After 750, the Abbasid caliphate established its authority across the Middle East.
- Between the eighth and thirteenth centuries, the great centers of Muslim urban life—Baghdad in Iraq, Córdoba in Spain, and Cairo in Egypt—surpassed the cities of Western Europe in learning and the arts. Their cultural primacy was

shattered at the hands of the Mongols, who destroyed Baghdad in 1258.

- Until the mid-fourteenth century, Muslims dominated a system of world trade that stretched from Western Europe to China.

Islamic Culture

- The Muslims created the first global culture—a culture united by a single system of belief, but embracing a wide variety of regions, languages, and customs.
- Muslim scholars produced original work in the fields of mathematics, optics, philosophy, geography, and medicine. They translated into Arabic the valuable corpus of Greek writings, which they transmitted to the West along with the technological and scientific inventions of Asian civilizations.
- Themes of unrequited love were popular in Arab lyric verse. The poetry of the Islamic mystics known as the Sufi drew on the intuitive and mystical dimensions of religious experience. Lyrical repetition and infinite extension are notable features of the classic collection of prose tales *The Thousand and One Nights*.
- The Great Mosque in Córdoba and the Dome of the Rock in Jerusalem are two examples of Islamic architectural ingenuity: the first for its inventive disposition of horseshoe-shaped arches, the second for its dome, octagonal plan, and dazzling mosaics.
- Resistant to image-making, Islamic religious art is dominated by geometric, floral, and calligraphic motifs, often interlaced in patterns of infinite extension. Secular manuscripts, such as herbals and chronicles, feature lively scenes of everyday activities.
- Islamic music, confined to secular rather than religious purposes, is rich in song and unique in the invention of early instrumental ensembles. Treatises on composition and theory, and encyclopedic collections of Arab music and poetry, date from the ninth to eleventh centuries.

Music Listening Selections

- Islamic Call to Prayer.
- Anonymous, Twisya No. 3 of the Nouba.

Glossary

arabesque a type of ornament featuring intertwined leaf and flower forms

bismillah the invocation that precedes the chapters of the Qur'an and many Muslim prayers: "In the name of God [Allah], God of Mercy, the Giver of Mercy"

caliph (Arabic, "deputy") the official successor to Muhammad and theocratic ruler of an Islamic state

frame tale a narrative technique by which a main story incorporates a group of shorter stories

gilded (or **gilt**) gold-surfaced; covered with a thin layer of gold, gold paint, or gold foil

hajj pilgrimage to Mecca, the fifth Pillar of the Faith in Islam

hijra (Arabic, "migration" or "flight") Muhammad's journey from Mecca to Medina in the year 622

illuminated manuscript a handwritten and ornamented book, parts of which (the script, illustrations, or decorative devices) may be embellished with gold or silver paint or with gold foil, hence "illuminated"

imam a Muslim prayer leader

infidel a nonbeliever

jihad (Arabic, "struggle" [to follow God's will]) the struggle to lead a virtuous life and to further the universal mission of Islam through teaching, preaching, and, when necessary, warfare

Kaaba (Arabic, "cube") a religious sanctuary in Mecca; a square shrine containing the sacred Black Stone thought to have been delivered to Abraham by the archangel Gabriel

Kufic the earliest form of Arabic script; it originated in the Iraqi town of Kufa

madrasa an Islamic school affiliated with a mosque

mihrab a special niche in the wall of a mosque that indicates the direction of Mecca

minaret a tall, slender tower usually attached to a mosque and surrounded by a balcony from which the *muezzin* summons Muslims to prayer

minbar a stepped pulpit in a mosque

mosque the Muslim house of worship

muezzin a "crier" who calls the hours of Muslim prayer five times a day

mullah a Muslim trained in Islamic law and doctrine

polygyny the marriage of one man to several women at the same time

qadi a Muslim judge

qibla the direction that should be faced when a Muslim prays

shahadah ("witness") the Muslim declaration of faith testifying to the oneness of Allah and his messenger Muhammad

sharia the body of Muslim law based on the Qur'an and the *Hadith*

stucco fine plaster or cement used to coat or decorate walls

Patterns of Medieval Life

ca. 500–1300

"When they mount chargers, take up their swords and shields,
Not death itself could drive them from the field.
They are good men; their words are fierce and proud."
Song of Roland

Figure 11.1 *French Knights under Louis IX Besieging Damietta*, Egypt, Seventh Crusade, 1249. After the Muslims recaptured Jerusalem in 1244, King Louis IX of France (better known as "Saint Louis") led the last major Crusade, capturing the Egyptian seaport of Damietta in 1249. But the following year the Egyptians trapped the Crusaders by opening sluice gates for reservoirs on the Nile and surrounding them with floodwater. To secure their escape, Louis had to surrender Damietta and pay a large ransom.

Scholars once described the five centuries following the fall of Rome as a "dark age" whose cultural achievements fell far short of those of ancient Greece and Rome. Our present understanding suggests otherwise: the Early Middle Ages (ca. 500–1000) was one of the most creative periods in Western history. During this time, three distinct traditions—Classical, Germanic, and Christian—came together to produce a vigorous new culture. While Germanic invasions (Map **11.1**) contributed to the decline and decentralization of the Roman Empire, Germanic practices slowly blended with those of ancient Rome and rising Christianity. In the territories that would come to be called "Europe," the political and military system known as feudalism would shape the social and cultural patterns of early medieval life.

Ushering in the new mobility of Europe's High Middle Ages (ca. 1000–1300), the Christian Crusades altered these patterns. The Crusades encouraged the rise of towns and trade dominated by a rising middle class whose values differed from those of the feudal nobility. The patterns of medieval secular life reflect the shift from a feudal society to a more centralized and urbanized one: a society distinguished by complex social interaction between lord and vassal, farmer and merchant, male and female.

The Germanic Tribes

The Germanic peoples were a tribal folk who followed a migratory existence. Dependent on their flocks and herds, they lived in pre-urban village communities throughout Asia and frequently raided and plundered nearby lands for material gain, yet they settled no territorial state. As early as the first century B.C.E., a loose confederacy of Germanic tribes began to threaten Roman territories, but it was not until the fourth century C.E. that these tribes, driven westward by the fierce Central Asian nomads known as Huns, pressed into the Roman Empire. Lacking the hallmarks of civilization—urban settlements, monumental architecture, and the art of writing—the Germanic tribes struck the Romans as inferiors, as outsiders, hence, as "barbarians." Ethnically distinct from the Huns, the

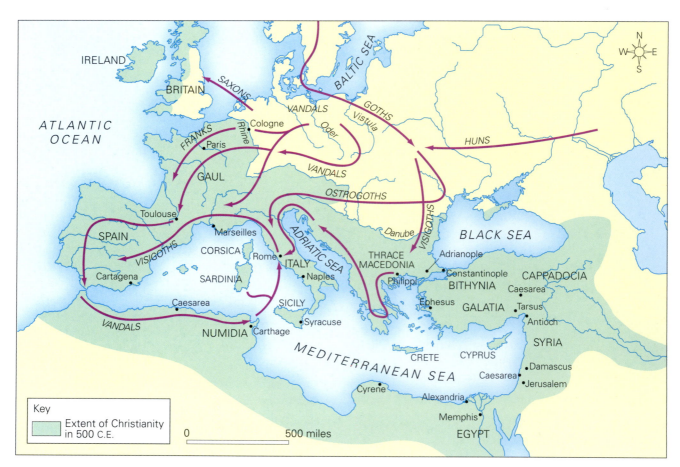

Map 11.1 The Early Christian World and the Barbarian Invasions, ca. 500. The map indicates the routes of the Germanic tribes as they invaded the Roman Empire. Note that many of the tribes came into Italy in the early to mid-fifth century; the Visigoths attacked Rome in 410; the Vandals sacked the city in 455.

Science and Technology

568	Germanic tribes introduce stirrups (from China) into Europe
600	a heavy iron plow is used in Northern Europe
770	iron horseshoes are used widely in Western Europe

Germanic folk, including East Goths (Ostrogoths), West Goths (Visigoths), Franks, Vandals, Burgundians, Angles, and Saxons, belonged to one and the same language family, dialects of which differed from tribe to tribe. The Ostrogoths occupied the steppe region between the Black and Baltic seas, while the Visigoths settled in territories closer to the Danube River (see Map 11.1). As the tribes pressed westward, an uneasy alliance was forged: the Romans allowed the barbarians to settle on the borders of the Empire, but in exchange the Germanic warriors were obliged to protect Rome against other invaders. Antagonism between Rome and the Visigoths led to a military showdown. At the Battle of Adrianople (130 miles northwest of Constantinople, near modern Edirne in Turkey) in 378, the Visigoths defeated the "invincible" Roman army, killing the East Roman emperor Valens and dispersing his army. Almost immediately thereafter, the Visigoths swept across the Roman border, raiding the cities of the declining West, including Rome itself in 410.

The Battle of Adrianople opened the door to a sequence of barbarian invasions. During the fifth century, the Empire fell prey to the assaults of many Germanic tribes, including the Vandals, whose willful, malicious destruction of Rome in 455 produced the English word "vandalize." In 476, a Germanic commander named Odoacer deposed the reigning Roman emperor in the West, an event that is traditionally taken to mark the official end of the Roman Empire. Although the Germanic tribes leveled the final assaults on an already declining empire, they did not utterly destroy Rome's vast resources, nor did they ignore the culture of the late Roman world. The Ostrogoths embraced Christianity and sponsored literary and architectural enterprises modeled on those of Rome and Byzantium, while the Franks and the Burgundians chose to commit their legal traditions to writing, styling their codes of law on Roman models.

Germanic culture differed dramatically from that of Rome: in the agrarian and essentially self-sufficient communities of these nomadic peoples, fighting was a way of life and a highly respected skill. Armed with javelins and shields, Germanic warriors fought fiercely on foot and on horseback. Superb horsemen, the Germanic cavalry would come to borrow from the Mongols spurs and foot stirrups—devices (originating in China) that firmly secured the rider in his saddle and improved his driving force. In addition to introducing to the West superior methods of fighting on horseback, the Germanic tribes imposed their own long-standing traditions on medieval Europe.

Every Germanic chieftain retained a band of warriors that followed him into battle, and every warrior anticipated sharing with his chieftain the spoils of victory. At the end of the first century, the Roman historian Tacitus (see chapter 6) wrote an account of the habits and customs of the Germanic peoples. He observes:

> All [men] are bound, to defend their leader . . . and to make even their own actions subservient to his renown. If he dies in the field, he who survives him survives to live in infamy. . . . This is the bond of union, the most sacred obligation. The chief fights for victory; the followers for their chief. . . . The chief must show his liberality, and the follower expects it. He demands, at one time this warlike horse, at another, that victorious lance drenched with the blood of the enemy.

The bond of **fealty**, or loyalty, between the Germanic warrior and his chieftain and the practice of rewarding the warrior would become fundamental to the medieval practice of feudalism.

Germanic Law

Germanic law was not legislated by the state, as in Roman tradition, but was, rather, a collection of customs passed orally from generation to generation. The Germanic dependence on custom would have a lasting influence on the development of law, and especially **common law**, in parts of the West. Among the Germanic peoples, tribal chiefs were responsible for governing, but general assemblies met to make important decisions: fully armed, clan warriors demonstrated their assent to propositions "in a military manner," according to Tacitus—by brandishing their javelins. Since warlike behavior was commonplace, tribal law was severe, uncompromising, and directed toward publicly shaming the guilty. Tacitus records that punishment for an adulterous wife was "instant, and inflicted by the husband. He cuts off the hair of his guilty wife, and having assembled her relations, expels her naked from his house, pursuing her with stripes through the village. To public loss of honor no favor is shown. She may possess beauty, youth, and riches; but a husband she can never obtain."

As in most ancient societies—Hammurabi's Babylon, for instance—penalties for crimes varied according to the social standing of the guilty party. Among the Germanic tribes, however, a person's guilt or innocence might be determined by an ordeal involving fire or water; such trials reflected the faith Germanic peoples placed in the will of nature deities. Some of the names of these gods came to designate days of the week; for example, the English word "Wednesday" derives from "Woden's day" and "Thursday" from "Thor's day."

Germanic Literature

Germanic traditions, including those of personal valor and heroism associated with a warring culture, are reflected in the epic poems of the Early Middle Ages. The three most famous of these, *Beowulf, The Song of the Nibelungen,* and the *Song of Roland,* were transmitted orally for hundreds of years before they were written down some time between the tenth and thirteenth centuries. *Beowulf*, which originated among the Anglo-Saxons around 700, was recorded in Old English—the Germanic language spoken in the British Isles between the fifth and eleventh centuries. *The Song of the Nibelungen*, a product of the Burgundian tribes, was recorded in Old German; and the Frankish *Song of Roland* in Old French. Celebrating the deeds of warrior-heroes, these three epic poems have much in common with the *Iliad*, the *Mahabharata*, and other orally transmitted adventure poems.

The 3000-line epic known as *Beowulf* is the first monumental literary composition in a European vernacular language. The tale of a daring Scandinavian prince, *Beowulf* brings to life the heroic world of the Germanic people with whom it originated. In unrhymed Old English verse embellished with numerous two-term metaphors known as **kennings** ("whale-path" for "sea," "ring-giver" for "king"), the poem recounts three major adventures: Beowulf's encounter with the monster Grendel, his destruction of Grendel's hideous and vengeful mother, and (some five decades later) his effort to destroy the fire-breathing dragon that threatens his people. These stories—the stuff of legend, folktale, and fantasy—immortalize the mythic origins of the Anglo-Saxons. Composed in the newly Christianized England of the eighth century, the poem was not written down for another two centuries. Only a full reading of *Beowulf* conveys its significance as a work of art. However, the passage that follows—from a modern translation by Burton Raffel—offers an idea of the poem's vigorous style and narrative. The excerpt (lines 2510–2601 of the work), which describes Beowulf's assault on the fire-dragon, opens with a "battle-vow" that broadcasts the boastful courage of the epic hero. Those who wish to know the outcome of this gory contest must read further in the poem.

READING 11.1 From *Beowulf*

And Beowulf uttered his final boast: 1
  "I've never known fear; as a youth I fought
In endless battles. I am old, now,
But I will fight again, seek fame still,
If the dragon hiding in his tower dares 5
To face me."
  Then he said farewell to his followers,
Each in his turn, for the last time:
  "I'd use no sword, no weapon, if this beast
Could be killed without it, crushed to death
Like Grendel, gripped in my hands and torn 10
Limb from limb. But his breath will be burning
Hot, poison will pour from his tongue.
I feel no shame, with shield and sword
And armor, against this monster: when he comes to me
I mean to stand, not run from his shooting 15
Flames, stand till fate decides
Which of us wins. My heart is firm,
My hands calm: I need no hot
Words. Wait for me close by, my friends.

We shall see, soon, who will survive 20
This bloody battle, stand when the fighting
Is done. No one else could do
What I mean to, here, no man but me
Could hope to defeat this monster. No one
Could try. And this dragon's treasure, his gold 25
And everything hidden in that tower, will be mine
Or war will sweep me to a bitter death!"
  Then Beowulf rose, still brave, still strong,
And with his shield at his side, and a mail shirt on his breast,
Strode calmly, confidently, toward the tower, under 30
The rocky cliffs: no coward could have walked there!
And then he who'd endured dozens of desperate
Battles, who'd stood boldly while swords and shields
Clashed, the best of kings, saw
Huge stone arches and felt the heat 35
Of the dragon's breath, flooding down
Through the hidden entrance, too hot for anyone
To stand, a streaming current of fire
And smoke that blocked all passage. And the Geats'[1]
Lord and leader, angry, lowered 40
His sword and roared out a battle cry,
A call so loud and clear that it reached through
The hoary rock, hung in the dragon's
Ear. The beast rose, angry,
Knowing a man had come—and then nothing 45
But war could have followed. Its breath came first,
A steaming cloud pouring from the stone,
Then the earth itself shook. Beowulf
Swung his shield into place, held it
In front of him, facing the entrance. The dragon 50
Coiled and uncoiled, its heart urging it
Into battle. Beowulf's ancient sword
Was waiting, unsheathed, his sharp and gleaming
Blade. The beast came closer; both of them
Were ready, each set on slaughter. The Geats' 55
Great prince stood firm, unmoving, prepared
Behind his high shield, waiting in his shining
Armor. The monster came quickly toward him,
Pouring out fire and smoke, hurrying
To its fate. Flames beat at the iron 60
Shield, and for a time it held, protected
Beowulf as he'd planned; then it began to melt,
And for the first time in his life that famous prince
Fought with fate against him, with glory
Denied him. He knew it, but he raised his sword 65
And struck at the dragon's scaly hide.
The ancient blade broke, bit into
The monster's skin, drew blood, but cracked
And failed him before it went deep enough, helped him
Less than he needed. The dragon leaped 70
With pain, thrashed and beat at him, spouting
Murderous flames, spreading them everywhere.
And the Geats' ring-giver did not boast of glorious
Victories in other wars: his weapon
Had failed him, deserted him, now when he needed it 75
Most, that excellent sword. Edgetho's

---

[1] The Scandinavian tribe led by Beowulf.

Famous son stared at death,
Unwilling to leave this world, to exchange it
For a dwelling in some distant place—a journey
Into darkness that all men must make, as death   80
Ends their few brief hours on earth.
    Quickly, the dragon came at him, encouraged
As Beowulf fell back; its breath flared,
And he suffered, wrapped around in swirling
Flames—a king, before, but now   85
A beaten warrior. None of his comrades
Came to him, helped him, his brave and noble
Followers; they ran for their lives, fled
Deep in a wood. And only one of them
Remained, stood there, miserable, remembering,   90
As a good man must, what kinship should mean. . . .

Q How does the poet bring color and excitement to Beowulf's assault on the fire-dragon?

Germanic Art

The artistic production of nomadic peoples consists largely of easily transported objects such as carpets, jewelry, and weapons. Germanic folk often buried the most lavish of these items with their deceased chieftains in boats that were cast out to sea (as described in *Beowulf*). In 1939, archeologists at Sutton Hoo in eastern England excavated a seventh-century Anglo-Saxon grave that contained weapons, coins, utensils, jewelry, and a small lyre. These treasures were packed, along with the corpse of their chieftain, into an 89-foot-long ship that served as a tomb.

Among the remarkable metalwork items found at Sutton Hoo were gold buckles, shoulder clasps, and the lid of a purse designed to hang from the chieftain's belt (Figure 11.2). These objects are adorned with semiprecious stones and *cloisonné*—enamelwork produced by pouring molten colored glass between thin gold partitions (Figure 11.3). The purse lid is ornamented with a series of motifs: interlaced fighting animals, two frontal male figures between pairs of rampant beasts (compare Figure 1.3), and two curved-beaked predators attacking wild birds.

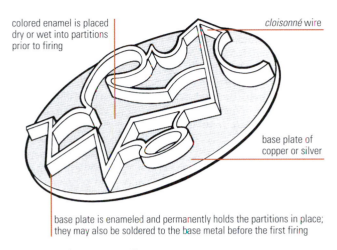

colored enamel is placed dry or wet into partitions prior to firing

cloisonné wire

base plate of copper or silver

base plate is enameled and permanently holds the partitions in place; they may also be soldered to the base metal before the first firing

Figure 11.3 *Cloisonné* enameling process.

These motifs explore the interface between man and beast in what was primarily a hunting society. A 5-pound gold belt buckle is richly ornamented with a dense pattern of interlaced snakes incised with a black sulfurous substance called **niello** (see Figure 11.4).

The high quality of so-called barbarian art, as evidenced at Sutton Hoo and elsewhere, shows that technical sophistication and artistic originality were by no means the monopoly of "civilized" societies. It also demonstrates the continuous diffusion and exchange of styles across Asia and into Europe. The **zoomorphic** (animal-shaped) motifs found on the artifacts at Sutton Hoo, along with many of the metalwork techniques used in their fabrication, are evidence of contact between the Germanic tribes and the nomadic populations of Central Asia, who perpetuated the decorative traditions of ancient Persian, Scythian, and Chinese craftspeople.

As the Germanic tribes poured into Europe, their art and their culture commingled with that of the people with whom they came into contact. A classic example is the fusion of Celtic and Anglo-Saxon styles. The Celts were a non-Germanic, Iron Age folk that had migrated throughout

Figure 11.2 Sutton Hoo purse cover, East Anglia, England, ca. 630. Gold with garnets and *cloisonné* enamel, 8 in. long. The Germanic tribes carried west techniques and motifs popular in the arts of the nomadic peoples of Mesopotamia and the Russian steppes. Compare the frontal male figures flanked by animals on the purse lid with the image of Gilgamesh standing between two human-headed bulls (see Figure 1.3).

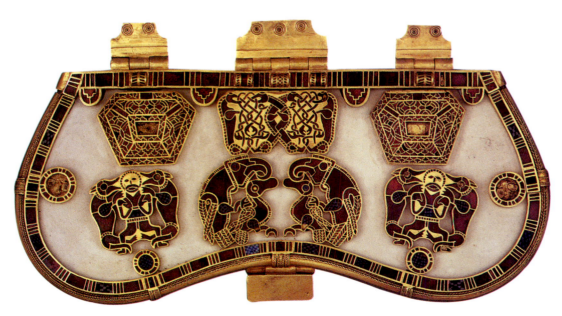

The influence of Anglo-Saxon art on early medieval manuscript illumination is evident in the comparison of the Sutton Hoo buckle (Figure **11.4**) and the Book of Kells, an eighth-century Latin Gospel book. Produced by monks in either Britain or Ireland, and housed for centuries at the Irish monastery of Kells, 40 miles north of Dublin, this magnificent manuscript is the most richly ornamented of all Celtic prayer books. At the beginning of each chapter, elaborate capital letters make up designs that dominate the page. The initial page of the Gospel of Matthew features the letters (*chi, rho, iota*) of the Greek word *Christos*, which opens the Gospel (Figure **11.5**). Like a sheet of metal engraved with the decorative devices of Anglo-Saxon weapons and jewelry, the parchment page is covered with a profusion of spirals, knots, scrolls, interlaced snakes, and, here and there, human and animal forms. As early as the eleventh century, this manuscript was known as "the chief relic of the Western world."

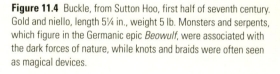

Figure 11.4 Buckle, from Sutton Hoo, first half of seventh century. Gold and niello, length 5¼ in., weight 5 lb. Monsters and serpents, which figure in the Germanic epic *Beowulf*, were associated with the dark forces of nature, while knots and braids were often seen as magical devices.

Figure 11.5 Monogram XPI, first page of Matthew's Gospel, Book of Kells, ca. 800. Manuscript illumination, 13 × 9½ in. Because of its similarities to the techniques and devices of Germanic metalwork, this and other folios in the Book of Kells have inspired historians to dub its artist "the Goldsmith."

Europe between the fifth and third centuries B.C.E., settling in the British Isles before the time of Christ. A great flowering of Celtic art and literature occurred in Ireland and England following the conversion of the Celts to Christianity in the fifth century C.E. The instrument of this conversion was the fabled Saint Patrick (ca. 385–461), the British monk who is said to have baptized more than 120,000 people and founded 300 churches in Ireland. In the centuries thereafter, Anglo-Irish monasteries produced a number of extraordinary illuminated manuscripts, whose decorative style is closely related to the dynamic linear ornamentation of the Sutton Hoo artifacts.

The syncretic union of Germanic, Asiatic, and Mediterranean techniques and motifs influenced both the illumination of Christian manuscripts and the production of Christian liturgical objects, such as the **paten** (Eucharistic plate) and the **chalice** (Eucharistic cup). Used in the celebration of the Mass, these objects usually commanded the finest and most costly materials; and, like the manuscripts that accompanied the sacred rites, they received inordinate care in execution. The Ardagh Chalice, which is made of silver, gilded bronze, gold wire, glass, and enamel, displays the technical virtuosity of early eighth-century metalworkers in Ireland (Figure **11.6**). On the surface of the vessel, a band of interlaced designs is offset by raised roundels worked in enamel and gold thread. Clearly, in the liturgical objects and illuminated manuscripts of the Early Middle Ages, the abstract, ornamental Germanic style provided Christian art with an aesthetic alternative to Classical modes of representation.

Charlemagne and the Carolingian Renaissance

From the time he came to the throne in 768 until his death in 814, the Frankish chieftain Charles the Great (in French, "Charlemagne") pursued the dream of restoring the Roman Empire under Christian leadership. A great warrior and an able administrator, the fair-haired heir to the Frankish kingdom conquered vast areas of land (Map 11.2). His holy wars resulted in the forcible conversion of the Saxons east of the Rhine River, the Lombards of northern Italy, and the Slavic peoples along the Danube. Charlemagne's campaigns also pushed the Muslims back beyond the Pyrenees into Spain.

In the year 800, Pope Leo III crowned Charlemagne "Emperor of the Romans," thus establishing a firm relationship between Church and state. But, equally significantly, Charlemagne's role in creating a Roman Christian or "Holy" Roman Empire cast him as the prototype of Christian kingship. For the more than thirty years during which he waged wars in the name of Christ, Charlemagne sought to control conquered lands by placing them in the hands of local administrators—on whom he bestowed the titles "count" and "duke"—and by periodically sending out royal envoys to carry his edicts abroad. He revived trade

Figure 11.6 Ardagh Chalice, from Ireland, early eighth century. Silver, gilt bronze, gold wire, glass, and enamel, 6¼ × 7½ × 7 in.

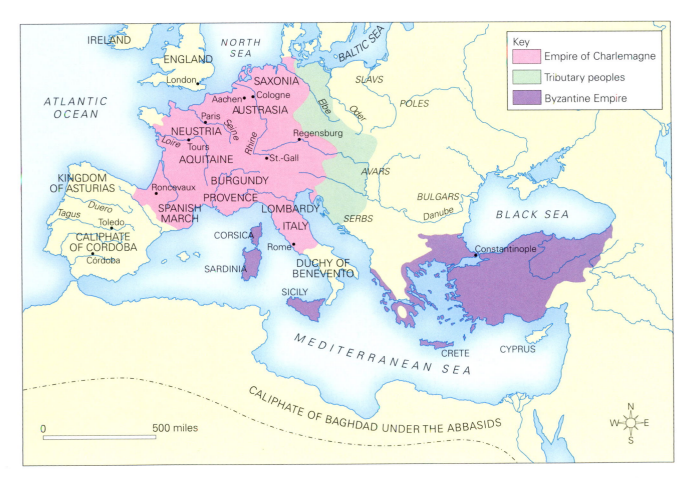

Map 11.2 The Empire of Charlemagne, 814. It required thirty-two campaigns to subdue the Saxons living between the Rhine and Elbe rivers. The eastern frontier brought Slavs, Avars, and other Asiatic peoples under Charlemagne's rule in an area that later became Austria. The Spanish March (or Mark) established a frontier against the Muslims.

with the East, stabilized the currency of the realm, and even pursued diplomatic ties with Baghdad, whose caliph, Harun al-Rashid, graced Charlemagne's court with the gift of an elephant.

Charlemagne's imperial mission was animated by a passionate interest in education and the arts. Having visited San Vitale in Ravenna (see Figures 9.14 and 9.15), he had its architectural plan and decorative program imitated in the Palatine Chapel at Aachen (Figure 11.7). The topmost tier, crowned by a mosaic dome, represented Heaven and the bottom tier the earth, where priest and congregation met for worship; enthroned in the gallery between, which was connected by a passageway to the royal palace, Charlemagne assumed his symbolic role as mediator between God and ordinary mortals. Alert to the legacy of his forebears, he revived the bronze-casting techniques of Roman sculptors, although on a small scale (Figure 11.8). Despite the fact that he himself could barely read and write—his sword hand was, according to his biographers, so callused that he had great difficulty forming letters—he sponsored a revival of learning and literacy. To initiate this **renaissance** or "rebirth," Charlemagne invited to his court missionaries and scholars from all over Europe. He established schools at Aachen (Aix-la-Chapelle), in town centers throughout the Empire, and in Benedictine monasteries such as that at Saint-Gall in Switzerland (see Figure 11.12). In Carolingian **scriptoria** (monastic writing rooms), monks and nuns copied religious manuscripts, along with texts on medicine, drama, and other secular subjects. The scale of the Carolingian renaissance is evident in that 80 percent

Figure 11.7 ODO OF METZ, Palatine Chapel of Charlemagne, Aachen, Germany, 792–805.

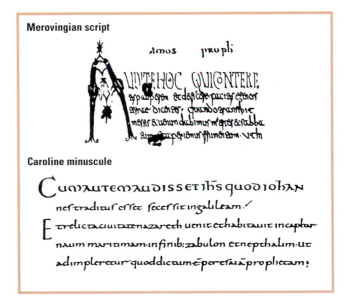

Merovingian script

Caroline minuscule

Figure 11.9 Comparison of Merovingian (pre-Carolingian) book script and Caroline (Carolingian) minuscule.

Figure 11.8 Equestrian statuette of Charlemagne, from Metz, ninth century. Bronze with traces of gilt, height 9½ in. Although this sculpture is less than 10 inches high, it shares the monumental presence of its Classical predecessor, the equestrian statue of Marcus Aurelius (see Figure 6.23).

Figure 11.10 *The Ascension*, from the Sacramentary of Archbishop Drogo of Metz, ca. 842.

of the oldest surviving Classical Latin manuscripts exist in Carolingian copies.

Carolingian copyists rejected the Roman script, which lacked punctuation and spaces between words, in favor of a neat, uniform writing style known as the minuscule (Figure 11.9), the ancestor of modern typography. The decorative programs of many Carolingian manuscripts reflect the union of late Roman Realism and Germanic stylization. The former is revealed in the pictorial narrative that fills (or "historiates") the capital letter in Figure 11.10, while the latter is seen in the ribbonlike pattern of the initial itself. But the Carolingian Renaissance was not limited to the copying of manuscripts. Among the most magnificent artifacts of the period were liturgical and devotional objects, often made of ivory or precious metals. Dating from the decades after Charlemagne's death, the book cover for the Lindau Gospels testifies to the superior technical abilities of Carolingian metalsmiths (Figure 11.11). The surface of the back cover, worked in silver gilt, inlaid with *cloisonné* enamel, and encrusted with precious gems,

consists of an ornate Greek cross that dominates a field of writhing, interlaced creatures similar to those found in Anglo-Saxon metalwork (see Figure 11.4) and Anglo-Irish manuscripts. At the corners of the inner rectangle of the book cover are four tiny scenes showing the evangelists at their writing desks. These realistically conceived representations contrast sharply with the more stylized figural

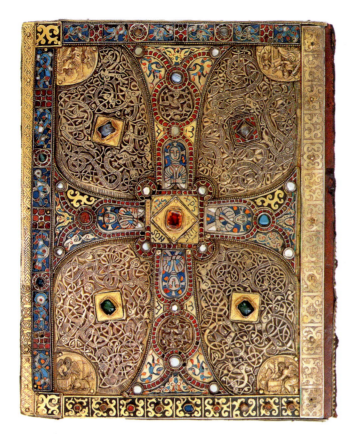

Figure 11.11 Back cover of the *Lindau Gospels*, ca. 870. Silver gilt with *cloisonné* enamel and precious stones, 13⅜ × 10⅜ in.

images that appear in the arms of the cross. The integration of Germanic, Roman, and Byzantine stylistic traditions evident in the cover of the *Lindau Gospels* typifies the Carolingian Renaissance, the glories of which would not be matched for at least three centuries.

The Abbey Church

During the Carolingian Renaissance, Charlemagne authorized the construction of numerous Benedictine monasteries, or abbeys. Central to each abbey was a church that served as a place of worship and as a shrine that housed sacred relics. Although built on a smaller scale than that of Early Christian churches, most abbey churches were simple basilicas with square towers added at the west entrance and at the crossing of the nave and transept.

In the construction of the abbey church, as in the arrangement of the monastic complex as a whole, Carolingian architects pursued a strict geometry governed by Classical principles of symmetry and order. The plan for an ideal monastery (Figure **11.12**) found in a manuscript in the library of the monastery of Saint-Gall reflects these concerns: each part of the complex, from **refectory** (dining hall) to cemetery, is fixed on the gridlike plan according to its practical function. Monks gained access to the church, for example, by means of both the adjacent dormitory and the cloister. At the abbey church of Saint-Gall, where a second transept provided longitudinal symmetry, the monks added chapels along the aisles and transepts to house relics of saints and martyrs whose bones had been exhumed from the Roman catacombs.

Early Medieval Culture

Feudal Society

When Charlemagne died, in the year 814, the short-lived unity he had brought to Western Europe died with him. Although he had turned the Frankish kingdom into an empire, he failed to establish any legal and administrative machinery comparable with that of imperial Rome. There was no standing army, no system of taxation, and no single code of law to unify the widely diverse population. Following his death, the fragile stability of the Carolingian Empire was shattered by Scandinavian seafarers known as Vikings. Charlemagne's sons and grandsons could not repel the raids of these fierce invaders, who ravaged the northern coasts of the Empire; at the same time, neither were his heirs able to arrest the repeated forays of the Muslims along the Mediterranean coast. Lacking effective leadership, the Carolingian Empire disintegrated.

In the mid-ninth century, Charlemagne's three grandsons divided the Empire among themselves, separating French- from German-speaking territories. Increasingly, however, administration and protection fell to members of the local ruling aristocracy—heirs of the counts and dukes whom Charlemagne had appointed to administer portions of the realm, or simply those who had taken land by force. The fragmentation of the Empire and the insecurity

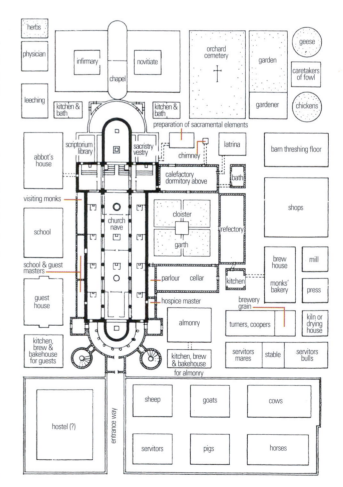

Figure 11.12 Plan for an ideal Benedictine monastery, ninth century. 13½ × 10¼ in.

generated by the Viking invasions caused people at all social levels to attach themselves to members of a military nobility who were capable of providing protection. These circumstances enhanced the growth of a unique system of political and military organization known as **feudalism**.

Derived from Roman and Germanic traditions of rewarding warriors with the spoils of war, feudalism involved the exchange of land for military service. In return for the grant of land, known as a **fief** or *feudum* (the Germanic word for "property"), a **vassal** owed his **lord** a certain number of fighting days (usually forty) per year. The contract between lord and vassal also involved a number of other obligations, including the lord's provision of a court of justice, the vassal's contribution of ransom if his lord were captured, and the reciprocation of hospitality between the two. In an age of instability, feudalism provided a rudimentary form of local government while answering the need for security against armed attack.

Those engaged in the feudal contract constituted roughly the upper 10 percent of European society. The feudal nobility, which bore the twin responsibilities of military defense and political leadership, was a closed class of men and women whose superior status was inherited at birth. A male member of the nobility was first and foremost a mounted man-at-arms—a *chevalier* (from the French *cheval*, for "horse") or knight (from the Germanic *Knecht*, a youthful servant or soldier). The medieval knight was a cavalry warrior equipped with stirrups, protected by **chain mail** (flexible armor made of interlinked metal rings), and armed with such weapons as broadsword and shield.

The knight's conduct and manners in all aspects of life were guided by a strict code of behavior called **chivalry**. Chivalry demanded that the knight be courageous in battle, loyal to his lord and fellow warriors, and reverent toward women. Feudal life was marked by ceremonies and symbols almost as extensive as those of the Christian Church. For instance, a vassal received his fief by an elaborate procedure known as **investiture**, in which oaths of fealty were formally exchanged (Figure **11.13**). In warfare, adversaries usually fixed the time and place of combat in advance. Medieval warfare was both a profession and a pastime, as knights entertained themselves with **jousts** (personal combat between men on horseback) or war games that imitated the trials of combat (Figure **11.14**).

Women played an active role in the chivalric society of the Middle Ages. In many parts of Europe they inherited land,

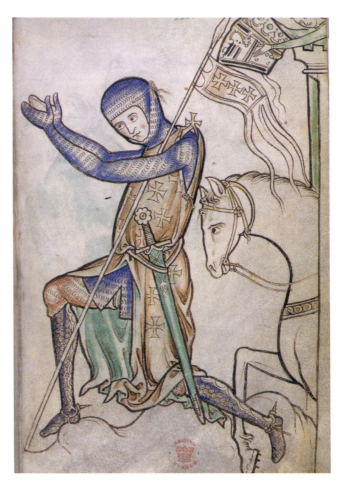

Figure 11.13 MATTHEW PARIS, *Vassal Paying Homage to His Lord*, from the Westminster Psalter, ca. 1250. The feudal status (or aristocratic lineage) of the medieval European soldier was usually indicated by heraldic devices painted on his shield or helmet, embroidered on his tunic (worn here over his protective chain mail), or displayed on flags.

which they usually defended by means of hired soldiers. A woman controlled her fief until she married, and regained it upon becoming a widow. Men and women took great pride in their aristocratic lineage and advertised the family name by means of heraldic devices emblazoned on tunics, pennants, and shields (see Figure 11.13).

Figure 11.14 French plaque from a casket, fourteenth century. Ivory, 3⅞ × ⅝ in.

The Literature of the Feudal Nobility

The ideals of the fighting nobility in a feudal age are best captured in the oldest and greatest French epic poem, the *Song of Roland*. It is based on an event that took place in 778—the ambush of Charlemagne's rear guard, led by Charlemagne's nephew Roland, as they returned from an expedition against the Muslims in Spain. This 4000-line *chanson de geste* ("song of heroic deeds") was transmitted orally for three centuries and not written down until the early 1100s. Generation after generation of *jongleurs* (professional entertainers) wandered from court to court, chanting the story (and possibly embellishing it with episodes of folklore) to the accompaniment of a lyre. Although the music for the poem has not survived, it is likely that it consisted of a single, highly improvised line of melody. The tune was probably syllabic (setting just one note to each syllable) and—like folk song—dependent on simple repetition.

As with other works in the oral tradition (the *Epic of Gilgamesh* and the *Iliad*, for instance), the *Song of Roland* is grandiose in its dimensions and profound in its lyric power. Its rugged Old French verse describes a culture that prized the performance of heroic deeds that brought honor to the warrior, his lord, and his religion. The strong bond of loyalty between vassal and chieftain that characterized the Germanic way of life also resonates in Roland's declaration of unswerving devotion to his temporal overlord, Charlemagne.

The *Song of Roland* brings to life such aspects of early medieval culture as the practice of naming one's battle gear and weapons (often considered sacred), the dependence on cavalry, the glorification of blood-and-thunder heroism, and the strong sense of comradeship among men-at-arms. Women play almost no part in the epic. The feudal contract did not exclude members of the clergy; hence Archbishop Turpin fights with lance and spear, despite the fact that church law forbade members of the clergy to shed another man's blood. (Some members of the clergy got around this law by arming themselves with a **mace**—a spike-headed club that could knock one's armored opponent off his horse or do damage short of bloodshed.) Roland's willingness to die for his religious beliefs, fired by the archbishop's promise of admission into paradise for those who fall fighting the infidels (in this case, the Muslims), suggests that the militant fervor of Muslims was matched by that of early medieval Christians. Indeed, the *Song of Roland* captures the powerful antagonism between Christians and Muslims that dominated all of medieval history and culminated in the Christian Crusades described later in this chapter.

The descriptive language of the *Song of Roland* is stark, unembellished, and vivid: "he feels his brain gush out," reports the poet in verse 168. Such directness and simplicity lend immediacy to the action. Gruesome episodes may be retold numerous times with varying details (verses 168 and 174). Characters are stereotypical ("Roland's a hero, and Oliver is wise," verse 87), and groups of people are characterized with epic expansiveness: *all* Christians are good and *all* Muslims are bad. The figure of Roland epitomizes the ideals of physical courage, religious devotion, and personal loyalty. Yet, in his refusal to call for assistance from Charlemagne and his troops, who have already retreated across the Pyrenees, he exhibits a foolhardiness—perhaps a "tragic flaw"—that leads him and his warriors to their deaths.

READING 11.2 From the *Song of Roland*

81

Count Oliver has climbed up on a hill;	1
From there he sees the Spanish lands below,	
And Saracens[1] assembled in great force.	
Their helmets gleam with gold and precious stones,	
Their shields are shining, their hauberks[2] burnished gold,	5
Their long sharp spears with battle flags unfurled.	
He tries to see how many men there are:	
Even battalions are more than he can count.	
And in his heart Oliver is dismayed;	
Quick as he can, he comes down from the height,	10
And tells the Franks what they will have to fight.	

82

Oliver says, "Here come the Saracens—	
A greater number no man has ever seen!	
The first host carries a hundred thousand shields,	
Their helms are laced, their hauberks shining white,	15
From straight wood handles rise ranks of burnished spears.	
You'll have a battle like none on earth before!	
Frenchmen, my lords, now God give you the strength	
To stand your ground, and keep us from defeat."	
They say, "God's curse on those who quit the field!	20
We're yours till death—not one of us will yield." AOI[3]	

83

Oliver says, "The pagan might is great—	
It seems to me, our Franks are very few!	
Roland, my friend, it's time to sound your horn;	
King Charles[4] will hear, and bring his army back."	25
Roland replies, "You must think I've gone mad!	
In all sweet France I'd forfeit my good name!	
No! I will strike great blows with Durendal,[5]	
Crimson the blade up to the hilt of gold.	
To those foul pagans I promise bitter woe—	30
They all are doomed to die at Roncevaux!"[6] AOI	

---

[1] Another name for Muslims.
[2] Long coats of chain mail.
[3] The letters AOI have no known meaning but probably signify a musical appendage or refrain that occurred at the end of each stanza.
[4] Charlemagne.
[5] Roland's sword.
[6] "The gate of Spain," a narrow pass in the Pyrenees where the battle takes place.

84

"Roland, my friend, let the Oliphant[7] sound!
King Charles will hear it, his host will all turn back,
His valiant barons will help us in this fight."
Roland replies, "Almighty God forbid   35
That I bring shame upon my family,
And cause sweet France to fall into disgrace!
I'll strike that horde with my good Durendal;
My sword is ready, girded here at my side,
And soon you'll see its keen blade dripping blood.   40
The Saracens will curse the evil day
They challenged us, for we will make them pay."   AOI

85

"Roland, my friend I pray you, sound your horn!
King Charlemagne, crossing the mountain pass,
Won't fail, I swear it, to bring back all his Franks."   45
"May God forbid!" Count Roland answers then.
"No man on earth shall have the right to say
That I for pagans sounded the Oliphant!
I will not bring my family to shame.
I'll fight this battle; my Durendal shall strike   50
A thousand blows and seven hundred more;
You'll see bright blood flow from the blade's keen steel.
We have good men; their prowess will prevail,
And not one Spaniard shall live to tell the tale."

86

Oliver says, "Never would you be blamed;   55
I've seen the pagans, the Saracens of Spain.
They fill the valleys, cover the mountain peaks;
On every hill, and every wide-spread plain,
Vast hosts assemble from that alien race;
Our company numbers but very few."   60
Roland replies, "The better, then, we'll fight!
If it please God and His angelic host,
I won't betray the glory of sweet France!
Better to die than learn to live with shame—
Charles loves us more as our keen swords win fame."   65

87

Roland's a hero, and Oliver is wise;
Both are so brave men marvel at their deeds.
When they mount chargers, take up their swords and shields,
Not death itself could drive them from the field.
They are good men; their words are fierce and proud.   70
With wrathful speed the pagans ride to war.
Oliver says, "Roland, you see them now.
They're very close, the king too far away.
You were too proud to sound the Oliphant:
If Charles were with us, we would not come to grief.   75
Look up above us, close to the Gate of Spain:
There stands the guards—who would not pity them!
To fight this battle means not to fight again."

Roland replies, "Don't speak so foolishly!
Cursed be the heart that cowers in the breast!   80
We'll hold our ground; if they will meet us here,
Our foes will find us ready with sword and spear."   AOI

88

When Roland sees the fight will soon begin,
Lions and leopards are not so fierce as he.
Calling the Franks, he says to Oliver: 85
"Noble companion, my friend, don't talk that way!
The Emperor Charles, who left us in command
Of twenty thousand he chose to guard the pass,
Made very sure no coward's in their ranks.
In his lord's service a man must suffer pain,   90
Bitterest cold and burning heat endure;
He must be willing to lose his flesh and blood.
Strike with your lance, and I'll wield Durendal—
The king himself presented it to me—
And if I die, whoever takes my sword   95
Can say its master has nobly served his lord."

89

Archbishop Turpin comes forward then to speak.
He spurs his horse and gallops up a hill,
Summons the Franks, and preaches in these words:
"My noble lords, Charlemagne left us here,   100
And may our deaths do honor to the king!
Now you must help defend our holy Faith!
Before your eyes you see the Saracens.
Confess your sins, ask God to pardon you;
I'll grant you absolution to save your souls.   105
Your deaths would be a holy martyrdom,
And you'll have places in highest Paradise."
The French dismount; they kneel upon the ground.
Then the archbishop, blessing them in God's name,
Told them, for penance, to strike when battle came.   110

. . . .

91

At Roncevaux Count Roland passes by,
Riding his charger, swift-running Veillantif[8]
He's armed for battle, splendid in shining mail.
As he parades, he brandishes his lance.
Turning the point straight up against the sky,   115
And from the spearhead a banner flies, pure white,
With long gold fringes that beat against his hands.
Fair to behold, he laughs, serene and gay.
Now close behind him comes Oliver, his friend,
With all the Frenchmen cheering their mighty lord.   120
Fiercely his eyes confront the Saracens;
Humbly and gently he gazes at the Franks,
Speaking to them with gallant courtesy:
"Barons, my lords, softly now, keep the pace!
Here come the pagans looking for martyrdom.   125
We'll have such plunder before the day is out,

---

[7] A horn made from an elephant's tusk.

[8] Roland's horse.

As no French king has ever won before!"
And at this moment the armies join in war.   AOI

. . . .

161

The pagans flee, furious and enraged,
Trying their best to get away in Spain.   130
Count Roland lacks the means to chase them now,
For he has lost his war-horse Veillantif;
Against his will he has to go on foot.
He went to give Archbishop Turpin help,
Unlaced his helmet, removed it from his head,   135
And then took off the hauberk of light mail;
The under-tunic he cut into long strips
With which he stanched the largest of his wounds.
Then lifting Turpin, carried him in his arms
To soft green grass, and gently laid him down.   140
In a low voice Roland made this request:
"My noble lord, I pray you, give me leave,
For our companions, the men we held so dear,
Must not be left abandoned now in death.
I want to go and seek out every one,   145
Carry them here, and place them at your feet."
Said the archbishop, "I grant it willingly.
The field belongs, thank God, to you and me."

162

Alone, Count Roland walks through the battlefield,
Searching the valleys, searching the mountain heights.   150
He found the bodies of Ivon and Ivoire,
And then he found the Gascon Engelier.
Gerin he found, and Gerier his friend,
He found Aton and then Count Bérengier,
Proud Anseïs he found, and then Samson,   155
Gérard the Old, the Count of Roussillon.
He took these barons, and carried every one
Back to the place where the archbishop was,
And then he put them in ranks at Turpin's knees.
Seeing them, Turpin cannot restrain his tears;   160
Raising his hand, he blesses all the dead.
And then he says, "You've come to grief, my lords!
Now in His glory, may God receive your souls,
Among bright flowers set you in Paradise!
It's my turn now; death keeps me in such pain,   165
Never again will I see Charlemagne."

163

Roland goes back to search the field once more,
And his companion he finds there, Oliver.
Lifting him in his arms he holds him close,
Brings him to Turpin as quickly as he can,   170
Beside the others places him on a shield;
Turpin absolves him, signing him with the cross,
And then they yield to pity and to grief.
Count Roland says, "Brother in arms, fair friend,
You were the son of Renier, the duke   175
Who held the land where Runers valley lies.
For breaking lances, for shattering thick shields,

Bringing the proud to terror and defeat,
For giving counsel, defending what is right,
In all the world there is no better knight."   180

164

When Roland sees that all his peers are dead,
And Oliver whom he so dearly loved,
He feels such sorrow that he begins to weep;
Drained of all color, his face turns ashen pale,
His grief is more than any man could bear,   185
He falls down, fainting whether he will or no.
Says the archbishop, "Baron, you've come to woe."

. . . .

168

Now Roland knows that death is very near.
His ears give way, he feels his brain gush out.
He prays that God will summon all his peers;   190
Then, for himself, he prays to Gabriel.
Taking the horn, to keep it from all shame,
With Durendal clasped in his other hand,
He goes on, farther than a good cross-bow shot,
West into Spain, crossing a fallow field.   195
Up on a hilltop, under two lofty trees.
Four marble blocks are standing on the grass.
But when he comes there, Count Roland faints once more,
He falls down backward; now he is at death's door.

. . . .

174

Count Roland feels the very grip of death   200
Which from his head is reaching for his heart.
He hurries then to go beneath a pine;
In the green grass he lies down on his face,
Placing beneath him the sword and Oliphant;
He turns his head to look toward pagan Spain.   205
He does these things in order to be sure
King Charles will say, and with him all the Franks,
The noble count conquered until he died.
He makes confession, for all his sins laments.
Offers his glove to God in penitence.   AOI 210

Q **What aspects of European feudalism are brought to life in the Song of Roland?**

The Norman Conquest and the Arts

As early as the eighth century the seafarers known as Vikings (but also as Norsemen, Northmen, and, later, Normans) had moved beyond the bounds of their Scandinavian homelands. They constructed long wooden ships equipped with sailing gear that allowed them to tack into the wind (Figure **11.15**). Expert ship builders, sailors, and navigators, they soon came to control the North Atlantic. The western Vikings were the first to colonize Iceland, and they set up a colony in Greenland before the year 1000. The eastern Vikings sailed across the North Sea to establish trading centers at Kiev and Novgorod. Known among Arab traders of this area as "*rus*," they gave their name to Russia.

Figure 11.15 *William Duke of Normandy's Fleet Crossing the Channel*, detail from the Bayeux Tapestry, late eleventh century. Wool embroidery on linen, depth 20 in. (approx.), entire length 231 ft. The ship pictured here is typical of the wooden vessels that carried the Vikings across the North and Mediterranean seas. Some 70 feet in length, they were propelled by sails and oars.

They traded animal hides, amber, and other valued items, including captive Eastern Europeans—Slavs—from which the English word "slave" derives.

The Vikings began their raids on England with an attack on the Lindisfarne monastery in 793, and by the end of the ninth century, they had settled throughout Northern Europe. Within a hundred years, they made Normandy one of the strongest fiefs in France. In 1066, under the leadership of William of Normandy, some 5000 men crossed the English Channel; at the Battle of Hastings, William defeated the Anglo-Saxon duke Harold and seized the throne of England. The Norman Conquest had enormous consequences for the histories of England and France, for it marked the transfer of power in England from Anglo-Saxons to Normans, who, already vassals of the king of France, were now also the ruling lords of England.

The Normans brought feudalism and the techniques of stone fortification to England (Figures **11.16** and **11.17**). To raise money, William ordered a detailed census of all property in the realm—the *Domesday Book*—which laid the basis for the collection of taxes. King William controlled all aspects of government with the aid of the *Curia Regis*—the royal court and council consisting of his feudal barons. Under the Norman kings, England would become one of Europe's leading medieval states.

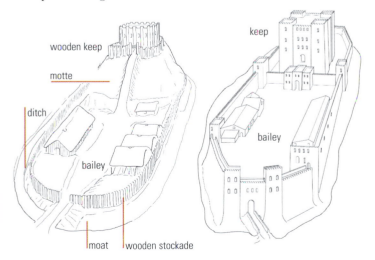

Figure 11.16 Dover Castle, Kent, England, twelfth century. While William's first stone fortification was the Tower of London, he constructed an earthwork castle at Dover, a defensive site that earlier held a Roman lighthouse and an Anglo-Saxon fortress. During the twelfth century, Henry II rebuilt the castle in stone.

Figure 11.17 Development of the Norman castle between eleventh-century timber and twelfth-century stone construction.

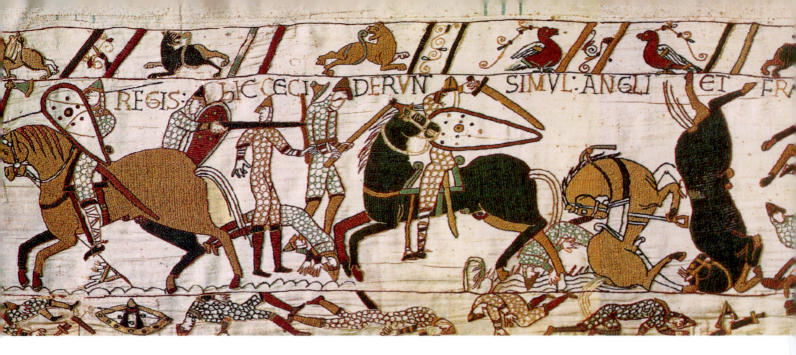

Figure 11.18 *The Battle Rages*, detail from the Bayeux Tapestry, late eleventh century. Wool embroidery on linen, depth 20 in. (approx.), entire length 231 ft. The Latin script embroidered above the action reads: "Here the English and French have fallen together in battle." At the far right, Bishop Odo (on a black stallion) ;rallies the Norman cavalry with a swinging mace. The bottom register is filled with fallen soldiers, shields, weapons, and a bodiless head.

The Normans led the way in the construction of stone castles and churches. Within a 20-mile radius of London, King William constructed no fewer than nine castles. At such vulnerable sites as Dover on the southeast coast of England, he erected the largest of England's austere castle-fortresses (see Figure 11.16). Dover castle featured a **keep** (square tower) containing a dungeon, a main hall, and a chapel, and incorporated a central open space with workshops and storehouses (see Figure 11.17). The enclosing stone walls were usually surmounted by turrets with **crenellations** that provided archers with protection in defensive combat. A **moat** (a trench usually filled with water) often surrounded the castle walls to deter enemy invasion. The brilliance of the Normans' achievements in architecture, apparent in their fortresses and churches (see chapter 13), lies in the use of stone to replace earlier timber fortifications and in the clarity with which the form of the building reflects its function.

The Bayeux Tapestry

One of the most famous Norman artifacts is the Bayeux Tapestry. Not an actual tapestry, but an embroidery, it is an unusual visual record of the conquest of England by William of Normandy. Named for the city in northwestern France where it was made and where it is still displayed today, it documents the history and folklore of the Normans with the same energetic spirit that animates the *Song of Roland.* Sewn into the bleached linen cloth, some 20 inches high and 231 feet long, are lively representations of the incidents leading up to and including the Battle of Hastings (see Figure 11.15 and Figure **11.18**). Above and alongside the images are Latin captions that serve to identify characters, places, and events. The seventy-nine scenes in this wall-hanging progress in the manner of a parchment scroll or a cartoon comic strip (they also call to mind the style of ancient Assyrian narrative reliefs, pictured in chapter 1). Rendered in only eight colors of wool yarn,

the ambitious narrative includes 626 figures, 190 horses, and over 500 other animals. Since embroidery was almost exclusively a female occupation, it is likely that the Bayeux Tapestry was the work of women—although women are depicted only four times in the entire piece.

The *Song of Roland* and the Bayeux Tapestry have much in common: both are epic in theme and robust in style. Both consist of sweeping narratives whose episodes are irregular rather than uniform in length. Like the stereotypical (and almost exclusively male) characters in the *chanson*, the figures of the tapestry are delineated by means of expressive gestures and simplified physical features; the Normans, for instance, are distinguished by the shaved backs of their heads. Weapons and armor in both epic and embroidery are described with loving detail. Indeed, in the Bayeux Tapestry, scenes of combat provide a veritable encyclopedia of medieval battle gear: kite-shaped shields, conical iron helmets, hauberks, short bows, double-edged swords, battle axes, and lances. Both the *Song of Roland* and the Bayeux Tapestry offer a vivid record of feudal life in all its heroic splendor.

The Lives of Medieval Serfs

Although the feudal class monopolized land and power within medieval society, this elite group represented only

a tiny percentage of the total population. The majority of people—more than 90 percent—were unfree peasants or **serfs** who, along with freemen, farmed the soil. Medieval serfs lived quite differently from their landlords. Bound to large farms or manors, they, like the farmers of the old Roman *latifundia* (see chapter 6), provided food in exchange for military protection furnished by the nobility. They owned no property. They were forbidden to leave the land, although, on the positive side, they could not be evicted. Their bondage to the soil assured them the protection of feudal lords who, in an age that lacked effective central authority, were the sole sources of political power.

During the Middle Ages, the reciprocal obligations of serfs and lords and the serf's continuing tenure on the land became firmly fixed. At least until the eleventh century, the interdependence between the two classes was generally beneficial to both; serfs needed protection and feudal lords, whose position as gentlemen-warriors excluded them from menial toil, needed food. For upper and lower classes alike, the individual's place in medieval society was inherited and bound by tradition.

A medieval fief usually included one or more manors. The average manor community comprised fifteen to twenty families, while a large manor of 5000 acres might contain some fifty families. The lord usually appointed the local priest, provided a court of justice, and governed the manor from a fortified residence or castle. Between the eighth and tenth centuries, such residences were simple wooden structures, but by the twelfth century, elaborate stone manor houses with crenellated walls and towers became commonplace. On long winter nights, the lord's castle might be the scene of reveling and entertainment by

jongleurs singing epic tales like the *Song of Roland* (see Reading 11.2).

The typical medieval manor consisted of farmlands, woodland, and pasture, and included a common mill, winepress, and oven (Figure **11.19**). Serfs cultivated the major crops of oats and rye on strips of arable land. In addition to the food they produced from fields reserved for the lord, they owed the lord a percentage—usually a third—of their own agricultural yield. They also performed services in the form of labor. In the medieval world, manor was isolated from manor, and a subsistence economy similar to that of the Neolithic village prevailed. The annual round of peasant labor, beset by a continuing war with the elements, was harsh and demanding. Nevertheless, during the Early Middle Ages, serfs made considerable progress in farm technology and agricultural

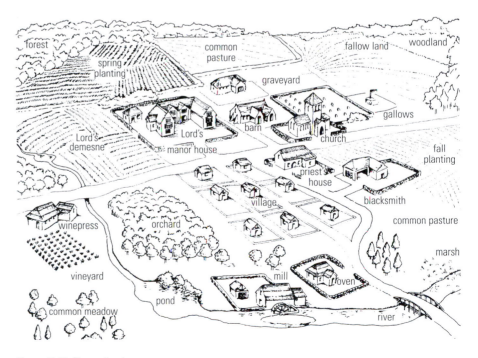

Figure 11.19 The medieval manor.

Figure 11.20 *Women and Men Reaping*, from the Luttrell Psalter, ca. 1340.

practices. They developed the heavy-wheeled plow and the tandem harness, utilized wind and water mills, recovered land by dredging swamps and clearing forests, and offset soil exhaustion by devising systems of crop rotation. The "three-field system," for example, left one-third of the land fallow to allow it to recover its fertility. Such innovations eventually contributed to the production of a food surplus, which in turn stimulated the revival of trade.

Medieval serfs were subject to perennial toil and constant privations, including those of famine and disease. Most could neither read nor write. Unfortunately, art and literature leave us little insight into the lives and values of the lower classes of medieval society. Occasionally, however, in the sculptures of laboring peasants found on medieval cathedrals, in stained glass windows, and in medieval manuscripts, we find visual representations of lower-class life. As illustrations from the Luttrell Psalter indicate, peasant women worked alongside men in raising crops: sowing, reaping, gleaning, threshing, and assisting even in the most backbreaking of farming tasks (Figure **11.20**). Medieval women were associated with the professions that involved food preparation (milking, raising vegetables, brewing, and baking) and the making of cloth (sheep-shearing, carting, spinning, and weaving). The distaff, the pole on which fibers were wound prior to spinning, came to be a symbol of women's work and (universally) of womankind. But lower-class women also shared their husbands' domestic tasks and day-to-day responsibilities that few noblewomen shared with their upper-class partners.

High Medieval Culture

The Christian Crusades

During the eleventh century, numerous circumstances contributed to a change in the character of medieval life. The Normans effectively pushed the Muslims out of the Mediterranean Sea and, as the Normans and other marauders began to settle down, Europeans enjoyed a greater degree of security. At the same time, rising agricultural productivity and surplus encouraged trade and travel. The Crusades of the eleventh to thirteenth centuries were a symptom of the increased freedom and new mobility of Western Europeans during the High Middle Ages. They

were also the product of idealism and religious zeal. The Byzantine emperor had pressed the Catholic Church to aid in delivering the East from the Muslim Turks, who were threatening the Byzantine Empire and denying Christian pilgrims access to the Holy Land.

In 1095, Pope Urban II preached a fiery sermon that called on Christians to rescue Jerusalem from the "accursed race" who had invaded Christian lands. Thousands of laymen and clergy "took up the Cross" and marched across Europe to the Byzantine East (Map **11.3**). Well before reaching their destination, a combination of avarice and religious fervor inspired some of the Crusaders to plunder the cities along the Rhine, robbing and murdering all "enemies" of Christ, including the entire Jewish populations of Cologne and Mainz. While the First Crusade succeeded in recapturing some important cities, including Jerusalem, the Crusades that followed were generally unsuccessful (see Figure **11.1**).

It soon became apparent that the material benefits of the Crusades outweighed the spiritual ones, especially in that the campaigns provided economic and military advantages for the younger sons of the nobility. While the eldest son of an upper-class family inherited his father's fief under the principle of **primogeniture**, his younger brothers were left to seek their own fortunes. The Crusades stirred the ambitions of these disenfranchised young men who had been schooled in warfare. Equally ambitious were

Chronology

378	Battle of Adrianople
410	the Visigoths attack Rome
455	the Vandals sack Rome
476	Odoacer deposes the reigning Roman emperor
768–814	Carolingian Empire
1066	Norman Conquest of England
1095–1204	major Christian Crusades
1215	the Magna Carta

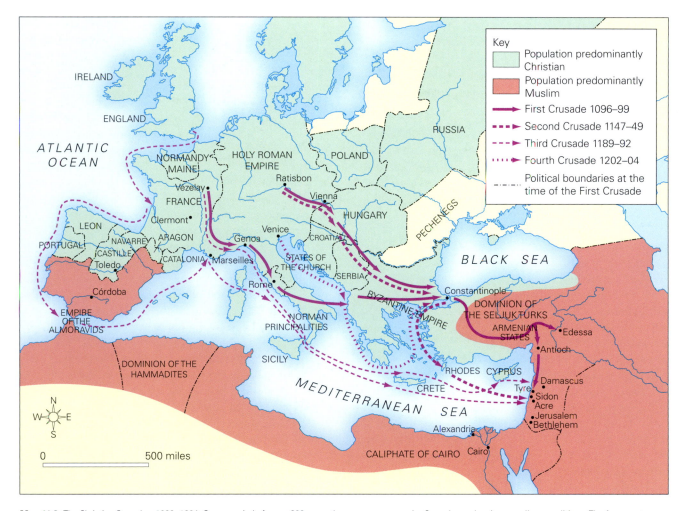

Map 11.3 The Christian Crusades, 1096–1204. Over a period of some 200 years there were seven major Crusades and various smaller expeditions. The four most significant Crusades are shown here: the first departed from central France and proceeded overland, while the fourth, a maritime venture, began in Venice.

the Italian city-states Genoa, Pisa, and Venice. Eager to expand their commercial activities, they encouraged the Crusaders to become middlemen in trade between Italy and the East. In the course of the Fourth Crusade, when the Crusaders could not pay the Venetians for the fleet of ships that was contracted to carry them east, profit-seekers persuaded them to take over (on behalf of Venice) trading ports in the Aegean; from there, the Crusaders went on to plunder and sack Constantinople. Moral inhibitions failed to restrain greed, and in 1204, the Fourth Crusade deteriorated into a contest for personal profit. A disastrous postscript to the Fourth Crusade was the Children's Crusade of 1212, in which thousands of children, aged between ten and fourteen, set out to recapture Jerusalem. Almost all died or were taken into slavery before reaching the Holy Land.

Aside from such economic advantages as those enjoyed by individual Crusaders and the Italian city-states, the gains made by the seven major Crusades were slight. By 1291, all recaptured lands, including the city of Jerusalem, were lost again to the Muslims. Indeed, in more than 200 years of fighting and seven major Crusades, the Crusaders did not secure any territory permanently, nor did they stop the westward advance of the Turks. Constantinople finally fell in 1453 to a later wave of Muslim Turks.

Despite their failure as religious ventures, the Crusades had enormous consequences for the West: the revival of trade between East and West enhanced European commercial life, encouraging the rise of towns and bringing great wealth to the Italian cities of Venice, Genoa, and Pisa. Then, too, in the absence or at the death of crusading noblemen, feudal lords (including emperors and kings) seized every opportunity to establish greater authority over the lands within their domains, thus consolidating and centralizing political power in the embryonic nation-states of England and France. Finally, renewed contact with Byzantium promoted an atmosphere of commercial and cultural exchange that had not existed since Roman times. Luxury goods, such as saffron, citrus, silks, and damasks, entered Western Europe, as did sacred relics associated with the lives of Jesus, Mary, and the Christian saints. And, to the delight of the literate, Arabic translations of Greek manuscripts poured into France, along with all genres of Islamic literature (see chapter 10).

The Medieval Romance and the Code of Courtly Love

The Crusades inspired the writing of chronicles that were an admixture of historical fact, Christian lore, and stirring fiction. As such histories had broad appeal in an age of increasing upper-class literacy, they came to be written in the everyday language of the layperson—the vernacular—rather than in Latin. The Crusades also contributed to the birth of the **medieval romance**, a fictitious tale of love and adventure that became the most popular form of literary entertainment in the West between the years 1200 and 1500. Medieval romances first appeared in twelfth-century France in the form of rhymed verse, but later ones were written in prose. While romances were probably recited before a small, courtly audience rather than read individually, the development of the form coincided with the rise of a European "textual culture," that is, a culture dependent on written language rather than on oral tradition. In this textual culture, vernacular languages gained importance for intimate kinds of literature, while Latin remained the official language of Church and state.

The "spice" of the typical medieval romance was an illicit relationship or forbidden liaison between a man and woman of the upper class. During the Middle Ages, marriage among members of the nobility was usually an alliance formed in the interest of securing land. Indeed, noble families might arrange marriages for offspring who were still in the cradle. In such circumstances, romantic love was more likely to flourish outside marriage. An adulterous affair between Lancelot, a knight of King Arthur's court, and Guinevere, the king's wife, is central to the popular twelfth-century verse romance *Lancelot*. Written in vernacular French by Chrétien de Troyes (d. ca. 1183), *Lancelot* belongs to a cycle of stories associated with a semi-legendary sixth-century Welsh chieftain named Arthur. Chrétien's poem (a portion of which appears in prose translation in the following pages) stands at the beginning of a long tradition of Arthurian romance literature. Filled with bloody combat, supernatural events, and romantic alliances, medieval romances introduced a new and complex picture of human conduct and courtship associated with the so-called code of courtly love.

Courtly love, as the name suggests, was a phenomenon cultivated in the courts of the medieval nobility. Characterized by the longing of a nobleman for a (usually unattainable) woman, the courtly love tradition, with its "rules" of wooing and winning a lady, laid the basis for concepts of romantic love in Western literature and life. Popularized in twelfth-century manuals of conduct for European aristocrats, the code held that love (whether requited or not) had a purifying and ennobling influence on the lover. To love was to suffer; witness, in the excerpt that follows, Queen Guinevere's distress upon hearing the false report of Lancelot's death. Courtly love was also associated with a variety of distressing physical symptoms, such as an inability to eat or sleep. The tenets of courtly love required that a knight prove his love for his lady by performing daring and often impossible deeds; he must even be willing to die for her. In these features, the medieval romance is far removed from the rugged, bellicose spirit of earlier literary works like the *Song of Roland*. Indeed, *Lancelot* dramatizes the feminization of the chivalric ideal. The *Song of Roland* pictures early medieval culture in terms of heroic idealism and personal loyalty between men. The Arthurian romance, however, redefined these qualities in the direction of sentiment and sensuality. Lancelot fights not for his country, nor even for his lord, but to win the affections of his mistress. His prowess is not exercised, as with Roland, on a field of battle, but as individual combat undertaken in the courtyard of his host. While Roland is motivated by the ideal of glory in battle, Lancelot is driven by his love for Guinevere.

The courtly love tradition contributed to shaping modern Western concepts of gender and courtship. It also worked to define the romantic perception of women as objects, particularly objects of reward for the performance of brave deeds. For although courtly love elevated the woman (and her prototype, the Virgin Mary) as worthy of adoration, it defined her exclusively in terms of the interests of men. Nevertheless, the medieval romance, which flattered and exalted the aristocratic lady as an object of desire, was directed toward a primarily female audience. A product of the aristocratic (and male) imagination, the lady of the medieval romance had no counterpart in the lower classes of society, where women worked side by side with men in the fields (see Figure 11.20) and in a variety of trades. Despite its artificiality, however, the theme of courtly love and the romance itself had a significant influence on Western literary tradition. In that tradition, even into modern times, writers have tended to treat love more as a mode of spiritual purification or as an emotional affliction than as a condition of true affection and sympathy between the sexes.

READING 11.3 From Chrétien de Troyes' *Lancelot* (ca. 1170)

[Gawain and Lancelot, knights of King Arthur's court, set out in quest of Queen Guinevere. In the forest, they meet a damsel, who tells them of the Queen's whereabouts.]

Then the damsel relates to them the following story: "In truth, my lords, Meleagant, a tall and powerful knight, son of the King of Gorre, has taken her off into the kingdom whence no foreigner returns, but where he must perforce remain in servitude and banishment." Then they ask her: "Damsel, where is this country? Where can we find the way thither?" She replies: "That you shall quickly learn; but you may be sure that you will meet with many obstacles and difficult passages,   1

Figure 11.21 *Lancelot Crossing the Sword-Bridge and Guinevere in the Tower*, from the *Romance of Lancelot*, ca. 1300. 10 × 13½ in.

for it is not easy to enter there except with the permission of the king, whose name is Bademagu; however, it is possible to 10 enter by two very perilous paths and by two very difficult passage-ways. One is called 'the water-bridge,' because the bridge is under water, and there is the same amount of water beneath it as above it, so that the bridge is exactly in the middle; and it is only a foot and a half in width and in thickness. This choice is certainly to be avoided, and yet it is the less dangerous of the two. . . . The other bridge is still more impracticable and much more perilous, never having been crossed by man. It is just like a sharp sword, and therefore all the people call it 'the sword-bridge.' Now I have 20 told you all the truth I know. . . ."

[They reach the sword-bridge.]

At the end of this very difficult bridge they dismount from their steeds and gaze at the wicked-looking stream, which is as swift and raging, as black and turgid, as fierce and terrible as if it were the devil's stream; and it is so dangerous and bottomless that anything falling into it would be as completely lost as if it fell into the salt sea. And the bridge, which spans it, is different from any other bridge; for there never was such a one as this. If any one asks of me the truth, there never was such a bad bridge, nor one whose flooring was so bad. The 30 bridge across the cold stream consisted of a polished, gleaming sword; but the sword was stout and stiff, and was as long as two lances. At each end there was a tree-trunk in which the sword was firmly fixed. No one need fear to fall because of its breaking or bending, for its excellence was such that it could support a great weight . . . . [Lancelot] prepares, as best he may, to cross the stream, and he does a very marvelous thing in removing the armor from his feet and hands. He will be in a sorry state when he reaches the other side [Figure **11.21**]. He is going to support himself with his 40 bare hands and feet upon the sword, which was sharper than a scythe, for he had not kept on his feet either sole or upper[1] or

hose. But he felt no fear of wounds upon his hands or feet; he preferred to maim himself rather than to fall from the bridge and be plunged in the water from which he could never escape. In accordance with this determination, he passes over with great pain and agony, being wounded in the hands, knees, and feet. But even this suffering is sweet to him: for Love, who conducts and leads him on, assuages and relieves the pain. Creeping on his hands, feet, and knees, he proceeds 50 until he reaches the other side. . . .

[Lancelot confronts the Queen's captors: King Bademagu's son, Meleagant, refuses to make peace with Lancelot and promptly challenges him to battle.]

. . . Very early, before Prime[2] had yet been sounded, both of the knights fully armed were led to the place, mounted upon two horses equally protected. Meleagant was very graceful, alert, and shapely; the hauberk with its fine meshes, the helmet, and the shield hanging from his neck—all these became him well. . . . Then the combatants without delay make all the people stand aside; then they clash the shields with their elbows, and thrust their arms into the straps, and spur at each other so violently that each sends his lance two 60 arms' length through his opponent's shield, causing the lance to split and splinter like a flying spark. And the horses meet head on, clashing breast to breast, and the shields and helmets crash with such a noise that it seems like a mighty thunder-clap; not a breast-strap, girth, rein or surcingle[3] remains unbroken, and the saddle-bows, though strong, are broken to pieces. The combatants felt no shame in falling to earth, in view of their mishaps, but they quickly spring to their feet, and without waste of threatening words rush at each other more fiercely than two wild boars, and deal great blows 70 with their swords of steel like men whose hate is violent.

[1] Parts of the shoe or boot.

[2] The second of the canonical hours, around 6 a.m. The devout recited special devotional prayers at each of the canonical hours: Lauds, Prime, Terce, Sext, None, Vespers, and Compline.

[3] A band passing around a horse's body to bind the saddle.

Repeatedly they trim the helmets and shining hauberks so fiercely that after the sword the blood spurts out. They furnished an excellent battle, indeed, as they stunned and wounded each other with their heavy, wicked blows. Many fierce, hard, long bouts they sustained with equal honor, so that the onlookers could discern no advantage on either side. But it was inevitable that he who had crossed the bridge should be much weakened by his wounded hands. The people who sided with him were much dismayed, for they notice that his strokes are growing weaker, and they fear he will get the worst of it; it seemed to them that he was weakening, while Meleagant was triumphing, and they began to murmur all around. But up at the window of the tower there was a wise maiden who thought within herself that the knight had not undertaken the battle either on her account or for the sake of the common herd who had gathered about the list, but that his only incentive had been the Queen; and she thought that, if he knew that she was at the window seeing and watching him, his strength and courage would increase. . . . Then she came to the Queen and said: "Lady, for God's sake and your own as well as ours, I beseech you to tell me, if you know, the name of yonder knight, to the end that it may be of some help to him." "Damsel," the Queen replies, "you have asked me a question in which I see no hate or evil, but rather good intent; the name of the knight, I know, is Lancelot of the Lake." "God, how happy and glad at heart I am!" the damsel says. Then she leans forward and calls to him by name so loudly that all the people hear: "Lancelot, turn about and see who is here taking note of thee!"

When Lancelot heard his name, he was not slow to turn around: he turns and sees seated up there at the window of the tower her whom he desired most in the world to see. From the moment he caught sight of her, he did not turn or take his eyes and face from her, defending himself with backhand blows. . . . Lancelot's strength and courage grow, partly because he has love's aid, and partly because he never hated any one so much as him with whom he is engaged. Love and mortal hate, so fierce that never before was such hate seen, make him so fiery and bold that Meleagant ceases to treat it as a jest and begins to stand in awe of him, for he had never met or known so doughty a knight, nor had any knight ever wounded or injured him as this one does. . . .

[Lancelot spares Meleagant but thereafter is taken prisoner. Rumor reaches the Queen that Lancelot is dead.]

The news of this spread until it reached the Queen, who was sitting at meat. She almost killed herself on hearing the false report about Lancelot, but she supposes it to be true, and therefore she is in such dismay that she almost loses the power to speak; but, because of those present, she forces herself to say: "In truth, I am sorry for his death, and it is no wonder that I grieve, for he came into this country for my sake, and therefore I should mourn for him." Then she says to herself, so that the others should not hear, that no one need ask her to drink or eat, if it is true that he is dead, in whose life she found her own. Then grieving she rises from the table, and makes her lament, but so that no one hears or notices her. She is so beside herself that she repeatedly grasps her throat

with the desire to kill herself; but first she confesses to herself, and repents with self-reproach, blaming and censuring herself, for the wrong she had done him, who, as she knew, had always been hers, and would still be hers, if he were alive. . . . "Alas how much better I should feel, and how much comfort I should take, if only once before he died I had held him in my arms! What? Yes, certainly, quite unclad, in order the better to enjoy him. If he is dead, I am very wicked not to destroy myself. Why? Can it harm my lover for me to live on after he is dead, if I take no pleasure in anything but in the woe I bear for him? In giving myself up to grief after his death, the very woes I court would be sweet to me, if he were only still alive. It is wrong for a woman to wish to die rather than to suffer for her lover's sake. It is certainly sweet for me to mourn him long. I would rather be beaten alive than die and be at rest."

[Once freed, Lancelot makes his way to the castle and Guinevere agrees to meet with him secretly that evening. They are separated physically by the iron bars in the castle window.]

...Then Lancelot asserts that, with the Queen's consent, he will come inside to be with her, and that the bars cannot keep him out. And the Queen replies: "Do you not see how the bars are stiff to bend and hard to break? You could never so twist, pull or drag at them as to dislodge one of them." "Lady," says he, "have no fear of that. It would take more than these bars to keep me out. . . ."

Then the Queen retires, and he prepares to loosen the window. Seizing the bars, he pulls and wrenches them until he makes them bend and drags them from their places. But the iron was so sharp that the end of his little finger was cut to the nerve, and the first joint of the next finger was torn; but he who is intent upon something else paid no heed to any of his wounds or to the blood which trickled down. Though the window is not low, Lancelot gets through it quickly and easily . . . then he comes to the bed of the Queen, whom he adores and before whom he kneels, holding her more dear than the relic of any saint. And the Queen extends her arms to him and, embracing him, presses him tightly against her bosom, drawing him into the bed beside her and showing him every possible satisfaction: her love and her heart go out to him. It is love that prompts her to treat him so; and if she feels great love for him, he feels a hundred thousand times as much for her. For there is no love at all in other hearts compared with what there is in his; in his heart love was so completely embodied that it was niggardly toward all other hearts. Now Lancelot possesses all he wants, when the Queen voluntarily seeks his company and love, and when he holds her in his arms, and she holds him in hers. Their sport is so agreeable and sweet, as they kiss and fondle each other, that in truth such a marvellous joy comes over them as was never heard or known. But their joy will not be revealed by me, for in a story it has no place. Yet, the most choice and delightful satisfaction was precisely that of which our story must not speak. That night Lancelot's joy and pleasure was very great. But, to his sorrow, day comes when he must leave his mistress' side. It cost him such pain to leave her that he

suffered a real martyr's agony. His heart now stays where the   180
Queen remains; he has not the power to lead it away, for it
finds such pleasure in the Queen that it has no desire to leave
her: so his body goes, and his heart remains . . .

Q How do Roland (Reading 11.2) and
Lancelot compare as medieval heroes?
And what "brave deeds" does each
undertake to achieve his goal?

Lancelot's worship of Guinevere and his repeated references to her "saintliness" illustrate the confusion of sensual
and spiritual passions that characterized the culture of the
High Middle Ages. The fact that Lancelot uses the termi-
nology of religious worship to flatter an unfaithful wife
suggests the paradoxical nature of the so-called religion
of love associated with courtly romance. However one
explains this phenomenon, *Lancelot* remains representative
of the climate of shifting values and the degeneration of
feudal ideals, especially those of honor and loyalty among
gentleman-warriors.

The Poetry of the *Troubadours*

During the Early Middle Ages, few men and women could
read or write. But by the eleventh century, literacy was
spreading beyond the cathedral schools and monasteries.
The popularity of such forms of vernacular literature as
lyric poetry, the chronicle, and the romance gives evidence of increasing lay literacy among upper-class men
and women. To entertain the French nobility, *trouvères* (in
the north) and *troubadours* (in the south) composed and
performed poems devoted to courtly love, chivalry, religion, and politics. The most famous collection of such lyric
poems, the *Carmina Burana*, came from twelfth-century
France. In German-speaking courts, *Minnesingers* provided
a similar kind of entertainment, while *Meistersingers*, masters of the guilds of poets and musicians, flourished somewhat later in German towns.

Unlike the minstrels of old, *troubadours* were usually
men and women of noble birth. Their poems, like the
chansons of the Early Middle Ages, were monophonic and
syllabic, but they were more expressive in content and
more delicate in style, betraying their indebtedness to Arab
poetic forms. Often, *troubadours* (or the professional musicians who recited their poems) accompanied themselves
on a lyre or a lute (see Figure 10.15). Many of the 2600
extant *troubadour* poems exalt the passionate affection of a
gentleman for a lady, or, as in those written by the twenty
identifiable *trobairitzes* (female *troubadours*), the reverse
(Figure **11.22**).

Influenced by Islamic verse such as that found in
chapter 10, *troubadour* poems generally manifest a positive, even joyous, response to physical nature and the
world of the senses. An eleventh-century poem by
William IX, duke of Aquitaine and one of the first
troubadours, compares the anticipation of sexual fulfillment with the coming of spring. It opens with these
high-spirited words:

Figure 11.22 *Konrad von Altstetten Smitten by Spring and His Beloved*, from
the Manesse Codex, Zürich, ca. 1300. Manuscript illumination, 14 × 9⅞ in. This
richly illuminated manuscript is the single largest collection of medieval German
love songs. The poems of over 140 *Minnesingers* are represented here, along
with colorful illustrations and the heraldic devices of the poets.

> In the sweetness of the new season
> when woods burst forth and birds
> sing, each in its own voice
> to the lyrics of a new song,
> *then* should one seize
> the pleasures one most desires.

In a more melancholic vein, the mid-twelfth-century poet
Bernart de Ventadour explored the popular theme of
unrequited love in the poem "When I behold the lark."
Occasionally, *troubadour* verse gives evidence of hostility
between upper and lower social classes. Such is the case
with the second of the poems printed here, in which
the *troubadour* Peire Cardenal levels a fierce attack on
social inequity and upper-class greed. The third voice
represented below is that of a woman: the countess of Dia
(often called "Beatriz") was a twelfth-century *trobairitz*; her
surviving four songs are filled with personal laments for
lost love ("I've been in great anguish") and impassioned
enticements of physical pleasure.

🎵 See Music Listening Selections at end of chapter.

Bernart de Ventadour's "When I behold the lark"

When I behold the lark arise   1
with wings of gold for heaven's height,
to drop at last from flooded skies,
lost in its fullness of delight,
such sweetness spreads upon the day   5
I envy those who share the glee.
My heart's so filled with love's dismay
I wait its breaking suddenly.

I thought in love's ways I was wise,
yet little do I know aright.   10
I praised a woman as love's prize
and she gives nothing to requite.
My heart, my life she took in theft,
she took the world away from me,
and now my plundered self is left   15
only desire and misery.

Her rule I'm forced to recognize
since all my broken joys took flight.
I looked within her lifted eyes,
that mirror sweet with treacherous might: 20
O mirror, here I weep and dream
of depths once glimpsed and now denied.
I'm lost in you as in the stream
comely Narcissus looked and died.

Now trust in indignation dies   25
and womanhood I henceforth slight.
I find that all her worths are lies.
I thought her something made of light.
And no one comes to plead for me
with her who darkens all my days.   30
Woman I doubt and now I see
that she like all the rest betrays.

Aye, pity women all despise.
Come face the truth and do not fight.
The smallest kindness she denies,   35
yet who but she should soothe my plight?
So gentle and so fair is she,
it's hard for others to believe.
She, who could save, in cruelty
watches her wasting lover grieve.   40

My love has failed and powerless lies;
devotion bears for me no right.
She laughs to hear my deepest sighs—
then silently I'll leave her sight.
I cast my love of her away.   45
She struck and I accept the blow.
She will not speak and I must stray
in exile. Where, I do not know.

Tristan, I've made an end, I say.
I'm going—where, I do not know.   50

My song is dying, and away
all love and joy I cast, and go.

Peire Cardenal's "Lonely the rich need never be"

Lonely the rich need never be,   1
they have such constant company.
For Wickedness in front we see,
behind, all round, and far and wide.
The giant called Cupidity   5
is always hulking at their side.
Injustice waves the flag, and he
is led along by Pride . . .

If a poor man has snitched a bit of rag,
he goes with downcast head and frightened eye.   10
But when the rich thief fills his greedy bag,
he marches on with head still held as high.
The poor man's hanged, he stole a rotten bridle.
The man who hanged him stole the horse. O fie.
To hang poor thieves the rich thieves still aren't idle.   15
That kind of justice arrow-swift will fly . . .

The rich are charitable? Yes,
as Cain who slew his brother Abel.
They're thieves, no wolves as merciless.
They're liars, like a whoreshop-babel.   20
O stick their ribs, O stick their souls!
No truth comes bubbling from the holes,
but lies. Their greedy hearts, abhorrent,
are rabid as a mountain-torrent . . .

With loving-kindness how they quicken,   25
what hoards of charity they spread.
If all the stones were loaves of bread,
if all the streams with wine should thicken,
the hills turn bacon or boiled chicken,
they'd give no extra crumb. That's flat,   30
    Some people are like that.

The Countess of Dia's "I've been in great anguish"

I've been in great anguish   1
over a noble knight I once had,
and I want everyone to know, for all time,
that I loved him—too much!
Now I see I'm betrayed   5
because I didn't yield my love to him.

For that I've suffered greatly,
both in my bed and when I'm fully clad.

How I'd yearn to have my knight
in my naked arms for one night!   10
He would feel a frenzy of delight
only to have me for his pillow.
I'm more in love with him
than Blancheflor ever was with Floris.[1]

---

[1] The lovers in a popular medieval romance.

To him I'd give my heart, my love,   15
my mind, my eyes, my life.

Beautiful, gracious, sweet friend,
when shall I hold you in my power?
If I could lie with you for one night,
and give you a kiss of love,   20
you can be sure I would desire greatly
to grant you a husband's place,
as long as you promised
to do everything I wished!

Q **On what specific topics and themes are these songs focused?**

Q **What do these themes reveal about the culture that produced the *troubadours*?**

The Origins of Constitutional Monarchy

The new social consciousness voiced by Peire Cardenal was a reflection of political and economic change, especially in England. In the year 1215, the barons of the realm forced the English king John (1167–1216) to sign the landmark document known as the Magna Carta ("great charter"). The document forbade the king to levy additional feudal taxes without the consent of his royal council. It also guaranteed other privileges, such as trial by jury. Although it was essentially a feudal agreement between English noblemen and their king, it became one of the most significant documents in the history of political freedom: by asserting the primacy of the law over the will of the ruler, the Magna Carta established the principle that paved the way for the development of constitutional monarchy.

Some fifty years after the signing of the Magna Carta, the English nobility, demanding equal authority in ruling England, imprisoned King Henry III (1207–1272) and invited representatives of a new class of people "midway" between serfs and lords—the middle class—to participate in the actions of the Great Council (Parliament). The Council was the first example of representative government among the rising nation-states of the West.

The Rise of Medieval Towns

Medieval kings looked for financial support from the middle class, and especially from the taxes provided by commercial activity. Increased agricultural production and the reopening of trade routes encouraged urban development, a process that usually began with the establishment of the local market. By the end of the eleventh century, merchants—often the disenfranchised younger sons of the nobility—were engaging in commercial enterprises that required local trade markets. Usually located near highways or rivers, outside the walls of a fortified castle (*bourg* in French, *burg* in German, *borough* in English), the market (*faubourg*) became part of manorial life. The permanent market eventually grew into the medieval town—an urban center that attracted farmers and artisans who might buy freedom from their lord or simply run away from the manor. "City air makes a man free" was the cry of those who had discovered the urban alternative to manorial life.

In the newly established towns, the middle class pursued profit from commercial exchange. Merchants and craftspeople in like occupations formed **guilds** for the mutual protection of buyers and sellers. The guilds regulated prices, fixed wages, established standards of quality in the production of goods, and provided training for newcomers in each profession. During the eleventh and twelfth centuries, urban dwellers purchased charters of self-government from lords in whose fiefs their towns were situated. Such charters allowed townspeople (*bourgeois* in French; *Burghers* in German) to establish municipal governments and regulate their own economic activities. Such commercial centers as Milan, Florence, and Venice became completely self-governing city-states similar to those of ancient Greece and Rome. The self-governing Flemish cities of Bruges and Antwerp exported fine linen and wool to England and to towns along the Baltic Sea. The spirit of urban growth was manifested in the construction of defensive stone walls that protected the citizens, as at Carcassonne in southwestern France (Figure **11.23**), and in the building of cathedrals and guildhalls that flanked the open marketplace. Although by the twelfth century town-dwellers constituted less than 15 percent of the total European population, the middle class continued to expand and ultimately it came to dominate Western society.

Middle-class values differed considerably from those of the feudal nobility. Whereas warfare and chivalry preoccupied the nobility, financial prosperity and profit were

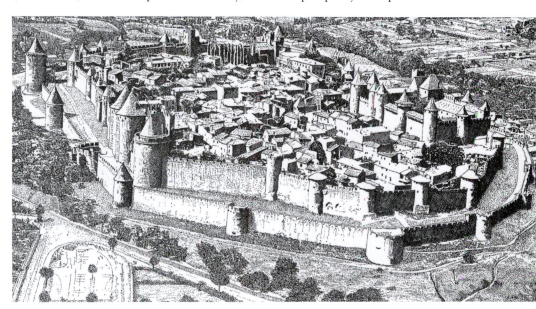

Figure 11.23 The walled city of Carcassonne, France, twelfth to thirteenth centuries.

the principal concerns of the middle class. In European cities, there evolved a lively vernacular literature expressive of middle-class concerns. It included humorous narrative tales (*fabliaux*) and poems (*dits*) describing urban occupations, domestic conflict, and street and tavern life (Figure **11.24**). These popular genres, which feature such stereotypes as the miserly husband and the lecherous monk, slyly reflect many of the social tensions and sexual prejudices of the day. A favorite theme of medieval *fabliaux* and *dits* was the antifemale diatribe, a denunciation of women as bitter as Juvenal's (see chapter 6), and one that was rooted in a long tradition of misogyny (the hatred of women). While medieval romances generally cast the female in a positive light, *fabliaux* and *dits* often described women as sinful and seductive. The hostile attitude toward womankind, intensified perhaps by women's increasing participation in some of the commercial activities traditionally dominated by men, is readily apparent in both urban legislation and the popular literature of the late thirteenth century. The following verse, based on a widely circulated proverb, voices a popular male complaint:

> He who takes a wife trades peace for strife,
> Long weariness, despair, oppress his life,
> A heavy load, a barrel full of chatter,
> Uncorkable, her gossip makes a clatter,
> Now, ever since I took a wife,
> Calamity has marred my life.

Figure 11.24 *Young Lady Shopping for Belts and Purses,* from the Manesse Codex, Zürich, ca. 1315–1333. Purses such as those hanging on the rod were usually handsomely embroidered and worn at the lady's waist.

LOOKING BACK

The Germanic Tribes

- The westward migrations of the Germanic tribes threatened the stability of the already waning Roman Empire. Nevertheless, these peoples introduced customs and values that came to shape the character of the European Middle Ages.
- Germanic languages, laws, and forms of artistic expression fused with those of the late Roman and newly Christianized world to fix the patterns of early medieval life. Germanic bonds of fealty and cavalry warfare gave rise to the medieval practice of feudalism, while Germanic custom would have lasting influence on the development of law in the West.
- The Anglo-Saxon epic *Beowulf* and the art of Sutton Hoo are landmarks of Germanic cultural achievement. Metalwork techniques and the decorative zoomorphic style influenced the evolution of early medieval religious art and artifacts.

Charlemagne and the Carolingian Renaissance

- Charlemagne's hope of restoring the Roman Empire under Christian leadership led to the conquest of vast areas of land; his holy wars resulted in the forcible conversion of the Saxons east of the Rhine River, the Lombards of northern Italy, and the Slavic peoples along the Danube.
- By the ninth century, the Holy Roman Empire had become the cultural oasis of the West. Under Charlemagne's influence, much of Europe converted to Christianity, while members of his court worked to encourage education and the arts.
- Charlemagne cast himself as the prototype of Christian kingship. He controlled conquered lands by placing them in the hands of local administrators. He revived trade with the East, stabilized currency, and pursued diplomatic ties with Baghdad.

- The Carolingian Renaissance saw the rebirth of monumental architecture, bronze casting, and manuscript illumination. The Carolingian abbey church became the focal point of monastic life as well as the repository of sacred relics that drew pilgrims from neighboring areas. In the construction of the abbey church, as in the arrangement of the monastic complex as a whole, Classical principles of symmetry and order prevailed.

Early Medieval Culture

- In the turbulent century following the fragmentation of the Carolingian Empire, feudalism—the exchange of land for military service—gave noblemen the power to rule locally while providing protection from outside attack.
- The artistic monuments of the Early Middle Ages—the *Song of Roland,* the Norman castle, and the Bayeux

Tapestry—all describe a heroic age that glorified feudal combat, male prowess, and the conquest of land.

- Manorialism, the economic basis for medieval society, offered the lower classes physical protection in exchange for food production.

High Medieval Culture

- The Christian Crusades altered the patterns of economic and cultural life, even as they marked the revival of European mobility. While no territorial gains were made in the Muslim East, the Crusades encouraged the rise of towns and trade dominated by a new middle class, whose ambitions were materialistic and profit-oriented.
- Changing patterns of secular life between the years 700 and 1300 reflect the shift from a feudal society to an urban one. The values of merchants and craftspeople differed from those of the feudal nobility, for whom land had provided the basis of wealth, and chivalry had dictated manners and morals.
- In the courtly literature of the High Middle Ages, sentiment and sensuousness replaced the heroic idealism and chivalric chastity of the early medieval era. Romantic love, a medieval invention, dominated both the vernacular romance and *troubadour* poetry. Vernacular tales and poems often satirized inequality between classes and antagonism between the sexes.

Music Listening Selection

- Bernart de Ventadour, "Can vei la lauzeta mouver" ("When I behold the lark"), ca. 1150, excerpt.

Glossary

chain mail a flexible medieval armor made of interlinked metal rings

chalice a goblet; in Christian liturgy, the Eucharistic cup

chanson de geste (French, "song of heroic deeds") an epic poem of the Early Middle Ages

chivalry a code of behavior practiced by upper-class men and women of medieval society

cloisonné (French, *cloison*, meaning "fence") an enameling technique produced by pouring molten colored glass between thin metal strips secured to a metal surface; any object ornamented in this manner (see Figure 11.2)

common law the body of unwritten law developed primarily from judicial decisions based on custom and precedent; the basis of the English legal system and that of all states in the United States with the exception of Louisiana

crenellations tooth-shaped battlements surmounting a wall and provided protection during defensive combat

fealty loyalty; the fidelity of the warrior to his chieftain

feudalism the system of political organization prevailing in Europe between the ninth and fifteenth centuries and having as its basis the exchange of land for military defense

fief in feudal society, land or property given to a warrior in return for military service

guild an association of merchants or craftspeople organized according to occupation

investiture the procedure by which a feudal lord granted a vassal control over a fief

jongleur a professional entertainer who wandered from court to court in medieval Europe

joust a form of personal combat, usually with lances on horseback, between men-at-arms

keep a square tower, the strongest and most secure part of the medieval castle (see Figure 11.17)

kenning a two-term metaphor used in Old English verse

lord any member of the feudal nobility who invested a vassal with a fief

mace a heavy, spike-headed club used as a weapon in medieval combat

medieval romance a tale of adventure that deals with knights, kings, and ladies acting under the impulse of love, religious faith, or the desire for adventure

moat a wide trench, usually filled with water, surrounding a fortified place such as a castle (see Figure 11.17)

niello a black sulfurous substance used as a decorative inlay for incised metal surfaces; the art or process of decorating metal in this manner

paten a shallow dish; in Christian liturgy, the Eucharistic plate

primogeniture the principle by which a fief was passed from father to eldest son

refectory dining hall

renaissance (French, "rebirth") a revival of the learning of former and especially Classical culture

scriptorium (plural **scriptoria**) a monastic writing room

serf an unfree peasant

vassal any member of the feudal nobility who vowed to serve a lord in exchange for control of a fief

zoomorphic animal-shaped; having the form of an animal

Chapter 12

Christianity and the Medieval Mind

ca. 1000–1300

"All earthly things is but vanity:
Beauty, Strength, and Discretion, do man forsake,
Foolish friends and kinsmen, that fair spake,
All fleeth save Good Deeds . . ."
Everyman

Figure 12.1 *The Mouth of Hell*, from the Psalter of Henry of Blois, Bishop of Winchester, twelfth century, 12⅔ × 8¾ in. An angel locks the gate that opens into the mouth of a fanged dragon; among the souls being tormented by demons are three royal figures (wearing gold crowns). Note the protruding serpentine creatures—survivals of Anglo-Saxon and Viking art.

There is much about the medieval world—its knights in shining armor, its walled castles, and its bloody Crusades—that provides the stuff of modern fantasy. In reality, however, the Middle Ages had a powerful influence on the evolution of basic Western values, beliefs, and practices. The geographic contours of modern European states, as well as their political and linguistic traditions, emerged during this era. As Europe's population rose from 27 million in 700 to 73 million in 1300, the High Middle Ages saw the rise of new urban institutions, including the medieval university. At the same time, the Roman Catholic Church reached its peak as the dominant political, religious, and cultural authority. Its doctrines and its liturgy gave coherence and meaning to everyday life. Its earthly ministers, the priesthood, shepherded Christians through the rites of passage that marked the soul's pilgrimage to salvation. Its view of the terrestrial world as divinely ordered by an all-knowing God dominated all aspects of medieval expression.

The Medieval Church

During the High Middle Ages, the Catholic Church exercised great power and authority not only as a religious force, but also as a political institution. The papacy asserted the Church of Rome as the sole authority in Christendom, a position strongly opposed by the patriarchs of the Greek Orthodox Church in Constantinople. This disagreement, complicated by long-standing doctrinal and liturgical differences, led to a permanent breach in 1054 between the Eastern and Western churches. In the West, the papacy took strong measures to ensure the independence of the Church from secular interference, especially by the emerging European states. In 1022, the Church formed the College of Cardinals as the sole body responsible for the election of popes. Medieval pontiffs functioned much like secular monarchs, governing a huge and complex bureaucracy that incorporated financial, judicial, and disciplinary branches. The Curia, the papal council and highest church court, headed a vast network of ecclesiastical courts, while the Camera (the papal treasury) handled financial matters. The medieval Church was enormously wealthy. Over the centuries, Christians had donated and bequeathed to Christendom so many thousands of acres of land that, by the end of the twelfth century, the Catholic Church was the largest single landholder in Western Europe.

Among lay Christians of every rank the Church commanded religious obedience. It enforced religious conformity by means of such spiritual penalties as **excommunication** (exclusion from the sacraments) and **interdict**, the excommunication of an entire city or state—used to dissuade secular rulers from opposing papal policy. In spite of these spiritual weapons, **heresy** (denial of the revealed truths of the Christian faith) spread rapidly within the increasingly cosmopolitan centers of twelfth-century Europe. Such anticlerical groups as the Waldensians (followers of the thirteenth-century French reformer Peter Waldo) denounced the growing worldliness of the Church. Waldo proposed that lay Christians administer the sacraments and that the Bible—sole source of religious authority—should be translated into the vernacular.

Condemning such views as threats to civil and religious order, the Church launched antiheretical crusades that were almost as violent as those advanced against the Muslims. Further, in 1233, the pope established the Inquisition, a special court designed to stamp out heresy. The Inquisition brought to trial individuals whom local townspeople denounced as heretics. Deprived of legal counsel, the accused were usually tried in secret. Inquisitors might use physical torture to obtain confession, for the Church considered injury to the body preferable to the eternal damnation of the soul. If the Inquisition failed to restore accused heretics to the faith, it might impose such penalties as exile or excommunication, or it might turn over the defendants to the state to be hanged or burned at the stake—the latter being the preferred punishment for female heretics. With the same energy that the Church persecuted heretics, it acted as a civilizing agent. It preserved order by enforcing periods in which warfare was prohibited. It assumed moral and financial responsibility for the poor, the sick, and the homeless; and it provided for the organization of hospitals, refuges, orphanages, and other charitable institutions.

The power and prestige of the Church were enhanced by the outstanding talents of some popes as diplomats, canon lawyers, and administrators. Under the leadership of the lawyer-pope Innocent III (d. 1216), one of Christendom's most influential popes, the papacy emerged as the most powerful political institution in Western Europe. Pope Innocent enlarged the body of canon law and refined the bureaucratic machinery of the Church. He used his authority to influence secular rulers and frequently intervened in the political, financial, and personal affairs of heads of state.

The Christian Way of Life and Death

Christianity made the promise of personal salvation central to the medieval world-view. It provided a unique system by which medieval Christians might achieve final victory over death. Through the **sacraments**, a set of sacred rites that impart **grace** (the free and unearned favor of God), medieval Christians were assured of the soul's redemption from sin and, ultimately, of eternal life in the world to come. The seven sacraments—the number fixed by the Fourth Lateran Council of 1215—touched every significant phase of human life: at birth, baptism purified the recipient of

The Conflict Between Church and State

As secular rulers grew in power among the burgeoning nation-states of medieval Europe, the early medieval alliance between Church and state slowly deteriorated. The attempts of kings and emperors to win the allegiance of their subjects—especially those in the newly formed towns—and to enlarge their financial resources often interfered with papal ambitions and Church decrees. When, for example, King Philip IV ("the Fair") of France (1268–1314) attempted to tax the clergy as citizens of the French realm, Pope Boniface VIII (ca. 1234–1303) protested, threatening to excommunicate and depose the king. In the dispute that followed, Pope Boniface issued the edict *Unam sanctam* ("One [and] Holy

[Church]"), the boldest assertion of spiritual authority ever published. The edict rested upon the centuries-old papal claim that the Church held primacy over the state, since, while the Church governed the souls of all Christians, the state governed only their bodies. In the ensuing struggle between popes and kings, the latter would emerge victorious. By the end of the fourteenth century, as European rulers freed themselves of papal interference in temporal affairs, the separation of Church and state—each acting as sole authority in its own domain—would become established practice in the West. Nevertheless, *Unam sanctam* remained the classic justification for Church supremacy in both temporal and spiritual realms.

Original Sin; confirmation admitted the baptized to full church privileges; ordination invested those entering the clergy with priestly authority; matrimony blessed the union of man and woman; penance acknowledged repentance of sins and offered absolution; Eucharist—the central and most important of the sacraments—joined human beings to God by means of the body and blood of Jesus; and finally, just prior to death, extreme unction provided final absolution from sins.

By way of the sacraments, the Church participated in virtually every major aspect of the individual's life, enforcing a set of values that determined the collective spirituality of Christendom. Since only church officials could administer the sacraments, the clergy held a "monopoly" on personal salvation. Medieval Christians thus looked to representatives of the Mother Church as shepherds guiding the members of their flock on their long and hazardous journey from cradle to grave. Their conduct on earth determined whether their souls went to Heaven, Hell, or Purgatory (the place of purification from sins). But only by way of the clergy might they receive the gifts of grace that made salvation possible.

By the twelfth century, Christian concepts of sin and salvation had become ever more complex: church councils identified Purgatory as an intermediate realm occupied by the soul after death (and before the Last Judgment). In Purgatory punishment was imposed for the unexpiated but repented sins committed in mortal life. While ordinary Christians might suffer punishment in Purgatory, they might also benefit from prayers and good works offered on their behalf. The role of the priesthood in providing such forms of remission from sin would give the medieval Church unassailable power and authority.

The Franciscans

At the Fourth Lateran Council (1215), Pope Innocent III endorsed the establishment of a new monastic order

that would revive the humane candor and devotional simplicity of the Sermon on the Mount. The Franciscans took their name from their founder, Giovanni Bernardone (1181–1226), whose father had nicknamed

Figure 12.2 GIOTTO, *Sermon to the Birds*, ca. 1290. Fresco, 8 ft. 10⅓ in. × 6 ft. 8⅔ in. Upper Church of San Francesco, Assisi, Italy. The humanized devotionalism of the Franciscans would be reflected as well in Giotto's tender and realistic depictions of sacred subjects (see Figures 15.8 and 15.10).

him "Francesco." The son of a wealthy Italian cloth merchant, Francis renounced a life of luxury and dedicated himself to preaching and serving the poor. In imitation of the apostles, he practiced absolute poverty and begged for his food and lodging as he traveled from town to town. Unlike Saint Benedict (see chapter 9) and other cloistered followers of Christ, Francis chose to evangelize among the citizens of the rapidly rising Italian city-states. His mendicant (begging) lifestyle made him an icon of humility; and his attention to the poor and the sickly revived the compassionate ideals of Early Christianity and of Jesus himself. Some of the legends written after the death of Francis reported that the body of the saint bore stigmata, the marks of crucifixion. Others described Francis as a missionary to all of God's creation, hence the popular depiction of the saint sermonizing to the beasts and the birds (Figure **12.2**). In the song of praise written by Francis two years before his death, his reverence for nature is displayed with a forthright simplicity that resembles both the hymns of Ambrose (see Reading 9.2) and the ritual prayers chanted by Native Americans in praise of nature (see Reading 18.5).

READING 12.1 Saint Francis' *The Canticle of Brother Sun* (1224)

Most High, all-powerful, good Lord,	1
Yours are the praises, the glory, the honor, and all blessing.	
To You alone, Most High, do they belong,	
and no man is worthy to mention Your name.	
Praised be You, my Lord, with all your creatures,	
especially Sir Brother Sun,	
Who is the day and through whom You give us light.	
And he is beautiful and radiant with great splendor;	
and bears a likeness of You, Most High One.	
Praised be You, my Lord, through Sister Moon and the stars,	10
in heaven You formed them clear and precious and beautiful.	
Praised be You, my Lord, through Brother Wind,	
and through the air, cloudy and serene, and every kind of weather	
through which You give sustenance to Your creatures.	
Praised be You, my Lord, through Sister Water,	
which is very useful and humble and precious and chaste.	
Praised be You, my Lord, through Brother Fire,	
through whom You light the night	
and he is beautiful and playful and robust and strong.	
Praised be You, my Lord, through our Sister Mother Earth,	20
who sustains and governs us,	
and who produces varied fruits with colored flowers and herbs.	
Praised be You, my Lord, through those who give pardon for Your love	
and bear infirmity and tribulation.	
Blessed are those who endure in peace	
for by You, Most High, they shall be crowned.	
Praised be You, my Lord, through our Sister Bodily Death,	
from whom no living man can escape.	
Woe to those who die in mortal sin.	
Blessed are those whom death will find in Your most holy will,	30
for the second death shall do them no harm.	

Praise and bless my Lord and give Him thanks
and serve Him with great humility.

Q **What is the relationship between God and nature in this song of praise?**

The Franciscans were not the sole exemplars of the wave of humanitarianism that swept through the Christian West during the thirteenth century: in 1216 the followers of the well-educated Spanish priest Saint Dominic (ca. 1170–1221) founded a second mendicant order devoted to teaching and preaching. Deeply committed to the study of theology, the Dominicans educated many renowned scholars, including Thomas Aquinas, discussed later in this chapter. The Franciscan and Dominican friars ("brothers") earned longlasting respect and acclaim for educating the young, fighting heresy, and ministering to the sick and needy.

Saint Francis and Saint Dominic drew many into their folds, but their female followers had a difficult time establishing orders in their name. The Fourth Lateran Council had confirmed Church restrictions prohibiting nuns from hearing confession, preaching, and singing the Gospel—measures that limited the freedom and privileges of Benedictine nuns and other holy women. The new orders denied female participation, since neither Francis nor Dominic considered the apostolic life suitable for women. Nevertheless, one of the followers of Saint Francis, Clare Affreduccio (1193–1253), a young noblewoman from Assisi, renounced a life of aristocratic privilege to establish a community of women modeled on the practice of poverty and humility. Initially denied papal approval for a monastic order, Clare had her rule endorsed only days before she died. She was the first woman to write a rule for a religious order; the Order of Poor Ladies came to be called the Order of Saint Clare, or the "Poor Clares."

Medieval Literature

The Literature of Mysticism

Most of the religious literature of the Middle Ages was didactic—that is, it served to teach and instruct. Visionary literature, however, functioned in two other ways. It reflected an individual's intuitive and direct knowledge of God (thus constituting a form of autobiography); and it conjured vivid images of the supernatural (thus providing a vocabulary by which the unknowable might actually be known). The leading mystic of the twelfth century, Hildegard of Bingen (1098–1179), was an extraordinary individual. Entering a Benedictine convent at the age of eight, she went on to become its abbess. A scholar of both Latin and her native German, she wrote three visionary tracts, treatises on natural science, medicine, and the treatment of disease, an allegorical dialogue between the vices and the virtues, and a cycle of seventy-seven songs for devotional performance (see chapter 13). While some regard Hildegard as the *first* of the female visionaries, she actually follows a long line of mystics and seers whose history begins in antiquity (most famously represented by the Delphic priestesses and the Roman sibyls). One of the first great Christian mystics, however, Hildegard produced original works on such topics as the nature of the universe, the meaning of Scripture, and the destiny of the Christian soul. The Church confirmed the divine source of her visions and, along with most of her contemporaries, acknowledged her prophetic powers. In the following selection from *Scivias*, short for *Scito vias domini* (*Know the Ways of the Lord*), her encounter with the "voice from Heaven" is followed by two of her most compelling visions. The miniature accompanying one of these visions (Figure **12.3**)—like all those that illustrate her manuscripts—was supervised by Hildegard herself.

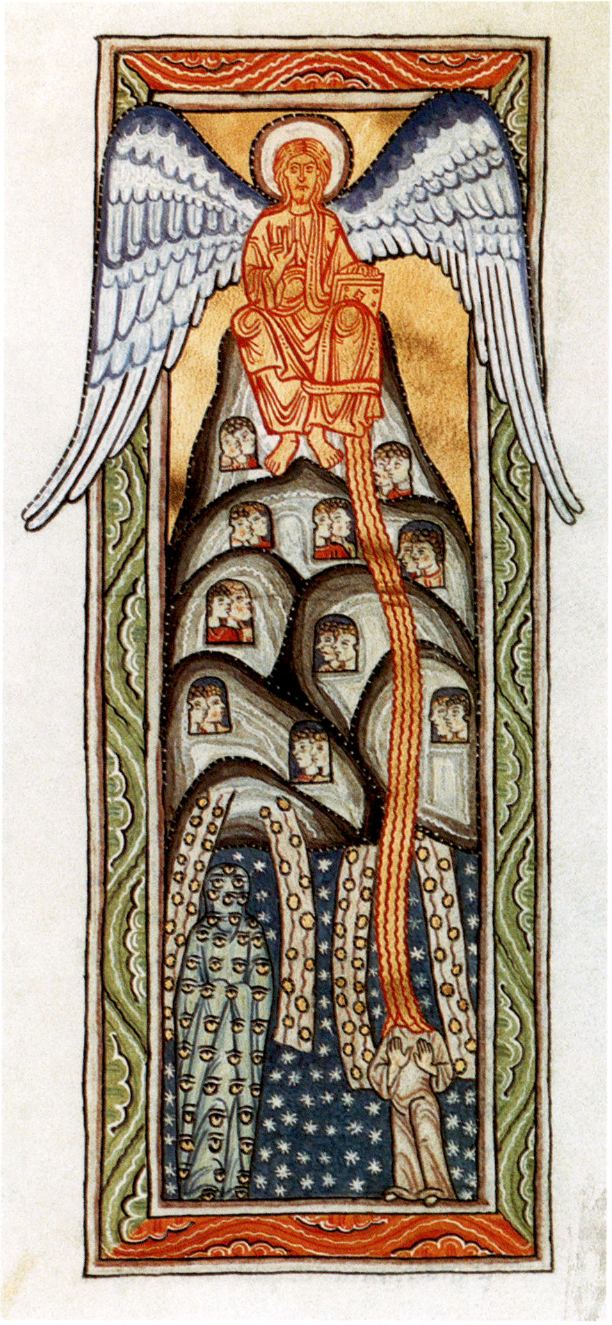

Figure 12.3 HILDEGARD OF BINGEN, *Scivias*, ca. 1146. Height 12⅖ in. The revelation is pictured as a burst of "fiery light" that flows from the angelic figure of Jesus at the top of the illustration to the small image of Hildegard (bottom right). The voice from Heaven orders Hildegard: "Speak," in a manner similar to the command ("Recite") of the archangel Gabriel to Muhammad (see chapter 10).

READING 12.2 From Hildegard of Bingen's *Know the Ways of the Lord* (ca. 1146)

1. A Solemn Declaration Concerning the True Vision Flowing from God: *Scivias*. Protestificatio

Lo! In the forty-third year of my temporal course, when I clung to a celestial vision with great fear and tremulous effort, I saw a great splendor. In it came a voice from heaven, saying: [1]

"O frail mortal, both ash of ashes, and rottenness of rottenness, speak and write down what you see and hear. But because you are fearful of speaking, simple at expounding, and unlearned in writing—speak and write, not according to the speech of man or according to the intelligence of human invention, or following the aim of human composition, but according to what you see and hear from the heavens above [10] in the wonders of God! Offer explanations of them, just as one who hears and understands the words of an instructor willingly makes them public, revealing and teaching them according to the sense of the instructor's discourse. You, therefore, O mortal, speak also the things you see and hear. Write them, not according to yourself or to some other person, but according to the will of the Knower, Seer, and Ordainer of all things in the secrets of their mysteries."

And again I heard the voice from heaven saying to me: "Speak these wonders and write the things taught in this [20] manner—and speak!"

It happened in the year 1141 of the Incarnation of the Son of God, Jesus Christ, when I was forty-two years and seven months old, that a fiery light of the greatest radiance coming from the open heavens flooded through my entire brain. It kindled my whole breast like a flame that does not scorch but warms in the same way the sun warms anything on which it sheds its rays.

Suddenly I understood the meaning of books, that is, the Psalms and the Gospels; and I knew other catholic books of [30] the Old as well as the New Testaments—not the significance of the words of the text, or the division of the syllables, nor did I consider an examination of the cases and tenses.

Indeed, from the age of girlhood, from the time that I was fifteen until the present, I had perceived in myself, just as until this moment, a power of mysterious, secret, and marvelous visions of a miraculous sort. However, I revealed these things to no one, except to a few religious persons who were living under the same vows as I was. But meanwhile, until this time when God in his grace has willed these things to be revealed, [40] I have repressed them in quiet silence.

But I have not perceived these visions in dreams, or asleep, or in a delirium, or with my bodily eyes, or with my external mortal ears, or in secreted places, but I received them awake and looking attentively about me with an unclouded mind, in open places, according to God's will. However this may be, it is difficult for carnal man to fathom. . . .

2. The Iron-Colored Mountain and the Radiant One: *Scivias*. Book I, Vision 1

I saw what seemed to be a huge mountain having the color of iron. On its height was sitting One of such great radiance that it stunned my vision. On both sides of him extended a gentle shadow like a wing of marvelous width and length. And in front of him at the foot of the same mountain stood a figure full of eyes everywhere. Because of those eyes, I was not able to distinguish any human form.

In front of this figure there was another figure, whose age was that of a boy, and he was clothed in a pale tunic and white shoes. I was not able to look at his face, because above his head so much radiance descended from the One sitting on the mountain. From the One sitting on the mountain a great many living sparks cascaded, which flew around those figures with great sweetness. In this same mountain, moreover, there seemed to be a number of little windows, in which men's heads appeared, some pale and some white.

And see! The One sitting on the mountain shouted in an extremely loud, strong voice, saying: "O frail mortal, you who are of the dust of the earth's dust, and ash of ash, cry out and speak of the way into incorruptible salvation! Do this in order that those people may be taught who see the innermost meaning of Scripture, but who do not wish to tell it or preach it because they are lukewarm and dull in preserving God's justice. Unlock for them the mystical barriers. For they, being timid, are hiding themselves in a remote and barren field. You, therefore, pour yourself forth in a fountain of abundance! Flow with mystical learning, so that those who want you to be scorned because of the guilt of Eve may be inundated by the flood of your refreshment!

"For you do not receive this keenness of insight from man, but from that supernal and awesome judge on high. There amidst brilliant light, this radiance will brightly shine forth among the luminous ones. Arise, therefore, and shout and speak! These things are revealed to you through the strongest power of divine aid. For he who potently and benignly rules his creatures imbues with the radiance of heavenly enlightenment all those who fear him and serve him with sweet love in a spirit of humility. And he leads those who persevere in the path of justice to the joys of everlasting vision!"

3. The Fall of Lucifer, the Formation of Hell, and the Fall of Adam and Eve: *Scivias*. Book I, Vision 2

Then I saw what seemed to be a great number of living torches, full of brilliance. Catching a fiery gleam, they received a most radiant splendor from it. And see! A lake appeared here, of great length and depth, with a mouth like a well, breathing forth a stinking fiery smoke. From the mouth of the lake a loathsome fog also arose until it touched a thing like a blood vessel that had a deceptive appearance.

And in a certain region of brightness, the fog blew through the blood vessel to a pure white cloud, which had emerged from the beautiful form of a man, and the cloud contained within itself many, many stars. Then the loathsome fog blew and drove the cloud and the man's form out of the region of brightness.

Once this had happened, the most luminous splendor encircled that region. The elements of the world, which previously had held firmly together in great tranquility, now, turning into great turmoil, displayed fearful terrors. . . .

Now "that lake of great length and depth" which appeared to you is Hell. In its length are contained vices, and in its deep abyss is damnation, as you see. Also, "it has a mouth like a well, breathing forth a stinking, fiery smoke" means that drowning souls are swallowed in its voracious greed. For although the lake shows them sweetness and delights, it leads them, through perverse deceit, to a perdition of torments. There the heat of the fire breathes forth with an outpouring of the most loathsome smoke, and with a boiling, death-dealing stench. For these abominable torments were prepared for the Devil and his followers, who turned away from the highest good, which they wanted neither to know nor to understand. For this reason they were cast down from every good thing, not because they did not know them but because they were contemptuous of them in their lofty pride. . . .

Q **What role does revelation play in Hildegard's visions?**

Q **Which of her visionary images do you find most vivid?**

Sermon Literature

While the writings of Hildegard of Bingen addressed individual, literate Christians, medieval sermons, delivered orally from the pulpit of the church, were directed to the largely illiterate Christian community. Both visionary tracts and sermon literature, however, described grace and salvation in vivid terms. The classic medieval sermon *On the Misery of the Human Condition* (ca. 1200) was written by Innocent III. This sermon is a compelling description of the natural sinfulness of humankind and a scathing condemnation of the "vile and filthy [human] condition." Such motifs, like those found in Hildegard's visions, proceeded from prevailing views of the human condition: weighed down by the burden of the flesh, the body is subject to corruption, disease, and carnal desire. As the temple of the soul, the body will be resurrected on Judgment Day, but not before it suffers the trials of mortality. Warning of the "nearness of death," Innocent's sermon functioned as a *memento mori*, a device by which listeners in a predominantly oral culture might "remember death" and thus prepare themselves for its inevitable arrival. Innocent's portrayal of the decay of the human body reflects the medieval disdain for the world of matter, a major theme in most medieval didactic literature. During the Late Middle Ages, especially after the onslaught of the bubonic plague (see chapter 15), the motif of the body as "food for worms"—one of Innocent's most vivid images—became particularly popular in gruesomely forthright tomb sculptures (Figure **12.4**).

Innocent's vivid account of the Christian Hell transforms the concept of corruption into an image of eternal punishment for unabsolved sinners—a favorite subject for medieval artists (see Figures **12.1** and **12.8**). The contrast

Figure 12.4 Detail of *transi* (effigy of the dead) of François de la Sarra, ca. 1390. La Sarraz, Switzerland. Length 5 ft. (approx.). Worms crawl into the flesh of the deceased, while toads gnaw at his eyes and mouth.

that Innocent draws between physical death and spiritual life has its visual counterpart in the representations of the Last Judgment depicted in medieval manuscripts and on Romanesque and Gothic church portals (see Figure 13.8).

READING 12.3 From Pope Innocent III's *On the Misery of the Human Condition* (ca. 1200)

Of the Miserable Entrance upon the Human Condition

. . . Man was formed of dust, slime, and ashes: what is even more vile, of the filthiest seed. He was conceived from the itch of the flesh, in the heat of passion and the stench of lust, and worse yet, with the stain of sin. He was born to toil, dread, and trouble; and more wretched still, was born only to die. He commits depraved acts by which he offends God, his neighbor, and himself; shameful acts by which he defiles his name, his person, and his conscience; and vain acts by which he ignores all things important, useful, and necessary. He will become fuel for those fires which are forever hot and burn forever bright; food for the worm which forever nibbles and digests; a mass of rottenness which will forever stink and reek. . . . [10]

On the Nearness of Death

A man's last day is always the first in importance, but his first day is never considered his last. Yet it is fitting to live always on this principle, that one should act as if in the moment of death. For it is written: "Remember that death is not slow."[1] Time passes, death draws near. In the eyes of the dying man a thousand years are as yesterday, which is past. The future is forever being born, the present forever dying, and what is past is utterly dead. We are forever dying while we are alive; we only cease to die when we cease to live. Therefore it is better to die to life than to live waiting for death, for mortal life is but a living death. . . . [20]

On the Putrefaction of the Dead Body

. . . Man is conceived of blood made rotten by the heat of lust; and in the end worms, like mourners, stand about his corpse. In life he produced lice and tapeworms; in death he will produce worms and flies. In life he produced dung and vomit; in death he produces rottenness and stench. In life he fattened one man; in death he fattens a multitude of worms. What then is more foul than a human corpse? What is more horrible than [30] a dead man? He whose embrace was pure delight in life will be a gruesome sight in death.

Of what advantage, then, are riches, food, and honors? For riches will not free us from death, neither food protect us from the worm, nor honors from the stench. That man who but now sat in glory upon a throne is now looked down on in the grave; the dandy who once glittered in his palace lies now naked and vile in his tomb; and he who supped once on delicacies in his hall is now in his sepulcher food for worms. . . .

That Nothing Can Help the Damned

. . . O strict judgment!—not only of actions, but "of every idle [40] word that men shall speak, they shall render an account";[2] payment with the usurer's interest will be exacted to the last penny. "Who hath showed you to flee from the wrath to come?"[3]

"The Son of Man shall send his angels and they shall gather out of his kingdom all scandals, and them that work iniquity, and they will bind them as bundles to be burnt, and shall cast them into the furnace of fire. There shall be weeping and gnashing of teeth,"[4] there shall be groaning and wailing, shrieking and flailing of arms and screaming, screeching, and [50] shouting; there shall be fear and trembling, toil and trouble, holocaust and dreadful stench, and everywhere darkness and anguish; there shall be asperity, cruelty, calamity, poverty, distress, and utter wretchedness; they will feel an oblivion of loneliness and namelessness; there shall be twistings and piercings, bitterness, terror, hunger and thirst, cold and hot, brimstone and fire burning, forever and ever world without end. . . .

Q How does Innocent describe the nature and the destiny of humankind?

Q How does this sermon compare with the Sermon on the Mount (Reading 8.2)?

---

[1] Ecclesiastes 14:12.

[2] Matthew 12:36.
[3] Luke 3:7.
[4] Matthew 13:41–42.

The Medieval Morality Play

While medieval churches rang with sermons, town squares (often immediately adjacent to a cathedral) became open-air theaters for the dramatization of Christian history and legend. To these urban spaces, townspeople flocked to see dramatic performances that might last from sunrise to sunset. The **mystery play** dramatized biblical history from the fall of Lucifer to the Last Judgment, while the **miracle play** enacted stories from the Life of Christ, the Virgin, or the saints. The **morality play**, the third type of medieval drama, dealt with the struggle between good and evil and the destiny of the soul in the hereafter. The first medieval morality play, Hildegard of Bingen's *Ordo virtutum* (*Play of the Virtues*) was a twelfth-century allegorical dialogue between vice and virtue. All these types of play were performed by members of the local guilds, and mystery plays were usually produced on **pageants** (roofed wagon-stages) that were rolled into the town square. Medieval plays were a popular form of entertainment, as well as a source of religious and moral instruction.

Medieval drama, like Greek drama, had its roots in religious performance. The Catholic Mass, the principal rite of Christian worship, admitted all the trappings of theater: colorful costumes, symbolic props, solemn processions, dramatic gestures, and ceremonial music. It is likely that the gradual dramatization of church liturgy (see chapter 13) influenced the genesis of mystery and miracle plays. The morality play, however, had clear precedents in allegorical poetry and sermon literature. Allegory—a literary device we have encountered in Plato's *Republic* (Reading 4.6) and in Augustine's *City of God* (Reading 9.4)—uses symbolic figures to capture the essence of a person, thing, or idea. The characters in the morality play are personifications of abstract qualities and universal conditions. In the play *Everyman*, for instance, the main character represents *all* Christian souls, Fellowship stands for friends, Goods for worldly possessions, and so forth.

Although *Everyman* has survived only in fifteenth-century Dutch and English editions, plays similar to it originated considerably earlier. The most popular of all medieval morality plays, *Everyman* symbolically recreates the pilgrimage of the Christian soul to its ultimate destiny. The play opens with the Messenger, who expounds on the transitory nature of human life. The subsequent conversation between Death and God, somewhat reminiscent of that between Satan and God in the Book of Job (see chapter 1), shows God to be an angry, petulant figure who finds human beings "drowned in sin." If left to their own devices, he opines, "they will become much worse than beasts." As the action unfolds, Everyman realizes that Death has come for him. Frightened and unprepared, he soon discovers that his best friends, his kin, his worldly possessions—indeed, all that he so treasured in life—will not accompany him to the grave. Knowledge, Five-Wits, Beauty, and Discretion may point the way to redemption, but they cannot save him. His only ally is Good-Deeds, which, with the assistance of the Catholic priesthood, will help him win salvation. *Everyman* is essentially a moral allegory that dramatizes the pilgrimage of the Christian soul from earthly existence to Last Judgment. Like Innocent's sermon, it teaches that life is transient, that worldly pleasures are ultimately valueless, and that sin can be mitigated solely by salvation earned through grace as dispensed by the Church.

─ READING 12.4 From *Everyman* (ca. 1500)

Characters

Messenger	Cousin	Strength
God (Adonai)	Goods	Discretion
Death	Good-Deeds	Five-Wits
Everyman	Knowledge	Angel
Fellowship	Confession	Doctor
Kindred	Beauty	

HERE BEGINNETH A TREATISE HOW THE HIGH FATHER OF HEAVEN SENDETH DEATH TO SUMMON EVERY CREATURE TO COME AND GIVE ACCOUNT OF THEIR LIVES IN THIS WORLD AND IS IN MANNER OF A MORAL PLAY.

Messenger: I pray you all give your audience,	1
And hear this matter with reverence,	
By figure a moral play—	
The Summoning of Everyman called it is,	
That of our lives and ending shows	
How transitory we be all day.[1]	
This matter is wondrous precious,	
But the intent of it is more gracious,	
And sweet to bear away.	
The story saith—Man, in the beginning,	10
Look well, and take good heed to the ending,	
Be you never so gay!	
Ye think sin in the beginning full sweet,	
Which in the end causeth thy soul to weep,	
When the body lieth in clay.	
Here shall you see how *Fellowship* and *Jollity*,	
Both *Strength*, *Pleasure*, and *Beauty*,	
Will fade from thee as flower in May.	
For ye shall hear, how our heaven king	
Calleth *Everyman* to a general reckoning:	20
Give audience, and hear what he doth say.	
God: I perceive here in my majesty,	
How that all creatures be to me unkind,[2]	
Living without dread in worldly prosperity:	
Of ghostly[3] sight the people be so blind,	
Drowned in sin, they know me not for their God:	
In worldly riches is all their mind,	
They fear not my right wiseness, the sharp rod:	
My law that I shewed, when I for them died,	
They forget clean, and shedding of my blood red:	30
I hanged between two, it cannot be denied:	
To get them life I suffered to be dead:	
I healed their feet, with thorns hurt was my head:	

---

[1] Always.
[2] Ungrateful.
[3] Spiritual.

I could do no more than I did truly,
And now I see the people do clean forsake me,
They use the seven deadly sins damnable;
As pride, covetise, wrath, and lechery,
Now in the world be made commendable;
And thus they leave of angels the heavenly company;
Everyman liveth so after his own pleasure,   40
And yet of their life they be nothing sure:
I see the more that I them forbear
The worse they be from year to year;
All that liveth appaireth[4] fast,
Therefore I will in all the haste
Having a reckoning of Everyman's person
For and[5] I leave the people thus alone
In their life and wicked tempests,
Verily they will become much worse than beasts;
For now one would by envy another up eat;   50
Charity they all do clean forget.
I hoped well that Everyman
In my glory should make his mansion,
And thereto I had them all elect;
But now I see, like traitors deject,
They thank me not for the pleasure that I to them meant
Nor yet for their being that I them have lent;
I proffered the people great multitude of mercy,
And few there be that asketh it heartily;
They be so cumbered with worldly riches,   60
That needs of them I must do justice,
On Everyman living without fear.
Where art thou, Death, thou mighty messenger?
    Death: Almighty God, I am here at your will,
Your commandment to fulfil.
    God: Go thou to Everyman,
And show him in my name
A pilgrimage he must on him take,
Which he in no wise may escape:
And that he bring with him a sure reckoning   70
Without delay or any tarrying.
    Death: Lord, I will in the world go run over all,
And cruelly outsearch both great and small;
Every man will I beset that liveth beastly
Out of God's laws, and dreadeth not folly:
He that loveth riches I will strike with my dart,
His sight to blind, and from heaven to depart,
Except that alms be his good friend,
In hell for to dwell, world without end.
Lo, yonder I see Everyman walking;   80
Full little he thinketh on my coming;
His mind is on fleshly lusts and his treasure,
And great pain it shall cause him to endure
Before the Lord Heaven King.
Everyman, stand still; whither art thou going
Thus gaily? Hast my Maker forgot?
    Everyman: Why askst thou?
Wouldest thou wete?[6]

    Death: Yea, sir, I will show you;
In great haste I am sent to thee   90
From God out of his majesty.
    Everyman: What, sent to me?
    Death: Yea, certainly.
Though thou have forget him here,
He thinketh on thee in the heavenly sphere,
As, or [ere] we depart, thou shalt know.
    Everyman: What desireth God of me?
    Death: That shall I show thee;
A reckoning he will needs have
Without any longer respite.   100
    Everyman: To give a reckoning longer leisure I crave;
This blind matter troubleth my wit.
    Death: On thee thou must take a long journey:
Therefore thy book of count with thee thou bring:
For turn again thou can not by no way.
And look thou be sure of thy reckoning:
For before God thou shalt answer, and show
Thy many bad deeds and good but a few;
How thou hast spent thy life, and in what wise,
Before the chief lord of paradise.   110
Have ado that we were in that way,
For, wete thou well, thou shalt make none attournay.[7]
    Everyman: Full unready I am such reckoning to give.
I know thee not: what messenger art thou?
    Death: I am Death, that no man dreadeth.
For every man I rest[8] and no man spareth;
For it is God's commandment
That all to me should be obedient.
    Everyman: O Death, thou comest when I had thee least
        in mind,
In thy power it lieth me to save,   120
Yet of my good[s] will I give thee, if ye will be kind,
Yea, a thousand pound shalt thou have,
And defer this matter till another day.
    Death: Everyman, it may not be by no way;
I set not by gold, silver, nor riches,
Ne by pope, emperor, king, duke, ne princes,
For and I would receive gifts great,
All the world I might get;
But my custom is clean contrary.
I give thee no respite: come hence, and not tarry.   130
    Everyman: Alas, shall I have no longer respite?
I may say Death giveth no warning:
To think on thee, it maketh my heart sick,
For all unready is my book of reckoning.
But twelve year and I might have abiding,
My counting book I would make so clear,
That my reckoning I should not need to fear.
Wherefore, Death, I pray thee, for God's mercy.
Spare me till I be provided of remedy.
    Death: Thee availeth not to cry, weep, and pray: 140
But haste thee lightly that you were gone the journey.
And prove thy friends if thou can.
For, wete thou well, the tide abideth no man,

---

[4] Decays.
[5] If.
[6] Know.

[7] Mediator.
[8] Arrest.

And in the world each living creature
For Adam's sin must die of nature.

    Everyman: Death, if I should this pilgrimage take,
And my reckoning surely make,
Show me, for saint charity,
Should I not come again shortly?

    Death: No, Everyman; and thou be once there, 150
Thou mayst never more come here,
Trust me verily.

    Everyman: O gracious God, in the high seat celestial,
Have mercy on me in this most need;
Shall I have no company from this vale terrestrial
Of mine acquaintance that way me to lead?

    Death: Yea, if any be so hardy,
That would go with thee and bear thee company.
Hie thee that you were gone[9] to God's magnificence,
Thy reckoning to give before his presence. 160
What, weenest[10] thou thy life is given thee,
And thy worldly goods also?

    Everyman: I had wend[11] so, verily.

    Death: Nay, nay; it was but lent thee;
For as soon as thou art go,
another awhile shall have it, and then go therefrom
Even as thou has done.
Everyman, thou art mad; thou hast thy wits five,
And here on earth will not amend thy life,
For suddenly I do come. 170

    Everyman: O wretched caitiff,[12] whither shall I flee,
That I might scape this endless sorrow!
Now, gentle Death, spare me till to-morrow,
That I may amend me
With good advisement.

    Death: Nay, thereto I will not consent,
Nor no man will I respite,
But to the heart suddenly I shall smite
Without any advisement.
And now out of thy sight I will me nie; 180
See thou make thee ready shortly,
For thou mayst say this is the day
That no man living may scape away.

    Everyman: Alas, I may well weep with sighs deep,
Now have I no manner of company
To help me in my journey, and me to keep;
And also my writing is full unready.
How shall I do now for to excuse me?
I would to God I had never be gete![13]
To my soul a full great profit it had be; 190
For now I fear pains huge and great.
The time passeth; Lord, help that all wrought;
For though I mourn it availeth nought.
The day passeth, and is almost a-go;
I wot not well what for to do.
To whom were I best my complaint to make?

[9] Hurry and go.
[10] Do you suppose.
[11] Supposed.
[12] a cowardly or contemptible person
[13] Been born.

What, and I to Fellowship thereof spake,
And showed him of this sudden chance?
For in him is all mine affiance;[14]
We have in the world so many a day 200
Be on good friends in sport and play.
I see him yonder, certainly;
I trust that he will bear me company;
Therefore to him will I speak to ease my sorrow.
Well met, good Fellowship, and good morrow!

    Fellowship: Everyman, good morrow by this day.
Sir, why lookest thou so piteously?
If any thing be amiss, I pray thee, me say,
That I may help to remedy.

    Everyman: Yea, good Fellowship, yea. 210
I am in great jeopardy.

    Fellowship: My true friend, show to me your mind;
I will not forsake thee, unto my life's end,
In the way of good company.

    Everyman: That was well spoken, and lovingly.

    Fellowship: Sir, I must needs know your heaviness;
I have pity to see you in any distress;
If any have ye wronged he shall revenged be,
Though I on the ground be slain for thee—
Thou that I know before that I should die. 220

    Everyman: Verily, Fellowship, gramercy.[15]

    Fellowship: Tush! by thy thanks I set not a straw;
Show me your grief, and say no more.

    Everyman: If I my heart should to you break,
And then you to turn your mind from me,
And would not me comfort, when you hear me speak,
Then should I ten times sorrier be.

    Fellowship: Sir, I say as I will do in deed.

    Everyman: Then be you a good friend at need:
I have found you true here before. 230

    Fellowship: And so ye shall evermore;
For, in faith, and thou go to Hell,
I will not forsake thee by the way!

    Everyman: Ye speak like a good friend: I believe you well;
I shall deserve[16] it, and I may.

    Fellowship: I speak of no deserving, by this day.
For he that will say and nothing do
Is not worthy with good company to go;
Therefore show me the grief of your mind,
As to your friend most loving and kind. 240

    Everyman: I shall show you how it is;
Commanded I am to go a journey,
A long way, hard and dangerous,
And give a strait count without delay
Before the high judge Adonai.[17]
Wherefore I pray you, bear me company,
As ye have promised, in this journey.

    Fellowship: That is matter indeed! Promise is duty,
But, and I should take such a voyage on me,
I know it well, it should be to my pain: 250

[14] Trust.
[15] Many thanks.
[16] Repay.
[17] God.

Also it make me afeard, certain.
But let us take counsel here as well as we can,
For your words would fear[18] a strong man.
  Everyman: Why, ye said, if I had need,
Ye would me never forsake, quick nor dead,
Though it were to Hell truly.
  Fellowship: So I said, certainly,
But such pleasures be set aside, thee sooth to say:
And also, if we took such a journey,
When should we come again?   260
  Everyman: Nay, never again till the day of doom.
  Fellowship: In faith, then will not I come there!
Who hath you these tidings brought?
  Everyman: Indeed, Death was with me here.
  Fellowship: Now, by God that all hath bought,
If Death were the messenger,
For no man that is living today
I will not go that loath journey—
Not for the father that begat me!
  Everyman: Ye promised other wise, pardie.[19]   270
  Fellowship: I wot well I say so truly
And yet if thou wilt eat, and drink, and make good cheer,
Or haunt to women, the lusty company,
I would not forsake you, while the day is clear,
Trust me verily!
  Everyman: Yea, thereto ye would be ready;
To go to mirth, solace, and play
Your mind will sooner apply
Than to bear me company in my long journey.
  Fellowship: Now, in good faith, I will not that way.   280
But and thou wilt murder, or any man kill,
In that I will help thee with a good will!
  Everyman: O that is a simple advice indeed!
Gentle fellow: help me in my necessity;
We have loved long, and now I need,
And now, gentle Fellowship, remember me.
  Fellowship: Whether ye have loved me or no,
By Saint John, I will not with thee go.

. . . .

[Everyman next turns to members of his family, but both Kindred
and Cousin refuse to accompany him to the grave. He then seeks
out Goods, his worldly possessions. Goods explains that money
and treasure were only "lent" to Everyman and should have been
shared with the poor. Knowledge guides Everyman to Confession,
Discretion, Strength, Beauty, and Five-Wits, who direct him to
receive the sacrament of extreme unction.]

. . . .

Knowledge: Everyman, hearken what I say;
Go to priesthood, I you advise,   290
And receive of him in any wise
The holy sacrament and ointment together;
Then shortly see ye turn again hither;
We will all abide you here.
  Five-Wits: Yea, Everyman, hie[20]

you that ye ready were, There is no emperor, king, duke, ne baron,
That of God hath commission,
As hath the least priest in the world being;
For of the blessed sacraments pure and benign,
He beareth the keys and thereof hath the cure   300
For man's redemption, it is ever sure;
Which God for our soul's medicine
Gave us out of his heart with great pine;[21]
Here in this transitory life, for thee and me
The blessed sacraments seven there be.
Baptism, confirmation, with priesthood good,
And the sacrament of God's precious flesh and blood,
Marriage, the holy extreme unction, and penance;
These seven be good to have in remembrance,
Gracious sacraments of high divinity.   310

. . . .

[All but Good-Deeds then abandon Everyman.]

Everyman: Methinketh, alas, that I must be gone
To make my reckoning and my debts pay,
For I see my time is nigh spent away.
Take example, all ye that this do hear or see,
How they that I loved best do forsake me,
Except my Good-Deeds that bideth truly.
  Good-Deeds: All earthly things is but vanity:
Beauty, Strength, and Discretion, do man forsake,
Foolish friends and kinsmen, that fair spake,
All fleeth save Good-Deeds, and that am I.   320
  Everyman: Have mercy on me, God most mighty;
And stand by me, thou Mother and Maid, holy Mary.
  Good-Deeds: Fear not, I will speak for thee.
  Everyman: Here I cry God mercy.
  Good-Deeds: Short our end, and minish[22] our pain;
Let us go and never come again.
  Everyman: Into thy hands, Lord, my soul I commend; Receive it,
Lord, that it be not lost;
As thou me boughtest, so me defend,
And save me from the fiend's boast,   330
That I may appear with that blessed host
That shall be saved at the day of doom.
In manus tuas—of might's most
For ever—commendo spiritum meum.[23]

. . . .

Q **What key aspects of the medieval mind are
represented in this play?**

Dante's *Divine Comedy*

The medieval view of life on earth as a vale of tears was
balanced by a triumphant belief in the divine promise of
deliverance and eternal bliss. By far the most profound
statement of these ideas is the epic poem known as the
Commedia Divina or *Divine Comedy*, by the Florentine

---

[18]Terrify.
[19]By God.
[20]Hasten.

[21]Suffering.
[22]Diminish.
[23]Into your hands I commend my spirit.

Figure 12.5 DOMENICO DI MICHELINO, *Dante and His Poem*, 1465. Fresco, 9 ft. 7 in. × 10 ft. 6 in. Florence Cathedral, Italy. Dante, with an open copy of the *Commedia*, points to Hell with his right hand. The Mount of Purgatory with its seven terraces is behind him. The walled city of Florence and its cathedral (with its newly finished dome) are pictured on Dante's left. Above, the painter has depicted Paradise as a series of colored arcs complete with planets, after which each heavenly ring is named (see Figure 12.7).

poet Dante Alighieri (1265–1321). Begun ca. 1308, the *Commedia* records, on the literal level, an adventure-packed journey through the realm of the dead (Figure **12.5**). On a symbolic level, the poem describes the spiritual pilgrimage of the Christian soul from sin (Hell), through purification (Purgatory), and ultimately, to salvation (Paradise; Figures **12.6** and **12.7**). The *Divine Comedy* is the quintessential expression of the medieval mind in that it gives dramatic form to the fundamental precepts of the Christian way of life and death. The structure of the poem reflects the medieval view of the universe as the mirror of God's plan (Figure **12.8**), while the text provides an invaluable picture of the context: the ethical, political, and theological concerns of Dante's time.

Every aspect of Dante's *Commedia* carries symbolic meaning. For instance, Dante is accompanied through Hell by the Roman poet Virgil, who stands for human reason. Dante deeply admired Virgil's great epic, the *Aeneid*, and was familiar with the hero's journey to the underworld included in the sixth book of the poem. As Dante's guide, Virgil may travel only as far as the top of Mount Purgatory, for while human reason serves as the pilgrim's initial guide to salvation, it cannot penetrate the divine mysteries

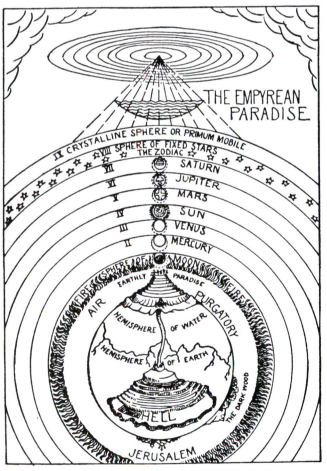

Figure 12.6 Plan of Dante's Universe.

of the Christian faith. In Paradise, Dante is escorted by Beatrice, the symbol of Divine Wisdom, modeled on a Florentine woman who had, throughout the poet's life, been the object of his physical desire and spiritual devotion. Dante structured the *Commedia* according to a strict moral hierarchy. The three parts of the poem correspond to the Aristotelian divisions of the human psyche: reason, will, and love. They also represent the potential moral conditions of the Christian soul: perversity, repentance, and grace.

Sacred numerology—especially the number 3, symbolic of the Trinity—permeates the design of the *Commedia*. The poem is divided into three canticles (books), and each canticle has thirty-three **cantos**, to which Dante added one introductory canto to total a sublime one hundred (the number symbolizing plenitude and perfection). Each canto consists of stanzas composed in *terza rima*—interlocking lines that rhyme a/b/a, b/c/b, c/d/c. There are three guides to escort Dante, three divisions of Hell and Purgatory, three main rivers in Hell. Three squared (9) are the regions of sinners in Hell, the circles of penitents in Purgatory, and the spheres of Heaven.

The elaborate numerology of the *Commedia* is matched by multileveled symbolism that draws into synthesis theological, scientific, and historical information based in ancient and medieval sources. Given this wealth of symbolism, it is remarkable that the language of the poem is so sharply realistic. For, while the characters in the *Commedia*, like those in *Everyman*, serve an allegorical function, they are, at the same time, convincing flesh-and-blood creatures. The inhabitants of Dante's universe are real people, some drawn from history and legend, others from his own era—citizens of the bustling urban centers of Italy through which Dante had wandered for nineteen years after his exile from his native Florence for political offenses. By framing the poem on both a literal level and an allegorical one, Dante reinforces the medieval (and essentially Augustinian) bond between the City of Man and the City of God. At the same time, he animates a favorite theme of medieval sermons: the warning that actions in this life bring inevitable consequences in the next.

Well versed in both Classical and Christian literature, Dante had written Latin treatises on political theory and on the origins and development of language. But for the poem that constituted his epic masterpiece, he rejected the Latin of churchmen and scholars and wrote in his native Italian, the language of everyday speech. Dante called his poem a comedy because the piece begins with affliction (Hell) and ends with joy (Heaven). Later admirers added the adjective "divine" to the title, not simply to describe its religious character, but also to praise its sublime lyrics and its artful composition.

The most lively of the canticles, and the one that best manifests Dante's talent for creating realistic images with words, is the "Inferno," the first book of the *Commedia*. With grim moral logic, sinners are assigned to one of the nine rings in Hell, where they are punished according to the nature of their sins: the violent are immersed for eternity in boiling blood, for example, and the gluttons wallow like pigs in their own excrement. By the law of symbolic retribution, the sinners are punished not *for* but *by* their sins. Those condemned for sins of passion—the least grave of sins—inhabit the conical rings at the top of Hell, while those who have committed sins of the will lie farther down. Those guilty of sins of the intellect are imprisoned still lower, deep within the pit ruled by Satan (Figure 12.9). Thus, Dante's Hell pictures a moral hierarchy in which the damned suffer the destiny they have earned.

In the last canto of the "Inferno," Dante visits the ninth circle of Hell, the very bottom of the infernal pit. Lodged in ice up to his chest, a three-faced Satan beats his six batlike wings to create a chilling wind—the setting provides sharp contrast with the flaming regions of Upper Hell. Surrounding Satan, whom Dante calls "the Emperor of the Universe of Pain," those guilty of treachery—the most foul of all sins, according to Dante—are imprisoned in the ice, "like straws in glass." Satan, weeping tears "mixed with bloody froth and pus," chews with "rakelike teeth" on the bodies of the three most infamous traitors of Christian and Classical history: Judas, Brutus, and Cassius. The dark and brooding despair that pervades the "Inferno" reflects the medieval view of Hell as the condition of the soul farthest from the light of God. Nevertheless, the last canto of the "Inferno" ends with Dante and Virgil climbing from the frozen pit "into the shining world," a motif of ascent that pervades the second and third canticles.

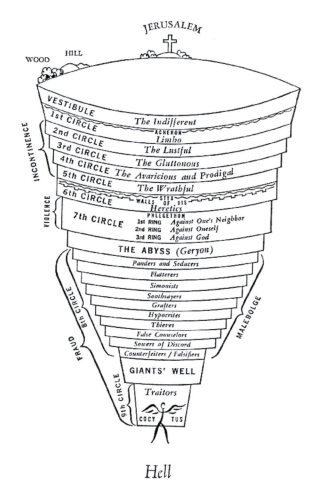

Hell

Figure 12.7 Plan of Dante's "Inferno."

Satan's domain stands in grim contrast to the blissful experience of God enjoyed by those in Paradise. Light, the least material of natural elements, is a prime image in Dante's evocation of Heaven, and light imagery—as central to the *Commedia* as it is to Saint Ambrose's hymn (see Reading 9.2)—pervades Dante's vision of the mystery and majesty of God. The last stanzas of Canto 33 of "Paradiso" are the culminating phase of that vision. In the perfect shape of the circle, as in a cathedral's rose window, Dante sees the image of humankind absorbed into the substance of God. And as that wheel of love turns, the poet discovers the redemptive radiance of God.

It is impossible to recreate the grandeur of the *Commedia* by means of two cantos, especially since, in English, a great deal of the richness of the original Tuscan dialect is lost. Nevertheless, some of the majesty of Dante's poem may be conveyed by the excerpts reproduced here.

Figure 12.8 *God as Architect of the Universe*, from the *Bible Moralisée*, thirteenth century. 13½ × 8¼ in. The Divine Geometer uses a compass to bring order to a mass of unformed matter flanked by the sun and moon. This popular medieval manuscript paired each biblical event with an illustration that explained its moral significance.

READING 12.5 From Dante's *Divine Comedy*

(ca. 1308–1321)

The Dark Wood of Error ("Inferno," Canto 1)

Midway in our life's journey, I went astray
   from the straight road and woke to find myself
   alone in a dark wood. How shall I say   3

what wood that was! I never saw so drear,
   so rank, so arduous a wilderness!
   Its very memory gives a shape to fear.   6

Death could scarce be more bitter than that place!
   But since it came to good, I will recount
   all that I found revealed there by God's grace.   9

How I came to it I cannot rightly say,
   so drugged and loose with sleep had I become
   when I first wandered there from the True Way.   12

But at the far end of the valley of evil
   whose maze had sapped my very heart with fear!
   I found myself before a little hill   15

and lifted up my eyes. Its shoulders glowed
   already with the sweet rays of that planet
   whose virtue leads men straight on every road,   18

and the shining strengthened me against the fright
   whose agony had wracked the lake of my heart
   through all the terrors of that piteous night.   21

Just as a swimmer, who with his last breath
   flounders ashore from perilous seas, might turn
   to memorize the wide water of his death—   24

so did I turn, my soul still fugitive
   from death's surviving image, to stare down
   that pass that none had ever left alive.   27

And there I lay to rest from my heart's race
   till calm and breath returned to me. Then rose
   and pushed up that dead slope at such a pace   30

each footfall rose above the last. And lo!
   almost at the beginning of the rise
   I faced a spotted Leopard, all tremor and flow   33

and gaudy pelt. And it would not pass, but stood
   so blocking my every turn that time and again
   I was on the verge of turning back to the wood.   36

This fell at the first widening of the dawn
   as the sun was climbing Aries with those stars
   that rode with him to light the new creation.   39

Thus the holy hour and the sweet season
   of commemoration did much to arm my fear

Yet not so much but what I shook with dread
   at sight of a great Lion that broke upon me
   raging with hunger, its enormous head   45

held high as if to strike a mortal terror
   into the very air. And down his track,
   a She-Wolf drove upon me, a starved horror   48

ravening and wasted beyond all belief.
   She seemed a rack for avarice, gaunt and craving.
   Oh many the souls she has brought to endless grief!   51

She brought such heaviness upon my spirit
   at sight of her savagery and desperation,
   I died from every hope of that high summit.   54

And like a miser—eager in acquisition
   but desperate in self-reproach when Fortune's wheel
   turns to the hour of his loss—all tears and attrition   57

I wavered back; and still the beast pursued,
   forcing herself against me bit by bit
   till I slid back into the sunless wood.   60

And as I fell to my soul's ruin, a presence
   gathered before me on the discolored air,
   the figure of one who seemed hoarse from long silence.   63

At sight of him in that friendless waste I cried:
   "Have pity on me, whatever thing you are,
   whether shade or living man." And it replied: 66

"Not man, though man I once was, and my blood
   was Lombard, both my parents Mantuan.
   I was born, though late, sub Julio, and bred   69

in Rome under Augustus in the noon
   of the false and lying gods. I was a poet
   and sang of old Anchises' noble son   72

who came to Rome after the burning of Troy.
   But you—why do you return to these distresses
   instead of climbing that shining Mount of Joy   75

which is the seat and first cause of man's bliss?"
   "And are you then that Virgil and that fountain
   of purest speech?" My voice grew tremulous: 78

"Glory and light of poets! now may that zeal
   and love's apprenticeship that I poured out
   on your heroic verses serve me well!   81

For you are my true master and first author,
   the sole maker from whom I drew the breath
   of that sweet style whose measures have brought me honor.   84

See there, immortal sage, the beast I flee.

For my soul's salvation, I beg you, guard me from her,
for she has struck a mortal tremor through me."   87

And he replied, seeing my soul in tears:
    "He must go by another way who would escape
    this wilderness, for that mad beast that fleers*   90

before you there, suffers no man to pass.
    She tracks down all, kills all, and knows no glut,
    but, feeding, she grows hungrier than she was.   93

She mates with any beast, and will mate with more
    before the Greyhound comes to hunt her down.
    He will not feed on lands nor loot, but honor   96

and love and wisdom will make straight his way.
    He will rise between Feltro and Feltro, and in him
    shall be the resurrection and new day   99

of that sad Italy for which Nisus died,
    and Turnus, and Euryalus, and the maid Camilla.
    He shall hunt her through every nation of sick pride   102

till she is driven back forever to Hell
    whence Envy first released her on the world.
    Therefore, for your own good, I think it well   105

you follow me and I will be your guide
    and lead you forth through an eternal place.
    There you shall see the ancient spirits tried   108

in endless pain, and hear their lamentation
    as each bemoans the second death of souls.
    Next you shall see upon a burning mountain   111

souls in fire and yet content in fire,
    knowing that whensoever it may be
    they yet will mount into the blessed choir.   114

To which, if it is still your wish to climb,
    a worthier spirit shall be sent to guide you.
    With her shall I leave you, for the King of Time,   117

who reigns on high, forbids me to come there
    since, living, I rebelled against his law.
    He rules the waters and the land and air   120

and there holds court, his city and his throne.
    Oh blessed are they he chooses!" And I to him:
    "Poet, by that God to you unknown,   123

lead me this way. Beyond this present ill
    and worse to dread, lead me to Peter's gate
    and be my guide through the sad halls of Hell."   126

And he then: "Follow." And he moved ahead
in silence, and I followed where he led.

* sneers.

Notes to "Inferno" (Canto 1)

line 1 *midway in our life's journey*: The biblical life span is three-score years and ten. The action opens in Dante's thirty-fifth year, i.e., 1300.

line 17 *that planet*: The sun. Ptolemaic astronomers considered it a planet. It is also symbolic of God as He who lights man's way.

line 31 *each footfall rose above the last*: The literal rendering would be: "So that the fixed foot was ever the lower." "Fixed" has often been translated as "right," and an ingenious reasoning can support that reading, but a simpler explanation offers itself and seems more competent: Dante is saying that he climbed with such zeal and haste that every footfall carried him above the last despite the steepness of the climb. At a slow pace, on the other hand, the rear foot might be brought up only as far as the forward foot. This device of selecting a minute but exactly centered detail to convey the whole of a larger action is one of the central characteristics of Dante's style.

lines 33, 44, 48 *Leopard, Lion, She-Wolf*: These three beasts are undoubtedly taken from Jeremiah 5:6. Many additional and incidental interpretations have been advanced for them, but the central interpretation must remain as noted. They foreshadow the three divisions of Hell (incontinence, violence, and fraud) that Virgil explains at length in Canto 11, 16–111. I am not at all sure but what the She-Wolf is better interpreted as Fraud and the Leopard as Incontinence. Good arguments can be offered either way.

lines 38–39 *Aries . . . that rode with him to light the new creation*: The medieval tradition had it that the sun was in Aries at the time of the Creation. The significance of the astronomical and religious conjunction is an important part of Dante's intended allegory. It is just before dawn of Good Friday 1300 when he awakens in the Dark Wood. Thus his new life begins under Aries, the sign of creation, at dawn (rebirth), and in the Easter season (resurrection). Moreover the moon is full and the sun is in the equinox, conditions that did not fall together on any Friday of 1300. Dante is obviously constructing poetically the perfect Easter as a symbol of his new awakening.

line 69 *sub Julio*: In the reign of Julius Caesar.

lines 95–98 *the Greyhound . . . Feltro and Feltro*: This almost certainly refers to Can Grande della Scala (1290–1329), a great Italian leader born in Verona, which lies between the towns of Feltre and Montefeltro.

lines 100–101 *Nisus, Turnus, Euryalus, Camilla*: All were killed in the war between the Trojans and the Latians when, according to legend, Aeneas led the survivors of Troy into Italy. Nisus and Euryalus (*Aeneid IX*) were Trojan comrades-in-arms who died together. Camilla (*Aeneid XI*) was the daughter of the Latian king and one of the warrior women. She was killed in a horse charge against the Trojans after displaying great gallantry. Turnus (*Aeneid XII*) was killed by Aeneas in a duel.

line 110 *the second death*: Damnation. "This is the second death, even the lake of fire." (Revelation 20:14)

lines 118–119 *forbids me to come there since, living, etc.*: Salvation is only through Christ in Dante's theology. Virgil lived and died before the establishment of Christ's teachings in Rome, and therefore cannot enter Heaven.

line 125 *Peter's gate*: The gate of Purgatory. (See "Purgatorio" 9, 76 ff.) The gate is guarded by an angel with a gleaming sword. The angel is Peter's vicar (Peter, the first pope, symbolized all popes;

i.e., Christ's vicar on earth), and is entrusted with the two great keys.

Some commentators argue that this is the gate of Paradise, but Dante mentions no gate beyond this one in his ascent to Heaven. It should be remembered, too, that those who pass the gate of Purgatory have effectively entered Heaven.

The three great gates that figure in the entire journey are: the gate of Hell (Canto 3, 1–11), the gate of Dis (Canto 8, 79–113, and Canto 9, 86–87), and the gate of Purgatory, as above.

The Ninth Circle of Hell ("Inferno," Canto 34)

"On march the banners of the King of Hell,"
   my Master said. "Toward us. Look straight ahead:
   can you make him out at the core of the frozen shell?"   **3**

Like a whirling windmill seen afar at twilight,
   or when a mist has risen from the ground—
   just such an engine rose upon my sight   **6**

stirring up such a wild and bitter wind
   I cowered for shelter at my Master's back
   there being no other windbreak I could find.   **9**

I stood now where the souls of the last class
   (with fear my verses tell it) were covered wholly:
   they shone below the ice like straws in glass.   **12**

Some lie stretched out; others are fixed in place
   upright, some on their heads, some on their
   soles; another, like a bow, bends foot to face.   **15**

When we had gone so far across the ice
   that it pleased my Guide to show me the foul creature
   which once had worn the grace of Paradise,   **18**

he made me stop, and, stepping aside, he said:
   "Now see the face of Dis! This is the place
   where you must arm your soul against all dread."   **21**

Do not ask, Reader, how my blood ran cold
   and my voice choked up with fear. I cannot write it:
   this is a terror that cannot be told.   **24**

I did not die, and yet I lost life's breath:
   imagine for yourself what I became,
   deprived at once of both my life and death.   **27**

The Emperor of the Universe of Pain
   jutted his upper chest above the ice;
   and I am closer in size to the great mountain   **30**

the Titans make around the central pit,
   than they to his arms. Now starting from this part,
   imagine the whole that corresponds to it.   **33**

If he was once as beautiful as now
   he is hideous, and still turned on his Maker,
   well may he be the source of every woe!   **36**

With what a sense of awe I saw his head
   towering above me! for it had three faces:
   one was in front, and it was fiery red,   **39**

the other two, as weirdly wonderful,
   merged with it from the middle of each shoulder
   to the point where all converged at the top of the skull;   **42**

the right was something between white and bile;
   the left was about the color that one finds
   on those who live along the banks of the Nile.   **45**

Under each head two wings rose terribly,
   their span proportioned to so gross a bird:
   I never saw such sails upon the sea.   **48**

They were not feathers—their texture and their form
   were like a bat's wings—and he beat them so
   that three winds blew from him in one great storm: **51**

it is these winds that freeze all Cocytus [the final pit of Hell].
   He wept from his six eyes, and down three chins
   the tears ran mixed with bloody froth and pus.   **54**

In every mouth he worked a broken sinner
   between his rakelike teeth. Thus he kept three
   in eternal pain at his eternal dinner.   **57**

For the one in front the biting seemed to play
   no part at all compared to the ripping: at times
   the whole skin of his back was flayed away.   **60**

"That soul that suffers most," explained the Guide,
   "is Judas Iscariot, he who kicks his legs
   on the fiery chin and has his head inside.   **63**

Of the other two, who have their heads thrust forward,
   the one who dangles down from the black face
   is Brutus: note how he writhes without a word.   **66**

And there, with the huge and sinewy arms, is the soul
   of Cassius. But the night is coming on
   and we must go, for we have seen the whole."   **69**

Then, as he bade, I clasped his neck, and he,
   watching for a moment when the wings
   were opened wide, reached over dexterously   **72**

and seized the shaggy coat of the king demon;
   then grappling matted hair and frozen crusts
   from one tuft to another, clambered down.   **75**

When we had reached the joint where the great thigh
   merges into the swelling of the haunch,
   my Guide and Master, straining terribly,   **78**

turned his head to where his feet had been
   and began to grip the hair as if he were climbing;
   so that I thought we moved toward Hell again.   **81**

"Hold fast!" my Guide said, and his breath came shrill
   with labor and exhaustion. "There is no way
   but by such stairs to rise above such evil." 84

At last he climbed out through an opening
   in the central rock, and he seated me on the rim;
   then joined me with a nimble backward spring. 87

I looked up, thinking to see Lucifer
   as I had left him, and I saw instead
   his legs projecting high into the air. 90

Now let all those whose dull minds are still vexed
   by failure to understand what point it was
   I had passed through, judge if I was perplexed. 93

"Get up. Up on your feet," my Master said.
   "The sun already mounts to middle tierce,
   and a long road and hard climbing lie ahead." 96

It was no hall of state we had found there,
   but a natural animal pit hollowed from rock
   with a broken floor and a close and sunless air. 99

"Before I tear myself from the Abyss,"
   I said when I had risen, "O my Master,
   explain to me my error in all this: 102

where is the ice? and Lucifer—how has he
   been turned from top to bottom: and how can the sun
   have gone from night to day so suddenly?" 105

And he to me: "You imagine you are still
   on the other side of the center where I grasped

the shaggy flank of the Great Worm of Evil 108

which bores through the world—you were while I climbed down,
   but when I turned myself about, you passed
   the point to which all gravities are drawn. 111

You are under the other hemisphere where you stand;
   the sky above us is the half opposed
   to that which canopies the great dry land. 114

Under the mid-point of that other sky
   the Man who was born sinless and who lived
   beyond all blemish, came to suffer and die. 117

You have your feet upon a little sphere
   which forms the other face of the Judecca [named
      for Judas Iscariot].
   There it is evening when it is morning here. 120

And this gross Fiend and Image of all Evil
   who made a stairway for us with his hide
   is pinched and prisoned in the ice-pack still. 123

On this side he plunged down from heaven's height,
   and the land that spread here once hid in the sea
   and fled North to our hemisphere for fright; 126

and it may be that moved by that same fear,
   the one peak that still rises on this side
   fled upward leaving this great cavern here." 129

Down there, beginning at the further bound
   of Beelzebub's dim tomb, there is a space
   not known by sight, but only by the sound 132

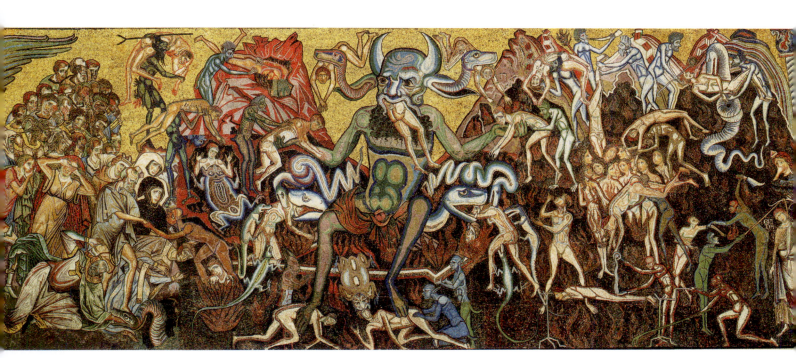

Figure 12.9 Attributed to **SCHOOL OF COPPO DI MARCOVALDO**, *Last Judgment* (detail), thirteenth century. Florence Baptistery. Mosaic, 12 × 40 ft. (approx.)

of a little stream descending through the hollow
it has eroded from the massive stone
in its endlessly entwining lazy flow.   135

My Guide and I crossed over and began
to mount that little known and lightless road
to ascend into the shining world again.   138

He first, I second, without thought of rest
we climbed the dark until we reached the point
where a round opening brought in sight the blest   141

and beauteous shining of the Heavenly cars.
And we walked out once more beneath the Stars.

———

Notes to "Inferno" (Canto 34)

line 1 *On march the banners of the King*: The hymn ("Vexilla regis
prodeunt") was written in the sixth century by Venantius Fortunatus,
bishop of Poitiers. The original celebrates the Holy Cross, and is
part of the service for Good Friday, to be sung at the moment of
uncovering the Cross.

line 17 *the foul creature*: Satan.

line 38 *three faces*: Numerous interpretations of these three faces
exist. What is essential to all explanations is that they be seen as
perversions of the qualities of the Trinity.

line 54 *bloody froth and pus*: The gore of the sinners he chews,
which is mixed with his slaver.

line 62 *Judas*: His punishment is patterned closely on that of the
Simoniacs whom Dante describes in Canto 19.

line 67 *huge and sinewy arms*: The Cassius who betrayed Caesar
was more generally described in terms of Shakespeare's "lean and
hungry look." Another Cassius is described by Cicero (*Catiline III*) as
huge and sinewy. Dante probably confused the two.

line 68 *the night is coming on*: It is now Saturday evening.

line 82 *his breath came shrill*: Cf. Canto 23, 85, where the fact that
Dante breathes indicates to the Hypocrites that he is alive. Virgil's
breathing is certainly a contradiction.

line 95 *middle tierce*: In the canonical day tierce is the period from
about 6 to 9 a.m. Middle tierce, therefore, is 7:30. In going through
the center point, they have gone from night to day. They have moved
ahead twelve hours.

line 128 *the one peak*: The Mount of Purgatory.

line 129 *this great cavern*: The natural animal pit of line 98. It is also
"Beelzebub's dim tomb," line 131.

line 133 *a little stream*: Lethe. In Classical mythology, the river of
forgetfulness, from which souls drank before being born. In Dante's
symbolism it flows down from Purgatory, where it has washed away
the memory of sin from the souls who are undergoing purification.
That memory it delivers to Hell, which draws all sin to itself.

line 143 *Stars*: As part of his total symbolism, Dante ends each of the
three divisions of the *Commedia* with this word. Every conclusion of
the upward soul is toward the stars, God's shining symbols of hope

and virtue. It is just before dawn of Easter Sunday that the Poets
emerge—a further symbolism.

**Q Why is Dante's Commedia considered a
medieval epic?**

**Q Whom does Dante find in the ninth circle of Hell?
Why are they there?**

The Medieval University

Of the many medieval contributions to modern Western
society, one of the most significant is the university.
Education in medieval Europe was almost exclusively a
religious enterprise, and monastic schools had monopolized learning for many centuries. By the twelfth century,
however, spurred by the resurgence of economic activity,
the rise of towns, and the influx of heretofore unavailable
Classical texts, education shifted from monastic and parish settings to cathedral schools located in the new urban
centers of Western Europe. Growing out of these schools,
groups of students and teachers formed guilds for higher
learning; the Latin word *universitas* describes a guild of
learners and teachers.

In medieval Europe, as in our own day, universities were
arenas for intellectual inquiry and debate. At Bologna,
Paris, Oxford, and Cambridge, to name but four among
some eighty universities founded during the Middle Ages,
the best minds of Europe grappled with the compelling ideas of their day, often testing those ideas against
the teachings of the Church. The universities offered a
basic Liberal Arts curriculum divided into two parts: the
trivium, consisting of grammar, logic, and rhetoric; and
the *quadrivium*, which comprised arithmetic, geometry,
astronomy, and music. Programs in professional disciplines, such as medicine, theology, and law, were also available. Textbooks—that is, handwritten manuscripts—were
expensive and difficult to obtain, so teaching took the
form of oral instruction, and students took copious notes
based on class lectures (Figure **12.10**). Exams for the bach-
elor of arts (B.A.) degree, usually taken upon completion
of a three-to-five-year course of study, were oral. Beyond
the B.A. degree, one might pursue additional study leading
to mastery of a specialized field. The master of arts (M.A.)
degree qualified the student to teach theology or practice

Chronology

1054	split between Roman Catholic and Greek Orthodox churches
1159	University of Bologna founded
1215	Fourth Lateran Council
1215	Franciscan order established
1302	*Unam sanctam*

law or medicine. Still another four years of study were usually required for the doctoral candidate, whose efforts culminated in his defense of a thesis before a board of learned masters. (Tradition required the successful candidate to honor his examiners with a banquet.)

Among the first universities was that founded at Bologna in northern Italy in 1159. Bologna was a center for the study of law. Its curriculum was run by students who hired professors to teach courses in law and other fields. University students brought pressure on townsfolk to maintain reasonable prices for food and lodging. They controlled the salaries and teaching schedules of their professors, requiring a teacher to obtain permission from his students for even a single day's absence and docking his pay if he was tardy. In contrast to the student-run university at Bologna, the university in Paris was a guild of teachers organized primarily for instruction in theology. This institution, which grew out of the cathedral school of Notre Dame, became independent of Church control by way of a royal charter issued in the year 1200. Its respected degree in theology drew an international student body that made Paris the intellectual melting pot of the medieval West.

Until the thirteenth century, upper-class men and women received basically the same kind of formal education. But with the rise of the university, women were excluded from receiving a higher education, much as they were forbidden from entering the priesthood. Ranging between the ages of seventeen and forty, students often held minor orders in the Church. The intellectual enterprise of the most famous of the theologically trained schoolmen (or *Scholastics*, as they came to be called) inspired an important movement in medieval intellectual life known as Scholasticism.

Medieval Scholasticism

Before the twelfth century, intellectuals (as well as ordinary men and women) considered Scripture and the writings of the church fathers to be the major repositories of knowledge. Faith in these established sources superseded rational inquiry and preempted the empirical examination of the physical world. Indeed, most intellectuals upheld the Augustinian credo that faith preceded reason. They maintained that since both faith and reason derived from God, the two could never stand in contradiction. In the late

Figure 12.10 *University Lecture by Henry of Germany*, from a medieval German edition of Aristotle's *Ethics*, second half of fourteenth century. Manuscript illumination, parchment, 7 × 8¾ in. In this all-male classroom, most of the students follow the lecturer attentively, but some appear bored, others distracted, and at least one has fallen asleep.

twelfth century, however, Arab transcriptions of the writings of Aristotle and Arab commentaries on some of his works filtered into the West from Muslim Spain and Southwest Asia. By 1200, Aristotle's *Physics* and some of his treatises on natural science were in circulation among scholars. And, within a few decades, new and better Latin translations—many surpassing those that had been translated from Arabic—were made from Greek manuscripts brought west from Constantinople. The impact of Aristotelian thought presented new intellectual and theological challenges to churchmen and scholars. How might they reconcile Aristotle's rational and dispassionate views on natural phenomena with the supernatural truths of the Christian faith? The Church's initial reaction was to ban Aristotle's works (with the exception of the *Logic*, which had long been available in the West), but efforts at censorship were futile. Indeed, in 1255, the University of Paris endorsed as required reading the entire corpus of the venerated Greek philosopher. For the next hundred years, the Scholastics engaged in an effort to reconcile the two primary modes of knowledge: faith and reason, the first as defended by theology, the second as exalted in Greek philosophy.

Even before the full body of Aristotle's works was available, a brilliant logician and popular teacher at the University of Paris, Peter Abelard (1079–ca. 1144), had inaugurated a rationalist approach to church dogma—one that emphasized the freedom to doubt and to question authority. In his treatise *Sic et Non* (*Yes and No*), written several years before the high tide of Aristotelian influence, Abelard puts into practice one of the principal devices of the Scholastic method—that of balancing opposing points of view. *Sic et Non* presents 150 conflicting opinions on important religious matters from such sources as the Old Testament, the Greek philosophers, the Latin church fathers, and the decrees of the Church. Abelard's methodical compilation of Hebrew, Classical, and Christian thought is an expression of the Scholastic inclination to collect and reconcile vast amounts of information. This impulse toward synthesis also inspired the many *compendia* (collections), *specula* ("mirrors" of knowledge), and *summa* (comprehensive treatises) that were written during the twelfth and thirteenth centuries.

The impulse toward Scholastic synthesis was shared by scholars elsewhere. In Spain, home to a large Jewish population, the brilliant rabbi and physician Moses Maimonides (1135–1205) assembled the rabbinical history of Hebrew law to produce a fourteen-volume summary known as the *Torah Mishnah*. While this work was written in Hebrew, Maimonides' more famous *Guide to the Perplexed* was written in Arabic. This effort to harmonize faith and reason drew on both the works of Aristotle (as rendered in Arabic translations) and the teachings of rabbinical Judaism. The *Guide* examines such traditional matters as free will and the existence of evil, but argues that the truths of revelation are beyond rational demonstration.

Thomas Aquinas

Maimonides' *Guide* would influence the writings of the greatest of the Scholastics, Thomas Aquinas (1225–1274). A Dominican theologian and teacher, Aquinas lectured and wrote on a wide variety of theological and biblical subjects, but his major contribution was the *Summa Theologica*, a vast compendium of virtually all the major theological issues of the High Middle Ages. In this unfinished work, which exceeds Abelard's *Sic et Non* in both size and conception, Aquinas poses 631 questions on topics ranging from the nature of God to the ethics of money lending. The comprehensiveness of Aquinas' program is suggested by the following list of queries drawn arbitrarily from the *Summa*:

Whether God exists
Whether God is the highest good
Whether God is infinite
Whether God wills evil
Whether there is a trinity in God
Whether it belongs to God alone to create
Whether good can be the cause of evil
Whether angels assume bodies
Whether woman should have been made in the first production of things
Whether woman should have been made from man
Whether the soul is composed of matter and form
Whether man has free choice
Whether paradise is a corporeal place
Whether there is eternal law
Whether man can merit eternal life without grace
Whether it is lawful to sell a thing for more than it is worth

In dealing with each question, Aquinas follows Abelard's method of marshaling opinions that seem to oppose or contradict each other. But where Abelard merely mediates, Aquinas offers carefully reasoned answers; he brings to bear all the intellectual ammunition of his time in an effort to prove that the truths of reason (those proceeding from the senses and from the exercise of logic) are compatible with the truths of revelation (those that have been divinely revealed). Aquinas begins by posing an initial question—for instance, "Whether woman should have been made in the first production of things"; then he offers objections or negations of the proposition, followed by positive responses drawn from a variety of authoritative sources (mainly Scripture and the works of the early church fathers; see chapter 9). The exposition of these "seeming opposites" is followed by Aquinas' own opinion, a synthesis that invariably reconciles the contradictions. Finally, Aquinas provides "reply objections" answering the original objections one by one. So, for example, Objection 3, which argues that woman should not have been created because she constituted an "occasion for sin," is countered by Reply Objection 3, which asserts God's power to "direct any evil (even that of womankind) to a good end."

In the following excerpt, Aquinas deals with the question of whether and to what purpose God created women, whom most medieval churchmen regarded as the "daughters of Eve" and hence the source of humankind's depravity. Following Aristotle, Aquinas concludes that, although inferior to man in "the discernment of reason," woman was created as man's helpmate in reproducing the species. Significantly, however, Aquinas denies Aristotle's claim that woman is a defective male, and, elsewhere in the *Summa*, he holds that women should retain property rights and their own earnings. Even this brief examination of the *Summa Theologica* reveals its majestic intellectual sweep, its hierarchic rigor, and its power of synthesis—three of the principal characteristics of medieval cultural expression.

READING 12.6 From Thomas Aquinas' *Summa Theologica* (1274)

Whether Woman Should Have Been Made in the First Production of Things? We proceed thus to the First Article:

Objection 1. It would seem that woman should not have been made in the first production of things. For the Philosopher[1] says, that "the female is a misbegotten male." But nothing misbegotten or defective should have been in the first production of things. Therefore woman should not have been made at that first production.

Objection 2. Further, subjection and limitation were a result of sin, for to the woman was it said after sin (*Gen.* iii. 16): "Thou shalt be under the man's power;" and Gregory[2] says that, "Where there is no sin, there is no inequality." But woman is naturally of less strength and dignity than man; "for the agent is always more honorable than the patient," as Augustine says. Therefore woman should not have been made in the first production of things before sin.

Objection 3. Further, occasions of sin should be cut off. But God foresaw that the woman would be an occasion of sin to man. Therefore He should not have made woman.

On the contrary, It is written (*Gen.* ii. 18): "It is not good for man to be alone; let us make him a helper like to himself."

I answer that, It was necessary for woman to be made, as the Scripture says, as a "helper" to man; not, indeed, as a helpmate in other works, as some say, since man can be more efficiently helped by another man in other works; but as a helper in the work of generation.... Among perfect animals, the active power of generation belongs to the male sex, and the passive power to the female. And

[1] Aristotle.
[2] Gregory the Great (see chapter 9).

as among animals there is a vital operation nobler than generation, to which their life is principally directed; therefore the male sex is not found in continual union with the female in perfect animals, but only at the time of coition; so that we may consider that by this means the male and female are one, as in plants they are always united; although in some cases one of them preponderates, and in some the other. But man is yet further ordered to a still nobler vital action, and that is intellectual operation. Therefore there was greater reason for the distinction of these two forces in man; so that the female should be produced separately from the male; although they are carnally united for generation. Therefore directly after the formation of woman, it was said: "And they shall be two in one flesh" (*Gen.* ii. 24).

Reply to Objection 1. As regards the individual nature, woman is defective and misbegotten, for the active force in the male seed tends to the production of a perfect likeness in the masculine sex; while the production of woman comes from defect in the active force, or from some material indisposition, or even from some external influence; such as that of a south wind, which is moist, as the Philosopher observes. On the other hand, as regards human nature in general, woman is not misbegotten, but is included in nature's intention as directed to the work of generation. Now the general intention of nature depends on God, Who is the universal Author of nature. Therefore, in producing nature, God formed not only the male but also the female.

Reply to Objection 2. Subjection is twofold. One is servile, by virtue of which a superior makes use of a subject for his own benefit; and this kind of subjection began after sin. There is another kind of subjection, which is called economic or civil, whereby the superior makes use of his subjects for their own benefit and good; and this kind of subjection existed even before sin. For good order would have been wanting in the human family if some were not governed by others wiser than themselves. So by such a kind of subjection woman is naturally subject to man, because in man the discretion of reason predominates. Nor is inequality among men excluded by the state of innocence, as we shall prove.

Reply to Objection 3. If God had deprived the world of all those things which proved an occasion of sin, the universe would have been imperfect. Nor was it fitting for the common good to be destroyed in order that individual evil might be avoided; especially as God is so powerful that He can direct any evil to a good end....

Q What does this reading reveal about the potential conflict between reason and authority?

The Scholastics aimed at producing a synthesis of Christian and Classical learning, but the motivation for and the substance of their efforts were still largely religious. Despite their attention to Aristotle's writings and their respect for his methods of inquiry, medieval Scholastics created no system of knowledge that completely dispensed with supernatural assumptions. Nevertheless, the Scholastics were the humanists of the medieval world; they held that the human being, the noblest and most rational of God's creatures, was the link between the created universe and divine intelligence. They believed that human reason was the handmaiden of faith, and that reason—although incapable of transcending revelation—was essential to the understanding of God's divine plan.

The Medieval Church

- The Catholic Church was the dominant political, religious, and cultural force of the European Middle Ages. Wealthy and powerful, it governed vast lands, a complex bureaucracy, and a large body of secular and regular clergymen.
- By means of excommunication, interdict, and the Inquisition, the Church challenged a rising tide of heresy. Despite increasingly powerful secular rulers among the European states, the Church maintained a position of political dominance in the West.
- At the Fourth Lateran Council (1215), Pope Innocent III authorized the Franciscan order, the first of the mendicant orders that worked to revive Early Christian ideals of poverty, compassion, and humility.
- The Christian immortality ideology taught that life on earth was transient and that, depending on their conduct on earth, Christian souls would reap reward or punishment in an eternal hereafter. These concepts colored all aspects of medieval expression.

- By way of the sacraments, the Church participated in virtually every major aspect of the individual's life, enforcing a set of values that determined the collective spirituality of Christendom. Only the clergy could dispense the means by which the medieval Christian achieved personal salvation.

Medieval Literature

- The visionary tracts of Hildegard of Bingen brought the Scripture to life in dazzling allegorical prose. Medieval sermons and morality plays warned Christians of the perpetual struggle between good and evil and reminded them of the need to prepare for death.
- The morality play *Everyman* is a medieval allegory. It teaches that life is transient, that worldly goods are ultimately valueless, that only one's good works accompany one to the grave, and, finally, that in the soul's pilgrimage to salvation, the Church is the sole guide.
- The medieval mind perceived the visible world as a reflection of invisible truths, which, in God's universal scheme,

followed a predesigned and unchanging order. The late medieval work that best reflects these ideas is Dante's *Commedia*. Written in the medieval Italian vernacular, this tripartite epic poem describes the Christian pilgrimage through Hell, Purgatory, and Paradise.

The Medieval University

- With the rise of universities in twelfth-century Bologna, Paris, and elsewhere, intellectual life flourished. The leading teachers at the University of Paris, Abelard and Aquinas, were proponents of Scholasticism, a movement aimed at reconciling faith and reason.
- The effort to collect and reconcile vast amounts of information, in part a response to the influx of medieval Arabic transcriptions of Aristotle, complemented the move toward intellectual synthesis. Among Scholastics, matters concerning the eternal destiny of the soul and the fulfillment of God's design became the focus of humanist inquiry.

Glossary

canto one of the main divisions of a long poem

excommunication ecclesiastical censure that excludes the individual from receiving the sacraments

grace the free, unearned favor of God

heresy the denial of the revealed truths or orthodox doctrine by a baptized member of the Church; an opinion or doctrine contrary to Church dogma

interdict the excommunication of an entire city, district, or state

memento mori (Latin, "remember death") a warning of the closeness of death and the need to prepare for one's own death

miracle play a type of medieval play that dramatized the lives of, and especially the miracles performed by, Christ, the Virgin Mary, or the saints

morality play a type of medieval play that dramatized moral themes, such as the conflict between good and evil

mystery play a type of medieval play originating in church liturgy and dramatizing biblical history from the fall of Satan to the Last Judgment

pageant a roofed wagon-stage on which medieval plays and spectacles were performed

sacrament a sacred rite or pledge; in medieval Christianity, a visible sign (instituted by Jesus Christ) of God's grace

The Medieval Synthesis in the Arts

ca. 1000–1300

*"That which is united in splendor, radiates in splendor
And the magnificent work inundated with the new light shines."*
Abbot Suger

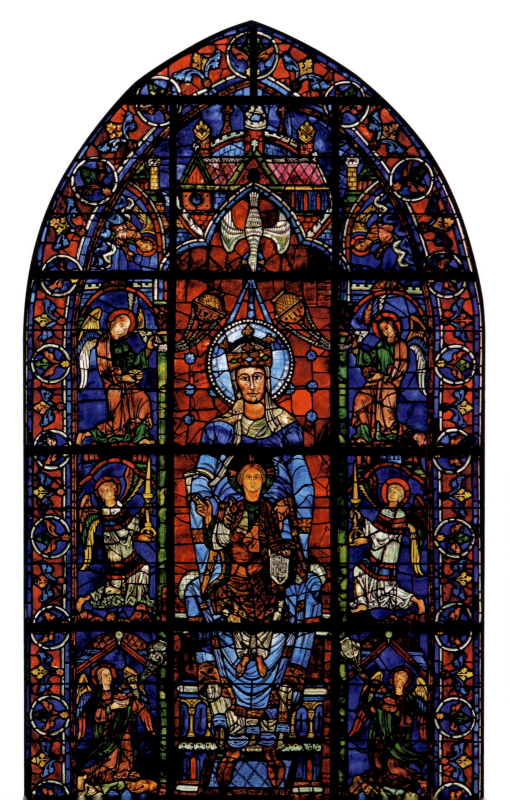

Figure 13.1 *Notre Dame de la Belle Verrière* ("Our Lady of the Beautiful Glass"), twelfth century. Stained glass, height 7ft. 4⅔ in. Chartres Cathedral. Heavily restored in recent centuries, the central panel of this magnificent stained glass window was one of the few treasures to survive the fire of 1194. Here, the stiffly posed Mother of God shares the stylized features of Romanesque sculpture, while the angels surrounding her, added in the thirteenth century, reflect the lively realism of the Gothic style.

If the Catholic Church was the major source of moral and spiritual instruction, it was also the patron and wellspring of artistic creativity. Its great monastic complexes, majestic cathedrals, painted altarpieces, illuminated manuscripts, and liturgical music all reflect the irrepressible vitality of an age of faith. While each of these genres retained its distinctive quality, each contributed to a grand synthesis, the all-embracing "whole" of Christian belief and worship. As with Dante's *Commedia* and Aquinas' *Summa*, the enterprise of synthesis involved the reconciliation of many diverse components. It drew inspiration from the idea of God as Master Architect (see Figure 12.8). If the macrocosm (the lesser universe) was designed by God so that no part stands independent of the whole, then the microcosm (the lesser universe of the Christian on earth) must mirror that design. The medieval architect, artist, and composer served the Christian community by recreating the majesty of God's plan. While operating to point the way to salvation, their creations worked to unite the temporal and divine realms.

The Romanesque Church

After the year 1000, devout Christians, who had expected the return of Jesus at the end of the millennium, reconciled themselves to the advent of a new age. The Benedictine abbey of Cluny in southeastern France launched a movement for monastic revitalization that witnessed—within a period of 150 years—the construction of more than a thousand monasteries and abbey churches throughout Western Europe. The new churches, most of which were modeled on Cluny itself, enshrined relics brought back from the Holy Land by the Crusaders or collected locally. Such relics—the remains of saints and martyrs, a piece of the Cross on which Jesus was crucified, and the like—became objects of holy veneration. They were housed in ornamented containers, or **reliquaries**, some in the shape of the body part they held. The reliquary statue pictured in Figure **13.2** held the cranium of the child martyr and favorite local saint of Conques. On feast days, the image, sheathed in thin sheets of gold and semiprecious stones, was carried through the streets in sacred procession. The monastic churches that housed the holy relics of saints and martyrs attracted thousands of Christian pilgrims. Some traveled to the shrine to seek pardon for sins or pay homage to a particular saint. Supplicants afflicted with blindness, leprosy, and other illnesses often slept near the saint's tomb in hope of a healing vision or a miraculous cure.

There were four major pilgrimage routes that linked the cities of France with the favorite shrine of Christian pilgrims: the cathedral of Santiago de Compostela in northwestern Spain (Map **13.1**). Santiago—that is, Saint James Major (brother of Saint John the Evangelist)—was said to have brought Christianity to Spain. He was martyred upon his return to Judea, but his body was miraculously recovered in the early ninth century and buried at Compostela, where repeated miracles made his shrine a major pilgrimage center. Along the roads that carried pilgrims from Paris across to the Pyrenees, old churches were rebuilt and new churches erected, prompting one eleventh-century chronicler to observe: "The whole world seems to have shaken off her slumber, cast off her old rags, and clothed herself in a white mantle of new churches."

Figure 13.2 Reliquary statue of Sainte Foy, Conques, France, late tenth to eleventh century. Gold and gemstones over a wooden core, height 33½ in.

Map 13.1 Romanesque and Gothic Sites in Western Europe, ca. 1000–1300.

The medieval architects' return to stone barrel and groin vaults of the kind first used by the Romans (see chapter 6) inaugurated the *Romanesque style*. Romanesque architects employed round arches and a uniform system of stone vaults in the upper zones of the nave and side aisles. While the floor plan of the typical Romanesque church preserved the Latin cross design of the Early Christian and Carolingian basilica (see Figure 9.8), the new system of stone vaulting allowed medieval architects to build on a grander scale than ever before. In the construction of these new, all-stone structures, the Normans led the way. The technical superiority of Norman stonemasons, apparent in their castles (see Figure 11.16), is reflected in the abbey churches at Caen and Jumièges in northwestern France. At the abbey of Jumièges, consecrated in 1067 in the presence of William the Conqueror, little remains

other than the **westwork** (west façade), with its 141-foot-high twin towers (Figure **13.3**). This austere entrance portal, with its **tripartite** (three-part) division and three round arches, captures the geometric simplicity and rugged severity typical of the Romanesque style in France and England. It also anticipates some of the main features of medieval church architecture: massive towers pointing heavenward made the church visible from great distances; stone portals separated the secular from the divine realm and dramatized the entrance door as the gateway to salvation.

Like the medieval Crusades, the pilgrimage phenomenon was an expression of increased mobility and economic revitalization (see chapter 11). Since pilgrims, like modern tourists, constituted a major source of revenue for European towns and churches, parishes competed for them by enlarging church interiors and by increasing

Figure 13.3 West façade of the abbey of Jumièges, on the lower Seine near Rouen, France, 1037–1067. Height of towers 141 ft.

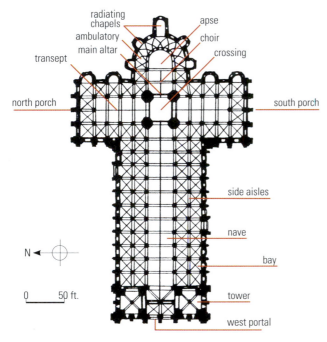

Figure 13.4 Plan of Saint-Sernin, Toulouse.

the number of reliquary chapels. The practical requirement for additional space in which to house these relics safely and make them accessible to Christian pilgrims determined the plan of the pilgrimage church. To provide additional space for shrines, architects gradually enlarged the eastern end of the church to include a number of radiating chapels. They also extended the side aisles around the transept and behind the apse to form an ambulatory (walkway). The ambulatory allowed lay visitors to move freely into the chapels without disturbing the monks at the main altar (Figure **13.4**). In the Early Christian church (see Figure 9.8), as in the Carolingian abbey (see Figure 11.12), the width of the nave was limited by the size and availability of roofing timber, and the wooden superstructure itself was highly susceptible to fire. The use of cut stone as the primary vaulting medium provided a solution to both of these problems.

The church of Saint-Sernin at Toulouse, on the southernmost pilgrimage route to Compostela, is one of the largest of the French pilgrimage churches (Figure **13.5**). Constructed of magnificent pink granite, Saint-Sernin's spacious nave is covered by a barrel vault divided by ornamental transverse arches (Figure **13.6**). Thick stone walls and heavy piers carry the weight of the vault and provide lateral (sideways) support (see Figure 13.18). Since window openings might have weakened the walls that buttressed the barrel vault, the architects of Saint-Sernin eliminated the clerestory. Beneath the vaults over the double side aisles, a gallery that served weary pilgrims as a place of overnight refuge provided additional lateral buttressing.

The formal design of Saint-Sernin follows rational and harmonious principles: the square represented by the crossing of the nave and transept is the module for the organization of the building and its parts (see Figure 13.4). Each nave **bay** (vaulted compartment) equals one-half the module, while each side-aisle bay equals one-fourth of the module. Clarity of design is also visible in the ways in which the exterior reflects the geometry of the interior:

Figure 13.5 Saint-Sernin, Toulouse, France, ca. 1080–1120 (tower enlarged in the thirteenth century).

Figure 13.6 Nave and choir of Saint-Sernin, Toulouse. Pink granite, length of nave 377 ft. 4 in.

at the east end of the church, for instance, five reliquary chapels protrude uniformly from the ambulatory, while at the crossing of the nave and transept, a tower (enlarged in the thirteenth century) rises as both a belfry and a beacon to approaching pilgrims (see Figure 13.5). Massive and stately in its exterior, dignified and somber in its interior, Saint-Sernin conveys the overall effect of a monumental spiritual fortress.

Romanesque architects experimented with a wide assortment of regional variation in stone vaulting techniques. At the pilgrimage church of Sainte-Madeleine (Mary Magdalene) at Vézelay in France—the site from which the Second Crusade was launched—the nave was covered with groin vaults separated by pronounced transverse arches. The concentration of weight along the arches, along with lighter masonry, allowed the architect to enlarge the width of the nave to 90 feet and to include a clerestory that admitted light into the dark interior (Figure **13.7**). The alternating light and dark stone **voussoirs** (wedges) in the arches of this dramatic interior indicate the influence of Muslim architecture (see Figure 10.10) on the development of the Romanesque church.

Figure 13.7 Nave of Sainte-Madeleine, Vézelay, France, ca. 1104–1132. Width 90 ft.

A Romanesque Last Judgment

Framed by a **mandorla** (an almond-shaped halo) that surrounds his body, Jesus displays his wounds and points to the realms of the afterlife: Heaven (on his right) and Hell (on his left). Surrounding the awesome Christ, flamelike saints and angels await the souls of the resurrected. Saint Michael weighs a soul in order to determine its eternal destiny, a motif that recalls late Egyptian art (see Figure 2.14), while a wraithlike devil tries to tip the scales in his own favor (see Figure 13.10). In the

lintel (the horizontal band below the tympanum), the resurrected are pictured rising from their graves. Just beneath the mouth of Hell, a pair of disembodied claws clutch at the damned, who cower in anticipation of eternal punishment. The **archivolts** that frame the tympanum hold roundels with signs of the zodiac and depictions of the labors of the months, symbols of the calendar year, and the passage of time between the First and Second Coming of Christ.

Figure 13.8 GISLEBERTUS, *Last Judgment*, ca. 1130–1135. West tympanum, Autun Cathedral, France. Height of Christ figure 10 ft.

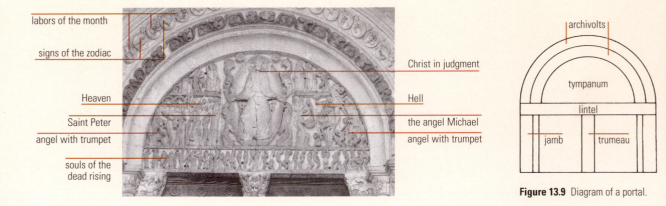

labors of the month

signs of the zodiac

Heaven

Saint Peter

angel with trumpet

souls of the
dead rising

Christ in judgment

Hell

the angel Michael

angel with trumpet

archivolts

tympanum

lintel

jamb   trumeau

Figure 13.9 Diagram of a portal.

Figure 13.10 GISLEBERTUS, detail of *Last Judgment*, ca. 1130–1135. Autun Cathedral.

Romanesque Sculpture

Pilgrimage churches of the eleventh and twelfth centuries heralded the revival of monumental stone sculpture—a medium that, for the most part, had been abandoned since Roman antiquity. Scenes from the Old and New Testaments—carved in high relief and brightly painted—usually appeared on the entrance portals of the church, as well as in the capitals of columns throughout the basilica and its cloister. The entrance portal, normally at the west end of the church, marked the dividing point between the earthly city and the City of God. Passage through the portal marked the beginning of the symbolic journey from sin (darkness/west) to salvation (light/east). On the carved west portal of the cathedral of Saint Lazarus at Autun in France, medieval Christians were greeted by the forbidding image of Christ as Judge from the center of the **tympanum** (the semicircular space within the arch of the portal) just above their heads (see LOOKING INTO, Figures **13.8** and **13.9**). Like a medieval morality play, the tympanum served as a *memento mori*, reminding Christians as they passed beneath it of the inevitability of death and judgment (Figure **13.10**). Indeed, under his signature, the artist Gislebertus added the warning: "Let this terror frighten those bound by earthly sin."

Among the most intriguing examples of Romanesque sculpture are those that adorn the capitals of columns in churches and cloisters. These so-called **historiated capitals** feature narrative scenes depicting the life of Christ. One of the largest extant groups of historiated capitals comes from Autun Cathedral. In *The Flight to Egypt*, a moon-faced Mary sits awkwardly upon a toylike donkey led by a bearded Joseph (Figure **13.11**). The six-pointed star above Mary's right shoulder and the naively shortened figures—altered to fit into the shape of the capital—give the scene

Figure 13.11 *The Flight to Egypt*, late eleventh century. Capital, Autun Cathedral. Height 2 ft. (approx.).

Romanesque sculpture shares with Romanesque painting a distinctive style marked by abstract stylization and linear movement. In carved Romanesque portals, as in painted illustrations for all types of religious and secular manuscript, the figures are lively and elongated; they bend and twist, as if animated by the restless energy of the age—one of pilgrimage and crusades. The carved sculptures at the abbey church of Saint Pierre at Moissac, France (Figure **13.12**), are similar to the painted illustrations for the Psalter of Saint Swithin (Figure **13.13**); both feature thin, dancelike figures, their bodies defined by rhythmic, concentric folds of drapery that emphasize movement. At Moissac, the Hebrew prophet Jeremiah stretches like taffy to conform to the shape of the **trumeau** (the central post supporting the superstructure). Both sculpture and painting preserve the graphic features of early medieval metalwork techniques (see chapter 11), as well as the decorative draftsmanship of Byzantine and Islamic art.

Figure 13.12 *Jeremiah the Prophet*, early twelfth century. Trumeau of south portal, Saint-Pierre, Moissac, France. Height 12 ft. (approx.). The placement of this figure is symbolic. It illustrates the Christian claim that Old Testament prophets "supported" New Testament revelation.

Figure 13.13 *Capture and Flagellation of Christ*, from the Psalter of Saint Swithin, ca. 1250. 12½ × 8¾ in. The gestures and facial expressions of the figures in these scenes are exaggerated to emphasize contrasting states of arrogance and humility.

a whimsical quality. Romanesque artisans plumbed their imaginations to generate the legions of fantastic beasts and hybrid demons that embellish church portals and capitals. The popularity of such imagery moved some medieval churchmen to debate whether the visual arts inspired or distracted the faithful from contemplation and prayer. Nevertheless, the fusion of dogma and fantasy that characterizes Romanesque sculpture must have made a tremendous impact on the great percentage of people who could neither read nor write.

The Gothic Cathedral

Seventeenth-century Neoclassicists coined the term "Gothic" to condemn a style they judged to be a "rude and barbarous" alternative to the Classical style. But modern critics have recognized the *Gothic style* as a sophisticated and majestic expression of the age of faith.

The Gothic style was born in northern France and spread quickly throughout medieval Europe. In France alone, eighty Gothic cathedrals and nearly 500 cathedral-class churches were constructed between 1170 and 1270. Like all Christian churches, the Gothic cathedral was a sanctuary for the celebration of the Mass. But, reflecting a shift of intellectual life from the monastery to the town, the Gothic cathedral was also the administrative seat (*cathedra*)

of a bishop, the site of ecclesiastical authority, and an educational center—a fount of theological doctrine and divine precept. The Gothic cathedral honored one or more saints, including and especially the Virgin Mary—the principal intercessor between God and the Christian believer. Indeed, most of the prominent churches of the Middle Ages were dedicated to Notre Dame ("Our Lady"). On a symbolic level, the church was both the Heavenly Jerusalem (the City of God) and a model of the Virgin as Womb of Christ and Queen of Heaven. In the cathedral, the medieval synthesis was realized: sculpture appeared in its portals, capitals, and choir screens; stained glass diffused divine light through its windows; painted altarpieces embellished its chapels; religious drama was enacted both within its walls and outside its doors; liturgical music filled its choirs.

Finally, the Gothic cathedral, often large enough to hold the entire population of a town, was the municipal center of gravity. If the Romanesque church constituted a rural retreat for monastics and pilgrims, the Gothic cathedral served as the focal point for an urban community. Physically dominating the town, its spires soaring above the houses and shops below (Figure **13.14**), the cathedral attracted civic events, public festivals, and even local business. Its construction was usually a town effort, supported by the funds and labor of local citizens and guild members,

Figure 13.14 Chartres Cathedral, France, begun 1194. This aerial view shows the south porch of the cathedral, which was added in the thirteenth century. The double sets of flying buttresses at the west end of the building are also visible.

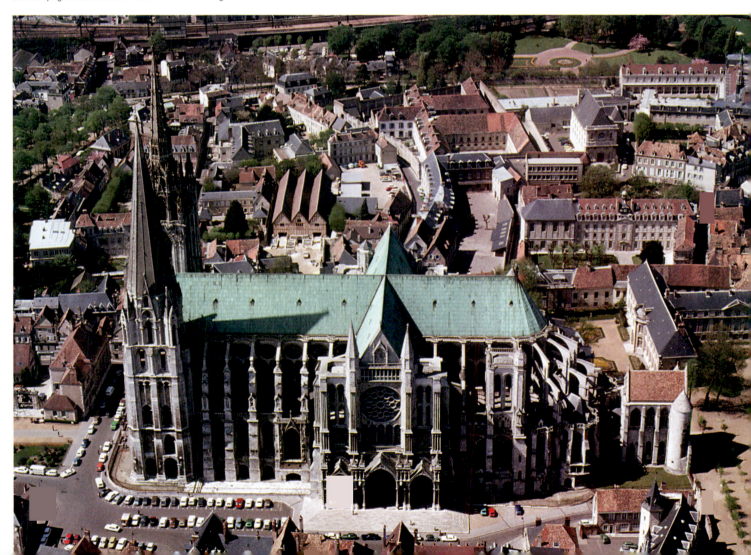

Figure 13.15 *Thirteenth-Century Masons*, French miniature from an Old Testament building scene, ca. 1240. 15⅓ × 11⅞ in. Stones, shaped by the two men (bottom right), are lifted by a hoisting engine powered by the treadwheel on the left. The man climbing the ladder carries mortar on his back.

Figure 13.16 Choir and ambulatory of the abbey church of Saint-Denis, France, 1140–1144. The wooden church pews shown in photographs of medieval churches are modern additions. In the High Middle Ages, as the liturgy expanded in length and complexity, benches and stalls for members of the choir came into use in the area behind the altar; but parishioners normally stood in the nave before the altar during the Mass.

including stonemasons (Figure **13.15**), carpenters, metalworkers, and glaziers.

In contrast with the Romanesque church, which drew on Greco-Roman principles and building techniques, Gothic architecture represented a clear break with the Classical past. Unlike the Classical temple, which seemed to hug the earth, the Gothic cathedral soared heavenward. It rejected the static, rationalized purity of the Classical canon in favor of a dynamic system of thrusts and counterthrusts; and it infused form with symbolic meaning.

The definitive features of the Gothic style were first assembled in a monastic church just outside the gates of Paris: the abbey church of Saint-Denis—the church that held the relics of the patron saint of France and, for centuries, the burial place of French royalty. Between 1122 and 1144, Abbot Suger (1085–1151), a personal friend of and adviser to the French kings Louis VI and VII, enlarged and remodeled the old Carolingian structure. Suger's designs for the east end of the church called for a combination of three architectural innovations that had been employed only occasionally or experimentally: the pointed arch, the rib vault, and stained glass windows. The result was a spacious choir and ambulatory, free of heavy stone supports and flooded with light (Figure **13.16**).

While Gothic cathedrals followed Saint-Denis in adopting a new look, their floor plan—the Latin cross—remained basically the same as that of the Romanesque church; only the transept might be moved further west to create a larger choir area to accommodate the ever-increasing number of priestly officiates and liturgical rituals (Figure **13.17**). The ingenious combination of rib vault and pointed arch, however, had a major impact on the size and elevation

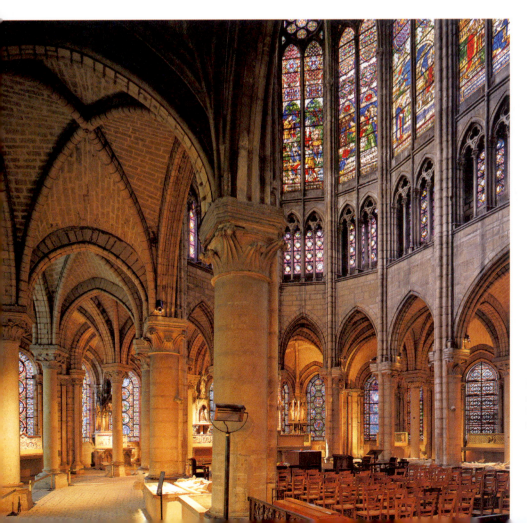

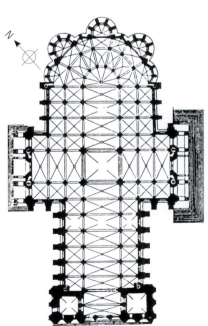

Figure 13.17 Floor plan of Chartres Cathedral. A comparison with Figure 13.4 reveals that the transept has been moved farther west so as to provide a larger choir area for the performance of church ritual.

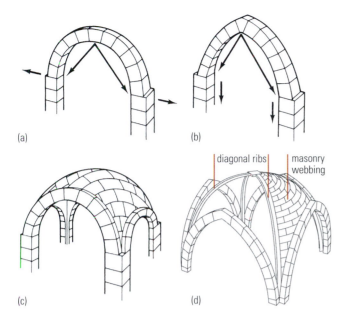

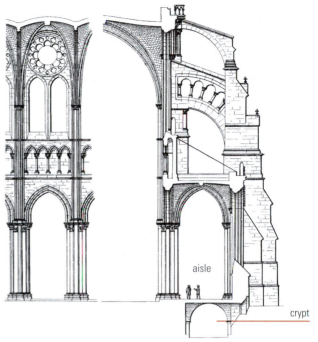

(a)

(b)

diagonal ribs | masonry webbing

(c)

(d)

Figure 13.18 Round and pointed arches and vaults. The round arch (a) spreads the load laterally, while the pointed arch (b) thrusts its load more directly toward the ground. The pointed arch can rise to any height, while the height of the semicircular arch is governed by the space it spans. Round arches create a dome-shaped vault (c). The Gothic rib vault (d) permits a lighter and more flexible building system with larger wall openings that may accommodate windows.

aisle

crypt

Figure 13.19 Elevations and sections of Chartres Cathedral nave.

of Gothic structures. Stone ribs replaced the heavy stone masonry of Romanesque vaults, and pointed arches raised these vaults to new heights. Whereas the rounded vaults of the Romanesque church demanded extensive lateral buttressing, the steeply pointed arches of the Gothic period, which directed weight downward, required only the combination of slender vertical piers and thin lateral ("flying") buttresses (Figures **13.18** and **13.19**). In place of masonry, broad areas of glass filled the interstices of this "cage" of stone. The nave wall consisted of an arcade of pier bundles that swept from floor to ceiling, an ornamental **triforium** gallery (the arcaded passage between the nave arcade and the clerestory), and a large clerestory consisting of **rose** (from the French *roue*, "wheel") and **lancet** (vertically pointed) windows (see Figure 13.19). Above the clerestory hung elegant canopies of **quadripartite** (four-part; Figure **13.20**, also frontispiece) or **sexpartite** (six-part) rib vaults.

Science and Technology

1122	Abbot Suger combines pointed arches and rib vaults in remodeling the abbey church of Saint-Denis
ca. 1175	flying buttresses are first used, in the cathedral of Notre Dame in Paris
ca. 1225	Villard de Honnecourt (French) begins a sketchbook of architectural plans, elevations, and engineering devices
1291	Venetian glassmakers produce the first clear (as opposed to colored) glass

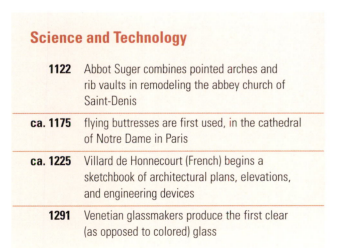

Figure 13.20 Nave facing east, Chartres Cathedral. Nave completed in 1220. Height of nave 122 ft.

Figure 13.21 West façade of Chartres Cathedral, lower parts 1134–1150, mainly after 1194.

Lighter and more airy than Romanesque churches, Gothic interiors seem to expand and unfold in vertical space. The pointed arch, the rib vault, and stained glass windows, along with the flying buttress (first used at the cathedral of Notre Dame in Paris around 1170), became the fundamental ingredients of the Gothic style.

Medieval towns competed with one another in the grandeur of their cathedrals: at Chartres, a town 50 miles southwest of Paris (see Map 13.1), the nave of the cathedral rose to a height of 122 feet (Figure **13.21**; see also Figures 13.14 and 13.20); architects at Amiens took the space from the floor to the apex of the vault to a breathtaking 144 feet. At Beauvais, the 157-foot vault of the choir (the equivalent of a fourteen-story high-rise) collapsed twelve years after its completion and had to be reconstructed over a period of forty years. These major enterprises in engineering design and craftsmanship often took decades to build, and many were never finished. In contrast to the Romanesque church, with its well-defined cubic volume and its simple geometric harmony, the Gothic cathedral was an intricate web of stone, a dynamic network of open and closed spaces that evoked a sense of unbounded extension. Despite its

Figure 13.23 Grotesques and a gargoyle waterspout on a tower terrace of Notre Dame, Paris, as restored in the nineteenth century.

visual complexity, however, the Gothic interior obeyed a set of proportional principles aimed at achieving harmonious design: at Chartres, for instance, the height of the clerestory and the height of the nave arcade are each exactly three times the height of the triforium (see Figure 13.20). At the cathedral of Notre Dame in Paris, these interior sections are mirrored in the three-story elevation of the façade: the height of the nave arcade corresponds to that of the west portals; the triforium arcade is echoed in the rows of saints standing above those portals; and the clerestory is marked by a majestic rose window (Figure **13.22**).

Gothic architects embellished the structural extremities of the cathedral with stone **crockets** (stylized leaves) and **finials** (crowning ornamental details). At the upper portions of the building, **gargoyles**—waterspouts in the form of grotesque figures or hybrid beasts—were believed to ward off evil (Figure **13.23**). During the thirteenth century and thereafter, cathedrals increased in structural and ornamental complexity. Flying buttresses became ornate stone wings terminating in minichapels that housed individual statues of saints and martyrs. Crockets and finials sprouted in greater numbers from gables and spires, and sculptural details became more numerous. But, like an Aquinan proposition, the final design represents the reconciliation of all individual parts into a majestic and harmonious synthesis.

Figure 13.22 West façade of Notre Dame, Paris, ca. 1200–1250.

Figure 13.24 Royal Portal, west façade, Chartres Cathedral, ca. 1140–1150.

Gothic Sculpture

The sculpture of the Gothic cathedral was an exhaustive compendium of Old and New Testament history, Classical and Christian precepts, and secular legend and lore. The sculptural program of the cathedral—that is, the totality of its carved representations—conveyed Christian doctrine and liturgy in terms that were meaningful to both scholars and laity. Learned churchmen might glean from these images a profound symbolic message, while less educated Christians might see in them a history of their faith and a mirror of daily experience. Designed to be "read" by the laity, the Gothic façade was both a "Bible in stone" and an encyclopedia of the religious and secular life of an age of faith.

In the sculpture of the cathedral, as in the stained glass windows, the Virgin Mary holds a prominent place. This is especially so at Chartres Cathedral, which, from earliest times, had housed the tunic that the Virgin Mary was said to have worn at the birth of Jesus. When, in 1194, the tunic survived the devastating fire that destroyed most of the old cathedral, it was taken as a miracle indicating the Virgin's desire to see her shrine gloriously rebuilt. Financial contributions for its reconstruction poured in from all of Christendom. Chartres' west portal, which survived the fire, is called the Royal Portal for its jamb figures of the kings and queens of the Old Testament (Figure **13.24**).

Its central tympanum features Christ in Majesty. Rigidly posed, he is flanked by symbols of the four evangelists and framed in the archivolts by the Elders of the Apocalypse. In the lintel below, the apostles are ordered into formal groups of three.

On the right tympanum, the Mother of God is pictured as the Seat of Wisdom and honored as the Queen of the Liberal Arts (Figure **13.25**). The bottom register of the tympanum shows (from left to right) the Annunciation, the Visitation, the Nativity, and the Annunciation to the Shepherds. The upper register depicts the Presentation of Jesus in the Temple with an image of Jesus standing on the sacrificial altar directly below the seated Virgin. Framing the tympanum, the archivolts include allegorical representations of the *trivium* and the *quadrivium* (see chapter 12). Here, each of the disciplines is accompanied by the appropriate historical authority. On the lower right, for instance, the allegorical figure of Music, holding on her lap a **psaltery** (a stringed instrument), strikes a set of bells. Below her, Pythagoras (celebrated for having discovered the numerical relation between the length of strings and musical tones) is shown hunched over his lap desk.

On cathedral façades, the Virgin Mary appears frequently as Mother of God and Queen of Heaven. The central trumeau of the west portal at Notre Dame in Paris shows the regal Mary carrying the Christ Child

Figure 13.25 *Scenes from the Life of the Virgin Mary*, between 1145 and 1170. Right tympanum of the Royal Portal, west façade, Chartres Cathedral. Height 10 ft (approx.).

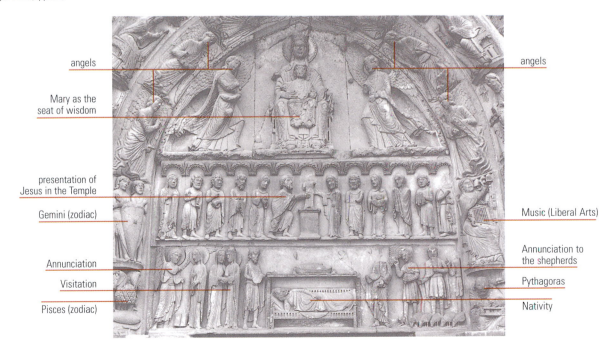

angels

angels

Mary as the
seat of wisdom

presentation of
Jesus in the Temple

Music (Liberal Arts)

Gemini (zodiac)

Annunciation to
the shepherds

Annunciation

Pythagoras

Visitation

Pisces (zodiac)

Nativity

From the earliest years of its establishment as a religion, Christianity exalted the Virgin Mary as an object of veneration. Long revered as the "second Eve," Mary was honored as the woman who redeemed humankind from damnation and death, the twin consequences of the first Eve's disobedience. The image of Mary as a paragon of virtue and chastity constituted an ideal feminine type not unlike that held by Isis in the ancient world (Figure **13.26**). The great cathedrals, most of which were dedicated to the Virgin, portrayed her as Mother of God, Bride of Christ, and Queen of Heaven. Enthroned alongside Jesus—often no smaller in size—she appears as his equal in authority. During the twelfth century, as emphasis came to be placed on the humanity of Jesus, Mary was depicted as the suffering mother and compassionate intercessor, and her virtues were praised in literature and song. As legends of her miracles proliferated, the cult of the Virgin inspired worship at shrines in her honor (Figure **13.27**) and special prayers of supplication. Increasingly, images of Mary and depictions of her life came to adorn church portals, stained glass windows, altarpieces, and illuminated manuscripts.

Figure 13.26 *Isis and Horus Enthroned*, Middle Egyptian, fourth century C.E. Limestone, height 35 in.

Figure 13.27 *Yolande de Soissons Kneeling before a Statue of the Virgin and Child*, from Psalter and Book of Hours, northern France, ca. 1290. 7⅕ × 5¼ in.

(Figure **13.28**). Beneath her feet is an image of the fallen Eve, standing alongside Adam in the Garden of Eden. The conjunction of Mary and Eve alluded to the popular medieval idea that Mary was the "new Eve," who brought salvation as a remedy for the sentence of death resulting from the disobedience of the "old Eve."

The thousands of individually carved figures on the façades of the cathedrals at Chartres, Paris, Amiens, and elsewhere required the labor of many sculptors working over long periods of time. Often, a single façade reflects a variety of styles, the efforts of different workshops and different eras. The present cathedral at Chartres, at least the fifth on that site, was the product of numerous building campaigns. The Royal Portal retains the linear severity of the Romanesque style (see Figure 13.24), while the figures on its north and south portals, added in the early thirteenth century, seem to detach themselves from the stone frame. Like the sculptures on the west façade of Notre Dame, they are weighty and lifelike (see Figure 13.28). Their robes reflect the movements of their bodies,

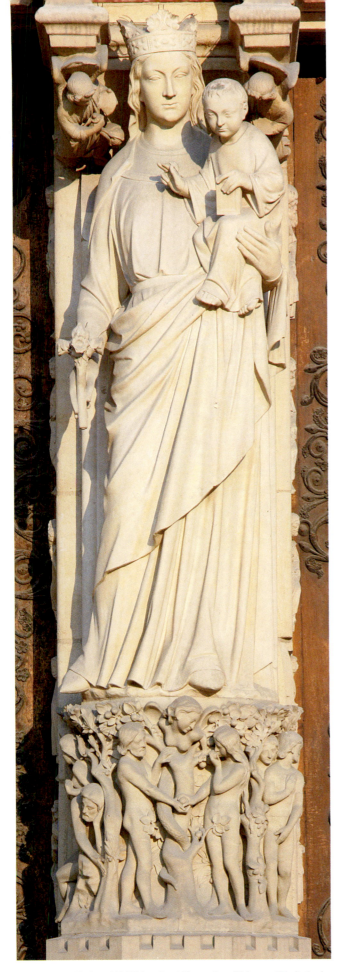

and their gestures are varied and subtle. Clearly, between the eleventh and thirteenth centuries, medieval sculpture moved in the direction of heightened Realism. This trend accompanied a proliferation of religious imagery and architectural detail that turned some Late Gothic church façades into encyclopedias in stone.

Stained Glass

Stained glass was to the Gothic cathedral what mosaics were to the Early Christian church: a source of religious edification, a medium of divine light, and a delight to the eye. Produced on the site of the cathedral by a process of mixing metal oxides into molten glass, colored sheets of glass were cut into fragments to fit preconceived designs. They were then fixed within lead bands, bound by a grid of iron bars, and set into stone **mullions** (vertical frames). Imprisoned in this lacelike armature, the glass vibrated with color, sparkling in response to the changing natural light and casting rainbows of color that seemed to dissolve the stone walls. The faithful of Christendom regarded the cathedral windows as precious objects—glass tapestries that clothed the House of God with radiant light. They especially treasured the windows at Chartres, with their rich blues, which, in contrast to other colors, required an ingredient—cobalt oxide—that came from regions far beyond France. Legend had it that Abbot Suger, the first churchman to exploit the aesthetic potential of stained glass, produced blue glass by grinding up sapphires—a story that, although untrue, reflects the popular equation of precious gems with sacred glass.

Suger exalted stained glass as a medium that filtered divine revelation. To the medieval mind, light was a symbol of Jesus, who had proclaimed to his apostles, "I am the light of the world" (John 8:12). Drawing on this mystical bond between Jesus and light, Suger identified the *lux nova* ("new light") of the Gothic church as the symbolic equivalent of God and the windows as mediators of God's love. But for Suger, light—especially as it passed through the stained glass windows of the church—also signified the sublime knowledge that accompanied the progressive purification of the ascending human spirit (a theme that also dominates Dante's "Paradiso"; see chapter 12). Suger's mystical interpretation of light, inspired by his reading of Neoplatonic treatises (see chapter 8), sustained his belief that contemplation of the "many-colored gems" of church glass could transport the Christian from "the slime of this earth" to "the purity of heaven." On the wall of the ambulatory at Saint-Denis, Abbot Suger had these words inscribed: "That which is united in splendor, radiates in splendor/And the magnificent work inundated with the new light shines."

The light symbolism that Suger embraced was as distinctive to medieval sermons and treatises as it was to the everyday liturgy of the Church. It permeates the writings of Hildegard of Bingen (see Reading 12.2), who referred to God as "the Living Light," and it is the principal theme in Saint Ambrose's sixth-century song of praise, the "Ancient Morning Hymn" (see Reading 9.2).

Figure 13.28 *Virgin and Child* (above) and *Temptation of Adam and Eve* (below), thirteenth century. Central trumeau of the west portal, Notre Dame, Paris. Height 5 ft. (approx.).

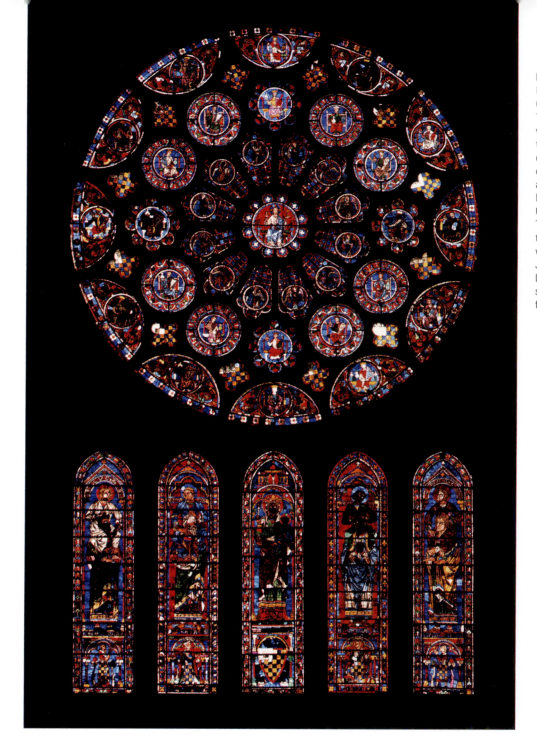

Figure 13.29 South rose and lancets, thirteenth century. Chartres Cathedral. 57 ft. 6¾ in. × 34 ft. 7¾ in. One of the three great rose windows at Chartres Cathedral, the south rose centers on the image of Christ, surrounded by symbols of the evangelists, censing angels, and the elders of the Apocalypse. In the lancet windows, Mary and the Christ Child stand between four Old Testament prophets who carry on their shoulders the four evangelists, visually representing the idea that Jesus had come to fulfill the Hebrew Law (Matthew 5:17). The donors are shown kneeling at the base of the five lancets.

The Windows at Chartres

The late twelfth and early thirteenth centuries were, without doubt, the golden age of stained glass. At Chartres, the 175 surviving glass panels with representations of more than 4000 figures comprise a cosmic narrative of humankind's religious and secular history. Chartres' windows, which were removed for safekeeping during World War II and thereafter returned to their original positions, follow a carefully organized theological program designed, as Abbot Suger explained, "to show simple folk . . . what they ought to believe." In one of Chartres' oldest windows, whose vibrant combination of reds and blues inspired the title *Notre Dame de la Belle Verrière* ("Our Lady of the Beautiful Glass"), the Virgin appears in her dual role as Mother of God and Queen of Heaven (see Figure 13.1). Holding the Christ Child on her lap and immediately

adjacent to her womb, she also signifies the Seat of Wisdom (compare Figure 13.25).

Among the glories of Chartres Cathedral are its three rose windows. While the term "rose window" did not come into use until the seventeenth century, the wheel-like design was already included in many Romanesque churches. Light passing through the circular and semi-circular glass elements in Chartres' south rose window produces magnificent shifting visual effects (Figure **13.29**). In the lancet windows below the rose of the south transept wall, Mary and the Christ Child are flanked by four Old Testament prophets who carry on their shoulders the four evangelists, a symbolic rendering of the Christian belief that the Old Dispensation (the Hebrew Law) upheld the New Dispensation (the Gospels; compare Figure 13.12). Often, the colors chosen for the contents of the design carry symbolic value. For instance, in scenes of the Passion from the west-central lancet window, the Cross carried by Jesus is green—the color of vegetation—symbolizing rebirth and regeneration.

Many of Chartres' windows were donated by members of the nobility, who may be shown kneeling in prayer (see Figure 13.29). The activities of bakers, butchers, stonemasons, and other laborers regularly appear in the windows commemorating the patron saints of the guilds.

Sainte-Chapelle: Medieval "Jewelbox"

The art of stained glass reached its height in Sainte-Chapelle, the small palace chapel commissioned for the Ile de France by King Louis IX ("Saint Louis") (Figure **13.30**). Executed between 1245 and 1248, the chapel was designed to hold the Crown of Thorns, a prized relic that Christian Crusaders claimed to have recovered along with other symbols of Christ's Passion. The lower level of the chapel is richly painted with frescoes that imitate the canopy of Heaven, while the upper level consists almost entirely of 49-foot-high lancet windows dominated by ruby red and purplish blue glass (Figure **13.31**). More than a thousand individual stories are depicted in the windows that make up two-thirds of the upper chapel walls. In its vast iconographic program and its dazzling, ethereal effect, this medieval "jewelbox" is the crowning example of French Gothic art.

Figure 13.30 Sainte-Chapelle, Paris, from the southwest, 1245–1248.

Figure 13.31 Upper chapel of Sainte-Chapelle, Paris. Height of lancet windows 49 ft.

Medieval Painting

Responsive to the combined influence of Germanic, Islamic, and Byzantine art, medieval artists cultivated a taste for decorative abstraction through line. In fresco, manuscript illumination, and panel painting, line worked to flatten form, eliminate space, and enhance the iconic nature of the image. The artist who painted the *Crucifixion and Deposition of Christ* for the Psalter of Blanche of Castile (the mother of Saint Louis) recreates the geometric compositions and strong, simple colors of stained glass windows (Figure **13.32**). The Church (representing the New Dispensation) and the Synagogue (representing the Old Dispensation) are depicted to the right and left of the two interlocked roundels. Book illuminators might make use of pattern books filled with stock representations of standard historical and religious subjects, a practice that encouraged stylistic conservatism. Nevertheless, in the execution of thousands of miniatures and marginal illustrations for a wide variety of secular and religious manuscripts, the imagination of medieval artists seems unbounded.

The preparation of medieval manuscripts was a time-consuming and expensive enterprise, usually shared by many different workers. The production of a Bible might require the slaughter of some 200 sheep or calves, whose hides were then scraped, bleached, and carefully processed before becoming the folded sheets of parchment

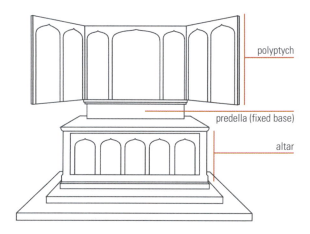

Figure 13.33 Diagram of an altar and altarpiece. The medieval altarpiece was a devotional object set on or behind an altar. Two hinged panels made up a **diptych**; three a **triptych**; and many panels (seen here) a **polyptych**.

Figure 13.32 *Crucifixion and Deposition of Christ with the Church and the Synagogue,* from the Psalter of Blanche of Castile, ca. 1235. 11 × 7⅝ in.

Figure 13.34 CIMABUE, *Madonna Enthroned*, ca. 1280–1290. Tempera on wood, 12 ft. 7½ in. × 7 ft. 4 in.

Figure 13.35 SIMONE MARTINI, *Annunciation*, 1333. (Saints in side panels by **LIPPO MEMMI**.) Tempera on wood, 8 ft. 8 in. × 10 ft.

(or, if derived from calves, vellum) that made up the book itself. Gold was used lavishly to "illuminate" the images, while rich colors, such as the blue used in Figure 13.32, might come from places as far away as Afghanistan, hence the name "ultramarine" ("beyond the sea") to designate a shade of blue.

Some of the finest examples of medieval painting appear in altarpieces installed on or behind chapel altars dedicated to the Virgin or one of the saints (Figures **13.33, 13.34,** and **13.35**). The typical Gothic altarpiece consisted of a wooden panel or group of panels coated with **gesso** (a chalky white plaster), on which figures were painted in **tempera** (a powdered pigment that produces dry, flat surface colors), and embellished with gold leaf that reflected the light of the altar candles. The object of devotional prayer, the altarpiece usually displayed scenes from the life of Jesus, the Virgin Mary, or a favorite saint or martyr. A

late thirteenth-century altarpiece by the Florentine painter Cimabue (1240–1302) shows the Virgin and Child elevated on a monumental seat that is both a throne and a tower (see Figure 13.34). Angels cluster around the throne, while, beneath the Virgin's feet, four Hebrew prophets display scrolls predicting the coming of Jesus. To symbolize their lesser importance, angels and prophets are pictured considerably smaller than the enthroned Mary. Such hierarchic grading, while typical of medieval art, also characterized Egyptian and Byzantine compositions.

Cimabue's lavishly gilded devotional image has a schematic elegance: line elicits the sharp, metallic folds of the Virgin's dark blue mantle, the crisp wings of the angels, the chiseled features of the Christ Child, and the decorative surface of the throne. The figure of the Virgin combines the hypnotic grandeur of the Byzantine icon and the weightless, hieratic clarity of Gislebertus' Christ in Majesty at Autun (see Figure 13.8). Although Cimabue's Virgin is more humanized than either of these, she is every bit as regal.

Medieval altarpieces integrated the ornamental vocabulary of Gothic architecture and the bright colors of stained glass windows. The Sienese painter Simone Martini (1284–1344) made brilliant use of Gothic architectural motifs in his *Annunciation* altarpiece of 1333 (see Figure 13.35). The frame of the altarpiece consists of elegant Gothic spires and heavily gilded **ogee** arches (pointed arches with S-shaped curves near the apex) sprouting finials and crockets. Set on a gold-leaf ground, the petulant Virgin, the angel Annunciate, and the vase of lilies (symbolizing Mary's purity) seem suspended in time and space. Martini's composition depends on a refined play of lines: the graceful curves of the archangel Gabriel's wings are echoed in his fluttering vestments, in the contours of the Virgin's body as she shrinks from the angel's greeting, and in the folds of her mantle, the pigment for which was ground from semiprecious lapis lazuli.

Medieval Music

Early Medieval Music and Liturgical Drama

The major musical developments of the Early Middle Ages, like those in architecture, came out of the monasteries. In Charlemagne's time, monastic reforms in church liturgy and in sacred music accompanied the renaissance in the visual arts. Early church music took the form of unaccompanied monophonic chant (see chapter 9), a solemn sound that inspired one medieval monk to write in the margin of his songbook: "The tedious plainsong grates my tender ears." Perhaps to remedy such complaints, the monks at Saint-Gall enlarged the range of expression of the classical Gregorian chant by adding **antiphons**, or verses sung as responses to the religious text. Carolingian monks also embellished plainsong with the **trope**, an addition of music or words to the established liturgical chant. Thus, "Lord, have mercy upon us" became "Lord, omnipotent Father, God, Creator of all, have mercy upon us." A special kind of trope, called a **sequence**, added words to the long, melismatic passages—such as the alleluias and amens—that occurred at the end of each part of the Mass (Figure **13.36**).

By the tenth century, singers began to divide among themselves the parts of the liturgy for Christmas and Easter, now embellished by tropes and sequences. As more and more dramatic incidents were added to the texts for these Masses, fully fledged music-drama began to emerge. Eventually, these liturgical plays broke away from the liturgy and were performed in the intervals between the parts of the Mass. Such was the case with the twelfth-century *Play of Daniel*, whose dramatic "action" brought to life episodes from the Book of Daniel (in the Hebrew Bible) that Christians took to prophesy the birth of the Messiah—a story that was therefore appropriate to the Christmas season.

By the twelfth century, spoken dialogue and possibly musical instruments were introduced. At the monastery of the German abbess Hildegard of Bingen, Benedictine nuns may have performed her *Ordo virtutum*

Figure 13.36 *An Angel Tells Joachim that Anna Will Conceive* (tropes with musical notation above), England, ca. 1050. Parchment, 12⅖ × 8⅔ in.

♪ See Music Listening Selections at end of chapter.

(see chapter 12). In this music-drama, the earliest known morality play in Western history, the Virtues contest with the Devil for the Soul of the Christian. The Devil's lines are spoken, not sung, consistent with Hildegard's belief that satanic evil was excluded from knowing music's harmony and order. Hildegard's most important musical compositions, however, were liturgical. Her monophonic hymns and antiphons in honor of the saints, performed as part of the Divine Office, are exercises in musical meditation. Some offer praise for womankind and for the virgin saints, while others, such as the chant *O Successores,* celebrate the holy confessors—Christ's "successors," who hear confession and give absolution.

Medieval Musical Notation

Musical notation was invented in the monasteries. As with Romanesque architecture, Benedictine monks at Cluny were especially influential in the development of medieval musical theory and practice. Cluny's second abbot, Odo of Cluny (878–942), is said to have devised a system of musical notation using the letters A through G to designate the seven notes of the Western scale. Building on Odo's efforts, the Italian Benedictine, Guido of Arezzo (ca. 990–ca. 1050), introduced a staff of colored lines (yellow for C, red for F, and so on) on which he registered neumes—notational signs traditionally written above the words to indicate tonal ascent or descent (see chapter 9). Guido's system established a precise means of indicating shifts in pitch. Instead of relying on memory alone, singers could consult songbooks inscribed with both words and music. Such advances facilitated the performance and transmission of liturgical music, and anticipated the kinds of compositional complexity represented by medieval polyphony.

Medieval Polyphony

Although our knowledge of early medieval music is sparse, there is reason to believe that, even before the year 1000, choristers were experimenting with multiple lines of music as an alternative to the monophonic style of Gregorian chant. **Polyphony** (music consisting of two or more lines of melody) was a Western invention; it did not make its appearance in Asia until modern times. The earliest polyphonic compositions consisted of Gregorian melodies sung in two parts simultaneously, with both voices moving note-for-note in parallel motion (parallel **organum**), or with a second voice moving in contrary motion (free organum), perhaps also adding many notes to the individual syllables of the text (melismatic organum). Consistent with rules of harmony derived from antiquity, and with the different ranges of the voice, the second musical part was usually pitched a fourth or a fifth above or below the first, creating a pure, hollow sound.

Throughout the High Middle Ages, northern France—and the city of Paris in particular—was the center of polyphonic composition. From the same area that produced the Gothic cathedral came a new musical style that featured several lines of melody arranged in counterpoised rhythms. The foremost Parisian composer was Pérotin (ca. 1160–1240). A member of the Notre Dame School, Pérotin enhanced the splendor of the Christian Mass by writing three- and four-part polyphonic compositions based on Gregorian chant. Pérotin's music usually consisted of a principal voice or "tenor" (from the Latin *tenere,* meaning "to hold"), which sang the chant or "fixed song" (Latin, *cantus firmus*), and one or more voices that moved in shorter phrases and usually faster tempos. The combination of two or three related but independent voices, a musical technique called **counterpoint**, enlivened late twelfth- and thirteenth-century music. Indeed, the process of vertical superimposition of voice on voice enhanced sonority and augmented the melodic complexity of medieval music much in the way that the thrusts and counterthrusts of the Gothic structure enriched its visual texture.

As medieval polyphony encouraged the addition of voices and voice parts, the choir areas of Gothic cathedrals were enlarged to accommodate more singers. Performed within the acoustically resonant bodies of such cathedrals as Notre Dame in Paris, the polyphonic Mass produced an aural effect as resplendent as the multicolored light that shimmered throughout the interior. Like the cathedral itself, the polyphonic Mass was a masterful synthesis of carefully arranged parts—a synthesis achieved in *time* rather than in *space.*

The "Dies Irae"

One of the best examples of the medieval synthesis, particularly as it served the Christian immortality ideology, is the "Dies irae" ("Day of Wrath"). This fifty-seven-line hymn, which originated among the Franciscans during the thirteenth century, was added to the Roman Catholic **requiem** (the Mass for the Dead) and quickly became a standard part of the Christian funeral service. Invoking a powerful vision of the end of time, the "Dies irae" is the musical counterpart of the apocalyptic sermons and Last Judgment portals that issued solemn warnings of final doom. The hymn opens with the words:

> Day of Wrath! O day of mourning!
> See fulfilled the prophets' warning,
> Heaven and earth in ashes burning!

But, as with most examples of apocalyptic art, including Dante's *Commedia,* the hymn holds out hope for absolution and deliverance:

> With Thy favored sheep, oh, place me!
> Nor among the goats abase me,
> But to Thy right hand upraise me.
>
> While the Wicked are confounded,
> Doomed to flames of woe unbounded,
> Call me, with Thy saints surrounded.

Like so many other forms of medieval expression, the "Dies irae" brings into vivid contrast the eternal destinies

---

See Music Listening Selections at end of chapter.

See Music Listening Selections at end of chapter.

Figure 13.37 *Music and Her Attendants*, from **BOETHIUS**, *De Institutione Musica*, fourteenth century. Holding a portable pipe organ, the allegorical figure of Music is surrounded by an ensemble of court musicians. 9 × 6½ in. (approx.).

of sinners and saints. In later centuries, it inspired the powerful requiem settings of Mozart, Berlioz, and Verdi, and its music remains a familiar symbol of death and damnation.

The Motet

The thirteenth century also witnessed the invention of a new religious musical genre, the **motet**—a short, polyphonic choral composition based on a sacred text. Performed both inside and outside the church, it became the most popular kind of medieval religious song. Like the trope, the motet (from the French *mot*, meaning "word") developed from the practice of adding words to the melismatic parts of a melody. Medieval motets usually juxtaposed two or more uncomplicated themes, each with its own lyrics and metrical pattern, in a manner that was both lilting and lively. Motets that were designed to be sung outside the church often borrowed secular tunes with vernacular words. A three-part motet might combine a love song in the vernacular, a well-known hymn of praise to the Virgin, and a Latin liturgical text in the *cantus firmus*. Thirteenth-century motets were thus polytextual as well as polyphonic and polyrhythmic. A stock of melodies (like the stock of images in medieval pattern books) was available to musicians for use in secular and sacred songs, and the same one might serve both types of song. Subtle forms of symbolism occurred in many medieval motets, as for instance where a popular song celebrating spring might be used to refer to the Resurrection of Jesus, the awakening of romantic love, or both.

♪ See Music Listening Selections at end of chapter.

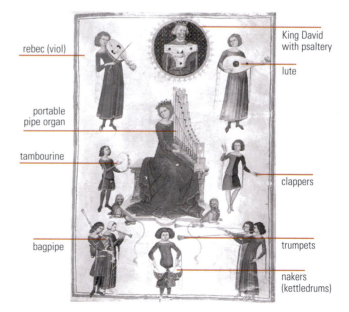

rebec (viol)

King David with psaltery

lute

portable pipe organ

tambourine

clappers

bagpipe

trumpets

nakers (kettledrums)

Instrumental Music

Musical instruments first appeared in religious music not for the purpose of accompanying songs, as with *troubadour* poems and folk epics, but to substitute for the human voice in polyphonic compositions. Medieval music depended on **timbre** (tone color) rather than volume for its effect, and most medieval instruments produced sounds that were gentle and thin by comparison with their modern (not to mention electronically amplified) counterparts. Medieval string instruments included the harp, the psaltery, and the lute (all three are plucked), and bowed fiddles such as the vielle and the rebec (Figure **13.37**). Wind instruments included portable pipe organs, recorders, and bagpipes. Percussion was produced by chimes, cymbals, bells, tambourines, and drums. Instrumental music performed without voices accompanied medieval dancing. Percussion instruments established the basic rhythms for a wide variety of high-spirited dances, including the estampie, a popular round dance consisting of short, repeated phrases.

 See Music Listening Selections at end of chapter.

LOOKING BACK

The Romanesque Church

- After the year 1000, Romanesque pilgrimage churches were constructed in great numbers throughout Western Europe. Their stone portals and capitals displayed Christian themes of redemption and salvation.
- Largely rural, the churches were gathering points for pilgrims who traveled to visit the holy relics of saints and martyrs enshrined in church chapels.
- Since pilgrims constituted a major source of revenue for European towns and churches, parishes competed for them by enlarging church interiors. They revived the systems of stone vaulting used by the Romans. Built on a Latin cross plan, the Romanesque church features round arches and thick barrel and groin vaults.
- The Romanesque style, characterized by lively linearity and vivid imagination, is apparent in the stone sculpture of entrance portals and historiated capitals, as well as in illuminated manuscripts.

The Gothic Cathedral

- The Gothic cathedral was the focus and glory of the medieval town. First developed in the region of Paris, the cathedral was an ingenious synthesis of three structural elements: rib vaults, pointed arches, and flying buttresses.
- Often large enough to hold the entire population of a town, the Gothic cathedral was the center of the urban community. It attracted civic events, public festivals, theatrical performances, and local business.

- The great cathedrals, most of which were dedicated to the Virgin, portrayed her as Mother of God, Bride of Christ, and Queen of Heaven. The image of Mary as a paragon of virtue and chastity constituted an ideal feminine type.
- The medieval cathedral represents the point of synthesis at which all the arts—visual, literary, and musical—served a common, unified purpose.

Gothic Sculpture

- The sculpture of the Gothic cathedral was an exhaustive compendium of Old and New Testament history, Classical and Christian precepts, and secular legend and lore. The totality of its carved representations conveyed doctrine in terms that were meaningful to scholars and laity alike.
- During the thirteenth century, figural representation became more detailed and lifelike. Figures assume natural poses, and cease to conform to the architectural framework. The trend toward greater Realism in Gothic sculpture accompanied the proliferation of religious imagery and architectural details.

Stained Glass

- Stained glass was a source of religious edification and a delight to the eye. Following Abbot Suger, the faithful Christian regarded cathedral windows as glass tapestries that served the House of God by filtering the light of divine truth.
- The windows at Chartres Cathedral and at Sainte-Chapelle in Paris constitute the high point of medieval stained glass ornamentation.

Medieval Painting

- Responsive to the combined influence of Germanic, Islamic, and Byzantine arts, medieval painting styles were generally abstract and symbolic; they reveal an expressive linearity, the use of bright colors, and a decorative treatment of form.
- Thousands of medieval manuscripts were handwritten and richly illuminated during the Middle Ages. Their production was time-consuming, despite the fact that the illuminators often used pattern books with stock representations of historical and religious subjects.
- Installed on or behind the chapel altar, the medieval altarpiece featured an image of the Virgin and/or the saints as objects of devotional prayer. Lavishly gilded, medieval Italian altarpieces reveal a humanized Byzantine style.

Medieval Music

- As with the visual arts, the music of the Middle Ages was closely related to religious ritual. In Carolingian times, tropes and sequences came to embellish Christian chant, a process that led to the birth of liturgical drama.
- By the eleventh century, Benedictine monks had devised a system of musical notation that facilitated performance and made possible the accurate transmission of music from generation to generation.

- Medieval polyphony, consisting of multiple independent lines of melody, introduced a new richness to both religious and secular music. Polyphonic

religious compositions known as motets often integrated vernacular texts and secular melodies.

- A combination of many medieval instruments provided music for dance and secular entertainment.

Music Listening Selections

- Medieval liturgical drama, *The Play of Daniel*, "Ad honorem tui, Christe," "Ecce sunt ante faciem tuam."
- Hildegard of Bingen, *O Successores* ("Your Successors"), ca. 1150.
- Two examples of early medieval polyphony: parallel organum, "Rex caeli, Domine," excerpt; melismatic organum,

"Alleluia, Justus ut palma," ca. 900–1150, excerpts.
- Pérotin, three-part organum, "Alleluia" (Nativitas), twelfth century.
- Anonymous, motet, "En non Diu! Quant voi; Eius in Oriente," thirteenth century, excerpt.

- French dance, "Estampie," thirteenth century.

Glossary

antiphon a verse sung in response to the text

archivolt a molded or decorated band around an arch or forming an archlike frame for an opening (see Figure 13.9)

bay a regularly repeated spatial unit of a building; in medieval architecture, a vaulted compartment

counterpoint a musical technique that involves two or more independent melodies; the term is often used interchangeably with "polyphony"

crocket a stylized leaf used as a terminal ornament

diptych a two-paneled painting

finial an ornament, usually pointed and foliated, that tops a spire or pinnacle

gargoyle a waterspout usually carved in the form of a grotesque figure

gesso a chalky white plaster used to prepare the surface of a panel for painting

historiated capital the uppermost member of a column, ornamented with figural scenes

lancet a narrow window topped with a pointed arch

lintel a horizontal beam or stone that spans an opening (see Figure 13.9)

mandorla a halo that surrounds the entire figure

motet a short, polyphonic religious composition based on a sacred text

mullion the slender, vertical pier dividing the parts of a window, door, or screen

ogee a pointed arch with an S-shaped curve on each side

organum the general name for the oldest form of polyphony: In *parallel organum*, the two voices move exactly parallel to one another; in *free organum*, the second voice moves in contrary motion; *melismatic organum* involves the use of multiple notes for each individual syllable of the text

polyphony (Greek, "many voices") a musical texture consisting of two or more lines of melody that are of equal importance

polyptych a multipaneled painting

psaltery a stringed instrument consisting of a flat soundboard and strings that are plucked

quadripartite consisting of or divided into four parts

reliquary a container for a sacred relic or relics

requiem a Mass for the Dead; a solemn chant to honor the dead

rose (from the French *roue*, "wheel") a large circular window with stained glass and stone tracery

sequence a special kind of trope consisting of words added to the melismatic passages of Gregorian chant

sexpartite consisting of or divided into six parts

tempera a powdered pigment that produces dry, flat colors

timbre tone color; the distinctive tone or quality of sound made by a voice or a musical instrument

triforium in a medieval church, the shallow arcaded passageway above the nave and below the clerestory (see Figure 13.19)

tripartite consisting of or divided into three parts

triptych a three-paneled painting

trope an addition of words, music, or both to Gregorian chant

trumeau the pillar that supports the superstructure of a portal (see Figure 13.9)

tympanum the semicircular space enclosed by the lintel over a doorway and the arch above it (see Figure 13.9)

voussoir (French, "wedge") a wedge-shaped block or unit in an arch or vault

westwork (from the German, *Westwerk*) the elaborate west end of a Carolingian or Romanesque church

Chapter 14

The World Beyond the West: India, China, and Japan

ca. 500–1300

"Heaven is my father and earth is my mother, and even such a small creature as I finds an intimate place in their midst."
Zhang Zai

Figure 14.1 *Guanyin*, tenth to early twelfth century. Wood with painted decoration, height 7 ft. 11 in. Brightly painted and gilded, this Chinese wood-carved *bodhisattva* wears sumptuous robes, a profusion of jewels, and an ornate headdress. Guanyin is equally popular in Japan, where he is known as Kannon.

Western students often overlook the fact that Europe—home of the culture that is most familiar to them—occupies only a tiny area at the far western end of the vast continental landmass of Asia. At the eastern end of that landmass lie two geographic and cultural giants, India and China, and the small but mighty Japan. During the European Middle Ages, East and West had little contact with each other, apart from periodic exchanges of goods and technology facilitated by Muslim intermediaries.

Between 500 and 1300 C.E., India produced some of the finest Sanskrit literature ever written. Hindu temple architecture and sculpture reached new levels of imagination and complexity,

and Indian music flourished. In China, during roughly the same period, the Tang and Song dynasties fostered a golden age in poetry and painting. The Chinese surpassed the rest of the world in technological invention and led global production in fine pottery and textiles. Medieval Japan produced the world's oldest prose fiction, as well as a unique form of theatrical performance known as Nō drama. In both secular and religious art, the Japanese cultivated a style governed by elegance and artless simplicity. A brief examination of the artistic record of these three civilizations puts our study of the medieval era in global perspective.

India

Although the term "medieval" does not apply to the history of India in the Western sense of an interlude between Classical and early modern times, scholars have used that term to designate the era between the end of the Gupta dynasty (ca. 500) and the Mongol invasion of India in the fourteenth century—a thousand-year period approximate to the Western Middle Ages. The dissolution of the Gupta Empire at the hands of Central Asian Huns, an event that paralleled the fall of Rome in the West and the collapse of the Han Empire in China, destroyed the remains of South Asia's greatest culture. Following this event, amidst widespread political turmoil and anarchy, India reverted to a conglomeration of fragmented rival kingdoms dominated by a warrior caste (not unlike the feudal aristocracy of medieval Europe). Ruling hereditary chiefs or *rajputs* ("sons of kings") followed a code of chivalry that set them apart from the lower classes.

The caste system (see chapter 3), which had operated in India for many centuries, worked to enforce the distance between rulers and the ruled. And as groups were subdivided according to occupation and social status, caste distinctions became more rigid and increasingly fragmented. Extended families of the same caste were ruled by the eldest male, who might take a number of wives. Children were betrothed early in life and women's duties—to tend the household and raise children (preferably sons)—were carefully prescribed. In a society where males were masters, a popular Hindu proverb ran: "A woman is never fit for independence." The devotion of the upper-caste Hindu woman to her husband was dramatically expressed in *sati*, a custom by which the wife threw herself on her mate's funeral pyre.

Early in the eighth century, Arab Muslims entered India and began to convert the native population to Islam. Muslim authority took hold in northern India, and Muslims rose to power as members of the ruling caste. During the tenth century, the invasions of Turkish Muslims brought further chaos to India, resulting in the

capture of Delhi (Map **14.1**) in 1192 and the destruction of the Buddhist University of Nalanda in the following year. Muslim armies destroyed vast numbers of Hindu and Buddhist religious statues, prohibited by Islamic law. Islam ultimately supplanted Hinduism and Buddhism in the Indus valley (modern Pakistan) and in Bengal (modern Bangladesh). Elsewhere, however, the native traditions of

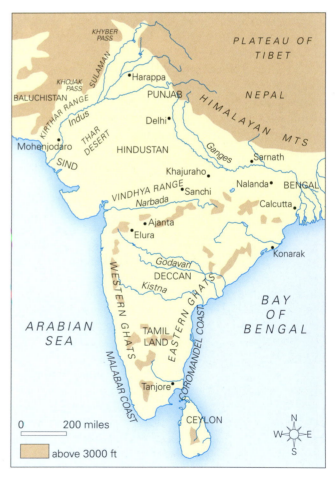

Map 14.1 India in the Eleventh Century.

India itself prevailed. Indeed, most of India—especially the extreme south, which held out against the Muslims until the fourteenth century—remained profoundly devoted to the Hindu faith. Today, approximately 85 percent of India's population is Hindu. Buddhism, on the other hand, would virtually disappear from India by the thirteenth century.

Hinduism

Unique in having no historical founder, Hinduism teaches that all individual aspects of being belong to the same divine substance: the impersonal, all-pervading Absolute Spirit known as Brahman. Pantheistic Hinduism, as defined in the principal religious writings, the *Upanishads* and the *Bhagavad-Gita* (see chapter 3), would seem to be contradicted by the sheer number of Hindu gods and goddesses worshiped in India. The growing devotion to the gods in the fourteenth and fifteenth centuries was the result of a process of **syncretism** by which Hinduism accommodated a wide variety of local and regional deities, along with the ancient nature gods and mythological beings of the *Vedas*. Although the worship of many gods suggests that Hindus are polytheistic, in reality, India's gods are perceived as individual aspects of the One; more specifically, as **avatars** ("incarnations") of Brahman, that is, metaphorically, as facets of a diamond. Much in the way that Christians regard Jesus as the incarnate form of God, Hindus believe that the avatars of Brahman assume various names and physical forms, even those of animals. They freely honor the Buddha and Jesus as human forms of the Absolute Spirit.

In that Hinduism embraces a multitude of religious sects, there exists no monolithic Hindu authority (comparable, for instance, to the Church in the Christian West), nor is there a prescribed or uniform liturgy. Hinduism encourages its devotees to seek union with Brahman in their own fashion, or in the fashion taught by their *guru* (spiritual guide), placing a fundamental faith in the concept that there are infinite ways of reaching the godhead.

Hindu devotional practice involves visiting the shrines of the gods, and offering prayers, flowers, or food. Gazing at the image of a deity is essential: the god is present in its representation. Thus, visual contact with an image of the deity is a form of direct contact with the divine; this is known as *darshan* (literally, "seeing and being seen by the god"). The very act of beholding the image is an act of worship and an expression of intense personal devotion by which divine blessings are received.

Out of the host of deities that characterized Hindu worship in medieval India, three principal gods dominate: Brahma, Vishnu, and Shiva. Hindus associate this "trinity" with the three main expressions of Brahmanic power: creation, preservation, and destruction. They honor Brahma—his name is the masculine form of Brahman—as the creator of the world. They prize Vishnu (identified with the sun in ancient Vedic hymns) as the preserver god. Hindu mythology recounts Vishnu's appearance on earth in nine different incarnations, including that of Krishna, the hero-god of the *Mahabharata* (see chapter 3). The conically crowned Vishnu pictured in Figure **14.2** holds in his upper right hand a flaming solar disk; his upper left hand displays a conch shell, a reminder of his association with the primeval ocean, but also a symbol of the ancient war trumpet used by Vishnu to terrorize his enemies. With his lower right hand, he makes the *mudra* of protection (see Figure 9.25), while his lower left hand points to the earth and the sacred lotus, symbol of the cosmic womb. Ritual icons like this one, cast in bronze by the lost-wax method (see Figure 0.19), are among the finest free-standing figural sculptures executed since Golden Age Greece. Produced in large numbers in tenth-century Tamil Nadu in south India, bronze effigies of the god were often bedecked with flowers and carried in public processions. (Note the rings

Figure 14.2 *Standing Vishnu*, from southern India, Chola period, tenth century. Bronze, with greenish blue patination, height 33¾ in. Icons of Vishnu often resemble those of the Buddha, who is accepted by Hindus as an avatar of Vishnu.

Shiva: Lord of the Dance

Framed in a celestial ring of fire, Shiva enacts the dance of creation and destruction, the cosmic cycle of birth and death. His serpentine body bends at the neck, waist, and knees in accordance with India's specific and prescribed dance movements. Every part of the statue has symbolic meaning (and some parts have multiple meanings): Shiva's earrings are mismatched to represent the male/female duality; the cobra, symbolizing the celestial force (*kundalini*), embodies various kinds of divine energy. Shiva's right hand holds a small drum, the symbol of creation; a second right hand performs the *mudra* meaning protection from evil (see Figure 9.25); one left hand holds a flame, the symbol of destruction; the second left hand points toward Shiva's feet, the left "released" from worldliness, the right one crushing a demon-dwarf symbolizing egotism and ignorance. Utterly peaceful in countenance, Shiva embodies the five activities of the Hindu godhead: creation, protection, destruction, release from destiny, and enlightenment. By these activities, the god dances the universe in and out of existence.

Figure 14.3 *Shiva Nataraja, Lord of the Dance,* from southern India, Chola period, eleventh century. Bronze, 35 × 28 in. Dallas Museum of Art. Surrounded by a ring of fire, Shiva dances the eternal rhythms of the universe: birth, death, and rebirth.

skull (victory over death)

crescent moon (cyclical time)

Goddess Ganga (sacred river Ganges)

locks of hair

third eye

drum (creation/the passage of time)

flame (destruction)

mudra (protection from evil)

halo of fire (cosmic ring)

mismatched earrings (male/female)

cobra (regeneration/cosmic force)

uplifted foot (release from worldliness)

mudra (release from worldliness)

lotus platform (primordial creation)

demon-dwarf (ignorance/ego)

at the four corners of the base of the *Standing Vishnu* in Figure 14.2, which once held poles for transporting the statue.) As a ninth-century Tamil poet explained, "The god comes within everyone's reach."

The third god of the trinity, Shiva, is the Hindu lord of regeneration. A god of destruction and creation, of disease and death, and of sexuality and rebirth, Shiva embodies the dynamic rhythms of the universe. While often shown in a dual male and female aspect, Shiva is most commonly portrayed as Lord of the Dance, an image that evokes the activity of the universe and the Hindu notion of time. Unlike the Western view of time, which is linear and progressive, the Hindu perception of time is cyclical: comparable to an ever-turning cosmic wheel. The four-armed figure of Shiva as Lord of the Dance is one of medieval India's most famous Hindu icons (see LOOKING INTO, Figure **14.3**)—so popular, in fact, that Tamil sculptors cast multiple editions of the subject, widely known as a "visual sermon."

Indian Religious Literature

Medieval Indian literature drew heavily on the mythology and legends of early Hinduism as found in the Vedic hymns and in India's two great epics, the *Mahabharata* and the *Ramayana* (see chapter 3). This body of classic Indian literature was recorded in Sanskrit, the language of India's educated classes. Serving much the same purpose that Latin served in the medieval West, Sanskrit functioned for centuries as a cohesive force amidst India's diverse regional vernacular dialects.

Among the most popular forms of Hindu literature are the *Puranas* (Sanskrit, "old stories"), a collection of eighteen religious books that preserve the myths and legends of the Hindu gods. Transmitted orally for centuries, they were not written down until well after 500 C.E. Many of the tales in the *Puranas* illustrate the special powers of Vishnu and Shiva or their avatars. In the *Vishnu Purana*, for instance, Krishna (the eighth and most venerated incarnation of Vishnu) is pictured as the "cosmic lover" who courts his devotees with sensual abandon, seducing them to become one with the divinity. Over the next five centuries, as the devotional aspects of Hinduism came to overshadow the metaphysical aspects of the faith, Krishna became increasingly humanized. His seduction of Radha, his principal consort, became the focus of religious poems, the most notable of which is the twelfth-century *Gita Govinda*, written by Jayadeva (fl. 1200). This epic poem, which holds an important place in Indian devotional music and art, tells of the enduring romance between Govinda (Krishna) and Radha, the most enticing of his 16,000 wives and lovers (Figure **14.4**).

In both the *Puranas* and the *Gita*, intense earthly passion serves as a metaphor for the Self (Atman) seeking union with the Absolute (Brahman). Unlike the medieval Christian condemnation of erotic sensuality, Hinduism values the physical union of male and female as symbolic of the eternal mingling of flesh and spirit, a state of spiritual unity that would lead believers out of the cycle of reincarnation. The *Upanishads* make clear the analogy:

Figure 14.4 Page from *Gita Govinda*, "Krishna and Radha with their Confidantes," India, ca. 1635–1640. Ink and opaque watercolor on paper, 10¼ × 8⅜ in. Krishna (his name means "dark" or "dark blue") declares his love for Radha, symbol of human longing for the divine. Her servants are shown on the right; below is a garden bower set with refreshments.

In the embrace of his beloved a man forgets the whole world—everything both within and without. In the same manner, he who embraces the Self knows neither within nor without.

In the following passage from the *Vishnu Purana*, Krishna's cajoling and sensuous courtship, culminating in the circle of the dance, symbolizes the god's love for the human soul and the soul's unswerving attraction to the One.

READING 14.1 From the *Vishnu Purana*

(recorded after 500)

. . . [Krishna], observing the clear sky, bright with the autumnal moon, and the air perfumed with the fragrance of the wild water-lily, in whose buds the clustering bees were murmuring their songs, felt inclined to join with the milkmaids [Gopis] in sport. . . . 1

Then Madhava [Krishna], coming amongst them, conciliated some with soft speeches, some with gentle looks; and some he took by the hand: and the illustrious deity sported with them in the stations of the dance. As each of the milkmaids, however, attempted to keep in one place, close to the side of Krishna, the circle of the dance could not be constructed; and he, therefore, took each by the hand, and when their eyelids were shut by the effects of such touch, the circle was formed. Then proceeded the dance, to the music of their clashing 10 bracelets, and songs that celebrated, in suitable strain, the charms of the autumnal season. Krishna sang of the moon of autumn—a mine of gentle radiance; but the nymphs repeated the praises of Krishna alone. At times, one of them, wearied by the revolving dance, threw her arms, ornamented with tinkling bracelets, round the neck of the destroyer of Madhu [Krishna]; another, skilled in the art of singing his praises, embraced him. The drops of perspiration from the arms of Hari [Krishna] were like fertilizing rain, which produced a crop of down upon the temples of the milkmaids. Krishna sang the strain that was appropriate to the dance. The milkmaids repeatedly exclaimed "Bravo, Krishna!" to his song. When leading, they followed him; when returning they encountered him; and whether he went forwards or backwards, they ever attended on his steps. Whilst frolicking thus, they considered every instant without him a myriad of years; and prohibited (in vain) by husbands, fathers, brothers, they went forth at night to sport with Krishna, the object of their affection. 20 30

Thus, the illimitable being, the benevolent remover of all imperfections, assumed the character of a youth among the females of the herdsmen of [the district of] Vraja; pervading their natures and that of their lords by his own essence, all-diffusive like the wind. For even as the elements of ether, fire, earth, water, and air are comprehended in all creatures, so also is he everywhere present, and in all . . .

Q **How do "seduction" and "the dance" function as metaphors of Hindu spirituality?**

Indian Poetry

If the religious literature of India is sensuous in nature, so too is the secular literature, much of which is devoted to physical pleasure. Sanskrit lyric poetry is the most erotic of all world literatures. Unlike the poetry of other ancient cultures, that of India was meant to be spoken, not sung. On the other hand, Sanskrit poetry shares with most ancient Greek and Latin verse a lack of rhyme. It makes use of such literary devices as **alliteration** (the repetition of initial sounds in successive words, as in "panting and pale") and **assonance** (similarity between vowel sounds, as in "lake" and "fate").

In Sanskrit verse, implication and innuendo are more important than direct statement or assertion. The multiplicity of synonyms in Sanskrit permits a wide range of meanings, puns, and verbal play. And although this wealth of synonyms and near-synonyms contributes to the richness of Indian poetry, it makes English translation quite difficult. For example, there are some fifty expressions in Sanskrit for "lotus"; in English there is but one. Sanskrit poets employ a large number of stock similes: the lady's face is like the moon, her eyes resemble lotuses, and so on. Classical rules of style dictate that every poem must exhibit a single characteristic sentiment, such as anger, courage, wonder, or passion. Grief, however—the emotion humans seek to avoid—may not dominate any poem or play.

A great flowering of Indian literature occurred between the fourth and tenth centuries, but it was not until the eleventh century and thereafter that the renowned anthologies of Sanskrit poetry appeared. One of the most honored of these collections, an anthology of 1739 verses dating from between 700 and 1050, was compiled by the late eleventh-century Buddhist monk Vidyakara. It is entitled *The Treasury of Well-Turned Verse*. As with most Indian anthologies, poems on the subject of love outnumber those in any other category, and many of the love lyrics feature details of physical passion. As suggested by the selection that follows, Indian poetry is more frank and erotic than ancient or medieval European love poetry and less concerned with the romantic aspects of courtship than most Islamic verse.

READING 14.2 From *The Treasury of Well-Turned Verse* (ca. 1050)

"When we have loved, my love"

When we have loved, my love,
Panting and pale from love,
Then from your cheeks my love,
Scent of the sweat I love:
And when our bodies love
Now to relax in love
After the stress of love,
Ever still more I love
Our mingled breath of love.

"When he desired to see her breast"

When he desired to see her breast
She clasped him tight in an embrace;
And when he wished to kiss her lip
She used cosmetics on her face.
She held his hand quite firmly pressed
Between her thighs in desperate grip;
   Nor yielded to his caress,
   Yet kept alive his wantonness.

"If my absent bride were but a pond"

If my absent bride were but a pond,
her eyes the water lilies and her face the lotus,
her brows the rippling waves, her arms the lotus stems;
then might I dive into the water of her loveliness
and cool of limb escape the mortal pain
exacted by the flaming fire of love.

Q **How do these poems compare with similar expressions of love in Egypt (Reading 2.2), Greece (Reading 5.2), and Rome (Reading 6.6)?**

Indian Architecture

Hinduism generated some of the finest works of art and architecture in India's long history. Buddhist imagery influenced the style of medieval Hindu art, and Buddhist rock-cut temples and shrines provided models for Hindu architects. Between the sixth and fourteenth centuries, Hindus built thousands of temple-shrines to honor Vishnu and Shiva. These structures varied in shape from region

Figure 14.5 Kandariya Mahadeo temple, Khajuraho, India, ca. 1000. Stone, height approx. 102 ft.

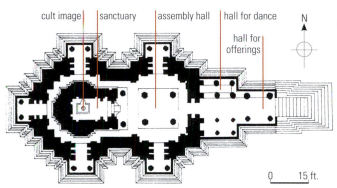

Figure 14.6 Plan of Kandariya Mahadeo temple, Khajuraho.

to region, but generally they took the shape of a mound (often square or rectangular) topped with lofty towers or spires. Such structures were built of stone or brick with iron dowels frequently substituted for mortar. As with the early Buddhist *stupa* (see Figure 9.20), the Hindu temple symbolized the sacred mountain. Some temples were even painted white to resemble the snowy peaks of the Himalayas.

The Buddhist *stupa* was invariably a solid mound; however, the Hindu temple, more akin to the *chaitya* hall (see Figures 9.22 and 9.23), encloses a series of interior spaces leading to a shrine—the dwelling place of the god on earth. Devotees enter the temple by way of an ornate porch or series of porches, each porch having its own roof and spire. Beyond these areas lies a large hall, and, finally, the dim, womblike sanctuary that enshrines the cult image of the god. The Hindu temple does not serve as a place for congregational worship (as does the medieval church); rather, its basic function is as a place of private, individual devotion, a place in which the devotee may visit and make offerings to the god. Often the focus of pilgrimage, at particular times of the year it hosts religious festivals specific to the god (or gods) to which it is dedicated. The design of the Hindu temple is based on the cosmic mandala (the diagrammatic map of the universe) and governed by divine numerology. The sacred space at the center is the primordial Brahman; the surrounding squares correspond to gods, whose roles in this context are as guardians of the Absolute Spirit. Although the Hindu temple and the Gothic cathedral were

Figure 14.7 Sculpted figures on the Kandariya Mahadeo temple, Khajuraho.

very different in terms of design and function, both signified the profoundly human impulse to forge a link between heaven and earth and between matter and spirit.

The Kandariya Mahadeo temple in Khajuraho is but one of twenty-five remaining Hindu temple-shrines that rise like cosmic mountains out of the dusty plains of central north India (see Map 14.1). Dedicated in the early eleventh century to the god Shiva, the temple rests on a high masonry terrace and is entered through an elevated porch (Figures **14.5** and **14.6**). Like most Indian temples, Kandariya Mahadeo consists of a series of extensively ornamented horizontal cornices that ascend in narrowing diameter to their lotus-shaped peaks. At each tier of the beehivelike tower is a row of high-relief sculptures: human beings and animals drawn from India's great epics appear at the lower levels, while divine nymphs and celestial deities adorn the upper sections. The ornamental ensemble comprises a total of some 600 figures (Figure **14.7**).

Like the Gothic cathedral, the Hindu temple was a kind of "bible" in stone. Yet no two artistic enterprises could have been further apart: whereas the medieval Church discouraged the depiction of nudity as suggestive of sexual pleasure and sinfulness, Hinduism exalted the representation of the human body as symbolic of abundance, prosperity, and regeneration. The sinuous nudes that animate the surface of the Kandariya Mahadeo temple assume languid, erotic poses. Deeply carved, and endowed with supple limbs and swelling breasts and buttocks, their bodies signify the divine attributes of life-breath and "fullness." The loving couples (known as *mithunas*)—men and women locked in passionate embrace (Figure **14.8**)—call to mind the imagery of the dance in the *Vishnu Purana*. They symbolize the interdependence of male and female forces in the universe, and the ultimate union of human and divine love.

Indian Music and Dance

The music of India is inseparable from religious practice. A single musical tradition—one that goes back some 3000 years—dominates both secular and religious music. In ancient times, India developed a system of music characterized by specific melodic sequences (*ragas*) and rhythms (*talas*). The centuries have produced thousands of *ragas*, sixty of which remain in standard use; nine are considered primary. Each *raga* consists of a series of seven basic tones arranged in a specific order. The performer may improvise on a chosen *raga* in any manner and at any length. As with the Greek modes, each of the basic Indian *ragas* is associated with a different emotion, mood, or time of day. A famous Indian anecdote tells how a sixteenth-century court musician, entertaining at midday, once sang a night *raga* so beautiful that darkness instantly fell where he stood. Governing the rhythmic pattern of an Indian musical composition is the *tala*, which, in union with the *raga*, shapes the mood of the piece. Indian music divides the octave into twenty-two principal tones and many more microtones, all of which are treated equally. There is, therefore, no tonal center and no harmony in traditional Indian music. Rather, the character of a musical composition depends on the choice of the *raga* and on its exposition. A typical *raga* opens with a slow portion that establishes a particular mood, moves into a second portion that explores rhythmic variations, and closes with rapid, complex, and often syncopated improvisations that culminate in a frenzied finale.

India developed a broad range of stringed instruments that were either bowed or plucked. The most popular of these was the **sitar**, a long-necked stringed instrument with a gourd resonator, which came into use during the thirteenth century (Figure **14.9**). Related to the kithara, an instrument used in ancient Greece (see chapter 5), the sitar provided a distinctive rhythmic "drone," while its strings were plucked for melody. Accompanied by flutes, drums, bells, and horns, sitar players were fond of improvising patterns of notes in quick succession against a resonating bass sound.

Figure 14.8 *Mithuna* couple, from Orissa, India, twelfth to thirteenth centuries. Stone, height 6 ft. On the exterior of Hindu temples, interspersed with figures of the gods, the erotically linked *mithunas* represent the soul's yearning for union with Brahman. The canopy of leaves above the couple may also suggest fertility.

See Music Listening Selections at end of chapter.

Figure 14.9 Ravi Shankar (1920–2012) playing the sitar (right); the other musicians play the tabla (hand drums) and a tamboura (plucked string instrument).

The Sanskrit word for music (*sangeeta*) means both "sound" and "rhythm," suggesting that the music of India, like that of most ancient cultures, was inseparable from the art of the dance. Indian dance, like the *raga* that accompanied it, set a mood or told a story by way of rigidly observed steps and hand gestures (*mudra*). India trained professional dancers to achieve difficult leg and foot positions, some of which may be seen on the façades of Indian temples (see Figure 14.7). Each of some thirty traditional dances requires a combination of complex body positions, of which there are more than a hundred. The close relationship among the arts of medieval India provides something of a parallel with the achievement of the medieval synthesis in the West. On the other hand, the sensual character of the arts of India distinguishes them sharply from those of Christian Europe.

China

Nowhere else in the world has a single cultural tradition dominated so consistently over so long a period as in China. When European merchants visited China in the thirteenth century, the Chinese had already enjoyed 1700 years of civilization. China's agrarian landmass, rich in mineral, vegetable, and animal resources, readily supported a large and self-sufficient population, the majority of which constituted a massive land-bound peasantry. Despite internal shifts of power and repeated attacks from its northern nomadic neighbors, China experienced a single form of government—imperial monarchy—and a large degree of political order until the invasion of the Mongols in the thirteenth century. Even after the establishment of Mongol rule under Kublai Khan (1215–1294), the governmental bureaucracy on which China had long depended remained intact, and Chinese culture continued to flourish. The wealth and splendor of early fourteenth-century China inspired the awe and admiration of Western visitors, such as the famous Venetian merchant-adventurer Marco Polo (1254–1324) (see Chapter 18). Indeed, in the two centuries prior to Europe's rise to economic dominion (but especially between 1250 and 1350), China was "the most extensive, populous, and technologically advanced region of the medieval world."

China in the Tang Era

Tang China (618–907) was a unified, centralized state that had no equal in Asia or the medieval West. In contrast with India, class distinctions in China were flexible and allowed a fair degree of social mobility: thanks to the imperial examination system, even commoners could rise to become members of the ruling elite. Nevertheless, in China as in all Asian and European civilizations of premodern times, the great masses of peasants had no voice in political matters.

Under the rule of the Tang emperors, China experienced a flowering of culture that was unmatched anywhere in the world. Often called the greatest dynasty in Chinese history, the Tang brought unity and wealth to a vast Chinese empire (Map **14.2**). Tang emperors perpetuated the economic policies of their immediate predecessors, but they employed their vast powers to achieve a remarkable series of reforms. They completed the Grand

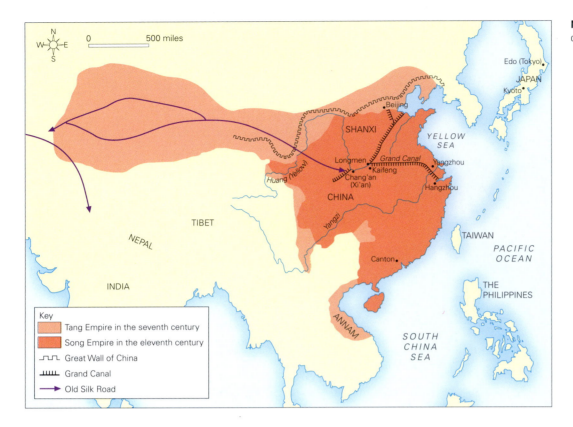

Map 14.2 East Asia, ca. 600–1300.

Canal connecting the lower valley of the Yellow River to the eastern banks of the Yangzi, a project that facilitated shipping and promoted internal cohesion and wealth. Arab merchants who reached China by either land or sea reported the equitable standards of commercial exchange, as well as the wealth of luxury goods—silks, pearls, gold, and silver—transacted with the aid of China's copper coins. The emperors also initiated a full census of the population (some four centuries before a similar survey was undertaken in Norman England), which was repeated

Figure 14.10 Attributed to the Song emperor **HUIZONG** (reigned 1101–1125), but probably by court academician, after a lost painting by Zhang Xuan (fl. 713–741), *Women Combing Silk*, detail of *Court Ladies Preparing Newly Woven Silk*, Northern Song dynasty, early twelfth century. Ink, color, and gold on silk handscroll, height 14½ in., length 4 ft. 9¼ in.

Figure 14.11 Attributed to **GU HONGZHONG**, detail of *Night Revels of Han Xizai*, ca. twelfth-century copy of a tenth-century composition. Ink and color on silk handscroll, 11¼ in. × 11 ft. 1 in. The tenth-century emperor Li Yu, angry with one of his officials who had been lax in attending court, is said to have assigned the artist to spy on him at the all-night parties in his private quarters. The courtier's misdeeds apparently continued even after the "evidence" was brought before the emperor. On the left, a young girl plays a *pipa*, the Chinese equivalent of the lute.

every three years. They also humanized the penal code and tried to guarantee farmlands to the peasants. They stimulated agricultural production, encouraged silk production (Figure **14.10**) and the flourishing silk trade, launched a tax reform that based assessments on units of land rather than agricultural output, and they commuted payments from goods to coins.

The Tang Empire dwarfed the Carolingian Empire in the West not only in terms of its geographic size and population but also with respect to its intellectual and educational accomplishments. Tang bureaucrats, steeped in Confucian traditions and rigorously trained in the literary classics, were members of an intellectual elite that rose to service on the basis of merit. Beginning in the seventh century (but rooted in a long tradition of leadership based on education and ability), every government official was subject to a rigorous civil service examination. A young man gained a political position by passing three levels of examinations (district, provincial, and national) that tested his

familiarity with the Chinese classics as well as his grasp of contemporary politics. For lower-ranking positions, candidates took exams in law, mathematics, and calligraphy. As in the Islamic world and the Christian West, higher education in China required close familiarity with the basic religious and philosophical texts. But because Chinese characters changed very little over the centuries, students could read 1500-year-old texts as easily as they could read contemporary ones. Chinese classics were thus accessible to Chinese scholars in a way that the Greco-Roman classics were not to Western scholars. Training for the arduous civil service examinations required a great degree of memorization and a thorough knowledge of the Chinese literary tradition, but originality was also important: candidates had to prove accomplishment in the writing of prose and poetry, as well as in the analysis of administrative policy. Strict standards applied to grading, and candidates who failed the exams (only 1 to 10 percent passed the first level) could take them over and over, even into middle and old age.

During the seventh century, the imperial college in the capital city of Chang'an (present-day Xi'an) prepared some 3000 men for the civil service examinations. (As in the West, women were excluded from education in colleges and universities.) Such scholar officials constituted China's highest social class. And while the vast population of Chinese peasants lived in relative ignorance and poverty, the aristocratic bureaucracy of the Tang generally enjoyed lives of wealth and position (Figure **14.11**). Nowhere else in the world (except perhaps ninth-century Baghdad) was such prestige attached to scholarship and intellectual achievement. Despite instances in which family connections influenced political position, the imperial

Science and Technology

700	the Chinese perfect the making of porcelain, which reaches Europe as "china"
725	the Chinese build a water clock with a regulating device anticipating mechanical clocks
748	the first printed newspaper appears in Beijing
868	the *Diamond Sutra*, the first known printed book, is produced in China

examination system remained the main route to official status in China well into the twentieth century.

A less enlightened Chinese practice survived into the modern period: the binding of women's feet. From earliest times, Chinese women participated in agricultural activities as well as in the manufacture of silk (see Figure 14.10); many were trained in dance and musical performance. In the early 900s, however, as women seem to have assumed a more ornamental role in Chinese society, footbinding became common among the upper classes. To indicate that their female offspring were exempt from common labor, prosperous urban families bound the feet of their infant daughters—a practice that broke the arch and dwarfed the foot to half its normal growth. Footbinding, a cruel means of signifying social status, persisted into the early twentieth century.

Confucianism

During the Tang Era, Confucianism remained China's foremost moral philosophy. Confucian teachings encouraged social harmony and respect for the ruling monarch, whom the Chinese called the "Son of Heaven." While Tang rulers drew on Buddhism and Daoism to legitimize their office, political counsel remained Confucian. Confucian culture held firmly to a secular ethic that emphasized proper conduct (*li*) and the sanctity of human life on earth. These tenets challenged neither the popular worship of Chinese nature deities, nor the ancient rites that honored the souls of the dead. Confucian ideals of order, harmony, and filial duty were easily reconciled with holistic Daoism. Tolerant of all religions, the Chinese never engaged in religious wars or massive crusades of the kind that disrupted both Christian and Islamic civilizations.

Buddhism

The Tang Era was the golden age of Chinese Buddhism. Buddhist monasteries flourished and Buddhist sects proliferated. These sects emphasized various aspects of the Buddha's teachings or practices, the first of which was meditation.

Figure 14.12 *Luohan*, China, tenth to thirteenth centuries. Pottery with three-color glaze, height 3 ft. 10½ in.

Figure 14.13 **ZHANG ZEDUAN**, detail from *Life Along the River on the Eve of the Qing Ming Festival*, late eleventh to early twelfth century. Handscroll, ink on silk, 10 in. × 17 ft. 3 in.

The image of the Buddhist **luohan** (or *arhat*, "worthy one"), transfixed in a state of deep meditation (Figure **14.12**), became a popular model of self-control and selflessness—an ideal type not unlike the Christian saint.

The most famous of Tang China's Buddhist sects was the Pure Land sect, presided over by Amitabha, the Buddha of Infinite Light. In the Mahayana tradition, this sect emphasized faith (and the repeated invocation of the Buddha's name) as a means of achieving rebirth in the Pure Land, or Paradise. Simply uttering his name many times a day assured the faithful of salvation. Followers of Amitahba were assisted by the *bodhisattva* of mercy known as Guanyin (see Figure **14.1**). Chan Buddhism ("Zen" in Japan) became equally influential. Rejecting other popular practices, such as the study of Scriptures or the performance of meritorious deeds, it held meditation as the sole means of achieving enlightenment—deliverance in a sudden illuminating flash.

While Confucianism was generally tolerant of popular religious practice, it disapproved of Buddhist celibacy, which contravened the Confucian esteem for family. The vast wealth and political influence accumulated by the Buddhist community and the loss of large numbers of talented men to Buddhism moved some emperors to restrict the number of Buddhist monasteries and to limit the ordination of new monks and nuns. This culminated in a brief but catastrophic ban of the religion in the year 845; Buddhist temples and monasteries were closed, and monks and nuns were forced to return to the population at large. The ban, however, was short in duration; and the vigor of Buddhist religion became ever greater in subsequent years.

China in the Song Era

After a brief period of political turmoil resulting from the collapse of the Tang dynasty and attacks by nomadic tribes, the Song dynasty (960–1279) reestablished a unified Chinese empire. Although its territory was much reduced compared to that of the Tang Empire, and it had powerful and land-hungry neighbors to the north and west, the Song nevertheless presided over a period of great advancement both in terms of culture and technology. The three centuries of Song rule corresponded roughly to the golden age of Muslim learning, the waning of the Abbasid Empire, and the era of Norman domination in Europe (see chapters 10 and 11).

The Song Era enjoyed population growth, agricultural productivity, and vigorous commercial trade centering on the exportation of tea, silk, and ceramics. China's new economic prosperity caused a population shift from the countryside to the city, where social mobility was on the rise. The imperial capitals of Kaifeng and Hangzhou (see Map 14.2), with populations of over one million people, boasted a variety of restaurants, teahouses, temples, gardens, and shops, including bookstores and pet shops (Figure **14.13**). Chinese cities were larger and more populous than those in the West, and city dwellers enjoyed conditions of safety that are enviable even today—in Hangzhou, the streets were patrolled at night, and bridges and canals were guarded and fitted with balustrades to prevent drunken revelers from falling into the water.

Given the constant threat posed by the Song's northern neighbors, a ready army was a necessity. Mercenaries, however, characterize the military of the Song state. Where medieval Islam and the feudal West prized heroism and the art of war, the Chinese despised military life. A Chinese proverb warned that just as good steel should not be made into common nails, good men should not become soldiers. Chinese poets frequently lamented the disruption of family life as soldiers left home to defend remote regions of the Empire. In combat, the Chinese generally preferred starving out their enemies to confronting them in battle. The peaceful nature of the Chinese impressed their first Western visitors: arriving in China a half-century after the end of the Song Era, Marco Polo observed with some astonishment that no one carried arms. Well into the twentieth century, China espoused the notion of cosmic harmony best expressed in the writings of the Neo-Confucian philosopher Zhang Zai (1020–1077):

> Heaven is my father and earth is my mother, and even such a small creature as I finds an intimate place in their midst. Therefore that which extends throughout the universe I regard as my body and that which directs the universe I consider as my nature. All people are my brothers and sisters, and all things are my companions.

Confucian, Daoist, and Buddhist practices continued to flourish during the Song Era. It was at this time that the image and person of the *bodhisattva* of compassion, Guanyin, became feminized (see Figure 14.1). This beloved icon, like that of the Virgin Mary in medieval Christendom, embodied the loving, forgiving aspect of devotional faith.

Technology in the Tang and Song Eras

Chinese civilization is exceptional in the extraordinary number of its technological inventions, many of which came into use elsewhere in the world long after their utilization in China. A case in point is printing, which originated in ninth-century China but was not perfected in the West until the fifteenth century. The earliest printed document, the *Diamond Sutra*, dated 868, is a Buddhist text produced from large woodcut blocks (Figure **14.14**). In the mid-eleventh century, the Chinese invented movable type and, by the end of the century, the entire body of Buddhist

and Confucian classics, including the commentaries, were available in printed editions. One such classic (a required text for civil service candidates) was the *Book of Songs*, a venerable collection of over 300 poems dating from the first millennium B.C.E. By the twelfth century, the Chinese were also printing paper money—a practice that inevitably gave rise to the "profession" of counterfeiting. Although in China movable type did not inspire a revolution in the communication of ideas (as it would in Renaissance Europe), it encouraged literacy, fostered scholarship, and facilitated the preservation of the Chinese classics.

Chinese technology often involved the intelligent application of natural principles to produce labor-saving devices. Examples include the water mill (devised to grind tea leaves and to provide power to run machinery), the wheelbarrow (used in China from at least the third century but not found in Europe until more than ten centuries

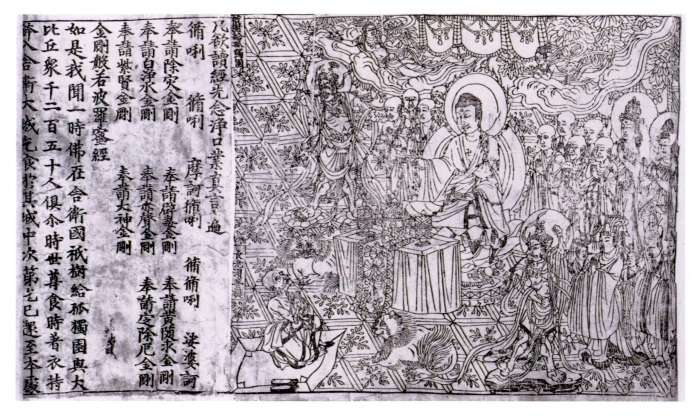

Figure 14.14 The *Diamond Sutra*, the world's earliest printed book, dated 868. 30 in. × 6 ft. In 1900, the *Diamond Sutra* was found along with hundreds of other scrolls sealed in a Chinese cave. It records the Buddha's teachings on the nature of perception.

Science and Technology

1045	Su Song builds a giant water clock and mechanical armillary sphere
1100	the Chinese use coke in iron smelting
1145	illustrations of the internal organs and circulatory vessels are published in China
1221	the Chinese devise shrapnel bombs with gunpowder

later), and the stern-post rudder and magnetic compass, both of which originated in the Han Era (see chapter 3), but were improved by the Song to facilitate maritime trade. The last two devices had revolutionary consequences for Western Europeans, who used them to inaugurate an age of exploration and discovery (see chapter 18). Gunpowder, invented by the Chinese as early as the seventh century and used in firework displays, was employed (in the form of fire-arrow incendiary devices) for military purposes in the mid-tenth century, but arrived in the West only in the fourteenth century. Other contrivances, such as the abacus and the hydromechanical clock, and such processes as iron casting (used for armaments, for suspension bridges, and for the construction of some Tang and Song pagodas) were unknown in the West for centuries, or were invented independently of Chinese prototypes. Not until the eighteenth century, for instance, did Western Europeans master the technique of steel casting, which had been in use in China since the sixth century C.E.

Some of China's most important technological contributions, such as the foot stirrup (in use well before the fifth century) and gunpowder, improved China's ability to withstand the attacks of Huns, Turks, and other tribal peoples who repeatedly attacked its northern frontiers. In the West, however, these devices had revolutionary results: the former ushered in the military aspect of medieval feudalism; and the latter ultimately undermined siege warfare and inaugurated modern forms of combat. While thirteenth-century China was far ahead of the medieval West in science and technology, its wealth in manpower—a population of some hundred million people—may have made industrial technology unnecessary.

In addition to their ingenuity in engineering and metallurgy, the Chinese advanced the practice of medicine. From the eleventh century on, they used vaccination to prevent diseases, thus establishing the science of immunology. Their grasp of human anatomy and the theory that illness derives from an imbalance of *qi* (life energy) gave rise to acupuncture—the practice of applying needles to specific parts of the body to regulate and restore proper energy flow. Chinese medical encyclopedias dating from the twelfth century were far in advance of any produced in the medieval West. In both India and China, the belief in the unity of mind and body encouraged healing practices (such as meditation and yoga) that have met with an enthusiastic reception in the West only in recent decades.

Chinese Literature

Chinese literature owes little to other cultures. It reflects at every turn a high regard for native traditions and for the concepts of universal harmony expressed in Confucian and Daoist thought. Philosophic in nature, it is, however, markedly free of religious sentiment. Even between the fifth and ninth centuries, when Buddhism was at its height, Chinese literature was largely secular, hence quite different from most of the writings of medieval Europe and the rest of Asia.

The Tang and Song eras saw the production of a wide variety of literary genres, including treatises on history, geography, religion, economics, and architecture; monographs on botany and zoology; essays on administrative and governmental affairs; drama, fiction, and lyric poetry. Experts in the art of compiling information, the Chinese produced a vast assortment of encyclopedias, manuals of divination and ritual, ethical discourses, and anthologies based on the teachings of Confucius and others. Like the medieval Scholastics in the West, Chinese scholars esteemed their classical past, but, unlike the Europeans, they acknowledged no conflict between (and therefore no need to reconcile) faith and reason.

During the twelfth and thirteenth centuries, in Song urban centers, storytelling flourished, and popular theater arose in the form of dramatic performance. Popular genres included comedy, historical plays, and tales of everyday life—many of which featured love stories. As dramatists began to adapt literary plots to music, **opera** (musical drama) became the fashionable entertainment among ordinary townspeople and at the imperial court. The first Chinese **novels**—products of a long tradition of oral narrative—also appeared during the twelfth century, focusing on the adventures of contemporary heroes.

The novel, however, was not original to China. Rather, it was a product of the aristocratic and feudal culture of medieval Japan (discussed later in this chapter). In China, early fiction reached a high point with the monumental historical novel entitled *Three Kingdoms* (attributed to the fourteenth-century playwright Luo Guanzhong). This 1000-page work, filled with hundreds of characters and lengthy descriptions of martial prowess, brings alive the turbulent era (220–280) that followed the breakup of the Han dynasty.

Chinese Music and Poetry

To the Chinese, music functioned to imitate and sustain the harmony of nature. Both Daoists and Confucians regarded music as an expression of cosmic order, and Daoists even made distinctions between *yin* and *yang* notes. Like most of the music of the ancient world, that of China was monophonic, but it assumed a unique timbre produced by nasal tones that were often high in pitch and subtle in inflection. The sliding nasal tones that typify Chinese music resemble those of the zither. Frequently used for Buddhist chant (see chapter 9), the zither was

See Music Listening Selections at end of chapter.

the favorite Chinese instrument, and musical notation to guide the performer was devised as early as the second century B.C.E. Chinese instrumental ensembles included the zither, the *pipa* (a short-necked lute), and a variety of flutes, bells, and chimes (see Figure 14.11).

The most popular Chinese musical genre was the solo song, performed with or without instrumental accompaniment. A close kinship between Chinese music and speech was enforced by the unique nature of the Chinese language. Consisting of some 50,000 characters, spoken Chinese demands subtle intonations: the pitch or tonal level at which any word is pronounced gives it its meaning. A single word may have more than a hundred meanings, depending on how it is uttered. In this sense, all communication in the Chinese language is musical—a phenomenon that has particular importance for Chinese poetry. Chinese poetry is a kind of vocal music: a line of spoken poetry is—like music—essentially a series of tones that rise and fall in various rhythms. Moreover, since Chinese is a monosyllabic language with few word endings, rhyme is common to speech. All Chinese verse is rhymed, often in long runs that are almost impossible to imitate in English. Equally difficult to capture in translation are the extraordinary kinds of condensation and innuendo that most characterize Chinese verse.

During the Tang Era, China produced some of the most beautiful poetry in world literature. The poems of the eighth and ninth centuries—an era referred to as the golden age of Chinese poetry—resemble diary entries that record the intimate experience of everyday life. Unlike the poetry of India, Chinese lyrics are rarely sensuous or erotic and only infrequently attentive to either physical affection or romantic love. Restrained and sophisticated, the poetry of the Tang period was written by scholar-poets (the so-called literati) who considered verse-making, along with calligraphy and painting, the mark of educational and intellectual refinement. From earliest times, nature and natural imagery played a large part in Chinese verse. Tang poets continued this long tradition: their poems are filled with the meditative spirit of Daoism and a sense of oneness with nature.

Two of the greatest poets of the Tang period, Li Bo (ca. 700–762) and Du Fu (712–770), belonged to the group of cultivated individuals who made up China's cultural elite. Although Li Bo was not a scholar-official, as was his friend Du Fu, he was familiar with the Chinese classics. Both Li Bo and Du Fu were members of the Eight Immortals of the Wine Cup, an informal association of poets who celebrated the kinship of ink and drink and the value of inebriation to poetic inspiration. Du Fu, often regarded as China's greatest poet, wrote some 1400 poems, some that recorded the dynastic wars that plagued mid-eighth-century China, and others that infused autobiographical reflection with genuine emotion and humor. In contrast, the ninth-century poet Bo Zhuyi, who headed the Tang Bureau of War, brought to his poems a note of cynicism and worldliness that is particularly typical of the late Tang period and that of the succeeding Song. Like most of the poets of his time, he was a statesman,

a calligrapher, an aesthetician, and a moralist. He thus epitomized the ideal well-rounded individual long before that concept became important in Renaissance Europe.

READING 14.3 Poems of the Tang and Song Eras
(750–900)

Li Bo's "Watching the Mount Lushan Waterfall"

Incense-Burner Peak shimmers in the sun,   1
Purple mist slowly rising.
A flying stream, seen from below,
Hangs like clouds down the crag.
The waterfall pours itself   5
Three thousand feet straight down,
Roaring like the Milky Way
Tumbling from high heaven.

Li Bo's "Zhuang Zhou and the Butterfly"

Zhuang Zhou[1] in dream became a butterfly,   1
And the butterfly became Zhuang Zhou at waking.
Which was the real—the butterfly or the man?
Who can tell the end of the endless changes of things?
The water that flows into the depth of the distant sea   5
Returns anon to the shallows of a transparent stream.
The man, raising melons outside the green gate of the city,
Was once the Prince of the East Hill,[2]
So must rank and riches vanish.
You know it, still you toil and toil,—What for?   10

Du Fu's "Spring Rain"

Oh lovely spring rain!   1
You come at the right time, in the right season.
Riding the night winds you creep in,
Quietly wetting the world.
Roads are dark, clouds are darker.   5
Only a light on a boat, gleaming.
And in the morning the city is drunk with red flowers,
Cluster after cluster, moist, glistening.

Du Fu's "Farewell Once More"
(To my friend Yan at Feng Ji Station)

Here we part.   1
You go off in the distance,
And once more the forested mountains
Are empty, unfriendly.
What holiday will see us   5
Drunk together again?
Last night we walked
Arm in arm in the moonlight,

---

[1] A fourth-century follower of Lao Zi (see chapter 3), whose writings describe how, in a dream, he became a butterfly.

[2] The marquis of Dongling, a third-century B.C.E. official, lost his exalted position at court after the fall of the Qin dynasty, and retired to grow melons outside of the city of Chang'an.

Singing sentimental ballads
Along the banks of the river.   10
Your honor outlasts three emperors.
I go back to my lonely house by the river,
Mute, friendless, feeding the crumbling years.

Bo Zhuyi's "On His Baldness"

At dawn I sighed to see my hairs fall;   1
At dusk I sighed to see my hairs fall.
For I dreaded the time when the last lock should go . . .
They are all gone and I do not mind at all!
I have done with that cumbrous washing and getting dry;   5
My tiresome comb forever is laid aside.
Best of all, when the weather is hot and wet,
To have no topknot weighing down on one's head!
I put aside my dusty conical cap;
And loose my collar fringe,   10
In a silver jar I have stored a cold stream;
On my bald pate I trickle a ladle-full.
Like one baptized with the Water of Buddha's Law,
I sit and receive this cool, cleansing joy.
Now I know why the priest who seeks repose   15
Frees his heart by first shaving his head.

Bo Zhuyi's "Madly Singing in the Mountains"

There is no one among men that has not a special failing: 1
And my failing consists in writing verses.
I have broken away from the thousand ties of life:
But this infirmity still remains behind.
Each time that I look at a fine landscape: 5
Each time that I meet a loved friend,
I raise my voice and recite a stanza of poetry
And am glad as though a god had crossed my path.
Ever since the day I was banished to Xunyang
Half my time I have lived among the hills.   10
And often, when I have finished a new poem,
Alone I climb the road to the Eastern Rock.
I lean my body on the banks of white stone:
I pull down with my hands a green cassia[3] branch.
My mad singing startles the valleys and hills: 15
The apes and birds all come to peep.
Fearing to become a laughing-stock to the world,
I choose a place that is unfrequented by men.

Q What themes dominate these six poems?

Q How do these poems differ from those of medieval India (Reading 14.2)?

Chinese Landscape Painting

During the Tang Era, figural subjects dominated Chinese art, but by the tenth century, landscape painting became the favorite genre. The Chinese, and especially the literati

---

[3] A tree whose bark is used as a source of cinnamon.

of Song China, referred to landscape paintings as wordless poems and poems as formless paintings; such metaphors reflect the intimate relationship between painting and poetry in Chinese art. In subjects dealing with the natural landscape, both Chinese paintings and Chinese poems evoke a mood rather than provide a literal, objective description of reality. Chinese landscapes work to convey a spirit of harmony between heaven and earth. This cosmic approach to nature, fundamental to Confucianism, Daoism, and Buddhism, asks the beholder to contemplate, rather than simply to view the painted image. It requires that we integrate multiple viewpoints, shifting between foreground, middleground, and background in ways that resemble the mental shifts employed in reading lines of verse.

Chinese paintings generally assume one of three basic formats: the handscroll, the hanging scroll, and the album leaf (often used as a fan). Between 1 and 40 feet long, the handscroll is viewed continuously from right to left. An object of lingering contemplation and delight, such a scroll would have been unrolled privately and read one section at a time. Like a poem, the visual "action" unfolds in time. The hanging scroll, on the other hand, is vertical in format and is meant to be read from the bottom up—from earth to heaven, so to speak (see Figure 14.15). The third format, the album leaf, usually belongs to a book that combines poems and paintings in a sequence. Both leaves and scrolls are made of silk or paper and ornamented with ink or thin washes of paint applied in monochrome or in muted colors. An interesting Chinese practice is the addition of the seals or signatures of collectors who have owned the work of art. These appear along with occasional marginal comments or brief poems inspired by the visual image. The poem may serve as an extension of the content of the work of art. Transmitted from generation to generation, the Chinese painting, then, becomes a repository of the personal expressions of both artist and art lover.

By comparison with the art of the medieval West, much of which is religious in subject matter, Chinese painting draws on everyday human activities. Yet Chinese artists rarely glorify human accomplishments. Their landscapes often dwarf the figures so that human occupations seem mundane and incidental.

A Solitary Temple Amid Clearing Peaks, attributed to Li Cheng (fl. 940–967), is meditative in mood and subtle in composition (see Figure **14.15**). There is no single viewpoint from which to observe the mountains, trees, waters, and human habitations. Rather, we perceive the whole from what one eleventh-century Chinese art critic called the "angle of totality." We look down upon some elements, such as the rooftops, and up to others, such as the tree tops. The lofty mountains and gentle waterfalls seem protective of the infinitely smaller images of temples, houses, and people. Misty areas provide transition between foreground, middleground, and background, but each plane—even the background—is delineated with identical precision. Here, as elsewhere, Chinese painting style displays a remarkable economy of line and color—that is, a limited number of brushstrokes bring the scene to life. Li Cheng's hanging scroll fulfills the primary aim of the Chinese landscape painter (as defined by Song critics): to capture the whole universe within a few inches of space.

More intimate in detail but equally subtle in its organization of positive and negative space, *Five-Colored Parakeet on a Branch of Apricot Blossom*, traditionally ascribed to the emperor Huizong (1082–1135), reflects the Song court taste for decorative works featuring bird-and-flower motifs (Figure **14.17**). In contrast with the traditional panoramic landscape, refined nature studies like this one, executed in ink and delicate colors on silk, present individual natural elements in flattened airless settings. The inscription at the right, a poem and signature inscribed by the emperor, associates the bird with beauty and nobility; it rehearses the "message" of the image as an exotic gift "from far away," an

MAKING CONNECTIONS

Figure 14.15 Attributed to **LI CHENG**, *A Solitary Temple Amid Clearing Peaks*, Northern Song dynasty, ca. 950. Ink and slight color on silk hanging scroll, 3 ft. 8 in. × 22 in. Mountains, Chinese symbols of immortality, were often described as living organisms that issued the life force (*qi*) in the form of cloud vapor.

Chinese Landscape—Tattoo (1999) by the multimedia artist Huang Yan (b. 1966) pays tribute to the genre of landscape painting, the quintessential expression of Chinese traditional culture (Figures **14.15** and **14.16**). Using the body as a canvas, Huang creates a living version of the typical Song landscape. He transposes images of mountains, trees, and water to the surface of the skin, then records his work in the form of large chromogenic prints. His "living landscape" is a reimagined body that may become a moving participant in modern performance art (see chapter 37). "Landscape is a place to store my body . . . a way of releasing my Chan [Buddhist] ideas," explains Huang. Making the body a site of creativity, Huang fuses his East Asian heritage with the contemporary (and primarily Western) emphasis on the human body as a vehicle of theatrical display.

Figure 14.16 HUANG YAN, *Chinese Landscape—Tattoo*, 1999. Chromogenic print, 31½ × 39⅜ in. Collection Artur Walther.

Figure 14.18 *Standing Court Lady*, Tang dynasty, mid-seventh century. Pottery with painted decoration, height 15⅛ in. Filled with pottery figures like this one, showing a court dancer, Tang graves provide a record of the various roles played by women in Chinese society.

auspicious sign from Heaven endorsing the enlightened rule of an emperor who actively patronized the arts.

The earliest treatises on Chinese painting appeared in the Song Era. They describe the integration of complementary pictorial elements: dark and light shapes, bold and muted strokes, dense and sparse textures, large and small forms, and positive and negative shapes, each pair interacting in imitation of the *yin/yang* principle that underlies cosmic wholeness. A unique type of calligraphy, the artist's brushstrokes are the "bones" of Chinese painting. Specific brushstrokes, each bearing an individual name, are prescribed for depicting different natural phenomena: pine needles, rocks, mountains, and so forth. Economy of line and color, gestural expressiveness, and spontaneity are hallmarks of the finest Chinese paintings, as they are of the best Chinese poems. Tradition rather than originality was prized: artists freely copied the works of the masters, honoring their forebears by "quoting" from their poems or paintings.

Chinese Crafts

From earliest times, the Chinese excelled in the production of ceramic wares. They manufactured fine terracotta and earthenware objects for everyday use and for burial in the tombs of the dead (see chapter 7). During the Tang Era, Chinese craftspeople produced thousands of realistic clay images: a terracotta court dancer wears an elegant dress with long sleeves designed to sway with her body movements (Figure **14.18**). Other female figures are shown playing polo or performing on musical instruments—evidence of the wide range of activities enjoyed by aristocratic women. Representations of horsemen and horses—the treasured animals of China—appear in great numbers in Tang graves (as they had in the tombs of earlier dynasties; see Figure 7.7). Such figures were usually cast from molds, assembled in sections, and glazed with green, yellow, and brown colors (Figure **14.19**).

Tang and Song craftspeople perfected various types of stoneware, the finest of which was **porcelain**—a hard, translucent ceramic fired at extremely high heat. Glazed with delicate colors, and impervious to water, porcelain vessels display a level of sophistication that is not merely technical; their elegant shapes, based on natural forms, such as lotus blossoms and buds, are marvels of calculated simplicity in formal design (Figure **14.20**). Describing the magnificent porcelain vessels of the Tang Era, a ninth-century merchant marveled that one could see the sparkle of water through Chinese bowls that were "as fine as glass." International trade in porcelain did not begin, however, until the Song Era. Exported along with silk, lacquer-ware, and carved ivory, porcelain became one of the most sought-after of Chinese luxury goods—indeed, it was so popular that Westerners still refer to dishes and plates as "china." Classic porcelains reflect the refinement of age-old traditions: their shapes often drew inspiration from those conceived by early bronzeworkers of the Shang Era (see chapter 3), while the cool blues and yellowish greens of the finest Chinese porcelains recall the color and texture of Chinese jades. Still other types, such as the cobalt blue and white porcelains that influenced Islamic art, originated in the thirteenth century.

The somber restraint of Chinese pottery stands in sharp contrast to the ornate richness of Chinese metal-work, inlaid wood, carved lacquers, and textiles. Weavers of the Song Era produced exquisite silks embroidered to imitate bird-and-flower paintings. Luxury silks and Chinese embroideries were so highly valued that they were often buried, along with fine ceramics and gold and silver objects, in the graves of wealthy Asians found along the Silk Road, that 8000-mile trade route from Constantinople on the Black Sea to Chang'an on the Pacific Ocean.

Chinese Architecture

Chinese architects embraced a building system that reflect-ed the practice of *feng shui* (see chapter 7) and the ancient Daoist quest for harmony with nature. Structures were emphatically horizontal—built to hug the earth. Whole towns and individual buildings were laid out according to a cosmic axis that ran from north to south. Celestial symbol-ism governed design: for instance, four doors represented the seasons, eight windows signified the winds, and twelve halls stood for the months of the year. House doors faced the "good" southerly direction of the summer sun, and rear walls were closed to the cold north, homeland of the barbarian hordes that threat-ened China throughout its history. Chinese residences were normally self-enclosed and looked inward to courtyards or gardens.

In the Tang Era, the classical period of Chinese archi-tecture, Buddhist temple complexes attracted scores of pilgrims. The complex featured a hall for the veneration of the Buddha-image, and a multistoried pagoda (see Figure 9.28) erected over Buddhist relics. Despite China's

Figure 14.19 *Horse and Rider*, Tang dynasty, early eighth century. Pottery with three-color glaze and painted decoration, height 15 in.

Figure 14.20 Ru ware, cup stand in the shape of a lotus, Northern Song dynasty, ca. 1086–1125. Stoneware, height 3 in. The stoneware bowl-stand with a flange shaped like a five-petalled flower has a subtle gray-blue glaze. Such pieces are known as the classic expression of Chinese ceramics.

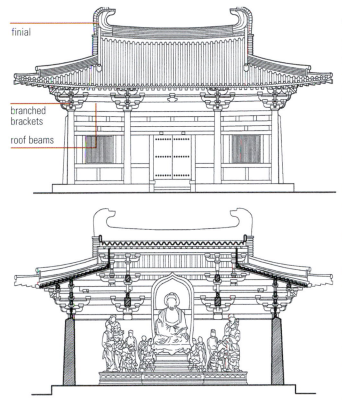

finial

branched
brackets

roof beams

Figure 14.21 Elevation and transverse section through the main hall of Nanchan Monastery, Shanxi province, 782. In one of China's earliest surviving wooden Buddhist temple halls, architects used layered (or branched) brackets to support the roof beams. The cantilevered brackets allow the roof to overhang the exterior, thus giving the building a sense of lightness and grace, while affording protection from foul weather.

proficiency in iron casting, Buddhist temples and shrines of the Tang and Song eras continued to be constructed of wood, a material that was plentiful in China and one that was highly valued for its natural beauty. Chinese architectural ingenuity lay in the invention of a unique timber frame that—in place of walls—bore the entire weight of the roof while making the structure earthquake-resistant (Figure **14.21**).

Perfected during the Tang Era, the Chinese system of vaulting consisted of an intricate series of wooden cantilevers (horizontal brackets extending beyond the vertical supports) that provided support for centrally pitched, shingled, or glazed-tile roofs. By the tenth century, the aesthetics of wood construction were firmly established, and during the following century, scholars enshrined these principles in China's first manual on architecture. Because wooden buildings were very vulnerable to fire—almost all examples of early Chinese shrines had been destroyed by the end of the first millennium—Chinese architects began to build in brick, stone, and cast iron. Regardless of medium, however, Chinese pagodas, temples, and domestic structures, with their projecting upturned eaves, became models of elegant design. The many magnificent pagodas found in Japan (see Figure 14.22) and Southeast Asia testify to China's influence in disseminating an architectural style dependent on the wooden cantilever.

Japan

Buddhism entered Japan from China by way of Korea in the early sixth century, bringing in its wake a restructuring of the government on Chinese imperial models. Japan's elite embraced all things Chinese: the Chinese system of writing, record keeping, and governing, as well as the fundamentals of Chinese art and architecture. By the eighth century, Japan had absorbed both Buddhism and Chinese culture. For roughly four centuries (794–1185), Japan enjoyed a cultural golden age centered on the imperial capital of Heian (modern Kyoto), from which came Japan's first wholly original literature and a set of aesthetic norms that left a permanent mark on Japanese culture.

It was Japan that introduced to world literature the prose form known as the novel. *The Tale of Genji* (ca. 1004), a Japanese classic, tells the story of the "shining prince" of the Heian court. Because the novel exposes the inner life of Genji and other characters, it has been called the world's first psychological novel. However, it also paints a detailed picture of Japanese life within a small segment of the population: the aristocracy. The men and women of this class prized elegant clothes (women usually wore five to twelve layers of silk robes), refined manners, and poetic versatility: the inability to compose the appropriate on-the-spot poem was considered a serious social deficiency. The Heian aristocracy regarded as essential education in the Confucian classics and the cultivation of dance, music, and fine calligraphy—in all, a set of values that prefigured by some five hundred years the Renaissance ideal of the well-rounded courtier.

The author of *The Tale of Genji*, Murasaki Shikibu (978–1016), was one of a group of outstanding female writers and a member of Heian court society. Upper-class women like Murasaki were prized in East Asian literary history: their fame in writing polished intimate prose was so great that one tenth-century male diarist pretended his work had been penned by a woman. Their achievement is all the more remarkable because (like their Chinese counterparts) they were excluded from the world of scholarly education and therefore, from training in written Chinese. Nevertheless, using a system of phonetic symbols derived from Chinese characters, these women produced the outstanding monuments of medieval Japanese prose.

The Tale of Genji—in English translation some six volumes long—cannot be represented adequately here. But it is possible to gain insight into both the talents of Murasaki Shikibu and the character of the Heian court by means of a brief look at her *Diary*. Written between 1008 and 1010, it reveals her keen eye for visual detail, evident in this vivid description of court attire:

> . . . the older women wore plain jackets in yellow-
> green or dark red, each with five damask cuffs.
> The brightness of the wave pattern printed on their
> trains caught the eye, and their waistlines too were
> heavily embroidered. They had white robes lined
> with dark red in either three or five layers but of

plain silk. The younger women wore jackets with five cuffs of various colors, white on the outside with dark red on yellow-green, white with just one green lining, and pale red shading to dark red with one white layer interposed; they were all arranged most intelligently.

Beyond its importance as a historical record, Murasaki's *Diary* is significant as an exercise in self-analysis. Not an autobiography, it is, rather, a series of reminiscences, anecdotes, and experiences. Nevertheless, it documents the author's quest to understand her role as a writer and her place in the highly artificial imperial court. As such, the *Diary* displays a dimension of self-consciousness that has long been considered an exclusively Western phenomenon.

READING 14.4 From *The Diary of Lady Murasaki*
(ca. 1000)

The wife of the Governor of Tanba is known to everyone in the 1
service of Her Majesty and His Excellency as Masahira Emon. She
may not be a genius but she has great poise and does not feel that
she has to compose a poem on everything she sees, merely
because she is a poet. From what I have seen, her work is most
accomplished, even her occasional verse. People who think so
much of themselves that they will, at the drop of a hat, compose
lame verses that only just hang together, or produce the most
pretentious compositions imaginable, are quite odious and
rather pathetic. 10

Sei Shōnagon,[1] for instance, was dreadfully conceited. She
thought herself so clever and littered her writings with Chinese
characters; but if you examined her closely, they left a great deal
to be desired. Those who think of themselves as being superior to
everyone else in this way will inevitably suffer and come to a bad
end, and people who have become so precious that they go out
of their way to try and be sensitive in the most unpromising
situations, are bound to look ridiculous and superficial.
How can the future turn out well for them?

Thus do I criticize others from various angles—but here is one 20
who has survived this far without having achieved anything of
note. I have nothing in particular to look forward to in the future
that might afford me the slightest consolation, but I am not the
kind of person to abandon herself completely to despair. And yet,
by the same token, I cannot entirely rid myself of such feelings.
On autumn evenings, which positively encourage nostalgia,
when I go out to sit on the veranda and gaze, I seem to be always
conjuring up visions of the past—"and did they praise the beauty
of this moon of yore?" Knowing full well that I am inviting the kind
of misfortune one should avoid, I become uneasy and move 30
inside a little, while still, of course, continuing to recall the past.
And when I play my *koto*[2] rather badly to myself in the cool

breeze of the evening, I worry lest someone might hear me and
recognize how I am just "adding to the sadness of it all";[3] how
vain and sad of me. So now both my instruments, the one with
thirteen strings and the one with six, stand in a miserable, sotty
little closet still ready-strung. Through neglect—I forgot, for
example, to ask that the bridges be removed on rainy days—they
have accumulated dust and lean against a cupboard. Two *biwa*[4]
stand on either side, their necks jammed between the 40
cupboard and the pillar.

There is also a pair of larger cupboards crammed to bursting
point. One is full of old poems and tales that have become the
home for countless insects which scatter in such an unpleasant
manner that no one cares to look at them any more; the other
is full of Chinese books that have lain unattended ever since he
who carefully collected them passed away. Whenever my
loneliness threatens to overwhelm me, I take out one or two of
them to look at; but my women gather together behind my back.
"It's because she goes on like this that she is so miserable. 50
What kind of lady is it who reads Chinese books?" they whisper.
"In the past it was not even the done thing to read sutras!"[5]
"Yes," I feel like replying, "but I've never met anyone who lived
longer just because they believed in superstitions!" But that
would be thoughtless of me. There is some truth in what they say.

Each one of us is quite different. Some are confident, open and
forthcoming. Others are born pessimists, amused by nothing, the
kind who search through old letters, carry out penances, intone
sutras without end, and clack their beads, all of which makes
one feel uncomfortable. So I hesitate to do even those things 60
I should be able to do quite freely, only too aware of my own
servants' prying eyes. How much more so at court, where I have
many things I would like to say but always think the better of it,
because there would be no point in explaining to people who
would never understand. I cannot be bothered to discuss matters
in front of those women who continually carp and are so full of
themselves: it would only cause trouble. It is so rare to find
someone of true understanding; for the most part they judge
purely by their own standards and ignore everyone else.

So all they see of me is a façade. There are times when 70
I am forced to sit with them and on such occasions I simply
ignore their petty criticisms, not because I am particularly shy
but because I consider it pointless. As a result, they now look
upon me as a dullard.

"Well, we never expected this!" they all say. "No one liked her.
They all said she was pretentious, awkward, difficult to approach,
prickly, too fond of her tales, haughty, prone to versifying,
disdainful, cantankerous and scornful; but when you meet her,
she is strangely meek, a completely different person altogether!"

How embarrassing! Do they really look upon me as such a 80
dull thing, I wonder? But I am what I am. Her Majesty has also
remarked more than once that she had thought I was not the kind

---

[3] A reference to Poem 985 in the *Kokinshū* by Yoshimine no Munesada (Bishop Henjō): "While on his way to Nara he heard a woman playing a *koto* in a dilapidated house. He wrote this poem and sent it in: It seemed to be a dwelling where you might expect someone dejected to be living; and now I hear the sound of a *koto* that adds to the sadness of it all."

[4] A short-necked lute, similar to the Chinese *pipa*.

[5] Buddhist discourses (see chapter 8).

---

[1] Female writer (ca. 968–1025) famous for her *Pillow Book*, a long collection of notes, stories, and descriptions of everyday life among members of the Heian upper class.

[2] A Japanese musical instrument of the zither family.

of person with whom she could ever relax, but that I have now become closer to her than any of the others. I am so perverse and standoffish. If only I can avoid putting off those for whom I have a genuine regard.

To be pleasant, gentle, calm, and self-possessed: this is the basis of good taste and charm in a woman. No matter how amorous or passionate you may be, as long as you are straightforward and refrain from causing others embarrassment, no one will mind. 90

But women who are too vain and act pretentiously, to the extent that they make others feel uncomfortable, will themselves become the object of attention; and once that happens, people will always find fault with whatever they say or do: whether it be how they enter a room, how they sit down, how they stand up, or how they take their leave. Those who end up contradicting themselves and those who disparage their companions are also carefully watched and listened to all the more. As long as you are free from such faults, people will surely refrain from listening to tittle-tattle and will want to show you sympathy, if only for the 100 sake of politeness.

I am of the opinion that when you intentionally cause hurt to another, or indeed if you do ill through mere thoughtless behavior, you fully deserve to be censured in public. Some people are so good-natured that they can still care for those who despise them, but I myself find it very difficult. Did the Buddha himself in all his compassion ever preach that one should simply ignore those who

slander the Three Treasures?[6] How in this sullied world of ours can those who are hard done by be expected not to reciprocate in kind? And yet people react in very different ways. 110

Some glare at each other face to face and fling abuse in an attempt to gain the upper hand; others hide their true intent and appear quite friendly on the surface—thus are true natures revealed.

Q **What does this reading reveal about the court culture of medieval Japan, and about the role of women in that culture?**

Buddhism in Japan

As Buddhism spread throughout Japan, it inspired the construction of hundreds of shrines and temples, the oldest of which are found just outside Japan's early capital city of Nara. The site of the oldest wooden buildings in the world, the eighth-century temple complex at Yakushiji, with its graceful five-storied pagoda (Figure **14.22**), preserves the

---

[6] The Three Treasures without which the teachings would not survive were the Buddha himself, the Buddhist Law, and the community of monks who preserved that law. Slander of these three treasures was one of the gravest offences.

Figure 14.22 East pagoda of Yakushiji, Nara, Japan, ca. 720.

timber style that originated in China. The Buddhism that arrived in sixth-century Japan was of the Mahayana variety (see chapter 8). It coexisted with Japan's native Shinto religion, which venerated the divinity of the emperor as well as the host of local and nature spirits of the countryside. The two faiths, Buddhism and Shintoism, formed a vigorous amalgam that accommodated many local beliefs and practices. The aspiration of the Buddhist faithful to be reborn in a Buddhist paradise proving very popular in Japan, the Pure Land sect venerated Amitabha (known in Japanese as Amida).

One of Japan's most famous tributes to Amida belongs to an imperial chapel (the Byodoin) that served as part of the recreated Pure Land Paradise located in Uji, outside of Kyoto. Central to the chapel's Amida Hall (also known as the Phoenix Hall) is the dazzling, gilded and lacquered image of Amida seated on a richly carved lotus throne (Figure 14.23). Music-making angels adorn the elaborate halo that backs the golden Buddha. Richly detailed with murals and an open-work canopy inlaid with mother-of-pearl, the Byodoin hall is among the most lyrical sculptural expressions of religious art in East Asia.

Figure 14.23 JOCHO *Amida Buddha*, Phoenix Hall, Byodoin, Late Heian period, ca. 1053. Gold leaf and lacquer on wood, height 9 ft. 8 in. Amida's hands make the *mudra* of welcome. The master sculptor of his day, Jocho explored a variety of mid-eleventh-century wood-joining techniques in the design and assembly of Japan's religious shrines.

Although not identical with European feudalism, the Japanese feudal system flourished between the ninth and twelfth centuries—the age of medieval warfare in the West (Figure **14.24**). As with Western feudalism, skilled warriors, known in Japan as **samurai** (literally, "those who serve"), held land in return for military service to local landlords. The strength of the Japanese clan depended on the allegiance of the *samurai*.

Outfitted with warhorses and elaborate armor (Figure **14.25**), and trained in the arts of archery and swordsmanship, *samurai* clans competed for position and power. Their code of honor, known as *bushido* ("the way of the warrior"), exalted fierce loyalty to one's overlord, selflessness in battle, and a disdain for death. The code called for ritual suicide, usually by disembowelment, if the *samurai* fell into dishonor. Not surprisingly, the sword was the distinctive symbol of this warrior class.

Figure 14.24 MATTHEW PARIS, *Vassal Paying Homage to His Lord*, from the Westminster Psalter, ca. 1250. 9 × 6⅛ in. The chain mail shown here consisted of thousands of individually joined metal links. By the fourteenth century, plate mail came to replace chain mail.

Figure 14.25 YOSHIHISA MATAHACHIRO, suit of armor. Muromachi period, ca. 1550. Steel, blackened and gold-lacquered; flame-colored silk braid, gilt bronze, stenciled deerskin, bear pelt, and gilt wood; approx. height 5 ft. 6 in., approx. weight 48 lb. Japanese armor was made of iron, plated with lacquer to protect against the rain. In contrast with the rigidity of European plate armor, *samurai* armor was notable for its flexibility.

The Age of the *Samurai*:
The Kamakura Shogunate (1185–1333)

Toward the mid-twelfth century, Heian authority gave way to a powerful group of local clans that competed for political and military preeminence. Two in particular—the Taira and the Minamoto—engaged in outright war, fought by the military nobility known as *samurai* (see Box on previous page). When the civil wars came to an end in 1192, the generals of the Minamoto clan became the rulers of Japan. They established the seat of their government at Kamakura, near present-day Tokyo. Minamoto no Yoritomo (1147–1199) adopted the title of *shogun* ("general-in-chief") and set up a form of military dictatorship that ruled in the emperor's name. The events of the turbulent Kamakura Era were recorded in the Japanese war epic known as the *Heiji Monogatari Emaki* (*Tale of the Heiji Rebellion*), a thirteenth-century picture-scroll version of which shows the Minamoto attack on the palace at Kyoto

and the capture of the Taira clan leader (Figure **14.26**). Read from right to left, the visual narrative, enlivened by realistic details, is accompanied by written portions of the epic.

In the domain of sculpture, the Japanese were master woodcarvers. During the Kamakura Era they cultivated a style of intense pictorial Realism. The late twelfth-century sculptor Jokei executed a series of painted wood temple guardians that reveal the Japanese fascination with the human figure in violent action (Figure **14.27**). These superhuman sentinels, with their taut muscles and their grimacing faces, direct their wrath toward those who would oppose the Buddhist law. By means of exaggeration and forthright detail, Jokei achieved a balletic union of martial-arts grace and *samurai* fierceness. The Kamakura shogunate remained the source of Japanese government only until 1333, but the values of the *samurai* prevailed well into modern times.

Figure 14.26 Attributed to **SUMIYOSHI KEION**, *Heiji Monogatari Emaki* (*Tale of the Heiji Rebellion*). Picture-scroll, thirteenth century, detail. Colored ink on paper, 1 ft. 4⅔ in. × 31 ft. 3⅕ in. Reminiscent of the Bayeux Tapestry (see Figures 11.15 and 11.18), this illustrated handscroll commemorates an important chapter in Japanese national history.

gestures, dance, and music (usually performed on flute and drum), the play explored a given story to expose its underlying meaning.

Nō plays—still flourishing in modern-day Japan—are performed on a square wooden stage that opens to the audience on three sides and is connected by a raised passageway to an offstage dressing room. Although roofed, the stage holds almost no scenery, and that which does appear serves a symbolic function. As in ancient Greek drama, all roles are played by men. A chorus that sits at the side of the stage expresses the thoughts of the actors. Elegant costumes and masks, often magnificently carved and painted (Figure **14.28**), may be used to represent individual characters. This mask of a young woman reveals the classic Heian preference for the white-powdered face, plucked eyebrows, and blackened teeth—marks of high fashion among medieval Japanese females. A single program of Nō drama (which lasts some six hours) consists of a group of plays, with a selection from each of the play types, such as god-plays, warrior-plays, and women-plays. Comic interludes are provided between them to lighten the serious mood.

The formalities of Nō drama were not set down until the early fifteenth century, when the playwright and actor Zeami Motokiyo (1363–1443) wrote an instructional

Figure 14.27 **JOKEI**, *Kongorikishi*, Kamakura period, ca. 1288. Painted wood, height 5 ft. 4 in.

Nō Drama

Nō drama, the oldest form of Japanese theater, evolved from performances in dance, song, and mime popular in the Heian Era and possibly even earlier. Like Greek drama, the Nō play treats serious themes drawn from a legacy of history and literature. Just as Sophocles recounted the history of Thebes, so Nō playwrights recalled the civil wars of the *samurai*. They also drew on episodes from *The Tale of Genji*. Nō drama, however, was little concerned with character development or the realistic reenactment of actual events. Rather, by means of a rigidly formalized text,

Figure 14.28 *Ko-omote* Nō mask, Azuchi-Momoyama period, ca. 1573–1615. Painted wood, height approx. 8 in.

manual for Nō actors. Zeami's manual, the *Kadensho*, prescribes demanding training exercises for the aspiring actor; it also analyzes the philosophic and aesthetic purposes of Nō theater. In the excerpt that follows, certain hallmarks of Japanese culture emerge, including a high regard for beauty of effect and a melancholic sensitivity to the pathos of human life.

READING 14.5 From Zeami's *Kadensho* (ca. 1400)

Sometimes spectators of the Nō say, "The moments of 'no-action' are the most enjoyable." This is an art which the actor keeps secret. Dancing and singing, movements and the different types of miming are all acts performed by the body. Moments of "no-action" occur in between. When we examine why such moments without actions are enjoyable, we find that it is due to the underlying spiritual strength of the actor which unremittingly holds the attention. He does not relax the tension when the dancing or singing come to an end or at intervals between the dialogue and the different types of miming, but maintains an unwavering inner strength. This feeling of inner strength will faintly reveal itself and bring enjoyment. However, it is undesirable for the actor to permit this inner strength to become obvious to the audience. If it is obvious, it becomes an act, and is no longer "no-action." The actions before and after an interval of "no-action" must be linked by entering the state of mindlessness in which one conceals even from oneself one's intent. This, then, is the faculty of moving audiences, by linking all the artistic powers with one mind.

> Life and death, past and present—
> Marionettes on a toy stage.
> When the strings are broken,
> Behold the broken pieces.

This is a metaphor describing human life as it transmigrates between life and death. Marionettes on a stage appear to move in various ways, but in fact it is not they who really move—they are manipulated by strings. When these strings are broken, the marionettes fall and are dashed to pieces. In the art of the Nō too, the different sorts of miming are artificial things. What holds the parts together is the mind. This mind must not be disclosed to the audience. If it is seen, it is just as if a marionette's strings were visible. The mind must be made the strings which hold together all the powers of the arts. If this is done the actor's talent will endure. This resolution must not be confined to the times when the actor is appearing on the stage. Day or night, wherever he may be, whatever he may be doing, he should not forget this resolution, but should make it his constant guide, uniting all his powers. If he unremittingly works at this his talent will steadily grow. This article is the most secret of the secret teachings. . . .

Q **What is "no-action"? How does it serve Nō theater?**

Chronology

India:	550–1192	era of regional states
	1192	Muslim conquest of Delhi
China:	618–907	Tang dynasty
	960–1279	Song dynasty
Japan:	794–1185	Heian Era
	1185–1333	Kamakura shogunate

LOOKING BACK

India

- Following the collapse of the Gupta Empire, local kingdoms competed for power in India. In the early eighth century, Arab Muslims entered India and began to convert members of the native population to Islam. By the early twelfth century, the Muslims had become the ruling caste.
- Nevertheless, Hinduism prevailed as the dominant faith in most of India, ultimately overshadowing Buddhism, which virtually disappeared by the thirteenth century.

- Hinduism developed a growing devotion to the many gods and goddesses of Vedic mythology. The three principal gods, Brahma, Vishnu, and Shiva, were regarded as avatars of the regenerative Brahmanic powers of creation, preservation, and destruction. Bronze images of the gods were central to devotional practice, which involved viewing the image as a form of contact with the god.
- Popular Indian religious literature, the *Puranas*, drew heavily on the mythology and legends of early Hinduism as found

in the Vedic hymns and in India's great epics, the *Mahabharata* and the *Ramayana*.
- Sensuality is a key feature of India's vast body of Sanskrit poetry.
- Modeled on Buddhist *chaitya* halls, Hindu temples honoring the gods rose like stone mountains across India. Like the medieval cathedrals, these temples were adorned with hundreds of high-relief sculptures; but unlike medieval religious statuary, the Hindu figures—mostly nude and locked in erotic

embrace—are symbols of the union of human and divine love.

- A single musical tradition dominates secular and religious music in India. Prescribed melodic sequences (*ragas*) and rhythmic patterns (*talas*) are associated with specific moods and emotions. Similarly, the art of dance prescribes specific gestures and steps that signify distinct states of mind.

China

- Ruled by the Tang dynasty, China was a unified, centralized state without equal in Asia or the West. Steeped in Confucian tradition and trained in the literary classics, its administrators were members of an intellectual elite.
- The Tang Era, a golden age of Chinese Buddhism, saw the proliferation of Buddhist monasteries and sects that encouraged the popularity of Buddhist statuary. Buddhist temples and shrines made use of earthquake-resistant wooden cantilevers that supported elegant pitched roofs.
- The Song Era, which followed the collapse of the Tang, was a period of population growth, agricultural productivity, and vigorous commercial trade centering on the export of tea, silk, and ceramics.
- Chinese technology often involved the intelligent application of natural principles to produce labor-saving devices. Their inventions include the water mill, the wheelbarrow, the foot stirrup, steel casting, gunpowder, movable type, and the stern-post rudder.
- Chinese literature and music are closely related. Musical drama (or opera) and prose fiction were popular. Tang and Song scholar-poets (literati) left hundreds of lyrics that are refined in style and filled with human emotion.
- The Chinese invented the genre of landscape painting: on silk scrolls and album leaves, master calligraphers created cosmic views of natural surroundings whose majesty dwarfed the presence of human beings.
- Silk and porcelain, traded with other luxury goods along the Silk Road, brought wealth and prestige to China.

Japan

- By the eighth century, Japan had absorbed the Buddhist faith and the Chinese system of writing, governing, and record keeping, as well as the fundamentals of Chinese art and architecture.
- Japan introduced the first novel to world literature. Written by Murasaki Shikibu, *The Tale of Genji* tells the story of the "shining prince" of the Heian court. Because the novel exposes the inner life of its protagonist, it has also been called the world's first psychological novel.
- Buddhism and Shintoism formed an amalgam that accommodated Japan's local beliefs and practices. Mahayana Buddhist sects embraced Indian and East Asian deities and temple guardians, whom they represented in realistically carved and painted wooden sculptures.
- The *samurai* culture that began with the Kamakura shogunate belonged to a feudal tradition that produced magnificent weapons, armor, and palace portraits.
- The Japanese preference for refined form and beauty of effect is illustrated in the visual arts, in literature, and (perhaps most distinctively) in Nō theater, the classic drama of Japan.

Music Listening Selections

- Indian music, *Thumri*, played on the sitar by Ravi Shankar.
- Chinese music: Cantonese music drama for male solo, zither, and other instruments, "Ngoh wai heng kong" ("I'm Mad About You").

Glossary

alliteration a literary device involving the repetition of initial sounds in successive or closely associated words or syllables

assonance a literary device involving a similarity in sound between vowels followed by different consonants

avatar (Sanskrit, "incarnation") the incarnation of a Hindu deity

luohan (Chinese, "worthy one") a term for enlightened being, portrayed as a sage or mystic

mithuna the Hindu representation of a male and a female locked together in passionate embrace

novel an extended fictional prose narrative

opera a drama set to music and making use of vocal pieces with orchestral accompaniment

pipa a short-necked lute

porcelain a hard, translucent ceramic ware made from clay fired at high heat

raga a mode or melodic form in Hindu music; a specific combination of notes associated with a particular mood or atmosphere

samurai (Japanese, "those who serve") the warrior nobility of medieval Japan

sitar a long-necked string instrument popular in Indian music

syncretism the effort or tendency to combine or reconcile differing beliefs

tala a set rhythmic formula in Hindu music

Book

3

The European Renaissance, the Reformation, and Global Encounter

Adversity and Challenge: The Fourteenth-Century Transition

ca. 1300–1400

"So many bodies were brought to the churches every day that the consecrated ground did not suffice to hold them . . ."
Boccaccio

Figure 15.1 JEAN, POL, AND HERMAN LIMBOURG, *February*, plate 3 from the *Très Riches Heures* (*Very Precious Hours*) *du Duc de Berry*, ca. 1413–1416. Illumination, 8¾ × 5⁵⁄₁₆ in. Into this very small space, the artists packed a wealth of details depicting the everyday chores of farm laborers and servants of wealthy upper-class patrons.

The fourteenth century brought Western Europe out of the Middle Ages and into the early modern era. Three cataclysmic events wrenched medieval customs and practices out of their steady, dependable rhythms, radically altering all aspects of life and cultural expression: a long and debilitating war between England and France; the Avignon Papacy, Great Schism, and the ensuing decline of the Roman Catholic Church; and the persistent struggle for survival against the onslaught of the bubonic plague.

In economic life, manorialism slowly gave way to entrepreneurial capitalism. In political life, the feudal hierarchy was replaced by centralized forms of government among rising nation-states. In the arts, there were distinct signs of a revitalized self-consciousness, increasing fidelity to nature, and a growing attention to gender and class. The cultural developments of this transitional century would come to shape a modern world-system dominated by the West.

Europe in Transition

The Hundred Years' War

 The feudal histories of France and England provided the context for a war (more accurately a series of wars) that would last for more than 100 years (1337–1453). Larger and more protracted than any medieval conflict, the Hundred Years' War was the result of the long-standing English claim to continental lands held by the Norman rulers of England, whose ancestors were vassals of the French king. French efforts to wrest these feudal territories from English hands ignited decades of hostility and chronic resentment between the two burgeoning nation-states. But the immediate cause of the war was the English claim to the French throne, occasioned by the death of Charles IV (1294–1328), the last of the male heirs in a long line of French kings that had begun with Hugh Capet in 987.

The war that began in 1337 was marked by intermittent battles, in many of which the French outnumbered the English by three or four to one. Nevertheless, the English won most of the early battles of the war, owing to their use of three new "secret" weapons: the foot soldier, the longbow, and gunpowder—the invisible enemy that would ultimately eliminate the personal element in military combat. Along with the traditional cavalry, the English army depended heavily on foot soldiers armed with longbows (Figure 15.2). The thin, steel-tipped arrows of the 6-foot longbow could be fired more quickly and at a longer range than those of the traditional crossbow. Because the thin arrows of the longbow easily pierced the finest French chain mail, plate mail soon came to replace chain mail. However, within the next few centuries, even plate mail became obsolete, since it proved useless against artillery that employed gunpowder.

Introduced into Europe by the Muslims, who acquired it from the Chinese, gunpowder was first used in Western combat during the Hundred Years' War. In the first battle of the war, however, the incendiary substance proved too potent for the poorly cast English cannons, which issued little more than terrifying noise. Still, gunpowder, which could lay waste to a city, constituted an extraordinary advance in military technology.

Throughout the Hundred Years' War the English repeatedly devastated the French armies; nevertheless, the financial and physical burdens of garrisoning French lands ultimately proved too great for the English. Facing a revitalized army under the charismatic leadership of Joan of Arc, England finally withdrew from France in 1450. Of peasant background, the sixteen-year-old Joan begged the French king to allow her to obey the voices of the Christian saints who had directed her to expel the English (Figure 15.3). Donning armor and riding a white horse, she led the French into battle. Her success forced the English to withdraw from Orléans, but initiated her martyrdom. Betrayed by her supporters in 1431, she was condemned as a heretic and burned at the stake.

The Hundred Years' War dealt a major blow to feudalism. The use of gunpowder and the longbow, which put physical distance between combatants, worked to outmode hand-to-hand combat, thus rendering obsolete the medieval code of chivalry. Further, because the French were greatly outnumbered by the English, they resorted to ambush, a tactic that violated the "rules" of feudal warfare. While contemporary literary accounts of the war glorified the performance of chivalric deeds, the new military tactics clearly inaugurated the impersonal style of combat that has come to dominate modern warfare.

By the mid-fifteenth century, the French nobility was badly depleted, and those knights who survived the war found themselves "outdated." In France, feudal allegiances

Science and Technology

1300	eyeglasses come into use in Europe
1310	mechanical clocks appear in Europe
1346	gunpowder and longbows are utilized by the English army at the Battle of Crécy
1370	the steel crossbow is adopted as a weapon of war
1377	the first quarantine station for plague victims is established in Ragusa (modern-day Dubrovnik)

Figure 15.2 *The End of the Siege of Ribodane: English Soldiers Take a French Town*, late fifteenth century. Manuscript illumination, 8 × 12 in. (approx.). Wooden siege machines like that on the left, cannons, and longbows gave the English great advantage in attacking French towns. The miniature also shows the heavy plate mail worn by both the French and the English.

Figure 15.3 Joan of Arc, from **ANTOINE DUFOUR**'s *Lives of Famous Women*, 1504. French manuscript illustration, 5 × 4 in. (approx.). Immediately after her death, the so-called Maid of Orléans became the national heroine of France, and was declared a martyr in 1455. While she has become a semilegendary figure, numerous transcripts of her trial attest to her strong personality.

were soon superseded by systems of national conscription. The English Parliament, which had met frequently during the war in order to raise taxes for repeated military campaigns, used the opportunity this provided to bargain for greater power, including the right to initiate legislation. By the end of the fourteenth century, the English had laid the groundwork for a constitutional monarchy that bridged the gap between medieval feudalism and modern democracy. In the decades following the war, England and France were ready to move in separate directions, both politically and culturally.

The Decline of the Church

The growth of the European nation-states contributed to the weakening of the Christian commonwealth, especially where Church and state competed for influence and authority. The two events that proved most damaging to the prestige of the Catholic Church were the Avignon Papacy (1309–1377) and the Great Schism (1378–1417). The term "Avignon Papacy" describes the relocation of the papacy from Rome to the city of Avignon in southern France (see Map 13.1) in response to political pressure from the French king Philip IV ("the Fair"). Attempting to compete in prestige and political influence with the secular rulers of Europe, the Avignon popes established a luxurious and powerful court, using stringent (and occasionally corrupt) means to accomplish their purpose. The increasing need for church revenue led some of the Avignon popes to sell church offices (a practice known as **simony**), to levy additional taxes upon clergymen, to elect members of their own families to ecclesiastical office, and to step up the sale of **indulgences** (pardons from temporal penalties for sins committed by lay Christians). From the twelfth century on, the Church had sold these certificates of grace—drawn from the "surplus" of good works left by the saints—to lay Christians who bought them as a means of speeding their own progress to Heaven or to benefit their relatives and friends in Purgatory. While the seven popes who ruled from Avignon were able administrators, their unsavory efforts at financial and political aggrandizement damaged the reputation of the Church.

The return of the papacy to Rome in 1377 was followed by one of the most devastating events in church history: a rift between French and Italian factions of the College of Cardinals led to the election of two popes, one who ruled from Avignon, the other who ruled from Rome. This schism produced two conflicting claims to universal sovereignty and violent controversy within the Church. As each pope excommunicated the other, lay people questioned whether any Christian soul might enter Heaven. The Great Schism proved even more detrimental to Church prestige than the Avignon Papacy, for while the latter had prompted strong anticlerical feelings—even shock—in Christians who regarded Rome as the traditional home of the papacy, the schism violated the very sanctity of the Holy Office. The ecumenical council at Pisa in 1409 tried to remedy matters by deposing both popes and electing another (the "Pisan pope"), but, when the popes at Rome and Avignon refused to step down, the Church was rent by *three* claims to the throne of Christ, a disgraceful situation that lasted for almost a decade.

Anticlericalism and the Rise of Devotional Piety

In 1417, the Council of Constance healed the schism, authorizing Pope Martin V to rule from Rome, but ecclesiastical discord continued. Fifteenth-century popes refused to acknowledge limits to papal power, thus hampering the efforts of church councils to exercise authority over the papacy. The Avignon Papacy and the Great Schism drew criticism from uneducated Christians and intellectuals alike. Two of the most vocal church critics were the Oxford scholar John Wycliffe (ca. 1330–1384) and the Czech preacher Jan Hus (ca. 1373–1415). Wycliffe and Hus attacked papal power and wealth. They called for the abolition of pilgrimages and the worship of relics, insisting that Christian belief and practice must rest solidly in the Scriptures, which they sought to translate into the vernacular. The Church vigorously condemned Wycliffe and his bands of followers, who were called Lollards. Hus stood trial for heresy and was burned at the stake in 1415. Disenchanted with the institutional Church, lay Christians increasingly turned to private forms of devotional piety and to mysticism—the effort to know God directly and intuitively.

Popular mysticism challenged the authority of the institutional Church and threatened its corporate hold over Catholicism. Throughout the Middle Ages, mystics—many of whom came from the cloister—had voiced their passionate commitment to Christ. The twelfth-century mystic Hildegard of Bingen (see chapter 12), whose visionary interpretations of Scripture were intensely personal, received the approval of the institutional Church. By the thirteenth century, however, as churchmen sought to centralize authority in the hands of male ecclesiastics, visionary literature was looked upon with some suspicion. The Church condemned the lyrical descriptions of divine love penned by the thirteenth-century mystic Marguerite of Porete, for instance, and Marguerite herself was burned at the stake in 1310. Nonetheless, during the fourteenth century a flood of mystical and devotional literature engulfed Europe. The writings of the great fourteenth-century German mystics Johannes Eckhart (ca. 1260–1327) and Heinrich Suso (ca. 1295–1366), of the English Julian of Norwich (1342–ca. 1416), and of the Swedish Saint Bridget (ca. 1303–1373) describe—in language that is at once intimate and ecstatic—the heightened personal experience of God. Such writings—the expression of pious individualism—mark an important shift from the Scholastic reliance on religious authority to modern assertions of faith based on inner conviction.

The Black Death

While warfare, religious turmoil, and peasant unrest brought havoc to fourteenth-century Europe, their effects were compounded by a devastating natural catastrophe: the bubonic plague struck Europe in 1347, destroying 50 percent of its population in less than a century. Originating in Asia and spread by the Mongol tribes that dominated that vast area, the disease devastated China and the Middle East, interrupting long-distance trade and cross-cultural encounters that had flourished for two centuries.

The plague was carried into Europe by flea-bearing black rats infesting the commercial vessels that brought goods to Mediterranean ports. Within two years of its arrival it ravaged much of the Western world. In its early stages, it was transmitted by the bite of either the infected flea or the host rat; in its more severe stages, it was passed on by those infected with the disease. The symptoms of the malady were terrifying: buboes (or abscesses) that began in the lymph glands of the groin or armpits of the afflicted slowly filled with pus, turning the body a deathly black, hence the popular label "the Black Death." Once the boils and accompanying fever appeared, death usually followed within two to three days. Traditional treatments, such as the bleeding of victims and fumigation with vapors of vinegar, proved useless. No connection was perceived between the ubiquitous rats and the plague itself, and in the absence of a clinical understanding of bacterial infection, the medical profession of the day was helpless. (The bacillus of the bubonic plague was not isolated until 1894.)

The plague hit hardest in the towns, where the concentration of population and the lack of sanitation made the infestation all the more difficult to contain. Four waves of bubonic plague spread throughout Europe between 1347 and 1375, attacking some European cities several times and nearly wiping out their entire populations (Figure **15.4**). The virulence of the plague and the mood of mounting despair horrified the Florentine writer Giovanni Boccaccio (1313–1375). In his preface to the *Decameron*,

Figure 15.4 *The Black Death*, miniature from a rhymed Latin chronicle of the events of 1349–1352 by Egidius, abbot of Saint-Martin's, Tournai, France, ca. 1355. Manuscript illumination, 4 × 8 in. (approx.).

a collection of tales told by ten young people who abandoned plague-ridden Florence for the safety of a country estate, Boccaccio described the physical conditions of the pestilence, as well as its psychological consequences. He recorded with somber precision how widespread death had forced Florentine citizens to abandon the traditional forms of grieving and forego the age-old rituals associated with death and burial. Boccaccio's stirring vernacular prose captured the mood of dread that prevailed in Florence, as people fled their cities, their homes, and even their families.

READING 15.1 From Boccaccio's Introduction to the *Decameron* (1351)

In the year of Our Lord 1348 the deadly plague broke   **1**
out in the great city of Florence, most beautiful of Italian
cities. Whether through the operation of the heavenly
bodies or because of our own iniquities which the just
wrath of God sought to correct, the plague had arisen
in the East some years before, causing the death of
countless human beings. It spread without stop from one
place to another, until, unfortunately, it swept over the
West. Neither knowledge nor human foresight availed
against it, though the city was cleansed of much filth by   **10**
chosen officers in charge and sick persons were
forbidden to enter it, while advice was broadcast for the
preservation of health. Nor did humble supplications

serve. Not once but many times they were ordained in the
form of processions and other ways for the propitiation of
God by the faithful, but, in spite of everything, toward the
spring of the year the plague began to show its ravages in
a way short of miraculous.

It did not manifest itself as in the East, where if a man
bled at the nose he had certain warning of inevitable   **20**
death. At the onset of the disease both men and women
were afflicted by a sort of swelling in the groin or under
the armpits which sometimes attained the size of a
common apple or egg. Some of these swellings were
larger and some smaller, and all were commonly called
boils. From these two starting points the boils began in a
little while to spread and appear generally all over the
body. Afterwards, the manifestation of the disease
changed into black or livid spots on the arms, thighs and
the whole person. In many these blotches were large and   **30**
far apart, in others small and closely clustered. Like the
boils, which had been and continued to be a certain
indication of coming death, these blotches had the same
meaning for everyone on whom they appeared.

Neither the advice of physicians nor the virtue of any
medicine seemed to help or avail in the cure of these
diseases. Indeed, whether the nature of the malady did
not suffer it, or whether the ignorance of the physicians
could not determine the source and therefore could take
no preventive measures against it, the fact was that not   **40**
only did few recover, but on the contrary almost everyone
died within three days of the appearance of the signs—

some sooner, some later, and the majority without fever or other ill. Moreover, besides the qualified medical men, a vast number of quacks, both men and women, who had never studied medicine, joined the ranks and practiced cures. The virulence of the plague was all the greater in that it was communicated by the sick to the well by contact, not unlike fire when dry or fatty things are brought near it. But the evil was still worse. Not only did conversation and familiarity with the diseased spread the malady and even cause death, but the mere touch of the clothes or any other object the sick had touched or used, seemed to spread the pestilence. . . .

Because of such happenings and many others of a like sort, various fears and superstitions arose among the survivors, almost all of which tended toward one end— to flee from the sick and whatever had belonged to them. In this way each man thought to be safeguarding his own health. Some among them were of the opinion that by living temperately and guarding against excess of all kinds, they could do much toward avoiding the danger; and forming a band they lived away from the rest of the world. Gathering in those houses where no one had been ill and living was more comfortable, they shut themselves in. They ate moderately of the best that could be had and drank excellent wines, avoiding all luxuriousness. With music and whatever other delights they could have, they lived together in this fashion, allowing no one to speak to them and avoiding news either of death or sickness from the outer world.

Others, arriving at a contrary conclusion, held that plenty of drinking and enjoyment, singing and free living and the gratification of the appetite in every possible way, letting the devil take the hindmost, was the best preventative of such a malady; and as far as they could, they suited the action to the word. Day and night they went from one tavern to another drinking and carousing unrestrainedly. At the least inkling of something that suited them, they ran wild in other people's houses, and there was no one to prevent them, for everyone had abandoned all responsibility for his belongings as well as for himself, considering his days numbered. Consequently most of the houses had become common property and strangers would make use of them at will whenever they came upon them even as the rightful owners might have done. Following this uncharitable way of thinking, they did their best to run away from the infected.

Meanwhile, in the midst of the affliction and misery that had befallen the city, even the reverend authority of divine and human law had almost crumbled and fallen into decay, for its ministers and executors, like other men, had either died or sickened, or had been left so entirely without assistants that they were unable to attend to their duties. As a result everyone had leave to do as he saw fit.

[Others, in an effort to escape the plague, abandoned the city, their houses, their possessions, and their relatives.] The calamity had instilled such horror into the hearts of men and women that brother abandoned brother, uncles, sisters and wives left their dear ones to perish, and, what is more serious and almost incredible,

50

60

70

80

90

100

parents avoided visiting or nursing their very children, as though these were not their own flesh. . . . So great was the multitude of those who died in the city night and day, what with lack of proper care and the virulence of the plague, that it was terrible to hear of, and worse still to see. Out of sheer necessity, therefore, quite different customs arose among the survivors from the original laws of the townspeople.

It used to be common, as it is still, for women, friends and neighbors of a dead man, to gather in his house and mourn there with his people, while his men friends and many other citizens collected with his nearest of kin outside the door. Then came the clergy, according to the standing of the departed, and with funereal pomp of tapers and singing he was carried on the shoulders of his peers to the church he had elected before death. Now, as the plague gained in violence, these customs were either modified or laid aside altogether, and new ones were instituted in their place, so that, far from dying among a crowd of women mourners, many passed away without the benefit of a single witness. Indeed, few were those who received the piteous wails and bitter tears of friends and relatives, for often, instead of mourning, laughter, jest and carousal accompanied the dead—usages which even naturally compassionate women had learned to perfection for their health's sake. It was a rare occurrence for a corpse to be followed to church by more than ten or twelve mourners—not the usual respectable citizens, but a class of vulgar grave-diggers who called themselves "sextons" and did these services for a price. They crept under the bier and shouldered it, and then with hasty steps rushed it, not to the church the deceased had designated before death, but oftener than not to the nearest one. . . .

More wretched still were the circumstances of the common people and, for a great part, of the middle class, for, confined to their homes either by hope of safety or by poverty, and restricted to their own sections, they fell sick daily by thousands. There, devoid of help or care, they died almost without redemption. A great many breathed their last in the public streets, day and night; a large number perished in their homes, and it was only by the stench of their decaying bodies that they proclaimed their death to their neighbors. Everywhere the city was teeming with corpses. A general course was now adopted by the people, more out of fear of contagion than of any charity they felt toward the dead. Alone, or with the assistance of whatever bearers they could muster, they would drag the corpses out of their homes and pile them in front of the doors, where often, of a morning, countless bodies might be seen. Biers were sent for. When none was to be had, the dead were laid upon ordinary boards, two or three at once. It was not infrequent to see a single bier carrying husband and wife, two or three brothers, father and son, and others besides. . . .

So many bodies were brought to the churches every day that the consecrated ground did not suffice to hold them, particularly according to the ancient custom of giving each corpse its individual place. Huge trenches were dug in the crowded churchyards and the new dead were piled in them, layer upon layer, like merchandise in the hold of a

110

120

130

140

150

160

ship. A little earth covered the corpses of each row, and the procedure continued until the trench was filled to the top.

Q What aspects of Boccaccio's Introduction to the *Decameron* reflect a shift to Realism in prose literature?

Q Are there any modern analogies to the pandemic that Boccaccio describes?

The Effects of the Black Death

Those who survived the plague tried to fathom its meaning and purpose. Some viewed it as the manifestation of God's displeasure with the growing worldliness of contemporary society, while others saw it as a divine warning to all Christians, but especially to the clergy, whose profligacy and moral laxity were commonly acknowledged facts. Those who perceived the plague as God's scourge urged a return to religious orthodoxy; some endorsed fanatic kinds of atonement. Groups of flagellants, for instance, wandered the countryside lashing their bodies with whips in frenzies of self-mortification. At the other extreme, there were many who resolved to "eat, drink, and be merry" in what might be the last hours of their lives. Still others, in a spirit of doubt and inquiry, questioned the very existence of a god who could work such evils on humankind.

The abandonment of the church-directed rituals of funeral and burial described by Boccaccio threatened tradition and shook the confidence of medieval Christians. Inevitably, the old medieval regard for death as a welcome release from earthly existence began to give way to a gnawing sense of anxiety and a new self-consciousness. Some of these changes are mirrored in the abundance of death-related pictorial images, including purgatorial visions and gruesome depictions of death and burial. Of all the plague-related themes depicted in the arts, the most popular was the "Dance of Death," or *danse macabre*. Set forth in both poetry and the visual arts, the Dance of Death portrayed death as a grinning skeleton or cadaver shepherding a procession of his victims to the grave (Figure **15.5**).

In the medieval morality play *Everyman* (see chapter 12), Death is a powerful antagonist. But in visual representations,

Figure 15.5 GUY MARCHANT, *Dance of Death*, 1486. Woodcut illustration, 4 × 6 in. (approx.).

he assumes subtle guises—ruler, predator, and seducer—and is a sly and cajoling figure who mocks the worldly pursuits of his unsuspecting victims. The Dance of Death procession (which might have originated in conjunction with popular dances) included men, women, and children from all walks of life and social classes: peasants and kings, schoolmasters and merchants, priests and nuns—all succumb to Death's ravishment. This objectified the new regard for death as "the Great Equalizer," that is, as an impartial phenomenon threatening every individual, regardless of status or wealth. The sense of vulnerability is a prevailing motif in fourteenth- and fifteenth-century verse. Note, for example, these lines written by François Villon (1431–ca. 1463), the greatest French poet of his time.

> I know this well, that rich and poor
> Fools, sages, laymen, friars in cowl,
> Large-hearted lords and each mean boor,[1]
> Little and great and fair and foul,
> Ladies in lace, who smile or scowl,
> From whatever stock they stem,
> Hatted or hooded, prone to prowl,
> Death seizes every one of them.

If the psychological impact of the Black Death was traumatic, its economic effects were equally devastating. Widespread death among the poor caused a shortage of labor, which in turn created a greater demand for workers. The bargaining power of those who survived the plague was thus improved. In many parts of Europe, workers pressed to raise their status and income. Peasants took advantage of opportunities to become tenant farmers on lands leased by lords in need of laborers. Others fled their rural manors for cities where jobs were readily available. This exodus from the countryside spurred urban growth and contributed to the slow disintegration of manorialism.

All of Europe, however, was disadvantaged by the climatic disasters that caused frequent crop failure and famine, and by the continuing demands of financially threatened feudal overlords. Violent working-class revolts—the first examples of labor rebellion in Western history—broke out in France and England in the mid-fourteenth century. In 1358, French peasants (known as *jacques*) staged an angry protest (the *Jacquerie*) that took the

---

[1] Peasant; a rude and illiterate person.

lives of hundreds of noblemen before it was suppressed by the French king. In England, the desperation of the poor was manifested in the Peasants' Revolt of 1381, led by Wat Tyler and described in the *Chronicles* of the French historian Jean Froissart (1338–1410). Despite their ultimate failure, these revolts left their imprint on the social history of the West. They frightened landowners everywhere and lent an instability to class relationships that hastened the demise of the old feudal order.

Literature in Transition

The Social Realism of Boccaccio

Fourteenth-century Europeans manifested an unprecedented preoccupation with differences in class, gender, and personality. Both in literature and in art, there emerged a new fidelity to nature and to personal experience in the everyday world. This close, objective attention to human society and social interaction may be described as "Social Realism." The New Realism is evident in the many woodcuts of the Dance of Death (see Figure 15.5), where class differences are clearly drawn, and in the one hundred lively vernacular tales that make up Boccaccio's *Decameron* (part of the preface to which appeared earlier in this chapter). The context for this frame tale is, of course, the plague-ravaged city of Florence: eager to escape the contagion, seven young women and three young men, ages eighteen to twenty-eight, retreat to a villa in the suburbs of Florence, where, to pass the time, each tells a story on each of ten days. The stories, designed as distractions from the horrors of the pandemic, are, in effect, amusing secular entertainments. They provide insight, however, into the social concerns and values of both the fictional narrators and Boccaccio's reading public.

With the *Decameron*, Boccaccio established the Italian language as an affective narrative medium. He borrowed many of its stories from popular fables, *fabliaux* (humorous narrative tales), and contemporary incidents. His characters resemble neither the allegorical figures of *Everyman* nor the courtly stereotypes of *Lancelot*. Rather, they are realistically conceived, high-spirited individuals who prize cleverness, good humor, and the world of the flesh over the classic medieval virtues of chivalry, piety, and humility. A case in point is the "Tale of Filippa," a delightful story that recounts how a woman from the Italian town of Prato shrewdly escapes legal punishment for committing adultery. The heroine, Madame Filippa, candidly confesses that she has a lover; however, she bitterly protests the city ordinance that serves a double standard of justice: one law for men, another for women. Filippa's proposal that women should not waste the passions unclaimed by their husbands but, rather, be allowed to enjoy the "surplus" with others—a view that might enlist the support of modern-day feminists—rings with good-humored defiance. Boccaccio's Filippa strikes a sharp note of contrast with the clinging heroines of the medieval romance. While Guinevere, for instance, wallows in longing for Lancelot (see Reading 11.3), Filippa boldly defends her right to

sexual independence. Like many a male protagonist, she fearlessly challenges and exploits fortune to serve her own designs.

The *Decameron* must have had special appeal for men and women who saw themselves as the heroes and heroines of precarious and rapidly changing times. Toward the end of his life, Boccaccio repented writing what he himself called his "immoral tales"; nevertheless, his stories, as the following example illustrates, remain a lasting tribute to the varieties of human affection and desire.

READING 15.2 From Boccaccio's "Tale of Filippa" from the *Decameron* (1351)

Once upon a time, in the town of Prato, there used to be   1
a law in force—as pernicious, indeed, as it was cruel, to
the effect that any woman caught by her husband in the
act of adultery with a lover, was to be burned alive, like
any vulgar harlot who sold herself for money.

   While this statute prevailed, a beautiful lady called
Filippa, a devout worshiper of Cupid, was surprised in
her bedroom one night by her husband, Rinaldo de'
Pugliesi, in the arms of Lazzarino de' Guazzagliotri, a
high-born Adonis of a youth of that city, whom she   10
loved as the apple of her eye.

   Burning with rage at the discovery, Rinaldo could
scarcely forbear running upon them, and slaying them
on the spot. Were it not for the misgivings he had for his
own safety, if he gave vent to his wrath, he would have
followed his impulse. However, he controlled his evil
intent, but could not abandon his desire to demand of
the town's statute, what it was unlawful for him to bring
about—in other words, the death of his wife. As he had
no lack of evidence to prove Filippa's guilt, he brought   20
charges against her, early in the morning, at daybreak,
and without further deliberation, had her summoned
before the court.

   Now Filippa was a high-spirited woman, as all women
are who truly love, and though many of her friends and
relatives advised her against going, she resolved to appear
before the magistrate, preferring a courageous death, by
confessing the truth, to a shameful life of exile, by a
cowardly flight that would have proved her unworthy of
the lover in whose arms she had lain that night.   30

   Accordingly, she presented herself before the provost,
with a large following of men and women who urged her
to deny the charges. She asked him firmly and without
moving a muscle what he desired of her. The provost,
seeing her so beautiful, courteous and so brave—as her
words demonstrated—felt a certain pity stirring in his
heart at the thought that she might confess a crime for
which he would be obliged to sentence her to death to
save his honor. But then, seeing he could not avoid
cross-questioning her on the charge proffered against   40
her, he said:

   "Madam, here as you see, is Rinaldo, your husband,
who is suing you on the grounds of finding you in the act

of adultery with another man, and who therefore demands that I sentence you to death for it, as the law, which is in force, requires. I cannot pass sentence if you do not confess your guilt with your own lips. Be careful of your answers, then, and tell me if what your husband charges you with is true."

Filippa, not at all daunted, replied in a very agreeable voice: "Your honor, it is true *that* Rinaldo is my husband, and that last night he found me in the arms of Lazzarino, where I had lain many another time, out of the great and true love I bear him. Far be it from me ever to deny it.

"As you are doubtless aware, laws should be equal for all, and should be made with the consent of those whom they affect. Such is not the case with this particular statute, which is stringent only with us poor women, who, after all, have it in our power to give pleasure to many more people than men ever could. Moreover, when this law was drawn up, not a single woman gave her consent or was so much as invited to give it. For all these reasons, it surely deserves to be considered reprehensible. If you insist upon enforcing it, not at the risk of my body, but of your immortal soul, you are at liberty to do so; but before you proceed to pass judgment, I beg you to grant me a small request. Simply ask my husband whether I have ever failed to yield myself to him entirely, whenever he chose, and as often as he pleased."

Without waiting for the magistrate to question him, Rinaldo immediately answered that there was no doubt Filippa had always granted him the joy of her body, at each and every request of his.

"That being the case, your honor," she went on, directly, "I'd like to ask him, since he has always had all he wanted of me and to his heart's content, what was I to do with all that was left over? Indeed, what am I to do with it? Throw it to the dogs? Isn't it far better to let it give enjoyment to some gentleman who loves me more than his life, than to let it go to waste or ruin?"

As it happened, the whole town had turned out to attend the sensational trial that involved a lady of such beauty and fame, and when the people heard her roguish question, they burst into a roar of laughter, shouting to a man that she was right and had spoken well.

That day, before court was adjourned, that harsh statute was modified at the magistrate's suggestion to hold only for such women as made cuckolds of their husbands for love of money.

As for Rinaldo, he went away crest-fallen at his mad venture, while Filippa returned home victorious, feeling in her joy that she had, in a sense, been delivered from the flames.

Q **How does Boccaccio's tale illustrate new attitudes toward women in Italian society?**

The Feminism of Christine de Pisan

Just decades after Boccaccio took the woman's view in the "Tale of Filippa," the world's first feminist writer, Christine de Pisan (1364–1430?), came on the scene. The daughter of an Italian physician, Christine wedded a French nobleman when she was fifteen—medieval women usually married in their mid- to late teens. Ten years later, when her husband died, Christine was left to support three children, a challenge she met by becoming the first female professional writer. Christine attacked the long antifemale tradition that had demeaned women and denied them the right to a university education. She criticized her literary contemporaries for creating negative stereotypes that slandered the female image. Her feminism is all the more significant because it occurred in a time in which men were making systematic efforts to restrict female inheritance of land and female membership in the guilds. In an early poem, the "Epistle to the God of Love" (1399), Christine protested the persistent antifemale bias of churchmen and scholars with these spirited words:

Some say that many women are deceitful,
Wily, false, of little worth;
Others that too many are liars,
Fickle, flighty, and inconstant;
Still others accuse them of great vices,
Blaming them much, excusing them nothing,
Thus do clerics, night and day,
First in French verse, then in Latin,
Based on who knows what books
That tell more lies than drunkards do.

Christine was keenly aware of the fact that Western literary tradition did not offer a representative picture of women's importance to society. Eager to correct this inequity, she became a spokesperson for women, both Christian and pagan. Her chauvinistic poem celebrating Joan of Arc emphasizes the heroism of a sixteen-year-old girl ("stronger and more resolute than Achilles or Hector") whose leadership brought France to victory when thousands of men had failed to do so. In her *Book of the City of Ladies*, Christine attacks male misogyny and exalts the accomplishments of famous women throughout the ages. Patterned as an allegorical debate, *The City of Ladies* pictures Christine herself "interviewing" three goddesses—Lady Reason, Lady Rectitude, and Lady Justice (Figure **15.6**). She seeks moral guidance on matters such as whether women can and should be educated in the same manner as men (I.27) and why men claim it is not good for women to be educated at all (II.36). Excerpts from these two portions of Christine's landmark feminist work follow.

READING 15.3 From Christine de Pisan's *Book of the City of Ladies* (1405)

Part I.27 Christine asks Reason if God has ever blessed woman's mind with knowledge of the highest branches of learning, and Reason's reply

". . . if you don't mind, please tell me if, amongst all the other favors He has shown to women, God ever chose to honor any of them with great intelligence and knowledge. Do they indeed have an aptitude for learning?

Figure 15.6 Anonymous, *La Cité des Dames de Christine de Pizan*, ca. 1410. Illumination on parchment, 3 × 6 in. (approx.). In this miniature, Christine is pictured in conversation with the allegorical figures of Reason, Rectitude, and Justice. On the right, she assists in building the City of Ladies.

I'd really like to know why it is that men claim women to be so slow-witted."

Reason's reply was: "Christine, from what I've already told you, it should be obvious that the opposite of what they say is true. To make the point more clearly for you, I'll give you some conclusive examples. I repeat – and don't doubt my word – that if it were the custom to send little girls to school and to teach them all sorts of different subjects there, as one does with little boys, they would grasp and learn the difficulties of all the arts and sciences just as easily as the boys do. Indeed, this is often the case because, as I mentioned to you before, although women may have weaker and less agile bodies than men, which prevents them from doing certain tasks, their minds are in fact sharper and more receptive when they do apply themselves."

"My lady, what are you saying? If you please, I'd be grateful if you would expand on this point. No man would ever accept this argument if it couldn't be proved, because they would say that men generally know so much more than women."

She replied, "Do you know why it is that women know less than men?"

"No, my lady, you'll have to enlighten me."

"It's because they are less exposed to a wide variety of experiences since they have to stay at home all day to look after the household. There's nothing like a whole range of different experiences and activities for expanding the mind of any rational creature."

"So, my lady, if they have able minds which can learn and absorb as much as those of men, why don't they therefore know more?"

"The answer, my dear girl, is that it's not necessary for the public good for women to go around doing what men are supposed to do, as I informed you earlier. It's quite adequate that they perform the tasks for which they are fitted. As for this idea that experience tells us that women's intelligence is inferior to that of men simply because we see that those around us generally know less than men do, let's take the example of male peasants living in remote countryside or high mountains. You could give me plenty of names of places where the men are so backward that they seem no better than beasts. Yet, there's no doubt that Nature made them as perfect in mind and body as the cleverest and most learned men to be found in towns and cities. All this comes down to their lack of education, though don't forget what I said before about some men and women being more naturally endowed with intelligence than others …"

Part II.36 Against those who claim that it is not good for women to be educated

After hearing these words I, Christine, said, "My lady, I can clearly see that much good has been brought into the world by women. Even if some wicked women have done evil things it still seems to me that this is far outweighed by all the good that other women have done and continue to do. This is particularly true of those who are wise and well educated in either the arts or the sciences, whom we mentioned before. That's why I'm all the more amazed at the opinion of some men who state that they are completely opposed to their daughters, wives or other female relatives engaging in study, for fear that their morals will be corrupted."

Rectitude replied, "This should prove to you that not all men's arguments are based on reason, and that these men in particular are wrong. There are absolutely no grounds for assuming that knowledge of moral disciplines, which actually inculcate virtue, would have a morally corrupting effect. Indeed, there's no doubt whatsoever that such forms of knowledge correct one's vices and improve one's morals. How could anyone possibly think that by studying good lessons and advice one will be any the worse for it? This view is completely unthinkable and untenable. I'm not saying that it's a good idea for men or women to study sorcery or any other type of forbidden science, since the Holy Church did not ban people for practicing them for nothing. However, it's just that it's not true to say that women will be corrupted by knowing what's right and proper.

"Quintus Hortensius,[1] who was a great rhetorician and a fine orator of Rome, did not subscribe to this opinion. He had a daughter named Hortensia, whom he loved dearly for her keen wits. He educated her himself, teaching her the science of rhetoric in which, states Boccaccio, she so excelled that she not only resembled her father in her intelligence, agile memory and excellent diction, but in fact surpassed him in her marvelous eloquence and command of oratory. On the subject of what we said before about all the benefits that women have brought, the good that this lady did is especially worthy of note. It was at the time when a triumvirate ruled over Rome that this Hortensia decided to take up the cause of women, thus performing a task which no man dared to do. As Rome was in great financial straits, it was proposed to levy certain charges on women and, in particular, to put a tax on their valuables. This Hortensia spoke so persuasively that she was listened to as attentively as if it had been her father speaking, and won her case.

"If we discuss more recent times, rather than going back to ancient history, Giovanni Andrea, the famous legist who taught at Bologna nearly sixty years ago, similarly opposed the view that women should not be educated. He gave his beloved daughter Novella, a fine and lovely girl, such a good education and detailed knowledge of the law that, when he was busy with other tasks which prevented him from lecturing to his students, he could send his daughter in his place to read to them from his professorial chair. In order not to distract the audience by her beauty, Novella had a little curtain put up in front of her. Thus she lightened her father's load and relieved him of some of his duties. In his devotion to her, he chose to preserve her name for posterity by writing an important commentary on a legal text which he named *La Novella* in her honor.

"Therefore, it is not all men, especially not the most intelligent, who agree with the view that it is a bad idea to educate women. However, it's true that those who are not very clever come out with this opinion because they don't want women to know more than they do. Your own father, who was a great astrologer and philosopher, did not believe that knowledge of the sciences reduced a woman's worth. Indeed, as you know, it gave him great pleasure to see you take so readily to studying the arts. Rather, it was because your mother, as a woman, held the view that you should spend your time spinning like the other girls, that you did not receive a more advanced or detailed initiation into the sciences. But, as that proverb which we've already had occasion to quote says, 'What is in our nature cannot be taken away.' Despite your mother's opposition, you did manage to glean some grains of knowledge from your studies, thanks to your own natural inclination for learning. It's obvious to me that you do not esteem yourself any less for having this knowledge: in fact, you seem to treasure it, and quite rightly so."

I, Christine, then replied, "Without a doubt, what you're saying, my lady, is as true as the Lord's Prayer itself."

Q With what arguments does Lady Reason defend the intelligence of women?

Q What role does education play in matters of gender equality?

The Social Realism of Chaucer

The master of fourteenth-century English vernacular literature, Geoffrey Chaucer (1340–1400), was a contemporary of Boccaccio and Christine de Pisan. A middle-class civil servant and diplomat, a soldier in the Hundred Years' War, and a citizen of the bustling city of London, Chaucer left an indelible image of his time in a group of stories known as the *Canterbury Tales*. Modeled broadly on Boccaccio's *Decameron*, this versified frame tale recounts the stories told by a group of pilgrims to entertain one another while traveling from London to the shrine of Saint Thomas à Becket in Canterbury. Chaucer's twenty-nine pilgrims, who include a miller, a monk, a plowman, a knight, a priest, a scholar, and a prioress, provide a literary cross section of late medieval society. Although they are type characters, representative of the nobility, the clergy, the merchant, and the commoner, they are also individual personalities. The effeminate Pardoner, the lusty Wife of Bath, and the belligerent Miller are creatures of flesh and blood, whose interaction throughout the journey contributes to our perception of them as participants in Chaucer's human comedy. Chaucer characterizes each pilgrim by descriptive detail, by their lively and humorous conversations, and by the twenty stories they tell, which range from moral tales and beast fables to *fabliaux* of the most risqué and bawdy sort.

Like his medieval predecessors, Chaucer tended to moralize, reserving special scorn for clerical abuse and human hypocrisy. But unlike his forebears, whose stories were often peopled by literary stereotypes, Chaucer brought his characters to life by means of vivid detail. His talent in this direction is best realized through a brief comparison. In a twelfth-century verse narrative called *Equitan*, written by Marie de France, a notable poet in the Norman court of England, we find the following description of the heroine:

> Very desirable was the lady; passing tender of body and sweet of vesture, coiffed and fretted with gold. Her eyes were blue, her face warmly colored, with a fragrant mouth, and a dainty nose. Certainly she had no peer in all the realm.

---

[1] Quintus Hortensius (114–50 B.C.E.).

Compare Chaucer's descriptions of the Wife of Bath and the Miller (from the "Prologue"). Then, in direct comparison with the lines from *Equitan*, consider Chaucer's evocation of Alison (the Miller's wife) in "The Miller's Tale" which, though too long to reproduce here, is recommended to all who might enjoy a spicy yarn.

READING 15.4 From Chaucer's "Prologue" and "The Miller's Tale" in the *Canterbury Tales* (ca. 1390)

Here begins the Book of the Tales of Canterbury: When   1
April with its gentle showers has pierced the March
drought to the root and bathed every plant in the moisture
which will hasten the flowering; when Zephyrus with his
sweet breath has stirred the new shoots in every wood and
field, and the young sun has run its half-course in the Ram,
and small birds sing melodiously, so touched in their hearts
by Nature that they sleep all night with open eyes—then
folks long to go on pilgrimages, and palmers to visit foreign
shores and distant shrines, known in various lands; and   10
especially from every shire's end of England they travel to
Canterbury, to seek the holy blessed martyr who helped
them when they were sick.

    One day in that season when I stopped at the Tabard in
Southwark, ready to go on my pilgrimage to Canterbury
with a truly devout heart, it happened that a group of
twenty-nine people came into that inn in the evening. They
were people of various ranks who had come together by
chance, and they were all pilgrims who planned to ride to
Canterbury. The rooms and stables were large enough for   20
each of us to be well lodged, and, shortly after the sun had
gone down, I had talked with each of these pilgrims and
had soon made myself one of their group. We made our
plans to get up early in order to start our trip, which I am
going to tell you about. But, nevertheless, while I have time
and space, before I go farther in this account, it seems
reasonable to tell you all about each of the pilgrims, as
they appeared to me; who they were, and of what rank,
and also what sort of clothes they wore.

. . . .

There was a good Wife from near Bath, but she was   30
somewhat deaf, which was a shame. She had such skill in
clothmaking that she surpassed the weavers of Ypres and
Ghent. In all her parish there was no woman who could go
before her to the offertory; and if someone did, the Wife
of Bath was certainly so angry that she lost all charitable
feeling. Her kerchiefs were of fine texture; those she wore
upon her head on Sunday weighed, I swear, ten pounds.
Her fine scarlet hose were carefully tied, and her shoes
were uncracked and new. Her face was bold and fair and
red. All of her life she had been an estimable woman: she   40
had had five husbands, not to mention other company in
her youth—but of that we need not speak now. And three
times she had been to Jerusalem; she had crossed many
a foreign river; she had been to Rome, to Bologna, to

St. James' shrine in Galicia, and to Cologne. About journeying
through the country she knew a great deal. To tell the truth
she was gap-toothed. She sat her gentle horse easily, and
wore a fine headdress with a hat as broad as a buckler or
a shield, a riding skirt about her large hips, and a pair of
sharp spurs on her heels. She knew how to laugh and joke   50
in company, and all the remedies of love, for her skill was
great in that old game.

. . . .

The Miller was a very husky fellow, tremendous in bone
and in brawn which he used well to get the best of all
comers; in wrestling he always won the prize. He was
stocky, broad, and thickset. There was no door which he
could not pull off its hinges or break by ramming it with his
head. His beard was as red as any sow or fox, and as
broad as a spade. At the right on top of his nose he had a
wart, from which there grew a tuft of hairs red as the   60
bristles of a sow's ears, and his nostrils were wide and
black. A sword and a shield hung at his side. His mouth
was as huge as a large furnace, and he was a jokester
and a ribald clown, most of whose jests were of sin and
scurrility. He knew quite well how to steal grain and charge
thrice over, but yet he really remained reasonably honest. The
coat he wore was white and the hood blue. He could play the
bagpipe well and led us out of town to its music.

. . . .

The young wife was pretty, with a body as neat and graceful
as a weasel. She wore a checked silk belt, and around her   70
loins a flounced apron as white as fresh milk. Her smock
was white also, embroidered in front and in back, inside and
outside and around the collar, with coal-black silk. The
strings of her white hood were of the same material as her
collar; her hair was bound with a wide ribbon of silk set
high on her head. And, truly, she had a wanton eye. Her
eyebrows were plucked thin and were arched and black as
any sloe.[1] She was even more delightful to look at than a
young, early-ripe pear tree, and she was softer than lamb's
wool. A leather purse, with a silk tassel and metal   80
ornaments, hung from her belt. In all the world there is no
man so wise that, though he looked far and near, he could
imagine so gay a darling or such a wench. Her coloring was
brighter than that of a coin newly forged in the Tower, and
her singing was as loud and lively as a swallow's sitting on
a barn. In addition, she could skip about and play like any
kid or calf following its mother. Her mouth was as sweet as
honey or mead, or a pile of apples laid up in hay or heather.
She was as skittish as a young colt, and tall and straight
as a mast or wand. On her low collar she wore a brooch as   90
broad as the boss on a shield. Her shoes were laced high on
her legs. She was a primrose, a trillium,[2] fit to grace the bed of
any lord or to marry any good yeoman.

Q **Which of Chaucer's descriptive devices are most effective in evoking character and personality?**

---

[1] A small, dark berry.
[2] A lily.

Chaucer uses sprightly similes ("graceful as a weasel," "as sweet as honey") and vivid details ("a checked silk belt," shoes "laced high") to bring alive the personality and physical presence of the Miller's wife. (He also hints at the contradiction between her chaste exterior and her sensual nature, a major feature in the development of the story in which she figures.) By comparison, Marie de France's portrait is a pallid and stereotypical adaptation of the standard medieval female image: the courtly lady, the Virgin Mary, and the female saint. Chaucer's humanizing techniques bring zesty realism to both his pilgrim-narrators and the characters featured in their tales. Writing in the everyday language of his time (Middle English, as distinguished from the more Germanic Old English that preceded it), Chaucer shaped the development of English literature, much as Dante, a century earlier, had influenced the course of Italian poetry.

Art and Music in Transition

Giotto's New Realism

The shift to Realism evidenced in the works of Boccaccio and Chaucer was anticipated in painting by the Florentine artist Giotto (1266–1337). The follower of Cimabue, Giotto was hailed by his contemporaries as the leader of a new direction in visual representation.

MAKING CONNECTIONS

A comparison of Cimabue's *Madonna Enthroned*, completed around 1290 (Figure **15.7**; see also color photo Figure 13.34), with Giotto's rendering of the same subject some twenty years later (Figure **15.8**) provides evidence of the shift to Realism that accompanied the transition from the medieval to the modern era. Both are huge, iconic images, well over 10 feet in height. Like Cimabue, Giotto shows an oversized Virgin on a Gothic throne set against an airless gold background. But Giotto renounces the graceful Gothic line and flat, decorative stylization reminiscent of the Byzantine icons that inspired Cimabue's late medieval painting. Instead, he models the form by way of gradations of light and shade, a technique known as **chiaroscuro**, which gives the Madonna an imposing three-dimensional presence. (Note the forward projection of her knees, which provide support for the baby Jesus—here more childlike than Cimabue's toga-clad infant.) Rather than placing the angels one above another on either side of the throne, Giotto arranges them in positions that suggest their presence in three-dimensional space.

The kneeling angels at the foot of the throne, like those on the sides, bring dramatic attention to the central figures. In contrast with Cimabue's idealized Madonna, Giotto has created a robust and lifelike image that anticipates the pictorial Realism of Italian Renaissance art (see chapter 17).

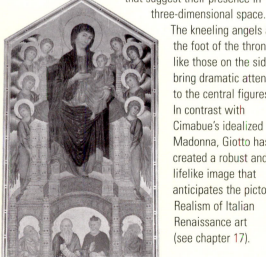

Figure 15.7 CIMABUE, *Madonna Enthroned*, ca. 1280–1290. Tempera on wood, 12 ft. 7½ in. × 7 ft. 4 in.

Figure 15.8 GIOTTO, *Madonna Enthroned*, ca. 1310. Tempera on panel, 10 ft. 8 in. × 6 ft. 8 in.

Figure 15.9 GIOTTO, Arena Chapel (Cappella Scrovegni), Padua, interior looking toward the choir. Height 42 ft., width 27 ft. 10 in., length 96 ft. Unlike the artists of ancient Egyptian frescoes, who applied paint to a dry surface, Giotto made use of the technique known as ***buon fresco*** ("true fresco"), in which the artist applied earth pigments onto the wet lime or gypsum plaster surface.

rocks and a single barren tree. Two foreground mourners viewed from behind enhance the illusion of spatial depth and call attention to the poignant expression of the Mother of God. Dramatic expression is also heightened by gestures of lament that vary from the tender remorse of Mary Magdalene, who embraces the feet of Jesus, to the impassioned dismay of John the Evangelist, who flings back his arms in astonished grief, a sentiment echoed among the weeping angels that flutter above the scene. Giotto gives weight, volume, and emotional resonance to figures whose gravity and dignity call to mind Classical sculpture. Like the characters in Boccaccio's *Decameron* and Chaucer's *Canterbury Tales*, those in Giotto's paintings are convincingly human: while they are not individualized to the point of portraiture, neither are they stereotypes. Giotto advanced the trend toward Realism already evident in Late Gothic art. At the same time, he gave substance to the spirit of lay piety and individualism that marked the fourteenth century.

Devotional Realism and Portraiture

In religious art, Realism enhanced the devotional mood of the age. Traditional scenes of the lives of Christ and the Virgin became at once more pictorial and more detailed, a reflection of the new concern with Christ's human nature and his suffering. Images of the Crucifixion and the *Pietà* (the Virgin holding the dead Jesus), which had been a popular object of veneration since the tenth century, were now depicted with a new expressive intensity. One anonymous German artist of the mid-fourteenth century rendered the *Pietà* (the word means both "pity" and "piety") as a traumatic moment between a despairing Mother and her Son, whose broken torso and elongated arms are as rigid as the wood from which they were carved (Figure **15.11**). This votive sculpture captures the torment of Christ's martyrdom with fierce energy.

In the domain of fourteenth-century monumental sculpture the most notable personality was the Dutch artist Claus Sluter (ca. 1350–1406). Sluter's *Well of Moses*, executed between 1395 and 1406 for the Carthusian monastery at Champmol, just outside Dijon, France, was originally part of a 25-foot-tall stone fountain designed to celebrate the sacraments of Eucharist and baptism.

Giotto brought an equally dramatic naturalism to his frescoes. In 1303, the wealthy banker and money lender Enrico Scrovegni commissioned him to paint a series of frescoes for the family chapel in Padua. On the walls of the Arena Chapel, Giotto illustrated familiar episodes from the narrative cycle that recounts the lives of the Virgin and Christ (Figure **15.9**). While wholly traditional in subject matter, the enterprise constituted an innovative approach that transformed the tiny barrel-vaulted chamber into a theater in which the individual scenes, lit from the west and viewed from the center, appear to take place in real space.

In the *Lamentation* (Figure **15.10**), the figures appear in a shallow but carefully defined space delimited by craggy

Figure 15.10 GIOTTO, *Lamentation*, 1305–1306. Fresco, 7 ft. 7 in. × 7 ft. 9 in. In one of the most moving frescoes from the Arena Chapel, Giotto has transformed a traditional episode from the Passion of Christ into a theatrical drama. His staging of the event reflects the trend toward realistic representation that characterized the fourteenth century.

The Crucifixion group that made up the superstructure is lost, but the pedestal of the fountain with its six Old Testament prophets—Moses, David, Jeremiah, Zachariah, Daniel, and Isaiah—survives in its entirety (Figure **15.12**). Carrying scrolls engraved with their messianic texts, the life-sized prophets are swathed in deeply cut, voluminous draperies. Facial features are individualized so as to render each prophet with a distinctive personality. As in Giotto's *Lamentation*, mourning angels (at the corners of the pedestal above the heads of the prophets) cover their faces or wring their hands in gestures of anguish and despair. So intensely theatrical is the Realism of the Champmol ensemble that scholars suspect Sluter might have been inspired by contemporary mystery plays, where Old Testament characters regularly took the stage between the acts to "prophesy" New Testament events.

Devotional Realism is equally apparent in illuminated manuscripts, and especially in the popular prayer book known as the Book of Hours. This guide to private prayer featured traditional recitations for the canonical hours—the sets of prayers recited daily at three-hour intervals: Matins, Lauds, Prime, Terce, Sext, None, Vespers, and Compline—as well as prayers to the Virgin and the saints. As manuals for personal piety and alternatives to daily church ritual, Books of Hours were in great demand, especially among prosperous Christians. In the miniatures of these prayer books, scenes from sacred history are filled with realistic and homely details drawn from everyday life. Even miraculous events are made more believable as they are presented in lifelike settings and given new dramatic fervor. Such is the case with the animated ***grisaille*** (gray-toned) miniatures found in a prayer book executed around

1325 for Jeanne d'Evreux, queen of France, by the French court painter Jean Pucelle (Figure **15.13**). In contrast with the stylized treatment of the Betrayal of Christ in the thirteenth-century *Psalter of Saint Swithin* (see Figure 13.13), Pucelle's figures are accurately proportioned and, modeled in subtle *chiaroscuro*, substantial in form. In the *Annunciation*, pictured on the *recto* (right) folio, the artist engaged receding diagonal lines to create the illusion of a "doll's house" that holds an oversized Madonna.

Pucelle's experiments in empirical perspective and his lively renderings of traditional subjects were carried further by the three brothers Jean, Pol, and Herman Limbourg, who flourished between 1385 and 1415. Their generous patron Jean, duke of Berry and brother of the king of France, commissioned from them a remarkable series of Books of Hours illustrated with religious and secular subjects. For the calendar pages of the *Très Riches Heures* (*Very Precious Hours*), the Limbourgs painted scenes illustrating the mundane activities and labors peculiar to each month of the year. In the scene for the month of February—the first snowscape in Western art—three peasants warm themselves

Figure 15.11 Anonymous, *The Röttgen Pietà*, ca. 1300–1325. Painted wood, height 35 in.

Figure 15.12 CLAUS SLUTER, figure of Moses on the *Well of Moses*, 1395–1406. Painted stone, height approx. 6 ft. Moses is seen here in the center with King David on his left. Time has robbed this piece of the brightly colored paint and metal accessories—the scholarly Jeremiah (far left) bore a pair of copper spectacles—that once gave it a startlingly lifelike presence.

by the fire, while others hurry to complete their chores (see Figure **15.1**). The Limbourgs show a new fascination with natural details: dovecote and beehives covered with new-fallen snow, sheep that huddle together in a thatched pen, smoke curling from a chimney, and even the genitalia of two of the laborers who warm themselves by the fire.

Devotional Realism also overtook the popular subject of the Madonna and Child: the new image of the Virgin as a humble matron tenderly nurturing the Infant Jesus (Figure **15.14**) replaced earlier, more hieratic representations of Mary Enthroned (see Figures 13.1, 13.34, and

15.8). In paintings of the Virgin as "Nursing Madonna," the Infant is shown as a lively baby, not as the miniature adult of earlier renderings. Fourteenth-century artists frequently introduced descriptive details from mystery plays and from the writings of mystics like Saint Bridget of Sweden. Indeed, the interchange of imagery between devotional literature, medieval drama, and the visual arts was commonplace.

In light of the growing interest in the human personality—so clearly revealed in the literature of Boccaccio and Chaucer—it is no surprise that fourteenth-century artists produced the first portrait paintings since Classical antiquity. Most such portraits appear in manuscripts. In panel painting, the anonymous portrait of John the Good, king of France (Figure **15.15**), documents the new consciousness of the particular as opposed to the generalized image of humankind.

The *Ars Nova* in Music

The cultural transformation that characterizes the fourteenth century is apparent in its music, which composers of that era perceptively called the **ars nova** ("new art"). The *ars nova* is a musical style that, in its aural expressiveness, parallels the richly detailed Realism apparent in fourteenth-century literature and the visual arts. The new

art features a distinctive rhythmic complexity, achieved in part by **isorhythm** (literally "same rhythm"): the close repetition of identical rhythmic patterns in different portions of a composition. Isorhythm, an expression of the growing interest in the manipulation of pitches and rhythms, gave unprecedented unity to musical compositions.

In France, the leading proponent of the *ars nova* was the French poet, priest, and composer Guillaume de Machaut (1300–1377). In his day, Machaut was more widely known and acclaimed than Chaucer and Boccaccio. Like the Limbourg brothers, he held commissions from the French aristocracy, including the duke of Berry. Machaut penned hundreds of poems, including a verse drama interspersed with songs, but his most important musical achievement was his *Messe de Notre Dame* (*Mass of Our Lady*). Departing from the medieval tradition of treating the Mass as five separate compositions (based on Gregorian chant), he unified the parts into a single polyphonic composition, adding a sixth movement, the "Ite missa est" ("Go, the Mass is ended") that dismissed the congregation. Distinctive to our listening selection of the "Ite missa est" is the diversity of rhythmic style, the appearance of **syncopation**, and the use of instruments, either doubling or playing the lower parts of the four-voice setting. Machaut's efforts at coherence of design are clear evidence that composers had

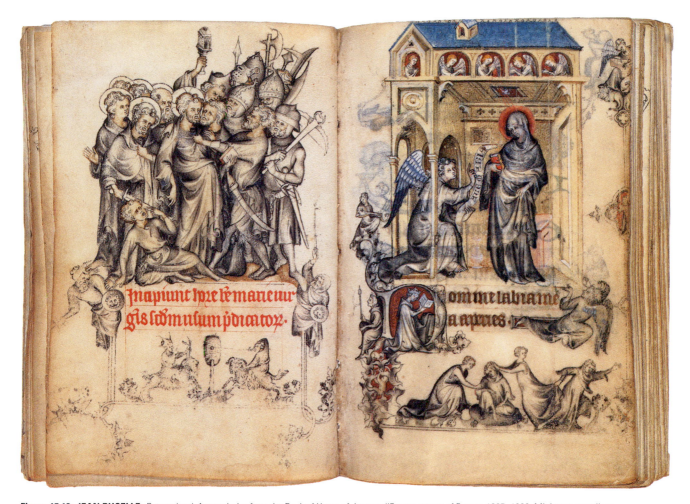

Figure 15.13 JEAN PUCELLE, *Betrayal* and *Annunciation* from the Book of Hours of Jeanne d'Evreux, queen of France, 1325–1328. Miniature on vellum, each folio 3½ × 2⁷⁄₁₆ in. Note the lively secular scenes of commonplace activities in the *bas-de-page* (bottom of the page) illustrations.

Outside France, polyphonic music flourished. The blind Italian composer Francesco Landini (ca. 1325–1397) produced graceful instrumental compositions and eloquent two- and three-part songs. Landini's 150 works constitute more than one-third of the surviving music of the fourteenth century—evidence of his enormous popularity. Italian composers favored florid polyphonic works that featured a close relationship between musical parts. The *caccia* (Italian for "chase"), for instance, which dealt with such everyday subjects as fishing and hunting, was set to lively music in which one voice part "chased" another. Another popular polyphonic composition, the **round**, featured several voices that enter one after the other, each repeating the same words and music (as in "Row, Row, Row Your Boat"). The Middle English round "Sumer is icumen in" is an example of polyphony at its freshest and most buoyant. Although fourteenth-century polyphony involved both voices and instruments, manuscripts of the period did not usually specify whether a given part of a piece was instrumental or vocal. Custom probably dictated the performance style, not only for vocal and instrumental ensembles, but for dance as well.

Figure 15.14 AMBROGIO LORENZETTI, *Madonna del Latte* (*Nursing Madonna*), ca. 1330. Oil on board, 35⅓ × 19 in. Only a few decades after Giotto's regal *Madonna Enthroned* (see Figure 15.8), Lorenzetti renders a more humanized version.

begun to rank musical effect as equal to liturgical function. This new treatment of the Catholic liturgy set a precedent for many composers, including the sixteenth-century Palestrina and the Baroque master Johann Sebastian Bach (see chapters 20 and 23).

Machaut's sacred compositions represent only a small part of his total musical output. His secular works include 142 polyphonic **ballades** that look back to the vernacular songs of the *trouvères*, but their attention to expressive detail is unique. They introduce new warmth and lyricism, as well as vivid poetic imagery—features that parallel the humanizing currents in fourteenth-century art and literature. "One who does not compose according to feelings," wrote Machaut, "falsifies his work and his song."

See Music Listening Selections at end of chapter.

Figure 15.15 *King John the Good*, ca. 1356–1359 (?). Canvas on panel, 21⅞ × 13⅜ in. Following the tradition of Classical and medieval coins and medals, the earliest portraits in Western painting feature the human profile.

Europe in Transition

- The fourteenth century witnessed the transition from medieval to early modern culture in the West. During this era, violence uprooted tradition, corruption bred cynicism, and widespread death generated insecurity and fear.
- The two great catalysts of the age—the Hundred Years' War and the Black Death—brought about a collapse of the medieval order, along with political, military, and economic unrest. A new kind of warfare, featuring the use of gunpowder, outmoded older methods of combat. By the end of the century, the population of Western Europe had declined by approximately 50 percent.
- The relocation of the papacy to Avignon, and the Great Schism, which divided the papacy and produced two conflicting claims to universal sovereignty, led to controversy within the Church and widespread popular criticism.

Literature in Transition

- In Italy, Boccaccio penned vernacular tales to entertain urban audiences. Rejecting literary stereotypes, allegorical intent, and religious purpose, he brought to life the personalities of self-motivated men and women.
- In France, Christine de Pisan attacked the antifemale tradition in life and letters, and ushered in the birth of feminism in Western literature.
- Geoffrey Chaucer, an English middle-class civil servant and soldier, left an indelible image of his time in the *Canterbury Tales*. This versified human comedy was framed in the setting of a pilgrimage whose participants tell stories to entertain one another while traveling to Canterbury.

Art and Music in Transition

- Giotto pioneered the new direction in realistic representation. His robust, lifelike figures, posed in three-dimensional space, anticipated the art of the Italian Renaissance.
- The New Realism was also evident in the rise of portraiture and in a more humanized approach to traditional religious subjects.
- In the sculpture of Claus Sluter and in manuscript illumination, as in panel and fresco painting, true-to-life detail and emotional expressiveness came to replace Gothic abstraction and stylization.
- Promoted by Guillaume de Machaut, the *ars nova* brought warmth and lyricism to secular and religious music that featured increased rhythmic complexity and aural expressiveness.

Music Listening Selections

- Machaut, *Messe de Notre Dame* (*Mass of Our Lady*), "Ite missa est, Deo gratias," 1364.
- Anonymous, English round, "Sumer is icumen in," fourteenth century.

Glossary

ars nova (Latin, "new art") a term used for the music of fourteenth-century Europe to distinguish it from that of the old art (*ars antiqua*); it featured new rhythms, new harmonies, and more complicated methods of musical notation

ballade a secular song that tells a story in simple verse, usually repeating the same music for each stanza

buon fresco (Italian, "true fresco") the technique of applying earth pigments onto a wet lime or gypsum plaster surface

caccia (Italian, "chase") a lively fourteenth-century Italian musical form that deals with everyday subjects, such as hunting and fishing

chiaroscuro (Italian, "light–dark") in drawing and painting, the technique of modeling form in gradations of light and shade to produce the illusion of three-dimensionality

grisaille (French, "gray-toned") the use of exclusively gray tones in painting or drawing

indulgence a church pardon from the temporal penalties for sins; the remission of purgatorial punishment

isorhythm the close repetition of identical rhythmic patterns in different sections of a musical composition

round a type of polyphonic composition that features successive voices that enter one after another, each repeating exactly the same melody and text

simony the buying or selling of church office or preferment (see Simon Magus, Acts of the Apostles 8:9–24)

syncopation a musical effect of uneven rhythm resulting from changing the normal pattern of accents and beats

Classical Humanism in the Age of the Renaissance

ca. 1300–1600

". . . man is, with complete justice, considered and called a great miracle and a being worthy of all admiration."
Pico della Mirandola

Figure 16.1 The *studiolo* of Federico da Montefeltro in the Palazzo Ducale, Urbino, Italy, 1476. In the panels that line the walls of the study, the illusion of real books, scientific devices, musical instruments, and military equipment—objects related to Federico's intellectual and civic accomplishments—was created by way of **intarsia** (inlaid wood), a technique perfected in Renaissance Florence. The half-length portraits (above) represent Christian notables, and Classical and Renaissance humanists.

Classical humanism, the movement to recover and revive Greco-Roman culture, was the phenomenon that gave the Renaissance (the word literally means "rebirth") its distinctive, secular stamp. Classical humanists were the cultural archeologists of their age. They uncovered lost evidence of the splendor of Greco-Roman antiquity and avidly consumed the fruits of the Classical legacy. Unattached to any single school or university, this new breed of humanists pursued what the ancient Romans had called *studia humanitatis*, a program of study that embraced grammar, rhetoric, history, poetry, and moral philosophy. These branches of learning fostered training in the moral and aesthetic areas of human knowledge—the very areas of experience with which this textbook is concerned. While such an educational curriculum was assuredly not antireligious—indeed, most Renaissance humanists were devout Catholics—its focus was secular. For the humanists, life on earth was not a vale of tears but, rather, an extended occasion during which human beings might cultivate their unique talents and abilities. Classical humanists saw no conflict between humanism and religious belief. They viewed their intellectual mission as both pleasing to God and advantageous to society in general. Humanism, then, grounded in a reevaluation of Classical literature and art, represented a shift in emphasis rather than an entirely new pursuit; it involved a turning away from exclusively otherworldly preoccupations to a robust, this-worldly point of view.

Italy: Birthplace of the Renaissance

The Renaissance designates that period in European history between roughly 1300 and 1600, during which time the revival of Classical humanism spread from its birthplace in Florence, Italy, throughout Western Europe. Italy was the homeland of Roman antiquity, the splendid ruins of which stood as reminders of the greatness of Classical civilization. The least feudalized part of the medieval world and Europe's foremost commercial and financial center, Italy had traded with Southwest Asian cities even in the darkest days of the Middle Ages. It had also maintained cultural contacts with Byzantium, the heir to Greek culture. The cities of Italy, especially Venice and Genoa (Map **16.1**), had profited financially from the Crusades (see chapter 11) and—despite the ravages of the plague—continued to enjoy a high level of commercial prosperity. In fourteenth-century Florence, shopkeepers devised a practical system (based on Arab models) of tracking debits and credits: double-entry bookkeeping helped merchants to maintain systematic records of transactions in what was the soundest currency in the West, the Florentine gold florin. Fifteenth-century handbooks on arithmetic, foreign currency, and even good penmanship also encouraged the commercial activities of traders and bankers.

Map 16.1 Renaissance Italy, 1300–1600.

Figure 16.2 **AMBROGIO LORENZETTI**, *Effects of Good Government in the City and the Country*, from *The Allegory of Good Government*, 1338–1339. Fresco, total length 46 ft. (approx.). Peace and prosperity are the themes of this urban landscape, a view of Siena's bustling commune: merchants sell their wares at storefronts, classes are in progress in a schoolroom, revelers dance in the street, and builders work on rooftop construction.

The pursuit of money and leisure, rather than a preoccupation with feudal and chivalric obligations, marked the lifestyle of merchants and artisans who lived in the bustling city-states of Italy. In a panoramic cityscape commissioned for the Palazzo Pubblico (Town Hall) of Siena, Ambrogio Lorenzetti (whom we met in chapter 15) celebrated the positive effects of good government on urban life (Figure **16.2**), while a matching fresco illustrated the evil effects of bad government. Throughout Italy, the Avignon Papacy and the Great Schism had produced a climate of anticlericalism and intellectual skepticism. Middle-class men and women challenged canonical sources of authority that frowned on profit-making and the accumulation of wealth. In this materialistic and often only superficially religious society, the old medieval values no longer made sense, while those of pre-Christian antiquity seemed more compatible with the secular interests and ambitions of the rising merchant class. The ancient Greeks and Romans were indeed ideal historical models for the enterprising citizens of the Italian city-states.

Politically, Renaissance Italy had much in common with ancient Greece. Independent and disunited, the city-states of Italy, like those of ancient Greece, were fiercely competitive. As in Golden Age Greece, commercial rivalry among the Italian city-states led to frequent civil wars.

In Italy, however, such wars were not always fought by citizens (who, as merchants, were generally ill prepared for combat), but by *condottieri* (professional soldiers) whose loyalties, along with their services, were bought for a price. The papacy, a potential source of political leadership, made little effort to unify the rival Italian communes. Rather, as temporal governors of the Papal States (the lands located in central Italy), Renaissance popes joined in the game of power politics, often allying with one group of city-states against another.

The Medici

Italian Renaissance cities were ruled either by members of the petty nobility, by mercenary generals, or—as in the case of Florence and Venice—by wealthy middle-class families. In Florence, a city of approximately 50,000, some one hundred families dominated political life. The most notable of these was the Medici, a wealthy banking family that rose to power during the fourteenth century and gradually took over the reins of state. Partly because the commercial ingenuity of the Medici enhanced the material status of the Florentine citizens, and partly because strong, uninterrupted leadership guaranteed local economic stability, the Medici ruled Florence for four generations. The Medici merchant-princes, Cosimo (1389–1464),

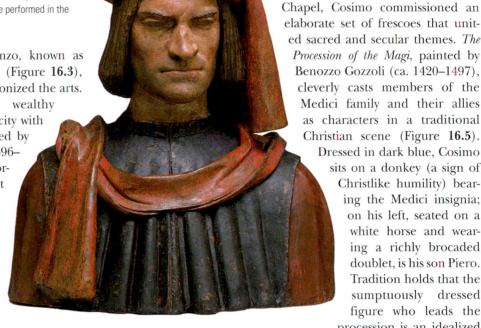

Figure 16.3 ANDREA DEL VERROCCHIO, *Lorenzo de' Medici,* ca. 1478. Terracotta, 25⅞ × 23¼ × 12⅞ in. The patron of Ficino, Botticelli, and Michelangelo, Lorenzo followed in the footsteps of his grandfather Cosimo, the first of the great Medici humanists. Personally engaged in humanist studies, he also wrote vernacular poems and songs that were performed in the popular street pageants of Florence.

Piero (1416–1468), and Lorenzo, known as "the Magnificent" (1449–1492) (Figure **16.3**), supported scholarship and patronized the arts.

The Medici, like many wealthy Florentines, embellished their city with a private stone palace. Designed by Michelozzo di Bartolomeo (1396–1472) to resemble both a fortress and a private home, it attracted foreign ambassadors, artists, and notable humanists. Roughly cut masonry appears on the ground floor, and the windows are located high up for purposes of security. The upper stories, topped by a Classically inspired cornice, are lighter and more elegant, their windows divided by Corinthian colonettes (Figure **16.4**). For the walls of the Medici Chapel, Cosimo commissioned an elaborate set of frescoes that united sacred and secular themes. *The Procession of the Magi,* painted by Benozzo Gozzoli (ca. 1420–1497), cleverly casts members of the Medici family and their allies as characters in a traditional Christian scene (Figure **16.5**). Dressed in dark blue, Cosimo sits on a donkey (a sign of Christlike humility) bearing the Medici insignia; on his left, seated on a white horse and wearing a richly brocaded doublet, is his son Piero. Tradition holds that the sumptuously dressed figure who leads the procession is an idealized portrait of Lorenzo, who would have been only ten years old at the time the fresco was painted.

Affluence coupled with intellectual discernment and refined taste inspired the Medici to commission works from some of the greatest artists of the Renaissance: Brunelleschi, Botticelli, Verrocchio, and Michelangelo. For almost two centuries, scholars, poets, painters, and civic leaders shared common interests, acknowledging one another as leaders of a vigorous cultural revival.

Classical Humanism

Classical culture did not disappear altogether with the fall of Rome in 476 C.E. It was preserved by countless Christian and Muslim scholars, revived by Charlemagne in the Early Middle Ages, and championed by such medieval intellectuals as Aquinas (who took Aristotle as his master) and Dante (who chose Virgil as his guide). But the Classical humanists of the Renaissance generated a deeper and more all-embracing appreciation of Greco-Roman antiquity than any of their predecessors. They advocated the recovery and uncensored study of the entire body of Greek and Latin manuscripts and the self-conscious imitation of Classical art and architecture. They regarded Classical authority not exclusively as a means of clarifying Christian truths, but as the basis for a new appraisal of the role of the individual in the world order. Thus, although Renaissance humanists still prized the Liberal Arts as the basis for intellectual advancement, they approached the Classics in a way that differed from that of their Scholastic predecessors. Whereas the Scholastics had studied the Greco-Roman legacy as the foundation for Christian dogma and faith, Renaissance humanists discovered in the Greek and Latin Classics a rational guide to the fulfillment of the human

Figure 16.4 MICHELOZZO DI BARTOLOMEO, exterior of the Medici Palace, 1444–1460. The Medici coat of arms, consisting of seven balls, is seen at the corner of the second course of the palace. The meaning of the balls is variously interpreted: most likely, they represent the coins signifying the Medici as bankers and pawnbrokers.

Figure 16.5 BENOZZO GOZZOLI, *Procession of the Magi*, 1459. Fresco, 8 × 10 ft. (approx.). East wall of the Medici Chapel, Medici Palace, Florence. In the upper left corner is a self-portrait of the artist, who identifies himself with an inscription on the headband of his red hat. Some scholars see the faces of the six-year-old Giuliano de' Medici and the ten-year-old Lorenzo de' Medici in the figures just below the artist.

potential. Moreover, the Renaissance revival of human-ism differed from earlier revivals because it attracted the interest of a broad base of the population and not a mere handful of theologians, as was the case, for instance, in Carolingian or later medieval times.

Petrarch: "Father of Humanism"

The most famous of the early Florentine humanists was the poet and scholar Francesco Petrarch (1304–1374). Often called the "father of humanism," Petrarch devoted his life to the recovery, copying, and editing of Latin manuscripts. In search of these ancient sources of wisdom, he traveled all over Europe, hand-copying manuscripts he could not beg or buy from monastic libraries, borrowing others from friends, and gradually amassing a private library of more than 200 volumes. Petrarch was a tireless popularizer of Classical studies. Reviving the epistolary (letter-writing) tradition that had practically disappeared after Roman antiquity, he wrote hundreds of letters describing his

admiration for antiquity and his enthusiasm for the Classics, especially the writings of the Roman statesman Cicero (see chapter 6). In his letters, Petrarch eulogized and imitated Cicero's polished prose style, which stood in refined contrast to the corrupt Latin of his own time.

The intensity of Petrarch's passion for antiquity and his eagerness to rescue it from neglect come across powerfully in a letter addressed to his friend Lapo da Castiglionchio. Here, he laments the scarcity and incompetence of copy-ists, bemoans the fact that books that are difficult to understand have "sunk into utter neglect," and defends his ambition to preserve them, despite the inordinate amount of time it takes to copy them. (Such fervor, shared by his successors, surely motivated the invention of printing technology within a hundred years of his death.) In the letter to Lapo, part of which is reproduced below, Petrarch vows to sacrifice the precious hours of his old age to the pleasures of copying Cicero (whom he calls fondly by his middle name, Tullius).

READING 16.1 From Petrarch's *Letter to Lapo da Castiglionchio* (ca. 1351)

Your Cicero has been in my possession four years and
more. There is a good reason, though, for so long a delay;
namely, the great scarcity of copyists who understand
such work. It is a state of affairs that has resulted in an
incredible loss to scholarship. Books that by their nature
are a little hard to understand are no longer multiplied,
and have ceased to be generally intelligible, and so have
sunk into utter neglect, and in the end have perished.
This age of ours consequently has let fall, bit by bit,
some of the richest and sweetest fruits that the tree of
knowledge has yielded; has thrown away the results of
the vigils and labors of the most illustrious men of genius,
things of more value, I am almost tempted to say, than
anything else in the whole world. . . .

But I must return to your Cicero. I could not do without
it, and the incompetence of the copyists would not let me
possess it. What was left for me but to rely upon my own
resources, and press these weary fingers and this worn
and ragged pen into service? The plan that I followed was
this. I want you to know it, in case you should ever have
to grapple with a similar task. Not a single word did I read
except as I wrote. But how is that, I hear someone say;
did you write without knowing what it was that you were
writing? Ah! but from the very first it was enough for me to
know that it was a work of Tullius, and an extremely rare
one too. And then as soon as I was fairly started I found
at every step so much sweetness and charm, and felt so
strong a desire to advance, that the only difficulty which
I experienced in reading and writing at the same time came
from the fact that my pen could not cover the ground so
rapidly as I wanted it to, whereas my expectation had
been rather that it would outstrip my eyes, and that my
ardor for writing would be chilled by the slowness of my
reading. So the pen held back the eye, and the eye drove
on the pen, and I covered page after page, delighting in
my task, and committing many and many a passage to
memory as I wrote. For just in proportion as the writing is
slower than the reading does the passage make a deep
impression and cling to the mind.

And yet I must confess that I did finally reach a point
in my copying where I was overcome by weariness; not
mental, for how unlikely that would be where Cicero was
concerned, but the sort of fatigue that springs from
excessive manual labor. I began to feel doubtful about this
plan that I was following, and to regret having undertaken
a task for which I had not been trained; when suddenly
I came across a place where Cicero tells how he himself
copied the orations of—someone or other; just who it was
I do not know, but certainly no Tullius, for there is but one
such man, one such voice, one such mind. These are his
words: "You say that you have been in the habit of reading
the orations of Cassius[1] in your idle moments. But I," he

1
10
20
30
40
50

jestingly adds, with his customary disregard of his
adversary's feelings, "have made a practice of copying
them, so that I might have no idle moments." As I read this
passage I grew hot with shame, like a modest young soldier
who hears the voice of his beloved leader rebuking him.
I said to myself, "So Cicero copied orations that another
wrote, and you are not ready to copy his? What ardor! What
scholarly devotion! what reverence for a man of godlike
genius!" These thoughts were a spur to me, and I pushed
on, with all my doubts dispelled. If ever from my darkness
there shall come a single ray that can enhance the splendor
of the reputation which his heavenly eloquence has won
for him, it will proceed in no slight measure from the fact
that I was so captivated by his ineffable sweetness that
I did a thing in itself most irksome with such delight and
eagerness that I scarcely knew I was doing it at all.

So then at last your Cicero has the happiness of
returning to you, bearing you my thanks. And yet he also
stays, very willingly, with me; a dear friend, to whom I give
the credit of being almost the only man of letters for whose
sake I would go to the length of spending my time, when
the difficulties of life are pressing on me so sharply and
inexorably and the cares pertaining to my literary labors
make the longest life seem far too short, in transcribing
compositions not my own. I may have done such things in
former days, when I thought myself rich in time, and had
not learned how stealthily it slips away: but I now know
that this is of all our riches the most uncertain and
fleeting; the years are closing in upon me now, and there
is no longer any room for deviation from the beaten path.
I am forced to practice strict economy; I only hope that
I have not begun too late. But Cicero! he assuredly is worthy
of a part of even the little that I have left. Farewell.

60
70
80

Q In what ways does Petrarch's letter exemplify the aims and passions of the Renaissance humanist?

Nothing in the letter to Lapo suggests that Petrarch
was a devout Christian; yet, in fact, Petrarch's affection
for Cicero was matched only by his devotion to Saint
Augustine and his writings. Indeed, in their introspective tone and their expression of intimate feelings and
desires, Petrarch's letters reveal the profound influence
of Augustine's *Confessions*, a work that Petrarch deeply
admired. Torn between Christian piety and his passion for
Classical antiquity, Petrarch experienced recurrent psychic
conflict. In his writings there is a gnawing and unresolved
dissonance between the dual imperatives of his heritage:
the Judeo-Christian will to believe and the Classical will to
reason. Such self-torment—evident in Petrarch's poems,
over 300 examples of which make up the *Canzoniere*
(*Songbook*)—implies that Petrarch remained, in part, a
medieval man. Yet it did not prevent him from pursuing
worldly fame. At Rome in 1341, he proudly received the
laurel crown for outstanding literary achievement. The tradition, which looks back to the ancient Greek practice of
honoring victors in the athletic games with wreaths made
from the foliage of the laurel tree, survives in our modern
honorary title "poet *laureate*."

---

[1] More probably Lucius Licenius Crassus (140–91 B.C.E.), one of
the great Roman orators and a principal figure in Cicero's treatise
On Oratory.

The object of Petrarch's affection and the inspiration for the *Canzoniere* was a married Florentine woman named Laura de Sade. Petrarch dedicated hundreds of love lyrics to Laura, many of which were written after she died of bubonic plague in 1348. While Petrarch used Latin, the language of learning, for his letters and essays, he wrote his poems and songs in vernacular Italian. His favorite poetic form was the **sonnet**, a fourteen-line lyric poem (see LOOKING INTO). Influenced by the "sweet style" of his Italian forebears and, more generally, by *troubadour* songs and Islamic lyric verse, Petrarch's sonnets are a record of his struggle between the flesh and the spirit. In their reflective and even self-indulgent tone, they are strikingly modern, especially where they explore Petrarch's own moods, his love for Laura—and for love itself.

In his own time, Petrarch was acclaimed as the finest practitioner of the sonnet form. His sonnets were translated by Chaucer and set to music by Landini (see chapter 15). During the sixteenth century, Michelangelo Buonarroti in Italy and the English poets Thomas Wyatt, Edmund Spenser, and William Shakespeare (see chapter 19) wrote sonnets modeled on those of Petrarch. Petrarch's influence as a Classical humanist was equally significant: he established the standards for the study of the Latin classics, and, by insisting on the union of ethics and eloquence, he pioneered the modern ideal of the educated individual. Although Petrarch never learned to read Greek, he encouraged his contemporaries and friends (including Boccaccio) to master the language of the first philosophers. Petrarch's passion for Classical learning initiated

LOOKING INTO

Petrarch's Sonnet 134 (ca. 1350)

The fourteen-line lyric poem known as the sonnet originated among the poets of medieval Sicily, but it was Petrarch who brought the form to perfection. As shown in the original Italian version of Sonnet 134 below, Petrarch favored a rhyme scheme of abab/abab for the octave (the first eight lines), and cde/cde for the sestet (last six lines).

In Sonnet 134, Petrarch explores the conflicting emotional states evoked by his unfulfilled desire for Laura, the Florentine woman who served as his spiritual guide and the "laurel" of his poetry,

but also as the object of his physical passion. The poet's anguish is phrased intriguingly in antithetical sets: peace/war, burn/freeze, rise/fall, as well in the use of the **oxymoron**, a figure of speech that juxtaposes apparently contradictory elements, such as the phrase "no eyes yet see." While it is difficult to capture the music of the original Italian and to replicate the rhyme scheme in an English translation, the author (with the assistance of Giuliano Ceseri) has rendered the sonnet in an English version that is faithful to the Petrarchan sonnet form.

(a)	*Pace non trovo, et non ò da far guerra;*
(b)	*e temo, et spero; et ardo, et son un ghiaccio;*
(a)	*et volo sopra 'l cielo, et giaccio in terra;*
(b)	*et nulla stringo, et tutto 'l mondo abbraccio.*
(a)	*Tal m'à in pregion, che non m'apre né serra,*
(b)	*né per suo mi riten né scioglie il laccio;*
(a)	*et non m'ancide Amore, et non mi sferra,*
(b)	*né mi vuol vivo, né mi trae d'impaccio.*
(c)	*Veggio senza occhi, et non ò lingua et grido;*
(d)	*et bramo di perir, et cheggio aita;*
(e)	*et ò in odio me stesso, et amo altrui.*
(c)	*Pascomi di dolor, piangendo rido;*
(d)	*egualmente mi spiace morte et vita:*
(e)	*in questo stato son, donna, per voi.*

(a)	I find no peace, yet I am not at war;
(b)	I fear and hope, I burn and freeze;
(a)	I rise to heaven, and fall to earth's floor
(b)	Grasping at nothing, the world I seize.
(a)	My jailer opens not, nor locks the door,
(b)	Nor binds me to herself, unbinds nor frees;
(a)	Love does not kill, nor bids me to endure,
(b)	Love takes my life, but will not grant me ease.
(c)	I have no eyes yet see, no tongue yet scream;
(d)	I long to perish, and seek release;
(e)	I hate myself, and love another.
(c)	I feed on grief, and in my laughter weep;
(d)	Both death and life displease me;
(e)	Lady, because of you, I suffer.

Q **What are the main features of the Petrarchan sonnet?**

Figures 16.6 and **16.7 PIERO DELLA FRANCESCA**, *Battista Sforza, duchess of Urbino* and *Federico da Montefeltro, duke of Urbino*, after 1475. Oil and tempera on panel, each 18½ × 13 in. The two profile portraits made up a diptych that commemorated the marital union of the two rulers. Federico became wealthy as a *condottiere* and diplomat. Battista, who died at the age of twenty-six, bore eight daughters and one son. The two are shown against an expansive landscape designating the lands they ruled in central Italy.

something of a cult, which at its worst became an infatuation with everything antique, but which at its best called forth a diligent examination of the Classical heritage.

Civic Humanism

The effort to recover, copy, and produce accurate editions of Classical writings dominated the early history of the Renaissance in Italy. By the middle of the fifteenth century, almost all the major Greek and Latin manuscripts of antiquity were available to scholars. Throughout Italy, the small study retreat, or *studiolo*, filled with manuscripts, musical instruments, and the artifacts of scientific inquiry, came to be considered essential to the advancement of intellectual life. Wealthy patrons like Federico da Montefeltro, duke of Urbino, and his wife, Battista Sforza (Figures **16.6** and **16.7**), encouraged humanistic education, commissioning private studies for their villas and for the ducal palace itself (see Figure **16.1**).

Among the humanists of Italy, Classical writings kindled new attitudes concerning the importance of active participation in civic life. Aristotle's view of human beings as "political animals" (see chapter 4) and Cicero's glorification of duty to the state (see chapter 6) encouraged humanists to perceive that the exercise of civic responsibility was the hallmark of the cultivated individual. Such civic humanists as Leonardo Bruni and Coluccio Salutati, who served Florence as chancellors and historians during the Renaissance, defended the precept that one's highest good was activity in the public interest.

Alberti and Renaissance *Virtù*

A formative figure of the Early Renaissance was the Florentine humanist Leon Battista Alberti (1404–1474) (Figure **16.8**), a mathematician, architect, engineer, musician, and playwright. Alberti's most original literary contribution (and that for which he was best known in his own time) was his treatise *On the Family*. Published in 1443, it is the first sociological inquiry into the structure, function, and responsibilities of the family. It is also a moralizing treatise that defends the importance of a Classical education and hard work as prerequisites for worldly success. In Alberti's view, skill, talent, fortitude, ingenuity, and the ability to determine one's destiny—qualities summed up in the single Italian word *virtù*—are essential to human enterprise. *Virtù*, Alberti observes, is not inherited; rather, it must be cultivated. Not to be confused with the English word "virtue," *virtù* describes the self-confident vitality of the self-made individual.

In *On the Family*, Alberti warns that idleness is the enemy of human achievement, while the performance of "manly tasks" and the pursuit of "fine studies" are sure means to worldly fame and material fortune. Pointing to the success of his own family, he defends the acquisition of wealth as the reward of free-spirited *virtù*. The buoyant optimism so characteristic of the age of the Renaissance is epitomized in Alberti's statement that "man can do anything he wants." The multitalented Alberti himself was living proof of that viewpoint.

READING 16.2 From Alberti's *On the Family* (1443)

Let Fathers . . . see to it that their sons pursue the   1
study of letters assiduously and let them teach them to
understand and write correctly. Let them not think they
have taught them if they do not see that their sons have
learned to read and write perfectly, for in this it is almost
the same to know badly as not to know at all. Then let
the children learn arithmetic and gain a sufficient

Figure 16.8 LEON BATTISTA ALBERTI, *Self-Portrait*, ca. 1435. Bronze, 7²⁹⁄₃₂ × 5¹¹⁄₃₂ in. This bronze self-portrait of Alberti revives the tradition of the Roman medals that commemorated the achievements of notable rulers. The artist includes his personal emblem, a winged eye that resembles an Egyptian hieroglyph.

knowledge of geometry, for these are enjoyable sciences suitable to young minds and of great use to all regardless of age or social status. Then let them turn once more to   10 the poets, orators, and philosophers. Above all, one must try to have good teachers from whom the children may learn excellent customs as well as letters. I should want my sons to become accustomed to good authors. I should want them to learn grammar from Priscian and Servius and to become familiar, not with collections of sayings and extracts, but with the works of Cicero, Livy, and Sallust above all, so that they might learn the perfection and splendid eloquence of the elegant Latin tongue from the very beginning. They say that the same   20 thing happens to the mind as to a bottle: if at first one puts bad wine in it, its taste will never disappear. One must, therefore, avoid all crude and inelegant writers and study those who are polished and elegant, keeping their works at hand, reading them continuously, reciting them often, and memorizing them. . . .

Think for a moment: can you find a man—or even imagine one—who fears infamy, though he may have no strong desire for glory, and yet does not hate idleness and sloth? Who can ever think it possible to achieve   30 honors and dignity without the loving study of excellent arts, without assiduous work, without striving in difficult manly tasks? If one wishes to gain praise and fame, he must abhor idleness and laziness and oppose them as deadly foes. There is nothing that gives rise to dishonor and infamy as much as idleness. Idleness has always been the breeding-place of vice. . . .

Therefore, idleness which is the cause of so many evils must be hated by all good men. Even if idleness were not a deadly enemy of good customs and the cause of every   40 vice, as everyone knows it is, what man, though inept, could wish to spend his life without using his mind, his limbs, his every faculty? Does an idle man differ from a tree trunk, a statue, or a putrid corpse? As for me, one who does not care for honor or fear shame and does not act with prudence and intelligence does not live well. But one who lies buried in idleness and sloth and completely neglects good deeds and fine studies is altogether dead. One who does not give himself body and soul to the quest for praise and virtue is to be deemed   50 unworthy of life. . . .

[Man] comes into this world in order to enjoy all things, be virtuous, and make himself happy. For he who may be called happy will be useful to other men, and he who is now useful to others cannot but please God. He who uses things improperly harms other men and incurs God's displeasure, and he who displeases God is a fool if he thinks he is happy. We may, therefore, state that man is created by Nature to use, and reap the benefits of, all things, and that he is born to be happy. . . .   60

I believe it will not be excessively difficult for a man to acquire the highest honors and glory, if he perseveres in his studies as much as is necessary, toiling, sweating, and striving to surpass all others by far. It is said that man can do anything he wants. If you will strive with all your strength and skill, as I have said,

I have no doubt you will reach the highest degree of perfection and fame in any profession. . . .

To those of noble and liberal spirit, no occupations seem less brilliant than those whose purpose is to make money. If you think a moment and try to remember which are the occupations for making money, you will see that they consist of buying and selling, lending and collecting. I believe that these occupations whose purpose is gain may seem vile and worthless to you, for you are of noble and lofty spirit. In fact, selling is a mercenary trade; you serve the buyer's needs, pay yourself for your work, and make a profit by charging others more than you yourself have paid. You are not selling goods, therefore, but your labors; you are reimbursed for the cost of your goods, and for your labor you receive a profit. Lending would be a laudable generosity if you did not seek interest, but then it would not be a profitable business. Some say that these occupations, which we shall call pecuniary, always entail dishonesty and numerous lies and often entail dishonest agreements and fraudulent contracts. They say, therefore, that those of liberal spirit must completely avoid them as dishonest and mercenary. But I believe that those who judge all pecuniary occupations in this manner are wrong. Granted that acquiring wealth is not a glorious enterprise to be likened to the most noble professions. We must not, however, scorn a man who is not naturally endowed for noble deeds if he turns to these other occupations in which he knows he is not inept and which, everyone admits, are of great use to the family and to the state. Riches are useful for gaining friends and praise, for with them we can help those in need. With wealth we can gain fame and prestige if we use it munificently for great and noble projects.

Q **What is Alberti's opinion of the business of money-making? What, according to him, is the value of wealth?**

Ficino: The Platonic Academy

After the fall of Constantinople to the Ottoman Turks in 1453, Greek manuscripts and Byzantine scholars poured into Italy, contributing to the efflorescence of what the humanist philosopher Marsilio Ficino (1433–1499) called "a golden age." Encouraged by the availability of Greek resources and supported by his patron Cosimo de' Medici, Ficino translated the entire corpus of Plato's writings from Greek into Latin, making them available to Western scholars for the first time since antiquity. Ficino's translations and the founding of the Platonic Academy in Florence (financed by Cosimo) launched a reappraisal of Plato and the Neoplatonists that had major consequences in the domains of art and literature. Plato's writings—especially the *Symposium*, in which love is exalted as a divine force—advanced the idea, popularized by Ficino, that "platonic" (or spiritual) love attracted the soul to God. Platonic love became a major theme among Renaissance poets and painters, who held that spiritual love was inspired by physical beauty.

Pico della Mirandola

While Ficino was engaged in popularizing Plato, one of his most learned contemporaries, Giovanni Pico della Mirandola (1463–1494), undertook the translation of various ancient literary works in Hebrew, Arabic, Latin, and Greek. Humanist, poet, and theologian, Pico sought not only to bring to light the entire history of human thought, but also to prove that all intellectual expression shared the same divine purpose and design. This effort to discover a "unity of truth" in all philosophic thought—similar to but more comprehensive than the medieval quest for synthesis and so dramatically different from our own modern pluralistic outlook—came to dominate the arts and ideas of the High Renaissance.

Pico's program to recover the past and his reverence for the power of human knowledge continued a tradition that looked back to Petrarch; at the same time, his monumental efforts typified the activist spirit of Renaissance *individualism*—the affirmation of the unique, self-fashioning potential of the human being. In Rome, at the age of twenty-four, Pico boldly challenged the Church to debate some 900 theological propositions that challenged the institutional Church in a variety of theological and philosophical matters. The young scholar did not get the opportunity to debate his theses; indeed, he was persecuted for heresy and forced to flee Italy. As an introduction to the disputation, Pico had prepared the Latin introduction that has come to be called the *Oration on the Dignity of Man*. In this "manifesto of humanism," Pico drew on a wide range of literary sources to build an argument for free will and the perfectibility of the individual. Describing the individual's position as only "a little lower than the angels," he stressed man's capacity to determine his own destiny on the hierarchical "chain of being" that linked the divine and brute realms. Although Pico's *Oration* was not circulated until after his death, its assertion of free will and its acclamation of the unlimited potential of the individual came to symbolize the collective ideals of the Renaissance humanists. The Renaissance view that the self-made individual occupies the center of a rational universe is nowhere better described than in the following excerpt.

READING 16.3 From Pico's
Oration on the Dignity of Man (1486)

Most esteemed Fathers,[1] I have read in the ancient writings of the Arabians that Abdala the Saracen[2] on being asked what, on this stage, so to say, of the world, seemed to him most evocative of wonder, replied that there was nothing to be seen more marvelous than man. And that celebrated exclamation of Hermes Trismegistus,[3] "What a great miracle

---

[1] The assembly of clergymen to whom the oration was to be addressed.
[2] The Arabic philosopher and translator Abd-Allah Ibn al Muqaffa (718–775).
[3] The Greek name (Hermes Thrice-Great) for the Egyptian god Thoth, the presumed author of a body of occult philosophy that mingled Neoplatonism, alchemy, and mystical interpretations of the Scriptures.

is man, Asclepius,"[4] confirms this opinion.

And still, as I reflected upon the basis assigned for these estimations, I was not fully persuaded by the diverse reasons advanced by a variety of persons for the preeminence of human nature; for example: that man is the intermediary between creatures, that he is the familiar of the gods above him as he is lord of the beings beneath him; that, by the acuteness of his senses, the inquiry of his reason and the light of his intelligence, he is the interpreter of nature, set midway between the timeless unchanging and the flux of time; the living union (as the Persians say), the very marriage hymn of the world, and, by David's testimony,[5] but little lower than the angels. These reasons are all, without question, of great weight; nevertheless, they do not touch the principal reasons, those, that is to say, which justify man's unique right to such unbounded admiration. Why, I asked, should we not admire the angels themselves and the beatific choirs more?

At long last, however, I feel that I have come to some understanding of why man is the most fortunate of living things and, consequently, deserving of all admiration; of what may be the condition in the hierarchy of beings assigned to him, which draws upon him the envy, not of the brutes alone, but of the astral beings and of the very intelligences which dwell beyond the confines of the world. A thing surpassing belief and smiting the soul with wonder. Still, how could it be otherwise? For it is on this ground that man is, with complete justice, considered and called a great mir●cle and a being worthy of all admiration.

Hear then, oh Fathers, precisely what this condition of man is; and in the name of your humanity, grant me your benign audition as I pursue this theme.

God the Father, the Mightiest Architect, had already raised, according to the precepts of His hidden wisdom, this world we see, the cosmic dwelling of divinity, a temple most august. He had already adorned the supercelestial region with Intelligences, infused the heavenly globes with the life of immortal souls and set the fermenting dung-heap of the inferior world teeming with every form of animal life. But when this work was done, the Divine Artificer still longed for some creature which might comprehend the meaning of so vast an achievement, which might be moved with love at its beauty and smitten with awe at its grandeur. When, consequently, all else had been completed, . . . in the very last place, He bethought Himself of bringing forth man. Truth was, however, that there remained no archetype according to which He might fashion a new offspring, nor in His treasure-houses the wherewithal to endow a new son with a fitting inheritance, nor any place, among the seats of the universe, where this new creature might dispose himself to contemplate the world. All space was already filled; all things had been distributed in the highest, the middle and the lowest orders. Still, it was not in the nature of the power of the Father to fail in this last creative élan; nor was it in the nature of that supreme Wisdom to hesitate

through lack of counsel in so crucial a matter; nor, finally, in the nature of His beneficent love to compel the creature destined to praise the divine generosity in all other things to find it wanting in himself.

At last, the Supreme Maker decreed that this creature, to whom He could give nothing wholly his own, should have a share in the particular endowment of every other creature. Taking man, therefore, this creature of indeterminate image, He set him in the middle of the world and thus spoke to him:

"We have given you, Oh Adam, no visage proper to yourself, nor any endowment properly your own, in order that whatever place, whatever form, whatever gifts you may, with premeditation, select, these same you may have and possess through your own judgment and decision. The nature of all other creatures is defined and restricted within laws which We have laid down; you, by contrast, impeded by no such restrictions, may, by your own free will, to whose custody We have assigned you, trace for yourself the lineaments of your own nature. I have placed you at the very center of the world, so that from that vantage point you may with greater ease glance round about you on all that the world contains. We have made you a creature neither of heaven nor of earth, neither mortal nor immortal, in order that you may, as the free and proud shaper of your own being, fashion yourself in the form you may prefer. It will be in your power to descend to the lower, brutish forms of life; [or] you will be able, through your own decision, to rise again to the superior orders whose life is divine."

Oh unsurpassed generosity of God the Father, Oh wondrous and unsurpassable felicity of man, to whom it is granted to have what he chooses, to be what he wills to be! The brutes, from the moment of their birth, bring with them, as Lucilius[6] says, "from their mother's womb" all that they will ever possess. The highest spiritual beings were, from the very moment of creation, or soon thereafter, fixed in the mode of being which would be theirs through measureless eternities. But upon man, at the moment of his creation, God bestowed seeds pregnant with all possibilities, the germs of every form of life. Whichever of these a man shall cultivate, the same will mature and bear fruit in him. If vegetative, he will become a plant; if sensual, he will become brutish; if rational, he will reveal himself a heavenly being; if intellectual, he will be an angel and the son of God. And if, dissatisfied with the lot of all creatures, he should recollect himself into the center of his own unity, he will there become one spirit with God, in the solitary darkness of the Father, Who is set above all things, himself transcend all creatures.

Who then will not look with awe upon this our chameleon, or who, at least, will look with greater admiration on any other being? This creature, man, whom Asclepius the Athenian, by reason of this very mutability, this nature capable of transforming itself, quite rightly said was symbolized in the mysteries by the figure of Proteus. This is the source of those metamorphoses, or transformations, so celebrated among the Hebrews and among the Pythagoreans;[7]

---

[4] The Greek god of healing and medicine.
[5] In Psalms 8.6.

[6] A Roman writer of satires (180–102 B.C.E.).
[7] Followers of the Greek philosopher and mathematician Pythagoras (fl. 530 B.C.E.); see chapter 4.

. . . . while the Pythagoreans transform men guilty of crimes into brutes or even, if we are to believe Empedocles,[8] into plants; and Mohamet,[9] imitating them, was known frequently to say that the man who deserts the divine law becomes a brute. And he was right; for it is not the bark that makes the tree, but its insensitive and unresponsive nature; nor the hide which makes the beast of burden, but its brute and sensual soul; nor the orbicular form which makes the heavens, but their harmonious order. Finally, it is not freedom from a body, but its spiritual intelligence, which makes the angel. If you see a man dedicated to his stomach, crawling on the ground, you see a plant and not a man; or if you see a man bedazzled by the empty forms of the imagination, as by the wiles of Calypso,[10] and through their alluring solicitations made a slave to his own senses, you see a brute and not a man. If, however, you see a philosopher, judging and distinguishing all things according to the rule of reason, him shall you hold in veneration, for he is a creature of heaven and not of earth; if, finally, a pure contemplator, unmindful of the body, wholly withdrawn into the inner chambers of the mind, here indeed is neither a creature of earth nor a heavenly creature, but some higher divinity, clothed with human flesh.

120

130

Q **In what ways, according to Pico, is man "a great miracle" (line 6)?**

Q **Why does he call man "our chameleon" (line 110)?**

Castiglione: The Well-Rounded Person

By far the most provocative analysis of Renaissance individualism is that found in *The Book of the Courtier*, a treatise written between 1513 and 1518 by the Italian diplomat and man of letters Baldassare Castiglione (1478–1529) (Figure **16.9**). Castiglione's *Courtier* was inspired by a series of conversations that had taken place among a group of sixteenth-century aristocrats at the court of Urbino, a mecca for humanist studies located in central Italy. The subject of these conversations, which Castiglione probably recorded from memory, concerns the qualifications of the ideal Renaissance man and woman. Debating this subject at length, the members of the court arrive at a consensus that affords the image of *l'uomo universale*: the well-rounded person. Castiglione reports that the ideal man should master all the skills of the medieval warrior and display the physical proficiency of a champion athlete. But he also must possess the refinements of a humanistic education. He must know Latin and Greek (as well as his own native language), be familiar with the Classics, speak and write well, and be able to compose verse, draw, and play a musical instrument. Moreover, all that the Renaissance gentleman does, he should do with an air of nonchalance and grace, a quality summed up in the Italian

[8] A Greek philosopher and poet (495–435 B.C.E.).
[9] The prophet Muhammad (570–632); see chapter 10.
[10] In Greek mythology, a sea nymph who lured Odysseus to remain with her for seven years.

Figure 16.9 RAPHAEL, *Portrait of Baldassare Castiglione*, ca. 1515. Oil on canvas, 30 × 26 in. (approx.)

word *sprezzatura*. This unique combination of breeding and education would produce a cultured individual to serve a very special end: the perfection of the state. For, as Book Four of the *Courtier* explains, the primary duty of the well-rounded person is to influence the ruler to govern wisely.

Although, according to Castiglione, the goal of the ideal gentleman was to cultivate his full potential as a human being, such was not the case with the Renaissance gentlewoman. The Renaissance woman should have a knowledge of letters, music, and art—that is, like the gentleman, she should be privileged with a humanistic education—but in no way should she violate that "soft and delicate tenderness that is her defining quality." Castiglione's peers agreed that "in her ways, manners, words, gestures, and bearing, a woman ought to be very unlike a man." Just as the success of the courtier depends on his ability to influence those who rule, the success of the lady rests with her skill in entertaining the male members of the court.

Castiglione's handbook of Renaissance etiquette was based on the views of a narrow, aristocratic segment of society. But despite its selective viewpoint, it was immensely popular: in 1527, the Aldine Press in Venice printed it in an edition of more than a thousand copies. It was translated into five languages and went through fifty-seven editions before the year 1600. Historically, *The Book of the Courtier* is an index to cultural changes that were taking place between medieval and early modern times. It departs from exclusively feudal and Christian educational ideals and formulates a program for the cultivation of both mind *and* body that has become fundamental to modern Western education. Representative also of the shift from medieval to modern values is Castiglione's preoccupation with manners rather than morals; that is, with *how* individuals act and how their actions may impress their peers, rather than with the intrinsic moral value of those actions.

READING 16.4 From Castiglione's *The Book of the Courtier* (1518)

[Count Ludovico de Canossa says:] "I am of opinion that the principal and true profession of the Courtier ought to be that of arms; which I would have him follow actively above all else, and be known among others as bold and strong, and loyal to whomsoever he serves. And he will win a reputation for these good qualities by exercising them at all times and in all places, since one may never fail in this without severest censure. And just as among women, their fair fame once sullied never recovers its first lustre, so the reputation of a gentleman who bears arms, if once it be in the least tarnished with cowardice or other disgrace, remains forever infamous before the world and full of ignominy.[1] Therefore the more our Courtier excels in this art, the more he will be worthy of praise. . . . 1

"Then coming to the bodily frame, I say it is enough if this be neither extremely short nor tall, for both of these conditions excite a certain contemptuous surprise, and men of either sort are gazed upon in much the same way that we gaze on monsters. Yet if we must offend in one of the two extremes, it is preferable to fall a little short of the just measure of height than to exceed it, for besides often being dull of intellect, men thus huge of body are also unfit for every exercise of agility, which thing I should much wish in the Courtier. And so I would have him well built and shapely of limb, and would have him show strength and lightness and suppleness, and know all bodily exercises that befit a man of war; whereof I think the first should be to handle every sort of weapon well on foot and on horse, to understand the advantages of each, and especially to be familiar with those weapons that are ordinarily used among gentlemen; for besides the use of them in war, where such subtlety in contrivance is perhaps not needful, there frequently arise differences between one gentleman and another, which afterwards result in duels often fought with such weapons as happen at the moment to be within reach; thus knowledge of this kind is a very safe thing. Nor am I one of those who say that skill is forgotten in the hour of need; for he whose skill forsakes him at such a time, indeed gives token that he has already lost heart and head through fear. 40

"Moreover I deem it very important to know how to wrestle, for it is a great help in the use of all kinds of weapons on foot. Then, both for his own sake and for that of his friends, he must understand the quarrels and 10

20

30

differences that may arise, and must be quick to seize an advantage, always showing courage and prudence in all things. Nor should he be too ready to fight except when honor demands it. . . . 50

"There are also many other exercises, which although not immediately dependent upon arms, yet are closely connected therewith, and greatly foster manly sturdiness; and one of the chief among these seems to me to be the chase [hunting], because it bears a certain likeness to war: and truly it is an amusement for great lords and befitting a man at court, and furthermore it is seen to have been much cultivated among the ancients. It is fitting also to know how to swim, to leap, to run, to throw stones, for besides the use that may be made of this in war, a man often has occasion to show what he can do in such matters; whence good esteem is to be won, especially with the multitude, who must be taken into account withal. Another admirable exercise, and one very befitting a man at court, is the game of tennis, in which are well shown the disposition of the body, the quickness and suppleness of every member, and all those qualities that are seen in nearly every other exercise. Nor less highly do I esteem vaulting on horse, which although it be fatiguing and difficult, makes a man very light and dexterous more than any other thing; and besides its utility, if this lightness is accompanied by grace, it is to my thinking a finer show than any of the others. 60

70

"Our Courtier having once become more than fairly expert in these exercises, I think he should leave the others on one side: such as turning somersaults, rope-walking, and the like, which savor of the mountebank and little befit a gentleman.

"But since one cannot devote himself to such fatiguing exercises continually, and since repetition becomes very tiresome and abates the admiration felt for what is rare, we must always diversify our life with various occupations. For this reason I would have our Courtier sometimes descend to quieter and more tranquil exercises, and in order to escape envy and to entertain himself agreeably with everyone, let him do whatever others do, yet never departing from praiseworthy deeds, and governing himself with that good judgment which will keep him from all folly; but let him laugh, jest, banter, frolic and dance, yet in such fashion that he shall always appear genial and discreet, and that everything he may do or say shall be stamped with grace." 80

90

[Cesare Gonzaga says:] "But having before now often considered whence this grace springs, laying aside those men who have it by nature, I find one universal rule concerning it, which seems to me worth more in this matter than any other in all things human that are done or said: and that is to avoid affectation to the uttermost and as it were a very sharp and dangerous rock; and, to use possibly a new word, to practice in everything a certain nonchalance that shall conceal design and show that what is done and said is done without effort and almost without thought[2]. . . ." 100

---

[1] Shame, dishonor.

[2] That is, with nonchalance (in Italian, *sprezzatura*).

[Count Ludovico says:] "I think that what is chiefly important and necessary for the Courtier, in order to speak and write well, is knowledge; for he who is ignorant and has nothing in his mind that merits being heard, can neither say it nor write it.

"Next he must arrange in good order what he has to say or write; then express it well in words, which (if I do not err) ought to be precise, choice, rich and rightly formed, but above all, in use even among the masses; because such words as these make the grandeur and pomp of speech, if the speaker has good sense and carefulness, and knows how to choose the words most expressive of his meaning, and to exalt them, to mould position and order that they shall at a glance show and make known their dignity and splendor, like pictures placed in good and proper light.

"And this I say as well of writing as of speaking: in which however some things are required that are not needful in writing—such as a good voice, not too thin and soft like a woman's, nor yet so stern and rough as to smack of the rustic's—but sonorous, clear, sweet and well sounding, with distinct enunciation, and with proper bearing and gestures; which I think consist in certain movements of the whole body, not affected or violent, but tempered by a calm face and with a play of the eyes that shall give an effect of grace, accord with the words, and as far as possible express also, together with the gestures, the speaker's intent and feeling.

"But all these things would be vain and of small moment, if the thoughts expressed by the words were not beautiful, ingenious, acute, elegant and grave—according to the need.

"I would have him more than passably accomplished in letters, at least in those studies that are called the humanities, and conversant not only with the Latin language but with the Greek, for the sake of the many different things that have been admirably written therein. Let him be well versed in the poets, and not less in the orators and historians, and also proficient in writing verse and prose, especially in this vulgar[3] tongue of ours; for besides the enjoyment he will find in it, he will by this means never lack agreeable entertainment with ladies, who are usually fond of such things. And if other occupations or want of study prevent his reaching such perfection as to render his writings worthy of great praise, let him be careful to suppress them so that others may not laugh at him. . . .

"My lords, you must know that I am not content with the Courtier unless he be also a musician and unless, besides understanding and being able to read notes, he can play upon divers[4] instruments. For if we consider rightly, there is to be found no rest from toil or medicine for the troubled spirit more becoming and praiseworthy in time of leisure, than this; and especially in courts, where besides the relief from tedium that music affords us all, many things are done to please the ladies, whose

110

120

130

140

150

tender and gentle spirit is easily penetrated by harmony and filled with sweetness. Thus it is no marvel that in both ancient and modern times they have always been inclined to favor musicians, and have found refreshing spiritual food in music. . . .

"I wish to discuss another matter, which I deem of great importance and therefore think our Courtier ought by no means to omit: and this is to know how to draw and to have acquaintance with the very art of painting.

"And do not marvel that I desire this art, which to-day may seem to savor of the artisan and little to befit a gentleman; for I remember having read that the ancients, especially throughout Greece, had their boys of gentle birth study painting in school as an honorable and necessary thing, and it was admitted to the first rank of liberal arts; while by public edict they forbade that it be taught to slaves. Among the Romans too, it was held in highest honor. . . ."

[The discussion turns to defining the court lady. Giuliano de' Medici addresses the company of ladies and gentlemen:] ". . . although my lord Gaspar has said that the same rules which are set the Courtier serve also for the Lady, I am of another mind; for while some qualities are common to both and as necessary to man as to woman, there are nevertheless some others that befit woman more than man, and some are befitting man to which she ought to be wholly a stranger. The same I say of bodily exercises; but above all, methinks that in her ways, manners, words, gestures and bearing a woman ought to be very unlike a man; for just as it befits him to show a certain stout and sturdy manliness, so it is becoming in a woman to have a soft and dainty tenderness with an air of womanly sweetness in her every movement. . . .

"Now, if this precept be added to the rules that these gentlemen have taught the Courtier, I certainly think she ought to be able to profit by many of them, and to adorn herself with admirable accomplishments, as my lord Gaspar says. For I believe that many faculties of the mind are as necessary to woman as to man; likewise gentle birth, to avoid affectation, to be naturally graceful in all her doings, to be mannerly, clever, prudent, not arrogant, not envious, not slanderous, not vain, not quarrelsome, not silly, to know how to win and keep the favor of her mistress and of all others, to practice well and gracefully the exercises that befit women. I am quite of the opinion, too, that beauty is more necessary to her than to the Courtier, for in truth that woman lacks much who lacks beauty. . . .

[The Court Lady] must have not only the good sense to discern the quality of him with whom she is speaking, but knowledge of many things, in order to entertain him graciously; and in her talk she should know how to choose those things that are adapted to the quality of him with whom she is speaking, and should be cautious lest occasionally, without intending it, she utter words that may offend him. Let her guard against wearying him by praising herself indiscreetly or by being too prolix. Let her not go about mingling serious matters with her

160

170

180

190

200

210

---

[3] Common speech; that is, Italian.
[4] Various.

playful or humorous discourse, or jests and jokes with her serious discourse. Let her not stupidly pretend to know that which she does not know, but modestly seek to do herself credit in that which she does know—in all things avoiding affectation, as has been said. In this way she will be adorned with good manners, and will perform with perfect grace the bodily exercises proper to women; her discourse will be rich and full of prudence, virtue and pleasantness; and thus she will be not only loved but revered by everyone, and perhaps worthy to be placed side by side with this great Courtier as well in qualities of the mind as in those of the body. . . . 230

"Since I may fashion this Lady as I wish, not only am I unwilling to have her practice such vigorous and rugged manly exercises, but I would have her practice even those that are becoming to women, circumspectly and with that gentle daintiness which we have said befits her; and thus in dancing I would not see her use too active and violent movements, nor in singing or playing those abrupt and oft-repeated diminutions[5] which show more skill than sweetness; likewise the musical instruments that she uses ought, in my opinion, to be appropriate to this intent. Imagine how unlovely it would 240 be to see a woman play drums, fifes or trumpets, or other like instruments; and this because their harshness hides and destroys that mild gentleness which so much adorns every act a woman does. Therefore when she starts to dance or make music of any kind, she ought to bring herself to it by letting herself be urged a little, and with a touch of shyness which shall show that noble shame which is the opposite of effrontery. . . .

"And to repeat in a few words part of what has been already said, I wish this Lady to have knowledge of 250 letters, music, painting, and to know how to dance and make merry; accompanying the other precepts that have been taught the Courtier with discreet modesty and with the giving of a good impression of herself. And thus, in her talk, her laughter, her play, her jesting, in short, in everything, she will be very graceful, and will entertain appropriately, and with witticisms and pleasantries befitting her, everyone who shall come before her. . . ."

Q **What are the primary characteristics of Castiglione's courtier? What are those of his court lady?**

Q **How do Castiglione's views of the well-rounded individual compare with your own?**

Renaissance Women

As *The Book of the Courtier* suggests, the Renaissance provided greater opportunities for education among upper-class women than were available to their medieval counterparts. The Renaissance woman might have access

---

[5] Rapid ornamentation or variation of a line of music, here implying excessive virtuosity.

to a family library and, if it pleased her parents, to a humanistic education. The Bolognese painter Lavinia Fontana (1552–1614), a product of family tutelage in painting and the arts, continued her career well after her marriage to a fellow artist, who gave up his own career and helped to rear their eleven children. Noted for her skillful portraits, Fontana received numerous commissions for works that commemorated the luxurious weddings of the nobility. Her *Portrait of a Noblewoman* depicts a lavishly dressed young bride (whose identity is unknown) adorned with gold earrings, headdress, belt, and pectoral chains, all of which are encrusted with pearls and rubies (Figure **16.10**). A bodice of shimmering satin ribbons and a red velvet dress enhance the image of wealth, marital fidelity (symbolized by the dog), and gentility—virtues that (along with her dowry) the young woman would likely bring to the marriage. Once married, Renaissance women's roles and rights were carefully limited by men, most of whom considered women their social and intellectual inferiors. Even such enlightened humanists as Alberti perpetuated old prejudices that found women "almost universally timid by nature, soft, and slow." Indeed, according to Alberti, nature had decreed "that men should bring things home and women care for them." Although Renaissance women were held in high esteem as housekeepers and mothers, they were not generally regarded as respectable models for male children, who, Alberti explained, should be "steered away from womanly customs and ways." Married (usually between the ages of thirteen and sixteen) to men considerably older than themselves, women often inherited large fortunes and lucrative businesses; and, as they came into such positions, they enjoyed a new sense of independence that often discouraged them from remarrying.

Renaissance women's occupations remained limited to service tasks, such as midwifery and innkeeping, but there is ample evidence that by the sixteenth century they reaped the advantages of an increasingly commercialized economy in which they might compete successfully with men. If, for centuries, women had dominated the areas of textiles, food preparation, and healthcare, many also rose to prominence in positions of political power. Elizabeth, queen of England, and Caterina Sforza of Milan are but two of the more spectacular examples of women whose strong will and political ingenuity shaped history.

The seeds of feminism planted by Christine de Pisan (see chapter 15) flowered among increasing numbers of women writers and patrons. Battista Sforza, niece of Francesco Sforza, the powerful ruler of Milan, shared the efforts of her husband Duke Federico da Montefeltro in making Urbino a cultural and intellectual center. The duchess of Urbino (see Figure 16.6) was admired for her knowledge of Greek and Latin and for her role as patron of the arts. In nearby Mantua, Isabella d'Este (1474–1539), wife of the ruler Federigo Gonzaga, commissioned and collected sculptures and paintings with Classical themes. Displaying ancient and modern artworks together in her castle at Mantua, this eminent patron of the arts may be said to have anticipated the modern concept of the museum.

Figure 16.10 LAVINIA FONTANA, *Portrait of a Noblewoman*, ca. 1580. Oil on canvas, 3 ft. 9¼ × 2 ft 11¼ in.

Women Humanists

Women humanists, a small but visible group of wealthy aristocrats, often had to choose between marriage, the convent, and the pursuit of a Liberal Arts education. The humanist study of Greek and Latin and (in particular) intellectual inquiry into the moral philosophy of Plato, Aristotle, and Cicero attracted a small group of women, mostly from northern Italy. To her patrons and friends throughout Europe, the Venetian humanist Cassandra Fedele (1465–1558) penned elegant Latin letters in the tradition of Petrarch (see Reading 16.1). The Roman humanist Vittoria Colonna (1490–1547) wrote religious verse and vernacular poems mourning the loss of her husband. Her passionate admirer, Michelangelo, compared her to "a block of marble whose talent was hidden deep within" (Figure **16.11**). Most female humanists, however, had to contend with the criticism of their male peers. In their writings they repeatedly defend their own efforts by citing the achievements of famous women who preceded them—a theme that earlier appeared in the writings of Boccaccio and Christine de Pisan (see Reading 15.3). Such was the case with Laura Cereta (1468–1499), the daughter of a Brescian aristocrat, who married at the age of fifteen and continued her studies even after the death of her husband (some eighteen months later). In her letters, she denounces the frivolous attention to outward forms of luxury among the women of her time. She also describes the difficulties encountered by intelligent women.

The letter known as the *Defense of Liberal Instruction of Women* (1488) is Cereta's bitter counterattack against a critic who had praised her as a prodigy, implicitly condemning her female humanist contemporaries. "With just cause," objects Cereta, "I am moved to demonstrate how great a reputation for learning and virtue women have won by their inborn excellence." To the conventional list of famous women—Babylonian sibyls, biblical heroines, ancient goddesses, and notable Greek and Roman writers and orators—Cereta adds the female humanists of her own time. Finally, she tries to explain why outstanding women are so few in number:

The explanation is clear: women have been able by nature to be exceptional, but have chosen lesser goals. For some women are concerned with parting their hair correctly, adorning themselves with lovely dresses, or decorating their fingers with pearls and other gems. Others delight in mouthing carefully composed phrases, indulging in dancing, or managing spoiled puppies. Still others wish to gaze at lavish banquet tables, to rest in sleep, or, standing at mirrors, to smear their lovely faces. But those in whom a deeper integrity yearns for virtue, restrain from the start their youthful souls, reflect on higher things, harden the body with sobriety and trials, and curb their tongues, open their ears, compose their thoughts in wakeful hours, their minds in contemplation, to letters bonded to righteousness. For knowledge is not given as a gift, but [is gained] with diligence. The free mind, not shirking effort, always soars zealously toward the good, and the desire to know grows ever more wide and deep. It is because of no special holiness, therefore, that we [women] are rewarded by God the Giver with the gift of exceptional talent. Nature has generously lavished its gifts upon all people, opening to all the doors of choice through which reason sends envoys to the will, from which they learn and convey its desires. The will must choose to exercise the gift of reason.

[But] where we [women] should be forceful we are [too often] devious; where we should be confident we are insecure.

Lucretia Marinella

The most extraordinary of sixteenth-century female humanists, the Venetian writer Lucretia Marinella (1571–1653), was neither devious nor insecure. The daughter and the wife of physicians, Marinella published a great many works, including religious verse, madrigals, a pastoral drama, a life of the Virgin, and an epic poem that celebrated the role of Venice in the Fourth Crusade (see chapter 11). However, the work that marks Marinella's dual importance as humanist and feminist is her treatise *The Nobility and Excellence of Women and the Defects and Vices of Men*. This formal polemic (the first of its kind written by a woman)

Figure 16.11 SEBASTIANO DEL PIOMBO, Portrait of Vittoria Colonna, ca. 1520–1525. Oil on wood, 37⅕ × 28½ in. National Art Museum of Catalonia, Barcelona.

was a direct response to a contemporary diatribe on the defects of women—an attack that rehearsed the traditional misogynistic litany that found woman vain, jealous, lustful, fickle, idle, and inherently flawed.

The first part of Marinella's treatise observes the standard model for dispute and debate (employed by Christine de Pisan, Laura Cereta, and others) in which womankind is defended by a series of examples of illustrious women drawn from history. More remarkable—indeed, unique to its time—is Marinella's attack on what she perceived as the defects and vices of men. Using the very techniques that prevailed in humanist polemics, Marinella presents each defect—brutality, obstinacy, ingratitude, discourtesy, inconstancy, vanity—and proceeds to illustrate each by the evidence of illustrious men from Classical and biblical antiquity. Moreover, and in a manner worthy of modern feminists, she attempts to analyze the psychological basis for misogyny, contending that certain flaws—specifically anger, envy, and self-love—drive even the wisest and most learned men to attack women. The following excerpts suggest that while humanism was an enterprise dominated by men, it provided women with the tools by which they might advance their intellectual status and voice their own complaints.

READING 16.5 From Marinella's *The Nobility and Excellence of Women and the Defects and Vices of Men* (1600)

A reply to the flippant and vain reasoning adopted by men in their own favor

It seems to me that I have clearly shown that women are far nobler and more excellent than men. Now it remains for me to reply to the false objections of our slanderers. These are of two sorts, some founded on specious reasonings and others solely on authorities and their opinions. Commencing with the latter, I maintain that I am not obliged to reply to them at all. If I should affirm that the element of air does not exist, I would not be obliged to reply to the authority of Aristotle or of other writers who say that it does. [1]

I do not, however, wish to wrong famous men in denying their conclusions, since certain obstinate people would regard this as being unjust. I say, therefore, that various reasons drove certain wise and learned men to reprove and vituperate women. They included anger, self-love, envy, and insufficient intelligence. It can be stated therefore that when Aristotle or some other man reproved women, the reason for it was either anger, envy, or too much self-love. [10]

It is clear to everyone that anger is the origin of indecent accusations against women. When a man wishes to fulfill his unbridled desires and is unable to because of the temperance and continence of a woman, he immediately becomes angry and disdainful and in his rage says every bad thing he can think of, as if the woman were something evil and hateful. The same can be said of the envious man, who when he sees someone worthy of praise can only look at them with a distorted view. And thus when a man sees that a woman is superior to him, both in virtue and in beauty, and that she is justly honored and loved even by him, he tortures himself and is consumed with envy. Not being able to give vent to his emotions in any other way, he resorts with sharp and biting tongue to false and specious vituperation and reproof. The same occurs as a result of the too great love that men bear for themselves, which causes them to believe that they are more outstanding in wit and intelligence and by nature superior to women—an exaggerated arrogance and over-inflated and haughty pride. But if with a subtle intelligence they should consider their own imperfections, oh how humble and low they would become! Perhaps one day, God willing, they will perceive it. [20][30]

All these reasons therefore induced the good Aristotle to blame women—the principal among them, I believe, being the envy he bore them. For three years, as Diogenes Laertius[1] relates, he had been in love with a lady concubine of Hermias[2] who, knowing of his great and mad love for her, gave her to him as his wife. He, arrogant with joy, made sacrifices in honor of his new lady and goddess— as it was the custom in those times to make to Ceres of [40]

---

[1] The third century C.E. author of *Lives and Opinions of Eminent Philosophers*.
[2] The ruler of Atarneus, whom Aristotle was said to have tutored.

Eleusis[3]—and also to Hermias who had given her to him. Pondering then on all those worthy and memorable matters, he became envious of his wife and jealous of her state, since, not being worshiped like a god by anyone, he could not equal it. Thus he turned to reviling women even though he knew they were worthy of every praise.

It can also be added that, like a man of small intelligence (pardon me you Aristotelians who are reading this . . .) he attributed the reasons for his long error to Hermias's lady, and not to his own unwise intellect, and proceeded to utter shameful and dishonorable words in order to cover up the error he had committed and to lower the female sex, which was an unreasonable thing to do.

To these two motives can also be added self-love, since he judged himself to be a miracle of nature and grew so excessively conceited that he reputed every other person in the world to be unworthy of his love. Therefore, whenever he remembered the time when he had been subservient to women and was secretly ashamed of it, he sought to cover up his failing by speaking badly of them.

The fact that it was disdain against certain women that induced him to injure the female sex is something that must of necessity be believed. He had been a lover, and as I have shown above, an unbridled lover. These were the reasons that induced poor Aristotle to say that women were more dishonest and given to gossiping than men, and more envious and slanderous. He did not see that in calling them slanderous, he too was joining the ranks of the slanderers.

In *History of Animals*, book IX, and in other places, he says that women are composed of matter, imperfect, weak, deficient and poor-spirited—things we have discussed. It could also be thoughtlessness that caused him to deceive himself about the nature and essence of women. Perhaps a mature consideration of their nobility and excellence would have proved too great a burden for his shoulders. As we know, there are many people who believe that the earth moves and the sky remains still,[4] others that there are infinite worlds,[5] still others that there is only one, and some that the fly is nobler than the heavens. Each and every person defends his or her opinion obstinately and with infinite arguments, and these are the replies that we give to those who vituperate the female sex.

There have also been some men who, on discovering a woman who was not very good, have bitingly and slanderously stated that all women are bad and wicked. They have made the grave error of basing a universal criticism on one particular case. It is true, however, that, having realized their error, they have then astutely praised good women. One reply is sufficient for the moral philosophers and poets

who, when they criticize women are merely criticizing the worst ones. . . .

Of men who are ornate, polished, painted, and bleached

For men born to politics and civil life it is becoming, to a certain extent, to be elegant and polished. Everyone knows this, and it has been verified by Della Casa, Guazzo, Sabba, and *The Book of the Courtier*.[6] If, according to these authors' reasoning, this is right for men, we must believe that it is even more right for women, since beauty shines brighter among the rich and elegantly dressed than among the poor and rude. Tasso[7] demonstrates this in *Torrismondo*, by means of the Queen's speech to Rosmonda:

Why do you not adorn your pleasing limbs and with pleasing clothes augment that beauty which heaven has given you courteously and generously? Unadorned beauty in humble guise is like a rough, badly polished gem, which in a humble setting shines dully.

Since beauty is woman's special gift from the Supreme Hand, should she not seek to guard it with all diligence? And when she is endowed with but a small amount of that excellent quality, should she not seek to embellish it by every means possible, provided it is not ignoble? I certainly believe that it is so. When man has some special gift such as physical strength, which enables him to perform as a gladiator or swagger around, as is the common usage, does he not seek to conserve it? If he were born courageous, would he not seek to augment his natural courage with the art of defense? But if he were born with little courage would he not practice the martial arts and cover himself with plate and mail and constantly seek out duels and fights in order to demonstrate his courage rather than reveal his true timidity and cowardice?

I have used this example because of the impossibility of finding a man who does not swagger and play the daredevil. If there is such a one people call him effeminate, which is why we always see men dressed up like soldiers with weapons at their belts, bearded and menacing, and walking in a way that they think will frighten everyone. Often they wear gloves of mail and contrive for their weapons to clink under their clothing so people realize they are armed and ready for combat and feel intimidated by them.

What are all these things but artifice and tinsel? Under these trappings of courage and valor hide the cowardly souls of rabbits or hunted hares, and it is the same with all their other artifices. Since men behave in this way, why should not those women who are born less beautiful than the rest hide their less fortunate attributes and seek to augment the little beauty they possess through artifice, provided it is not offensive?

Why should it be a sin if a woman born with considerable

---

[3] A nature deity whose cult was celebrated annually in Greece.

[4] A reference to the heliocentric theory defended by Copernicus in his treatise *On the Revolution of the Heavenly Spheres*, published in 1543 (see chapter 23).

[5] A reference to the claim made by Giordano Bruno (1548–1600) that the universe was infinite and might contain many solar systems. Bruno was burned at the stake in Rome the year that Marinella's treatise was published.

---

[6] A reference to four famous sixteenth-century handbooks on manners.

[7] The Italian poet Torquato Tasso (1495–1544), whose tragedy *Torrismondo* was published in 1586.

beauty washes her delicate face with lemon juice and the water of beanflowers and privets[8] in order to remove her freckles and keep her skin soft and clean? Or if with columbine, white bread, lemon juice, and pearls she creates 150 some other potion to keep her face clean and soft? I believe it to be merely a small one. If roses do not flame within the lily pallor of her face, could she not, with some art, create a similar effect? Certainly she could, without fear of being reproved, because those who possess beauty must conserve it and those who lack it must make themselves as perfect as possible, removing every obstacle that obscures its splendor and grace. And if writers and poets, both ancient and modern, say that her golden hair enhances her beauty, why should she not color it blonde and make ringlets and curls in it so 160 as to embellish it still further?. . . .

But what should we say of men who are not born beautiful and who yet make great efforts to appear handsome and appealing, not only by putting on clothes made of silk and cloth of gold as many do, spending all their money on an item of clothing, but by wearing intricately worked neckbands? What should we say of the medallions they wear in their caps, the gold buttons, the pearls, the pennants and plumes and the great number of liveries[9] that bring ruin on their houses? They go around with their hair waved, greased, 170 and perfumed so that many of them smell like walking perfumeries. How many are there who go to the barbers every four days in order to appear close-shaven, rosy-cheeked, and like young men even when they are old? How many dye their beards when the dread arrival of old age causes them to turn white? How many use lead combs to tint their white hairs? How many pluck out their white hairs in order to make it appear that they are in the flower of youth? I pass over the earrings that Frenchmen and other foreigners wear and the necklaces, of Gallic invention, 180 which we read of in Livy.

How many spend three or four hours each day combing their hair and washing themselves with those balls of soap sold by mountebanks in the piazza?[10] Let us not even mention the time they spend perfuming themselves and putting on their shoes and blaspheming against the saints because their shoes are small and their feet are big, and they want their big feet to get into their small shoes. How ridiculous!

Q What, according to Marinella, motivates men to slander women?

Q How does Marinella defy traditional male attacks on female vanity?

Machiavelli

The modern notion of progress as an active process of improving the lot of the individual was born during the Renaissance. Repeatedly, Renaissance humanists asserted

---

[8] Flowering shrub.
[9] Servants.
[10] A broad, open public space.

that society's leaders must exercise *virtù* in order to master Fate (often personified in Western art and literature as a female) and fashion their destinies in their own interests. Balanced against the ideals of human perfectibility championed by Castiglione and Pico were the realities of human greed, ignorance, and cruelty. Such technological innovations as gunpowder made warfare increasingly impersonal and devastating, while the rise of strong national rulers occasioned the worst kinds of aggression and brute force. Even the keepers of the spiritual kingdom on earth—the leaders of the Church of Rome—had become notorious for their self-indulgence and greed, as some Renaissance popes actually took mistresses, led armed attacks upon neighboring states, and lived at shocking levels of luxury.

The most acute critic of these conditions was the Florentine diplomat and statesman Niccolò Machiavelli (1469–1527). A keen political observer and a student of Roman history, Machiavelli lamented Italy's disunity in the face of continuous rivalry among the city-states. He anticipated that outside powers might try to take advantage of Italy's internal weaknesses. The threat of foreign invasion became a reality in 1494, when French armies marched into Italy, thus initiating a series of wars that left Italy divided and impoverished. Exiled from Florence upon the collapse of the republican government he had served from 1498 to 1512, and eager to win favor with the Medici now that they had returned to power, Machiavelli wrote *The Prince*, a political treatise that called for the unification of Italy under a powerful and courageous leader. This notorious little book laid out the guidelines for how an aspiring ruler might gain and maintain political power.

In *The Prince*, Machiavelli argued that the need for a strong state justified strong rule. He pictured the secular prince as one who was schooled in war and in the lessons of history. The ruler must trust no one, least of all mercenary soldiers. He must imitate the lion in his fierceness, but he must also act like a fox to outsmart his enemies. Finally, in the interest of the state, he must be ruthless, and, if necessary, he must sacrifice moral virtue. In the final analysis, the end—that is, the preservation of a strong state—will justify the means of maintaining power, however cunning or violent. As indicated in the following excerpts, Machiavelli formulated the idea of the state as an entity that remains exempt from the bonds of conventional morality.

READING 16.6 From Machiavelli's *The Prince* (1513)

XII How Many Different Kinds of Soldiers There Are, and of Mercenaries

. . . a Prince must lay solid foundations since otherwise he will inevitably be destroyed. Now the main foundations of all States, whether new, old, or mixed, are good laws and good arms. But since you cannot have the former without the latter, and where you have the latter, are likely to have the former, I shall here omit all discussion on the subject of laws, and speak only of arms.

I say then that the arms wherewith a Prince defends his State are either his own subjects, or they are mercenaries, or they are auxiliaries, or they are partly one and partly another. Mercenaries and auxiliaries are at once useless and dangerous, and he who holds his State by means of mercenary troops can never be solidly or securely seated. For such troops are disunited, ambitious, insubordinate, treacherous, insolent among friends, cowardly before foes, and without fear of God or faith with man. Whenever they are attacked defeat follows; so that in peace you are plundered by them, in war by your enemies. And this because they have no tie or motive to keep them in the field beyond their paltry pay, in return for which it would be too much to expect them to give their lives. They are ready enough, therefore, to be your soldiers while you are at peace, but when war is declared they make off and disappear. I ought to have little difficulty in getting this believed, for the present ruin of Italy is due to no other cause than her having for many years trusted to mercenaries, who though heretofore they may have helped the fortunes of some one man, and made a show of strength when matched with one another, have always revealed themselves in their true colors as soon as foreign enemies appeared. . . .

XIV Of the Duty of a Prince in Respect of Military Affairs

A Prince, therefore, should have no care or thought but for war, and for the regulations and training it requires, and should apply himself exclusively to this as his peculiar province; for war is the sole art looked for in one who rules and is of such efficacy that it not merely maintains those who are born Princes, but often enables men to rise to that eminence from a private station; while, on other hand, we often see that when Princes devote themselves rather to pleasure than to arms, they lose their dominions. And as neglect of this art is the prime cause of such calamities, so to be proficient in it is the surest way to acquire power. . . .

XV Of the Qualities in Respect of which Princes Are Praised or Blamed

It now remains for us to consider what ought to be the conduct and bearing of a Prince in relation to his subjects and friends. And since I know that many have written on this subject, I fear it may be thought presumptuous in me to write of it also; the more so, because in my treatment of it I depart widely from the views that others have taken.

But since it is my object to write what shall be useful to whosoever understands it, it seems to me better to follow the real truth of things than an imaginary view of them. For many Republics and Princedoms have been imagined that were never seen or known. It is essential, therefore, for a Prince who would maintain his position, to have learned how to be other than good, and to use or not to use his goodness as necessity requires.

Laying aside, therefore, all fanciful notions concerning a Prince, and considering those only that are true, I say that all men when they are spoken of, and Princes more than others from their being set so high, are noted for certain of those qualities which attach either praise or blame. Thus one is accounted liberal, another miserly . . . ; one is generous, another greedy; one cruel, another tender-hearted; one is faithless, another true to his word; one effeminate and cowardly, another high-spirited and courageous; one is courteous, another haughty; one lewd, another chaste; one upright, another crafty; one firm, another facile; one grave, another frivolous; one devout, another unbelieving; and the like. Every one, I know, will admit that it would be most laudable for a Prince to be endowed with all of the above qualities that are reckoned good; but since it is impossible for him to possess or constantly practice them all, the conditions of human nature not allowing it, he must be discreet enough to know how to avoid the reproach of those vices that would deprive him of his government, and, if possible, be on his guard also against those which might not deprive him of it; though if he cannot wholly restrain himself, he may with less scruple indulge in the latter. But he need never hesitate to incur the reproach of those vices without which his authority can hardly be preserved; for if he well consider the whole matter, he will find that there may be a line of conduct having the appearance of virtue, to follow which would be his ruin, and that there may be another course having the appearance of vice, by following which his safety and well-being are secured.

XVII Whether It is Better to Be Loved Than Feared

[We now consider] the question whether it is better to be loved rather than feared, or feared rather than loved. It might perhaps be answered that we should wish to be both; but since love and fear can hardly exist together, if we must choose between them, it is far safer to be feared than loved. For of men it may generally be affirmed that they are thankless, fickle, false, studious to avoid danger, greedy of gain, devoted to you while you are able to confer benefits upon them, and ready, as I said before, while danger is distant, to shed their blood, and sacrifice their property, their lives, and their children for you; but in the hour of need they turn against you. The Prince, therefore, who without otherwise securing himself builds wholly on their professions is undone. For the friendships which we buy with a price, and do not gain by greatness and nobility of character, though they be fairly earned are not made good, but fail us when we have occasion to use them.

Moreover, men are less careful how they offend him who makes himself loved than him who makes himself feared. For love is held by the tie of obligation, which, because men are a sorry breed, is broken on every whisper of private interest; but fear is bound by the apprehension of punishment which never relaxes its grasp.

Nevertheless a Prince should inspire fear in such a fashion that if he do not win love he may escape hate. For a man may very well be feared and yet not hated, and this will be the case so long as he does not meddle with the property or with the women of his citizens and subjects. And if constrained to put any to death, he should do so only when there is manifest cause or reasonable justification. But, above all, he must abstain from the property of others. For men will sooner forget the death of their father than the loss of their property. . . .

XVIII How Princes Should Keep Faith

Every one understands how praiseworthy it is in a Prince to keep faith, and to live uprightly and not craftily. Nevertheless, we see from what has taken place in our own days that Princes who have set little store by their world, but have known how to overreach men by their cunning, have accomplished great things, and in the end got the better of those who trusted to honest dealing.

Be it known, then, that there are two ways of contending, one in accordance with the laws, the other by force; the first of which is proper to men, the second to beasts. But since the first method is often ineffectual, it becomes necessary to resort to the second. A Prince should, therefore, understand how to use well both the man and the beast . . . of beasts [the Prince should choose as his models] both the lion and the fox; for the lion cannot guard himself from traps, nor the fox from wolves. He must therefore be a fox to discern traps, and a lion to drive off wolves.

To rely wholly on the lion is unwise; and for this reason a prudent Prince neither can nor ought to keep his word when to keep it is hurtful to him and the causes which led him to pledge it are removed. If all men were good, this would not be good advice, but since they are dishonest and do not keep faith with you, you, in return, need not keep faith with them; and no Prince was ever at a loss for plausible reasons to cloak a breach of faith. Of this numberless recent instances could be given, and it might be shown how many solemn treaties and engagements have been rendered inoperative and idle through want of faith in Princes, and that he who has best known to play the fox has had the best success.

It is necessary, indeed, to put a good disguise on this nature, and to be skillful in simulating and dissembling. But men are so simple, and governed so absolutely by their present needs, that he who wishes to deceive will never fail in finding willing dupes. . . .

And you are to understand that a Prince, and most of

110

120

130

140

150

160

all a new Prince, cannot observe all those rules of conduct in respect whereof men are accounted good, being often forced, in order to preserve his Princedom, to act in opposition to good faith, charity, humanity, and religion. He must therefore keep his mind to shift as the winds and tides of Fortune turn, and, as I have already said, he ought not to quit good courses if he can help it, but should know how to follow evil courses if he must. . . . Moreover, in the actions of all men, and most of all Princes, where there is no tribunal to which we can appeal, we look to results. Therefore if a Prince succeeds in establishing and maintaining his authority, the means will always be judged honorable and be approved by every one. For the vulgar are always taken by appearances and by results, and the world is made up of the vulgar, the few only finding room when the many have no longer ground to stand on. . . .

170

Q **What are the primary qualities of the Machiavellian ruler?**

Q **Why is Machiavelli often called "the first political realist"?**

The advice Machiavelli gives in his handbook of power politics is based on an essentially negative view of humankind: if, by nature, human beings are "thankless," "fickle," "false," "greedy," "dishonest," and "simple" (as Machiavelli describes them), how better to govern them than by ruthless unlimited power that might keep this "sorry breed" in check? Machiavelli's treatise suggests, furthermore, that personal morality, guided by the principles of justice and benevolence, differs from the morality of the collective entity, the state. It implies, further, that the state, itself an impersonal phenomenon, may be declared amoral, that is, exempt from any moral judgment. In either case, Machiavelli's separation of the value-principles of governance from the principles of Christian morality stunned the European community. The rules of power advertised in *The Prince* appeared to Renaissance thinkers not as idealized notions, but, rather, as expedient solutions based on a realistic analysis of contemporary political conditions. Indeed, Machiavelli's political theories rested on an analysis of human nature not as it should be, but as it was. Throughout *The Prince*, Machiavelli cites examples of power drawn from Roman history and contemporary politics. In defending the successful use of power, for instance, his favorite role model was Cesare Borgia (the illegitimate son of the Renaissance pope Alexander VI), who, along with other thoroughly corrupt and decadent members of his family, exercised a ruthless military campaign to establish a papal empire in central Italy. In such figures, Machiavelli located the heroic aspects of *virtù*: imagination, resilience, ingenuity, and canny intelligence. He provided ample evidence to justify his denunciation of the secular ruler as the divinely appointed model of moral rectitude—a medieval conception staunchly defended by Castiglione.

Machiavelli's profound grasp of past and present history, which he summed up as "knowledge of the actions of man," made him both a critic of human behavior and modern Europe's first political scientist. While his longer and more detailed works—the *History of Florence*, the *Art of War*, and the *Discourses on the First Ten Books of Livy*—summed up his practical experience in government and diplomacy, *The Prince* brought him notoriety. Widely circulated in manuscript form (it was not published until 1532), it was hailed as both a cynical examination of political expediency and as an exposé of real-life politics—so much so that the word "Machiavellian" became synonymous with the evils of political duplicity.

LOOKING BACK

Italy: Birthplace of the Renaissance

- The Renaissance designates that period in European history between roughly 1300 and 1600, during which time the revival of Classical humanism spread from its birthplace in Florence, Italy, throughout Western Europe.
- Florence, a thriving commercial and financial center dominated by a prosperous middle class, found political and cultural leadership in the wealthy and sophisticated Medici family.
- In the climate of intellectual skepticism created by the Great Schism, middle-class men and women challenged canonical sources of authority that frowned upon the accumulation of wealth.
- While Renaissance Italy flourished in the soil of ancient Rome, its political circumstances had much in common with ancient Greece. Independent and disunited, the city-states of Italy, like those of ancient Greece, were fiercely competitive.

Classical Humanism

- Classical humanism, the movement to recover, edit, and study ancient Greek and Latin manuscripts, took shape in fourteenth-century Italy, where it marked the beginnings of the Renaissance.
- Petrarch, the father of humanism, provided the model for Renaissance scholarship and education. He glorified Ciceronian Latin, encouraged the preservation and dissemination of Classical manuscripts, and wrote introspective sonnets that were revered and imitated for centuries afterward.
- Classical humanism helped to cultivate a sense of civic pride, a new respect for oral and written eloquence, and a set of personal values that sustained the ambitions of the rising merchant class. Alberti stressed the importance of Classical education and hard work in the cultivation of *virtù*. Ficino translated the entire body of Plato's writings, while Pico della Mirandola applied his vast study of ancient literature to defend free will and the unlimited potential of the individual.
- Renaissance humanists cultivated the idea of the good life. They applied the moral precepts of the Classical past to diplomacy, politics, and the arts. Castiglione's *Book of the Courtier* established a modern educational ideal in the person of *l'uomo universale*—the well-rounded individual.

Renaissance Women

- The Renaissance provided greater opportunities for education and power among upper-class women than were available to their medieval counterparts. While Renaissance women's roles and rights were carefully limited by men, most of whom considered women their social and intellectual inferiors, many reaped the advantages of an increasingly commercialized economy. Some even rose to fame as political figures, writers, and portraitists.
- Women humanists usually had access to a family library and a private education. The notable northern Italian humanists, Laura Cereta and Lucretia Marinella, defended women in the face of contemporary misogyny. They brought attention to the achievements of educated women and compared the frivolous pursuits of both sexes.

Machiavelli

- The West's first political scientist, Machiavelli lamented Italy's disunity amidst continuous rivalry among the city-states. He anticipated the invasion of foreign powers that might try to take advantage of Italy's internal weaknesses. His canonical text, *The Prince*, argued the need for a strong state ruled by a strong leader.
- Machiavelli envisioned the secular ruler as ruthless. If necessary, he must sacrifice moral virtue for the good of the state. In his view, the state, an impersonal entity, could not be judged by the standards of human morality.
- The views of Machiavelli and other of the Renaissance humanists would come to shape the modern character of the European West.

Glossary

condottiere (plural *condottieri*) a professional soldier; a mercenary who typically served the Renaissance city-state

intarsia the decoration of wood surfaces with inlay

oxymoron a figure of speech juxtaposing two seemingly contradictory terms

sonnet a fourteen-line lyric poem with a fixed scheme of rhyming

Chapter

17

Renaissance Artists: Disciples of Nature, Masters of Invention

ca. 1400–1600

"The eye, which is called the window of the soul, is the chief means whereby the understanding may most fully and abundantly appreciate the infinite works of nature."
Leonardo da Vinci

Figure 17.1 LEON BATTISTA ALBERTI, Santa Maria Novella, Florence, completed 1470. Green and gray marble. In designing this façade, Alberti applied the mathematical ratios of the musical octave established by the ancient Greeks, as well as the basic Vitruvian principles of geometric harmony. He ingeniously added the **volutes** (scrolls) in order to conceal the disjunction between the high nave and the lower side aisles of the Gothic interior.

The Renaissance produced a flowering in the visual arts rarely matched in the annals of world culture. Artists embraced the natural world with an enthusiasm that was equalled only by their ambition to master the lessons of Classical antiquity. The result was a unique and sophisticated body of art that set the standard for most of the painting, sculpture, and architecture produced in the West until the late nineteenth century.

During the Early Renaissance, the period from roughly 1400 to 1490, Florentine artists worked side by side with literary humanists to revive the Classical heritage. These artist–scientists combined their interest in Greco-Roman art with an impassioned desire to understand the natural world and imitate its visual appearance. As disciples of nature, they studied its operations and functions; as masters of invention, they devised new techniques by which to represent the visible world more realistically. In the years of the High Renaissance—approximately 1490 to 1530—the spirit of individualism reached heroic proportions, as artists such as Leonardo da Vinci, Raphael, and Michelangelo integrated the new techniques of naturalistic representation with the much-respected principles of Classical art.

While the subject matter of Renaissance art was still largely religious, the style was more lifelike than ever. Indeed, in contrast with the generally abstract and symbolic art of the Middle Ages, Renaissance art was concrete and realistic. Most medieval art served liturgical or devotional ends; increasingly, however, wealthy patrons commissioned paintings and sculptures to embellish their homes and palaces or to commemorate secular and civic achievements. Portrait painting, a genre that glorified the individual, became popular during the Renaissance, along with other genres that described the physical and social aspects of urban life. These artistic developments reflect the needs of a culture driven by material prosperity, civic pride, and personal pleasure.

Renaissance Art and Patronage

In the commercial cities of Italy and the Netherlands, painting, sculpture, and architecture were the tangible expressions of increased affluence. In addition to the traditional medieval source of patronage—the Catholic Church—merchant princes and petty despots vied with growing numbers of middle-class patrons and urban-centered guilds whose lavish commissions brought prestige to their businesses and families. Those who supported the arts did so at least in part with an eye on leaving their mark upon society or immortalizing themselves for posterity. Thus art became evidence of material well-being as well as a visible extension of the ego in an age of individualism.

Active patronage enhanced the social and financial status of Renaissance artists. Such artists were first and foremost craftspeople, apprenticed to studios in which they might achieve mastery over a wide variety of techniques, including the grinding of paints, the making of brushes, and the skillful copying of images. While trained to observe firmly established artistic convention, the more innovative amongst them moved to create a new visual language. Indeed, for the first time in Western history, artists came to wield influence as humanists, scientists, and poets: a new phenomenon of the artist as hero and genius was born. The image of the artist as hero was promoted by the self-publicizing efforts of these artists, as well as by the adulation of their peers. The Italian painter, architect, and critic Giorgio Vasari (1511–1574) immortalized hundreds of Renaissance artists in his monumental biography *The Lives of the Most Excellent Painters, Architects, and Sculptors*, published in 1550. Vasari drew to legendary proportions the achievements of notable Renaissance figures, many of whom he knew personally. Consider, for instance, this characterization of the most magnetic figure of the Italian Renaissance, Leonardo da Vinci:

> . . . He might have been a scientist if he had not been so versatile. But the instability of his character caused him to take up and abandon many things. In arithmetic, for example, he made such rapid progress during the short time he studied it that he often confounded his teacher by his questions. He also began the study of music and resolved to learn to play the lute, and as he was by nature of exalted imagination, and full of the most graceful vivacity, he sang and accompanied himself most divinely, improvising at once both verses and music. He studied not one branch of art only, but all. Admirably intelligent, and an excellent geometrician besides, Leonardo not only worked in sculpture . . . but, as an architect, designed ground plans and entire buildings; and, as an engineer, was the one who first suggested making a canal from Florence to Pisa by altering the river Arno. Leonardo also designed mills and water-driven machines. But, as he had resolved to make painting his profession, he spent most of his time drawing from life. . . .

The Early Renaissance

The Revival of the Classical Nude

Like the Classical humanists, artists of the Renaissance were the self-conscious beneficiaries of ancient Greek and Roman culture. One of the most creative forces in Florentine sculpture, Donato Bardi, known as Donatello (1386–1466), traveled to Rome to study antique statuary.

The works he observed there inspired his extraordinary likeness of the biblical hero David (Figure **17.2**). Completed in 1432, Donatello's bronze was the first free-standing, life-sized nude sculpture since antiquity. While not an imitation of any single Greek or Roman statue, the piece reveals an indebtedness to Classical models in its correct anatomical proportions and gentle **contrapposto** stance (compare the *Kritios Boy* and *Doryphorus* in chapter 5). However, the sensuousness of the youthful figure—especially apparent in the surface modeling—surpasses that of any antique statue. Indeed, in this tribute to male beauty, Donatello rejected the medieval view of the human body as the wellspring of sin and anticipated the modern Western exaltation of the body as the seat of pleasure.

The Renaissance revival of the Classical nude was accompanied by a quest to understand the mechanics of the human body. Antonio Pollaiuolo (ca. 1431–1498) was among the first artists to dissect human cadavers in order

Figure 17.3 ANTONIO POLLAIUOLO, *Hercules and Antaeus*, ca. 1475. Bronze, height 18 in. with base.

Figure 17.2 DONATELLO, *David*, completed 1432. Bronze, height 5 ft. 2 in.

to study anatomy. The results of his investigations are documented in a bronze sculpture depicting the combat between Hercules and Antaeus, a story drawn from Greco-Roman legend (Figure **17.3**). This small but powerful sculpture in the round is one of many examples of the Renaissance use of Classical mythology to glorify human action, rather than as an exemplum of Christian morality. The wrestling match between the two legendary strongmen of antiquity, Hercules (the most popular of all Greek heroes) and Antaeus (the son of Mother Earth), provided Pollaiuolo with the chance to display his remarkable understanding of the human physique, especially as it responds to stress. Pollaiuolo concentrates on the moment when Hercules lifts Antaeus off the ground, thus divesting him of his maternal source of strength and crushing him in a "body lock." The human capacity for tension and energy is nowhere better captured than in the straining muscles and tendons of the two athletes in combat.

The Classically inspired nude fascinated Renaissance painters as well as sculptors. In the *Birth of Venus* (Figure **17.4**) by Sandro Botticelli (1445–1510), the central image is an idealized portrayal of womankind based on an antique model (Figure **17.5**). Born of sea foam (according to the Greek poet Hesiod), Venus floats on a pearlescent scallop shell to the shore of the island of Cythera. To her right, blowing the shell to shore, are the wind gods Zephyr and Chloris, locked in sensuous embrace; to her left is the welcoming figure of Pomona, the ancient Roman goddess of fruit trees and fecundity. Many elements in

Figure 17.4 SANDRO BOTTICELLI, *Birth of Venus*, after 1482. Tempera on canvas, 5 ft. 9 in. × 9 ft. ½ in.

Florentine artists, humanists, and their patrons collected Classical statuary, examples of which were recovered and revered during the age of the Renaissance. The life-sized Hellenistic marble sculpture known as the *Medici Venus* (Figure **17.5**), depicting Aphrodite, the Greek goddess of love—probably a copy of a bronze original—is said to have been found (in fragments) in Rome during the fifteenth century. (Its exact origin and date of recovery

are disputed by scholars.) The dolphin at the foot of the sculpture is a reference to the legendary origins of the goddess, who, according to Hesiod (see chapter 4), was generated by the sea foam (or semen) of her mythical father, Uranus. Botticelli's goddess of love (Figure 17.4) retains the graceful *contrapposto* stance and the modest gesture of the *Medici Venus*, suggesting that he had probably seen the restored sculpture or a copy.

Figure 17.5 *Medici Venus*, first century C.E. Marble, height 5 ft. ¼ in.

the painting—water, wind, flowers, trees—suggest procreation and fertility, powers associated with Venus as herald of spring and goddess of earthly love. But Botticelli, inspired by a contemporary Neoplatonic poem honoring Aphrodite/Venus as goddess of divine love, renders her also as an object of ethereal beauty and spiritual perfection. He pictorializes ideas set forth at the Platonic Academy of Florence (see chapter 16), particularly the

Neoplatonic notion that objects of physical beauty move the soul to desire union with God, divine fount of goodness and truth. Botticelli's wistful goddess assumes the double role accorded her by the Neoplatonists: goddess of earthly love and goddess of divine (or Platonic) love.

Botticelli executed the *Birth of Venus* in tempera on a large canvas. He rendered the figures with a minimum of shading, so that they seem weightless, suspended in space. An undulating line animates the windblown hair, the embroidered robes, and the delicate flowers that lie on the tapestrylike surface of the canvas. Gold accents and pastel colors (including the delicious lime of the water) further remove this idyllic vision from association with the mundane world.

Early Renaissance Architecture

The art of the Early Renaissance was never a mere imitation of antique models (as was often the case with Roman copies of Greek sculpture), but rather an original effort to reinterpret Greco-Roman themes and principles. The same is true of Renaissance architecture. The revival of Classical architecture was inaugurated by the architect, sculptor, and theorist Filippo Brunelleschi (1377–1446). In 1420, Brunelleschi won a civic competition for the

Figure 17.6 Florence Cathedral. Brunelleschi's dome became a legend in its time. It remains an architectural landmark, the defining feature of the Florentine skyline.

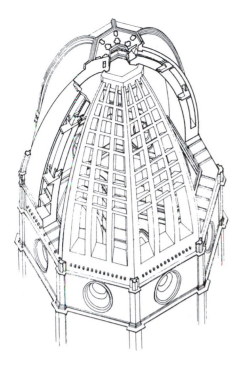

Figure 17.7 Axonometric section of the dome of Florence Cathedral. Cross section at base 11 × 7 ft.

Figure 17.8 FILIPPO BRUNELLESCHI, Pazzi Chapel, cloister of Santa Croce, Florence, ca. 1441–1460.

design of the dome of Florence Cathedral (Figure **17.6**). His ingeniously conceived dome—the largest since that of the Pantheon in Rome—consisted of two octagonal shells. Each incorporated eight curved panels joined by massive ribs that soar upward from the octagonal **drum**—the section immediately beneath the dome—to converge at an elegant **lantern** through which light enters the interior. In the space between the two shells, Brunelleschi designed an interlocking system of ribs that operate like hidden flying buttresses (Figure **17.7**). At the base of the dome, reinforced by stone chains, he constructed a double wall made of sandstone bricks laid in herringbone fashion. To raise the dome, he devised new methods of hoisting stone and new masonry techniques, all of which won him acclaim in Florence. Indeed, Brunelleschi's younger colleague Leon Battista Alberti hailed the completed dome as "a feat of engineering . . . unknown and unimaginable among the ancients."

Brunelleschi was among the first architects of the Renaissance to defend Classical principles of symmetry and proportion in architectural design. In the graceful little chapel he produced for the Pazzi family of Florence (Figure **17.8**), he placed a dome over the central square of the inner hall and buttressed the square with two short barrel vaults. Since the exterior of this self-contained structure was later modified by the addition of a portico, it is in the interior that Brunelleschi's break with the medieval past is fully realized (Figure **17.9**). Here, the repetition of geometric shapes

Figure 17.9 FILIPPO BRUNELLESCHI, Pazzi Chapel, Santa Croce, ca. 1441–1460.

enforces a new kind of visual clarity wherein all parts of the structure are readily accessible to the eye and to the mind. Gray stone moldings and gray Corinthian **pilasters**—shallow, flattened, rectangular columns that adhere to the wall surface—emphasize the "seams" between the individual segments of the stark white interior, producing a sense of order and harmony that is unsurpassed in Early Renaissance architecture. Whereas the medieval cathedral coaxes one's gaze heavenward, the Pazzi Chapel fixes the beholder decisively on earth.

Brunelleschi's enthusiasm for an architecture of harmonious proportions was shared by Alberti, a multitalented Florentine humanist (see chapter 16). Alberti's scientific treatises on painting, sculpture, and architecture reveal his admiration for Roman architecture and his familiarity with the writings of the Roman engineer Vitruvius (see Reading 5.1). In his *Ten Books on Architecture* (modeled after Vitruvius' *De architectura*), Alberti argued that architectural design should proceed from the square and the circle, the two most perfect geometric shapes. This proposition was the guiding precept for all Alberti's buildings (a total of only six); it would become the definitive principle of High Renaissance composition (see Figures 17.23, 17.29, and 17.30).

In the townhouse Alberti designed for the wealthy Rucellai family of Florence (Figure **17.10**), all the details of the building conform to an elegant uniformity of style that stands in contrast with Michelozzo's more rugged

Figure 17.10 LEON BATTISTA ALBERTI (designer) and **BERNARDO ROSSELLINO** (architect), Palazzo Rucellai, Florence, 1446–1451.

Medici Palace (see Figure 16.4). Lacking direct antique precedents for palace architecture, Alberti reconceived the Classical principles of regularity, symmetry, and proportion. Each story of the palace is identical in height, and each is ornamented with a different Classical order (see chapter 5). Rows of crisply defined arcaded windows appear on the upper stories, while square windows placed well above the street (for safety and privacy) accent the lowest level. From the Roman Colosseum (see chapter 6), Alberti borrowed the device of alternating arches and engaged columns, flattening the latter into pilasters. Here the principles of clarity and proportion prevail. Alberti's building quickly became the model for Renaissance palace architecture.

For the west front of Santa Maria Novella, his second major architectural project in Florence (see Figure 17.1), Alberti produced a striking pattern of geometric shapes ordered by a perfect square: the height of the green and white marble façade (from the ground to the tip of the pediment) exactly equals its width. All parts are related by harmonic proportions based on numerical ratios; for instance, the upper portion of the façade is one-fourth the size of the square into which the entire face of the church would fit. Huge volutes—imitated by generations of Western architects to come—unite the upper and lower divisions of the façade, while the motif of a triumphal arch dominates the central entrance. At Santa Maria Novella, as in the churches he designed at Rimini and Mantua, Alberti imposed the motifs and principles of Classical architecture upon the brick Latin cross basilica, thus uniting Greco-Roman and Christian traditions.

Both Alberti and Brunelleschi espoused the Hellenic theory that the human form mirrored the order inherent in the universe. Indeed, a central tenet of Renaissance thought was the belief that the human microcosm (or "lesser world") was the natural expression of the divine macrocosm (or "greater world"). Accordingly, the study of nature and the understanding and exercise of its underlying harmonies put one in touch with the macrocosm. Rational architecture, reflecting natural laws, would help to cultivate rational individuals. Just as the gentler modes in music elicited refined behavior (the Doctrine of Ethos; see chapter 5), so harmoniously proportioned buildings might produce ideal citizens.

The Renaissance Portrait

The revival of portraiture during the Renaissance was an expression of two impulses: the desire to immortalize oneself by way of one's physical appearance and the wish to publicize one's greatness in the traditional manner of Greek and Roman antiquity. Like biography and autobiography—two literary genres that were revived during the Renaissance—portraiture and self-portraiture were hallmarks of a new self-consciousness. The bronze self-portrait of Alberti, a medal bearing the artist's personal emblem of a winged eye (see Figure 16.8), looks back to the small fourteenth-century portrait profile of King John of France (see Figure 15.15). But the former is more deliberate in its effort to recreate an accurate likeness and, at the same time, more clearly imitative of Roman coins and medals.

While the profile view tended to draft a distinctive likeness (see Figures 16.6 and 16.7), the three-quarter and full-face views gave artists the opportunity to capture the physical presence of the sitter (see Figures 16.9 and 16.10). One of the earliest efforts at realistic representation along these lines came from the Netherlandish artist Jan van Eyck (ca. 1380–1441), discussed more fully in chapter 19. Jan's pioneering use of the technique of thin, transparent glazes of pigments bound with linseed oil recreated the naturalistic effects of light, and consequently achieved a high degree of realism. In his penetrating self-portrait (Figure **17.11**), whose level gaze and compressed lips suggest the

Figure 17.11 JAN VAN EYCK, *Man in a Turban (Self-Portrait?)*, 1433. Tempera and oil on panel, 13⅛ × 10⅛ in. The three-quarter view gives the figure an aggressive spatial presence that is enhanced by the complex folds of crimson fabric in the turban.

personality of a shrewd realist, facial features are finely, almost photographically, detailed. To the Renaissance passion for realistic representation, van Eyck introduced the phenomenon of the psychological portrait—the portrait that probed the temperament, character, or unique personality of the subject.

While Early Renaissance artists usually represented their sitters in domestic interiors, High Renaissance masters preferred to situate them in *plein-air* (outdoor) settings, as if to suggest human consonance with nature. Leonardo da Vinci's *Mona Lisa* (Figure **17.12**), the world's best-known portrait, brings figure and landscape into exquisite harmony: the pyramidal shape of the sitter (possibly the wife of the Florentine banker Francesco del Giocondo) is echoed in the rugged mountains; the folds of her tunic are repeated in the curves of distant roads and rivers. Soft

Figure 17.12 LEONARDO DA VINCI, *Mona Lisa*, ca. 1503–1505. Oil on panel, 30¼ × 21 in. Scientific analysis of the painting in 2004 revealed that the figure originally wore a large transparent robe favored by expecting or nursing mothers in Renaissance Italy, a detail that some scholars take to support the thesis that the painting commemorated the birth of the third child of Lisa Gherandini, wife of a Florentine silk merchant.

Figure 17.13 ANDREA DEL VERROCCHIO
(completed by Alessandro Leopardi), equestrian
statue of Bartolommeo Colleoni, ca. 1481–1496.
Bronze, height 13 ft. (approx.).

golden tones, achieved by the application of thin layers of transparent oil paint, bathe the figure, which, like the landscape, is realized in soft, smoky (in Italian, *sfumato*) gradations of light and shade. The setting, a rocky and ethereal wilderness, is as elusive as the sitter, whose eyes and mouth are delicately blurred to produce a facial expression that is almost impossible to decipher—a smile both melancholic and mocking. While the shaved eyebrows and plucked hairline are hallmarks of fifteenth-century female fashion, the figure resists classification by age and (in the opinion of some) by gender. Praised by Renaissance copyists for its "lifelikeness," the *Mona Lisa* has remained an object of fascination and mystery for generations of beholders.

Renaissance portraits often took the form of life-sized sculptures in the round, some of which were brightly painted to achieve naturalistic effects. Such is also the case with the polychrome terracotta likeness of Lorenzo de' Medici (see Figure 16.3), executed by the Florentine sculptor

Andrea del Verrocchio (1435–1488), which reveals a spirited naturalism reminiscent of Roman portraiture (see chapter 6). Verrocchio (a nickname meaning "true eye") was the Medici court sculptor and the close companion of Lorenzo, whose luxurious lifestyle and opulent tastes won him the title "Il Magnifico" ("the Magnificent"). Verrocchio immortalized the physical appearance of the Florentine ruler, who was also a humanist, poet, and musician. At the same time, he captured the willful vitality of the man whose *virtù* made him a legend in his time.

Renaissance sculptors revived still another antique genre: the equestrian statue. Verrocchio's monumental bronze statue of the *condottiere* Bartolommeo Colleoni (Figure **17.13**), commissioned to commemorate the mercenary soldier's military victories on behalf of the city of Venice, recalls the Roman statue of Marcus Aurelius on horseback (see Figure 6.23) as well as the considerably smaller equestrian statue of Charlemagne (see Figure 11.8).

However, compared with these works, Verrocchio's masterpiece displays an unprecedented degree of scientific naturalism and a close attention to anatomical detail—note the bulging muscles of Colleoni's mount. Verrocchio moreover makes his towering mercenary twist dramatically in his saddle and scowl fiercely. Such expressions of *terribilità*, or awe-inspiring power, typify the aggressive spirit that fueled the Renaissance.

Early Renaissance Artist–Scientists

If Renaissance artists took formal and literary inspiration from Classical antiquity, they were equally motivated by a desire to recreate the appearance of the natural world. The empirical study of the physical world—the reliance on direct observation—was the first step in their effort to capture in art the "look" of nature. Medieval artists had little motivation to simulate the world of the senses, a world they

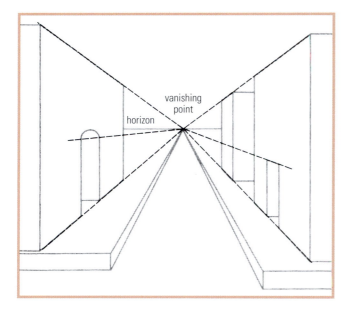

Figure 17.14 One-point perspective.

regarded as the imperfect reflection of the divine order. For Renaissance artist–scientists, however, the visible, physical world could be mastered only if it were understood. To this end, they engaged in a program of examination, analysis, and record keeping. They drew from live studio models, studied human and animal anatomy, and analyzed the effects of natural light on objects in space. Art became a form of rational inquiry or, as in the case of Leonardo, of scientific analysis.

For Renaissance artists, the painting constituted a window on nature: the **picture plane**, that is, the two-dimensional surface of the panel or canvas, was conceived as a transparent glass: a window through which one might perceive the three-dimensional world. Various techniques aided artists in the task of recreating the illusion of reality. The technique of oil painting, refined by Jan van Eyck, was among the first of these. The application of thin oil glazes, which also became popular in Italy, produced a sense of atmospheric space rarely achieved in fresco (see Figure 15.9) or tempera (see Figure 17.4). But the more revolutionary "breakthrough" in Renaissance painting was the invention of **linear perspective**, an ingenious tool for the translation of three-dimensional space onto a two-dimensional surface. Around 1420, inspired, in all likelihood, by Latin translations of Arab-Muslim treatises on optics and optical devices, Brunelleschi formulated the first laws of linear perspective. These laws describe the manner by which all parallel lines in a given visual field appear to converge at a single vanishing point on the horizon (an illusion familiar to anyone who, from the rear of a train, has watched railroad tracks "merge" in the distance). Brunelleschi projected the picture plane as a cross section through which diagonal lines (orthogonals) connected the eye of the beholder with objects along those lines and hence with the vanishing point (Figure **17.14**; see also Figure 17.16). The new perspective system, stated mathematically and geometrically by Alberti in 1435 and advanced thereafter by Leonardo and by Albrecht Dürer

Renaissance Art and Optics

One of the most intriguing debates of the early twenty-first century concerns the question of whether Renaissance artists made use of optical devices in the preparation of their paintings. The artist David Hockney, the physicist Charles M. Falco, and the architect Philip Steadman (among others) have argued that, as early as the 1430s, artists were able to achieve astounding accuracy of visual representation by using either concave mirrors or refractive lenses to project images onto paper, wooden panels, or canvas. Such optical devices, they argue, enabled artists to trace these projected images before painting them. An early version of the *camera lucida*,

a portable lens and prism device (traditionally associated with later centuries; see chapter 23), would have allowed them to transcribe with ease the contours and details of their models onto a two-dimensional surface. The opponents of this thesis contend that there is no corroboratory evidence in literature or legend for such devices during the Renaissance. They maintain that numerous nonoptical factors, such as the new science of geometric perspective, experimentation with the medium of oils, and a growing passion for the realistic representation of the physical world, are more likely explanations for the heightened accuracy of Renaissance painting.

(see chapter 19), enabled artists to represent objects "in depth" at various distances from the viewer and in correct proportion to one another. Linear perspective satisfied the Renaissance craving for an exact and accurate description of the physical world. It also imposed a fixed relationship—in both time and space—between the image and the eye of the beholder, making the latter the exclusive point of reference within the spatial field, and thus, metaphorically, placing the individual at the center of the world.

Masaccio

The first artist to master Brunelleschi's new spatial device was the Florentine painter Tommaso Guidi, called Masaccio, or "Slovenly Tom" (1401– 1428). Before his untimely death (possibly by poison) at age twenty-seven, Masaccio demonstrated his remarkable artistic talent in frescoes he painted for the churches of Florence. His *Trinity with the Virgin, Saint John the Evangelist, and Donors* (Figure **17.15**), in Santa Maria Novella, reflects the artist's mastery of the new perspective system: the lines of the painted barrel vault above the *Trinity* recede and converge at a vanishing point located at the foot of the Cross, thus corresponding precisely with the eye-level of viewers standing below the scene in the church itself (Figure **17.16**). Masaccio further enhanced the illusion of real space by placing the figures of the kneeling patrons "outside" the Classical architectural forms that frame the sacred space.

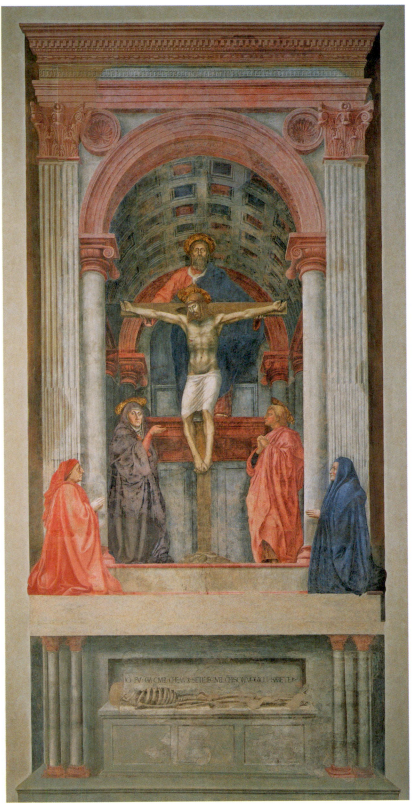

Figure 17.15 MASACCIO, *Trinity with the Virgin, Saint John the Evangelist, and Donors*, ca. 1426–1427. Fresco (now detached from wall), 21 ft. 10⅝ in. × 10 ft. 4¾ in.

Figure 17.16 MASACCIO, *Trinity with the Virgin, Saint John the Evangelist, and Donors*, showing perspective lines.

Figure 17.17 MASACCIO, *The Tribute Money*, ca. 1425. Fresco (after restoration), 8 ft. 4 in. × 19 ft. 8 in. Seeking to entrap Jesus, a group of Pharisees asked him whether taxes should be paid to Rome. To avoid offending the divergent authorities, Jewish and Roman, Jesus replied, "Render unto Caesar the things that are Caesar's, and unto God the things that are God's" (Matthew 22:21).

The cycle of frescoes Masaccio executed for the Brancacci Chapel in Santa Maria del Carmine in Florence represents an even more elaborate synthesis of illusionistic techniques. In *The Tribute Money*, a scene based on the Gospel story in which Jesus honors the demands of the Roman state by paying a tax or "tribute," the artist combined three related scenes: on the left, the apostle Peter gathers money from the mouth of a fish, as instructed by Jesus, who stands in the center; on the right, Peter is shown delivering the coins to the Roman tax collector (Figure 17.17). Masaccio's application of linear perspective—the orthogonals of the building on the right meet at a vanishing point just behind the head of Jesus—provides spatial unity to the three separate episodes. Tonal unity is provided by means of **aerial perspective**—the subtle blurring of details and diminution of color intensity in objects perceived at a distance. Refining the innovative spatial techniques explored by Giotto at the Arena Chapel in Padua (see Figures 15.9 and 15.10), Masaccio also made use of light and shade (*chiaroscuro*) to model his figures as though they actually stood in the light of the chapel window located to the right of the fresco (Figure 17.18).

Eager to represent nature as precisely as possible, Masaccio worked from live models as well as from the available antique sources. From Classical statuary he borrowed the graceful stance of the Roman tax collector, who is shown twice in the fresco—viewed from front and back. Antique sculpture also probably inspired the Roman togas and the head of John the Evangelist (on Jesus' right). In the Brancacci Chapel frescoes, Masaccio anticipated the three principal features of Early Renaissance painting: the adaptation of Classical prototypes, the empirical study of nature, and the application of the new techniques of spatial illusionism.

Figure 17.18 Brancacci Chapel (after restoration). Masaccio was in his early twenties when he began work in the chapel. *The Tribute Money*, a subject that may have been chosen as a reference to the recent establishment of income tax in Florence, is pictured on the upper left wall.

Figure 17.19 LORENZO GHIBERTI, "Gates of Paradise," 1425–1442. The east portal of the Florentine Baptistry contains Lorenzo Ghiberti's immense (18 ft. 6 in. tall) gilt-bronze doors, brilliantly depicting in low relief ten episodes from the Old Testament. Ghiberti pictured himself in the roundel at the middle of the left door. Other figures represent his son Vittorio, biblical prophets, and heroines. In 1990, the doors were removed for restoration. They now reside in the Museo del Duomo in Florence; copies have replaced the originals on the baptistry.

Ghiberti

Masaccio was not alone in the rush to explore the new illusionism. Artists throughout Italy found numerous opportunities to devise *trompe l'oeil* ("fool-the-eye") illusions such as those that delighted visitors to the *studiolo* of Federico da Montefeltro (see Figure 16.1). In the domain of sculpture, the Early Renaissance master of pictorial illusionism was the Florentine goldsmith Lorenzo Ghiberti (1378–1455). After winning the civic competition (his competitor was the eminent Brunelleschi) for a set of bronze relief panels to adorn the north door of the Florentine baptistry of San Giovanni, Ghiberti was commissioned to prepare a second set for the east doorway of the building, which faced the Duomo.

He spent twenty-seven years creating the ten panels for the monumental 3-ton, 20-foot-tall door (Figure **17.19**).

The panels were executed by means of the lost-wax process (see Figure 0.19): each detailed beeswax model was embedded in a clay mold; when the mold was fired and the wax melted away, liquid bronze was poured into the mold. The panels bring to life ten milestones of the Hebrew Bible, from the creation of Adam and Eve to the reign of Solomon. They make brilliant use of linear perspective to stage dramatic narratives filled with graceful figures and fine atmospheric details. The bottom panel on the right, which depicts the meeting of Solomon and Sheba (Figure **17.20**), engages one-point perspective to give dramatic focus

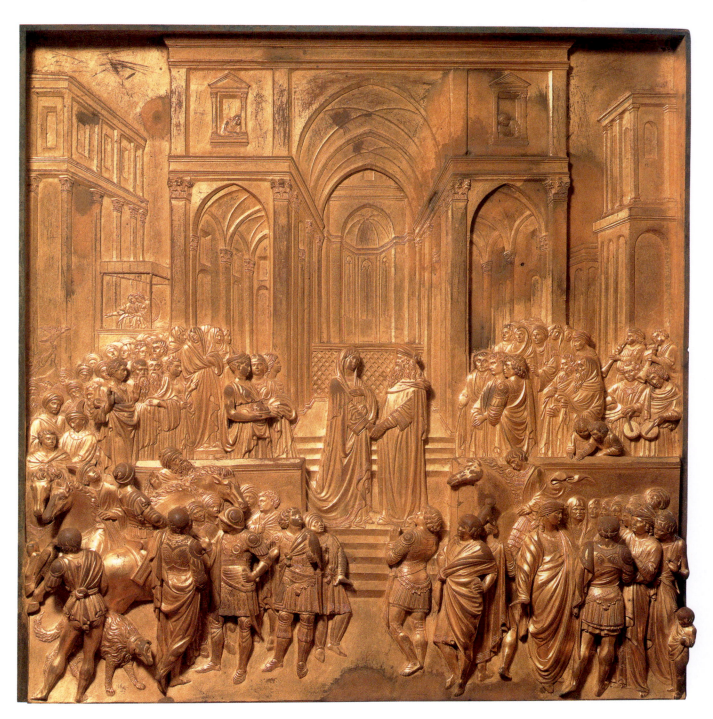

Figure 17.20 LORENZO GHIBERTI, *Meeting of Solomon and Sheba* (single panel of the "Gates of Paradise," Figure 17.19). Gilt-bronze relief, 31¼ × 31¼ in.

to the event. Overwhelmed by the majesty of these doors, the great sculptor of the next generation, Michelangelo, pronounced them worthy of being the Gates of Paradise. In their splendid union of naturalism and idealization, and in their masterful casting, Ghiberti's doors established a benchmark in the art of Renaissance sculpture.

Leonardo da Vinci as Artist–Scientist

Among the artist–scientists of the Renaissance, Leonardo da Vinci (1452–1519) best deserves that title. A diligent investigator of natural phenomena, Leonardo examined the anatomical and organic functions of plants, animals, and human beings. He also studied the properties of wind and water and invented several hundred ingenious mechanical devices, including an armored tank, a diving bell, and a flying machine, most of which never left the notebook stage. Between 1489 and 1518, Leonardo produced thousands of drawings accompanied by notes (Figure 17.21) written in mirror-image script (devised perhaps to discourage imitators and plagiarists). This annotated record of the artist–scientist's passion to master nature includes anatomical drawings whose accuracy remained unsurpassed until 1543, when the Flemish physician Andreas Vesalius published the first medical illustrations of the human anatomy. Some of Leonardo's studies explore ideas—for example, the mechanics of flight (Figure 17.22)—and the standardization of machine parts that were far in advance of their time. Although Leonardo's notebooks (unpublished until 1898) had little influence on European science, they remain a symbol of the Renaissance imagination and a timeless source of inspiration.

Following Alberti, Leonardo maintained that a universal system of proportion governed both nature and art. Indeed, Leonardo's quest for a governing order led him to examine the correspondence between human proportions and ideal geometric shapes, as Vitruvius and his followers had advised. Leonardo's so-called Vitruvian Man (Figure 17.23), whose strict geometry haunts the compositions of High Renaissance painters and architects, is the metaphor for the Renaissance view of the microcosm as a mirror of the macrocosm. Yet, more than any other artist of his time, Leonardo exalted the importance of dependence on the senses for discovering the general rules of nature. Critical of abstract speculation bereft of sensory confirmation, he held that the human eye was the most dependable instrument for obtaining true knowledge of nature. When Leonardo wrote, "That painting is the most to be praised which agrees most exactly with the thing imitated," he was articulating the Renaissance view of art as the imitation of nature. Although Leonardo never established a strict methodology for the formulation of scientific laws, his insistence on direct experience and experimentation made him the harbinger of the Scientific Revolution that would sweep through Western Europe during the next two centuries. In the following excerpts from his notebooks, Leonardo defends the superiority of sensory experience over "book-learning," and argues that painting surpasses poetry as a form of human expression.

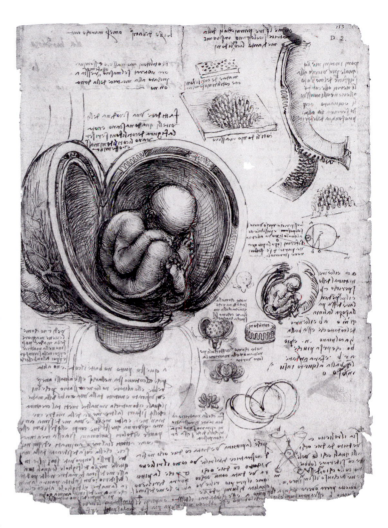

Figure 17.21 LEONARDO DA VINCI, *Embryo in the Womb*, ca. 1510. Pen and brown ink, 11¾ × 8½ in. Some 40,000 of Leonardo's drawings survive in notebooks and in loose sheets; this is probably a fraction of the total number he produced during his lifetime.

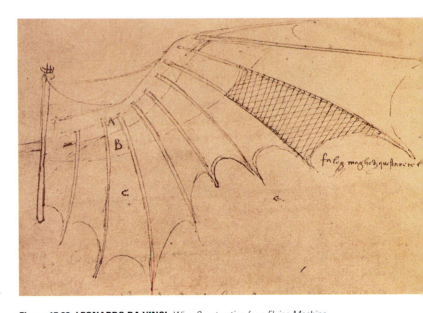

Figure 17.22 LEONARDO DA VINCI, *Wing Construction for a Flying Machine*, ca. 1500. Pen and brown ink. The comic-book hero Batman, according to his twentieth-century creator, Bob Kane, was born when Kane first viewed Leonardo's notebook drawings describing the mechanics of flight.

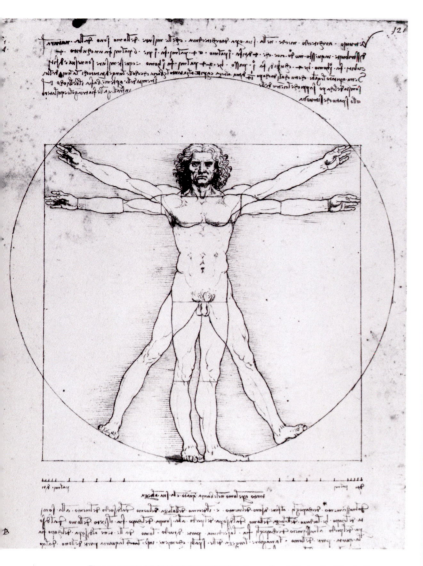

Figure 17.23 LEONARDO DA VINCI, *Proportional Study of a Man in the Manner of Vitruvius*, ca. 1487. Pen and ink, 13½ × 9⅝ in. Leonardo's famous figure indicates that man's proportions are regular, reflecting Vitruvian "divine" geometry: the outstretched arms make the figure a square; at a diagonal they center a circle.

READING 17.1 From Leonardo da Vinci's *Notes* (ca. 1510)

I am fully aware that the fact of my not being a man of letters may cause certain arrogant persons to think that they may with reason censure me, alleging that I am a man ignorant of book-learning. Foolish folk! Do they not know that I might retort by saying, as did Marius to the Roman Patricians, "They who themselves go about adorned in the labor of others will not permit me my own." They will say that because of my lack of book-learning, I cannot properly express what I desire to treat of. Do they not know that my subjects require for their exposition experience rather than the words of others? And since experience has been the mistress of whoever has written well, I take her as my mistress, and to her in all points make my appeal.

I wish to work miracles. . . . And you who say that it is better to look at an anatomical demonstration than to see

these drawings, you would be right, if it were possible to observe all the details shown in these drawings in a single figure, in which, with all your ability, you will not see nor acquire a knowledge of more than some few veins, while, in order to obtain an exact and complete knowledge of these, I have dissected more than ten human bodies, destroying all the various members, and removing even the very smallest particles of the flesh which surrounded these veins without causing any effusion of blood other than the imperceptible bleeding of the capillary veins. And, as one single body did not suffice for so long a time, it was necessary to proceed by stages with so many bodies as would render my knowledge complete; and this I repeated twice over in order to discover the differences. . . .

The eye, which is called the window of the soul, is the chief means whereby the understanding may most fully and abundantly appreciate the infinite works of nature; and the ear is the second inasmuch as it acquires its importance from the fact that it hears the things which the eye has seen. If you historians, or poets, or mathematicians had never seen things with your eyes you would be ill able to describe them in your writings. And if you, O poet, represent a story by depicting it with your pen, the painter with his brush will so render it as to be more easily satisfying and less tedious to understand. If you call painting "dumb poetry," then the painter may say of the poet that his art is "blind painting." Consider then which is the more grievous affliction, to be blind or be dumb! Although the poet has as wide a choice of subjects as the painter, his creations fail to afford as much satisfaction to mankind as do paintings, for while poetry attempts with words to represent forms, actions, and scenes, the painter employs the exact images of the forms in order to reproduce these forms. Consider, then, which is more fundamental to man, the name of man or his image? The name changes with change of country; the form is unchanged except by death.

And if the poet serves the understanding by way of the ear, the painter does so by the eye which is the nobler sense. I will only cite as an instance of this how if a good painter represents the fury of a battle and a poet also describes one, and the two descriptions are shown together to the public, you will soon see which will draw most of the spectators, and where there will be most discussion, to which most praise will be given and which will satisfy the more. There is no doubt that the painting which is by far the more useful and beautiful will give the greater pleasure. Inscribe in any place the name of God and set opposite to it his image, you will see which will be held in greater reverence!. . .

If you despise painting, which is the sole imitator of all the visible works of nature, it is certain that you will be despising a subtle invention which with philosophical and ingenious speculation takes as its theme all the various kinds of forms, airs, and scenes, plants, animals, grasses and flowers, which are surrounded by light and shade. And this truly is a science and the true-born daughter of nature, since painting is the offspring of nature. But in order to speak more correctly we may call it the grandchild of nature; for all visible things derive their existence from nature, and from these same things is born painting. So therefore we may justly speak of it as the grandchild of nature and as related to God himself.

Q How does this reading illustrate Leonardo's role as an artist–scientist?

Q In what ways is painting, according to Leonardo, superior to poetry?

The High Renaissance

Leonardo

By the end of the fifteenth century, Renaissance artists had mastered all the fundamental techniques of visual illusionism, including linear and aerial perspective and the use of light and shade. They now began to employ these techniques in ever more heroic and monumental ways. To the techniques of scientific illusionism they wedded the Classical principles of clarity, symmetry, and order, arriving at a unity of design that would typify High Renaissance art. The two artists whose paintings best represent the achievements of the High Renaissance are Leonardo da Vinci and Raphael.

In his few (and largely unfinished) religious narratives, Leonardo da Vinci fused narrative and symbolic content to achieve an ordered, grand design. The classic example is his *Last Supper*, executed in the late 1490s to adorn the wall of the refectory (the monastery dining room) of Santa Maria delle Grazie in Milan (Figures **17.24** and **17.25**). The *Last Supper* is one of the great religious paintings of all time. Leonardo intended that the sacred event (appropriate for meditation by the monks at table) *appear* to take place within the monastic dining room. The receding lines of the ceiling beams and side-wall tapestries create a sense of spatial depth and link the scene illusionistically with the interior walls of the refectory. Leonardo fixed the vanishing point at the center of the composition directly behind the head of Jesus (see Figure 17.14). Topped by a pediment, the open doorway (one of three, symbolic of the Trinity) acts as a halo, reinforcing the centrality of Christ and his mission as "light of the world." The formal elements of the composition thereby underscore the symbolic aspects of the religious narrative. To this masterful rationalization of space, Leonardo

Science and Technology

1494	Leonardo devises plans to harness the waters of the Arno River
1508	Leonardo records the results of cadaver dissections and analyzes the movements of birds in flight, in unpublished manuscripts
1513	Leonardo undertakes scientific studies of botany, geology, and hydraulic power

added high drama: he divided the apostles into four groups of three who interact in response to the Master's declaration that one of his followers would betray him (Matthew 26:21). The somber mood, enhanced by Christ's meditative look and submissive gesture indicating the bread and wine as symbols of the Eucharist, is heightened by the reactions of the apostles—astonishment, anger, disbelief—appropriate to their biblical personalities. (The quick-tempered Peter, for instance—fifth from the left—wields the knife he later uses to cut off the ear of Christ's assailant, Malchus.)

Leonardo seems to have completed the figures of all the apostles before portraying Jesus and Judas. A chronic procrastinator, he often came into the refectory and gazed thoughtfully at the work for hours, sometimes without picking up a brush, a habit that infuriated the monastery's prior. Vasari, the enthusiastic admirer of Leonardo's fresco, recounts the details.

READING 17.2 From Vasari's *Lives of the Most Excellent Painters, Architects, and Sculptors* (1550)

Biography of Leonardo da Vinci

Having depicted the heads of the Apostles full of splendor [1] and majesty, he deliberately left the head of Christ unfinished, convinced he would fail to give it the divine spirituality it demands. This all-but-finished work has ever since been held in the greatest veneration by the Milanese and others. In it Leonardo brilliantly succeeded in envisaging and reproducing the tormented anxiety of the Apostles to know who had betrayed their master; so in their faces one can read the emotions of love, dismay, and anger, or rather sorrow, at their failure to grasp the meaning of Christ. And this excites [10] no less admiration than the contrasted spectacle of obstinacy, hatred, and treachery in the face of Judas [fourth figure from the left] or, indeed, than the incredible diligence with which every detail of the work was executed. The texture of the very cloth on the table is counterfeited so cunningly that the linen itself could look no more realistic.

It is said that the prior used to keep pressing Leonardo in the most importunate [annoying] way, to hurry up and finish the work, because he was puzzled by Leonardo's habit of sometimes spending half a day at a time contemplating [20] what he had done so far; if the prior had had his way, Leonardo would have toiled like one of the laborers hoeing in the garden and never put his brush down for a moment. Not satisfied with this, the prior then complained to the duke, making such a fuss that the duke was constrained to send for Leonardo and, very tactfully, question him about the painting, although he showed perfectly well that he was only doing so because of the prior's insistence. Leonardo, knowing he was dealing with a prince of acute and discerning intelligence, was willing (as he never had been with the prior) to explain his mind at length; and so he talked to the duke for a long time about the art of painting. He explained that men of genius sometimes [30] accomplish most when they work the least; for, he added, they

The *Last Supper*: Restoration or Ruin?

Slow in his working methods, Leonardo rejected the traditional (fast-drying) *buon fresco* technique of applying paint to a wet-plastered wall. Instead, he experimented with a mixture of oil, tempera, and varnish that proved not to be durable. The use and abuse of the Santa Maria delle Grazie refectory over the centuries—especially after it was hit by an Allied bomb in 1943—further precipitated the deterioration of the *Last Supper*. Between the eighteenth and twentieth centuries, the fresco underwent much retouching, repainting, and cleaning, the most recent of which was a twenty-two-year Italian-led rehabilitation enterprise (completed in 1999) that made use of various technologies,

Figure 17.24 LEONARDO DA VINCI, *Last Supper*, ca. 1485–1498. Fresco: oil, tempera, and varnish on plaster, 15 ft. 1⅛ in × 28 ft. 10½ in. This photograph shows the fresco before restoration.

are thinking out inventions and forming in their minds the perfect ideas which they subsequently express and reproduce with their hands. Leonardo then said that he still had two heads to paint: the head of Christ was one, and for this he was unwilling to look for any human model, nor did he dare suppose that his imagination could conceive the beauty and divine grace that properly belonged to the incarnate Deity. Then, he said, he had yet to do the head of Judas, and this troubled him since he did not think he could imagine the features that would form the countenance of a man who, despite all the blessings he had been given, could so cruelly steel his will to betray his own

master and the creator of the world. However, added Leonardo, he would try to find a model for Judas, and if he did not succeed in doing so, why then there was the head of the tactless and importunate prior. The duke roared with laughter at this and said that Leonardo had every reason in the world for saying so. The unfortunate prior retired in confusion to worry the laborers in his garden, and he left off worrying Leonardo.

40

Q **What aspects of Leonardo's *Last Supper* does Vasari admire? What does this suggest about Renaissance standards in the visual arts?**

but left many of the figures with almost no facial features (Figure 17.25). Bitter controversy surrounded the issue of restoring this and other landmark works, such as the Sistine Chapel ceiling (see Figure 17.33). While some scholars praise the restoration of the *Last Supper*, others claim that the cleaning has done additional damage and has distorted Leonardo's colors beyond repair. Some art historians vehemently refuse to show the restored version in their books and classrooms, claiming that the precleaned fresco (see Figure 17.24) is closer to Leonardo's original intentions. Most agree, however, that what is left of the masterpiece is not much more than a ghost of the original.

Figure 17.25 LEONARDO DA VINCI, *Last Supper*, ca. 1485–1498. This photograph shows the fresco in Figure 17.24 after the restoration was completed in 1999.

Raphael

The second of the great High Renaissance artists was Urbino-born Raphael (Raffaello Sanzio; 1483–1520). Less devoted to scientific speculation than Leonardo, Raphael was first and foremost a master painter. His fashionable portraits were famous for their verisimilitude and incisiveness. A case in point is the portrait of Raphael's lifelong friend Baldassare Castiglione (see Figure 16.9), which captures both the self-confidence and thoughtful intelligence of this celebrated personality of the Italian Renaissance.

Raphael's compositions are notable for their clarity, harmony, and unity of design. In *The Alba Madonna* (Figure **17.26**), one of Raphael's popular renderings of the Madonna and Child, the artist sets the figures in a landscape framed by the picturesque hills of central Italy. Using clear, bright colors and precise draftsmanship, he organized the **tondo** (round picture) by way of simple geometric shapes: the triangle (formed by the Virgin, the Christ Child, and the infant John the Baptist), the circle (the head of the Virgin), and the trapezoid (one length of which is formed by the Virgin's outstretched leg).

Figure 17.26 RAPHAEL, *The Alba Madonna*, ca. 1510. Oil on wood transferred to canvas, diameter 37¼ in.

Despite the formality of the composition and the nobility of the figures, the scene might be construed as a record of an ordinary woman with two children in a landscape, for Raphael has avoided obvious religious symbolism, such as the traditional halo. Raphael's religious figures, notable for their serenity and grace, occupy a world of sweetness and light. His female saints, often posed theatrically, are idealized creatures with gentle expressions. Such features were often taken to sentimental extremes by the artist's many imitators.

In 1510 Pope Julius II, the greatest of Renaissance church patrons, commissioned Raphael to execute a series of frescoes for the Vatican Stanza della Segnatura—the pope's personal library and the room in which official church papers were signed. The paintings were to represent the four domains of human learning: theology, philosophy, law, and the arts. To illustrate philosophy, Raphael painted *The School of Athens* (see LOOKING INTO, Figure **17.27**). In this landmark fresco, the artist immortalized the company of the great philosophers and scientists of ancient history.

In the restrained nobility of the near life-sized figures and the measured symmetry of the composition, the work marked the culmination of a style that had begun with Giotto and Masaccio; here, Raphael gave concrete vision to a world purged of accident and emotion. Monumental in conception and size and flawless in execution, *The School of Athens* advanced a set of formal principles that came to epitomize the *Grand Manner*: spatial clarity, decorum (that is, propriety and good taste), balance, unity of design, and grace (the last especially evident in the subtle symmetries of line and color). These principles remained touchstones for Western academic art until the late nineteenth century.

Raphael's *School of Athens*

At the center of *The School of Athens* appear, as if in scholarly debate, the two giants of Classical philosophy: Plato, who points heavenward to indicate his view of reality as fixed in universal Forms, and Aristotle, who points to the earth to indicate that universal truth depends on the study of nature. Framed by a series of receding arches, the two philosophers stand against the bright sky, beneath the lofty vaults of a Roman basilica that resembles the newly remodeled Saint Peter's Cathedral. Between their heads lies the invisible vanishing point at which all the principal lines of sight converge. On either side of the great hall appear historical figures belonging to each of the two philosophic "camps": the Platonists (left) and the Aristotelians (right).

The School of Athens constitutes a portrait gallery of Renaissance artists whose likenesses Raphael borrowed to depict his Classical heroes. The stately, bearded Plato is an idealized portrait of Leonardo, who was visiting Rome while Raphael was at work in the Vatican. The balding Euclid, seen bending over his slate in the lower right corner of the composition, resembles Raphael's good friend, the architect Bramante. In the far right corner, Raphael himself (wearing a dark hat) appears discreetly among the Aristotelians. And in final revisions of the fresco, Raphael added to the left foreground the likeness of Michelangelo in the guise of the brooding and solitary Greek philosopher Heraclitus. *The School of Athens* is the ultimate tribute to the rebirth of Classical humanism in the age of the Renaissance, for here, in a unified, imaginary space, the artists of Raphael's day are presented as the incarnations of the intellectual titans of antiquity.

Figure 17.27 RAPHAEL, *The School of Athens*, 1509–1511. Fresco, 18 × 26 ft.

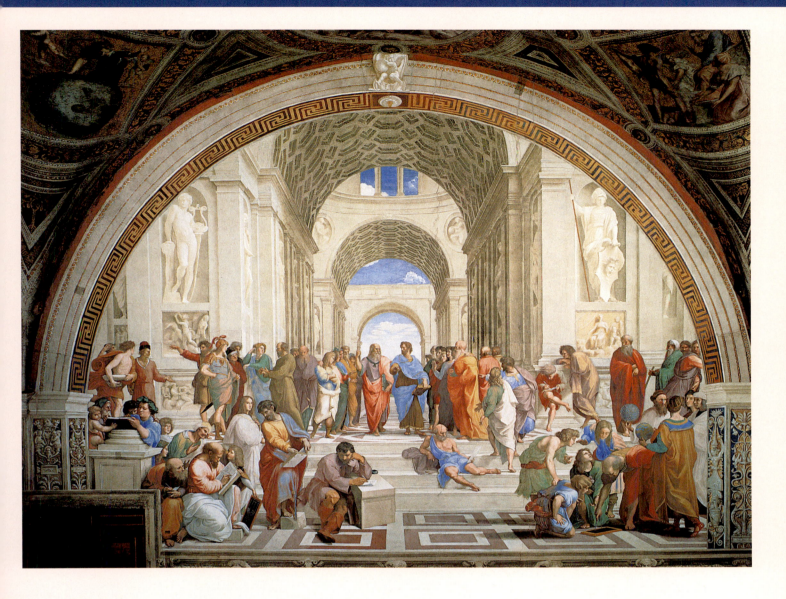

1 Apollo
2 Alcibiades or Alexander
3 Socrates
4 Plato (Leonardo)
5 Aristotle
6 Minerva
7 Sodoma
8 Raphael
9 Ptolemy
10 Zoroaster (Pietro Bembo?)
11 Euclid (Bramante)
12 Diogenes
13 Heraclitus (Michelangelo)
14 Parmenides, Xenocrates, or Aristossenus
15 Francesco Maria della Rovere
16 Telauges
17 Pythagoras
18 Averhöes
19 Epicurus
20 Federigo Gonzaga
21 Zeno

Architecture of the High Renaissance: Bramante and Palladio

During the High Renaissance, the center of artistic activity shifted from Florence to Rome as the popes undertook a campaign to restore the ancient city of Rome to its original grandeur as the capital of Christendom. When Pope Julius II commissioned Donato Bramante (1444–1514) to rebuild Saint Peter's Cathedral, the architect designed a monumentally proportioned, centrally planned church to be capped by an immense dome. Bramante's plan was much modified in the 120 years it took to complete the new Saint Peter's. But his ideal building—organized so that all structural elements were evenly disposed around a central point—took shape on a smaller scale in his Tempietto, the "little temple" that marked the site of Saint Peter's martyrdom in Rome (Figure **17.28**). Modeled on the Classical tholos (see chapter 5), Bramante's free-standing circular stone chapel is ringed by a simple Doric colonnade and topped by a dome elevated upon a niched drum. Although the interior affords little light and space, the exterior gives the appearance of an elegant marble reliquary. It embodies the High Renaissance ideals of clarity, mathematical order, and unity of design.

The Renaissance passion for harmonious design had an equally powerful influence on the history of domestic architecture, a circumstance for which the Italian architect Andrea Palladio (Andrea di Pietro della Gondola; 1518–1580) was especially responsible. In his *Four Books on Architecture*, published in Venice in 1570, Palladio defended symmetry and centrality as the controlling elements of architectural design. He put his ideals into practice in a number of magnificent country houses he built for patrons in northern Italy. The Villa Rotonda near Vicenza—a centrally planned, thirty-two-room country house—is a perfectly symmetrical structure featuring a central room (or rotunda) covered by a dome (Figure **17.29**). All four façades of the villa are identical, featuring a projecting Ionic portico approached by a flight of steps (Figure **17.30**). In its geometric clarity, its cool elegance, and its dominance over its landscape setting, the Villa Rotonda represents the Renaissance distillation of Classical principles as applied to secular architecture. With this building, Palladio established the definitive ideal in domestic housing for the wealthy, and provided a model of solemn dignity that would inspire generations of Neoclassical architects in England and America (see chapter 26).

Figure 17.28 DONATO BRAMANTE, Tempietto, San Pietro in Montorio, Rome, 1502. Height 46 ft., external diameter 29 ft.

Figure 17.29 ANDREA PALLADIO, Villa Rotonda, Vicenza, Italy, completed 1569.

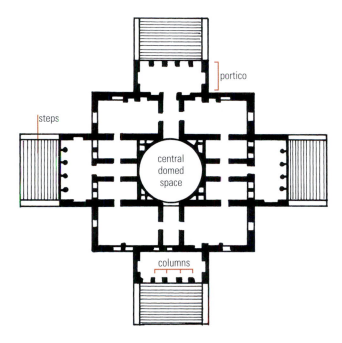

Figure 17.30 Plan of the Villa Rotonda. Palladio's illustrations for an Italian translation of Vitruvius in 1556 provided the historical model of the illustrated architectural book.

Michelangelo and Heroic Idealism

The works of the High Renaissance master Michelangelo Buonarroti (1475–1564) are some of the most heroic in Renaissance art. An architect, poet, painter, and engineer, Michelangelo regarded himself first and foremost as a sculptor. At the age of twenty-one, he launched his career with a commission for a marble *Pietà* that would serve as a tomb monument in Old Saint Peter's Cathedral in Rome (Figure **17.31**). Boasting that he would produce the most beautiful marble sculpture in Rome, Michelangelo carved the image of the young Virgin holding the lifeless body of Jesus (as was traditional to this subject), but, at the same time, caught in a moment of sorrowful meditation. The figure of Mary, disproportionately large in comparison with that of Jesus, creates a protective pyramidal shape that not only supports, but also enfolds the Son. All elements of the composition—the position of the left arm of Jesus, the angles formed by his knees, and the folds of Mary's drapery—work toward a gentle unity of design that contrasts sharply with earlier versions of the subject (see Figure 15.11). Indeed, Michelangelo's *Pietà* transformed the late medieval devotional image into a monumental statement on the meaning of Christian sacrifice.

Michelangelo went on to establish his reputation in Florence at the age of twenty-seven, when he undertook to carve a free-standing larger-than-life statue of the biblical David from a gigantic block of Carrara marble that no other sculptor had dared to tackle (Figure **17.32**). When Michelangelo completed the statue in 1504, the rulers of Florence placed it at the entrance to the city hall as a symbol of Florentine vigilance. Compared to Donatello's lean and introspective youth (see Figure 17.2), Michelangelo's *David* is a defiant presence—the offspring of a race of giants. While indebted to Classical tradition, Michelangelo deliberately violated Classical proportions by making the head and hands of his figure too large for the trunk. The body of the fearless adolescent, with its swelling veins

and taut muscles, is tense and brooding, powerful rather than graceful. Indeed, in this image, Michelangelo drew to heroic proportions the Renaissance ideals of *terribilità* and *virtù*.

Although Michelangelo considered himself primarily a sculptor, he spent four years fulfilling a papal commission to paint the 5760-square-foot ceiling of the Vatican's Sistine Chapel (Figure **17.33**). The scope and monumentality of this enterprise reflect both the ambitions of Pope Julius II and the heroic aspirations of Michelangelo himself. Working from scaffolds poised some 70 feet above the floor, Michelangelo painted a vast scenario illustrating the Creation and Fall of Humankind as recorded in Genesis (1:1 through 9:27). In the nine principal scenes, as well as

Figure 17.31 MICHELANGELO, *Pietà*, 1497–1500. Marble, 15 ft 8½ in.

in the hundreds of accompanying prophets and sibyls, he used high-keyed, clear, bright colors (restored by recent cleaning). He overthrew many traditional constraints, minimizing setting and symbolic details and maximizing the grandeur of figures that—like those he carved in stone—seem superhuman in size and spirit.

A significant archeological event influenced Michelangelo's treatment of the figure after 1506: in that year, diggers working in Rome uncovered the *Laocoön* (see Figure 5.34), the celebrated Hellenistic sculpture that had been known to Western scholars only by way of the Roman writer Pliny. The sculpture—with its bold contortions and its powerfully rendered anatomy—had as great an impact on Michelangelo and the course of High Renaissance art as Cicero's prose had exercised on Petrarch and Early Renaissance literature. Indeed, the twisted torsos, taut muscles, and stretched physiques of the Sistine Chapel figures reflect the influence of the *Laocoön* and other recovered Classical antiquities. In the *Creation of Adam* (Figure **17.34**), God and Man—equal in size and muscular grace—confront each other like partners in the divine plan. Adam reaches longingly toward God, seeking the moment of fulfillment, when God will charge his languid body with celestial energy. If the image depicts Creation, it is also a metaphor for the Renaissance belief in the potential divinity of humankind—the visual analogue of Pico's *Oration on the Dignity of Man* (see chapter 16).

Creation and creativity are themes that dominate Michelangelo's sonnets. In some of the sonnets, he likens the creative act to the workings of Neoplatonic love, which move to purge the base (or lower) elements of the human being. In others, he suggests that the task of the sculptor is to "liberate" the "idea" that is embedded within the marble block. Hailed as a major poet even in his own time,

Figure 17.32 MICHELANGELO,
David, 1501–1504. Marble, height 13 ft. 5 in.

Figure 17.33 MICHELANGELO, Sistine Chapel ceiling (after cleaning), Vatican, Rome, 1508–1512. Fresco, 45 × 128 ft.

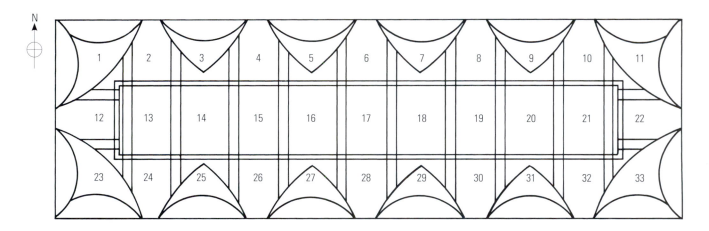

Sistine Chapel ceiling, plan of scenes (after Hibbard).

1	death of Haman	**14**	creation of Sun, Moon, planets	**27**	Asa
2	Jeremiah	**15**	separation of land from water	**28**	Cumaean Sibyl
3	Salmon	**16**	creation of Adam	**29**	Ezekias
4	Persian Sibyl	**17**	creation of Eve	**30**	Isaiah
5	Roboam	**18**	temptation and expulsion	**31**	Josiah
6	Ezekiel	**19**	sacrifice of Noah	**32**	Delphic Sibyl
7	Ozias	**20**	the Flood	**33**	Judith and Holofernes
8	Eritrean Sibyl	**21**	drunkenness of Noah		
9	Zorobabel	**22**	Zacharias		
10	Joel	**23**	Moses and the serpent of brass		
11	David and Goliath	**24**	Libyan Sibyl		
12	Jonah	**25**	Jesse		
13	separation of light from darkness	**26**	Daniel		

Figure 17.34 MICHELANGELO, *Creation of Adam*, detail of Figure 17.33. In this iconic portion of the fresco, the languid Adam, Father of Humankind, is about to receive the spiritual energy and creative authority invested by God the Father.

Michelangelo considered all aspects of the creative life; reflecting on the Sistine Chapel ceiling, he describes his hardships with comic eloquence:

In this hard toil I've such a goiter grown,
Like cats that water drink in Lombardy,
(Or wheresoever else the place may be)
That chin and belly meet perforce in one.
My beard doth point to heaven, my scalp its place
Upon my shoulder finds; my chest, you'll say,
A harpy's is, my paint-brush all the day
Doth drop a rich mosaic on my face.
My loins have entered my paunch within,
My nether end my balance doth supply,
My feet unseen move to and fro in vain.
In front to utmost length is stretched my skin
And wrinkled up in folds behind, while I
Am bent as bowmen bend a bow in [Spain].

In 1546, Michelangelo accepted the papal commission to complete the dome and east end of the new Saint Peter's Cathedral in Rome—a project that followed numerous earlier efforts to make the basilica a centrally planned, domed church (Figure **17.35**). For Saint Peter's, Michelangelo designed an elliptically shaped dome on a huge drum ornamented with double columns of the "colossal order" (Figure **17.36**). He lived to build the drum, but it was not until 1590 that the dome was completed. Rising some 450 feet from the floor of the nave to the top of its tall lantern, Michelangelo's dome was heroic in size and dramatic in contour. But its enormous double shell of brick and stone proved impractical: cracks in the substructure

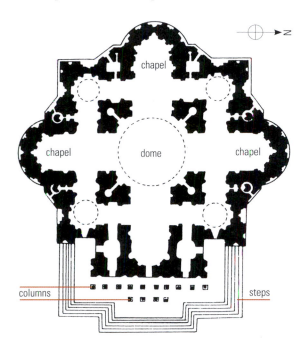

Figure 17.35 MICHELANGELO, plan for the new Saint Peter's, Vatican, Rome, ca. 1537–1550. Michelangelo revived the Greek cross plan originally projected by Bramante. He brought drama to the façade by adding a portico with two sets of columns and a massive flight of steps.

Figure 17.36 MICHELANGELO, dome of Saint Peter's, Vatican, Rome, ca. 1546–1564 (view from the south). Dome completed by Giacomo della Porta, 1590.

appeared less than ten years after completion, and the superstructure had to be bolstered repeatedly over the centuries, most recently by means of chains. Nevertheless, the great dome inspired numerous copies, such as that of Saint Paul's Cathedral in London (see Figure 22.3) and the United States Capitol in Washington, D.C.

Michelangelo shared the Neoplatonic belief that the soul, imprisoned in the body, yearned to return to its sacred origins. In his last works of art, as in his impassioned sonnets, he explored the conflict between flesh and spirit that had burdened many humanists, including Petrarch. The restless, brooding figures of Michelangelo's late works, especially those conceived for the Last Judgment fresco of the Sistine Chapel (see Figure 20.4)—unveiled twenty-nine years after the completion of the ceiling—mark a new direction in his art. As if burdened by a deeply troubled spirituality, these figures writhe and twist, like spirits trying to free themselves of physical matter. Ever the master of invention, the aging Michelangelo moved the gravity and solemnity of High Renaissance art in the direction of mannered theatricality.

The High Renaissance in Venice

The most notable artworks of the High Renaissance did not come from Florence, which suffered severe political upheavals at the end of the fifteenth century, but from the cities of Rome, Milan, and Venice. Venice, the Jewel of the Adriatic and a thriving center of trade, was a cluster of islands whose main streets consisted of canals lined with

richly ornamented palaces. The pleasure-loving Venetians, governed by a merchant aristocracy, regularly imported costly tapestries, jewels, and other luxury goods from all parts of Asia. During the sixteenth century, Venice outshone all the other city-states of Italy in its ornate architecture and its taste for pageantry. Both of these features are recreated in the *Procession of the Reliquary of the Cross in Piazza San Marco* (Figure **17.37**) painted by one of Venice's leading artists, Gentile Bellini (1429?–1507). In this panoramic canvas, Bellini employed the new system of one-point perspective to dramatize the union of civic and religious ritual: the annual celebration of the feast day of Saint Mark, patron saint of Venice, and the elevation of the True Cross, the prized relic said to have miraculously cured a dying Venetian child. At the far end of the *piazza* stands the cathedral of Saint Mark, a monumental counterpart of the ornate reliquary shrine carried in the foreground.

A symbol of Venetian opulence and one of the city's most prized architectural treasures, San Marco epitomizes the cross-cultural heritage of Byzantine, Islamic, and Western Christian decorative styles. The multidomed cathedral was begun during the eleventh century and ornamented over many centuries with dazzling mosaics that adorn both the interior and the exterior. As befitting this city of jeweled altarpieces, radiant mosaics, and sparkling lagoons, Renaissance Venice produced an art of color and light. While Florentine artists depended primarily on *line* as fundamental to design and the articulation of form, the Venetians delighted in the affective power of *color*.

Figure 17.37 GENTILE BELLINI, *Procession of the Reliquary of the Cross in Piazza San Marco*, 1496. Oil on canvas, 12 ft. ½ in. × 24 ft. 5¼ in. The white-robed members of the religious confraternity dedicated to Saint John the Evangelist are shown in the foreground. In the middle- and background are seen groups of ambassadors from Germany, Bohemia, and elsewhere. The red-robed father of the boy cured by the miraculous True Cross kneels in thanks just behind the canopied relic.

Figure 17.38 **TITIAN** (begun by **GIORGIONE**), *Pastoral Concert*, ca. 1505. Oil on canvas, 3 ft. 7¼ in. × 4 ft. 6¼ in. Some scholars interpret this painting as an allegory on the creation of poetry. The nude women, who seem to be invisible to the poets, may be viewed as their muses.

In preference to fresco-painting and tempera applied on wood panels, they favored the oil medium, to build up thin color glazes on rough canvas surfaces.

Giorgione and Titian

The two greatest Venetian colorists were Giorgio Barbarelli, known as Giorgione (ca. 1477–1511), and Tiziano Vecelli, called Titian (ca. 1488–1576). Little is known of Giorgione's life, but his influence on his younger colleague was significant. The *Pastoral Concert* (Figure **17.38**), a work that some scholars hold to be an early Titian, was probably begun by Giorgione and completed by Titian. This intriguing canvas shows two magnificently dressed Venetian courtiers—one playing a lute—in the presence of two female nudes. One woman holds a recorder, while the other pours water into a well. The precise subject of the painting is unclear, but its sensuousness—a product more of mood than of narrative content—is enhanced by textural and color contrasts: the red satin costume of the lute player versus the soft golden flesh of the women, the dense green foliage of the middleground versus the thin gray atmosphere on the distant horizon, and so forth. In its evocation of untroubled country life, *Pastoral Concert* may be considered the visual equivalent of pastoral verse, a genre that became popular among Renaissance humanists. But the painting also introduces a new subject that would become fashionable in Western art: the nude in a landscape setting.

During the sixteenth century, the female nude—often bearing the name of a Classical goddess—became a favorite subject of patrons seeking sensuous or erotic art for private enjoyment. The most famous of such commissions, the so-called *Venus of Urbino* (Figure **17.39**), was painted for Guidobaldo della Rovere, the duke of Urbino, during the last stage of Titian's artistic career. Here, a curvaceous nude reclines on a bed in the curtained alcove of a typical upper-class Venetian palace. The tiny roses in her hand, the myrtle plant (a symbol of Venus, goddess of love and fertility) on the window sill, the smooth dog at her feet (symbolic of fertility), and the servants who rummage in the nearby wedding chest all suggest impending marriage, while her seductive pose and arresting gaze are manifestly sexual. Titian enhanced the sensuality of the image by means of exquisitely painted surfaces: the delicate nuances of creamy skin modeled with glowing pinks, the reddish blond locks of hair, the deep burgundies of tapestries and cushions, and the cooler bluish whites of the sheets—all bathed in a pervasive golden light. Titian, who worked almost exclusively in oils, applied paint loosely, building up forms with layers of color so that contours seem to melt into one another, a technique best described as "painterly."

Figure 17.39 TITIAN, *Venus of Urbino*, 1538–1539. Oil on canvas, 3 ft. 11 in. × 5 ft. 5 in. Microscopic analysis of Venetian oil painting reveals that artists often mixed pulverized glass into their paints; these small bits of colored glass reflect and disperse light prismatically, giving the paintings their "glowing" appearance.

He preferred broken and subtle tones of color to the flat, bright hues favored by such artists as Raphael. Titian's painterly style became the definitive expression of the coloristic manner in High Renaissance painting and a model for such artists as Rubens in the seventeenth century and Delacroix in the nineteenth.

The Music of the Renaissance

Like Renaissance art, Renaissance music was increasingly secular in subject matter and function. However, the perception of the Renaissance as a time when secular music overtook ecclesiastical music may be caused by the fact that after 1450, more secular music was committed to paper. The printing press, perfected in Germany in the mid-fifteenth century, encouraged the preservation and dissemination of all kinds of musical composition. With the establishment of presses in Venice in the late fifteenth century, printed books of lute music and partbooks for individual instruments appeared in great numbers. (Most music was based on preexisting melodies, and manuscripts normally lacked tempo markings and other indications as to how a piece was to be performed.) Publishers also sold handbooks that offered instructions on how to play musical instruments. It is no surprise, then, that during the Renaissance, music was composed by both professional and amateur musicians. Indeed, Castiglione observed that making music was the function of all well-rounded individuals. Music was an essential ingredient at intimate gatherings, court celebrations, and public festivals (Figure **17.40**). And virtuosity in performance, a hallmark of Renaissance music, was common among both amateurs and professionals. Along with the poets of his court, the talented Lorenzo de' Medici took pleasure in writing lively vernacular songs for the carnivals that traditionally preceded the Lenten season. On pageant wagons designed for holiday spectacles in Florence and other cities, masked singers, dancers, and mimes enacted mythological, religious, and contemporary tales in musical performance.

While the literary and visual evidence of Classical antiquity was readily available to the humanists of the Renaissance, few musical examples had survived, and none could be accurately deciphered. For that reason, medieval tradition maintained a stronger influence in the development of music than it did in art and literature. (Not until the late sixteenth century did composers draw on Greek drama as the inspiration for a new genre: opera—discussed in chapter 20.) Moreover, perhaps because performing music was believed to be within everyone's reach, musicians were not held in such high esteem as painters, sculptors, or architects of the Renaissance. Most theorists, including Leonardo da Vinci (himself a musician

Figure 17.40 LORENZO COSTA, *The Concert*, ca. 1485–1495. Oil on poplar, 3 ft. 1½ in. × 29¾ in.

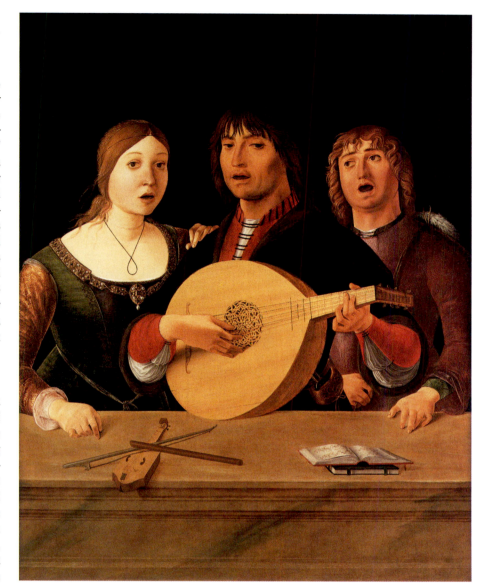

of some renown), as we have seen, considered poetry—and by extension, music—inferior to painting. Nevertheless, just as Renaissance artists pursued a more "natural-looking" art, Renaissance composers sought a more "natural-sounding" music. By the early fifteenth century, the trend toward consonant sounds encouraged the use of **intervals** of thirds in place of the traditional medieval (and ancient) intervals of fourths and fifths. And in the lighthearted songs that were written by Lorenzo de' Medici, an emphasis on melody and clear harmonic structure—a dramatic departure from complex polyphony—are apparent.

Early Renaissance Music: Dufay

While in the visual arts Italy took the lead, in music, French and Franco-Flemish composers outshone their Italian counterparts. During the fifteenth and much of the sixteenth centuries, composers from Burgundy and Flanders dominated the courts of Europe, including those of Italy. The leading Franco-Flemish composer of the fifteenth century, Guillaume Dufay (1400–1474), spent more than thirteen years of his career in Italy, during which time he set to music the verses of Petrarch and Lorenzo de' Medici (unfortunately, the latter compositions have been lost). In Dufay's more than 200 surviving vocal and instrumental compositions, including motets, Masses, and *chansons* (secular songs), he made extensive use of late medieval polyphonic techniques. At the same time, he introduced a close melodic and rhythmic kinship between all parts of a musical composition.

Just as religious subject matter inspired much of the art of Renaissance painters and sculptors, so religious music—and especially compositions for the Mass—held a prominent place in Dufay's output. However, sacred and secular themes are often indistinguishable in Dufay's works, and both are suffused by warmth of feeling. For his Mass settings, Dufay followed the common practice of borrowing melodies from popular folk tunes. In the *Missa L'homme armé*, for instance, he employed the best known of all fifteenth-century French folk songs, "The Armed Man," as the *cantus firmus* for all sections of the piece.

The Madrigal

During the sixteenth century, the most popular type of vernacular song was the **madrigal**, a composition for three to six unaccompanied voices. Usually polyphonic in texture, the madrigal often incorporated a large degree of vocal freedom, including the playful use of imitation and word painting. An intimate kind of musical composition, the madrigal might develop a romantic theme from a sonnet by Petrarch or give expression to a trifling and whimsical complaint. The Flemish composer Roland de Lassus (Orlando di Lasso; 1532–1594), who graced princely courts throughout Renaissance Europe, produced almost 200 madrigals among his more than 2000 compositions. In 1550, at age eighteen, Lassus wrote one of the most delightful vernacular songs of the Renaissance: "Matona, mia cara" ("My lady, my beloved"). The piece, a *villanella* (a light, dancelike song similar to the madrigal), describes a suitor's effort to seduce his lady friend; it ends each stanza with a frivolous group of nonsense syllables.

 See Music Listening Selections at end of chapter.

 See Music Listening Selections at end of chapter.

CHAPTER 17   Renaissance Artists: Disciples of Nature, Masters of Invention   **431**

My lady, my beloved,
Such pleasure would I choose
To sing beneath your window
Of love you'll never lose.

> *Dong, dong, dong, derry, derry,*
> *Dong, dong, dong, dong.*

I beg you, only hear me,
This song of sweetest news,
My love for you is boundless
Like lovebirds I enthuse.

> *Dong, dong, dong, derry, derry,*
> *Dong, dong, dong, dong.*

For I would go a-hunting
And falcons I would use
To bring you spoils a-plenty
Plump woodfowl as your dues.

> *Dong, dong, dong, derry, derry,*
> *Dong, dong, dong, dong.*

But though my words should fail me,
Lest fear my cause should lose,
E'en Petrarch could not help me
Nor Helicon's fair Muse.

> *Dong, dong, dong, derry, derry,*
> *Dong, dong, dong, dong.*

But only say you'll love me
And if you'll not refuse
I'll boldly sing of my love
Night long until the dews.

> *Dong, dong, dong, derry, derry,*
> *Dong, dong, dong, dong.*

Madrigals flourished primarily in the courts of Italy and England. At the fashionable court of Queen Elizabeth I of England, the madrigal became the rage. Usually based on Italian models, the English madrigal was generally lighter in mood than its Italian counterpart and often technically simple enough to be performed by amateurs. Two of the most popular Elizabethan composers, John Dowland (1563–1626) and Thomas Morley (1557–1602), composed English-language solo songs and madrigals that are still enjoyed today.

High Renaissance Music: Josquin

The outstanding figure in High Renaissance music was Josquin des Prez (ca. 1440–1521). Josquin followed the example of his Franco-Flemish predecessors by serving at the courts of France and Italy, including that of the papacy. A master of Masses, motets, and secular songs, he earned international recognition as "the prince of music." Like Dufay, Josquin unified each polyphonic Mass around a single musical theme, but, more in the grand style of the painter Raphael, Josquin contrived complex designs in which melody and harmony were distributed symmetrically and with "geometric" clarity. He might give focus to a single musical phrase in the way that Raphael might center

See Music Listening Selections at end of chapter.

the Virgin and Child within a composition. And, in an effort to increase compositional balance, he might group voices into pairs, with the higher voices repeating certain phrases of the lower ones.

The expressive grace of Josquin's music followed from the attention he gave to the relationship between words and music. He tailored musical lines so that they followed the natural flow of the words, a device inspired perhaps by his appreciation of the classical kinship of song and text. Josquin was among the first to practice **word painting**, the manipulation of music to convey the literal meaning of the text—as, for example, where the text describes a bird's ascent, the music might rise in pitch. Word painting characterized both the religious and the secular music of the Renaissance.

In music, as in the visual arts, composers of the Renaissance valued unity of design. Josquin achieved a homogeneous musical texture by the use of **imitation**, a technique whereby a melodic fragment introduced in the first voice is repeated closely (though usually at a different pitch) in the second, third, and fourth voices, so that one overlaps the next. Simple rhythmic lines and the ingenious use of imitation contributed to the smooth and sonorous style of such motets as "Tulerunt Dominum meum," his eight-voice setting of a New Testament text from the Gospel of John. A master of the integration of multiple voice lines—one of his motets has as many as twenty-four parts—Josquin wrote motets that featured a continuous flow of interwoven melodies and a graceful design that was comparable to the best of Raphael's High Renaissance compositions.

Women and Renaissance Music

Following the tradition of the female *troubadours* (see chapter 11) and the recommendations of Castiglione, many Renaissance women were accomplished in both playing and composing music. The Venetian aristocrat Maddalena Casulana (ca. 1540–ca. 1590) was the first professional female composer to witness the publication of her works, mainly madrigals. In these vernacular songs, she made active use of word painting to heighten the text in mood and meaning.

Women also played a significant role as professional performers. The *Concerto delle donne* (Consort of Ladies) was a group of professional singers who entertained at the late sixteenth-century court of Ferrara. Famous for their technical and artistic virtuosity, and for such musical innovations as the multiplication of ornamented upper voice parts, they became the model for similar all-female ensembles in Florence and elsewhere. By 1600, talented women, who were often brought to court to train as professional musicians, held independent careers in musical performance and composition. They sang their own repertory of songs from memory and sight-read others from popular partbooks.

Instrumental Music of the Renaissance

One of the liveliest records of fifteenth-century musical instruments is a set of sculptures executed by the

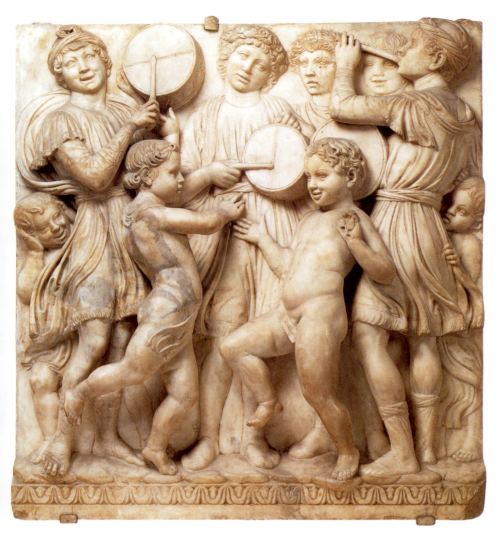

Figure 17.41 LUCA DELLA ROBBIA, *Drummers* (detail of the *Cantoria*). Marble, 3 ft. 6⅛ in. × 3 ft. 4¹⁹⁄₂₀ in. This marble relief panel is one of eight commissioned by Lorenzo de' Medici to adorn the 17-foot-long music gallery of the cathedral of Florence. The drummers seem to have produced enough volume of sound to offend the child at the far left, who covers his ears.

Florentine artist Luca della Robbia (1400–1482). Luca would become famous for his brightly polychromed terracotta religious figures; but in his first documented commission, the *Cantoria* ("Singing Gallery") for the cathedral of Florence, he exhibited his talents as a keen observer of secular entertainments involving musical instruments (Figure **17.41**). Greco-Roman techniques of high and low relief are revived in the eight panels representing choristers, instrumentalists, and dancers—the last drawn both from keen observation and from antiquity (the plump nude boys are based on Classical *putti* depicting Cupid). In a spirited display of song, dance, and jubilant music-making, Luca brought to life Psalm 150, which enjoins one to praise God with "trumpet sound," "lute and harp," "strings and pipe," and "loud clashing cymbals," to which Luca added drummers, a favorite instrument of Renaissance street pageants.

Although most Renaissance music was composed to be sung, the sixteenth century made considerable advances in the development of instrumental music. Music for solo instruments became more common, with the lute still the favorite. In London, its popularity as a solo instrument and to accompany madrigals (see Figure 17.40) warranted the importation of almost 14,000 lute strings in the one-year period between 1567 and 1568. A wide variety of other instruments, such as shawms, cromornes, cornets, trumpets, trombones, stringed instruments, and drums, were used for accompaniment and in small instrumental ensembles (Figure **17.42**).

Renaissance composers wrote music for portable **organs** (popular in private homes and princely courts) and for two other types of keyboard instrument: the **clavichord** and the **harpsichord** (also called the *spinet*, the *clavecin*, and the *virginal*—the last possibly after the "Virgin Queen," Elizabeth I of England, who was an

Figure 17.42 **HANS BURGKMAIR**, *The Music Room*, from *Der Weiss Kunig*, late sixteenth century. Woodcut, 8⅓ × 7⅔ in. This woodcut illustrates the musical education of the Holy Roman emperor Maximilian I (1459–1519). The instruments shown include the organ (lower left), harp, trumpet, drums, recorders, crumhorn (a curved reed instrument), and violin.

accomplished musician). Harpsichord sounds are made by quills that pluck a set of strings, while clavichord notes are produced by metal tangents that strike the strings. Such instruments create bright, sharp sounds, somewhat more robust in the harpsichord. Since Renaissance instruments produce a less dynamic and smaller range of sound than do modern instruments, they demand greater attention to nuances of *timbre*—the "color" or quality of musical sound.

During the Late Middle Ages, instruments occasionally took the place of one or more voice parts. It was not until the Renaissance, however, that music for instruments alone regularly appeared. Instrumental compositions developed out of dance tunes with strong rhythms and distinctive melodic lines. Indeed, the earliest model for the instrumental suite was a group of dances arranged according to contrasting rhythm and style. Instrumental music was characterized by the same kind of complex invention that marked the vocal compositions of Josquin, and the skillful performance of difficult instrumental passages brought acclaim to both performer and composer.

Renaissance Dance

In the Renaissance, dance played an important role in all forms of entertainment: town pageants, courtly rituals, festal displays sponsored by trade and merchant guilds, and almost all nonecclesiastical celebrations. Folk dancing, of the kind illustrated by the Flemish painter Pieter Bruegel (see Figure 19.15), was a collective public experience that fostered a powerful sense of community. In contrast with folk dances, court dances stressed individual grace and poise. Renaissance dancing masters distinguished folk dance from courtly dance, a move that would eventually result in the development of dance as a form of theatrical entertainment.

The Renaissance witnessed the first efforts to establish dance as an independent discipline. Guglielmo Ebreo (1439–1482), dancing master at the court of Urbino, wrote one of the first treatises on the art of dancing. He emphasized the importance of grace, the memorization of fixed steps, and the coordination of music and motion. Guglielmo also choreographed a number of lively dances or *balli*—the Italian word from which the French *ballet* derives. Three favorite forms of Italian court dance were the *basse* (a slow, solemn ceremonial dance), the *saltarello* (a vigorous, three-beat dance featuring graceful leaps), and the *piva* (a dance in rapid tempo with double steps). In Guglielmo's day, such dances were still performed by members of the court, rather than by professional dancers.

LOOKING BACK

Renaissance Art and Patronage

- In the commercial cities of Italy and the Netherlands, the arts became tangible expressions of increased affluence. Merchant princes and petty despots vied with growing numbers of middle-class patrons and urban guilds whose lavish commissions brought prestige to their cities, their businesses, and their families.
- No longer regarded as a mere craftsperson, the artist was now seen as a hero and genius, celebrated for his talents and powers of invention.

The Early Renaissance

- Renaissance artists were disciples of nature: they brought scientific curiosity to the study of the natural world and worked to understand its operations.
- The Early Renaissance artists Donatello, Masaccio, Ghiberti, and Brunelleschi studied the mechanics of the human body, the effects of light on material substances, and the physical appearance of objects in three-dimensional space.
- Renaissance artists were also masters of invention: they perfected the technique of oil painting, formulated laws of perspective, and applied the principles of Classical art to the representation of Christian and contemporary subjects.

The High Renaissance

- The art of the High Renaissance marks the culmination of a hundred-year effort to wed the techniques of naturalistic representation to Classical ideals of proportion and order.
- Leonardo da Vinci, the quintessential artist–scientist, tried to reconcile empirical experience with abstract principles of design. The art of Raphael, characterized by monumental grace and unity of design, provided the standard for the Grand Manner, the touchstone of academic art for centuries to come.
- Architect, sculptor, and painter, Michelangelo brought a heroic

dimension, both in size and in execution, to the treatment of traditional Christian and Classical subjects.

- The centrally planned buildings of Bramante and Palladio exemplified the ideals set forth by their predecessors Brunelleschi and Alberti for an architecture of harmony, balance, and clarity.
- In Venice, Giorgione and Titian achieved fame for their painterly renderings of sensuous female nudes occupying landscapes and rich interiors.

The Music of the Renaissance

- During the Renaissance, secular compositions began to outnumber religious ones. Printed sheet music helped to popularize the madrigal and other vernacular song forms.
- The Franco-Flemish composers Guillaume Dufay and Josquin des Prez outshone their Italian counterparts, providing religious and secular compositions for Church and court patrons.
- The techniques of imitation and word painting invested both religious and secular music with homogeneity and increased expressiveness. Madrigals and other vernacular songs regularly employed these techniques.
- The sixteenth century saw the emergence of women as professional composers and professional performers.
- The development of instrumental music as an independent genre went hand in hand with the refinement of musical instruments, such as the clavichord and the harpsichord. During the Renaissance, dance emerged as an independent genre, and the first treatises were written on the art of dancing.

Music Listening Selections

- Guillaume Dufay, *Missa L'homme armé* (Mass on "The Armed Man"), "Kyrie I," ca. 1450.
- Roland de Lassus (Orlando di Lasso), madrigal, "Matona, mia cara" ("My lady, my beloved"), 1550.
- Thomas Morley, madrigal, "My bonnie lass she smileth," 1595.
- Josquin des Prez, motet, "Tulerunt Dominum meum," ca. 1520.

Glossary

aerial perspective the means of representing distance that relies on the imitation of the ways atmosphere affects the eye—outlines are blurred, details lost, contrasts of light and shade diminished, hues bluer, and colors less vivid; also called "atmospheric perspective"

clavichord (French, *clavier*, meaning "keyboard") a stringed keyboard instrument widely used between the sixteenth and eighteenth centuries; when the player presses down on a key, a brass tangent or blade rises and strikes a string

contrapposto (Italian, "counterpoised") a position assumed by the human body in which one part is turned in opposition to another part

drum the cylindrical section immediately beneath the dome of a building

harpsichord a stringed keyboard instrument widely used between the sixteenth and eighteenth centuries; when the player presses down on a key, a quill, called a plectrum, plucks the string

imitation a technique whereby a melodic fragment introduced in the first voice of a composition is repeated closely (though usually at a different pitch) in the second, third, and fourth voices, so that one voice overlaps the next; the repetition may be exactly the same as the original, or it may differ somewhat

interval the distance between the pitches of two musical tones

lantern a small, windowed tower on top of a roof or dome that allows light to enter a building

linear perspective (or **optical perspective**) a method of creating the semblance of three-dimensional space on a two-dimensional surface; it derives from two optical illusions: (1) parallel lines appear to converge as they recede toward a vanishing point on a horizon level with the viewer's eye, and (2) objects appear to shrink and move closer together as they recede from view

madrigal a vernacular song, usually composed for three to six unaccompanied voices

organ a keyboard instrument in which keyboards and pedals are used to force air into a series of pipes, causing them to sound

picture plane the two-dimensional surface of a panel or canvas

pilaster a shallow, flattened, rectangular column or pier attached to a wall surface

tondo a circular painting or relief sculpture

villanella a light, dancelike song related to the madrigal

volute a scroll-shaped architectural ornament

word painting the manipulation of music to convey a specific object, thought, or mood—that is, the content of the text

Cross-Cultural Encounters: Asia, Africa, and the Americas

ca. 1300–1600

". . . the world is old, but the future springs from the past."
Sundiata: An Epic of Old Mali

Figure 18.1 Benin plaque showing a Portuguese warrior surrounded by *manillas* (horseshoe-shaped metal objects used as a medium of exchange), Nigeria, sixteenth century. Bronze, 18 × 13⁵⁄₁₆ in. The warrior's sword symbolizes the military authority of the Portuguese, who arrived in Benin in 1486. The trident indicates the popular legend that the invaders belonged to a semidivine race of spirits who came from the land of the dead beneath the sea.

A constellation of circumstances drove Westerners to undertake a program of exploration and expansion in the fifteenth century. The threat to previously established overland trade routes posed by the expanding Ottoman Empire was a major concern to the West. But other, more positive developments were equally significant: the growing enthusiasm for travel (made possible by advances in the science of navigation and the technology of shipbuilding), rising ambition for the accumulation of personal wealth, and the fundamental spirit of intellectual curiosity that marked the Age of the Renaissance.

Europe's overseas ventures would lead ultimately to a more accurate understanding of world geography. The proliferation of commercial exchange would work to establish a new set of trade networks. But perhaps the most compelling aspect of the enterprise of Western exploration was its human dimension: the cross-cultural encounters between Europe, Africa, East Asia, and the Americas. These encounters would set in motion a pattern of colonialism that disrupted older traditions and inaugurated new social, political, and cultural institutions. Sadly, some aspects of that contact would transform and even devastate the populations of Africa and the Americas. Ultimately, cross-cultural exchange brought massive economic transformation to all parts of the modern world. In order to better understand how the populations of Africa and the Americas were affected by European intrusion, it is necessary to examine the cultures of each in the centuries immediately prior to their contact with the Europeans.

Global Travel and Trade

The period between 1400 and 1600 was the greatest age of trans-Eurasian travel since the days of the Roman Empire. However, even earlier, and especially after 1000 C.E., long-range trade, religious pilgrimage, missionary activity, and just plain curiosity had stimulated cross-cultural contact between East and West. Arab merchants dominated North African trade routes. Converts to Islam—especially Turks and Mongols—carried the Muslim faith across Asia into India and Anatolia. Mongol tribes traversed the vast overland Asian Silk Road, which stretched from Constantinople to the Pacific Ocean. Enterprising families, like that of the Venetian merchant Marco Polo (1254–1324), established cultural and commercial links with the court of the Mongol emperor of China, Kublai Khan. Crossing the Asian continent with his father and uncle, he served the Mongol ruler for seventeen years before returning to Italy, where he eventually narrated the details of his travels. The fabulous nature of his account, much of which made the West seem like the poor, backward relation of a great Eastern empire, brought Marco instant fame. The best-selling *The Travels of Marco Polo* came to be known as *Il Milione* (*The Million*), a nickname that described both Marco's legendary wealth and the lavishness of his tales. Its significance, however, lies in the fact that it opened Europeans, poised for global expansion, to an interest in the "exotic" East. For his part, Kublai Khan also encouraged long-distance travel and cross-cultural dialogue, boasting that "brotherhood among peoples" had reached a new height during his rule (1260–1294).

The same roads that brought thirteenth-century Franciscan and Dominican monks into China sped the exchange of goods and religious beliefs between Muslims and Hindus, Confucians and Buddhists. Although the great plague that swept through Asia and Europe interrupted long-established patterns of East–West exchange, the appearance of fourteenth-century handbooks, such as that written by the Florentine merchant Francesco Pegolotti, suggests that global travel did not completely disappear (Pegolotti journeyed as far as China). Nor did regional travel cease: Chaucer's pilgrims traveled to local Christian shrines, while Buddhists visited their sanctuaries throughout East Asia, and Muslims often made even longer journeys to participate in the ritual of the *hajj*, that is, the pilgrimage to Mecca.

China's Treasure Ships

While the Mongols had encouraged long-distance travel, their policy of outreach took a bold direction under their followers. Eager to reinstate foreign trade and unite "the four seas," the young prince Zhu Di (1368–1424) of the newly established Ming dynasty (1368–1644) ordered the construction of a fleet larger than any in history: 317 wooden treasure ships, each more than 400 feet long (four times the length of Columbus' *Santa Maria*), were constructed between 1405 and 1433. Boasting tall prows, nine masts, and red silk sails, and painted with dragons and phoenixes, the "Dragon Ships"—the largest sail-powered fleet ever constructed—carried cargoes of silk, porcelain, iron, and tea, which were traded for spices, precious gems, incense, exotic animals, ivory, and rare woods. Along with translators and astrologers, 28,000 Chinese sailors crossed the Indian Ocean to trade at the port cities of Africa, India, and Arabia; eastward, they worked the ports of China, Sumatra, and Borneo. The death of Zhu Di and his followers brought an abrupt end to the enterprise, but their ambitious legacy endures in a document that boasts, "We have set eyes on barbarian regions far away . . . traversing the savage waves as if we were treading a public thoroughfare."

European Expansion

In 1453, the highly disciplined armies of the Ottoman Empire, using new gunpowder weaponry, captured Constantinople, renaming it Istanbul. By the end of the century, this Islamic empire had become the greatest power bloc in the world (see chapter 21). Stretching from

1405	China launches the first of seven overseas expeditions with over 300 of the largest wooden ships ever built
1418	Prince Henry of Portugal opens a school of navigation
1420	the Portuguese develop the three-masted caravel for ocean travel
1448	Andreas Walsperger (Flemish) uses the coordinates of longitude, latitude, and climatic divisions in his *mappa mundi* (world map)
1522	the circumnavigation of the globe (begun by Magellan) is completed

Eastern Europe across the Eurasian steppes, and into sub-Saharan Africa, it threatened the safety of European overland caravans to the East. Western rulers explored two main offensive strategies: warfare against the Ottoman Turks and the search for all-water routes to the East. The first strategy yielded some success when the allied forces of Venice, Spain, and the papacy defeated the Ottoman navy in western Greece at the Battle of Lepanto in 1571. Although this event briefly reduced the Ottoman presence in the Mediterranean—the Turks quickly rebuilt their navy—it did not answer the need for faster and more efficient trade routes to the East. Greed for gold, slaves, and spices—the major commodities of Africa and Asia—also encouraged the emerging European nations to compete with Arab and Turkish traders for control of foreign markets.

The technology of navigation was crucial to the success of these ventures. With the early fifteenth-century Latin translation of Ptolemy's *Geography*, mapmakers began to order geographic space with the coordinates of latitude and longitude. The Portuguese, encouraged by Prince Henry the Navigator (1394–1460), came to produce maps and charts that exceeded the accuracy of those drafted by Classical and Muslim cartographers. Renaissance Europeans improved such older Arab navigational devices as the compass and the astrolabe (an instrument that measures the angle between the horizon and heavenly bodies and thus fixes latitude; see chapter 10).

Portugal and Spain adopted the Arab lateen sail and built two- and three-masted caravels with multiple sails—ships that were faster, safer, and more practical for rough ocean travel than the oar-driven galleys that sailed the Mediterranean Sea (Figure 18.2). The new caravels were outfitted with brass cannons and sufficient firepower to fend off severe enemy attack. Christopher Columbus (1451–1506), a Genoese explorer in the employ of Spain, sailed west in search of an all-water route to China and India. His discovery of the Americas—the existence of which no Europeans had ever suspected—was to change the course of world history.

While the Spanish sought to reach China by sailing across the Atlantic Ocean, the Portuguese set off down

the coast of Africa (Map **18.1**). In 1488, Bartholomeu Dias (1450–1500) rounded the southernmost tip of Africa and entered the Indian Ocean; the sixteen-month journey confirmed that India could be reached by sailing east. By 1498, Vasco da Gama (1460–1524) made a similar journey that allowed him to establish Portuguese trading posts in India.

When, in the 1540s, a Portuguese vessel was blown off course by a typhoon, sailors found their way to the southernmost tip of Japan. Soon after, Portuguese vessels, carrying exotic cargo for trade and small groups of Jesuit missionaries (see chapter 20), arrived in Japan. The presence of these "barbarians from the south" (in Japanese, *nanbanjin*), was recorded in at least seventy multipaneled screens, painted for Japan's wealthy merchants between the 1590s and 1630s (Figure **18.3**). European firearms had a major impact on Japanese warfare, as musket-bearing foot soldiers came to replace earlier modes of combat. These enterprises initiated an era of global travel and cross-cultural encounter the consequences of which would

Figure 18.2 ALEJO FERNANDEZ, *Our Lady of the Navigators*, 1535. Oil on canvas 7 ft. 4½ in. × 4 ft. 5⅛ in. The painting, which celebrates the Spanish conquest of the Americas, was commissioned for a chapel in Seville. Pictured as the Madonna of Mercy, the Virgin shelters the faithful within her cloak. While none of the figures has been securely identified, the worshiper kneeling at the far left is probably Christopher Columbus.

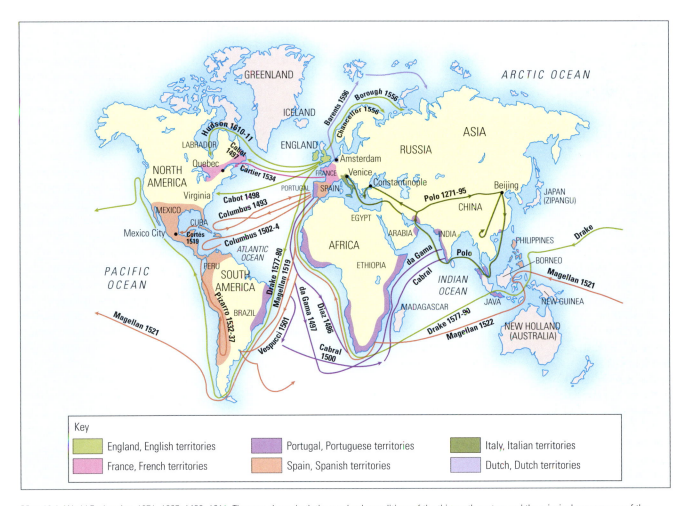

Map 18.1 World Exploration, 1271–1295; 1486–1611. The map shows both the overland expeditions of the thirteenth century and the principal sea voyages of the fifteenth and sixteenth centuries. The date of each expedition follows the name of the navigator.

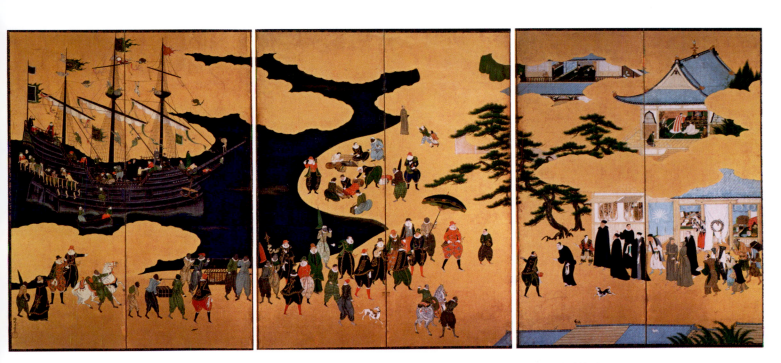

Figure 18.3 KANO NAIZEN, *Arrival of Portuguese Merchants in Japan*, 1593–1600. One of a pair of six-panel screens, color and gold leaf on paper, 5 ft. 1¼ in. × 11 ft. 11½ in. In the panels on the left side of this six-fold *nanban* screen, the Japanese are seen greeting a three-masted Portuguese vessel. Richly dressed Portuguese traders, Jesuit missionaries, and African slaves take part in this unique cross-cultural encounter. Small ships carry to shore cargo, which is unloaded by Africans (dressed in Western style), and eagerly examined by Japanese merchants.

transform the destinies of Asia, Africa, and the Americas. Indeed, the age of expansion would mark the beginning of a modern world-system dominated by the West.

The African Cultural Heritage

Diversity characterizes all aspects of Africa's history and culture. A vast continent, Africa comprises widely varying geographic regions: the sub-Sarahan region alone is host to more than 800 different spoken languages. From Southern Africa came our earliest known ancestors; and in the northeast, the ancient civilizations of Egypt and Nubia flourished thousands of years ago. For centuries, most of Africa consisted of farming villages like that of Nok (discussed in chapter 2), located at the Niger River in present-day Nigeria (Map 18.2). After ca. 1000, however, some of these villages grew into city-states that controlled the surrounding countryside; groups of villages might form a district, while others consolidated to emerge as local kingdoms or regional states, and, by the fourteenth century, empires. These societies, much like the complex societies of Eurasian states, involved clearly defined classes: a ruling elite, military and administrative nobility, religious authorities, merchants, commoners, peasants, and slaves.

Despite their geographic and linguistic diversity, African societies share some distinct cultural characteristics that provide a context for our understanding of African culture prior to the European encounter. The most notable of these is a kinship system that emphasizes the importance and well-being of the group as essential to that of the individual. Historically, the African kinship system was based on the extended family, a group of people who were both related to one another and dependent on one another for survival. A village might consist of several extended families or clans ruled by chiefs or elders—either hereditary or elected—who usually held semidivine status. All those who belonged to the same family, clan, or tribe—the living, the dead, and the yet unborn—made up a single cohesive community irrevocably linked in time and space. While this form of social organization was not unique to Africa—indeed, it has characterized most agricultural societies in world history—it played an especially important role in shaping the character of African society and culture. While African social structures might differ from century to century, these kin-based societies did not disappear with the emergence of regional states or empires, nor with the arrival of Muslims (see chapter 10) and Christians.

From earliest times, most African societies maintained the animistic belief that powerful spirits inhabit the natural world. They honored a single creator god, but they

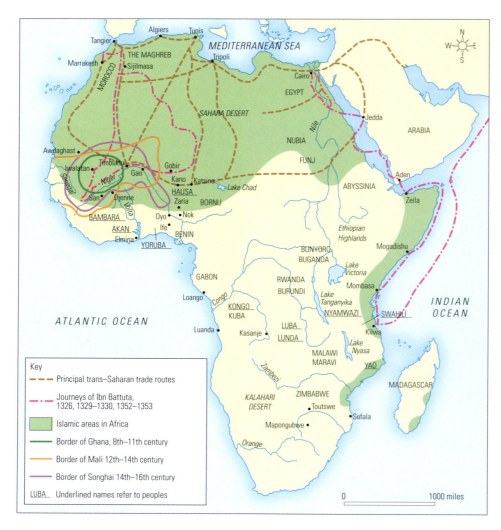

Map 18.2 Africa, 1000–1500. While the text focuses on the history of West African kingdoms and empires, the map shows the entire continent. Note that the kingdoms of Ife and Benin lay outside of direct Muslim influence.

addressed his powers indirectly through spirits associated with nature and the souls of departed ancestors. The spirits of the deceased, as well as local divinities, were called on in rituals designed to seek protection, resolve conflicts, or fulfill the special needs of the community. Ceremonies marking crucial life transitions—birth, puberty, marriage, death—were orchestrated by shamans or priests who held prominent positions in African society.

Ghana

In the ninth century, a number of African states emerged in the *Sudan* (the word means "Land of the Blacks"): the region that stretches across Africa south of the Sahara Desert (see Map **18.2**). Encouraged by the activities of Muslim merchants and lucrative trans-Saharan trade, some of West Africa's commercial centers grew into regional states. The first of these was Ghana (the name means "war chief"), whose empire came to flourish under the influence of powerful rulers, who extended their authority over the surrounding villages. Located in the forested region between the Senegal and Niger rivers, Ghana was the center of the gold trade. Its rulers, who were presumed to have divine ancestors, regulated the exportation of gold to the north and the importation of salt from the desert fringes. These two products—gold and salt—along with iron, slaves, and ivory were the principal African commodities.

After Ghana fell to the Muslims in the eleventh century, its native kings, along with much of the local culture, came under Muslim influence. The history of Ghana and other ancient African kingdoms is recorded primarily in Arabic sources describing the courts of kings, but little is known of African life in areas removed from the centers of power.

Mali and Songhai

During the thirteenth century, West Africans speaking the Mande language brought much of the Sudan under their dominion to form the Mali Empire. This dramatic development is associated with the powerful warrior-king Sundiata, who ruled Mali from around 1230 to 1255. The wealth and influence of the Mali Empire, which reached its zenith in the early fourteenth century, derived from its control of northern trade routes. On one of these routes lay the prosperous city of Timbuktu (see Map 18.2), the greatest of early African trans-Saharan trading centers and the site of a flourishing Islamic university that by the fourteenth century housed thousands of manuscripts ranging from poetry and history to scientific, legal, and theological texts. In Mali, as in many of the African states, the rulers were converts to Islam; they employed Muslim scribes and jurists and used Arabic as the language of administration. The hallmarks of Islamic culture—its great mosques (Figure **18.4**) and libraries and the Arabic language itself—did

Figure 18.4 Great Mosque, Djenne, Mali, 1906–1907. Djenne is the oldest known city in sub-Saharan Africa; under the Muslims it became a center of trade and learning. Originally built around 1220, the mosque pictured here dates from 1907 and is the third on this site.

Figure 18.5 The *oba* (ruler) of Ife wearing a beaded crown and plume, from Benin, twelfth to fourteenth centuries. Cast brass with red pigment, height 14⅛ in. The holes around the mouth once probably held hair or hairlike additions. Because many of the Benin male portraits bear similar features, it is likely that an idealized notion of a royal face was favored over specific characterization.

not penetrate deeply into the vast interior of Africa, however, where native African traditions dominated everyday life.

When the Mali Empire began to weaken in the fifteenth century, the small state of Songhai within its borders broke away, soon to emerge as the ruling power in the central Niger valley. With his capital at Gao, the first king of Songhai took control of the critical trade routes and major cities, including Timbuktu. At its height in the early sixteenth century, Songhai, under the leadership of its Muslim emperors, dominated all of West Africa in wealth and power.

Benin

Prior to the fourteenth century, neither Arabs nor Europeans traveled to the thickly vegetated area of tropical rainforest south of the great savanna. Here, at the mouth of the Niger, in present-day Nigeria, emerged the kingdom of Benin. Governed, beginning in the late twelfth century, by the young son of the Yoruba ruler at Ife, Benin came to dominate most of the West African territories north of the Niger delta. The Benin *obas* (rulers) established an impressive royal tradition, building large walled cities and engaging in trade with other African states. Guilds of artists, trained in the techniques of lost-wax bronze and copper casting, served the court, immortalizing the *oba* and members of the royal family in portraits that capture their dignity and authority. These works perpetuated a tradition of

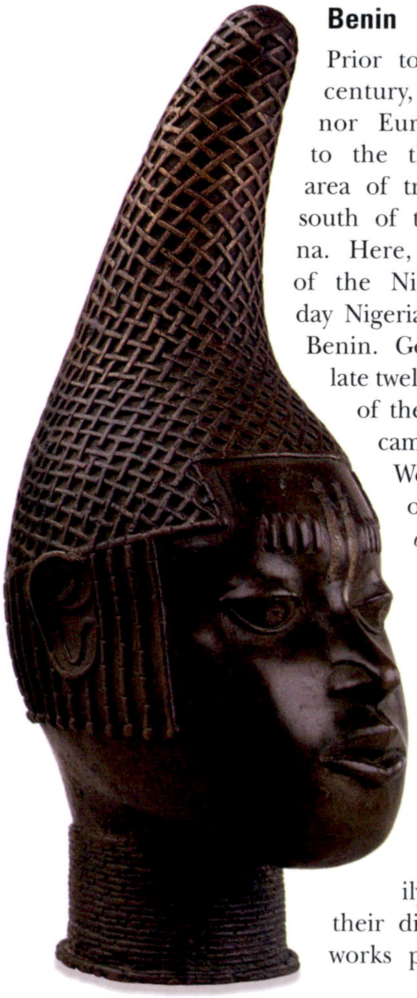

Figure 18.6 Queen mother head, from Benin, ca. 1500–1550. Brass, height 15½ in. In its subtle blend of realism and idealization, the portrait calls to mind the ancient Egyptian head of Nefertiti (see Figure 2.16). Images like this one stood on the royal altar for some 300 years after Benin culture reached its peak in the sixteenth century.

portraiture that can be traced back to the terracotta figures found in the ancient village of Nok (see Figure 2.23) and, more immediately, to the highly refined metal-cast portraits produced in Ife. The *oba* pictured in Figure 18.5, wearing a beaded crown and a plume, bears the thin, parallel lines of **scarification** (the process of incising the skin) that functioned as a type of body art, but also often designated membership of, or status within, a particular group.

Yet another kind of scarification is seen in the metal-cast image of the highest-ranking female member of the royal court, the queen mother (Figure 18.6). Those who bore this title were greatly valued as advisors, and numerous likenesses of them were enshrined on royal altars. In this example, the queen mother wears a tall, conical, netted headdress and a regal collar, both made of coral beads; vertical strands of coral beads also frame the face. The unique coiffure, known as the "chicken's beak," was being worn by royal wives well into the 1990s.

The Arts of Africa

Sundiata

Africa transmitted native folk traditions orally rather than in writing. As a result, the literary contributions of Africans remained unrecorded for hundreds of years—in some cases until the nineteenth century and thereafter. During the tenth century, Arab scholars in Africa began to transcribe popular native tales and stories into Arabic. Over time, several of the traditional African languages have developed written forms and produced a literature of note. Even to this day, however, a highly prized oral tradition dominates African literature.

Ancient Africa's oral tradition was the province of *griots*, a special class of professional poet–historians who preserved the legends of the past by chanting or singing them from memory. Like the *jongleurs* of the Early Middle Ages, *griots* transmitted the history of the people by way of stories that had been handed down from generation to generation. The most notable of these narratives is *Sundiata*, an epic describing the formative phase of Mali history. *Sundiata* originated around 1240, in the time of Mali's great empire, but it was not until the twentieth century that it was transcribed—first to written French and then to English. Recounted by a *griot*, who identifies himself in the opening passages, the epic immortalizes the adventures of Sundiata, the champion and founder of the Mali Empire. In the tradition of such Western heroes as Gilgamesh, Achilles, Alexander, and Roland, the "lion-child" Sundiata performs extraordinary deeds that bring honor and glory to himself and peace and prosperity to his people. The following excerpt includes the *griot's* introduction to the poem, the story of the Battle of Tabon, and a brief description of the lively festival that celebrates Sundiata's triumphs. In the final passages of the poem, Mali is pictured as a place of peace and prosperity; it is eternal in the memory of those who know its history.

READING 18.1 From *Sundiata: An Epic of Old Mali*

I am a griot. It is I, Djeli Mamoudou Kouyaté, son of Bintou Kouyaté and Djeli Kedian Kouyaté, master in the art of eloquence. Since time immemorial the Kouyatés have been in the service of the Keita[1] princes of Mali; we are vessels of speech, we are the repositories which harbor secrets many centuries old. The art of eloquence has no secrets for us; without us the names of kings would vanish into oblivion, we are the memory of mankind; by the spoken word we bring to life the deeds and exploits of kings for younger generations. **10**

I derive my knowledge from my father Djeli Kedian, who also got it from his father; history holds no mystery for us; we teach to the vulgar just as much as we want to teach them, for it is we who keep the keys to the twelve doors of Mali.[2]

I know the list of all the sovereigns who succeeded to the throne of Mali. I know how the black people divided into tribes, for my father bequeathed to me all his learning; I know why such and such is called Kamara, another Keita, and yet another Sibibé or Traoré; every **20** name has a meaning, a secret import.

I teach kings the history of their ancestors so that the lives of the ancients might serve them as an example, for the world is old, but the future springs from the past.

My word is pure and free of all untruth; it is the word of my father; it is the word of my father's father. I will give you my father's words just as I received them; royal griots do not know what lying is. When a quarrel breaks out between tribes it is we who settle the difference, for we are the depositaries of oaths which the **30** ancestors swore.

Listen to my word, you who want to know; by my mouth you will learn the history of Mali.

By my mouth you will get to know the story of the ancestor of great Mali, the story of him who, by his exploits, surpassed even Alexander the Great; he who, from the East, shed his rays upon all the countries of the West.

Listen to the story of the son of the Buffalo, the son of the Lion.[3] I am going to tell you of Maghan Sundiata, **40** of Mari-Djata, of Sogolon Djata, of Naré Maghan Djata; the man of many names against whom sorcery could avail nothing.

. . . .

[1] The ruling Muslim family, the Mali emperors identified themselves as descendants of the prophet Muhammad.
[2] The twelve provinces of which Mali was originally composed.
[3] According to tradition, the buffalo was the totem of Sundiata's mother, Sogolon, while the lion was the totem of his father.

Kings have prescribed destinies just like men, and seers who probe the future know it. They have knowledge of the future, whereas we griots are depositaries of the knowledge of the past. But whoever knows the history of a country can read its future.

Other peoples use writing to record the past, but this invention has killed the faculty of memory among them. **50** They do not feel the past any more, for writing lacks the warmth of the human voice. With them everybody thinks he knows, whereas learning should be a secret. The prophets did not write and their words have been all the more vivid as a result. What paltry learning is that which is congealed in dumb books!

I, Djeli Mamoudou Kouyaté, am the result of a long tradition. For generations we have passed on the history of kings from father to son. The narrative was passed on to me without alteration and I deliver it without **60** alteration, for I received it free from all untruth.

. . . .

Every man to his own land! If it is foretold that your destiny should be fulfilled in such and such a land, men can do nothing against it. Mansa Tounkara could not keep Sundiata back because the destiny of Sogolon's son was bound up with that of Mali. Neither the jealousy of a cruel stepmother, nor her wickedness, could alter for a moment the course of great destiny.

The snake, man's enemy, is not long-lived, yet the serpent that lives hidden will surely die old. Djata[4] was **70** strong enough now to face his enemies. At the age of eighteen, he had the stateliness of the lion and the strength of the buffalo. His voice carried authority, his eyes were live coals, his arm was iron, he was the husband of power.

Moussa Tounkara, king of Mema, gave Sundiata half of his army. The most valiant came forward of their own free will to follow Sundiata in the great adventure. The cavalry of Mema, which he had fashioned himself, formed his iron squadron. Sundiata, dressed in the **80** Muslim fashion of Mema, left the town at the head of his small but redoubtable army. The whole population sent their best wishes with him. He was surrounded by five messengers from Mali and Manding Bory rode proudly at the side of his brother. The horsemen of Mema formed behind Djata a bristling iron squadron. The troops took the direction of Wagadou, for Djata did not have enough troops to confront Soumaoro directly, and so the king of Mema advised him to go to Wagadou and take half of the men of the king, Soumaba Cissé. A swift messenger had **90** been sent there and so the king of Wagadou came out in person to meet Sundiata and his troops. He gave Sundiata half of his cavalry and blessed the weapons. Then Manding Bory said to his brother, "Djata, do you think yourself able to face Soumaoro now?"

"No matter how small a forest may be, you can always find there sufficient fibers to tie up a man. Numbers mean nothing; it is worth that counts. With my cavalry

[4] Sundiata.

I shall clear myself a path to Mali."

Djata gave out his orders. They would head south, skirting Soumaoro's kingdom. The first objective to be reached was Tabon, the iron-gated town in the midst of the mountains, for Sundiata had promised Fran Kamara that he would pass by Tabon before returning to Mali. He hoped to find that his childhood companion had become king. It was a forced march and during the halts the divines, Singbin Mara Cissé and Mandjan Bérété, related to Sundiata the history of Alexander the Great[5] and several other heroes, but of all of them Sundiata preferred Alexander, the king of gold and silver, who crossed the world from west to east. He wanted to outdo his prototype both in the extent of his territory and the wealth of his treasury. . . .

In the evening, after a long day's march, Sundiata arrived at the head of the great valley which led to Tabon. The valley was quite black with men, for Sosso Balla had deployed his men everywhere in the valley, and some were positioned on the heights which dominated the way through. When Djata saw the layout of Sosso Balla's men he turned to his generals laughing.

"Why are you laughing, brother, you can see that the road is blocked."

"Yes, but no mere infantrymen can halt my course towards Mali," replied Sundiata.

The troops stopped. All the war chiefs were of the opinion that they should wait until the next day to give battle because, they said, the men were tired.

"The battle will not last long," said Sundiata, "and the men will have time to rest. We must not allow Soumaoro the time to attack Tabon."

Sundiata was immovable, so the orders were given and the war drums began to beat. On his proud horse Sundiata turned to right and left in front of his troops. He entrusted the rearguard, composed of a part of the Wagadou cavalry, to his younger brother, Manding Bory. Having drawn his sword, Sundiata led the charge, shouting his war cry.

The Sossos were surprised by this sudden attack for they all thought that the battle would be joined the next day. The lightning that flashes across the sky is slower, the thunderbolts less frightening and floodwaters less surprising than Sundiata swooping down on Sosso Balla and his smiths.[6] In a trice, Sundiata was in the middle of the Sossos like a lion in the sheepfold. The Sossos, trampled under the hooves of his fiery charger, cried out. When he turned to the right the smiths of Soumaoro fell in their tens, and when he turned to the left his sword made heads fall as when someone shakes a tree of ripe fruit. The horsemen of Mema wrought a frightful slaughter and their long lances pierced flesh like a knife sunk into a paw-paw.[7] Charging ever forwards, Sundiata looked for

100

110

120

130

140

150

Sosso Balla; he caught sight of him and like a lion bounded towards the son of Soumaoro, his sword held aloft. His arm came sweeping down but at that moment a Sosso warrior came between Djata and Sosso Balla and was sliced like a calabash.[8] Sosso Balla did not wait and disappeared from amidst his smiths. Seeing their chief in flight, the Sossos gave way and fell into a terrible rout. Before the sun disappeared behind the mountains there were only Djata and his men left in the valley.

160

. . . .

The festival began. The musicians of all the countries were there. Each people in turn came forward to the dais under Sundiata's impassive gaze. Then the war dances began. The sofas[9] of all the countries had lined themselves up in six ranks amid a great clatter of bows and spears knocking together. The war chiefs were on horseback. The warriors faced the enormous dais and at a signal from Balla Fasséké, the musicians, massed on the right of the dais, struck up. The heavy war drums thundered, the bolons[10] gave off muted notes while the griot's voice gave the throng the pitch for the "Hymn to the Bow."[11] The spearmen, advancing like hyenas in the night held their spears above their heads; the archers of Wagadou and Tabon,[12] walking with a noiseless tread, seemed to be lying in ambush behind bushes. They rose suddenly to their feet and let fly their arrows at imaginary enemies. In front of the great dais the Kéké-Tigui, or war chiefs, made their horses perform dance steps under the eyes of the Mansa.[13] The horses whinnied and reared, then, overmastered by the spurs, knelt, got up and cut little capers, or else scraped the ground with their hooves.

170

180

The rapturous people shouted the "Hymn to the Bow" and clapped their hands. The sweating bodies of the warriors glistened in the sun while the exhausting rhythm of the tam-tams[14] wrenched from them shrill cries. But presently they made way for the cavalry, beloved by Djata. The horsemen of Mema threw their swords in the air and caught them in flight, uttering mighty shouts. A smile of contentment took shape on Sundiata's lips, for he was happy to see his cavalry maneuver with so much skill. . . .

190

. . . .

After a year Sundiata held a new assembly at Niani, but this one was the assembly of dignitaries and kings of the empire. The kings and notables of all the tribes came to Niani. The kings spoke of their administration and the dignitaries talked of their kings. Fakoli, the nephew of Soumaoro, having proved himself too independent, had to flee to evade the Mansa's anger. His lands were confiscated and the taxes of Sosso were paid directly

---

[5] In Mali tradition, it is said that Alexander was the second great conqueror and Sundiata the seventh and last.

[6] Metalsmiths, within the clan, a powerful caste of men who were noted as makers of weapons and sorcerers or soothsayers.

[7] Papaya.

[8] The common bottle gourd.

[9] Sudanese infantrymen or soldiers.

[10] Large harps with three or four strings.

[11] A traditional song among the people of Mali.

[12] Kingdoms near Mali.

[13] Emperor.

[14] Large circular gongs.

into the granaries of Niani. In this way, every year, Sundiata gathered about him all the kings and notables; so justice prevailed everywhere, for the kings were afraid of being denounced at Niani.

Djata's justice spared nobody. He followed the very word of God. He protected the weak against the strong and people would make journeys lasting several days to come and demand justice of him. Under his sun the upright man was rewarded and the wicked one punished.

In their new-found peace the villages knew prosperity again, for with Sundiata happiness had come into everyone's home. Vast fields of millet, rice, cotton, indigo and fonio[15] surrounded the villages. Whoever worked always had something to live on. Each year long caravans carried the taxes in kind[16] to Niani. You could go from village to village without fearing brigands. A thief would have his right hand chopped off and if he stole again he would be put to the sword.

New villages and new towns sprang up in Mali and elsewhere. "Dyulas," or traders, became numerous and during the reign of Sundiata the world knew happiness.

There are some kings who are powerful through their military strength. Everybody trembles before them, but when they die nothing but ill is spoken of them. Others do neither good nor ill and when they die they are forgotten. Others are feared because they have power, but they know how to use it and they are loved because they love justice. Sundiata belonged to this group. He was feared, but loved as well. He was the father of Mali and gave the world peace. After him the world has not seen a greater conqueror, for he was the seventh and last conqueror. He had made the capital of an empire out of his father's village, and Niani became the navel of the earth. In the most distant lands Niani was talked of and foreigners said, "Travelers from Mali can tell lies with impunity," for Mali was a remote country for many peoples.

The griots, fine talkers that they were, used to boast of Niani and Mali saying: "If you want salt, go to Niani, for Niani is the camping place of the Sahel[17] caravans. If you want gold, go to Niani, for Bouré, Bambougou and Wagadou work for Niani. If you want fine cloth, go to Niani, for the Mecca road passes by Niani. If you want fish, go to Niani, for it is there that the fishermen of Maouti and Djenné come to sell their catches. If you want meat, go to Niani, the country of the great hunters, and the land of the ox and the sheep. If you want to see an army, go to Niani, for it is there that the united forces of Mali are to be found. If you want to see a great king, go to Niani, for it is there that the son of Sogolon lives, the man with two names."

This is what the masters of the spoken word used to sing. . . .

How many piled-up ruins, how much buried splendor! But all the deeds I have spoken of took place long ago

and they all had Mali as their background. Kings have succeeded kings, but Mali has always remained the same.

Mali keeps its secrets jealously. There are things which the uninitiated will never know, for the griots, their depositaries, will never betray them. Maghan Sundiata, the last conqueror on earth, lies not far from Niani-Niani at Balandougou, the weir town.

After him many kings and many Mansas reigned over Mali and other towns sprang up and disappeared. Hajji Mansa Moussa, of illustrious memory, beloved of God, built houses at Mecca for pilgrims coming from Mali, but the towns which he founded have all disappeared, Karanina, Bouroun-Kouna—nothing more remains of these towns. Other kings carried Mali far beyond Djata's frontiers, for example Mansa Samanka and Fadima Moussa, but none of them came near Djata.

Maghan Sundiata was unique. In his own time no one equaled him and after him no one had the ambition to surpass him. He left his mark on Mali for all time and his taboos still guide men in their conduct.

Mali is eternal. To convince yourself of what I have said go to Mali.

. . . .

Men of today, how small you are beside your ancestors, and small in mind too, for you have trouble in grasping the meaning of my words. Sundiata rests near Niani-Niani, but his spirit lives on and today the Keitas still come and bow before the stone under which lies the father of Mali.

To acquire my knowledge I have journeyed all round Mali. At Kita I saw the mountain where the lake of holy water sleeps; at Segou, I learnt the history of the kings of Do and Kri; at Fadama, in Hamana, I heard the Kondé griots relate how the Keitas, Kondés and Kamaras conquered Wouroula. At Keyla, the village of the great masters, I learnt the origins of Mali and the art of speaking. Everywhere I was able to see and understand what my masters were teaching me, but between their hands I took an oath to teach only what is to be taught and to conceal what is to be kept concealed.

— **Q** **How does Sundiata compare with other epic heroes: Gilgamesh, Achilles, and Roland?**

— **Q** **What does the *griot* mean by the statement "the future springs from the past"?**

As lines 161–191 of this excerpt suggest, in African ritual celebration, the arts of music, dance, poetry, and decorative display formed a synthesis that mirrored shared spiritual and communal values. Similarly, within the African community, the telling of stories was a group enterprise and an expression of social unity. Seated around the communal fire, the members of the tribe recited tales serially and from memory. Traditionally, such tales were told only after sundown, because, as favored entertainments, they might otherwise distract the group from daily labor.

---

[15] A crabgrass with seeds that are used as a cereal.
[16] In produce or goods instead of money.
[17] A region of the Sudan bordering the Sahara.

African Myths and Proverbs

Among the many genres of African literature was the mythical tale that accounted for the origins of the universe, of the natural forces, and of the community. African creation myths—like those of the Hebrews, Egyptians, and Mesopotamians—explained the beginnings of the world, the creation of human beings, and the workings of nature, while still other myths dealt with the origin of death. The following brief examples, which come from three different parts of Africa, represent only a sampling of the many African tales that explain how death came into the world.

READING 18.2 Three African Myths on the Origin of Death

1

In the beginning, Nzambi slid down to earth on a rainbow, and there created the animals and the trees. After this he also created a man and a woman, and he told them to marry and have children. Nzambi imposed only one prohibition upon men, that they should not sleep when the moon was up. If they disobeyed this command, they would be punished with death. When the first man had become old and had poor eyesight, it once happened that the moon was veiled behind the clouds, so that he could not see it shine. He went to sleep and died in his sleep. Since then all men have died, because they are unable to keep awake when the moon is up.

(Lunda)

2

One day God asked the first human couple who then lived in heaven what kind of death they wanted, that of the moon or that of the banana. Because the couple wondered in dismay about the implications of the two modes of death, God explained to them: the banana puts forth shoots which take its place, and the moon itself comes back to life. The couple considered for a long time before they made their choice. If they elected to be childless they would avoid death, but they would also be very lonely, would themselves be forced to carry out all the work, and would not have anybody to work and strive for. Therefore they prayed to God for children, well aware of the consequences of their choice. And their prayer was granted. Since that time man's sojourn is short on this earth.

(Madagascar)

3

Formerly men had no fire but ate all their food raw. At that time they did not need to die for when they became old God made them young again. One day they decided to beg God for fire. They sent a messenger to God to convey their request. God replied to the messenger that he would give him fire if he was prepared to die.

The man took the fire from God, but ever since then all men must die.

(Darasa, Gada)

Q **What aspects of ancient African culture do these myths reflect?**

Q **What do these myths have in common with those in Reading 0.1?**

These myths offer valuable insights into ancient African culture. The directness with which the characters in these tales address the gods suggests the basic intimacy between Africans and the spirit world. Moreover, the tales stress human fallibility (as in the disastrous blunder of the nearly blind "first man"), rather than (as in most Christian literature) human sinfulness. They describe a gentle and casual, rather than a forbidding and patriarchal, relationship between divine and human realms. Finally, as the second myth suggests, Africans placed great value on their children; as was the case in most agricultural societies, children were prized as helpers and as perpetuators of tradition. One African proverb reads, "There is no wealth where there are no children." Another asserts, "Children are the wisdom of the nation."

Africans invented a huge and colorful literature of tales, proverbs, and riddles. The animal tale explains why certain creatures look and act as they do. In the trickster tale, a small animal, such as a hare or spider, outwits a larger one, such as a hyena or elephant. Explanatory tales treat such themes as "Why some people are good-looking" and "Why one never tells a woman the truth." African tales, proverbs, and riddles—often playfully swapped—functioned as sources of instruction and entertainment. Like most forms of African expression, they were characterized by animism: consider, for instance, the riddle "who goes down the street and passes the king's house without greeting the king?" The answer is "rainwater." Many proverbs call attention to the immutability of nature's laws. One states, "When it rains, the roof always drips in the same way." Africans used their riddles and proverbs to help teach moral values and even to litigate tribal disputes.

African Poetry

In ancient Africa, religious rituals and rites of passage featured various kinds of chant. Performed by shamans and priests, but also by nonprofessionals, and often integrated with mime and dance, the chant created a unified texture not unlike that of modern rap and Afro-pop music. Poets addressed the fragility of human life, celebrated the transition from one stage of growth to another, honored the links between the living and the dead, praised heroes and rulers, and recounted the experiences of everyday life. African poetry does not share the satiric thrust of Roman verse, the erotic mood of Indian poetry, the intimate tone of the Petrarchan or Shakespearean sonnet, or the reclusive spirit of Chinese verse; it is, rather, a frank and intensely personal form of vocal music.

African poetry is generally characterized by strong percussive qualities, by **anaphora** (the repetition of a word or words at the beginning of two or more lines), and by tonal patterns that—much like Chinese poetry—are based on voice inflections. Repetition of key phrases and **call-and-response** "conversations" between narrator and listeners add texture to oral performance. The rhythmic energy and raw vitality of African poetry set it apart from most other kinds of world poetry, including Chinese, which seems controlled and intellectualized by comparison. The poem of praise for the *oba* of Benin, reproduced in Reading 18.3, throbs with rhythms that invite accompanying drumbeats or hand-clapping of the kind familiar to us in gospel singing and contemporary rock music.

African poetry is also notable for its inventive similes and metaphors. In the Yoruba poem "The God of War," warfare is likened to a needle "that pricks at both ends," a vivid image of the perils of combat—compare the plain-spoken ode "On Civil War" by the Roman poet Horace (see chapter 6). And in the "Song for the Sun," the Hottentot poet invents the memorable image of God collecting the stars and piling them into a basket "like a woman who collects lizards and piles them into her pot."

READING 18.3 Selections from African Poetry

Song for the Sun that Disappeared behind the Rainclouds

The fire darkens, the wood turns black.	1
The flame extinguishes, misfortune upon us.	
God sets out in search of the sun.	
The rainbow sparkles in his hand,	
the bow of the divine hunter.	5
He has heard the lamentations of his children.	
He walks along the milky way, he collects the stars.	
With quick arms he piles them into a basket	
piles them up with quick arms	
like a woman who collects lizards	10
and piles them into her pot, piles them up	
until the basket overflows with light.	

(Hottentot)

Longing for Death

I have been singing, singing I have cried bitterly	1
I'm on my way.	
How large this world!	
Let the ferryman bring his boat	
on the day of my death.	5
I'll wave with my left hand,	
I'm on my way.	
I'm on my way,	
the boat of death is rocking near,	
I'm on my way,	10
I who have sung you many songs.	

(Ewe)

The Oba of Benin

He who knows not the Oba	1
let me show him.	
He has mounted the throne,	
he has piled a throne upon a throne.	

Plentiful as grains of sand on the earth	5
are those in front of him.	
Plentiful as grains of sand on the earth	
are those behind him.	
There are two thousand people	
to fan him.	10
He who owns you	
is among you here.	
He who owns you	
has piled a throne upon a throne.	
He has lived to do it this year;	15
even so he will live to do it again.	

(Bini)

The God of War

He kills on the right and destroys on the left.	1
He kills on the left and destroys on the right.	
He kills suddenly in the house and suddenly in the field.	
He kills the child with the iron with which it plays.	
He kills in silence.	5
He kills the thief and the owner of the stolen goods.	
He kills the owner of the slave—and the slave runs away.	
He kills the owner of the house—and paints the hearth with his blood.	
He is the needle that pricks at both ends.	
He has water but he washes with blood.	10

(Yoruba)

The Poor Man

The poor man knows not how to eat with the rich man.	1
When they eat fish, he eats the head.	
Invite a poor man and he rushes in	
licking his lips and upsetting the plates.	
The poor man has no manners, he comes along	5
with the blood of lice under his nails.	
The face of the poor man is lined	
from the hunger and thirst in his belly.	
Poverty is no state for any mortal man.	
It makes him a beast to be fed on grass.	10
Poverty is unjust. If it befalls a man,	
though he is nobly born, he has no power with God.	

(Swahili)

A Baby is a European

A baby is a European	1
he does not eat our food:	
he drinks from his own water pot.	
A baby is a European	
he does not speak our tongue:	5
he is cross when the mother understands him not.	
A baby is a European	
he cares very little for others;	
he forces his will upon his parents.	

A baby is a European   10
he is always very sensitive:
the slightest scratch on his skin results in an ulcer.

(Ewe)

The Moon

The moon lights the earth   1
it lights the earth but still
the night must remain the night.
The night cannot be like the day.
The moon cannot dry our washing.   5
Just like a woman cannot be a man
just like black can never be white.

(Soussou)

Q **Based on these poems, how might one describe the African's response to nature? To the community? To European culture?**

African Music and Dance

African music shares the vigorous rhythms of poetry and dance. In texture, it consists of a single line of melody without harmony. As with most African dialects, where pitch is important in conveying meaning, variations of musical effect derive from tonal inflection and timbre. The essentially communal spirit of African culture is reflected in the use of call-and-response chants similar to those of African poetry. The most distinctive characteristic of African music, however, is its polyrhythmic structure. A single piece of music may simultaneously engage five to ten

🎼 See Music Listening Selections at end of chapter.

different rhythms, many of which are repeated over and over. African dance, also communally performed, shares the distinctively dense polyrhythmic qualities of African music. The practice of playing "against" or "off" the main beat provided by the instruments is typical of much West African music and is preserved in the "off-beat" patterns of early modern jazz (see chapter 36).

A wide variety of percussion instruments, including various types of drum and rattle, is used in the performance of African ritual (Figure **18.7**). Also popular are the *balafo* (a type of xylophone), the *bolon* or *kora* (a large harp), and the *sansa* (an instrument consisting of a number of metal tongues attached to a small wooden soundboard). The last two of these instruments, used to accompany storytelling, were believed to contain such potent supernatural power that they were considered dangerous and were outlawed among some African tribes, except for use by *griots*. Africa was the place of origin of the banjo, which may have been the only musical instrument permitted on the slave ships that traveled across the Atlantic in the sixteenth century (bells, drums, and other instruments were forbidden). African culture is notably musical, and the dynamic convergence of poetry, dance, and music generates a singularly dramatic experience.

The African Mask

African masks and headdresses were part of the amalgam of poetry, music, and dance that served a ceremonial or ritual event. The mask was usually part of a larger costume (made of cloth or fiber) that covered the body (see Figure 18.7). It functioned not simply to disguise the wearer's identity, but to channel the spirit of an animal, god, or ancestor. The masker embodied the spirit of the being he

Figure 18.7 Bambara ritual Chi Wara dance, Mali.

The Chi Wara headdress pictured in Figure **18.8** dates from the nineteenth century, but it belongs to a much older tradition honoring Mali's ancestral founders: its predecessors consisted of a wickerwork cap, antelope horns, and a leather face-mask. African sculpture had a major impact on European art of the early twentieth century, when numerous examples of this genre were introduced into Europe (see chapter 31). The Spanish artist Pablo Picasso was among the first to recognize the aesthetic power of African masks, which he referred to as "magical objects." To this day, the African legacy continues to inspire the creative arts. In the sculpture entitled *Speedster Tji Wara* (Figure **18.9**), the African-American artist Willie Cole (b. 1955) gives the Chi Wara headdress a new, Postmodern identity. Assembling scavenged bicycle parts, Cole recasts the Mali totem as a symbol of popular urban culture.

Figure 18.8 Bambara antelope headpiece, from Mali, nineteenth century, based on earlier models. Wood, height 35¾ × 15¾ in.

Figure 18.9 WILLIE COLE, *Speedster Tji Wara*, 2002. Bicycle parts, 3 ft. 10½ in. × 1 ft. 3 in.

---

represented. By the transformative power of the mask, he became the agent of the supernatural. Masked dancers took part in rituals of exorcism, initiation, purification, and burial. They functioned regularly in ceremonies that marked the transition from one stage of being to another. Such ceremonies might feature a **totem**, the heraldic emblem of a specific family or clan.

The people of Mali have long regarded the antelope as their mythical ancestor, Chi Wara, who taught humankind how to cultivate the land. Chi Wara dance rituals incorporate movements that imitate those of the antelope (see Figure 18.7). The performers wear headdresses with huge

Figure 18.10 Songe mask, from Zaire, nineteenth century, based on earlier models. Wood and paint, height 17 in.

crests that combine the features of the antelope, the anteater, and local birds (see Figure 18.8). In these magnificently carved headpieces, the triangular head of the antelope is repeated in the chevron patterns of the neck and the zigzags of the mane. The Chi Wara totem (which has become the logo for modern Mali's national airline) epitomizes the African taste for expressive simplification and geometric design.

While there exists a wide variety of mask types and styles, most African masks do not share the naturalism of the metal-cast and terracotta portraits from Ife and Benin; rather, they reflect a tradition of expressive abstraction. A case in point is the Songe mask from Zaire in Central Africa (Figure 18.10). Worn at ceremonies for the death or installation of a king, its facial distortions and scarification seem to compress emotion and energy. A comparison of this mask with that of the portrait of an Ife *oba* (see Figure 18.5) reminds us that African artists developed a wide variety of styles ranging from idealized portraiture to stylized abstraction. The object that channeled spiritual energy clearly required a style more powerful than that which recreated the optical illusion of the natural world. Feathers, shells, teeth, beads, raffia, hair, and other materials were often added to a mask to enhance its vital powers. The color red might be used to symbolize danger, blood, or power; black suggested chaos and evil; and white represented death.

Throughout world history, the religious rites and festivals of numerous cultures—from the Dionysian festivals of ancient Greece to the modern-day Catholic Mardi Gras—have involved the act of masking, usually as part of a larger ceremonial performance that includes music and dance. Among the African-American Mardi Gras "Indians" of New Orleans, such traditions prevail to this day.

African Sculpture

Over the course of centuries, African artisans mastered a wide variety of media. The techniques of terracotta modeling, ivory carving, and metal casting were well known to Africans before the end of the first millennium B.C.E. Works in these enduring media seem to have been produced mainly in the western and southern portions of Africa. The greater part of African sculpture was executed, however, in the less durable medium of wood. Using axes, knives, and chisels, professional sculptors—almost exclusively male—carved images from green or semidry timber. Unlike works in other media, few examples of Africa's wood sculpture survived the sixteenth century. Most were destroyed or damaged by Africa's corrosive climate, by termites, or by Muslims and Christians who deemed these objects sacrilegious or idolatrous. Among some African peoples, masks of soft wood seem to have been discarded after ritual use. Nevertheless, eleventh-century Arab chronicles confirm the existence of a rich native tradition of wood sculpture; this tradition is described as well by the Portuguese in the sixteenth century.

African figural sculpture served many functions: grave figures were designed

Figure 18.12 Standing male figure (*nkisi nkondi*, Mangaaka type), nineteenth century. Wood, iron, raffia, pigment, kaolin, and red camwood (tukula), 44 × 15⅝ × 1⅜ in. Condemned as pagan fetishes, such sculptures were destroyed by Christian missionaries following the colonial invasion of the Congo. An English trader in this area between 1607 and 1610 described similar figures; however, in that there is no mention of the use of nails, some scholars argue that this aspect of the genre was influenced by Christian representations of the Crucifixion.

Figure 18.11 Bamana people, *Mother and Child*, Bougouni-Dioila area, Mali, fifteenth to twentieth century. Wood, height 48⅝ in. Like the trunks of the trees from which they were carved, African sculptures like this one are rigid and tubular. Bamana figures often wear tokens of their physical powers, such as the knife strapped to this woman's left arm, and the amulets on her hat.

to watch over the dead, while fertility images were invoked to promote pregnancy or assist in childbirth; still other sculptures served in rituals of divination and healing. In style, such objects range from realistic to abstract. The 4-foot-tall wooden sculpture of a mother and child was one of a group of sculptures displayed by the Bamana people at annual ceremonies associated with fertility and childbirth (Figure **18.11**). The woman's full breasts, which invert the shape of her conical cap, point down toward the child she tenderly embraces.

African Wood Sculpture: Text and Context

The fact that almost all surviving examples of African wood sculpture date from the nineteenth and twentieth centuries gives rise to some important questions. Should African art executed during the early modern era be considered in the context of modern Africa, or does such art, by its adherence to older traditions and practices, reflect the values of an earlier culture? How might we interpret the relationship of text (an African sculpture) to context (a specific culture or time period) if we are dealing with a modern object that perpetuates premodern traditions and practices?

The fact that the literature of both eleventh-century Muslims and sixteenth-century Portuguese describes Africa's amazing wood sculptures confirms the longevity of this tradition. Such records suggest that many types of nineteenth- and twentieth-century

African sculpture—such as the wooden mask and the *nkisi*—have histories that go back centuries before foreign intervention. More recently created, they nevertheless embody age-old traditions, both in their fabrication and in their function.

Little effort was made to preserve African sculptures as aesthetic objects prior to the development of **ethnography** in late nineteenth-century Europe (see chapter 31). In our own day, however, such objects have become commercialized. Attractive to art dealers, tourists, and collectors, they are often produced and marketed by Africans who have long since discontinued the ritual practices to which their ancestors (and the sculptures themselves) were bound. Given these considerations, to what cultural context does "modern" African art belong?

Another type of African sculpture, the *nkisi*, describes a type of power object produced throughout the Congo basin in Central Africa (Figure **18.12**). Employed in rituals designed to channel spiritual energy, some *nkisi* were used to heal the sick, while others served functions ranging from sealing agreements to warding off evil spirits. On behalf of a client, a diviner or priest prepared "medicinal" ingredients (possibly hair or nail clippings) that were placed inside the *nkisi* or tied to it in packets. With ritual oversight, the client drove a nail or sharp object into the *nkisi* to activate its power. Such objects were among the first to be identified by sixteenth-century Europeans, who referred to them as "idols" and "**fetishes**" (a word derived from the Portuguese *feiticoa*, meaning "charm" or "spell"), that is, objects believed to have magical powers.

African Architecture

As with the sculpture of pre-colonial Africa, little survives of its native architecture, and that which does suggests a wide diversity of structural forms. A survey of traditional African house forms lists almost three dozen different types of structure. Construction materials consist of mud, stones, and brushwood, or adobe brick—a sun-dried mixture of clay and straw. Outside of Benin and a few urban centers, Africans seem to have had little need for monumental religious or administrative buildings. But at the ancient trade center of Zimbabwe (the name means "House of Stone"), in South Central Africa, where a powerful kingdom developed before the year 1000, the remains of huge stone walls and towers, constructed without mortar, indicate the presence of a royal residence or palace complex—the largest structures in Africa after the pyramids.

Africa's Muslim-dominated cities display some of the most visually striking structures in the history of world architecture. The adobe mosques of Mali, for instance,

with their organic contours, bulbous towers, and conical finials (native symbols of fertility), resemble fantastic sand castles (see Figure 18.4). They have proved to be almost as impermanent: some have been rebuilt (and replastered) continuously since the twelfth century. Their walls and towers bristle with sticks or wooden beams that provide a permanent scaffolding for restoration. African mosques are testimonials to the fusion of Muslim, Asian, and local ancestral traditions. Their domical contours, similar to the temple-shrines and burial mounds of early cultures, recall the primordial mountain and the womb—sites of spiritual renewal. Africa's vernacular architecture calls to mind the sacred link between Mother Earth and the human community. Even the wooden pickets (see Figure 18.4) that serve as scaffolding have symbolic significance: used at Bambara initiation ceremonies and often buried with the dead, such tree branches are symbols of rebirth and regeneration.

Cross-Cultural Encounter

Ibn Battuta in West Africa

Islam was present in West Africa from at least the eighth century, and the religion increased in influence as Muslims came to dominate trans-Saharan trade. Occasional efforts to spread Islam by force were generally unsuccessful, yet the Islamization of the Sudan ultimately succeeded as the result of the peaceful and prosperous activities of Muslim merchants, administrators, and scholars. Mali's most famous ruler, Mansa ("King") Musa (1312–1337), came to symbolize the largesse of the African Muslim elite when, during his *hajj* of 1324, he and his retinue scattered large amounts of gold from Mali to Mecca. West African rulers like Musa patronized the arts, commissioned the construction of mosques, and encouraged conversion to Islam.

Nowhere in the literature of the age are the realities of cross-cultural encounter so well expressed as in the journal of the fourteenth-century Muslim traveler–scholar Ibn Battuta (1304–1369). Born into an upper-class Muslim family in the North African city of Tangier, Battuta was educated in law and Arabic literature before he made the first of his seven pilgrimages in 1325. Over the course of his lifetime, this inveterate tourist journeyed on foot or by camel caravan some 75,000 miles, visiting parts of China, Indonesia, Persia, India, Burma, Spain, Arabia, Russia, Asia Minor, Egypt, and East and West Africa. Although his initial motives for travel were religious, he shared with other itinerant Muslim scholars an interest in Islamic law and a curiosity concerning the customs of Muslim communities throughout the world. In 1354, Battuta narrated the history of his travels, including his two-year trip from Morocco to Mali—his last recorded journey—to a professional scribe who recorded it in a *ribla* ("book of travels"). That portion of the *ribla* that recounts Battuta's visit to Mali is the only existing eyewitness account of the kingdom at the height of its power. It documents Battuta's keen powers of observation and reveals his efforts to evaluate social and cultural practices that differed sharply from his own.

READING 18.4 From Ibn Battuta's *Book of Travels* (1354)

We reached the city of Īwālātan[1] at the beginning   1
of the month of Rabi'I[2] after a journey of two full months
from Sijilmāsa. It is the first district of the country of the
Blacks. . . .
    When we arrived the merchants deposited their goods
in an open space and the Blacks took responsibility for
them. The merchants went to the Farbā who was sitting
on a rug under a shelter; his officials were in front of him
with spears and bows in their hands. The Massūfa[3]
notables were behind him. The merchants stood in front   10
of him and he spoke to them through an interpreter as a
sign of his contempt for them, although they were close
to him. At this I was sorry I had come to their country,
because of their bad manners and contempt for white
people. I made for the house of the Ibn Baddā', a kind
man of Salā to whom I had written asking him to let[4] a
house to me, which he did. . . .
    . . . I stayed in Īwālātan about fifty days. Its people
treated me with respect and gave me hospitality. Among
them were the qāḍī[5] of the town Muḥammad b. 'Abdallāh   20
b. Yanūmar, and his brother the jurist and professor
Yahyā. The town of Īwālātan is extremely hot. There are a
few small palms and they sow melons in their shade.
Water comes from underground sources. Mutton is
plentiful. Their clothes are of fine quality and Egyptian

origin. Most of the inhabitants belong to the Massūfa.
The women are of outstanding beauty and are more
highly regarded than the men.
    Conditions among these people are remarkable and
their life style is strange. The men have no jealousy. No   30
one takes his name from his father, but from his maternal
uncle. Sons do not inherit, only sister's sons![6] This is
something I have seen nowhere in the world except
among the infidel Indians of al-Mulāibar. Nevertheless
these people are Muslims. They are strict in observing the
prayers, studying the religious law, and memorizing the
Qur'ān. Their women have no shame before men and do
not veil themselves, yet they are punctilious about their
prayers. Anyone who wants to take a wife among them
does so, but they do not travel with their husbands, and   40
even if one of them wished to, her family would prevent
her. Women there have friends and companions among
men outside the prohibited degrees for marriage, and in
the same way men have women friends in the same
category. A man goes into his house, finds his wife with
her man friend, and does not disapprove.
    One day I called upon the qāḍī at Īwālātan after he had
given permission for me to enter. I found him with a
young and exceptionally beautiful woman. When I saw her
I hesitated and was going to go back, but she laughed at   50
me and showed no embarrassment. The qāḍī said to me:
"Why are you turning back? She is my friend." I was
astonished at them, for he was a jurist and a Ḥājj.[7]
I learnt that he had asked the Sultan's permission to go on
pilgrimage that year with his female companion. I do not
know whether this was the one or not, but permission was
not given.
    One day I called on Abū Muḥammad Yandakān
al-Massūfi, in whose company we had arrived, and found
him sitting on a rug. In the middle of the room was a   60
canopied couch and upon it was a woman with a man
sitting and talking together. I said to him: "Who is this
woman?" He said: "She is my wife." I said: "What about
the man who is with her?" He said: "He is her friend."
I said: "Are you happy about this, you who have lived in
our country and know the content of the religious law?"
He said: "The companionship of women and men among
us is a good thing and an agreeable practice, which
causes no suspicion; they are not like the women of your
country." I was astonished at his silliness. I left him and   70
did not visit him again. Afterwards he invited me a
number of times but I did not accept. . . .
    The Blacks are the most respectful of people to their
king and abase themselves most before him. . . . If he
summons one of them at his session in the cupola we
have mentioned, the man summoned removes his robe
and puts on a shabby one, takes off his turban, puts on a
dirty skull-cap and goes in with his robe and his trousers
lifted half way to his knees. He comes forward humbly
and abjectly, and strikes the ground hard with his   80

---

[1] Near Timbuktu in Mali.
[2] April 1352.
[3] A Berber people of the western Sahara.
[4] Rent.
[5] Muslim judges.

[6] In the matrilineal sub-Saharan tribes, the mother's brother is considered the most important male.
[7] One who has made the pilgrimage to Mecca.

elbows. He stands as if he were prostrating himself in prayer, and hears what the Sultan says like this. If one of them speaks to the Sultan and he answers him, he takes his robe off his back, and throws dust on his head and back like someone making his ablutions with water. I was astonished that they did not blind themselves.

When the Sultan makes a speech in his audience those present take off their turbans from their heads and listen in silence. Sometimes one of them stands before him, recounts what he has done for his service, and says: "On such and such a day I did such and such, and I killed so and so on such and such a day." Those who know vouch for the truth of that and he does it in this way. One of them draws the string of his bow, then lets it go as he would do if he were shooting. If the Sultan says to him: "You are right" or thanks him, he takes off his robe and pours dust on himself. That is good manners among them. . . .

Among their good practices are their avoidance of injustice; there is no people more averse to it, and their Sultan does not allow anyone to practice it in any measure; the universal security in their country, for neither the traveler nor the resident there has to fear thieves or bandits; they do not interfere with the property of white men who die in their country, even if it amounts to vast sums; they just leave it in the hands of a trustworthy white man until whoever is entitled to it takes possession of it; their punctiliousness in praying, their perseverance in joining the congregation, and in compelling their children to do so; if a man does not come early to the mosque he will not find a place to pray because of the dense crowd; it is customary for each man to send his servant with his prayer-mat to spread it out in a place reserved for him until he goes to the mosque himself; their prayer-mats are made of the leaves of a tree like the date-palm, but which has no fruit. They dress in clean white clothes on Fridays; if one of them has only a threadbare shirt he washes it and cleans it and wears it for prayer on Friday. They pay great attention to memorizing the Holy Qur'ān. If their children appear to be backward in learning it they put shackles on them and do not remove them till they learn it. I called on the qāḍī on the Feast Day. His children were in shackles. I said to him: "Are you not going to free them?" He said: "Not till they learn the Qur'ān by heart." One day I passed by a handsome youth, who was very well dressed, with a heavy shackle on his foot. I said to the person with me: "What has he done? Has he killed someone?" The youth understood what I said and laughed. I was told: "He has been shackled to make him memorize the Qur'ān."

Among their bad practices are that the women servants, slave-girls, and young daughters appear naked before people, exposing their genitals. I used to see many like this in Ramaḍān,[8] for it is customary for the fararīs[9] to break the fast in the Sultan's palace, where their food is brought to them by twenty or more slave-girls, who are naked. Women who come before the Sultan are naked and unveiled, and so are his daughters. On the night of the twenty-seventh of Ramaḍān I have seen about a hundred naked slave-girls come out of his palace with food; with them were two daughters of the Sultan with full breasts and they too had no veil. They put dust and ashes on their heads as a matter of good manners. There is the clowning we have described when poets recite their works. Many of them eat carrion, dogs, and donkeys.[10]

Q What aspects of African life did Ibn Battuta find congenial? Which did he find most unusual?

The Europeans in Africa

European commercial activity in Africa was the product of the quest for new sea routes to the East, and for control of the markets in gold, salt, and slaves. For thousands of years, slavery in Africa had been no different from that which had prevailed elsewhere in the ancient world: free people normally became slaves as captives of war, debtors, or convicted criminals. They made up a class of men and women used, for the most part, as laborers. Although some rose to high positions within society or were able to purchase their freedom, most were regarded as chattel, that is, property to be bought and sold. In the economies of ancient Mesopotamia, Greece, and Rome, as in Africa, slave-holding and slave-trading enhanced one's wealth and social status. With the arrival of Islam in North Africa, the slave trade expanded greatly. During the ninth century, East Africans (known as the Zanj) were brought to Basra (in present-day Iraq) to work as slaves in the salt mines. Their bitter fourteen-year revolt (839–883) was the first and only major uprising against a Muslim caliphate. Scholars estimate that the number of African slaves transported to foreign lands in the years between 750 and 1500 may have exceeded ten million.

During the sixteenth century, Portugal intruded upon the well-established Muslim-dominated trans-Saharan commercial slave trade. The Portuguese slave trade in West Africa, the Congo, and elsewhere developed according to the pattern that had already been established by Muslim traders: that is, in agreement with local African leaders who reaped profits from the sale of victims of war or raids on neighboring African territories. Alarmed at the damage caused by Portuguese merchants who (he claimed) were depopulating the Kingdom of Congo by trafficking slaves, King Afonso I of Congo (1456–1543) sent official letters of protest to the kings of Portugal. He welcomed Christian missionaries (Congo had made Christianity its state religion), but condemned the trade in human chattel. The *obas* of Benin accommodated the Portuguese, establishing a royal monopoly over trade in ivory, cloth, and pepper. Benin prohibited the exportation of male slaves, while importing and reselling slaves purchased by Europeans elsewhere in West Africa.

---

[8] The Muslim month of fasting; the daily fast ends at sunset.
[9] Chiefs.

[10] The Qur'an forbids the eating of unclean meat.

By the year 1500, the Portuguese controlled the flow of both gold and slaves to Europe. Transatlantic slave trade commenced in 1551, when the Portuguese began to ship thousands of slaves from Africa to work in the sugar plantations of Brazil, a "New World" territory claimed by Portugal. European forms of slavery were more brutal and exploitative than any previously practiced in Africa: slaves shipped overseas were branded, shackled in chains like beasts, underfed, and—if they survived the ravages of dysentery and disease—conscripted into oppressive kinds of physical labor (see chapter 25).

In their relations with the African states, especially those in coastal areas, the Europeans were equally brutal. They often ignored the bonds of family and tribe, the local laws, and religious customs; they pressured Africans to adopt European language and dress and fostered economic rivalry. While in a spirit of missionary zeal and altruism they introduced Christianity and Western forms of education, they also brought ruin to some tribal kingdoms, and, in parts of Africa, they almost completely destroyed native cultural life. These activities were but a prelude to the more disastrous forms of exploitation that prevailed during the seventeenth and eighteenth centuries, when the transatlantic slave trade, now dominated by the Dutch, the French, and the English, reached massive proportions. By the mid-seventeenth century, a triangular trade route had developed: European ships carried to Africa goods that were traded for African prisoners; the latter were transported to the Americas, where they were sold or traded for goods that were then brought to Europe. The notorious "Middle Passage" of this route (Africa to the Americas) came to describe the system of forced transportation (by some estimates, fifteen to twenty million Africans) that flourished between 1450 and 1850 (see chapter 25).

Considering the repeated intrusion of outsiders over the centuries, it is remarkable that local traditions in the arts of Africa continued to flourish. Native traditions in literature and music remained intact. African metalworkers, enjoying an influx of European copper and brass, refined the techniques of metal casting that had brought them centuries of renown. Hundreds of bronze low-relief wall plaques decorated the royal palace at Benin. One shows a Portuguese warrior with a sword and trident, surrounded by *manillas* (from the Portuguese word for "bracelets"), the horseshoe-shaped metal objects that were the earliest form of currency used in West Africa (see Figure 18.1). First manufactured in the West, *manillas* were exchanged for pepper, ivory, and slaves, the primary commodities of the transatlantic trade system. Sixteenth-century carved ivories reflect a high degree of expertise, and many individual ivories record the European presence. On the crown and collar of a small ivory mask, bearded Portuguese heads alternate with symbolic mudfish, emblematic of Benin royalty, who, like these creatures, dominated (thus "ruled") both land and sea; and possibly of the foreign invaders themselves, who were perceived as semidivine creatures emerging from the sea (Figure **18.13**). A skillfully executed blend of naturalism and stylization characterizes the portrait, whose eyes and forehead scarification were originally inlaid with iron. This commanding portrait, along with some 2000 other Benin artworks, were appropriated by the British in 1897 and transported to London.

The Americas

Native American Cultures

Native cultures in the territories of North, Central, and South America began to develop at least 20,000 years ago, following nomadic migrations across a land bridge that once linked Siberia and Alaska at the Bering Strait, by way of Scandinavian ice sheets, and possibly via small boats that brought them across the Pacific (see chapter 3). During the centuries prior to the first European contact with the Americas, well over a thousand migrant groups established independent communities throughout North, South, and Middle (or Meso-) America (parts of present-day Mexico and South America (Map **18.3**). Like pre-colonial Africans, Native Americans were culturally and linguistically diverse. Individual societies shared deeply felt ethnic loyalties and an animistic view of the world as being infused with living spirits. The indigenous peoples of North America ranged culturally from the relative socioeconomic simplicity of some Pacific coast tribes to the complexity of the Iroquois town-dwellers.

Many Native American cultures produced illustrious histories, and several achieved the status of empire. In Middle

Figure 18.13 Mask, sixteenth century, Court of Benin, Nigeria. Ivory, height 9¾ in. While it is possible that the mask was used as a belt ornament, the lugs above the ears on either side of the head suggest that it was worn around the neck of the *oba*.

Map 18.3 The Americas Before 1500.

America and on the western coast of South America, villages grew into states that conquered or absorbed their rivals. Settlers of essentially tropical areas, these agricultural peoples traded only regionally and made frequent war on one another. They fashioned their tools and weapons out of wood, stone, bone, and pieces of volcanic glass. They had no draft animals and no wheeled vehicles. Although after the ninth century copper came into use in Meso-America, iron was unknown until the arrival of the Spaniards in the fifteenth century. These facts make all the more remarkable the material achievements of the Maya, Inca, and Aztec civilizations, all three of which developed into empires of considerable authority in the pre-Columbian era.

Native North American Arts: The Northwest

There is no word for "art" in any Native American language; the aesthetically compelling objects produced among Native Americans were either items of daily use or power-objects associated with ceremony and ritual. Moreover, the modern distinction between craft and fine art is nonexistent among those who practice weaving, beadwork, ceramics, and jewelry-making. The Haida folk of the Queen Charlotte Islands, near British Columbia, continue the ancient practice of raising wooden poles carved and painted with totems—heraldic symbols of social status, spiritual authority, and ancestral pride. Other peoples of the Northwest Coast make portrait masks of spirits and ancestors whose powers help to cure the sick and predict events. Dance masks and clan helmets—which, like African masks, draw on the natural elements of wood, human hair and teeth, animal fur, seashell, and feathers—invoke the metamorphic powers of legendary creatures

such as the raven (see Reading 18.6). Masks with hidden strings connected to moving parts that "become" different creatures or spirits are themselves vehicles of transformation (Figure **18.14**). Such "performance masks" are used in the orchestration of mythic cycles—often lasting many days—that enact the encounters of ancestors, totemic figures, and supernatural beings.

Native North American Arts: The Southwest

In various parts of the American Southwest, Native Americans raised communal villages, called "pueblos" by the Spanish. These communities consisted of flat-roofed structures built of stone or adobe arranged in terraces to accommodate a number of families. Among the most notable of the pueblo communities was that of the Anasazi (a Navajo word meaning "ancient ones"). Their settlements at Mesa Verde and Chaco Canyon in southwestern Colorado, which flourished between the eleventh and fourteenth centuries, consisted of elaborate multistoried living spaces with numerous rooms, storage areas, and circular underground ceremonial centers, known as *kivas*. Large enough to hold all the male members of the community (women were not generally invited to attend sacred ceremonies), *kivas* served as cosmic symbols of the underworld and as theaters for rites designed to maintain harmony with nature. The Cliff Palace at Mesa Verde, Colorado, positioned under an overhanging canyon wall, whose horizontal configuration it echoes, is one of the largest cliff dwellings in America (Figure **18.15**). Its inhabitants—an estimated 250 people—engineered the tasks of quarrying sandstone, cutting logs (for beams and posts), and hauling water, sand, and clay (for the adobe core structure)

Figure 18.14 Transformation mask, Kwakiutl, British Columbia. Carved wood, pigment, and feathers, 24 × 18 in. The mask, made by the Kwakiutl people of the Queen Charlotte Strait, features a large mythic bird with a huge beak. It is worn high on the head, while the body is covered with a costume of cedar bark.

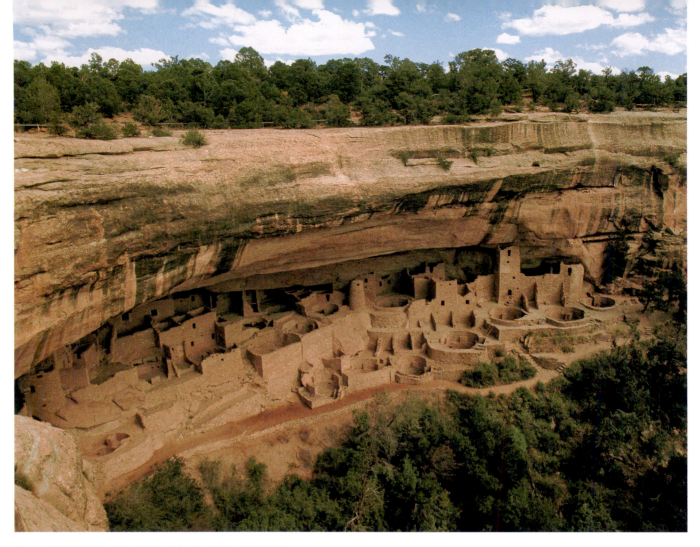

Figure 18.15 Cliff Palace, Mesa Verde, Colorado, inhabited 1073–1272.

entirely without the aid of wheeled vehicles, draft animals, or metal tools.

The pueblo tribes of the American Southwest produced some of the most elegant ceramic wares in the history of North American art. Lacking the potter's wheel, women handbuilt vessels for domestic and ceremonial uses. Beginning in the late tenth century until ca. 1130, they embellished jars and bowls with black-on-white designs that vary from a stark, geometric abstraction to stylized human, animal, and plant forms. One Mimbres bowl shows a mythological creature, the rabbit-man, carrying a basket on his back (Figure **18.16**): the shape of the creature, which subtly blends human and animal features, works harmoniously with the curves of the bowl and animates the negative space that surrounds the image. Mimbres pottery—usually pierced or ritually "killed" before being placed with its owner in the grave—testifies to the rich imagination and sophisticated artistry of pueblo culture.

For centuries, the Hopi people of Arizona and the Zuni of New Mexico, both of the pueblo culture, have fabricated the small wooden figures known as *kachinas* (Figure **18.17**). Literally "life-bringers," *kachinas* are spirit-beings that embody ancestral spirits. They are presented to Hopi children during initiation ceremonies designed to familiarize them with the spirits that oversee agricultural productivity. Among the highly prized creations of the Hopi,

Figure 18.16 Classic Mimbres bowl showing rabbit-man with burden basket, from Cameron Creek village, New Mexico, 1000–1150. Black-on-white pottery, height 4⅜ in., diameter 10¾ in.

Figure 18.17 Butterfly maiden, Hopi *kachina*. Carved wood, pigment, and feathers, height 13 in. During Hopi ceremonies, *kachina* maidens, representing the wives and sisters of the *kachinas*, are impersonated by male dancers, who wear painted wooden headdresses like the one seen on this doll.

Zuni, and Navajo peoples of the American Southwest are richly patterned textiles, hand-woven baskets, and silver jewelry, often embellished with turquoise and other semi-precious stones.

Native American religious rituals, like those of all ancient societies, integrated poetry, music, and dance. The sun dance was a principal part of the annual ceremony that celebrated seasonal renewal. In the Navajo tribal community of the American Southwest, the shaman still conducts the healing ceremony known as the Night Chant. Beginning at sunset and ending some nine days later at sunrise, the Night Chant calls for a series of meticulously executed sand paintings and the recitation of song cycles designed to remove evil and restore good. Characterized by monophonic melody and hypnotic repetition, the Night Chant is performed to the accompaniment of whistles and percussive instruments such as gourd rattles, drums, and rasps. Its compelling rhythms are evident in both the Music Listening Selection and in the "Prayer of the Night Chant" reproduced below. Rituals like the Night Chant are not mere curiosities but, rather, living practices that remain sacred to the Navajo people.

♪ See Music Listening Selections at end of chapter.

READING 18.5 "A Prayer of the Night Chant" (Navajo)

Tségihi.	1
House made of dawn.	
House made of evening light.	
House made of the dark cloud.	
House made of male rain.	5
House made of dark mist.	
House made of female rain.	
House made of pollen.	
House made of grasshoppers.	
Dark cloud is at the door.	10
The trail out of it is dark cloud.	
The zigzag lightning stands high upon it.	
Male deity!	
Your offering I make.	
I have prepared a smoke for you.	15
Restore my feet for me.	
Restore my legs for me.	
Restore my body for me.	
Restore my mind for me.	
This very day take out your spell for me.	20
Your spell remove for me.	
You have taken it away for me.	
Far off it has gone.	
Happily I recover.	
Happily my interior becomes cool.	25
Happily I go forth.	
My interior feeling cool, may I walk.	
No longer sore, may I walk.	
Impervious to pain, may I walk.	
With lively feelings may I walk.	30
As it used to be long ago, may I walk.	
Happily may I walk.	
Happily, with abundant dark clouds, may I walk.	
Happily, with abundant showers, may I walk.	
Happily, with abundant plants, may I walk.	35
Happily, on a trail of pollen, may I walk.	
Happily may I walk.	
Being as it used to be long ago, may I walk.	
May it be beautiful before me.	
May it be beautiful behind me.	40
May it be beautiful below me.	
May it be beautiful above me.	
May it be beautiful all around me.	
In beauty it is finished.	

Q **What is the purpose of repetition in the Night Chant?**

Q **What similarities do you detect between this chant (Music Listening Selection I-23), Gregorian chant (MLS I-2), and Buddhist chant (MLS I-3)?**

Native American Literature

Myths and folktales, transmitted orally for generations (and recorded only since the seventeenth century), feature themes that call to mind those of Africa. Creation myths,

myths of destruction (or death), and myths that describe the way things are, provided explanations of the workings of nature (see Readings 0.1 and 18.2). Usually told by men who passed them down to boys, myths and tales often traveled vast distances, and, thus, may appear in many variant versions. As with African folklore, Native American myths feature heroes or heroines who work to influence or dominate nature; the heroes/tricksters may themselves be humans who are transformed into ravens, spiders, coyotes, wolves, or rabbits (see Figure 18.16), or vice-versa: animals who are physically transformed into human beings. As with the African trickster tale, which usually points to a moral, the Native American trickster story means to teach or explain; nonetheless, heroes whose strategies involve deceit and cunning are often held in high regard.

READING 18.6 Two Native American Tales

How the Sun Came

There was no light anywhere, and the animal people stumbled around in the darkness. Whenever one bumped into another, he would say, "What we need in the world is light." And the other would reply, "Yes, indeed, light is what we badly need."

At last, the animals called a meeting, and gathered together as well as they could in the dark. The red-headed woodpecker said, "I have heard that over on the other side of the world there are people who have light." "Good, good!" said everyone. 10

"Perhaps if we go over there, they will give us some light," the woodpecker suggested.

"If they have all the light there is," the fox said, "they must be greedy people, who would not want to give any of it up. Maybe we should just go there and take the light from them."

"Who shall go?" cried everyone, and the animals all began talking at once, arguing about who was strongest and ran fastest, who was best able to go and get the light.

Finally, the 'possum said, "I can try. I have a fine big 20 bushy tail, and I can hide the light inside my fur."

"Good! Good!" said all the others, and the 'possum set out.

As he traveled eastward, the light began to grow and grow, until it dazzled his eyes, and the 'possum screwed his eyes up to keep out the bright light. Even today, if you notice, you will see that the 'possum's eyes are almost shut, and that he comes out of his house only at night.

All the same, the 'possum kept going, clear to the other side of the world, and there he found the sun. He 30 snatched a little piece of it and hid it in the fur of his fine, bushy tail, but the sun was so hot it burned off all the fur, and by the time the 'possum got home his tail was as bare as it is today.

"Oh, dear!" everyone said. "Our brother has lost his fine, bushy tail, and still we have no light."

"I'll go," said the buzzard. "I have better sense than to put the sun on my tail. I'll put it on my head."

So the buzzard traveled eastward till he came to the place where the sun was. And because the buzzard flies 40 so high, the sun-keeping people did not see him, although now they were watching out for thieves. The buzzard dived straight down out of the sky, the way he does today, and caught a piece of the sun in his claws. He set the sun on his head and started for home, but the sun was so hot that it burned off all his head feathers, and that is why the buzzard's head is bald today.

Now the people were in despair. "What shall we do? What shall we do?" they cried. "Our brothers have tried hard; they have done their best, everything a man can 50 do. What else shall we do so we can have light?"

"They have done the best a man can do," said a little voice from the grass, "but perhaps this is something a woman can do better than a man."

"Who are you?" everyone asked. "Who is that speaking in a tiny voice and hidden in the grass?"

"I am your Grandmother Spider," she replied. "Perhaps I was put in the world to bring you light. Who knows? At least I can try, and if I am burned up it will still not be as if you had lost one of your great warriors." 60

Then Grandmother Spider felt around her in the darkness until she found some damp clay. She rolled it in her hands, and molded a little clay bowl. She started eastward, carrying her bowl, and spinning a thread behind her so she could find her way back.

When Grandmother Spider came to the place of the sun people, she was so little and so quiet no one noticed her. She reached out gently, gently, and took a tiny bit of the sun, and placed it in her clay bowl. Then she went back along the thread that she had spun, with the sun's 70 light growing and spreading before her, as she moved from east to west. And if you will notice, even today a spider's web is shaped like the sun's disk and its rays, and the spider will always spin her web in the morning, very early, before the sun is fully up.

"Thank you, Grandmother," the people said when she returned. "We will always honor you and we will always remember you."

And from then on pottery making became woman's work, and all pottery must be dried slowly in the shade 80 before it is put in the heat of the firing oven, just as Grandmother Spider's bowl dried in her hand, slowly, in the darkness, as she traveled toward the land of the sun.

(Cheyenne)

Raven and the Moon

One day Raven learnt that an old fisherman, living alone 1 with his daughter on an island far to the north, had a box containing a bright light called the moon. He felt that he must get hold of this wonderful thing, so he changed himself into a leaf growing on a bush near to the old fisherman's home. When the fisherman's daughter came to pick berries from the wild fruit patch, she pulled at the twig on which the leaf stood and it fell down and entered into her body. In time a child was born, a dark-complexioned boy with a long, hooked nose, almost like 10 a bird's bill. As soon as the child could crawl, he began to cry for the moon. He would knock at the box and keep calling, "Moon, moon, shining moon."

At first nobody paid any attention, but as the child became more vocal and knocked harder at the box, the old fisherman said to his daughter, "Well, perhaps we should give the boy the ball of light to play with." The girl opened the box and took out another box, and then another, from inside that. All the boxes were beautifully painted and carved, and inside the tenth there was a net 20 of nettle thread. She loosened this and opened the lid of the innermost box. Suddenly light filled the lodge, and they saw the moon inside the box; bright, round like a ball, shining white. The mother threw it toward her baby son and he caught and held it so firmly they thought he was content. But after a few days he began to fuss and cry again. His grandfather felt sorry for him and asked the mother to explain what the child was trying to say. So his mother listened very carefully and explained that he wanted to look out at the sky and see the stars in the 30 dark sky, but that the roof board over the smoke hole prevented him from doing so. So the old man said, "Open the smoke hole." No sooner had she opened the hole than the child changed himself back into the Raven. With the moon in his bill he flew off. After a moment he landed on a mountain top and then threw the moon into the sky where it remains, still circling in the heavens where Raven threw it.

(Northwest Coast)

Q **What creatures assume importance in these tales?**

The Arts of Meso- and South America

Until recently, scholars regarded the Olmecs as the largest and most advanced of early Meso-American cultures (see chapter 3). In the last ten years, however, archeologists have excavated sites near Peru's west coast that may have flourished as early as 3500 B.C.E. Clearly, the ancient history of the Americas is yet to be written. While it is difficult to generalize on the unique features of Middle and South American cultures before the fifteenth century, the abundance of objects created in a single medium—gold—suggests that this rare metal held great significance: The sheer number and quality of works produced in gold surpassed that of most world cultures. Over thousands of years, the techniques of metalwork, and especially goldworking, passed from generation to generation to attain remarkable levels of proficiency. Gold was associated with the sun, whose radiance gave life to the crops, and with the gods, whose blood (in the form of rain) was considered procreative and thus essential to the survival of the community. The medium of choice for the glorification of gods and their earthly representatives, gold was used to produce extraordinary artworks ranging from small items of jewelry to masks and weapons, especially those associated with rituals of blood sacrifice (Figure **18.18**).

In the sacrificial rites and royal ceremonies of pre-Columbian communities, human blood was shed to feed

and appease the gods, thus saving the world from destruction. This fundamental sense of interdependence between earthly and spiritual realms is nowhere more clearly illustrated than in the civilization of the Maya.

Figure 18.18 Ceremonial knife, from the Lambayeque valley, Peru, ninth to eleventh centuries. Hammered gold with turquoise inlay, 13 × 5⅛ in.

Early Empires in the Americas

The Maya

Maya civilization reached its classic phase between 250 and 900 C.E. and survived with considerable political and economic vigor until roughly 1600. At sites in southern Mexico, Honduras, Guatemala, and the Yucatán peninsula, the Maya constructed fortified cities consisting of elaborate palace complexes that are hauntingly reminiscent of those from ancient Mesopotamia (Figure **18.19**). Like the Mesopotamian ziggurat (see Figure 3.12), the Maya temple was a terraced pyramid with a staircase ascending to a platform capped by a multiroomed superstructure (Figure **18.20**). A shrine and sanctuary, it also served as a burial place for priests or rulers. On the limestone façades of such structures, the Maya carved and painted scenes of religious ceremonies and war, as well as images of their gods: Quetzalcoatl, the creator god—a hybrid of the Meso-American bird (*quetzal*) and the serpent (*coatl*)—hence, "Feathered Serpent" (see Figure 18.27); and Tlaloc, the long-snouted rain deity. Ceremonial complexes often include reclining stone figures known as "chacmools," which functioned as altars or bearers of sacrificial offerings (see Figure 18.20, left foreground).

The Maya were the only known Native American culture to produce a written language. Their ancient script, comprised of hieroglyphs, was decoded during the second half of the twentieth century. Only since 1995 have the glyphs been recognized as a system of phonetic signs that operate like spoken syllables—a discovery made, in part,

Figure 18.19
Reconstruction drawing of post-classic Maya fortress city of Chutixtiox, Quiche, Guatemala, ca. 1000, from Richard Adams, *Prehistoric Mesoamerica*.

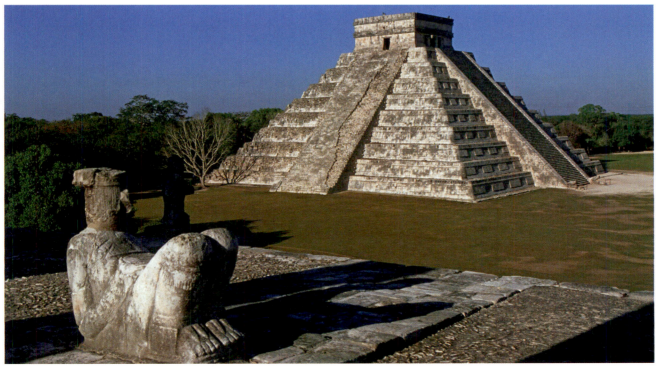

Figure 18.20 Castillo, with chacmool in the foreground, Chichén Itzá, Yucatán, Mexico. Maya, ninth to thirteenth centuries.

by studying the living language of modern-day descendants of the Maya who inhabit the Guatemalan highlands and the Yucatán. Despite the survival of some codices and many stone inscriptions, nearly all of the literary evidence of this people was destroyed during the sixteenth century by Spanish missionaries and colonial settlers. Newly deciphered glyphs on ceramic vessels and elaborate murals offer additional insight into Maya culture. Perhaps the most important source of Meso-American mythology, however, survives in the form of an oral narrative believed to date from the Maya classic period, transcribed into the Quiche language around 1500. This narrative, known as the *Popol Vuh* (see Reading 0.1), recounts the creation of the world. According to the Maya, the gods fashioned human beings out of maize—the principal Native American crop—but chose deliberately to deprive them of perfect understanding. Reenactments of the event of creation are still performed in ritual dances among Maya descendants.

As if to challenge the gods, the Maya became accomplished mathematicians and astronomers. Carefully observing the earth's movements around the sun, they devised a calendar that was more accurate than any used in medieval Europe before the twelfth century. Having developed a mathematical system that recognized "zero," they computed planetary and celestial cycles with some accuracy, tracked the paths of Venus, Jupiter, and Saturn, and successfully predicted eclipses of the sun and moon. They recorded their findings in stone, on the limestone-covered bark pages of codices, and on the façades of temples, some of which may have functioned as planetary observatories. At the principal pyramid at Chichén Itzá in the Yucatán (see Figure 18.20), the ninety-one steps on each of four sides, plus the platform on which the temple stands, correspond to the 365 days in the solar calendar. According to the Maya, the planets (and segments of time itself) were ruled by the gods, usually represented in Maya art as men and women carrying burdens on their shoulders. The Maya and the various Meso-American peoples who followed them believed in the cyclical creation and destruction of the world, and they prudently entrusted the sacred mission of timekeeping to their priests.

A key feature of almost all Meso-American sacred precincts was an I-shaped, high-walled stone court that served as a ballpark. It was used for the performance of ceremonial games played by two teams of nine to eleven men each. The ballgame was not exclusively a sport, but an age-old religious pageant whose symbolism was embedded

Figure 18.21 Lintel relief, Yaxchilan, Chiapas, Mexico, late classic period, 725. Limestone, 43½ × 31¾ in. Traces of red, green, and yellow pigments on this and other lintels from Yaxchilan confirm that many Maya sculptures were once brilliantly painted.

in the mythic narrative of the *Popol Vuh*. It enacted a life-and-death ritual that maintained the regenerative power of the sun, thus securing cosmic order. The object of the game was to propel a 5-pound rubber ball, representing the sun, through the stone rings at either side of the court. Members of the losing team lost more than glory: they were sacrificed to the sun god, their hearts torn from their bodies on ritual altars adjacent to the court.

Blood sacrifice and bloodletting were ritual practices of the Maya nobility. A low-relief lintel from Yaxchilan in Chiapas, Mexico, shows a royal bloodletting ceremony that, according to hieroglyphs carved on the upper and left edges of the stone, took place in 709 C.E. (Figure 18.21). It identifies King Shield Jaguar (the jaguar was a favorite symbol of military strength) and his queen, Lady Xoc. The king, holding a staff and wearing a feathered headdress adorned with the shrunken head of a sacrificial victim, witnesses the ritual by which the queen pulls a thorn-lined rope through her tongue. The blood-soaked rope falls into a basket filled with slips of paper that absorb the royal blood. These would be burned in large sacrificial vessels, so that the smoke might lure the gods. Such ceremonies were performed on the accession of a new king, prior to waging war, and at ceremonies celebrating victory in battle. They served to honor the gods and confirm the political legitimacy of the ruler. A sophisticated blend of

Science and Technology

1500	Maya in the Yucatán use vegetable-based molds to treat wounds and infections
1568	Gerhard Kremen (Flemish) produces the first Mercator projection map
1596	Korean naval architects launch the first ironclad warship

Figure 18.22 Machu Picchu, Peru, ca. 1500.

realistic detail and abstract design, the Yaxchilan lintel reveals the Maya genius for uniting representational and symbolic modes of expression.

The Inca

Until the fifteenth century, the Inca state was only one of many regional states that occupied the coastal areas of Andean South America. By way of a series of military campaigns that the Inca launched around 1438, it soon became an empire that, at its height at the end of the century, extended almost 3000 miles (from present-day Ecuador to Chile; see Map 18.3) to incorporate some sixteen million inhabitants. Ruling Peru's coastal plains and the mountains and valleys of the Andes, the Inca absorbed the traditions of earlier Peruvian cultures.

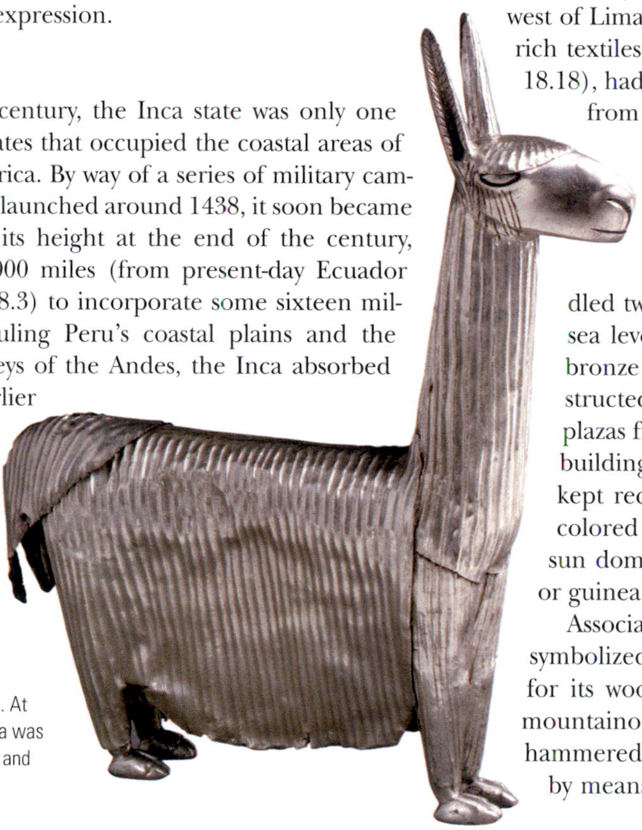

Figure 18.23 Silver long-haired Inca llama, ca. fifteenth century, 9⅓ × 8 in. The figure may represent the sacred white llama honored by Inca rulers. At ritual festivals, a white llama was dressed in a bright red tunic and wore gold ear ornaments.

Some of these, like Caral (discussed in chapter 3), flourished as early as 3500 B.C.E. in the coastal region northwest of Lima. Others, notable for their fine ceramics, rich textiles, and sophisticated goldwork (see Figure 18.18), had occupied the valleys of rivers that flowed from the Andes to the Pacific Ocean.

Like the ancient Romans, the Inca constructed thousands of miles of roads and bridges in order to expedite trade and communication. At Machu Picchu, they built a 3-square-mile city that straddled two mountain peaks some 9000 feet above sea level (Figure 18.22). With heavy stone and bronze tools (but without mortar), they constructed fortresslike walls and large ceremonial plazas filled with temples, terraces, and two-story buildings. While lacking the written word, they kept records by way of a system of knotted and colored cords known as *quipu*. The cult of the sun dominated religious festivals at which llamas or guinea pigs were daily sacrificed.

Associated with rain and fertility, the llama symbolized royal authority; it was also treasured for its wool and as a source of transportation in mountainous terrain. Images of the llama were hammered from sheets of gold and silver or cast by means of the lost-wax method (Figure 18.23).

A sixteenth-century chronicler reported that life-sized gold and silver llamas guarded the Temple of the Sun, itself ornamented with hundreds of sheets of jewel-embedded gold.

The arts of feather ornamentation and textile weaving were also brought to remarkable heights by the Inca. Essential to the cold climate of the Andes, tunics and blankets were made of fibers spun, dyed with bright colors, and woven by highly skilled female weavers. Royal textiles often included complex geometric designs (Figure **18.24**).

The Aztecs

Small by comparison with the Inca civilization, that of the Aztecs—the last of the three great Meso-American empires—is estimated to have numbered between three and five million people. In their earliest history, the Aztecs (who called themselves *Mexica*) were an insignificant tribe of warriors who migrated to central Mexico in 1325. Driven by a will to conquer, matched perhaps only by that of the ancient Romans, they created in less than a century an empire that encompassed all of central Mexico and

Figure 18.24 Tapestry-weave Inca tunic, from the south coast of Peru, 1440–1540. Camelid fiber and cotton, 35⅞ × 30 in. Members of the camel family, llamas and alpacas provided fibers that were used for tunics like this one. Its designs belong to a heraldic or totemic code that remains undeciphered.

Meso-America as far south as Guatemala. Their capital at Tenochtitlán ("Place of the Gods"), a city of some 250,000 people, was constructed on an island in the middle of Lake Texcoco. It was connected to the Mexican mainland by three great causeways and watered by artificial lakes and dams. The Aztecs were masterful engineers, whose roads, canals, and aqueducts astounded the Spaniards who arrived in Mexico in 1519. Upon encountering Tenochtitlán, with its huge temples and palaces connected by avenues and ceremonial plazas, Spanish soldiers reported that it rivaled Venice and Constantinople—cities that were neither so orderly nor so clean.

Aztec civilization absorbed the cultural traditions of earlier Meso-Americans, including the Maya. They honored the pantheon of nature deities centering on the sun and extended the practice of blood sacrifice to the staggering numbers of victims captured in their incessant wars. They preserved native traditions of temple construction, ceramics, weaving, metalwork, and stone carving. During the fifteenth century, the Aztecs raised to new heights the art of monumental stone sculpture, carving great basalt statues that ranged from austere, realistic portraits to fantastic and terrifying icons of gods and goddesses such as Coatlicue, Lady of the Skirt of Serpents and ancient Earth Mother of the Gods (Figure **18.25**). Combining feline and human features, the over-life-sized "she-of-the-serpent-skirt" bears a head consisting of two snakes, clawed hands and feet, and a necklace of excised hearts and severed hands. Renaissance Europeans, whose idea of female divinity was shaped by Raphael's gentle Madonnas, found these blood-drenched "idols" outrageous; they destroyed as many as they could find.

The Aztecs believed in the cyclical death and rebirth of the universe. They carried on the traditions of time-keeping begun by the Maya. Like the Maya, they devised a solar calendar of 365 days. The "Calendar Stone" functioned not as an actual calendar, but as a symbol of the Aztec cosmos (Figure **18.26**). Central to the stone is the face of the sun god, whose tongue is a sacrificial knife; his outstretched claws hold severed human heads. The four square panels that surround the face of the god represent the four previous creations of the world. Arranged around these panels are the twenty signs of the days of the month in the eighteen-month Aztec year, and embracing the entire cosmic configuration are two giant serpents that bear the sun on its daily journey. The stone is the pictographic counterpart of Aztec legends that bind human beings to the gods who govern the irreversible wheel of time.

Some of the most interesting records of Aztec culture are preserved in the form of codices, that is manuscripts—usually made of deer hide—with pictographic representations that recount tribal genealogy, history, and mythology. The most complex surviving Meso-American codex (known as the Borgia Codex), which is housed today at the Vatican Library in Rome, illustrates the history of Quetzalcoatl in the underworld. The folio illustrated in Figure **18.27** recounts the life–death dualism that is fundamental to Aztec thought.

Figure 18.25 *Coatlique, Mother of the Gods*, Aztec, 1487–1520. Andesite, height 8 ft. 3¼ in. According to Aztec mythology, the children of the pregnant mother goddess Coatlicue, jealous of the offspring she would produce, cut off her head. The two streams of blood took the form of snakes leaping from her severed neck, as seen here.

Figure 18.26 Sun disk, known as the "Calendar Stone," Aztec, fifteenth century. Diameter 13 ft., weight 24½ tons.

The Clash of Cultures

When Ibn Battuta visited Mali, he was startled by the strange customs of its inhabitants, which differed from those of his own country. The same is true of Hernán Cortés (see below), who, while marveling at the glories of the Aztec city of Tenochtitlán, found the religious practices of its inhabitants "barbarous" (see Reading 18.7). However, the European outreach took a different course from that of individual travelers. It also differed from the trading expeditions of the Chinese, in that Western overseas expansion ultimately involved the colonization of foreign lands and, in some cases, the enslavement of foreign peoples.

In their exploration of Africa and the Americas, Europeans encountered people very different from themselves. Because these human beings did not resemble them in appearance, religious beliefs, or technological sophistication, they were regarded as "Other." Just as the ancient Greeks considered non-Greeks "barbarians," so Renaissance Europeans perceived Africans and Native Americans as barbarous savages or, at the least, as inferiors. Observing that despite many similarities to the way the Spanish lived, the Aztecs were "cut off from all civilized nations" (Reading 18.7), Cortés concluded that such people were in need of enlightenment. This, in turn, became justification for the evangelical efforts of Catholic missionaries who worked to convert the "savages" to Christianity. It was, as well, sufficient justification for seeking dominion, or control, over them. The questions persist. Was the European colonization of Africa and the Americas rationalized by a belief in the inferiority of the "Other"? To what extent might such rationalization contribute to the age-old imperialistic ambitions (still with us today) of powerful groups of people to dominate the less powerful—or, for that matter, simply those who are unlike themselves?

Figure 18.27 Aztec peoples, *Mictlantecuhtli and Quetzalcoatl*. Parchment, 11 × 11 in (detail of a 35-ft.-long codex). The inverted skull beneath the two gods may represent the land of the dead or the bones that, according to legend, Quetzalcoatl dropped and scattered prior to his returning them to earth.

Depicted on the left is the god of death, holding a blood-splattered skeleton; he is challenged by the creator god, Quetzalcoatl, whom legend describes as having stolen the bones of older gods and returned them to earth in order to repopulate the land of the living. Pictographic signs representing twenty thirteen-day weeks are shown on either side of the scene.

Cross-Cultural Encounter

The Spanish in the Americas

Columbus made his initial landfall on one of the islands now called the Bahamas, and on successive voyages he explored the Caribbean islands and the coast of Central America. At every turn, he encountered people native to the area—people he called "Indians" in the mistaken belief that he had reached the "Indies," the territories of India and China. Other explorers soon followed and rectified Columbus' misconception. Spanish adventurers, called *conquistadores*, sought wealth and fortune in the New World. Although vastly outnumbered, the force of 600 soldiers under the command of Hernán Cortés (1485–1547), equipped with fewer than twenty horses and the superior technology of gunpowder and muskets, overcame the Aztec armies in 1521. Following a seventy-five-day siege, the Spanish completely demolished the island city of Tenochtitlán, from whose ruins Mexico City would eventually rise. While the technology of gunpowder and muskets had much to do with the

Spanish victory, other factors contributed, such as religious prophecy (that Quetzalcoatl would return as a bearded white man), support from rebellious Aztec subjects, and an outbreak of smallpox among the Aztecs.

The Spanish destruction of Tenochtitlán and the melting down of most of the Aztec goldwork left little tangible evidence of the city's former glory. Consequently, the description that is the subject of Cortés' second letter to Spain is doubly important: not only does it offer a detailed picture of Aztec cultural achievement, but also it serves as a touchstone by which to assess the conflicted reactions of Renaissance Europeans to their initial encounters with the inhabitants of strange and remote lands.

READING 18.7 From Cortés' Letters from Mexico (1520)

This great city of Temixtitan[1] is built on the salt lake, and no matter by what road you travel there are two leagues from the main body of the city to the mainland. There are four artificial causeways leading to it, and each is as wide as two cavalry lances. The city itself is as big as Seville or Córdoba. The main streets are very wide and very straight; some of these are on the land, but the rest and all the smaller ones are half on land, half canals where they paddle their canoes. All the streets have openings in places so that the water may pass from one canal to another. Over all these openings, and some of them are very wide, there are bridges made of long and wide beams joined together very firmly and so well made that on some of them ten horsemen may ride abreast.

Seeing that if the inhabitants of this city wished to betray us they were very well equipped for it by the design of the city, for once the bridges had been removed they could starve us to death without our being able to reach the mainland, as soon as I entered the city I made great haste to build four brigantines, and completed them in a very short time. They were such as could carry three hundred men to the land and transport the horses whenever we might need them.

This city has many squares where trading is done and markets are held continuously. There is also one square twice as big as that of Salamanca,[2] with arcades all around, where more than sixty thousand people come each day to buy and sell, and where every kind of merchandise produced in these lands is found; provisions as well as ornaments of gold and silver, lead, brass, copper, tin, stones, shells, bones, and feathers. They also sell lime, hewn and unhewn stone, adobe bricks, tiles, and cut and uncut woods of various kinds. There is a street where they sell game and birds of every species found in this land: chickens, partridges and quails, wild ducks, flycatchers, widgeons, turtledoves, pigeons, cane birds, parrots, eagles and eagle owls, falcons, sparrow hawks and kestrels, and they sell the

1
10
20
30

skins of some of these birds of prey with their feathers, heads and claws. They sell rabbits and hares, and stags and small gelded dogs which they breed for eating.

There are streets of herbalists where all the medicinal herbs and roots found in the land are sold. There are shops like apothecaries', where they sell ready-made medicines as well as liquid ointments and plasters. There are shops like barbers' where they have their hair washed and shaved, and shops where they sell food and drink. There are also men like porters to carry loads. There is much firewood and charcoal, earthenware braziers and mats of various kinds like mattresses for beds, and other, finer ones, for seats and for covering rooms and hallways. There is every sort of vegetable, especially onions, leeks, garlic, common cress and watercress, borage, sorrel, teasels and artichokes; and there are many sorts of fruit, among which are cherries and plums like those in Spain.

They sell honey, wax, and a syrup made from maize canes, which is as sweet and syrupy as that made from the sugar cane. They also make syrup from a plant which in the islands is called *maguey*,[3] which is much better than most syrups, and from this plant they also make sugar and wine, which they likewise sell. There are many sorts of spun cotton, in hanks of every color, and it seems like the silk market at Granada, except here there is a much greater quantity. They sell as many colors for painters as may be found in Spain and all of excellent hues. They sell deerskins, with and without the hair, and some are dyed white or in various colors. They sell much earthenware, which for the most part is very good; there are both large and small pitchers, jugs, pots, tiles, and many other sorts of vessel, all of good clay and most of them glazed and painted. They sell maize both as grain and as bread and it is better both in appearance and in taste than any found in the islands or on the mainland. They sell chicken and fish pies, and much fresh and salted fish, as well as raw and cooked fish. They sell hen and goose eggs, and eggs of all the other birds I have mentioned, in great number, and they sell tortillas made from eggs.

Finally, besides those things which I have already mentioned, they sell in the market everything else to be found in this land, but they are so many and so varied that because of their great number and because I cannot remember many of them nor do I know what they are called I shall not mention them. Each kind of merchandise is sold in its own street without any mixture whatever; they are very particular in this. Everything is sold by number and size, and until now I have seen nothing sold by weight. There is in this great square a very large building like a courthouse, where ten or twelve persons sit as judges. They preside over all that happens in the markets, and sentence criminals. There are in this square other persons who walk among the people to see what they are selling and the measures they are using; and they have been seen to break some that were false.

40
50
60
70
80
90

---

[1] Tenochtitlán.
[2] A Spanish university town.

[3] Fermented aloe or *pulque*, a powerful liquor still popular today in Mexico.

There are, in all districts of this great city, many temples or houses for their idols. They are all very beautiful buildings, and in the important ones there are priests of their sect who live there permanently; and, in addition to the houses for the idols, they also have very good lodgings. All these priests dress in black and never comb their hair from the time they enter the priesthood until they leave; and all the sons of the persons of high rank, both the lords and honored citizens also, enter the priesthood and wear the habit from the age of seven or eight years until they are taken away to be married; this occurs more among the first-born sons, who are to inherit, than among the others. They abstain from eating things, and more at some times of the year than at others; and no woman is granted entry nor permitted inside these places of worship.

Amongst these temples there is one, the principal one, whose great size and magnificence no human tongue could describe, for it is so large that within the precincts, which are surrounded by a very high wall, a town of some five hundred inhabitants could easily be built. All round inside this wall there are very elegant quarters with very large rooms and corridors where their priests live. There are as many as forty towers, all of which are so high that in the case of the largest there are fifty steps leading up to the main part of it; and the most important of these towers is higher than that of the cathedral of Seville. They are so well constructed in both their stone and woodwork that there can be none better in any place, for all the stonework inside the chapels where they keep their idols is in high relief, with figures and little houses, and the woodwork is likewise of relief and painted with monsters and other figures and designs. All these towers are burial places of chiefs, and the chapels therein are each dedicated to the idol which he venerated.

There are three rooms within this great temple for the principal idols, which are of remarkable size and stature and decorated with many designs and sculptures, both in stone and in wood. Within these rooms are other chapels, and the doors to them are very small. Inside there is no light whatsoever; there only some of the priests may enter, for inside are the sculptured figures of the idols, although, as I have said, there are also many outside.

The most important of these idols, and the ones in whom they have most faith, I had taken from their places and thrown down the steps; and I had those chapels where they were cleaned, for they were full of the blood of sacrifices; and I had images of Our Lady and of other saints put there, which caused Mutezuma[4] and the other natives some sorrow. First they asked me not to do it, for when the communities learnt of it they would rise against me, for they believed that those idols gave them all their worldly goods, and that if they were allowed to be ill treated, they would become angry and give them nothing and take the fruit from the earth leaving the people to die of hunger. I made them understand through the interpreters how deceived they were in placing their trust in those idols which they had made with their hands from unclean things. They must know that there was only one

God, Lord of all things, who had created heaven and earth and all else and who made all of us; and He was without beginning or end, and they must adore and worship only Him, not any other creature or thing. And I told them all I knew about this to dissuade them from their idolatry and bring them to the knowledge of God our Saviour. All of them, especially Mutezuma, replied that they had already told me how they were not natives of this land, and that as it was many years since their forefathers had come here, they well knew that they might have erred somewhat in what they believed, for they had left their native land so long ago; and as I had only recently arrived from there, I would better know the things they should believe, and should explain to them and make them understand, for they would do as I said was best. Mutezuma and many of the chieftains of the city were with me until the idols were removed, the chapel cleaned and the images set up and I urged them not to sacrifice living creatures to the idols, as they were accustomed,[5] for, as well as being most abhorrent to God, Your Sacred Majesty's laws forbade it and ordered that he who kills shall be killed. And from then on they ceased to do it, and in all the time I stayed in that city I did not see a living creature killed or sacrificed.

. . . .

Q What aspects of Aztec life and culture favorably impressed Cortés? Of what was he critical?

The Aftermath of Conquest

Mexican gold and (after Spain's conquest of the Incas) Peruvian silver were not the only sources of wealth for the conquerors; the Spanish soon turned to the ruthless exploitation of the native populations, enslaving them for use as miners and field laborers. During the sixteenth century, entire populations of Native Americans were destroyed as a result of the combined effects of such European diseases as smallpox and measles and decades of inhumane treatment. When Cortés arrived, for example, Mexico's population was approximately twenty-five million; in 1600, it had declined to one million. Disease traveled from America to Europe as well: European soldiers carried syphilis from the "New World" to the "Old." Guns and other weaponry came into the Americas, even as Christian missionaries brought a pacifistic Catholicism to the native populations. The impact of colonialism is described in the following eyewitness account from a *History of the New World* (1565) by the Italian Girolamo Benzoni (1519–1570), who spent fifteen years in the Americas:

> After the death of Columbus, other governors were sent to Hispaniola;* both clerical and secular,

---

4 Moctezuma II, the last Aztec monarch, who ruled from 1502 to 1520.
5 In 1488, at the dedication of the Great Pyramid at Tenochtitlán, Aztec priests sacrificed more than 20,000 war captives.
* The name Columbus gave to the island in the West Indies that now comprises Haiti and the Dominican Republic.

Figure 18.28 THEODORE DE BRY, *Spanish Cruelties Cause the Indians to Despair,* from *Grands Voyages.* Frankfurt, 1594. Copper engraving, 13⅓ × 16 in.

till the natives, finding themselves intolerably oppressed and overworked, with no chance of regaining their liberty, with sighs and tears longed for death. Many went into the woods and having killed their children, hanged themselves, saying it was far better to die than to live so miserably serving such ferocious tyrants and villainous thieves. The women terminated their pregnancies with the juice of a certain herb in order not to produce children, and then following the example of their husbands, hanged themselves. Some threw themselves from high cliffs down precipices; others jumped into the sea and rivers; others starved themselves to death. Sometimes they killed themselves with their flint knives; others pierced their bosoms or sides with pointed stakes. Finally, out of two million inhabitants, through suicides and other deaths occasioned by the excessive labor and cruelties imposed by the Spaniards, there are not a hundred and fifty now to be found.

Such reports of Spanish imperialism in the Americas, brought to life by the illustrations of the Flemish engraver Theodore de Bry (1528–1598; Figure **18.28**), fueled the so-called Black Legend of Spanish cruelty toward the "Indians" and fed the heated debate that questioned the humanity of so-called savage populations. In this debate, the Spanish missionary-priest Bartolomé

de Las Casas (1474–1566), author of the infamous *Very Brief Account of the Destruction of the Indies* (1552), roundly denounced Spanish treatment of the "Indians." His humanitarian position prompted Pope Paul III to declare officially in 1537 that "the said Indians and all other people who may later be discovered by Christians, are by no means to be deprived of their liberty or . . . property." (The papal edict, it is worth noting, failed to extend such protection to Africans.) Las Casas, known as the "Apostle to the Indians," pleaded, "all the peoples of the world are men, and the definition of all men collectively and severally, is one: that they are rational beings. All possess understanding and volition, being formed in the image and likeness of God."

Unlike the civilizations of India, China, and Africa, which have each enjoyed a continuous history from ancient times until the present, none of the empires that once flourished in ancient America has survived into modern times. The European invasion of the Americas severely arrested the cultural evolution of native tribal populations. Remnants of these populations, however, exist today among such groups as the Hopi and the Pueblo of the Southwestern United States, the Maya of the Yucatán, and the Inuit of the Pacific Northwest. Among these and other tribes, the ancient crafts of pottery, weaving, beadwork, and silverwork still reach a high degree of beauty and technical sophistication.

The Columbian Exchange

While the immediate effect of European expansion and cross-cultural encounter was a dramatic clash of traditions and values, the long-range effects were more positive, especially in the realms of commerce and culture. The so-called Columbian Exchange describes the interchange of hundreds of goods and products between Western Europe and the Americas. The Europeans introduced into the Americas horses, cattle, pigs, sheep, chickens, wheat, barley, oats, onions, lettuce, sugar cane, and various fruits, including peaches, pears, and citrus. From America, Western Europe came to enjoy corn, potatoes, tomatoes, peppers, chocolate, vanilla, tobacco, avocados, peanuts, pineapples, pumpkins, and a variety of beans.

One of the most illustrious results of cross-cultural encounter occurred in the production and exchange of textiles. From the late fifteenth century on, the Portuguese engaged in vigorous trade with both China and India; the result was an interchange of native textile techniques and motifs. Dyed and painted fabrics from India, Chinese silks, and (eventually) Peruvian weavings and unique Mexican dyes generated a flourishing market in exotic textiles that reflected the energies of a new globalism.

The most important aspect of the Columbian Exchange, however, may be said to lie in the creation of vibrant new cultures and new peoples. The biological mix of Europeans, Native Americans, and Africans would alter the populations of the world to introduce the *mestizo* (a person of mixed European and Native American ancestry) and the various *creole* ("mixed") inhabitants of the Americas. Consequently, the Columbian Exchange generated new developments in all aspects of life, ranging from technology and industry to language, diet, and dance. On the threshold of modernity, the Euro-African and Euro-American exchanges opened the door to centuries of contact and diffusion that shaped the future of a brave new world.

Chronology

1404–1424	Zhu Di sponsors China's naval expeditions
1492	Columbus' first voyage
1498	Vasco da Gama reaches India
1519	Cortés enters Mexico
1531	Pizarro conquers Peru
1551	transatlantic slave trade begins
1571	Battle of Lepanto (defeat of Ottoman navy)

LOOKING BACK

Global Travel and Trade

- Ming China initiated a policy of global outreach that took some 300 wooden treasure ships to the shores of Africa, India, and Arabia.
- The period between 1400 and 1600 was the greatest age of trans-Eurasian travel since the days of the Roman Empire. European exploration was motivated by the fall of Constantinople in 1453 to the Ottoman Turks, who now dominated overland trade routes to the East.
- The technology of navigation was crucial to the success of European ventures. The Portuguese produced maps and charts that exceeded the accuracy of those drafted by Classical and Muslim cartographers. Renaissance Europeans improved such older Arab navigational devices as the compass and astrolabe.
- By 1498, Vasco da Gama had navigated around Southern Africa to establish Portuguese trading posts in India.

- Christopher Columbus, an Italian in the employ of Spain, sailed west in search of an all-water route to China; his discovery of the Americas would change the course of world history.

The African Cultural Heritage

- Diversity characterizes all aspects of Africa's history and culture, from language to geography to political organization. Two features that distinguish the history of this vast continent are the dominance of a kinship system that forms the basis of social and communal organization, and an animistic view of nature.
- Even after the Muslim conquest of North Africa in the seventh century, many parts of Africa, such as the kingdom of Benin, remained independent of foreign domination. Nevertheless, the West African empires of Ghana, Mali, and Songhai all came under the influence of Muslim culture.

The Arts of Africa

- From the epic *Sundiata* to tales, proverbs, and poems of praise, the great body of African literature emerges out of an oral tradition. Like African music and art, these works are characterized by strong rhythms and inventive imagery.
- African music, marked by a polyrhythmic structure and responsorial (call-and-response) patterns, reflects the communal spirit of African societies.
- African sculpture, including masks, royal portraits, and power-objects, manifests diverse styles, ranging from realistic representation to expressive abstraction. Inseparable from the rituals for which they were made, masks function as transformative objects that work to channel spiritual energy.

Cross-Cultural Encounter

- The fourteenth-century travels of the scholar Ibn Battuta document a cross-cultural encounter between peoples—Muslims and native North Africans—of vastly different customs and beliefs.
- European commercial activity in Africa was the product of the quest for new sea routes to the East, and for control of the markets in gold, salt, and slaves that had long made Africa a source of wealth for Muslim merchants.
- By the year 1500, the Portuguese controlled the flow of both gold and slaves to Europe. The transatlantic slave trade commenced in 1551, when the Portuguese began to ship thousands of slaves from Africa to work on the sugar plantations of Brazil.
- European forms of slavery were more brutal and exploitative than any previously practiced in Africa: slaves shipped overseas were conscripted into oppressive physical labor.

The Americas

- Similar to early African societies, Native Americans were culturally and linguistically diverse. Animistic and polytheistic, they maintained deep connections to nature and to the spirits associated with their kinship groups.
- Carved and painted wooden totems and masks are among the rich output of the native populations of the Northwest.
- Ceramics, textiles, baskets, metalwork, and *kachina* images, as well as the remains of pueblo architecture, testify to the vitality and originality of the native Southwest peoples.
- Orally transmitted, Native American folktales and myths explain natural phenomena and pass down moral truths. They often feature hero/trickster figures who work to transform nature.

Early Empires in the Americas

- The first of the great Meso-American empires, the Maya built civic centers with stone temples, palaces, and ballcourts. Ceremonies honoring the gods involved rituals of blood sacrifice. Accomplished mathematicians and astronomers, the Maya were the only Native American people to leave a system of writing.
- At their height in the late fifteenth century, the Inca ruled a Peruvian empire of some sixteen million people. They left monumental architecture, textiles, and ritual objects in silver and gold.
- The last of the Native American empires, that of the Aztecs, was centered in Mexico. Absorbing the cultural traditions and artistic practices of earlier native civilizations, they established a capital at Tenochtitlán that is notable for its stone architecture and sculpture.

Cross-Cultural Encounter

- The Spanish destruction of Tenochtitlán left little tangible evidence of the city's former glory. When Cortés first arrived, Mexico's population was approximately twenty-five million; in 1600 it had declined to one million.
- Mexican gold and Peruvian silver fueled foreign exploitation of native peoples. Unlike the civilizations of India, China, and Africa, which have enjoyed a continuous history from ancient times to the present, none of the empires that once flourished in ancient America has survived into modern times.
- The positive aspects of the European–American encounter lay in the exchange of goods and products, and in the biological mix of Africans, Native Americans, and Europeans that would produce the creolized cultures of the "New World."

Music Listening Selections

- Music of Africa, Senegal, "Greetings from Podor."
- Music of Africa, Angola, "Gangele Song."
- Music of Native America, "Navajo Night Chant," male chorus with gourd rattles.

Glossary

anaphora the repetition of a word or words at the beginning of two or more lines of verse

call-and-response a vocal pattern in which the soloist raises a song and the chorus responds

ethnography the sociocultural study of human societies

fetish an object believed to have magical powers

griot a class of poet-historians who preserved the legends and lore of Africa by chanting or singing them from memory

kiva the underground ceremonial center of the Southwest Indian pueblo community

scarification the act or process of incising the flesh as a form of identification and rank, and/or for aesthetic purposes

totem an animal or other creature that serves as a heraldic emblem of a tribe, family, or clan

Chapter 19

Protest and Reform: The Waning of the Old Order

ca. 1400–1600

"Now what else is the whole life of mortals but a sort of comedy, in which the various actors, disguised by various costumes and masks, walk on and play each one his part, until the manager waves them off the stage?"
Erasmus

Figure 19.1 ALBRECHT DÜRER, *The Four Horsemen of the Apocalypse*, ca. 1496. Woodcut, 15½ × 11 in. This illustration from the Revelation of Saint John, the last book of the New Testament, might be considered a grim prophecy of the sixteenth century, in which five million people would die in religious wars.

By the sixteenth century, the old medieval order was crumbling. Classical humanism and the influence of Italian Renaissance artist–scientists were spreading throughout Northern Europe (Map **19.1**). European exploration and expansion were promoting a broader world-view and new markets for trade. The rise of a global economy with vast opportunities for material wealth was inevitable. Europe's population grew from 69 million in 1500 to 188 million in 1600. As European nation-states tried to strengthen their international influence, political rivalry intensified. The "superpowers"—Spain, under the Hapsburg ruler Philip II (1527–1598), and England, under Elizabeth I (1533–1603)—contended for advantage in Atlantic shipping and trade. In order to resist the encroachment of Europe's stronger nation-states, the weaker ones formed balance-of-power alliances that often provoked war. The new order took Europe on an irreversibly modern course.

While political and commercial factors worked to transform the West, the event that most effectively destroyed the old medieval order was the Protestant Reformation. In the wake of Protestantism, the unity of European Christendom would disappear forever. Beginning in the fifteenth century, the Northern Renaissance, endorsed by middle-class patrons and Christian humanists, assumed a religious direction that set it apart from Italy's Classical revival. Its literary giants, from Erasmus to Shakespeare, and its visual artists, Flemish and German, shared little of the idealism of their Italian Renaissance counterparts. Their concern for the reality of human folly and for the fate of the Christian soul launched a message of protest and a plea for Church reform expedited by way of the newly perfected printing press.

The Temper of Reform

The Impact of Technology

In the transition from medieval to early modern times, technology played a crucial role. Gunpowder, the light cannon, and other military devices made warfare more impersonal and ultimately more deadly. At the same time, Western advances in navigation, shipbuilding, and maritime instrumentation propelled Europe into a dominant position in the world.

Just as the musket and the cannon transformed the history of European warfare, so the technology of mechanical printing revolutionized learning and communication. Block printing originated in China in the ninth century and movable type in the eleventh, but print technology did not reach Western Europe until the fifteenth century. By 1450, in the city of Mainz, the German goldsmith Johannes Gutenberg (ca. 1400–ca. 1468) perfected a printing press that made it possible to fabricate books more cheaply, more rapidly, and in greater numbers than ever before (Figure **19.2**). As information became a commodity for mass production, vast areas of knowledge—heretofore the exclusive domain of the monastery, the Church, and the university—became available to the public. The printing press facilitated the rise of popular education and encouraged individuals to form their own opinions by reading for themselves. It accelerated the growing interest in vernacular literature, which in turn enhanced national and individual self-consciousness. Print technology proved to

Figure 19.2 An early sixteenth-century woodcut of a printer at work.

Science and Technology

1320	paper adopted for use in Europe (having long been in use in China)
1450	the Dutch devise the first firearm small enough to be carried by a single person
1451	Nicolas of Cusa (German) uses concave lenses to amend nearsightedness
1454	Johannes Gutenberg (German) prints the Bible with movable metal type

Map 19.1
Renaissance Europe,
ca. 1500.

Key — Northward spread of the Renaissance

be the single most important factor in the success of the Protestant Reformation, as it brought the complaints of Church reformers to the attention of all literate folk.

Christian Humanism and the Northern Renaissance

The new print technology broadcast an old message of religious protest and reform. For two centuries, critics had attacked the wealth, worldliness, and unchecked corruption of the Church of Rome. During the early fifteenth century, the rekindled sparks of lay piety and anticlericalism spread throughout the Netherlands, where religious leaders launched the movement known as the *devotio moderna* ("modern devotion"). Lay Brothers and Sisters of the Common Life, as they were called, organized houses in which they studied and taught Scripture. Living in the manner of Christian monks and nuns, but taking no monastic vows, these lay Christians cultivated a devotional lifestyle that fulfilled the ideals of the apostles and the church fathers. They followed the mandate of Thomas à Kempis (1380–1471), himself a Brother of the Common Life and author of the *Imitatio Christi* (*Imitation of Christ*), to put the message of Jesus into daily practice. After the Bible, the *Imitatio Christi* was the most frequently published book in the Christian West well into modern times.

The *devotio moderna* spread quickly throughout Northern Europe, harnessing the dominant strains of anticlericalism, lay piety, and mysticism, even as it coincided with the revival of Classical studies in the newly established universities of Germany. Although Northern humanists, like their Italian Renaissance counterparts, encouraged learning in Greek and Latin, they were more concerned with the study and translation of Early Christian manuscripts than with the Classical and largely secular texts that preoccupied the Italian humanists. This critical reappraisal of religious texts is known as Christian humanism. Christian humanists studied the Bible and the writings of the church fathers with the same intellectual fervor that the Italian humanists had brought to their examination of Plato and Cicero. The efforts of these Northern scholars gave rise to a rebirth (or renaissance) that focused on the late Classical world and, specifically, on the revival of church life and doctrine as gleaned from Early Christian literature. The Northern Renaissance put Christian humanism at the service of evangelical Christianity.

The leading Christian humanist of the sixteenth century—often called "the Prince of Humanists"—was Desiderius Erasmus of Rotterdam (1466–1536; Figure 19.3). Schooled among the Brothers of the Common Life and learned in Latin, Greek, and Hebrew, Erasmus was a superb scholar and a prolific writer (see Reading 19.2). The first humanist to make extensive use of the printing press, he once dared a famous publisher to print his

Figure 19.3 ALBRECHT DÜRER, *Erasmus of Rotterdam*, 1526. Engraving, 9¾ × 7½ in. The Latin inscription at the top of the engraving reports that Dürer executed the portrait from life. The Greek inscription below reads, "The better image [is found] in his writings." The artist wrote to his friend that he felt the portrait was not a striking likeness.

words as fast as he could write them. Erasmus was a fervent Neoclassicist—he held that almost everything worth knowing was set forth in Greek and Latin. He was also a devout Christian. Advocating a return to the basic teachings of Christ, he criticized the Church and all Christians whose faith had been jaded by slavish adherence to dogma and ritual. Using four different Greek manuscripts of the Gospels, he produced a critical edition of the New Testament that corrected Jerome's mistranslations of key passages. Erasmus' New Testament became the source of most sixteenth-century German and English vernacular translations of this central text of Christian humanism.

The Protestant Reformation

During the sixteenth century, papal extravagance and immorality reached new heights, and Church reform became an urgent public issue. In the territories of Germany, loosely united under the leadership of the Holy Roman emperor Charles V (1500–1558), the voices of protest were more strident than anywhere else in Europe. Across Germany, the sale of indulgences (see chapter 15) for the benefit of the Church of Rome—specifically for the rebuilding of Saint Peter's Cathedral—provoked harsh criticism, especially by those who saw the luxuries of the papacy as a betrayal of apostolic ideals. As with

most movements of religious reform, it fell to one individual to galvanize popular sentiment. In 1505, Martin Luther (1483–1546), the son of a rural coal miner, abandoned his legal studies to become an Augustinian monk (Figure **19.4**). Thereafter, as a doctor of theology at the University of Wittenberg, he spoke out against the Church. His inflammatory sermons and essays offered radical remedies to what he called "the misery and wretchedness of Christendom."

Luther was convinced of the inherent sinfulness of humankind, but he took issue with the traditional medieval view—as promulgated, for instance, in *Everyman*—that salvation was earned through the performance of good works and grace mediated by the Church and its priesthood. Inspired by the words of Saint Paul, "the just shall live by faith" (Romans 1:17), Luther argued that salvation could be attained only by faith in the validity of Christ's sacrifice: human beings were saved by the unearned gift of God's grace, not by their good works on earth. Purchasing indulgences, venerating relics, making pilgrimages, and seeking the intercession of the saints were useless, because only the grace of God could save the Christian soul. Justified by faith alone, Christians should assume full responsibility for their own actions and intentions.

In 1517, in pointed criticism of Church abuses, Luther posted on the door of the collegiate church at Wittenberg a list of ninety-five subjects he intended for dispute with the leaders of the Church of Rome. The *Ninety-Five Theses*, which took the confrontational tone of the sample below, were put to press and circulated throughout Europe:

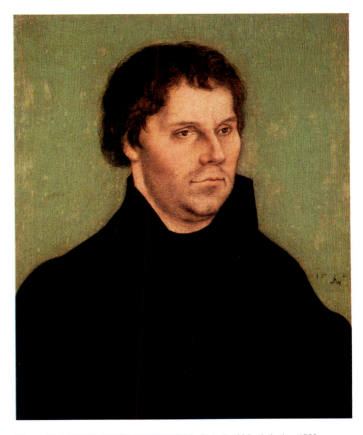

Figure 19.4 LUCAS CRANACH THE ELDER, *Portrait of Martin Luther*, 1533. Panel, 8 × 5¾ in.

27 They are wrong who say that the soul flies out of Purgatory as soon as the money thrown into the chest rattles.

32 Those who believe that, through letters of pardon [indulgences], they are made sure of their own salvation will be eternally damned along with their teachers.

37 Every true Christian, whether living or dead, has a share in all the benefits of Christ and of the Church, given by God, even without letters of pardon.

43 Christians should be taught that he who gives to a poor man, or lends to a needy man, does better than if he bought pardons.

44 Because by works of charity, charity increases, and the man becomes better; while by means of pardons, he does not become better, but only freer from punishment.

45 Christians should be taught that he who sees any one in need, and, passing him by, gives money for pardons, is not purchasing for himself the indulgences of the Pope but the anger of God.

49 Christians should be taught that the Pope's pardons are useful if they do not put their trust in them, but most hurtful if through them they lose the fear of God.

50 Christians should be taught that if the Pope were acquainted with the exactions of the Preachers of pardons, he would prefer that the Basilica of Saint Peter should be burnt to ashes rather than that it should be built up with the skin, flesh, and bones of his sheep.

54 Wrong is done to the Word of God when, in the same sermon, an equal or longer time is spent on pardons than on it.

62 The true treasure of the Church is the Holy Gospel of the glory and grace of God.

66 The treasures of indulgences are nets, wherewith they now fish for the riches of men.

67 Those indulgences which the preachers loudly proclaim to be the greatest graces, are seen to be truly such as regards the promotion of gain.

68 Yet they are in reality most insignificant when compared to the grace of God and the piety of the cross.

86 . . . why does not the Pope, whose riches are at this day more ample than those of the wealthiest of the wealthy, build the single Basilica of Saint Peter with his own money rather than with that of poor believers? . . .

Luther did not set out to destroy Catholicism, but rather to reform it. Gradually he extended his criticism of Church abuses to criticism of Church doctrine. For instance, because he found justification in Scripture for only two Roman Catholic sacraments—baptism and Holy Communion—he rejected the other five. He attacked monasticism and clerical celibacy. (Luther himself married, and fathered six children.) Luther's boldest challenge to the old medieval order, however, was his unwillingness to accept the pope as the ultimate source of religious authority. Denying that the pope was the spiritual heir to Saint Peter, he claimed that the head of the Church, like any other human being, was subject to error and correction. Christians, argued Luther, were collectively a priesthood of believers; they were "consecrated as priests by baptism." The ultimate source of authority in matters of faith and doctrine was Scripture, as interpreted by the individual Christian. To encourage the reading of the Bible among his followers, Luther translated the Old and New Testaments into German.

Luther's assertions were revolutionary because they defied both church dogma and the authority of the Church of Rome. In 1520, Pope Leo X issued an edict excommunicating the outspoken reformer. Luther promptly burned the edict in the presence of his students at the University of Wittenberg. The following year, he was summoned to the city of Worms in order to appear before the Diet—the German parliamentary council. Charged with heresy, Luther stubbornly refused to back down, concluding, "I cannot and will not recant anything, for to act against our conscience is neither safe for us, nor open to us. On this I take my stand. I can do no other. God help me. Amen." Luther's confrontational temperament and down-to-earth style are captured in this excerpt from his *Address to the German Nobility*, a call for religious reform written shortly before the Diet of Worms and circulated widely in a printed edition.

READING 19.1 From Luther's *Address to the German Nobility* (1520)

It has been devised that the Pope, bishops, priests, and monks are called the *spiritual estate*; princes, lords, artificers, and peasants are the *temporal estate*. This is an artful lie and hypocritical device, but let no one be made afraid by it, and that for this reason: that all Christians are truly of the spiritual estate, and there is no difference among them, save of office alone. As Saint Paul says (1 Cor.:12), we are all one body, though each member does its own work, to serve the others. This is because we have one baptism, one Gospel, one faith, and are all Christians alike; for baptism, Gospel, and faith, these alone make spiritual and Christian people. 1 10

As for the unction by a pope or a bishop, tonsure, ordination, consecration, and clothes differing from those of laymen—all this may make a hypocrite or an anointed puppet, but never a Christian or a spiritual man. Thus we are all consecrated as priests by baptism. . . .

And to put the matter even more plainly, if a little company of pious Christian laymen were taken prisoners and carried away to a desert, and had not among them a priest consecrated by a bishop, and were there to agree to elect one of them, born in wedlock or not, and were to order him to baptize, to celebrate the Mass, to absolve, and to preach, this man would as truly be a priest, as if all the bishops and all the popes had consecrated him. That is why in cases of necessity every man can baptize and absolve, which would not be possible if we were not all priests. . . . 20

[Members of the Church of Rome] alone pretend to be considered masters of the Scriptures; although they learn nothing of them all their life. They assume authority, and juggle before us with impudent words, saying that the Pope cannot err in matters of faith, whether he be evil or good, albeit they cannot prove it by a single letter. That is why the canon law contains so many heretical and unchristian, nay unnatural, laws. . . .

And though they say that this authority was given to Saint Peter when the keys were given to him, it is plain enough that the keys were not given to Saint Peter alone, but to the whole community. Besides, the keys were not ordained for doctrine or authority, but for sin, to bind or loose; and what they claim besides this from the keys is mere invention. . . .

Only consider the matter. They must needs acknowledge that there are pious Christians among us that have the true faith, spirit, understanding, word, and mind of Christ: why then should we reject their word and understanding, and follow a pope who has neither understanding nor spirit? Surely this were to deny our whole faith and the Christian Church. . . .

Therefore when need requires, and the Pope is a cause of offence to Christendom, in these cases whoever can best do so, as a faithful member of the whole body, must do what he can to procure a true free council. This no one can do so well as the temporal authorities, especially since they are fellow-Christians, fellow-priests, sharing one spirit and one power in all things . . . Would it not be most unnatural, if a fire were to break out in a city, and every one were to keep still and let it burn on and on, whatever might be burnt, simply because they had not the mayor's authority, or because the fire perchance broke out at the mayor's house? Is not every citizen bound in this case to rouse and call in the rest? How much more should this be done in the spiritual city of Christ, if a fire of offence breaks out, either at the Pope's government or wherever it may! The like happens if an enemy attacks a town. The first to rouse up the rest earns glory and thanks. Why then should not he earn glory that decries the coming of our enemies from hell and rouses and summons all Christians?

But as for their boasts of their authority, that no one must oppose it, this is idle talk. No one in Christendom has any authority to do harm, or to forbid others to prevent harm being done. There is no authority in the Church but for reformation. Therefore if the Pope wished to use his power to prevent the calling of a free council, so as to prevent the reformation of the Church, we must not respect him or his power; and if he should begin to excommunicate and fulminate, we must despise this as the doings of a madman, and, trusting in God, excommunicate and repel him as best we may.

Q **Which of Luther's assertions would the Church of Rome have found heretical? Why?**

Q **Which aspects of this selection might be called anti-authoritarian? Which might be called democratic?**

The Spread of Protestantism

Luther's criticism constituted an open revolt against the institution that for centuries had governed the lives of Western Christians. With the aid of the printing press, his "protestant" sermons and letters circulated throughout Europe. His defense of Christian conscience worked to justify protest against all forms of dominion. In 1524, under the banner of Christian liberty, German commoners instigated a series of violent uprisings against the oppressive landholding aristocracy. The result was full-scale war, the so-called Peasant Revolts that resulted in the bloody defeat of thousands of peasants. Although Luther condemned the violence and brutality of the Peasant Revolts, social unrest and ideological warfare had only just begun. His denunciation of the lower-class rebels brought many of the German princes to his side; and some used their new religious allegiance as an excuse to seize and usurp Church properties and revenues within their own domains. As the floodgates of dissent opened wide, civil wars broke out between German princes who were faithful to Rome and those who called themselves Lutheran. The wars lasted for some twenty-five years, until, under the terms of the Peace of Augsburg in 1555, it was agreed that each German prince should have the right to choose the religion to be practiced within his own domain. Nevertheless, religious wars resumed in the late sixteenth century and devastated German lands for almost a century.

Calvin

All of Europe was affected by Luther's break with the Church. The Lutheran insistence that enlightened Christians could arrive at truth by way of Scripture led reformers everywhere to interpret the Bible for themselves. The result was the birth of many new Protestant sects, each based on its own interpretation of Scripture. In the independent city of Geneva, Switzerland, the French lawyer and theologian John Calvin (1509–1564) set up a government in which elected officials, using the Bible as the supreme law, ruled the community.

Calvin held that Christians were predestined from birth for either salvation or damnation, a circumstance that made good works irrelevant. The "Doctrine of Predestination" encouraged Calvinists to glorify God by living an upright life, one that required faith, obedience, and abstention from dancing, gambling, swearing, drunkenness, and all forms of public display. Although one's status was known only by God, Protestant Christians manifested that they were among the "elect" by their display of moral rectitude. Further, since Calvin taught that wealth was a sign of God's favor, Calvinists extolled the "work ethic" as consistent with the divine will. Calvin's treatise *Institutes of the Christian Religion* (1536) was hugely influential in transforming Luther's teachings into a rational legal system, while his model city, Geneva, became a missionary center for Calvinist followers in Germany, England, the Netherlands, Scotland, and elsewhere.

Humanism and Religious Fanaticism: The Persecution of Witches

The age of Christian humanism witnessed the rise of religious fanaticism, the most dramatic evidence of which is the witch hunts that infested Renaissance Europe and Reformation Germany. While belief in witches dates back to humankind's earliest societies, the practice of persecuting witches did not begin until the late fourteenth century. Based in the medieval practice of finding evidence of the supernatural in natural phenomena, and fueled by the popular Christian belief that the Devil is actively engaged in human affairs, the first mass persecutions occurred at the end of the fifteenth century, reaching a peak approximately one hundred years later. Among Northern European artists, witches and witchcraft became favorite subjects (Figure **19.5**).

In 1484, two German theologians published the *Malleus Maleficarum* (*The Witches' Hammer*), an encyclopedia that described the nature of witches, their collusion with the Devil, and the ways in which they might be recognized and punished. Its authors reiterated the traditional claim that women—by nature more feeble than men—were dangerously susceptible to the Devil's temptation. As a result, they became the primary victims of the mass hysteria that prevailed during the so-called age of humanism. Women—particularly those who were single, old, or eccentric—constituted four-fifths of the roughly 70,000 witches put to death between the years 1400 and 1700. Females who served as midwives might be accused of causing infant deaths or deformities; others were condemned as witches at the onset of local drought or disease. One recent study suggests that witches were blamed for the sharp drops in temperature that devastated sixteenth-century crops and left many Europeans starving.

The persecution of witches may be seen as an instrument of post-Reformation religious oppression, or as the intensification of antifemale sentiment in an age when women had become more visible politically and commercially. Nevertheless, the witchcraft hysteria of the early modern era dramatizes the troubling gap between humanism and religious fanaticism.

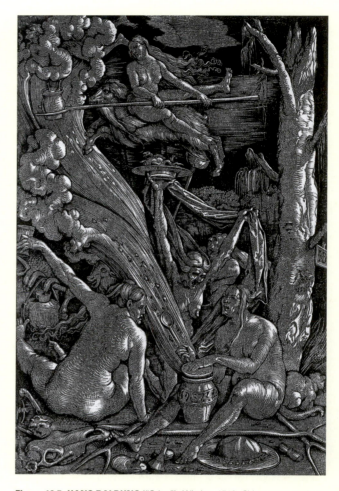

Figure 19.5 HANS BALDUNG ("Grien"), *Witches*, 1510. *Chiaroscuro* woodcut, 15⅞ × 10¼ in. Three witches, sitting under the branches of a dead tree, perform a black Mass. One lifts the chalice, while another mocks the Host by elevating the body of a dead toad. An airborne witch rides backward on a goat, a symbol of the Devil.

The Anabaptists

In nearby Zürich, a radical wing of the Protestant movement emerged: the Anabaptists (given this name by those who opposed their practice of "rebaptizing" adult Christians) rejected all seven of the sacraments (including infant baptism) as sources of God's grace. Placing total emphasis on Christian conscience and the voluntary acceptance of Christ, the Anabaptists called for the abolition of the Mass and the complete separation of Church and state: holding individual responsibility and personal liberty as fundamental ideals, they were among the first Westerners to offer religious sanction for political disobedience. Many Anabaptist reformers met death at the hands of local governments—the men were burned at the stake and the women were usually drowned. English off-shoots of the Anabaptists—the Baptists and the Quakers—would come to follow Anabaptist precepts, including the rejection of religious ritual (and imagery) and a fundamentalist approach to Scripture.

The Anglican Church

In England, the Tudor monarch Henry VIII (1491–1547) broke with the Roman Catholic Church and established a church under his own leadership. Political expediency colored the king's motives: Henry was determined to leave England with a male heir, but when eighteen years of marriage to Catherine of Aragon produced only one heir (a daughter), he attempted to annul the marriage and take a new wife. The pope refused, prompting the king—formerly a staunch supporter of the Catholic Church—to break with Rome. In 1526, Henry declared himself head of the Church in England. In 1536, with the support of Parliament, he closed all Christian monasteries and sold Church lands, accumulating vast revenues for the royal treasury. His actions led to years of dispute and hostility between Roman Catholics and Anglicans (members of the new English Church). By the mid-sixteenth century, the consequences of Luther's protests were evident: the religious unity of Western Christendom was shattered forever. Social and political upheaval had become the order of the day.

Music and the Reformation

Since the Reformation clearly dominated the religious and social history of the sixteenth century, it also touched, directly or indirectly, all forms of artistic endeavor, including music. Luther himself was a student of music, an active performer, and an admirer of Josquin des Prez (see chapter 17). Emphasizing music as a source of religious instruction, he encouraged the writing of hymnals and reorganized the German Mass to include both congregational and professional singing. Luther held that all religious texts should be sung in German, so that the faithful might understand their message. The text, according to Luther, should be both comprehensible and appealing.

Luther's favorite musical form was the **chorale**, a congregational hymn that served to enhance the spirit of Protestant worship. Chorales, written in German, drew on Latin hymns and German folk tunes. They were characterized by monophonic clarity and simplicity, features that encouraged performance by untrained congregations. The most famous Lutheran chorale (the melody of which may not have originated with Luther) is "Ein' feste Burg ist unser Gott" ("A Mighty Fortress is our God")—a hymn that has been called "the anthem of the Reformation." Luther's chorales had a major influence on religious music for centuries. And although in the hands of later composers the chorale became a complex polyphonic vehicle for voices and instruments, at its inception it was performed with all voices singing the same words at the same time. It was thus an ideal medium for the communal expression of Protestant piety.

Other Protestant sects, such as the Anabaptists and the Calvinists, regarded music as a potentially dangerous distraction for the faithful. In many sixteenth-century churches, the organ was dismantled and sung portions of the service edited or deleted. Calvin, however, who encouraged devotional recitation of psalms in the home, revised church services to include the congregational singing of psalms in the vernacular.

This Lutheran chorale inspired Johann Sebastian Bach's Cantata No. 80, an excerpt from which is included among the Listening Selections for Chapter 22.

Northern Renaissance Art

Jan van Eyck

Prior to the Reformation, in the cities of Northern Europe, a growing middle class joined princely rulers and the Church to encourage the arts. In addition to traditional religious subjects, middle-class patrons commissioned portraits that—like those painted by Italian Renaissance artists (see chapter 17)—recorded their physical appearance and brought attention to their earthly achievements. Fifteenth-century Northern artists, unlike their Italian counterparts, were relatively unfamiliar with Greco-Roman culture; many of them moved in the direction of detailed Realism, already evident in the manuscript illuminations of the Limbourg brothers (see Figure 15.1).

The pioneer of Northern realism was the Flemish artist Jan van Eyck (ca. 1380–1441). Van Eyck, whom we met in chapter 17, was reputed to have perfected the art of oil painting (see Figure 17.11). His application of thin glazes of colored pigments bound with linseed oil achieved the impression of dense, atmospheric space, and simulated the naturalistic effects of light reflecting off the surfaces of objects. Such effects were almost impossible to achieve in fresco or tempera. While van Eyck lacked any knowledge of the system of linear perspective popularized in Florence, he achieved an extraordinary level of realism both in the miniatures he executed for religious manuscripts and in his panel paintings.

Van Eyck's full-length double portrait of 1434 is the first painting in Western art to have portrayed a secular couple in a domestic interior (see LOOKING INTO, Figure **19.6**). The painting has long been the subject of debate among scholars who have questioned its original purpose, as well as the identity of the sitters. It was long thought to represent the marriage of Giovanni di Nicolao Arnolfini (an Italian cloth merchant who represented the Medici bank in Bruges) to Jeanne Cenami, but it has recently been discovered that Jeanne died in 1433, a year before the date of the painting. Since so many elements in the painting suggest a betrothal or wedding vow, however, it is speculated that Giovanni, who knew van Eyck in Bruges for many years, might have remarried in 1434 and commissioned the artist to record the union.

In the painting, the richly dressed Arnolfini raises his right hand as if to greet or vow, while the couple joins hands, a gesture traditionally associated with engagement or marriage. Behind the couple, an inscription on the back wall of the chamber reads "*Johannes de Eyck fuit hic*" ("Jan van Eyck was here"); this testimonial is reiterated by the presence of two figures, probably the artist himself and a second observer, whose painted reflections are seen in the convex mirror below the inscription. Van Eyck's consummate mastery of minute, realistic details—from the ruffles on the young woman's headcovering to the whiskers of the monkey-faced dog—demonstrate the artist's determination to capture the immediacy of the physical world. This attention to detail and deliberate

Van Eyck's *Arnolfini Double Portrait*

lack of idealization, typical of Northern painting, sets it apart from most Italian Renaissance art.

Bosch

The generation of Flemish artists that followed Jan van Eyck produced one of the most enigmatic figures of the Northern Renaissance: Hieronymus Bosch (1460–1516). Little is known about Bosch's life, and the exact meaning of some of his works is much disputed. His career spanned the decades of the High Renaissance in Italy, but comparison of his paintings with those of Raphael or Michelangelo underscores the enormous difference between Italian Renaissance art and that of the European North: whereas Raphael and Michelangelo elevated the natural nobility of the individual, Bosch detailed the fallibility of humankind, its moral struggle, and its apocalyptic destiny.

Bosch's most famous work, the triptych known as *The Garden of Earthly Delights* (Figure **19.7**), was executed around 1510, the very time that Raphael was painting *The School of Athens*. A work of astonishing complexity, the imagery of Bosch's painting has baffled and intrigued viewers for centuries. For, while it seems to describe the traditional Christian theme of the Creation, Fall, and Punishment of humankind, it does so by means of an assortment of wildly unconventional images. When the wings of the altarpiece are closed, one sees an image of God hovering above a huge transparent globe: the planet earth in the process of creation. An accompanying inscription reads: "He spoke, and it came to be; he commanded and it was created" (Psalm 33.9). When the triptych is opened, the left wing shows the Creation of Eve, but the event takes place in an Eden populated with fabulous and predatory creations (such as the cat at lower left). In the central panel, amidst a cosmic landscape, hordes of youthful nudes cavort in a variety of erotic and playful pastimes. They frolic with oversized flora and fruit, real and imagined animals, gigantic birds, and strangely shaped vessels. In the right wing, Bosch pictures Hell as a dark and sulfurous inferno where the damned are tormented by an assortment of sinister creatures and infernal machines that inflict punishment on sinners appropriate to their sins (as in Dante's *Inferno*; see chapter 12). The hoarder (at the lower right), for instance, pays for his greed by excreting gold coins into a pothole, while the nude nearby, punished for the sin of lust, is fondled by demons.

The Garden of Earthly Delights has been described by some as an exposition on the decadent behavior of the descendants of Adam and Eve, but its distance from conventional religious iconography has made it the subject of endless scholarly interpretation. Bosch, a Roman Catholic, seems to have borrowed imagery from a variety of medieval and contemporary sources, including the Bible, popular proverbs, marginal grotesques in illuminated manuscripts, and pilgrimage badges, as well as the popular pseudo-sciences of his time: astrology, the study of the influence of heavenly bodies on human affairs (the precursor of astronomy); and alchemy, the art of transmuting base metals into gold (the precursor of chemistry). The egg-shaped vessels, beakers, and transparent tubes that appear in all parts of the

Figure 19.6 JAN VAN EYCK, *Arnolfini Double Portrait*, 1434. Tempera and oil on panel, 32¼ × 23½ in.

The *Arnolfini Double Portrait* is typical of the Northern sensibility in the way in which the physical details "speak" to the function of the painting as a visual document related to marriage: the burning candle (traditionally carried to the marriage ceremony by the bride) suggests the all-seeing presence of Christ; the ripening fruit lying on and near the window sill both symbolizes fecundity and alludes to the union of the First Couple in the Garden of Eden; the carved image on the chairback near the bed represents Saint Margaret, the patron saint of childbirth.

The objects in this domestic interior suggest a world of material comfort and pleasure: the brass chandelier, convex mirror, and oriental carpet were luxuries in fifteenth-century Flanders, while the ermine and sable-trimmed outer garments and the very abundance of rich fabrics worn by both the merchant and his partner would have been recognized as signs of great wealth and prosperity. At the same time, however, many of these details make symbolic reference to a less tangible, spiritual reality. In this effort to reconcile the visible world with the invisible legacy of faith, van Eyck anticipated the unique character of Northern Renaissance art.

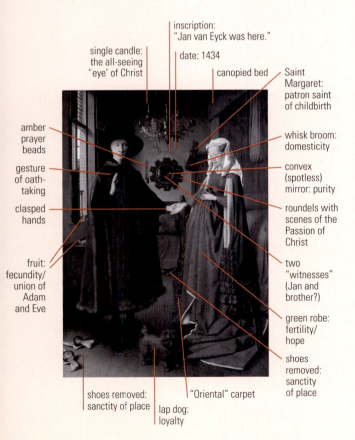

- inscription: "Jan van Eyck was here."
- date: 1434
- single candle: the all-seeing "eye' of Christ
- canopied bed
- Saint Margaret: patron saint of childbirth
- amber prayer beads
- whisk broom: domesticity
- gesture of oath-taking
- convex (spotless) mirror: purity
- clasped hands
- roundels with scenes of the Passion of Christ
- fruit: fecundity/ union of Adam and Eve
- two "witnesses" (Jan and brother?)
- green robe: fertility/ hope
- shoes removed: sanctity of place
- shoes removed: sanctity of place
- "Oriental" carpet
- lap dog: loyalty

Figure 19.7 HIERONYMUS BOSCH, *The Creation of Eve: The Garden of Earthly Delights: Hell* (triptych), ca. 1510–1515. Oil on wood, 7 ft. 2⅝ in. × 12 ft. 8¾ in. Bosch probably painted this moralizing work for lay patrons. Many of its individual images would have been recognized as references to the Seven Deadly Sins, for instance: the bagpipe (a symbol of Lust) that sits on a disk crowning the Tree-Man (upper center) and the man who is forced to disgorge his food (symbolic of Gluttony) depicted beneath the enthroned frog (lower right).

triptych were commonly used in alchemical transmutation. The latter process may have been familiar to Bosch as symbolic of creation and destruction, and, more specifically, as a metaphor for the biblical Creation and Fall.

Regardless of how one interprets Bosch's *Garden*, it is clear that the artist transformed standard Christian iconography to suit his imagination. Probably commissioned by a

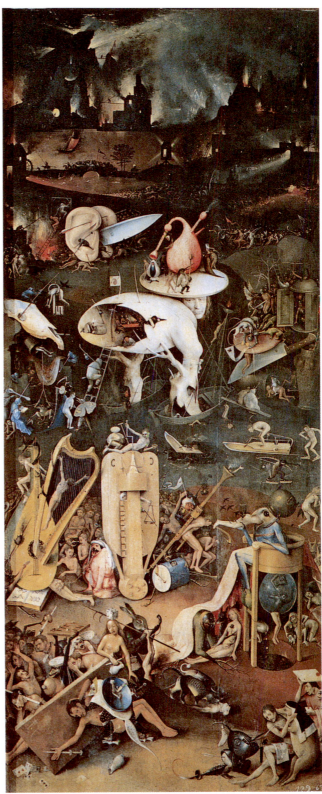

private patron, Bosch may have felt free to bring fantasy and invention to traditional subject matter. The result is a moralizing commentary on the varieties of human folly afflicting sinful creatures hopeful of Christian salvation.

More conventional in its imagery, Bosch's *Death and the Miser* (Figure **19.8**) belongs to the tradition of the *memento mori* (discussed in chapter 12), which warns the beholder of the inevitability of death. The painting also shows the influence of popular fifteenth-century handbooks on the art of dying (the *ars moriendi*), designed to remind Christians that they must choose between sinful pleasures and the way of Christ. As Death looms on the threshold, the miser, unable to resist worldly temptations even in his last minutes of life, reaches for the bag of gold offered to him by

Figure 19.8 HIERONYMUS BOSCH,
Death and the Miser, ca. 1485–1490. Oil on oak,
3 ft. ⅝ in. × 12⅛ in.

a demon. In the foreground, Bosch depicts the miser storing gold in his money chest while clutching his rosary. Symbols of worldly power—a helmet, sword, and shield—allude to earthly follies. The depiction of such still-life objects to symbolize vanity, transience, or decay would become a genre in itself among seventeenth-century Flemish artists.

Printmaking

The Protestant Reformation cast a long shadow upon the religious art of the North. Protestants rejected the traditional imagery of medieval piety, along with church relics and sacred images, which they associated with superstition and idolatry. Protestant iconoclasts stripped the stained glass from cathedral windows, shattered religious sculpture, whitewashed church frescoes, and destroyed altarpieces. At the same time, however, the voices of reform encouraged the proliferation of private devotional art, particularly that which illustrated biblical themes. In the production of portable devotional images, the technology of printmaking played a major role. Just as movable type had facilitated the dissemination of the printed word, so the technology of the print made devotional subjects available more cheaply and in greater numbers than ever before.

The two new printmaking processes of the fifteenth century were **woodcut**, the technique of cutting away all parts of a design on a wood surface except those that will be inked and transferred to paper (Figure **19.9**), and **engraving** (Figure **19.10**), the process by which lines are incised on a metal (usually copper) plate that is inked and run through a printing press. Books with printed illustrations

became cheap alternatives to the hand-illuminated manuscripts that were prohibitively expensive to all but wealthy patrons.

Dürer

The unassailed leader in Northern Renaissance printmaking, and one of the finest graphic artists of all time, was Albrecht Dürer of Nuremberg (1471–1528). Dürer earned international fame for his woodcuts and metal engravings. His mastery of the laws of linear perspective and human anatomy and his investigations into Classical principles of proportions (enhanced by two trips to Italy) equaled those of the best Italian Renaissance artist–scientists. In the genre of portraiture, Dürer was the match of Raphael, but, unlike Raphael, he recorded the features of his sitters with little idealization. His portrait engraving of Erasmus (see Figure 19.3) captures the concentrated intelligence of the Prince of Humanists.

Dürer brought to the art of his day a desire to convey the spiritual message of Scripture. His series of woodcuts illustrating the last book of the New Testament, the Revelation According to Saint John (also called the "Apocalypse"), reveals the extent to which he achieved his purpose. *The Four Horsemen of the Apocalypse*—one of fifteen woodcuts in the series—brings to life the terrifying events described in Revelation 6.1–8 (see Figure 19.1). Amidst billowing clouds, Death (in the foreground), Famine (carrying a pair of scales), War (brandishing a sword), and Pestilence (drawing his bow) sweep down upon humankind; their victims fall beneath

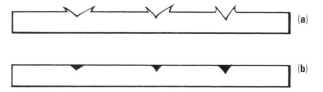

Figure 19.10 Engraving. An intaglio method of printing. The cutting tool, a *burin* or *graver*, is used to cut lines in the surface of metal plates. (**a**) A cross section of an engraved plate showing burrs (ridges) produced by scratching a burin into the surface of a metal plate; (**b**) the burrs are removed and ink is wiped over the surface and forced into the scratches. The plate is then wiped clean, leaving ink deposits in the scratches; the ink is forced from the plate onto paper under pressure in a special press.

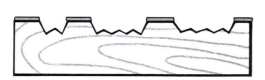

Figure 19.9 Woodcut. A relief printing process created by lines cut into the plank surface of wood. The raised portions of the block are inked and transferred by pressure to the paper by hand or with a printing press.

Figure 19.11 ALBRECHT DÜRER, *Knight, Death, and the Devil*, 1513. Engraving, 9⅝ × 7½ in. Dürer's engraving is remarkable for its wealth of microscopic detail. Objects in the real world—the horse, the dog, and the lizard—are depicted as precisely as those imagined: the devil and the horned demon.

the horses' hooves, or, as with the bishop in the lower left, are devoured by infernal monsters.

Dürer was a humanist in his own right and a great admirer of both the moderate Erasmus and the zealous Luther. In one of his most memorable engravings, *Knight, Death, and the Devil*, he depicted the Christian soul in the allegorical guise of a medieval knight (Figure **19.11**), a figure made famous in a treatise by Erasmus entitled *Handbook for the Militant Christian* (1504). The knight, the medieval symbol of fortitude and courage, advances against a dark and brooding landscape. Accompanied by his loyal dog, he marches forward, ignoring his fearsome companions: Death, who rides a pale horse and carries an hourglass, and the devil, a shaggy, cross-eyed, horned demon. Here is the visual counterpart of Erasmus' message that the Christian must hold to the path of virtue, and in

spite of "all those spooks and phantoms" that come upon him, he must "look not behind." The knight's dignified bearing (probably inspired by heroic equestrian statues Dürer had seen in Italy) contrasts sharply with the bestial and cankerous features of his forbidding escorts. In the tradition of Jan van Eyck, but with a precision facilitated by the new medium of metal engraving, Dürer records every leaf and pebble, hair and wrinkle; and yet the final effect is not a mere piling up of minutiae but, like nature itself, an astonishing amalgam of organically related elements.

In addition to his numerous woodcuts and engravings, Dürer produced hundreds of paintings: portraits and large-scale religious subjects. His interest in the natural world inspired the first landscapes in Western art (Figure **19.12**). These detailed panoramic views of the countryside, executed in watercolor during his frequent travels to Italy and elsewhere, were independent works, not mere studies for larger, more formal subjects. To such landscapes, as well as to his meticulously detailed renderings of plants, animals, and birds, Dürer brought the eye of a scientific naturalist and a spirit of curiosity not unlike that of his Italian contemporary Leonardo da Vinci.

Grünewald

Dürer's German contemporary Matthias Gothardt Neithardt, better known as "Grünewald" (1460–1528), did not share Dürer's Classically inspired aesthetic ideals, nor his quest for realistic representation. The few paintings and drawings left by Grünewald (as compared with the hundreds of works left by Dürer) do not tell us whether the artist was Catholic or Protestant. In their spiritual intensity and emotional subjectivity, however, they are among the most striking devotional works of the Northern Renaissance.

Grünewald's landmark work, the Isenheim Altarpiece, was designed to provide solace to the victims of disease and especially plague at the Hospital of Saint Anthony in

Figure 19.12 ALBRECHT DÜRER, *Wire Drawing Mill*, undated. Watercolor, 11¼ × 16¾ in.

Figure 19.13 MATTHIAS GRÜNEWALD, Isenheim Altarpiece, ca. 1510–1515. Oil on panel, central panel 8 ft. × 10 ft. 1 in. The opened wings of the altarpiece show Saint Sebastian (left) and Saint Anthony (right), both protectors against disease and plague. Those afflicted with disease (including leprosy, syphilis, and poisoning caused by ergot, a cereal fungus), were able to contemplate the altarpiece daily in the hospital chapel.

Isenheim, near Colmar, France (Figure **19.13**). Like the *Imitatio Christi*, which taught Christians to seek identification with Jesus, this multipaneled altarpiece reminded its beholders of their kinship with the suffering Jesus, depicted in the central panel. Following the tradition of the devotional German *Pietà* (see Figure 15.11), Grünewald made use of expressive exaggeration and painfully precise detail: the agonized body of Jesus is lengthened to emphasize its weight as it hangs from the bowed cross, the flesh putrefies with clotted blood and angry thorns, the fingers convulse and curl, while the feet—broken and bruised—contort in a spasm of pain. Grünewald reinforces the mood of lamentation by placing the scene in a darkened landscape. He exaggerates the gestures of the attending figures, including that of John the Baptist, whose oversized finger points to the prophetic Latin inscription that explains his mystical presence: "He must increase and I must decrease" (John 3:30).

Cranach and Holbein

The German cities of the sixteenth century produced some of the finest draftsmen in the history of Western art. Dürer's contemporary Lucas Cranach the Elder (1472–1553) was a highly acclaimed court painter at Wittenberg

and, like Dürer, a convert to the Protestant reform. In 1522, he produced the woodcuts for the first German edition of the New Testament. Although he also worked for Catholic patrons, he painted and engraved numerous portraits of Protestant leaders, the most notable of whom was his friend Martin Luther, whose likeness he recreated several times. In the portrait illustrated in Figure 19.4, Cranach exercised his skill as a master draftsman, capturing both the authoritative silhouette and the confident demeanor of the famous reformer.

Hans Holbein the Younger (1497–1543), celebrated as the greatest of the German portraitists, was born in Augsburg, but spent much of his life in Switzerland, France, and England. With a letter of introduction from his friend Erasmus, Holbein traveled to England to paint the family of Sir Thomas More (see Figure 19.16)—Western Europe's first domestic group portrait (it survives only in drawings and copies). On a later trip to England, Holbein became the favorite of Henry VIII, whose likeness he captured along with portraits of the king's current and prospective wives. In common with Dürer and Cranach, Holbein was a master of line. All three artists manifested the integration of brilliant draftsmanship and precise, realistic detail that characterizes the art of the Northern Renaissance. Holbein, however, was unique in his minimal use of line to evoke a penetrating sense of the sitter's personality. So lifelike are some of Holbein's portraits that modern scholars have suggested that he made use of technical aids, such as the *camera lucida*, in their preparation (see chapter 17, Exploring Issues).

Bruegel

The career of the last great sixteenth-century Flemish painter, Pieter Bruegel the Elder (1525–1569), followed the careers of most other Northern Renaissance masters by a generation. Like Dürer, Bruegel had traveled to Italy and absorbed its Classical culture; his style, however, would remain relatively independent of Italian influence. Closer in temperament to Bosch, he was deeply concerned with human folly, especially as it was manifested in the everyday life of his Flemish neighbors. Among his early works were crowded panoramas depicting themes of human pride and religious strife. Bruegel's *Triumph of Death* may be read as an indictment of the brutal wars that plagued sixteenth-century Europe (Figure **19.14**). In a cosmic landscape that resembles the setting of a Last Judgment or a Boschlike underworld, Bruegel depicts throngs of skeletons relentlessly slaughtering all ranks of men and women. The armies of the dead are without mercy. In the left foreground, a cardinal collapses in the arms of a skeleton; in the left corner, an emperor relinquishes his hoards of gold; on the right, death interrupts the pleasure of gamblers and lovers. Some of the living are crushed beneath the wheels of a death cart, others are hanged from scaffolds or subjected to torture. Bruegel's apocalyptic vision transforms the late medieval Dance of Death into a universal holocaust.

Many of Bruegel's best-known works were inspired by biblical parables or local proverbs, popular expressions of universal truths concerning human behavior. In his drawings, engravings, and paintings, he rendered these as visual narratives set in the Flemish countryside. His treatment of the details of rustic life, which earned him the title "Peasant Bruegel," and his landscapes illustrating the labors appropriate to each season were the culmination of a tradition begun in the innovative miniatures of the Limbourg brothers (see Figure 15.1). However, Bruegel's **genre paintings**

Figure 19.14 PIETER BRUEGEL THE ELDER, *Triumph of Death*, ca. 1562–1564. Oil on panel, 3 ft. 10 in. × 5 ft. 3¾ in.

Figure 19.15 **PIETER BRUEGEL THE ELDER**, *The Wedding Dance*, 1566. Oil on panel, 3 ft. 11 in. × 5 ft. 2 in.

(representations of the everyday life of ordinary folk) were not small-scale illustrations, but monumental (and sometimes allegorical) transcriptions of rural activities. *The Wedding Dance* (Figure **19.15**) depicts peasant revelry in a country setting whose earthiness is reinforced by rich tones of russet, tan, and muddy green. At the very top of the panel, an improvised wedding table appears among the trees. The red-haired bride, clothed in black (center left), has joined the villagers, who cavort to the music of the bagpipes (right foreground). Although Bruegel's figures are clumsy and often ill-proportioned, they share an ennobling vitality. In his art, as in that of other Northern Renaissance painters, we discover an unvarnished perception of human beings in mundane and unheroic circumstances—a sharp contrast to the idealized conception of humankind found in the art of Renaissance Italy.

Sixteenth-Century Literature

Erasmus: *The Praise of Folly*

European literature of the sixteenth century was marked by heightened individualism and a progressive inclination to clear away the last remnants of medieval orthodoxy. It was,

in many ways, a literature of protest and reform, and one whose dominant themes reflect the tension between medieval and modern ideas. European writers were especially concerned with the discrepancies between the noble ideals of Classical humanism and the ignoble reality of human behavior. Religious rivalry and the horrors of war, witch hunts, and religious persecution all seemed to contradict the optimistic view that the Renaissance had inaugurated a more enlightened phase of human self-consciousness.

Science and Technology

1540	the Swiss physician Paracelsus (Philippus von Hohenheim) pioneers the use of chemistry for medical purposes
1543	Copernicus (Polish) publishes *On the Revolution of the Heavenly Spheres*, announcing his heliocentric theory
1553	Michael Servetus (Spanish) describes the pulmonary circulation of the blood

Satire, a literary genre that conveys the contradictions between real and ideal situations, was especially popular during the sixteenth century. By means of satiric irony, Northern Renaissance writers held up prevailing abuses to ridicule, thus implying the need for reform.

The learned treatises and letters of Erasmus won him the respect of scholars throughout Europe; but his single most popular work was *The Praise of Folly*, a satiric oration attacking a wide variety of human foibles, including greed, intellectual pomposity, and pride. *The Praise of Folly* went through more than two dozen editions in Erasmus' lifetime, and influenced other humanists, including his lifelong friend and colleague Thomas More, to whom it was dedicated (in Latin, *moria* means "folly").

A short excerpt from *The Praise of Folly* offers some idea of Erasmus' keen wit as applied to a typical Northern Renaissance theme: the vast gulf between human fallibility and human perfectibility. The reading opens with the image of the world as a stage, a favorite metaphor of sixteenth-century painters and poets—not the least of whom was William Shakespeare. Dame Folly, the allegorical figure who is the speaker in the piece, compares life to a comedy in which the players assume various roles: in the course of the drama (she observes), one may come to play the parts of both servant and king. She then describes each of a number of roles (or disciplines), such as medicine, law, and so on, in terms of its affinity with folly. Erasmus' most searing words were reserved for theologians and church dignitaries, but his insights expose more generally (and timelessly) the frailties of all human beings.

READING 19.2 From Erasmus' *The Praise of Folly* (1511)

Now what else is the whole life of mortals but a sort of   1
comedy, in which the various actors, disguised by various
costumes and masks, walk on and play each one his
part, until the manager waves them off the stage?
Moreover, this manager frequently bids the same actor
go back in a different costume, so that he who has but
lately played the king in scarlet now acts the flunkey in
patched clothes. Thus all things are presented by
shadows; yet this play is put on in no other way. . . .

[The disciplines] that approach nearest to common   10
sense, that is, to folly, are held in highest esteem.
Theologians are starved, naturalists find cold comfort,
astrologers are mocked, and logicians are slighted. . . .
Within the profession of medicine, furthermore, so far
as any member is eminently unlearned, impudent, or
careless, he is valued the more, even in the chambers of
belted earls. For medicine, especially as now practiced
by many, is but a subdivision of the art of flattery, no
less truly than is rhetoric. Lawyers have the next place
after doctors, and I do not know but that they should   20
have first place; with great unanimity the philosophers—
not that I would say such a thing myself—are wont to
ridicule the law as an ass. Yet great matters and little
matters alike are settled by the arbitrament of these

asses. They gather goodly freeholds with broad acres,
while the theologian, after poring over chestfuls of the
great corpus of divinity, gnaws on bitter beans, at the
same time manfully waging war against lice and fleas.
As those arts are more successful which have the greatest
affinity with folly, so those people are by far the happiest   30
who enjoy the privilege of avoiding all contact with the
learned disciplines, and who follow nature as their only
guide, since she is in no respect wanting, except as a
mortal wishes to transgress the limits set for his status.
Nature hates counterfeits; and that which is innocent of
art gets along far the more prosperously.

What need we say about practitioners in the arts? Self-
love is the hallmark of them all. You will find that they
would sooner give up their paternal acres than any piece
of their poor talents. Take particularly actors, singers,   40
orators, and poets; the more unskilled one of them is,
the more insolent he will be in his self-satisfaction, the
more he will blow himself up. . . . Thus the worst art
pleases the most people, for the simple reason that the
larger part of mankind, as I said before, is subject to
folly. If, therefore, the less skilled man is more pleasing
both in his own eyes and in the wondering gaze of the
many, what reason is there that he should prefer sound
discipline and true skill? In the first place, these will
cost him a great outlay; in the second place, they will   50
make him more affected and meticulous; and finally,
they will please far fewer of his audience. . . .

And now I see that it is not only in individual men that
nature has implanted self-love. She implants a kind of it
as a common possession in the various races, and even
cities. By this token the English claim, besides a few other
things, good looks, music, and the best eating as their
special properties. The Scots flatter themselves on the
score of high birth and royal blood, not to mention their
dialectical skill. Frenchmen have taken all politeness for   60
their province; though the Parisians, brushing all others
aside, also award themselves the prize for knowledge of
theology. The Italians usurp *belles lettres* and eloquence;
and they all flatter themselves upon the fact that they
alone, of all mortal men, are not barbarians. In this
particular point of happiness the Romans stand highest,
still dreaming pleasantly of ancient Rome. The Venetians
are blessed with a belief in their own nobility. The Greeks,
as well as being the founders of the learned disciplines,
vaunt themselves upon their titles to the famous heroes of   70
old. The Turks, and that whole rabble of the truly
barbarous, claim praise for their religion, laughing at
Christians as superstitious. . . .

[Next come] the scientists, reverenced for their beards
and the fur on their gowns, who teach that they alone are
wise while the rest of mortal men flit about as shadows.
How pleasantly they dote, indeed, while they construct
their numberless worlds, and measure the sun, moon,
stars, and spheres as with thumb and line. They assign
causes for lightning, winds, eclipses, and other   80
inexplicable things, never hesitating a whit, as if they

were privy to the secrets of nature, artificer of things, or as if they visited us fresh from the council of the gods. Yet all the while nature is laughing grandly at them and their conjectures. For to prove that they have good intelligence of nothing, this is a sufficient argument: they can never explain why they disagree with each other on every subject. Thus knowing nothing in general, they profess to know all things in particular; though they are ignorant even of themselves, and on occasion do not see the ditch or the stone lying across their path, because many of them are blear-eyed or absent-minded; yet they proclaim that they perceive ideas, universals, forms without matter. . . . Perhaps it were better to pass over the theologians in silence, [for] they may attack me with six hundred arguments, in squadrons, and drive me to make a recantation; which if I refuse, they will straightway proclaim me an heretic. By this thunderbolt they are wont to terrify any toward whom they are ill-disposed.

90

They are happy in their self-love, and as if they already inhabited the third heaven they look down from a height on all other mortal men as on creatures that crawl on the ground, and they come near to pitying them. They are protected by a wall of scholastic definitions, arguments, corollaries, implicit and explicit propositions; . . . they explain as pleases them the most arcane matters, such as by what method the world was founded and set in order, through what conduits original sin has been passed down along the generations, by what means, in what measure, and how long the perfect Christ was in the Virgin's womb, and how accidents subsist in the Eucharist without their subject.

100

110

But those are hackneyed. Here are questions worthy of the great and (as some call them) illuminated theologians, questions to make them prick up their ears—if ever they chance upon them. Whether divine generation took place at a particular time? Whether there are several sonships in Christ? Whether this is a possible proposition: God the Father hates the Son? Whether God could have taken upon Himself the likeness of a woman? Or of a devil? Of an ass? Of a gourd? Of a piece of flint? Then how would that gourd have preached, performed miracles, or been crucified? . . . .

120

Coming nearest to these in felicity are the men who generally call themselves "the religious" and "monks"— utterly false names both, since most of them keep as far away as they can from religion and no people are more in evidence in every sort of place. . . . For one thing, they reckon it the highest degree of piety to have no contact with literature, and hence they see to it that they do not know how to read. For another, when with asinine voices they bray out in church those psalms they have learned, by rote rather than by heart, they are convinced that they are anointing God's ears with the blandest of oil. Some of them make a good profit from their dirtiness and mendicancy, collecting their food from door to door with importunate bellowing; nay, there is not an inn, public

130

conveyance, or ship where they do not intrude, to the great disadvantage of the other common beggars. Yet according to their account, by their very dirtiness, ignorance, these delightful fellows are representing to us the lives of the apostles.

140

Q What disciplines does Dame Folly single out as having "the greatest affinity with folly"?

Q How does Erasmus attack the religious community of his day?

More's *Utopia*

In England, Erasmus' friend the scholar and statesman Sir Thomas More (1478–1535) served as chancellor to King Henry VIII at the time of Henry's break with the Catholic Church (Figure **19.16**). Like Erasmus, More was a Christian humanist and a man of conscience. He denounced the evils of acquisitive capitalism and religious fanaticism and championed religious tolerance and Christian charity. Unwilling to compromise his conviction as a Roman Catholic, he opposed the actions of the king and was executed for treason in 1535.

Figure 19.16 HANS HOLBEIN THE YOUNGER, *Sir Thomas More*, ca. 1530. Oil on panel, 29½ × 23¼ in. In his attention to minute detail and textural contrast—fur collar, velvet sleeves, gold chain, and Tudor rose pendant—Holbein refined the tradition of realistic portraiture initiated by Jan van Eyck (compare van Eyck's self-portrait, Figure 17.11).

In 1516, More completed his classic political satire on European statecraft and society, a work entitled *Utopia* (the Greek word meaning both "no place" and "a good place"). More's *Utopia*, the first literary description of an ideal state since Plato's *Republic*, was inspired, in part, by accounts of wondrous lands reported by sailors returning from the "New World" across the Atlantic (see chapter 18). More's imaginary island ("discovered" by a fictional explorer–narrator) is a socialistic state in which goods and property are shared, war and personal vanity are held in contempt, learning is available to all citizens (except slaves), and freedom of religion is absolute. Work, while essential to moral and communal well-being, is limited to six hours a day. In this ideal commonwealth, natural reason, benevolence, and scorn for material wealth ensure social harmony.

More's society differs from Plato's in that More gives to each individual, rather than to society's guardians, full responsibility for the establishment of social justice. Writing both a social critique and a satire, More draws the implicit contrast between his own corrupt Christian society and that of his ideal community. Although his Utopians are not Christians, they are guided by Christian principles of morality and charity. They have little use, for instance, for precious metals, jewels, and the "trifles" that drive men to war.

┌ READING 19.3 From More's *Utopia* (1516)

[As] to their manner of living in society, the oldest man   1
of every family . . . is its governor. Wives serve their
husbands, and children their parents, and always the
younger serves the elder. Every city is divided into
four equal parts, and in the middle of each there is a
marketplace: what is brought thither, and manufactured
by the several families, is carried from thence to houses
appointed for that purpose, in which all things of a sort
are laid by themselves; and there every father goes and
takes whatsoever he or his family stand in need of,   10
without either paying for it or leaving anything in
exchange. There is no reason for giving a denial to any
person, since there is such plenty of everything among
them; and there is no danger of a man's asking for more
than he needs; they have no inducements to do this,
since they are sure that they shall always be supplied.
It is the fear of want that makes any of the whole race of
animals either greedy or ravenous; but besides fear, there
is in man a pride that makes him fancy it a particular
glory to excel others in pomp and excess. But by the   20
laws of the Utopians, there is no room for this. . . .

[Since the Utopians] have no use for money among
themselves, but keep it as a provision against events
which seldom happen, and between which there are
generally long intervening intervals, they value it no
farther than it deserves, that is, in proportion to its use.
So that it is plain they must prefer iron either to gold or
silver; for men can no more live without iron than
without fire or water, but nature has marked out no use
for the other metals so essential and not easily to be   30

dispensed with. The folly of men has enhanced the value
of gold and silver, because of their scarcity. Whereas,
on the contrary, it is their opinion that nature, as an
indulgent parent, has freely given us all the best things
in great abundance, such as water and earth, but has
laid up and hid from us the things that are vain and
useless. . . .

. . . They eat and drink out of vessels of earth, or glass,
which make an agreeable appearance though formed of
brittle materials: while they make their chamber-pots   40
and close-stools[1] of gold and silver, and that not only
in their public halls, but in their private houses: of the
same metals they likewise make chains and fetters for
their slaves; to some [slaves], as a badge of infamy, they
hang an ear-ring of gold, and [they] make others wear a
chain or coronet of the same metal; and thus they take
care, by all possible means, to render gold and silver of
no esteem. And from hence it is that while other nations
part with their gold and silver as unwillingly as if one
tore out their bowels, those of Utopia would look on   50
their giving in all they possess of those [metals] but
as the parting with a trifle, or as we would esteem the
loss of a penny. They find pearls on their coast, and
diamonds and carbuncles on their rocks; they do not
look after them, but, if they find them by chance, they
polish them, and with them they adorn their children,
who are delighted with them, and glory in them during
their childhood; but when they grow to years, and see
that none but children use such baubles, they of their
own accord, without being bid by their parents, lay   60
them aside; and would be as much ashamed to use them
afterward as children among us, when they come to
years, are of their puppets and other toys. . . .

They detest war as a very brutal thing; and which, to the
reproach of human nature, is more practiced by men than
by any sort of beasts. They, in opposition to the sentiments
of almost all other nations, think that there is nothing more
inglorious than that glory that is gained by war. And
therefore though they accustom themselves daily to
military exercises and the discipline of war—in which   70
not only their men but their women likewise are trained up,
that in cases of necessity they may not be quite useless—
yet they do not rashly engage in war, unless it be either to
defend themselves, or their friends, from any unjust
aggressors; or out of good-nature or in compassion
assist an oppressed nation in shaking off the yoke of
tyranny. They indeed help their friends, not only in
defensive, but also in offensive wars; but they never do
that unless they had been consulted before the breach
was made, and being satisfied with the grounds on which   80
they went, they had found that all demands of reparation
were rejected, so that a war was unavoidable. . . .

If they agree to a truce, they observe it so religiously that
no provocations will make them break it. They never lay
their enemies' country waste nor burn their corn, and even

---

[1] A covered chamber pot set in a stool.

in their marches they take all possible care that neither horse nor foot may tread it down, for they do not know but that they may have for it themselves. They hurt no man whom they find disarmed, unless he is a spy. When a town is surrendered to them, they take it into their protection; and when they carry a place by storm, they never plunder it, but put those only to the sword that opposed the rendering of it up, and make the rest of the garrison slaves, but for the other inhabitants, they do them no hurt; and if any of them had advised a surrender, they give them good rewards out of the estates of those that they condemn, and distribute the rest among their auxiliary troops, but they themselves take no share of the spoil.

Q **What sort of social organization does More set forth in his Utopia?**

Q **How would you describe More's views on precious metals and on war?**

Cervantes: *Don Quixote*

While Erasmus and More wrote primarily in Latin—*Utopia* was not translated into English until 1551—other European writers preferred the vernacular. The language of everyday speech was favored for such literary genres as the medieval romance (see chapter 11) and the more realistic and satiric **picaresque novel**, which emerged as a popular form of literary entertainment in sixteenth-century Spain. Narrated by the hero, the picaresque novel recounted the comic misadventures of a *picaro* ("rogue"). Its structure—a series of episodes converging on a single theme—anticipated the emergence of the novel in Western literature.

As a genre, the novel, a large-scale prose narrative, had its origins in eleventh-century Japan, with Murasaki Shikibu's *Tale of Genji*. However, in the West, the first such work in this genre was *Don Quixote*, written in two volumes (over a decade apart) by Miguel de Cervantes (1547–1616). *Don Quixote* resembles the picaresque novel in its episodic structure and in its satiric treatment of Spanish society, but the psychological complexity of its hero and the profundity of its underlying theme—the conflict between reality and the ideal—set it apart from the picaresque.

The fifty-year-old Alonso Quixado, who assumes the title of a nobleman, Don Quixote de la Mancha, sets out to roam the world as a knight errant, defending the ideals glorified in medieval books of chivalry. (Cervantes himself had fought in the last of the crusades against the Muslim Turks.) Seeking to bring honor to himself and his imaginary ladylove, he pursues a long series of adventures in which he repeatedly misperceives the ordinary for the sublime: he attacks a flock of sheep as a hostile army, advances on a group of windmills that he mistakes for giants. (The expression "tilting at windmills" has come to represent the futility of self-deluding action.) The hero's eternal optimism is measured against the practical realism of his potbellied sidekick, Sancho Panza, who tries to expose the Don's illusions of grandeur. In the end, the Don laments in self-reflection that the world "is nothing but schemes and plots."

Cervantes' masterpiece, *Don Quixote* attacks outworn medieval values, especially as they reflect sixteenth-century Spanish society. In Spain, on the eve of the early modern era, New World wealth was transforming the relationship between peasants and aristocrats; the tribunal of Catholic orthodoxy known as the Inquisition worked to expel the large populations of Jews and Muslims that had powerfully influenced earlier Iberian culture. While the novel emerged from this context of transformation and (often misguided) reform, it left a timeless, universal message, captured in the English word "quixotic," which means "foolishly idealistic" or "impractical."

READING 19.4 From Cervantes' *Don Quixote* (1605–1615)

The great success won by our brave Don Quijote[1] *in his dreadful, unimaginable encounter with two windmills, plus other honorable events well worth remembering*

Just then, they came upon thirty or forty windmills, which (as it happens) stand in the fields of Montiel, and as soon as Don Quijote saw them he said to his squire:

"Destiny guides our fortunes more favorably than we could have expected. Look there, Sancho Panza, my friend, and see those thirty or so wild giants, with whom I intend to do battle and to kill each and all of them, so with their stolen booty we can begin to enrich ourselves. This is noble, righteous warfare, for it is wonderfully useful to God to have such an evil race wiped from the face of the earth." 10

"What giants?" asked Sancho Panza.

"The ones you can see over there," answered his master, "with the huge arms, some of which are very nearly two leagues long."

"Now look, your grace," said Sancho, "what you see over there aren't giants, but windmills, and what seem to be arms are just their sails, that go around in the wind and turn the millstone."

"Obviously," replied Don Quijote, "you don't know much about adventures. Those are giants—and if you're frightened, take yourself away from here and say your prayers, while I go charging into savage and unequal combat with them." 20

Saying which, he spurred his horse, Rocinante, paying no attention to the shouts of Sancho Panza, his squire, warning him that without any question it was windmills and not giants he was going to attack. So utterly convinced was he they were giants, indeed, that he neither heard Sancho's cries nor noticed, close as he was, what they really were, but charged on, crying: 30

"Flee not, oh cowards and dastardly creatures, for he who attacks you is a knight alone and unaccompanied."

Just then the wind blew up a bit, and the great sails began to stir, which Don Quijote saw and cried out:

---

[1] A variant spelling of Quixote is Quijote, as in this excerpt.

"Even should you shake more arms than the giant Briareus himself, you'll still have to deal with me."

As he said this, he entrusted himself with all his heart to his lady Dulcinea, imploring her to help and sustain him at such a critical moment, and then, with his shield held high and his spear braced in its socket, and Rocinante at a full gallop, he charged directly at the first windmill he came to, just as a sudden swift gust of wind sent its sail swinging hard around, smashing the spear to bits and sweeping up the knight and his horse, tumbling them all battered and bruised to the ground. Sancho Panza came rushing to his aid, as fast as his donkey could run, but when he got to his master found him unable to move, such a blow had he been given by the falling horse.

"God help me!" said Sancho. "Didn't I tell your grace to be careful what you did, that these were just windmills, and anyone who could ignore that had to have windmills in his head?"

"Silence, Sancho, my friend," answered Don Quijote. "Even more than other things, war is subject to perpetual change. What's more, I think the truth is that the same Frestón the magician, who stole away my room and my books, transformed these giants into windmills, in order to deprive me of the glory of vanquishing them, so bitter is his hatred of me. But in the end, his evil tricks will have little power against my good sword."

"God's will be done," answered Sancho Panza.

Then, helping his master to his feet, he got him back up on Rocinante, whose shoulder was half dislocated. After which, discussing the adventure they'd just experienced, they followed the road toward Lápice Pass, for there, said Don Quijote, they couldn't fail to find adventures of all kinds, it being a well-traveled highway. But having lost his lance, he went along very sorrowfully, as he admitted to his squire, saying:

"I remember having read that a certain Spanish knight named Diego Pérez de Vargas, having lost his sword while fighting in a lost cause, pulled a thick bough, or a stem, off an oak tree, and did such things with it, that day, clubbing down so many Moors that ever afterwards they nicknamed him Machuca [Clubber], and indeed from that day on he and all his descendants bore the name Vargas y Machuca. I tell you this because, the first oak tree I come to, I plan to pull off a branch like that, one every bit as good as the huge stick I can see in my mind, and I propose to perform such deeds with it that you'll be thinking yourself blessed, having the opportunity to witness them, and being a living witness to events that might otherwise be unbelievable."

"It's in God's hands," said Sancho. "I believe everything is exactly the way your grace says it is. But maybe you could sit a little straighter, because you seem to be leaning to one side, which must be because of the great fall you took."

"True," answered Don Quijote, "and if I don't say anything about the pain it's because knights errant are never supposed to complain about a wound, even if their guts are leaking through it."

"If that's how it's supposed to be," replied Sancho, "I've got nothing to say. But Lord knows I'd rather your grace told me, any time something hurts you. Me, I've got to groan, even if it's the smallest little pain, unless that rule about knights errant not complaining includes squires, too."

Don Quijote couldn't help laughing at his squire's simplicity, and cheerfully assured him he could certainly complain any time he felt like it, voluntarily or involuntarily, since in all his reading about knighthood and chivalry he'd never once come across anything to the contrary. Sancho said he thought it was dinner-time. His master replied that, for the moment, he himself had no need of food, but Sancho should eat whenever he wanted to. Granted this permission, Sancho made himself as comfortable as he could while jogging along on his donkey and, taking out of his saddlebags what he had put in them, began eating as he rode, falling back a good bit behind his master, and from time to time tilting up his wineskin with a pleasure so intense that the fanciest barman in Málaga might have envied him. And as he rode along like this, gulping quietly away, none of the promises his master had made were on his mind, nor did he feel in the least troubled or afflicted—in fact, he was thoroughly relaxed about this adventure-hunting business, no matter how dangerous it was supposed to be.

In the end, they spent that night sleeping in a wood, and Don Quijote pulled a dry branch from one of the trees, to serve him, more or less, as a lance, fitting onto it the spearhead he'd taken off the broken one. Nor did Don Quijote sleep, that whole night long, meditating on his lady Dulcinea—in order to fulfill what he'd read in his books, namely, that knights always spent long nights out in the woods and other uninhabited places, not sleeping, but happily mulling over memories of their ladies. Which wasn't the case for Sancho Panza: with his stomach full, and not just with chicory water, his dreams swept him away, nor would he have bothered waking up, for all the sunlight shining full on his face, or the birds singing—brightly, loudly greeting the coming of the new day—if his master hadn't called to him. He got up and, patting his wineskin, found it a lot flatter than it had been the night before, which grieved his heart, since it didn't look as if they'd be making up the shortage any time soon. Don Quijote had no interest in breakfast, since, as we have said, he had been sustaining himself with delightful memories. They returned to the road leading to Lápice Pass, which they could see by about three that afternoon.

"Here," said Don Quijote as soon as he saw it, "here, brother Sancho Panza, we can get our hands up to the elbows in adventures. But let me warn you: even if you see me experiencing the greatest dangers in the world, never draw your sword to defend me, unless of course you see that those who insult me are mere rabble, people of low birth, in which case you may be permitted to help me. But if they're knights, the laws of knighthood make it absolutely illegal, without exception, for you to help me, unless you yourself have been ordained a knight."

"Don't worry, your grace," answered Sancho Panza. "You'll find me completely obedient about this, especially since I'm a very peaceful man—I don't like getting myself into quarrels and fights. On the other hand, when it comes to someone laying a hand on me, I won't pay much attention to those laws, because whether they're divine or human they permit any man to defend himself when anyone hurts him."   160

"To be sure," answered Don Quijote. "But when it comes to helping me against other knights, you must restrain your natural vigor."

"And that's what I'll do," replied Sancho. "I'll observe this rule just as carefully as I keep the Sabbath."

Q **What rules of chivalry forbid Sancho's assisting his master in battle, and with what exception?**

Rabelais and Montaigne

Another master of vernacular prose, the French humanist François Rabelais (1495–1553), mocked the obsolete values of European society. Rabelais drew upon his experiences as a monk, a student of law, a physician, and a specialist in human affairs to produce *Gargantua and Pantagruel*, an irreverent satire filled with biting allusions to contemporary institutions and customs. The world of the two imaginary giants, Gargantua and Pantagruel, is one of fraud and folly drawn to fantastic dimensions. It is blighted by the absurdities of war, the evils of law and medicine, and the failure of Scholastic education. To remedy the last, Rabelais advocates education based on experience and action, rather than rote memorization. In the imaginary abbey of Thélème, the modern version of a medieval monastery, he pictures a coeducational commune in which well-bred men and women are encouraged to live as they please. *Gargantua and Pantagruel* proclaims Rabelais' faith in the ability of educated individuals to follow their best instincts for establishing a society free from religious prejudice, petty abuse, and selfish desire.

The French humanist Michel de Montaigne (1533–1592) was neither a satirist nor a reformer, but an educated aristocrat who believed in the paramount importance of cultivating good judgment. Trained in Latin, Montaigne was one of the leading proponents of Classical learning in

Renaissance France. He earned universal acclaim as the "father" of the personal **essay**, a short piece of expository prose that examines a single subject or idea. The essay—the word comes from the French *essayer* ("to try")—is a vehicle for probing or "trying out" ideas.

Montaigne regarded his ninety-four vernacular French essays as studies in autobiographical reflection—in them, he confessed, he portrayed himself. Addressing such subjects as virtue, friendship, old age, education, and idleness, he examined certain fundamentally humanistic ideas: that contradiction is a characteristically human trait, that self-examination is the essence of true education, that education should enable us to live more harmoniously, and that skepticism and open-mindedness are sound alternatives to dogmatic opinion. Like Rabelais, Montaigne defended a kind of teaching that posed questions rather than provided answers. In his essay on the education of children, he criticized teachers who might pour information into students' ears "as though they were pouring water into a funnel" and then demand that students repeat that information instead of exercising original thought.

Reflecting on the European response to overseas expansion (see chapter 18), Montaigne examined the ways in which behavior and belief vary from culture to culture. In his essay *On Cannibals*, a portion of which appears below, he weighted the reports of "New World" barbarism and savagery against the morals and manners of "cultured" Europeans. War, which he calls the "human disease," he finds less vile among "barbarians" than among Europeans, whose warfare is motivated by colonial expansion. Balancing his own views with those of Classical Latin writers, whom he quotes freely throughout his essays, Montaigne questions the superiority of any one culture over another. Montaigne's essays, an expression of reasoned inquiry into human values, constitute the literary high-water mark of the French Renaissance.

Science and Technology

1556	Georg Agricola (German) publishes *On the Principles of Mining*
1571	Ambroise Paré (French) publishes five treatises on surgery
1587	Conrad Gesner (Swiss) completes his *Historiae Animalum*, the first zoological encyclopedia
1596	Sir John Harington (English) invents the "water closet," providing indoor toilet facilities

READING 19.5 From Montaigne's *On Cannibals* (1580)

I had with me for a long time a man who had lived for   1
ten or twelve years in that other world which has been
discovered in our century, in the place where Villegaignon
landed, and which he called Antarctic France.[1] This
discovery of a boundless country seems worthy of
consideration. I don't know if I can guarantee that some
other such discovery will not be made in the future, so
many personages greater than ourselves having been
mistaken about this one. I am afraid we have eyes bigger
than our stomachs, and more curiosity than capacity.   10
We embrace everything, but we clasp only wind. . . .
      This man I had was a simple, crude fellow—a character

---

[1] *La France antarctique* was the French term for South America. In 1555, Nicolas Durand de Villegaignon founded a colony on an island in the Bay of Rio de Janeiro, Brazil. The colony collapsed some years later, and many of those who had lived there had returned to France.

fit to bear true witness; for clever people observe more things and more curiously, but they interpret them; and to lend weight and conviction to their interpretation, they cannot help altering history a little. They never show you things as they are, but bend and disguise them according to the way they have seen them; and to give credence to their judgment and attract you to it, they are prone to add something to their matter, to stretch it out and amplify it. We need a man either very honest, or so simple that he has not the stuff to build up false inventions and give them plausibility; and wedded to no theory. Such was my man; and besides this, he at various times brought sailors and merchants, whom he had known on that trip, to see me. So I content myself with his information, without inquiring what the cosmographers say about it.

We ought to have topographers who would give us an exact account of the places where they have been. But because they have over us the advantage of having seen Palestine, they want to enjoy the privilege of telling us news about all the rest of the world. I would like everyone to write what he knows, and as much as he knows, not only in this, but in all other subjects; for a man may have some special knowledge and experience of the nature of a river or a fountain, who in other matters knows only what everybody knows. However, to circulate this little scrap of knowledge, he will undertake to write the whole of physics. From this vice spring many great abuses. Now to return to my subject, I think there is nothing barbarous and savage in that nation, from what I have been told, except that each man calls barbarism whatever is not his own practice; for indeed it seems we have no other test of truth and reason than the example and pattern of the opinions and customs of the country we live in. *There* is always the perfect religion, perfect government, the perfect and accomplished manners in all things. Those people are wild, just as we call wild the fruits that Nature has produced by herself and in her normal course; whereas really it is those that we have changed artificially and led astray from the common order, that we should rather call wild. The former retain alive and vigorous their genuine, their most useful and natural, virtues and properties, which we have debased in the latter in adapting them to gratify our corrupted taste. And yet for all that, the savor and delicacy of some uncultivated fruits of those countries is quite as excellent, even to our taste, as that of our own. It is not reasonable that art should win the place of honor over our great and powerful mother Nature. We have so overloaded the beauty and richness of her works by our inventions that we have quite smothered her. Yet wherever her purity shines forth, she wonderfully puts to shame our vain and frivolous attempts.

> Ivy comes readier without our care;
> In lonely caves the arbutus grows more fair;
> No art with artless bird song can compare.
> Propertius

All our efforts cannot even succeed in reproducing the nest of the tiniest little bird, its contexture, its beauty

and convenience; or even the web of the puny spider. All things, say Plato, are produced by nature, by fortune, or by art; the greatest and most beautiful by one or the other of the first two, the least and most imperfect by the last.

These nations, then, seem to me barbarous in this sense, that they have been fashioned very little by the human mind, and are still very close to their original naturalness. The laws of nature still rule them, very little corrupted by ours, and they are in such a state of purity that I am sometimes vexed that they were unknown earlier, in the days when there were men able to judge them better than we.

. . . .

They have their wars with the nations beyond the mountains, further inland, to which they go quite naked, with no other arms than bows or wooden swords ending in a sharp point, in the manner of the tongues of our boar spears. It is astonishing what firmness they show in their combats, which never end but in slaughter and bloodshed; for as to routs and terror, they know nothing of either.

Each man brings back as his trophy the head of the enemy he has killed, and sets it up at the entrance to his dwelling. After they have treated their prisoners well for a long time with all the hospitality they can think of, each man who has a prisoner calls a great assembly of his acquaintances. He ties a rope to one of the prisoner's arms, by the end of which he holds him, a few steps away, for fear of being hurt, and gives his dearest friend the other arm to hold in the same way; and these two, in the presence of the whole assembly, kill him with their swords. This done, they roast him and eat him in common and send some pieces to the absent friends. This is not, as people think, for nourishment, as of old the Scythians used to do; it is to betoken an extreme revenge.[2] And the proof of this came when they saw the Portuguese, who had joined forces with their adversaries, inflict a different kind of death on them when they took them prisoner, which was to bury them up to the waist, shoot the rest of their body full of arrows, and afterward hang them. They thought that these people from the other world, being men who had sown the knowledge of many vices among their neighbors and were much greater masters than themselves in every sort of wickedness, did not adopt this sort of vengeance without some reason, and that it must be more painful than their own; so they began to give up their old method and to follow this one.

I am not sorry that we notice the barbarous horror of such acts, but I am heartily sorry that, judging their faults rightly, we should be so blind as to our own. I think there is more barbarity in eating a man alive than in eating him dead; and in tearing by tortures and the rack a body still full of feeling, in roasting a man bit by bit, in having him bitten and mangled by dogs and swine (as we have not only read but seen within fresh memory, not among ancient enemies, but among neighbors and fellow citizens, and

---

2 Montaigne overlooks the fact that ritual cannibalism might also involve the will to consume the power of the opponent, especially if he were a formidable opponent.

what is worse, on the pretext of piety and religion), than in roasting and eating him after he is dead.

. . . .

So we may well call these people barbarians, in respect of the rules of reason, but not in respect of ourselves, who surpass them in every kind of barbarity.

Their warfare is wholly noble and generous, and as excusable and beautiful as this human disease can be; its only basis among them is their rivalry in valor. They are not fighting for the conquest of new lands, for they still enjoy that natural abundance that provides them without toil and trouble with all necessary things in such profusion that they have no wish to enlarge their boundaries. They are still in that happy state of desiring only as much as their natural needs demand; any thing beyond that is superfluous to them.

130

Q **"Each man calls barbarism whatever is not his own practice," writes Montaigne. What illustrations does he offer? Does this claim hold true in our own day and age?**

Shakespeare

No assessment of the early modern era would be complete without some consideration of the literary giant of the age: William Shakespeare (1564–1616; Figure **19.17**).

A poet of unparalleled genius, Shakespeare emerged during the golden age of England under the rule of Elizabeth I (1533–1603). He produced thirty-seven plays—comedies, tragedies, romances, and histories—as well as 154 sonnets and other poems. These works, generally considered to be the greatest examples of English literature, have exercised an enormous influence on the evolution of the English language and the development of the Western literary tradition.*

Little is known about Shakespeare's early life and formal education. He grew up in Stratford-upon-Avon in the English Midlands, married Anne Hathaway (eight years his senior), with whom he had three children, and moved to London sometime before 1585. In London, a city of some 80,000 inhabitants, he formed an acting company, the Lord Chamberlain's Company (also called "the King's Men"), in which he was shareholder, actor, and playwright. Like fifteenth-century Florence, sixteenth-century London (and especially the queen's court) supported a galaxy of artists, musicians, and writers who enjoyed a mutually stimulating interchange of ideas. Shakespeare's theater company performed at the court of Elizabeth I and that of her successor James I (1566–1625). But its main activities took place in the Globe, one of a handful of playhouses built

* The complete works of Shakespeare are available at the following website: http://shakespeare.mit.edu/works.html

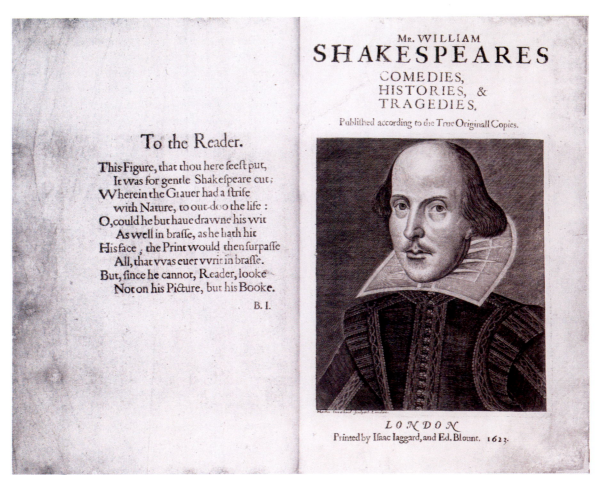

Figure 19.17 DROESHOUT, First Folio edition portrait of William Shakespeare, 1623. 13 × 18 in. (approx.).

just outside London's city limits—along with brothels and taverns, theaters were generally relegated to the suburbs.

Shakespeare's Sonnets

While Shakespeare is best known for his plays, he also wrote some of the most beautiful sonnets ever produced in the English language. Indebted to Petrarch (see LOOKING INTO in chapter 16), Shakespeare nevertheless devised most of his own sonnets in a form that would come to be called "the English sonnet": **quatrains** (four-line stanzas) with alternate rhymes, followed by a concluding **couplet**. Shakespeare's sonnets employ—and occasionally mock—such traditional Petrarchan themes as the blind devotion of the unfortunate lover, the value of friendship, and love's enslaving power. Some, like Sonnet 18, reflect the typically Renaissance (and Classical) concern for immortality achieved through art and love. In Sonnet 18, Shakespeare contrives an extended metaphor: like the summer day, his beloved will fade and die. But, exclaims the poet, she will remain eternal in and through the sonnet; for, so long as the poem survives, so will the object of its inspiration remain alive. Stripped of sentiment, Sonnet 116 defends the unchanging nature of love, its constancy and its ability to withstand adversity and the test of time. The poem exalts the "marriage of true minds" that most Renaissance humanists perceived as only possible among men. Sonnet 130, on the other hand, pokes fun at the literary conventions of the Petrarchan love sonnet. Satirizing the fair-haired, rosy-lipped heroine as object of desire, Shakespeare celebrates the real—though somewhat ordinary—features of his beloved.

READING 19.6 From Shakespeare's Sonnets (1609)

Sonnet 18

Shall I compare thee to a summer's day?	1
Thou art more lovely and more temperate.	
Rough winds do shake the darling buds of May,	
And summer's lease[1] hath all too short a date.	
Sometime too hot the eye[2] of heaven shines,	5
And often is his gold complexion dimm'd;	
And every fair from fair sometime declines,[3]	
By chance or nature's changing course untrimm'd;[4]	
But thy eternal summer shall not fade	
Nor lose possession of that fair thou ow'st,	10
Nor shall Death brag thou wand'rest in his shade,	
When in eternal lines to time thou grow'st.[5]	
So long as men can breathe or eyes can see,	
So long lives this[6] and this gives life to thee.	

---

[1] Allotted time.
[2] The sun.
[3] Beautiful thing from beauty.
[4] Stripped of beauty.
[5] Your fame will grow as time elapses.
[6] The sonnet itself.

Sonnet 116

Let me not to the marriage of true minds	1
Admit impediments. Love is not love	
Which alters when it alteration finds,	
Nor bends with the remover to remove.[7]	
O, no, it is an ever-fixed mark,[8]	5
That looks on tempests and is never shaken;	
It is the star to every wand'ring bark,	
Whose worth's unknown, although his height be taken.[9]	
Love's not Time's fool, though rose lips and cheeks	
Within his bending sickle's compass come;	10
Love alters not with his brief hours and weeks,	
But bears it out even to the edge of doom.[10]	
If this be error, and upon me proved,	
I never writ, nor no man ever loved.	

Sonnet 130

My mistress' eyes are nothing like the sun;	1
Coral is far more red than her lips' red:	
If snow be white, why then her breasts are dun;	
If hairs be wires, black wires grow on her head.	
I have seen roses damasked, red and white,	5
But no such roses see I in her cheeks;	
And in some perfumes is there more delight	
Than in the breath that from my mistress reeks.	
I love to hear her speak, yet well I know	
That music hath a far more pleasing sound:	10
I grant I never saw a goddess go,—	
My mistress, when she walks, treads on the ground:	
And yet, by heaven, I think my love as rare	
As any she belied with false compare.	

Q **What does each of these sonnets convey about the nature of love?**

The Elizabethan Stage

In the centuries following the fall of Rome, the Church condemned all forms of pagan display, including the performance of comedies and tragedies. Tragedy, in the sense that it was defined by Aristotle ("the imitation of an action" involving "some great error" made by an extraordinary man), was philosophically incompatible with the medieval world-view, which held that all events were predetermined by God. If redemption was the goal of Christian life, there was no place for literary tragedy in the Christian cosmos. (Hence Dante's famous journey, though far from humorous, was called a "comedy" in acknowledgment of its "happy" ending in Paradise.) Elizabethan poets revived secular drama, adapting Classical and medieval texts to the writing of contemporary plays. While the context and the characters of such plays might be Christian, the plot and the dramatic action were secular in focus and in spirit.

---

[7] Changes as the beloved changes.
[8] Sea mark, an aid to navigation.
[9] Whose value is beyond estimation.
[10] Endures to the very Day of Judgment.

The rebirth of secular drama, Renaissance England's most original contribution to the humanistic tradition, unfolded during an era of high confidence. In 1588, the English navy defeated a Spanish fleet of 130 ships known as the "Invincible Armada." The victory gave clear advantage to England as the dominant commercial power in the Atlantic. The routing of the Spanish Armada was a victory as well for the partisans of Protestantism over Catholicism. It encouraged a sense of national pride that found its counterpart in a revival of interest in English history and its theatrical recreation. It also contributed to a renewed spirit of confidence in the ambitious policies of the "Protestant Queen," Elizabeth I (Figure **19.18**). In its wake followed a period of high prosperity, commercial expansion, and cultural vitality, all of which converged in London.

Elizabethan London played host to groups of traveling actors (or "strolling players") who performed in public spaces or for generous patrons. In the late sixteenth century, a number of playhouses were built along the River Thames across from the City of London. Begun in 1599,

the Globe, which held between 2000 and 3000 spectators, offered all levels of society access to professional theater (Figure **19.19**). The open-air structure consisted of three tiers of galleries and standing room for commoners (known as "groundlings") at the cost of only a penny—one-sixth of the price of a seat in the covered gallery. The projecting, rectangular stage, some 40 feet wide, included balconies (for musicians and special scenes, as in *Romeo and Juliet*), exits to dressing areas, and a trapdoor (used for rising spirits and for burial scenes, as in *Hamlet*). Stage props were basic, but costumes were favored, and essential for the male actors who played the female roles, since women were not permitted on the public stage. Performances were held in the afternoon and advertised by flying a flag above the theater roof. A globe, the signature logo, embellished the theater, along with a sign that read "*Totus mundus agit histrionem*" (loosely, "All the World's a Stage"). The bustling crowd that attended the theater—some of whom stood through two or more hours of performance—often ate and drank as they enjoyed the

Figure 19.18 GEORGE GOWER, *"Armada" Portrait of Elizabeth I*, ca. 1588. Oil on panel, 3 ft. 6 in. × 4 ft. 5 in. Bedecked with jewels, the queen rests her hand on the globe, an allusion to its circumnavigation by her vice-admiral, Sir Francis Drake. In the background at the right, the Spanish Armada sinks into the Atlantic amidst the "Protestant winds" of a fierce storm.

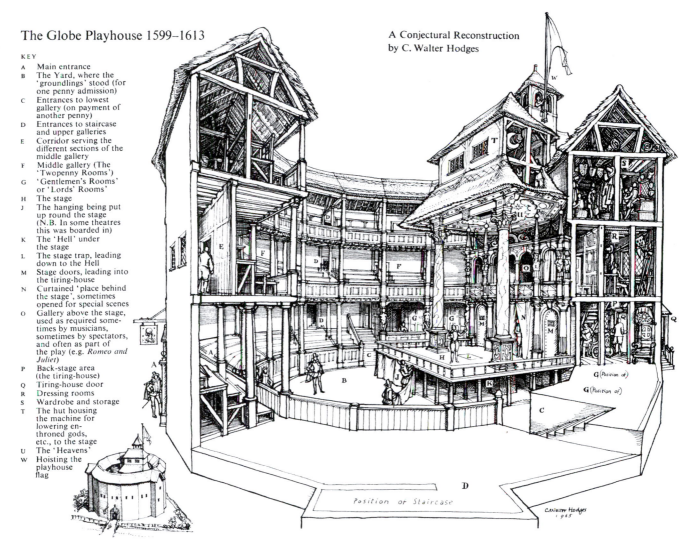

The Globe Playhouse 1599–1613

A Conjectural Reconstruction
by C. Walter Hodges

KEY

A   Main entrance
B   The Yard, where the 'groundlings' stood (for one penny admission)
C   Entrances to lowest gallery (on payment of another penny)
D   Entrances to staircase and upper galleries
E   Corridor serving the different sections of the middle gallery
F   Middle gallery (The 'Twopenny Rooms')
G   'Gentlemen's Rooms' or 'Lords' Rooms'
H   The stage
J   The hanging being put up round the stage (N.B. In some theatres this was boarded in)
K   The 'Hell' under the stage
L   The stage trap, leading down to the Hell
M   Stage doors, leading into the tiring-house
N   Curtained 'place behind the stage', sometimes opened for special scenes
O   Gallery above the stage, used as required sometimes by musicians, sometimes by spectators, and often as part of the play (e.g. *Romeo and Juliet*)
P   Back-stage area (the tiring-house)
Q   Tiring-house door
R   Dressing rooms
S   Wardrobe and storage
T   The hut housing the machine for lowering enthroned gods, etc., to the stage
U   The 'Heavens'
W   Hoisting the playhouse flag

Figure 19.19 Globe Playhouse, London, 1599–1613. Architectural reconstruction by **C. WALTER HODGES**, 1965.

most cosmopolitan entertainment of their time. A reconstruction of the Globe playhouse, located on the south bank of the Thames, opened in 1997.

Shakespeare's Plays

In Shakespeare's time, theater ranked below poetry as a literary genre. As popular entertainment, however, Shakespeare's plays earned high acclaim in London's thriving theatrical community. Thanks to the availability of printed editions, the Bard of Stratford was familiar with the tragedies of Seneca and the comedies of Plautus and Terence. He knew the popular medieval morality plays that addressed the contest between good and evil, as well as the popular improvisational form of Italian comic theater known as the *commedia dell'arte*, which made use of stock or stereotypical characters. All these resources came to shape the texture of his own plays. For his plots, Shakespeare drew largely on Classical history, medieval chronicles, and contemporary romances.

Like Machiavelli, Shakespeare was an avid reader of ancient and medieval history, as well as a keen observer of

his own complex age; but the stories his sources provided became mere springboards for the exploration of human nature. His history plays, such as *Henry V* and *Richard III*, celebrate England's medieval past and its rise to power under the Tudors. The concerns of these plays, however, are not exclusively historical; rather, they explore the ways in which individuals behave under pressure: the weight of kingly responsibilities on mere humans and the difficulties of reconciling royal obligations and human aspirations.

Shakespeare's comedies, which constitute about one-half of his plays, deal with such popular themes as the battle of the sexes, rivalry among lovers, and mistaken identities. But here too, in such plays as *Much Ado About Nothing*, *All's Well That Ends Well*, and *The Taming of the Shrew*, it is Shakespeare's characters—their motivations exposed, their weaknesses and strengths laid bare—that command our attention.

It is in the tragedies, and especially the tragedies of his mature career—*Hamlet*, *Macbeth*, *Othello*, and *King Lear*— that Shakespeare achieved the concentration of thought and language that has made him the greatest English playwright of all time. Human flaws and failings—jealousy, greed, ambition, insecurity, and self-deception—give substance to most of Shakespeare's plays, but in these last tragedies they become definitive: they drive the action of the play. They are, in short, immediate evidence of the playwright's efforts to probe the psychological forces that motivate human action.

No discussion of Shakespeare's plays can substitute for the experience of live performance. Yet, in focusing on two of the late tragedies, *Hamlet* and *Othello*, it is possible to isolate Shakespeare's principal contributions to the humanistic tradition. These lie in the areas of character development and in the brilliance of the language with which characters are brought to life. Despite occasional passages in prose and rhymed verse, Shakespeare's plays were written in **blank verse**. This verse form was popular among Renaissance writers because, like Classical poetry, it was unrhymed, and it closely approximated the rhythms of vernacular speech. In Shakespeare's hands, the English language took on a breadth of expression and a majesty of eloquence that has rarely been matched to this day.

Shakespeare's *Hamlet*

Hamlet, the world's most quoted play, belongs to the popular Renaissance genre of revenge tragedy; the story itself came to Shakespeare from the history of medieval Denmark. Hamlet, the young heir to the Danish throne, learns that his uncle has murdered his father, the king of Denmark, and married his mother in order to assume the throne; the burden of avenging his father falls squarely on his shoulders. The arc of the play follows Hamlet's inability to take action—his melancholic lack of resolve that, in due course, results in the deaths of his mother (Gertrude), his betrothed (Ophelia), her father (Polonius), the king (Claudius), and, finally, Hamlet himself.

Shakespeare's protagonist differs from the heroes of ancient and medieval times: Hamlet lacks the sense of obligation to country and community, the religious loyalties, and the clearly defined spiritual values that impassioned Gilgamesh, Achilles, and Roland. He represents a new, multidimensional, and essentially modern hero, afflicted (even tormented) by self-questioning and brooding skepticism. Although sunk in melancholy, Hamlet shares Pico della Mirandola's view (see Reading 16.3) that human nature is freely formed by human beings themselves: He marvels, "What a piece of work is a man! How noble in reason! How infinite in faculty! In form and moving how express and admirable! In action how like an angel! In apprehension how like a god! The beauty of the world! The paragon of animals." Nevertheless, he qualifies this optimistic view of humankind with personal despair, concluding on a note of utter skepticism: "And yet, to me, what is this quintessence of dust?" (Act II, ii, ll. 303–309). It is by way of the oral examination of his innermost thoughts—a literary device known as the *soliloquy*—that Hamlet most fully reveals himself. He questions the motives for meaningful action and the impulses that prevent him from action; at the same time, he contemplates the futility of all human action. In the following excerpt

from the third act of this great play, two aspects of Hamlet's character come into focus: his deeply conflicted and self-reflective personality, and his peevish and dissembling behavior toward Ophelia.

┌─ READING 19.7 From Shakespeare's *Hamlet* (1602)

Hamlet, Act III, Scene 1
[The King, Queen, Polonius, Rosencrantz, and Guildenstern seek to determine the nature of Hamlet's recent changes in behavior by arranging his "accidental" meeting with Ophelia.]

King: Sweet Gertrude, leave us too,   1
  For we have closely sent for Hamlet hither,
  That he, as 'twere by accident, may here
  Affront Ophelia.
  Her father and myself, lawful espials,
  Will so bestow ourselves that seeing, unseen,
  We may of their encounter frankly judge,
  And gather by him, as he is behaved,
  If 't be th' affliction of his love or no
  That thus he suffers for.   10
Queen: I shall obey you.
  And for your part, Ophelia, I do wish
  That your good beauties be the happy cause
  Of Hamlet's wildness. So shall I hope your virtues
  Will bring him to his wonted way again,
  To both your honors.
Ophelia: Madam, I wish it may.
                            [Exit Queen.]
Polonius: Ophelia, walk you here.—Gracious, so please you,
  We will bestow ourselves. [*To Ophelia.*] Read on this
    book,   [*giving her a book*] 20
  That show of such an exercise may color
  Your loneliness. We are oft to blame in this—
  'Tis too much proved—that with devotion's visage
  And pious action we do sugar o'er
  The devil himself.
King [*aside*]: O, 'tis too true!
  How smart a lash that speech doth give my conscience!
  The harlot's cheek, beautied with plastering art,
  Is not more ugly to the thing that helps it
  Than is my deed to my most painted word.   30
  O heavy burden!
Polonius: I hear him coming. Let's withdraw, my lord.
          [The King and Polonius withdraw.]
       Enter Hamlet. [Ophelia pretends to read a book.]
Hamlet: To be, or not to be, that is the question:
  Whether 'tis nobler in the mind to suffer

III.1. Location: The castle.
2 closely privately **4 Affront** confront, meet **5 espials** spies
15 wonted accustomed **18 Gracious** Your Grace (i.e., the king)
19 bestow conceal **21 exercise** religious exercise (the book she reads is one of devotion) **color** give a plausible appearance to **22 loneliness** being alone **23 too much proved** too often shown to be true, too often practiced **29 to** compared to **the thing** i.e., the cosmetic **32 s.d. withdraw** the King and Polonius may retire behind an arras. The stage directions specify that they "enter" again near the end of the scene.

The slings and arrows of outrageous fortune,
Or to take arms against a sea of troubles
And by opposing end them. To die, to sleep—
No more—and by a sleep to say we end
The heartache and the thousand natural shocks
That flesh is heir to. 'Tis a consummation   40
Devoutly to be wished. To die, to sleep;
To sleep, perchance to dream. Ay, there's the rub,
For in that sleep of death what dreams may come,
When we have shuffled off this mortal coil,
Must give us pause. There's the respect
That makes calamity of so long life.
For who would bear the whips and scorns of time,
Th' oppressor's wrong, the proud man's contumely,
The pangs of disprized love, the law's delay,
The insolence of office, and the spurns   50
That patient merit of th' unworthy takes,
When he himself might his quietus make
With a bare bodkin? Who would fardels bear,
To grunt and sweat under a weary life,
But that the dread of something after death,
The undiscovered country from whose bourn
No traveler returns, puzzles the will,
And makes us rather bear those ills we have
Than fly to others that we know not of?
Thus conscience does make cowards of us all;   60
And thus the native hue of resolution
Is sicklied o'er with the pale cast of thought,
And enterprises of great pitch and moment
With this regard their currents turn awry
And lose the name of action.—Soft you now,
The fair Ophelia. Nymph, in thy orisons
Be all my sins remembered.

Ophelia: Good my lord,
How does your honor for this many a day?

Hamlet: I humbly thank you; well, well, well.   70

Ophelia: My lord, I have remembrances of yours,
That I have longèd long to redeliver.
I pray you, now receive them.   [*She offers tokens.*]

Hamlet: No, not I, I never gave you aught.

Ophelia: My honored lord, you know right well you did,
And with them words of so sweet breath composed
As made the things more rich. Their perfume lost,
Take these again, for to the noble mind
Rich gifts wax poor when givers prove unkind.
There, my lord.   [*She gives tokens.*]   80

Hamlet: Ha, ha! Are you honest?

Ophelia: My lord?

Hamlet: Are you fair?

Ophelia: What means your lordship?

Hamlet: That if you be honest and fair, your honesty
should admit no discourse to your beauty.

Ophelia: Could beauty, my lord, have better commerce
than with honesty?

Hamlet: Ay, truly, for the power of beauty will sooner
transform honesty from what it is to a bawd than the   90
force of honesty can translate beauty into his likeness.
This was sometime a paradox, but now the time gives
if proof. I did love you once.

Ophelia: Indeed, my lord, you made me believe so.

Hamlet: You should not have believed me, for virtue
cannot so inoculate our old stock but we shall relish of
it. I loved you not.

Ophelia: I was the more deceived.

Hamlet: Get thee to a nunnery. Why wouldst thou be a
breeder of sinners? I am myself indifferent honest, but   100
yet I could accuse me of such things that it were better
my mother had not borne me: I am very proud,
revengeful, ambitious, with more offenses at my beck
than I have thoughts to put them in, imagination to
give them shape, or time to act them in. What should
such fellows as I do crawling between earth and
heaven? We are arrant knaves all; believe none of us.
Go thy ways to a nunnery. Where's your father?

Ophelia: At home, my lord.

Hamlet: Let the doors be shut upon him, that he may   110
play the fool nowhere but in 's own house. Farewell.

Ophelia: O, help him, you sweet heavens!

Hamlet: If thou dost marry, I'll give thee this plague for
thy dowry: be thou as chaste as ice, as pure as snow,
thou shalt not escape calumny. Get thee to a nunnery,
farewell. Or, if thou wilt needs marry, marry a fool, for
wise men know well enough what monsters you
make of them. To a nunnery, go, and quickly too.
Farewell.

Ophelia: Heavenly powers, restore him!   120

Hamlet: I have heard of your paintings too, well
enough. God hath given you one face, and you make
yourselves another. You jig, you amble, and you
lisp, you nickname God's creatures, and make your
wantonness your ignorance. Go to, I'll no more on 't;

---

66 orisons prayers **81 honest** (1) truthful (2) chaste **83 fair** (1) beautiful (2) just, honorable **85 your honesty** your chastity **86 discourse to** familiar dealings with **87–88 commerce** dealings, intercourse **91 his** its **92 sometime** formerly **a paradox** a view opposite to commonly held opinion **the time** the present age **96 inoculate** graft, be engrafted to **96–97 but . . . it** that we do not still have about us a taste of the old stock, i.e., retain our sinfulness **99 nunnery** convent (with possibly an awareness that the word was also used derisively to denote a brothel) **100 indifferent honest** reasonably virtuous **103 beck** command **117 monsters** an illusion to the horns of a cuckold **you** i.e., you women **123 jig** dance **amble** move coyly **124 you nickname . . . creatures** i.e., you give trendy names to things in place of their God-given names **124–125 make . . . ignorance** i.e., excuse your affectation on the grounds of pretended ignorance **125 on 't** of it

---

35 slings missiles **42 rub** literally, an obstacle in the game of bowls **44 shuffled** sloughed, cast **coil** turmoil **45 respect** consideration **46 of . . . life** so long-lived, something we willingly endure for so long (also suggesting that long life is itself a calamity) **48 contumely** insolent abuse **49 disprized** unvalued **50 office** officialdom **spurns** insults **51 of . . . takes** receives from unworthy persons **52 quietus** acquittance; here, death **53 a bare bodkin** a mere dagger, unsheathed **fardels** burdens **56 bourn** frontier, boundar **61 native hue** natural color, complexion **62 cast** tinge, shade of color **63 pitch** height (as of a falcon's flight) **moment** importance **64 regard** respect, consideration **currents** courses **65 Soft you** i.e., wait a minute, gently

it hath made me mad. I say we will have no more
marriage. Those that are married already—all but
one—shall live. The rest shall keep as they are. To a
nunnery, go. *Exit.*

Ophelia: O, what a noble mind is here o'erthrown!   130
The courtier's, soldier's, scholar's, eye, tongue,
sword,
Th' expectancy and rose of the fair state,
The glass of fashion and the mold of form,
Th' observed of all observers, quite, quite down!
And I, of ladies most deject and wretched,
That sucked the honey of his music vows,
Now see that noble and most sovereign reason
Like sweet bells jangled out of tune and harsh,
That unmatched form and feature of blown youth   140
Blasted with ecstasy. O, woe is me,
T' have seen what I have seen, see what I see!

**Q What profound question does Hamlet address in
his soliloquy?**

**Q What conclusion does Ophelia reach at the end of
her conversation with Hamlet?**

Shakespeare's *Othello*

The Tragedy of Othello, the Moor of Venice was based on a story
from a collection of tales published in Italy in the sixteenth
century. The life of the handsome and distinguished
Othello, an African soldier whose leadership in the
Venetian wars against the Turks has brought him heroic
esteem, takes a tragic turn when his ensign Iago beguiles
him into thinking that his beautiful wife Desdemona has
betrayed him with another man. Enraged with jealousy,
Othello destroys the person he loves most in the world,
his wife; and, in the unbearable grief of his error, he takes
his own life as well. While Othello's jealousy is the flaw
that brings about his doom, it is Iago whose unmitigated
evil drives the action of the plot. Conniving Iago is the
Machiavellian villain, "a demi-devil," as he is called in the
play. In contrast, Desdemona is the paragon of virtue and
beauty. Such characters hark back to the allegorical figures
in medieval morality plays, but Shakespeare transforms
these figures into complex personalities, allowing them
full freedom to falter and fail through their own actions.

That Shakespeare made a black man the hero of one of
his tragedies is significant, since his treatment of the character seems to have challenged Elizabethan stereotypes.
Medieval and Renaissance literature described anyone
who was black as vengeful, hot-blooded, and evil, black
being the color traditionally associated with the Devil.
But in Shakespeare's play, the Moor (the Elizabethan
name for any African) is unwitting, ingenuous, and pure,
while Iago, the white man who confounds him, is the

personification of evil. Perhaps more significant than this
irony is Shakespeare's implication that underlying the
most untainted acts of heroism and the purest emotions
of love is the dark possibility of misguided action that
leads to self-defeat. Shakespeare's plays generally preach
no explicit moral; rather, they suggest that, in a universe
in which order and disorder coexist, human choices play
a vital and potentially destructive part. The nihilism that
darkens *Othello*, *Macbeth*, and *Hamlet* was unthinkable
before the modern era.

READING 19.8 From Shakespeare's *Othello* (1604)

Othello, Act IV, Scene III
Enter Othello, Lodovico, Desdemona, Emilia, and Attendants.

Lodovico: I do beseech you, sir, trouble yourself no further.   1
Othello: O, pardon me; 'twill do me good to walk.
Lodovico: Madam, good night. I humbly thank your
ladyship.
Desdemona: Your honor is most welcome.
Othello: Will you walk, sir?
O, Desdemona!
Desdemona: My lord?
Othello: Get you to bed on th' instant; I will be return'd
forthwith. Dismiss your attendant there. Look 't be done.
Desdemona: I will, my lord.
                    Exit [*Othello, with Lodovico and Attendants*].
Emilia: How goes it now? He looks gentler than he did.   10
Desdemona: He says he will return incontinent,
And hath commanded me to go to bed,
And bade me to dismiss you.
Emilia: Dismiss me?
Desdemona: It was his bidding; therefore, good Emilia,
Give me my nightly wearing, and adieu.
We must not now displease him.
Emilia: I would you had never seen him!
Desdemona: So would not I. My love doth so approve him,
That even his stubbornness, his checks, his frowns—
Prithee unpin me—have grace and favor in them.   20
                    [*Emilia prepares Desdemona for bed.*]
Emilia: I have laid those sheets you bade me on the bed.
Desdemona: All's one. Good faith, how foolish are our
minds!
If I do die before thee, prithee shroud me
In one of those same sheets.
Emilia: Come, come, you talk.
Desdemona: My mother had a maid call'd Barbary.
She was in love, and he she lov'd prov'd mad
And did forsake her. She had a song of "Willow,"
An old thing 'twas, but it express'd her fortune,
And she died singing it. That song tonight

---

133 **expectancy** hope **rose** ornament 134 **The glass . . . form** the
mirror of true self-fashioning and the pattern of courtly behavior 135
Th' observed . . . observers i.e., the center of attention and honor
in the court 137 **music** musical, sweetly uttered 140 **blown**
blooming 141 **Blasted** withered **ecstasy** madness

IV. iii Location: The citadel.
11 **incontinent** immediately 19 **stubbornness** roughness **checks**
rebukes 26 **mad** wild, i.e., faithless

Will not go from my mind; I have much to do   30
   But to go hang my head all at one side
   And sing it like poor Barbary. Prithee, dispatch.
Emilia: Shall I go fetch your nightgown?
Desdemona: No, unpin me here.
   This Lodovico is a proper man.
Emilia: A very handsome man.
Desdemona: He speaks well.
Emilia: I know a lady in Venice would have walk'd barefoot
   to Palestine for a touch of his nether lip.
Desdemona [*Singing*]:
   "The poor soul sat sighing by a sycamore tree,
      Sing all a green willow;   40
   Her hand on her bosom, her head on her knee,
      Sing willow, willow, willow.
   The fresh streams ran by her, and murmur'd her moans;
      Sing willow, willow, willow;
   Her salt tears fell from her, and soft'ned the stones"—
   Lay by these.
[*Singing*]: "Sing willow, willow, willow"—
   Prithee, hie thee; he'll come anon.
[*Singing*] "Sing all a green willow must be my garland.
      Let nobody blame him; his scorn I approve"—   50
   Nay, that's not next.—Hark! Who is 't that knocks?
Emilia: It's the wind.
Desdemona [*Singing*]
   "I call'd my love false love; but what said he then?
      Sing willow, willow, willow;
   If I court moe women, you'll couch with moe men"—
   So, get thee gone; good night. Mine eyes do itch;
   Doth that bode weeping?
Emilia: '   Tis neither here nor there.
Desdemona: I have heard it said so. O, these men, these
   men!
   Dost thou in conscience think—tell me, Emilia—
   That there be women do abuse their husbands   60
   In such gross kind?
Emilia: There be some such, no question.
Desdemona: Wouldst thou do such a deed for all the world?
Emilia: Why, would not you?
Desdemona: No, by this heavenly light!
Emilia: Nor I neither by this heavenly light; I might do
   't as well i' th' dark.
Desdemona: Wouldst thou do such a deed for all the
   world?
Emilia: The world's a huge thing. It is a great price
   For a small vice.
Desdemona: Good troth, I think thou wouldst not.
Emilia: By my troth, I think I should; and undo 't when I
   had done. Marry, I would not do such a thing for a joint-   70
   ring, nor for measures of lawn, nor for gowns, petticoats,
   nor caps, nor any petty exhibition; but, for all the whole
   world—'ud's pity, who would not make her husband a
   cuckold to make him a monarch? I should venture
   purgatory for 't.

Desdemona: Beshrew me if I would do such a wrong for the
   whole world.
Emilia: Why, the wrong is but a wrong i' th' world; and
   having the world for your labor, 'tis a wrong in your own
   world, and you might quickly make it right.   80
Desdemona: I do not think there is any such woman.
Emilia: Yes, a dozen; and as many to th' vantage as
   would store the world they play'd for.
   But I do think it is their husbands' faults
   If wives do fall. Say that they slack their duties,
   And pour our treasures into foreign laps,
   Or else break out in peevish jealousies,
   Throwing restraint upon us? Or say they strike us,
   Or scant our former having in despite?
   Why, we have galls, and though we have some grace,
   Yet have we some revenge. Let husbands know   90
   Their wives have sense like them. They see, and smell,
   And have their palates both for sweet and sour,
   As husbands have. What is it that they do
   When they change us for others? Is it sport?
   I think it is. And doth affection breed it?
   I think it doth. Is 't frailty that thus errs?
   It is so too. And have not we affections,
   Desires for sport, and frailty, as men have?
   Then let them use us well; else let them know,
   The ills we do, their ills instruct us so.   100
Desdemona: Good night, good night. God me such uses
   send,
   Not to pick bad from bad, but by bad mend!   *Exeunt.*

**Q How do Emilia's views on women as wives
compare with those of Desdemona?**

Chronology

1450	Gutenberg perfects the printing press
1517	Luther posts the *Ninety-Five Theses*
1524	German Peasant Revolts
1526	Henry VIII establishes the Anglican Church
1588	England defeats the Spanish Armada

30–31 I . . . hang I can scarcely keep myself from hanging **48 hie thee** hurry **70–71 joint-ring** a ring made in separate halves **71 lawn** fine linen **72 exhibition** gift **73 'ud's** i.e., God's

82 to th' vantage in addition, to boot **store** populate **85 pour . . . laps** i.e., are unfaithful, give what is rightfully ours (semen) to other women **88 scant . . . despite** reduce our allowance to spite us **89 have galls** i.e., are capable of resenting injury and insult **91 sense** physical sense **101 uses** habit, practice **102 Not . . . mend** i.e., not to learn bad conduct from others' badness (as Emilia has suggested women learn from men), but to mend my ways by perceiving what badness is, making spiritual benefit out of evil and adversity

The Temper of Reform

- The printing press facilitated the rise of popular education and encouraged individuals to form their own opinions by reading for themselves. The new print technology would be essential to the success of the Protestant Reformation.
- The Netherlandish religious movement known as the *devotio moderna* harnessed the dominant strains of anticlericalism, lay piety, and mysticism, even as it coincided with the revival of Classical studies in Northern Europe.
- Erasmus, the leading Christian humanist, led the critical study of the Bible and writings of the church fathers. Northern humanists brought to their efforts the same intellectual fervor that the Italian humanists had applied to their examination of Plato and Cicero.

The Protestant Reformation

- Across Germany, the sale of indulgences to benefit the Church of Rome provoked harsh criticism, especially by those who saw the luxuries of the papacy as a betrayal of apostolic ideals.
- Martin Luther was the voice of the Protestant Reformation. In his sermons and essays he criticized the worldliness of the Church and bemoaned "the misery and wretchedness of Christendom."
- Luther's greatest attempt at reforming the Catholic Church came in the form of his *Ninety-Five Theses* (1517), which listed his grievances against the Church and called for reform based on scriptural precedent.
- Luther's teachings, with the aid of the printing press, circulated throughout Europe, giving rise to other Protestant sects, including Calvinism and Anabaptism, and, in England, the Anglican Church.
- The Lutheran chorale became the vehicle of Protestant piety.

Northern Renaissance Art

- Even before the North felt the impact of the Italian Renaissance, Netherlandish artists initiated a painting style rich in realistic detail. Jan van Eyck's pioneering use of thin oil glazes captured the naturalistic effects of light on objects that, while tangible, also functioned as symbols.
- The paintings of Hieronymus Bosch infused traditional religious subjects with a unique combination of moralizing motifs drawn from illuminated manuscripts, pilgrimage badges, and the popular pseudo-sciences: astrology and alchemy.
- The Protestant Reformation, which rejected relics and sacred images as reflections of superstition and idolatry, favored devotional, and especially biblical, subjects. The two new graphic techniques, woodcutting and engraving, facilitated the mass production of devotional images that functioned as book illustrations and individual prints.
- A growing middle class provided patronage for portraiture, landscapes, and scenes of everyday life, subjects that were pursued by Albrecht Dürer, Lucas Cranach, Hans Holbein, and Pieter Bruegel. Nevertheless, deeply felt religious sentiment persisted in many Northern artworks, such as Matthias Grünewald's rivetingly expressive Isenheim Altarpiece.

Sixteenth-Century Literature

- Northern Renaissance writers took a generally skeptical and pessimistic view of human nature. Erasmus, More, and Rabelais lampooned individual and societal failings and described the ruling influence of folly in all aspects of human conduct.
- In France, Montaigne devised the essay as an intimate form of rational reflection, while in Spain, Cervantes' novel, *Don Quixote*, wittily attacked feudal values and outmoded ideals.
- Northern Renaissance literature was, in many ways, a literature of protest and reform, and one whose dominant themes reflect the tension between medieval and modern ideas.

Shakespeare

- Shakespeare emerged during the golden age of England, which flourished under the rule of Elizabeth I. He produced thirty-seven plays—comedies, tragedies, romances, and histories—as well as 154 sonnets and other poems. His work, along with that of other Northern artists and writers, brought the West to the threshold of modernity.
- The most powerful form of literary expression to evolve in the late sixteenth century was secular drama. In the hands of William Shakespeare, Elizabethan drama became the ideal vehicle for exposing the psychological forces that motivate human behavior.

Glossary

blank verse unrhymed lines of iambic pentameter, that is, lines consisting of ten syllables each with accents on every second syllable

chorale a congregational hymn, first sung in the Lutheran church

couplet two successive lines of verse with similar end-rhymes

engraving the process by which lines are incised on a metal plate, then inked and printed; see Figure 19.10

essay a short piece of expository prose that examines a single subject

genre painting art depicting scenes from everyday life; not to be confused with "genre," a term used to designate a particular category in literature or art, such as the essay (in literature) and portraiture (in painting)

picaresque novel a prose genre that narrates the comic misadventures of a roguish hero

quatrain a four-line stanza

woodcut a relief printing process by which all parts of a design are cut away except those that will be inked and printed; see Figure 19.9

Picture Credits

The author and publishers wish to thank the following for permission to use copyright material. Every effort has been made to trace or contact copyright holders, but if notified of any omissions, Laurence King Publishing would be pleased to insert the appropriate acknowledgement in any subsequent edition of this publication.

Bold indicates Figure number or page/position of the image.

Cover

Top left: Image © The Metropolitan Museum of Art, New York/Art Resource, NY/Scala, Florence; **Top right:** Dallas Museum of Art, gift of Mrs. Eugene McDermott, the Hamon Charitable Foundation, and an anonymous donor in honor of David T. Owsley, with additional funding from The Cecil and Ida Green Foundation and the Cecil and Ida Green Acquisition Fund; **Bottom left**: Sonia Halliday Photographs; **Bottom right:** National Anthropological Museum, Mexico/Gianni Dagli Orti/The Art Archive

Frontispiece and page xvi: © English Heritage (J870257)

page xix: © The Trustees of the British Museum, London

Introduction

0.1 Photo by Dean R. Snow; **0.2** Sisse Brimberg/National Geographic Creative; **0.3** © Goran Burenhult/Heritage-Images; **0.4** Naturhistorisches Museum, Wien; **0.5** Erich Lessing/akg-images; **0.6** Courtesy of the Oriental Institute of the University of Chicago; **0.7** Photo © RMN-Grand Palais (Musée du Louvre). Photo: Gérard Blot; **0.8** Image © The Metropolitan Museum of Art, New York/Art Resource, NY/Scala, Florence; **0.10** Ancient Art & Architecture Collection Ltd.; **0.11** Photo: Klaus Schmidt. Deutsches Archäologisches Institut; **0.12** Fernando G. Baptista/National Geographic Creative; **0.13** © English Heritage (J940113); **0.14** © English Heritage (A910713 & A910714); **0.15** Adapted from Samuel Noah Kramer, The Sumerians, © 1957 by Scientific American, Inc.; **0.16** Ashmolean Museum, University of Oxford/Bridgeman Images; **0.17** © The Trustees of the British Museum, London; **0.18** Photo © RMN-Grand Palais (Musée du Louvre). Photo: Hervé Lewandowski; **0.20** Private Collection/Photo © Dirk Bakker/Bridgeman Images; **0.21** Prisma Bildagentur AG/Alamy

Chapter 1

1.1 Photo © RMN-Grand Palais (Musée du Louvre); **1.2** © The Trustees of the British Museum, London, **1.3** Courtesy of The University of Pennsylvania Museum of Archaeology & Anthropology, Philadelphia (Image #150082); **1.4** © The Trustees of the British Museum, London; **1.5** Photo Scala, Florence; **1.6** © The Trustees of the British Museum, London; **1.7** Photo © RMN-Grand Palais (Musée du Louvre). Photo: Franck Raux; **1.8** Silvio Fiore/SuperStock; **1.9** Courtesy of the Oriental Institute of the University of Chicago; **1.10** Erich Lessing/akg-images; **1.11** www.BibleLandPictures.com/Alamy; **1.12** Courtesy of the Oriental Institute of the University of Chicago; **1.14** Erich Lessing/akg-images; **1.15** © The Trustees of the British Museum, London; **1.16** Image © The Metropolitan Museum of Art, New York/Art Resource, NY/Scala, Florence

Chapter 2

2.1 De Agostini Picture Library/SuperStock; **2.2** Andrea Jemolo/akg-images; **2.3** Egyptian Museum, Cairo/Werner Forman Archive; **2.4** Photograph © 2015 Museum of Fine Arts, Boston. Harvard University - Boston Museum of Fine Arts Exhibition 11.1738; **2.5** © The Trustees of the British Museum, London; **2.6** © Paul M.R. Maeyaert; **2.7** Heritage Image Partnership Ltd./Alamy; **2.11** Photo © RMN-Grand Palais (Musée du Louvre). Photo: Franck Raux; **2.12** © J. Paul Getty Trust. Wim Swaan Photograph Collection. The Getty Research Institute, Los Angeles (96.P.21); **2.13** Image © The Metropolitan Museum of Art, New York/Art Resource, NY/Scala, Florence; **2.14** © Araldo de Luca; **2.15** Andrea Jemolo/akg-images; **2.16** BPK, Bildagentur für Kunst, Kultur und Geschichte, Berlin/Photo Scala, Florence; **2.17** Image © The Metropolitan Museum of Art, New York/Art Resource, NY/Scala, Florence; **2.18** © The Trustees of the British Museum, London; **2.21** Photo Jean Vertut; **2.22** National Museum, Athens. Photo: Stournaras. © Hellenic Ministry of Culture and Sports/Archaeological Receipts Fund; **2.23** Private Collection/Photo © Dirk Bakker/Bridgeman Images

Chapter 3

3.1 Image © The Metropolitan Museum of Art, New York/Art Resource, NY/Scala, Florence; **3.2** National Museum, New Delhi; **3.3** Robert Harding Productions; **3.4** The Nelson-Atkins Museum of Art, Kansas City, Missouri. Purchase: William Rockhill Nelson Trust, 33-81. Photo: John Lamberton; **3.5** Freer Gallery, Smithsonian Institution, Washington, D.C./Bridgeman Images; **3.6** Cultural Relics Press, Beijing; **3.7** Courtesy of C. V. Starr. East Asian Library, Columbia University; **3.8** Courtesy of the Institute of History and Philology, Academia Sinica; **3.10** George Steinmetz/Corbis; **3.13** Stock Connection/SuperStock; **3.14** Anthropology Museum, Veracruz University, Jalapa/Werner Forman Archive

Chapter 4

4.1 Image © The Metropolitan Museum of Art, New York/Art Resource, NY/Scala, Florence; **4.2** Gloria K. Fiero; **4.3** Ancient Art & Architecture Collection Ltd.; **4.4** © Craig & Marie Mauzy, Athens; **4.5** © Craig & Marie Mauzy, Athens; **4.6** Musée du Louvre, Paris/Giraudon/Bridgeman Images; **4.7** Photo Spectrum/Heritage Images/Scala, Florence; **4.8** © Craig & Marie Mauzy, Athens; **4.9** Courtesy of the Ministero Beni e Att. Culturali/Photo Scala, Florence; **4.10** Photograph © 2015 Museum of Fine Arts, Boston. Henry Lillie Pierce Fund 98.923; **4.11** G. Nimatallah/DeA Picture Library/The Art Archive; **4.12** JFB/The Art Archive; **4.13** © Vincenzo Pirozzi, Rome; **4.14** Marka/SuperStock; **4.16** A. Dagli Orti/De Agostini Picture Library/Getty Images; **4.17** Image © The Metropolitan Museum of Art, New York/Art Resource, NY/Scala, Florence; **4.18** "line drawing of the cave, page 316", from THE GREAT DIALOGUES OF PLATO by Plato, translated by W.H.D. Rouse, translation copy © 1956, renewed © 1984 by J.C.G. Rouse. Used by permission of Dutton Signet, a division of Penguin Group (USA) LLC.

Chapter 5

5.1 Photo Scala, Florence; **5.2** © Fotografica Foglia, Naples; **5.3** Galleria dell'Accademia, Venice; **5.4** Image © The Metropolitan Museum of Art, New York/Art Resource, NY/Scala, Florence; **5.5** Photo Scala, Florence; **5.6** © The Trustees of the British Museum, London; **5.7** Image © The Metropolitan Museum of Art, New York/Art Resource, NY/Scala, Florence; **5.8** Photograph © 2015 Museum of Fine Arts, Boston. Harvard University - Boston Museum of Fine Arts Exhibition 11.1738; **5.9** Universal Images Group/SuperStock; **5.10** De Agostini Picture Library/SuperStock; **5.11** © Craig & Marie Mauzy, Athens; **5.12** © Craig & Marie Mauzy, Athens; **5.13** © Craig & Marie Mauzy, Athens; **5.14** Photo Scala, Florence; **5.15** Paul Stepan/Photo Researchers, Inc./Science Photo Library; **5.16** The American School of Classical Studies at Athens; **5.18** The American School of Classical Studies at Athens; **5.20** Sayre, Henry M., The Humanities: Culture, Continuity and Change, Volume 1: Prehistory to 1600, 2nd edition, © 2012, p. 142. Reprinted by permission of Pearson Education, Inc., Upper Saddle River, NJ.; **5.21** © The Trustees of the British Museum, London; **5.22** Peter Connolly/akg-images; **5.23** British Museum, London/Bridgeman Images; **5.24** Peter Barritt/SuperStock; **5.25** RIA Novosti/akg-images; **5.26** Image © The Metropolitan Museum of Art, New York/Art Resource, NY/Scala, Florence; **5.27** Image © The Metropolitan Museum of Art, New York/Art Resource, NY/Scala, Florence; **5.28** Universal Images Group/SuperStock; **5.29** BPK, Bildagentur für Kunst, Kultur und Geschichte, Berlin/Photo Scala, Florence; **5.30** E. Lessing/De Agostini Picture Library/Getty Images; **5.31** Erich Lessing/akg-images; **5.32** White Images/Scala, Florence; **5.33** Photo © RMN-Grand Palais (Musée du Louvre). Photo: Gérard Blot/Christian Jean; **5.34** Araldo de Luca/Corbis

Chapter 6

6.1 Courtesy of the Ministero Beni e Att. Culturali/Photo Scala, Florence; **6.2** akg-images; **6.3** BPK, Bildagentur für Kunst, Kultur und Geschichte, Berlin/Photo Scala, Florence; **6.4** Photo Scala, Florence; **6.5** Museo Capitolino, Rome/Collection Dagli Orti/The Art Archive; **6.7** © Paul M.R. Maeyaert; **6.8** Reconstruction by I. Gismondi. Image courtesy the Museum of Roman Civilization, Rome; **6.9** Alinari Archives/Corbis; **6.10** Galleria Borghese, Rome/Collection Dagli Orti/The Art Archive; **6.11** McGraw-Hill Education; **6.12** © Vincenzo Pirozzi, Rome; **6.13** Courtesy of The Library of Virginia; **6.14** Courtesy National Gallery of Art, Washington, D.C., Samuel H. Kress Collection (1939.1.24); **6.15** Bjanka Kadic/age fotostock/SuperStock; **6.16** Jerry Driendl/Photodisc/Getty Images; **6.18** Courtesy of the Ministero Beni e Att. Culturali/Photo Scala, Florence; **6.20** Courtesy of the Ministero Beni e Att. Culturali/Photo Scala, Florence; **6.21** Courtesy of the Ministero Beni e Att. Culturali/Photo Scala, Florence; **6.22** Erich Lessing/akg-images; **6.23** Photo Scala, Florence; **6.24** Mondadori Portfolio/Electa/akg-images; **6.25** Photo © Tarker/Bridgeman Images; **6.26** Image © The Metropolitan Museum of Art, New York/Art Resource, NY/Scala, Florence; **6.27** © Fotografica Foglia, Naples; **6.28** Photo Scala, Florence

Chapter 7

7.1 Photo Spectrum/Heritage Images/Scala, Florence; **7.2** Jean-Pierre De Mann/Robert Harding World Imagery; **7.3** Zhang Shui Cheng/Bridgeman Images; **7.4** Cultural Relics Press, Beijing; **7.5** The Nelson-Atkins Museum of Art, Kansas City, Missouri. Purchase: William Rockhill Nelson Trust, 33–521. Photo: John Lamberton; **7.6** Cultural Relics Press, Beijing; **7.7** Cultural Relics Press, Beijing; **7.8** Cultural Relics Press, Beijing; **7.9** Cultural Relics Press, Beijing; **7.10** Cultural Relics Press, Beijing

page 181: © The Board of Trinity College, Dublin/Bridgeman Images

Chapter 8

8.1 Fondo Edifici di Culto - Min. dell'Interno/Photo Scala, Florence; **8.2** BPK, Bildagentur für Kunst, Kultur und Geschichte, Berlin/Photo Scala, Florence; **8.3** Image © The Metropolitan Museum of Art, New York/Art Resource, NY/Scala, Florence; **8.4** Oratorio di Galla Placidia, Ravenna/Giraudon/Bridgeman Images; **8.5** Cleveland Museum of Art, Ohio; Leonard C. Hanna Jr. Fund/Bridgeman Images; **8.6** Photograph © 2015 Museum of Fine Arts, Boston. Helen and Alice Colburn Fund 37.99

Chapter 9

9.1 Fondo Edifici di Culto - Min. dell'Interno/Photo Scala, Florence; **9.2** Sant'Apollinare in Classe, Ravenna/Bridgeman Images; **9.4** Photo Scala, Florence; **9.5** Photo Scala, Florence; **9.6** Photo Scala, Florence; **9.7** Courtesy of the Ministero Beni e Att. Culturali/Photo Scala, Florence; **9.9** Ken Kaminesky/Corbis; **9.11** Sonia Halliday Photographs; **9.12** Erich Lessing/akg-images; **9.14** Gianni Dagli Orti/The Art Archive; **9.15** Photo Scala, Florence; **9.16** © CAMERAPHOTO Arte, Venice; **9.17** © CAMERAPHOTO Arte, Venice; **9.18** Courtesy of the Ministero Beni e Att. Culturali/Photo Scala, Florence; **9.19** Erich Lessing/akg-images; **9.20** De Agostini Picture Library/Scala, Florence; **9.21** Adam Woolfitt/Robert Harding World Imagery; **9.22** Dinodia Photos/Alamy; **9.24** Freer Gallery, Smithsonian Institution, Washington, D.C./Bridgeman Images; **9.26** Luca Tettoni/Robert Harding World Imagery; **9.27** Jean-Louis Nou/akg-images; **9.28** Lowell Georgia/Corbis; **9.29** Ursula Gahwiler/Robert Harding World Imagery; **9.30** The Nelson-Atkins Museum of Art, Kansas City, Missouri. Purchase: William Rockhill Nelson Trust, 40-38; **9.31** Image © The Metropolitan Museum of Art, New York/Art Resource, NY/Scala, Florence

Chapter 10

10.1 De Agostini Picture Library/SuperStock; **10.2** Nabil Mounzer/EPA/Corbis; **10.3** The Nelson-Atkins Museum of Art, Kansas City, Missouri. Purchase: William Rockhill Nelson Trust, 44-40/2. Photo: Jamison Miller; **10.4** Image © The Metropolitan Museum of Art, New York/Art Resource, NY/Scala, Florence; **10.5** © The Trustees of the British Museum, London; **10.6** Image © The Metropolitan Museum of Art, New

Literary Credits

The author and publishers wish to thank the following for permission to use copyright material. Every effort has been made to trace or contact copyright holders, but if notified of any omissions or errors, Laurence King Publishing would be pleased to insert the appropriate acknowledgement in any subsequent edition of this publication.

Introduction
READING:
0.1 (pp. 15–16): A.L. Basham, "The Song of Creation" translated from the Rig Veda, from *The Wonder That Was India*, copyright © A.L. Basham, 1985. Reproduced by permission of Pan Macmillan and Namita Catherine Basham; Dennis Tedlock, from *Popol Vuh*, copyright © 1985, 1996 Dennis Tedlock. Reprinted with the permission of Simon & Schuster Publishing Group and The Ward & Balkin Agency, Inc.

Chapter 1
1.1 (pp. 19–20): from *Poems of Heaven and Hell from Ancient Mesopotamia*, translated and introduced by N. K. Sandars (Penguin Classics, 1971), copyright © N. K. Sandars, 1971. Reproduced by permission of Penguin Books Ltd.

1.2 (pp. 23–24): from *The Epic of Gilgamesh*, translated with an introduction by N. K. Sandars (Penguin Classics, 1960, Third edition 1972), copyright © N. K. Sandars, 1960, 1964, 1972. Reproduced by permission of Penguin Books Ltd.

1.4a–e (pp. 31–39): Scripture quotations taken from the New American Standard Bible, copyright © 1960, 1962, 1963, 1968, 1971, 1972, 1973, 1975, 1977, 1995 by The Lockman Foundation. Used by permission. (www.Lockman.org).

Chapter 2
2.1 (p. 55): "The Hymn to the Aten" from *The Literature of Ancient Egypt*, 1973, ed William Kelley Simpson, Yale University Press. Reproduced by permission of the publisher;

2.2 (p. 58): Mariam Lichtheim, "My Sister Has Come" from *Ancient Egyptian Literature: Volume II: The New Kingdom*, copyright © 2006 by the Regents of the University of California. Published by the University of California Press.

Chapter 3
3.1 (pp. 66–67): *The Song of God: The Bhagavad-Gita*, translated by Swami Prabhavanda and Christopher Isherwood (Vedanta Press, 1951). Reprinted by permission of the publisher.

3.2 (p. 72): Lao Tzu, "Thirty spokes will converge (11)", from *The Way of Life*, translated by Raymond B. Blakney, translation copyright © 1955 by Raymond B. Blakney, renewed © 1983 by Charles Philip Blakney. Used by permission of Dutton Signet, a division of Penguin Group (USA) LLC; and Dorrie and Charles Blakney for the Estate of Raymond B. Blakney.

Chapter 4
4.1 (pp. 82–85): *The Iliad of Homer*, translated by Richmond Lattimore, University of Chicago Press, copyright © 2011, CCC Republication.

4.2 (pp. 88–90): Thucydides, from *The History of the Peloponnesian War*, translated by Rex Warner with an introduction and notes by M. I. Finley (Penguin Classics 1954, Revised edition 1972). Translation copyright © Rex Warner, 1954. Introduction and Appendices copyright © M. I. Finley, 1972. Reproduced by permission of Penguin Books Ltd and Curtis Brown Group Ltd, London on behalf of the Estate of Rex Warner.

4.3 (pp. 92–98): Sophocles, from "Antigone", from ANTIGONE, OEDIPUS THE KING, ELECTRA, edited by Edith Hall, translated by H. D. F Kitto (Oxford University Press, 2008) pp.3-6, 8-19, 23-27, 39-45. By permission of Oxford University Press.

4.4 (pp. 99–100): Aristotle, from "De Poetica" translated by Ingram Bywater from *Rhetoric & Poetics* from The Oxford Translation of Aristotle edited by W. D. Ross (Volume II, 1925). By permission of Oxford University Press.

4.5 (p. 103–104): Plato, from *EUTHYPHRO, APOLOGY, CRITO*, translated by F.J. Church, copyright ©1956. Printed and Electronically reproduced by permission of Pearson Education, Inc., Upper Saddle River, New Jersey.

4.6 (pp. 105–107): Plato, from *The Republic*, translated by F. M. Cornford (1975) from "Allegory of the Cave". By permission of Oxford University Press.

Chapter 5
5.1 (pp. 114–116): Vitruvius, from *Ten Books on Architecture*, translated by Morris Hicky Morgan, 1960. Reprinted by permission of Dover Publications, Inc.

5.2 (p. 128): *Sappho: A New Translation*, translated by Mary Barnard, copyright © 1986 by Mary Barnard. Published by the University of California Press. By permission of the publisher.

5.3 (pp. 128–129): *Pindar*, by C. M. Bowra (1964) from Nemean Ode VI & Pythian Ode VII. By permission of Oxford University Press.

Chapter 6
6.1 (p.140): *Josephus: Volume III, The Jewish War, Books III–IV*, Loeb Classical Library Volume 487, translated by H. St. J. Thackeray, pp.25, 27, 29, 31, 33, 35, 37, Cambridge, Mass.: Harvard University Press, 1927. Loeb Classical Library® is a registered trademark of the President and Fellows of Harvard College. Reprinted by permission of the publishers and the Trustees of the Loeb Classical Library.

6.2 (pp. 144–145): Seneca, from *The Stoic Philosophy of Seneca*, by Moses Hadas, translation copyright © 1958 by Moses Hadas. Used by permission of Doubleday, an imprint of the Knopf Doubleday Publishing Group, a division of Random House LLC. All rights reserved.

6.3 (pp. 145–146): *Cicero: Volume XXI, De Officiis*, Loeb Classical Library Volume 30, translated by Walter Miller, pp.81, 83, 85, Cambridge, Mass.: Harvard University Press, 1913. Loeb Classical Library® is a registered trademark of the President and Fellows of Harvard College. Reprinted by permission of the publishers and the Trustees of the Loeb Classical Library.

6.4 (p. 146): *Tacitus: Volume I, Dialogue On Oratory*, translated by William Peterson, revised by M. Winterbottom, Loeb Classical Library Volume 35, pp.329, 331, 333, Cambridge, Mass.: Harvard University Press, copyright © 1970 by the President and Fellows of Harvard College. Loeb Classical Library® is a registered trademark of the President and Fellows of Harvard College. Reprinted by permission of the publishers and the Trustees of the Loeb Classical Library.

6.5 (pp. 147–148): *The Aeneid of Virgil*, translated by Rolfe Humphries, 1951. Reproduced by permission of Archives & Special Collections, Amherst College Library.

6.6 (pp. 148–149): *Poems of Catullus*, translated by Horace Gregory (W. W. Norton, 1972) copyright © 1956, 1972 by the Estate of Horace Gregory. Used with permission from Alison Bond Associates.

6.8a,b (pp. 150–152): "Against the City of Rome" and "Against Women" from *The Satires of Juvenal*, translated by Rolfe Humphries, copyright © 1960, Indiana University Press. Reprinted with permission of Indiana University Press.

Chapter 7
7.1 (pp. 169–170): *The Analects of Confucius*, translated by Simon Leys, copyright © 1997 by Pierre Ryckmans. Used by permission of W. W. Norton & Company, Inc.

7.3 (p.176): Liu Xijun, "Song of Sorrow", "I Watered My Horse at the Long Wall Caves" and "Nineteen Old Poems of the Han" from *The Columbia Book of Chinese Poetry*, translated by Burton Watson, copyright © 1984, Columbia University Press. Reprinted with permission of the publisher.

Chapter 8
8.1 (p. 185): Apuleius, from *Apuleius: Volume II, Metamorphoses, Books VII–XI*, Loeb Classical Library Volume 453, translated by Arthur Hansen, pp.283, 285, (Cambridge, Mass.: Harvard University Press), copyright © 1989 by the President and Fellows of Harvard College. Loeb Classical Library® is a registered trademark of the President and Fellows of Harvard College.

8.4a, 8.4b (pp. 194–195): Lin Yutang, from Buddha's "Sermon at Benares" and "Sermon on Abuse" from *The Wisdom of China and India* (Random House, 1970), copyright 1942 and renewed © 1970 by Random House, Inc. Reprinted by permission of Hsiang Ju Lin, Jill Chih-wen Lai Miller and Larry Chih-yi Lai.

Chapter 9
9.1 (p. 200): from "The Nicene Creed" from *Documents of Christian Church, 3rd Edition*, edited by Henry Bettenson and Chris Maunder , (Oxford University Press, 1999). By permission of Oxford University Press.

9.3 (pp. 201–202): Saint Augustine, from *The Confessions*, translated by Henry Chadwick, pp.203–204, 210–212, 214–215, (Oxford University Press, 2008). By permission of Oxford University Press.

9.4 (pp. 203–204): Saint Augustine from St. Augustine: Volume IV, City of God, Books XII–XV Loeb Classical Library Volume 414, translated by Phil Levine, pp.405, 407, 565, 567, (Cambridge, Mass.: Harvard University Press), copyright © 1966 by the President and Fellows of Harvard College. Loeb Classical Library® is a registered trademark of the President and Fellows of Harvard College.

Chapter 10
10.1 (pp. 230–232): from *The Qur'an*, translated by Maulana Wahiduddin Khan (Goodword Books, 2009).

10.2 (pp. 237–238): from Tarafa, "Praise for His Camel", Al-Asmai, "Romance of Antar", Ibn Zaydun "Two Fragments" and Ibn Abra, "The Beauty-Spot" from *Anthology of Islamic Literature from the Rise of Islam to the Modern World*, (Henry Holt, 1964), copyright © 1964 edited by James Kritzeck. Used by permission of Henry Holt and Company, LLC. All rights reserved.

10.4 (pp. 240–243): "Prince Behram and the Princess Al-Datma" from *Arabian Nights*, translated by Jack Zipes (Dutton Signet, 1991), translation copyright © 1991 by Jack Zipes. Used by permission of Dutton Signet, a division of Penguin Group (USA) LLC.

Chapter 11
11.1 (pp. 252–253): from *Beowulf*, translated by Burton Raffel (Dutton Signet, 1963), copyright © 1963, renewed © 1991 by Burton Raffel. Used by permission of Dutton Signet, a division of Penguin Group (USA) LLC; and Russell & Volkening as agents for the author.

11.4 (pp. 272–273): Bernart de Ventadour, "When I Behold a Lark"; Peire Cardenal, "Lonely the rich need never be", The Countess of Dia, "I've been in great anguish" from *The Troubadours and Their World*, translated by Jack Lindsay (Frederick Muller, 1976). Reprinted by permission of David Higham Associates.

Chapter 12
12.1 (pp. 279): from Saint Francis', 'The Canticle of Brother Sun, from *Francis and Clare: The Complete Works*, translated by Regis J Armstrong and Ignatius C Brady, (Paulist Press, 1982). Reprinted by permission of Copyright Clearance Center.

12.3 (p. 282): from *On the Misery of the Human Condition*, ed by Donald, R. Howard, translated by Mary Margaret Dietz, (The Bobbs Merrill Company, 1969) copyright © 1969. Reprinted by permission of Pearson Education, Inc. Upper Saddle River, NJ.

12.5 (pp. 290–294): Dante Alighieri, from *The Divine Comedy*, translated by John Ciardi (W. W. Norton, 1970), copyright 1954, 1957, 1959, 1960, 1961, 1965, 1967, 1970 by the Ciardi Family Publishing Trust. Used by permission of W. W. Norton & Company, Inc.

Chapter 14

14.2 (p. 330): Vidyakara, Subhasitaratnakosa "From the swaying of their equal commerce", "When his eyes seek out her breast" and "If my absent bride were but a pond" from *An Anthology of Sanskrit Court Poetry*, translated by Daniel H. H. Ingalls, Harvard Oriental Series, 44, pp.204, 227, 248, (Cambridge, Mass.: Harvard University Press), copyright © 1965 by the President and Fellows of Harvard College.

14.3 (pp. 340–341): Du Fu, "Spring Rain" from *The Collected Shorter Poems*, copyright © 1971 by Kenneth Rexroth, and "Farewell Once More" from *One Hundred Poems from the Chinese*, edited by Kenneth Rexroth (New Directions, 1971), copyright © 1956 by New Directions Publishing Corp. Reprinted by permission of New Directions Publishing Corp.

14.4 (pp. 346–347): Professor Richard Bowring for an extract from *The Diary of Lady Murasaki*, translated by Richard Bowring, pp.54–57, (Penguin Classics, revised 2005 edition), copyright © Richard Bowring. Reproduced with permission of the translator.

14.5 (p. 353): Zeami Motokiyo, from "Kadensho" from *Sources of Japanese Tradition*, edited by William Theodore de Bary (Columbia University Press, 1958), copyright © Columbia University Press, 1958. Reprinted by permission of the publisher.

Chapter 15

15.1, 15.2 (pp. 361–365): Giovanni Boccaccio, from *The Decameron*, translated by Frances Winwar, (New York: Modern Library, 1955). Reproduced with permission of MBI, Inc.;

15.3 (p.365): Christine de Pisan, from *The Book of the City of Ladies,* translated by Rosalind Brown-Grant (Penguin Classics, 1999), translation copyright © Rosalind Brown-Grant, 1999. Reproduced by permission of Penguin Books Ltd.

Chapter 16

16.2 (pp. 384–385): Leon Battista Alberti , from "On the Family" from *The Albertis of Florence*, translated by Guido A Guarino (Associated University Press, 1971), copyright © Associated University Presses, 1971. Reproduced by permission of the publisher.

16.3 (pp. 385–387): Pico della Mirandola, from *Oration on the Dignity of Man*, translated by A. Robert Caponigri, (Regnery Gateway), copyright © 1956, 1996 printing. All rights reserved. Reprinted by special permission of Regnery Publishing, Washington, D.C.

16.5 (pp. 392–394.): Lucrezia Marinella, from *The Nobility and Excellence of Women and the Defects and Vices of Men*, edited and translated by Anne Dunhill, pp.119–121, (University of Chicago Press, 1999). Reprinted by permission of Copyright Clearance Center.

Chapter 17

17.2 (pp. 415–416): Giorgio Vasari, from *Lives of the Artists, Vol I*, translated by George Bull (Penguin Classics, 1987), copyright © George Bull, 1965. Reproduced by permission of Penguin Books Ltd.

Chapter 18

18.1 (pp. 443–445): Djibril Tamsir Niane, from *Sundiata: An Epic of Old Mali, 2nd edition*, (Présence Africaine, 2001).

Reprinted by permission of Présence Africaine and Pearson Education Ltd.

18.3 (pp. 447–448): Ulli Beier, from *African Poetry: An Anthology of Traditional African Poems*, compiled and edited by Ulli Beier (Cambridge University Press, 1966). Reprinted by permission of Tunji Beier.

18.4 (pp. 452–453): Ibn Battuta, from "Book of Travels" from *The Travels of Ibn Battuta A.D. 1325–1354, Vol IV*, translated by H.A.R. Gibb, (The Hakluyt Society, 1994). Reproduced by permission of David Higham Associates Ltd.

18.7 (pp. 467–468): Hernan Cortés, from *Hernan Cortés: Letters from Mexico*, edited by Anthony Pagden (Yale University Press, 1986). Reproduced by permission of the publisher.

Chapter 19

19.2 (pp. 489–490): Desiderius Erasmus, from *The Praise of Folly*, translated by Hoyt H. Hudson, (Princeton University Press, 1941),copyright © 1941, 1969 Princeton University Press. Reprinted by permission of Princeton University Press.

19.4 (pp. 492–494): Miguel de Cervantes, from *Don Quixote: A Norton Critical Edition*, edited by Diana de Armas Wilson, translated by Burton Raffel (W. W. Norton), copyright © 1999 by W. W. Norton & Company, Inc. Used by permission of W. W. Norton & Company, Inc.

19.5 (pp. 494–496): Michel de Montaigne, from "On Cannibals" from *The Complete Essays on Montaigne: Essays, Travel Journal. Letters*, translated by Donald M Frame, (Stanford University Press), copyright © 1943 by Donald M. Frame, copyright © 1948, 1957 by the Board of Trustees of the Leland Stanford Junior University. Renewed © 1971, 1976. All rights reserved. With the permission of Stanford University Press, www.sup.org.

Index

Numbers in **bold** refer to figure numbers.
Text excerpts are indicated by (quoted).